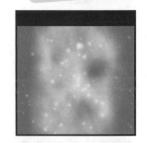

CORBA 3
Fundamentals and Programming
Second Edition

Written and Edited by

Jon Siegel, PhD

Wiley Computer Publishing

John Wiley & Sons, Inc.

NEW YORK · CHICHESTER · WEINHEIM · BRISBANE · SINGAPORE · TORONTO

Publisher: Robert Ipsen
Editor: Robert Elliott
Associate Developmental Editor: Kathryn A. Malm
Managing Editor: Micheline Frederick
Electronic Products, Associate Editor: Brian Snapp
Text Design & Composition: Benchmark Productions, Inc.

Designations used by companies to distinguish their products are often claimed as trademarks. In all instances where John Wiley & Sons, Inc., is aware of a claim, the product names appear in initial capital or ALL CAPITAL LETTERS. Readers, however, should contact the appropriate companies for more complete information regarding trademarks and registration.

This book is printed on acid-free paper. ♾

Published by John Wiley & Sons, Inc.

Published simultaneously in Canada.

Chapter 21, "Modeling CORBA Applications with UML," from the book *Modeling Software Architectures with UML* by Cris Kobryn, copyright 2000, Addison Wesley Longman., used by permission.

This publication is designed to provide accurate and authoritative information in regard to the subject matter covered. It is sold with the understanding that the publisher is not engaged in professional services. If professional advice or other expert assistance is required, the services of a competent professional person should be sought.

Library of Congress Cataloging-in-Publication Data:

ISBN 0-471-29518-3

Printed in the United States of America.

10 9 8 7 6 5 4 3 2

OMG Press Advisory Board

OMG Press Books in Print

(For complete information about current and upcoming titles, go to www.wiley.com/
compbooks/omg/)

Building Business Objects by Peter Eeles and Oliver Sims, ISBN: 0471-191760.

Business Component Factory: A Comprehensive Overview of Component-Based Development for the Enterprise by Peter Herzum and Oliver Sims, ISBN: 0471-327603.

Business Modeling with UML: Business Patterns at Work by Hans-Erik Eriksson and Magnus Penker, ISBN: 0471-295515.

CORBA 3 Fundamentals and Programming, 2nd Edition by Jon Siegel, ISBN: 0471-295183.

CORBA Design Patterns by Thomas J. Mowbray and Raphael C. Malveau, ISBN: 0471-158828.

Developing C++ Applications with UML by Michael Sandberg, ISBN: 0471-38304X.

Enterprise Application Integration with CORBA: Component and Web-Based Solutions by Ron Zahavi, ISBN: 0471-32704.

The Essential CORBA: Systems Integration Using Distributed Objects by Thomas J. Mowbray and Ron Zahavi, ISBN: 0471-106119.

Instant CORBA by Robert Orfali, Dan Harkey and Jeri Edwards, ISBN: 0471-183334.

Integrating CORBA and COM Applications by Michael Rosen and David Curtis, ISBN: 0471-198277.

Java Programming with CORBA, 2nd Edition by Andreas Vogel and Keith Duddy, *The Object Technology Casebook: Lessons from Award-Winning Business Applications* by Paul Harmon and William Morrisey, ISBN: 0471-147176.

The Object Technology Revolution by Michael Guttman and Jason Matthews, ISBN: 0471-606790.

Programming with Enterprise JavaBeans, JTS and OTS: Building Distributed Transactions with Java and C++ by Andreas Vogel and Madhavan Rangarao, ISBN: 0471-319724.

Programming with Java IDL by Geoffrey Lewis, Steven Barber and Ellen Siegel, ISBN: 0471-247979.

UML Toolkit by Hans-Erik Eriksson and Magnus Penker, ISBN: 0471-191612.

About the OMG

The Object Management Group (OMG) was chartered to create and foster a component-based software marketplace through the standardization and promotion of object-oriented software. To achieve this goal, the OMG specifies open standards for every aspect of distributed object computing from analysis and design, through infrastructure, to application objects and components.

The well-established CORBA (Common Object Request Broker Architecture) standardizes a platform- and programming-language-independent distributed object computing environment. It is based on OMG/ISO Interface Definition Language (OMG IDL) and the Internet Inter-ORB Protocol (IIOP). Now recognized as a mature technology, CORBA is represented on the marketplace by well over 70 ORBs (Object Request Brokers) plus hundreds of other products. Although most of these ORBs are tuned for general use, others are specialized for real-time or embedded applications, or built into transaction processing systems where they provide scalability, high throughput and reliability. Of the thousands of live, mission-critical CORBA applications in use today around the world, over 300 are documented on the OMG's success-story Web pages at www.corba.org.

CORBA 3, the OMG's latest release, adds a Component Model, quality-of-service control, a messaging invocation model, and tightened integration with the Internet, Enterprise Java Beans and the Java programming language. Widely anticipated by the industry, CORBA 3 keeps this established architecture in the forefront of distributed computing, as will a new OMG specification integrating CORBA with XML. Well-known for its ability to integrate legacy systems into your network, along with the wide variety of heterogeneous hardware and software on the market today, CORBA enters the new millennium prepared to integrate the technologies on the horizon.

Augmenting this core infrastructure are the CORBAservices which standardize naming and directory services, event handling, transaction processing, security, and other functions. Building on this firm foundation, OMG Domain Facilities standardize common objects throughout the supply and service chains in industries such as Telecommunications, Healthcare, Manufacturing, Transportation, Finance/Insurance, Electronic Commerce, Life Science, and Utilities.

The OMG standards extend beyond programming. OMG Specifications for analysis and design include the Unified Modeling Language (UML), the repository standard Meta-Object Facility (MOF), and XML-based Metadata Interchange (XMI). The UML is a result of fusing the concepts of the world's most prominent methodologists. Adopted as an OMG specification in 1997, it represents a collection of best engineering practices that have proven successful in the modeling of large and complex systems and is a well-defined, widely -accepted response to these business needs. The MOF is OMG's standard for metamodeling and metadata repositories. Fully integrated with UML, it uses the UML notation to describe repository metamodels. Extending this work, the XMI standard enables the exchange of objects defined using UML and the MOF. XMI can generate XML Data Type Definitions for any service specification that includes a normative, MOF-based metamodel.

In summary, the OMG provides the computing industry with an open, vendor-neutral, proven process for establishing and promoting standards. OMG makes all of its specifications available without charge from its Web site, www.omg.org. With over a decade of standard-making and consensus-building experience, OMG now counts about 800 companies as members. Delegates from these companies convene at week-long meetings held five times each year at varying sites around the world, to advance OMG technologies. The OMG welcomes guests to their meetings; for an invitation, send your email request to info@omg.org.

Membership in the OMG is open to end users, government organizations, academia and technology vendors. For more information on the OMG, contact OMG headquarters by phone at +1-508-820 4300, by fax at +1-508-820 4303, by email at info@omg.org, or on the Web at www.omg.org.

To Nancy

Trademarks

CORBA, The Information Brokerage, CORBA Academy, IIOP and the Object Management Group logo are registered trademarks of the Object Management Group. OMG, Object Management Group, the CORBA Logo, ORB, Object Request Broker, the CORBA Academy logo, XMI, MOF, OMG Interface Definition Language, IDL, CORBAservices, CORBAfacilities, CORBAmed, CORBAnet, UML, the UML Cube Logo, and Unified Modeling Language are trademarks of the Object Management Group.

BEA, Object Broker, TOP END, and TUXEDO are registered trademarks of BEA Systems, Inc. BEA Builder, BEA Connect, BEA eLink, BEA Manager, BEA MessageQ, Jolt, M3, The E-Commerce Transactions Company, and WebLogic are trademarks of BEA Systems, Inc.

Expersoft is a registered trademark and PowerBroker and CORBAplus are trademarks of Vertel Corporation. The pyramid logo with Vertel, Vertel, The TMN Company, Vertel Cougar, Vertel Jaguar, Vertel Panther and Vertel Tigress are trademarks of the Vertel Corporation.

AIX, Component Broker, DB2, DB2 Universal Database, Encina, IBM, MQSeries, TXSeries, VisualAge, and WebSphere are trademarks or registered trademarks of the IBM Corporation in the United States, and/or other countries.

Tivoli and Tivoli Ready are trademarks or registered trademarks of the Tivoli Systems Inc., an IBM company, in the United States, and/or other countries.

All Inprise and Borland brands and product names are trademarks or registered trademarks of Inprise Corporation.

The following are trademarks of IONA Technologies Plc: Orbix, OrbixNames, OrbixCOMet, WonderWall, OrbixWeb, OrbixSSL, OrbixOTM, OrbixManager, OrbixOTS, OrbixTalk, MessageStore, OrbixNotification, and "Making Software Work Together".

MERANT and NetExpress are registered trademarks of MERANT International Ltd.

DAIS is a trademark of International Computers Limited. PeerLogic and the PeerLogic logo are registered trademarks of PeerLogic, Inc.

Adobe, Acrobat, Acrobat Reader, FrameMaker, FrameReader, Frame Technology, and Post-Script are registered trademarks of Adobe Systems, Inc.

Sun, Sun Microsystems, the Sun Logo, SunOS and Solaris are trademarks or registered trademarks of Sun Microsystems, Inc. in the United States and other countries.

All SPARC trademarks are used under license by Vertel/Expersoft and other companies, and are trademarks or registered trademarks of SPARC International, Inc. in the United States and other countries. Products bearing SPARC trademarks are based upon an architecture developed by Sun Microsystems, Inc.

Enterprise Java Beans, Java, JavaServer Pages, and JDBC are trademarks or registered trademarks of Sun Microsystems, Inc, in the United States, and/or other countries.

Microsoft, DriveSpace, MS, MS-DOS, Windows, Windows NT, Visual C++, Developer Studio, and the Windows logo are either registered trademarks or trademarks of Microsoft Corporation in the United States and/or other countries.

Oracle is a registered trademark of the Oracle Corporation, in the United States, and/or other countries.

FLEXlm and Globetrotter Software are either trademarks or registered trademarks of Globetrotter Software, Inc.

HP-UX is a registered trademark of the Hewlett-Packard Company.

UNIX is a registered trademark, licensed by X/Open Corp. Ltd.

All other trademarks are the property of their respective owners.

About the Authors

Dr. Jon Siegel is Director of Technology Transfer for the Object Management Group (OMG). At OMG, he heads OMG's technology transfer program with the goal of teaching the technical aspects and benefits of the Object Management Architecture including CORBA, the CORBAservices, the Domain specifications in vertical markets ranging from healthcare, life sciences, and telecommunications to manufacturing and retail systems, and the modeling specifications UML, MOF and XMI. In this capacity, he presents tutorials, seminars, and company briefings around the world, and writes magazine articles and books. With OMG since 1993, Siegel was founding chair of the Domain Technology Committee responsible for OMG specifications in the vertical domains.

Before joining OMG, Dr. Siegel performed research and development in Computer Science for Shell Oil Company where he championed the use of standards to reduce software development time and cost, and was an early developer of distributed object software. While at Shell, he served as its representative to the Open Software Foundation for four years, and to the Object Management Group for two years. He holds a Ph.D. in Theoretical Chemistry from Boston University.

Dr. Dan Frantz, BEA Systems, Inc. Dan is an architect in the E-commerce Servers division of BEA Systems, developing CORBA-related products for the last five years. He served on the OMG's Architecture Board for three years and contributed to several OMG specifications including the POA, Messaging, and Interoperable Naming, as well as the CORBA 2.2 and 2.3 revisions. Dan holds a Ph.D. in Computer Science from the University of Michigan.

Patrick Ryan, for Expersoft Corp. Patrick was a Senior Systems Architect for Expersoft Corporation and is now a consultant specializing in CORBA and distributed systems. Patrick has been involved with distributed systems since 1992 and is currently working on C++ and Java CORBA applications. Patrick can be reached at distributedsolutions@yahoo.com

Virgil Albaugh, IBM Corp. Virgil is a Senior Programmer at IBM, and was the team lead for the design and implementation of the CORBA 2.0 compliant C++ ORB in WebSphere. Virgil is a graduate of the University of Akron and Rensselaer Polytechnic Institute.

Dr. Michael Cheng, IBM Corp. Michael has been a key contributor to IBM's ORB technology, including C++ emitters, Objects by Value, and IBM's Interlanguage Object Model. He is currently involved in supporting EJBs on Websphere Enterprise Edition. Michael holds a Ph.D. in Computer Science from the University of Wisconsin-Madison.

Alan Conway, IONA Technologies PLC Alan is a Senior Consultant with IONA Technologies, where he has four years experience in helping IONA's customers develop CORBA systems. He has also been involved in design and development of some of the Orbix product range.

Jim O'Leary, for IONA Technologies PLC Jim graduated from University of Limerick, Ireland with a Bachelors of Engineering in Computer Engineering. His time at IONA Technologies Professional Services department, where he was a consultant/trainer for Orbix and OrbixWeb, was sandwiched between stints designing and developing SW for Real Time GSM mobile phone systems and developing financial software for a bank. He is now an independent consultant with his own company, Anhid Technology, specializing in designing and developing Distributed Systems in EJB and CORBA.

Frederic Desjarlais, for Inprise Corp Frederic has been working with distributed systems for 8 years and is now lead technologist at Enjiva Corporation (www.enjiva.com) where he does research and development as well as consulting. Frederic holds an Honours Computer Science degree from Carleton University, Ottawa, Canada.

David Gamble, MERANT PLC Dave has been active in the industry since 1977 and currently works for Merant as a Technical Architect on e-commerce solutions. He also chairs the ORB/OS task force at OMG and has contributed to several OMG specifications including the COBOL language mapping. Dave may be contacted at dave.gamble@merant.com.

Martin Tonge, PeerLogic, Inc. After graduating with Honours in Computer Information Systems Science at the University of Bradford, Martin Tonge joined International Computers Ltd in 1989, working with rapidly evolving RDBMS technologies. Starting in 1991, he helped productize the research and development project that matured into the DAIS Object Request Broker. Since then, he has been a leading consultant on CORBA and was the chief architect for training on DAIS. He represented ICL on OMG initiatives such as the IIOP Demonstrations and CORBA Academy. Martin moved to PeerLogic in 1999, and is currently responsible for PeerLogic's Object Transaction Service and Java Transaction Service implementations.

Cris Kobryn, EDS Cris is a Chief Technologist for the E.solutions unit of EDS where he specializes in software architectures and methods for e-business. Cris has broad international experience leading high-productivity software development teams, and has architected many distributed systems and software packages. Cris is a co-author of the Unified Modeling Language (UML) specification and co-chair of the UML Revision Task Force at the OMG. Cris may be contacted at ckobryn@acm.org .

Sridhar Iyengar, Unisys Corp. Sridhar, a Unisys Fellow, leads the advanced development of object technologies for Unisys corporation (www.unisys.com). He is the chief architect of the OMG Meta Object Facility (MOF) and XML Metadata Interchange (XMI) specifications and the Metamodeling architecture of OMG, which unifies UML, MOF, and XMI with the OMA. He is the chief architect of Unisys Universal Repository (UREP), the industry's first commercial object repository framework. Sridhar currently serves on the OMG Architecture Board, chairs the MOF Revision Task Force and previously chaired the OMG Object Analysis and Design Task Force.

Acknowledgments

It's not possible to acknowledge all of the people who contributed to this book. It's based on all of the OMG specifications, and hundreds of skilled people from hundreds of companies around the world have participated in their creation. Five times every year, more than five hundred CORBA experts gather at a hotel somewhere in the world at an OMG meeting to advance OMG's suite of standards. We can't name them all here, but we can at least start by acknowledging our debt to these people for their fine work.

Enthusiastic support from the Object Management Group made this book possible. In particular, we want to thank OMG CEO Dr. Richard Soley and Technical Director Andrew Watson, who provided advice as well as technical review although Jon Siegel takes full responsibility for any errors or omissions, of course. Jon Siegel also takes full responsibility for the opinions expressed here and there in the book; they're his, and neither OMG's nor anyone else's. Others around the OMG offices who provided support and/or encouragement include COO Bill Hoffman, VP of Marketing Cheryl Rocheleau, Wayne Haughey, Henry Lowe, Mark Lowenstein, Dody Keefe, and the rest of the staff.

We also want to give special thanks to all of the contributing companies: BEA Systems, Inc.; Expersoft Corp.; IBM Corp.; IONA Technologies PLC; Inprise Corp.; MERANT plc; and PeerLogic, Inc. By making time available for their contributing authors, and giving them encouragement, they made possible the example section. We are not aware of any other standard that is illustrated by a single example worked directly in so many different products, programming languages, and platforms. We are proud to be associated with an effort in which so many competing companies worked so well together for the benefit of their end users and the computing industry as a whole.

The contributing authors worked far beyond the call of duty: Dan Frantz, Patrick Ryan, Virgil Albaugh, Michael Cheng, Alan Conway, Jim O'Leary, Frederic Desjarlais, David Gamble, and Martin Tonge. Although we expected that they would work on the book on company time, many additional hours were squeezed in under deadline pressure, and every minute is greatly appreciated.

We also have to thank the original crew who created and worked the example for the first edition: Dan Frantz (the only returning star!), Raghu Hudli, Alex Thomas, Wilf Coles, Hal Mirsky, Peter deJong, Sean Baker, Maurice Balick, Alan Klein, and Brent Wilkins. Bart Hanlon of HP suggested and outlined the POS example early in the development cycle of the first edition; we're happy to acknowledge this contribution and sorry that his other duties did not allow him to continue working with on the first edition with us, back in 1994 and 1995.

Dan Frantz wrote and updated the original analysis and design chapter, and updated it for this edition. Hal Mirsky wrote the IDL chapter for the first edition, and did such a good job that little change was necessary although Dan did update the IDL to conform to OMG's IDL Style Guide, which he also wrote. Special thanks to Dan for also contributing the section on scalability and the writeup of the technical details of the POA.

Many thanks to Ed Cobb (BEA Systems, Inc.), Patrick Thompson (Rogue Wave Software, Inc.), and Patrick Ravenel (Persistence Software, Inc.), who wrote the code for the mini-example in the CORBA Components section of Chapter 5 and reviewed my text for that section so many times, they might as well have written some of it themselves. Patrick Ravenel also wrote the PSDL code and reviewed the PSS section of Chapter 17, and so gets double thanks. Our other double-dipper is Ed Cobb, who reviewed the chapter on Transactions and helped by pointing out what was new since the first edition. Thanks also go to Mike Greenberg of NEC (http://www.nec.com) for his review of the Notification Service writeup, Polar Humenn of Adiron Software, Inc. (http://www.adiron.com) for his review of the Security chapter, to David Zenie of Genesis Development, Inc. (http://www.gen-dev.com) for his review of the workflow section of Chapter 20, and to Carol Burt of 2AB, Inc. (www.2ab.com) for her review of the PIDS section of that same chapter.

On the Analysis and Design side, thanks to Cris Kobryn of EDS (http://www.eds.com) for contributing Chapter 21 on UML. Cris is one of the authors of the specification, and chairs the current UML Revision Task Force at OMG. Also, thanks to Sridhar Iyengar of Unisys, Inc. (http://www.unisys.com) for Chapter 22 on the MOF and XMI. Sridhar is the principal author of these specifications, and known around OMG as "Mr. MOF". We're proud to have these two authorities contribute to this book.

We kept the example moving and synchronized with twice-weekly teleconferences. With participants spread over eight time zones from the British Isles to California, these teleconferences were not simple to set up or coordinate. We want to acknowledge our teleconference service, Connex International, and especially Diane, who provided personalized service setting up our recurring intercontinental conversations.

Since books tend to be written during evening, weekends, and even vacations, authors' families contribute noticeably to the success of a project such as this one. I want to thank my wife Nancy, and our children Joshua and Adam, for their support and patience during the writing and editing of this book. Their help and forbearance made this work possible.

Dave Gamble acknowledges his wife Sara and also their children, who gracefully tolerated his presence in body but absence in spirit while he wordcrafted his humble contribution to this distillation of CORBA wisdom. Alan Conway thanks the many folks at IONA who supported and helped him in his professional development, and his wife Denise for her support and help in everything else. Michael Cheng sends special thanks to Kim Rochat, who's always ahead on the Java knowledge curve. Pat Ryan would like to thank these people at Expersoft: Gail Slemon, Terri Liebowitz, Shahzad Aslam-Mir, Joey Garon and Scott Herscher. Pat also thanks his wife Claire for her support. Dan Frantz would like to thank Jeri Edwards for helping with the product description by giving permission to adapt her material at BEA Systems, Inc. and from her book "3-Tier Client/Server At Work", Revised Edition, Wiley, 1999. Jim O'Leary acknowledges his wife Fiona and son Aodh. Sridhar Iyengar thanks his parents, A. N. Srinivasa Iyengar and Ranganayakammal who inspired his passion for introspection and semantics (which turned into the MOF!), and Dick Ulmer of Unisys who started the Advanced Object Technology labs where many of these ideas were implemented. Sridhar is also grateful to his wonderful wife Sumathi and her parents Sundararajan and Janakavalli who nurtured his children Mangala, Apoorva, and Amalan during his many hours away from home.

We're sure you'll agree with us, as you read through the example implementation on the eight ORBs, that this is a remarkable book based on a number of remarkable achievements: the shared example presented here and the OMG specifications that make it possible. The cooperative spirit of the OMG carried through our teleconferences into this book where it is on display in every chapter. All of the authors and contributors are proud to be associated with this effort, and hope that it contributes greatly to your understanding of CORBA.

Enjoy!

Jon Siegel
Director, Technology Transfer
Object Management Group

Contents

About the Fonts

We've used only two special fonts in this book:

This font is used for the three languages specified by OMG: OMG IDL (Interface Definition Language), OMG PSDL (Persistent State Definition Language), and OMG CIDL (Component Implementation Definition Language). Because the context makes clear which of these is intended everywhere they occur, it was not necessary to flag any of these languages with its own unique font.

`This font` is used for code (in any programming language, particularly C++, Java, and COBOL as presented in the example chapters), and for commands that you may type into a terminal window, for example at a command prompt.

List of Figures

Introduction

This book presents all of the Object Management Group's (OMG) specifications: While concentrating on the Common Object Request Broker Architecture (CORBA) and the Object Management Architecture (OMA), it also introduces OMG's specifications supporting analysis and design: the Unified Modeling Language (UML), the Meta-Object Facility (MOF), and XML Metadata Interchange Format (XMI).

If you're new to CORBA, we want to reassure you, right here at the front of the book, that we really do begin at the beginning. The first chapter covers the benefits of CORBA and interoperability, while the second surveys the OMG's overall architecture, before we get down to the technical and programming details that start in Chapter 3 and are covered from the ground up. CORBA—the Common Object Request Broker Architecture—as well as the CORBAservices, and the horizontal and domain CORBAfacilities, are all described in a way that lets you understand what they are, how they work, and most importantly, what they do for you.

If you have some CORBA experience, or are an experienced programmer and pick up new things quickly, we'd like to tell you that this book covers *all* of the new areas included in the now-extensive OMG specification suite: the additions called CORBA 3 including the CORBA Component Model (CCM), the new and revised CORBAservices including Persistence, the domain CORBAfacilities, and in a new specifications area for OMG, the Unified Modeling Language (UML), Meta-Object Facility (MOF), and XML-based Model Interchange facility (XMI). And, these were worked into the organization of the book from the beginning; not tacked on in an appendix or final chapter.

This is a second edition of the successful *CORBA Fundamentals and Programming*, which introduced CORBA to tens of thousands of readers. It continues in the same informal style of the first edition (which so many readers told us they liked), bringing it up to date by adding new specifications (CORBA 3 and a suite of new and revised CORBAservices), new standards areas (UML, the MOF, and Domain Facilities), and new languages working the programming example (Java and COBOL replace C and Smalltalk).

People use the term "CORBA 3" is used in two different ways: Commonly, it is used as a shorthand expression to refer to "the new stuff" in this latest CORBA release, but officially it is the designation of an entire release of the CORBA specification—all of the old stuff, plus the new, combined into a single formal document and released (with some fanfare, perhaps) on the OMG Web site. In this book, when we say "CORBA 3" we're usually referring to the new stuff. As we went to press in late 1999, OMG's formal CORBA 3 book had not been issued and was not expected until mid- or late-2000 since a new OMG procedure postpones this step until the initial drafts of new specifications have been proven in products that reach the marketplace. Nevertheless, all of these new specifications are presented here in extensive chapters or sections, worked into the overall structure of the book in their proper places.

There are a number of reasons you might be reading this book. For instance, you might be the architect responsible for selecting the interoperability architecture for your enterprise, and someone told you to find out more about CORBA. Or, you might be assigned to a prototype CORBA project, and you need to find out as much as you can about it in order to start your project and evaluation. Or, perhaps your company produces software, and you're considering CORBA as a platform that will let you market on a wide range of networked platforms with minimal porting. Or, there might not be any decision involved: You've been assigned to a CORBA-based development project, and you need a jump-start to find out about CORBA and learn to develop applications that take advantage of the interoperability and portability that the OMA provides.

It turns out that a lot of people need to find out more about CORBA, and there's even more about CORBA to find out about than there was when we wrote the first edition. We've been writing about this topic in magazines for years and covered a lot of ground, but we really needed a book format to answer the questions people have about such a large topic. This book collects in one place the information you need. Here's how the book is arranged:

The OMG produces *specifications*, but you buy *products*. In order to cover both, we've divided this book into two major sections:

The first section, Chapters 1 through 22, presents the OMG specifications: CORBA, the CORBAservices, the CORBAfacilities including the Domain Facilities, UML, the MOF, and XMI. The discussion builds the environment from the architectural foundations of the Interface Definition Language (IDL) and Object Request Broker to the services and facilities that round out the programming and interoperability environment.

The second section, Chapters 23 through 36, presents a single programming example worked in eleven ORBs, from seven vendors, in three programming languages. Because the example in the first edition was so successful, we haven't changed it much. Dan Frantz has revised the IDL to conform to OMG's IDL Style Guide (which he wrote), and we've substituted two different languages: We now work the example in C++, Java, and COBOL, instead of C, C++, and Smalltalk. (Why COBOL, I can hear some of you ask? Half of the world's programs, and half of the world's programmers, use COBOL. Someone has to put this important enterprise language into a CORBA book, and we figured OMG ought to do it.)

The discussion of each OMG specification starts from an architectural viewpoint: What does this component do, and how does it contribute to the OMA environment? Then, most topics continue with a more detailed discussion. Usually, this part of the presentation concludes with selected programming details, since we've found that almost everyone wants to see how developers will work with CORBA in real life. Other topics, for example the ORB and interoperability, go into detail because we've found that potential CORBA users want to know how location transparency really works, or how the object invocations are transmitted over the wire from one ORB to another, even though this functionality is automatic and not accessed directly by either end user or programmer. We've put the most detail into topics about which people have been the most curious; if your reaction to a claim is ``How do they do that?'' you'll probably find the answer later in the chapter where you can either analyze it yourself, or pass the section on to a technical colleague. When you finish reading this part of the book, you'll understand how CORBA and the OMA work together to enable the transparencies that applications need to work in today's networked world: transparencies to programming language, platform, operating system, network protocol, and more.

The products that implement CORBA cover a lot of ground: programming languages from C and C++ to COBOL and Ada; platforms from mainframes to micros to desktops; networks from fiber to satellite links. The tutorial programming example in this book showcases both the diversity and the commonality of the ORBs and CORBA development environments on the market today. It is worked here in eleven ORBs, from seven vendors, in the three programming languages C++, Java, and COBOL. More ORB vendors have worked the example as well; this book's web page (http://www.omg.org/library/corfun/corfun.html) includes pointers to all that we know about. The programmers and authors who wrote the example worked hard to maximize commonality; the analysis and design and the IDL file, are common to every implementation; within each language, almost all of the code is as well. Common code is presented only once; ORB-specific sections detail product-specific portions and go on to explain how to use each programming environment to generate your executable objects. When you finish reading about and working the example, you'll have both overview and detailed programming-level knowledge of CORBA products and programming, which spans the range of products on the market today.

Chapter 1 discusses objects, and their benefits, in general. If objects are new to you, this material will help fill in the gaps in your knowledge (and if this isn't enough, check out the references in Appendix A for entire books devoted to this topic). Chapter 2 is a technical overview, covering all of CORBA and the OMA at an architectural level.

Chapters 3 through 9 detail CORBA, and Chapters 10 through 22 detail the rest of the OMA. Chapter 3 is devoted exclusively to OMG's Interface Definition Language (OMG IDL), the cornerstone of interoperability and transparency. We wanted to start out with ORB structure—what it does and how it works—but we had to organize this way because all of the ORB interfaces are defined in IDL. If you're never going to program to these interfaces, you can skip most of this chapter and go to the Object Request Broker (ORB) description—-Chapters 4 and 5—after reading the introductory material. The section on the CORBA Component Model is in Chapter 5; the mini CCM programming example in the section was written by Ed Cobb of BEA Systems, Patrick Thompson of Rogue Wave, and Patrick Ravenel of Persistence Software, authors of the specifications. The section on the new Asynchronous Invocation specification and Quality of Service Control appears in Chapter 6 along with Interoperability. Chapters 7 through 9 present mappings from IDL to the programming languages C++, Java, and COBOL. This is where the world of the OMA meets your application code. Chapters 10 through 18 present the CORBAservices, and Chapters 19 and 20 cover the CORBAdomains both in general and in specific.

Most of these chapters are organized in ``drill-down'' style—architectural and user-level material toward the front; technical and programming-level details following. If you're not a programmer or a ``techie,'' you can still learn a lot from the first section or two of each chapter up through Chapter 14, and Chapters 17, 19 and 20 as well. If you're technically inclined, just read everything straight through. (If you're really technical, of course, you can buy the OMG specifications and read them, or join the OMG and *write* them)

Chapter 21 covers the Unified Modeling Language (UML), written by Kris Cobryn, one of the specification's authors. Chapter 22 covers the Meta-Object Facility (MOF) and the XML-Based Model Interchange (XMI) specification, written by Sridhar Iyengar, the main author of those specifications. We're pleased to have these two authorities contributing to this book.

The rest of the book deals with the programming example. Chapter 23 is the problem statement: We have a retail domain with a depot or warehouse, a store, and a number of point-of-sale (POS) terminals, and our job is to design and implement a distributed computing system to handle sales and inventory. Chapter 24 follows up with a semi-formal object-oriented analysis and design: the objects in our system, what each one does, and which parameters are provided and returned in each invocation. Chapter 25 describes the ORB products and environments used to work the example in the rest of the book, presented by the companies in their own words. These are not the only ORBs on the market, of course; for information on more ORB products (including additional ORBs that implement this example in this book), check out this book's Web page, and the CORBA links collections referenced in Appendix A. .

Chapter 26 presents the common IDL file used by every ORB to work the example. Following this, the three modules Depot, Store, and POS Terminal are worked in three-chapter groupings, one chapter each for C++, Java, and COBOL. There's a roadmap in the beginning of Chapter 23; Figure 23.1 maps the path through the example for each language and ORB. When your development is complete, Chapter 36 shows how to fire up your example objects and run your retail empire. The diskette contains the common OMG IDL file, plus all the source code and supplemental files (makefiles or whatever) you need to run the example on all of the listed ORBs. This book's Web page contains pointers to other ORBs that support the example on-line.

The example here is long on CORBA and short on functionality (although it includes enough to demonstrate that CORBA really does useful work); after all, every reader is interested in CORBA, but only a minority will ever run a retail chain. Most of the code demonstrates how CORBA works and exercises key features that developers need to know to make effective use of object-oriented distributed computing. Objects in the example represent, and work like, objects in the real world, and best-practice programming technique is used throughout (and the text points out places where this makes a difference).

So, how should you read this book? It depends on who you are and what you need to know. If you're an executive more concerned with corporate directions and budget than with electronic plumbing, start by reading Chapters 1 and 2. Then read the beginning few sections of each chapter from 3 through 13 and 17, as much as you need of 14 (Security), and all of 20 (the CORBAdomains). Then skim Chapter 23 (example description) and any other part of the example that interests you. If you're a technical manager or supervisor who will never (or almost never) program a CORBA application yourself, read the first part of the book the same way, but spend more time on the product descriptions (Chapter 25) and example programming in the second part. If you're on a team evaluating CORBA for your company, you (or someone on the team, anyhow) probably needs to understand almost everything in here. If you're a programmer and you're already sitting at your machine, you can spin the CD-ROM and start at Chapter 23 if you don't mind working ahead of the explanations——the text will guide you through the example whether you understand the overall architecture or not. Then you can read the hows and whys when you're home, away from your machine, or by candlelight during a power failure.

Thanks for picking up this book. The authoring team has done its best to give you everything you need to really understand CORBA, all tucked between two covers and on one CD-ROM. All of us hope you'll like what you find here.

CHAPTER

1

Introducing CORBA
and the OMA

WHAT ABOUT CORBA 3?

First, let's be precise about what we're discussing. CORBA 3 officially refers to the recent release of *all* of CORBA—updated versions of CORBA 2.3, plus a significant suite of new specifications and capabilities. Some people use the term CORBA 3 when they really mean just the new stuff, and we agree that it's an easy way to refer to the new parts of CORBA.

But this book is still a primer on *all* of CORBA, so we're not going to describe the new parts in their own chapter apart from everything else. Instead, you'll find them in many different chapters right next to the parts of pre-existing CORBA that they extend or modify. (For example, the new messaging and asynchronous invocation service is covered in Chapter 6 on interoperability.) The result, we think, is a coherent picture of all of CORBA, with old and new parts treated equally.

If you're new to CORBA, you'll find this organization holds together well and presents each part of the suite of OMG specifications where you expect it. If you're an old hand looking for the new stuff, you'll need a roadmap. We put the roadmap, with pointers to both the sections in this book and the OMG specifications on their Web site, into a sidebar at the beginning of Chapter 2. If you're mainly interested in new CORBA 3 material, you can look there now; otherwise, continue here with our general introduction.

This book contains the information you need to get started with CORBA—the Common Object Request Broker Architecture from the Object Management Group (OMG). The first half of the book, Chapters 1–22, presents and explains CORBA and the Object

Management Architecture (OMA). This chapter is an executive summary, presenting Corba's benefits but only referencing the supporting details. Chapter 2 presents a technical overview, while Chapters 3–22 fill in technical details about CORBA, the CORBAservices, and the CORBAfacilities. Chapters 23–36 present a single tutorial programming example, demonstrated in eight CORBA environments representing three programming languages and seven different vendors. If you're only interested in programming (unlikely, we presume), you can skip to Chapter 23 right now, fire up one of the CORBA environments on our list, spin the CD, and start coding. But if you want to find out about CORBA first, keep reading here.

Of course, there is more to object-oriented development than CORBA. First, there is a lot more that can be said about the business case for object orientation (OO), and an excellent presentation of this is given in *The Object Revolution* by Michael Guttman and Jason Matthews (see Appendix A for references). Second, many folks recommend a thorough object-oriented analysis and design as the first step for all but the smallest development projects. The Unified Modeling Language (UML) is the OMG specification that helps you out here. Cris Kobryn, one of the authors of the UML specification, introduces this in Chapter 21 and provides references in Appendix A. In this book, we will focus on *interoperability, architecture,* and *implementation.*

1.1 Heterogeneous Distributed Computing

Diversity in hardware and software is a fact of life, and our networked computing environment is becoming more diverse as computers evolve. At the high end, super-

NEW BREADTH OF SCOPE TO OMG SOLUTIONS

A few years ago, the OMG was concerned with solving the interoperability problem and had only one solution to offer: CORBA. Since solving the interoperability problem a couple of years ago, the OMG has extended beyond its basic architecture to solve other problems. You'll have an easier time figuring out our explanations of each part if you keep in mind what it's supposed to do. The following list spells out the basics. Use it to refresh your memory if you get a little confused; there's a lot of good detail in this book but it won't make sense if you lose your way.

COMPUTING PROBLEM	CORBA/OMA SOLUTION
Analysis and design interoperability, Metadata	UML®, Meta-Object Facility (MOF)
Overcoming interoperability barriers: platform, operating system, programming language, network	CORBA®: IDL® interfaces, language mappings, ORBs, Object Reference, IIOP protocol, asynchronous invocation modes
Server resource control, scalability	POA (Portable Object Adapter)
Server-side programming and runtime support; software distribution	CCM
COTS (Commercial off-the-shelf) software functionality and interoperability	CORBAdomain standards: transportation, telecommunications, healthcare, interoperability, and more

computers working in teams perform complex scientific and engineering calculations, or serve massive databases such as airline reservation systems. In the midrange, powerful servers and surprisingly capable desktop machines provide an increasingly complex array of services. And at the low end, embedded systems, which we may not even think of as computers, interact with each other and with conventional systems to provide automation of tasks at home and work: TV sets and VCRs interacting with programming services; thermostats and alarm sensors acting as components of building automation systems; PDAs, pagers, and more. You know from scanning this list that these computers will use a range of operating systems and a number of programming languages. But the need for interoperability spans machine size and type. For example, PDAs and pagers are more valuable when they can receive and reply to messages from machines anywhere on the network, not just desktop machines, but also large mainframes serving, for example, financial data (a service available today) or airline schedules.

If you're responsible for all or part of the information technology (IT) in an enterprise, you may have recognized your company's computer and network configuration in the preceding paragraph—a collection of diverse computers, performing different functions or storing different data in different places, loaded with immovable legacy applications storing legacy data in legacy formats, and hampered from working together by incompatible operating systems, network hardware and protocols, thus preventing you from getting your work done. But you know that the computing paradigm has changed: No longer satisfied with using their computers to count their money, companies like yours want to use their computers to *make* money by having them work together to recognize and respond to new opportunitites in increasingly rapid and flexible ways.

Let's focus on the problems that such an integrated environment creates:

- *It's difficult to get the hardware—computers and networks—to work together.* We need varied types of computer and network hardware and operating systems to get our work done and meet our price/performance expectations, but a complex computing environment makes this task difficult.

- *It's even more difficult to get the software to work together.* Today's enterprise is a collection of diverse parts (hopefully!) working smoothly together toward a common goal. We need the same attributes in our software, but different pieces bought by different departments to work on different systems don't speak the same language, and it costs time and money to integrate them.

- *Software development takes too long and costs too much.* Typically, each project starts from scratch. This approach was acceptable when projects were small and relatively simple, but it will not work for large applications that model the enterprise. We need a way to build all of our software on a common foundation, modeled after the assembly line instead of the craftsman, to cut down on time and cost.

Component software is making solutions to these problems possible. Applications are changing; customers are less willing to accept huge, monolithic applications, and are looking for smaller components that they can combine flexibly and dynamically to create tools focused on their particular business needs. And components will work together only if they have been designed and built on **standard interfaces**.

Since interoperability must span the enterprise and even go beyond it to customer and supplier systems, these interfaces must be independent of platforms, operating systems, programming languages, even network protocols; anything less will create "islands of interoperability" insulated from each other by arbitrary technological barriers that keep us from realizing the full benefits of our computing investments.

1.2 The Internet

You're concerned with at least one of the two primary targets for heterogeneous distributed computing, and many companies are concerned with both. The two targets are your company's internal network, which may extend to several continents and be extremely large and complex, and the Internet, with its millions of attached (and relatively unaccounted-for) computers of every type.

The Internet connects computers around the world and allows them to interoperate at three levels: The lowest level provides basic functions such as e-mail and file transfer. The second level features the World Wide Web. And the third level offers program-specific functionality. Which of these levels gives us true interoperability? Let's examine each in turn:

Basic functionality such as file transfer protocol (ftp) and e-mail is undoubtedly useful and important. E-mail may even have a significant effect on your life; it surely does for the authors! But computers can do much more than shuffle letters around, and the interoperability provided by e-mail and FTP is extremely limited compared to the possibilities.

What about the World Wide Web, with its multicolored displays, sound, and even video? Consider this: If you were a computer programmer in the early 1980s, you probably worked with a 3278 terminal (unless you worked with a VT-100, of course). The 3278 displayed uppercase letters only, plus numbers and punctuation, 80 columns across and 24 columns tall, with a status line at the bottom of the screen. These terminals didn't scroll; they displayed a full screen of data and waited for you to press a key to erase everything and display the next full screen. To program for these terminals, you defined fields, which the user filled in by typing and then tabbing from one to the next. When the user had filled in all the fields, he or she pressed "enter" to send the entire screenful of data to your program.

The main difference between this approach and filling in Web forms is that the Web forms appear in color. Sure, now we have animated Java "eye candy" applets in the borders and music to entertain us while we type into a field and tab to the next, 3278-style, in our on-screen shopping cart, but the level of interoperability is limited to what some of us old-timers were getting in 1982. Computing has come a long way since the 1980s, and we deserve better than this!

The bright spot here is program-specific interoperability. By writing a program with a client-side piece and a server-side piece, we can have any degree of interoperability that we want. Some of the most obvious commercial examples on the Internet are computer games, where the client-side software is sold on CD-ROM and the user pays a fee to cover server use, but business applications make up another big part of this segment.

Programs written to this high level of interoperability have a richness of interaction that Web browser displays never achieve, even with their downloadable audio and video. In online computer games, client characters visible in the screen, in full medieval armor, interact with word and sword not only with characters programmed on the server, but also with characters controlled by other remote users through their client programs. In comparable business applications, data displays itself graphically in interactive windows on your computer screen where both local and remote components respond in synch with your mouse clicks and keyboard input.

If the interfaces to these program-specific components could be written in a standard way, and companies agreed to use these interfaces for their programs, then we could extend this level of interoperability from a single program into a whole Internet of programs working together at the highest level of integration that computing can support. And that, it turns out, is what CORBA does, how it does it, and what this book is about.

1.3 Object Technology

What we need is a new way of looking at the entire problem—from problem statement and analysis through solution design and implementation to deployment, use, maintenance, and extension—that integrates every component and takes us in orderly fashion from one step to the next. *Object technology* is this new way, and in this book, we'll begin to see how.

Since object technology is too big a topic for a single book, we'll concentrate on the areas concerned with implementation, where the OMG's contributions provide the most benefit. In this section, we'll discuss the concept of object technology and why it has become the new computing paradigm. But first, let's take a look at how we got here. From the beginning of business computing in the 1950s until desktop computing became well established in the late '80s, computing was such a costly endeavor that programs and systems focused on conserving resources such as memory, persistent storage, and input/output. This approach led to batch-oriented systems that updated periodically instead of continuously, and produced weekly and monthly reports. In many cases, these reports were out of date before they were even printed.

That is, computing focused on the data rather than its uses, and on computing procedures rather than business processes. Computers, not people, were in the driver's seat, and computer users had to translate data to the program's structure on input, and translate back from the program's structure to their needs when they received the output.

1.3.1 Modeling the Real World

Hardware has changed a lot since its early days; in fact, the rapid pace of change sometimes seems like a problem itself. But there's no denying that abundant computing power, memory, storage, and data communications give us an environment where we can mold computing to our needs rather than adapt to it.

In a nutshell, object technology means computing that models the real world. An object in a computer program corresponds to a real object, both to the programmer when he or she implements it, and to the user when he or she creates, manipulates, and uses it. And, computer objects work together to model the interactions of real-world objects. For instance, a storage tank object in a computer-modeled petroleum refinery might be connected through pipe and valve objects to chemical reactor objects, distiller objects, and other refinery components in an integrated application, which, taken as a whole, simulates refinery operation very closely even though no single part represents the entire system.

1.3.2 Dealing with Complexity

Complexity is the word that best describes the problems we're facing today. The simple computing problems have been solved during the past several decades, and companies that can't handle the complex problems are going to fall by the wayside in the future. Fortunately, the tools to deal with these complex problems are available now, and that's what the rest of this book is about.

Generations of problem-solving experience have shown that the best way of dealing with complexity is to split a huge problem into a number of smaller, more manageable parts. But, we have to be careful how we do this, because the wrong split will make our problem more complex instead of simpler. For instance, some approaches split data from functionality; if we started with basically a data problem or a functionality problem, this simplifies our task by letting us focus on the core without distraction from the rest. But if we actually started with an integrated problem, this division leaves us holding only half the clues and half the tools, but still trying to solve the whole thing.

By splitting our computing problem into objects that model the real world, we build on things that are familiar to us. Objects will be easier for customers, analysts, programmers, and users to grasp, and interactions between objects will appear logical and well-founded.

But object orientation does more than give us a real-world model. It also helps solve the three major problems of programming:

- *Programs are difficult to change or extend.* When programs are implemented as discrete objects, many changes will turn out to affect only a single object or a small group of related ones. The "house of cards" problem is reduced or eliminated.

- *Programs are difficult to maintain.* Old-paradigm programs scattered related functionality or data throughout a program, almost guaranteeing that maintenance changes would have far-reaching and unanticipated consequences. By basing our programming on modules formulated on real-world objects, we limit the scope of these unwanted effects.

- *Programs take too long to write.* Well-conceived objects invite reuse, making new programs faster and cheaper to write. Sometimes, objects can be reused as written; in other cases, the objects provide a basis that can be extended. Of course, this advantage isn't evident right away—you need to generate the reusable code before you can benefit from it. But even new project teams benefit from class libraries that provide basic functionality, and more vendor-provided objects are coming on the market every week.

1.4 Object-Oriented Software Integration

The next three sections sum up our object-oriented solution to the software integration problem: First, we'll define a CORBA object; second, we'll look at the basic architecture (that is, CORBA) that allows all of the objects on our system to communicate; and third, we'll examine the higher-level architecture for the objects themselves, which allows applications to communicate—the OMG's Object Management Architecture. The rest of the book builds on this introduction: Chapters 2–22 give details on all three parts; then the example in Chapters 23–36 demonstrates the interoperability solution.

Without a doubt, our ultimate goal is application integration. But, in order to get there, OMG had to solve the interoperability problem first to create a foundation for the work on integration. The OMG's solution is CORBA, and it's described in Chapters 2–9, and illustrated in the tutorial example. The integration solution is a work in progress: The base layer of CORBAservices is described in Chapters 10–18, and the higher-level CORBAfacilities, including the Domain CORBAfacilities, are described in Chapters 19 and 20.

1.4.1 What Is an Object?

Objects are discrete software units—they contain data, and can manipulate it (see Chapter 2 for a more complete definition). Usually, they model real-world objects, although sometimes it's useful to create objects specifically for things we want to compute. Other software units send messages to objects with requests; the objects send other messages back with their responses.

In an enterprise, many objects model real-world entities. For example, an oil company's refinery control program might contain a number of Storage Tank objects. Each of these would know what type of liquid it contains (because it had received this information in a message and stored it), how full it was (perhaps by reading a sensor), and how big it was. In response to a request, the tank could respond by telling what it contained—type of liquid and amount. In a modeling calculation, the tank object could "deliver" the liquid to a pipe or valve object by sending it a message, stopping the flow when it became empty, just like a real tank. And it would probably sound an alarm (by sending a message to an alarm system object) if its fill level exceeded a preset safe level.

Usually objects in the computer are created from a template. For our tank object, the template knows all of the properties that a tank might have: size, location, content type, content amount, connections, and so forth. When we use the template to create a tank object "instance," we place values in the placeholders the template provides in order to make this object represent a particular tank. (In object-speak, this template is termed a *class*.)

The template also knows all the things that a tank can do—that is, the messages that we can send it, and ones that it can send to other objects. Each particular tank object instance that we create has the same set of capabilities.

From the template, we can create as many tank objects as we need or want. Each one has the same set of quantities that it can store, the same set of messages that it will respond to, and the same set of functions that it can perform. What if this template is almost, but not quite, what we need? We can derive a new template from this one using inheritance. (For details, look ahead to Section 2.2.1.2.)

Flexibility is built in, since one of the things an object can do is send messages to other objects. We would expect, for instance, that our tank object would talk to pipe or valve objects, and possibly to sensors that monitor fill level or possibly temperature. Since each tank can connect to its own set of other objects—pipes, valves, sensors—a small set of templates representing these different object types will let us model a refinery of any size and complexity!

A spreadsheet cell is another good example of an object. It contains data: probably a numerical value; perhaps instead some text or a formula. It can perform operations: It can manipulate the data by displaying them on the screen or a printed page, perhaps in a particular font, size, and format; or by performing calculations; and it can deliver its contents on request (perhaps to a linked document). Like many (but not all) objects, there can be many cells, all identical except for contents and address, and each created from the same template.

The spreadsheet program with its loaded spreadsheet data—a collection of objects—is an object itself. The additional operations it can perform include displaying, printing, or formatting ranges of cells, or the entire spreadsheet.

In this book, we won't consider passive collections of data to be objects. That means that your spreadsheet data file, or document data file, are not objects when they're stored on disk. Neither is a CD-ROM disk, nor the files on it. But the spreadsheet data file and document data file become intrinsic parts of objects (or collections of objects) when they are loaded into the programs that manipulate them, and the CD-ROM disk may become the data part of an object when it's loaded into a drive and its data are read into an operating program module. Why this distinction? Because to us, an object is something that can take part in our component software environment, and that means that an object has to be more than just data.

1.4.2 CORBA: Object Interoperability

In order for objects to plug and play together in a useful way, clients have to know exactly what they can expect from every object they might call upon for a service. In CORBA, the services that an object provides are expressed in a contract that serves as the interface between it and the rest of our system. This contract serves two distinct purposes:

- It informs potential clients of the services the object provides and tells them how to construct a message to invoke the service.

- It lets the communications infrastructure know the format of all messages the object will receive and send, allowing the infrastructure to translate data formats where necessary to provide transparent connection between sender and receiver.

Each object needs one more thing: a unique handle that a client can pass to the infrastructure to route a message to it. We're deliberately not calling it an address—object instances keep the same handle when they move from one location to another, as they might do for load-balancing in a heavily used server. Think of the handle as a kind of address with automatic forwarding.

Now we have a complete conceptual picture of our networked computing environment. Each node is an object with a well-defined interface, identified by a unique handle. Messages pass between a sending object and a target object; the target object is identified by its handle, and the message format is defined in an interface known to the system. This information enables the communications infrastructure to take care of all of the details.

1.4.3 And Now, Add Components

With this architecture, we've truly broken down the barriers to interoperability. Any CORBA client on any connected network can access any CORBA object instance regardless of location, platform, operating system, programming language, or even network protocol (since CORBA network messages can bridge from one protocol to another). This is great, but two things are missing: a standard environment that provides the basic services—transactions, security, event-handling, and persistence—that enterprise server applications need; and software distribution technology to enable a multiplatform software marketplace. The CORBA Component Model (CCM) environment fills these needs.

Mission-critical enterprise applications typically run in an environment that is transactional and secure. In addition, they must save their state (including non-transactional variables) to persistent storage, and generate and receive events that are transmitted about the system. Although the CORBAservices provide these functions in a standard way, they do so at such a low level that application-level programmers have found the services somewhat opaque and difficult to use. The CCM packages these four services into a container; CORBA components (which are special CORBA objects that have been programmed to a special style of interface) may be installed into a CORBA component container and access these four services in a simple, nearly automatic way.

Two new declarative languages automate application-building in the CCM. One declares persistent state, while the other handles server structure. Through its infrastructure and these new languages, the CCM packages up the most successful patterns that experienced programmers use to write scalable servers, and makes them accessible to business programmers.

To enable a multiplatform component marketplace, CCM establishes a distribution standard that specifies formats for installation and configuration data in addition to executable program files, allowing vendors to put multiple platform installation files onto a single CD-ROM. Upon installation, the configuration files tell the container which interfaces and events the component provides and which it requires, enabling the container to "connect up" interacting components to each other even though they may have come from different vendors. You can even assemble applications using a combination of CORBA Components and Enterprise JavaBeans (EJB), because these two component varieties have been designed to work together.

These simple yet powerful concepts provide the foundation for CORBA's component software revolution. The interfaces are expressed in OMG Interface Definition Language—OMG IDL—making them accessible to objects written in virtually any programming language, and the cross-platform communications architecture is the Common Object Request Broker Architecture—CORBA. The CCM container provides support for the application builder, and the distribution format enables a multiplatform software marketplace.

1.4.4 The OMA: Application-Level Integration

CORBA is a great accomplishment but it connects only objects, not applications. Enterprise integration requires a lot more integration, and OMG provides it in the OMA (Figure 1.1). Of course, it's based on CORBA, but this is just a starting point.

The Object Management Architecture embodies OMG's vision for the component software environment. One of the organization's earliest products, this architecture shows how standardization of component interfaces will penetrate up to—although not into—application objects in order to create a plug-and-play component software environment based on object technology. Application objects, although not standardized by OMG, will access CORBAservices and CORBAfacilities through standard interfaces to provide benefits to both providers and end users: for providers, lower development costs and an expanded market base; for end users, a lower-cost software environment that can easily be configured to their company's specific needs.

Based on the CORBA architecture we just discussed, the OMA specifies a set of standard interfaces and functions for each object. Different vendor implementations of the interfaces and their functionality then plug-and-play on customer networks, allowing integration of additional functionality from purchased modules or in-house development.

The OMA is divided into two major components: lower-level CORBAservices and intermediate-level CORBAfacilities.

The CORBAservices provide basic functionality that almost any object might need: object lifecycle services such as move and copy, naming and directory services, and other basics. Basic does not necessarily mean simple, however; included in this category are object-oriented access to online transaction processing (OLTP, the mainstream

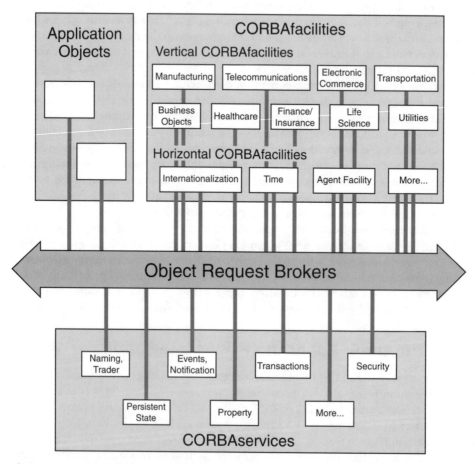

Figure 1.1   OMG's Object Management Architecture. Each service (boxes) is composed of a number of CORBA objects, each accessed by a standard IDL interface. Clients access all services through the Object Request Broker.

application for business accounting) and a sophisticated object trader service—kind of a "yellow pages" where objects advertise the availability (and price!) of their services. The Trader Service has the potential to revolutionize distributed computing. (See Chapter 12 for details.)

Where the CORBAservices provide services for objects, the CORBAfacilities provide services for applications. For instance, the Patient Identifier Service (PIDS) Domain CORBAfacility gives applications a standard way to match a patient's identity information with entries in any one of a healthcare provider's patient databases. Implemented with a variety of matching algorithms on an array of databases, PIDS enables any CORBA-based application to request and receive a match, with the flexibility that today's business environment demands.

It is the CORBAfacilities that give meaning to our promise of application integration. The CORBAfacilities architecture has two major components: one horizontal, including facilities such as the print facility, which can be used by virtually every business; and the other vertical or domain-oriented, standardizing management of information specialized to particular industry groups. So large is the scope of this effort that the CORBAfacilities—especially the Domain facilities—will eventually dwarf CORBA and the CORBAservices in size. However, OMG does not produce the CORBAfacility standards all by itself. The organization has put in place procedures to incorporate other consortia standards as CORBAfacilities as long as they conform to the rest of the OMA. Industries such as healthcare, finance, and others are participating now; for details, look ahead to Chapters 19 and 20.

1.5 CORBA Benefits

So, why move to CORBA and the OMA? Here's a summary of the benefits from two points of view: First, for your developers—the people who design and produce your applications; and second, for your users—not just the people who run your applications (and your business!), but also your business itself, for it is a user in its own right, with its own complex set of requirements.

1.5.1 For Your Developers

For developers, there are many reasons to move to CORBA. For example:

CORBA is the only environment that lets you take advantage of all the tools you've bought, from hardware to development software: There's a reason for all of that diversity in the marketplace (and probably around your company as well)—different tools are tuned for different jobs, and it's not practical to limit your choices in the face of limited budgets, high expectations, and competition hot on your heels. You need an architecture that can run on every hardware platform and network, and an interoperability architecture that links every programming language from Java and C++ through COBOL and Ada to almost every other, including productivity-building interactive development tools.

The object-oriented paradigm meshes with software "best practice" from the start of the development cycle to the end: Object-oriented analysis and design in the beginning stages, implemented in object-oriented languages and object-oriented databases using object-oriented user interfaces, deployed in a distributed object environment.

Give them an IDL interface and a thin layer of wrapper code, and legacy applications come into the CORBA environment on an equal basis with your new software components: Since you have to keep your business going full speed while you bring in distributed computing and object orientation, this is essential to enabling enterprises to make the transition.

The CORBA/Components/OMA environment maximizes programmer productivity: CORBA provides a sophisticated base, with transparent distribution and easy access to objects around your network. Drop your objects into a CCM container and they find each other, connect up, and work in the secure, transactional environment that business software needs in today's networked world. Use standardized, off-the-shelf Domain objects and components as the foundation for your application, and let your developers create or assemble application objects for them, taking advantage of all of the components available on the network.

This standard CORBA/OMA environment provides three advantages:

- Your programmers don't have to build the tools; they're provided for you.

- The same set of CORBAservices and CORBAfacilities is available with every CORBA environment, so both your applications and your programmers port from one platform or ORB to another.

- Interoperability results because clients on one platform know how to invoke standard operations on objects on any other platform.

Code reuse comes into play in two ways: First, components get reused as-is in new or dynamically reconfigured applications; and second, your programmers can build new objects by making incremental modifications to existing ones without having to recode the parts that already work. Since these build on what you already have, the boost from reuse starts out small but snowballs as libraries of components and code accumulate. Experience shows, companies that code for reuse realize savings of 50 to 80 percent after a few projects' library-building.

Prior to CORBA components, one barrier to reuse was the "tweaking" or adjusting that every piece of software seems to need when it's moved from one application to the next. CORBA components are, therefore, *configurable*—written to be flexible, and configured at installation time for different environments. The new standard provides interfaces for visual configuration tools, with settings that can be modified at different stages of development, installation, and runtime.

You can mix and match tools within a project—develop a desktop component using an interactive builder, for instance, while you write its server module in a lower-level language like C++. CORBA will allow the two to interoperate smoothly.

1.5.2 For Your Users and Your Company

You need to solve the entire integration problem in order to survive, but you also need to devote maximum resources to widening your technological edge in order to compete. There's only one way to do this: Use industry standards to get your company onto the playing field quickly and inexpensively; then devote the resources you saved toward building an edge that beats your competition hands-down.

For your users, a CORBA/OMA application is a dynamic collection of client and object implementation components, configured and connected at runtime to attack the problem at hand. It may include and integrate:

- Components located in different departments or divisions.

- Components located both inside and outside your enterprise, including sites of customers, suppliers, and service providers.

- Components from multiple software vendors.

- Components from both in-house developers and outside vendors.

- Components embedded in other elements—automated production facilities or monitoring systems in the enterprise; TVs, VCRs, and alarm systems in the home.

- Additional types of components, all working together in an integrated way.

By the time you or your programmers have finished the example in this book, you will (depending on which or how many CORBA environments you complete) be able to demonstrate many of these integration modes and benefits for yourself!

There are many reasons—some good, some unavoidable—you might have to integrate such diverse platforms. For instance, in most companies, office desktops run PC- or Apple-compatible architectures, while technical and engineering desktops run open-systems workstations; the integration problem from this involves (at least) two or three operating systems and two networks. Many companies are just now trying to integrate equipment acquired by different departments or divisions over the past few decades, chosen with no consideration for ease of possible integration down the road (that is, now). And other enterprises have to integrate hardware and software from companies that they acquire during the course of their own business.

You will have to integrate these diverse platforms and systems, because you need them all in order to run your business at a price you can afford. And you will have to solve the complexity problem in order to survive, because some of your competitors will, and your company's future depends on your doing it better and faster than they do.

1.6 What Is the OMG?

The Object Management Group is a consortium of computing-involved companies. Its 800-plus members include most of the major systems and software vendors from around the world, as well as independent software vendors, consulting companies, and an increasing number of end-user companies primarily involved in setting specifications for the vertical CORBAfacilities. OMG is an international organization, with one-third of its members coming from outside the United States, most from Europe, but about 5 percent from other countries, chiefly in the Asian Pacific Rim, but also including Australia, Africa, and South America.

Unlike some other consortia, the OMG does not produce software—only specifications. The specifications are freely available for any company (OMG member or not) to implement; explicit permission is not required. Implementations have already come from more than 70 companies or institutions (since many universities and research labs, as well as commercial companies, produce ORBs). The numerous ORBs in this book, and the dozens more not included here, demonstrate that this expectation is already a reality.

Members of the OMG meet five times a year to advance the standards process. Task forces reporting to the OMG Platform and Domain technical committees (TCs) write and issue Requests For Proposals (RFPs), requirements documents for each standard. Responding companies, which must be members of the OMG at the contributing, platform, or domain level, submit their software specifications for consideration. A period of time is allowed for member evaluation and revision of submissions. Sometimes, revisions target requirements that were not met; other times, different submitters merge proposals where differences were found to be minor or resolved easily. A voting process moving successively through the task force, technical committee, and finally, the OMG Board of Directors declares the successful proposal an official OMG specification. Along the way, an Architecture Board certifies that the new specification is consistent with the OMG's architecture and existing suite of specifications.

This process is noteworthy because it drives all of the participating companies toward consensus. Although submitting companies tend to work individually or in small groups at the beginning of the specification process, by the end, they are typically working in concert, concentrating on the production of a final specification that will withstand the scrutiny of all of their peers in the task force and technical committee. As a result, published OMG specifications tend to bear the names of many submitting companies; for example, the original CORBA specification was a consensus submission from six companies, and the first set of CORBAservices was cosubmitted by eleven.

The companies that submit the successful proposal must market a commercial implementation within a year. This requirement serves both to keep companies' proposals realistic, and to ensure that OMG specifications become a reality in the marketplace. In fact, it is market opportunity, and not this requirement, that leads to many companies, not just submitters, getting compliant products to market as quickly as they can.

The OMG is an open organization, and welcomes any company to join. Prospective members frequently attend a meeting as guests to find out firsthand about the benefits of membership. For information on how to contact the OMG, see Appendix A.

CHAPTER

2

Technical Overview

2.1 Introduction

This chapter introduces all of the important OMA- and CORBA-related concepts, the benefits of each, and the total benefit that accrues when all work together to provide true intra-enterprise and inter-enterprise distributed computing. The first section presents the big picture, introducing all of the components and how they interconnect. Subsequent sections fill in key details. Although the presentation here is more technical than Chapter 1, it does not include programming aspects. For these, continue with Chapters 3 through 22, which examine the CORBA architecture and the OMA one component at a time.

WHAT'S NEW AT OMG: UML, CORBA 3, AND THE OMA

There's a lot new at OMG since the first edition of this book. CORBA 3 is the development that gets the most attention, but there are two other important development areas: One is the CORBAdomains, specifications in vertical markets such as healthcare and telecommunications, which now constitute half of OMG members' efforts and arrive on the scene at the rate of a dozen new specifications each year. The other area concentrates in Analysis and Design with three specifications so far: The Unified Modeling Language (UML), the Meta-Object Facility (MOF), and XML Metadata Interchange (XMI).

CORBA 3, the first major addition to the Common Object Request Broker Architecture (CORBA) from OMG since the IIOP protocol added interoperability in 1996, was officially released as this book went to press, allowing us to use primarily adopted specifications but also some final submissions as sources (CORBA Component Model and the new Persistent State Service, just adopted as we went to press in early 2000, fall into this last category). The heading *CORBA 3* actually refers to a suite of specifications which, taken together, add a new dimension of capability and ease of use to CORBA. In this sidebar, we list the parts of CORBA 3 and tell a little about each one. As we touch each one, we give the chapter and section where we discuss it in this book, and give the URL where information was available for it on the OMG Web site as we went to press. (In the rest of this book, we've put references in Appendix A, but in this sidebar, we'll embed the URLs in the text so you can read and surf with minimal page-flipping. In addition, all of the CORBA specifications, including CORBA 3, are included on the CD-ROM that accompanies this book.) After we've finished summarizing CORBA 3, we'll give pointers to the new Domain specifications and some new CORBAservice developments.

Here are some other Web pages with CORBA 3 information: First, a summary we wrote for the OMG Web site appears at www.omg.org/news/pr98/compnent.html. While CORBA 3 is new, we'll keep this article and its embedded URLs up to date so you can use it to find the specification for any part of CORBA 3. (It is, in a sense, this sidebar with continually updated URLs.) When CORBA 3 is established and no longer "news," the specification will still appear on the OMG's Web site, but without the banners and exclamation points; just follow the "CORBA/IIOP" link on the left-hand column of the OMG homepage, about halfway down the page, to find it. Second, this book's Web page will also maintain a pointer to the current version of CORBA 3, so check us out at www.omg.org/library/corfun/corfun.html.

Introduction to CORBA 3

The specifications included in the designation CORBA 3 divide into three major categories:

- Java and Internet Integration
- Quality of Service Control
- The CORBA Component Model

In this sidebar, we'll cover them in that order:

1. Java and Internet Integration

Three specifications enhance CORBA integration with the increasingly popular language Java, and the Internet:

Java-to-IDL Mapping

CORBA 3 adds a Java-to-IDL mapping to the "normal" IDL-to-Java mapping that you're familiar with if you've done any CORBA programming. This new mapping defines IDL interfaces for Java objects, with two effects: It lets Java programmers use the OMG standard protocol IIOP for their remote invocations, and it allows Java servers to be invoked by CORBA clients written in any CORBA-supported programming language. Since Enterprise JavaBeans (EJB) are based on this specification, EJBs interoperate on the wire using IIOP.

This specification comprises two documents: a main part at www.omg.org/cgi-bin/doc?orbos/98-04-04, plus an erratum at www.omg.org/cgi-bin/doc?orbos/98-03-16. A maintenance revision, not voted as we went to press, appears at www.omg.org/cgi-bin/doc?ptc/99-03-09. We discuss this new specification in Chapter 8, Section 4.

Firewall Specification

The CORBA 3 Firewall Specification defines transport-level firewalls, application-level firewalls, and (perhaps most interesting) a bidirectional GIOP connection useful for callbacks and event notifications.

Transport-level firewalls work at the TCP level. By defining (courtesy of IANA) well-known ports 683 for IIOP and 684 for IIOP over SSL, the specification allows administrators to configure firewalls to cope with CORBA traffic over the IIOP protocol. There is also a specification for CORBA over SOCKS.

In CORBA, objects frequently need to call back or notify the client that invoked them; for this, the objects act as clients and the client-side module instantiates an object that is called back in a reverse-direction invocation. Because standard CORBA connections carry invocations only one way, a callback typically requires the establishment of a second TCP connection for this traffic heading in the other direction, which is a no-no to virtually every firewall in existence. Under the new specification, an IIOP connection is allowed to carry invocations in the reverse direction under certain restrictive conditions that don't compromise the security at either end of the connection.

The Firewall Specification comprises two documents: www.omg.org/cgi-bin/doc?orbos/98-05-04 and an erratum, www.omg.org/cgi-bin/doc?orbos/98-07-04. We present the Firewall Specification in Chapter 14.

Interoperable Naming Service

The CORBA object reference is a cornerstone of the architecture. Because the computer-readable IOR was (until this specification) the only way to reach an instance and invoke it, there was no way to reach a remote instance—even if you knew its location and that it was up and running—unless you could get access to its object reference. The easiest way to do that was to get a reference to its Naming Service, but what if you didn't have a reference for even that?

The Interoperable Naming Service (INS) defines one URL-format object reference, corbaloc, that can be typed into a program to reach defined services at a remote location, including the Naming Service. A second URL format, corbaname, actually invokes the remote Naming Service using the name that the user appends to the URL, and retrieves the IOR of the named object.

For example, a corbaloc identifier

corbaloc://www.omg.org/NameService

would resolve to the CORBA Naming Service running on the machine whose IP address corresponded to the domain name www.omg.org (if we had a Name Server running here at OMG).

The URL for the Interoperable Naming Service Specification is //www.omg.org/cgi-bin/doc?orbos/98-10-11.

We discuss the INS in Chapter 11, Section 2.3.

2. Quality of Service Control
Asynchronous Messaging and Quality of Service Control

If every computer in the world were powerful enough to keep its queues short all the time, and every network had the speed and bandwidth to transmit your requests instantly, we wouldn't need Quality of Service (QoS) control—every invocation would execute at the highest possible QoS regardless of its setting. However, queues fill up, networks become congested, and clients (and users!) end up waiting for "instant" response from your servers. If it's your network or server that's filling up, you might want to assign the highest priorities to the customers who spend the most money, or to your biggest accounts, or whatever. CORBA 3 defines a number of specifications that allow you to do this.

Policies defined by the Asynchronous Invocation and Messaging Specification allow control of Quality of Service of invocations. Clients and objects may control ordering (by time, priority, or deadline); set priority, deadlines, and time-to-live; set a start time and end time for time-sensitive invocations; and control routing policy and network routing hop count.

This new specification also defines a number of asynchronous and time-independent invocation modes for CORBA, and allows both static and dynamic invocations to use every mode. Asynchronous invocations' results may be retrieved by either polling or callback, with the choice made by the form used by the client in the original invocation.

The URL for the this specification is www.omg.org/cgi-bin/doc?orbos/98-05-05. We discuss this new specification in Chapter 6, Sections 6.4, 6.5, and 6.6.

Minimum, Fault-Tolerant, and Real-Time CORBA

Minimum CORBA is primarily intended for embedded systems. Embedded systems, once they are finalized and burned into chips for production, are fixed and their interactions with the outside network are predictable—they have no need for the dynamic aspects of CORBA, such as the Dynamic Invocation Interface or the Interface Repository that supports it, which are therefore not included in Minimum CORBA. The URL for the Minimum CORBA specification is www.omg.org/cgi-bin/doc?orbos/98-08-04.

Real-Time CORBA standardizes resource control—threads, protocols, connections, and so on—using priority models to achieve predictable behavior for both hard and statistical real-time environments. Departing from the absolute transparency that has characterized CORBA since its inception, Real-Time CORBA allows client and object control of communications including dedicated connections, priority-banded connections, and choice of network protocol. Dynamic scheduling, not a part of the current specification, is being added via a separate RFP. The URL for the Real-Time CORBA specification is www.omg.org/cgi-bin/doc?orbos/99-02-12; an erratum is www.omg.org/cgi-bin/ doc?orbos/99-03-29.

Fault-tolerance for CORBA is being addressed by an RFP, currently in process, for a standard based on entity redundancy and fault management control. The URL for all information on this RFP is:

www.omg.org/techprocess/meetings/schedule/Fault_Tolerance_RFP.html.

We discuss Real-Time CORBA in Chapter 6. We haven't included a section on Minimum CORBA because it's devoted to a specialized market, and we omitted Fault-Tolerant CORBA because the specification wasn't ready when we went to press.

3. CORBA components Package

CORBA Objects Passable by Value

Termed *valuetypes*, objects passable by value add a new dimension to the CORBA architecture, which previously supported passing and invocation only by reference. Like conventional CORBA objects, these entities have state and methods; unlike CORBA objects, they do not (typically) have object references and are invoked in-process as programming language objects. It is only when they are included in parameter lists of CORBA invocations that they show their talent of packaging up their state in the sending context, sending it over the wire to the receiving context, creating a running instance of the object there, and populating it with the transmitted state. Frequently used to represent nodes in binary trees or cyclically linked lists, valuetypes have been specified and implemented to faithfully represent these important constructs.

Mentioned here because of its use in the CORBA Component Model, the valuetype specification is actually part of the CORBA 2.3 release and may be downloaded from www.omg.org/library/c2indx.html, where it comprises Chapters 5 and 6 of CORBA 2.3.

The CORBA Component Model (CCM)

One of the most exciting developments to come out of OMG since the IIOP protocol defined CORBA 2, the CORBA Component Model (CCM) represents a multipronged advance with benefits for programmers, users, and consumers of component software. The three major parts of the CCM are:

- A container environment that packages transactionality, security, and persistence, and provides interface and event resolution
- Integration with Enterprise JavaBeans
- A software distribution format that enables a CORBA component software marketplace

The CCM container environment is persistent, transactional, and secure. For the programmer, these functions are prepackaged and provided at a higher level of abstraction than the CORBAservices provide. This leverages the skills of business programmers who are not necessarily skilled at building transactional or secure applications, who can now use their talents to produce business applications that acquire these necessary attributes automatically.

Containers know the event types emitted and consumed by the component they contain, and provide event channels to carry events. The containers also keep track of interfaces provided and used by the components they contain, and connect one to another where they fit. The CCM supports multiple interfaces, and the architecture supports navigation among them.

CORBA components and Enterprise JavaBeans (EJBs) are designed to work with each other. EJBs are Java-language basic level CORBA components, and applications can be built up from any combination of EJBs and CORBA components. Unlike EBJs, of course, CORBA components can be written in multiple languages and support multiple interfaces.

The specification defines a multiplatform software distribution format, including an installer and XML-based configuration tool, and a separate Scripting specification will map CORBA and component assembly to a number of established scripting languages.

As we go to press, the CORBA Component Model has just been completed and is under final vote at OMG; members expect a quick approval. The main documents under vote are

www.omg.org/cgi-bin/doc?orbos/99-07-01

www.omg.org/cgi-bin/doc?orbos/99-07-02

www.omg.org/cgi-bin/doc?orbos/99-07-03

Our main discussion of the CCM is in Chapter 5, Sections 5.4 through 5.6.

What's New in the Object Management Architecture?

There's so much new in CORBA 3 that you might think that OMG members couldn't spare the time or effort for another major development, but you'd be wrong. Organizationally, OMG divides into two parts: Platform and Domain. While the Platform (or infrastructure) side was working on CORBA 3, the Domain side was taking shape (it was constituted in early 1996) and expanding so quickly that, as we finished up this edition in late 1999, it was equal to the Platform side in number of members and turning out specifications at the rate of a dozen or more per year. With Task Forces in Business Objects, Telecommunications, Manufacturing, Healthcare, Transportation, Finance, Electronic Commerce, and Utilities, OMG's Domain members are rapidly populating the Domain Facilities part of the Object Management Architecture.

We describe the new structure of OMG in Chapter 19, and describe a sample of Domain specifications in Chapter 20.

What about the CORBAservices and CORBAfacilities? There's a new release of the Persistent State Service that we describe in Chapter 17, and a new Print Management Facility that we mention in Chapter 15 but don't cover in detail. For Business Object people, there's the start of a new Business Object facility supported by three RFPs that you can find at these URLs:

www.omg.org/techprocess/meetings/schedule/UML_Profile_for_EDOC_RFP.html

www.omg.org/techprocess/meetings/schedule/UML_Profile_for_CORBA_RFP.html

www.omg.org/techprocess/meetings/schedule/UML_Textual_Notation_RFP.html

The envisioned Business Object Facility will be based on UML and the CCM, and so could not take shape until the CORBA Component Model Specification was released. Unfortunately, that means that we did not have enough information to describe it in this book.

Analysis and Design Support

Wait, there's more: Analysis and design experts have been working on standards at OMG also, and have come up with three important ones so far. Their major contribution is the Unified Modeling Language (UML), which standardizes model expression. Also in this area are the Meta-Object Facility (MOF) and XML Metadata Interchange (XMI). Cris Kobryn, one of the authors of UML, describes this language's structure and features in Chapter 21, and Sridhar Iyengar, an author of the MOF and XMI specifications, describes these in Chapter 22. The UML specification is on the Web at www.omg.org/cgi-bin/doc?ad/99-06-09. The URL for the MOF specification is www.omg.org/cgi-bin/doc?ad/99-09-04, and for XMI it is ftp://ftp.omg.org/pub/docs/ad/98-10-07.zip. These UML, MOF, and XMI specifications are also included on this book's CD-ROM.

2.2 CORBA and the OMA

Figure 2.1 shows a request passing from a client to an object implementation in the CORBA architecture. Two aspects of this architecture stand out:

■ Both client and object implementation are isolated from the Object Request Broker (ORB) by an IDL interface. CORBA requires that every object's interface be expressed in OMG IDL. Clients see only the object's interface, never any implementation detail. This guarantees substitutability of the implementation behind the interface—our plug-and-play software environment. And, on the server side, it allows ORBs to be engineered for scalability.

■ The request does not pass directly from client to object implementation; instead, every request is passed to the client's local ORB, which manages it. The standard form of the CORBA object invocation is *location transparent*; that is, its form is the same whether the target object is local (in the same process, or at least in the same memory space) or remote. This simplifies your programming, since object location has almost no effect at the application level—effects show primarily at the systems management level, where they belong. In CORBA 2, this was the whole story. However, because business and computing realities sometimes require greater client control of resources, CORBA 3 provides several different services that expose remoteness to your application, each with its own invocation format: objects passable by value, client control of quality of service, asynchronous and time-independent invocation modes, and detailed control allowed in real-time environments. We'll discuss all of these services as we work our way through this book.

Regardless of the mode and form of the invocation, distribution details remain in the ORB where they are handled by software you bought, not software you built. Application code, no longer required to manage distribution details, concentrates on the problem at hand.

It takes more than a flexible request-passing mechanism to build an enterprise-spanning object-based distributed computing system. If, in addition, all components

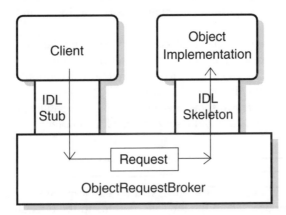

Figure 2.1 A request passing from client to object implementation.

share a common architecture and set of standard IDL interfaces, the resulting system achieves a coherence and synergy that provides many benefits. To the enterprise, the common architecture makes possible a unified enterprise computing environment composed of interoperating components from multiple vendors and inhouse developers; to vendors, it provides quick passage from the building of basic components to product differentiation through value-added features and functionality.

OMG's CORBA Component Model (CCM) and Object Management Architecture (OMA, Figure 1.1) define this common architecture. The OMA defines multiple levels of standard services provided by CORBA objects (and, in the future, components) with standard IDL interfaces: a basic level of CORBAservices, including the persistence, transaction, event handling, and security services, and above it the CORBAfacilities and Domain facilities. Building on this, the CCM standardizes a persistent, transactional, event-handling, secure development and runtime environment. In the container, components discover and connect to each other, working together as an application with more functionality than any of the components individually. (For more on CORBA components, look ahead to Section 2.7.3.)

The first thing we do in this chapter is go over the characteristics of a CORBA object. Then we examine the role of the IDL interface, not only because it enables our modular software environment, but also because the ORB uses IDL in its operation. We'll learn details about the ORB next. Then we'll put the two together and see how the combination of IDL interfaces and ORB infrastructure combine to give the benefits of the basic CORBA architecture.

With this part of the plumbing in place, before we cover CORBA 3 additions, we'll cover the Object Management Architecture (OMA) that builds on these basics, since several of the CORBAservices are packaged up and served to components as part of the CCM environment. We cover CORBA 3 additions last. You'll find this a satisfying way of pulling the entire environment together into a coherent picture.

2.2.1 What Is a CORBA Object?

In Section 1.3.1, we defined objects in a general way. Here we'll go further, and examine the characteristics that let a software module plug-and-play as an object in the CORBA environment. There are four keys: **encapsulation**, **inheritance**, **polymorphism**, and **instantiation**.

In the original CORBA specification, every CORBA object was passed by reference. CORBA 3 adds a new type of object, an object passable by value, termed a valuetype. Valuetypes adhere to the key principles of OO similar to the way that conventional CORBA objects do; we fill in details about valuetypes in Chapter 3.

A CORBA component is a CORBA object with some very nice extended capabilities. We review their basic architecture in Section 2.7.3, but reserve details for Chapter 5.

2.2.1.1 Encapsulation

Encapsulation enables plug-and-play software. An encapsulated software module consists of two distinct parts: its interface, which the module presents to the outside world; and its implementation, which it keeps private. The interface represents a contract or promise by the object: If a client sends the object one of the messages specified in the interface, with the proper input arguments in their agreed-upon formats, the object will provide the response message with the results in their proper places. How the response was calculated or produced and the results placed into their proper places in the return message is of concern only to the object itself; the client is not allowed to examine the process, nor to obtain any additional information.

If we have more than one implementation of an object with the same interface—written in a different programming language, for instance, or using a different database or file format for its persistent storage—we could substitute one for another on our system. A client would neither know nor care, since the responses to its messages would not change. This substitutability is the key to our component software environment.

Encapsulation also enables CORBA to provide server-side scalability. Once the server-side ORB accepts a client's invocation, it can do anything it needs to provide robust service without disturbing the client's view of the classic object always "at your service." Supported by the Portable Object Adapter specification (POA, Chapter 5) and the CCM, ORBs provide load balancing, redundancy, and flexible resource management, enabling CORBA applications to handle Internet and enterprise load levels. What about CORBA components and encapsulation? Components work together using standardized IDL interfaces, so encapsulation is not broken. In fact, encapsulation is the principle that makes components work.

Encapsulation is enough to make our environment modular, but not object oriented. We can substitute equivalent encapsulated implementations, and move them around the network almost at will. However, in order to benefit from object-oriented software engineering and development concepts, we also need inheritance, polymorphism, and instantiation.

2.2.1.2 Inheritance

Sometimes, we can create a new object template more easily by adapting an existing one than by creating it from scratch. For instance, a department manager object is an employee object that knows which department it manages. **Inheritance** is the object-oriented concept that allows us to actually create the manager object template from the employee template in this way.

Inheritance saves designers and programmers a lot of work, since existing object templates can serve as the basis for new ones. It requires forethought, though, since inheritance works better when the fundamental objects are constructed with these extensions in mind. Object-oriented languages like C++ and Smalltalk have inheritance built in, and object-oriented design tools take advantage of it whenever they can, so CORBA includes it too. There's a key difference between the inheritance in C++ and Smalltalk, which is *implementation inheritance*, compared to CORBA inheritance in IDL, which is *interface inheritance*. We'll bring out the technical differences between these two types of inheritance as we fill in details about IDL and its programming language mappings in Chapters 3, 7, 8, and 9.

2.2.1.3 *Polymorphism*

Some operations naturally belong to more than one kind of object. For instance, you would expect to be able to invoke the draw operation on just about any graphics object—a square, or circle, or line, or whatever—and have it draw itself on a screen or a printer. But the client invoking the same operation on a set of objects actually results in different things happening, since each object has its own methods, which get executed when it receives the order to draw itself. Moreover, if we added a new graphics object to our program—a house, let's say—our client would already know how to draw it: just send it the message draw, and it draws itself! This is **polymorphism**.

2.2.1.4 *Instantiation*

Of the OO principles we're covering here, this is the one you may not see in other texts but we believe that it belongs in this group. We said, back in Chapter 1, that object-oriented computing is computing that models the real world and, to do this, we're going to use individual CORBA objects in our computer to represent individual real-world objects. That is, each paper sales order that a salesman writes becomes an individual, running, CORBA object in our computer; and each fighter plane or tank in our military simulation is a CORBA object, acting on its own but interacting, through its IDL interfaces, with the other objects in the simulation. In the new world of Internet commerce, the electronic shopping cart is a good candidate for representation as a CORBA object: It has state—that is, it remembers what we put into it, and who its owner is, and it does things—it accepts items into itself, or allows them to be removed, and carries out the "checkout" process that completes a sale. In our electronic storefront, our system can **instantiate** a cart for each customer as he or she starts to shop.

Many aspects of CORBA support this use: Its basis is the object reference—the system gives each running instance its own unique object reference, and the Naming Service lets us keep track of them all in a directory-like structure, so this is a natural way to program. The POA and Persistent State Service (Chapters 5 and 17) complete the picture. **Instantiation** is the name we give to this process of creating a new, individual object instance for each real-world counterpart.

Clearly, there are some CORBA objects where it makes sense to use instantiation and create new instances at a user's bidding (shopping carts, sales orders, document objects), and others where it does not (your company's main accounting system, running on the mainframe in Tulsa).

2.2.1.5 *Summary*

These four key characteristics of object orientation play different roles in CORBA. Encapsulation is the cornerstone. By itself, it enables plug-and-play modular software and location transparency. It is also the concept that comes into play when you wrap a legacy application in OMG IDL so it can be accessed from your CORBA clients. Instantiation, which lets us model the sets of real-world objects that we use in our business, comes next. In a sense, these are user-level tools (and your user does, in a very real sense, instantiate object instances directly). In contrast, inheritance and polymorphism are programmer tools: they help CORBA work with object-oriented tools and languages; some analysis and design tools use them automatically, as do object-oriented languages like C++ and Smalltalk. So they're built into OMG IDL, but you don't have to use them in order for your software to plug-and-play in the CORBA environment.

What about *scalability*? Since these concepts deal with objects one at a time, this topic hasn't come up, but it's the difference between success and failure to enterprise and Internet applications. CORBA has a great story here, too, but it's not built using only these four concepts (although they provide the foundation, to be sure). We discuss it, without getting too technical, in this chapter in Section 2.5 on Server Scalability and Section 2.7.3 on the CCMs, give details in Section 5.3 on the Portable Object Adapter, and give technical details on CORBA components in Sections 5.4 through 5.6.

2.2.2 OMG IDL

In CORBA, an object's interface is defined in OMG IDL—Interface Definition Language. The interface definition specifies the operations the object is prepared to perform, the input and output parameters required, and any exceptions that may be generated along the way. This interface constitutes a contract with clients of the object, who use the same interface definition to build and dispatch invocations as the object implementation uses to receive and respond. Client and object implementation are then isolated by at least three parts of the basic CORBA architecture: an IDL stub on the client end, an ORB (or several, as we shall see later, if we are interoperating with a remote system), and a corresponding IDL skeleton on the object implementation end. This isolation provides a great deal of flexibility, and many benefits.

Now you can see how CORBA enforces encapsulation: Clients can only access an object as defined by its IDL interface; there is no way in the architecture to get around the interface and access the implementation directly.

Contrast this approach to invocation of objects in programming languages. C++ clients call C++ objects directly: The "interface" consists of C++ statements that invoke methods on the objects. Similarly, Smalltalk clients invoke methods on Smalltalk objects directly through Smalltalk statements. This approach, although straightforward, does not have the flexibility of CORBA: There is no standard way, for example, for a C++ client to invoke a method on a Smalltalk object, or vice versa.

The CORBA architecture separates the interface, written in OMG IDL, from the implementation, which must be written in some programming language. To the client or user, the interface represents a *promise*: When the client sends a proper message to the interface, the response will come back. To the object implementor, the interface represents an *obligation*: He or she must implement, in some programming language, all of the operations specified in the interface. Writing the contract (in OMG IDL) and fulfilling it (in a programming language such as C++, Java, or Smalltalk) are usually two separate steps in the writing of a CORBA application, although some ORB environments generate IDL automatically from your programming language file in various languages. This "reverse mapping" is not a standard for most languages, but OMG has specified the IDL and stub that correspond to an Java RMI object. We present this reverse Java mapping in the last section of Chapter 8.

By the way, OMG IDL is also an ISO and ITU-T standard; in fact, we write it OMG/ISO IDL when we're being precise. The ISO standard number is 14750, and it corresponds to the IDL specified in CORBA 2.2. For a copy of the ISO document (which you'll have to pay for, unlike the OMG specifications which you can download free from our Web site), point your browser to www.iso.ch/cate/d25486.html. In ITU-T, OMG IDL is Recommendation X.920; you can order it at www.itu.int/itudoc/itu-t/rec/x/x500up/x920.html.

2.3 Building a CORBA Object

Let's say we're going to build a new CORBA object. The first thing we do is figure out (by performing an analysis and design using a UML-based tool, if we're following good programming practice) exactly what it's going to do. We'll skip that part here, since our object in this chapter is hypothetical, but we do want to point out that analysis and design is a crucial step for the success of your object-oriented project. (To learn about the Universal Modeling Language [UML], OMG's standard for Analysis and Design model representation, look ahead to Chapter 21; to see the analysis and design for the example in this book, take a look at Chapter 24.)

Since this is a CORBA object, the next thing we need to do is define its interface in OMG IDL. The IDL interface specifies all of the operations the object is going to perform, their input and output parameters and return values, and interface-specific exceptions that may be generated. Chapter 3 describes OMG IDL in more detail, including object-oriented aspects such as inheritance. The IDL file for the example worked in this book appears in Chapter 26.

By the way, there wouldn't be much difference if we were building an object from an existing legacy application instead of starting from scratch. Most of our program would already be written, but we'd still have to generate an IDL interface to represent the module's functions, and code a thin "wrapper" to connect our IDL layer to the legacy app.

2.3.1 Making Choices

Notice that, although we have fixed the functionality and syntax for invoking our object, we have not fixed any other aspect at this point. Specifically, we have not yet fixed:

- The programming language we will use to implement it
- The platform or operating system it will run on
- The ORB it will connect to
- Whether it will run local to its clients or remotely
- The network hardware or protocol it will use, if remote
- Other aspects including, for example, security levels and provisions

The flexibility remaining is a major benefit of the CORBA standard. The CORBA architecture allows these important choices to be postponed until later stages of the development process. Although the choice of programming language will happen very early (in fact, that's the next step), the interoperability built in to CORBA allows the selection of local or remote access and network protocol to be postponed until runtime. In this chapter, we point out the decisions that focus on our specific implementation environment.

Even though these important aspects remain undetermined, we already have all the information we need to construct a client of the object. In CORBA, all a client developer needs to know is the IDL interface definition and the description of what the object does. This is how CORBA and IDL enable our plug-and-play component software environment. At runtime, only one other piece of information will be needed to invoke a method on the object: its object reference. (More on this a little later.)

2.3.2 Choosing an Implementation Language

As we saw in Figure 2.1, the IDL skeleton connects to our ORB on one end and our object implementation on the other. (There is a similar configuration at the client end as well.) Each connection requires a decision on our part: On the object implementation end, we need to select a programming language; on the ORB end, we need to select a vendor and product. We'll discuss the language issues first, ORB selection next.

In selecting a programming language, you need to consider two things: suitability and availability. A programming language is suitable if it can do the things your application needs, using only the computing resources you have available, and if you and your programming team know it or can learn it. At your site, there may be other considerations. For instance, some companies have administrative preferences or restrictions covering certain languages. And for availability, not all ORBs support IDL mappings for every programming language. You will have to check ORBs for availability on the hardware platforms you plan to run on; you will have more freedom (and more decisions to make) if you are able to select hardware platform and ORB software together. Chapter 25 introduces the 11 ORB products covered in this book, including the platforms covered and languages implemented by each. They're a great place to start your investigation. For pointers to even more ORBs, check out the OMG homepage and other CORBA URL collections referenced in Appendix A.

For every major programming language, an OMG standard language mapping specifies how IDL types, method invocations, and other constructs convert into language function or method calls. This is how the IDL skeleton and the object implementation come together, as shown in Figure 2.2. The IDL compiler uses the mapping specifications to generate a set of function calls from the IDL operations. Your programmer, probably assisted by an automated or semiautomated tool, refers to the IDL file and uses the language mapping to generate the corresponding set of function statements. After compilation and linking, these resolve so that the skeleton makes the right calls to invoke operations on your object implementation.

Since the language mapping is an OMG standard, every vendor's IDL compiler (for a particular language) will generate the same set of function or method calls from a given IDL file. This guarantees that, whichever vendor's ORB you select for a particular language, your object implementation accesses the skeleton using the same syntax. If you deploy on multiple vendors' ORBs, your code will port from one to another. The example presentation in this book brings this out. Thus, you may select a programming language and complete your implementation with the knowledge that you still

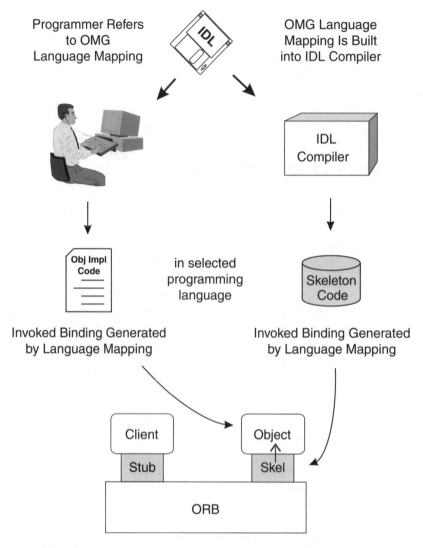

Figure 2.2   Role of the OMG language mapping standard. (Generated components are shown shaded.)

have freedom to switch ORBs down the road. (The original OMG specification for the binding of your object implementation to the ORB was termed the BOA, and was so loose that server-side code did not port from one vendor's ORB to another. However, the BOA specification has been deprecated in favor of the new Portable Object Adaptor, or POA specification, which solves this problem and provides a lot more functionality than the BOA ever could. We cover the POA in Chapter 5.)

The current CORBA specification includes standard IDL language mappings for the programming languages C, C++, Java, COBOL, Smalltalk, and Ada; a mapping for LISP is in process. Mappings for the scripting languages Python and IDL script are under vote. Mappings don't have to be standardized by OMG in order to be useful; products implementing nonstandard mappings are available now for objective C, Eiffel, Perl, and other languages. (Check out the URLs referenced in Appendix A for these ORBs.)

2.3.2.1 Connecting to the ORB

The two ends of the implementation skeleton are truly opposite: The connection to the client, governed by OMG IDL, is standard and provides portability; the connection to the ORB on the other end is proprietary (except for Java, as we explain in detail in Chapter 8). This freedom in the specification allows the vendor to implement the connection with the performance characteristics customers demand.

The connections to the ORB, one for each interface in our IDL file, are generated automatically by the IDL compiler. Since the ORB-skeleton interface is proprietary, ORBs and IDL compilers come in matched sets. You must use the IDL compiler with its companion ORB; the skeleton from vendor A will not mate with the ORB from vendor B (again, except for Java). Since the language mapping provides a standard junction between object implementation and ORB, and the stubs are generated automatically by the IDL compiler, you can switch ORBs just by recompiling your IDL file and linking with the new stub this produces—no changes to source code will be necessary. (On the server end, this claim assumes your ORB implements the new POA specification, and not the now-deprecated BOA.)

Why is Java different? For other languages, the programmer assembles all of the components into a single file termed an *executable*. For Java, the parts are assembled in a Java Virtual Machine at runtime, which removes this element of control from the programmer. By standardizing the interface between skeleton and ORB for Java, OMG ensured that your Java e-commerce application will always work for all of your customers regardless of the other Java applets they may have run before they visited your Web site.

2.3.3 Summary: Object Implementation End

We've covered the complete development process on the object implementation end. Here's a summary of how we narrowed down to our specific ORB and languages environment: We started with an IDL interface definition, which was usable with any programming language and ORB (Figure 2.2). We selected a programming language, and, using the OMG standard language mapping, determined the corresponding function calls in that language. Then, using the IDL compiler that came with our ORB, we input the IDL file and generated a skeleton that joins to our chosen ORB. Portability assured by the standard language mapping will allow us to also compile with a different vendor's IDL compiler and generate a skeleton with the same function calls that connects to the new vendor's ORB.

2.3.4 Client End: Single-ORB Version

Keeping in the spirit of "first things first," in this section, we'll assume that both client and object implementation are written in the same programming language and connected to the same ORB. Soon, in Section 2.5, we'll relax these restrictions and show how client and object implementation can be written in different languages and connected to different ORBs around our network. But first, this important foundation material.

The same execution of the IDL compiler that generated our implementation skeleton also generated a client stub (Figure 2.3). Where the skeleton contained function calls, the stub contains function declarations; in our client, we write the corresponding function calls that resolve to the stub. These are the same declarations as on the implementation end, generated by the standard language mapping. Like our implementation, our client code ports from one ORB to any other that supports the programming language we used. (By the way, this isn't the only way to connect to the ORB. There's also a dynamic connection, which we describe in Section 2.3.5.4.) And, as you might expect, the stub joins to the ORB with a proprietary interface.

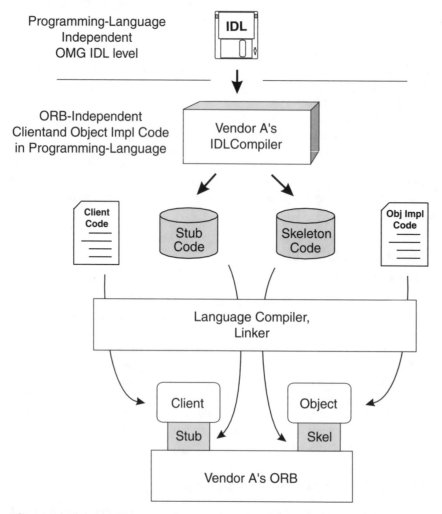

Figure 2.3   Producing an IDL file, client, and object implementation. (Shading indicates generated components.)

2.3.4.1 Summary: Both Ends, Single ORB

Now we know all about how CORBA works, at least with a single ORB. It's all summed up in Figure 2.3: We write a single IDL file, a client, and an object implementation. The IDL compiler generates a stub for the client end, and a skeleton for the object implementation end. Our client and implementation (for POA ORBs) port among ORBs using the programming language we chose, so we can recompile with different ORB's IDL compilers to switch from one ORB to another.

2.3.5 The Object Request Broker

If you're familiar with the remote procedure call (RPC) paradigm, you may think we're done. (If you're not, bear with us for a second.) All we would need to do to run the above as an RPC would be to establish a network connection between the client stub and the implementation skeleton, and make the call between them. However, this would require each stub to resolve individually to its corresponding skeleton, and the CORBA architecture instead resolves all of the stubs to the ORB. There are a lot of good reasons for this, and we examine them in this section.

2.3.5.1 Foundations for Interoperability

Our objective is to use a web of ORB-to-ORB communications pathways to enable interoperability among all of the CORBA objects on a network. The two problems we have to overcome are *location*—how do we address our invocation to a particular object implementation—and *translation*—how does our invocation get translated to a foreign ORB's data format on the way over, and the response get translated on the way back?

We define an object reference to solve the first problem. You already know the solution to the second problem: it's IDL. Here's how the object references and IDL work with the ORB to provide the interoperability we promised.

2.3.5.2 The Object Reference

Some objects in our enterprise will have extremely long lifetimes, and will be required to maintain their state persistently from creation to the last day of an enterprise's existence. An example might be the main account object of our accounting system, which keeps track of our enterprise's net worth. Other objects might have intermediate lifetimes, such as a sales order object that could be created in response to an actual sale and destroyed after the merchandise was delivered and payment received. Smaller objects might have short, transitory lifetimes, such as a pushbutton on a dialog box that appears only for a single mouse-click response.

Every CORBA object in a system, regardless of its lifetime, has its own object reference. This is assigned by its ORB at object creation and remains valid until the object is explicitly deleted. Clients obtain object references in various ways, and associate them with the invocation according to the mapping of the language they are using. This association enables the ORB to direct the invocation to the specified target object.

The OMA places certain requirements on the validity of the object reference. For instance, a client is able to store the reference for a particular object in a file or database.

When the client retrieves the reference from storage later, the OMA requires that its invocation execute successfully even if the target object has been moved in the interim (although not if the target object has been explicitly deleted).

Protocols permitting (as we explain in Chapter 6), the OMA allows any ORB to understand any object reference at any time. Thus, object reference plays a key role in getting user and resource together in our widespread distributed object system. Object references can be passed around your enterprise—or beyond, to your suppliers, customers, and prospects—using a database, naming or trading service, publicized file location, or any other means. Any application using any ORB on the network can retrieve them and pass them to its own ORB to invoke the object.

Since only ORBs can interpret object references, there's no reason other than curiosity for you to be concerned about their form and how they work. However, since there seems to be a lot of curiosity around, we've put an explanation in Chapter 6 on interoperability.

Since you're in the fortunate position of being an ORB user instead of an ORB builder, the concept of object reference for you is straightforward: You hand the object reference to the ORB, and the ORB gets your invocation to the target object. And, if you're passing it or receiving it as a parameter, the ORB takes care of the details regardless of where, or how far, it's going. It's as simple as that.

2.3.5.3 IDL and the ORB

If you've ever written a distributed application for a heterogeneous network, you know how much trouble it is to interoperate among a group of platforms with different data formats and byte ordering. The OMA requires that the ORB take care of these details for you, just as simply as it took care of addressing using the object reference. Fortunately, we've already given it the tool it needs.

That tool, of course, is OMG IDL. The OMG had good reason to make IDL a strongly typed language: Besides using IDL to create the client stub and implementation skeleton, CORBA requires that the Object Request Broker store the IDL definition for all of its objects in an Interface Repository (IR). This collection of interface definitions is a key resource in the distributed object system. It must be available, not only to the ORB itself, but also to clients and object implementations, and utilities such as object hierarchy browsers and debuggers. Using IDL interfaces defined by OMG standards, interface definitions can be added to the IR, modified, deleted, or retrieved; the contents of the IR may be searched; and inheritance trees in it may be traced to determine the exact type of an object.

The obvious use of the IR is for interoperability: Knowing the types and order of the arguments in a message enables communicating ORBs to translate byte order and data format wherever necessary. The other major use of the IR is in the Dynamic Invocation Interface and dynamic skeleton interface, enabling bridges, gateways, debuggers, and performance monitors.

2.3.5.4 The Dynamic Invocation Interface

If there is any notable limitation of the object architecture we've sketched so far, it would be inflexibility at runtime. In order to invoke an operation on an object, a client has to call, and be statically linked to, the stub for its type. (Remember that this one stub lets the client access *any* instance of this type, no matter how many millions there might be, since the client can associate any object reference of the proper type with its invocation.) Since the developer determines which stubs a client contains when he or she writes its code, clients built on this interface (termed the Static Invocation Interface, or SII) cannot access new object types that are added to the system later. However, sophisticated users of dynamic distributed object systems demand more than this: They want to use new objects as soon as they are added to any ORB on their network, without having to wait for or install a new release of the client software on their desktop.

The Dynamic Invocation Interface (DII) provides this capability, and it's built in to every CORBA-compliant ORB. The DII enables a properly written client at runtime to:

- Discover new objects
- Discover their interfaces
- Retrieve their interface definitions
- Construct and dispatch invocations
- Receive the resulting response or exception information

to and from objects whose client stubs are not linked in to its module—for instance, objects that were added to the system after the client was written. The DII is actually an ORB interface defined in OMG IDL (of course!) that includes routines to allow the client and ORB, working together using interface definitions from the IR, to construct and invoke operations on any available object.

How does a client figure out which object or interface it wants to retrieve from the IR? This is not the same job as putting together a request. Although a client could browse the IR and select an interface, there are other, more straightforward ways. At installation time, for instance, new server objects could create entries in a file known to the client, listing their interface names along with extra information that the client could display in a menu. This provides the user with the information he or she needs to select the object, and the client with the information it needs to retrieve the interface definition from the IR. Standard ways to find out about objects on the system include the Naming and Trader Services, discussed in Section 2.6.2 and Chapter 11.

Before Java, the flexibility of the DII was just about the only way to provide access to new object types as they were created, without getting into the hassle of distributing platform-specific client code. Now that the Java Virtual Machine is available on virtually every platform and automatic download makes distribution automatic, the administrative drawbacks associated with providing new clients for your server have been largely overcome. You can put your CORBA server on the Internet (or any network), write a client for it in Java, and highlight the client application's URL on a Web page. Users click on the URL to download and run the client, including its ORBlet (an ORB that runs in a browser sandbox) in their Java virtual machine, invoking your server. Because this scenario involves no system administration burden, it also strips DII clients of one of their benefits.

Why use the DII, then? The DII (and its corresponding server-side analog, the Dynamic Skeleton Interface, or DSI) is used by bridges and gateways to interconnect domains of different network hardware or software, as well as by systems and network administration tools and desktop managers, which must contend with or manage constantly-changing suites of objects. These system-level applications need to create interface-specific proxies that look like skeletons on one side, and clients on the other; the only way to do this is by creating stubs and skeletons on-the-fly, which they do using the DII and DSI. In fact, this is becoming the major use of these dynamic tools. If you need either the DII or DSI for some other reason in your CORBA application, you may use them with confidence: They're not going to go away.

2.4 CORBA-Based Interoperability

The section on interoperability in this chapter is short for two reasons: First, we're building on the firm foundation laid in previous sections, and second, most of the remaining details occur "under the covers," so they are properly postponed until Chapter 6.

2.4.1 Accessing an Object on a Remote ORB

Interoperability in CORBA, as shown in Figure 2.4, is based on ORB-to-ORB communication. The client does nothing different for a remote invocation compared to the local case. It passes its usual IDL-based invocation to its local ORB. If the invocation contains the object reference of a local object implementation, the ORB routes it to its target object; if not, the ORB routes the invocation to the remote ORB that hosts the target object. The remote ORB then routes the invocation to the target object.

The client cannot tell from either the form of the invocation or the object reference whether the target object is local or remote. The user may be aware that the target is, for example, an accounting object that resides on a networked mainframe, or a printer on the third floor of an adjoining building, but this does not affect the invocation. All details of the invocation are taken care of by the ORB: resolving the object reference to a specific remote ORB and object, translating data byte order and format where necessary, and whatever other chores arise.

Of course, there's a lot going on under the covers. Each ORB is required to maintain an IR with its collection of interface definitions, and this becomes a significant distributed database application in itself as your system grows to large numbers of ORBs and interfaces. Communications details must be synchronized as well—ORB network protocols must match, or gateways must translate between them.

However, the CORBA architecture removes this layer from the concern of not only the end user, but from the application programmer as well. The client and object implementation make or receive only local function calls, since their communication is through the stub to their local ORB. OMG standards guarantee that any ORB that bears the CORBA brand will interoperate over the network with any other CORBA 2-branded ORB. For more on the CORBA certification and branding process, see Section 3.2.

Implementation details have been taken care of by the ORB implementors. Some protocol-related decisions will affect network administrators—the people at your site who install and configure your networked ORB environment. These people should read the technical details of interoperability presented in Chapter 6.

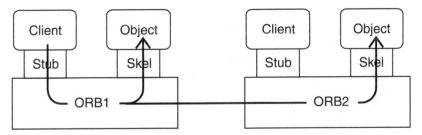

Figure 2.4   Interoperability uses ORB-to-ORB communication.

2.4.2 Reuse: Integrating a Purchased Object Implementation

In this section, we show how the CORBA architecture makes it easy to integrate a purchased object implementation into your distributed object system. Of course the implementation does not have to be purchased for these steps to work; you could have obtained it from another department at your company, or from any of a number of sources. The point is, this process is the key to *reuse*—gaining maximum benefit (for the user) and return on investment (for the vendor) from an implementation, and reuse only works if you can integrate the software quickly and easily.

This structure is a necessary and basic building block in our architecture; a lot of the rest of the book builds on it, or relates to it in one way or another. If distributed object computing is new to you, it will add a new dimension to your concept of application architecture. We're going to oversimplify in order to make this a good starting example, by showing only a single client invoking a single object. In order to scale to the enterprise or the Internet, a server needs to manage hundreds of thousands, or perhaps millions, of objects. CORBA has the machinery to do this, but we need to establish the foundation first and that's what we're doing here. Later in this chapter, we discuss scalable servers and then extend this scenario to CORBA components to give a hint of what else we'll need to succeed in the real world, and where the tools come from in CORBA. So, if it occurs to you that this example is a little too simple, you're right, but bear with us for now and we'll fix that as soon as we can.

Inter-ORB communication is the key feature that gives CORBA its unparalleled flexibility. Client and object implementation may:

- Reside on different vendors' ORBs
- Reside on different platforms
- Reside on different operating systems
- Reside on different networks
- Be written in different programming languages by programmers who never saw or spoke to each other

and they will still interoperate perfectly as long as client and object use the same IDL syntax and underlying semantics.

All your programmer needs in order to write a client that accesses a remote object is a copy of its IDL file, the description of what each operation does, and at runtime an object reference. This makes it easy to integrate, for example, purchased software implementations, objects written by other programmers in your company, or objects generated by interactive tools that provide IDL interfaces. Forward-looking companies are widening their competitive advantage by purchasing basic software modules implementing common knowledge in their field, then extending this functionality with modules written inhouse. Here we show how to access these objects.

The process is diagrammed in Figure 2.5. When you purchase the software, you will receive both an executable object implementation and an IDL file from the vendor. Install the object on the ORB on the server node where it will reside. The installation process will produce an object reference, which may be automatically placed in a directory or Naming Service for you, or may be written to a file where you can access it.

Now you're ready to write the client. Move to your development platform. Remember, this does not need to be the same platform or ORB as the one running the object implementation. Load the IDL file, and compile it with the local IDL compiler. It doesn't matter which language the vendor used to write the object you purchased. You can write your client in any language you want, so choose the IDL compiler that supports your desired development environment.

The IDL compilation step will yield both a client stub and an implementation skeleton. Discard the implementation skeleton—you don't need it. Use the client stub to access the ORB from your client. In your client code, retrieve the object reference from the Naming Service or file where it was stored, and use it to invoke operations on the purchased object, wherever it might reside.

2.4.3 Distributing Both Client and Object

It's a simple conceptual jump to go from the process we just described to building a distributed client/object system with different ORBs and platforms for client and object implementation. The client-side process would be the same as shown in Figure 2.5. The object implementation process would be the analog executed on the server development platform, keeping the IDL skeleton and building the code that runs behind it.

When the client and object have been completed, and the object is running, the client can retrieve the object reference from the Naming Service or wherever it was stored and invoke operations on the object just by passing an invocation to its local ORB.

2.5 Scalable Servers

Some CORBA objects will be large; others will be small. In other terms, architects speak of *fine-grained* and *coarse-grained* object systems. A coarse-grained system might be your company's main accounting system, wrapped in a thin layer of code and given OMG IDL interfaces that represent it as one or a few CORBA objects, and put onto your network so that different departments could make entries and retrieve results interactively online instead of batch. A fine-grained system, on the other hand, might be the set of shopping carts on an e-commerce Web site. Shopping carts are a great use of CORBA:

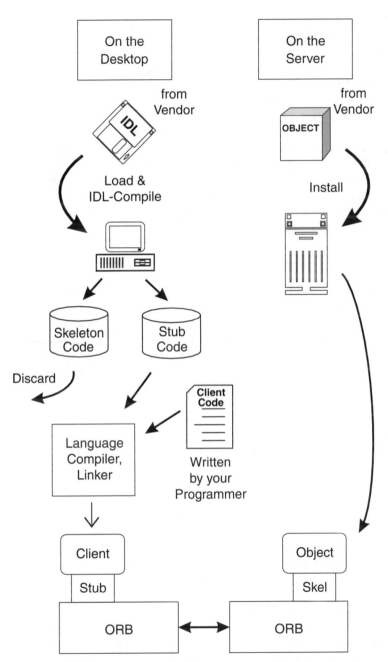

Figure 2.5   Integrating a purchased object into your software environment.

each shopper needs his or her own, and every cart has both methods (shoppers can put stuff into it or remove stuff, review the contents, and check out) and state (the stuff that's in it, and the shopper's name and address information).

When we build our CORBA-based e-commerce Web site, we have to address the problem of *scalability*. That is, how will we service the load that we expect, using the resources that we have? After all, we're expecting millions of people to come shop our Web site, and each will have his or her own shopping cart. CORBA has a great set of tools you can use to build scalable servers, and we'll introduce some of them now.

We've already covered the concept of *instantiation*: When a new customer starts shopping, we're going to instantiate a new shopping cart object for this shopping trip. Once created, it stays around, holding the items the customer puts into it, until the customer checks out at the cashier (yes, even if the customer logs out and leaves our site for a while). When the customer checks out, he "turns in" the shopping cart (just like at a real supermarket); when he comes back, we'll instantiate a new one for him.

When the customer returns for a visit after being away for a long time, what does the client program have to do to use the shopping cart again? Nothing special, it turns out: just use the object reference (perhaps saved in a cookie) to invoke operations on it, and they work. There are no activation or deactivation operations in CORBA; the client's view is that an object, once instantiated, runs continuously until it is explicitly destroyed (and once that happens, all operations on that object will fail since destroyed objects cannot be re-created). All the client has to do is invoke whatever operation it wants on the object reference; the object will perform it and the result will return.

This is fine from the client's point of view, but what about the server—does it have to keep a shopping cart object running continuously for every one of our millions of customers, so it can service an invocation whenever it happens to come in? Between visits, a cart may not be used for days or weeks, and this would waste computing resources that could be used to service active customers.

What we need is a server-side infrastructure that allows us to swap CORBA objects into and out of our execution space. If the object instance has persistent state, we'll need to save its state when we swap it out, and retrieve it when we swap it in again. CORBA has this infrastructure: It's called the Portable Object Adapter (POA), and it's discussed in Chapter 5. The CORBA Component Model, which is also a server infrastructure, builds on the POA so it takes care of swapping too.

Of course there's a lot more to the POA than we've said here. Even the concept of swapping that we've presented is an oversimplification of what really happens, but we'll postpone the details until Chapter 5. The point to remember now is that CORBA gives you the tools to create scalable servers with objects as fine-grained as shopping carts or bank accounts, so you can design your systems around them.

This concludes the overview of CORBA (except for CORBA 3, which we discuss briefly in Section 2.7). In just a few pages, we've gone from object basics to scalable, heterogeneous interoperabilty. But don't think that interoperability—electronic plumbing, really—is all there is to OMG standards. The people who wrote the OMA knew that this was only the beginning. By the time the CORBAservices and CORBAfacilities are fully populated with OMG standards, CORBA will be a small fraction of the whole.

2.6 The Object Management Architecture

If we compare CORBA, with its communications links, to a telephone line, then it's tempting to also think of IDL as a language, but this is not quite right. Instead, IDL

WHAT'S NEW IN THE OMA

Here's the "big picture" view of how the OMA has changed since we wrote the first edition of this book: There have been two major changes, both at the CORBAfacilities level. The horizontal Common Facilities have been deemphasized, probably because fewer OMG members decided to participate in those parts of the architecture; and the Domain Facilities (Chapters 19 and 20) have grown into a force that rivals the platform effort. Changes at the CORBAservices level have been evolutionary rather than revolutionary: The services that receive the most use—Naming (Chapter 11), Events (Chapter 12), Transactions (Chapter 13), and Security (Chapter 14)—have been augmented with additional capability, and the old Persistent Object Service has just (as we go to press) been replaced with a totally new version (Chapter 17) that addresses the same problem space. Most other services remain stable in their original form.

plays the role of an alphabet: In the same way that different languages use the same alphabet, different applications could all use IDL interfaces but not be able to interoperate if each one created its own IDL interface for a particular function.

There must be a common language for all applications, or our vision of plug-and-play component software will not be realized. That common language is the OMG's Object Management Architecture. A foundation of standard services invoked using standard interfaces, the OMA defines an environment where interoperability penetrates upward from the system level into application components.

2.6.1 Goal of the OMA

The goal of the OMA is simple: When applications provide basic functionality, let them provide it via a standard interface. This enables a component software market both above and below the level of the interface. Below it, multiple implementations of the basic functionality (Object Transaction Services, for instance) may still provide differences in performance, price, or adaptation to run on specialized platforms, while above it, specialized components (transactional e-commerce software, for example) come to market which can work with any compliant implementation of the service.

For each component of the OMA, the OMG provides a formal specification—a published document prescribing the syntax (how to invoke each operation on each object) in OMG IDL—and semantics (what each operation does) in English text. Vendors of OMA-compliant systems then implement and sell the services (some bundled with an ORB package, others ORB-independent), where they are accessed via the specified IDL interfaces. Vendors do not have to provide every service, but every service they provide must conform to the OMG specifications in order to bear the CORBA brand.

Since each service stands alone and is accessed through standard IDL interfaces, you do not have to obtain all of your services from the same vendor. Standardization enables a high level of mix-and-match. Your enterprise may, for instance, decide to use the same implementation of object services on all platforms and all ORBs to maximize homogeneity. Another enterprise may choose a different vendor for a particular service for another reason—licensing terms, perhaps, or a special compatability with a legacy system or application. However, we notice a trend toward ORB packages offering basic

CORBAservices, either bundled or optional. This provides a very easy way to provide your developers with all they need to build CORBA applications. In Appendix A, we give you URLs with pointers to ORBs and services from dozens of companies.

2.6.2 The CORBAservices

The CORBAservices (still referred to within OMG as the Object Services) provide fundamental, nearly system-level services to OO applications and their components. In this book, we will refer to 16 OMG specifications as CORBAservices. They are

- Naming Service
- Trader Service
- Event Service
- Notification Service (actually a Telecommunications Domain Facility, but plays the role of a CORBAservice in the architecture)
- Object Transaction Service
- Security Service
- LifeCycle Service
- Relationship Service
- Persistent State Service
- Externalization Service
- Object Query Service
- Object Properties Service
- Concurrency Service
- Licensing Service
- Secure Time Service
- Object Collection Service

If you're interested in the details about any of these services, you'll have to look ahead to Chapters 10 through 18. In this overview chapter, we preview only the big four service types (actually six individual CORBAservices). They are the Naming and Object Trader Services, which provide access to object references around your enterprise; the Event and Notification Services, which broadcast events to objects that subscribe to their event channels; the Object Transaction Service, which provides distributed transactional semantics (two-phase commit and rollback) and transaction-monitor scalability to your CORBA system; and the Security Service, for security whatever your environment (governmental, business, banking, or e-commerce). When we finish, we'll introduce the Domain Facilities.

How does your application get the object references for the objects it needs to invoke? The OMA provides two ways. First is the **Naming Service**. When you create a new CORBA object, you can store its object reference in the Naming Service along with a name of your choice. (Pick a logical one!) Then later, you or someone else can use the name to retrieve the object reference and invoke operations on that object, similar to the way you use filenames today to retrieve files and documents. The Interoperable Naming Service, new in CORBA 3, allows you to type in a URL-like string and access the Naming Service at a remote site without having to retrieve its machine-format object reference first, for sites that decide to support this type of access. Second is the **Trader Service**, a sophisticated service that may yet evolve into the core of the dynamic distributed object environment. It's the service to use when you know what sort of object you want, although not exactly, since the Trader Service stores ancillary data associated with every object reference that will let you zero in on exactly the object you want to invoke. You can browse the Trader Service for an amortization object to calculate depreciation, or for a printer in your building on the third or fourth floor in an accessible area that prints double-sided sheets faster than 10 pages per minute, and ask it to return you that object's reference. This important service was standardized by ISO (the International Organization for Standardization) in an OMA-compliant form, so the Trader Service that OMG adopted is also an ISO standard.

Distributed CORBA systems use events to synchronize the activity of their different objects, and there are two versions of the system that handles this. The simpler one is the original **Event Service**, which provides channels where supplier objects can input events, and consumer objects can receive them. The **Notification Service** adds sophisticated event typing and filtering to the basic event service functionality.

The **Transaction Service**, and the **Concurrency Service** that supports it with file and resource locking, provide CORBA systems with object-oriented access to the mainstream of business accounting systems, OLTP (OnLine Transaction Processing). Developed by a cooperating group that included every major TP vendor, this OMG-standard set of IDL interfaces provides access to major OLTP systems.

Security is essential—without it, CORBA would not be usable in areas such as business, commerce, and defense. How do you get end-to-end security in multivendor object networks? How do you protect communications over open channels such as commercial phone lines or wireless links? The **Security Service** defines an architecture and interfaces that answer these questions, and implementations are available now.

By now, you should be starting to develop a picture in your mind of how this is all going to work together: CORBA and OMG IDL provide the telephone line and alphabet that our apps will use to link up. Then the OMA standardizes the language they use to speak to each other, and provides "matchmaking" services like Naming and Trader to get clients and object implementations together when they need it. When you're ready to use a service, you can find it, you can talk to it, and you can use it.

There's one more layer that we can standardize without penetrating the uppermost reaches where competition adds value and (after all) provides the resource that produces the products we all benefit from. OMG calls this layer the CORBAfacilities and it now comes in two parts: the Horizontal CORBAfacilities and the Domain CORBAfacilities.

2.6.3 The Horizontal CORBAfacilities

In the first edition of this book, we wrote expectantly about the Horizontal CORBAfacilities with their four-part architecture: User Interface, Information Management, Task Management, and Systems Management. Since then, a number of things have happened: The OpenDoc specification, which filled parts of the User Interface and Information Management parts of the architecture, was abandoned by CI Labs when it folded, although IBM continues to make OpenDoc C++ source code available for free (see Appendix A for the URL). More recently, the XCMF Systems Management Facility was deprecated by OMG members when they realized that many of its functions would be replaced by superior versions in the CCM specification. The Common Facilities Task Force was disbanded by OMG members in mid-1997 and its work partitioned among the ORBOS Task Force and various Domain Task Forces. The Common Facilities Architecture document with its four-part architecture was deprecated in early 1999.

Nevertheless, the box labeled Horizontal Common Facilities persists in the Object Management Architecture, and a recent revision of the Object Management Architecture document written by an OMG committee confirms that it's not going away. It's a place for facilities that don't fit into a specialized vertical market but are still at too high a level to be called a CORBAservice. The Printing, Mobile Agent, and Internationalization and Time Facilities fit in this category now; other specifications will join them (albeit at a slow pace) in the years to come.

What's the story? Some of the CORBAfacilities areas (User Interface, primarily) concentrated on the client side, and CORBA has not been as successful on the client side as on the server in spite of its potential there (we talk about this in a sidebar at the end of this chapter). Other parts of the CF Architecture (Task Management, Systems Management) may have been too poorly defined to lead to definite standards, or lacked market support. Printing is one area where management tools use OMG standards, and this level of use and experience shows in the well-designed Printing Facility. There is a lot of CORBA in network management also, but the standards reside in OMG's Telecommunications Domain Facilities and not here.

As we've mentioned, there are three specifications in the Horizontal CORBAfacilities book as we go to press. Here's the bulleted list for readers who are paging through, looking for highlighted text:

- Internationalization Service
- Print Facility
- Mobile Agents Facility

2.6.4 The Domain CORBAfacilities

In order to unify the enterprise, we must be able to share functionality and data. CORBA and the CORBAservices make a great set of pipes, but we need a lot more than plumbing to make good on the promises set out in Chapter 1.

As we showed in Figure 1.1, the Domain CORBAfacilities fill in the architecture between the basic CORBAservices and the visible, competitive Application Objects.

The basic structure of the OMG domain architecture is shown in Figure 2.6. When the full architecture is realized in off-the-shelf products, you'll be able to share the application-level data and functionality you need to in order to integrate your company's IS. Since top-level Application Objects will not be standardized, the mid-level CORBAfacilities will be accessed either by innovative clients you buy from a competitive software marketplace, or by targeted modules your developers or integrators tailor specifically to your company's needs. And development will be hastened because the basic and intermediate functionality comes from the CORBAservices and CORBAfacilities; only incremental capability and integration need to be provided at the top.

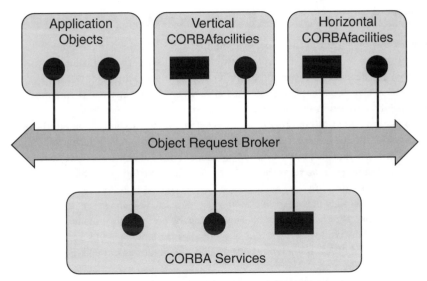

Figure 2.6   OMG's Object Management Architecture (OMA).

At the base, the CORBAservices provide basic functionality that allows CORBA objects and components to find each other (Naming and Trader), ping each other (events and notification), keep order (persistence, transactions, security), and in general stay organized. Above this, the Components specification has just extended the architecture to support advanced server-side functionality, opening the way for future extensions by the BODTF and Analysis and Design Task Force (A&DTF) to add business semantics support. (We know that many readers are interested in OMG support for Business Objects; for a discussion, see Section 19.4.2.1.) Basic business objects in the various fields populate the next level, while the top layer of boxes represents frameworks of either CORBA objects or components that have been designed together to provide server-side functionality in various areas.

Currently, nine Domain Task Forces are working in OMG: Business Objects, Finance/Insurance, Electronic Commerce, Manufacturing, Healthcare, Telecommunications, Transportation, Life Science Research, and Utilities. In the formative stage are groups representing Call Center and other customer interaction technology and service, Statistics and Analytical Data Management, Retail, Space and Satellite Science, Printing and Publishing, and several other areas. In late 1999, about 20 domain specifications had been completed and another 30 or so were under way. For details about the completed specs, see Chapters 19 and 20. We've put a snapshot of work in progress into Chapter 19 as things stood when we went to press; for an updated look, surf to the OMG URLs listed in Appendix A for this chapter.

As we end this chapter, we should mention how closely OMG works with other organizations. If an outside organization is producing standards in an area where an OMG Domain Task Force plans to work, OMG encourages its members to form a liaison relationship with the organization. There are dozens of active liaisons, overseen by a full-time Liaison Manager on the OMG staff. Besides the general liaisons with ISO and other IT-related standards organizations, there are many with industry-specific groups in such areas as Telecommunications, Finance, and more.

OMG AND CORBA DIRECTIONS

We've already covered, in our introductory way, all the parts of CORBA and the Object Management Architecture. We've seen some new efforts that are successful (Domain specifications) and likely to be successful (CORBA components and the other CORBA 3 enhancements). We've also identified some past efforts that did not succeed (Compound Document Facility) or never even got started (User Interface Common Facility).

There's a pattern here: OMG efforts on the *server side* tend to succeed, while efforts on the *client side* tend to be ignored by the marketplace regardless of their technical merit. Why is this? We think it's because client-side and server-side environments have very different dynamics (and we think that CORBA would improve things on the client side, of course). Here's the story:

Consider the overall view of the world's computing infrastructure shown in Figure 2.7. We've only shown one set of servers from a single company on the slide, but suppose they represent all of the world's servers, and similarly that the individual PCs, set-top boxes, telephones, and PDAs on the left represent all of the hundreds of millions of connected devices in the world.

The rightmost two columns correspond to the bottom two tiers of a conventional three-tier architecture: storage at the base, and business logic next to it.

We've expanded the top client tier into the two columns on the left. The second column from the left is a mediating layer that relays requests from the various client machines to the business logic layer, and formats and delivers the replies from the business layers to the various clients. Although we've shown this layer running on its own hardware, this is not a requirement; after all, your database (bottom tier) and business logic (middle tier) share hardware resource without any problem today. If the mediating

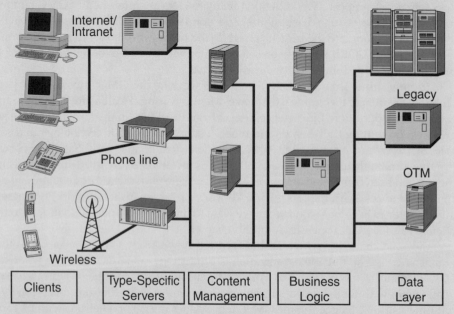

Figure 2.7 A view of today's enterprise/Internet computing architecture.

software runs on the same infrastructure as the servers, this layer will be very thin (or absent); if not, it will have more to do.

At the extreme left is a column of clients. Do not assume that "client" and "PC" are synonomous; companies are realizing that *any* device capable of connecting to a digital network is a potential client, and there are a lot more television sets, telephones, and pagers in use than there are PCs. We admit that the infrastructure supporting the lower left corner of this picture is not fully realized now; although some pagers, cell phones, and other devices integrate with the Internet and customer-accessible computer networks, most connect only to private networks and are accessed painfully through, for example, telephone touchpads. More general interoperability is coming, however.

There are a couple of big differences between the environment of servers on the right, and of clients on the left. About the servers on the right, we notice that:

- They are outnumbered by client machines by many orders of magnitude, even though there are many servers and a greater variety.
- When a server fails, even for a short time, impact may be severe both on the business that owns it and on the potentially large number of clients it was serving.
- Because of this, server hardware and software are designed and run to be reliable even though this is costly.
- Servers typically run in controlled environments and are administered by trained staff.
- Although a server may count millions of other machines as its clients, it works with only a few other (also closely controlled) machines as peers, relying on them for help in getting its business done.

About the clients on the left, we notice that:

- There are many of them—in the hundreds of millions or more; certainly too many to count.
- When a client machine fails, the impact is confined to itself and its user.
- Because of this, and because client hardware and software are typically bought by households, small businesses, or individual offices (without their own IT support), the economic model for this end of the network connection favors low cost over reliability. Using this model, vendors have expanded this market to a nearly unbelievable size.
- Client machines may run in any environment, typically uncontrolled, and may be administered by their users who are untrained in this task, or not administered at all.
- They may access a number of servers, in the role of client, but they depend on no other machine as a peer. Instead, whatever work they do without calling on a server, they do entirely on their own.

Seen in this light, it's evident why the common Web-browser client model is so thin: It's uneconomic and impractical to move functionality from a single, reliable, administered server to many types of unreliable, uncontrolled client machines. However, you can sell a lot of merchandise with the same type of block-data-transfer interaction that we got used to in the 1970s and 1980s. (Do you remember 3270-type terminals? Do you get a sense of *déjà-vu* when you fill in a CGI form and press "enter"? My kids play Internet-based games and enjoy much richer interoperability than I ever get filling out CGI forms and sending them to a server over http.)

Where is CORBA in this diagram? It's holding together the enterprise, where reliability is important and many different platforms and operating systems must work together to get the job done in the most robust way possible. Even though the desktop corner in the upper left dominates in sheer numbers of machines, the enterprise portion is where the action (and the money!) concentrates: *All* of the requests from *all* of the clients on the left, of every machine type, execute on the far smaller number of enterprise machines on the right.

These machines are going to be stressed: High volumes of network traffic and requests, coming from millions of machines of various types and shapes, over radio, cable, and copper links, funnel down to these servers. If you're a provider of a service in this part of the diagram, you need two things: First, you need the freedom to pick the *best possible* hardware and software for your job, since second-rate just won't cut it in this high-pressure environment. Second, you need platform-independent, scalable, robust interoperability so that your best-of-breed hardware and software integrate smoothly with the rest of your enterprise. CORBA gives this to you, and enterprise architects already realize this. If you can get this in an infrastructure that is transactional and secure, which CORBA is, so much the better.

What about the link from the data preparation layer to the client? As we head further into the year 2000, there is no single protocol that covers all of the various client machine types we've shown in Figure 2.7. For PCs and equivalent machines (WebTVs, mainly), the Internet economy is based on html over http: from the server to the client we have html, a data display format; from the client back to the server we augment this with a cgi block-data-transfer reverse channel.

We've run CORBA applications over the Internet. We noticed, right away, a richer experience due to the much tighter integration with the server. In fact, we didn't have the sense of being outside the server looking in through a data display window; instead, we felt that our computer, and we ourselves, had become part of the server environment—on the other side of the thin link to the client, as it were. And, in a very real sense, this was true. Computers built for home and office use have a lot of power, and downloadable code removes some of the system-administration obstacles to thicker clients. We don't think that every application needs a thick client; the success of the Internet shows how much you can do with data display and block data transfer. But, this doesn't mean that this is enough. When you need a richer level of interaction with your user, think of CORBA on the client as the way to deliver it.

What about other types of devices? Pagers and PDAs use device-type-specific or proprietary formats over their intrinsically unreliable wireless links, and cellular telephones use more protocols than we can count. We'd like to see more CORBA in this link too. There already is some; probably more than you imagine. The telecommunications industry has been relying on CORBA for years, primarily for network management, and is moving it into devices. Some set-top boxes are CORBA based. As we write this, the infrastructure supporting the lower-left corner of this picture is not fully realized, and some of the blanks are being filled in with CORBA. We've spoken to and, we hope, influenced some of the people who are deciding what pieces of this layer will look like a few years down the road. We hope that our words, and this book, have some effect there, too.

2.7 CORBA 3 Additions to This Architecture

In the sidebar at the beginning of this chapter, we summarized the CORBA 3 additions but mainly as a list. Now that we've covered the CORBA 2 architecture, let's review these new features and see what they add to it. In this section, we highlight the CORBA 3 features that change client-object interaction in a fundamental way: objects passable by value, quality of service control, asynchronous communications, and CORBA components. As we go over each one, we'll point out the chapter and section where it's discussed in more detail. The sidebar at the beginning of this chapter lists every addition in CORBA 3; look back to it if you want to see how the rest of CORBA 3 adds onto the basics that we've just covered.

2.7.1 CORBA Objects Passable by Value

In the architecture we've just described, all CORBA objects have object references and every client invokes the *same* copy of the object, wherever it happens to be, every time it needs to. On the plus side, this architecture is very straightforward from the client's point of view; if there's a negative, it's that every invocation requires a network round-trip for objects that reside remote from the client (and most, although certainly not all, CORBA objects are not on the same machine or in the same process as the client that calls them). For some objects, especially ones that represent a collection of data (whether or not they also bear methods that act on the data), it makes sense to pass them *by value*; that is, to package up the whole object, data, methods, and all, send it over the wire, and recreate it as a running object at the far end of the invocation. This allows a client to make subsequent invocations on the local object, avoiding the round-trip delay. The new CORBA type that does this is the valuetype.

There is no magic in CORBA, and the running copy of the object does not miraculously spring to life in the process it was passed to. The machinery to create the new running object on the receiving end must be present in its process; the ORB triggers its creation and stuffs the state variable values (which just came down the wire) into it. For details, check out Chapter 3, Section 3.3.

This addition lets CORBA handle applications that would otherwise have had trouble scaling to their data-handling requirements. Already, OBV has played a role in new OMG specifications including those for asynchronous invocation, the reverse Java-to-IDL mapping, and CORBA components.

2.7.2 Asynchronous Invocation and Quality of Service Control

If every computer in the world were powerful enough to keep its queues short all the time, and every network had the speed and bandwidth to transmit all of its users' requests instantly, location transparency (the only invocation paradigm available in CORBA 2) would be the way to go. Its architectural elegance still makes it the mode of choice where load and usage conditions allow. However, computers have queues and networks have capacity limitations, and sometimes (usually in your most critical applications, since these get the most use) we need to take these into account in order to get our work done. The additions to CORBA that allow us to do this are client-specified quality of service and asynchronous invocation modes (Sections 6.4 through 6.6). Valuetypes, just discussed, help out here as well.

Location Transparency means that, for an invocation it's about to make, the client literally doesn't care where the object target lives—the client just makes the invocation and the response comes back. Preserving the illusion that the object is local, this mode also means that the client has no concept of quality of service. However, when a server is stressed and the response doesn't come back for several seconds or minutes—forever, in computer time—this illusion breaks down anyhow. CORBA 3 faces up to this problem and opens up to the client, for the first time, a number of invocation options that allow it to see and deal with network conditions as it dispatches remote invocations.

One of these additions to CORBA 3 allows the client and server to negotiate and establish Quality of Service (QoS) levels. Depending on the QoS in effect on a connection, clients may specify either priority or time-out values for their invocations; routers on the network along the way, and the server at the remote end, work together to provide the agreed-upon QoS. The routers, by the way, optionally render the network connection *reliable*, passing invocations from one to the next with a handshake that doesn't release the sender until the receiver acknowledges that it has stored all data persistently, which it does before it passes it to the next stop along its way.

Like valuetypes, this is a big plus for CORBA, allowing it to serve well when resources are stressed which, we know, is most of the time for successful applications.

Also like valuetypes, QoS changes the CORBA architecture in a fundamental way since it exposes to the client that its invocation may not stay local. Point by point, our client is changing as we add features. Asynchronous invocation continues this trend, exposing the networked nature of the client-object connection.

Under CORBA 2, static (that is, stub-based) invocations could only be made in *synchronous* mode: Invocations block execution of the client thread until the operation completes and the results return. Dynamic invocations could be made in *deferred-synchronous* mode, allowing the client to continue execution and retrieve the results later. This distinction between static and dynamic modes was confusing, and the lack of non-synchronous invocation mode for static invocations forced CORBA clients (or at least the invoking thread of those clients) to sit idle while remote invocations executed on another machine, even if they had useful calculations or user interface functions to do during that time.

The CORBA Messaging Specification (which also defines the QoS modes covered earlier) fixes all this by defining a number of new asynchronous modes that are not only rich in features and flexibility, but also symmetric with respect to static and dynamic invocation, eliminating the need to make dynamic invocations in order to keep the client thread executing (that is, doing some other useful work) during a remote invocation.

Going still further, the specification combines asynchronous invocation with reliable network QoS to define the Time-Independent Invocation (TII), CORBA-based messaging. These provide the flexibility of disconnected client and server operation but, even in connected mode, provide a reliability that opens up new dimensions to CORBA applications.

2.7.3 The CORBA Component Model

The CORBA Component Model (CCM) takes the most important of the server-side application tools that we've introduced in this chapter and combines them into a package that your developers use to build, and your administrators use to deploy and run, enterprise-scalable distributed object applications. The CCM specification itself is huge—over 700 pages—and the secret to understanding it is to realize that only parts of it are truly new; much of CCM consists of the basic concepts we've already covered, packaged in a standard way. Do not sell this packaging effort short: Of the many ways to combine CORBA and the OMA into an application, only the most effective are included in CCM, selected and standardized by more than a dozen of the world's best CORBA and ORB programmers.

The core of the CCM is the *container*: a running piece of code that you buy from a vendor and install on your server machine. The container includes an ORB with a POA. CORBA components are server-side objects; your system administrator installs components into the container, which takes charge of them when they run.

Transactionality, security, and *persistence* change, under CCM, from coding-time concepts to runtime concepts. CCM containers are transactional, secure, and persistent. When your system administrator installs a container on your server machine, he also installs its transaction, security, and persistence systems; any component installed within it will use these container services to run transactional, secure, and with persistent state. Of course, interfaces to these and other container services are standardized, allowing any vendor's component to be installed into any other vendor's container.

This packaging simplifies coding of components, compared to coding of CORBA objects. Your business programmers, familiar with your business rules but unskilled in the concepts of transactions and security, can program enterprise components that become transactional and secure, and store their state persistently, because of the environment in which they run, instead of the way they were coded. This leverages the skills of your key programming staff, making the most of their business skills while compensating for technical weaknesses that are not going to help them program to your core business anyhow.

Another thing the CCM provides are connections, of two kinds: First, the container provides *event channels*; components declare the types of events they provide, and the types that they consume; the container creates event channels for them and connects suppliers to consumers. Second, similar to events, components declare the interfaces that they provide and the others that they require; the container connects these up too.

This lets you build an application out of multiple component types that work together, one providing a service through an interface that's invoked by another. Building on this concept, the specification also defines component *assemblies*: an application (or part of an application) consisting of multiple component types, assembled and packaged together, that can be installed later just as easily as a single component. This lets a vendor (or you), for example, package up a shopping cart component, an order check-out component, and an order billing component into a single component-based application that can be installed in a single operation. We present nearly complete code for this 3-component e-commerce CCM application in Chapter 5.

CORBA components, unlike CORBA objects, may bear *more than one* IDL interface, each with its own object reference; the CCM defines interfaces that allow clients to navigate among them. (We'll see in Chapter 5 that these multiple interfaces are referred to as *facets*.) The navigation services are implemented by the container, of course, and allow component-aware clients to navigate from any interface on any component up to the component's *home* interface, where the client can discover all of the interfaces available on that component. To component-unaware clients, each interface on a component appears identical to a CORBA object and may be invoked in the usual way.

The CCM also packages up the POA's instance-swapping mechanisms. This lets you define a shopping-cart component (in place of the shopping cart object we've discussed so far), and let the container manage the swapping of individual carts in and out of execution space as customers come and go. We think that this mode of resource control will be more popular than programming to the POA directly, but we do want to point out that POA programming isn't as difficult as some people think, and that it gives more flexibility than CCM, which isolates an (admittedly popular and successful) subset.

If you think this sounds a lot like Enterprise JavaBeans (EJB), you're right. In fact, the CCM defines two levels of components: a basic model that corresponds nearly exactly to EJB, and a higher level that adds multiple interfaces, navigation, event handling, and advanced persistence. Of course, CCM is programming-language independent as is all of CORBA, while EJB is restricted to Java only; sorry, but if you want to program components in C++ or some other language, you'll have to use CORBA and not EJB. However, the correspondence between EJB and CORBA components' container APIs is so close that EJBs can function as Level 1 CORBA components, and Java-language Level 1 CORBA components can function as EJBs. In addition, EJB clients can invoke operations on EJBs and CORBA components equivalently, as can CORBA clients.

If you buy a CCM-based e-commerce application to run on your Web site, with shopping carts and services to support them, what do you actually buy? At the beginning of this subsection we used the phrase "installs CORBA components into a container," implying that you're buying a bunch of shopping carts, since each one is a CORBA component. What you would actually buy in this case, however, would be a base application that, among other things, *instantiates* shopping carts. It also manages them, working with the container and the services it provides. Later in the book, we use the term *factory* for this kind of object-creating object, so we'll introduce it here and start to get used to it; a factory object is just a regular CORBA object (or component) that happens to, as its job, instantiate other CORBA objects (or components).

Components are configurable, allowing a single executable to serve in applications that need sort of the same thing, but not exactly. Experience with CORBA objects showed that totally immutable objects do not get reused even in situations where the fit is nearly exact; configurable components are flexible enough to overcome this barrier.

How do you buy a CCM-based application? The specification takes care of that too, defining a multiplatform software distribution format suitable for CD-ROM or other media. Component vendors create, and you buy and install, software in this format, which includes executables for multiple platforms plus configuration files in XML format. Included in the container is an *installer* that reads the CD-ROM, selects and installs the executable for the proper platform, reads the configuration files, presents a menu of install-time options for customization, and then finishes the installation.

Finally, a separate scripting language specification provides yet another way to combine separate components into an application.

The CCM is a revolutionary specification with the potential to change the way software is written and distributed. Before we sum up the effect of CORBA 3 on the architectural framework that we've been building throughout this chapter, let's speculate on some of these possible effects:

OMG members originally thought, back when CORBA was first standardized in the early 1990s, that IDL interfaces and CORBA interoperability were enough to establish a market where vendors would write and sell, and customers would buy and use, CORBA objects. Although many implementations of the CORBAservices were built and sold this way, the component market didn't expand beyond this, probably because it needed a little more support. Then, during late 1997 and 1998, Enterprise Java Beans (EJB) showed how to establish a marketplace for components for a single-language environment and, finally, in early 1999, OMG members established the foundation for a multilanguage, multiplatform component market with the CCM.

As the CCM becomes established over the next year or two, we expect three things to happen:

- Vendors will start writing and selling components, and a healthy market will develop. It's straightforward to develop enterprise components in the transactional, secure environment provided by the CORBA component container, and the standardized distribution format and installer ease the transition from development to shrink-wrap.

- OMG Domain Task Forces will standardize components instead of plain CORBA objects, where component traits are needed or helpful. Working synergistically, components already on the market will define OMG standards in some fields, while OMG domain standards efforts will hasten the maturation process in other fields.

- In an effort that started during the third quarter of 1998, OMG Business Objects proponents began standardizing a business object environment that extends from UML modeling, through IDL, to a Business Object Facility based on the CCM (Section 19.4.2.1). Although it was too early to tell exactly what functions would be added to the base container in this effort, candidate items included pre- and post-conditions, lifecycle support including queries across extents, and some association and relationship management (although the group is unlikely to resolve the formal problems associated with referential integrity in large distributed systems!).

2.7.4 CORBA 3 Architecture Summary

There's a lot to CORBA 3, and the CCM is only a part of it. To gain an overview, let's just look at the changes to the client, since these mirror the additions to the overall architecture.

A CORBA 2 client holding an object reference could make an invocation and get a response back in one of only two basic ways: synchronously using either static or dynamic invocation, or deferred-synchronous using dynamic mode only. Deferred-synchronous invocation was the only operation available to the client that acknowledged that there might be a network connection between it and the object it was invoking.

A CORBA 3 client has a lot more possibilities:

- It can negotiate a quality-of-service level with the server.
- It can make the invocation in synchronous, asynchronous, or time-independent mode.
- It can pass and invoke CORBA objects by value.
- It can discover that an interface belongs to a component, and navigate among its interfaces and those related to it.

These possibilities allow us to create a client—and an overall environment—that is *network aware*. No longer hidden, the network has become a tool that both client and server can use to their advantage, although in a way that preserves the fundamental advantages of object orientation. As the Internet, and large corporate networks, move to a dominant position in computer architectures everywhere, these capabilities bring CORBA into the forefront, supporting applications that run on modern infrastructures and take advantage of every feature they provide.

CHAPTER

3

Introducing OMG IDL

3.1 About This Part of the Book

There are many reasons to read this book. For instance, you might have to help pick an interoperability architecture for your already-networked company, and you need to find out more about CORBA. Or, you might be assigned to a prototype CORBA project, and you need to find out as much as you can about every aspect in order to complete the project and evaluation. Or, perhaps your company produces software, and you're considering CORBA as a platform that will let you market on a wide variety of networked platforms with minimal porting.

This means you have to learn enough about CORBA to reach a valid decision, but you're not about to plow through a bunch of highly technical OMG specifications to do it. (And the OMG specs are written for ORB and service implementors anyway, not for users.) If there's a prototype in your future, you probably want to see how to program for CORBA, using more than one vendor's ORB since multivendor portability and interoperability are the main reasons you're considering CORBA in the first place.

These are the needs we've taken into account in the rest of this book. Chapters 3–9 detail the parts of CORBA that have only been summarized so far. How much detail? Certainly enough to let you make your architectural decision with confidence, and enough to give you a concrete idea of what programming for CORBA is like, but probably not enough to get you all the way through your first independent programming project, and certainly not enough to enable you to build your own ORB from scratch. For the programming project, you will at least need the documentation that comes with the ORB product you select (and we recommend a good book or two on OO analysis and design using UML, too). To build an ORB, you will have to refer to the original OMG specifications.

Chapters 10–22 detail the rest of the OMA. Chapter 10 is an architectural introduction, which discusses design using the CORBAservices and facilities. We then highlight the four OMA functions essential for business computing—object reference passing, event passing, transactions, and security—each in its own chapter. Other services are discussed in Chapters 15–18, and the CORBA Domain specifications, which are actually a larger collection than the rest in terms of pages of spec, are featured in Chapters 19 and 20. UML and the MOF, which are used in the initial stages of programming projects, get the last word in this part of the book, in Chapters 21 and 22.

This chapter is devoted exclusively to the OMG's Interface Definition Language (OMG IDL), the cornerstone of interoperability and transparency. We wanted to start out with Object Request Broker (ORB) details—what an ORB does and how it works—but we have to present IDL first because all ORB interfaces are defined in IDL. If you're never going to program to these interfaces, you can skip most of this chapter and go straight to the ORB description in Chapter 4 *after* you read the introductory material. (There's a note telling you when to skip ahead.)

Each chapter is organized in "drill-down" style—architectural and user-level material first, followed by technical and programming-level details. If you're not a programmer or a "techie," you can still learn a lot from the first section or two of most of the chapters on OMA services and facilities, as well as Chapters 10, 19, and 21, and 22. If you're technically inclined, just read everything straight through. (If you're really technical, of course, you can download the OMG specifications for free and read them, or join the OMG and *write* them.)

3.2 CORBA Compliance and Testing

CORBA and the OMA are defined by many separate specifications, all interdependent in various ways. Because products differ in the number and assortment of specifications that they implement, you will have to draw up a list of points that are important to you and compare it to the features of an ORB product to determine if it meets your needs. This section will give you a good start.

Therefore, CORBA users (and potential users) have to consider two questions:

1. Which specifications from the suite do I want my ORB product to comply with?

2. Has anyone—preferably a neutral, unbiased, experienced testing organization— written and run a test to see if it really complies?

Of course the answer to the second question is "Yes"—otherwise we wouldn't have brought it up. The OMG and The Open Group's (TOG) testing laboratory have teamed up to create and administer CORBA compliance testing. The test suite, funded partly by the initial ORB vendors who signed up for testing with the remainder contributed by a European Commission ESPRIT project, covers CORBA but not (yet) any of the CORBAservices.

The Open Group provided us this description of their testing and branding program:

The Open Brand for CORBA Program provides, through its Trademark License Agreement (TMLA), the ability for vendors to demonstrate to users of the CORBA technology their support for the OMG standard. By signing the TMLA, vendors commit to the users that their products conform to the OMG Standard. Successfully running the test suites required for registration provides an "Indicator of Conformance" for each of the vendors products. Should any issue be reported, by whatever means, the vendor is legally bound to resolve the issue within the guidelines provided by the TMLA. This guarantee of conformance to the standards covers both the Application Programming Interfaces (API) as well as the Interoperability of implementations from more than one vendor. Failure to resolve an issue will result in the vendor losing their Brand registration.

In the current implementation of the Open Brand for CORBA Program, the Product Standard calls for products to support OMG's CORBA 2.1 standard in the product registration. At its launch in May 1999, 3 products were registered as conformant to the CORBA 2.1 standard. Further projects are now in place to enhance the conformance indicators and registrations, for the CORBA Version 2.3 standard recently published, and the new CORBA Version 3.0 standard which will include the CORBA Component Model.

Since the list of ORBs that passed the test changes as more products come into full compliance, we're not going to publish it here. Vendors will trumpet their compliance by putting a special logo on their product (see Figure 3.1). We suspect that magazine articles, which have a much shorter shelf life than a book like this, will print up-to-date lists from time to time as well, as will various Web sites.

Figure 3.1   Logo awarded to ORB products that pass the compliance test.

What about products that haven't passed the test? Passing the TOG test suite is a lot of work, so many ORBs are unlikely to ever get tested. What if the ORB you like best fits in this category? Don't despair; even before the testing program began, ORBs interoperated successfully just by relying on the CORBA specification documents. Chances are, the ORB you want to use will work and interoperate well for just about everything you need and if it doesn't, vendors will fix whatever is wrong without needing a test result to prod them. Of course, this is something that you will have to discover for yourself. If you have any questions about a particular vendor's point of view toward interoperability, ask the vendor directly.

3.2.1 CORBA Compliance Points

Since one aspect of putting together a test suite is figuring out, and setting down in a formal statement, exactly what you're going to test, the effort also produced a CORBA Product Definition that helps with the first question. Here is the TOG's definition of a CORBA-compliant product (copyright by The Open Group, reprinted with permission):

Products which conform to this Product Standard include an implementation of the OMG abstract object model which includes the following:

- Object Request Broker (ORB), including interfaces that allow access to the ORB without dependencies on the Basic Object Adapter (BOA).
- Interface Definition Language (IDL), which is used to describe the interfaces that client objects call and object implementations provide.
- Dynamic Invocation Interface (DII), which describes the client side of the interface that allows dynamic creation and invocation of requests to objects.
- Dynamic Skeleton Interface (DSI), which describes the server-side interface that can deliver requests from an ORB to an object implementation that does not have compile-time knowledge of the type of object it is implementing.

Products which conform to this Product Standard may optionally include an implementation of the OMG abstract object module which includes the following:

- Interface Repository (IR), which describes the component of the ORB that manages and provides access to a collection of object definitions.

The detailed Technical Standard specifying the functionality in CORBA-compliant products, including specification of the CORBA architecture and components, is detailed in The Common Object Request Broker: Architecture and Specification (OMG document formal/97-09-01) and the associated IDL/Java Language Mapping (OMG document orbos/98-01-16). Hereafter, these documents are referred to as "the Specification."

In addition to the core ORB technology, these products supply an implementation of the ORB interoperability architecture that supplies the framework for ORB interoperability, including the General Inter-ORB Protocol (GIOP) and the Internet Inter-ORB Protocol (IIOP). Products described by this Product Standard correspond to Interoperability-compliant ORBs, as defined by Section 9.3.4 of the Specification.

Each implementation also includes one or more of the following language mappings of OMG IDL:

- C Language
- C++ Language
- Java
- Smalltalk
- COBOL
- ADA

This Product Standard includes core ORB functionality, DII, DSI, IIOP Version 1.0, and at least one of the OMG IDL language mappings.

This Product Standard optionally includes the core ORB functionality of the Interface Repository (IR).

This Product Standard does not require inclusion of the following components of the CORBA specification:

- Basic Object Adapter (BOA)
- Portable Object Adapter (POA)
- COM/CORBA interworking functionality
- Any specific object facilities or services

Support for IIOP Version 1.0 is required. Support for IIOP Version 1.1 is optional.

Based on this section, when you go ORB shopping, you can expect to get an ORB that supports the basic CORBA architecture, and an IDL compiler for at least one programming language from the preceding list. The IDL compiler will generate stubs and skeletons according to the spec. In addition, the ORB will support the DII and DSI (Dynamic Invocation Interface and Dynamic Skeleton Interface, described in Chapter 4) and have an IR (Interface Repository, also in Chapter 4), which bears the standard interfaces. The other interfaces discussed in the first paragraph include interface Object, discussed in Section 3.4.

You can use other programming languages with CORBA. Many besides the six on this list have been implemented in IDL compilers and are perfectly useful even though their mappings lack OMG-standard status. We've run across ORBs with IDL compilers for Lisp, Perl, Tcl, Eiffel, Python, and Objective-C; we're sure there are others that you can find if you look hard enough. (If you find an ORB with a FORTRAN IDL compiler, let me know.) If these languages can help your implementation, go ahead and use them if the product you find meets your company's criteria for reliability—the only caveat you have to keep in mind is that, because there is no OMG standard language mapping, you might have to do a little work if you need to port your client and object-implementation code from one vendor's ORB to another. Of course, if there's only one vendor and one ORB for your language, this won't even come up. Interoperability relies on the standard network protocol IIOP, and this will be the same regardless of programming language.

As we write this, ORB vendors are transitioning the server side of their products from the BOA to the POA. There are many advantages to the POA, and you should adopt or switch to it as early as you can. But, it will be a while before it is universally available so you will have to pay attention to which object adaptor an ORB comes with as you make your selection.

Some IDL datatypes, notably long long, long double, fixed, and the wide character and string types, are not universally available. If your application needs high precision, or relies on wide character sets (a universal requirement in many countries around the world), you will have to limit your search to ORBs that support these features.

The CORBA 3 features that we discussed in the first section of this book are too new to appear in products as we write this, but you will be able to buy them all "real soon now." We think that means in early to mid-2000 for first-generation products, and about a year later for second-generation, for all CORBA 3 features including Asynchronous and Messaging-capable ORBs with client control of Quality of Service and CORBA components. Also in this category are specialized CORBA implementations for real-time, embedded, and fault-tolerant systems.

There are many Web sites that list ORBs that are available on the market or downloadable. We've collected some on this book's Web site; see Appendix A.

3.2.2 The CORBAservices

Each CORBAservice is a separate compliance point. In principle, vendors may choose individually whether to offer each service, but most vendors are offering a set of CORBAservices including all or some of the basics. In our survey of available services, Naming and Events (and possibly Notification) were the most common, followed by Trader. Transactions is also widely available although this is usually a separate product with its own price tag; Security is also available with a number of ORBs, but this feature is not always a full implementation of the OMG specification. Persistence is another desirable service, but the OMG had just replaced the deprecated Persistent Object Service as we went to press, and implementations of the new Persistent State Service (Chapter 17) were not out yet.

Here's a list of the specified CORBAservices, arranged in the order we present them in the book—that is, by how basic, important, or interesting they are. We've grouped two services under each of the first two bullets because the pair perform similar functions. We admit, Notification is a Domain facility from the Telecoms Task Force, but it's really the Event Service on steroids so we list it here. In the third bullet, we also list concurrency because its function is to support the Transaction service. When we organized and wrote these chapters, there was no persistence CORBAservice. As we finished up, OMG members adopted the new Persistent State Service (PSS). They did a good job: not only is the PSS destined to be used frequently as a standalone service, it's incorporated into the CCM as the basis for built-in persistence. If the specification had been available earlier, we would have put it higher up on our list.

- Naming and Trader
- Event Management and Notification
- Transactions and Concurrency
- Security Services
- LifeCycle
- Relationships
- Persistence

- Externalization
- Property
- Collections
- Query
- Time
- Licensing

3.2.3 The Horizontal CORBAfacilities

The CORBAfacilities are, almost without exception, too big to be bundled with an ORB product. Instead, you would search out and purchase these separately. The CORBAfacilities are split into two groups: Horizontal, which are generally useful, and Vertical or Domain, which are typically adopted and used by a particular industry (healthcare, finance, manufacturing, etc.) as we describe in Chapters 19 and 20. However, there is a Business Objects Domain Task Force that has adopted a Workflow Facility, so you see that this categorization is not absolute.

There are a few horizontal CORBAfacilities—that is, facilities that don't belong in any particular domain, and that weren't adopted by an OMG Domain Task Force. These are:

- Mobile Agents Facility
- Printing Facility
- Internationalization Facility

The Printing Facility was written in large part by Xerox Corporation. It's a comprehensive collection of document management and printing functions with CORBA interfaces. When we asked them, Xerox said they plan to make an implementation available to System Integrators and other vendors, although they didn't give out any specific information about availability dates or terms. There is at least one implementation on the market for each of these specifications. (Because there are only these few horizontal CORBAfacilities, and also because the OMG has disbanded the horizontal CORBAfacilities Task Force, we don't have a chapter on them. Therefore, if you're interested in any of these specifications, you'll have to download it from the OMG Web site and read it yourself. These are all available from OMG's *Technology Adoptions* Web page, listed with the other references in Appendix A.)

3.2.4 The Domain CORBAfacilities

When we wrote the first edition of this book, the OMG's Domain Technology Committee was newly formed and every Domain specification was a distant thought. But the Domain Task Forces have been working long enough to issue 18 specifications, with about 20 more in the works. Again, these are typically large specifications and would not be bundled with an ORB, but you would want to find out about system compatabilities for any of these services that you wanted to buy and use. Because they're all CORBA-based, of course, the incompatibilities will be minimal!

We discuss the Domain facilities in Chapters 19 and 20, so we won't even list them here. Look ahead for details.

3.2.5 Specifying Your CORBA Environment

What do you need to buy to have a complete CORBA environment? Section 3.2.1 says that you'll need an ORB with all of the functionality mentioned, paying particular attention to the choice of BOA or POA functionality on the server side. With your ORB you will get an IDL compiler for at least one of the languages listed, but you should also request (and pay for, if you have to) compilers for other languages that your site or application configuration requires. If you're shopping in mid-2000 or beyond, consider getting some of the CORBA 3 enhancements that should be available in products by then. Add the services you need to your shopping cart: basic ones such as Naming, Trader, Events, and Notification, and the not-so-basic pair Transactions and Security. When you're done with these, look at the list in this chapter and compare it to your vendor's catalog and see what else you can get that will be helpful with your application.

Where should you start looking? We'd suggest Chapter 25, which contains condensed descriptions of the ORB products represented in the programming example in this book, listing the services and facilities that were available as we went to press. For more up-to-date information, you can either check individual vendors' Web sites or go to the book Web site listed in Appendix A under References and surf from there.

3.3 OMG IDL by Example

The easiest way to learn IDL basics is by working through an example. We'll use a short excerpt from the tutorial example demonstrated in this book. In this section, we're going to focus on the IDL grammar and capabilities, but pay little attention to what these objects actually do; that discussion occurs in Chapter 23.

The example deals with a store with point-of-sale (POS) terminals. Here's the interface the POS terminal object uses to communicate with its barcode-reader object, keypad object, and receipt-printer object:

```
//POS Object IDL example
module POS {
    typedef string Barcode;

    interface InputMedia {
        typedef string OperatorCmd;
        void      barcode_input(in Barcode item);
        void      keypad_input(in OperatorCmd cmd);
    };

    interface OutputMedia {
        boolean output_text(in string string_to_print );
    };
```

```
interface POSTerminal {
        void    end_of_sale();
        void    print_POS_sales_summary();
    };
};
```

Before we start to worry about the exact syntax of this IDL declaration, let's consider the highest level view—what it does. *This file declares the interfaces for all of the objects in our Point-of-Sale Terminal computer, in a programming-language independent way.* In our "store," other objects will invoke these objects on the Point-of-Sale Terminal Computer through these interfaces. In addition, these objects will invoke operations on other objects using *their* interfaces, which we can't see here because we've only reprinted part of the IDL for the system. (To see the rest, skip ahead to Chapter 26.)

Even without any knowledge of programming, you can tell a lot from this file. There are three objects (called "interfaces," which we'll discuss later in the chapter): Input-Media, OutputMedia, and POSTerminal. InputMedia does two things: a barcode input thing, and a keypad input thing. OutputMedia outputs a string but we can't tell why, where, or what from this file alone. You can tell POSTerminal to end a sale, or to print a summary of its sales (presumably on the OutputMedia, wouldn't you think?). Variable type and instance names give us a lot of insight into what the variables mean, too: Barcode, OperatorCmd. Hmm—maybe IDL isn't quite as hard or opaque as you thought, right?

This is where the details start. If you're only looking for a high-level overview, now is the time to skip ahead to Chapter 4 and start looking at the Object Request Broker. You've seen an example—if you need to learn more details about IDL, keep reading here. Otherwise, skip to the next chapter.

We'll take this example apart as we work our way through the language. But first, some IDL basics.

3.3.1 IDL Basics

Although IDL interfaces are programming language-independent, the IDL language itself has the appearance (but not the semantics) of ANSI C++. Notable resemblances include:

- C++-like preprocessing
- Lexical rules (with new keywords for distribution concepts)
- Grammar, which is a subset of C++ and incorporates syntax for constant, type, and operation declarations; but lacks algorithmic structures and variables

And differences:

- Function return type is required (but may be void)
- Each formal parameter in an operation declaration must have a name
- and others

Comments may be placed between /* and */; lines that start with a double-slash (//) also constitute a comment.

Since some programming languages are case-sensitive, while others are not, OMG IDL is *restrictive* with respect to case: You're not allowed to define two identifiers in the same scope that differ only in case. If you try, they collide and give a compilation error. For example, you can't have a module named MyCompany that contains an operation myCompany in the same scope. (Scope is defined in the next section.)

3.3.1.1 IDL Types, Modules, and Scoping

OMG IDL is a strongly typed language; that is, every variable must be declared to be a particular type (but see the discussion of the **any** type, later in this section). This feature enables ORBs to convert variables from one platform format to another as they transfer messages around your heterogeneous network.

In order to ensure interoperability, OMG's official language mappings map *every* IDL type to something in every mapped language—either a language type, or something more complex (such as a **struct** or even a class)—if that's necessary. The reverse is not true, however, and many IDL-mapped programming languages have language types that do not map directly to IDL types. If you need to use one of these types in a CORBA operation, however, chances are you can figure out a reasonable IDL type or construct to use for the purpose—most likely a string, or some kind of **struct**.

IDL defines *basic, constructed,* and *template* types. Here's a tour:

IDL basic types include the integer types **short** and **unsigned short** (16 bits), **long** and **unsigned long** (32 bits), and **long long** and **unsigned long long** (64 bits). Floating-point IDL types are **float** (corresponding to IEEE single-precision floating point), **double** (IEEE double-precision), and **long double** (IEEE double-extended). **char** is an 8-bit quantity; graphic characters are defined by the ISO 8859-1 (Latin1) standard. **wchar** encodes wide characters from any character set; its size is undefined so be careful if you need to pass **wchars** or **wchar** strings from one vendor's ORB to another. **boolean** can only take on the values **TRUE** and **FALSE**. **octet** is guaranteed not to undergo any conversion when it passes over the wire.

Constructed types are defined in IDL files (yours and the OMG's), using the basic types as building blocks. The palette of constructed IDL types is very rich. We will only sample it here; the example demonstrates and uses many of these in a realistic way. Consult the documentation that came with your IDL compiler for the rest of the details, or download the IDL specification from the OMG's Web site.

An IDL **struct** may contain any combination of IDL types, primitive or constructed; you just list them in a declaration or **typedef** statement to define the new **struct**. (There's no **struct** in this module, but you can see one in the example IDL in Chapter 26.) **valuetype**s, defined by the new Objects-by-Value specification, will be used frequently in place of **struct**s once they become widely available; we discuss **valuetype**s starting in Section 3.3.3. The IDL discriminated **union** is a cross between the C union and switch statements, and uses a typed tag field to determine which of the alternative formats is contained in any particular instance of the field. The **enum** is an ordered list of identifiers; you can test in a case or switch statement in your code to determine which listed value a variable corresponds to. Since our example uses an **enum** to demonstrate both what they're good for and how to use them, we won't go into any more detail here.

There are four template types: **sequence, string, wstring**, and **fixed. sequence** is a one-dimensional array of any IDL type (even a **struct** that you defined, so you see that even sequences can be complicated), or you could put **sequence**s into **struct**s. You may either set the maximum length of your **sequence** in your IDL (bounded **sequence**) or not (unbounded **sequence**). Language mappings for unbounded **sequence**s may require you to fill in some size information, or provide storage adequate to hold the **sequence**, so that your program is ready to cope with whatever gets sent down the wire.

string and **wstring** are basically arrays of **char** and **wchar**, respectively, but IDL defines them as strings so that ORB implementations can take advantage of string-processing support already available on many systems, typically as library routines, for faster and more flexible manipulation.

The **fixed** type represents a fixed-point number with up to 31 significant digits. Mappings attempted to define extended-precision decimal quantities in different programming languages, but OMG members agree that this part of the specification contains significant flaws. If your ORB implements **fixed** for the programming language you use most, take advantage of it, but don't count on it interoperating with other vendors' ORBs in the near future.

Finally, you can define a multidimensional array of any IDL quantity but, in order for this to work, all array dimensions must be fixed in your IDL file—that is, no array dimension may be a parameter. There's no IDL keyword for this; you simply follow your IDL identifier with a series of integer constants, each enclosed in square brackets, when you define it.

What about the CORBA object reference? It's also an IDL type but it's neither primitive, constructed, nor template. Where semantic considerations allow (basically, if it makes sense), an object reference may appear in IDL declaration with any other IDL type—in **struct**s, **sequence**s, **array**s, all by itself, or whatever. In the example later in this book, we define and use a **struct** that includes an object reference.

IDL's **any** type provides an alternative format to the restrictions that strong typing imposes. (Object purists will insist, correctly it turns out, that there are very few cases—perhaps none—where the **any** type is actually required, but we won't get into that here.) A variable of the **any** type may be used anywhere another IDL type would be allowed; since an **any** may represent literally any IDL type, including constructed types and variable-length arrays, and may be cast to any type dynamically at runtime, clients and object implementations enjoy the freedom of dynamic typing. Internally, ORBs associate an **any**'s type with its value, allowing them to provide the same level of service for an **any** as they do for all of the other IDL types. On the network, a standard set of typecodes accompanies the **any**s as they pass from one ORB to another so they can be interpreted correctly. At the receiving end, though, your client or object implementation code will have to extract the **any**'s contents so you'll probably need instances of whatever language types are available to receive these contents (since few languages allow you to create new instances of language types at runtime).

The **DynAny** (short for Dynamic Any) type allows programs to traverse and extract language types from **any** values that they might not have compiled into their code. The **DynAny** is not intended for casual application use—it's really aimed at system programmers who use it for constructing bridges, debuggers, and monitors, which justify the additional skilled programming required to be able to cope with *anything* that comes over the wire. We recommend that you control the types you use, so your programs can either avoid use of **any**, or at least use it to contain one of only a few different types. If you really need to use a **DynAny**, check your vendor's documentation for the howto's.

IDL provides multiple nested levels of scope: At the highest level, each IDL file constitutes a scope. Within a file, the **module**, **interface**, **valuetype**, **struct**, **union**, **operation**, and **exception** each defines a smaller scope. (We'll define each of these terms later in this chapter.) IDL scopes these identifiers: types, constants, enumeration values, **exception**s, **interface**s, **valuetype**s, **attribute**s, and operations. All of these identifiers are valid only within the scope in which they are defined and invisible outside it, unless their definition is specifically imported into another scope through the import operator "**::**" (double colon). When you import from a separate IDL file, you'll have to **#include** it so the IDL compiler knows where to find the definitions. In the future, an **input** statement added by the CORBA components specification will provide an alternative to **#include**.

In this example, the variables **Barcode** and **POSid** are scoped to the module **POS**. In this module, **Barcode** is used in two interfaces: **Interface InputMedia** and **Interface POSTerminal**. The scoping ensures that the definition is valid (and identical) for both cases. **POSid** is scoped to the module for a different reason; in fact, it is not used here. But it is used later in another module where it is included and referred to as **POS::POSid**. It is proper programming practice to define it in this module, which defines all of the characteristics of the POSTerminal object. The external module expects only to use it, not to define it.

3.3.1.2 Defining an Interface

Typically, an **interface** construct in an IDL file collects a number of operations that form a natural group. Most objects will bear a single interface, but some objects, and many CCMs, will bear more than one so this may not be all of the operations of a particular object or component but rather some subset. One of the most important aspects of the **interface** is that it is the unit of inheritance, but we'll postpone this discussion until Section 3.3.2.3.

The keyword **interface** starts a new scope; inside its curly brackets we get a chance to define yet another set of scoped quantities and finally a set of operations. Of course, this time, the quantities are defined only for the interface.

This example module defines three interfaces: **InputMedia** with two operations, **OutputMedia** with one, and **POSTerminal** with three. **InputMedia** also defines the new type, **OperatorCmd**.

3.3.1.3 Operations

The format of the operation statement has three required parts, as well as three optional parts that do not appear in this particular example.

First, the three required parts. Look at the operation **output_text** in interface **OutputMedia**. The statement starts by declaring a return type. This operation returns a **boolean** (**TRUE** or **FALSE**) value; note that most of the other operations in our example return **void**, which is an allowed return type. You can't omit the return type declaration just because it's **void**.

The second part is the operation name; the IDL compiler will use this name to construct a name for the language mapping. The third part is the list of parameters. Each parameter declaration consists of a parameter attribute, which must be either **in**, **out**, or **inout**; a type declaration; and the parameter name. ORBs use these type declarations in the operation statements to manipulate data as requests fly about your enterprise.

By the way, the target object reference does not appear in the IDL; the binding of invocation to target is handled by each language in the way that fits it most naturally. However, other object references may be included as parameters to operations. The ORBs that transmit the request will recognize these as they pass by; if they are transmitted to a remote ORB, they will first be put into a form that it can recognize and use.

3.3.1.4 Exceptions

The **exception** is the first optional operation parameter we'll discuss. Operation declarations may optionally contain **exception**s. As you might expect, we can scope **exception** definitions across either our file, module, or interface. (This capability allows us, for instance, to define one global set of exceptions for our entire "application"—that is, across all of our objects and interfaces—and additional sets of exceptions that apply only to certain interfaces.) Exceptions are associated with operations using the **raises** expression, and may have one or more values associated with them. For example:

> **exception input_out_of_range { long dummy };**

> **void operation1(in long arg1) raises (input_out_of_range);**

You can specify multiple exceptions in a list, separated by commas.

OMG defines a set of standard exceptions, covering primarily communications failures. Any operation may raise one of these. You don't have to declare these exceptions (in fact, you can't), but your invoking code must be prepared to deal with them because they may be raised by any invocation of a remote object. And, since the client side of an invocation is the same whether the target is local or remote, you should check the standard exceptions after virtually every invocation. We'll show why in the next few chapters as we go over the rest of the CORBA architecture.

When an operation raises an exception during its execution, the ORB is responsible for transmitting this information back to the client and notifying it. Notification is accomplished through the language mappings in various ways; we will discuss this in more detail in Chapters 7–9 and in the example.

3.3.2 Oneway Declaration

The second optional operation parameter is the **oneway** declaration. Operations may optionally be declared **oneway** by prepending to their declaration:

> **oneway void SendMyMessage (in string MyMessage);**

A **oneway** operation must specify a **void** return type; only input parameters are allowed, and no exceptions may be declared. (However, some of the standard exceptions may be raised by a **oneway** invocation attempt.) Invocation semantics are being redefined by the OMG: The original CORBA specification (and your ORB, if it's pre-CORBA 3) says that **oneway** invocations are "ORB best effort" *without* defining "best effort"—that is, ORB vendors decide the level of reliability they engineer into a **oneway** invocation. However, things are better for CORBA 3 ORBs: The messaging specification also defines quality of service for **oneway** invocations and actually provides for a client choice of four different levels. See Chapter 6 for a description of the messaging service and the qualities of service including **oneway**. Operations not declared **oneway** may return results in **out** or **inout** parameters and the return value. You still get a choice of semantics and quality of service, also discussed in Chapter 6.

3.3.2.1 Context Objects

A **context** object contains a list of name-value pairs called properties. Currently, the OMG specification restricts the values to **string**s, but you can put a number into a string and convert back when you need to, so this isn't a showstopper. There is no limit to the number of pairs a **context** object may contain, and context objects may be chained together. **context** objects are the CORBA equivalent of the environment in Unix or PC-DOS—a set of user and application preferences, which may or may not affect a particular operation, in a format that a module can scan for items that it needs to take into account. Some environments will have a system **context** object, a separate **context** object for each user, and another for each application that requires it. These could be chained together and propagated at runtime so that remote executions would occur in the environment you expect.

In IDL, you declare a context for an operation with the expression:

```
context (context1, context2, ...)
```

right after the **raises** expression in your operation definition. You add and manipulate **context** properties using operations addressed to the ORB. Only the ORB can create a **context**, so there's an operation to do that. Then there are operations to add, set, get, and delete properties, as you might expect. These are not the same properties as those defined by the properties service, so don't confuse them.

3.3.2.2 Attribute Variables

CORBA objects have state—that is, the variables in your implementation must retain the values they're set to, until they are explicitly changed or the object is deleted or destroyed. Consequently, setting and retrieving values of variables is done frequently. To make this easier, OMG IDL provides the **attribute**, a variable with a pair of implicit functions that allow clients to **set** and **get** its value. There is also a **readonly attribute**, which lacks the **set** function. This is handy for variables that are set by the object—perhaps in response to some condition or event—to a value that must then be read by its clients. The accessor functions, implicit in the IDL, are made real by each language mapping. You can read about their form in Chapters 7–9.

The CORBA components specification has added attribute-specific exceptions to the **set** and **get** operations of IDL attributes. This omission should have been corrected sooner, since the lack of exception capability rendered attributes unsuitable for use in many OMG specifications and a lot of user IDL as well. Once products implement this advance, IDL can be written more simply. Remember, this is a recent change to the OMG specification; products may not implement it until mid or late 2000.

Here's what an **attribute** looks like in IDL, including the new **exception** capability:

```
interface MyInterface {
        attribute float radius
            get_raises ( get_ exception_list )
            set_raises ( set_exception_list )
};
```

The language mapping for this will be the same as if we had written (still in IDL):

```
interface MyInterface {
        float  _get_radius() raises ( get_ exception_list );
        void  _set_radius(in float r) raises ( set_exception_list );
}
```

since the accessor function names are generated by prepending **_get_** and **_set_** to the name of the attribute variable. Attributes are just a more convenient way of setting up a variable or struct with a **get/set** operation pair.

3.3.2.3 Inheritance

Using inheritance, you can derive a new interface from one or more existing interfaces. The derived interface inherits all of the elements of the interfaces it is based upon; it then adds whatever new elements (constants, types, attributes, operations, and so forth) that it needs. The new interface starts out with all of the operations of the base interfaces, and can add new ones. You are not allowed to redefine the base interfaces, although other base elements may be redefined. This means that a client written originally to invoke the base class is guaranteed to be able to invoke the derived interface, since all the operations that it expects are included. However, a client written to access the derived interface cannot necessarily work with the base interface, since it may invoke operations that were newly added to the derived interface and do not appear in the base interface.

The syntax for introducing inheritance in IDL is the colon. Here is an example:

```
interface example1 {
        long operation1 (in long arg1);
};
interface example2:example1 {
        void operation2 (in long arg2, out long arg3);
};
```

interface example2 also includes, through inheritance, **operation1**. Even though it does not appear explicitly in the IDL, the language mappings will generate code for it, and the object implementation for **example2** must be prepared to respond to invocations of **operation1**, as well as **operation2**. (We use this brief example to illustrate inheritance in each language mapping. Look for it in Chapters 7, 8, and 9.)

Multiple inheritance is allowed. For example, in the interface declaration

```
interface example4:example3, example1 {
    . . .
}
```

interface example4 includes not only all of **example3**, but also **example1**. The language mappings will generate code for all the operations of both **example3** and **example1** in the stub for **example4**, plus its own operations; its object implementation must be prepared to respond to them.

3.3.3 Objects Passable by Value: The valuetype

The introduction of objects passable by value was the first major change that OMG members have made to the CORBA architecture since its inception. Like the Asynchronous and Messaging Interfaces that followed this specification, the **valuetype** exposes aspects of the remoteness of object instances to the client, and either allows or requires a client to treat objects differently depending on location. Following the principle of *location transparency* in our application code, we have treated objects without regard to their location whether local or remote. But in our design, installation, and administration, we have always paid careful attention to remoteness because we know that network transmission is never free—bandwidth is limited and latency is frequently longer than users want to wait. The point is, these problems have nothing to do with any particular application—they're characteristic of the network environment, and should be dealt with in the infrastructure layer.

In one sense, issuing the RFP for objects passable by value was an admission on the OMG's part that some objects—with their states—need to be operated on in multiple locations with the performance you can only get with local invocations. Where resources are stressed, this may be the only way to get your work done with the service levels that your users expect. It doesn't matter whether your data structure is huge—gigabytes or more—or the network is so overloaded that even small payloads travel slowly. Whatever the reason, this is another tool in your CORBA programmer's toolbox that you can use to cope in special situations. We'll discuss later that recursive and cyclic graphs such as btrees, when represented by valuetypes, are guaranteed to transfer properly over the wire and so receive both the speed and assurance they need to be programmed well.

The IDL keyword for an object passable by value is **valuetype**. The **valuetype** is also useful in other situations. Java programmers, especially those programming in Java and accessing CORBA through the reverse language mapping (see Chapter 8), generate serializables that will encode as **valuetype**s over the wire and only be accessible in CORBA using this specification. In general, this specification enhances the interworking between CORBA and the Java language, a benefit because of both the undeniable popularity of Java and the close parallels between their two programming and execution environments.

You can think of a **valuetype** as a "struct with functionality"—you can put any IDL datatypes that you want (including constructed types) into a **valuetype**. When you pass the **valuetype** as a parameter to a CORBA call, the ORB at the receiving end constructs a *local copy* with whatever data was contained in the original at the instant you made the invocation or sent the reply that contained it (since **valuetype**s can be either **in**, **out**, **inout**, or return value parameters). At the receiving end, it becomes a *local programming-language object*, where it is invoked through the language mechanism and not through the ORB. Data at the two locations is *not* synchronized by any CORBA mechanism—as far as the system is concerned, there is no relationship between source and copy once the transferred data finishes its trip over the wire. If you want the data at the two ends to remain synchronized, you'll have to do all the work for this yourself.

valuetypes are *not* CORBA objects—they do not inherit from **CORBA::Object**; instead they have their own base class, **ValueBase**. This allows **valuetype** implementations to stay lightweight, avoiding the baggage required by CORBA interface semantics: marshaling, POA support, and so forth—they don't even have object references. **valuetype**s can inherit singly (but not multiply) from other **valuetype**s, but can only "support" interfaces. We'll discuss this a little more at the end of this subsection.

Since there is no magic in CORBA (or anywhere else except on TV), you can't just pass a **valuetype** to any application and expect it to work. At the receiving end, the ORB must have a factory that it can invoke to create a running instance of the **valuetype**. After the factory creates it, the instance accepts the stream of state data that the ORB received over the wire and uses it to reconstruct its state, making it ready to accept calls. If you're using Java, you'll be pleased to know that the protocol provides for a look over the wire for downloadable code to create the running instance, although the ORB also looks for a local factory even in Java.

Although **valuetype**s are active objects with callable methods, many applications will use them to represent objects which mainly encapsulate data, or to pass large or complicated structs. If your application passes the same struct data over the wire in repeated calls, the **valuetype** gives you an easy way to re-create the struct in the remote context where it remains accessible after the call that created it. As soon as the **valuetype** became official, new OMG specifications started using it in place of structs wherever they could.

Does this mean that you should start using **valuetype**s in your applications right away? In mid-1999 when we wrote this, **valuetype**s were a new part of CORBA; so new that they were not present in any vendor's product, so this wasn't even a question for us. But, they were such an important addition to the architecture that almost every vendor (including those represented in this book) was already working on bringing their **valuetype**-enabled IDL compiler to market. However, ORB builders acknowledge that the **valuetype** implementation is a complex piece of code to write—there's a lot to do in the sending ORB, and even more in the marshaling/de-marshaling code that transmits your valuetypes over the wire, and the receiving ORB that has to re-create them. It wouldn't be much of a surprise to anybody if it took two generations of product for robust, interoperable implementations of **valuetype** to become generally available, at about a year (or maybe a little less since we like to be optimistic) per generation. So, our advice to most readers is to design for valuetypes but program with **struct**s until your ORB vendor delivers a robust implementation, and then start your migration to this new technology. But, if your application manipulates recursive or cyclic graphs (see the rest of this section and the next section), or if you interoperate a lot between CORBA and Java, you might want to become an early adopter because of the particular advantages the **valuetype** has in these areas. (As we go to press, the first implementations of **valuetype** are reaching the market from both large and small ORB vendors, representing both Java and C++.)

valuetype implementations depend on the mapping of the new IDL to different programming languages. Although only C++ and Java had completed mappings when we wrote this in mid-1999, new mappings were already under way for Smalltalk and Ada, ensuring that applications using these languages will be able to participate in the full suite of CORBA features. A mapping for C may take a little longer, and we don't know of plans to map this feature to COBOL. And finally, getting back to the technical side, if you're one of those techies who writes btree routines or the like, operating on recursive or cyclic graphs (lists, trees, lattices, etc.), you'll be pleased to know that the authors of the OBV spec took your needs into account. Graphs are replicated at the receiving end exactly as they were originally, with cycles and internal references intact. Our example in the next section demonstrates this capability. Another specialization: For Java and any other language that requires transmission of nulls, **valuetype**s do this as well. (IDL does not transmit empty strings or sequences as nulls in CORBA object invocations.)

3.3.3.1 valuetype Example

Let's analyze a **valuetype** definition, to figure out what's in there and how it works. This example, from the specification, also demonstrates the use of recursion, but first we'll concentrate on the three major parts of the declaration.

```
typedef sequence<unsigned long> WeightSeq;

valuetype WeightedBinaryTree {
    // state definition
      unsigned long weight;
      WeightedBinaryTree left;
      WeightedBinaryTree right;
    // initializer
      init(in unsigned long w);
    // local operations
      WeightSeq pre_order();
      WeightSeq post_order();
};
```

Following the single line typedef'ing **WeightSeq** comes our definition of a **value-type** named **WeightedBinaryTree**. The three components of a **valuetype** declaration are, as shown here, its state, zero or more initializers, and local operations.

When we defined CORBA objects, declarations served only to define types for use in invocations, which was the only place that these declared variables were realized. In a **valuetype**, this part of the declaration defines the type's actual *state*—that is, the state variables whose values will be sent over the wire when the **valuetype** is passed as a parameter of an invocation. These declarations commit us to declare space for these variables, and make them our implementation's state, when we write it—far different from the situation when we wrote an implementation of an IDL interface. Don't get carried away though: This state only exists in memory, and does not persist. When your process terminates, it all goes away.

Following the state declaration comes zero or more initializer declarations. Language mappings will define a constructor for each initializer you write. Unlike the IDL interface declarations, the operation **init** will be overloaded if you have more than one (all initializers are named **init**); this is OK since it's not a CORBA call (that is, it will only be callable from within your local language implementation). Watch out for different

IDL type arguments that map to the same language type because they can generate colliding constructors. The specification recommends that you vary the number of parameters to avoid this. (No, it doesn't give you another alternative.)

The final component of the declarations are the *local* language operations on a local language object in your running code.

Let's take a closer look at the recursion in this declaration, since it shows the unique advantage of **valuetype**s so well. A weighted binary tree is composed of nodes, each of which is another weighted binary tree. This makes its declaration simple—what you see is all there is. In realization, at one end of the tree one node will be the root (no other nodes will point to it); at the other end of the tree will be many leaves (**left** and **right** will be null; that is, pointing to no other nodes). All other nodes will have at least one member (**left** or **right**) that is actually another node.

If each node were a CORBA object, using it would be extremely slow: Every reference would be one or more round trips. And an attempt to copy all these objects, keeping (or re-establishing) referential integrity at the end of the process, would be complicated.

In contrast, passing the tree as a set of **valuetype**s is easy. When you pass the root node of your tree as a **valuetype**, its state gets passed automatically. (That's what **valuetype**s are for—right?) Its state, it turns out, are the two WeightedBinaryTree nodes **left** and **right**, which are **valuetype**s in their own right, and they get passed too. When they do, their state nodes get passed, and so on down the line until all leaf nodes are passed. The system guarantees that, when the tree is reconstructed at the receiving end, the copy is an exact local replica of the original structure. You do have to be careful to pass the root node when you start this process, of course; if you start in the middle, all you get are the branches off the node from which you started.

3.3.3.2 *valuetype Details*

Several advanced aspects of **valuetype**s are interdependent. First, **valuetype**s can be either concrete or abstract. Concrete **valuetype**s are the form that we just discussed—with state, constructors, and operations. Abstract **valuetype**s have no state or constructors, and are declared **abstract** instead of **valuetype**. (If you declare a **valuetype** with no state variables, it's not abstract—it's just a degenerate stateful **valuetype**.)

valuetypes can inherit. Concrete **valuetype**s can single-inherit only; the authors of the specification believed (correctly, most likely) that the complications of statefulness make multiple inheritance impractical. **abstract** interfaces can multiple inherit.

Suppose your application deals with something with lots of instances—a **stockaccount** type, let's say—and it makes sense for some of these **stockaccount** instances to be CORBA objects and others to be **valuetype**s. (The **valuetype**s can be passed to traders' computers, while the CORBA instances work well on the trading company's own network, for example.) In this situation, you will have many operations that should accept *either* the valuetype or CORBA object form of **stockaccount**.

To make this work, you can create an abstract type named **stockaccount** that has all of the needed operations but no state. You can then inherit this abstract type in both your **valuetype** and CORBA object definitions. When you define the signature of processing objects that need to accept both forms interchangeably, you place the abstract interface into the signature instead of either concrete form. At runtime, you can place either an object reference or a **valuetype** in the slot, and the system will do the right thing with either one.

A valuebox is a **valuetype** with only one data member and no inheritance, initializers, or methods (the opposite of an abstract interface, which has methods but no data). There's a one-line shorthand for declaring a valuebox. For example,

valuetype mystring string

is all it takes to declare the valuebox **mystring** to be a **string**. If all you're doing is encapsulating data, this form can save you a lot of typing. But, try to resist the temptation to replace all your database entries with valueboxes and think that you're object oriented—that's not what they're for, and it certainly isn't a good architecture. You need active CORBA objects with methods and state, and a well-designed architecture, to be object oriented and gain the benefits.

The specification also allows a **valuetype** to "support" an interface. **supports** means that the **valuetype** does what you would expect if it had inherited the interface, but the mechanism is not the same as inheritance so the authors of the specification use the word "support" to avoid confusion. As an example, you could declare

valuetype Example3 supports ThisInterface { . . . }

and your IDL definition would incorporate, through the **supports** mechanism, the types and operations of **ThisInterface**, in addition to everything that you declared in your IDL here, and the valuetype would have included them in its implementation. In Java, the IDL compiler uses a tie mechanism (defined in the language mapping in a standard way) to couple the implementations; in C++, a combination of virtual base classes and a POA skeleton provide the functionality. Why not inherit? Using CORBA inheritance would allow **widen** operations to move between valuetypes and objects, a type-system error since the valuetype was defined to be a totally new type, and not derive from **CORBA::object**.

Should you use **supports**? It's an advanced feature, and not one with an obvious use advantage that we can see in most applications. (Maybe that's why we didn't mention it until the end of the chapter.) This means the risks (for example, spending time programming and debugging, and maybe never getting it to work right, or not having it port) are high, and the potential reward is low. If you have some spare time, and a robust OBV implementation to play with sometime in 2002 or later after products have matured, then go ahead and fool around with **supports** and see if you can get it to work. But we don't think it's a tool you'll use every day.

3.3.3.3 *valuetype Summary*

That's it for **valuetype**s. We've covered the new capabilities as thoroughly as we could, even though this meant leaving out some programming details. This way, you leave this chapter with a good understanding of **valuetype**s. Later, when your vendor delivers a product that includes them, you can read the doc set to learn the programming details.

We'll conclude this chapter with an overview of **interface Object**, the OMG's collection of interfaces that operate on the object reference via the ORB. Once we're done, we'll be ready to tackle the ORB itself in Chapter 4.

3.4 The Object Interface

interface Object defines some operations that are performed on object references. You can think of it as an interface inherited by every object, but that's not how it's implemented—these operations are actually performed by the ORB. This means you don't have to take them into account when you build your object implementation, but you can use them anyhow.

In CORBA parlance, these operations are implemented by a pseudo-object; that is, not by an actual CORBA object. Their interfaces are defined in OMG IDL, but there are some differences: A pseudo-object may not be specified as a parameter in an operation on an ordinary object, may not be accessed using the DII, and does not have definitions in the interface repository. The IDL that defines them is termed pseudo-IDL or PIDL.

The OMG is moving away from PIDL to specify operations with these characteristics. The latest development is the declaration **<local>**, defined in the CORBA Component Model specification. For more on this, see the end of Chapter 5.

Here's the PIDL for **interface Object**:

```
interface Object {                                        // PIDL
        InterfaceDef get_interface ();
        boolean is_nil();
        Object duplicate ();
        void release ();
        boolean is_a (
                in string logical_type_id
        );
        boolean non_existent();
        boolean is_equivalent (
                in Object other_object
        );
        unsigned long hash(
                in unsigned long maximum
        );
        void create_request (
                in Context ctx
                in Identifier operation,
                in NVList arg_list,
                inout NamedValue result,
                out Request request,
                in Flags req_flag
        );
        Policy get_policy (
                in PolicyType policy_type
        );
        DomainManagersList get_domain_managers ();
```

```
Object set_policy_overrides(
        in PolicyList policies,
        in SetOverrideType set_add
    );
};
```

We'll use the operation **get_interface** to show how these operations work. You invoke **get_interface** targeted to the object with the interface definition you want. The invocation gets to the ORB, which recognizes it as one that the ORB is equipped to handle itself. Your ORB uses the object reference, not as the target for the invocation, but instead to identify the object whose interface you want—think of the object reference as an input parameter instead of the target. For more on the interface repository, see Chapter 4.

duplicate and **release** are operations performed by the ORB on object references because only the ORB is able to do this kind of thing. When your client creates and uses a **duplicate** object reference, the target object implementation cannot tell past that point whether the original or the copy was used to invoke a request. **release** reclaims storage for the object reference. This operates only on the object reference; the target object is not involved, nor are any other references to that particular target object.

Is_nil checks an object reference to see if it denotes **OBJECT_NIL**, that is, no object.

You invoke **is_a** on an object, with an interface repository ID as the input parameter, and the operation returns **TRUE** if the object is that type. To determine the response to your inquiry, the ORB performs basically the same operation that it does when you do a type-safe **narrow** operation in an object-oriented language. If your language does not have compile-time type checking, you can use this to maintain type safety.

non_existent is another operation that probes for object existence, but this one probes for existence of the instance, not the object reference. It returns **TRUE** (and does not, as you might have expected, raise the **OBJECT_NOT_EXIST** exception) if the ORB knows authoritatively that the object instance does not exist, and **FALSE** if it can not confirm. This operation may involve your ORB contacting the remote ORB, but it never invokes any operation on the remote instance itself. If the remote invocation fails and your ORB cannot make a reliable determination of existence, the operation raises an error. This operation is not really intended for end-user applications (which can just make their invocation and deal with **OBJECT_NOT_EXIST** exceptions if the instance has been destroyed); rather, it's intended for bridges and event channels that can use idle time to look for nonexistent objects and garbage-collect their own tables, stubs, and skeletons.

There's a **hash** operation that applications can use to establish that two object references are *not* identical. (You can't just compare copies of an object reference; even within a session, your ORB may give you two different pointers that actually refer to the same object.) You hash two object references, and if the hash values are different, then the object references are definitely different. If the hash values are the same, then you don't know anything because hash values are not guaranteed to be unique. (Two different object references may, by coincidence, return the same hash value. But two references to the same object will *always* return the same value.)

is_equivalent tries to establish that two object references *are* equivalent; that is, that they refer to the same object instance. (The two object references are the one that you input, and the one that is the target of the invocation.) This could be because they are truly identical—that is, the same value (since the ORB can determine this). But, two object references with different values can also refer to the same object. ORBs are allowed to expend resource to determine this, but a return value of FALSE doesn't mean that the two objects are truly different—just that the ORBs couldn't determine that they were the same. Again, this operation is intended more for bridges and gateways than for clients.

Don't be tempted to be existentialist and spend a lot of time in your programs trying to figure out if two objects or object references are the same or not. It turns out that the answer to the question, "Are these two object references the same?" is, "Who's asking, and why do they want to know?" For example, suppose we have an accounting object that's performing slowly, so our system administrator builds a monitor object, which he places in front of it. The monitor object passes requests through unchanged, but collects usage and performance data along the way. So there are two object references—one for the monitor object, and another for the accounting object—and some users invoke the monitor object while others invoke the accounting object. To a user of the accounting object, these two object references are *the same*—it doesn't matter which one he or she uses, the *same* instance does the *same* calculations, ends up in the *same* state, and returns the *same* result. To the system administrator, the two objects are *different*: one collects usage data, and the other doesn't. Replace monitor object with bridge or gateway object (more on this in Chapter 6) and you'll see even more places where object reference comparison is basically meaningless without more information. The bottom line: These operations have their place in bridges and gateways where they enable garbage-collecting during idle time, but they're time-wasters at best, and damaging to your architecture at worst, if you use them to break encapsulation and build location knowledge into your system. Since you've decided to follow object-oriented principles, go all the way and leave the implementation and topological knowledge out of your application and in the administrative layer where it belongs.

create_request is the operation you perform to start the process of building an invocation for the DII. This operation has many parameters, which are defined in Section 4.3.

get_policy returns a policy object. We'll talk more about policy objects when we describe the POA in Chapter 5, and Security in Chapter 14. **set_policy_overrides and get_domain_managers** also manipulate or concern policies. Since policies are also used for security, one kind of managed domain is a security domain.

Now, on to the ORB.

CHAPTER

4

Understanding the ORB, Part 1: Client Side

We've discussed a lot about what the ORB does, but very little about how it does it. In the next three chapters, we'll fill in some of the details. Since the ORB—or, more precisely, our network of intercommunicating ORBs—is the nerve center of our distributed object system, there's a lot to cover.

Fortunately for us, the ORB Core specification is divided into a number of parts that we can examine separately. On the client side, and discussed later in this chapter, we have:

- The Client Stubs
- The Dynamic Invocation Interface (DII)

Available to both client and object and also discussed in this chapter are

- The Orb Interface and ORB core, including
- Interface Repository (IR), operations on the object reference, and other miscellaneous services

On the object implementation (server) side and discussed in the next chapter are:

- The Portable Object Adapter (POA)
- The static IDL skeleton(s)
- The Dynamic Skeleton Interface (DSI)
- The CORBAcomponents container

Connecting client and object, and presented separately in Chapter 6, is:

- The CORBA 2.0 Interoperability specification, now extended with

- The new CORBA 3 asynchronous invocation and quality-of-service spec

What about the client side of the CCM? The CCM presents a navigation interface to the client, but we'll discuss that in Chapter 5 where we'll present it alongside its server-side part. It doesn't make sense to put it here when all of the underlying rationale won't be presented until later.

In the first section of this chapter, we'll present an overview of the client side of the ORB. Then, in Sections 4.2–4.5, we'll fill in the details, including some of the IDL interfaces of these features.

4.1 ORB and Client-Side Overview

Figure 2.1 showed an extremely simplified view of a request passing from a client, through its IDL stub, the ORB, and the target object's skeleton, and finally arriving at the object implementation, where it is executed and the result returned by the corresponding return route. From this, we learned that the definition of all interfaces in OMG IDL allows the ORBs to handle all the details of request/response passing, including format translation when client and target object reside on different systems; and that the client possesses an object reference for each target, which it passes to the ORB in each request to denote the particular object instance that is the target of that request.

It turns out that the two ORB interfaces that were shown in Figure 2.1 are now not sufficient to handle all of the logistics that CORBA users require. A more complete diagram of client, ORB, and object implementation components is shown in Figure 4.1. This figure shows six ORB interfaces and eight ORB parts. Two interfaces communicate only with the client, and two others only with the object implementation, while the ORB interface provides services for both. The Dynamic Skeleton Interfaces usually communicate with remote ORBs, although they may be used in other ways as well. Interface and Implementation Repository services are accessed directly through the ORB interface, and indirectly through method invocations via the SII and DII, which rely on this information in various ways. (We realize that both Interface Repository and Implementation Repository abbreviate to IR. In this book, and almost every other CORBA-related publication, IR refers to the Interface Repository. When we want to refer to the Implementation Repository, we'll spell it out.)

The client initiates requests, which may be passed to the ORB via either a static IDL stub (Static Invocation Interface, SII) or the DII. There are a number of important differences between the SII and the DII; the major one is that the DII lets you postpone selection of object *type* and *operation* until runtime, while the SII requires this selection to be made at compile time. Formally, we say that the DII allows *dynamic typing* while the SII requires *static typing*. (Both allow *dynamic binding*; that is, you don't have to select the target object *instance* until runtime.)

There are additional differences: As a consequence of dynamic typing, the DII cannot check argument type correctness at compile time while the SII can. Structurally, the ORB requires a separate stub for each static interface (generated by the IDL compiler, as we saw in Chapter 2), but only one DII interface that is provided by the ORB itself.

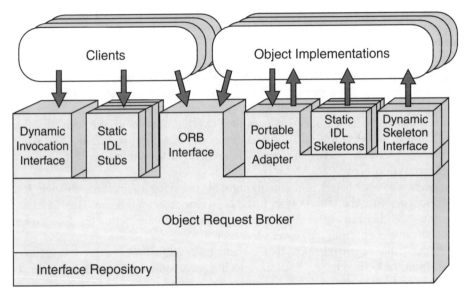

Figure 4.1   Structure of the Object Request Broker. Interfaces between ORB components and its clients and object implementations (shown by arrows) are expressed in OMG IDL and standardized by the OMG. Interfaces between ORB components (where component boxes abut in the figure) are proprietary except for Java (see Chapter 8).

A final difference has been erased by recent developments at OMG: It used to be that only the DII provided non-synchronous invocation; as we detail in Chapter 6, the new messaging specification not only equalizes invocation modes under SII and DII; it also enhances the available options.

The ORB interfaces provide access to the Interface and Implementation Repositories, and some operations on object references that only the ORB can perform. These are discussed in Section 4.5.

4.2 Client Structure and IDL Stubs

In CORBA, the roles of client and object implementation have meaning only with respect to a particular request; unlike in "client-server" architectures, they are not roles to which components commit. A software element that accepts an invocation (that is, an object implementation) may, if its developer wished, turn around and invoke the services of another object (thus playing the role of client) as part of the processing it does to service the request. Since the original request is still outstanding, the module is simultaneously client and object implementation; this does not bother the ORB in the slightest. This flexibility allows developers to use the full power of the system and all of the available elements to solve their problems and is a major benefit of CORBA. Most of the units in our programming example are both client and object—this is a configuration which arises naturally, again and again, as you design your system.

The role of the client, then, is simply to request services by invoking operations. There are no standard CORBA operations for object instance management; object activation, deactivation, suspension, and so on are performed either automatically by the ORB or by customized services located outside the client, for example in a management tool. Client code deals exclusively with the problem at hand, resulting in maximum portability and interoperability. (In Chapter 5 we will see that the simplicity on the client side results in a plethora of functionality and options on the object side, and that some options become noticeably complex. On the other hand, the scalablity that the POA and CCM bring to CORBA through these options is superb. The CCM packages the most successful server resource management patterns into an easy-to-use programming environment.)

The client accesses object implementations by invoking them through their IDL interfaces, specifying the target object instance via its object reference. The IDL interface isolates the client from the object's implementation details, while the object reference isolates the client from the object's location.

At runtime, the object reference that a client holds is just an opaque token that it received from the ORB as the result of some CORBA invocation—either an invocation of the naming or trading service, or a de-stringification of a "stringified" object reference. (We'll explain all of these terms and operations, but you'll have to wait until Section 4.5.) This token is valid only for a single session; at your next session, you'll obtain a new token to refer to the same object instance, again by invoking the naming service, or de-stringifying a stringified object reference, which remains valid from one session to the next.

CORBA standardizes only what the session object reference does, and not how it does it. That's why you can't examine this token and learn anything about the object to which it refers. To your ORB, it's probably a pointer to information about the object, but you don't know what's stored there, or what format it's in, so that's not much help to you.

But, this allows each ORB designer to optimize or tune object reference handling in the way he or she thinks is best. Some ORBs will be optimized for remote invocations, others will be tuned for quick response from local objects, and still others may compromise or tune for some alternative variable. And performance is one characteristic of an ORB product that you may expect to improve from one release to another. If performance is important to you, look for reviews in recent magazines with performance figures, then confirm in your own environment that the product meets your needs. The CORBA specification gives ORB builders the freedom to design and build implementations to meet your needs, and the resulting products are coming to market with excellent characteristics. (When ORBs pass object references from one to another, they use a different form—the Interoperable Object Reference—which is standard. We cover the different forms of object reference in Chapter 6.)

The stub joins to the client at one end and to the ORB at the other. Since the stub is generated by the IDL compiler, and not written by a programmer, it is not necessary for most stubs to be interchangeable—since the IDL is interchangeable, you just run it through the IDL compiler to generate the stub for the ORB you're using. Standardization is not necessary here; therefore, OMG standards allow vendors to construct this junction for performance and reliability. This means that you cannot use stubs from vendor A's IDL compiler with vendor B's ORB. IDL compilers and ORBs come in sets; you cannot mix and match (not that we can think of any benefit from this even if you could, for most languages). But, because Java is assembled dynamically at runtime, it is necessary for Java stubs to be interchangeable, and they are—see Chapter 8.

The client-to-stub interface is defined by the standard OMG IDL language mapping for the programming language you chose. This means that your source code ports from one vendor's ORB to another for the same language, since the bindings generated by your IDL file are defined by this standard rather than by any particular vendor.

The example in this book demonstrates this; most of the code is common to every ORB of a particular language and is presented only once in common sections of the example chapters. Client-side code ports intact, while object-side code portability is marred by differences in BOA (Basic Object Adapter) interfaces from one ORB to another. The POA specification, which replaces the BOA, solves this problem but POA *products* had not completely replaced BOA products when we wrote this book. Because BOA is no longer an OMG specification, Chapter 5 presents only the POA. But, to be useful with current products, the example section in this book presents both POA and BOA versions for C++ and Java. Thanks to its high level of standardization, POA code (and explanations) will port to other vendors' POA ORBs as they come to market.

Coding to the SII is simple; in addition, this method provides type-checking at compile time, thus avoiding surprises when you run. We present examples for each language mapping; check out Chapters 7, 8, and 9 to see how this works.

4.3 The Dynamic Invocation Interface

Almost everything in life involves a trade-off. In the DII, you trade off a few more lines of code for each initial object invocation for complete freedom in picking your target object type, interface, and operation at runtime.

The DII allows a client, at any time, to invoke any operation on any object that it may access over the network. (We admit, it would take a lot of clever programming to produce this super-client, but the principle is the same.) This includes objects for which the client has no stub—objects newly added to the network or discovered through a Naming or Trading service. (Since this includes every object in your system, you could program exclusively in the DII, something you could not do in the SII without restricting access to new objects.)

Object implementations cannot detect, when they receive an invocation, whether the invocation came into the ORB via the SII or the DII. The ORB is responsible for preparing dynamic requests so that they have exactly the same form as static requests, before it transmits the request to the target object instance. The choice is entirely up to the client, and the work is done by the ORB; object builders have nothing extra to do to prepare for requests coming from the DII.

Even though many programmers will never program in the DII, we present some of the details here for a couple of reasons: First, it's a key part of CORBA and you should keep in mind that you may be able to use the DII to solve some future problem that won't yield any other way. And second, since you have to assemble a DII invocation yourself, this presentation lays out the anatomy of an invocation much more transparently than our SII explanation did Therefore, if you're curious about the details of how CORBA works, this is one place to learn them.

4.3.1 Identifying a Target Object

There are four steps to a dynamic invocation:

1. Identify the object you want to invoke.
2. Retrieve its interface definition from the IR.
3. Construct the invocation.
4. Invoke the request, and receive the results.

In a dynamic distributed object environment, users will probably consult an Object Trading Service to locate object implementations. Described in more detail in Chapter 11, the Trader Service is like a combination Yellow Pages and mail-order catalog that lists available service instances with ancillary information such as features, location, or cost. Most users will access Trader via their browser, clicking through services until they find one they like; additional use will come from programs written to access Trader directly. But there will be no OMG standard for the browser itself; standard programmatic interfaces to the Trader enable browsers to operate interchangeably on different Trader implementations, and OMG expects services like the browser to be produced in a competitive environment. On request, the Trader Service furnishes the object reference of the service provider object, allowing the client to follow up its successful shopping trip with an immediate use (which might be called a purchase, if the service has an associated cost) of the service.

We argued, in the first edition of this book, that the DII would enable the production of ubiquitous, flexible clients that could invoke almost any CORBA object they encountered on a network, whether discovered via a Trader or some other way. Since then, the popularity of the Web browser has demonstrated that you don't need sophisticated functionality to be popular—all you need to do is display text and graphics, and let people fill in forms. And, when clients need to execute code more sophisticated than a browser, they turn increasingly to Java modules downloaded from a URL. Since this combines the "just-in-time" adaptability of the DII with the specificity of a specialized application, downloadable Java clients are a more popular way for service providers to make their CORBA objects available to new users.

4.3.2 Retrieving the Target Interface

Retrieving the target object's interface is straightforward, although information will come from several locations since the primary source, the Interface Repository (see Section 4.4), contains only syntax information. First, using the object reference obtained from the Naming or Trading Service, the client invokes the ORB operation **get_interface**. This returns, not the interface itself, but an object reference that returns the top-level elements of the interface when passed to the IR. Additional calls return all of the interface's operations (by name), their parameters, and their types.

We'll need more information in order to construct an invocation: what each operation does, the function of each parameter, allowed parameter ranges, allowable sequence of operations, and anything else that might be helpful (or necessary). This information won't come from the IR, but it may come from the Trader or your MOF-based metadata repository if you have one, although there is no standard location or format for these metadata.

4.3.3 Constructing the Invocation

The DII provides standard interfaces for constructing a request. As noted earlier, the request is referred to as a pseudo-object in the OMG specifications, and its interface is described in pseudo-IDL or PIDL. The interface to create a request is named (of course) **create_request**.

We've already seen the operation **create_request**; it's part of interface **Object** inherited by every object and was introduced in Section 3.4. The request that is created by this operation will always be directed to the object that was the target of the **create_request**. (What about polymorphism? You can reuse the code you write to create a DII request with the same operation name on a different object, but you cannot reuse the same request object on a series of different targets, even if they all support the same operation with the same signature, because there's no way to change the target object reference on a request object.) The full definition of **create_request** is:

```
Typedef unsigned long ORBStatus;
ORBStatus create_request (          // PIDL
        in Context          ctx,        // context object for
                                        // operation
        in Identifier       operation,  // intended operation on
                                        // object
        in NVList           arg_list,   // args to operation
        inout NamedValue    result,     // operation result
        out Request         request,    // newly created request
        in Flags            req_flags   // request flags
);
```

We already defined Context in Section 3.3.7. **operation**, **NVList**, and **Flags** are defined as follows:

operation is the same name as the one in the original IDL file used to create the skeleton for the object.

There are two ways to specify the arguments of the operation. You can use either one, but you cannot combine them. You either pass all of the arguments in **arg_list** when you call **create_request**, or you specify **arg_list** as null and use calls to **add_arg** (discussed in the next section).

NVList is a list of named values representing the parameter list in our IDL definition; the values in an **NVList** can be of any type. The client invokes an ORB operation to create an **NVList**:

```
ORBStatus create_list (
        in long         count,
        out NVList      new_list
);
```

Each element in the list is a **NamedValue**:

```
typedef unsigned long Flags;
struct NamedValue {
        Identifier   name;          // argument name
```

```
        any        argument;        // argument
        long       len;             // length/count of argument
                                    // value
        Flags      arg_modes;       // argument mode flags
};
```

This struct can represent any component of a parameter list.

Flags do just what you think: You can set the flags to **ARG_IN**, **ARG_OUT**, or **ARG_INOUT**.

4.3.4 The Request Interface

Now that we've created a **request**, there are many useful things we can do with (or to) it, all defined in the **request** interface. Even though **request** is a pseudo-object, you map these IDL definitions specifying your **request** as the target, and the ORB knows exactly what to do.

If you didn't specify values in **arg_list**, you add them to the **request** with calls to **add_args**, one call per argument:

```
ORBStatus add_arg (
        in Identifier     name,          // argument name
        in TypeCode       arg_type,      // argument datatype
        in void           * value,       // argument value to be added
        in long           len,           // length/count of argument
                                         // value
        in Flags          arg_flags      // argument flags
                     );
```

You can delete a request with **ORBStatus delete ();**.

4.3.5 Invoking a DII Request

The new Messaging specification replaces the original DII deferred-synchronous invocation signatures. Because the original signatures are deprecated, we're not going to present them in this book. (They were presented in the original edition.) Details for the various nonsynchronous invocation methods and signatures are presented under interoperability, in Chapter 6, for SII but not for DII; to see the DII interfaces, download the message specification from the OMG Web site. For a synchronous invocation, you invoke **invoke**:

```
ORBStatus invoke (
        in Flags  invoke_flags      //invocation flags
);
```

This operation, specified with the request as the target, directs the ORB to marshal the target request and route it to the referenced object, which was the target of the original **create_request**. Since **invoke** is the synchronous form, when control returns to your client, **inout** and **out** values will be in their proper places in **arg_list**, and the return value (if any) will be in **result**.

This completes the discussion of the SII and DII. Next, we'll take a look at the Interface Repository.

4.4 The Interface Repository

The Interface Repository (IR) is crucial to the operation of CORBA. CORBA requires that each ORB bear and implement the interfaces defined for the IR, allowing the IDL definitions for all of the objects it knows about to be stored, retrieved, and modified. These definitions can be used for many different purposes, both by the ORB to provide functionality promised by the specification, and by CORBA programmers. The CORBA specification manual defines three ways the ORB can use IR definitions directly:

- To provide interoperability between different ORB implementations.
- To type-check request signatures at runtime, whether a request was issued through the DII or through a stub.
- To check the correctness of inheritance graphs.

In addition, the information is helpful for clients and users, which can use the IR in the following ways:

- To construct DII invocations.
- To manage installation and distribution of interface definitions around your network.
- To implement components of a CASE environment (for example, an interface browser).
- To browse or modify interface definitions or other information stored in IDL during the development process.
- To compile stubs and skeletons directly from the IR instead of from the IDL files, since all of the information required for compilation is contained in both formats.

4.4.1 Using the IR

There are two basic ways to access the IR: You can use utilities provided by your ORB vendor, or you can write code that invokes the standard IR IDL interfaces mandated by the OMG. The advantage of the IDL interfaces is that they are a standard, allowing the same code to access any compliant IR. The disadvantage, of course, is that you have to write code to use them, while the vendor utilities eliminate this step. (Of course, these utilities use IR APIs, although you can't tell whether they use the standard OMG interfaces or additional ones available only on your particular vendor's ORB. Vendors are expected to extend the OMG basics; the only requirement is that their extensions not break any of the standard mechanisms.)

This means you'll probably start accessing IRs through your vendor's utilities. Each vendor will provide its own way of doing this; you'll find details in each products' documentation. Some ORBs have a command or command-line option for inserting an IDL definition into the IR; others store automatically when the IDL is compiled. However you do it, storing an interface definition in an IR is a simple operation for every ORB.

4.4.2 Identifying Interfaces in a Repository

Do not assume that there is a one-to-one correspondence between IRs and ORBs. The OMG specifications are much more flexible than this; the only requirement is that every ORB be able to access at least one IR. So, a particular IR may be shared by more than one ORB; and an ORB may access more than one IR.

IRs are CORBA objects, and (of course) each one has its own object reference. You can always get your main IR reference from the ORB at startup by calling **list_initial_services** (which will hopefully tell you that an IR is available) followed by **resolve_initial_references** (which returns the object reference of the IR). If there is more than one IR available, you will be able to get the object references of the others in some implementation- or site-specific way.

However, since our distributed environment spans the entire world (and beyond, since CORBA already runs on many satellites already), CORBA doesn't require that client and invoked object instance share the same IR—rather, interoperability requires that they share the same *definition* of the invoked interface. To this end, the OMG specifies an identification mechanism, the *RepositoryID*. There is (or can be) a unique RepositoryID for *every* IDL identifier within an IR—modules, interfaces, variables, anything in an IDL file that has a name.

The domain of RepositoryIDs is the universe, although the responsibility for ensuring that RepositoryID names are unique and do not collide is placed, explicitly, on application developers (you, perhaps) and system administrators. Any string is a legal RepositoryID, but the OMG spec defines and strongly recommends four conventional formats. For the remainder of this discussion, we're going to assume that you'll use only these formats, which are named *IDL, RMI Hashed, DCE,* and *LOCAL.*

The **IDL format** consists of three parts separated by colons. It starts with the initials IDL and the first colon. This is followed by a series of identifiers separated by (forward) slash marks; after the last identifier comes the second colon. The format ends with a major and minor version number separated by a period. So, the RepositoryID for one of our example operations might be

IDL:Primer/POS/OutputMedia/OutputText:1.0

The **RMI Hashed** format is defined automatically from Java code when IDL interfaces are generated using the reverse Java to IDL mapping (Chapter 8). The generated RepositoryID changes when the Java code (and therefore the interface) changes. It starts with "RMI:", continues with the scoped name of the identifier, and ends with a hash code defined in the specification.

The **DCE format** consists, mainly, of a DCE UUID. There's the prefix you might expect, "DCE:", before the UUID, which is followed by a colon and a minor version number.

The **LOCAL format** starts with "LOCAL:". You're not supposed to refer to local RepositoryIDs outside of your little workgroup, so there's no restriction on what you can put in the rest of it.

The most important use of RepositoryIDs is to identify interfaces. You can assign a RepositoryID to an interface (or to any IDL identifier) using the **#pragma ID** directive:

```
module MyModule {
    interface MyInterface  {
            //  interface stuff goes here ...
    }
    #pragma ID MyInterface "IDL:MyCompany/PrinterStuff/SpoolingOps:1.0"
}
```

There are two other **#pragma** directives that you can use to define the prefix and version fields for automatically generated IDL format RepositoryIDs. For example, the following IDL:

```
#pragma prefix "MyCompany"
#pragma version "1.3"
module MyModule {
    interface MyInterface  {
            //  interface stuff goes here ...
    }
}
```

would generate the following ID for interface MyInterface:

IDL:MyCompany/MyModule/MyInterface:1.3

There's a set of rules for **#pragma prefix** and **version** assignment when you **#include** files, which will, of course, have their own **#pragma prefix** and **version** assignments, but we won't go over them here. As you might expect, **#pragma ID** overrides **prefix** and **version** assignment.

You *are not allowed* (by convention) to revise someone else's IDL interface and increment their version number. If this were allowed, every (different!) next revision of any particular ID'd interface, regardless of who revised it, would share the *same* RepositoryID—the same strings with the next increment of the version number. The OMG is very firm on this: *Only the originator of the RepositoryID can increment the version number*; everyone else must create a new RepositoryID with his or her own prefix to identify his or her own version of the modified interface.

4.4.3 What's Stored in an IR?

In Chapter 3, we said that an IDL module can contain other modules, as well as interfaces, components, valuetypes, attributes, operations, typedefs, and other IDL definitions, and most of these types can, in turn, contain lower types in a well-defined hierarchy.

Internally, the structure of the IR mirrors this hierarchy. Each type is represented by a CORBA object whose data structure and operations represent its position in the hierarchy as well as identify its type and characteristics. The name of the IR object type that represents an IDL type is given by its name followed by the suffix "def," for example, inside the IR, an **interface** is represented by an **InterfaceDef** object.

We don't have space to go over the definition of every "def" type, but here's some insight into the **InterfaceDef** type as an example: In structs defined in the IR, it stores its own name, its type, a sequence containing all of its base interfaces (identified as their **InterfaceDef**s, of course), its own RepositoryID, the RepositoryID of whatever it's defined (that is, contained) in so you can go up the containment hierarchy, its version, its operations and attributes, and a boolean telling whether or not it's abstract. There's a **contents** operation that returns all of the IDL identifiers that it contains; fortunately this operation has a flag we can set to turn off the listing of everything contained in the inherited interfaces.

Although it's not mandated by the OMG specification, many IRs store IDL structure and comments in addition to the required "def" types. This capability allows them to reproduce and output the IDL file, in addition to compiling it. This feature also provides a certain amount of convenience, certainly, but storing IDL files is not so daunting a chore that we'd consider this trick a big differentiator compared to other differences that exist between the various ORBs on the market.

4.4.4 Retrieving Information from the IR

First, here's how to retrieve something based on its RepositoryID. In **module CORBA**, the spec defines the operation

Contained lookup_id (in RepositoryId search_id);

on the Interface Repository, where **Contained**, typedef'd in the IR IDL module, is the object reference of the thing identified by the RepositoryID **search_id** that we input—that is, an **InterfaceDef**, **ModuleDef**, **ComponentDef**, or whatever other "def" we requested.

The **get_interface** operation retrieves, from the IR, the interface definition that corresponds to an object reference. Its syntax is

InterfaceDef get_interface ();

and it returns the **InterfaceDef** which represents the interface we want. How did we specify which interface we wanted? We invoked **get_interface** on the object reference of the instance for which we requested the interface definition. Although this appears, to us, to be an operation on the object itself, it's really carried out by the ORB (and is most likely local, although the specification is silent on where the work is actually done), which invokes the IR on our behalf, retrieves the **InterfaceDef** corresponding to the object's type, and returns it to us.

To retrieve the object reference of a CORBA component, you use **ComponentDef get_component_def()**, since **get_component** was used for one of the component interface navigation operations. For more on this, see the components section in Chapter 5.

4.4.5 How Do IRs Work?

An implementation of an IR requires some form of persistent object store. For an ORB serving thousands or more different interfaces, regardless of whether their source is local or remote, this can grow to be a substantial piece of software. Fortunately for ORB implementors, the OMG specification allows vendors the freedom to implement the IR in the best way for their target platform and operating system, while the standard set of IDL interfaces maintains interoperability and portability.

For example, an IR may be implemented on top of a database, either written specifically for the ORB or purchased and installed separately. The distribution characteristics of this database will determine how the separate ORBs see their contents. If the database is distributed and replicated, remote ORBs will retrieve interfaces quickly from local copies, but changes will propagate with a latency characteristic of the underlying database implementation.

When you evaluate an ORB product, check out how it manages the information in its IRs. Your needs will differ depending on how much developing and beta testing you plan to do, so beware of blanket recommendations about IRs that may assume a set of requirements very different from yours. Scalability is a big factor here; ORB vendors know this and are working hard to provide products that retain both responsiveness and flexibility even when systems grow to thousands of ORBs and interfaces or more. Clearly, this is an area where users will benefit in the long run.

We didn't cover the IDL interfaces to the IR in detail because most users will access the IR through their vendors' interfaces, and there isn't a lot of curiosity about how this component works "under the covers" (unlike, for example, interoperability). But do not underestimate the value of the IR to your enterprise's distributed object environment. Pay attention to the setup of the IR on your network, and leverage it to maximize the interoperability you get from your investment in CORBA.

4.5 The ORB Interface

interface object is a part of the ORB interface. We covered it in Section 3.4, so we don't have to go over it again here.

The most important part of the ORB interface is the initialization component. There's a part for the client, which we'll cover here, and another for the object implementation, which we'll put off until Chapter 5.

When your first client starts up, it needs object references for its ORB, a Naming Service, and the Interface Repository. The OMG felt that these common initialization operations should be standardized since every client has to invoke them, and the format had to allow the client to specify which ORB, Naming Service, or Interface Repository it wants since CORBA allows clients to connect to as many of these as they like. The Initialization Specification meets these requirements.

4.5.1 Initializing a Client at Startup

There are a few things your client will have to do at startup.
Find and connect to its local ORB, and locate services, including:

- Naming
- Security
- Transactions

These operations are performed by the ORB. All except the first can look like normal CORBA operations, but the initial connection to the ORB has to be made via a language call, of course. Following this, the client can call **list_initial_services** and then, as many times as needed, **resolve_initial_references**, which returns the object reference for each service, one per call.

Initialization is an operation on the ORB pseudo-object—the client holds a token that appears, to it, to be a normal object reference. However, this token cannot be passed to a remote program and invoked by it, nor can it be stringified and used in a later session.

In addition, the language mappings do not follow the general principles we'll cover later on, because the normal components of a mapped operation won't be fully defined until we've obtained our first few object references. Instead, initialization calls for each language are defined in that language only.

The following pseudo-IDL invocation will allow you to obtain your initial ORB reference:

```
typedef  string  ORBid;  //PIDL
typedef  sequence <string> arg_list;
```

```
ORB ORB_init (inout arg_list argv, in ORBid orb_identifier);
```

Before we explain this, we'll look at the somewhat unconventional language mappings. First, for C and C++, we have:

```
/* C Language Mapping - Contacting the ORB  */
typedef CORBA_string  CORBA_ORBid;
extern CORBA_ORB CORBA_ORB_init (int *argc,
        char **argv,
        CORBA_ORBid orb_identifier,
        CORBA_Environment *env);
  and
//C++ Language Mapping - Contacting the ORB
namespace CORBA
    typedef string ORBid;
    ORB_ptr ORB_init (int& argc,
        char** argv,
        ORBid orb_identifier);
```

In C and C++, ORBs are identified by strings, typed as ORBid. These names will be locally scoped, like filenames; there will not be a formal registry for ORB names. When your site starts to interoperate on a wide scale, someone will appoint an administrator who will register or assign ORB names in a way that avoids collisions between different departments or whatever. Or you can set ORBid to NULL and pass a parameter pair tagged ORBid, which specifies the ORBid string (-ORBid "ORB_depot", for example).

The ORB initialization function will remove parameters from the argument list once they are used, in the standard way of C and C++.

The **ORB_init** function may be called multiple times, and will return the *same* pseudo-object reference if the same parameters are used. This allows, for example, multithreaded applications to access the same ORB from multiple threads, or alternatively, for ORBs to be implemented as a shared library.

For Java, things are different. The language mapping defines three initialization methods as the overloaded Java function init:

```
// Java: static methods for ORB initialization
// Java
package org.omg.CORBA;
abstract public class ORB {
// Application init
      public static ORB init(String[] args,
            java.util.Properties props) {
         // call to: set_parameters(args, props);
...
}
// Applet init
      public static ORB init(java.applet.Applet app,
            java.util.Properties props) {
         // call to: set_parameters(app, props);
...
// Default (singleton) init
      public static ORB init()
{...}
// Implemented by subclassed ORB implementations
// and called by init methods to pass in their params
      abstract protected void set_parameters(String[] args,
            java.util.Properties props);
      abstract protected void set_parameters(Applet app,
            java.util.Properties props);
```

Both application and applet initialization methods return a *new, distinct* ORB instance each time they are called, unlike the C and C++ calls. The ORBs will differ in the security they provide, in keeping with the assumption that applications are local and can be trusted, while applets are probably downloaded and cannot.

The default method returns what's called the "singleton" ORB—there's only one of them, and every call to this init returns an object reference to it. This is a very minimal-functioning ORB, which functions mainly as a factory for typecodes for helper and holder classes. (Look in the Java language mapping Chapter 8 for an explanation of what these are.)

Since this ORB serves multiple untrusted applets and must keep them isolated from each other, it does not make invocations—you'll need an Application or Applet ORB for this in addition to the singleton ORB. You get these from the other init methods; as the code fragment above shows, the operation is overloaded (this is Java, not IDL, and it supports overloading!) so you use argument types to tell the system which call you mean.

4.5.2 Obtaining Initial References

Now, in any language, you can invoke operations on the ORB, but you still need your first object reference in order to do anything useful. The standard way to do this is via the Naming Service, but since the CORBAservices are optional components of the standard, the OMG did not want to mandate including a full-blown service with every ORB just to get things started. (There's a good reason for this. ORBs may be built into just about anything in the future, and some hardware that contains embedded ORBs will be really small—those on wristwatch-sized pagers, for example, or switches in a telephone network. Manufacturers of this equipment want the benefit of an industry standard, but have to keep memory footprint to an absolute minimum. The CORBA specifications take these needs into account.)

To meet these requirements, initial object references are provided by the ORB via operations that are modeled after the Naming Service. It's really a mini-Naming Service implemented within the ORB itself, with two operations. The first (**list_initial_services**) returns a list of available service names; you then pass each service name to the next operation (**resolve_initial_references**), and it returns an object reference that gets you started with that service. Currently, these service names are defined for return from **list_initial_services**:

- NameService

- TradingService

- InterfaceRepository

- SecurityCurrent

- TransactionCurrent

- DynAny Factory

- ORBPolicyManager

- PolicyCurrent

- RootPOA

- POACurrent

- Component HomeFinder

Clients will surely want the Naming Service, and may use any of the others except the two POA-related services, depending on their environment. Object instances may use all except the first two. (If an object instance uses the Naming or Trading Service, it's acting as a client, of course.) Clearly, **list_initial_services** is an ORB service that is useful to both clients and objects.

This service is implemented as a pseudo-object—a service provided by the ORB that looks like it's provided by a regular object. And, it's defined in pseudo-IDL:

```
//PIDL Interface to obtain initial services
        typedef string ObjectId;
        typedef sequence <ObectId> ObjectIdList;
        exception InvalidName;
        ObjectIdList list_initial_services ();
        Object resolve_initial_references (in ObjectId identifier)
                raises (InvalidName);
```

This maps to C and C++ in the following way:

```
/* C Mapping */
typedef CORBA_string CORBA_ORB_ObjectId;
typedef CORBA_sequence_CORBA_ORB_ObjectId
        CORBA_ORB_ObjectIdList;
```

```
typedef struct CORBA_ORB_InvalidName
        CORBA_ORB_InvalidName;
CORBA_ORB_ObjectIdList
        CORBA_ORB_list_initial_services (
        CORBA_ORB orb,
        CORBA_Environment *env);
CORBA_Object       CORBA_ORB_resolve_initial_references(
        CORBA_ORB orb,
        CORBA_ORB_ObjectId identifier,
        CORBA_Environment *env);
and
//C++ Language Mapping:
namespace CORBA
    class ORB
    public:
        typedef String ObjectId;
class InvalidName ...;
ObjectIdList_ptr
                list_initial_services();
        Object_ptr resolve_initial_references (
                ObjectId identifier);
```

Here's how it maps to Java:

```
//Java Language Mapping:
public abstract String[] list_initial_services();
public abstract org.omg.CORBA.Object
    resolve_initial_references(
        String object_name)
        throws org.omg.CORBA.ORBPackage.InvalidName;
```

Since Java lacks typedefs, the return value from list_initial_services is a string instead of a more heuristically named type. resolve_initial_references returns an Object type, which is defined in org.omg.CORBA.

resolve_initial_references operates on the ORB rather than on the Naming Service, which we'll define in Chapter 12, since the service is provided by a pseudo-object. And ObjectId (in the C++ mapping) is a string, not a name construct (a sequence of structs containing a string pair for each component of a name, as we'll see in Chapter 11).

In the example in this book, we use ORB_init to connect to the ORB, and resolve_initial_references to gain access to the Naming Service. The naming service is basic to CORBA, so we modified the example since the first edition to include it and wanted to gain access through this standard method. When we wrote the original example, some vendors had not had time to market their versions of the Naming Service. Since this functionality was essential to our application (as it is to virtually every CORBA application), we wrote our own, but now we use the standard service.

4.5.3 Stringifying Object References

Another part of the CORBA module manipulates object references. CORBA clients see two forms of the object reference: the opaque token "session reference" they associate with invocations, and the stringified form we are about to investigate. There's a third form, the one that ORBs pass over the wire in argument lists, but we'll postpone discussion of this form until Chapter 6.

In spite of its name, the stringified form is *not* simply the bytes of the opaque token, converted to an ASCII string by a conversion algorithm. Where the token is valid for only a single session, and only on the ORB that produced it, the stringified form is valid for any session as long as the object it refers to has not been deleted. In addition, the stringified form may be passed to, and used by, any other instance of the same vendor's ORB and in addition, if produced by an ORB that emits the OMG-standard protocol IIOP (see Chapter 6), it may be passed to and used by any other IIOP ORB. Since the stringified form may be passed by any method that handles ASCII text without mangling it—e-mail, storage in and retrieval from files or databases, even by fax— stringification is one of the most popular ways of passing object references, especially to friends or business clients who can't access your naming service. (Or, you could use this method to pass your friends the object reference of your naming service, which would give them access to more than just a single object.)

To preserve vendors' flexibility in optimizing their ORBs, the OMG specifications are silent on the format of the session object reference that clients pass to the ORB with invocations, and how these token object references are converted to strings. However, we can surmise that ORBs must use the session reference as a "key" to look up additional information about the target object. If the object reference is associated with an invocation, the ORB will use the information to route the invocation to the specified target. If the object reference is the argument in a "stringify" operation, the ORB will assemble the information into IOR format and convert it all to a string, following the OMG standard. And finally, if the object reference appears in an argument list or return value, the ORB will assemble the information into IOR format and marshal it into IIOP wire format for transmission.

Here are the operations that convert object references to strings and back, along with some list operations that also reside in this module:

```
interface ORB {                                // PIDL
    string              object_to_string (in Object obj);
    Object              string_to_object (in string str);

    Status          create_list (
                in long             count,
                out NVList          new_list
    );
    Status              create_operation_list (
                in OperationDef     oper,
                out NVList          new_list
    );
}
```

We already covered the list operations in Section 4.3.3, so we won't go over them again here.

Understanding the ORB, Part 2: Object Implementation (Server) Side, Including the CORBA Component Model

5.1 Introduction

Now that we've covered the (simpler!) client side, you're ready for the serious server-side stuff—right? As we'll see in this chapter, CORBA keeps your application architecture manageable by deliberately keeping the client side simple, but that means that all of the features for scalability and robustness live on the server side—the side that we're about to discuss. In addition, the CORBA Component Model (CCM) adds programmer convenience to the model, as we'll see starting with Section 5.4.

We have two things to do in this chapter: First, we have to cover the server side of CORBA—the implementation side of our invocation—concentrating on the Portable Object Adapter, or POA. This is a major topic in itself. Once we're done, we have a second task: describing the CCM. This embodies all of the server side including the POA, and adds much more: persistence, transactions, security, event handling, assemblies, configuration, and other features. What's special about the CCM? The way it packages up these low-level CORBA services and features into a higher-level programming environment, making CORBA programming simpler for our enterprise programmers, and accessible to our business programmers. But first we have to understand the POA, because that's what CCM is based on.

If you're already a CORBA programmer, or if you've read the first edition of this book, you're already familiar with the Basic Object Adapter, or BOA. This construct,

OMG's first server-side architecture, was a good start, but neither robust enough nor precisely enough described to serve in today's complex applications. In mid-1995, OMG members issued the Portable Server RFP, and two years later adopted the POA specification. The original impetus for the RFP was programmers' complaints (quite justified) that the BOA interfaces were not written precisely enough to allow server code to port from one vendor's ORB to another's; thus the name Portable Object Adapter for the overall standard. However, while the submitters were drawing up their specification, Internet computing outgrew its training wheels and entered the mainstream, and interactive networking replaced batch jobs in serious enterprise computing. With this in mind, the submitters added many scalability features to their specification, finally coming up with the POA that we present here. Mind you, we're not criticizing the authors of the BOA specification: At the time it was written, it was the only structure of its kind and represented a major advance over any other standard architecture. In the early 1990s when it was first described and implemented, networks did not support the traffic volumes or speeds that we have today, and few people had even conceived of applications needing to respond to the hit rates that today's servers handle with aplomb.

The POA specification deprecates the BOA; that is, it replaces that part of the specification, and requires future products to provide POA support in order to claim compliance. (Products can continue to offer BOA support alongside, so you don't have to recode your applications all at once. Even so, we'd recommend that you upgrade and recode as soon as you can since the POA architecture is so much better than the BOA.) Because POA is a complex specification to implement (far more than it is to use!), compliant implementations were only starting to come to market as we wrote this book. However, looking to the future, we discuss only the POA, and not the BOA, in this chapter. If you're using a BOA-based ORB and want to read about it, you can either look in your copy of our first edition, or download and print out the original server-side chapter from this book's Web site—we'll make it accessible there.

5.2 The CORBA Server-Side Computing Model

You could tell from Figure 4.1 that the server side of the ORB is more complicated than the client side, even though the figure shows the POA as a simple blob with no internal structure. In this section, we'll introduce the server-side CORBA computing model; the rest of the chapter will fill in the details.

To get started, let's consider two very different CORBA object types: One is an iterator object, created by another object during an invocation to provide access to a list of results that was too big to return in a single argument. The other is a customer object in our e-commerce database.

Although each of these is a CORBA object with its own unique object reference, their lifespans are very different: The iterator will spew out its list of results in a few calls and then be destroyed; neither the object nor its reference will work again after this. Because of its brief lifetime, the iterator object can keep its state in memory for the brief duration between calls; it does not need to use a persistent store. But we hope our customers will keep coming back to buy more at our electronic emporium, and so the customer objects that represent them in our system are expected to live forever. To support this, the persistent data that comprise their state are enshrined in our best database. As long as we remain in business, all of our customer objects remain active and their references remain valid, each object instance representing the same customer whose data are stored in the same row in our database.

These are quite different object-use patterns, and there are others besides. A shopping cart, for example, has a lifetime intermediate between our ephemeral iterator and robust customer objects, as we'll see in Section 5.5.3 in this chapter. To enable scalable applications, the POA supports a range of object lifetimes and activation patterns, as we'll see shortly. Before we do, however, let's consider a problem specific to object types with medium to long lifetimes.

CORBA intentionally keeps the client-side programming model simple. As we mentioned in the previous chapter, *no* object activation or deactivation operations are visible to it; *from the client's point of view, a CORBA object starts running as soon as it (and its object reference) are created, and the object runs constantly, always ready and waiting for invocations, until it is irrevocably destroyed.*

This model is great for the client: Its only interface to CORBA is the IDL for the object it invokes. When it wants to make an invocation, it just goes ahead and does it. When it doesn't, it doesn't. If it wants, a client can hold on to an object reference (or the name of an object in the Naming Service) for years without invoking it. Then, whenever it wants, it can just send an invocation and expect that the answer will come back. (That is, unless the object has been destroyed. Unlike deactivation, destruction of an object is irrevocable—once an object has been destroyed, it's totally gone and its object reference will *never* work again.)

The model does not look as good on the server side, however. Do we really have to keep all of our CORBA objects active, or at least the persistent long-lived ones, so we're prepared for the off-chance that a client will send us an invocation at some random time? Suppose we have 10 million customers, each with his own shopping cart object, but only 2000 of them are shopping now. We'd be overjoyed if the other 9+ million customers suddenly came back and started to shop all at once, but this is pretty unlikely, and we don't have enough computing power to run all 10 million carts at once anyhow. What can we do?

CORBA, and specifically the POA, deals with this situation by distinguishing the concept of CORBA object—the client's concept of an object that runs continuously from creation to destruction—from the concept of *servant*: a piece of running code that services an invocation. In the POA model, object references are mapped to running code dynamically when needed—sometimes only when an invocation comes in, although there are other patterns as well (and we'll describe the common ones later in this chapter). When the invocation is complete, the resources are freed and become available for whatever the ORB needs to do next. What's true is that the object is always *available*; what's not true is that it's always *running*.

This concept is necessary for scalability: the ability of an ORB to service millions of clients, using a reasonable number of computers. However, we've found that this concept is confusing or disconcerting to many when they hear about it for the first time. In the next section, we'll tell a short story to illustrate, by analogy, the difference between *object* and *servant*, and demonstrate that it's perfectly possible for the client to cling to its concept of "CORBA object running all the time, waiting for me to invoke" while the server allocates a servant for it only when an invocation needs to be serviced. If you're comfortable with this concept already, you can skip ahead to the following section. If you're still a little hazy, read on here.

5.2.1 Santa Claus Is a CORBA Object

Until just a year or two ago, my younger son (who is now 12) believed in Santa Claus. Santa Claus is a fat and jolly old man who wears a red coat and pants trimmed with white fur, and travels in a sleigh pulled by eight or nine reindeer (depending on the weather), delivering toys to children around the world by jumping down their chimneys and putting the toys into stockings hanging from the mantel. For a few days after Christmas, Santa recovers from this effort by soaking his feet in a hot bathtub and drinking hot chocolate; he spends the rest of the year making lists and collecting toys for the next Christmas. (This is the North American view of Santa Claus and the one we'll use in this story; if you're reading this book in another country with another view, please adopt our version for the sake of the analogy. We know that in Finland, for example, Father Christmas walks through the front door and hands presents directly to the children. If Father Christmas is also a CORBA object, his encapsulation boundary is very different from the one we're about to describe for Santa Claus!)

The Santa Claus CORBA object that my son believes in supports a single interface with a single, well-defined operation **GetPresents**. Here is the invocation:

- Wait until December 24, in the evening. Otherwise, the invocation fails and returns the **WrongNight** exception.

- Find a stocking, preferably a very large one with your name on it, and hang it from the mantel above the fireplace.

- Fill a glass with milk, and set it on the hearth beneath the stocking.

- Cover a small plate with cookies and set it next to the glass of milk.

- Optionally, put a note requesting specific toys next to the milk and cookies. (The milk, cookies, and note are the input parameters.)

- Go upstairs to bed, and go to sleep.

Going to sleep is very important, since it defines the *encapsulation boundary*. Clients are not allowed to peek beyond this boundary: The interface is defined on it, and once the invocation has been delivered to it, the invocation is in the realm of the implementation. In object orientation, one reason for encapsulation is to enable substitutable implementations. Fortunately, encapsulation also enables scalability, as we'll see shortly. For the Santa Claus object, encapsulation is the only thing that enables the invocation to work at all.

But this invocation is not going to work if we rely on the client's concept of CORBA Santa to fulfill it. However, if we use the POA concept of *servant*—that is, some resource that gets activated and configured when needed, services a single invocation, and then is released—things can work out well. Parents around the world will appreciate this next concept: In this story, my wife and I are *servants* (okay, at least in the POA sense!). Here's how the Santa invocation is serviced at our house:

- After son completes invocation, including going upstairs to bed, Mom and Dad stay up and wrap various presents until we are sure that encapsulation requirements have been met.

- Mom fetches bag with various small gifts, and commences stashing them in stocking. New England tradition requires an orange in the toe, and family tradition requires a stuffed animal reaching out from the top, even though Dad thinks son is much too old for this.

- Dad takes the glass of milk, pours it back into the bottle, fills the glass up with eggnog and rum, grates fresh nutmeg on the top, and drinks it down.

- While drinking the eggnog, Dad may eat a cookie or two. Most of the cookies get put back into the box. Part of one is crumbled on the plate, which remains on the hearth.

- Dad rinses the glass with milk to cover up the smell of the eggnog and rum, and places it back on the hearth next to the plate of cookie crumbs.

- Dad helps Mom put the last of the toys into the stocking and hangs it back up on the mantle.

- Dad and Mom clean up their mess, and go to sleep.

In the morning, son awakens and runs downstairs. Seeing the stocking full of toys and the empty glass and plate, he exclaims, "Wow, look at all the toys. Santa Claus must be real—he left all these toys, and drank the milk and ate the cookies!" And, from his point of view, this is true: The CORBA object accepted the input parameters (milk, cookies, optional note), and delivered the expected return value (toys).

Let's go over the CORBA lessons from this story:

- Client and server can have totally different viewpoints of the object *implementation*, but as long as invocations get serviced according to the agreed-upon definition of the operation, this inconsistency does not matter.

- In the story, Son thinks that Santa is real and always exists, as we described at the start. In reality, the Santa Claus servant comes into being only for a few minutes a year on Christmas Eve when it's needed.

- In CORBA, the client holds an object reference and acts as if the object always exists, making an invocation any time it wants and assuming that the object will maintain its state from one invocation to the next regardless of the time that elapses between invocations. In reality, in POA-based systems, *computing resources may not be allocated for an object until an invocation comes in, and may be freed as soon as the invocation has completed.* State is maintained on persistent storage between invocations, loaded on activation, and stored again with any changes on completion.

- There is a lesson here on scalability as well: The story about the jolly fat guy in the red suit may be charming, but as an implementation architecture, it just doesn't scale. Too many kids need presents on the same night for any one person to distribute them all, especially a fat old man who obviously doesn't keep in shape during his off-season, and the year between Christmases is too long for such a resource to sit around unused. The POA implementation, however, does not have either of these problems: Every household (well, almost) has a resource that can play the role of Santa Servant on one night a year, so there's no problem scaling to any number of households. And, the resource is flexible enough to play other servant roles during the rest of the year, whenever the household POA requires it.

The object-oriented principle that enables this is *encapsulation*: The implementation is encapsulated beneath a boundary that the client is not allowed to penetrate. Until now, we have only suggested that implementation details such as algorithm and coding reside on the far side of this boundary and may change unbeknownst to the client. Now we are adding that resource allocation efforts—some of them massive, supporting a huge enterprise application or a worldwide e-commerce shopping site—may also exist beneath this boundary.

Here's one more example of a difference between client and servant points of view: When a new object—for example, a new shopping cart or bank-account object for a first-time customer—is created, the client receives a new object reference and has the impression that the object "exists." However, on the implementation side, *no servant was activated for the object, and no resource was allocated for execution, when the object reference was created* (at least for the allocation patterns used in large, scalable applications). No servant will be allocated until the client uses the object reference in an invocation. You can "create" a new shopping cart object for every customer who browses your Website, allowing each client to invoke "add to shopping cart" without any setup, without consuming *any* resource in your server, including storage, since your POA and implementation can be configured to postpone setup until the first invocation on each reference. You can even allocate account numbers at creation. We'll see later how they can be stored without consuming resources in your system. (Actually, they will be stored *inside* the object reference, but invisible to the client. We'll give details later in this chapter.)

5.3 What Is a POA and How Is It Used?

A short definition of an object adapter is:

An object adapter is the mechanism that connects a request using an object reference with the proper code to service that request.

The POA is a particular type of object adapter specified by OMG to achieve the maximum amount of portability among ORBs that have widely differing design points.

5.3.1 Three-Part POA Definition

Let's analyze the three important pieces of the definition and apply them to the POA. They are:

- The object reference
- A mechanism that connects a request
- Code to service the request

It's worth anticipating the "mechanism" part of the discussion a bit. You should be aware that there isn't necessarily just one POA in a server. We'll talk about "the POA," but we really mean "the concept of the POA specified by the OMG of which there may be several instances with different characteristics." Yes, by golly, the POA itself is an object, albeit a strictly local object used only in a single server. A server programmer may create several POAs in a server, each of which helps the programmer implement objects. We'll see more details later, but for now you can think of a POA as being part of the implementation of your object, and that not all objects use the same POA.

With that introduction, let's look at the pieces of the definition.

5.3.1.1 Object Reference

An object reference is the center of all CORBA usage. It is the only means by which a client can do something with an object. We'll discuss it (again) in some detail because it is the basic concept around which all of CORBA (including the POA) is organized, and its meaning is very specific when considered by the POA.

While "object reference" is the generic term, we'll often talk about an "Interoperable Object Reference," or IOR, meaning an object reference that is understood by ORBs that can interoperate using the OMG defined protocols (GIOP/IIOP); look ahead to the next chapter for our discussion of interoperability. Most importantly, ORBs written by different people understand an IOR, and this is one of the strengths of CORBA. We'll use the term "IOR" when we want to emphasize interoperability, and "object reference" otherwise. Most vendors provide object references that are indeed IORs.

Where does an object reference come from? In a POA-based ORB, an object reference can be created only in server code that is using a POA. It is important to remember that object reference creation is server related rather than client related. Once created by a server, an object reference can be passed outside the server and can travel to any number of clients, any of which can then issue a request on it, but that's all clients can do with it.

An object reference can come only from server code because the act of creating and giving out the reference promises the recipient of the reference that some server, somewhere, is willing to service invocations on the object represented by the reference. The server code that creates the object reference puts information in the reference that reminds the server of what it promised.

So, what is an object reference? One thing it is not is something a client can manipulate directly or see into. It is opaque to clients. Only ORBs can manipulate it. The information in an object reference is meaningless to the client and is vital to the encapsulation, location transparency, and implementation independence of CORBA.

When a client makes a request using the object reference, the client's ORB extracts pieces from the reference and returns them to the server. Since the reference is the means by which a request is sent to the server (returned to the server from whence it came), the server (and the POA) must have created the object reference with enough information to tell the client-side ORB how to get back to the server code. So, logically (meaning we're skipping a lot of details), an object reference contains at least three pieces of information: an address for the benefit of the ORBs, and two pieces that are important for a server programmer. The three pieces are:

- Something like an address
- The name of the POA that created the object reference
- An Object ID

Since a client can't see any of these pieces, they are meaningful only to the client ORB, the server ORB, and the programmer-written server code.

- *Something like an address* is necessary so that the client ORB can find the right computer to which to send the request. The "something like" weasel words cover up a lot of trickery that sophisticated ORBs provide in order to achieve proper routing, failover, load balancing, and other features that are administrative in nature and that neither client nor server code need be aware of. Programmers can feel confident that requests will eventually make their way to an appropriate machine.

- *The name of the POA that created the object reference* is the first concrete piece of information about the POA that we've run into. Server-side programmer code must first create a POA (with particular characteristics) and specify a name for it before it can create an object reference. That name uniquely identifies the POA (and its characteristics) when requests are returned to a particular computer. That computer may have several servers (processes). A server that contains a POA with the given name is the server that will service the request. A request for service will come back to a POA with the same name as the POA that created the object reference. The important point is that every object implementation belongs to a POA, and the POA name is part of the identification of the code that services requests. The server programmer typically creates a named POA with the same characteristics each time it is created. This means that the POA that created an object reference has the same characteristics as the POA that will service invocations on the object.

So far, two of the three pieces of information in an object reference have gotten us to a particular computer node, to a particular server, and to a unique POA within that server. Up to this point, all the processing of a request has taken place through the "routing" function of the ORB. For example, if we have an object reference called "objref" and we invoke its "doit" operation, we might see the routing path shown in Figure 5.1 to arrive at the POA called "POA-X."

None of the routing involves programmer-written code. It is performed entirely by the infrastructure of a CORBA vendor's system (part of it even across vendors). Routing is the "Broker" part of an Object Request Broker: Its purpose is to find the right code to execute. The quality of the routing function is one of the primary determiners of the efficiency and scalability of a CORBA system, and one of the differentiators among CORBA vendors.

- The *Object ID* was assigned when the object reference was created. After a request is routed to the POA, the Object Id may be used for two purposes: even more routing, and object identification. The further routing occurs when the POA connects the request to the right piece of code that implements the object; that is, to a servant. (Remember the Santa Claus analogy from the introduction?

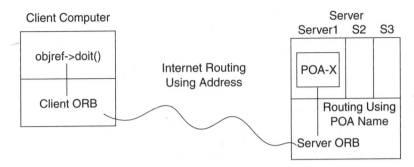

Figure 5.1   Routing as client invokes the "doit" operation on a servant on POA-X.

We'll discuss servant in more detail later.) "Making the connection" is the third of the three pieces of the POA definition and we'll discuss it in detail later too.

Once the servant has control, it typically (but not always) uses the Object Id for its second purpose: identification of the instance of the object. For example, the creating server may have set the Object Id to the key for a database containing the permanent state of the object. In this case, the servant receiving the request now uses that Object Id to access the permanent state.

To complete the routing picture shown in Figure 5.1 with the last piece of object reference information, we might show the logical contents of POA-X as seen in Figure 5.2.

Actually, this figure shows only one possible configuration for a POA and servants, but it illustrates the point. A POA is responsible for passing control for the request to the method of a servant that is prepared to handle the interface to an Object with a particular Object Id.

5.3.1.2 Code to Service the Request

In the discussion about the object reference, we've already had to start talking about servants. A servant is code written by a programmer, specifically by the server programmer, that contains the business logic of an object. All of the ORB, POA, and routing are merely administrative constructs to get a request from a client to the correct servant.

More precisely, a servant contains the methods for an OMG object, where a method is defined in CORBA as the programming language code that implements an operation defined in an IDL interface. In OO languages such as C++ and Java, a servant is an

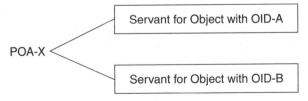

Figure 5.2   Logical contents of POA-X.

instance of a class, which is a declarational entity in those languages. Creating a servant in these languages requires knowing the declaration for the class and then using the language function `new` on the class name. Since a servant implements the operations of an IDL interface, it contains computational language entities in its class corresponding to operations on the IDL interface. The computational entity for Java is called a *class method*, and for C++ it's called a *member function*.

(Unfortunately, there isn't a single terminology for all of O-O. As another example of terminology confusion, OMG's concept of object is not the same as C++'s and Java's. Objects in those languages are instances of the language class, strictly local and temporary in nature, while OMG's object is location transparent and potentially persistent.)

For other languages, a servant might be a set of structures, pointers, and subroutines that are organized to achieve essentially the same effect. In all cases, control is transferred to code using some initialized data. For the rest of this discussion, we'll use the C++ and Java terminologies rather than that of procedural languages, but the techniques are essentially the same.

To understand servants a little better, let's review all of what an IDL interface corresponds to in, for example, the C++ language mapping. An IDL compiler first generates a definition file that is used by the client for invocations and by both client and server for access to the data types defined in the interface. Directly corresponding to that definition file, the IDL compiler also generates a stub, C++ code that intercepts object invocations on that interface and delivers them to the ORB. Programmers don't deal with stubs except to compile and include them in the client binary.

Getting closer to the servant, the IDL compiler next generates a skeleton, also called the *servant base class*: a class declaration and code that contains interface-specific details for runtime use on the server. A server programmer uses the servant base class in two ways: First, the servant base class code is compiled and linked into the server executable binary; like stubs, the programmer doesn't look at or modify this code. Then, after the IDL compiler has provided the servant base class declaration, the programmer codes the servant class, inheriting all the methods required for the object from the servant base class declaration and providing the code for them.

Figure 5.3 diagrams the relationship among IDL interfaces, CORBA Object, servants, and the servant base class. This diagram is not UML—it shows what files and classes are generated by the IDL compiler, and the inheritance relationships of those classes.

A new class and a couple of new methods appear in Figure 5.3. `ServantBase` is a class definition and code provided by an ORB vendor; it serves as the base class for all servants. Since the ORB vendor provides this code, it can have secrets in helping the ORB vendor deal with servants in general. (Note: We're skipping over some programmer-visible details in the definition of `ServantBase` that might be useful for advanced users.)

`POA_foo` is the name of the compiler-generated servant base class (aka skeleton); it contains specific, secret information about the foo interface, as well as the declaration of the operations of the foo interface for use by the servant inheriting from it. `POA_foo` inherits from `ServantBase`, and the real servant inherits from `POA_foo`.

Finally, `my_foo` is the programmer-selected name of the class for the real servant. The programmer must provide the code for all the **interface foo** operations (whose definitions are inherited from `POA_foo`) and may contain other useful, internal code as defined by the programmer, indicated here by `xyzzy`.

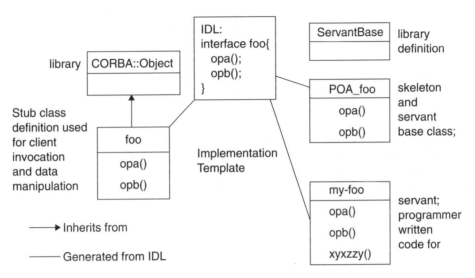

Figure 5.3   Relationships among IDL interfaces, the CORBA object, servants, and the servant base class.

In summary, a servant is an instance of a programming language class that contains at least the methods for an IDL interface. The IDL compiler cannot provide the business logic for the servant, but does provide the superstructure: a servant base class declaration (the skeleton). Many products also provide an example servant class declaration and an outline to be filled in with business logic, but that's only a convenience, saving a little typing.

At runtime, the class definition of a servant is made into an instance of a servant (something that can be executed) by the programming language new function.

After an instance of a servant is created, the programmer must communicate its existence to a POA so that the POA can route requests to it. That takes us to the last part of our POA definition.

5.3.1.3 A Mechanism that Connects

Finally, we arrive at the interesting part of the POA: How does it connect a request to a servant?

The first fact about POAs worth noting is that a POA is an object. It is created, has an object reference, is invoked, and is destroyed like other objects, with the only difference being that a POA is locality constrained. That means that the POA object reference makes sense only to the ORB on the server on which the POA was created. You can't pass a POA reference to any other computer because its entire job in life is to deal with servants and requests on a particular computer; it deals with addresses, entities meaningful only within a single process.

The first thing we can deduce from what we've already discussed is that a POA doesn't just connect the request to a servant and then get out of the way. A POA is part of the implementation of an object. That is, the implementation of an object is the combination of a POA and a servant.

This statement makes more sense when we consider again that there isn't just a single object called a POA like there is a single object called the ORB. We've already seen that a request is routed to one of many possible POAs, one with a particular identity (a name). The reason for a POA having a name is that when a server creates a POA, it assigns not only a name, but also some characteristics; that is, a POA is a stateful object. The routing function of the ORB goes to a lot of trouble to deliver a request to the correct POA because that POA has the characteristics necessary for the correct implementation of an interface, such as the ability to handle transactions. In addition, in servicing a request, a servant might need to create an object reference. A servant can't do this by itself; it must ask its POA to do it because an object reference is complex and has information meaningful only to ORBs and POAs. The way in which the POA creates the right kind of object reference depends on characteristics of the POA.

For this and many other reasons, the characteristics assigned to the POA at its creation time are vital to the implementation of an object. These creation-time characteristics are called the *policies* of the POA. Once a POA is created, its policies are immutable. The policies govern how the POA operates. For example, POA policies control:

- What kind of object references it creates (among other things, what kind of routing is done, and how long the object and object reference might exist)

- How an Object Id is assigned and used

- Whether the object is allowed to take part in transactions

- How the POA deals with servants (Must they be created and registered with the POA before the POA starts processing requests, or can they be created and destroyed dynamically, in one or more ways?)

In addition to policies that are assigned at POA creation, a POA has dynamically specifiable, optional behaviors that are largely administrative in nature. Finally, there are some POA features that are totally independent of a POA's role in implementations and are available primarily for convenience.

Some POA policies and optional behaviors are defined for situations that only a very small number of servers in the world will ever want to deal with. We won't discuss every possibility; a couple could take a page to set the context for the two alternatives it offers. When you get to the point that you can imagine an option, check your manual; it might already be there.

5.3.2 POA Usage Patterns

We will cover most of the important aspects of the POA by considering the most common patterns of usage. After you've seen one example of code for each of these, you can probably just keep re-using it as a template. You will probably keep a set of about for or five such templates and paste them into new applications. The default POA (available without worrying about options) is quite useful. We use it later in the book for one of the examples.

The most important of the POA characteristics are the policies controlling how POAs interact with servants. While there are slight variations on the theme, there are about five patterns concerning POAs and servants. These relate to the way the POA associates a servant with an Object Id so that the POA can dispatch control to the servant to service the request. These patterns are:

- Explicit object activation
- Single servant for all objects (with two variations)
- On-demand activation for the duration of a single method
- On-demand activation, indefinite duration

The last four patterns (including the two variations on single servant) are mutually exclusive. The first (explicit object activation) can be used by itself or combined with most of the others. We'll discuss each individually.

5.3.2.1 Explicit Object Activation

Explicitly activating an object means that programmer code creates a servant and tells the POA that the POA should use that servant whenever it sees a particular Object Id. The phrase *activating an object* comes from the name of the POA operations to do so: `activate_object` and `activate_object_with_id`. Programmer code can tell the POA to stop the association of a servant and an Object Id at any time by using the `deactivate_object` operation.

The two options for `activate_object` exist for alternate methods of assigning an Object Id. Most often, a programmer wants to specify the Object Id, but other times doesn't care about it. For example, the programmer might use a database key as the Object Id, to represent an object with a long lifetime. Whenever the request comes into a servant, the programmer looks at the Object Id and accesses that database record. The Object Id has meaning in this case. On the other hand, sometimes an object exists only a short time (say, for the duration of a session) and has no long-term meaning. In that case, the programmer doesn't care what the Object Id is, and lets the system assign it. This works because the object is unique and is identified by the system-assigned unique number (which has no other meaning than to cause a request to return to a particular servant). This choice is expressed by the POA policy called IdAssignmentPolicy. It has values USER_ID and SYSTEM_ID. No matter which of the patterns are used, the programmer has the choice of assigning Object Id in this fashion.

The advantage of activating an object explicitly is that the servant is always ready to service a request on the object. An object that is activated gives the fastest response time to a request because the POA can quickly find the servant and dispatch to it (by looking up the Object Id in an internal table called the *Active Object Map*). The disadvantage of having continuously active objects is resource usage: An active object is a stateful object. Since the servant always exists and has the state of the object in memory, it uses more memory than the other techniques that dynamically create a servant and activate an object only when needed. When there are more active objects, more memory is used, causing memory contention and reducing overall throughput.

A server main program might activate several objects when the process is started and then turn control over to the ORB. Explicit activation is typically used when the server has a predetermined set of objects (although the server may later deactivate such objects before server shutdown). Such a technique might be very useful for access to very frequently accessed objects in a stable environment, where speed of access is the primary consideration.

Rather than a main program preactivating many objects, a servant servicing a request on one object can explicitly activate another object so that the POA will be prepared to service the other object after this method completes. A method on the active object (or any other) might later deactivate the object. Explicitly activating and deactivating objects like this allows very strong programmer control over resource utilization decisions.

The technique of explicitly activating objects under control of another object is particularly well suited for temporary objects; that is, objects that are created and destroyed in a short period of time, such as an enumerator. During its lifetime, the object is stateful, but it is destroyed very quickly and has no permanent state or existence. This idea of a temporary object is further supported by the POA LifeSpanPolicy, which tells the POA to create an object reference taking into account the expected lifetime of the object and the object reference. A LifeSpanPolicy value of TRANSIENT tells the POA that any objects created have meaning only in the process in which they were created. When the process goes away, the object goes away, and the object reference is no longer valid, even if a client still holds it. An advantage of TRANSIENT is that the routing information in the object reference can be very limited. Only one process on one machine can service requests on the object reference. The routing function need make no decisions nor try to load balance or deal with failure. If the process still lives, the request can be served; if the process terminates, the request fails with no further attempts at finding an alternate server. A LifeSpanPolicy of PERSISTENT, on the other hand, means that the object is expected to be long-lived, certainly beyond the lifetime of the process creating it. The object reference must then contain more generalized routing information so that the routing function has more latitude in finding an appropriate server. The LifeSpanPolicy of TRANSIENT is used almost exclusively with Explicit Activation. (I can't think of any other reasonable usage. That's a dare.)

If a POA was created with a RequestProcessingPolicy of USE_ACTIVE_OBJECT_MAP_ONLY, the only way that POA can deal with servants is through this explicit object activation technique. It is more likely that a server will use a mixture of explicit object activation and of the POA-controlled, dynamic servant finding defined later. In the case of such a mixture, the POA checks its active objects first to see if there is a servant already dealing with the Object ID; if not, the POA performs its other servant finding techniques.

Example of Explicit Object Activation

How hard is it to use a POA pattern? Well, "explicit object activation" is the easiest, but it's still instructive to see how "regular" the pattern is.

The default (root) POA uses only the explicit activation pattern with a LifeSpanPolicy value of TRANSIENT and an IdAssignmentPolicy with value SYSTEM_ID. If these options are suitable for your application, you don't have to create a POA. You obtain the "root POA" from the ORB and start using it immediately, activating objects, creating references, and preparing your process to service requests. For example, in C++, you can get an ORB reference and a reference to the root POA with the following piece of code:

```
CORBA::ORB_ptr           orb_ptr;
CORBA::Object_ptr        obj;
PortableServer::POA_ptr rootPOA;

orb_ptr = CORBA::ORB_init(argc, argv, "");
obj = orb_ptr->resolve_initial_references("RootPOA");
rootPOA = PortableServer::POA::_narrow(obj);
```

The first three statements are declarations of data types. The first active statement retrieves a pointer to the ORB. The second asks the ORB for a reference to the root POA, and the third narrows the reference so returned to be type-specifically a POA. Now you've got a POA.

Let's say you want to provide a server for an object with interface Foo. You must activate the object; that is, tell the POA to get ready to service requests made on that object reference. To do that, you first need code to service requests, a servant. Let's say you have created such a class, FooServantClass, for this purpose. The next code might then be:

```
FooServantClass* foo_servant = new FooServantClass();
Foo_var foo_ref = foo_servant->_this();
```

The first statement creates a servant (an instance of FooServantClass), and the second tells the POA to activate it, using an Object Id assigned by the POA, and then to create an object reference for it and return it. You can now hand out that object reference (foo_ref) to clients (perhaps through a naming service).

The POA and ORB are now almost ready to start servicing requests for that object. We start the server proper by performing two administrative functions.

```
rootPOA->the_manager()->activate();
orb_ptr->run();
```

The first tells the POA that it's been properly initialized and it's okay to service requests. The second tells the ORB that it now has control of the process so it can process requests.

That wasn't so bad, was it? Only seven lines of code from the very beginning. You'll get used to just pasting this into your programs. Only the name of the interface and servant class will change in each usage. The other patterns described next require a few more lines of code, but they're just as regular.

5.3.2.2 Single Servant for All Objects

(We ignore for now the possibility that a server has explicitly activated an object. That possibility affects only one part of the POA as described previously.) If the POA was created with a RequestProcessing policy of USE_DEFAULT_SERVANT, the POA will dispatch control to a single servant that has been registered with it. To perform this registration, the programmer first creates a servant (using the new language function) and then calls the set_servant operation on the POA, passing the servant. This means that there is a single servant always ready to receive requests directed to the POA. Such a servant may or may not be stateful, but there is only one such servant for the entire POA, and its state is likely to be small.

The servant so registered can handle a multitude of objects, in one of two ways: servicing a single interface type in a stateless object fashion, or servicing many different interfaces in an extremely general fashion defined only by the server programmer. Which of these two cases applies depends on what kind of object references the programmer creates with the POA, and what kind of servant is registered with the POA. The latter requires more work.

Single Servant for All Objects of the Same Type

For the first case, if each `create_reference` operation invoked on this POA is for the same interface, it makes perfect sense for all invocations on this POA to be directed to the methods of a single servant. (It makes sense since every request is directed toward a servant designed to handle that interface.) That single servant can be written to service requests for any number of objects using that interface. Since each object reference created can have a different Object Id, this POA/servant combination can service an arbitrarily large number of objects, one object and one method at a time. While the servant itself exists between method invocations, it probably takes few resources. For each request that arrives, each of the servant's methods will find the request's Object Id, use it to read the object's state from permanent storage, perform the business logic on the state, and save the object's state at the end of the method invocation. This technique for POA/servant is very powerful and is explicitly designed for rapid access to stateless objects. That is, the servant is created only once; invoking it is quite cheap, and the state for the object uses memory only for the duration of a single method.

Single Servant for All Objects of Different Types

The second way of using the single servant for all objects technique is for the single servant to handle any of a variety of interfaces. For this to work, the servant must be a special kind of servant, a `DynamicImplementation` servant. (In particular, the servant must inherit from the class of that name, rather than directly from `Servant-Base`.) This is the CORBA notion of DSI (Dynamic Skeleton Interface, the server-side analog of the DII that we discussed in the previous chapter). When the POA dispatches control to this single servant, it obviously can't call the object's interface method directly since the only servant provided is going to handle multiple interfaces, each with potentially many methods. Instead, the POA invokes the DSI servant using a generic method and passes it an object that describes the request (the `Ser-vantRequest` pseudo-object). It is then the job of the DSI servant to take apart the `ServantRequest`, figure out what interface and method the request is intended for, do some internal processing to create a "second level" servant (for the target interface), and then invoke a method on that servant. If this sounds complicated, it is. This is a technique for use only by advanced programmers who seek the last ounce of resource usage. Actually, it remains to be seen if the DSI servant (originally defined in CORBA 2.0 as a resource optimization technique for use with the BOA) can yield better performance than the dynamically created servants defined in CORBA 2.2 for use with the POA.

5.3.2.3 On-Demand Activation for Duration of a Single Method

Stateless objects have no in-memory existence (state) except when a method is actively servicing the object. Since a servant is the keeper of in-memory object state, even the servant does not exist at the beginning of server processing. When a request arrives, the POA must cause object activation to occur. This is completely different from the Explicit Activation technique, because the POA (not the programmer) is in control at the time when the object must be activated. The POA itself cannot create a servant out of thin air because it doesn't know what servant to activate. Thus, the POA needs the help of programmer code to create a servant and initialize the state for an object before the POA can invoke the method for the request.

Activating an object on demand requires that the server programmer configure the POA with a "callback" object reference that the POA can invoke in order to create a servant. The callback is the entry to programmer written code, since only the programmer knows how to create the servant for a particular interface (and, perhaps, for a particular Object Id).

Configuring the POA for on-demand activation requires the server programmer to do the following:

- At runtime (probably in the main program for the server), the server creates a POA with two particular policy values. The first is a RequestProcessingPolicy value of USE_SERVANT_MANAGER, meaning that the POA should invoke a Servant-Manager object to ask the programmer-written code to create, initialize, and return a servant. The second is a ServerRetentionPolicy value of NON_RETAIN, meaning that any servant created on demand is to be discarded after the method invocation completes (remember, the goal is statelessness). Since the Server-RetentionPolicy is NON_RETAIN, the particular kind of `ServantManager` that the POA will invoke will be called a `ServantLocator`.

- The server programmer codes the `ServantLocator`. A `ServantLocator` has two operations, `preinvoke` and `postinvoke`. The server programmer codes `preinvoke` to create a servant by deciding what kind of servant is needed (possibly querying the Object ID), using the `new` command to bring an instance of that servant into existence, and initializing the state needed for the object. The `postinvoke` operation of the `ServantLocator` cleans up any state, perhaps writing it to permanent storage, and then most likely destroys the servant.

- At runtime (probably in the main program), the server programmer creates an instance of this `ServantLocator` and an object reference to it.

- A weird twist in creating the `ServantManager` callback object is that it is a real object so it has to be registered with a POA. This sounds a little strange at first, but it's really a mechanical procedure that, seen once, can just be copied into your own program. The root POA is designed with policies that are ideal for implementing `ServantManager` callback objects.

- The server programmer invokes `POA::set_servant_manager`, passing the `ServantLocator` object reference. This tells the POA how to get at the callback.

After the server programmer provides this setup and turns control over to the ORB, the ORB waits for requests. When it receives a request for a particular POA, the ORB passes control to that POA. If the POA doesn't already have an appropriate servant, the POA uses the `ServantLocator` callback to invoke the `ServantLocator::preinvoke` operation (that is, the programmer code), asking it to create a servant, initialize the object in memory, and return the servant. Upon return, the POA invokes the appropriate method on that servant. After return from the method, the POA invokes the callback's `ServantLocator::postinvoke` operation to let the programmer code clean up any state and destroy the servant.

5.3.2.4 On-Demand Activation, Indefinite Duration

This pattern is very similar in structure to "on-demand activation for duration of a single method," although it is intended for objects that are stateful over some period. The similarities are that the POA starts out without a servant for objects, and when a request comes in, the POA uses a callback to create a servant (as for the "... single method").

The difference is that, after calling the method on the object, the POA keeps the object activated instead of deactivating it immediately. The object thus remains activated until (most likely) programmer code deactivates it (using `POA::deactivate_object`), or the POA itself is shut down. If the POA is shutting down, all its constituents are also shut down in a graceful manner, resulting in the POA deactivating the objects that were activated on demand by invoking the callback object to do so (this is similar to the automatic deactivation for stateless, differing only in timing).

When a request for an active object arrives, the POA can find the servant for it and invoke the method on the servant directly, without having to create a new servant. Being active continuously has resource and responsiveness implications (it uses more resources, but responds faster). This statefulness is useful when the decreased response time is needed, or when the object takes part in a transaction that requires statefulness across multiple method invocations.

"On-demand activation, indefinite duration" differs from "explicit object activation" by not activating the object until it is needed. Even after this on-demand activation, the object can be deactivated and then activated on demand again later. Thus, the overall resource use may be lower because the object is active only while needed, while in Explicit Activation, the object is usually active all the time (subject to the discussion in that section).

As stated earlier, the basic programming structure of "on-demand activation, indefinite duration" is similar to stateless, with only two differences in the details:

- The POA is created with a different ServerRetentionPolicy value, RETAIN.

- The type of `ServantManager` used is a `ServantActivator`, and its two operations are `incarnate` (to create the servant and initialize state) and `etherealize` (to deactivate the object).

5.3.3 Code Wrappers and the POA

Given these patterns, how would you use the POA to write wrappers for existing applications, for code that was written before CORBA? (These are sometimes called *legacy applications*, but they're much more than "old-fashioned," which is what "legacy" often implies. They're usually applications that are vital to an enterprise and are not likely to be rewritten just to take advantage of a different technology. They're not broken and they don't need to be fixed. They just need to be used differently.) Maddeningly, as with most things, the answer is, "it depends." Each of the patterns is suitable for particular kinds of applications.

For example, if the existing application runs on a high rate transaction processing backend, it probably uses a stateless programming model within itself. That is, it doesn't keep information in memory between calls to the application. It might read records from one or more databases, modify them, write them back, and return, leaving nothing in memory. In this case, your CORBA object's methods are probably stateless: They repackage their parameters suitably for the existing application and call that application using the existing API. Depending on how difficult it is to repackage the parameters and how often the object gets invoked, you might use one of two patterns to achieve this stateless operation. If the servant is simple and the repackaging is easy, you could mirror the existing application by using the pattern on-demand activation for duration of a single method. Don't bother creating a servant until it's needed, and then get rid of it right away. Alternately, if the servant is complicated, takes a long time to set up, and is called quite frequently, you might use single servant for all objects. In this case, you would initialize the servant once and have the same servant field all requests. Such a servant wouldn't have to keep state—it uses only the parameters during a single method. It stays around because you want to avoid servant setup time to get better response, and you can afford to have the servant exist between calls.

The other POA patterns are likewise usable for fronting an existing application, depending on the characteristics of the application. Wrapping existing applications in CORBA and the POA isn't something that needs special treatment. The applications just need to be called correctly, and every one of them is different. That's true of new applications, too, so you can usually use the same analysis techniques for both kinds of applications.

5.3.4 The Dynamic Skeleton Interface

We have just one more topic to cover before we get to the CORBA Component Model, and that's the Dynamic Skeleton Interface (DSI). As we pointed out a few pages back, the DSI is the server-side analog to the Dynamic Invocation Interface (DII) that a cleverly programmed client can use to invoke *any* CORBA interface.

The DSI entered the CORBA architecture along with interoperability, and for good reason: It enables an ORB to act as a bridge that communicates an invocation to the remote object's ORB, and returns the response. Without the DSI, this would be possible only if the invoking ORB had linked a skeleton for the target object, an unlikely case for all of the objects on a dynamic network. Chapter 6 covers interoperability, so we'll postpone coverage of some details until then.

Like many good ideas, the DSI proved valuable for many additional uses beyond those originally intended. These include interactive development tools based on interpreters; debuggers, and monitors that dynamically interpose on objects; and support for dynamically typed languages such as LISP. These uses are so important that the DSI specification is considered part of the CORBA Core and not CORBA Interoperability.

The DSI is implemented via a Dynamic Implementation Routine, or DIR. The ORB invokes the *same* routine, the DIR, for *every* DSI request it makes. The target object is specified via the language binding, and the operation is specified as a parameter. DSI invocations do not enter the target via the same language-mapping constructs as the static skeleton; instead, the object implementation is required to support the DIR explicitly (analogous to the support the client gives the DII).

While object implementations are free to support the DSI if they prefer, your distributed object environment is much more dependent on all of your ORBs supporting it because the DSI is a key component of CORBA interoperability. This specification expects that DSI bridges will form to pass object invocations between ORBs, with one ORB playing the invoker while the other creates a proxy for the target object and becomes the invokee. The initiating ORB makes a standard remote invocation; the target is actually a proxy, but the initiating ORB does not have to make any adjustment for this. The request enters the receiving ORB through the proxy DSI target and is passed through to the target object (and at this stage it does not matter whether the object itself uses SSI or DSI). This is a *request-level bridge*, discussed in Section 6.8.3.1.

The DSI can be supported by any object adapter, and may include adapter-specific details. The POA specification includes provision for the DSI. The DSI is specified in terms of pseudo-IDL, pseudo-objects, and directly in terms of the standard mapped languages. All parameters and the return value (if any) are bundled in a single NVList.

We're not going to present the DSI or DIR interfaces here. Although they are a crucial component of CORBA interoperability, you won't have to write to them, and the explanation we've already given is enough to understand how they work.

5.4 What CORBA Components Does for You

The CORBA Component Model (CCM) takes the key services you use regularly—persistence, transactions, security, notification—combines them with the POA's servant handling capability, and wraps all of these tools with higher-level interfaces that correspond to the patterns that experienced programmers use to code enterprise and Internet server applications.

Here's what this means to you and your programmers:

- *CCM applications are very compact.* They comprise very little code, and the code that is required all devotes to business programming.

- *CCM applications are easier to code.* Only the best resource-usage patterns are included in the CCM solution space. Code for these patterns and for other recurring functions is generated automatically from declarations in specially designed new languages built upon the familiar OMG IDL.

- *CCM applications are modular.* They can be assembled from commercial CCM components, in-house programmed CCM components, or any combination. CCM components and Enterprise JavaBeans can be combined in a single application.

- *CCM applications scale to enterprise and Internet usage levels.* Years of vendor experience with current products are embodied in the resource-handling patterns built into CCM; your applications automatically reap the benefits—high throughput, great performance, robustness—even though your programmers didn't write a single line of infrastructure code. These infrastructure functions—storing data, activating and de-activating servants—are not only performed automatically, but *coded* automatically.

We're going to start our presentation of the CCM with an example of a realistic e-commerce application, and show how compactly it can be coded up. Second (and partly as we go along coding), we'll point out the automated code generation and functionality that the CCM provides. Finally, we'll review the CCM infrastructure; that is, all (well, perhaps most) of the functions that it provides, and how they fit together. There are a bunch of these, so this section will be kind of long and perhaps imposing. That's why we'll put it off until after the example: If you're familiar with some of the CCM functions before you start it, the rest will fall into place better.

Don't be put off just because you've heard that the CCM specification is 700 pages long and complicated: Most of that stuff is for the people who write CCM ORBs, and includes details on how they have to package up the infrastructure, so that your CCM applications not only work on one CCM ORB, but also port to any other that you might decide to use in the future. We'll spare you these implementor details—life is complicated enough without them.

5.5 CCM Shopping Cart Example

We're going to illustrate CCM programming with an e-commerce Website shopping cart application. We'll present the example as code, but it hasn't been tested: We wrote this just after the final draft of the CCM submission was being completed, and there were no compilers that we could use to check out our CIDL (Component Implementation Definition Language). When you get your CCM ORB and development environment (lucky you!), if you type this example in, you'll probably have to make some adjustments to get it to compile and run, but the basic structure will be right and the application really will have the scalability characteristics that we will describe later.

What's a CORBA component? Strictly speaking, it's any piece of functionality that runs in the CCM environment, and takes advantage of the services that the environment provides. But, are components large or small? A component can be any size you write, but *the most efficient applications will be built of relatively small components*. That's because the component (or, to use a word before we've defined it, the *segment*) is the smallest unit that our CCM runtime can swap in and out to optimize throughput; by keeping your components small, you give your runtime a leg up as it struggles to run your Internet or enterprise application, keeping up with your thousands of employees or millions of customers. By "small" we don't mean "tiny"; take a look at the size of the customer, shopping cart, and checkout components in our example to see what we think of as a good size.

That's not the whole story, though, because components are also the unit of re-use, and you can lose some of the benefits of re-use if your components are too fine-grained. Fortunately, the CCM gives you a number of ways to get around this: You can either keep your components small and group them into *assemblies*, which can be re-used just as components can, or you can make your components larger but divide them into segments (as we hinted in the previous paragraph), allowing your CCM runtime to activate and passivate segments instead of entire components for efficiency. We'll cover assemblies and segments as part of our CCM discussion.

You write components in different categories, depending on how long they and their object references are expected to last, whether or not they have persistent state, and how this state is exposed to the client. These have names like *service, session, entity,* and *process.* (Yes, some of these category names are the same as those used with EJBs, quite intentionally.) We'll use three in this example and describe each one as we introduce it; later in the section, we'll present a table with all of them and their characteristics.

In our example, we'll have a *Customer* component, a *Shopping Cart* component, and a *Checkout* component. Actually we'll have many of each of these, since each customer will have his own persistent customer component to maintain account information, and his own shopping cart whenever he's shopping. (A shopping session starts when a customer puts the first item into his shopping cart, and ends when he checks out.) The Checkout component generates a bill and a shipping order from the contents of the shopping cart, so its existence is fleeting. As with many component-based applications, our deployed application consists of component *factories*, and not the component instances themselves. At runtime, the factories create component instances on-the-fly as we need them. The ability to create, activate, passivate, and destroy components as needed is the key to the CCM's scalability.

Each component type (not instance) has its own Component Home type—kind of a class object for the type. Component Homes bear lifecycle interfaces for their type: create, find (for entity components only), and remove. We'll have to declare the ComponentHome types in our IDL file also, but we get a lot for our efforts: IDL *and code* for ComponentHome operations will be generated automatically from our simple declaration.

We'll start by defining our three CORBA components and their homes in an IDL file. We'll define the Customer component first. This component makes available the customer information that resides permanently in our database; when a customer comes to our site and logs in, the application will find his record and account number for use during the session, and return a component reference for a new shopping cart so he can start shopping.

We'll design the Shopping Cart component to last for one shopping session, regardless of how long the session lasts (even if the customer logs out, and logs back in again days or weeks later). The Cart component will only come into memory for execution when the customer adds something to it or checks out, and be swapped out in between times. When it's swapped out, its contents (the component's state) are stored persistently in our database. This allows us to service many more customers than any other pattern—a typical customer spends most of his time browsing, and relatively little time actually putting items into the cart. After the customer checks out—that is, buys the stuff in the cart—his particular Cart component is released and its resources reclaimed by the system. The next time he shops, he gets a new Shopping Cart component, just as he would at a physical store.

When our customer finishes shopping, he clicks the "purchase" button, which activates the Checkout component, charging his credit card and notifying the shipping department to send his stuff out. We'll design the Checkout component to be *stateless*—it does all of its work on a single invocation, using only the information we pass in at the start. This gives our CCM a lot of freedom in allocating resources, since it doesn't have to find a special servant for the task—any Checkout servant that's not busy can be pressed into service.

To illustrate how components can work together, we've tied the Shopping Cart component and Checkout component together with **uses** and **provides** statements, declaring that the Checkout component provides the CheckoutIntf interface, and the Shopping Cart component uses the CheckoutIntf interface. To illustrate that there are other ways to tie components together, we've used the client part of the application to tie the customer's account object to the shopping cart. To do this, we've used a number of new component capabilities, but we won't give details until later.

We've tied our three-component application into an *assembly*, comprising our executables, configuration information including how the shopping cart uses the checkout component, and installation information. Why does the CCM define the assembly? Because it will be rare for a component-based application to be complete with only a single component type. Most, like ours, will be composed of many component types working together. The commercial CCM applications you buy will surely be assemblies. You can combine purchased and inhouse programmed components in an assembly, for deployment as an application.

A component is not a CORBA object with super powers; instead, it's a new CORBA meta-type that *supports* or *provides* interfaces that you define separately in your IDL. This means we need to predeclare all of our interfaces before we declare their components, as you'll see in this file. Once we've declared its interface (or interfaces), we can declare our components using the new IDL keyword component. For each, we'll have to declare the interfaces they support or provide, and we'll need to declare a Component Home.

This IDL file looks a lot longer than it really is: When you use components, the CCM development environment generates a lot of IDL and code from your input. In this file, we present a lot of this generated IDL in comments, so you'll be prepared when we use it later. This makes the file about three times longer than it needs to be.

Here's the IDL for the three components and their homes:

```
// IDL

// First, some general typedefs:

    typedef  long    CustAcctNum;
    typedef  string  CustName;
    typedef  string  CustAddress;
    typedef  string  CustCity;
    typedef  long    CustZip;
    typedef  string  CustCredCdNum;

    typedef  long    ItemNum;
    typedef  long    ItemQty;
    typedef  float   ItemPrice;

    typedef struct CartItem {
    ItemNum    thisItem;
```

```
    ItemQty     thisQty;
    ItemPrice   thisPrice;
    };


    typedef sequence<CartItem> CartItemList;


// We need to define our customer interface
//  before we can declare its component:

interface  CustomerIntf {
    CustAcctNum        AcctNum();
    CustName           Name ();
    CustAddress        Address ();
    CustCity           City ();
    CustZip            Zip ();
    CustCredCdNum   CredCard ();
}

// Now we can define the customer Component:

component Customer  supports CustomerIntf { };

// The "equivalent IDL" for this declaration is:
//   Interface Customer : CustomerIntf, CCMObject {
// };

//  Next we declare a CustomerHome. This declaration will generate IDL
//  for operations to manage the lifecycle of our Customer components:
//  that is, to create, find, and destroy instances. We won't show the
//  equivalent IDL here.

home CustomerHome manages Customer primaryKey CustomerKey { };
// definition of the primary key for our Customer component.
   valuetype CustomerKey : Components::PrimaryKeyBase {
      public CustAcctNum custKey;
   };

// We need to define the operations for our ShoppingCart interface
// before we can declare its component:
interface ShoppingCartIntf {
      void setCust  (CustAcctNum cust);
      void addItem (ItemNum n, ItemQty q, ItemPrice p);
      void buyContents ( );
      // operations to remove items from cart, and list items,
      // have been left as an exercise for the reader!
   };
```

```
// Forward declaration – we'll define this fully afterwards:
interface CheckoutIntf;

// Now we can declare our Shopping Cart Component.
// It provides the ShoppingCartIntf interface on a separate facet,
// and uses the CheckoutIntf interface of the Checkout component,
// which we will define next:
component ShoppingCart {
     provides ShoppingCartIntf Cart1;
     uses CheckoutIntf CheckOut1;

// The ShoppingCart interface generates operations that permit
// the client to access the ShoppingCartIntf facet of the ShoppingCart
// component, and to connect to the Checkout component.
// In this case the generated operations look like:
// interface ShoppingCart : CCMObject {
//     ShoppingCartIntf provide_Cart1 ();
//     void connect_CheckOut1 ( in CheckoutIntf MyCheckout );
//     CheckoutIntf disconnect_CheckOut1 ();
//     CheckoutIntf get_connection_CheckOut1 ():
//   };
// }

// Next we declare a ShoppingCartHome. This declaration will generate IDL
// for operations to manage the lifecycle of our Shopping Cart components:
// that is, to create, and destroy instances. The Shopping Cart is a process
// component with no primary key, so no find operation is generated (unlike
// the CustomerHome, above). Again, we won't show the equivalent IDL here.

home ShoppingCartHome manages ShoppingCart { };

// Need to define the operation for our Checkout component:

Interface CheckoutIntf {
   boolean buy (in Customer cust, in CartItemList cartStuff);
};

// Now we can define our Checkout Component:
component Checkout  {
   provides CheckoutIntf  Check1 ;
// This is equivalent to the following IDL:
//   interface Checkout  : CCMObject {
// The Checkout interface supports an operation to access the
// CheckoutIntf facet. In this case the generated interface looks like:
//     CheckoutIntf provide_Check1();
//   };
```

```
};
```

home CheckoutHome manages Checkout { };

5.5.1 Making Our Components' State Persist

Our Customer component's state persists from session to session, hopefully for a long time (as long as we keep our customers happy!). Shopping carts' state may also persist. In CCM, persistence can be managed by the new Persistent State Service (PSS) and declared using Persistent State Definition Language (PSDL), which are defined and presented in Chapter 17. In IDL, a forward declaration lets us use a type before we define it, so in that spirit we're going to use the PSS here and refer you to Chapter 17 for the definitions and details, although we'll certainly present the basics here.

In our system, we represent the customer using a component with state that persists from every session to the next, and exposes its key (the account number) to the client. In the terminology of the CCM, this is an *entity* component. Architecturally, this is a departure for CORBA, which up to now has never used the infrastructure to maintain identity that was visible to the client: CCM clients may invoke **find_by_primary_key** on the ComponentHome (a part of the CCM that we'll define shortly), passing in a key that might be an account number or social security number, and receive the reference for that component instance in return. In the past, identity of this sort has been maintained by CORBAservices that are distinct from the infrastructure; in the CCM, this is no longer true.

Before we go into detail on persistent state, let's review objects and identity: We now have *four* ways to identify different aspects of an object or component's instance, and it's important to keep track. Here they are:

- *The CORBA object reference.* Every instance of a CORBA object, and every interface on a CORBA component, has its own unique object reference.

- *The POA ObjectId.* When we **create_reference_with_ID**, the POA lets us assign an ObjectID of our choosing to the instance. At activation time, the POA gives the key value to our servant, which uses it to find and restore the proper state for that instance. This applies regardless of the persistence method we're using.

- *The PSS Object Key.* If we're using the PSS for persistence, we get yet another key: The PSS key, which may be distinct from the ObjectId. This key identifies the instance to our PSS schema. If we're using both the POA and the PSS, it makes sense to assign the PSS key and the POA ObjectID to be identical. (They're both strings.)

- *The CCM Key.* For entity components only, the CCM supports component identity, letting us assign a key valuetype to each instance. The ComponentHome maintains a table of keys and component references, and supports an operation that accepts a key as input and returns the component's reference.

Of the three component types in our application, two have persistent state: the Customer, and the Shopping Cart. However, only the Customer is an entity component with a CCM key (and the other three identifiers also, of course); the Shopping Cart has a PSS key that identifies its persistent store, but no CCM key so you can't ask the Shopping Cart ComponentHome to pick your shopping cart out of the flock in the electronic parking lot by giving it a key! In the PSDL that follows, watch for the assignment of PSS keys to both Customer and Shopping Cart. Later in the CIDL, look for Customer to get a CCM key, while Shopping Cart does not.

We almost don't have to write the implementation of the customer entity component at all. In our abbreviated presentation of this example, we're not including the interactive I/O that asks a new customer for his name, address, and other data, but if we did, all we would have to do is assign these data to their variables in our component. Then, by declaring these variables to be the component's state using PSDL, we cause the CCM to generate code to store and retrieve the values whenever they're used; that is, to generate nearly our entire implementation.

Here are the PSDL declarations for the Customer component:

```
// PSDL:
// This defines the state variables of our customer account, in a way that
//  lets the PSS generate code to store and retrieve them automatically:

abstract storagetype CustomerState {
        state long   AcctNum;
        state string Name;
        state string Address;
        state string City;
        state string Zip;
        state string CreditCard;
};

// The PSS needs a storagetype object; this implements the abstract storage

storagetype PortableCustomerState implements CustomerState { };

typedef sequence <Customer> CustomerList;

// The primary key in this code is the PSS key:
abstract storagehome CustomerStorageHome of Customer {
        primary key AcctNum(AcctNum);
        factory create(AcctNum, Name, Address, City, Zip, CreditCardNum);
// You can define operations on the storage home. For example:
        CustomerList find_customers_by_zip(in string Zip);
// This is handy, but we won't explain it any further in this example.
// See Chapter 17 for more.
};

storagehome PortableCustomerStorageHome implements CustomerStateHome { };
```

Since the Customer component accepts, stores, and furnishes the customer's personal information and does nothing else, our CCM development environment can produce the *entire* implementation from these declarations.

The client side of our application will either log in an existing customer or initialize a new one. (We show some of this code in Section 5.5.6 about the client.) If this is a new customer, the client will find the CustomerHome and invoke its create operation, getting back a new component reference. At create time, the factory will assign a new account number, which it encapsulates in the component reference and simultaneously stores in the database as the key to that customer's record. Doing triple duty, the account number is also the primary key for the Customer component. The client then collects name, address, and credit card data from the customer and assigns each piece to a declared state variable by invoking the component using interfaces that we didn't show here. The CCM stores these state values automatically using code generated by the PSS. For an existing customer, the client application asks the customer to input his account number and then invokes **find_by_primary_key** on the CustomerHome component.

Now for the shopping cart. Since this is a *process* component, it does not have a CCM primary key, but since it's persistent, it will have a persistence key and a POA ObjectId. Fortunately for us, the PSS and CCM work together to generate these and use them to tie each shopping cart's state to its servant, so we don't have to do anything here—not even declare them. Here's the PSDL for the shopping cart:

```
// Embedded storagetype (no home definition)
// More on embedded storagetypes in Chapter 17.
abstract storagetype CartItem {
        state long item_number;
        state long quantity;
        state float price;
};


storagetype PortableCartItem implements CartItem { };


typedef sequence<CartItem> CartItemList;


abstract storagetype CartState {
        CustomerState get_Customer();
        CartItemList get_items();
        float calculate_total();
};


storagetype PortableCartState implements CartState {
        readonly state long AcctNum;
        state CartItemList  ItemList;
};


// Since we won't declare a primary PSS key on the
// ShoppingCartStateHome, the PSS and POA will
// automatically generate and use a common key that couples
// the state of our shopping cart instance with its component
// reference.
abstract storagehome ShoppingCartStateHome { };
```

```
catalog ShoppingCatalog {
    provides CustomerStateHome;
    provides ShoppingCartStateHome;
};
```

There is no PSS declaration for the Checkout component, which has no persistent state.

5.5.2 Implementing the Customer Component

Since we're not including the registration of a new customer as part of our abbreviated example, there isn't much to show here. Our client code (which we'll show last) invokes the Customer component to ensure that there really is a valid account associated with each shopping trip. We've shown the IDL and PSDL that maintains this state persistent. Here's the CIDL that declares our implementation to be an entity component:

```
// CIDL:

composition entity CustomerImpl {

    implements Customer;
    home executor CustomerHomeImpl delegatesTo
        abstractstoragehome CustomerStateStorageHome;
};
```

Finally, there's an XML-based component configuration file that tells the CCM about our component. This is where we declare its servant activation policy to be per-method, as well as other runtime info: Interface Repository ID, threading and transaction policies, and more. These files will be generated by interactive visual tools, and use a lot of defaults, so you'll never have to code one up yourself. But, they're in XML so you can read them if you're truly curious. Since we're writing this to satisfy curiosity, here's at least part of the file for the Customer component. Remember, you won't have to write this yourself!

```
<corbacomponent>
    <corbaversion> 3.0 </corbaversion>
    <componentrepid repid="IDL:Customer:1.0" />
    <homerepid repid="IDL:CustomerHome:1.0" />
    <componentkind>
        <entity>
            <servant lifetime="method" />
        </entity>
    </componentkind>
    <threading policy="multithread" />
    <configurationcomplete set="true" />

    <segment name="Customerseg" segmenttag="1">
        <segmentmember facettag="1" />
```

```
                    <containermanagedpersistence>
                        <storagehome id="PSDL:CustomerStorageHome:1.0" />
                        <pssimplementation id="ACME-PSS" />
                        <catalog type="PSDL:CustomerCatalog:1.0" />
                        <accessmode mode="READ_ONLY" />
                        <psstransaction policy="TRANSACTIONAL" >
                            <psstransactionisolationlevel
                                    level="SERIALIZABLE" />
                        </psstransaction>
                    </containermanagedpersistence>

            <homefeatures
             name="CustomerHome"
             repid="IDL:CustomerHome:1.0">
                <operationpolicies>
                    <operation name="*">
                        <transaction use="supported" />
                    </operation>
                </operationpolicies>
            </homefeatures>

            <componentfeatures name="Customer" repid="IDL:Customer:1.0">
                <supportsinterface repid="IDL:CustomerIntf:1.0">
                    <operationpolicies>
                        <operation name="*">
                            <transaction use="supported" />
                        </operation>
                    </operationpolicies>
                </supportsinterface>
            </componentfeatures>
```

5.5.3 Implementing the Shopping Cart Component

To conserve resources, we'll make ShoppingCart a *process* component and give it a *method* activation policy. While customers browse, their shopping carts are swapped out, so even millions of browsing customers won't consume any resources (for carts, at least) on our server. When a customer clicks the "Add to Shopping Cart" button on a product's Web page, the CCM runtime and PSS do everything we'd like them to do, automatically: The CCM activates our Shopping Cart component, assigning a servant, retrieving its state from persistent storage, and starting its execution. We're executing the addItem operation with parameters ItemNum, ItemQty, and ItemPrice. These are declared state variables in our PSDL, and come in as parameters in the invocation. All we need to do is increment the number of items in the cart, and assign the ItemNum, ItemQty, and ItemPrice to their corresponding state variables. Because the PSS couples state in execution space with its image in storage, this automatically updates our database. When this is done and we return, the cart is automatically deactivated by the CCM runtime, which then reclaims its resources.

To do this, the ShoppingCart component must also implement the **Components:: Basic::EntityComponent** interface. (Process and entity components, which both have persistent references and state, share the EntityComponent interface, which is defined by the CCM specification. Entity components have an additional interface that gives them their Primary Key, which we'll see later on.) When we declare ShoppingCart to be a process component, the CCM assigns it the **Components::Basic::EntityComponent** interface. Here's the CIDL for this:

```
//CIDL
    composition process ShoppingCartMgr {
        uses catalog {ShoppingCatalog Scart};
    };
    home executor ShoppingCartHomeImpl {
        implements ShoppingCartHome;
        bindsTo Scart1.ShoppingCartStateHome;
        manages ShoppingCartImpl;
    };
};


class ShoppingCartImpl implements ShoppingCart;


// PSEUDOCODE:
// You will have to fill the code for the business operations of
// your components into the skeletons that come from your IDL compilation,
// in your chosen programming language.  Here, in pseudocode, are the
// operations that you'll have to fill in:

// setCust imports the customer's account information into the
// ShoppingCart, based on the account number that came in
// as an input parameter:
setCust operation:
    sc.acct = cust.acctnum;
    sc.name = cust.name;
    sc.address = cust.address;
    sc.city = cust.city;
    sc.zip = cust.zip;
    sc.cc = cust.cc;

// addItem adds selected items to the cart:
addItem operation:
    for I=1 to number_of_items do;
        sc.item[I] = item[I];
        sc.qty[I] = qty[I];
        sc.price[I] = price[I];
    end;

// buyContents creates a Checkout component and buys the contents
```

```
//  of the ShoppingCart:

// This is the "Factory Pattern" and there are two ways to code it:
// Do everything explicitly ourselves, or let the CCM runtime take
// care of the details by declaring a connection. In either case, the
// Checkout ComponentHome is invoked to create a Checkout
// component instance whose reference is returned to the
// Shopping Cart component.
// In a real application, we'd only do this one way and most likely
// the easy way using a connection. Here, we'll show you both.

// Here's the easy way, using a Connection:

// buyContents creates a Checkout component and buys the contents
//  of the ShoppingCart:
buyContents operation;

// PSEUDOCODE, USING CCM CONNECTION:
    // This is the "Factory Pattern" using the connection declared
    // in the configuration file. At run time, the CCM will
    // locate the checkout Home, create an instance, and connect it
    // to the Checkout1 receptacle of our Shopping Cart:
    // We don't save the reference, which is not valid after
    // this single invocation since Checkout is a Service
    // component type.

    CheckoutIntf co = sc.get_connection_CheckOut1 ();

    // Buy the contents of the ShoppingCart;
    status = buy.co (in customer cust, in cartItemList list);

    // If we were building a robust application, we'd check the boolean
    //  status return value here.
    return;

// END OF CONNECTION FACTORY PATTERN.

// PSEUDOCODE, CREATING CHECKOUT COMPONENT OURSELVES:
    // This is the "Factory Pattern" coded explicitly: Our ShoppingCart
    // finds the Checkout ComponentHome which is a checkout component
    // factory, and invokes it to create a checkout component which it
    // invokes to check out.
    // It doesn't save the reference, which is not valid after this single
    // invocation since Checkout is a Service component type.

    // Locate a CheckoutHome;
```

```
HomeFinder hf = orb.resolve_initial_references("ComponentHomeFinder");

CheckoutHome coh = hf.find_home_by_comp_type
   (CheckoutHome co_repid);

// Create a Checkout component. This is implemented
//  as a Service component –

Checkout co = create.coh();

// Buy the contents of the ShoppingCart;
status = buy.co (in customer cust, in cartItemList list);

// If we were building a robust application, we'd check the boolean
//  status return value here.
return;
```

```
// END OF EXPLICIT FACTORY PATTERN.
```

```
class ShoppingCartStateMgr  implements  Components::Basic::EntityComponent;
```

```
// COMPONENT CALLBACK INTERFACES: The operations that follow are all
// callbacks: your component implements these interfaces, and they're called by the
// CCM when it is activated, or about to be passivated, or when it needs to load
// or store persistent state. Skeletons for these operations are generated by the
// CCM for process and entity components. Code for the persistence-related
// operations will be generated automatically by the PSS from your PSDL
// declarations. In our example here, the other operations don't need anything
// except for set_session_context, which needs its value saved. This is still
// pseudocode.
```

```
set_session_context  (in SessionContext ctx);
   sc = ctx; // save in local instance variable
return;
```

```
ccm_activate operation
// If we had anything to do on activation, in addition to the persistence operations,
// which are generated automatically, we'd put it here.
return;
```

```
ccm_load operation
// this code will be generated automatically from the PSDL
// declaration. It consists of a series of accessor operations
// for the defined fields.
return;
```

```
ccm_store operation
```

```
// this code will be generated automatically from the PSDL
// declaration. It consists of a series of accessor operations
// for the defined fields.
return;


ccm_passivate operation
// If we had operations to do before passivation, we'd put them here.
return;


ccm_remove operation
// Last chance to do anything (besides persistence, which is automatic) before
// our instance is destroyed!
return;
```

Because our shopping cart is persistent, we've made it a Process component. A Process component can have transactional persistent state, but does not expose it to its clients. It is intended to model business processes like the act of shopping at an e-commerce site. If we declare the activation policy to be *component*, the servant will stay in memory from the first invocation until the object is destroyed, but we think this will leave too many idle carts in memory. So, we'll declare the activation policy to be *method*. This allows our CCM product to swap out carts, except when shoppers are in the act of adding something to them or checking out, and, since we made it a process component, the code that is necessary to save the state on passivation, and restore it on activation, is generated automatically. We think it would be effective to create a permanent database table with a pool of rows for this temporary storage, and allocate from it as carts need. We haven't shown this level of detail in the example code, but your PSS documentation will tell you how to code up something like this.

There has to be an XML-based configuration file for the ShoppingCart, just as there was for our Customer component. In it, we declare the servant activation policy to be per-method, allowing inactive carts to move out of the way while others swap in to have stuff dropped into them.

We've taken good advantage of the Transaction Policy here, by requiring that everything the ShoppingCart does occurs in the context of an active transaction. Look for the line in the next code listing that reads `<operation name="*"=>`, and the few lines that follow, to see how this is done. With this declaration in the configuration file, the CCM will examine every invocation of every ShoppingCart component to see if it carries a transaction context. (For the definition of Transaction Context, look ahead to Chapter 13.) If it does—that is, if the operation is already transactional—the CCM does nothing. If it's not, the CCM creates a transaction that covers everything the Shopping-Cart component does during the invocation, and commits just before it returns. *Every* call to the Transaction Service is generated and executed automatically by the CCM.

The ShoppingCart component has only two operations (thus far, anyhow): addItem and buyContents. This simple declaration makes the adding of items, and the *entire* purchase procedure (including everything that happens in other components that get called, including the CheckOut component), transactional. If you follow our suggestion and add an operation to delete items from the ShoppingCart, that operation will automatically become transactional, too.

Let us point out one more time: You won't have to write this file yourself; it's generated automatically. Here it is:

```
<corbacomponent>
    <corbaversion> 3.0 </corbaversion>
    <componentrepid repid="IDL:ShoppingCart:1.0" />
    <homerepid repid="IDL:ShoppingCartHome:1.0" />
    <componentkind>
        <process>
            <servant lifetime="method" />
        </process>
    </componentkind>
    <threading policy="multithread" />
    <configurationcomplete set="true" />


    <segment name="ShoppingCartseg" segmenttag="1">
        <segmentmember facettag="1" />
        <containermanagedpersistence>
            <storagehome id="PSDL:ShoppingCartStateHome:1.0" />
            <pssimplementation id="ACME-PSS" />
            <catalog type="PSDL:ShoppingCatalog:1.0" />
            <accessmode mode="READ_WRITE" />
            <psstransaction policy="TRANSACTIONAL" >
                <psstransactionisolationlevel
                        level="SERIALIZABLE" />
            </psstransaction>
        </containermanagedpersistence>
    </segment>


    <componentfeatures name="ShoppingCart"
                repid="IDL:ShoppingCart:1.0">
        <ports>
          <provides providesname="Cart1"
                    repid="IDL:ShoppingCartIntf:1.0"
                    facettag="1">
            <operationpolicies>
              <operation name="*"=>
                <transaction use="required" />
              </operation>
            </operationpolicies>
          </provides>

          <uses usesname="Check1"
            repid="IDL:CheckOutIntf:1.0" />
        </ports>
    </componentfeatures>


    <homefeatures
     name="ShoppingCartHome"
     repid="IDL:ShoppingCartHome:1.0">
```

```
<operationpolicies>
    <operation name="*">
        <transaction use="supports" />
    </operation>
</operationpolicies>
</homefeatures>
```

5.5.4 Implementing the Checkout Interface

We've implemented Checkout as a service component—a very low-resource component with no state. The POA can keep a pool of initialized Checkout servants around, and assign an incoming request to any one of them since they're all the same, functionally. Based solely on information in the input parameters, the Checkout component will charge the amount of the sale to the credit card and produce a bill of lading, which the shipping department will use to assemble and ship the order. This is all encapsulated behind the **buyContents** operation that the client invokes on the Shopping Cart, which invokes the Checkout component.

```
// CIDL
    composition service CheckoutMgr {
        home executor CheckoutHomeMgr {
        implements CheckoutHome;
        manages CheckoutImpl;
        }:
    };


    class CheckoutImpl implements CheckoutIntf;


    //PSEUDOCODE:
    // Here, in pseudocode, are suggestions on how you would code up the Checkout
    // component functionality in your programming language, inserted into the
    // skeletons generated by the CCM from your IDL and CIDL.
    // The implementation of the buy operation is shown here as invocation of two
    // additional components which we won't show: A CreditInvoice component
    // which bills the customer's credit card, and a Lading component which generates
    // a bill of lading for the shipping department. Both of these are created and invoked
    // using the Factory pattern, since they're session components. We've assumed
    // that they were declared as used interfaces in our IDL, allowing us to find the
    // component home and create our instance in a single call for each one.
    // However, we haven't shown any of the declarations for the CreditInvoice
    // or Lading components in this oversimplified example.

    buy operation:
        // locate a CreditInvoiceHome and create a CreditInvoice component:
        CreditInvoice ci = co.get_connection_CreditInvoice1;
        // Copy billing information from ShoppingCart to CreditInvoice and submit.
```

```
// All of this is in the scope of the client's transaction;
submit.ci ();
//
// Create a Bill of Lading for the order;
Lading li = co.get_connection_Lading1();
// Copy order information from ShoppingCart to Bill of Lading and submit
// All of this is in the scope of the client's transaction:
submit.li ();
return;

class CheckoutStateMgr implements Components::Basic::SessionComponent;
    set_session_context (in SessionContext ctx);
    sc = ctx; // save in local instance variable
    return;


ccm_activate operation
    return; // nothing to do;


ccm_passivate operation
    return; // nothing to do;


ccm_remove operation
    return; // nothing to do;
```

5.5.5 Component Assembly

The last thing we need to do to the server side of our CCM application is assemble it into a single unit that we can deploy, install, and run. Like the component configuration file we examined earlier, this is a file that will be generated by an interactive tool using a lot of defaults, but it's in XML so we can read it if we want. If detail doesn't scare you, read through it and look for the location of the executable files, the partitioning information, and especially the details of how the "buy" invocation made by the Shopping Cart (through its receptacle) is connected to the interface and implementation provided by a Checkout component.

```xml
<componentassembly id="7823828d878a7878c">
    <description>Assembly descriptor for web store example
     </description>
    <componentfiles>
        <componentfile id="ShoppingCartFile">
            <fileinarchive name="shoppingcart.car"/>
        </componentfile>
        <componentfile id="CheckOutFile">
            <fileinarchive name="checkout.car"/>
        </componentfile>
        <componentfile id="CustomerFile">
            <fileinarchive name="customer.car"/>
        </componentfile>
```

```
    </componentfiles>

    <partitioning>
        <homeplacement id="ShoppingCartHome">
            <componentfileref idref="ShoppingCartFile"/>
        </homeplacement>

        <homeplacement id="CustomerHome">
            <componentfileref idref="CustomerFile"/>
        </homeplacement>

        <homeplacement id="CheckOutHome">
            <componentfileref idref="CheckOutFile"/>
            <componentinstantiation id="CheckOutSingleton"/>
            <registercomponent>
                <registerwithnaming name="CheckOut"/>
            </registercomponent>
        </homeplacement>
    </partitioning>

    <connections>
        <connectinterface>
            <!— connect the "uses" ports of all ShoppingCarts
                created out of ShoppingCartHome to the "provides"
                port of CheckOutSingleton —>
            <usesport>
                <usesidentifier>Check1</usesidentifier>
                <homeplacementref idref="ShoppingCartHome"/>
            </usesport>
            <providesport>
                <providesidentifier>Check1</providesidentifier>
                <componentinstantiationref
                    idref="CheckOutSingleton"/>
            </providesport>
        </connectinterface>
    </connections>

</componentassembly>
```

5.5.6 Coding the Client

Now that our application is complete, we can write a client to invoke it. (If we had completed an Analysis and Design before we started coding, we could have coded our client in a parallel effort, of course.)

In real life, the client will be a GUI application, but we won't show any of that here, nor will we show the small amount of coding that saves the ShoppingCart reference in a cookie, enabling a shopping trip to be spread over two or more logins. The server-side application is ready for this, but our client won't be. You can code this yourself, if you want, as an exercise.

Here's the client, in C++ with liberal comments:

```
// We need to start by using the finder pattern
// to get the CustomerHome for our customer
// account component.
//
// There are two ways for this client to find
// the CustomerHome: Through the Home Finder,
// or via the Naming Service. Of course for the
// Naming Service method to work, we had to save
// the reference of the Customer Home in the
// service beforehand.
//
// We've already shown how to find the CustomerHome
// using the initial service ComponentHomeFinder,
// so this time we'll use the Naming Service:

// Initialize the ORB
    CORBA::ORB_var orb = CORBA::ORB_init(argc, argv);

// Get initial naming context
    CORBA::Object_var obj;
    obj = orb->resolve_initial_references("NameService");
    CosNaming::NamingContext_var nameContext;
    nameContext = CosNaming::NamingContext::_narrow(obj);

// lookup up CustomerHome using our agreed-upon name:
    CosNaming::Name homeName;
    homeName.length(2);
    homeName[0].id = CORBA::string_dup("MyHomes");
    homeName[1].id = CORBA::string_dup("MyCustomerHome");
    obj = nameContext->resolve(homeName);
    CustomerHome custHome_var = CustomerHome::_narrow(obj);

// We need to get the Customer Account Number
// from the user to find his account component.
// This isn't very friendly, but it keeps the
// example short. You'll have to be friendlier
// than this in a real e-commerce application:
//
// Code to get customer acct from user goes here
// but we won't show it.
// Use acct number to find the customer's record:
// CustomerAcctKey holds valuetype which contains
// primary key.
    Customer_var cust =
        custHome->find_by_primary_key (CustomerAcctKey);

// Get a reference to the ComponentHomeFinder:
    obj = orb->resolve_initial_references("ComponentHomeFinder");
    Components::HomeFinder_var homeFinder;
```

```
      homeFinder = Components::Homefinder::_narrow(obj);

// Now use the Factory Pattern to get a shopping cart:
// Look up a ShoppingCartHome:
      Components::CCMHome_var ccmHome;
      ccmHome = homeFinder->find_home_by_component_type
        ( "IDL:ShoppingCartHome:1.0");
      ShoppingCartHome_var shopCartHome =
        ShoppingCartHome::_narrow(ccmHome);

// Create a ShoppingCartIntf:
      ShoppingCartIntf_var shoppingCart =
        shopCartHome->create();

// Tell it who the customer is:
      shoppingCart->setCust (CustAcctNum);

// Do some shopping. This is a loop, where our
// customer browses our website and occasionally
// drops something (or a number of somethings)
// into his cart. When that happens, the operation
// looks like this:
      for (i = 1; i < total_number_of_items; i++)
          shoppingCart->addItem
            (ItemNum n[i],
             ItemQty q[i],
             ItemPrice p[i]);

// This is the end of the shopping loop. If
// you were to allow shopping trips to be interrupted
// and re-started without losing the contents of the
// cart, code for this would go here too.

// When the customer finishes shopping and presses
// the "Purchase" button on our web page, buy the
// contents of the shopping cart:

        shoppingCart->buyContents();

// Now we're done with this shopping trip. In a clever
// application, we'd ask the customer if he wanted to
// do some more shopping, and loop back to create another
// shopping cart.
```

One important thing to remember: The client need not be a component! If the client is not a component, then it does not have receptacles, and cannot connect to our components automatically. It can, however, make full use of the factory and finder patterns.

There are some things a client *cannot* do if it is running on a CORBA 2.X ORB, including navigation operations. Such a client is referred to as *component-unaware*; it lacks the ability to do certain operations whose IDL is generated automatically from the component declaration. We'll discuss this more in Section 5.6.16.2. Clients must execute on CORBA 3 ORBs to access the full capabilities of the CCM.

In this client, we've used the Naming Service to find the **CustomerHome**, and the finder pattern to find the Customer component we want using the customer's account number as the primary key. We admit, it's not user friendly to require your customer to memorize his account number in order to log in, and we suggest that you save it in a cookie or something to save your customers from memorizing yet another string of seemingly random numbers.

The operation `find_by_primary_key` is a departure for CORBA: For the first time, the CORBA runtime is managing object identity *for, and visible to, the client*. It's as if the CCM is running its own mini Naming Service, at least for primary keys and only for components within the control of this particular CCM runtime. We'll discuss this further in a couple of places in the rest of this chapter.

Once we have the reference to our Customer component, we can use the factory pattern to create a shopping cart instance. We invoke `find_home_by_component_type` to find the `ShoppingCart` Home, which we invoke to create the cart. As soon as we have the cart, we invoke `setCust` so it knows that it's our cart. The cart will use this information when we check out. If we had coded this robustly, the cart would not accept items unless it had been set up with a valid customer account number. If we were resuming an interrupted shopping trip and already had a cart, we would retrieve its component reference here (probably from a cookie).

Now we browse away, dropping items into our shopping cart whenever we see something we like. The server-side code allows us to interrupt our shopping trip and come back to it later without losing the contents of our cart, but we're not going to show the client-side code for this here. We don't have to do anything special to save the contents of the cart, since it's saved automatically every time we drop anything into it. All we have to do is save the Cart component reference in a cookie, for retrieval when we resume shopping.

When we're done shopping, we trigger the `buyContents` operation, presumably by clicking the "purchase" button on our Web page, although we haven't shown the GUI code for this. The `buyContents` operation was defined on the ShoppingCart back in our IDL, and in our implementation it triggers the creation of an instance of a Checkout component that charges our credit card and creates a bill of lading for the shipping department.

Even though our entire shopping trip executes with transactional assurance, there is no invocation of the Transaction Service in the client. In fact, the only place we needed to specify transactionality was in the XML-based configuration files for our components. With these declarations in place, the CCM took care of all of the details.

5.5.7 Running Our Component Example

That's our component example—quite a compact bit of code for a scalable, Internet application. Here's what we did:

We started out by coding the interfaces to our components in OMG IDL, using the new keyword **component** instead of **interface**, and declaring a home to manage each of our various components. Using these declarations, our CCM product can start to set up a structure in which it can instantiate and manage each of our component types.

Next, we declared state for each of our components that have state, in PSDL. Our CCM product, perhaps working with a separate persistence product, will use these declarations to generate code to store and retrieve state variables during execution.

Then, we declared some implementation in CIDL. Our CCM implementation will use this to construct more of our implementation.

We weren't quite done; we also had to declare some configuration information in our XML-based component descriptor files. This file is where we declared runtime characteristics, including servant lifetime policy, security, transactions, and more.

Although the functionality of this shopping-cart application may be bare-bones, it's fully scalable just the way it's written: Our customer list will scale to the size of the database that holds it; if we buy a multiprocessor distributed database to implement our PSS, we can handle millions. Similarly, the scalability of our shopping site will depend on the CCM implementation we buy to run it, and these will come in load-balanced versions as well.

Scalable patterns are built into CCM implementations by the specification, and we've demonstrated how to use several of them in this brief example. Customer is an entity object with persistent state and a key (the account number) that is exposed to the client. Its operation is very simple: Once it has been properly filled in, all it does is pop into memory for an instant to trigger and sanction the creation of a shopping cart with its account number. This ensures that all shopping carts are associated with active accounts.

Shopping Cart is only slightly more complex, and we did this partly to demonstrate this server activation pattern. Carts are process components that save their state in a database when they are not active; this lets them activate only for the brief instant when a customer is adding something or checking out. (We've left the programming of "Remove item from shopping cart" and "List contents of shopping cart" for you, dear reader.) This pattern uses our server resource extremely economically; even with hundreds of thousands of customers actively shopping, there will be only a small fraction of that number of carts executing at any instant.

Alternatively, we could have implemented our shopping as a session component and kept intermediate values in memory. Session components maintain their values in memory across invocations in the same session (thus their name), from the time they are created until they are destroyed, so our values would be preserved if we gave our session carts the activation policy of component as well. This has the disadvantage that every shopping cart occupies memory—or at least virtual memory—from the time a customer starts shopping until he either checks out, logs out, or times out. If we're successful enough to have a million people shopping our site, this means a million active shopping carts compared to perhaps a couple of thousand using the activation-per-method pattern. For lower-traffic sites, however, per-session is a perfectly reasonable activation pattern to use.

For checkout, we used a service component. Service components are stateless—they have neither identity nor state; nothing persists from one call to the next. This makes them very cheap (in resources, at least) to activate (or create, actually), and just about free to deactivate, increasing your server's efficiency. Of course you can only use them with the factory pattern; there's nothing to find! We thought about using a process component for this step; this would have used more resource in exchange for a slight increase in robustness that we thought wasn't really necessary.

Once we've declared these component types to have these activation patterns, our role as programmer is done and our CCM implementation takes over. CCM products may range from small, single-machine implementations with simple datastores, to large multimachine, multiprocessor implementations that couple to distributed databases and transaction engines. Your CCM application will run with all of the power of your CCM engine, since the high-level code you write does not over-specify how it's supposed to run, and the engine has already been tuned for your environment.

As CCM applications go, this one is pretty simple: The CCM has features that we didn't use, quite intentionally, since this example was meant to be only an introduction. In the rest of this chapter, we'll introduce the entire CCM. It won't be a complete treatment—the specification itself runs over 700 pages, and we don't have space. We're sure that books devoted entirely to CCM will be out soon; in fact, we're planning one ourselves.

5.6 Description of the CCM

CCM is designed for large, distributed enterprise and Internet applications that need to run with transactional assurance, security, and high throughput. Although CORBA gives architects and developers everything they need to develop these applications (as we know from the large number of successful CORBA installations running now), it may give you too much because POA policies, transactions, security, and other resources combine in thousands of different ways, and it requires considerable skill to select the best combination out of all the alternatives. Of these combinations, a relatively few patterns have proven successful—so successful that it's usually not necessary to consider the others; all you have to do is pick one of these and get on with your development.

The CORBA Component Model packages up this subset of successful use patterns into a new OMG specification that defines a comprehensive server-side development and runtime architecture. Because component-based applications must fit the CCM's pattern space, they will be expressed very compactly in the new languages that the specification defines, plus a minimal amount of code in a language with a CORBA language mapping. (Vendors will support C++ or Java initially, adding more CORBA-mapped languages as CCM products mature.)

The CCM consists of a number of interlocking conceptual pieces that, taken together, comprise the complete server computing architecture. These pieces are:

- *The Components* themselves, including:

  An Abstract Component Model, expressed as extensions to IDL and the object model

  A Component Implementation Framework, centered on the new Component Implementation Definition Language (CIDL)

- *The Component Container Programming Model* expressed alternatively in the specification as:

The component implementer and client view

The container provider view

- *Integration with persistence, transactions, and events*

- *Component Packaging and Deployment*

- *Interworking with EJB 1.1*

- *Component MetaData Model*—Interface Repository and MOF extensions

In the rest of this chapter, we'll summarize most of these pieces. We'll skip the container provider's view; if you're a vendor building a CCM product, you'll need to read and understand the specification itself and not a summary like this one (or maybe you *wrote* the specification). We'll also skip the metadata model. We admit that it's important, but we just didn't have time to work on this part in the short time between delivery of the specification and our deadline for this chapter!

5.6.1 Stages in a CCM Development Project

Here are the steps in a CCM development project. For each one, we've listed the things you write, the CCM tools you use, and the artifacts that the step produces.

5.6.1.1 Analysis/Design Phase

CCM projects, in general, will be large so you'll want to do an analysis and design before you start to code. Chances are you'll use OMG's standard A&D language, UML, for this. (For a description of UML, turn to Chapter 21.) Right now, the connection from UML to CORBA and CCM hasn't been fully standardized: Although you can construct a UML model and use it for your CORBA or CCM application, you have to subset UML (which is a very general language) yourself, and map some of the UML constructs to coding constructs yourself.

OMG is working on this problem, and expects to have a connection within a year or two. The work goes under the name "Business Object Initiative"; currently there are three RFPs under way and one that will be issued when these complete since its piece builds on them. They were issued by OMG's Analysis and Design Task Force; you can watch their progress on the OMG Website. See Appendix A for the URLs.

This phase includes all the modeling and analysis work that happens before a developer is even ready to start designing CORBA components. This vital piece of work is outside of the scope of this submission, although ultimately its result has to be mapped and implemented via the CCM. The OMG has issued and is planning on issuing several RFPs (as part of the so-called Business Objective Initiative) whose goal is to integrate these analysis and design activities with the CCM.

This step produces a UML model of the application in several parts including an architecture, possibly a set of Use Cases, and other artifacts.

5.6.1.2 Component Declaration

As we've seen in our mini-example, you declare your CORBA component's methods and home (a type manager, basically) in OMG IDL using the component extensions.

Then you compile it using the CORBA 3 IDL compiler that came with your CCM product. (You'll declare its state and some additional aspects in PSDL and CIDL, but we'll cover those in their own steps.)

Because we're in the CCM environment and not just CORBA, our interfaces include more than the operations we declare. For example, every component interface includes operations to navigate around its various interfaces, and stubs for these were generated automatically when we compiled our IDL. When we code our clients, we're free to invoke any of these automatically generated methods, in addition to all of the ones we declare and write explicitly ourselves.

Server-side products of this step include skeletons, IR entries (in the new component keywords that we won't cover completely here), some automatically generated code, and an XML component description that we'll use later for packaging and deployment.

5.6.1.3 Component Implementation

The first part of the implementation step is to declare each component's persistent state in PSDL (an extension of OMG IDL, presented in Chapter 17), and some behavior in CIDL (an extension of PSDL). This integrates your components with the CCM's transaction, persistence, event handling, and other features.

You map components' declared state to your persistent store using an interactive tool, or by writing some simple code.

Compilation of the CIDL generates component skeletons that you fill in with business logic in your chosen programming language. Some CCM products may assist this step with interactive tools; others will let you use your favorite text editor. You may also have to write a few lines of code to tie together some of the CIDL declarations.

From this step, once we compile the code we and the CCM wrote, we get still more compiled libraries.

5.6.1.4 Component Packaging

Next, you generate a component *descriptor*: a file, in XML, that tells the CCM runtime how to connect up and manage the implementation that we've just created. Again, you may write this using a text editor, but many CCM products will provide an interactive tool that does most of the work and ensures that the file produced is error-free.

Then you package up the implementation and the component descriptor into a *Component Archive File* (*CAR*; the file extension is `.car`), using a packaging tool (again, probably interactive) provided with your CCM product.

The CAR is deployable, as is, but we can optionally use the CAR in an *assembly* as we point out in the next step.

5.6.1.5 Component Assembly

This optional step allow us to assemble a number of components into a *component assembly*—that is, an application or part composed of a number of components with predefined interaction pathways—that will be packaged in an assembly archive file (`.aar`) to be distributed and deployed together.

The specification says this step is optional, but it won't be left out of very many development projects. As we've already mentioned, efficient CCM applications will be made up of many different, small components, and they'll be put together in assemblies for distribution and deployment.

In this step, you custom-configure each component in the assembly, describe how it connects to the other included components, and tell how the different component types will be partitioned among a set of computers if the installation is designed for a multimachine execution environment for load balancing. You will probably do this using one or a set of interactive tools, but a text editor will work too, in a pinch.

The output is a component assembly archive file that contains a set of component archives and an XML-based descriptor that describes the assembly.

You can't nest assemblies, but you can extend an existing assembly by pulling it into your assembly tool, adding stuff to it, and saving the result as a new assembly.

5.6.1.6 Component Deployment and Installation

Now we leave the development space and enter the runtime environment. CCM product vendors must provide a runtime that supports transactions, security, and event handling. (In fact, many CCM runtime products will be built upon vendors' current TP, TM, or OTM products, packaging up the years of experience embodied in these products in the best possible wrapper.) These systems may support persistence as well, although the CCM specification allows a runtime to rely on a separate compliant PSS implementation.

Before you can install your components, you (or your system administrator) have to install and configure your component runtime, get its transaction processing system and security system working properly, and connect it up to your persistence service whether it's built in or separate.

CCM development and runtime products will be quite distinct, even though most CCM product vendors will provide both. Some component applications will be constructed in-house, built, deployed, and supported by the same crew. For these, it's likely that a site will deploy the runtime of the same vendor that provided their CCM development environment. But, many other component applications—perhaps most, if the specification is as successful as we hope—will be built by application vendors, packaged (perhaps even shrink-wrapped), and sold either at retail or through industrial channels, to be deployed and run at many different sites.

The component runtime includes an installer program that reads the CAR and installs the components or assemblies, connects up provided and required interfaces, and supplied and consumed events. When the installer tool is done, the component application is ready to run.

5.6.1.7 Runtime: Component Instance Activation

For most component-based applications, you won't deploy the components themselves. Remember, most components will be ephemeral beings: shopping carts (as in our example) or other objects that come and go along with the customers or other users that need them. What you really deploy are the component factories and managers that create and manage the components during their lifecycle. At runtime, components are activated by the container POA using the subset of modes available, and are invoked by clients via their IDL interfaces.

Once deployed and installed, the component instances are available to be activated and used via the standard CORBA ORB mechanisms.

5.6.2 The CORBA Component Model and CCM Extensions to OMG IDL

Component is a new basic meta-type in CORBA; when you define a component in IDL, you declare a **component** and not an **interface**. The CCM specification extends IDL and the IR with the new keywords and concepts required by its model. At runtime, a component is represented by a component reference, which is derived from the CORBA object reference.

There are two levels of components, *basic* and *extended*, that differ in the range of capabilities they support:

Basic components, whose characteristics correspond nearly exactly to those of Release 1.1 Enterprise JavaBeans, enable an extremely close relationship between CCM and EJB. They also provide a simple mechanism for converting existing CORBA objects into components.

Extended components add a number of new features, as we'll see later on. As in the specification, we'll tell you when we're describing basic components; if we don't say, we're referring to extended.

There's more about the difference between basic and extended components later in the chapter; the details involve CCM features we haven't covered yet.

Figure 5.4 summarizes the structure of a component and how it interacts with the outside world. We'll add to this as we work through the rest of this chapter, but the features on this diagram will get us started.

The various stubs and skeletons a component bears are referred to as *ports*. Four types have special names:

Facets are the potentially multiple interfaces that a component provides to its clients.

Receptacles are the client stubs that a component uses to invoke other components, as described in its configuration file.

Event sources are the named connection points that emit events of specified type to one or more interested consumers, or to an event channel.

Event sinks are the named connection points into which events of a specified type may be pushed by a supplier or an event channel.

A component may also incorporate client stubs used to invoke other (noncomponent) CORBA objects—for example, the naming or trader service. These interfaces do not have a special name.

Other new features of the model include:

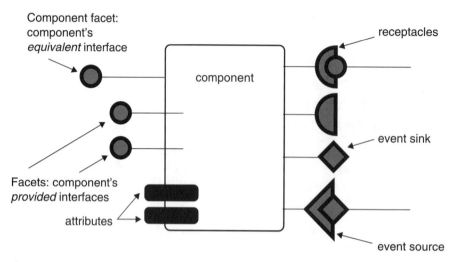

Component facet:
component's
equivalent interface

receptacles

component

Facets: component's
provided interfaces

event sink

attributes

event source

Figure 5.4   Structure of a component, showing the various ways that it can interact with the outside world.

Primary keys, values that components (that have persistent state; not all component types do) expose to their clients to help identify themselves—a customer account number or social security number might be a primary key.

Attributes and **configuration**, named values exposed through accessor and mutators, primarily used for component configuration.

Home interfaces that provide standard factory and finder operations.

At runtime, a CCM *container* supports components' lifecycles from instantiation, through execution (which may entail a number of activations and deactivations), to destruction. You can think of a container as a specialized POA with some added features, but you'll see as we work our way through the specification that it's sometimes hard to tell when one container stops and another one starts. (CCM allows applications to span machines, for load-balancing.) A CCM application will, almost always, include a number of component types with different activation and persistence characteristics, requiring a number of different POAs and, therefore, containers. Component types have names including "session" and "entity" that you remember from EJB. There are a total of seven types, as we'll detail soon.

5.6.3 Multiple Facets (interfaces) and Navigation

Here's the structure of the multiple interfaces—that is, facets—that an extended component may support, as shown in Figure 5.5.

The interface named in our component declaration—**component ShoppingCart** in our mini-example—is the component's *equivalent interface* and, for each instance as soon as it is created at runtime, bears its *distinguished reference*. We could have also declared that the component supports additional interfaces, related by inheritance,

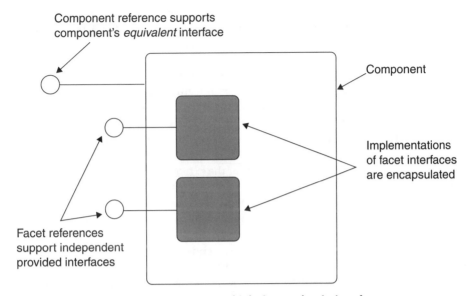

Component reference supports
component's *equivalent* interface

Component

Implementations
of facet interfaces
are encapsulated

Facet references
support independent
provided interfaces

Figure 5.5   A component supporting multiple facets; that is, interfaces.

defined elsewhere in our IDL file; each of these interfaces augments the equivalent interface by adding operations to the distinguished reference.

We can also declare that the component provides additional interfaces. Each is independent of the equivalent interface and has its own reference, and is referred to as a *facet*.

The entire implementation is encapsulated within the bold line that delineates the component, but you shouldn't assume that the implementation of each facet is distinct from all of the others, and from the distinguished interface, since this is up to the developer. In fact, we'll see later that there are two ways to program multifaceted components—segmented and nonsegmented—depending on whether or not you intermingle implementation of the various facets.

Component-aware clients can navigate from any component interface—distinguished or facet—to any other, using functionality provided by the CCM through standard interfaces.

Basic components only bear the equivalent interface; no additional facets allowed.

5.6.4 Component Homes: CORBA Finally Gets Some Class

For years, OMG members who write enterprise applications have been asking for standard operations on the extent of a type. (*Extent* is the set of instances of a type.) In an object-oriented language, these are typically class operations. With all instances residing in the same process, class operations are no problem: All instances are created within the process, and there's no way for one to get away. In CORBA, however, applications are distributed: Instances of a CORBA type can be created anywhere, coming and going at the whim of their clients. This makes the concept of extent so hazy that CORBA never bothered to define anything resembling a class operation. (Nothing prevented individual applications from providing this functionality for themselves, at least within a restricted domain; it was just not defined as a standard part of CORBA.)

With CCM, things are different: We know in advance that all of the instances are going to run in the scope of our CCM runtime. This may be spread across several machines to provide load-balancing and redundancy for fault tolerance, but at least our scope is well defined and managed. The architecture virtually demands that we define a factory to create these instances, making it easy to keep a list of their component references as they get created. If we can just cross them off the list as they're destroyed, we'll always know the extent, and it's easy to write an operation that lets an instance take itself off the list as it destroys itself. We do, indeed, have everything we need to define class-type operations, at least for the extent within the scope of our CCM runtime.

So, the CCM defines another new meta-type, the ComponentHome, that takes on these responsibilities—basically, a type manager for its instances. You declare the home type the same way (except using the keyword "home"), and at the same time, as you declare the component type. There must be at least one home type for each component type; you may define additional home types for the same component type if you want (for instance, homes defining different state variables as the primary key), but each component *instance* must consider only one of them to be its home at runtime.

The home bears lifecycle operations to manage instances of the type it was designed to manage: factory operations that create instances and associate a primary key value with each one; finder operations based on this key value; and destructor operations. These basic operations are defined and implemented by the CCM, via generated code. You can define and implement any other factory and finder operations you want.

You can also define operations—for example, queries—on a component home; on invocation, the home could contact every instance, query whatever you wanted to know, collate the answers, and report the result.

5.6.5 Receptacles

In one sense, we already know what a receptacle is: It's the client side of an interface, born by an object.

What's new in the CCM is the management of the connection. In your component IDL, you can declare that a component type uses one or more interfaces. CCM automatically generates a standard **connect** and **disconnect** operation for each interface, and generates code to manage the setting (**connect**) and unsetting (**disconnect**) of the object references at runtime. You can declare that instance connections be set up, for example at creation time, and the CCM will generate code to set the values at runtime too, although you'll have to do this yourself if program logic for this gets a little opaque. Then in your business application code, when your component is ready to invoke the interface, the object reference is already set.

5.6.6 Events

The CCM event model is based on publish/subscribe. It supports a subset of the semantics of the CORBA Notification Service, using simplified interfaces. Only push semantics are supported. We'll discuss events later, in Section 5.6.12.3 on CCM-provided services.

5.6.7 Component Usage Patterns

Everything that you do with the CCM is part of one or another pattern that it supports, but there is one place where this comes to the fore, and that is in the selection of *component category*. There are seven categories: four supported by the CCM, two by EJB, and an "empty" category that you can declare and support yourself, if you're up for the work.

Table 5.1 lists the four CCM categories. We'll define all of the new terms and explain everything in this section.

Every component type that you define (using IDL, PSDL, and CIDL) must have a category; you'll declare its category in its **composition** CIDL. You'll also declare its Container API Type; you declared its Container Category indirectly when you declared its category.

The component category is built up from a CORBA usage model and a Container API type, so we'll review those first.

> **Container API types.** There are two, and they differ depending on the durability of the component's object reference. *Session* container API types support transient references; these expire and are not valid across session boundaries. *Entity* container API types support persistent references, valid across session boundaries. Your container derives its API type from your component category declaration, following the third column of the chart. Session and Entity container APIs are defined in the CCM; they provide the services that the CCM defines for the type. Your CCM documentation will list the container APIs that you're allowed to use for each type.

> **CORBA usage models.** These refer to the interaction patterns between the component and its container on the one hand, and the rest of CORBA—especially persistence and transactionality—on the other. There are three: *Stateless* uses transient references, and the POA assigns an incoming request to any servant of the proper type. *Conversational* uses transient references, but the POA dedicates a specific servant to each component reference. This lets your client invoke an instance of a conversational component more than once, although not across a

Table 5.1 CCM Component Categories

COMPONENT CATEGORY	CORBA USAGE MODEL	CONTAINER API TYPE	PRIMARY KEY	EJB BEAN TYPE
Service	Stateless	Session	No	-
Session	Conversational	Session	No	Session
Process	Durable	Entity	No	-
Entity	Durable	Entity	Yes	Entity

session boundary. *Durable* uses persistent references and also dedicates a specific servant to each one.

Now for those component categories:

Service components have no state and no identity; every execution starts with a clean slate and has to finish everything it starts because nothing persists from one invocation of a service component to the next. In our mini-example, we used this category for the Checkout component and it fit well; in another application, a service component could execute a transaction, or a command. The *stateless* designation of its CORBA usage model indicates this. Its *Session* Container API type indicates that its component reference is transient: that is, clients cannot store it and use it again in a subsequent session. And, of course, service components cannot have a primary key since they don't have persistent storage.

Session components have transient state, and non-persistent identity. We could have used this category to implement a ShoppingCart component for an application where shopping trips are always limited to a single session; the client could hold onto its object reference and count on the component to maintain its state for that duration, but not much longer. This is indicated by the *conversational* designation of its CORBA usage model: The object reference is transient, but it is assigned to a specific POA servant. The *Session* container API type confirms that its object reference will not survive from one session to the next and, having no persistent state, it cannot have a primary key.

Process components have persistent identity and state that may span sessions, but no key is visible to the client. A client can save the reference for a process component and invoke it repeatedly to complete a task, but the instance and reference expire once the task is complete, so it doesn't make sense to register the reference in a Naming or Trader Service. Also, process components do not support the **find_by_primary_key** operation. They are useful to represent a process with a beginning and an end; we could have used a process component in our mini-example to collect name and address data from a new customer to create an account if we had included this stage of the customer interaction in the example. The account-creation piece would be a process component, while the resulting account would be represented by an entity component (presented next). The *entity* container API type supports persistent object references, and the *durable* CORBA usage model signifies in addition that the reference is assigned to a dedicated POA servant for execution. Process component may be transactional.

Entity components have persistent state and identity, visible to their client through a *primary key*. We used an entity component for our customer object, keyed by the customer's account number. Like the process component type, entity components use an *entity* container API type and *durable* CORBA usage model.

The CCM supports four *Servant Lifetime Policies*: *Method*, *Transaction*, *Component*, and *Container*.

Servants with a **method** lifetime policy are activated on every operation request, and passivated as soon as the operation has completed. For components that spend only a small fraction of their existence computing (such as our Shopping

Cart, that spends most of its time waiting for a customer to order something), this benefit of the memory savings outweighs the cost of the activation/passivation.

Servants with a **transaction** lifetime policy are activated at the beginning of a transaction, and passivated upon completion. Memory remains allocated for the duration of the transaction.

Servants with a **component** lifetime policy are activated on an operation request, and remain active until the component implementation asks to be passivated. This is useful when the executing servant has the information it needs to determine when passivation is in order.

Servants with a **container** lifetime policy are activated on an operation request, and passivated when the container decides that it's time. This is useful when information that the container has, which might include the active servant count, affects the decision. For example, you could leave container-policy servants in memory if only a few are active even if invocations come slowly, but passivate servants faster during busy times when memory is scarce.

Servants for service category components can only be assigned the method lifetime policy; all other categories of components can have any of these four lifetime policies. This makes sense; service components only live for a single invocation anyhow.

5.6.8 Component Attributes and Configuration

Components are *configurable*: You can design and write your components in a flexible way, and use features of the CCM to configure them to fit a particular application at install time (and, to a lesser extent, at runtime).

You can indicate which interfaces of a component are intended for configuration, and which are primarily for runtime use, although the distinction becomes blurry at times. There is an operation you can call at the end of installation, signaling that configuration is complete. Before the call, operations on configuration interfaces are allowed, and on operational interfaces are disallowed. After the call, the reverse is true.

IDL attributes hold configuration information, and the CCM recognizes their special role. Because of their critical role, the CCM adds exceptions to attributes' set and get operations. Any CORBA 3 application, and not just those using the CCM, can declare and use these exceptions.

The CCM collects all of the configuration information in a configurator object, which it saves. There's an operation to apply a configurator, with its collection of settings, to a component in a single operation.

5.6.9 Component Implementation

The CCM uses the term *Component Implementation Framework* (CIF) for the programming model that your programmers use to construct component implementations.

The core of the CIF is the CIDL, which we've already used in our mini-example. CIDL is an extension of PSDL, which adds persistent state declaration to OMG IDL.

The PSDL subset of CIDL allows the CCM to take care of your component's persistent state, through the mechanisms defined in the new Persistent State Service (PSS) described in Chapter 17. One thing PSDL lets you do is declare the implementation variables that make up your instances' persistent state; the PSS uses generated code and service functions to store and retrieve their values. (Since there's a pretty complete explanation in Chapter 17, we won't put much here; to find out about the PSS, skip ahead twelve chapters.)

At runtime, the CCM environment takes care of a lot of things for your components: navigation, identity (via the primary key), activation/deactivation, persistent state management, creation/destruction, and other functions. You declare these in CIDL; the CCM then generates code called *skeletons* (yes, an extension of the IDL skeletons that we've already discussed) that implements the automated CCM functions. You have to fill in the skeletons with code for the business part of your application—the only part that the CCM can't do for you!

5.6.10 Composition

For every component type that you define, you need to declare a *composition* that binds its various elements together. This is where you declare your component's name and category—service, session, process, or entity. This is also where you bind to its executor and home executor—the code for its behavior. There are optional parts to the composition: binding to PSS artifacts, and division into segments. Here are a few example composition declarations.

5.6.10.1 Minimal Composition

Here's an example minimal composition. (We took this example from the specification.) It declares a name for the composition, the component's category (service, session, process, or entity), the home type (which implicitly identifies the component type), the name of the generated home executor, and the name of the generated component executor.

A minimal composition definition (with no state management) looks like:

```
// CIDL
composition <category> MyComposition {
    home executor MyHomeExecutor {
        implements MyHomeType;
        manages MyExecutor;
    };
};
```

Figure 5.6 illustrates this composition. After declaring the category of the composition and its name, the definition identifies the Home Executor that defines the composition. The Home Executor is CCM-generated code in your programming language, that implements the operations of your Component Home—**create**, **remove**, and **find_by_primary_key** are provided and implemented by the CCM. You can add your own operations, as we show in the following sections.

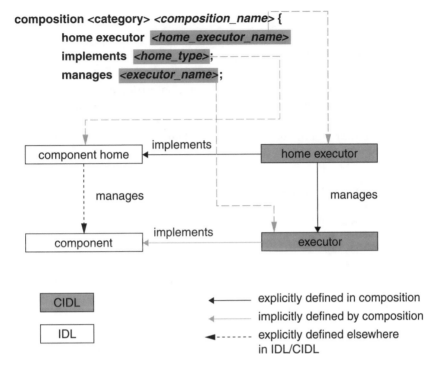

```
composition <category> <composition_name> {
        home executor <home_executor_name>
        implements <home_type>;
        manages <executor_name>;
```

Figure 5.6   A minimal composition.

5.6.10.2 State Management

Now we'll add persistent state management, still keeping things simple. Here's an example with a *catalog* (which, as we'll see in Chapter 17, manages a connection from our execution space to our storage space, which is probably in a database), and various types and homes that, together, manage our storage.

We won't explain all of these terms here; we're including this example to show that you can add persistent storage management with only a few lines of code. You'll find an explanation of Abstract Storage Homes and the like in Chapter 17.

```
// CIDL
composition <category> MyComposition {
  uses catalog {
    MyCatalogType MyCatalog;
  }
  home executor MyHomeExecutor {
    implements MyHomeType;
    bindsTo MyCatalog.MyAbstractStorageHome;
    manages MyExecutor;
  };
};
```

5.6.10.3 Home Operations

We've already mentioned that the **Component Home** acts as a type manager, providing factory, finder, and other operations on its extent. Here's an example of how you declare your own factory, finder, and other operations and delegate them to homes. Since the CIF cannot guess what you intend these operations to do, it (wisely!) does not attempt to generate implementation code. Instead, you use the **delegatesTo construct** to redirect these operations to, for example, an abstract storagehome (defined in Chapter 17) or an executor where they are either implemented or delegated one step further down. Here's a sample of the CIDL for this:

```
// CIDL:
composition <category> MyComposition {
   home executor MyHomeExecutor {
      ... // storage management specification goes here...
      delegatesTo abstract storagehome{
         MyHomeOp1 : MyStorageHomeOp1,
         ...
      };
      delegatesTo executor {
         MyHomeOp2 : MyExecutorOp2,
         ...
      abstract(MyHomeOp3, MyHomeOp4, ... );
      }
   };
};
```

5.6.10.4 Defining the Component Executor

Now that we've defined our home executor, it's time to define the component executor that it manages. There are two kinds of executors: A *monolithic* executor is a single programming artifact. Its persistent state is a single unit, and it is activated and deactivated all at once. In contrast, a *segmented* executor is made up of parts, each with its own defined persistent state and execution unit. A segment corresponds to one or more of a component's facets. This is one way to increase the efficiency of a heavily used server: The unit of activation/deactivation during execution is the segment. You can only segment entity and process components; there's no reason to use this trick on components without persistent state.

In the section of CIDL that declares your executor, you have to specify its name and one or more segments. Additional lines control code generation of receptacles (CCM-controlled client-side interfaces), and declare delegation relationships between component features and the PSS.

Here's a sample CIDL declaration of a component executor with a single segment, bearing two facets:

```
composition <category> MyComposition {
   ...
   home executor MyHomeExecutor {
      ... // storage management specification
```

```
        manages MyExecutor {
        segment MySegment0 {
          storedOn MyCatalog.MyAbstractStorageHome;
          provides ( MyFacet1, MyFacet2 );
      };
    ...
    };
  };
```

5.6.11 Container Programming Model

Now that we've defined the composition of our component, let's examine the programming environment that CCM gives us—that is, the container programming model. The container is the server's runtime environment for a CORBA component implementation— that is, how it offers CCM services to the components it services.

Figure 5.7 shows the container programming architecture. We'll go through its features one at a time.

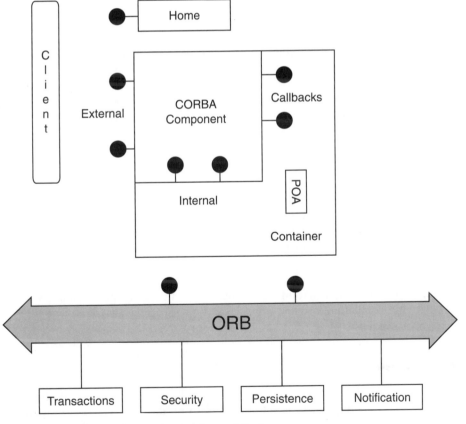

Figure 5.7   The container programming architecture.

External API Types (labeled "external" in Figure 5.7). These are the APIs that clients use to invoke operations on the component or its home. You defined the operational interfaces in your IDL; the standard factory and finder interfaces on the home were defined by the CCM, but (as we've already pointed out) you were able to define additional ones if you wanted.

Container API Types (labeled "Container" in Figure 5.7). These are local interfaces that allow either component-to-container or container-to-component invocations. Component-to-container invocations request the container-provided services shown in the diagram: Transactions, Security, Persistence, and Notification. Container-to-component invocations primarily concern activation/deactivation and informing the servant of its Primary Key so that it can restore the required state. The form of the container API types will vary depending on the type of your component: *session* or *entity*.

5.6.12 The CCM-Provided Services

The four services provided to components by the container are Transactions, Security, Event Handling, and Persistence. Here's a little more information about each one.

5.6.12.1 Transactions

You can manage the transactions your component takes part in yourself, or allow the container to do it. If you select self-managed transactions, you must declare the transactions' start and end boundaries yourself by invoking either the container's **UserTransaction** interface or the CORBA Transaction Service. If you select container-managed transactions, you declare transaction policies in the component's descriptor. The container follows these policies to make the right calls to the CORBA transaction service.

5.6.12.2 Security

The CCM container relies on CORBA security to retrieve security policy declarations from the deployment descriptor and to check the active credentials for invoking operations. You define your security policies at the operation level; in fact, it's done in the configuration file in the ComponentFeatures section, right next to the transaction declaration.

You define the access permissions for a component in its deployment descriptor. You've also defined a set of rights recognized by the CORBA security when you installed your CCM runtime. You have to align the component's permissions with the CCM security installation's rights; otherwise, the security system won't be able to process access requests.

5.6.12.3 Events

Your Component IDL (not your CIDL) generates operations for emitting and consuming events; the container maps these to the CORBA notification service. Components and component-aware clients can use either the CCM event APIs or the Notification Service APIs to publish and receive events. Component-unaware clients (described soon) must use the notification service APIs, and must stay within the subset supported by CCM. The CCM runtime includes an implementation of the notification service, or at least the subset required by the CCM.

The CCM defines two types of event channels: one shared, the target of the **publishes** designation; the other dedicated, and the target of the **emits** designation. The dedicated channel is intended primarily for use during configuration, while the shared channel is designed for runtime.

A component event is represented as a **valuetype** embedded in an **any**. This way, emitters and publishers can be matched to consumers by event type, but untyped channels can still be used. Containers set up the channels, accept a component event and push it to a channel as a structured event, and receive structured events and convert them to component events.

5.6.12.4 Persistence

There are two basic ways you can handle persistence, and they are:

> **Container-managed persistence**, selected in CIDL by connecting a state definition defined using PSDL (as specified in the CORBA Persistent State Service) to a component segment in CIDL. The container, using code generated from these declarations, automatically saves and restores state as required.

> **Self-managed persistence**, selected by suitable CIDL declarations (which we don't have space for in this chapter). The container still invokes defined interfaces when it needs to save or restore state, but in this case *you* are responsible for implementing the code that does the work.

If you're replacing an existing application with components and your database schema already exists, you'll have to use self-managed persistence and map the variables in your components to the database yourself. But, if you're starting from scratch, you can let the container manage the persistence and end up with an object-oriented schema that matches your object model.

5.6.13 Component Levels and Integration with Enterprise JavaBeans

Near the beginning of this section, we said that there were two levels of components: basic, corresponding to the EJB programming model, and extended. We didn't say much about it at the time, because the details involved concepts—segments and services, mostly—that we hadn't presented yet. Now we have, so it's time to add some detail.

> **A basic component** has only a single interface and may use transactions, security, and simple persistence for a single segment. It relies upon the container to manage the construction of CORBA object references, and uses only a single thread (the *serialize* threading model).

> **An extended component** has all the functionality of a basic component, plus multiple facets and advanced persistence assigned individually to multiple segments.

It may use the event model, participate in the construction of CORBA object references, and use multiple threads (the *multithreaded* threading model).

OMG members, including Sun (which is a supporter of the CCM specification), wanted to integrate Enterprise JavaBeans (EJBs) with CORBA Components as closely as possible. That, as things turned out, was extremely closely indeed, as we'll describe now: You will be able to mix EJBs and CORBA Components in the same application.

The basic level of the CCM specification corresponds, nearly feature for feature, to the 1.1 release of the EJB specification. In fact, the required programming API for Java CORBA Components is EJB 1.1. That release of the EJB specification also predicts that EJBs will be required to interoperate over the network using OMG's protocol IIOP, using equivalent IDL generated from Java objects via the reverse Java-to-IDL mapping (described in Section 8.4).

Building on this foundation, the CCM specification includes a comprehensive forward and reverse mapping of EJB operations and CCM operations. The correspondence, as you might expect, is extremely close; a thin bridge can span the gap. It encompasses not only method invocations, but also container, factory, finder, and other infrastructure operations.

With suitable bridges in place, an EJB running in a CORBA EJB container can look like a CCM component, and a CCM component running in a CCM container can look like an EJB. Figure 5.8 shows, conceptually at least, what such a system might look like.

This allows you to build up applications from both CCM components and EJBs, which is something you might want to do for many reasons. For example, staff skill levels may dictate use of one or the other environment, or you may find commercial components or EJBs that you can incorporate into your application.

You don't declare a component to be basic or extended; instead, the compiler identifies which one you mean by the format of your component declaration. The authors of the specification felt that, in the future, either CCM or EJB or both might develop in a way that renders this distinction moot, and IDL with the declarations of basic or extended obsolete.

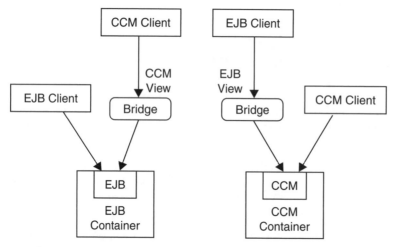

Figure 5.8 Interoperating between CORBA Components and EJBs.

5.6.14 Component Assembly and Packaging

Component applications with more than one component type—and that's every one that we can think of—have to be *assembled* into a unit that works together. You can do this in layers if you want, assembling assemblies into still larger assemblies, or do it all at once. (This comes in handy when you get an assembly from a vendor or other software supplier, and need to add more functionality to get what you need.)

When you're done, you need to *package* up everything for deployment. There is a component package, which you can use to deploy an implementation with a single component, but you may never use it. More useful is the component assembly package, that defines how to instantiate a set of components and homes, and couple them together into a running application.

The CCM defines, finally, a multiplatform software distribution format for CORBA. It's in layers, and can support the heterogeneous environments that the rest of CORBA handles so well. It's all built around a *component archive file*, which is a zip file with a prescribed contents.

The bottom layer is the *component package*. This centers around a descriptor file, written in XML, that points to the various files in the package and describes them in a standard way. The most important files in the package are the executables: You (or your vendor) can compile a component for different platforms and operating systems and put all of the executables into the package, telling in the descriptor file which platform each one supports. At deployment time, an installer in your CCM runtime will read the descriptor file and pull off the executable it needs. The descriptor for a component will also list and describe its ports, and how it wants to connect to other components, although the package descriptors (coming next) build on this.

You can install a component package into a CCM runtime, if the single component in it does something useful, or you can assemble it with other component packages into a *component assembly package*. This is a set of component packages with a package descriptor that describes them and the way they interconnect—provides/uses for receptacles and interfaces, and emits/publishes/consumes for events.

5.6.15 Component Deployment

The CCM specification places the onus onto CCM runtime vendors to build an installer that reads the component assembly archive file, including its descriptors at various levels, extracts and installs the proper executables, instantiates homes on the server, and registers them with the home finder that comes back from **resolve_initial_references**. Some ports can be connected at installation time, but ports on service, session, process, and dynamically created entity components will have to be connected at runtime based on information in these configuration files. Since the CCM explicitly allows assemblies to be deployed onto multiple-machine configurations for load balancing, you can expect installers to be fairly sophisticated pieces of software in their own right. The CCM expects that installers will gather some information at install time using interactive tools.

5.6.16 Client Programming Model

The CCM specification devotes some space and effort to differentiating and describing *component-aware* and *component-unaware* clients. Component-unaware clients are not somehow stupid or forgetful; they're the best you can write if you can only find a CORBA 2.X ORB on your client platform. Even though there are ways to compensate for the shortcomings you encounter, you'll still miss the client-side functions that the CORBA 3 ORB provides. We'll describe the more elegant component-aware client first, and follow up with the unaware and some ways to overcome its deficiencies.

5.6.16.1 Component-Aware Clients

CCM provides clients with many new ways to access remote functionality, but the basic component interface is still just a regular CORBA interface accessible via a regular CORBA object reference. The differences are in the additional things you can do, and not in changes to the stuff you've been doing already.

Service, session, and process components have to be created afresh for every use. Even entity components have to be created, although they stick around and can be used in later sessions. For this, CCM provides the *factory design pattern*: Our client starts by invoking **resolve_initial_references** for a **HomeFinder**. The **HomeFinder**, implemented by the CCM runtime, maintains a table of references and types of every **ComponentHome** in the system, and so is able to provide our client with the reference of the **Component-Home** for the type that we need. Our client then invokes the **create** operation on the **ComponentHome**, creating a new instance of the type we want and returning its reference to us. There may be several create operations on the **ComponentHome**, differing in signature. The **ComponentHome** acts as manager for its type in many ways, and not just as factory, so our client may use the reference for more than just create.

To locate existing instances of entity components, CCM provides the *finder design pattern*. To use it, our client still needs the reference for the **ComponentHome** which it finds the same way, but instead of invoking **create**, we invoke **find_by_primary_key**. Because entity components stick around, we can store their references in our Naming or Trader Service (described in Chapter 11) and retrieve them by name or characteristics.

You don't have to find your **ComponentHome** using the **HomeFinder**; homes have CORBA object references and can be registered with the Naming Service and found by clients that look them up using the name you establish in your application. EJBs use this pattern, substituting JNDI for the CORBA Naming Service.

Component-aware clients may use CCM-specific interfaces to delineate transaction boundaries, and manage security. They may also use the notification APIs defined by the CCM to post or consume events. Clients, no matter how component-aware, do *not* participate in persistence operations; only the component interacts with the PSS!

Finally, there are a number of operations provided by the CCM runtime: Navigation among multiple interfaces (for extended components); an operation to determine if a reference is a component or a CORBA object and another to determine if two references refer to the same component.

The component's equivalent interface bears operations for functionality declared using the **supports** clause, plus operations to discover and navigate to all of its facets.

Each facet bears operations declared using the **provides** clause, plus operations to navigate to its equivalent interface or any other facet.

5.6.16.2 Component-Unaware Clients

Because component interfaces are, under the covers, regular CORBA interfaces with CORBA object references, they can be invoked by a component-unaware client. One reason why you might end up writing component-unaware clients for your CCM application is CORBA version mismatch between client and server platforms; there are other reasons as well. Here's how this could happen:

It's likely that your CCM server-side application will run on a different platform than your clients, especially if it's aimed at a large enterprise or the Internet. If your CCM provider doesn't market a development environment on your client platform, you'll have to use a different ORB. Interoperability is no problem because client and server both generate the IIOP protocol, but if your client-platform ORB vendor hasn't upgraded his line to CORBA 3, you may have to write component-unaware clients for your first deployment. Remember, the keywords that generate the navigation and service stubs, and the stubs themselves, are defined in CORBA 3 and your CORBA 2.X client-side ORB doesn't know what they're for!

There are a few strategic things that a CORBA 2.X client cannot do in a CCM environment (navigation, HomeFinder operations, and a few other things) either because these operations are performed by the ORB at least in part, or because their stubs are generated automatically from the component IDL. These clients can use the factory pattern to create component instances, but only if the operations they need are on a supported interface. (There's no way for them to find and navigate to a provided interface.) They can find entity components using the Naming or Trader Services, but not by invoking **find_by_primary_key** on the **ComponentHome** because they won't have a stub for it.

In spite of the shortcomings of the CORBA 2.X clients that you'll have to field, we suggest that you design and build your CCM server for component-aware clients. If you designed your CCM server architecture for CORBA 2.X clients, avoiding client navigation operations and segmented servants, you would keep your CCM runtime from delivering the efficiency it's designed for.

To let your component-unaware client cope, you can split it in half: Put the CCM-specific calls in a wrapper component on the server. Register the wrapper factory with a Naming or Trader Service, so that the desktop part of your split client can find it easily and create a new wrapper component for each session. The interfaces between the true client and the wrapper client component may not be elegant, but at least they'll let you tread water until you get a CORBA 3 ORB on your client platform and can compile and deploy the client you wanted. And, even from the beginning, platforms with CORBA 3 ORBs can run the true client, bypassing the wrapper component and going straight to work.

5.6.17 Other IDL Extensions

That's all we're going to say about the CCM. There's a lot more to the specification, but our space is limited and this book is heavy enough already. But, before we turn to interoperability in the next chapter, there are a few general improvements that the CCM specification makes to CORBA, and we want to present them here:

Local Interfaces. Sometimes it's necessary to declare an object as "local"; that is, constrained to the same process as its ORB. Because references for these objects cannot be passed outside of their creating process, these objects can never be invoked remotely. These object types are typically used more to implement ORBs than to implement applications, so you may never need to use the new IDL declaration local interface that declares this characteristic.

Import. A new **import** statement imports only the declarations from another IDL scope or compilation into your IDL. Without import, you had to use **#include**, which brought in the IDL as well as the declarations.

Repository Id Declarations. The CCM adds **typeid** and **typePrefix** declarations to IDL, allowing you to declare repository ID values without using **#pragma**.

Exceptions for Attribute set and get operations. We already mentioned it, but this one fits here and is worth mentioning again. Attribute set and get operations raise exceptions: **getRaises**, and **setRaises**. No longer do you have to use the Property service (Chapter 18) to declare attributes that raise exceptions on **sets** and **gets**.

Architecting and Programming for CORBA Interoperability

6.1 What's New about CORBA Interoperability?

CORBA interoperability has come a long way since we wrote the first edition of this book. The original specification allowed only synchronous invocation unless you used the Dynamic Invocation Interface (DII), and CORBA objects could be passed by reference only. Even so, it required a substantial chapter to cover interoperability details.

CORBA 3 adds:

- The ability to control **quality of service** (QoS) for *any* remote invocation—synchronous or asynchronous, SII- or DII-invoked.

- A rich set of **asynchronous invocation modes** that cover both the SII and DII.

- An optional **messaging mode** that adds additional QoS settings, time-independent invocation, and the added assurance of messaging-oriented transport to CORBA through a standard set of interfaces.

- A special category of **objects that may be passed by value** (discussed in Chapter 3, but relevant here as well).

This means we have a lot more material to cover. To organize everything, let's consider the four primary roles or points of view you could adopt concerning interoperability, since your particular point of view will determine the aspects of interoperability you need to concentrate on:

- You might use the distributed objects yourself.

- You might configure, select, purchase, install, or maintain a network of distributed objects.

- You might program clients and objects for your system, a customer's system, or the software market.

- You might be an ORB implementor, and actually have to program ORB interoperability.

In the first edition of this book, we said that users would never see CORBA itself; all they would see is better application flexibility and connectivity, more convenience, at a lower cost. These delightful aspects are still there, but now some aspects of CORBA 3 interoperability peek through the location transparency curtain and reveal themselves to the user. However, you don't need an 800-plus page book to run CORBA. If your application lets you set priorities or time-outs, it will come with documentation or help files that tell you what to do. You can learn the hows behind the settings in this chapter, but you don't need this background in order to run the program!

This chapter is for architects, programmers, network administrators, and sophisticated users. Following a basic introduction to interoperability in Sections 6.2 and 6.3, we discuss QoS control in Sections 6.4 and 6.5 since it applies to every remote invocation. This leads to a discussion of the new asynchronous and messaging modes in Section 6.6, followed by a brief introduction to Real-Time CORBA in Section 6.7. The rest of the chapter examines interoperability from the ORB's and the wire's point of view. We've included this discussion mainly to satisfy curiosity, since the API for these aspects of interoperability are accessible only to ORB builders. We know there's a lot of curiosity from the many people who have told us that they appreciated the discussion in the first edition. Topics include marshaling, protocols, the interoperable object reference, connecting protocol domains via bridges and gateways, and finally some hints on how to use heterogeneity to advantage without letting it take over your life or your department.

6.2 Various Views of CORBA Interoperability

Let's examine the four user roles in a little more detail.

6.2.1 End Users

For end users, standard CORBA 2 interoperability is a transparent enabling technology. When you run a distributed application, there's nothing on your screen or printout that reveals the interoperability mode or network protocol. (This makes CORBA interoperability difficult to demonstrate: If it's working right, there's nothing special to see!) You may notice the freedom that results from transparent distribution at the application level, but individual applications could provide the same function (albeit with more work by the programmer) using other transports. For some invocations (where you can tell that there has been an invocation), you may be totally unaware of the location of the target object; where it's important to you, services such as Trader can tell you the physical location of objects such as a printer or scanner when they give you the object reference.

CORBA 3 enhancements include some things a user can see, the most important of which is Quality of Service (QoS) control—setting of priorities and timeouts, for example. New CORBA 3 specifications carry this through to the client; depending on your application design, these settings may be taken care of by your system adminstrator or may be left up to you. "Store and forward" messaging modes (termed **time-independent invocation**, or TII) let you make a CORBA invocation, disconnect, and obtain the result later when you reconnect to the network—you or someone else can even retrieve the result on another computer, in another location. The other enhancement we'll mention here (and that we've already discussed) is objects passed by value, which allow a user to perform an invocation that copies the object to his laptop or some other personal machine, for example, which can then continue to access the object even when disconnected from the network. Because synchronization of objects passed by value is left to the application and user, some of these applications will involve the user in their management as well.

So, if you're a user, the main thing you see is better and more flexible applications at a lower cost, but now you'll see the flexibility and enhancements of CORBA 3 peeking through the curtain as well.

6.2.2 System Administrators and ORB Purchasers

If you're purchasing, installing, configuring, or maintaining ORB environments, you will have to do the same type of analysis and configuration for CORBA that you would with any other interoperability system. CORBA can take the interoperability headaches out of the application, where they don't belong, but the traffic still appears on the network and you will have to configure for it.

Network protocol will make a difference to you, because you will have to configure your network for the protocols your users run, assuring adequate bandwidth and providing gateways when needed. You will also need to be concerned with security that interacts with the ORB interoperability protocol, and possibly with CORBA access to a transaction processing system. Real-Time CORBA, if you choose to install it, places additional demands on computing and network hardware and software. Our discussion of CORBA interoperability protocols will be helpful to you, because you will need to take advantage of the possibilities to meet your users' needs.

If your site fields a CORBA 3 application that takes advantage of time-independent invocation, you will have to configure host machines and routers (a new concept in CORBA, that we'll define in this chapter) to handle the protocol. Parameter lists and objects passed by value may usually be small, but some applications will pass large objects for which you will have to provide storage.

6.2.3 Object Programmers

CORBA 2 interoperability is totally transparent to your application. Once you give an object an OMG IDL interface, its location becomes transparent, allowing the administrator or installer to site it anywhere on the network.

CORBA 3 adds QoS control and client-visible asynchronous invocation modes. QoS control allows you to build programs that run well even when network or computing capacity is limited, or where execution times must be controlled. By adding four different messaging modes and objects-by-value to your toolbox, CORBA 3 increases your design and programming options. Real-Time CORBA, for applications that require it, contributes even more options. These tools will allow you to solve problems you couldn't any other way, but may complicate your life in cases where it's not obvious which mode provides the best solution to your particular problem.

Whether you use basic synchronous invocations, or the new asynchronous messaging modes and valuetypes, you will have to design and build your applications for distribution in order to get the combination of performance and functionality that your customers and users expect. The best design leaves room for flexibility at install or runtime, allowing the same set of executables to run well at multiple sites with differing requirements and resources. QoS control lets you fine-tune your good design for differing configurations, and keep it tuned as hardware and network configuratons evolve. Keep this in mind as you divide your application into objects.

Take advantage of good programming practices that you learned for non-CORBA distributed apps: Design to minimize network traffic, cache frequently used data, and use your good sense to ensure good performance and flexibility.

You will learn, as you work the example in the second half of this book, just how easy it is to program objects for distributed systems. CORBA was designed to be the easiest and most flexible distribution system, and OMG's membership believes that it has delivered on this promise. (We weren't able to put the new CORBA 3 features into the programming example because we wrote this book before any ORB product included them. However, we'll get a full-featured CORBA 3 example out in another book as soon as we can.)

6.2.4 ORB Builders

If you're planning to build an ORB, you'll need a lot more information than we can give you in this book. However, you're in good shape: The OMG specifications were written for you, which is one reason why object programmers and end users need a separate book—this one!—to tell them what's up. All you need to do is download the specs from the OMG Web site and get to work. We'll look for your ORB on the market when you're done.

6.3 Interoperability Basics: ORB-to-ORB Communication

CORBA 2 interoperability is based on ORB-to-ORB communication. We've been setting up for this ever since the first page: IDL interfaces, the Interface and Implementation Repositories, and all of the other aspects of CORBA have been designed with interoperability in mind.

Figure 6.1 shows how this works: An invocation from a client of ORB 1 passes through its IDL stub into the ORB core.

ORB 1 extracts the location of the object instance from the object reference where it is encapsulated. If the target instance is local, ORB 1 passes the invocation through the skeleton to the object for servicing. If the target is remote, ORB 1 marshals arguments for the wire and passes the invocation across the communication pathway to ORB 2, which unmarshals and routes everything to the object. Because the invocation must come into the implementation via either the skeleton or the DSI interface (and neither of these divulge client location), the object implementation (like the client) has no way of knowing whether the client is local or remote, nor does it care.

Don't get the impression that the ORB is an entity separate from the client or object because it's not, and the minimal processing we've described here adds only a small amount of overhead. The ORB is defined by the OMG in terms of the functions it performs and the interfaces it bears, *not* in terms of the way it is implemented. In the past, implementors have tried various ways to provide this functionality (including a brief try using a single, heavyweight ORB per machine running in its own separate process, an idea which fortunately did not last long!). Modern ORBs are provided to developers as library routines that link into the executable and run in-process with clients and objects, or as DLLs. For invocations that stay local, CORBA adds only a few extra instructions or so, and servicing of invocations is extremely fast. For remote invocations, most of the processing is local and only the actual invocation goes out over the wire unless the target object has moved; in this case, an extra round-trip or two are necessary to find its new location.

Notice that client and object implementation are not involved in the communication step. In CORBA, the communication always goes from one ORB to another. Granted, the client has specified the object reference of a remote target, but the object reference datatype is opaque to the client so, actually, it does not know or care whether the target is local or remote. (Of course, the user may care, for instance if the remote object is a printer or scanner, but that's not a reason to code location dependence into an application that will be used by lots of different folks in lots of different configurations.) Also, object implementations receive almost no information about the invoking client when they receive a request. (CORBAsecurity, of course, passes enough information to

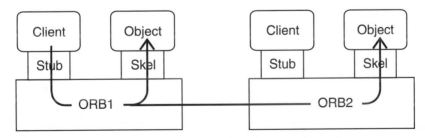

Figure 6.1 Interoperability via ORB-to-ORB communication. All of the clients connected to ORB 1 can access object implementations in both ORB 1 and ORB 2. The same condition holds for clients connected to ORB 2. The architecture scales to any number of connected ORBs.

make security access decisions, although this is separate from the application layer and does not break architectural transparencies. For a discussion of CORBAsecurity, see Chapter 14.

Because remote invocation works regardless of platform, protocol, and format differences that might exist between ORB 1 and ORB 2, it requires both ORBs to know enough about the invocation and response to allow them to translate data where necessary as they transfer the request from Platform 1 to Platform 2 and back. IDL interfaces are the key to this: Interface definitions are encoded in the stubs and skeletons, where they control marshaling and un-marshaling; for dynamic invocations, these details come from the Interface Repository. We've postponed this discussion until the second half of this chapter since it's not really a programming item.

6.4 Controlling Quality of Service

In principle always, and in real life most of the time, *location transparency* brings a host of benefits. It lets any client access any instance, anywhere, using the same invocation. At the server end, the object instance responds to every client in the same egalitarian way. This simplicity enables complex systems to be built using straightforward coding schemes. Designed into CORBA from the beginning, location transparency provides many benefits to programmer, administrator, and end user alike.

But, we all face limited resources from time to time, and the way we cope is to prioritize. For example, consider a company running a large accounting system on an overloaded mainframe or server. This machine should have been replaced years ago, but the company needed to upgrade its e-commerce servers for quicker response and didn't have resources to spare for back-office applications that were running well enough to get by. If this system treated all invocations equally, customers might have to wait while the market research department ran next year's projections, or the VP of marketing might have to wait for his reports while trial balances finish up for the clerks in the accounting department, since they got into the queue first.

This company needs to run customer transactions first in order to capture orders before customers get impatient and surf their browsers over to the competition. Remaining cycles need to be partitioned carefully, so that vital business functions get done before less important ones. In order to do this, they need to be able to prioritize requests.

There are other reasons to control QoS. Some operations need to be done *now*, or within a specified time interval. Examples include flight or engine control, plant security or building environmental control (heating, air conditioning), and data acquisition for scientific use or feedback in industrial systems. Financial quotes used in programmed trading may be worthless if delayed more than a certain time, sometimes measured in seconds or less. Architects and designers want to use CORBA in these systems, which almost always involve heterogeneous distributed hardware and software, but cannot unless they can control QoS.

These applications all require control of QoS. Some also require real-time aspects, a CORBA extension that has just completed, and, that we discuss in Section 6.7. (The QoS in the Messaging specification sets priorities, but does *not* define a real-time processing environment. There is a separate real-time specification that does this.)

So, to enable CORBA to play well in environments with limited resources or execution-time requirements, the Messaging Specification includes a comprehensive section on QoS. The Messaging Specification is a part of CORBA 3; its features will be incorporated in CORBA 3-compliant products when they come out.

6.5 QoS Framework

The QoS specification starts out by defining a general QoS framework based on *policies*, using the policy object defined in the CORBA module and covered in the previous chapter (primarily in our discussion of the POA, which uses policies heavily). The authors tried to formulate a comprehensive set of QoS policies but did not presume that they had covered everything, so they set up a framework that was extensible as well.

Both clients and servers can set policy values, although not for every policy type, of course. The specifications tell which policies are client-set, which are server-set, and which may be both (and, for these, how conflicts are resolved). We'll present some of these details later on in this section.

On the client side, QoS policy values are scoped to three levels. **ORB-level** QoS **policies** are the broadest. The ORB PolicyManager, returned by **ORB::resolve_initial_references** (described in Section 4.5.2), allows setting and retrieval of ORB-level policies. In your call to **resolve_initial_references**, you would ask for "**ORBPolicyManager.**" Your ORB may set default values here, but beware: OMG has *not* set standard defaults, so the values set by different vendors' ORBs will probably be, well, different as well. Remember this when you read the warning about defaults later in this section.

In the middle level are **thread-level QoS policies**, defined by a **PolicyCurrent** object, which override ORB-level policies. Again, you turn to **ORB::resolve_initial_references** for the reference to this object, asking for "**PolicyCurrent**"; this object bears interfaces that allow you to set policies at this level.

Finally, we have **object-reference-level QoS policies**, which override thread-level policies. These are set by extensions to interface **interface Object**, and affect individual instances. By starting with the ORB-level policy, and considering overrides at the thread level and object level in turn, your system comes up with what is termed the *effective client-side policy*; that is, the QoS value that your client wants to use, for each policy type, that controls invocation of a particular instance of a CORBA object. This evaluation is done separately for each policy type, for each instance, providing a high degree of control. However, clients cannot use any values they please—servers have rights too, and their policy values must be reconciled with clients' values in order to determine the actual values used for an invocation.

Server-side QoS policy is set the same way we handled every other type of server-side policy, by setting POA policy values at POA creation time. QoS settings derive from **interface Policy** for just this reason. Some server-side policy type settings affect client-side requests or constrain the values that client policies may use in requests; these are included in the object reference created by the POA and become available to the client's ORB and, through the call to **get_policy**, to the client itself. Other policy types affect the server only. The specification tells which affect what.

So, the actual set of policy values in effect for an invocation arises from a reconciliation of client-side and server-side policy values. To see how this is done, we need to consider the consequences of location transparency and the concept of **binding**.

In CORBA, there are a number of reasons why an object might break and reestablish its connection to a client. For example, the server may shut down the servant and start up a new one, which might be a new implementation or run on a different machine for better load balance. If it moves, it will leave a **LOCATION_FORWARD** instruction in effect at the original ORB. A CORBA 2 ORB will transparently follow the **LOCATION_FORWARD** instruction and invoke the object at its new location without notifying the client. (We'll cover this in Section 6.8.4.3, but we have to deal with its consequences here, so look ahead to that section if you're curious about the details.)

When a connection breaks and is re-established there may be a new servant running on a different POA, with different server-side QoS policies that change the way an invocation is processed. To prevent a QoS-concerned client from being surprised when an object changes its QoS settings, the specification introduces the concept of **binding** and allows QoS-concerned applications to evaluate settings at the forwarded location before the invocation is processed. (Careful: this "bind" is not the same as the vendor-specific "bind" call that some ORBs have you do to establish a link between client and object.)

An object instance is considered *bound* once the client's ORB has followed any **LOCATION_FORWARD** instructions and has a reference to the actual location of the running servant. Although binding occurs as the first step of an invocation, QoS-concerned applications will want to bind and determine true runtime server-side policies in effect *before* making any invocations. CORBA provides two routines—**validate_connection**, and **non_existent**—for this purpose. We'll tell you where to use them later in this section.

A subsequent reconnection of this bound object, which may have different QoS policies (since the policies are assigned at the POA level on the server side), is termed a *rebind*, whereas a simple reestablishment of a broken connection to the same instance at the same location is termed a *reconnect*.

If QoS is important to you, and the specification assumes that it may be critical, you will want to know if a rebind occurs, and be able to cope with any QoS differences that result. Now let's look at what the spec gives you for this situation.

First, your client may set its RebindPolicy to **TRANSPARENT, NO_REBIND**, or **NO_RECONNECT**. A setting of **TRANSPARENT** means "Either I don't care about QoS, or I'm positive that all locations will give satisfactory QoS, so if the instance moves, just keep processing as if nothing happened." A setting of **NO_REBIND** means "I'm concerned about QoS; if the instance moves, and the new instance has QoS settings incompatible with my client settings, raise a **NO_REBIND** exception and I'll follow up." Finally, a setting of **NO_RECONNECT** means "Not only should you let me know if policies are incompatible; I'm so concerned with QoS that I want to know if a new connection ever needs to be opened, so I can check things out myself."

Here are the tools that the spec gives you to check things out: First, a call to **get_client_policy** will tell you the policy values in effect for your client settings, by evaluating the ORB level, thread level, and finally the overriding client-side object instance level settings. (Most likely, the check will be made in the reverse order so processing for each policy type can stop when a policy setting is found.) Next, you'll want to find the policy that would actually be in effect if you made an invocation. This is where you'll want to invoke either **validate_connection** or **non_existent** on the object as a first step, to follow forwarding instructions to the location of the actual running servant and update the object reference that your client's ORB holds with the server-side policy values in effect. Then, a call to **get_policy** will determine and return the policy values that will actually be in effect for your invocation by comparing the client-side policy with corresponding updated values in the IOR for each policy type. Conflicts raise the **INV_POLICY** exception. The system will let you **get_policy** before you bind with a call to **validate_connection** or **non_existent**, but this will return indeterminate, implementation-dependent results—don't make this mistake if QoS is important to you!

Most QoS policies do *not* have CORBA-standardized defaults. If you do not set policy values at either the thread or object level, your system's ORB-level policies will determine the applied policy at runtime. ORB vendors will probably establish defaults of their own, in the absence of an OMG standard, but these will surely vary from one vendor to the next. *As a result, you (the programmer or administrator) will have to establish QoS policy values at either the thread or object level in order for your application to run identically on different vendors' ORBs. You cannot rely on the default values for this, because there are none.* Why not? There are so many policies, and they apply so differently to different situations and applications, that no set of default values made sense. In addition, the various CORBA 2 ORBs on the market exhibit different QoS behaviors since there was no QoS definition in the days before Messaging. By avoiding overall defaults, the specification allows each vendor's ORB to carry its CORBA 2 behavior into CORBA 3 as its ORB-specific default so that its established user base does not have to modify its code base to retain the behavior they're used to. The price you pay is, code that relies on defaults may not run identically on different vendors' ORBs. With capability comes responsibility, so straighten up and code this right!

6.5.1 QoS Policy Types

You can control a lot with CORBA 3 QoS policies. Some policy types are general enough to affect every invocation, while others either control or affect only messaging or asynchronous modes. We'll cover the general policy types next, and continue with the others as we cover the Messaging Specification.

If you're running a standard, nothing-special CORBA 3 ORB with the standard asynchronous and QoS capabilities, the only things you can control on a synchronous invocation are:

> **Timing and time-out policies.** You can specify lifetimes of requests and replies in three ways. There's also a **TIMEOUT** system exception, but you need to pay attention to its behavior: If your request does not reach its destination and start processing by the deadline, you get a **TIMEOUT** exception back. It looks like the specification requires that you get the same exception if the reply starts out from the server ORB in good shape but gets delayed en route and doesn't reach you by its deadline, but it's not clear what on the network is supposed to change the reply to an exception. (Something has to change the reply to an exception before it reaches the client or ReplyHandler, but routers aren't capable, and it doesn't make a lot of sense to send a reply all the way to the destination ORB just to get changed into an exception before it's delivered.) OMG members will clear this up

by the time products reach the market. We expect that **TIMEOUT** on reply will allow any agent handling the reply to drop it; this solution at least avoids cluttering your network with obsolete packets.

For policies:

First, you may specify *Start and End times for both Requests and Replies*. All may be specified as client-overrides only, and are valid for both synchronous and asynchronous invocations. Requests and replies will be held until the specified Start time. Requests will raise the **TIMEOUT** system exception if they miss their deadline; replies that miss the deadline will probably be dropped, undelivered (see above). Specify end times in your QoS settings to prevent cluttering the network with transmissions that are obsolete and would be discarded by the recipient even if they did manage to get through.

Second, there is also a *RelativeRequestTimeout Policy* that specifies the length of time that a request may be delivered. After the specified length of time, the request is canceled and the **TIMEOUT** exception is raised. For asynchronous invocations, the duration refers to the length of time during which the request may be processed—if processing completes in this interval, the reply will be delivered no matter how long the return transmission takes.

Finally, there is a *RelativeRoundtripTimeout policy* that covers the length of time when a request or its reply may be delivered. After this period, the request is canceled, or its reply is discarded. (For this particular policy, behavior of request and reply is prescribed in the specification.) This applies to both synchronous and asynchronous invocations. This would keep obsolete data from cluttering the network in, for example, financial or process-control invocations where results are useless after a predictable (and short!) time period.

If you've purchased and installed a messaging-enabled CORBA system, and configured routers around your system (as we'll explain in the next section on asynchronous invocations), you can also set two more things:

Queue ordering. The **QueueOrderPolicy** policy type controls routers that prioritize delivery of requests. The possible values are **ORDER_ANY** (client doesn't care about the order), **ORDER_TEMPORAL** (requests will be processed in the order they were issued, using timestamps), **ORDER_PRIORITY** (requests will be ordered for delivery according to their client-assigned priority values), and **ORDER_DEADLINE** (requests whose time-to-live is about to expire, as given by their End Times or Relative Timeouts, will move to the head of the queue). Both server and client may set a queue order policy range; server- and client-side ranges are intersected to determine the policy in effect. A null intersection raises the **INV_POLICY** exception, of course. We'll cover details in Section 6.6.2.4.)

Invocation priority values. These values are used by routers when the **QueueOrderPolicy** is set to **ORDER_PRIORITY**. A struct named **PriorityRange** controls priority range; you set both a maximum and minimum value at each end. The effective value is the intersection of the range set at the client end with the range at the server end. Both client and server may set a **RequestPriorityPolicy** and **ReplyPriorityPolicy**.

That's it for QoS independent of invocation mode, but there's a lot more QoS affecting the various deferred-synchronous, asynchronous, and messaging invocation modes, so stay tuned.

6.6 CORBA 3 Interoperability Modes

If you compiled your IDL into stubs and skeletons under CORBA 2, you could make the standard synchronous invocation or modify it to the *oneway* form in your IDL declaration. There was a *deferred synchronous* invocation that was available only for DII invocations, and that was all you got beyond standard synchronous.

Under CORBA 3, things have just gotten a whole lot better. The new Messaging Specification makes CORBA a fully equipped player in the asynchronous and messaging arena. If you want to do it asynchronously, now you can do it with CORBA. Here's what you get:

- A messaging architecture that cleanly separates the asynchronous programming model from the over-the-wire communications model.

- A flexible asynchronous **programming model** (described in Section 6.6.1) with automatically generated, standard interfaces for result retrieval by either callback or polling.

- A separate **communications model** (described in Section 6.6.2) with three distinct routing policies and types of network configurations, allowing the same application to automatically adapt to take best advantage of networks with different routing/staging capabilities and QoS support.

- QoS settings that let you tailor invocation characteristics to the needs of your application and your site.

- Callback-mode result return that allows "fire-and-forget" programming *and* optionally allows results to be returned to a different CORBA context than the client that made the invocation—even a totally separate application, running on another computer.

- Polling-mode result retrieval that allows a client to fetch results when it's ready for them, and optionally (depending on the features installed on the network) allows results to be retrieved in a different CORBA context than the one that made the invocation.

- An extended Transaction Service, able to handle asynchronous invocations within a transaction (Section 6.6.4).

- Clearly defined semantics for the ONEWAY invocation, with four different client-selected QoSs available (Section 6.6.5).

There's more good news: These additions have *no effect* on existing CORBA applications. If you're content with the synchronous invocations you've been making all along, you won't have to change anything. For non-transactional applications, all of the changes are on the client side so you can have asynchronous access to your existing CORBA servers just by rewriting the clients. The basic CORBA programming model is unchanged, and the new interfaces are defined in OMG IDL. GIOP remains the standard wire format, and IIOP remains the standard protocol, although GIOP receives a minor addition. However, the specification has been designed in a protocol-independent way so that it can be used with protocols other than IIOP.

The easiest way to learn how Asynchronous Method Invocation (AMI) works is by studying the programming model and the network communications model separately, since the specification was designed this way. We'll start with the programming model but only examine its architecture at first, leaving the programming details for the last part of our AMI discussion. Then we'll look at the communications model and see how the different policy settings interact with our programming model to deliver the flexibility that we need for modern distributed applications. We'll postpone the programming details until later, to allow the nonprogrammers to stay with us as long as possible. If you're not interested in the programming details, skip all of Section 6.6—when you get to it, move ahead to Section 6.7 and resume reading with Real-Time CORBA.

6.6.1 Asynchronous Programming Model

Under CORBA 2, you had to program using the DII using the deferred-synchronous invocation mode to get non-synchronous invocations. Under CORBA 3 using the AMI we're describing now, you have equal access to every asynchronous mode regardless of whether you use the SII or DII. Since most programmers use the SII when they have a choice, and now that they're equal in asynchronous access you have this choice all the time, we're only going to describe the SII interfaces for AMI in this book. That means that every asynchronous interface we describe is generated by your IDL compiler.

The taxonomy of the programming model is simple (Figure 6.2): At the top level, you can pick between the synchronous client-stub interfaces that we described in Chapter 3, and the asynchronous interfaces that we will describe here. If you pick **synchronous**, you have to program to your operation's stub, but there is still a choice left: You can declare the invocation to be **ONEWAY** in the IDL. If you don't (that is, you choose the default two-way), your invocation will block until it completes; when you get control back, the results will be in the return value, **out**, and **inout** parameters. If you choose **ONEWAY**, you will probably get control back sooner depending on the QoS you set (see Section 6.6.5 for details).

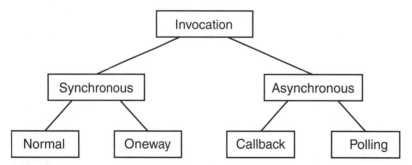

Figure 6.2   Synchronous/Asynchronous programming model taxonomy.

If you pick **asynchronous**, there's an additional level of choice: callback or polling mode result return. **Callback** is fire-and-forget programming for the invoking client. The advantage of callback is that you don't have to do anything; the result calls you when it's ready. However, if a result arrives when your program is busy doing something else, no matter how important, it will stop its processing and service the callback (or, at least, devote a thread to it if you're multithreaded). With **polling**, on the other hand, your program chooses when it wants to fetch and examine results. This suits some applications well, and others not so well. Architectural details on both are presented in the next two sections.

6.6.1.1 Callback-Mode Asynchronous Invocations

There's something unusual about how you get the response to a callback-mode AMI invocation. The CORBA model, up to now at least, is that a client makes a request, the target object receives it and does whatever while the client waits, and the object returns the result to the waiting client. In asynchronous mode, however, the client sends out the request and *doesn't wait*. The target object receives it, does whatever, and gets ready to return the result only to find that *nothing is waiting for it*. The original client is off doing something else, and there's no way to interrupt it with the response. How can we get the response to the client, or wherever it's needed?

Here's how: In Callback mode, we *turn the response into an invocation*. That's what callback mode is all about anyhow—calling something with the result so it doesn't have to keep polling to see if it's ready. Invocation is the mechanism we have in CORBA for calling something. By using it, we don't have to invent anything new.

The name for the CORBA object that receives the reply is the **ReplyHandler**. A CORBA 3 IDL compiler will generate skeletons for **ReplyHandler**s for every operation if you set the switch for it, but you have to program each **ReplyHandler** yourself to do whatever needs to happen when it is invoked with the result. It's a regular CORBA object with an object reference, created and instantiated on the POA in any of the usual ways. You have to create the object reference for it on your POA before you make the request, since that object reference is one of the arguments to the callback form of the AMI invocation.

When the AMI designers turned the response into an invocation, they created an opportunity and took advantage of it: Since the **ReplyHandler** is a regular CORBA object, it can be *anywhere on your network*, not just in the client process. This gives you a tremendous amount of flexibility in designing your distributed applications: Even if asynchrony is not an important aspect of an operation, you can use callback AMI to make an invocation whose result is routed to where it's needed by the system, instead of returning to your client where you will have to route it to wherever it's needed yourself.

There are two new aspects to exception handling here: First, because the system turns responses into invocations on a **ReplyHandler** object, exceptions raised in the invoked object during execution can't be handled in the usual way since exceptions can only be raised by a reply. To handle this, the system creates an **ExceptionHolder valuetype** that contains the exception as its state and has operations that raise the exception in the **ReplyHandler** context. You will have to do some of the programming that checks and calls the valuetypes to raise the exceptions. Second, even though you're used to throwing exceptions when you program a CORBA object and returning them to be raised in the client when the result returns, *you can't throw a CORBA exception in a ReplyHandler object* since it's never going to return anything anywhere, and it doesn't have a client. Remember, this object was called by an ORB or router with a result generated by an *object*, and not by a client, so the usual CORBA client-object relationship doesn't hold here! (Existentialists may want to pause here and ponder the ramifications of an object without a client. Where did the client go? If you wait long enough, will it show up? I know someone who programmed a client for a **ReplyHandler** object. He named it Godot. I don't know how he named a client. Isn't philosophy fun?)

There is one thing we haven't covered: What turns the response into an invocation on the **ReplyHandler**? This, it turns out, has no bearing on the programming model as long as it happens somewhere—it's actually part of the communications and messaging model, so we'll postpone discussion for now and meet up with it in Section 6.6.2.

6.6.1.2 Polling-Mode Asynchronous Invocations

Remember how we said that the AMI programming model and communications model were independent? Well, it's really true for callback mode, but only *almost* true for polling. There are two modes of polling. In the simpler one, this programming model takes advantage of the environment to allow lighter-weight clients suitable for small embedded systems, for example. (You select the extended model by setting your Routing QoS for Time-Independent Invocation; details later in this chapter.) Here is the programming model for the simpler case:

When your client invokes an operation using AMI polling mode, it immediately receives control back along with a **Poller valuetype** as the return value. While the client goes about its other business, the ORB (either using a separate thread, or another process—the specification doesn't dictate these implementation details) makes its usual invocation, gets the results back, and stores them somewhere in memory.

The IDL-compiler-generated **Poller valuetype** defines a separate operation for you to invoke to retrieve the results from each operation in the original interface. Your client can attempt to retrieve the results of an operation anytime after invoking it. You can make a retrieval attempt either block or not by specifying a time-out value in milliseconds: 0 (zero) means don't wait—return immediately whether the result is ready or not. If it is ready, you get it; if not, you get the error **CORBA::NO_RESPONSE** and you get to try again later. A timeout of $2^{32}-1$ tells the valuetype to block on this retrieval call until the result returns. Any value in between means you're willing to wait that many milliseconds for the result. When the result returns, the retrieval succeeds. You can only fetch the results once; subsequent attempts give the error **OBJECT_NOT_EXIST**.

In this simple mode, the **valuetype** is a locality-constrained object that will *not* work outside of the client process, so don't pass it to a friend somewhere else on your network and expect him to retrieve some result with it.

Why this constraint? The ORB libraries that we link with our CORBA applications are typically split into two, representing (small, lightweight) client-side functionality and (large, heavier) server-side stuff. In the simple Polling mode, there's no **Reply-**

Handler object so the client can link *without* the server-side libraries, making it lighter-weight as we promised at the beginning of this section.

We can instruct the ORB to generate a **ReplyHandler** object by requesting the highest value of the routing QoS as we'll show in a bit when we present the polling-mode AMI communications model. The **Poller valuetype** then contains the **ReplyHandler**'s object reference in its state, and can be passed out of process and still work. This flexibility is the advantage; the price is that the client may now require the server-side library and may no longer be the svelte lightweight as in the previous case. The **ReplyHandler** in this scenario is the same as the callback **ReplyHandler**, except that it's generated by the ORB and is hidden from the client, which can only invoke its **Poller valuetype** wrapper.

That covers the programming *architecture*. We haven't presented the IDL interfaces for asynchronous callback and polling invocations because we want to cover the communications model before we scare off the nonprogrammers. We'll cover the IDL details at the end of the AMI discussion in Section 6.6.6.

6.6.2 Asynchronous Communications Model

To get started, let's identify what we need to happen in order for AMI communication to work. Here's the fundamental principle:

Before AMI, the ORB expected to be invoked *synchronously* for *every* invocation. *AMI did not change this. The server-side ORB still expects to be invoked synchronously for every invocation.* (Only the client cares about the synchronous/asynchronous distinction, so the AMI specification avoided perturbing server-side architecture. This way, ORB and server implementations do not have to change. Only transactional server functions, that must synchronize with the client during a commit or rollback, are affected by AMI.)

Here's what happens during a synchronous invocation: The invoking ORB establishes a TCP connection with the server ORB. Connections are maintained, so many invocations may use the same one over time and even simultaneously. The client ORB receives an invocation from a client through its stub, applies a serial number to it, sends it to the server ORB over the connection, and waits for the response to come back over the same connection. If one or both ends are multithreaded, or if the connection is pooled for use by multiple ORBs, there may be multiple requests outstanding simultaneously on the same connection; responses are numbered with the same serial as the request to enable client ORBs to sort out results when they come back.

Contrast this with the asynchronous AMI invocation model (we'll consider only the callback case right now to keep things simple): The client makes its invocation and gets control back right away. The invocation contains the reference for a callback object, not necessarily in the client's process, that gets called back with the result when it's ready. There isn't any need to maintain a connection, or even a serial number for that matter, since the connection between the invocation and response is maintained by the *client*, and not by the ORB, in this model.

Clearly, we need an agent to translate from the asynchronous model on the client side to the synchronous model on the server side. That is, something that accepts the invocation from the client and takes charge of it, invoking the server over a maintained connection, receiving the response and matching it to the invocation using its serial number, and invoking the callback object whose reference was received with the invocation.

This can be done by the client's ORB: There's no reason why a multithreaded or multiprocess ORB couldn't return control to a client immediately upon receiving an asynchronous invocation, make a normal synchronous invocation of the server, and invoke the callback object when the result returns.

Alternatively, the agent could be separate from both the client's and the server's ORB; that is, it could be a *Router*. We'll present routers formally in Section 6.6.2.3, but introduce them briefly here. Routers are software agents that either store and forward asynchronous CORBA invocations, or (for the router closest to the server) transform the invocation from asynchronous to synchronous and invoke the server as we described. They may be co-located on the same hardware as the client or server, or on dedicated hardware strategically located on a network. Routers co-located with the client and server can perform special functions, as we'll show shortly.

CORBA routers come in two flavors: without, and with, persistent storage. Routers transfer invocations from one to another with a reliable hand-off that ensures that the data are passed correctly; by adding persistent storage, they combine to form a network that transmits data as reliably as an OTS processes it since invocations and responses are not lost even if power loss or other fault causes a router to shut down, even abruptly, and boot back up. Routers' functionality and the interfaces they use to transmit messages are defined in the AMI specification, but they are an optional conformance point. When you look at AMI implementations on the market, you will almost certainly find that routing capability—whether persistent or not—is an add-on to the basic product, although we detect an expectation that many AMI products will offer routing because of the additional capability that it offers.

There are three levels of QoS for routing of asynchronous invocations; as you might expect, you need to install routers to use any except the most basic. They are ranked, from minimum to maximum QoS, as **ROUTE_NONE**, **ROUTE_FORWARD**, and **ROUTE_STORE_AND_FORWARD**. You can set your **RoutingPolicy** to a range; if your minimum is **ROUTE_NONE** and your maximum is **ROUTE_STORE_AND_FORWARD**, your invocation will run anywhere and take advantage of the highest QoS of router it can. If your **RoutingPolicy** calls for a higher QoS than the physical network configuration can deliver, your invocation will fail with a **CORBA::INV_POLICY** exception (and it will serve you right!).

That's our introduction to asynchronous CORBA communications. Now we'll see how the various levels of QoS combine with the callback and polling invocation modes, starting with the simplest "no routers" case and building up from there.

6.6.2.1 No-Router Callback Communications

In this simplest case, the client makes a callback-mode invocation that includes the object reference of an already-created **ReplyHandler** in its parameter list. The client's ORB accepts the invocation and returns control to the client. Working either on a separate thread or in a separate process (the specification properly leaves these details to the implementor), the ORB places a serial number onto the request and invokes the server ORB over a stable connection. When the result comes back over the same connection, the client's ORB transforms it into an invocation of the **ReplyHandler** object which it executes, regardless of whether the **ReplyHandler** is local or remote. Keep in mind that CORBA does not define exactly where the "ORB" is, and the ORB may do its thing in a distributed way, so this transformation and invocation of the **ReplyHandler** may happen within the client process or elsewhere. Details are immaterial as long as everything happens according to the spec.

So this architecture meets all of our requirements: The client uses the callback-mode AMI programming model, the server sees a normal CORBA invocation, and no routers are involved. All of the pieces of the callback API are there, including callback to a remote **ReplyHandler** whenever you want. You get this behavior, or at least this observable functionality, when you make a callback-mode asynchronous invocation with **RoutingPolicy=ROUTE_NONE**.

As we've already mentioned, many vendors provide ORB functionality in two basic libraries, one for client functionality and the other for server stuff. (There may be additional libraries as well.) Client libraries are typically small, and executables that include only client functionality can be lightweight with a small memory footprint. In contrast, server libraries are much larger and add significantly to the memory footprint of an executable. If you've made callback-mode asynchronous invocations, your client process includes one or more ReplyHandlers and has to include the server libraries, which rules out lightweight clients. (Of course, such a lightweight client could not be called with events by the Event or Notification Services either, as we'll see in Chapter 12, so this may not be an option for you anyway.) However, if lightweight is a requirement, you can do it with polling, as we'll show in the next section.

6.6.2.2 No-Router Polling Communications

In this case, the client makes a callback-mode invocation that immediately returns control along with a **Poller valuetype** as the return value. Similarly to the callback case, the ORB (possibly in the same process on another thread, and possibly elsewhere; the specification does not dictate) proceeds in parallel to make a serialized invocation of the target object and receive the reply over the same connection.

Where is the **valuetype** operation implemented? The ORB does it by implementing the operations itself. Although you could imagine a "virtual" ReplyHandler object, there's no reason for any real CORBA object to be instantiated on the client side—the ORB just stores the return values itself when they come back, and hands them to your client when you invoke the fetch operation on the **Poller valuetype**. Remember, the AMI specification dictates that the Poller valuetype is constrained to your local process unless you've set **RoutingPolicy=ROUTE_STORE_AND_FORWARD**. There's a real advantage to this: As we just mentioned, most ORB products have you link a small, lightweight library for client-side functions, and a larger, heavier library for server-side functions. So, a client that makes only polling AMI calls and sets **RoutingPolicy= ROUTE_NONE or ROUTE_FORWARD** (that is, non-TII) links only the smaller client library, thereby keeping its memory footprint small. In order to make this work, the model for this case deviates from our client-side programming model (Section 6.6.3), which ordinarily allows the response to go anywhere instead of returning to the invoking client's process.

Of course this limits functionality: The Poller valuetype *cannot* be passed out of the client's process, since it has no state that refers back to the originating ORB so the retrieval functions won't work in a foreign process. And, the trick of switching from polling to callback mode while a request is outstanding will not work for the same reason. (We'll describe this in Section 6.6.6.5.) These limits go away if you have routers on your network and set **RoutingPolicy=ROUTE_STORE_AND_FORWARD**, but of course then you may have to link with the server-side library too, POA and all; details are coming up.

The bottom line on polling asynchronous invocations is this: Everything new happens on the client side, in process, small, and simple.

6.6.2.3 Adding Routers

As we hinted a few sections back, a *router* in CORBA AMI is a software agent with three possible functions:

- Routers store and forward AMI invocations and replies.

- Routers co-located with servers order and deliver invocations according to the QueueOrderPolicy in effect.

- Routers transform the asynchronous invocations that they receive from clients into synchronous invocations that they make on servers.

Some routers run on the same hardware as clients or servers, others run on separate hardware. Even routers on separate hardware may not have it all to themselves. Remember, routers are just applications with ORBs in them, the same as any other CORBA application.

Physically, CORBA AMI recognizes two different types of routers: those without persistent storage, and those with it. Routers with persistent storage participate in a reliable, end-to-end network configuration that gives a transaction-like assurance to the transport layer. Routers without persistent storage are really handy to keep network traffic flowing, but are regarded by the AMI specification as providing a lower level of assurance.

At the software level, you set **RoutingPolicy** to control the routing of your invocations. The policy takes a range, so you can set the minimum and maximum values. The choices are, from minimum to maximum, **ROUTE_NONE**, **ROUTE_FORWARD**, and **ROUTE_STORE_AND_FORWARD**. If your site has installed and configured routers with persistent storage, you may set your maximum value to any of these three levels. If your routers do not have persistent storage, the maximum you may set is **ROUTE_FORWARD**. Routing policy may be set at both the client and server ends; the policy used is the highest in the intersection of the two ranges. If you don't have any routers, the minimum you set must be **ROUTE_NONE** because this is the QoS you'll get and if it isn't in your range, your invocation will fail with an **INV_POLICY** exception.

If your network has persistent routers, and you set **RoutingPolicy=ROUTE_STORE_AND_FORWARD**, your invocations fall into the category of **Time-Independent Invocations** (TII). In TII, both callback and polling mode asynchronous invocations may return values to locations remote from the client that made them, and invocations will succeed even if both client and server are disconnected from the network when the invocation is made, and are never both connected to the network at the same time. The OMG specification document illustrates TII with a gee-whiz scenario in which a sporadically connected laptop client invokes an operation on a similarly sporadically connected laptop server over the Internet, using routers and staging in three places. We think this is a great demonstration of flexibility, but suggest that it's not a frequent enough use for routers to justify the cost of installing and maintaining them, so we'll use a different example. (Like downloading and uploading e-mail while you work offline, CORBA using a disconnected client can be really handy, and we think that people will use it a lot, for both enterprise and personal computing. However, we don't think that many applications will run disconnected at the server end.)

To get into it, we'll consider reasons to install and use routers in your CORBA network:

- With persistent routers, the robustness of your network matches that of your transactional servers.

- With persistent routers, invocations are preserved, not lost, when servers and network links/segments go down.

- With routers resident at or near your servers, invocations will be queued and delivered for processing in the order you specify, rather than the order in which they arrive.

- With persistent routers located at sites or enterprises located far apart and communicating over WANs or the Internet, all traffic is guaranteed to get through even though the interconnections may be slow, unreliable, or even totally down at times.

- With persistent routers, disconnected operation is supported at both the client and server ends of a CORBA invocation.

6.6.2.4 Example Router Configurations

Figure 6.3 shows a configuration consisting of two LANs with various computers and interconnections. We've shown only clients on the left and servers on the right for clarity although, of course, clients and servers can connect anywhere on the network. At the client end, we've shown a desktop machine and a laptop. The laptop is running a local router while the desktop is not. We think it will be typical to run a local router on a disconnected client but not on a connected one; the specification (of course) doesn't prescribe either way.

Each LAN has a router. The LANs are interconnected by either the Internet or a WAN; it doesn't matter what we call it, the effect is the same: This link is not quite as reliable or as fast as our corporate network, but it's pretty fast and usually up. The LAN on the left services our office complex, and on the right, our remote information center building. On the right, we show two servers, one on a fixed machine and the other on a laptop (yes, so we can work through the gee-whiz disconnected laptops illustration. It's neat, whether it's practical or not). Both servers have local routers. The local router plays such an important role in server request queuing that every server will want its own if it can get one.

Invocations and replies are transferred from one router to another in a reliable exchange. There's an IDL interface defined for the handshaking and transfer, but only ORB programmers write to it so we won't go into the details here. Suffice it to say that the sending ORB doesn't let go of its handshake until the receiving ORB acknowledges that it has received the entire message. Since we're describing only persistent routers in

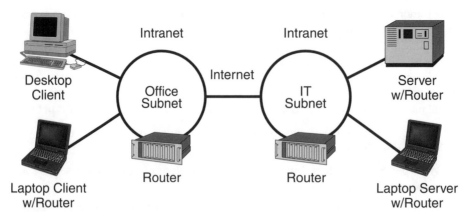

Figure 6.3 Enterprise network configuration with multiple LANs and WANs, showing CORBA routers at likely locations.

this section, that means the data are stored persistently while they await routing to their next stopover or their destination. (Techies take note: This IDL interface also gives you access to the ORB's marshaling engine, potentially useful for a host of purposes!)

To the laptop, the routers enable disconnected operation: While the machine is disconnected, CORBA clients may make any invocations they wish using asynchronous **STORE_AND_FORWARD** routing, in either callback or polling mode. All will go to the router where they are stored until the machine connects to the network. Even though client applications shut down in the interim, the invocations remain stored on the router and will be dispatched the next time the machine connects. If you've ever worked with an e-mail program that lets you type in messages while you're offline and "send" them to a queue where they wait until you connect up to your network or server, you understand how this works. And, responses that come back while you're connected to the network are stored by the router until you restart the clients that sent them. When the clients start, the router sends them the responses immediately if they went originally as callbacks, or waits for a poll if they went in polling mode.

The desktop client machine has no need for a local router if its physical network connection is reliable at least as far as the closest network router. Its invocations all go directly to the network. Depending on the QoS settings and the condition of the network, they may go directly to the invoked servers, or to routers that queue and order them before delivery.

To illustrate the benefits of routers, let's suppose that our fixed server is both important and overloaded, and that it processes both online customer transactions and bookkeeping requests. To keep customers happy (and coming back!), we decide to prioritize sale transactions higher than bookkeeping requests, and prioritize data analysis queries even lower than bookkeeping except at night when these have priority so that their results can be analyzed the next day.

We implement this by setting the QoS policy Ordering to **ORDER_PRIORITY** at both the server and all of its clients, and having each client assign a priority value to each invocation. The Maximum value for Routing must be at least **ROUTING_FORWARD**, but suppose we're using ROUTE_**STORE_AND_FORWARD** with persistent routers in this example.

Since the **ORDER_PRIORITY** Ordering policy requires queuing and prioritization, clients divert *all* invocations for the server to its local router, giving it a chance to arrange them in priority order. It doesn't matter whether the invocations were made synchronously or asynchronously, or on which network—they all go through the router and get sorted before they get to the server. The diversion to the server's router for prioritization is dictated by the routing specification in the AMI. Clients making synchronous invocations of this server will have to wait while their requests work their way up the queue; to them, the router acts like a bridge (which we explain in Section 6.8.3 later in this chapter). (We do have to point out one thing here: The AMI specification dictates that QoS settings apply equally to synchronous and asynchronous invocations, at least where it makes technical sense, but AMI itself is an optional conformance point and not all ORBs will choose to implement the full specification. If you plan to take advantage of priority queuing to order the synchronous hits on your enterprise transaction server, check with the vendor of your client ORB and confirm that it complies with this feature.)

By co-locating a router on the server machine, we avoid adding network hop overhead to asynchronous invocations even where queue ordering is performed. The client ORB addresses its asynchronous invocation to the server's router where it arrives without the use of intervening CORBA routers, and the reply heads directly to its destination (even if different from the client machine) directly from the server's router as well.

We expect that, eventually, some vendors will place routing functionality *inside* the server's ORB, avoiding even the interprocess communication step that occurs with co-located routers. Although this isn't required by the specification, which preserves the server-side ORB architecture and implementation, it moves queuing behavior into applications and allows them to respond directly to invocations according to users' preferences. We think this is a more natural way of providing this service to clients, even if it does require some rework of the server-network interface.

We can illustrate the use of the intermediate routers using this same figure and configuration. Suppose the fixed client attempts to invoke the server, but can't reach it or its router because the Internet connection is temporarily down. Failing to reach the router local to the server, the client's ORB next tries to reach the router on the distant WAN and fails again. Next it tries the router on the local WAN and succeeds, as far as it can; that is, the invocation is staged on the router and the client is free to go about its other business (assuming that it has made an asynchronous invocation). The local router now attempts, as routers do, to relay the invocation to either the server's co-located router or the router on the distant WAN, and eventually succeeds when the Internet link comes up after whatever interval. Most likely, access to both routers comes up simultaneously when the link is restored so the invocation is staged on the server's co-located router. From this point, the scenario proceeds exactly like the one before: When the invocation completes, the response routes directly back to the client unless some network link is down at that time as well.

Finally, here's the disconnected client-disconnected server example. Suppose we're running a CORBA client on the laptop on the left, and a CORBA server on the laptop on the right, and the client wants to invoke an operation on the server. The client may, at any time, make the invocation, which goes to his router if the laptop is not connected to the network at the time. (If made when connected, invocations bypass the router and go as far as they can to the server.)

When the user next connects his machine to the network, the router automatically goes to work, trying to execute all of the invocations it has stored up while offline. Presumably, any stored invocations for the fixed server, for example, execute during the session and the responses either go back to the clients if they are running, or get stored in the client's laptop's router if they are not. Invocations for the laptop server do not get executed because (we presume, in order to make this example interesting!) this machine is not connected when the client's machine is. The best that the client's Router can do is transmit the invocation to the router on the MainOffice network where it sits, awaiting the laptop server. The laptop chart now disconnects.

When the laptop server next connects, the IT network router notices, pulls the invocation out of its persistent store, and forwards it. (There is a protocol that routers use to contact each other that minimizes pinging, but we won't go into it in this book.) Depending on prioritization and queuing QoS levels in effect, the invocation may go either directly to the server or to its router where it is queued and delivered when its turn comes. Afterward, the server attempts to return the response directly to the laptop client but can't, since it's disconnected, so it routes the response as far as it can, which is the router on the office network where it sits until the laptop client next connects. You've already figured out what will happen when that machine connects, so we won't go over the details here. Right?

We think that the disconnected client part of this example is important, and will become a frequent pattern of CORBA use—if not quite as frequent as e-mail, almost as much. The application to a mobile sales force, already a frequent user of disconnected computing, is evident; so is the application to delivery services and other uses where work is done on a disconnected client machine and then uploaded to a business system. We don't think the disconnected server will be as prevalent, since companies will move all frequently accessed server applications to fixed machines where users do not have to wait for them to connect up. Nevertheless, the disconnected-server mode may be useful in some circumstances and requires little or nothing extra from the specification, so we're pleased that it's in there.

6.6.2.5 Callback Invocations with Routers

As we saw in the no-router callback example, something between the client and the server has to convert the asynchronous client invocation into a synchronous server invocation. Of course, the client and server are not involved in the siting of the conversion; we're discussing it here primarily to satisfy your curiosity about how AMI works, and perhaps also to enable your system administrator to configure your routers better.

In the no-router example, the conversion was done by the client's ORB. If we have routers installed on our system but have full connectivity and do not require queue ordering (**Order=ORDER_ANY**), the conversion could still be done by the client's ORB although there are now other possibilities. The most logical place is the server's co-located router, because this allows replies to go directly to their destination even when they're not going back to the client that originated them. If we use queue ordering (**Order≠ORDER_ANY**), the routing and ordering functions would both be performed at the same place.

Of course, the specification is silent on this, and ORB vendors are free to configure their systems to convert wherever they think best. Since this has nothing to do with any application, it does not affect client or server code. Some products will expose these decisions to your sysadmins, allowing them to tune your system for best performance.

6.6.2.6 Polling Invocations with Routers

When you make a TII polling invocation, the system creates a **PersistentRequest** object on your behalf, and returns a **Poller valuetype** that includes a method that queries the **PersistentRequest** object to obtain the result. Only if the invocation was made in TII mode (**RoutingPolicy=ROUTE_STORE_AND_FORWARD**) may the Poller be passed out of the client process and used *anywhere* on your connected system to obtain the result. This means that the **PersistentRequest** object must be accessible from anywhere, so your system will probably be configured to create it on a router on your corporate network. In this case, your polling client still does not need to link with the larger server-side library; however, if the **PersistentRequest** object gets created in your client process, you will need this library and your client will be larger.

The difference between polling in TII mode, which creates a **Poller valuetype** that functions anywhere including outside the client process, and polling in the other modes, where the poller only functions within, is this: In TII mode, the **Persistent Request** object is a true CORBA object with an object reference, accessible from anywhere on your system. In non-TII mode, its functionality is provided by code within the ORB and accessed—via **valuetype** APIs—but no true instance is created.

Of course the poller functions exactly the same in TII as before: You invoke it to obtain the result, using the same **Timeout** variable to control whether you get control right back or wait if the invocation has not completed. There is a way to collect pollers into a set and query them all with a single call, but we won't give details here.

6.6.2.7 Unchecked Narrow

As we've mentioned several times, CORBA uses the type system built into object-oriented languages to enforce type safety on CORBA objects. The programming tool you use to cast an object reference from the generic type Object to its specific type is the **narrow** operation. This operation may need to know the full type hierarchy of the object in order to confirm that the requested typecast is proper, but this information may only exist at the target. If your client is making TII invocations in disconnected mode, the server access to perform the **narrow** (done by the client ORB on your behalf, possibly requiring a synchronous invocation of the server) would not take place until the machine next connected to the network; until that time, no further processing could be done and no invocations could be queued on the router unless there were another way to perform the **narrow**. Timing constraints may even hamper program operation in situations where a response delay in a normal asynchronous call is acceptable but the **narrow** result is needed immediately.

To allow you to deal with this situation, the AMI specification defines a new operation, **unchecked_narrow**. Unlike the **narrow** function, **unchecked_narrow** does not check that the requested interface is supported by the target instance, and immediately returns an (apparently) valid object reference. If the target does not, in fact, support the interface, you will receive a **BAD_OPERATION** exception return from your invocation.

6.6.3 What about the Four Invocation Modes?

In some write-ups of CORBA AMI, you may see invocations divided into these four invocation modes:

- Synchronous invocations
- Deferred-synchronous invocations
- Asynchronous invocations
- Time-independent invocations

Although we've used these terms, we've avoided the assumption that every CORBA invocation fits neatly into just one of them. Instead, we've analyzed each invocation according to its programming model as we showed in Figure 6.2, and independently (well, mostly) on its communications model QoS as we discussed in Section 6.6.2 and its subsections. Overall, we found that it wasn't helpful to try to stuff all of this detail, permutations, and combinations into four overall categories, so we haven't done it. That's all; there's no mystery.

6.6.4 TII and Transactions

If you're not familiar with OLTP (online transaction processing), you can skip ahead and read Chapter 13 before you plow through this section if you want.

The classical transaction processing scenario involves a *synchronized* collection of actors and resources, all proceeding through a transaction (which may be financial but doesn't have to be) at the same time. This way, if one participant is unable to complete its part, it can notify the others that it is rolling back so that they do too. In this kind of transaction, either all participants commit, or none of them do.

OMG's Object Transaction Service (OTS) extended this pattern, which was first established on mainframes, to CORBA, following a standard set originally by X/Open. Established long before AMI, OTS executed over synchronous CORBA calls and spread the single transaction previously confined to the mainframe over a collection of distributed objects. This model didn't need a name at the time since it was the only model we had, but now we refer to it as the **shared transaction model**. That is, there is only one transaction and it is *shared* by all of the participants, regardless of where they are located.

It's pretty obvious that we can't run shared transactions over TII invocations. In a shared transaction, every player ties up resources while the transaction is pending, and releases them (hopefully in a new state) when it completes with either a commit or a rollback. When invocations are made via TII, there is no guarantee that the invocation will complete within any length of time—the originating machine may be a laptop that only connects for a few minutes each day, as we saw in one example in this chapter, and it is impractical for transaction systems to tie up resources for so long. (Remember, transaction systems that support successful businesses may run several tens or hundreds of millions of transactions per day!)

So, AMI adopted the **unshared transaction model** for use over TII. First we'll go over how it works, then we'll tell what it's good for. It's easy (now that we know how TII works), so hold on and here we go.

Recall that we said that invocation transfer with persistent routers was transactional. Now we get to take advantage of this. There is no single transaction that covers both the client and transactional server in this model. Instead, the client creates a transaction that only covers the transfer of its TII invocation to the network. The invocation transfers along the network transactionally, from router to router until it reaches the router closest to the server, which conducts a transactional invocation and waits (in its synchronous way, since the invocation is synchronous at this point) for it to complete. When this is done, the result snakes its way, transactionally again step by step, either back to the TII client or to wherever the TII client decided to route the result.

What is this good for? After all, it doesn't look anything like a shared transaction. As it turns out, it's good for lots of things.

One common purchase pattern that fits this model is the purchase of a vacation. Airline tickets, hotel room, and car rental must all be purchased for the same week. If you get the room and the car, but you can't get a hotel room for that week, you can't go, but the plane, hotel, and car rental all come from different companies so you know you can't involve them all in a single shared transaction. The solution is to conduct three separate transactions serially. As each succeeds, you go ahead to the next. If one fails, you go back and undo (*not* roll back; the previous transaction has already committed) the reservations you've made so far and start again on a different week.

Another common unshared transaction pattern is "memo posting." This is what a bank does when it records teller transactions durably (which used to mean recorded by hand) during the day and reconciles all of its accounts with a batch run of the accounting system overnight. The recording of the teller visit during the day is one transaction, while the adjustment to the customer's account at night is a separate one.

The unshared transaction model gives you a way to implement this type of scenario in your distributed CORBA applications.

One new characteristic of this model is the way you cope with failure. In a shared transaction, all of the parties roll back simultaneously, and when it's over, it's over. In the unshared model, each part finishes up and commits individually. When one part fails, the *application* has to go back and pick up the pieces, backing out whatever it needs to explicitly with application logic. Remember, each individual piece has committed as part of its own transaction, so it's too late to roll anything back.

This is clearly a different model from shared transactions, but no less useful. It is not designed to extend the original distributed transaction model to TII—if you need to roll back on failure, you'll have to conduct your business using a single shared transaction and stay connected long enough to invoke synchronously. Instead, the unshared transaction model lets you transactionalize new business dealings that already have some of the aspects of disconnected operation—between departments or enterprises with separate transactional systems, for example—with the reliability of CORBA transactions but the flexibility and freedom of TII.

6.6.5 ONEWAY Invocations

Under CORBA 2, the only way to make a stub-based invocation and get control back right away was to declare it **ONEWAY** *in your IDL*; that is (if you recall from Chapter 3), the operation had no output or inout parameters, and a **void** return value. Delivery was, according to the definition of **ONEWAY**, "ORB best effort," and the meaning of the phrase was defined by your ORB provider.

Why would you want to use **ONEWAY** invocations now that you have all of the asynchronous features that we've been discussing for the past however many pages? There's a common pattern that involves notifying an object somewhere that something happened, and not needing to get anything back, not even a confirmation. The event service is an example and its possible use of **ONEWAY** is a good example even if you probably won't implement this service yourself. Lots of applications need to notify specific objects about something, or send a couple of values when something happens, and they'd like to be able to send the information out and not worry about doing anything afterward.

However, the loose QoS (at least up 'til now) did not give programmers the feeling that they could regard **ONEWAY** as a mode for delivering notifications in code that might be run on different vendors' ORBs, since each vendor was free to interpret the phrase "best effort" however he wished.

To fix this shortcoming, the Messaging Specification introduced the QoS policy type **SyncScope**. There are four possible values; here they are, along with what they do:

SYNC_NONE. The client's ORB returns control to the client immediately on receiving the invocation from it, so there is not even a brief blocking of the client thread. On a separate thread, the ORB passes the **ONEWAY** invocation to the network and does not expect a reply. Since no reply returns from the server, no errors will be reported and location-forwarding cannot be done.

SYNC_WITH_TRANSPORT. The client's ORB returns control to the client only after the network transport has accepted the request. For the usual transports (e.g., TCP/IP), this is not much stronger than **SYNC_NONE** (although it does guarantee that your invocation will make it past a full TCP stack when your network is overloaded), but for reliable store-and-forward messaging protocols (that is, if you've installed persistent routers) it will provide a high degree of assurance without consuming client resources. No location-forwarding can be done in this mode either because no reply returns from the server.

SYNC_WITH_SERVER. The server-side ORB sends a reply after it has received the invocation, but before it invokes the target object; the client's ORB returns control only after it has received this acknowledgment. This form of guarantee is useful where the reliability of the network is substantially lower than that of the server. The client blocks until all location-forwarding has been completed.

SYNC_WITH_OBJECT. This is the same as a synchronous, non-oneway operation in CORBA 2.2. The server-side ORB doesn't send the reply message until the target has completed the invoked operation. Location-forwarding is no problem in this case, of course.

Before AMI, a major use of **ONEWAY** invocations was to trigger operations that returned results, when their execution was done, via a reverse **ONEWAY** invocation of an object in the originating client's application; that is, a callback-style asynchronous invocation constructed (painfully, perhaps) in application-level code. We think that most of these instances will be replaced by true asynchronous invocations now that CORBA provides them, even though **ONEWAY** has been improved so much. Use of **ONEWAY** for notification, however, will continue and probably rise now that this invocation form has determinate QoS.

Well, now we've covered all of the various architectural features of the invocation space and it's time to proceed on to programming details. In the next several sections, we'll cover interfaces for callback and polling invocations, reply handlers, and pollers. When we're finished with this, we'll also be finished discussing the new AMI specification and will go on to cover OMG's standard protocols, GIOP and IIOP.

6.6.6 Interfaces for Asynchronous Invocations

In CORBA 2, the IDL compiler generated a single synchronous stub for each operation you defined.

In CORBA 3, the IDL compiler will generate an additional *asynchronous* stub, with two additional signatures: one for callback-mode asynchronous invocations, and another for polling mode. You'll probably have to set a compiler switch to get these interfaces (since so many modules will not use them), but the compiler does all the interface generation, so it's no sweat for you. These stubs, and the ORB routines that support them, do most of the extra work that's necessary to make your asynchronous invocations go, but you will have to do a little more than you're used to for a simple synchronous invocation.

So, for both callback and polling-mode asynchronous invocations, we'll have to cover two aspects, each with its own distinct signature: making the invocation, and obtaining the result. That's because, while our synchronous invocations came back as the return to the same operation that made them, the return from asynchronous invocations will come back to a different routine, through a different interface, that has a different signature. In fact, even though asynchronous invocations are still made by clients, callback-mode responses come back to *servants*. Polling-mode responses don't come back at all—you have to go get them.

Before we get into the programming details, we want to remind you of a few things:

- Don't forget to set *all* of your QoS policies before you make your invocation.

- Remember that you'll probably have to reconcile client-side and server-side policies.

- You'll have to bind to the server first with a **validate_connection** call to get the actual server's actual policies. If you don't, and your client policies don't overlap with the server's, your invocation will fail with an **INV_POLICY** exception.

What if you want to use the DII? Since the DII doesn't use stubs, the IDL compiler isn't involved, and you don't get the invocation forms we're about to present. DII interfaces have been extended to access all of these invocation modes, and the old deferred-synchronous invocation is still valid, too. (Deferred-synchronous invocation is not exactly the same as any of the asynchronous cases we've presented so far.) Since the DII isn't used as much as the SII, we aren't going to present any of the DII interfaces and language mappings here. You can get the details in the documentation of your CORBA 3 ORB and that will tell you what to do.

6.6.6.1 Asynchronous Details—Callback Mode

For callback-mode invocations, you will have to program a **ReplyHandler** object to receive the results. Your IDL compiler will generate a skeleton and, optionally, a template for this object whose signature is defined by the AMI specification, but you'll have to fill in the working code. This is where you program in whatever your client-side application needs to do with the result. The **ReplyHandler**'s object reference is an input parameter to the invocation, of course, so that your ORB knows where to call when the reply completes. This means you'll have to get a reference for the object from your POA *before* you make your invocation. We'll examine the IDL interface of the **ReplyHandler** object when we see how to receive asynchronous replies.

Remember the two special aspects of a **ReplyHandler** object: Since it was called by an object, and not by a client, it cannot throw a CORBA exception, and it does not return.

As we just said, for asynchronous invocations there are two signatures that we have to be concerned about: one for the invocation, and another for the reply. The IDL compiler generates these signatures by converting your IDL to a specific form and then generating programming language code following each language mapping (Chapters 7–9). The specification refers to the generated invocation-side form as "implied IDL," since it never really exists although the IDL compiler generates programming-language code for it anyhow.

Why are these signatures called "Implied IDL"?

> **HERE'S SOME INSIGHT:**
>
> The asynchronous invocation signatures need to be defined in every programming language that supports CORBA—that is, every language with an IDL language mapping. The AMI specification can take care of this in one shot by expressing them in IDL, so that's what it does.
>
> Why "Implied"? If these were true IDL interfaces, they would map to both client-side and object-side signatures, and we'd have to implement them in our servant. But this isn't the case at all; instead, they're additional *client-side only* signatures that call the signatures on the object side that came from the mapping of the original "true" IDL. So, the client invokes the "implied IDL" signatures to make an asynchronous invocation, but the servant receives the invocation on the original, "true" IDL signature that it has used all along to receive synchronous invocations.
>
> Conversion from the client's asynchronous implied-IDL format invocation to the servant's true-IDL format invocation takes place either in the client's ORB or in a router, as we've seen. It's all automatic; you don't have to do any of the work.
>
> As we've stated before in this chapter, this has several advantages. The servant doesn't know or care whether an invocation is synchronous or asynchronous. And, servant programming style and existing servant code don't have to change to support asynchronous invocation. (Exception: Certain transactional invocations will notice the difference between synch and asynch, and these objects will have to be modified.)

6.6.6.2 Asynchronous Callback-Mode Invocations

The implied-IDL signature for asynchronous invocation of an IDL operation consists of:

- **void** return type (always); followed by
- **sendc_<opName>**; that is, an operation name that starts with **sendc** and concatenates an underscore and your operation name; followed by
- the object reference of your reply handler, with the parameter name **ami_handler**; followed by
- each **in** and **inout** parameter, with a parameter attribute of **in** and the type and parameter name as in the original IDL.
- **out** arguments do not appear. (**out** and **inout** parameters will be returned to the reply handler, as we'll see shortly.)

For attributes, the operation names are **sendc_get_<attributeName>**; and **sendc_set_<attributeName>**. The **get** form has no arguments except for the reply handler, while **set** has one named **attr_<attributeName>**. as you might expect.

As we pointed out just a few paragraphs back, the IDL compiler generates the skeleton for the reply handler. Its interface name is generated from the name of our interface, by prepending **AMI_** and appending **Handler**. The compiler also generates a set of operations for this interface, one for each operation in the original, and (easy enough for us) using the original operation names. We'll list the arguments in Section 6.6.6.3.

Here's an example to make this all concrete. In Chapter 3, our example IDL file included the **interface OutputMedia** with one operation:

```
interface OutputMedia {
boolean output_text (in string string_to_print );
{
```

If we ran this through a CORBA 3 IDL compiler (with the switch set to generate the additional asynchronous interfaces, of course), it would produce, in addition to the synchronous-invocation stub we're used to, an asynchronous stub *as if* we had also input this "implied" IDL operation:

```
void sendc_output_text (
        In AMI_OutputMediaHandler ami_handler,
        In string string_to_print );
```

So, each time we invoke the operation **output_text** in our client, we have a choice. We can either make a synchronous call by invoking the standard stub, or we can make an asynchronous callback-mode invocation by calling the stub **sendc_output_text**, which was also generated by the IDL compiler. (We could also make a polling-mode asynchronous call, as we'll see in the next section.)

6.6.6.3 Asynchronous Callback-Mode Replies

Here's our second new operation signature. For our reply, the IDL compiler has generated a complete new interface with operations. Its name is **AMI_<ifaceName>**, where **<ifaceName>** is the name we originally gave to this interface.

For every operation we defined on our original interface, the IDL compiler generates a new operation with a signature defined by this template:

- **void** return type (again, always); followed by

- The operation name which is the same as the original name of our operation; followed by

- If the original operation had a non-void return type, it is returned as the first parameter named **ami_return_val** and typed as it was in the original IDL. If the original return value was **void**, this parameter is omitted. This is followed by

- Each **inout** or **out** parameter, with its original type and name, as it was declared in the original IDL.

- **in** parameters do not appear.

So, an asynchronous call to **output_text** would result in a reply, after it completes, which causes the ORB to invoke the operation "**output_text**" on the **AMI_Output-MediaHandler** object running in our client code:

```
Interface AMI_OutputMediaHandler  {
void output_text (boolean ami_return_val);
}
```

The return value is the first parameter, with its original type and the name **ami_return_val** (since return values aren't assigned names in the IDL). Since we had no **out** or **inout** parameters in the original operation, nothing else appears inside the parentheses.

Some programming details: Since we're working in an asynchronous environment, we can have multiple calls outstanding, all returning to the same reply handler servant. To identify the calls when they return, even though all return to the same servant, we can use the POA to assign different **ObjectIDs** to the object references we generate. Since the **ObjectID** is accessible to the servant, it will have no trouble figuring out which reply is which.

If you're concerned with the details (and a little existentialism, as we mentioned), you'll want to consider this: The reply handler IDL generates a true object skeleton, but no client stub. In fact, even though the skeleton is invoked, no client ever exists for its IDL. Instead, this skeleton is invoked with a response from an object, that was transformed from response form to invocation form by an ORB or a router.

So, there are two normal "object-implementation" things that this object can never do: first, it can not `return`—there's no client for it to `return` to. When it finishes processing, it does `return` but this only returns control of its thread to the ORB; no output parameters or return value go anywhere. Second, it cannot raise CORBA exceptions, which are typically thrown in the object and caught in the client: There's no client to catch them!

If any exceptions were raised in the execution of the invocation, we want them raised in the **ReplyHandler** context. To enable this, the IDL compiler actually generates a separate operation for each exception. Since you never see either the IDL or the reply handler component that implements them, we won't show their forms here. You do have to write code to raise the exceptions once they come back this way.

6.6.6.4 Asynchronous
Polling-Mode Invocations

Just as with callback-mode invocations, polling-mode invocation signatures are defined by implied IDL converted from the original. In place of **sendc_,** polling-mode signatures start with **sendp_** (no surprise there, right?). Unlike the callback-mode signature, however, polling-mode signatures do have a return value: It's a **valuetype**, a CORBA object passed by value, which will contain the return values when the operation completes. We'll invoke an operation on this **valuetype** to check if our invocation has completed, and fetch the output values.

Why a **valuetype**? Because **valuetypes** execute as programming language objects that cannot be invoked remotely, and this fits the polling programming model. Since **valuetypes** have the operations and characteristics we need, they're a logical construct to use here. And, a **persistent poller** type can even be derived from them for TII invocations that allow responses to be obtained outside of the client process.

We'll define the **poller valuetype** more completely in Section 6.6.6.5. For now, we'll just say that its name is derived from the name of the original interface, and it bears operations with the same set of names, but with arguments rearranged in a manner similar to the asynchronous reply handler.

The signature of the implied-IDL operation in polling mode is:

- The **poller valuetype** for this operation as the return value, followed by

- The operation name, **sendp_<opName>**, where **_<opName>** is the name of the operation; followed by

- Each of the **in** and **inout** parameters, in their original order, all with the parameter attribute **in** and with their original types and names.

- The operation's original return value, if it has one, and **out** arguments do not appear. The **poller valuetype** will deliver them in the output.

For attributes, the operations are named **sendp_get_<attributeName>** and **sendp_set_<attributeName>.** The **set** operation has a single argument, **in <attr-Name>attributeName.**

Our same example in polling form would generate the implied IDL:

```
AMI_OutputMediaPoller sendp_output_text (
    in string string_to_print );
```

and the operation signatures in each programming language would follow the corresponding language mapping.

6.6.6.5 Asynchronous Polling-Mode Replies

The advantage of polling-mode invocations is that you can wait to fetch the reply until you're good and ready. The disadvantage is that you *have* to fetch the reply, since it's not delivered to your application, and you may have to try several (or many!) times if it hadn't come back when you asked for it the first time, or the next, or the time after that, or . . .

The base functionality that makes an object pollable is embodied in the **interface CORBA::Pollable**, from which all pollers derive. This interface has an operation **is_ready**, which returns **TRUE** if the reply is available, and **FALSE** if the reply has not yet returned from the target.

Generic poller functionality is embodied at the next level, which defines a generic poller valuetype. Poller has three interesting IDL attributes: the target object reference, the operation name as a **string**, and a **boolean is_from_poller**, which describes exception returns: **TRUE** means that a system exception was generated by the polling operation itself, and **FALSE** means that it was generated by your method execution. There's another attribute, **ReplyHandler**, which supports (of all things!) switching between polling and callback mode while the invocation processes. Not only can you do this, you can switch back and forth as many times as you can manage while your invocation is out there processing on the server machine, or waiting in the queue on your network. We haven't figured out why you'd even want to do it once, so we won't use any space in this book describing how. We will let on that you have to make your invocation in polling mode, and you have to code for both return modes yourself, in order to use this "feature."

Finally, our type-specific poller IDL is generated based on these types. The **valuetype** interface name is **AMI_<ifaceName>Poller**, where **<ifaceName>** is the name of the original interface. For each operation in our original IDL, this **valuetype** bears an operation with the following signature:

- The return type **void**; followed by

- The original name of the operation; followed by

- A timeout parameter, described below; followed by

- The original return value, as an **out** parameter, with its original type and the name **ami_return_val**; followed by

- Any **out** or **inout** parameters, all declared here as **out** parameters, in their original order with their original types and names; followed by

- A **raises** clause, citing any exceptions that were declared in the original IDL and one more, **CORBA::WrongTransaction**, which may be raised by certain transactional invocations.

The **timeout** parameter, an unsigned long representing milliseconds, lets you control how your polling executes:

- If you set **timeout** to **0** (zero), your poll is non-blocking and returns the exception **CORBA::NO_RESPONSE** if the reply is not available.

- If you set **timeout** to $2^{32}-1$, no **timeout** will be used. Your polling call will block until the reply is available.

- If you set **timeout** to some value in between, your poller will return the response to you as soon as it is available unless it is not available after **timeout** milliseconds, at which time the poller will return the exception **CORBA::TIMEOUT**.

Exceptions will be raised in your client on return from the poll, if any were raised during the invocation.

Here's our example, as a type-specific poller **valuetype**:

```
valuetype AMI_OutputMediaPoller : Messaging::Poller {
void output_text (
    In unsigned long timeout,
    Out boolean ami_return_val)
    Raises (CORBA::WrongTransaction)
}
```

Since this is a **valuetype**, we will invoke it locally as a programming-language object using the mapping for the language we use to implement.

This concludes our discussion of the AMI. We've spent a considerable amount of space on this, but we felt it would be worthwhile since communications is key to distributed computing and this is CORBA's (and your!) interface to the communications layer. We also believe that the specification is a good one, containing all of the enhancements that programmers and users have been asking for, wrapped up in a well-architected package. We're looking forward to working with some of these asynchronous invocation modes ourselves when products come on the market, presumably sometime during 2000.

There's one more CORBA specification that includes interfaces to QoS settings and the communications layer, and a lot more. It's Real-Time CORBA, a specialized but important and already well-established part of the distributed computing marketplace. We'll discuss it next, finishing up our examination of these related subjects.

Following the discussion of Real-Time CORBA, we'll cover (finally!) the basics of standard CORBA communications: the GIOP and IIOP protocols.

6.7 Real-Time CORBA

Before we get started, here are a few preliminary items to put Real-Time CORBA (which we'll abbreviate here as RT CORBA) into focus:

- First, RT CORBA is not just about interoperability, but its use of policies for scheduling and its reuse of some AMI time-out policies in particular make this the right part of the book in which to discuss it.

- Second, we're not going to devote enough space to satisfy real-time devotees and we know it. Real-time is a specialized topic, and all we can do here is give a flavor of what RT CORBA is capable of. If our description makes you curious, follow up by downloading the specification, or by investigating one of the many real-time ORB products on the market.

The goal of RT CORBA is to support end-to-end predictability. It tries to do this by:

- Respecting thread priorities between client and server during CORBA invocations
- Bounding the duration of thread priority inversions
- Bounding the latencies of operation invocations

You won't get predictable performance unless you control *every* aspect of your system; that is:

- Your Real-Time operating system's scheduling mechanism;
- Your Real-Time ORB;
- Your network communications; and
- Your application.

You're on your own here (and justly so) for the operating system and communications parts. The specification standardizes your Real-Time ORB and it's up to you to write your application, using all the tools we've just listed, to run predictably in your execution environment. You're also on your own for the explanation of basic real-time concepts so, if you're not already familiar with the field, you'll have to look somewhere else for the explanation of how the stuff in this section works together to deliver predictable operation. We're not going to explain any of it in this book.

Real-Time is a set of *optional extensions* to the standard CORBA ORB. Most likely, only a minority of specialized CORBA products will support these extensions and you will have to shop for them specifically, just as you shop for real-time operating systems now. RT CORBA is an established part of the computing world; real-time ORBs run many military, scientific, and industrial applications today and their use is increasing. The RT CORBA document was written and submitted jointly by 12 companies, a large number for such a specialized category, and 8 more put their names on it as supporters. Company names appear on the document, referenced in Appendix A.

6.7.1 Real-Time Basic Architecture

As Figure 6.4 shows, RT CORBA extends the client's **current** interface, the POA interface, and adds interfaces for Priority, a Threadpool, a Priority Mapping, Communications features, and a Manager. We'll present things in almost this way, except that we'll group Priority and Threading into a single section.

Real-Time reuses a lot from existing CORBA specifications: Its **policy** is the same as the POA **policy**, which it inherits, and it uses the AMI policies and interfaces for **Time-Out** of invocation. However, the Real-Time **priority** (which has its own interface definition and allows values from 0 to 32767) is *not* the same as the AMI **priority** (which allows –32768 to 32767), even though both store their value in a **short**.

6.7.2 Real-Time Priorities and Threading

RT CORBA needed a consistent, multiplatform representation for priorities. All Real-Time operating systems (on which RT CORBA runs) have priority representations too; the trouble is, each has its own. To enable interoperable and portable applications, RT CORBA defines an interface that maps from its own consistent, multiplatform scheme termed *Real-Time CORBA Priority* to the schemes on the platforms you run on.

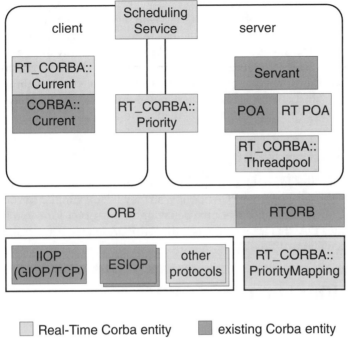

Figure 6.4 Real-time extensions (light shading) to CORBA.

There are two basic invocation priority models in RT CORBA: *Client Priority Propagation Model*, in which the client's priority is propagated to the server where its invocation executes at the corresponding reverse-mapped native priority; and the *Server-Set Priority Model*, where the server imposes its own priority on every request that it handles.

There are two basic ways to manipulate threads in RT CORBA. One set of interfaces, derived from **CORBA::Current**, affects threads for its object (that's what **Current** refers to, of course); the other set affects Threadpools. Threads in pools can be pre-allocated and partitioned amongst your active POAs. By preallocating threads, you minimize priority inversion, which occurs when the number of tasks exceeds the number of threads.

6.7.3 Real-Time Communications

Communications QoS is crucial to (or, perhaps, the bane of) end-to-end predictability, so RT CORBA gives you a lot of things to control. First, the folks who wrote this spec decided that the timeout *definitions* in the AMI spec were good enough for them too—after all, a millisecond is a millisecond everywhere, right? We guess they figure that a real-time network will take these values more seriously than your ISP does (or, at least, than *my* ISP does), and they're probably right. Since we've already covered these interfaces in this chapter, we got to leave the explanation out of this section, so be thankful.

RT CORBA introduces the concept of *priority-banded connections*. Your client can open up a number of connections with a server, each handling a restricted range of priorities. Once you've set this up, your client just makes invocations normally; the ORB takes care of the special handling. If you've tuned the ranges properly for the load in each range, this will keep lower-priority invocations from interfering with higher-priority work.

In addition, you can ask for a *non-multiplexed connection* from a client to a server. The network may block up, but at least your connection will be clear all the way through.

Finally, client and server may select and configure the protocols that they use to communicate. You can't do this from your app in standard CORBA (but your sysadmin can; controlling and tuning the network is his job), but in real-time work, communication details must be exposed to the application, so here they are.

6.7.4 Real-Time CORBA Management

There are a number of interfaces for setting up and managing all of the features we've just listed. Most are policies, derived from **POA::policy**, so they'll look familiar to you when you read the spec for yourself. For real-time behavior on the server side, you'll have to create a Real-Time POA; that is, one that uses the **RT::POA** interface and bears policies that make it execute in real-time mode.

6.8 GIOP and IIOP: Standard CORBA Communications

This concludes our discussion of the AMI and QoS control. Together with **valuetype**s, these CORBA 3 enhancements enlarge the scope of problems that can benefit from a CORBA solution, at some cost since they expose interoperability to the application— a fundamental change to the basic CORBA architecture, as we've pointed out several times. In the remainder of this chapter, we're going to discuss interoperability in a number of ways. We'll start with a discussion of interoperability in the enterprise and on the network: Building on the ORB-to-ORB communications pathway we defined back in the first pages of the chapter, we'll talk about how different aspects of interoperability and heterogeneity interact with your computing infrastructure to enable or inhibit different domains from working together. We'll examine how different kinds of bridges can overcome differences, but how simple, one-protocol installations have benefits above and beyond bridged interoperability (which, of course, is fine where it's the only possible solution, or at least the only possible technical solution). After the general discussion, we'll focus in on OMG's standard GIOP and IIOP protocols, and how optional additional protocols fit into the CORBA picture.

Why did we postpone this part of the discussion until now? These protocols run totally "under the covers," at least as far as programming is concerned: The API for GIOP and IIOP is your IDL interfaces, and we've already covered that. *There are no other interfaces to IIOP. Your CORBA Objects use IIOP automatically—or, perhaps, another protocol that your systems administrator has configured—when they invoke an object running on a remote server.* These protocols are what you get, automatically, when your ORB invokes an operation on a remote object (at least if you're using a CORBA-compliant ORB and you've configured for OMG's standard protocol), but programmers and users don't get any control over it. (Sysadmins have some control, of course.) So, we started with AMI for two reasons: First, it's new and everyone wants to know about it right away; and second, programmers and users can control it so it's something they need to know about.

6.8.1 Putting Heterogeneity into Perspective

There are two ways to get ORBs to talk to each other. We can either:

- Get all of the ORBs to speak the same protocol, so they can talk to each other directly; or

- If ORBs speak different protocols, we can install bridges to translate from one protocol to the other.

CORBA interoperability provides *both* solutions. The first is simple, streamlined, easy to administer, and efficient to use. Every CORBA-compliant ORB speaks the mandatory protocol IIOP (Section 6.8.4), allowing your enterprise to standardize on it and still choose from almost every ORB on the market with full interoperability. However, you may opt for some other single protocol instead.

This solution is inflexible. There will be times when a common protocol isn't possible, or isn't desirable for some reason—for example, if you find a product that isn't available on an ORB that speaks your enterprise's common protocol, or if you need to integrate a machine that is special somehow (a circuit breaker or thermostat, for example, with limited memory and bandwidth), or if you're working in a specialized domain (Real-Time or Telecommunications, for example). In these cases, *bridging* lets you provide transparent interoperability across domain boundaries. Frequently, hardware bridges are already in place at these boundaries, providing a natural location for a CORBA software bridge. The fact is, many (perhaps most) medium- to large-sized companies already use bridging in some form because it provides the flexibility to allow each part of a company to find its most cost-effective computing solution. And, as we'll see, the concept of domains is a general one, which can carry over from CORBA interoperability into other areas such as company organization, network administration, and security.

There is a trade-off here, simplicity versus flexibility, and someone at your company (you, perhaps?) will have to decide how much heterogeneity can be allowed before the costs outweigh the advantages. Or, perhaps your current installed base is already heterogeneous, giving you little room to maneuver. In any case, the material in this chapter will help you understand the alternatives, and place them into perspective. With this new knowledge, you will be in a better position to make decisions concerning, or possibly just better understand, this key issue.

6.8.2 CORBA 2 Domains

Let's identify the regions of our enterprise that share a common platform, operating system, network hardware and software, and so forth, and name this type of region a *technology domain*. Is this the only kind of domain we have to consider, or are there others?

It turns out that there are many different types of domains. Some result from technology differences, and others arise from the kind of work people do, the way they work together, and the way their computing resources are purchased and accounted for.

Perhaps you work in a company large enough to have departments, and your department has a number of networked computers, which might include "your" disk servers, "your" compute or database servers, and "your" printers. The money for these machines and their support comes from your department's budget, and you expect other departments in the company to have their own resources and avoid using yours. Your department's equipment constitutes a domain.

On the other hand, if you work for a government or military organization concerned with security, your work might be partitioned into *security domains*. In this case, you might have one window on your workstation that contains a document classified "Top Secret," while another window displays a document classified "Confidential." Even though both windows display on the same screen and are running on the same workstation, they belong to different security domains. Secure windowed operating systems will not allow a cut-and-paste between two windows that differ in security classification.

These are examples of *administrative domains*. There are also domains imposed by the technology, as we already discussed, and these come in many different varieties. For instance, a domain might share a common platform, network protocol or hardware, or operating system. Data or packet representations will differ across network domain boundaries, while commands will have to be translated across operating system boundaries.

The CORBA interoperability specification lists technology domains, administrative domains, and policy domains as just some of the different types that have to be taken into account.

We can draw some generalizations about domains: They exist for a reason. For instance, some people in your company or organization will be very concerned about the boundaries of a departmental domain, or the different security domains. While the reason for technical domains may not be as logical ("The Turbo-cooled 986 Multiprocessor Server had better price/performance, but it's little endian"), they're important enough to keep the domains distinct. Our interoperability solution must take this into account.

Applications and data will, in general, be shared across domain boundaries. We can make life simpler by keeping applications and data domain-independent, and providing domain-related services in an infrastructure layer. For example, a security attribute may restrict data to a particular security domain, but this is a property of the particular data and not something that should be coded into an application, where we would have to deal with it whether the dataset is marked secure or not. The CORBA architecture is a good start on this task.

If every quantity in one domain has a corresponding quantity in another domain (that is, the quantities "map" from one domain to the other), then we can render the boundary transparent by providing a bridge to perform translations where necessary. However, if a quantity or service that exists on one side has no equivalent on the other, then some aspect of the boundary will be apparent to the user under at least some circumstances no matter what we do in the bridge.

ORB boundaries define only a small fraction of the domains in a system. However, the ORB infrastructure is the best place to deal with almost all of the boundaries as enablers of interoperability. Taking these factors into consideration, the framers of CORBA interoperability based it on a concept of bridging far more general than inter-ORB communications. To get a general idea of what the specification is talking about and what it will let us do, we'll first present two different kinds of bridging, and then two kinds of bridges. The two kinds of bridging are *technological* and *policy-mediated bridging*. The two kinds of bridges are *immediate* and *mediated* bridges.

6.8.2.1 Technological and Policy-Mediated Bridging

There is a tendency to assume that domain boundaries should be rendered transparent everywhere, but this is strictly true only for technological boundaries—network protocol or data formats, for instance, or ORB platforms. Where technical differences like these prevent direct interoperation, bridges can map quantities on one side to those on the other and remove the barriers, keeping in mind that differences in service level can create boundaries where total interoperability is just not possible. Where the boundary is purely technological, this will (almost always) be fine with everyone.

However, some boundaries are administrative rather than technological. Administrative domain boundaries separate organizations that have different policies, goals, or resources. While some degree of interoperability may be desirable across these boundaries, the participants require control over the data flow for many important (at least to them) reasons. Bridging these domains requires policy mediation; that is, traffic across the boundaries must be monitored and controlled in ways that depend on its content. You're familiar with this type of control if your company uses a firewall to separate your corporate network from the external network; make the firewall concept object oriented, and it becomes policy-mediated CORBA bridging. In fact, since policy-mediated bridging requires that the bridge understand the traffic across the boundary, CORBA provides an ideal infrastructure for providing this type of control.

6.8.2.2 Immediate and Mediated Bridges

Now let's talk about different ways to build a bridge. The two major approaches are immediate bridging and mediated bridging. Figure 6.5 shows how each of these works.

The CORBA interoperability specification discusses bridging in very general terms, and ends up so abstract that it's difficult to form a mental picture unless you already know what it's talking about. In order to be more concrete, we'll talk specifically about bridging between different network protocols here; if you're interested in bridging something else (data format, let's say), then just substitute that in your mind as you read through the section.

In immediate bridging, two domains talk directly to each other over a single bridge that translates whatever parts of the message require it, as shown in the top half of Figure 6.5. Immediate bridging is a two-domain concept; the generalization of Figure 6.5 to multiple domains just contains many copies of the two-domain linkage, one for each connected domain pair.

This is fast and efficient, since each bridge can be designed specifically for the domain pair it serves. On the other hand, this approach is inflexible and may require a lot of bridges since the number required increases rapidly—as $(n^2-n)/2$, actually—with the number of domains. The top half of Figure 6.6 shows immediate bridging for an installation with four domains; this requires six bridges. Increasing the number of domains to six raises the number of bridges required to 15! In a few paragraphs we'll show how much simpler this is with mediated bridging.

Immediate-mode bridging is the preferred approach for policy-only bridging, since messages do not require translation. The bridge is actually a firewall, examining message contents to determine if they may pass through its barrier. If a bridge's policy is configurable, a single bridge type may be installed at various places around an enterprise to enforce any number of security policies and their domains. (This is not the same as the OMG Firewall specification. For more about CORBA and Firewalls, see Section 14.2.)

In mediated bridging, all domains bridge to a single common protocol (that is, for protocol domains. Remember, we might be bridging something else.). When a message passes over the first bridge from its originating domain, the parts that require it are translated into the common protocol. When the message passes from the common region into the destination domain, a second bridge translates it into the destination protocol. The bottom half of Figure 6.5 shows this for a 2-protocol installation.

The big advantage of mediated bridging is that the number of bridge types only grows as fast as the number of different domains (Figure 6.6, bottom), avoiding the exponential increase seen with immediate bridging. Another advantage is that this conforms to the backbone configuration of most large, multiprotocol networks; mediated bridging configures naturally in these networks since CORBA bridges will probably locate in the same position at which protocol bridges already exist. In an open market situation, if every vendor of an interoperability product makes available a

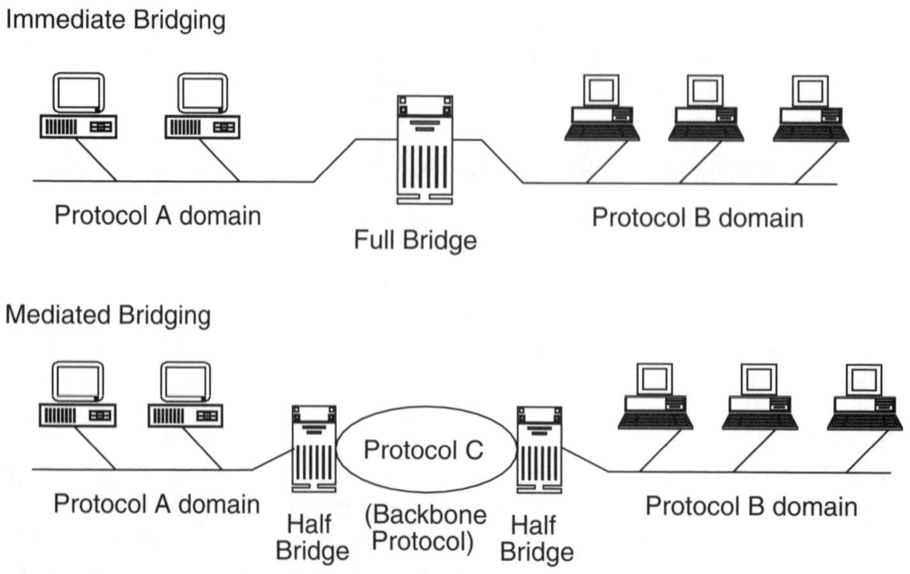

Immediate Bridging

Protocol A domain

Full Bridge

Protocol B domain

Mediated Bridging

Protocol A domain

Half Bridge

Protocol C

(Backbone Protocol)

Half Bridge

Protocol B domain

Figure 6.5 Immediate and mediated bridging.

Immediate Bridging

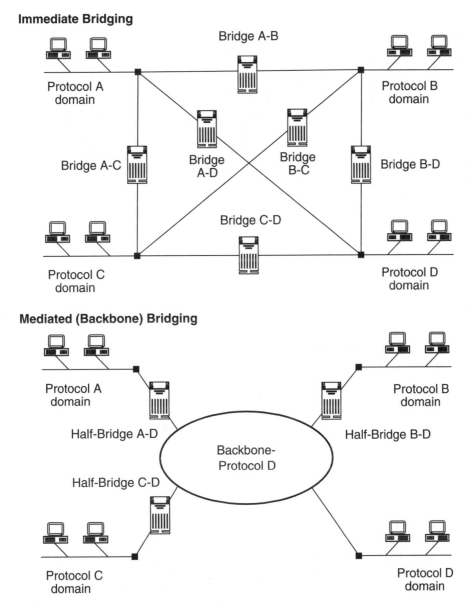

Figure 6.6 Four domains, immediate and mediated (backbone) bridging. The immediate bridging configuration requires six bridges, while the mediated (backbone) bridging configuration requires only three. The difference becomes proportionately greater as the number of domains increases.

bridge to an agreed-upon common protocol, customers can buy any of these products and know that the protocol will interoperate with every other one. This (by clever coincidence) is how CORBA guarantees out-of-the-box interoperability; the common protocol is the IIOP discussed in Section 6.8.4.5.

Disadvantages are, first, that it isn't as efficient for small numbers of domains (for instance, two, as shown in Figure 6.5); in this case, you would be better off using an immediate bridge. Second, almost every message gets translated twice. Why almost all, and not every one? Because messages to or from a domain that uses the same protocol as the common region will need to be translated only once. You can overcome this disadvantage by putting high-traffic services on domains that use the same protocol as the backbone, or by adding direct bridges for high-demand services that can't use that trick.

The mediated bridging (backbone) configuration with four domains, shown in Figure 6.6, requires only three bridges: Three domains require bridging to the backbone; one uses the backbone mode natively and does not require a bridge (this trick may not always be possible). Immediate bridging requires six bridges. The number of immediate-mode bridges increases as $(n^2 - n)/2$ with the number of domains; 6 domains would require 15 immediate bridges compared to only 5 in the mediated configuration.

What's the difference between a half bridge and a full bridge? Take another look at Figure 6.6 and trace the path from domain B to domain C in the mediated bridge configuration. It passes through two bridge components; each is a half bridge, since you need both to handle the general case of transmission from any one protocol to any other protocol. In the immediate bridge configuration, the path from domain E to F (or any other domain pair, for that matter) passes through only one bridge: a full bridge, of course.

6.8.3 Interoperable Object References (IORs)

Yes, Virginia, there really is a standard form for the object reference. Clients, object implementations, and their users may think that real object references are kind of like Santa Claus because they can never hold one or see one. It's not even used internally for single-ORB request routing and is never passed to a client or object implementation in its pure form, so you shouldn't expect to examine an object reference in your code and find that it looks anything like this. It's used in inter-ORB invocations, so it's emitted and accepted by ORBs speaking to the network, and used by the bridges between them. It's also the form that gets stringified and stored between sessions, or sent around your network in e-mail or via shared files. It's called an **Interoperable Object Reference**, or IOR.

We know you're curious about the stringified IOR, since almost everyone sends stringified IORs around the Net and Web in e-mail, passes them around using shared files, or gets them from Web pages by cut-and-paste. But, we need the upcoming example to bring out the reason for some common pitfalls in using the stringified form so we will postpone our explanation until the end of this section.

The information in the IOR lets invocations pass from one vendor's ORB to another's. It supports the building of bridges and gateways, and the passing of invocations from one vendor's ORB to another's. This requires the following information:

- *What type is the object?* ORBs may have to know the object's type in order to preserve the integrity of its type system.

- *What protocols may the invoking ORB use?* This is not as straightforward as you might think at first. As it leaves the originating ORB, the IOR lists the protocol or protocols accepted by that ORB. As it crosses a bridge, however, it becomes invocable only by protocols accepted by the bridge. This requires bridges to recognize IORs and update this information as they pass across. Remember, IORs are not just targets, they may be passed as parameters also. Every one needs to be recognized and updated.

- *What ORB services are available?* The invocation may involve extended ORB services; OMG specifications already allow these for invocations within a transaction, secure invocations, and other cases. By putting this information into the IOR, we can eliminate ORB-to-ORB negotiation of the context information.

- *Is the object reference null?* (That is, a special object reference signifying no object.) By recognizing nulls in advance, the bridge can avoid a lot of unnecessary work.

The IOR specified by OMG to meet these requirements consists of a type ID (the same as the Repository ID described in Section 4.4.2), followed by one or more tagged profiles.

Each protocol usable for CORBA 2 ORB-to-ORB communications has a tag and a profile. The tag is a 4-byte quantity, registered by OMG so ORB builders can avoid duplicate entries. Any company can register a protocol with OMG and receive a tag by sending e-mail to tag-request@omg.org—there are no requirements and no charge. This does not make the protocol an OMG standard, it justs registers it in OMG's publicly accessible database so that other ORB vendors will not use the same tag (at least, not if they're paying attention).

The profile contains all the information a remote ORB needs to perform an invocation using the protocol. Profiles come in two forms, *single-* or *multiple-component*. Single-component profiles have a profile ID (like the IIOP, just mentioned). Multiple-component profiles have a component ID for each part. They provide kind of a "smorgasbord" of protocol components, which an ORB can use to construct an invocation. The profile ID for a multicomponent protocol is 1 (one); then each component has its own component ID as well.

Some protocols are special: They are official OMG standards. So far there are two, which we'll cover later in this chapter: the IIOP, and the DCE-ESIOP. The tag for the IIOP is 0 (zero). The DCE ESIOP has a multicomponent profile.

The format of a profile is defined by the implementor or group that registered the tag. (The only requirement, after all, is that all users of the tag agree on the contents of the profile.) The implementor does not need to divulge the format and contents of the profile in order to register, but OMG will accept and make public the definition if it is given. Just as for the tag, registration does not make the profile an OMG standard; it only provides a convenient reference point for profile definitions.

Figure 6.7 shows how IORs provide interoperability across a domain boundary. We'll use actual protocol names even though we won't define them formally until later in the chapter; we think this sounds more realistic than "protocol A" and "protocol B." You can substitute your favorite protocol or domain attribute pair and things will fit together just about the same way.

We've drawn an enterprise with two network domains; suppose that one is TCP/IP and the other is Novell IPX. Each domain consists of several vendors' ORBs; suppose that all of the ORBs in the TCP/IP domain use the DCE CIOP inter-ORB protocol, and the ORBs in the Novell domain use GIOP over IPX. To keep things simple, suppose the two domains are joined by a single immediate bridge. (This example would be even more fun with an IIOP backbone and two half bridges. Try working this out for yourself.) Although each domain has its own Naming Service implementation, all of the information in each of them is accessible from the other. In our example, the system adminstrator set up the root of our *naming context* hierarchy (a kind of subdirectory of object names, defined in Chapter 11) with names that point to each of our domains: IPX, TCPIP, and so on. Using the CORBA IOR as a pointer, the Naming Service will automatically resolve any name to its proper domain.

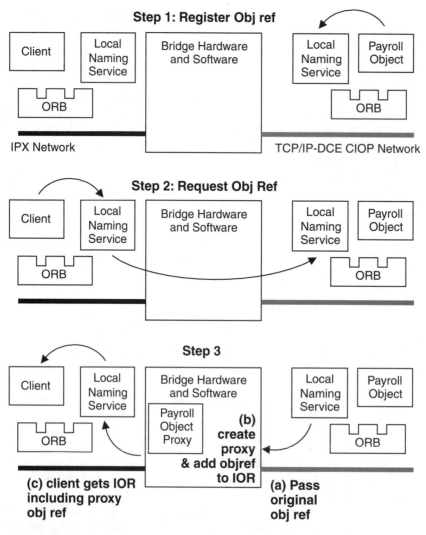

Figure 6.7 Illustration of bridging and IOR operation. Every invocation passes through an ORB (or more than one), although this part of the path is omitted for clarity.

What happens when we retrieve an object reference from a foreign domain and invoke an operation on the object? Let's install a server object named Payroll in the TCP/IP domain and register it with the Naming Service (step 1). Of course, this places our DCE CIOP IOR in the Naming Service in that domain. Name structure is hierarchical in the CORBA Naming Service, so let's suppose the full name of the object is /Object/TCPIP/DCECIOP/Accounting/PayrollObject. This is English, more or less (although it does show a touch of computerese), so it's easy to pass around to our friends anywhere in our enterprise, including other domains. (The original CORBA naming specification did not use slashes to separate name components; in fact, it was syntax independent. A refinement, the Interoperable Naming Specification, was adopted by the OMG as we wrote this book, and this new spec does, indeed, define a syntax and it does use forward slashes. We'll fill in the details in Chapter 11.)

In step 2, a client in the IPX domain passes the full name of the payroll object to its local Naming Service in a request for its object reference. As the Naming Service unravels the hierarchical name, the invocation passes automatically from the IPX domain where it started, to the TCP/IP domain where the object is registered. (For details of the **resolve** operation, see Chapter 11.) The object reference of the Payroll object is the return value of this invocation.

The object reference passes back over the bridge to the IPX domain in step 3. The bridge knows that this return value is an object reference from the operation signature, which it retrieved from its interface repository. The bridge must pass a usable object reference back to the client, and IPX clients cannot invoke operations directly on TCP/IP DCE CIOP objects. So, the bridge constructs a proxy skeleton using the Dynamic Skeleton Interface and adds its reference to the IOR. It doesn't need to remove the original reference; the IOR may be passed on to a domain where it will be valid, so it stays.

The object reference that the client just received is just an opaque pointer, of course; only the ORB knows that this is an IOR and not a local reference. Neither the client nor the ORB is aware that the IOR refers to a proxy, nor is it necessary for them to know. The client constructs an invocation for Payroll and passes it to its local ORB. The ORB examines the IOR and determines that the only IOR protocol component that the ORB can communicate with is the IPX component, which happens to be the proxy on the bridge, so it addresses the invocation there. The proxy and bridge translate the invocation from GIOP/IPX to DCE CIOP and route the invocation onto the DCE CIOP domain network to Payroll's ORB.

This concludes the example. We'll just point out here, for the technically inclined, that it is not necessarily the end of the route for the invocation; if the Payroll object has moved, then the invocation may yet bounce back to the bridge with a **LOCATION_FORWARD** return status and be automatically rerouted to Payroll's new location. We also realize that this discussion, and the specification itself, raises a few more questions than they answer; for example, about proxy lifetimes and housekeeping. At the current level of specification, these are considered implementation details.

We haven't heard a lot about bridge or gateway products on the market during the several years since this specification was issued. We know that many ORBs speak more than one protocol, and that multiprotocol CORBA is alive and well. However, we don't know of that many sites that are using CORBA on protocol-restricted network segments that would benefit from the kind of gateways that the specification describes.

One place this kind of bridge could play a role is where traffic goes from a TCP-based copper or fiber segment onto a wireless segment (especially during the next few years while wireless continues to run at far slower than copper or fiber speed). We are, at least, going to look for instances of this type of use as wireless transmission takes off in the beginning of the next milennium.

The CORBA specification points out that there are many reasons why an object reference stringified on one ORB may not work when destringified on another. For example,

- Identifiers embedded in the string form can belong to a different domain than the ORB attempting to destringify the object reference.

- The ORBs in question might not share a network protocol, or be connected at all.

- Security constraints may be placed on object reference destringification.

Since most ORBs running on both the Internet and large enterprise intranets run IIOP and are connected by continuous networks running TCP/IP, these pitfalls are not a major impediment. (They are the things to check when your stringified IOR doesn't work, though.) So, for invocations between any pair of IIOP-speaking ORBs on the same network, or for invocations between any two identical ORBs (i.e., same vendor, same model, same protocol, on the same network), you can stringify an object reference on one ORB, pass it to a client on the other any way you want, destringify it there, and successfully invoke operations on the remote object. We've seen object references stringified in Sydney, Australia, and e-mailed to Colorado where they were used, successfully, to invoke the object instance on the other side of the world via the Internet.

Our two-protocol bridging example showed all the reasons why you might not be able to invoke an object reference that you received in stringified form. Most reasons involve connectivity: In order for the invocation to work, your network needs to be connected, directly with the same protocol, to the network of the remote object that you're trying to invoke. If you e-mail the stringified object reference through a bridge or gateway, or (even harder to figure out) through two bridges and an intervening network segment of different protocols with like segments on either end, you don't have connectivity and the stringified reference will not work. Since IIOP works on TCP/IP, and so many invocations go over the Internet which runs on TCP/IP, people assume that these invocations will work anywhere. It's almost true, but not quite, so try to think through the configuration details if your invocation doesn't work and you can't figure out why.

If you're not sure about connectivity and you have a choice (that it, if you're the programmer, or if you're running a CORBA client and you can do a lookup in the Naming Service at the remote server), you should pass the object reference as a parameter from one system to the other and let the ORBs do the work. Naming and Trading Services do this automatically, but if you're writing both ends of the application yourself, you can always pass the object reference as a parameter in a call.

Before we leave this section, there's one more part of the IOR we need to cover. Some services require the cooperation of the ORB to pass information that is not included in the IDL definition. The first OMG standard service to require this is the Transaction Service: Every invocation between an **open transaction** call and its corresponding **commit** is part of a particular transaction. However, the Transaction Service may be taking care of operations for other clients at the same time, so the ORB ends up responsible for keeping track of a transaction identifier and passing it to the service with every invocation. This is certainly not in the IDL; the client is not even aware that his or her transaction *has* an identifier.

Consequently, CORBA interoperability defines a Service Context and a corresponding Service Context ID for this. OMG specifies Context IDs for services it standardizes; the Transaction Service got the first one, and its serviceID = 0 (zero). Other context indeces are for CodeSet handling, bidirectional IIOP, and other interoperability characteristics visible to ORBs only and not to your client or object. ORB implementors may register their own service context IDs with OMG the same way they register a profile or component ID.

6.8.3.1 Inline and Request-Level Bridging

If you think about it, you realize that nothing prevents ORB-to-ORB interoperability even without an OMG standard. Check out Figure 6.7 on page 202: Anyone with two ORBs and their IDL compilers can build a bridge that includes the skeleton from one ORB and the stub from the other and pass a request through, converting from one ORB's proprietary protocol to the other's. Use the DII and DSI and you don't even need the compiler. Split the bridge into two parts connected over the network and you're distributed, to boot. (In fact, this is such an appealing concept that an OMG member once suggested that no interoperability standard was necessary; vendors or users could just build bridges for objects that needed to interoperate. Fortunately, more practical heads prevailed, so we didn't end up with a network filled with thousands of do-it-yourself bridges, and ORBs spiked with stubs and skeletons for every interface type on the Internet.)

Figure 6.8 shows a *request-level bridge*, which is built using public ORB APIs; CORBA provides a number of APIs that are used in these bridges, including one, the DSI, that was standardized specifically for use here (although it has a number of other important uses). APIs and CORBA components useful or essential for bridging are the DII, the DSI, Interface Repositories, the POA, and object references including IORs.

The alternative to the request-level bridge is the *in-line bridge* (Figure 6.9). This is the bridge you would build if you needed the most streamlined possible implementation and you had the builders of both ORBs participating in the effort. In an in-line bridge, code inside the ORBs performs the translations and mappings to go from one to the

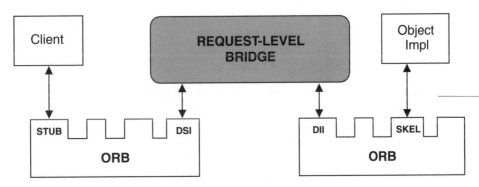

Figure 6.8   Request-level bridges are built using public ORB APIs.

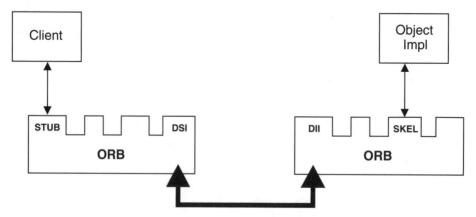

Figure 6.9   In-line bridges are built using ORB-internal APIs.

other, and there is no public API. Many vendors talk from one instance to another of their own ORBs using in-line bridges; typically, this interaction is invisible to the user and programmer. Since all internal representations are identical, this can be very efficient.

The fact is, you can't tell by using it whether an ORB employs a request-level bridge or an in-line bridge. The difference only has to do with the connection between the bridge and the ORB, and not with the message format or protocol that is output to the network; that is, either form of bridge could communicate using either a standard or proprietary protocol. In general, request-level bridges will be easier to build, while in-line bridges will be more efficient, although clever design can minimize the penalty associated with the request-level bridge. For now, we'll just note that in-line bridging provides ORB implementors with a known way to improve performance, always a worthy goal.

6.8.3.2 Interface-Specific and Generic Request-Level Bridges

Request-level bridges may be either:

Interface specific. Built using IDL compiler-generated stubs and skeletons, this type of bridge supports only interfaces that were incorporated into the bridge when it was constructed.

Generic. Taking full advantage of the DII, DSI, and interface repository, this type of bridge supports every interface known to the system.

Lack of flexibility is a notable disadvantage for the interface-specific bridge. Since stubs and skeletons must be built in, you must either replace or augment the interface-specific bridges in your system every time you add an object with a new interface. This bridge type compensates with a performance advantage over the generic bridge because it does not have to construct any components "on the fly." However, cleverly built generic bridges may construct and save stubs similar in function to those provided by the IDL compiler, so this penalty may be lessened in the future.

6.8.4 Structure of the Interoperability Specification

Figure 6.10 shows the structure of the CORBA Interoperablity Specification. In this section, we'll take a look at what's in each box and how they fit together; in the next two sections we'll take a closer look at the most interesting boxes, the ones that you can buy from your vendors.

We've emphasized the CORBA IDL API in the figure on purpose. *There is no API specifically for CORBA Interoperability accessible by client or object implementation:* If your target object reference is a local object, your invocation stays local; if it's remote, then your invocation goes remote. If your ORB uses CORBA-standard interoperablity including GIOP and IIOP, then that's what you get; if it doesn't, then you don't. That's because clients and object implementations talk to ORBs, and not to the network. All of the network communication is one ORB talking to another. That's the way CORBA works.

So, on to the boxes: The box labeled INTEROPERABILITY ARCHITECTURE contains most of what we've covered so far: the basic architecture built on bridging; the Interoperable Object Reference with its protocol profiles and components; the interoperability interfaces including the DSI; and the provisions for context-specific services.

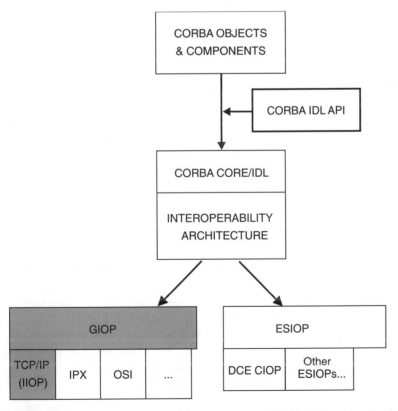

Figure 6.10 Structure of the CORBA Interoperability Specification. Shaded components are mandatory for CORBA Interoperability compliance.

GIOP, or General Inter-ORB Protocol, contains the specifications for the general, CORBA mandated inter-ORB messaging protocol, which has been designed to be implemented on any reliable network transport. In this box are the Common Data Representation, the eight GIOP messages and their formats, and a set of transport assumptions.

Underneath the GIOP box is a set of boxes representing reliable transport protocols on which GIOP can be carried. The first, TCP/IP, is mandatory. The others are easily implementable; it's very likely that implementations will be out by the time you read this.

ESIOP (pronounced Aesop) stands for Environment-Specific Inter-ORB Protocol. There isn't much in the box marked ESIOP; every ESIOP gets to define its protocol independently as long as it meets the requirements for ORB-to-ORB communication of object requests and responses.

There is only one OMG-standard ESIOP right now, the DCE CIOP. (The DCE ESIOP is officially designated the DCE Common Inter-ORB Protocol, or DCE-CIOP in the OMG specification; we discuss it briefly in Section 6.8.4.7.) ORBs can also communicate using proprietary protocols. There's nothing wrong with this; it may be the only way to achieve a necessary performance characteristic or cram functionality into a small or embedded system. However, proprietary protocols should stick as closely as possible to the GIOP structure to allow bridging to the standard IIOP and other GIOP-based protocols, as well as provide a bridge to the IIOP so that they can bear the CORBA 2 compliance brand and interoperate with other standard CORBA implementations.

6.8.4.1 General Inter-ORB Protocol (GIOP) and Internet Inter-ORB Protocol (IIOP)

IIOP, which is the GIOP over TCP/IP, is the one protocol *mandatory* for CORBA Interoperability compliance. The GIOP/IIOP specification was designed to meet these goals:

Widest possible availability. The IIOP is based on TCP/IP, the most widely used and flexible communications transport mechanism available, and defines only the minimum additional layers to transfer CORBA requests between ORBs.

Simplicity. Working within the other necessary goals, the GIOP was kept as simple as possible.

Scalability. It is designed to scale to the size of today's Internet, and beyond.

Low cost. Both ORB reengineering at implementation, and runtime support costs, were minimized as much as possible.

Generality. The GIOP was designed for implementation on any reliable, connection-oriented protocol, not just TCP/IP.

Architectural neutrality. GIOP makes minimal assumptions about the architecture and implementation of the ORBs and bridges that support it.

The GIOP consists of three specifications:

- The Common Data Representation (CDR) definition
- GIOP message formats
- GIOP transport assumptions

The IIOP specification adds:

- Internet IOP message transport

The IIOP is not a separate specification; it is a mapping of the GIOP to the specific transport TCP/IP (Figure 6.10). Other mappings are possible; mappings to several additional transports may be standardized at OMG during the next few years.

6.8.4.2 Common Data Representation (CDR)

The CDR defines representations for all OMG IDL datatypes, including typecodes and constructed types such as **struct**, **sequence**, and **enum**.

The specification takes into account byte ordering and alignment. *Receiver-makes-right* semantics avoids unnecessary translation of messages between machines of the same byte order.

We're not going to list any of the representations—there's nothing you can do with them unless you're building your own ORB; and if you are, then you need a copy of the spec and not just this book.

The point of the CDR is that all GIOPs share a common data representation, so bridging this part of the message should be easy.

6.8.4.3 GIOP Message Formats

GIOP defines eight distinct messages for ORB-to-ORB communications. These carry requests, locate object implementations, and manage communication channels. They support all of the functions and behavior required by CORBA, including exception reporting and passing of operation context.

These eight messages, and the accompanying list of message transfer characteristics, meet the needs of the object-oriented CORBA semantics in the most efficient way possible. A frequent comment about this mechanism is that it's "just another RPC," but, in fact, these eight messages with their associated characteristics are quite different from an RPC. You can program to these messages only if you build your own ORB. We're including this information because of the widespread curiosity about how remote CORBA invocations compare to an RPC mechanism. If you're still curious, keep reading here; if your curiosity was satisfied by these comments, feel free to skip ahead to the next section.

The eight messages simplify communications. Binding and format agreement are accomplished without negotiation. In most cases, messages from client ORB to object ORB can be sent as soon as a connection is established. Some characteristics of message transfer are described in the following:

The connection is asymmetric. Client and server roles are distinct, assigned at connection. The client originates the connection, and may send requests but not replies. The server accepts the connection, and may send replies but not requests. This simplifies the specification, and avoids some race conditions that might otherwise arise. (*Bidirectional GIOP*, an addition to the specification that helps CORBA work through firewalls, relaxes these restrictions under special circumstances; see Section 6.8.4.6 for details.)

Requests may be multiplexed. That is, multiple clients within an originating ORB may share a connection to a remote ORB. Information in the request differentiates it from others on the same connection.

Requests may overlap. If asynchronous, any order of requests and replies is supported through request/reply identifiers (the serial numbers we talked about in the AMI sections). Of the eight messages, three may be sent by the client: **Request**, **CancelRequest**, and **LocateRequest**. Three may be sent only by the server: **Reply**, **LocateReply**, and **CloseConnection**. Both may send **MessageError** and **Fragment**.

All GIOP messages start with a GIOP header. It's simple enough, so here it is in IDL:

```
struct MessageHeader {
    char            magic[4];
    Version         GIOP_version;
    boolean         byte_order;
    octet           message_type;
    unsigned long   message_size;
};
```

The magic number is GIOP encoded in ISO Latin-1—no surprise here. The version may be 1.0, 1.1, or 1.2. The byte order is specified next, and then the message type, which must be one of the eight we just listed. Finally, comes the message size in octets. Here are brief descriptions of the eight GIOP messages:

Request message. The **Request** message consists of the GIOP header, a request header, and a request body. The header contains the service context, a request ID, object identifier, operation, and some other information. The request body contains all of the **in** and **inout** parameters.

Reply message. The **Reply** message consists of the GIOP header, a reply header, and a reply body. The reply header contains a service context, the same request ID as the request, and a status code. If the status code contains **NO_EXCEPTION**, then the reply body contains the return value, if any, followed by all of the inout and out parameters. If the status code is **USER_EXCEPTION** or **SYSTEM_EXCEPTION**, the body contains encoded exception information. Finally, if the status code is **LOCATION_FORWARD**, the body contains an IOR to which the originating ORB should redirect the original request. This re-sending takes place without the knowledge of the originating client.

CancelRequest message. **CancelRequest** messages contain the usual GIOP header followed by a **CancelRequest** header with the request ID. This message notifies a server that the client is no longer expecting a reply for the specified pending **Request** or **LocateRequest** message.

LocateRequest message. **LocateRequest** messages are sent by a client to a server to determine whether a particular object reference is valid; whether the current server is capable of servicing requests; or, if not, a new address for requests for that object reference. **LocateRequest** provides a way to get the same information as a **LocationForward** reply from a **Request**, without having to transmit potentially large amounts of data.

LocateReply message. This is the server's reply to a **LocateRequest** message. It contains, besides the usual GIOP header, a **LocateReply** header with the request ID and a status value, and a **LocateReply** body that contains, if applicable, the IOR of the new target.

CloseConnection message. These messages are sent by servers to inform clients (or, more precisely, their ORBs) that the server intends to close the connection and will not provide further responses. The server is only allowed to send this when there are no pending requests, although requests may be received during the interval between the sending of **CloseConnection** and its acknowledgment at the receiving ORB. This also informs the ORBs that they will not receive replies to requests pending on that connection, and that these may safely be reissued on another connection. The ORB will send a **COMM_FAILURE** exception to the clients, with a completion status of **COMPLETED_MAYBE**. The **CloseConnection** message consists of only the GIOP header; the message type value says it all.

MessageError message. These messages are sent in response to any GIOP message that is, for some reason, uninterpretable. For example, the magic number may be wrong, or the version number unrecognized. This message consists of only the GIOP header as well; the sender is supposed to know what it did wrong.

Fragment message. If you send or return a lot of data with your invocation, your request or reply will have to be broken into multiple transmissions. In fact, it's possible that the sending ORB won't know the exact length of the message when it's finished marshaling the first fragment. So, GIOP allows multiple fragments to be sent using the **Fragment** message, with the total length not specified until the last fragment. Strict rules for breaking between fragments prevent the introduction of errors should the data need to be re-marshaled as they pass through a bridge or gateway between protocol domains. The **Fragment** message was introduced in GIOP 1.1.

Those are the eight messages. We've treated them summarily because you'll never need them unless you build your own ORB, and this is definitely not the book for that task. But these couple of pages let you know basically what's going on under the covers, and reassures you that there is, for instance, a version number in every message so that progress won't find your ORB totally unprepared.

6.8.4.4 GIOP Message Transport Requirements

GIOP message transport requirements were chosen specifically to map to TCP/IP, the most prevalent transport, as well as the widely used Novell IPX and OSI. Basically, GIOP requires:

- A connection-oriented transport protocol.

- Reliable delivery (byte order must be preserved, and acknowledgment of delivery must be available).

- Participants must be notified of disorderly connection loss.

- The model for initiating a connection must meet certain requirements (modeled after TCP/IP—no surprise here).

This concludes the description of the GIOP. Analogous to the way OMG IDL maps to various programming languages, the GIOP is not directly usable but becomes so when mapped to one of many possible transports, such as TCP/IP.

6.8.4.5 Internet Inter-ORB Protocol (IIOP)

The mapping of the GIOP onto TCP/IP is so straightforward that this section of the specification is extremely brief. It consists primarily of the specification for the IIOP IOR, which contains the hostname and port that listens for the client-initiated connection. If you're an ORB builder, chances are good that you already know exactly what to do.

6.8.4.6 Bidirectional GIOP

CORBA applications frequently run behind firewalls, which allow outgoing (that is, client-originated) connections with all of their associated traffic including replies, but block incoming connections. As we've seen, even an ordinary client-side CORBA application needs to receive push-style notification of events, or bear object-side interfaces for other services, and standard GIOP requires a reverse connection originated by the client-side component at the "server" end to carry this traffic.

Versions 1.0 and 1.1 of GIOP defined a connection-oriented, single-direction protocol: A client's ORB initiated a connection, and even though that connection could persist and be used for multiple invocations, every one had to go in the same direction—when the remote ORB needed to invoke an object on the client's ORB, it would have to open a separate connection for GIOP traffic going in the other direction. This was a characteristic of GIOP, and not of TCP/IP or any other transport protocol.

GIOP 1.2, the current version, introduces bidirectional connections. These allow operation through a firewall, but have limitations that you need to understand in order to take advantage. In order for an object to be invoked in the reverse direction on a connection, the client's application must create the object and sent its object reference to the remote ORB as a parameter in an invocation, *over the connection that is to become bi-directional*. Both ORBs must support bidirectional connections, and the client's ORB must send its request message with the bidirectional ServiceContext structure. The remote ORB will then invoke the referenced object using the same connection, in the reverse direction.

As is usual in all of these CORBA interoperability scenarios, there is nothing for the client or object instance to do in order for this to work, and there is no client or object API to invoke. If you buy and install an ORB on the client side that supports bidirectional connectivity, and you invoke a server on an ORB that also supports this, and you create an object and send its reference over the wire in an invocation, then invocations of this object from the remote ORB will come in over your open connection automatically, and the remote ORB will not attempt to open a new channel for the reverse direction invocation. That's all there is to it.

We won't go over the interfaces for this, since they're all ORB internal.

6.8.4.7 Environment-Specific Inter-ORB Protocols (ESIOPs)

A non-GIOP protocol is an ESIOP if it's based on the interoperability architecture including domains and bridging, the IOR, and the interoperability interfaces including the DSI. Not every inter-ORB protocol is an ESIOP; it is certainly possible to construct a proprietary protocol that does not include these components. In some demanding environments, this may be the only way to meet requirements for such specialized applications as guaranteed real-time response as in a fly-by-wire system or control for a nuclear power plant.

The DCE-based protocol adopted by OMG as part of CORBA 2 is an ESIOP. It conforms to all of the requirements that we listed. In addition, it uses the same CDR as the GIOP, a characteristic that will facilitate bridging between it and GIOP domains. It is every bit an OMG standard; even though it is not mandatory for all ORBs, it is the *only* compliant way to implement a DCE-based protocol in CORBA. That is, you don't *have* to do DCE, but if you do, you *have* to do it *this way* if you want to be branded CORBA compliant. In the specification, the name of the protocol is DCE Common Inter-ORB Protocol, abbreviated DCE-CIOP, so that's how we'll refer to it.

DCE-CIOP replaces the functionality of the eight GIOP messages with two DCE RPC calls, *locate* and *invoke*. It also replaces the GIOP transport assumptions with a reliance on the DCE RPC service to handle these two calls. Since the initials DCE figure so prominently in the name of this protocol, some people have misinterpreted the role of the DCE RPC in CORBA 2 communications. Here's the scoop, briefly:

The DCE-CIOP is a protocol for ORB-to-ORB communications, where it plays the same role as the IIOP. Client and object implementation still interact only with their local ORBs, and the fact that an invocation may have to go over the network is still hidden from them. This protocol does not make DCE servers accessible to CORBA clients, or CORBA servers accessible to DCE clients.

There is a new OMG specification for CORBA-DCE interworking. It's based on bridging technology, and gives CORBA clients access to legacy DCE servers implemented using the old, non-OO DCE IDL. Specifically, it does *not* address access from DCE clients to CORBA servers, nor any access either way with DCE OO extensions. For details, download the specification from the OMG Web site or ask your vendor.

6.8.5 One Last Word on Interoperability

We've devoted a lot of space to interoperability, especially considering that some of the interfaces covered in this chapter are not available to client and object programmers. Interoperability is serious business—our component software environment is based on it—so we have a lot of concern for what's going on under the covers when our objects get together over the network.

It's important to keep everything in perspective, and OMG has a good idea where the payoffs lie for both user and software vendor. In OMG's picture, the payoffs are in:

- A *common architecture* with common interface specifications and protocol (whether direct or bridged), a necessary enabling component

- A set of *common interfaces* to low- and intermediate-level components (the CORBAservices and, even more important, the CORBAfacilities) that enable the big payoff

- A dynamic *component software marketplace* based on infrastructure and domain standards, that enables off-the-shelf software purchases that function in your enterprise, and interoperate with your customers and suppliers, thanks to their reliance on OMG standards

CORBA 3 adds capabilities that address the needs of scalable, robust, enterprise applications: *Quality of Service control, asynchronous invocation,* and *objects passable by value.*

In this picture, the protocol lies hidden in the infrastructure. The reason CORBA 2 interoperability was such big news wasn't because it was such a great achievement, it was because it was a workable solution to a huge problem we created ourselves in the first place.

What's the best protocol? It depends on circumstances. You wouldn't use the same protocol in a miniature, wireless handheld as you would in a powerful workstation, and even the workstation may need a protocol change if it moves from a five-unit isolated LAN to a million-unit multinational enterprise. The framers of CORBA knew this; that's why the specification supports multiple protocols in such a natural and efficient way.

What should you look for in an interoperable ORB product? First, make sure that it conforms to the OMG specifications. Beyond that, there are a number of things to look for: reliability, robustness, scalability (how many ORBs, workstations, servers, etc., will you be running?), security, administrability, vendor company characteristics, and so on. You will not need the same ORB profile vis-à-vis these criteria as another company, so do your own evaluation, and make up your own mind.

CHAPTER

7

Language Mappings, Part 1: C++

7.1 Role of a Language Mapping

So far, we've only seen how to write our CORBA interface definitions in OMG IDL. Since these definitions are programming language independent, how are we going to access these interfaces from our code?

CORBA programming language mappings "map" (that is, define) one-to-one correspondences from OMG IDL constructs to programming language constructs. These constructs tell client and object-implementation writers what to write to invoke an operation on a CORBA object. In a non-object-oriented language such as C and COBOL, invocations typically map to function calls; in object-oriented languages like C++ and Smalltalk, mappings make CORBA invocations look like language-object invocations.

Some of the languages with IDL mappings are object oriented: C++, Java, Smalltalk. Others are not: C, COBOL, Ada. What's the difference?

- For every language, the mapping allows access to an object instance from any CORBA client.

- For object-oriented languages, the mappings use OO features to enhance programming and operational aspects such as type safety and inheritance.

In the first edition of this book, we spoke hypothetically of the advantages and disadvantages of a *reverse* language mapping; that is, one that took your language class definitions and generated an IDL file that you could use to write clients. This would automatically turn a programming-language object into a CORBA object, accessible remotely not only in its original programming language but also in any other language with a CORBA mapping—all you need to do is write a client to its reverse-mapping IDL interface. Well, there's no need to be hypothetical anymore because CORBA now has an official reverse mapping: it's for Java only, but works well and is the basis for CORBA-EJB interoperability. We'll discuss it in the next chapter along with the regular IDL-to-Java mapping.

The beginning part of this chapter, through Section 7.1.1, summarizes aspects common to all language mappings. The remainder of the chapter covers the C++ language mapping, followed by Chapter 8 on Java and Chapter 9 on COBOL.

What about other languages? Languages with pointers, structures, and dynamic memory allocation support IDL mappings most easily, but languages without them support mappings as well. C and Smalltalk have official mappings, and were presented in the first edition of this book. Ada also has an official mapping, and LISP is getting one. Mapping for two scripting languages, Python and IDL script, are being ratified as we go to press. Languages with unofficial mappings include Perl, Tcl, Objective-C, Eiffel, and others, but we don't have the space to discuss them here. You can find ORBs with these language mappings on the CETUS Web site mentioned in Appendix A.

7.1.1 Language Mapping Functions

A language mapping has a lot to do. First, it has to express all of the constructs of IDL, including:

- Basic and constructed datatypes, constants, and the CORBA object reference
- Operation invocations, including parameter passing
- Setting and retrieving attribute values
- Raising exceptions and handling exception conditions

To this list, CORBA 3 adds:

- Allowing a client to invoke every operation either synchronously or asynchronously
- Manipulating valuetypes

To ensure interoperability, every language mapping must provide a mapping for every IDL datatype. If some IDL datatypes were not supported by every language, operation signatures that used them would not interoperate everywhere.

There is also a converse problem, that of language datatypes that do not map directly to IDL datatypes. With the addition of fixed-point, double-long, and wide character and string types, IDL now handles most fundamental language types, although some types in some languages have to be defined as classes in order to support insertion, extraction, and proper handling of values on invocation and return. However, since interoperability does *not* require every language datatype to have a corresponding IDL type, we expect that some unusual language types will continue to lack directly comparable IDL types for a long time to come. For up-to-date information on this, check the OMG specs as they evolve.

There must be a datatype to represent the object reference. This representation is opaque; that is, the object reference is represented by a language-specific datatype, but CORBA programs do not (and, generally, can not) interpret the value that the type contains. Object references may be passed as input or output parameters or return values in CORBA invocations, and may be passed to ORB and POA operations. Object-oriented languages provide type safety to CORBA object references: Although the base reference is type **Object**, each CORBA type is kept separate by the language, which only allows operations on a reference that supports them. To cast object references to the proper type, you use the **narrow** operation provided by CORBA. An attempt to **narrow** an object reference to a type that it does not support will fail, but an attempt to **narrow** to a less-derived type is allowed. This leveraging of the type safety mechanism by CORBA is a key advantage to you, and the benefit increases as your applications become larger.

Object invocations are mapped in various ways. In C (which we won't present here), the static invocation interface mapping requires the client to insert an object reference into the mapped function call to specify the target. In C++, Java, and Smalltalk (object-oriented languages), a CORBA invocation looks like a language-object invocation. COBOL supports invocation in two different ways, including one that's almost all automatic.

For the DII, mappings vary. In C, the mapping follows the normal definitions even though the target is a pseudo-object. In C++, attribute operations replace **add_argument**. The CORBA 2.0 specification speculated that a mapping for a dynamic language like LISP could make a dynamic invocation look like an invocation of a language object.

The mapping must also provide access to ORB and POA functionality which, although expressed in PIDL, is not always accessed as the call that would be constructed from it. In fact, some of the PIDL definitions are left incomplete, to be fully defined only in the various language mappings. An application's first CORBA call, connecting to the ORB, is defined only by its language mapping as you might expect. Similarly, the mappings provide access to the DII including the various deferred invocation modes, and the DSI for the server side.

The last thing a language mapping does is fix responsibility for memory allocation and freeing among the client, the stub, and the ORB. We'll point out how this happens in the various languages as we work our way through the next three chapters.

Finally, remember that C and C++ are both generated by the same compiler in some implementations. Some ORB vendors required mappings for those two languages that coincided in the various functional areas, including memory management. This requirement, in the end, resulted in some changes in an older version of the C mapping being required by the C++ mapping.

We admit in advance that the simple examples we use to illustrate the three mappings are rather dry. We've done this on purpose: Since the second half of the book contains realistic examples worked in detail in all three languages, the illustrations in these three chapters have been kept as simple as possible to make the principles clear.

7.2 Language Mappings, Part 1: C++

C++ and Java, unlike C and COBOL, are object-oriented languages. Both languages include constructs to define objects and invoke operations on them. The OMG language mappings for C++ and Java take advantage of these constructs, and purposely make CORBA objects look as much like language objects as possible.

Applications vary widely in the size of the objects they define and manipulate. At one end of this scale are applications consisting of relatively few, coarse-grained objects with simple relationships and calling sequences. At the other end of the scale are applications with thousands (or more) of fine-grained objects, whose calling sequences interlock and intertwine as references to multiple objects and groups are passed through a sequence of intermediate objects and are not called until the end of the chain. In between is the type of application we talk about in most of our examples with medium-grained objects in our system (sales orders in a business system, planes and tanks in a military simulation, and the like) representing their real-life counterparts, one for one. We tend to like the middle ground—it allows business programmers to code business functionality while taking best advantage of the support CORBA provides for low-level system stuff. This scale of objects tends to run well, especially if you take advantage of POA features.

All of these styles are important, and CORBA supports them well. It turns out that the memory-management style that suits coarse-grained object systems is not acceptable for fine-grained systems, so CORBA provides both for C++. What we're talking about is allocation and freeing of memory for object references and dynamically allocated parameters in CORBA calls—whether you or the system allocates and frees this space as objects and variables come into and go out of scope. Programmer-controlled memory management can be optimized for each application, but is prone to errors as code grows large and memory leaks result. Inefficiencies in automatic memory management are typically not noticeable for a few operations or variables, but cause applications to bog down when they allocate or free hundreds or thousands of variables. So, for C++, CORBA provides both **_var** types, whose memory is automatically freed when they go out of scope, and **_ptr** types, which you must free yourself. IDL compilers generate **typedef**s for both, so you can pick the one you want each time you allocate a new object reference, **struct**, or whatever. Look for details in Section 7.3.2.1.

7.2.1 C++ Mapping and Your C++ Compiler

The OMG mapping is based on the C++ environment defined in *The Annotated C++ Reference Manual* by Ellis and Stroustrop, as adopted by the ANSI/ISO C++ standardization committee, including exception handling. It also relies on the namespace construct. This feature was almost impossible to resist, since it corresponds so closely with OMG IDL's scoping of names to file, module, interface, and so on. For compilers that do not support namespace, the mapping provides workarounds.

The OMG C++ Mapping specification mentions compatibility of the C and C++ mappings, specifically in call parameter memory management, as a feature. This is more important for ORB vendors than end users—it's almost impossible for you to notice whether your C and C++ code perform invocations use the same stub or different stubs. There are two advantages for coders, so we'll mention them briefly: First, memory management for call parameters in the C mapping was improved markedly when it was made compatible with C++ (okay, okay, some less-than-perfect decisions in the original mapping were fixed up). Second, since types are handled identically in C and C++, once you've learned memory management for one language, you automatically know the other one.

7.2.2 Changes from CORBA 2.1 to CORBA 2.2

Even though the title of this book is CORBA 3, there are a couple of changes to the C++ mapping from previous OMG updates that are only recently (as we publish in early 2000) showing up in IDL compiler products, so we need to go over them here. In fact, since the sample of C++ ORBs included in our example section includes some that already incorporate the changes and others that don't, you'll see **#ifdefs** in the code to allow for the first of the two changes.

The first addition is **_out** type parameters. Obviously added to enhance memory management (and, in fact, to allow the compiler and system to do more of it automatically and free you of the burden), mappings to **_out** types will show up in the argument list of your operations. All IDL types including the basic types have a corresponding **_out** mapping, as we'll see in the table in the next section.

The second change is a requirement for IDL compilers to provide a tie-type implementation option for every interface, in addition to the inheritance option. There are two ways that your implementation can acquire its CORBA functionality; that is, the ability to be called and to do all of the other things that CORBA provides. It can inherit them through inheritance from a base class generated by the IDL compiler called a *skeleton class*, or it can acquire them through a delegating class called a *tie*. Although inheritance is a more straightforward way to provide all of the functionality you need, it has problems when used to invoke wrappers built around legacy C++ applications that already have an inheritance hierarchy defined. Thus, the tie method is most often used with these wrappers, although it can be used for any C++ interface implementation. Prior to CORBA 2.2, IDL compilers did not have to provide the tie method. This meant that implementations that depended on it could only run on ORBs that provided this option. The portability provided to object implementations by the POA, coupled with this addition to the C++ mapping, takes care of just about all of the portability barriers that OMG knew about and gives you true server-side portability.

7.3 C++ Mapping Fundamentals

Now that we've taken care of all the preliminaries, it's time to get down to business. We'll start with the fundamentals: mappings for IDL basic datatypes, constructed types, and operations. With these done, we'll cover some specialized topics: the CORBA object reference, inheritance, IDL attributes, and exceptions. A section on **valuetype**s completes the chapter.

7.3.1 Mapping for Basic Datatypes

The most basic part of a mapping is how the primitive IDL types (Chapter 3) map to C++ types. Because the precision of IDL types is strictly defined, they cannot map directly to C++ types such as `long`, `short`, or `float`, whose precision differs on different systems. Therefore, the C++ mapping defines them in terms of `CORBA::types`, which are defined in a system-specific header file that ensures that the CORBA requirements are met. Here's the list:

OMG IDL	C++	C++ Out Type
short	`CORBA::Short`	`CORBA::Short_out`
long	`CORBA::Long`	`CORBA::Long_out`
long long	`CORBA::LongLong`	`CORBA::LongLong_out`
unsigned short	`CORBA::UShort`	`CORBA::UShort_out`
unsigned long	`CORBA::ULong`	`CORBA::ULong_out`
unsigned long long	`CORBA::ULongLong`	`CORBA::ULongLong_out`
float	`CORBA::Float`	`CORBA::Float_out`
double	`CORBA::Double`	`CORBA::Double_out`
long double	`CORBA::LongDouble`	`CORBA::LongDouble_out`
char	`CORBA::Char`	`CORBA::Char_out`
wchar	`CORBA::WChar`	`CORBA::WChar_out`
boolean	`CORBA::Boolean`	`CORBA::Boolean_out`
octet	`CORBA::Octet`	`CORBA::Octet_out`

Then a header file assures that `CORBA::long` maps to a 32-bit integer; a `CORBA::float` maps to an IEEE 32-bit floating point number, and so on through the list, ensuring that each CORBA type has its required precision.

7.3.2 Mapping for Constructed Types

The IDL provides mappings for **string** types, structured types (**struct, union**, and **sequence**), and **array**s. It also discusses use of **Typedef**s, and mapping for the **any** type. Although we will not go into the details in this chapter, the tutorial example deliberately includes a **struct**, a **sequence**, and an **enum** to illustrate their mapping.

7.3.2.1 `T_var` *Types*

The C++ mapping provides a `_var` type for almost every type, which automates memory management. Termed `T_var` types, their names are constructed by adding `_var` to the name of the type. Most helpful for variable-length structured types, `T_var` types are also defined for fixed-length structured types to allow a more consistent programming style. Thus, you can code in terms of `T_vars` for structured types uniformly, regardless of whether the underlying types are fixed- or variable-length. `T_vars` are designed specifically for allocation on the stack; when used this way, all storage used by the type is automatically freed when the variable goes out of scope.

One instance where the `T_var` type shows its benefit is the change of length of a variable-length type. This is helpful, for example, when simply copying a longer string into an existing string, but it really shows its worth when used for **out** and **inout** variables which change size during a CORBA invocation. Here, the automatic memory management provided by the _var type allows the client, the ORB, and the object implementation to work together to deallocate memory used by the **inout** and **out** parameters at the start of the call, and allocate exactly the memory required by the returning values for all of these types. (Although **out** parameters are not read by the object implementation before being set, they may contain values—and therefore occupy memory—left over from a previous call.) Without the help provided by the _var class, you would have to keep track of this memory, and perform at least some of this deallocation yourself.

An object of type T_var behaves similarly to the structured type T, except that members must be accessed indirectly. For a **struct**, this means using an arrow (->) instead of a dot (.):

```
// IDL
struct S { string name; float age; };
void f(out S p);
```

```
// C++
S a;
S_var b;
f(b);
a = b; // deep-copy
cout << "names " << a.name << ", " << b->name << endl;
```

T_var types are extremely helpful in the right places, but where should you avoid using T_var types? Keep in mind that T_vars are deallocated automatically when they go out of scope. If you're writing fine-grained code that passes through scope after scope, creating and destroying millions of T_vars along the way, you will pay a price in performance. Use conventional types for this style of code, allocating memory with new so it sticks around until you're ready to let it go. Use good coding practice to keep track of all of your allocated memory, and free it when you're done.

In our programming example in the second half of this book, watch for the use of the type string_var in several places, and _var structured types in the POS modules in Chapter 33.

7.3.3 Mapping an Operation

Here's a simple interface that we can use to demonstrate the C++ mapping:

```
interface example1 {
        long op1 (in long arg1);
}
```

In C++, the invocation looks object oriented. To C++ language programmers, it will even look familiar:

```
// C++
// Declare object reference:
    example1_var   myex1;
    CORBA::long    mylongin, mylongout;
```

```
// code to retrieve a reference to an
// example1 object and bind it to myex1  . . .

    mylongout = myex1->op1 ( mylongin );
```

The CORBA object reference in C++ can take one of two forms: pointer (_ptr) or variable (_var); the _var form is memory-managed automatically, analogous to the T_var structured variable types we just mentioned. If you're building relatively coarse-grained objects, the kind most applications end up distributing around the network, you should use the _var form because _var object references are automatically destroyed when they go out of scope. However, if you're building an application with many fine-grained objects (and using CORBA to ensure interlanguage portability, for example), you may have to use the _ptr form to avoid memory management operations that may hamper performance by occurring at inopportune moments. The cost of using _ptr object references is that you have to keep track of them, and free their memory yourself to avoid memory leaks.

7.3.4 Using Interface Class Members

An interface maps to a C++ class that contains public definitions of the types, constants, operations, and exceptions defined in the interface. C++ classes produced from your IDL are special. You can do many useful things with them, but some uses are forbidden. You cannot:

- Create or hold an instance of an interface class (automatic when you obtain an object reference)

- Derive from an interface class (derive in your IDL file instead)

- Use a pointer (A*) or a reference (A&) to an interface class (use _var or _ptr instead)

Of course, you can declare and use variables whose types are declared in the interface in the normal way.

These restrictions allow for a wide variety of implementations of the language mapping. For example, they ensure that interface classes can be implemented as abstract base classes. Keep in mind that an IDL compiler must produce, and we must use, a number of distinct classes in order to provide all of the CORBA functionality we've gone over so far. So, before we're done, we'll have at least a stub class, a skeleton class, a server class, and possibly an implementation class for each interface. By deriving all of these from an abstract base class, the IDL compiler automatically creates a consistency among all of these different components, which really helps when it comes time to code them up.

The C++ mapping results in portable C++ code on both the client and object implementation sides. However, if you ever compare the .h files produced by the same IDL from two different C++ IDL compilers, you'll find that they surely differ, possibly quite a bit in places. That's because the C++ mapping specification was deliberately written in a way that leaves flexibility to implementors to allow them to accommodate different C++ compilers, for instance, or derive from their own base class and have every object inherit functionality useful on their particular systems. However, this does not affect your code, which will port among all of these different compiled IDL stubs (on the client side) and skeletons (on the object side, POA ORBs only) without modification.

7.3.5 Passing and Narrowing an Object Reference

Next, we'll give an example of passing an object reference. The Naming Service (which we'll meet in Chapter 11) has an interface that looks like this:

Object resolve (in Name n);

That is, we pass **resolve** a **Name** (a sequence of **struct**s, each **struct** made up of two **strings** and defined in the Naming Service; for details, see Chapter 11) and it returns us an object reference—literally, since it is always of type **Object**. If the name of our instance was `MyInstance`, and it was of type `MyType`, the call would look like this:

```
// C++
// Declare object references:
    NameService_var   NameSvc;
    Object_ptr        MyObjPtr;
    MyType_ptr        MyInstancePtr;

// We won't show it, but we use "resolve_initial_references"
// to retrieve the object reference for the name service so
// now we can invoke . . .

    MyObjPtr = NameSvc->resolve ( MyInstanceName );

// now we have our MyInstance object reference
// bound to MyObjPtr
```

Why did we retrieve `MyObj` as a reference of type `Object` even though it's actually an instance of `MyType`? Because the Name Service operation **resolve** is defined to return a reference of type `Object`—if it didn't, we would be restricted in the types of object references we could use with it. However, C++ enforces type safety and will not allow us to invoke `MyType`'s operations on a reference of type `Object`, so we will have to convert- (that is, `narrow`-) this object reference to its true type. To do this, we invoke (no surprise here) the operation `narrow`, like this:

```
MyInstancePtr   =  MyType::_narrow ( MyObjPtr );
If (MyInstancePtr == NULL )   {
     //  code to print an error message and recover or abort
}
//  code continues . . .
```

The implementation of operation `MyType::_narrow` was created by the ORB and IDL compiler, and the object reference `MyObj` is the input parameter. If the object reference is the same type as, or a subtype of, type `MyType`, then the operation creates and returns an object reference `_ptr` of that type, and if it's not, it returns the `nil` object reference. This enforces type safety: If the `narrow` succeeds, then we are allowed to perform `MyType`'s operations on that object; if it doesn't, then we're not. This way, the language and CORBA work together to keep programs from invoking operations on objects that aren't expecting them. If you're thinking about a small CORBA project with a few programmers and a couple of types, totaling a few hundred lines of code, then this will seem like overkill. However, if you're talking about 15,000 programmers, thousands of types, millions of instances, thousands of nodes, and perhaps some with code burned into ROM and executing as embedded systems, it will be a big comfort to the project manager to know that there's more than programmer code review enforcing type safety.

7.3.6 Mapping for Inheritance

We'll use this three-line example to illustrate inheritance. It inherits from example1 (Section 7.3.3), like this:

```
#include "example1.idl"
interface example3:example1 {
      void op3 (in long arg3, out long arg4);
}
```

which we can use in C++ as follows:

```
// C++
// Declare object reference:
example3_var    myex3;
CORBA::long     mylongin, mylongout;

// code to retrieve a reference to an
// example3 object and bind it to myex3  . . .

// now we can invoke not only . . .

void = myex3->op3 ( mylongin, mylongout );

// but also, through inheritance,

mylongout = myex3->op1 ( mylongin );
```

7.3.7 Mapping for Attributes

Each read-write attribute maps to a pair of overloaded C++ functions, one to **set** the attribute's value and the other to **get** it. The **set** function takes a parameter with the same type as the attribute, while the **get** function takes no parameters but returns the same type as the attribute. If your attribute is declared read-only in its IDL, the compiler generates only the **get** function.

So, our attribute example

```
interface example4 {
      attribute float radius
}
```

would be used like this:

```
// C++
// Declare object reference:
    example4_var    myex4;
    CORBA::float    myfloatout;

// code to retrieve a reference to an
// example4 object and bind it to myex4  . . .

// set:
    example4->radius(3.14159);

// get:
    myfloatout = example4->radius();
```

7.3.8 Mapping and Handling Exceptions

We'll use the IDL from the example later in this book to illustrate basic exception handling. The IDL defines the exception **BarcodeNotFound** in module **AStore**:

module AStore {

   ...

   exception BarcodeNotFound {POS:: Barcode item;};

   ...

}

It's actually used in the **depot** module, in the following C++ code:

```
// various declarations not shown . . .
  item_info = new AStore::ItemInfo;
  if ( m_items.locate(item, *item_info) == 0)
  {
      throw AStore::BarcodeNotFound(item);
  }
}
```

m_items.locate returns a boolean indicating its success: if it returns 0 (zero) then it failed, and we pass this information back to our client by throwing the BarcodeNot-Found exception here in our object, with the item information as a parameter. This is all we have to do here to throw an exception that can be caught in the calling client.

This is about as simple as it gets, at least for the programmer. Behind the scenes, the exception maps to a C++ class defined in the **CORBA** module and is a variable-length **struct** that self-manages its storage. Declarations are in the .h file, so you don't have to declare the exception type in your code.

Recall that we have defined both systems exceptions and user exceptions in CORBA. There is a base **Exception** class, defined in the **CORBA** module. The **SystemException** and **UserException** classes both derive from this, and each specific system exception derives from **SystemException**. This hierarchy allows any exception to be caught simply by catching the **Exception** type.

```
//C++
try
  . . .
 catch (const Exception &exc)
  . . .
```

This approach looks simple so far, but you have to narrow to either **UserException** or **SystemException**. Alternatively, all user exceptions can be caught by catching the **UserException** type, and all system exceptions by catching the **SystemException** type.

```
//C++
try
  . . .
 catch (const UserException &ue)   . . .
```

7.4 Valuetypes

valuetypes are something new introduced in CORBA 2.3, as we pointed out in Chapter 3 where we presented them in the context of IDL and the CORBA architecture. One fundamental new characteristic is that they combine state and interface in a way no other IDL type does. Most IDL types—the primitive and constructed types that we've already discussed—are pure state. In contrast, the interface type is pure interface. And even though the object reference refers to an object with both state and interface, the language mapping doesn't have to deal with it. You'll see the consequences when you work with **valuetype**s in C++, since the mapping is more restrictive than it is for anything else.

The lifetimes of **valuetype**s are managed by reference counting. Unlike the reference counting for CORBA object references that is implemented on a remote ORB and deletes only the reference, and not the object, when the count reaches zero, the reference counting for **valuetype**s is implemented by the object itself. When the count reaches zero, the object itself is deleted. As you already suspected, a _var type automates all of this for you.

7.4.1 Using a Valuetype

Here's an example of a valuetype in IDL:

```
valuetype MyValueTypeExample {
    private unsigned long aLong;
    public boolean isMonday;
    void op1(in string val);
    public MyValueTypeExample myValType; // recursive definitions allowed
    factory init(in string defaultValue); //like a ctor
};
```

This valuetype maps to a number of C++ classes: First, the IDL compiler creates a C++ abstract base class with the same name as the **valuetype**. It has pure virtual accessor and modifier functions corresponding to the state members of the valuetype, and pure virtual functions corresponding to the operations of the valuetype:

```
class MyValueTypeExample : virtual public ::CORBA::ValueBase {

public:
    virtual  ::CORBA::Boolean   isMonday () const=0;
    virtual  void isMonday (::CORBA::Boolean _member) =0;
    virtual  ::MyValueTypeExample_ptr    myValType()
      const=0;
    virtual  void   myValType(
      ::MyValueTypeExample_ptr _member)=0;
    virtual  ::CORBA::Void op1(const char* val)=0;

    static MyValueTypeExample* _narrow
      (::CORBA::ValueBase *);

protected:
    virtual  ::CORBA::ULong aLong () const=0;
    virtual  void aLong (::CORBA::ULong _member) =0;

private:
    void   operator=(const MyValueTypeExample&);
      // private and unimplemented
};   // end of ::MyValueTypeExample
```

The mapping for valuetype data members follows the same rules as the C++ mapping for unions, except that the accessor and modifiers are pure virtual. Public state members are mapped to public pure virtual accessor and modifier functions of the C++ valuetype base class, and private state members are mapped to protected pure virtual accessor and modifier functions (so that derived concrete classes may access them).

The code that follows is just an example; vendors are allowed to differ in their implementations as long as they support the methods in the abstract base class My ValueTypeExample:

```
class OBV_MyValueTypeExample : virtual public MyValueTypeExample {

private:
    // states
    ::CORBA::ULong _aLong_;
    ::CORBA::Boolean _isMonday_;
    ::MyValueTypeExample_StructElem _myValType_;

public:
    virtual ::CORBA::Boolean isMonday () const;
    virtual void isMonday (::CORBA::Boolean _member) ;
    virtual ::MyValueTypeExample_ptr myValType() const;
    virtual void myValType(::MyValueTypeExample_ptr _member);

protected:
    virtual ::CORBA::ULong aLong () const;
    virtual void aLong (::CORBA::ULong _member) ;
```

```
protected:
    /* constructor */
    OBV_MyValueTypeExample();
    /* constructor */
    OBV_MyValueTypeExample(::CORBA::ULong _m_aLong, ::CORBA::Boolean
        _m_isMonday, ::MyValueTypeExample_ptr _m_myValType) ;
    /* destructor */
    virtual ~OBV_MyValueTypeExample();
private:
    void operator=(const OBV_MyValueTypeExample&);
}; // end of OBV_MyValueTypeExample
```

You subclass OBV_MyValueTypeExample to get a class that you fill in with your implementation of the virtual functions for the operations of the valuetype. OBV_MyValueTypeExample implements the state accessors and modifiers, so you do not need to reimplement them, although you may override them if you wish. For example, you could do this:

```
class MyValueTypeExampleImpl:
  virtual public OBV_MyValueTypeExample,
  virtual public ::CORBA:DefaultValueRefCountBase {
    // implement the operation op1
    void op1(const char *val){
        printf("op1: %s\n", val);
    }

    // over-ride the state setter for isMonday so that we
    // print a message whenever it's called.
    void isMonday(CORBA::Boolean isIt){
        printf("now calling isMonday %d\n", isIt);
        // parent call
        OBV_MyValueTypeExample::isMonday(isIt);
    }
};
```

The CORBA::DefaultValueRefCountBase is a mix-in class that supports simple reference counting for valuetype instances. This class will either be generated by your IDL compiler or available in your ORB library.

In C++, all factory <identifier> initializers declared for a **valuetype** map to pure virtual functions on a separate abstract C++ factory class. The class is named by appending "_init" to the name of the value type (e.g., type MyValueTypeExample has a factory class named MyValueTypeExample_init).

Here's the factory class for our example, as generated by the IDL compiler:

```
class  MyValueTypeExample_init:
  public ::CORBA::ValueFactoryBase {
  public:
    static MyValueTypeExample_init*
      _narrow(::CORBA::ValueFactoryBase *vf);

    virtual  MyValueTypeExample* init(const char*
      defaultValue)=0;
```

```
  protected:
    MyValueTypeExample_init();
};
```

You also have to subclass from `MyValueTypeExample_init` to provide a factory for the value. For example:

```
class  MyValueTypeExampleFactory:
  virtual public MyValueTypeExample_init{
  public:
    virtual  MyValueTypeExample* init(const char*
      defaultValue){
        MyValueTypeExample *newObj =
          new MyValueTypeExampleImpl();
        newObj->op1(defaultValue);
        return newObj;
    }
  private:
      virtual CORBA::ValueBase* create_for_unmarshal(){
        return new MyValueTypeExampleImpl();
      }
};
```

You register this factory with the ORB using the `register_value_factory()` method, passing in a RepositoryID and a factory instance as parameters. Before it unmarshals a new **valuetype**'s state, the ORB will locate the factory and call the `create_for_unmarshal()` method to create an instance of the **valuetype**. There is also a `lookup_value_factory()` method on the ORB that you can use to locate a value factory. Once it's located, you can call its factory methods to create your own instance of the valuetype.

7.4.2 Using a Valuebox

A valuebox is a shorthand that defines a **valuetype** with a single public state member. One advantage of using a valuebox is that you can pass along a NULL for the value, as expected by Java invocations. For example, you can pass a NULL in a string valuebox (or, if you wanted to do the extra work, in a string **valuetype**), but you can not pass a NULL in a CORBA::string.

If you are using a valuebox of **string**s, or **wstring**s, you will be interested in two types predefined in the CORBA module:

```
module CORBA {
    valuetype StringValue string;
    valuetype WStringValue wstring;
};
```

Here is the C++ mapping for `CORBA::StringValue`. The mapping for `CORBA::WStringValue` is similar:

```
namespace CORBA {
```

```
class  StringValue: virtual public ::CORBA::DefaultValueRefCountBase {

private:
    // state. Implemention may differ for ORB vendors
    char * _value_;
public:
    StringValue();
    StringValue(const StringValue& val);
    StringValue(char* str);
    StringValue(const char* str);
    StringValue(::CORBA::String_var& var);
    StringValue& operator=(char* str);
    StringValue& operator=(const char* str);
    StringValue& operator=(const ::CORBA::String_var& str);
    const char* _value() const;
    void _value( char* _member) ;
    void _value (const char* _member) ;
    void _value( const ::CORBA::String_var& _member);
    const char* _boxed_in()const;
    char*& _boxed_inout();
    char*& _boxed_out();
    char&operator[](::CORBA::ULong index);
    char operator[](::CORBA::ULong index)const;

    static StringValue* _narrow (::CORBA::ValueBase *);

protected:
    ~StringValue();
private:
    void operator=(const StringValue&);
}; // end of ::StringValue

};
```

This finishes our coverage of C++. In the next chapter we'll do Java, and then COBOL, before we proceed to the CORBAservices and CORBAfacilities.

Language Mappings, Part 2: Java

8.1 Java Mapping Basics

In this chapter, we look at the OMG IDL-to-Java language mapping. The Java language mapping is a little different than that of other languages, but it is not difficult to understand. Each IDL interface is mapped to several Java classes (and, hence, several files, because of the way Java classes are stored). In the latest versions of the mapping from OMG, virtually all of the filenames are mandated by the specification (in earlier versions, some names were not), and the names differ for BOA and POA ORBs. For example, the interface

```
interface MyExampleInterface {
    void op1(in string val);
};
```

would produce the following files after being translated by an IDL-to-Java compiler for a POA ORB:

```
MyExampleInterface.java
MyExampleInterfaceHolder.java
MyExampleInterfaceHelper.java
MyExampleInterfaceOperations.java
_MyExampleInterfaceStub.java
MyExampleInterfacePOA.java
```

The `MyExampleInterfaceOperations.java` file contains the methods supported by the interface.

`MyExampleInterface.java` inherits from `MyExampleInterfaceOperations.java`, and contains an interface called `MyExampleInterface` that supports the operation(s) defined in the IDL. The distinction between these last two interfaces is that `MyExampleInterface.java` is a `CORBA::Object`, while the ...`Operations.java` interface is not. This makes a difference for the POA, where the servants inherit from the `MyExampleInterfaceOperations`, while the object references inherit from `MyExampleInterface.java`. There will be a file named `_MyExampleInterfaceImplBase.java` for non-POA implementations, replacing the one named `MyExampleInterfacePOA.java`, which is for POA implementations only.

In CORBA 2.3, the name for the portable stub is `_MyExampleInterfaceStub.java`. The stub is responsible for marshaling and demarshaling on the client side, regardless of whether the target object is local or remote. In older versions of the mapping (which you may still be using in your work today), there were two stubs—one for local and the other for remote—but the new specification reduces this number to one.

`MyExampleInterfacePOA.java` is the POA skeleton that implements, among other things, `MyExampleInterfaceOperations`. It is responsible for marshaling and demarshaling on the server side, and provides a framework from which you derive your implementation classes. More specifically, `MyExampleInterfacePOA.java` extends `org.omg.PortableServer.Servant` and implements both `org.omg.CORBA.portable.InvokeHandler` and `MyExampleInterfaceOperations`.

The corresponding file for BOA ORBs is `_MyExampleInterfaceImplBase.java`, which is responsible for the marshaling and demarshaling on the server side, and provides the framework from which to derive the implementation classes.

We'll explain `Holder` and `Helper` classes later in the chapter.

Each IDL compiler should have an output similar to the one we just described. The Java language mapping does not provide much flexibility on this, so for applications defining many interfaces, you can expect many files to be generated.

8.1.1 Names

Every IDL name you specify in the IDL file (interface name, operation name, parameter name, etc.) will be directly mapped to Java without any modifications. If there is a conflict (e.g., a reserved word was used), then an underscore (_) will be added to the beginning of the name. Also, if you end a Java interface name with either "Helper" or "Holder", its generated class names will start with an underscore to avoid conflict with compiler-generated `Helper` and `Holder` class names. One more thing: Names that end with "Operations" or "Package" start with an underscore as well.

8.1.1.1 Reserved Names

The IDL mapping will produce several names from a single type. The reserved names are as follows:

- The Java class `<type>Helper`, where `<type>` is the name of an IDL-defined type.

- The Java class `<type>Holder`, where `<type>` is the name of an IDL-defined type (except where indicated in this chapter).

- The Java classes `<basicJavaType>Holder`, where `<basicJavaType>` is one of the primitive IDL types such as **string**, **short**, **float**, etc. The name will begin with a capital letter; e.g., the IDL **string** type will become Holder. These types will be in the package `org.omg.CORBA.*`.

- The Java classes `<interface>Operations`, `<interface>POA`, and (optionally) `<interface>POAtie`, where `<interface>` is the name of an IDL interface type.

- The nested scope Java package name `<interface>Package`.

- The keywords in the Java language.

- Operation or attribute declarations that collide with the methods declared in `java.lang.Object`.

8.1.2 Modules

An IDL module is simply mapped to a Java package. Every declaration within the module is also contained within the Java package. If no module is specified, then the types live in the global (unnamed) Java package.

8.1.3 Basic Types

The following table shows the mapping of IDL primitive types to Java types. Note that you (the programmer) are responsible for ensuring that large unsigned IDL type values

IDL TYPE	JAVA TYPE
boolean	boolean
char	char
wchar	char
octet	byte
string	java.lang.String
wstring	java.lang.String
short/unsigned short	short
long/unsigned long	int
long long/unsigned long long	long
float	float
Double	double
Fixed	java.math.BigDecimal

are handled correctly as negative integers in Java. This is because there is a mismatch between the unsigned IDL types and the signed Java types. For example, an unsigned IDL **short** corresponds to a primitive Java `short`. The highest value an unsigned IDL **short** can hold is 65536, which cannot be represented properly in Java as a `short` (maximum value of 32767).

NOTE: The long double IDL primitive type is not yet supported in Java.

8.1.4 The `null` Value

The Java `null` value can only be used to represent null object references. This is especially important to remember when using strings and arrays. Although in Java a `string` is an object, it is a primitive type in IDL and there is no wire format in GIOP for a null string. There is a way out, however: You can use a **string** valuebox; **valuetype**s are a recent IDL addition, and treat nulls consistently with Java usage. Arrays must be initialized to their declared size, and the elements of the array must be initialized to the correct value of the underlying type.

8.1.5 `Holder` Classes

The `Holder` classes mentioned in Section 8.1.1 are used for **out** and **inout** IDL operation parameters. `Holder` classes exist for all primitive Java types (in the `org.omg.CORBA` package) and for all named user-defined types except those that are defined by **typedef**s.

Each `Holder` class has two constructors and a public member variable. The first constructor is used to build a new instance from another instance (similar to a copy constructor), and the second is the default constructor (will initialize the value to a default value). The public member variable is always named value and you can get/set the value of the `Holder` variable class with it.

The memory management subsection of this chapter will also detail other uses of `Holder` classes.

8.1.6 `Helper` Classes

The generated `Helper` classes contain a number of static methods that are used to manipulate the type. The most important methods are the any insert and extract methods for that type, getting the RepositoryID, getting the typecode, and reading and writing the type from and to a stream.

Helper classes generated from an IDL interface also contain a static method called `narrow` that performs a safe down-casting (i.e., from `org.omg.CORBA.Object` to the interface type).

8.1.7 Constants

The mapping of IDL constants depends on the scope in which they appear. If the constant appears within an interface, it is mapped as a `public static final` field in the corresponding Java interface. If the constant does not appear within an interface, it is mapped as a `public interface` with the same name as the constant and will contain a `public static final` field named value. The value field will hold the constant's value.

8.1.8 Enumerations

An **enum** is mapped to a class in Java that contains one `value` method, two static data members per label, an integer conversion method, and a private constructor. One of the static member variables will have the same name as the label, and the other will have an underscore (_) added to the beginning of the name (this one is intended to be used with `switch` statements). The `value` method will return the integer value. The values are sequentially assigned, beginning with 0.

A Holder class is also generated for an **enum**.

8.1.9 Structures

The IDL **struct** type is mapped to a `final` class in Java. The Java class will have public member variables with the same name (and type) as the **struct** fields. There are also two constructors: the default constructor, and one to initialize each field to a nondefault value. A `Holder` class is also generated for each IDL **struct**.

8.1.10 Unions

An IDL **union** is also mapped to a `final` class. It has a default constructor, an accessor method for the discriminator (`discriminator()`), an accessor method for each branch, a modifier method for each branch, a modifier method for each branch that has more than one case label, and a default modifier method if needed.

The branch accessor and modifier methods are overloaded and named after the branch. If there is more than one case label corresponding to a branch, the simple modifier method for that branch sets the discriminant to the value of the first `case` label. An extra modifier method that takes an explicit discriminator parameter is also generated.

If the branch corresponds to the `default` case label, then the modifier method sets the discriminant to a value that does not match other case labels. A default modifier method (`_default()`) is created if there is no explicit default case label, and the set of case labels does not completely cover the possible values of the discriminant. The discriminant will be initialized to a value that does not match any other case labels. The value of the union is left uninitialized, but you must initialize it before you use it.

A Holder class is also generated for a **union**.

8.1.11 Sequences

Not surprisingly, an IDL **sequence** is mapped to a Java `array`. Bounds checking is always done on bounded sequences. A `Holder` class for the **sequence** is also generated.

8.1.12 Arrays

An IDL **array** is mapped the same way as a bounded IDL sequence. Bounds checking is always done. The length of the `array` can be made available in Java by bounding the array with an IDL constant, which will be mapped following the rules for constants (Section 8.1.7). A `Holder` class is also generated for the **array**.

8.1.13 Anys

The IDL **any** type maps to the `org.omg.CORBA.Any` Java class. Insertion and extraction operations differ depending on whether the contents are an IDL primitive type or not: Nonprimitive types are inserted into an **any** via the static methods provided in the `<type>Helper.java` class.

This isn't difficult. For example, to insert the CORBA object reference for an instance of `MyExampleInterface` into an any requires only the single line of code:

```
MyExampleInterfaceHelper.insert(any, obj);
      // obj is an instance of the interface
```

and to extract from the any,

```
obj = MyExampleInterfaceHelper.extract(any);
```

8.1.14 Exceptions

exceptions in IDL are mapped to a Java class that has instance variables for the fields of the exception. There will always be a default constructor, and there will be a constructor that allows you to initialize each field of the exception.

CORBA system **exception**s (e.g., `org.omg.CORBA.SystemException`) are (indirect) subclasses of `java.lang.RuntimeException`. User-defined **exception**s are (indirect) subclasses of `java.lang.Exception`.

User-defined **exception**s are final Java classes that extend `org.omg.CORBA.UserException` and are otherwise mapped just like an IDL struct. `Helper` and `Holder` classes are also generated.

8.2 Interfaces

An IDL **interface** maps to a Java `public interface`. A `Helper` (Section 8.1.6) is also generated. Each operation in the IDL interface maps to a method in the generated Java interface. **attribute**s declared within an **interface** map to a pair of accessor and modifier methods except for **readonly attribute**s, which have no modifier method. The accessor and modifier methods do *not* have `get` or `set` as a prefix. The name of the method(s) is/are the same as the IDL **attribute** name.

Interface inheritance is equivalently generated in Java: Multiple inheritance in IDL, where it occurs, maps to multiple inheritance of Java *interfaces*. However, since Java does not support multiple inheritance of implementation, you have to implement some other way, and there are basically two choices:

- You can implement all the methods of all the parent interfaces explicitly in the new class.

- You can delegate some of the methods.

If an interface has no supertype, then its Java interface has to extend `org.omg.CORBA.Object`.

A `Holder` class is also generated for the interface.

Although IDL allows type declarations nested within interfaces, Java does not permit classes to be nested within interfaces. The mapping for nested IDL types is to have a scope package generated to contain the mapped Java class declarations. The scope package name is constructed by adding the word "Package" at the end of the IDL type name. For example, if we have the following IDL:

```
interface MyInterface {
    exception MyException() {};
};
```

then the `MyException` type would live in the package `MyInterfacePackage`.

8.2.1 Parameter Passing Modes

There are three types of parameter passing modes in IDL: **in**, **out**, and **inout**. The most frequently used is the **in** parameter mode, which implements a call-by-value semantic (for the particular argument, not for the object as a whole). The return value of an operation is an **out** parameter by default. If an IDL parameter has mode **out**, then call-by-result is implied. The **inout** mode has both call-by-value and call-by-result semantics.

For example, consider the following IDL:

```
interface I {
    string get_SSN(in long authKey, inout string lastname, out short status);
};
```

For the purpose of this example, please ignore the fact that this may not represent good design(!). Since Java does not implement call-by-result semantics, the `Holder` classes come into play. The client of the operation that uses **in** and/or **inout** parameters creates an instance of the appropriate `Holder` class (e.g., in the case of a string it would be `org.omg.CORBA.StringHolder`) and passes it as the value of the **in** or **inout** parameter. The contents of the `Holder` instance (but not the instance itself) are modified by the operation implementation and can be used by the client.

There are a few rules that must be followed when passing parameters:

- Objects passed as IDL **in** parameters are created by and owned by the caller. The operation implementation (callee) must not modify the parameters, nor can it retain a reference to the parameter.

- Objects passed as IDL **out** parameters or return parameters are created by and owned originally by the callee. The ownership of these objects transfers to the caller upon completion of the invocation. The callee must not retain a reference to such objects beyond the duration of the call.

- Objects passed as IDL **inout** parameters combine both of the preceding semantics.

For **valuetype**s, the rules are slightly different:

- For in **valuetype**s, the caller creates the **valuetype**, but a copy is passed to the callee. The callee may modify or retain reference to the copy beyond the duration of the call.

- For **out** or **return** parameters, the callee creates a copy and transfers ownership to the caller. The callee must not retain a reference to the copy beyond the duration of the call. The callee still owns the original instance, of course.

- For **inout**, the **in valuetype** follows the **in** semantics and rules, and the **out valuetype** follows the **out** semantics and rules.

The preceding rules do not apply to Java primitive and immutable types (e.g., int, java.lang.String, double, etc.).

8.2.2 Context Parameters

If the IDL operation specifies a Context to be propagated with the operation, then an org.omg.CORBA.Context input parameter is added to the list of parameters to the Java interface method.

8.3 valuetypes (Object-by-Value)

An IDL **valuetype** is mapped to a public Java class of the same name. The class contains instance variables that correspond to the fields in the state definition in the IDL definition. Only private and public fields are supported in IDL. The public fields are mapped to public member variables, and private fields are mapped to default access instance variables (that is, package-level access). The operations defined in the IDL **valuetype** are correspondingly mapped to Java methods in the generated class. There is also a Java factory interface that declares methods used to create instances of the **valuetype**. Each factory <ident> declaration in IDL corresponds to a method of the same name in the factory interface.

For example, the Java language mapping for the following **valuetype** (which we've already seen in the previous chapter on C++):

```
valuetype MyValueTypeExample {
    private unsigned long aLong;
    public boolean isMonday;
    void op1(in string val);           // a method does not use "public" or "private"
    public MyValueTypeExample myValType; // recursive definitions allowed
    factory init(in string defaultValue);
};
```

is as follows:

```
abstract public class MyValueTypeExample implements
org.omg.CORBA.portable.StreamableValue
{
    int aLong;  // IDL unsigned long mapped to Java int.
            // Also note the default "package" protection
            // for private state members
    public boolean isMonday ;
    public MyValueTypeExample myValType; // Public -
```

```
        abstract public void op1 (String val) ;

          /* other emitted methods to help with marshaling/demarshaling*/

    };
```

```
    public interface MyValueTypeExampleFactory extends
    org.omg.CORBA.portable.ValueFactory {
        MyValueTypeExample init(String defaultValue);
    }
```

You extend the abstract base class to implement the **valuetype**:

```
    public class MyValueTypeExampleImpl extends MyValueTypeExample {

        public void op1(String val){
            /* user code */
        }
    };
```

You also have to provide a concrete factory:

```
    class MyValueTypeExampleDefaultFactory implements
    MyValueTypeExampleFactory {
        public MyValueTypeExample init(String val){
            /* just an example */
            MyValueTypeExample obj = new MyValueTypeExample();
            obj.op1(val);
            return obj;
        }
    };
```

A Java class supporting a **valuetype** must implement the `java.io.Serializable` interface. A **valuetype** that supports an IDL **interface** must use the TIE mechanism for its implementation.

`Holder` and `Helper` classes are also generated for the valuetype.

If you compare this to the C++ mapping for **valuetype**s, you will notice that the two are very similar. The two major differences are:

- C++ does not have introspection, so you have to register value factories. For Java, there is a set of rules that the ORB uses to find the value factory.

- The wire format for Java **valuetype**s may contain a pointer to the actual URL location of where the **valuetype** implementation is stored. This allows an ORB with missing Java **valuetype** implementations to automatically download the class files on the fly. Of course, you can't do this in C++.

8.4 Reverse Mapping: Java-to-IDL

There are many reasons why Java and CORBA work well together:

- Java, like CORBA, is object-oriented.

- Java has a distribution facility, RMI, with parallels to CORBA.

- Both work well over the Internet as well as over intranets.

On the other hand, each has things that the other lacks:

- CORBA is multilanguage, with all languages sharing the common protocol IIOP, while Java RMI is a single-language environment.

- Many programmers know Java RMI, but not CORBA and IDL, presumably just because they learned it first. (We're not going to say that CORBA interfaces are difficult to program; in fact, we think they're rather elegant, not to mention well-modeled and powerful.)

The reverse Java-to-IDL language mapping, termed RMI/IDL, lets Java programmers create servers that can be accessed by CORBA clients written in any programming language that has an IDL mapping, without having to learn IDL or CORBA themselves (or any of those other languages—horrors!). It also lets CORBA programmers access these Java servers through IDL interfaces using the standard IIOP protocol.

The Enterprise JavaBeans (EJB) specification is written on top of RMI/IDL. This will ensure that every EJB can communicate via IIOP, and that EJB servers will be accessible from any CORBA client. If you've studied both the EJB and RMI/IDL specifications, you may have noticed that the RMI/IDL type restrictions are built into EJB.

How should you use RMI/IDL in your enterprise? If you're thinking about developing servers in Java, it will be a lot easier to develop EJBs instead of building an infrastructure yourself. If you develop EJBs, and you purchase a CORBA/IIOP EJB container, you'll get the benefits of CORBA without worrying about even the slight restrictions in RMI/IDL. However, if you don't want to develop EJBs, or you don't have (and your company won't buy) an EJB container, and you'd rather develop in pure Java than in Java and CORBA, you should develop every server object that you build in the RMI/IDL subset. This costs you almost nothing at development time compared to working in pure Java RMI, and confers CORBA interoperability on your deployed servers. If your programming staff is skilled in Java but not CORBA, this path may be the one to take.

8.4.1 Mapping Details

Java programmers have to honor a few restrictions when they program their RMI servers to work over RMI/IDL and IIOP. CORBA programmers will discover that the IDL interfaces of these servers are somewhat restricted; for example, they will never include an **inout** or **out** parameter (all output comes back in the return value), or an **enum**. This is because Java doesn't allow **inout** or **out** parameters, and doesn't have an **enum**, so they never occur. Interfaces may have IDL **attribute**s, however, cleverly constructed by the reverse compiler from a pair of set and get invocations. Because RMI/IDL is a strict subset of Java RMI, it neither creates an additional distributed programming dialect nor adds an additional incompatible distributed environment.

The RMI/IDL Specification defines five "conforming" Java types, whose values may be transmitted across an RMI/IDL interface. They are an inclusive bunch, comprising:

- **All of the Java primitive types.** These are void, boolean, byte, char, short, int, long, float, and double.

- **A conforming remote interface.** Conforming remote interfaces must inherit from java.rmi.Remote (although this may be indirect). They must throw java.rmi.RemoteException or superclasses of it; method exceptions must conform to exception restrictions (see last bullet in this list). At runtime, only conforming types may be passed as arguments or results. In addition, there are some fairly evident (and not serious) restrictions on method names, constant definitions, and method and constant names.

- **A conforming valuetype.** Conforming valuetypes must implement java.io.Serializable, and not implement java.rmi.Remote. They may implement java.io.Externalizable. java.lang.String is a conforming RMI/IDL valuetype, but is handled specially in the mapping (although we won't give details here).

- **An array of conforming RMI/IDL types.** Arrays of conforming types are conforming types—'nuff said.

- **A conforming exception type.** Conforming RMI/IDL exceptions must inherit from java.lang.Exception, which extends java.lang.Throwable, which implements java.io.Serializable. Therefore, these exceptions do not have to implement java.io.Serializable directly since it's already done. Otherwise, all **valuetype** requirements apply.

If you've restricted your Java server interface and arguments to these types, and you're using a Java ORB, you can use your RMI compiler to get RMI-style bindings that talk to the Java ORB. If you use this method to access RMI/IDL, you'll never see any CORBA stuff even though the ORBs are talking IIOP underneath the covers.

Or, you can run your Java code through a reverse compiler to emit the IDL equivalent to your Java RMI interface, and from the IDL generate bindings that you can use in either Java or any other language to build CORBA clients that can access this Java object. Remember that any Serializable must have a corresponding implementation in the language of the binding. (This could be a big deal if you pass around lots of Serializable, which are mapped into **valuetype**s.) You have to use this method to access the object from nonJava clients, but you can use it for Java clients as well as long as the client and server are separated. (The RMI/IDL bindings conflict with the straight RMI bindings, and get in each other's way unless you have this separation.)

8.4.2 Writing and Calling an RMI/IDL Java Object

For each RMI/IDL interface, there is a stub class invoked by the client that extends javax.rmi.CORBA.Stub and supports stub methods for all of its remote methods.

For the server, there is a Tie class that implements javax.rmi.CORBA.Tie and is called by the ORB with the incoming call. In addition, Java provides a class javax.rmi.PortableRemoteObject that your implementation objects may inherit from, unless you want to use the exportObject method directly to register them as server objects.

Here's an example. Let's use this Java interface, which conforms to the requirements we just reviewed:

```
public interface MyInterface  extends java.rmi.Remote{
    int op(int param) throws java.rmi.RemoteException;
};
```

with this Java implementation, which also conforms to the RMI/IDL requirements:

```
public class MyInterfaceImpl extends javax.rmi.PortableRemoteObject
  implements MyInterface {
    MyInterfaceImpl() throws java.rmi.RemoteException{
    }

    public int op(int param) throws java.rmi.RemoteException{
        return param *2;
    }
};
```

First, you'll need to produce the .class files for the above, via

```
javac MyInterface.java
javac MyInterfaceImpl.java
```

Then you'll need to run the RMI compiler that came with your ORB to generate a special RMI stub for `MyInterface`, and a special RMI tie for `MyInterfaceImpl`. The stub is used by the client to make IIOP calls to the server. Its name is something like `MyInterface_Stub.java`. The Tie is used on the server side by the Java ORB to dispatch to your implementation. Its name might be `MyInterfaceImpl_Tie.java`.

On the server side, you'll have to create an instance of `MyInterfaceImpl`, and export its object reference to the client. We'll show an example using JNDI, but you'll want to register the name in your enterprise's CORBA Naming Service if you're planning to use cross-language invocations:

```
public class MyServer {
    public static void main(String args[]){
        try {
            /* ORB specific initialization */
            ...

            /* create an instance of MyInterfaceIMpl */
            MyInterfaceImpl impl = new MyInterfaceImpl();

            /* bind it to a naming context */
            javax.naming.InitialContext ctxt = new
                    javax.naming.InitialContext();
            ctxt.rebind("MyInterfaceServer", impl);
            ...
        }
        catch(Exception e){
            System.out.println("got exception " + e);
        }
    }
}
```

The Java client can use JNDI to locate the object that was exported:

```
public class MyClient {
    public static void main(String args[]){
        try {
            /* ORB specific initialization */
            ...

            /* lookup up the server object from a naming context */
            javax.naming.InitialContext ctxt = new
                    javax.naming.InitialContext();
            java.lang.Object obj = ctxt.lookup("MyInterfaceServer");

            // Use the RMI/IIOP version of narrow
            MyInterface myobj =
                    (MyInterface)javax.rmi.PortableRemoteObject.
                narrow(obj, MyInterface.class);

            int result = myobj.op(10); // call to method uses IIOP
            ...
        }
        catch(Exception e){
            System.out.println("got exception " + e);
        }
    }
}
```

Up to this point, no IDL is involved, but the method invocation uses the CORBA protocol IIOP, and the interface is accessible from nonJava CORBA clients. To access `MyInterface` from one of the CORBA languages, run the RMI-to-IDL compiler on `MyInterface`. This generates the following IDL:

```
interface MyInterface {
    long op( in long arg0 );
};
```

You can compile this IDL on any ORB in any programming language it supports, write your client in that language, and make calls on the RMI interface of your Java server using CORBA and IIOP.

In the next chapter, we'll look at our final language mapping: COBOL. Since COBOL is not an object-oriented language, it will look a lot different from the two we've just examined. (No, OMG did not map to OO-COBOL, because it's not used in the legacy COBOL applications that need and use CORBA the most.)

Language Mappings, Part 3: COBOL

9.1 COBOL and CORBA

There are several ways to categorize wrapped legacy applications. For example, we can categorize fine-grained objects as individual GUI elements such as the graphic units that form a pushbutton, and medium-grained objects as anything from an employee in your HR system to a sensor unit or storage tank in a refinery simulation. In this exercise in categorization, if we wrapped a legacy application such as an accounting or HR system with several interfaces and assigned it some object references, we would call it a coarse-grained object. Although the architecture of this system might not be object-oriented in a formal sense, it would certainly provide all the benefits of location, system, platform, and programming-language transparency that other systems do when they use CORBA.

CORBA systems built mostly of medium-grained objects (which, we admit, may vary in size) tend to work well: they don't bog down in millions of calls as can happen when you work with gazillions of fine-grained objects, but they're still flexible enough to model the things in your work environment, one per instance, as we've discussed for sales orders or employees, for example. Designed and programmed by skilled staff, they make the most of both system- and business-level expertise. Why, then, might we advocate building systems that include coarse-grained objects—so coarse, in fact, as to encompass a complete accounting or HR system?

Because your enterprise almost certainly owns, runs, and relies on these systems today, that's why. Most programmers call them "legacy applications," but we prefer to call them "applications that work," and they work even better when you integrate them into your distributed system with CORBA. And, since most of them are written in COBOL, that makes this language a necessity in the distributed architecture of your enterprise.

So, to ensure that you can retain the investment in your legacy applications written in COBOL, the OMG has adopted a COBOL language mapping. When you use this mapping in combination with services such as the Object Transaction service, you will find that it provides the ideal infrastructure for your distributed COBOL applications.

By the way—when you first heard of COBOL support for CORBA, did you assume that it was a reference to object-oriented COBOL? Languages don't have to be OO in order to map to CORBA—in fact, the original CORBA language was C and the mapping had to do some tricks to accommodate it (as we showed in the first edition of this book). And so, to enable enterprises to wrap legacy applications and bring them into today's distributed world, the OMG mapped IDL to standard COBOL—the language of applications that big business relies on.

9.2 COBOL Mapping Fundamentals

You'll notice many differences between the COBOL IDL mapping and the mappings we've just covered for C++ and Java. In part this is because COBOL is not an object-oriented language, but it's also due to the unique way that COBOL works with business problems. Watch for this as we go over details in the rest of the chapter.

9.2.1 The Latest COBOL Language Mapping Revision

As you examine the latest revision of the COBOL language mapping for CORBA, you will discover that it is divided into the following three subsections:

- Mapping of IDL to COBOL
- Dynamic COBOL mapping
- Type-specific COBOL mapping

The first part describes the mapping of IDL types to COBOL, and the other two parts are different mappings for COBOL. Dynamic mapping is an easy-to-use mapping for COBOL that uses a client-side object invocation that maps to the concepts contained within the CORBA Dynamic Invocation Interface (DII), and a server-side COBOL Object Adapter (COA) that maps to the concepts contained within the CORBA Dynamic Skeleton Interface (DSI). Type-specific Mapping is a version of the Portable Object Adapter (POA) for COBOL.

Because there are currently no commercial offerings available for the Type-specific COBOL mapping from any of the ORB vendors, your only implementation choice is the Dynamic COBOL mapping. As a result, we will focus only on Dynamic COBOL mapping in our examples.

9.2.2 Design Goals of the Mapping

Before we get into specific details, you should be familiar with the two principal goals behind the latest revision of the COBOL language mapping to understand why it works the way it does:

- As an application developer, you should be able to use the mapping easily.
- The COBOL syntax that you use should be standard ANSI85 COBOL—no special additions to the COBOL syntax should be used for CORBA support.

Both of these are important principles, so let's take a look at each of them in more detail.

9.2.2.1 Ease of Use

If you had attempted to use the initial COBOL Language mapping for CORBA, you would have discovered that the complexity involved in writing your distributed application was a bit daunting. To make it easier for you to use, the COBOL language mapping for CORBA was revised. It now provides a far simpler Dynamic COBOL Mapping alongside the original Type-specific Mapping. When we get down to the details of it, you will discover that it is basically a collection of routines that you can call using a standard COBOL CALL statement and is very easy for you to use. Bundled together as the Dynamic Mapping, these routines simplify your task of writing a distributed COBOL application by handling a lot of the distribution complexity for you. The result is an interface that reduces the burden you will face when crafting your distributed business solutions.

9.2.2.2 Support Pure ANSI85

What is ANSI85? It's actually a commonly used term that refers to a specific ISO standard for the COBOL language that was defined in 1985. Almost all commercially available implementations of COBOL support the ANSI85 COBOL syntax. Unfortunately, the initial COBOL language mapping defined by the OMG presented the ORB vendors with a difficulty because it included extensions to this standard, such as COBOL Typedefs. Since many of these extensions were not available within the COBOL compilers deployed on the mainframe platforms where COBOL normally resides, you would have found yourself rather restricted. To address this specific issue for you, the latest revision of the mapping of IDL types to COBOL, and the new Dynamic COBOL Mapping, were only allowed to use the standard ANSI85 syntax definition for COBOL.

9.2.3 COBOL Datatypes and IDL

By now, you realize that CORBA requires every IDL language mapping to provide a mapping for every IDL datatype and, of course, COBOL is no exception to this rule. If this were not universally true, and some datatypes were not available in a specific language, then it would not be possible for any of your components written in that language to handle IDL interfaces that used any of the unsupported types. However, the inverse principle does not hold true: While all IDL datatypes must be supported, CORBA does not dictate that every datatype within a specific language has to be supported. For you, this will be a specific concern because many of the older COBOL applications that you will be migrating into a CORBA environment may use some COBOL datatypes that cannot be described using IDL. How can you resolve this?

To solve this problem, you will have to place a COBOL adapter around any legacy COBOL that is being migrated. Inside each adapter you will code, not only the standard ORB initialization calls, but also code to convert any datatypes in the legacy code's interface into types that can be described using IDL. As a result, your IDL interface would actually describe the interface to your COBOL adapter.

In reality, the main job of your COBOL adapter is not the handling of COBOL-specific datatypes, but the definition of a well-designed interface. For example, you may choose to implement a business function within your IDL interface by invoking several CICS transactions. It would be sheer architectural madness for you to take any legacy application and CORBA-enable it directly.

9.2.4 Mapping for Basic Datatypes

In Chapters 3 and 7, we saw that CORBA specifies the precision of all the primitive IDL datatypes, but that C++ compilers (and C compilers as well, it turns out) do not map the corresponding language types to the same precision on every platform. As a result, we needed to **typedef** all the CORBA primitive types in order to guarantee portability.

The situation is handled more easily in COBOL, which is a much more portable language and does not have this vagueness in the representation of its datatypes. As a result, all the basic IDL datatypes map directly to specific COBOL datatypes. So, even though COBOL has no equivalent to a **typedef** or a class, we aren't at any disadvantage at least regarding the definitions of the IDL primitives.

Table 9.1 defines the COBOL mappings for all the primitive IDL datatypes.

There will be some inconsistencies from platform to platform in the binary representation of some types for COBOL. For example, PIC 9(10) BINARY may actually be big-endian on some platforms, and little-endian on others. However, it will always hold a 32-bit integer. The portability of COBOL itself will insulate you from such differences, and the ORB automatically converts any data that you need when it unmarshals your invocation parameters.

9.2.5 Mapping for Other Types

We have covered the mapping for the basic IDL datatypes, but what about the more complicated IDL types? The answer is that they are all mapped to a COBOL group item. For example, **struct** is mapped directly to the equivalent COBOL group item, and **union** maps to a COBOL group item with an initial discriminator and makes use of the REDEFINES clause for the union elements. There is no need to go into this in too much detail within this chapter, because the tutorial examples that you will encounter later on will illustrate this. Nevertheless, a couple of the structured types do deserve a bit of attention because they require the use of accessor functions to manipulate them. These specific types are **string, sequence,** and **any,** so we will now briefly look at each of them to see how they are handled.

Table 9.1 COBOL Mappings for IDL Primitive Types

IDL NAME	COBOL REPRESENTATION
short	PIC S9(05) BINARY
long	PIC S9(10) BINARY
long long	PIC S9(18) BINARY
unsigned short	PIC 9(05) BINARY
unsigned long	PIC 9(10) BINARY
unsigned long long	PIC 9(18) BINARY
float	COMP-1
double	COMP-2
char	PIC X
wchar	PIC G
boolean	PIC 9
octet	PIC X
enum	PIC 9(10) BINARY

9.2.5.1 Strings

The way you handle a **string** depends on whether it is a bounded string (a string with a specified limit, for example **string <8>**) or an unbounded **string** (a **string** without any specific size limit defined).

Bounded **string**s are simple—they are mapped directly to the equivalent COBOL PIC X(n) data item. For example, **string <12>** be mapped directly to COBOL PIC X(12).

However, for unbounded **string**s, this kind of mapping is just not possible because the actual length of the **string** is not known until runtime. So, you have to use string manipulation routines to handle the **string** values dynamically at runtime.

To keep it all simple, unbounded **string**s are mapped to a pointer to an opaque structure that you can manipulate using two accessor functions. These functions are **STRGET,** which extracts the actual string value from the opaque CORBA type and copies it into a COBOL PIC X(n) area within working storage, and **STRPUT** which copies a value out of a COBOL PIC X(n) working storage area and inserts it into the opaque CORBA type.

9.2.5.2 Sequences

Unlike **string**s, you handle both bounded and unbounded **sequence**s in the same way. Both map to a COBOL group item that contains one instance of the type being sequenced, and an opaque pointer to the **sequence** itself. The following example illustrates this:

```
Interface example {
    attribute sequence<float,10> vec10;

};
```

In COBOL, this is mapped to:

```
01 example-vec10.
   03 vec10                  COMPUTATIONAL-1.
   03 vec10-seq              POINTER.
```

Once again, your actual manipulation of the type is performed using a set of accessor functions. To start off, you have both SEQALLOC and SEQFREE to create or destroy the opaque sequence itself. You then have SEQGET and SEQSET to get or set a specific element within your sequence. Finally, you have several other routines, such as SEQLEN, which is used to obtain the actual number of elements currently within a sequence.

Because the COBOL tutorial example in the second half of the book uses an earlier implementation of **sequence** support for COBOL, it is a bit more complicated than this description. In the earlier mapping, the **sequence** type itself was not opaque, so we had to directly manipulate its contents. The memory management was also a lot more complicated. By making it opaque and automating the memory management, it has been made a lot easier for you to use. However, to enable you to run the example with a COBOL language mapping that is commercially available today, the tutorial uses the earlier version.

9.2.5.3 any

You might be tempted to consider the IDL **any** type to be the most difficult type to handle in any language mapping because of its dynamic nature. However, within a COBOL context, it is quite straightforward. Once again, it is mapped to a COBOL group item that contains a pointer to an opaque type that you manipulate using accessor routines. The following example illustrates this:

```
Interface example {
    attribute any temp;
};
```

In COBOL, this is mapped to:

```
01 example-temp                usage is pointer.
```

You can then manipulate this **any** type using accessor functions in the same way you managed **string** and **sequence** types. To handle the actual type code within **any**, your two accessor functions are TYPEGET and TYPESET. To manipulate the actual value of **sequence**, you use ANYSET and ANYGET.

9.2.6 Mapping the IDL Interface

Since we've covered the mapping of all the IDL types to COBOL, it's now time for us to think about how an entire IDL interface is handled within a COBOL context. Each of your IDL interfaces will be mapped to one COBOL copy file. Within this file you will have all the definitions you require, and you can use it in conjunction with the accessor functions to enable your COBOL applications to:

- Become a CORBA object implementation, and

- Access other CORBA object implementations

Within your interface's copy file, the IDL compiler generates data definitions for the arguments of each of your IDL attributes and operations. Since COBOL does not widely support the concept of COBOL **typedef**s, all of your IDL **typedef**s will be unrolled down to their basic types within the generated argument definitions. The following IDL illustrates this concept:

```
interface grid {
    readonly attribute short height;  // height of the grid
    readonly attribute short width;   // width of the grid

    // IDL operations

    // set the element [n,m] of the grid, to value:
    void set(in short n, in short m, in long value);

    // return element [n,m] of the grid:
    long get(in short n, in short m);
};
```

The COBOL mapping will generate a COBOL copy file called grid, which will look like this:

```
*
*  Attribute  : readonly short height
*
   01 GRID-HEIGHT-ARGS.
      03 RESULT          PICTURE S9(05) BINARY.


*
*  Attribute  : readonly short width
*
   01 GRID-WIDTH-ARGS.
      03 RESULT          PICTURE S9(05) BINARY.


*
*  Operation  :  set
*  Parameters :  in short n
*                in short m
*                in long value
*
   01 GRID-SET-ARGS.
      03 N               PICTURE S9(05) BINARY.
      03 M               PICTURE S9(05) BINARY.
      03 IDL-VALUE       PICTURE S9(10) BINARY.
```

```
    *
    *  Operation   :  get
    *  Parameters  :  in short n
    *                 in short m
    *  Returns     :  long
    *
     01 GRID-GET-ARGS.
        03 N                PICTURE S9(05) BINARY.
        03 M                PICTURE S9(05) BINARY.
        03 RESULT           PICTURE S9(05) BINARY.
```

9.2.7 Client-Side Mapping: Calling an Operation

Now that you have seen how IDL interfaces are mapped, you need to understand how you should actually use it. Let's move on now to look at the Dynamic COBOL mapping.

The Dynamic COBOL mapping enables you to invoke operations on a CORBA Object by using the IDL-generated COBOL copy file along with several auxiliary routines. The following sequence of routines will allow you to interface to a CORBA object from your COBOL program:

1. You start off with a call to the ORBSTAT function. This registers a status information block that is required for exception handling. Once registered, you can check the status of specific operation calls that will be stored within it when finished. "Ah, but what about the layout?" you might ask. It does in fact have a standard layout, and may be found within a special CORBA COBOL copy file that contains definitions for several common areas such as this. (We will look at this more closely when we get down to the details of how you should handle exceptions.)

2. The next call you make is to the ORBREG function, which registers the details of the interface you're about to call. The parameter you specify on this call provides the interface details, and is totally opaque to users. It is generated from your IDL interface description within the COBOL.

3. You are now almost ready to invoke an object that supports the interface you specified on the ORBREG call. What you have to do now is to obtain an object reference for one unique instance of an implementation of the registered interface. This is used in conjunction with the ORBEXEC auxiliary function to invoke operations on that specific instance of the interface. All of the ways we've used to obtain object references in other languages—the Naming and Trader Services, destringifying one cut from an e-mail, and so on—work in COBOL too, so just pick one.

4. Use the ORBEXEC function to invoke specific operations (or attributes) within a specific instance of the IDL interface that was previously registered using ORBREG. Your unique object reference for the interface object is the first parameter. The name of the specific operation you are calling is the second parameter, and the parameter area for your operation is the third parameter.

Let's look at an example to clarify this concept. The following segment of COBOL code is based upon the grid IDL that we used earlier when we discussed the mapping of IDL interfaces:

```
*
*       REGISTER STATUS INFORMATION BLOCK
*
        CALL "ORBSTAT"  USING ORB-STATUS-INFORMATION


*
*       REGISTER GRID INTERFACE
*
        CALL "COAREG"   USING GRID-INTERFACE.


*
*       CREATE THE OBJECT REFERENCE FOR THE GRID INTERFACE
*       (USE STRINGIFIED OBJECT REFERENCE IN OBJECT-NAME)
*
        CALL "OBJSET"   USING OBJECT-NAME
                              GRID-OBJ


*
*       USE ATTRIBUTE GET ACCESSOR FUNCTION TO GET ATTRIBUTE VALUE
*
        SET GRID-GET-HEIGHT      TO TRUE
        CALL "ORBEXEC"      USING GRID-OBJ
                                  GRID-OPERATION
                                  GRID-HEIGHT-ARGS
        DISPLAY "HEIGHT IS " RESULT IN GRID-HEIGHT-ARGS.
```

9.2.8 Server-Side Mapping: Operation Implementation

We shall now turn the coin over and look at the other side: How can you implement a CORBA Object for a specific interface in COBOL? The answer: Use the generated COBOL COPY file along with several auxiliary routines. All you need to do is to provide the following two COBOL programs to create your executable COBOL server:

- A server program within which you can run your object implementation
- A program that implements all of the IDL interface's operation and attribute accessor routines

9.2.8.1 The Server Program

To enable your Object Implementation to run, you need a server program that will register the IDL interface being implemented and then initiate the object. You do this using the following auxiliary functions:

1. Call ORBSTAT to register the standard status information block required for exception handling.

2. Use the ORBREG function to identify the IDL interface that your server will be supporting. If your server will be supporting more than one interface, you would register each of them in turn with successive calls to this routine.

3. Call the ORBINIT function to indicate that your server is ready to start receiving requests. This is pretty much the same as the **BOA::impl_is_ready** call that is used within the C++ mapping.

The following example illustrates what this actually looks like within a real server:

```
IDENTIFICATION DIVISION.
PROGRAM-ID. SERVER.

DATA DIVISION.
WORKING-STORAGE SECTION.

01 SERVER-NAME        PICTURE X(07)        VALUE "SERVER".
01 SERVER-NAME-LEN    PICTURE 9(09) BINARY VALUE 6.

    COPY CORBA.
    COPY GRID.

PROCEDURE DIVISION.

    CALL "ORBSTAT"    USING ORB-STATUS-INFORMATION
    CALL "ORBREG"     USING GRID-INTERFACE
    CALL "ORBINIT"    USING SERVER-NAME
                            SERVER-NAME-LEN

    STOP RUN.
```

9.2.8.2 The Interface Implementation

To complete your COBOL CORBA server you need a program that implements your IDL interface. This is almost always just a dispatcher that accepts incoming requests and dispatches them to the section of COBOL code that implements the specific operations or attribute accessors that have been requested. The language mapping requires that your dispatcher's entry point be named DISPATCH.

You will use the following auxiliary functions in your interface implementation:

1. A call to the standard ORBSTAT. As before, this call registers the status information area. You then call the ORBREQ function to obtain the details of the incoming request. (Every time your server receives a request, it calls DISPATCH.)

2. The request details returned by the call to ORBREQ contain the name of the called operation as an unbounded string. This is, of course, an opaque pointer to the actual value (as defined within the IDL mapping for COBOL), so you now need to use the STRGET function to extract the actual name. You then use this name to PERFORM the section of COBOL code that implements it.

3. Within each section that implements an operation (or attribute accessor function) you invoke two functions: At the start of processing, you call ORBGET to get the operation's **in** and **inout** parameters. When you've finished, you call ORBPUT to return the operation's **out**, **inout**, and return parameters.

The following example illustrates this three-step process:

```
ENTRY "DISPATCH".
*
*      GET DETAILS OF INCOMING REQUEST
*
      CALL "ORBSTAT" USING ORB-STATUS-INFORMATION
      CALL "ORBREQ"  USING REQUEST-INFO.


*
*      GET OPERATION NAME
*
      CALL "STRGET"  USING OPERATION-NAME
                           GRID-OPERATION-LENGTH
                           GRID-OPERATION.
*
*      DISPATCH TO APPROPRIATE SECTION
*
      EVALUATE TRUE
         ....
         WHEN GRID-GET-HEIGHT
            PERFORM DO-GRID-GET-HEIGHT
         ....
      END-EVALUATE
      ....

  DO-GRID-GET-HEIGHT.
      CALL "ORBGET" USING GRID-HEIGHT-ARGS.

*      Operation specific code here

      CALL "ORBPUT" USING GRID-HEIGHT-ARGS.
```

9.3 Additional COBOL Mapping Features

Now that we have covered the fundamentals of the mapping of IDL datatypes to COBOL, and the structure of a simple CORBA COBOL client and object implementation, we can build upon this basic knowledge. Within this section we will cover several other important topics that deserve some scrutiny at this stage: Object Reference Handling, Mapping for Attributes, Exception Handling, and Memory Management.

9.3.1 Object References

We've already covered the various ways to create and obtain object references, and learned how to manipulate them in other languages. Here are the corresponding routines in COBOL:

OBJTOSTR. The COBOL function that stringifies an object reference.

STRTOOBJ. The COBOL function that destringifies an object reference.

OBJDUP. The COBOL function that duplicates your object reference.

OBJREL. The COBOL function that releases an object reference.

OBJNEW. The COBOL function used within your servers to create a new unique object reference. It takes your server name, interface name, and string as input. Once your server starts, you would use this call to create your own unique object reference, then interface to a service such as the CORBA Naming Service, or Trader and place that unique reference there for your clients to find.

9.3.2 Mapping for Attributes

How do you handle **attribute**s within a COBOL context? IDL **attribute** declarations follow the normal conventions, implicitly mapping to a set of two operations: one to **get** the attribute value, and the other to **set** it. For example, the following IDL declaration:

```
interface example {
    attribute long   sum;
}
```

is implicitly equivalent to the following IDL declaration:

```
interface example {
    long _get_sum();
    void _set_sum(in long sum);

}
```

In the case of the preceding example, you would call your attribute accessor functions in the following manner:

```
SET EXAMPLE-GET-SUM  TO TRUE
    call "ORBEXEC" USING EXAMPLE-OBJ
                         EXAMPLE-OPERATION
                         EXAMPLE-SUM-ARGS

    ....
    SET EXAMPLE-SET-SUM  TO TRUE
    call "ORBEXEC" USING EXAMPLE-OBJ
                         EXAMPLE-OPERATION
                         EXAMPLE-SUM-ARGS
```

9.3.3 Exception Handling

Within the COBOL mapping you are required to register the ORB-STATUS-INFORMATION block at the start of each of your client and server programs using the ORBSTAT function. Once you have done this, the completion status of any object invocations or auxiliary functions that you make will be placed into this block. The actual definition of the block will be contained within the standard CORBA copy file that all of your CORBA COBOL programs must copy into their working storage. The following example illustrates the complete layout of this area:

```
01 ORB-STATUS-INFORMATION.
    03 EXCEPTION-NUMBER              PICTURE 9(9) BINARY.
    03 COMPLETION-STATUS             PICTURE 9(4) BINARY.
        88 COMPLETION-STATUS-YES       VALUE 0.
        88 COMPLETION-STATUS-NO        VALUE 1.
        88 COMPLETION-STATUS-MAYBE     VALUE 2.
    03 FILLER                        PICTURE X(02).
    03 EXCEPTION-TEXT                POINTER.
```

So how do you actually make use of this? In the following example, a COBOL client checks for exceptions after making an ORBEXEC call. When it detects an exception, it prints a text message giving the details of the exception:

```
*
*     REGISTER STATUS INFORMATION BLOCK
*
      CALL "ORBSTAT"  USING ORB-STATUS-INFORMATION
      . . . .


*
*     HANDLE EXCEPTION AFTER OPERATION CALL
*
      SET EXAMPLE-MY-FUNCTION    TO TRUE
      CALL "ORBEXEC"      USING EXAMPLE-OBJ
                                EXAMPLE-OPERATION
                                EXAMPLE-MY-FUNCTION-ARGS

      PERFORM CHECK-STATUS
      . . . .


*
*     CHECK STATUS ROUTINE
*
CHECK-STATUS.
      IF EXCEPTION-NUMBER NOT = 0
          DISPLAY "Exception = " EXCEPTION-NUMBER
          MOVE LENGTH OF WS-TXT TO WS-TXT-LTH
          CALL "STRGET" USING EXCEPTION-TEXT
                              WS-TXT-LTH
                              WS-TXT

          DISPLAY WS-TXT
          STOP RUN
      END-IF
      .
```

9.3.3.1 COBOL Mapping for IDL Exceptions

Since we have started to look at exception handling, we should also consider how IDL-defined **exception**s work in a COBOL context. It's really a simple process: IDL-defined **exception**s are mapped to a COBOL group item with a value that uniquely identifies it. The following example illustrates this concept:

```
interface example {
   exception err {
       long     value1;
   };

   void my_Function(in string arg)
       raises(err);
};
```

The **err** exception within the IDL maps to the following COBOL:

```
. . . .
01 EXAMPLE-ERR.
   03 VALUE1               PIC S9(09) BINARY.
01 EX-EXAMPLE-ERR          PIC X(14)
                              VALUE "EX-EXAMPLE-ERR".
01 EX-EXAMPLE-ERR-LENGTH   PIC 9(9) BINARY VALUE 14.
```

9.3.3.2 Raising an Exception

To enable you to raise an exception within your object implementations, the ORBERR function is provided. Before you call the ORBERR function, you should first set any used values required. The following example raises the exception **err** inside the COBOL object **my-function**:

```
MOVE 12     TO VALUE1 IN EXAMPLE-ERR
    CALL "ORBERR" USING EX-EXAMPLE-ERR
                        EX-EXAMPLE-ERR-LENGTH
                        EXAMPLE-ERR
```

9.3.4 Memory Management

In most cases, you will not have to worry about memory management because the dynamic manipulation of memory is not part of the standard ANSI85 COBOL syntax. In fact, the Dynamic COBOL Mapping for CORBA releases you from almost all memory management responsibilities. However, you should be aware that there are a couple of exceptions to this rule:

When using the Dynamic COBOL Mapping for CORBA, you need to specify the CORBA copy file within working storage along with the copy file that was specifically generated for the IDL interface you are handling. By doing this you have defined all the storage you will generally require. However, IDL types such as unbounded **string,**

sequences, and **any** do not have any known size until runtime. Therefore, you need to understand how memory is handled for these types, and what your responsibilities are.

9.3.4.1 string Memory Management

No memory management is required for bounded **string** types because they are mapped directly to the appropriate PIC X(nn) definition within the COBOL copy file for the IDL interface.

Memory management for unbounded **string** types is automated except in one instance: When your client receives an unbounded opaque **string** type in response to a call as either an **inout**, **out**, or **return** value, you are responsible for calling the STRFREE function to release the memory used to hold the string when it is no longer required.

9.3.4.2 sequence Memory Management

When a **sequence** type is to be sent, by either your client as an **in**, **inout**, or returned by your object implementation as an **inout**, **out**, or return, you need to first initialize your sequence using the SEQALLOC routine.

Once allocated, any further memory management for your **sequence** is automated except in one instance: When your client receives a **sequence** type in response to a call as either an **inout**, **out**, or return value, you are responsible for calling the SEQFREE function to release the memory used to hold the sequence when it is no longer required.

9.3.4.3 any Memory Management

Memory management for **any** types is automated except in one instance: When your client receives an opaque **any** type in response to a call as either an **inout**, **out**, or return value, you are responsible for calling the ANYFREE function to release the memory used to hold the value when it is no longer required.

CHAPTER

10

Designing with CORBAservices and CORBAfacilities

10.1 Introduction

In the first nine chapters, we've covered the entire CORBA architecture and seen what we can do with it. Summing up, we can:

- Design our interfaces in IDL, connecting to procedural programs written in non-OO languages, or programs in OO languages that let us take advantage of OO principles

- Build and run our clients, on almost any platform, in almost any programming language

- Build our object implementations, on almost any platform, in almost any programming language

- Invoke object from client, transparent to differences of platform, operating system, or programming language

- Make this invocation synchronously or asynchronously, controlling priority, timing, and other aspects of QoS

- Control and manipulate data transfer around the network using valuetypes

- Manage resources on the server side of the invocation using the POA

■ Assemble sophisticated application servers from multiple shrink-wrapped or home-built CORBA components

This is, you will have to admit, a rich and full environment that allows us to design, build, and execute our distributed applications. What more could we possibly want?

Well, back in the early days, the OMG members made up a list of some more things that they could possibly want, and it was a pretty long list. Here's what was on it. They wanted to:

■ Refer to objects using names, the same as they did with files

■ Browse lists of object instances, displaying information about each one, and clicking to invoke the one they liked

■ Have a running object notify other objects when something happened

■ Make invocations transactionally—that is, with the assurance of two-phase commit and rollback—and connect to existing transaction systems

■ Maintain a secure environment

■ Control and administer the object lifecycle—move, copy, delete—with standard invocations using standard tools

■ Establish and traverse relationships among objects

■ And more, invoking shrink-wrapped services using standard OMG interfaces

Many readers will recognize this (incomplete) list of Object Services; old-time OMG members will also recall that these services first appeared in the Object Services Architecture document some time before they came to be. The next ten chapters will cover them in detail. This chapter is an introduction, not so much to the contents of any particular service, but to the concept of designing and building applications using standard services, how to do it, and why.

10.2 Using an Object Service

Each CORBAservice provides a necessary piece of commonly needed functionality. To get started, we'll pick one: Naming. Our distributed applications will, of course, comprise objects running on different systems around our enterprise. Applications will differ, but we know that some functions will use sets of medium- or perhaps fine-grained objects to represent different aspects of things in our business—employees, supervisors, and executives of various ranks, purchase orders, and customer accounts, for example—while coarser-grained objects will provide their services through a CORBA-wrapped interface to a procedural system such as an accounting system or order-entry system, perhaps.

In either case, desktop clients will need to obtain the object references of either the objects or the services that they want to invoke. The Naming and Trader Services provide this functionality. We'll examine how they do this in the next chapter, but for now we're concerned only with how an application differs—in fact, benefits—when it uses a standard service for this function instead of a home-grown implementation.

To the project manager, services represent an opportunity to hire and get the most out of designers and programmers with expertise in *your business*. It's hard work to design and build scalable, robust system services, and you need the best since a poor set of services can bog down a system so much it becomes unusable. If your company has ever struggled with an overloaded directory service (your e-mail directory, or shared-file system, perhaps?), you already know that even some professionals have trouble delivering scalable implementations of these services. So how much should you expect from your company's IT department when this isn't even their core competency? Since IT is a cost center and not a profit center, it doesn't make sense to spend company resources building generic, system-level functionality. In contrast, if you take advantage of the CORBAservices, your designers and programmers who know your business can easily design and build distributed systems, which add their expertise to the basics that come prebuilt.

To architects and designers, each service represents a basic function that they can treat as a "black box." For the Naming and Trader Services, for example, their design can assume that they have a system that can accept and store an object reference along with either a name (for the Naming Service) or a set of ancillary information according to a schema (for the Trader Service), and return the object reference when queried for an association with the name or other information. Good design starts here: The experience of many great OO architects and builders is embodied in the architecture that defined the CORBAservices, and you build this experience into your system when you design around them. Before you start your design, know which services are available—Naming, Trader, Events, LifeCycle, Transactions, Security—and build these into your design tool before you start (or use a design tool that knows about them and includes them in your environment). Your design will be modular and clean, automatically, with system services providing lower-level functionality, while application objects contain only business-related logic and operations.

To programmers, each service represents an opportunity to deliver more functionality, in a quicker and more robust manner. There isn't much to add here—the design is already done when the programmer sees it (although iterative design technique allows programmers to improve on a first try as they implement), and the services have probably been selected and installed following a serious evaluation to ensure that they meet company needs for scalability, robustness, and conformance to the OMG standard. If the programmers on your project are rewarded for quick delivery of functionality and adherence to design (and not for lines of code!), they'll use the services and keep to the design, and your project will benefit.

The CORBA components environment, when it becomes available in mid to late 2000 or so, will leverage the services even more. The packaging of notification, persistence, transactionality, and security into the container, and the addition of interface navigation functions, will not only benefit your programmers who use the service, but will also bring more interchangeable shrink-wrapped application-level modules to market. Configurability will minimize the compromises your company might otherwise have to make in order to use purchased objects, and the standardized distribution format will make CORBA components easy to buy on whatever popular platforms your company uses.

To your users, the kindest way to use many of the CORBAservices is to keep the details "under the covers." Let's continue with our Naming Service example: When your system creates an object, register it in the Naming Service without exposing the programming details, or even anything about it, to the client or user. When a client needs an object, try to find its object reference in the Naming Service without any user intervention, using what you know about what the user is doing at the time. If the client needs to select a particular instance, do as much of the list-gathering and pruning as you can before you ask the user for input; when you do need input, keep it minimal. When the list is ready, present it in a menu or on a dialog box and let your user click on the object he or she wants. In summary, your architects and programmers see the Naming Service, while your users see an application that may have several different parts, all working together.

This, we think, is one secret to successful use of provided services: Designing the user interface to the function the client's specifications is designed to perform. Don't expose the service interface to the user through a thin wrapper; put the work into your code to transform from the service functions to user functions instead. Users will be able to concentrate on business, and you'll get credit for writing a natural and easy-to-use application. (Of course your users won't know what you saved them from, since they never knew what the service interfaces looked like, but you know and can feel smug about it.)

10.3 Designing Applications to Use Object Services

One advantage of OO is that you can design your distributed applications to mirror the real world. We did this, quite intentionally, in the programming example that makes up the second half of this book—for example, objects named Store and Depot perform store and depot functions. This is a key advantage of OO design, and the payback grows with your application as it grows larger and larger. This is the only thing we can think of besides trouble and effort that grows with (or faster than) your application, and we urge you to take advantage of it!

When you work the example, you'll see that the Naming Service is so fundamental that we use it in every module. In the first edition of this book, we didn't have a Naming Service available from every vendor so we wrote our own. Using the Naming Service is a good start, but what about the other services?

In a real store environment, we would have wanted more assurance that sales were recorded. For this, we probably would have used the Transaction Service, at least for the recording of totals. This is something we would have planned for at design time, if this were not just a programming example.

We might have used the Security Service also, although not on every object. The Point-of-Sales (POS) terminals talk to the store computer on a private, controlled network. We can probably get all the security we want with a simple logon procedure at each terminal. Things are different, however, for the store computer that will be accessed from our central office. The central office is out of our control, and we are beyond its influence as well, so a layer of security makes sense here. Therefore, if we were going to run a real retail empire on this application, we would design our objects on the store and central office computers to use CORBA security.

Because we haven't included any functionality in the central office computer beyond returning product name and price data for a barcode, we have no chance to use the Event Service. But, there are some "bells and whistles" that the office folks might like, and that we could do with it. For example, every time a POS terminal completes a sale and increments the store sales total, we could generate a CORBA event containing the new total. Several applications could subscribe to this event, and update a terminal display in the manager's office and a big LED display in the warehouse in near real time. We can think of many opportunities to use the Event Service when a new product comes into the warehouse—not only setting up administrative things such as line items on inventory lists, but also notifying managers to look for the new product and telling them how and where to set it up on display.

Administrative functions are the place to use lifecycle interfaces (Chapter 11). We didn't put any into the example in order to keep things simple, but you would need this functionality to keep your system running longer than a couple of hours, as rush times and cashier shifts come and go, and cashiers come in, work their shift, and leave to be replaced by a new set. When you write this, you should use the standard LifeCycle interfaces and consider using a system management tool when you have many managed objects.

10.4 Technical Advantages

So far, the reasons we've given for using the CORBAservices and CORBAfacilities in your application have been architectural, but there's more: solid technical reasons why applications built around the services and facilities are more robust than applications that do the same thing using home-grown functionality.

Suppose we're building an application for an enterprise that builds, sells, and services machine tools. They have a sales office with a staff of salespeople who sell on commission, and every time one of them makes a sale, he or she writes up a sales order. In their current paper-rich environment (which we have the job of replacing), these sales orders are paper forms with five copies: white, yellow, pink, blue, and orange. The salesperson keeps the white form and routes the yellow to shipping, the pink to accounting, the blue to marketing, and the orange to the head of the sales department for a departmental record. The form is numbered, so each sale is uniquely identified by its own number from the time it is entered.

Of course, any CORBA implementation will give all of these departments the *same* view of the sales order, so that updates made by one department are instantly available to all departments (unlike paper, where updates are routed as memos with a long delay). There are, at least, three ways we could design an application to automate sales order entry and processing using CORBA:

- First, we could make every sales order a unique CORBA object with its own object reference and implement each with its own servant in the POA.

- Second, we could keep the unique object reference for each sales order but use a default servant that keeps track of each sales order using its ObjectID.

- And finally, we could wrap a big accounting application in a CORBA wrapper that provides sales order processing functions, as well as other financial operations. Each time a request comes in, the application would have to figure out what type of operation to perform—sales order processing, purchase order processing, or human resources function, which might include pay calculations, salary adjustments, sick time, and so on.

First, let's take a look at what's wrong with the last alternative. When we're done, we'll see how the two CORBA-based solutions do the same work more elegantly and robustly.

If we built the thinnest possible wrapper around our accounting system, the entire system would be a single CORBA object with a single object reference and many, many operations. Some of the operations would perform sales order functionality. Since this architecture does not let us use the CORBA object reference or ObjectID to differentiate sales orders, every operation must include a sales order number as an input parameter. When we implement the method, we have to write the code that uses the sales order number as a key to retrieve the order's data from our persistent store, which might be a relational or OO database, or a flat file system if we had built the system from scratch. A user could, conceivably, confuse a sales order number with an employee number and, since there's no type system for these numbers, invoke an employee operation on a sales order number. Unless we had written robust code to protect against this kind of error, the user would get an unpredictable result and could conceivably corrupt the company's data.

Depending on how much of this we built ourselves, it may have fallen to us to build the code that sorts through all the sales order persistent data to find the information for the one in each invocation. This might be easy initially, but information stores increase and functions such as this start to drag down a system as they grow. Experienced architects know that scalability is something you want to buy, not build yourself.

(There are times when we might have to build this kind of system. For example, if we were called into a company that already owned the legacy core of this system, and only had time and resource to take this minimal step, we'd do it as best we could and try to build hooks into the design for an upgrade to a real OO architecture later. Otherwise, we'd be building a stopgap system without allowing for the next step, which we know will have to come sometime.)

In contrast, the first two designs assign a unique CORBA object reference and ObjectID to each sales order. Right away, this lets us use the CORBA Naming Service and POA ObjectID to keep track of everything: Our client code uses the sales order number to keep track, since that's what our staff is used to, but we've stored the object reference in the Naming Service using the number for its name. When it's time to make an invocation, our client code retrieves the object reference for the sales order. We also keep a master list of sales order numbers by customer company, in case we either forget a number or want to look up a company's order history.

There are many technical advantages to this architecture: For example, it encapsulates the ObjectID in the object reference, enabling us to automatically retrieve the proper data from storage using the Persistent State Service. Systems such as this one frequently grow more quickly than their designers ever dreamed. There are many reasons why the number of sales orders might grow: For example, sales of the expensive machine tools could peak in an economic boom, or our company could start making and selling a line of smaller power tools to keep going in a recession, or sales of repair parts could increase for any number of reasons. Regardless, we might have to move the system to a bigger and faster implementation in the future, and the easiest way to do this is by replacing the Naming Service and PSS implementations underneath the IDL interfaces since this doesn't require changes to any of our company's code. Both of these systems will be stressed as the system grows, so it's comforting to know that we can replace an increasingly inadequate Directory Service that underlies our Naming Service interfaces with a more robust implementation, perhaps by even switching vendors for this part of the system without changing the clients that invoke it.

Second, the system is type-safe. Since our sales order object has its type enforced by CORBA and our programming language's type system working together, we can only invoke sales order operations on it. Attempts to invoke employee or HR operations, for example, will raise the BAD_OPERATION system exception and fail, instead of performing incorrect operations on the wrong type of data. This is your payback for all of the narrows you had to insert when you retrieved object references from the Naming Service, before you were allowed to invoke the object's operations. In the context of a single type—sales order, in our example—this may seem like overkill, but try thinking of it instead in the context of your entire enterprise's distributed CORBA system, with hundreds or thousands of types and millions of instances, and it will be a real comfort to you as the project manager to know that CORBA will raise a flag each time a coder in a cubicle somewhere tries to invoke an inappropriate operation on an object instance.

10.5 The "Big Four" CORBAservices Functions

In the next four chapters, we'll describe the four CORBAservices functions, represented by six actual services, which are the most basic and frequently used. Each function will get its own chapter. The four functions are:

1. Passing object references around your system using the Naming Service and Trader Service (Chapter 11);

2. Notifying object instances when something happens, using the Event Service and the Notification Service (Chapter 12);

3. Performing invocations with the assuredness that business needs, using the Object Transaction Service (Chapter 13);

4. Controlling who gets access to your company's assets, using the Security Service (Chapter 14).

The passing of object references around your system is so fundamental that we had to write a service to do this in the first edition of this book when implementations of the Naming Service weren't universally available. The other three functions are also fundamental; in fact, they're the ones that come packaged in the CORBA components environment.

Following these four chapters, we'll describe some of the other commonly used services—LifeCycle, Relationship, Persistence, Externalization, Properties, and Collections—and summarize the rest. Then, we'll cover the CORBAfacilities including (and, in fact, concentrating on) the Domain Facilities—that is, CORBA standards in business areas such as finance, insurance, healthcare, manufacturing, telecommunications, and more. This is where the biggest payoff comes, and where the most exciting work is happening at the OMG. Look for this discussion in Chapters 19 and 20. Finally, before starting our programming example, we'll take a brief look at the UML and the MOF in Chapters 21 and 22.

CORBAservices, Part 1: Naming and Trader Services

When we wrote the first edition of this book, we started the Naming Service chapter with a section on sharing, and how the service was a necessary enabler for you to take advantage of your distributed object system. At the time, the Naming Service was pretty simple: You could put in a name (even a compound name, with a directory/subdirectory structure) and object reference together, and later put in the name and get back the object reference, or you could browse the names and retrieve references for any that seemed interesting. However, stashing names and object references in the Naming Service and getting them back out of it was all you could do. There was no standard string representation for object names so you couldn't send a name to a friend via e-mail or fax, nor could you initialize your ORB to access a service—not even the Naming Service—on a foreign system in a standard way, and sometimes you couldn't do it at all.

The stuff on sharing is still true, and we'll go over it in the next section. When the spec was originally written, its limitations weren't that serious, and, since the explosive growth of the Internet and enterprise intranets wasn't yet a concern, it was impossible to determine what else you might need.

But now our Internet- and intranet-based distributed systems are better defined and, just in the nick of time, the OMG has revised the Naming Service to provide the service level you need to make your enterprise and global distributed object systems work together. Specifically, the new service definition:

- Lets you configure an ORB to initialize using whichever Naming Service you want, so that all the ORBs in your company or department can see the same naming hierarchy

- Defines a standard stringified representation of the compound name, so you and all the CORBA 3 computers on the Net can read the same name in the same form, and the computers know what to do with it

- Defines two URL representations for the object reference that give your ORB access to the Naming Service, Trader Service, or any object that you know the name of, at any available remote site, using the standard DNS or IP address forms that you already know how to use (the CORBA equivalent of the Web's familiar format, http://www.omg.org)

In addition, the revision of the Naming Service also defined the extensions to the ORB's ability to configure initial references (discussed in Chapter 4, Section 4.5.2).

11.1 Sharing—What Distributed Computing Is All About

If you were to sum up, in one word, what makes distributed object systems unique and worthwhile, you might say, "sharing." It's the sharing of information, resources, and analysis that brings about the synergy that magnifies the efforts of the people who work together, leveraging your investment in both technology and people, and creating value for your enterprise.

And, if sharing is the key concept in distributed object systems, then this chapter is the key to the entire book because the two services described here, Naming and Trader, are the components that open up the environment to sharing.

Naming is so basic that it's mentioned first in the Initialization Service—as soon as a client connects to the ORB, it can invoke a standard call to retrieve the object reference for the Naming Service. From that it can get references to objects to do anything else that's available on the system. This makes the Naming Service a place that everyone knows how to get to, which makes it a great place for objects to meet.

But the Naming Service, even with its CORBA 3 extensions, is limited in what it can do. You can associate a name, or a hierarchy of names, with an object reference, but you can't store extra information such as syntax or specifications for what the object does, how much it costs to run, or the room where you pick up the output from the printer object (or, perhaps, the *city* where you pick up the output from the printer object!).

To do this, you need the Trader. Trader is like an electronic combination of the Yellow Pages and a mail-order catalog where you can look up any service you want, from every provider available. When you find one you like, Trader gives you the object reference and away you go. **list_initial_services** and **resolve_initial_references** will give you the object reference for the Trader, or you can get it from the Naming Service if you know its name.

In the first edition of this book, we predicted that Trader-based instance browsers would be an overwhelmingly popular way to access objects, but that it would take more than a few years for this to happen. It's a good thing we gave ourselves this leeway since it hasn't happened yet; but, it still might since many vendors provide implementations and Traders are getting a lot of use at some sites. Since we made that prediction, the growth of the Web has overshadowed other browsing sources, and Web-page embedded URLs are already a prime source of object references for folks who are "just browsing," or found exactly what they were looking for via a Web search engine. We still think that many sites will implement Trader so clients may look for a particular instance that provides a certain service. If there's any part of the prediction we'd change, it would be the part that predicted access to these objects through the DII. Now we think that a downloadable Java client is the likely way to invoke a newly discovered object, and the URL for this client could be stashed in the Trader so all you would need to do is click, download the client, and invoke.

Since we finished the first edition of this book, the Trader Service has been finalized at OMG so we've revised the chapter to reflect that. But first, let's discuss the newly expanded Naming Service.

11.2 The Naming Service

The IDL API is a mighty dry way of looking at the Naming Service. If this book were only for programmers, then it would be the only way we'd present it (like the CORBAservices specification published by OMG). However, this book is for both programmers and users—anyone who wants to benefit from distributed objects—so it's fitting to present here a few alternative and more reasonable ways of looking at the Naming Service.

Remember what we said in Chapter 10 about never exposing the API to a system service to the user through a thin layer of code? The Naming Service is a great opportunity to provide a service to the user by wrapping it with a thick layer of intelligent functionality. Users prefer to access names either as icons or via browsers, or through clients they run that utilize the Naming Service under the covers as they play traffic cop for all of the objects they invoke. Let your users drag and drop icons representing objects, activate or link objects with mouse clicks during the next few years, and (hopefully) use something more sophisticated like voice commands in the years to come. Minimize the use of dialog boxes that expose compound names in all their glory (even in their newly standardized CORBA-format glory) to the poor user who is too worried about getting the corporate tax return right to care about long techie-looking strings no matter what they represent.

The important thing about the Naming Service isn't how its IDL works, it's that the Naming Service *enables* these browsers and icons to make objects directly accessible to the user, and simultaneously give the client and object programmer a way to pass object references around the enterprise. Naming Service interoperability is the key to success here, because objects in one domain will have to resolve names of objects in other domains in order to invoke operations on them. So the OMG Naming Service specification allows services to *federate*, or share, their name databases so that all of the objects in remote name services can appear in results returned by your name service.

The architectural bottom line is that the Naming Service provides object names and references to your entire enterprise and beyond. In the next section, we'll look at the new features of the Interoperable Naming Service and how they let us create an enterprise object directory service accessible to clients everywhere on our network, so that everyone can share and use the same naming hierarchy. Following that, we'll look at the new forms for CORBA URLs and how they go the next step to integrate CORBA and the Web. Finally, with the architectural parts complete, we'll look at the IDL and programming interfaces.

11.2.1 Accessing the Naming Service

What we need is to be able to pass object names around using every medium we have—e-mail, Web pages, file transfer, fax, conversation, whatever—and make sure that anyone who receives them is able to resolve them to their object references without any hassle. One way to do this is to have a single, universal naming hierarchy so that all names have the same root and resolve the same way. However, this is impractical for at least two reasons: First, this kind of setup just begs for scalability problems, and second, we may want to restrict access to Naming Service instances if they, for example, contain references to security-restricted or developmental objects.

Even so, we can construct an enterprise or departmental directory that will be useful, and the additions to the Naming Service specification tell how an ORB can initialize to point to it (or any other service instance we want). We can also construct separate Naming Service instances for our department or development group and initialize to them when we need our own name "sandbox" to play in. What's new about this? Until the revised specification declared that the object reference for the Naming Service (and other non-locality-constrained service objects) had to be administratively configurable, there was no standard for what it could be or who could set it. Some vendors did allow administrative configuration in their own way (the best they could do without a standard, of course), while others imposed their own Naming Service that was local for some vendors and site-wide for others. This made it difficult to port name service clients from one ORB to another, and to establish an enterprise-wide object directory that all clients could access.

The flexibility to specify initial service references at ORB startup was added by the Interoperable Naming Service specification, which we discussed in Chapter 4. In this chapter, we'll only go over how this applies to the Naming Service. If your ORB conforms to the new specification, you'll be able to configure it to initialize with whatever name service instance you want. In fact, you can do this at three levels. At the highest level, you can specify an object reference for the Naming Service in the ORB initialization parameter `arg_list` to the operation `ORB_init`. The format for this is

```
-ORBInitRef NameService=<ObjectURL>
```

where the `<ObjectURL>` is an object reference in either one of the formats we present in the next section, or in `IOR:` format (that is, `IOR:` followed by a stringified object reference). Since this is a parameter you pass to the ORB yourself, you can set the value any way you want—keyboard input, command-line argument, read from a file or the environment, whatever. Standardization lets your code port from ORB to ORB without change. This setting overrides all the others: If your `<ObjectURL>` resolves, this is the name service you get. But if it doesn't resolve, or you don't specify anything at this level, the ORB looks at the next level.

At the second level, CORBA lets you establish a default source of initial references, which gets used if the one you specify at `ORBInitRef` level is not available. We discussed this in Chapter 4, so we won't repeat the details here. If the Naming Service instance we asked for in our `ORBInitRef` isn't available, our ORB will look for an alternative here.

At the third level is our administratively configured Naming Service.

11.2.2 String Form of CORBA Names

The original CORBA Naming Service specified how names were stored inside your program, but provided no standard format to print them out. That meant you couldn't print out a name and send it to a friend or coworker and expect him to use the literal string unless you both had the same ORB and used the same code. (Your friend could parse the name into pieces and enter each piece individually if his GUI allowed it, but this is not a friendly way to deal with names!) The revision of the Naming Service fixes this by specifying a string representation for CORBA names.

The bottom line is that CORBA object names are Unix-format directory and file names applied to objects. If you're more used to DOS directory and file names, change the backward slashes to forward slashes—it's the same. If you're used to Windows names, change the backward slashes to forward slashes *and* don't use spaces. There are some other differences but they're subtle, and you can skip them if you're only interested in the higher-level architecture. If you are interested in the details, read on.

The basic unit of the CORBA object naming structure is the naming context. You can think of a CORBA naming context as a subdirectory for names. A naming context has its own name and contains as many entries as you care to cram into it. Each entry in a naming context has a name and can be either another naming context or a CORBA object. As we just said, this is how your file system works if you're using any one of the popular computer operating systems.

Naming contexts are CORBA objects and are identified by CORBA object references. You can register a naming context in your Naming Service even if it resides in another Naming Service on another computer (and even though the naming context is already registered there too, probably under a different name!). This is called Federating, and the Naming Service will resolve a compound name by following its links wherever they lead.

Each part of the name—whether it's a naming context or an object name—consists of an identifier or ID (the main part of the name) and a kind (the minor part). In the standard name string, the two are separated by a dot and the different naming contexts are separated by slashes. Just in case you wanted to put dots and slashes into your object name, OMG defines *escape characters* you can use to tell the system that the next dot or slash is really part of the name and not a separator. Instead of telling you how to do this and what the escape character is, we're going to give you a piece of advice. Pardon us, we're going to shout so cover your ears: DO NOT EVER EVER ESCAPE DOTS OR SLASHES IN YOUR OBJECT NAMES!. It's a really stupid thing to do. If you ever feel like you really have to do this in a commercial or business system, take a long break instead. Go for a walk. Drink a non-caffeinated, non-alcoholic beverage slowly and deliberately. Don't go back to your terminal until the urge has totally passed. Your boss and your co-workers will appreciate your consideration.

When you represent a name as a string, if the kind field at a level is empty, you leave out the dot. If both the ID and kind fields are empty, you represent the missing level as a dot between the two bounding slashes. (This can happen if you're representing X.500 names, which are not hierarchical, in the CORBA scheme, which forces a hierarchical representation, albeit temporarily. X.500 names do not require an entry for every possible field. Don't worry, a Naming Service implementation based on X.500-format names will deal with this format properly.)

Two stringified names are equal if every identifier and every kind in one equals the corresponding name and kind in the other. If the two strings are equal, the names are equal. Simple enough?

11.2.3 Object URLs

One thing that's great about the Web is that you can guess the Web address of a place from its company name, type it in the address window of your browser, and get to the Web page right away. The best example I can think of is OMG—you know we're a not-for-profit organization, so you guess that our Web site would be at www.omg.org. You type this in and our homepage appears in your browser window. Wouldn't it be even nicer to be able to access a CORBA object by typing in a URL? The specification is in place, and soon you'll be able to do just that.

To see how this will work, first consider the analogy we made to the Web. On the Internet there's a network of domain name servers which your computer used to convert our domain name, www.omg.org, to our Web server's IP address, 192.67.184.81. By agreement, this computer is listening to http requests on its port number 80, so your browser sent its request to port 80 of our computer, asked for our homepage, and back it came.

11.2.3.1 URLs by Location for Standard Services

To make this work for CORBA, *almost* all we need to do is put a CORBA server on a well-known port of a machine with a domain name and address. What else do we need? Web servers hold lots of different pages and serve them up one at a time, identifying them by a page or file name ("specifications.html" or whatever) following the domain name and separated from it by a slash. Analogously, CORBA servers serve lots of different objects so we need to put an Object Key on to the end of our object URL. The Object Key identifies the service we want an object reference for.

The name of the CORBA URL format that corresponds to the object reference of a standard service at a location is `corbaloc`. Here's an example:

```
corbaloc://1.1@MyGiganticEnterprise.com:683/NamingService
```

The URL starts with the identifying string `corbaloc://`. It's followed, optionally, by the IIOP version number, which in this example is specified to be 1.1. If you leave out the version, it defaults to 1.0; if you put it in, you must follow it with the @ sign. Next comes the network address. This can either be a domain name (here, MyGigantic-Enterprise.com) or an IP address. Optionally, you can follow this with a colon and a port number. OMG has been assigned the standard port number 683 for IIOP, and 684 for Secure IIOP, so you will either want to specify one of those numbers, or let this field default. A forward slash and an Object Key follow all of this.

The Object Key in a standard (that is, non-URL-format) IOR is the part that the ORB uses to identify the object that is the target of the invocation. In CORBA 2, object keys were like elves: They lived in the Interoperable Object Reference and never came out where they could be seen in daylight even by programmers, never mind users. The new Naming Service specification defines URL-format object references with Object Keys that we can read. (The Object Keys that ORBs create are probably just long strings of computer numbers, but we'll never know for sure because they never come out into the light. Maybe they really *are* elves.) The keys for basic services will be the same strings as the ObjectIDs that come back from **list_initial_services** as we described in Chapter 4. There's nothing in the specification that restricts corbaloc-accessible objects to those that are included in the list of initial services, but we expect that ORB vendors will provide mainly those and few others.

So, now you can set up your CORBA server on a machine with a domain address, run the Naming Service, Trader Service, or another one of the standard services, and have anyone access it *without* having to obtain a stringified CORBA object reference first. Compared to the stringified object reference, which is a long, imposing stretch of hexadecimal characters, the corbaloc URL format is very user-friendly indeed.

In order for this to be useful, people must have clients for the objects that are served at these sites, but this isn't so far-fetched since most uses will be for standard CORBAservices: The first use will probably be for the Naming Service, which has standard interfaces so any CORBA programmer can write a client for it. The next common service will probably be Trader, because you can browse a Trader to see all the neat stuff that's available, and the Trader entry can point to a downloadable client so you can try it out right away. We talk about that in this chapter, section 11.3. OMG Task Forces have already defined standard services in finance, electronic commerce, telecommunications, manufacturing, transportation, and health care; standard CORBA clients written to these interfaces could easily be adapted to find services through CORBA URLs.

How do you code this into your client? Your ORB already has an interface to turn a string into an object reference—it's **string_to_object** (remember?), and OMG reused it for this function. You pass the URL object reference string to the ORB in **string_to_object**, and the ORB creates an IOR by doing whatever it needs to: converts the domain name to an IP address, creates IIOP/GIOP protocol identifiers and parameters, and inserts the Object Key—exactly the way you entered it—into the proper space in the IOR. It then passes you a session object reference for this IOR, which you can **narrow** to whatever it's supposed to be and then invoke.

More technical details: Remember how, for objects with persistent state, we stored their ObjectID and POA names in the IOR, back in Chapter 5? When you call **string_to_object** with an object URL and your ORB creates an object reference, it won't contain any of this information because there's no way to get it. Therefore, this technique can only create generic object references and is useful only to access standard services that run constantly and know what to do when they receive a simple request. So how do we access a specific named object on a foreign server if corbaloc won't let us? We use a URL to invoke the Naming Service on the server, get back a real

IOR for the object, and invoke it. `corbaname` is the new URL that we use for this. Here's how it works.

11.2.3.2 URLs for Objects by Name

It's great to be able to initialize our ORB to use our enterprise directory for object names, but sometimes we need to be able to resolve names on any server, anywhere, directly. For that, OMG has added a URL format that lets you invoke the Naming Service on a foreign computer—`corbaname`. All you do is take an `corbaloc` URL and make two changes: First, you change the initial string `corbaloc` to `corbaname`. (No surprise there!). Second, you remove the Object Key and put the object name in its place after the slash. So, if we were the outside auditor and wanted to make a secure invocation of a departmental account object at MyGiganticEnterprise and we knew its directory hierarchy, we might enter:

```
corbaname://1.1@MyGiganticEnterprise.com:684/RootObject
             /SalesDept/Accounts/1997/Receivables.obj
```

When you pass this to **string_to_object**, your ORB translates the domain name into an IP address (of course we could have entered an IP address instead, useful if the machine didn't *have* a domain name) and invokes the CORBA Naming Service on the named (or default) port at that IP address. For the name, it uses the string that you entered after the address. If it finds a Naming Service at that address, and the name resolves, the object reference comes back to your client's ORB and you get it as the return value from **string_to_object**.

For this example iiopname URL, your ORB would go to the computer at MyGiganticEnterprise.com, on port 684, using IIOP version 1.1, and ask the Naming Service there to resolve "/RootObject/SalesDept/Accounts/1997/Receivables.obj".

Here's a possibly more practical (or, at least, potentially more profitable) example: Suppose you've set up a company named "MyShoppingCompany" to sell widgets on line, and registered the domain. (No one had when I wrote this, but some reader may do it now to get free publicity in this book! But it sure is a dumb name for a company.) Let's say that we're running our OnlineShopping server. Now a potential customer of ours can go to the address window of his CORBA shopper client (not his Web browser!) and type

```
corbaname://MyShoppingCompany.com/OnlineShopping
```

and his CORBA shopper will invoke an operation on the e-commerce store object running on our server.

Don't get the impression that this is only useful with computers that have their own domain names. Although only a small fraction of computers have domain names, every machine on the Internet or on your company's enterprise network (if it's running TCP/IP) has an IP address. If you can find out the IP address and port number of the ORB running a Naming Service that you want to access, you can invoke it just by typing this information into an corbaname URL followed by the name you want to look up. For example, if we knew there was a Naming Service running at IP address 192.168.1.141 on the standard IIOP port 683, we could resolve the name /RootObj/Catalog/Clothing/Winter/Blouse1584389 .obj with the URL.

```
corbaname://192.168.1.141:683/RootObj/Catalog/Clothing
                /Winter/Blouse1584389.obj
```

Security permissions willing, *any* running Naming Service instance accessible to your client can be invoked this way. (By the way, the IP address we used for the example—191.168.1.141—is not an Internet address. It's part of a block of numbers restricted for private network use. If you attempt to invoke a service at that address and some machine responds, it's one on your company's private network and not on the Internet!)

11.2.4 Representing Names in Code

In Section 11.2.2, we saw that each level (which we'll now call a *component*) of a name consists of an ID and a kind. In the standard string, these are separated by slashes and dots, but in code they're different parts of a struct. Here's the IDL. Originally, **lstring** was a placeholder for a to-be-determined internationalized **string** type, but OMG has decided that it's too late to make this substitution (which would break every Naming Service implementation on the planet), so now **lstring** is just a typedef for **string**.

```
typedef string lstring
struct NameComponent {
 lstring id;
 lstring kind;
};
```

```
typedef sequence <NameComponent> Name;
```

So, a **Name** is a sequence of **NameComponents**, which is what we call the **struct** that contains the **id** and **kind string**s. All but the last component are bound to (that is, point to) Naming Contexts; the last one is bound to an object reference. If the sequence has more than one component (the only interesting case) then it is termed a *compound name*; you can pass a compound name to the service anywhere a name is called for, and the service will resolve all of the levels automatically.

You bind a name to an object using this IDL:

void bind (in Name n, in Object obj);

This operation establishes a correspondence in the Naming Service between the **Name n** and the **Object obj**. If you pass in a compound name, then all components except the last are resolved before the last one is bound to the object. This means that each call to bind can bind only one component of a compound name. If you have a five-component compound **name**, and none of the components has been bound, you'll make five calls before you're finished. However, this won't happen often in code; mostly you'll be adding components one at a time working from GUI input or in some loop on name components so you'll only have to code one call.

There's a special operation to bind a name to a Naming Context so that it can be resolved by the service:

void bind_context (in Name n, in NamingContext nc);

The **resolve** operation retrieves the object reference that we—or, more likely, someone else—bound to the name with a prior **bind.** If we pass in a compound name, it must match the bound name exactly in order for the operation to succeed:

Object resolve (in name n);

The Naming Service functions that let you display an entire naming context (subdirectory if you're still thinking in the analogy) are the list operation and BindingIterator interface. We won't go into the programming details; when you sit down to write your Naming Service GUI client, with your vendor's documentation in front of you, there won't be any problem figuring out what to do.

There are a few more operations in the standard: **rebind, rebind_context, unbind**; you create a new context with **new_context** or create and bind in one operation with **bind_new_context**. These complete the programmer's tool chest. We won't cover them in this book; when you need them, see the documentation that came with your Naming Service software product.

The Naming Service does not define any interfaces that convert name strings to sequences of name components, or vice versa. It doesn't need to; you can write this yourself easily enough if your Naming Service vendor doesn't provide it as an extra. The correspondence between fields in the standard string, and fields in the name struct, is obvious.

The Names Library, one of the least thought-out features of the original Naming Service, was removed from the specification by the revision. Not just deprecated, totally removed.

11.3 Trader Service

Telephone books provide us with a good analogy for the Naming and Trader services. The White Pages are our analogy to the Naming Service: When you know whom you want to call, you use the White Pages and look up the person or company by name; for example, Peter Smith on Elm Street, or The Cracker Barrel on Route 117. If, however, you just know that you want a store that sells dishwashers, the White Pages aren't much help because they list by name, and you want to search by category. Fortunately, there is a category listing of telephone customers called the Yellow Pages; you'll find most of the stores that sell dishwashers listed under Appliances. (Sorry, not under Dishwashers. We'll talk about schema standardization later in the chapter.) Staple a mail order catalog to the Yellow Pages and you have, in concept at least, the Object Trader Service: You use the schema to locate a category, and narrow down to an instance; finally the service hands you an object reference that you use to access the service.

The Trader Service lets you build an application that can go "object shopping" online. To get started, you set up a schema of **ServiceType**s in the Trader and register service instances. (In Trader jargon, this is called "exporting service offers.") Each entry in your schema declares a **ServiceTypeName**, an associated **InterfaceTypename**, and a set of named properties. The properties are **name-any** value pairs; each may be declared **mandatory** or **readonly** when you set up the schema. You create (that is, **export**) a service offer in this schema by providing the reference for a CORBA object that provides the service, values for all the mandatory properties, and values for any other properties you want. The good news about setting up a schema is that you can set up anything you want because the values are **any**s and you can have as many as you like. The other news is that you don't get any guidance from the spec, nor do we know of any industry-standard schema that you can either use or start from, so you really are on your own here unless your own company has already started a schema.

It's not difficult to construct a simple real-life example. Most people think of printers when they think of a computerized service offer, so that's what we'll use. We could start with a simple Printer service and subtype into ColorPrinter and BWPrinter (since Service Types follow the same kind of inheritance as CORBA interfaces); however, to keep this example simple, we won't. Our **ServiceTypeName** is **PrintService**, and the interface name (not visible to the human user) is **Print**. We could have some mandatory properties about location (Building, Floor, Department, PublicAccess [a **boolean**], etc.), some other mandatory properties about the printer itself (make, model, number of trays, available media, etc.) and a bunch of nonmandatory ones (PagesPerMinute, DoubleSided [another **boolean**], CostPerPage, PaperType, whatever).

The idea is that your Trader will contain multiple instances of whatever services you have, each with its own set of property values. Then when you invoke the Trader to retrieve the reference for a service, you can ask it to rank responses based on how well the offered service property values match the values you want, using a constraint language defined in the spec.

For our printer example, we probably have printers in different buildings, on various floors, departments, and so on, and some departments have printer rooms with different speed and quality printers in the same location.

Then, when you want to print something out, you input which building you're in, on what floor, and perhaps something about speed or quality. If you're printing a draft manuscript you will rank a close-by location higher than quality, but if you're printing the final copy of a color brochure for a big client, you'll go for quality even if the printer is across town. Your client program translates this into Trader Constraint Language and invokes the Trader, which ranks all of its PrintService offers by how well they meet your requirements and delivers an ordered list to your client program. It's up to your software whether it automatically invokes the best match or gives you some number of top picks and lets you make the final decision. Trader delivers the object reference of the service instance and all of the property name-value pairs with every offer, so you can get a property value if it's useful to you. (For the printer service, only the object reference counts so your client code uses it to direct your print job to the CORBA printer object, and you hike down the hall to pick up your output.)

OMG and the ISO Open Distributed Processing WG worked together very closely on the Trader. Preliminary versions of the ISO standard were used as the requirements document during the OMG specification process. Timetables for the two organizations' adoption process were synchronized so that the end product could be adopted simultaneously by both. The Trader standard is assigned ISO/IEC 13235-1, and ITU-T Recommendation X.950.

11.3.1 What Trader Is Good For

If you get a chance to read the Trader Service specification (or even your vendor's Trader documentation), you'll see that it's couched in the language of "Service Offers."

This is mighty prescriptive terminology for a general specification; after all, what it's really doing is storing object references associated with properties, and the properties are totally general, **name-any** value pairs. This means you can store and retrieve references for *any* kind of CORBA object, whether it provides a "service" (whatever that means) or not. In the most general sense, Trader is the thing to think of when you need to store and retrieve an object reference based on association with anything more than a name. Using Trader, you can store and retrieve object references based on any criteria you like.

How general is Trader (in spite of the persistent use of the term "service offer" in the specification)? It's totally general. In design and implementation, the Trader Service is a mini database: Each Service Type in your schema defines a table with declared property names and values. You can have as many different tables—pardon me, Service Types—as you want, and each accepts unlimited entries. The constraint-language-based ranked-list retrieval system is a lot more sophisticated and capable than SQL, unless you need to do a join, which is not possible because of the way the system is designed. If you declare one of the properties to act like a key, you can retrieve a specific record—pardon me, Service Offer—by requiring a match on "key" and giving its value. You could enter the nil object reference for every row, and use the system just for a database and not as a Trader! We're certainly not advocating this; the point is that Trader is a general CORBA object storage and retrieval facility that is useful for much more than objects that provide "services."

However, like anything this general, there are good ways and bad ways to use Trader.

One good architectural aspect of the printer example we used in the previous section is that the properties we stored in Trader—location, speed, price—were important aspects of a print server, but were not *software* aspects so they weren't duplicated in the Trader entry and the object instance's state. For objects that provide a concrete service, this is frequently the case—perhaps that's why the Trader documentation is couched in "service" terminology.

On the other hand, if we used Trader to store and retrieve object references for Employee CORBA objects for our HR system, we'd have to (for example) include Department information for each employee as a Trader property in order to retrieve object references sorted by department. Since employee-department affiliation has to be stored in our HR system as well, this design would require an endless synchronization effort to try to keep the Trader and database records identical—it's bad architecture. The better way to solve this problem is to avoid using Trader for this application, store department affiliation information in the HR Employee Record where it belongs (and only there), and design this tier of our application in a way that lets us efficiently sort employee records by attribute such as department. (We're presuming that our Trader implementation was not capable enough to hold and execute our entire HR employee database as we described in the fantasy a few paragraphs back.)

So, in general, Trader is a good way to store and retrieve object references based on ancillary information that is *not* also contained in the object instances' own state. Although this architecture corresponds closely to service offers, it applies in many other instances as well. However, if you want to select from a collection of CORBA objects based on their state values, try to do this without duplicating state information in another persistent store, which means avoiding Trader. Instead, you might set up a lightweight cache system to collect and store the data you need for the selection. If your set of objects looks like the employee records we used in the recent example, you could use the POA to set up a servant structure that allows cycling through records and sorting by department or other attribute without incurring I/O cost for each record.

11.3.2 Federating Traders and Designing Schemas

You can *federate* Trader instances; that is, connect them up so that offers contained in one are shared with others. The specification prescribes, in great detail, different ways to link Trader instances and control how far offers may propagate along a chain, and which types of offers are subject to which restrictions. We're not going to include the programming details here, since we're mainly interested in the architecture of a federated Trader system and what it allows you to do.

There are two conceivable reasons to federate Traders: First, you might have so many entries that a single instance becomes overloaded, so you create multiple instances and federate as a way to load balance. Second, you might establish Traders in truly distinct business domains (by department, division, or however your company is partitioned) and federate in order to share access to some identifiable subset of objects that are used on both sides of these boundaries. Related to this, you might have two preexisting but separately built Traders in domains that need to be linked long after they were established, due perhaps to a corporate merger or buyout, or customer-supplier cooperation across a corporate boundary. (This isn't so far-fetched; the concept of "virtual corporation" has been in the press a lot lately.)

We don't think that many sites will need to federate their traders for load-balancing. It's a lot more effective to run a single trader on a multiprocessor system that's designed for heavy loads; many of these systems are fault-tolerant as well. Architecturally, your first goal should be to keep your distributed systems as simple as you can and still get your job done, and there's no Trader configuration as simple as a single instance.

On the other hand, a well-designed federated system of independent Traders can work well in a large organization. You will want to balance convenience and administrative burden, which usually means minimizing the number of Trader instances especially if each needs to be duplicated for fault tolerance. Design and configure the system on paper first, and check how well it meets all of its clients' needs, before you purchase and install the hardware and software.

The main thing you will be concerned with is the Schema; that is, the list of Service Types, Properties, and their names that you build into your Trader installation. Together with the configuration of Traders that you install and how you link them up, the schema *is* your Trader architecture. The Trader specification gives you free rein here—you can have whatever Service Types with whatever names you want. You and a committee will probably meet to construct a list of Service Types and names that your company can agree to.

In order for federation to work, all of the linked Traders have to use the same schema for the service types they are going to share. There is no provision in the spec to translate or map from one schema to another as you pass over a Trader link. In large companies, it's going to be difficult to coordinate something as seemingly inconsequential as a Trader schema among dozens of independent departments that all have other things (such as core business!) on their minds. However, if you don't establish a company-standard schema right off the bat, you'll probably never get a system that integrates all of your company's traded objects smoothly. If establishing a single schema at rollout is difficult, reconciling multiple different established schemas later is impossible!

Of course, even if you succeed in getting your enterprise to develop and use a single schema, you won't be any closer to federating with outside companies and organizations. We don't know of any initiatives to standardize a schema to go along with the standard interfaces in the Trader specification. That's too bad because it limits your Trader horizon to your enterprise, pretty much, unless you have enough influence with either your customers or your suppliers to get them to cooperate. Perhaps this isn't surprising, considering the difficulties we face just getting departments in a single company to cooperate on anything, but it still impresses us as a lost opportunity. It will be a long time before virtual corporations can coalesce instantaneously by federating their Traders through a common schema.

11.3.3 Programming with Trader

We're not going to present any of the Trader IDL interfaces in this book. The main impact of Trader on your distributed system will come not from *how* it works, but just *that* it works; that is, Trader gives such easy access to objects and, yes, services, based on ancillary information through its ranked retrieval system that you can design your system around it.

On the technical side, Trader has many interfaces and, except for the few that import and export service offers, all relate to administrivia of schema definition, federation, and the like. If we described one interface, we'd have to describe them all and this book would turn into a text on Trader. If this introduction has inspired you to incorporate Trader into your enterprise architecture (and we certainly think that there's a good fit somewhere for most companies), we refer you to your Trader product's documentation to get started on the next steps.

chapter 12

CORBAservices, Part 2: Event and Notification Services

When we wrote the first edition of this book, we used a simple example of an event: a change in the value of a spreadsheet cell containing this year's calculated after-tax profit of our enterprise. The example presumed that the value would be used in a report to the board of directors, printed in the annual report and other places, and that all of the applications that used the number would want to be notified when the calculated value changed so they could update their output.

It turned out that this example was not only simple; it was truly naïve. Since those "early days" (only four years ago!), we've found out about many real-world uses of the Event Service that stress systems almost beyond recognition. For example, we know of a site that receives electronic news feeds from many hundreds of sources, using more varied protocols and formats than they can count. Thousands of stories come in every day, and each generates a CORBA event that carries the essence of the story to every editor's workstation; these workstations run a filtering application that receives the event and either displays or discards the story based on the individual user's profile. The telecommunications industry is another big user of CORBA events, especially in network administration and maintenance. In fact, it was their needs which led to the Notification Service specification which we're starting to describe.

The basic need is simple: In distributed systems, things happen, and when they do, many parts of the system all over the enterprise need to find out. The OMG members knew about these needs 'way back, and provided the original Event Service as one of the first four core parts of the Common Object Services. This is the specification that we described in the first edition of this book and in the first half of this chapter. They did a good job, producing a specification that was generally useful and flexible enough to handle a wide range of applications.

It did, however, leave many details to the implementor. For one thing, every aspect of QoS was left unspecified, explicitly—the document states:

> . . . Multiple implementations of event services are to be expected, with different services targeted toward different environments. As such, the event interfaces do not dictate **qualities of service**. Different implementations of the Event Service interfaces can support different qualities of service to meet different application needs.

What's wrong with this, more now than when it was written in 1993? Systems are growing larger, and are *relying on* event transmission because events don't just tell you that something happened, they tell you that *something important happened, and you'd better do something about it. Now!*

With the adoption of the Notification Service in mid-1998, CORBA Event Handling is ready for prime time. Building on the original Event Service interfaces, which provide a sound and proven foundation, the Notification Service adds:

- Quality of Service specification and administration, covering both reliability and speed

- Well-defined standards for Typed and Structured Events

- Dynamic Filtering of events based on type and QoS parameters

- Filtering at source, channel, channel proxy (event consumer group), and individual event consumer level

- Event discovery among source, channel, and client—a great efficiency booster, as we'll describe

In this chapter, we'll begin by discussing communication semantics and identifying which semantic of our set corresponds to event transmission. We'll continue with an explanation of the original Event Service, since it is both useful in itself as well as the foundation for the Notification Service. We'll finish up with an overview of the new service, as far as we can, but we have to point out that the Notification Service specification runs over 200 pages so we won't be able to include all the programming details you'll need to use it. We will describe all of its important capabilities, so you'll be able to figure out what you can do with it and how to design your distributed systems around it.

12.1 Communication Semantics

CORBA gives us many distinct invocation semantics, thanks to the refinement provided by the Messaging Specification. For all of these, one important characteristic is that a CORBA invocation is transmitted at-most-once. Some operations are *idempotent*; that is, the end state is the same no matter how many times the operation is sent and executed (for example, "delete the file myletter.doc," or "set count equal to 35"). Other operations are definitely not idempotent; for example, "subtract $10 from my bank account balance." (Ouch!) In some systems (but not CORBA), all operations are required to be idempotent. This is handy in distributed systems, since you can send another copy of a command if you're not sure the first got through. If a system is not idempotent, a good semantic (specified by CORBA for every invocation) is at-most-once, as you can tell from the bank balance example. Transactional semantics guarantee, if *commit* succeeds, that the operation executed *exactly* once.

For all CORBA invocations, regardless of semantics, two conditions always hold:

- The sender always selects the receiver.
- There is always a single receiver.

Before the messaging specification added routers, a third characteristic existed:

- There is no queue; if the receiver is not available, the communication attempt fails.

But what about communication semantics where one or more of these conditions does not hold? By turning off one or two of these conditions, we define additional communication semantics that are useful under certain circumstances. Even more interesting, some of these can be implemented using CORBA as the basic transport, so we can define them as CORBAservices.

If we turn off the first two—by *decoupling* the sender from the receiver with an intervening service—we get the Event Service. (In fact, some modes of the Event Service, even in its original form, turn off the third condition as well.) Interested recipients register their interest in receiving events, and the sender has no way of finding out where the events are going; multiple receivers may independently register to receive notification of the same event; and in "pull" mode, the event waits in a queue for the recipient to notify the service that it is ready.

If we turn off the third condition, we get messaging semantics. We described this in Chapter 6 where we added routers to our network in Section 6.6.2.3, but mention it here in context to point out the relationship between it and some of the Event Service and Notification Service execution modes.

The final semantics we'll discuss are *broadcast* and *multicast*. In the previous three cases, messages were addressed to a specific recipient. In broadcast and multicast, messages are addressed to more than one recipient. The difference between broadcast and multicast is that broadcast messages go to *everyone* on a network, while multicast messages go to a select group of recipients. The difference between multicast and the event service (at least the current incarnation of the event service) is that multicast sends the *same copy* of a message to a group of recipients, while the event service sends a separate copy to each one. If the recipient list is short or the message is small, individual copies won't clog modern high-speed networks, but if the list grows large or the message is a hundred-megabyte graphic, the impact can be severe. To remedy this, OMG has just issued and RFP for a new service termed "unreliable multicast," expected to be based on a layering of GIOP onto IP Multicast. Due to complete in mid to late 2000, the service will standardize this new semantic for CORBA. The new invocation mode may be applied to the event and notification services by this same RFP, or later in a separate process. Some ORB vendors already market proprietary extensions of the Event Service that implement multicast semantics, so you don't have to wait for this RFP to complete in order to test this out for yourself.

The real significance of the Event Service and Notification Service is that they let CORBA handle situations that require decoupled communication semantics in a natural way. The Event Service covers the straightforward cases (which may be large and complex in their own right as we pointed out in our real-life examples at the start of this chapter), while the Notification Service allows application to enterprise and Internet-scale distributed systems with clear reliability requirements.

12.2 Event Service Architecture

The Event Service standard uses inheritance to build up from the simplest case of two objects trading events, through an event channel that decouples the interactions, and finally to a typed event channel that replaces the generic **any** event data with your specific datatype before delivery. There are so many options that we can't possibly cover them all here (even for the Event Service, never mind for the Notification Service). We'll cover the event channel, which is the simplest part of the service that is truly useful, but we'll skip all except the most cursory of explanations of typed events which weren't used much even before the Notification Service defined Structured Events, a significant improvement.

The Event Service supports several options at each end of the event channel. The object that supplies the event is called the *supplier* (no surprise here); the objects that receive the event are called the *consumers*. You may connect as many suppliers and consumers as you want to an event channel.

The event channel object decouples communication between suppliers and consumers. To suppliers, it is a consumer; to consumers, it is a supplier. It accepts connections from one or many suppliers as we just pointed out, and one or many consumers, as shown in Figure 12.1. An event received from any one of the suppliers is transmitted to every consumer.

You can have as many event channel objects as you want, each working independently of the others. This, the crudest type of event filtering, at least keeps an object from being interrupted by events that don't concern it, but at a price: Every event type we want to segregate needs its own channel so, we suspect, channels will proliferate like rabbits in some installations.

Events include a piece of data, type **any**, that the receiver can examine to find out something about the event. Since the **any** could be a **struct** or **string**, for instance, you can send a lot of information. Remember, however, there's usually a price to be paid in performance for large data transfers so you don't want to be too casual about sending large **struct**s around with your events unless you're working with a department of desktop Crays connected with fiber links. Well, you know what we mean.

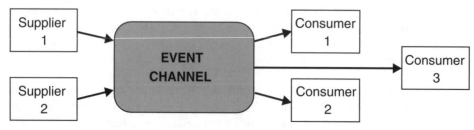

Figure 12.1 An event channel with multiple suppliers and consumers.

The Event Service supports both a **push** model and a **pull** model for events, independently at both ends of the channel. A push supplier sends an event to the channel whenever it wants by invoking a **push** operation; the channel must accept it. A pull supplier supports a **pull** server interface; the channel plays the role of client and solicits an event at the channel's discretion. (When, exactly? Perhaps when it receives a pull from a client at the far end of the channel, or at timed intervals. The service specification does not fix this.) At the consumer end, a push consumer supports the **push** server interface, which is invoked by the channel client, while a **pull** consumer invokes the pull operation on the channel that responds with the event if there is one on the queue. The pull operation comes in two flavors: pull blocks until an event is received, while **try_pull** returns immediately with a boolean that tells whether an event is waiting in the queue.

The channel has to store an event for some length of time if the supplier is using **push** mode and at least one consumer is using **pull**. In the original Event Service specification, there is no word on queue QoS, but (as we'll see shortly) the Notification Service fixes this nicely. Our advice (in case it's not obvious): If your setup includes any pull consumers, use the Notification Service, not the Event Service. This totally avoids reliance on undefined Event Service queue storage time and capacity.

That's it for a description of Event Service architecture. After a brief look at some of its IDL interfaces, we'll move on (finally!) to the Notification Service.

12.3 Event Service Interfaces

We're going to go over an example of an event channel with a single push-supplier object and two consumer objects, one in **push** mode and the other in **pull**. This will accomplish two things: First, it will fill in some details for readers who plan to program with the Event Service; and second, it will clarify the concepts of **push**, **pull**, and channel, even for those who never plan to program but still want to be clear on what's going on.

First let's go over what happens as an event is transmitted from the supplier to both consumers (shown in Figure 12.2). Here are the steps:

1. The supplier object sends the event to the channel object. Here, the supplier object is the client, and invokes the **push** operation on the channel that is the server.

2. When the same event is being sent to multiple objects, the Event Service does not specify the order in which it is sent, or how much time is allowed to elapse between the first notification and the last. These quality of service factors are considered to be implementation details, as we just pointed out. So the next two steps actually occur in indeterminate order, at least as far as the users of the service are concerned.

3. One is the **push** to the **push_consumer** object. The push consumer object must support (that is, inherit and implement) the **push_consumer** interface. This makes the object a *server*, to which the channel plays *client*. When the channel receives an event, it invokes the **push** operation on the consumer. The invocation mode is not specified, but it may have been invoked **oneway** to prevent the client from blocking execution of this channel thread by failing to return from the invocation immediately.

4. The channel object places the event on a queue where it waits for the **pull_consumer** object, which is a client here, to invoke the pull operation on the channel that is the server. How long does the event wait on the queue? As we pointed out a few pages back, the Event Service doesn't say. Look in the documentation for your Event Service implementation to find out how long your events will last. And, by the way, how many events can fit in the queue? Don't presume that event queues will always be small. Suppose your programmer sets up a single channel for all of the events from a spreadsheet, and a user sets it up for 1024 × 2048 cells and linked to every cell. Then he or she loops through 1000 different values for cell C3, recalculating the whole sheet with every iteration. You can multiply out how many events this generates if you're curious—it's a whole bunch. And if one of the receivers of these events registered to use the **pull** interface, and is iconified and fast asleep, every one of these events is accumulating on a queue in a channel somewhere and may stay there until the user turns off his or her machine to go home that evening. I know power users who do calculations like this five times before morning coffee. Check the documentation for your Event

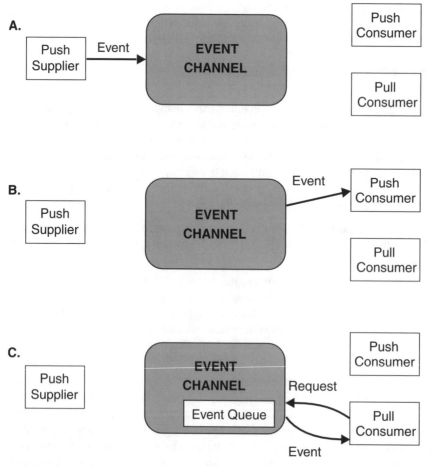

Figure 12.2 Operation of an event channel with both push and pull consumers.

Service implementation to make sure it can handle the load that some users provide without even thinking.

Here are the interfaces the objects use. We have two push consumer objects: the event channel, and the first true consumer object. They both support the **PushConsumer** interface:

```
interface PushConsumer {
        void push (in any data) raises (Disconnected);
        void disconnect_push_consumer ();
}
```

The channel implements this interface to allow it to receive events from the supplier object as a server. The consumer object, in order to receive push events from the channel, also has to inherit and implement this interface. This makes the object a server in the eyes of the Event Service.

The push supplier object also supports an interface:

```
interface PushSupplier {
        void disconnect_push_supplier ();
}
```

The symmetric disconnect operations allow either side to shut down communications. Since some configurations of Event Service implementations may include independent objects that may shut down arbitrarily (for instance, when a user quits his spreadsheet), this capability is a necessary part of the specification. Well-behaved objects will not shut down at times that will place an unnecessary burden on any user.

The channel supports the **PullSupplier** interface invoked by the pull consumer object:

```
interface PullSupplier {
        any pull () raises (disconnected);
        any try_pull ( out Boolean has_event)
            raises (disconnected);

        void disconnect_pull_supplier ();
}
```

This interface dishes out events stored on the queue we've been talking about. If there is an event on the queue, **pull** returns right away; otherwise, it blocks until an event is received by the channel and is available on the queue. **try_pull** returns immediately in either case. If there is an event, **has_event** will be **true** and the event value will be placed in the **any**; if not, **has_event** will be **false**.

12.3.1 Registering for Events on a Channel

There is a sophisticated set of interfaces for registering to send or receive events. The object that creates an event channel gets to control what gets to register as event supplier and consumer. This way, for instance, an object can ensure that it is the only one that can send events on a channel, while it makes the consumer end of the channel public so that any number of objects can receive events. Or, an object that creates a number of objects can also create a private event channel to connect them.

For details on registration interfaces, see either the OMG specification for the Event Service or the documentation that came with your Event Service implementation.

12.3.2 Typed Event Channels

All of the events we've passed so far include only an **any** datatype. What if you want to pass some particular type of data in your events?

You can do this using the Event Service as specified, but you have to create a specialized version of the channel and the objects that access it. The specification tells you what to do, and what the interfaces will look like when you're finished (with your particular datatypes inserted, of course).

This "specification" is more a piece of advice than a true specification, since the IDL interfaces include the application-specific type in their signature. Even the Notification Service specification points out that this part of the Event Service spec is a little obscure and difficult to follow. If you're generating a lot of events with a particular associated datatype, we recommend that you look at our write-up of the *structured event* feature of the Notification Service (Section 12.4.4), and use it instead.

12.4 Notification Service

In the introductory section of this chapter, we listed five key features that the Notification Service adds to our event delivery infrastructure. We're going to describe these features now, so you might want to flip back and review the list if you've forgotten it. First, though, we have to describe the basic Notification Service architecture so here we go:

12.4.1 Notification Service Architecture

Figure 12.3, reprinted from the specification, is the diagram of the Notification Service architecture.

The first thing you'll notice (besides that the service defines a lot of different parts!) is that a notification channel can accept both event-service-type and notification-channel-type connections, at both supplier and consumer ends, in both push and pull modes. Event-channel-connected objects are labeled EC in Figure 12.3, and notification-channel-connected objects are labeled NC. The ECA and NCA labels identify management objects defined in the **CosEventChannelAdmin** and **CosNotifyChannelAdmin IDL** modules.

Notification Service interfaces inherit from their corresponding Event Service interfaces. This enables current conformant Event Service applications to switch to the Notification Service without code change, although you would certainly want to change your code soon after switching to take advantage of the features of the new service. One place where this shows is in the administrative interfaces: In Figure 12.3, the old Event Service admin interfaces appear at the top, while the new Notification Service admin interfaces appear at the bottom. The ECA interfaces are pretty simple—basically factories that create Proxy Consumer and Supplier objects for new connections. In contrast, the NCA interfaces shown at the bottom provide access to all of the new QoS and filtering features.

About inheritance: Remember that this inheritance in the definition of the Notification Service means *only* that Event Service *interfaces* are inherited—this does *not* mean that your vendor's implementation of the Notification Service needs to inherit or use any part of their or anyone's *implementation* of the Event Service. This is just what you want, as a consumer and user. Your Event Service based application code continues to work without change, since all of the interfaces you used are still supported, but the implementation behind the service you buy—even of just the Event Service part—will be improved if your vendor needed to bring the service up to the standard of the new Notification Service.

You create a new notification event channel by invoking the **EventChannelFactory** interface. This is where you specify channel-level parameters including **MaxQueueLength**, **MaxConsumers**, and **MaxSuppliers**. (More on these later.)

The channel bears administrative interfaces that create other objects, including consumer and supplier admin objects. Every Notification Service object has an identifier unique within the scope of your installation (and likely, although not provably, unique everywhere else as well). Objects remember the IDs of objects they create, and can return their object references. Created objects retain back references to the object that created them. This allows full navigation around the service, from supplier proxy to

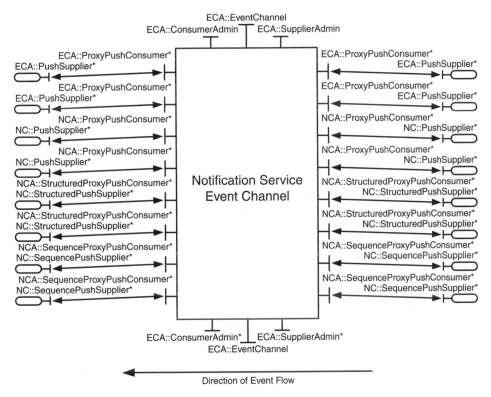

Figure 12.3 Overall architecture of the Notification Service.

channel to consumer proxy or back. For example, you can ask a channel for a list of its **ConsumerAdmin** instances, and each of these for its various **ProxyPushSupplier** objects (that push events onto push consumers). Because of this, it's easy to design and build objects to administer your notification service installation.

Each **NCA::ConsumerAdmin** or **NCA::SupplierAdmin** object on a channel can create, on request, one or more proxy objects to which event consumers or suppliers can connect. In the Notification Service, you can have as many of these Admin instances as you want, and each has its own set of QoS properties that are passed on to all of the proxy objects it creates. This lets you administer QoS properties, essentially, in group mode. You can have different QoS sets on the same channel, without having to administer QoS to many proxies at the individual client level—a worthy feature, especially for large installations such as Telecomms Management Networks. At the same time, this streamlines processing by allowing filter operations to be performed once for an entire group of consumers. By the way, you can also refine QoS settings at the proxy level for an individual client if you need to.

Three types of events are supported: First is the usual Event Service format with its accompanying **any**. Added by the Notification Service are one event with the newly defined Event structure and another with a sequence of Event structures. We'll describe the structure in its own section later in the chapter. The sequence of structures allows you to batch the handling of a large number of events, for efficiency. The service handles not only batching and separation of structures into and out of sequences, it even performs conversion of **any**-based events into structured events and the reverse for many forms of the contents of the **any.**

That covers the basic architecture: the pieces of the service, and how they fit together on a high level. Now let's look at the capabilities we've added beyond what we had in the Event Service, working our way down the list we drew up in the first section of this chapter.

12.4.2 Quality of Service Control

In the Notification Service, QoS is fixed by setting *Properties*, which the service defines as pairs of values of type **<string, any>**. Since this form was set before the POA and AMI defined their Policy format (which is an **unsigned long PolicyType** and an **any**), we'll have to live with the inconsistency. A number of properties can be assembled and passed as a sequence. The service defines some standard properties, but leaves the way open for vendors or users to create their own with the caveat that these, of course, will not interoperate with other installations unless they co-conspire to make this happen.

Here's the hierarchy of scope levels for QoS setup:

- At the highest level, you can set properties for a Notification Channel.

- At the next level, you can set properties for Admin objects connected to the channel.

- You can also set properties for individual proxies (which allows per consumer if you restrict each proxy to a single consumer).

- Orthogonal to this, you can set QoS property values for individual messages.

Table 12.1 Levels at which Notification Service QoS Property Settings Are Supported

PROPERTY	PER MESSAGE	PER PROXY	PER ADMIN	PER CHANNEL
EventReliability	X			X
ConnectionReliability		X	X	X
Priority	X	X	X	X
StartTime	X			
StopTime	X			
Timeout	X	X	X	X
StartTimeSupported		X	X	X
StopTimeSupported		X	X	X
MaxEventsPerConsumer		X	X	X
OrderPolicy		X	X	X
DiscardPolicy		X	X	X
MaximumBatchSize		X	X	X
PacingInterval		X	X	X

Table 12.1 shows which QoS properties can be set which way. We'll use the property list from the table to organize our presentation of the different QoS properties as follows:

- **EventReliability** and **ConnectionReliability** can be set to either **BestEffort** or **Persistent**. These two settings work together:

    EventReliability = ConnectionReliability = BestEffort: This combination gives no delivery guarantees—failures in the system may result in events not delivered to some consumers, or individual consumers receiving the same event more than once. The system will not automatically reestablish connections lost in a system failure.

    EventReliability = BestEffort and **ConnectionReliability = Persistent:** Connections will be remade when a channel comes up after a failure, but individual events are lost during a crash.

    EventReliability = Persistent and **ConnectionReliability = BestEffort:** This inconsistent setting combination is neither defined nor supported by the spec. (It doesn't make sense to save events because you can't deliver them when your connections stay down!)

    EventReliability = ConnectionReliability = Persistent: Channels store both connection and event information persistently. After a system failure, connections are automatically remade, and events are retrieved from storage and requeued for delivery.

- **Priority**: The channel delivers events in priority order. Priority values range from –32767 to +32767; zero is the default. Consumers can override the priority of an event.

- **StartTime**: For messages, this is a **TimeBase::UtcT** encoded value with the earliest time the event may be delivered, and may be specified per-message only. However, Proxies, Admins, and Channels have a boolean setting, **StartTimeSupported** (a little lower in our table), which tells whether or not they will honor the **StartTime** message setting.

- **StopTime**: May only be set per-message; as you expected, the **boolean StopTimeSupported** is the corresponding setting for Proxies, Admins, and Channels.

- **Timeout**: Since this is a relative time, it can be set at any level. Event consumers can override the value as well.

- **MaxEventsPerConsumer**: This can be set to prevent a single badly behaved consumer (Cher Whatsername from *Clueless*, perhaps?) from forcing a channel to queue its administrative limit of queued events, blocking further throughput. **MaxQueueLength**, the administrative limit, is a value representing just what it says; the default value of zero means no limit. Like QoS properties, administrative properties for a channel can only be set at creation time and cannot be changed.

- **OrderPolicy**: The following are defined: **AnyOrder**, **FifoOrder**, **PriorityOrder**, and **DeadlineOrder**. Like your father when you were young, these mean exactly what they say. Deadline order is based on impending Timeout , which we set two bullets up.

- **DiscardPolicy**: Queues and their associated buffers are maintained for channels, proxies, and individual event consumers; overflow and discard are therefore processed on all of these levels as well. Limits are **MaxQueueLength** for the channel, and **MaxEventsPerConsumer** for every other level. Proxies must keep track of different limits for different consumers, and process them properly. **DiscardPolicy** values are **AnyOrder**, **FifoOrder** (earliest events discard first), **LifoOrder** (opposite to **Fifo**), **PriorityOrder** (lower priority discards first), **DeadlineOrder** (shortest expiry discards first), and **RejectNewEvents**.

- **MaximumBatchSize**: Affects consumers that register to receive sequences of Structured Events. When the sequence reaches **MaximumBatchSize**, even if the time hasn't reached the **PacingInterval** (next), the sequence will be sent.

- **PacingInterval**: Also affects consumers that register to receive sequences of structured events: The period of time that events will be collected into a sequence before delivery.

You can set and validate QoS settings. We won't go over all of the various ways to do it, but will assure that validation operations can tell you the settings that would be in effect for an event in case you need to know before you send it. And if you use the system-defined event structure, you can insert QoS properties into the structure header yourself without using any service routines.

There is a set of exceptions defined in the service that covers just about anything that could possibly go wrong. There are also some clever operations that not only validate the QoS settings you ask about, but also suggest other valid settings you could use instead.

In addition to the **MaxQueueLength** administrative property we already mentioned, there are two more, **MaxConsumers** and **MaxSuppliers**, that can be set when you create a channel. The default of zero for these means no limit.

12.4.3 Typed and Structured Events

The Notification Service defines a general event structure as the basis for its event. The submitters' goal was to organize event data, especially metadata, without constraining applications from sending around the stuff they needed to get their job done. Their definition of a *structured event* is shown in Figure 12.4.

Basically, this divides into two main parts: Event Header, the first part, contains three major fields—**domain_type**, **type_name**, and **event_name**—followed by a series of optional minor header fields (designated **ohf** for Optional Header Field). Event Body, the second part, contains a series of filterable body fields (designated **fd** for Filterable Data), followed by **remainder_of_body**, which is an **any**. (Hey, we had to have one *somewhere!*)

The first three fields of the header identify the vertical industry domain, the category of the event, and the specific event; for example, **domain_type = Healthcare**, **type_name = VitalSigns**, and **event_name = NoPulse** (just to make up a heart-stopping example). If you use the first two fields to index into an event type repository such as the MOF-based one that the specification defines and recommends, your program can quickly and easily interpret and act on events it receives in this structured format. We won't describe the

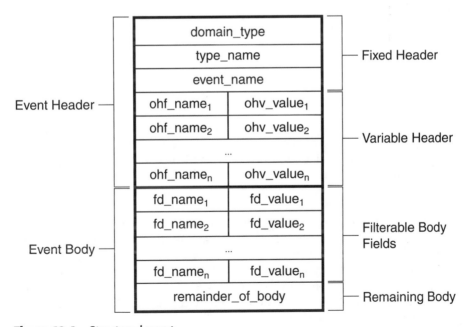

Figure 12.4   Structured event.

Notification Event Repository any more here, but it's a useful facility—if you're interested, see the original OMG specification, which contains a good write-up.

The Optional Header Fields contain per-message QoS settings. Although your enterprise can define its own names and values for these fields, they're most useful for the service-standard fields that go here: **EventReliability**, **Priority**, **StartTime**, **StopTime**, and **Timeout**.

The Filterable Data fields are the most interesting, if you have a well-defined and agreed-upon schema. You can put all of the interesting values here, identified with their proper names: PulseRate and RespirationRate, perhaps, continuing our health care example. With key datatypes identifiable in the event structure in this way, filters anywhere in the system can act on their values. This allows different parts of your organization to prioritize events their own way—a big help for large companies with well-defined areas of responsibility.

The authors of the specification encourage domains to standardize Event Types and their Filterable Data fields. We agree that this is a good idea, and suggest that the set of industry domain names and category names be standardized as well. The Trader Service isn't the only OMG specification that needs an agreed-upon schema to augment its standardized data structure.

The last part of the structure is the **any**. You can put your BLOB here, if you really have to. You could even define site-specific filters for data here.

12.4.4 Event Filtering

Event Filtering was the primary reason that OMG's Telecommunications Task Force defined the Notification Service—all the rest is gravy, at least as far as some users are concerned. The filtering infrastructure in the specification is flexible and powerful, allowing filtering at the channel, group (admin), and individual proxy levels. Filtering can be based on event content and priority settings. In our description, we'll concentrate on *what* you can do, more than *how* you do it, since a detailed documentation of this flexible and sophisticated filter facility is beyond the scope of this book.

12.4.4.1 Content Filtering

Filter Objects each support one or more constraints defined in an Object Constraint Language grammar specified by the service as an extension of the Trader's definition (see Chapter 11, "Naming and Trader Services"). Implementations may support additional constraint languages if they want, but all must support the one defined in the specification. Every Admin and Proxy object can create, define, and administer its own set of filter objects.

Constraints start with strings representing the domain and event type; for example, "Telecom" and "Communications Alarm." You can OR these to have the constraint that follows apply to multiple domains or event types, or use wild cards and then filter on the domain and event type in your boolean expression. The boolean expression operates, in its most transparent form, on the contents of the structured event. You can, in addition, define filters that operate on Event Service untyped and typed events as well, but we aren't going to describe them here.

Here's how filtering at Admin and Proxy level interact: First, you've created a set of filter objects associated with an Admin object. Each time an event comes in, it's filtered by all of these objects and the results are OR'd to produce a single TRUE or FALSE result at the Admin level. (Actually, it's filtered by each object in turn until one returns TRUE, or they all return FALSE, but conceptually it's an ORing of all the results.)

Second, you've also created a set of filter objects associated with individual proxy objects attached to that Admin. As with the Admin filtering, the results of all of the proxy-level filters are OR'd to produce a TRUE or FALSE result at the Proxy level.

You might assume that the Admin object would apply its filter result immediately, and only relay the event on to the proxy object if it passed (conceptually, this corresponds to ANDing the results of the two levels of filtering), but this isn't the case. Instead, there's an Admin-level policy that you can set to either AND or OR the results of the two levels of filtering. That is,

- All the Admin filters are applied and the set of results is OR'd to obtain an Admin-level result; and

- All the Proxy filters are applied and the results are OR'd to obtain a Proxy-level result; and then

- The Admin-level result and the Proxy-level result are either AND'd or OR'd with each other, depending on the Admin-level policy that the user had set at Admin creation time.

You can attach callbacks to filter objects. This supports the **subscription_change** operation, which we'll discuss shortly, that allows filter objects to notify interested objects when their constraint set is modified.

12.4.4.2 Priority Filtering

The two properties of an individual event most used for filtering are its priority and its expiration time. Unfortunately, it's possible that a supplier thinks that its events are of high priority and useful for a long time, while a particular consumer object thinks that those same events are not quite so important, and useful only for a shorter time. For cases such as this in which the supplier and consumer have different opinions on QoS settings, the Notification Service provides mapping filter objects that allow a client to override how these properties affect events' routing.

Consider, to be concrete, overriding the priority value of an event. You would set up a mapping filter on a proxy supplier, with an ordered set of constraint mapping-priority value pairs, and a default priority value that will be returned if none of the mappings is satisfied. Each time an event comes in, your proxy supplier calls the filter with the event. The filter applies the constraints in order and, as soon as one is satisfied, returns TRUE and the priority value associated with that constraint. If the filter gets to the end of the list and no constraints have been satisfied, the filter returns FALSE and the default priority value that you set. On return, if the result is TRUE, the proxy supplier treats the event as if its priority had been set to the value that was returned by the call; that is, the value that you wanted to be the override if this constraint was satisfied. If the result is FALSE, the proxy supplier treats the event according to its original priority value if it has one; otherwise, it uses the default value that you supplied via the filter. In either case, the values in the event header are not modified, only the treatment of the event is affected by the filter operation.

Filter on expiration time works analogously.

12.4.4.3 Filtering—Examples

Here are some examples, from the specification, of constraints in the defined Constraint Language.

- Accept all "CommunicationsAlarm" events but no "lost_packet" messages:

  $type_name == 'CommunicationsAlarm' and not
  ($event_name == 'lost_packet')

- Accept "CommunicationsAlarm" events with priorities ranging from 1 to 5:

  $type_name == 'CommunicationsAlarm' and
  $priority >= 1 and $priority <= 5

- Accept only recent events; that is, generated within about the last 15 minutes:

  $origination_timestamp.high + 2 < $curtime.high

12.4.4.4 Filtering—Summary

That's all we're going to mention about filtering. Hopefully, we've given you a good feel for the capability and flexibility of the system. If you have an implementation of the Notification Service, you can follow up by studying its documentation set; if not, check out the OMG specification, which you can download for free from the OMG Web site. See Appendix A for references.

12.4.5 Event Discovery

Consider an event channel, with its multiple event suppliers and consumers, *in toto*. Efficiency and quality both require coordination from end to end. For example, it doesn't make sense for suppliers to push thousands of CommunicationAlarm events onto a particular channel if no consumer is listening for them; conversely it doesn't make sense for a supplier to continue to withhold NodeFailure events that it could supply when a new consumer subscribes to the channel and wants to receive them.

To enable end-to-end coordination, a big step up from the simplistic Event Service model, the Notification Service provides several new operations organized into Offer and Subscription categories.

Offer Coordination. All Proxy Consumer objects and the SupplierAdmin objects support the **offer_change** operation; in addition, event consumers may support it as well. It has two parameters, one for newly offered event types and the other for newly withdrawn event types. To subscribe to **offer_change** calls when a channel's event list changes, objects call **attach_callback**. Notice that, if a particular event type has multiple suppliers on a channel, withdrawal by one supplier will not change the overall list of events available on that channel and **offer_change** calls will not be made.

- Consumers may also call **obtain_offered_types** for a complete list of event types on a channel.

Subscription Coordination. subscription_change is the analogous subscriber-side call, supported by all Proxy Supplier objects and the ConsumerAdmin object. Its arguments specify event types that are either newly required or no longer required. There is also an operation, **obtain_subscription_types**, analogous to **obtain_offered_types** described earlier.

Together, these operations allow the system to coordinate from end to end, so that event types with no subscribers are never loaded onto a channel, while newly requested event types are started soon after subscribers attach to a channel.

At every level of the system, CORBA continues to improve. In Chapter 6, we saw how the AMI specification added QoS control to invocations. Here, we've added not only QoS control but also typing, filtering, and subscription control to our event infrastructure through the Notification Service. Since event-passing is how distributed systems keep themselves organized, this is key to allowing us to rely on CORBA in our enterprise and on the Internet.

More important services are coming up in the next two chapters: First is the Transaction Service, one key to business operation. After that comes security, key to not only business but also to government, military, R&D, and other fields.

CHAPTER

13

CORBAservices, Part 3: Transaction and Concurrency Services

13.1 The Transaction Service

Online Transaction Processing (OLTP) is the foundation of the world's business computing. It is the system that ensures that the last 100 widgets are promised to only one customer; that the last two seats on flight 423 to Hawaii are assigned, together, to a honeymooning couple; that the balance printed on your ATM ticket in Taipei exactly matches the balance in the bank's central datastore in New York City. OLTP accomplishes this reliably, even in the face of (noncatastrophic) failure of hardware and software around the system.

In this chapter, we'll look at OLTP and OMG's Transaction Processing (TP) specification. First, we summarize the business problem, and see how transactional semantics require that all of the parties involved be prepared before allowing the transaction to be committed. If any of the parties cannot complete its part of the transaction, the entire transaction is rolled back. Then we'll review flat and nested transactions and, finally, summarize the TP specification itself.

The Object Transaction Service (OTS) extends transactional semantics to distributed, object-oriented applications. Using the service, our applications will have the reliability and robustness that business requires, in an environment where multiuser data access comes naturally. Transactional access can be appropriate for nonbusiness data, too; record-keeping is done in many contexts, and a TP system is almost always easier and less expensive in the long run than trying to code up equivalent reliability in-house.

A final benefit of the service is legacy systems integration. Key provisions of the service allow smooth integration of object and nonobject TP systems, on one or several ORBs or just out there on the network. These provisions allow your distributed, object-oriented TP clients and applications to integrate smoothly with your existing TP mainframes, providing a smooth transition from one world to the other. We'll give some details later, plus pointers to more information in some OMG references.

The OTS is a popular service with more than a dozen implementations on the market. A Japanese consortium has tested interoperability among four of them by running shared transactions to commit or roll back; their success indicates that the specification is sound, and that these implementations conform well.

13.1.1 What's New in OTS?

Although the OTS is a CORBAservice and therefore not part of the CORBA 3 specification, it has been revised twice since we wrote the first edition of this book. Three enhancements are important enough to discuss in this chapter, and they are:

- A new transaction model, *unshared transactions,* which extends the distribution model to asynchronous communications.

- In the original specification, you made an object transactional by inheriting the **TransactionalObject** interface; now, you make an instance transactional via a POA policy.

- A synchronization interface was added to give clients an opportunity to move data to their persistent database before the *prepare* step of a transaction.

We think the second item is fundamental: There are many CORBA object types that could usefully be run transactionally sometimes, but need to be run non-transactionally other times. Even the Naming and Trader Services could benefit from transactional assurance in high-reliability environments such as financial, military, or government applications. Using the original specification, an object could only be transactional if its interface inherited from **TransactionalObject**. This made *every* instance of the type transactional (although non-transactional invocations could be made of it); to create a non-transactional instance, you needed a separate implementation with an interface that did not inherit **TransactionalObject**. Using the revised specification, the object's interface has nothing to do with whether its instances are transactional or not, and architecturally this is much more sound. Now, if you create an object instance on a transactional POA, it's transactional; if you create it on a non-transactional POA, it's not. Of course, there's more to it than this; we tell all in Section 13.1.4.5.

The new unshared transaction model is also described in Section 13.1.4.5, and the synchronization interface in Section 13.1.4.8.

13.1.2 The Business Problem

OLTP refers to a class of applications critical to the operational needs of many businesses. OLTP systems control day-to-day activities—taking orders, operating production lines, transferring funds. It applies to all industries, private as well as the public sector.

The first OLTP applications were deployed to reduce costs by automating clerical tasks. As applications matured, they encompassed more business rules, becoming increasingly critical to daily operations so that, today, most businesses cannot operate without them. Their databases not only support operational applications, but also form the foundation for strategic decision-making.

OLTP applications inherently deal with shared data. For example:

- Accepted orders reduce product inventory, causing fewer items to be available for subsequent orders.

- Credit card payments reduce balances, enabling subsequent charges to be accepted.

Even when data are not updated, multiple users may read it and act on its contents. For example:

- When inventory falls below 100, order 1000 more from the wholesaler.

- When credit limit is exceeded, do not approve additional charges *and* send collection notice.

Allowing multiple users to read and update the same data requires a mechanism to protect its integrity. This mechanism must ensure that:

- Only one application can update the data at a time. This guarantees that the persistent copy reflects all activities that operate against it.

- Data seen by an application is consistent with the current state of the business. This guarantees that applications will follow business rules (for instance, taking orders only when there is sufficient inventory to fill them).

- Changes made to the data persist. This prevents decisions from being made with incorrect information (such as using last week's inventory rather than today's).

The mechanism that provides these guarantees is the *transaction*.

13.1.3 Transaction Concepts

The transaction is an important programming paradigm that simplifies the construction of reliable business applications. Initially deployed in commercial applications to protect data in centralized databases, it has been extended to the broader context of distributed computation. Today, transactions are considered the key to constructing reliable distributed applications.

Transaction semantics define the conditions that guarantee, for a sequence of operations, that the result always meets TP requirements. These requirements have become known by the acronym ACID, for *Atomicity, Consistency, Isolation*, and *Durability*. The transaction as a whole must demonstrate:

Atomicity. All changes are either completely done—committed—or completely undone—rolled back. Recoverable data changes uniformly and only at transaction boundaries (the beginning and end of a transaction).

Consistency. The effects of a transaction preserve invariant properties of your system. When you transfer funds at an ATM, your checking account is credited and your savings account is debited simultaneously. Recoverable data are visible to other applications only when committed.

Isolation. Intermediate states are not visible to other transactions. The two sides of your double-entry bookkeeping system change together, and never get out of synchronization. Transactions appear to execute serially, even if performed concurrently.

Durability. The effects of a completed transaction are persistent. Changes are never lost except for catastrophic failure.

Transaction semantics can be defined as part of any object that provides ACID properties. Examples are OODBMS and persistent objects. The value of a separate transaction service is that it allows:

- Transactions that include multiple, separately defined ACID objects
- Transactions that combine objects and nonobject resources

13.1.4 OTS Features

OMG required the writers of the OTS to meet a number of requirements targeted especially at the integration of legacy TP systems and simultaneous execution of parts of a single transaction on multiple TP systems. Legacy systems integration, especially, is crucial; if this had not been accomplished, businesses would not have a feasible pathway to move to object-oriented TP systems.

Here is a rundown of some of the features of the TP specification.

13.1.4.1 Support for Multiple Transaction Models

As we describe in detail in Sections 13.1.5.2 and 13.1.5.3, the OTS supports both the flat and nested transaction models. The flat transaction model, which is widely supported in the industry today, must be provided by every OTS supplier. The nested transaction model, which provides finer granularity isolation and facilitates object reuse in a transactional environment, is optional. The chained transaction model is not supported.

13.1.4.2 Evolutionary Deployment

The ability to wrap and integrate existing TP systems is a key feature of the OTS. OMG members knew that object technology would penetrate business computing much quicker if it could happen without disturbing current systems.

13.1.4.3 Model Interoperability

Especially during the transition from existing procedural TP systems to object-oriented systems, businesses need to make the two work together. Therefore, the OTS was designed to accommodate:

- A single transaction that includes ORB and non-ORB applications and resources
- Interoperability between the Object Transaction Service model and the X/Open Distributed Transaction Processing (DTP) model

- Access to existing (non-object) programs and resource managers by objects
- Access to objects by existing programs and resource managers
- Coordination by a single transaction service of the activities of both object and non-object resource managers
- The network case—a single transaction, distributed between an object and non-object system, each of which has its own transaction service

13.1.4.4 Network Interoperability

Businesses need to interoperate between systems offered by multiple vendors under a variety of conditions, including:

Single transaction service, single ORB. It must be possible for a single transaction service to interoperate with itself using a single ORB.

Multiple transaction services, single ORB. It must be possible for one transaction service to interoperate with a cooperating transaction service using a single ORB.

Single transaction service, multiple ORBs. It must be possible for a single transaction service to interoperate with itself using different ORBs.

Multiple transaction services, multiple ORBs. It must be possible for one transaction service to interoperate with a cooperating transaction service using different ORBs.

The OTS specifies all of the interactions required between cooperating transaction service implementations to support single-ORB interoperability. It relies on CORBA 2.0 interoperability to provide transaction service interaction between ORBs.

13.1.4.5 TII Support for Unshared Transactions

This is the recent addition we mentioned at the beginning of the chapter. The AMI specification made two changes to the Transaction Service: First, it changed the way objects become transactional, from inheritance to a POA policy. Second, it created a new kind of distributed transaction, the *unshared* transaction. Along the way, the modification provided a way for programmers and system administrators to control the transactionality of an object much more precisely than was possible before. Here's how and why:

In the original specification, an object participated in the transaction service by inheriting the **TransactionalObject** interface. This interface did not add any operations to the object; instead, the inherited traits notified its ORB that the object might be participating in transactions and provided hidden "hooks" that enabled the ORB to take care of the technical details. "Might be" is indeed the operative phrase here because, although invocations certainly could come in accompanied by a transaction context (indicating that they were part of a transaction that would be committed later), other invocations might come in that were not, and there was no way for an instance to indicate, should it wish, that it *required* invocations to be part of a transaction.

And, in the original model, transactions had to be *shared*; that is, client, object, and transaction system all participated in the same transaction, at the same time, within the same context. Since all (well, almost all) invocations were synchronous, every object knew what every other object was doing, and the shared model was effective and practical. Commit and rollback could be done over the network, with clients and objects staying together. (You could participate in a transaction using deferred-synchronous invocations, but the system did not help you keep coordinated. If a client got out of synch, it would receive the **Wrong_Transaction** exception and have to recover by itself.)

However, the shared model does not work over asynchronous communications links. Since TII runs over persistent routers that are reliable enough to support transactions, the AMI specification needed to define a new model—the *unshared transaction* —for transactions over TII. There are actually three transactions per TII invocation: The client starts a transaction, delivers its invocation (via the ORB, of course) to the reliable TII network routing system, and commits. In a second transaction, the object receives and processes the invocation, delivers the response to the network, and commits. Then (as you probably guessed) the client, finally, accepts the response from the network and processes it in a third transaction, which it commits. The unshared model allows the transaction processing system, along with the client and associated transactional objects, to cope with the TII environment where multiple requests may be outstanding and invocations may not be delivered in the order that they were sent. (In fact, if you use the "priority" delivery policy it may be *unlikely* that invocations are delivered in the order they were sent!)

This solves the problem of transactions over TII, but now we have to define whether an object supports shared transactions, unshared transactions, or both. In addition, the specifiers wanted, finally, to allow objects to declare that they *required* transactional invocation where previously they could only declare that they would *accept* those invocations if they came in.

To do this, the Messaging Specification moved the declaration of transactionality from inheritance of **TransactionalObject**, where it was imposed on every instance of the type, to a POA policy that allows transactionality to be defined individually for each instance at creation time by instantiating on a POA with whatever transactionality policy value. The POA transaction policy has a range of values that give you precise control of instances' transactionality. Specifically, a POA's servants may, by POA policy, either:

- *Allow* only shared transactions
- *Require* only shared transactions
- *Allow* only unshared transactions
- *Require* only unshared transactions
- *Allow* either shared or unshared transactions
- *Require* either shared or unshared transactions

And, of course, an object may be non-transactional.

The **TransactionalObject** interface is deprecated; that is, no longer a part of the specification. Although it's likely to stick around for a couple of years or more in at least some vendors' products (and we don't speak for any vendor, so check with yours to make sure), we like the new POA policy method so much better, both for its architecture and its precision, that we'd move our source code to it as soon as we could. Even if you don't run TII and shared transactions, you gain the ability to require transactional invocations of instances where you want, and to create transactional versions of types without changing their interfaces. But if you liked things the way they were before the change, you can continue to use your old code: The new specification was careful to make the default policy identical to the old way of doing things.

13.1.4.6 Flexible Transaction Propagation Control

Both client and object implementations can control transaction propagation:

- A client controls whether its transaction is propagated with an operation.
- A client can invoke operations on objects with transactional behavior and objects without transactional behavior within the execution of a single transaction.

An object can specify transactional behavior for its interfaces. The OTS supports both *implicit* (system-managed) propagation and *explicit* (application-managed) propagation, as described in Section 13.1.4.6. With implicit propagation, transactional behavior is not specified in the operation's signature. With explicit propagation, applications define their own mechanisms for sharing a common transaction.

13.1.4.7 Synchronization Interface

The new synchronization interface helps if you're using an X/Open XA Resource Manager or any similar system as the persistent storage for your transactional objects. (We'll define a transactional object in Section 13.1.5.) In the commit protocol, the transaction service issues a **prepare** command to all participating objects. On receiving this, the XA Resource Manager stores its data in preparation for the upcoming commit. A problem arises because *clients* of the Resource Manager are probably caching data that needs to be flushed *to* it first. The synchronization interface allows this: Any object may bear the synchronization methods **before_completion** and **after_completion**, and register to be notified by the transaction coordinator. On receiving a **before_completion**, the object flushes its own cache to the XA Resource Manager and returns. Thus, when the transaction coordinator issues **prepare** invocations after all registered synchronization objects have responded, all data in transactional objects are flushed to the Resource Manager and get properly stored.

13.1.4.8 Support for TP Monitors

Businesses deploy mission-critical applications on commercial transaction processing systems that use a TP monitor to provide both efficient scheduling and resource sharing for a large number of users. The OTS includes:

- The ability to execute multiple transactions concurrently
- The ability to execute clients, servers, and transaction services in separate processes

and can be used in a TP monitor environment.

13.1.4.9 Support for Existing TP Standards

The OTS uses a model similar to that of both the X/Open DTP model and the OSI TP protocol. This makes possible a mapping to the three major TP standards (for full references, see Appendix A):

- The X/Open TX interface

- The X/Open XA interface

- The OSI TP protocol

LU 6.2 protocol mapping is not supported where these TP systems use chained transactions, which are not part of the OTS specification.

13.1.5 Parts of OTS

Basically, here's how the OTS works: You can invoke any operation on any object during a transaction, but the object must be either *transactional* or *recoverable* for that operation to display transaction semantics.

A **recoverable object** is an object whose data are affected by the committing or rolling back of a transaction. The recoverable object owns the data, and implements a failure-recovery mechanism. Typically, the object places data into stable storage during the transaction. If failure occurs during the transaction, then during the restart procedure the transactional object reads its saved state data from stable storage, discovers that a transaction was in process, and participates in a commit/rollback protocol with the Transaction service. The recoverable object must be prepared to deal with messages from the transaction manager to commit or roll back the current transaction.

A **transactional object** is any object whose behavior is affected by being in the scope of the transaction. It may behave this way because it is itself a recoverable object (since all recoverable objects are transactional), or because it refers to data stored in recoverable objects. If it's not a recoverable object itself, it participates by passing the transaction context, invisibly, through from invocations it receives to those that it makes. At the end of the chain, the recoverable object and the transaction processing system use the transaction context to coordinate all of the different parts of the transaction for the commit or rollback.

Transactions are started and ended by declaration of an initiating client. Between the start and end, certain operations by that client and other clients will be handled by the transaction manager and acquire the ACID properties. Needless to say, these operations must all be invoked on transactional or recoverable objects in order for this to work. When the client declares the end of the transaction, the transaction manager asks all of the objects involved if they are ready to commit. If they all respond yes, the transaction manager gives the word to commit; if no, the manager gives the command to roll back, and the entire transaction fails.

This process is termed *two-phase commit*. It's invisible to the client, which just invokes a commit operation; the two-phase commit is carried out under the covers by the TP system itself. In case you're curious, we've exposed some of the interface to this in Section 13.1.7.

At any time before the final commit, any participant in a transaction can force the transaction to be rolled back (eventually). If a transaction is rolled back, all participants roll back their changes. Typically, a participant will request the rollback of the current transaction after encountering a failure. It is implementation specific whether the Transaction Service itself monitors the participants in a transaction for failures or inactivity.

Where do transactional and recoverable objects come from? Recoverable objects, the ones that actually store the transactional data, usually come from software suppliers; frequently, databases will have transactional modes, and some TP systems come with an integral datastore. Transactional objects—the modules that tell the database what to do—are usually written by your staff or integrator, since they deal with your business' unique schema. These objects are transactional rather than recoverable since they aren't affected by commit or rollback; the database owns the data and takes care of the two-phase commit/rollback procedure. Transactional objects are the ones that will use the new **synchronize** interface. There may be other objects involved behind the scenes, but these are the ones you will be most concerned about, at least at first. By the way, the OTS opens up your system and increases your options. If you discover an opportunity to use a recoverable object that you can write yourself, the interfaces are available for you to integrate it into your system.

13.1.5.1 Transaction Context

There's a well-established programming convention in TP that says that every operation executed between a begin transaction statement and an end transaction statement is part of the transaction, and that no explicit transactional declaration is required on the individual operations. Besides making for cleaner code, this allows functions that have no explicit transactional declarations to be executed in the scope of a transaction.

The OMG went to great lengths to preserve this environment in the OTS. Basically, it required the ORB to become "transaction-aware." The OTS specification marked the first time the ORB had ever become involved in any communication beyond just passing it through or converting datatypes' byte order. This is an indication of just how important the OMG believes OLTP is to the success of CORBA and the OMA. The operation to begin a transaction is actually executed by a pseudo-object located in the ORB (where every pseudo-object is located, of course). It sets up a *transaction context*, which the ORB automatically and invisibly inserts as a parameter to every invocation in the scope of the transaction until the client invokes the corresponding end transaction operation. This is termed *implicit transaction propagation*. Transactional and recoverable objects look for the transaction context to determine whether a request is part of a transaction and, if so, which one. If you plan to use the OTS, check with your ORB vendor to ensure that the ORB you buy supports the service. You don't have to buy the OTS from the same vendor as your ORB, but there is a component of ORB support that must be in there or else no OTS will work.

By the way, there is also a CORBA mode that supports *explicit* passing of the transaction context. This allows the originating client, or any other object that receives the context from that object, to extend the bounds of the transaction explicitly.

Believe it or not, we have passed over some of the details: how the initiating client can delegate authority to end the transaction; how other clients can perform operations in an implicitly propagated transaction; and how to tell which operations are transactional. Some of these details will come out in the rest of the chapter. If TP is new to you and this introduction piques your interest, you can follow up with the references to this chapter listed in Appendix A.

Now that we've covered the basics, let's go over the two types of transactions covered by the service, see how the service fits together, look at a brief example, and finish up with a sample of OTS IDL.

13.1.5.2 Flat Transactions

We'll deal with only two basic types of transactions: *flat*, and *nested*. There is also a *chained* transaction type, which is not supported by the OTS. We've already described a flat transaction; it has a single start and end, and a single level.

The flat transaction model is widely supported in the industry today in transaction processing systems such as IBM's CICS and BEA's TUXEDO as well as database systems from IBM, Oracle, and Sybase. It is the basis for the X/Open Distributed Transaction Processing model and the ISO OSI-TP standard.

13.1.5.3 Nested Transactions

Nested transactions permit creation of transactions embedded within an existing transaction to form a transaction hierarchy (Figure 13.1). The existing transaction is called the *parent* of the embedded transaction. The embedded transaction is a subtransaction and is called a *child* of the parent transaction.

Subtransactions can be embedded in other subtransactions to any level of nesting. The ancestors of a transaction are the parents of the subtransaction and the parents of its ancestors. The descendants of a transaction are the children of the transaction and

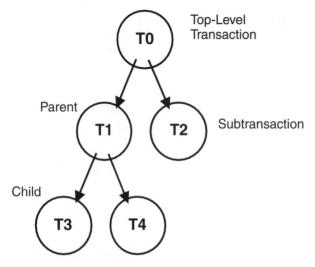

Figure 13.1 A transaction hierarchy.

the children of its descendants. Subtransactions are strictly nested. A transaction cannot commit unless all of its children have completed. When a transaction is rolled back, all of its children are rolled back.

A *top-level transaction* is a transaction without a parent. A flat transaction can be modeled as a top-level transaction without children. A top-level transaction and all of its descendants are called a *transaction family*.

Subtransactions are atomic; however, when a subtransaction commits, its changes remain pending until commitment of all its ancestors. Thus, subtransactions are not durable; only top-level transactions are durable.

Isolation also applies to subtransactions. When a transaction has multiple children, a child appears to execute serially to other siblings, even if they execute concurrently.

A subtransaction can fail without causing the entire transaction family to fail. This failure granularity aligns nicely with the partitioning of application function provided by encapsulation.

13.1.6 OMG's Object Transaction Service

Figure 13.2 shows the components of the OTS, and how they work together to execute a transaction. A transactional client makes requests (1) of the OTS to define the boundaries of a series of operations that constitute a transaction. It then invokes transactional operations (2) on transactional objects. During the transaction, requests can also be made (3) on recoverable objects.

Transactional objects are used to implement two types of application servers—*transactional* and *recoverable*. A transactional server is a collection of objects whose behavior is affected by the transaction, but has no recoverable state of its own. It implements recoverable changes using other objects. It does not participate in transaction completion, but may force transaction rollback.

A recoverable server is a collection of objects, at least one of which has recoverable state. It participates in transaction completion by registering (4) Resource objects. The Resource implements transaction completion by participating (5) in two-phase commit. For each active transaction, OTS maintains a transaction context that it associates with transactional operations. The transaction context is an implicit parameter of transactional operations and is transferred by the ORB along with the operation, as we pointed out in Section 13.1.5.

13.1.7 Transaction Service Example

Our goal here is to cover enough of the OTS to give you a basic understanding of what it can do, and perhaps some of how it works, so that you can decide if you're interested in buying and using it, and know enough to figure out what people tell you about various OTS implementations and programs. It's a complex service with many parts, and we don't have the space to cover all of them in enough detail to make sense. So, we'll cover the service by presenting an example and showing the parts of the OTS that come into play as the different stages of the example execute.

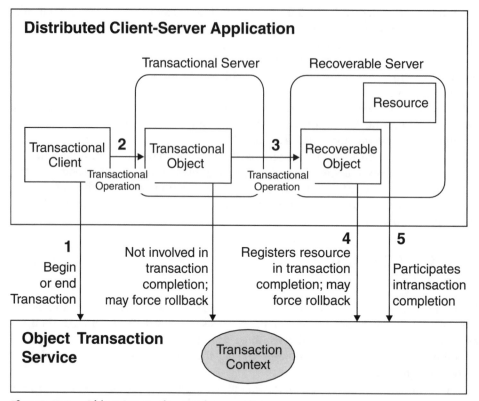

Figure 13.2 Object Transaction Service overview.

The client code following this paragraph implements an order entry application. It's shown in pseudo-code—operations are only shown if they are part of the flow; exception checking is omitted as are most declarations; and coding is, at best, imprecise. The inventory and the purchase order are implemented as objects: `Inventory` and `Purchase`. The transaction consists of a `reduce` operation on `Inventory` followed by an `add` operation on `Purchase`. If sufficient inventory is not available, the transaction is rolled back.

```
// Transaction Example  --  pseudocode
Boolean OrderEntry ( Amount quantity )

    Inventory   theInventory;
    Purchase    thePurchaseOrder;

    Current     theCurrentTransaction;

    theCurrentTransaction.begin();
      Amount balance = theInventory.query();
      if (balance > quantity)
         theInventory.reduce( quantity );
           thePurchaseOrder.add( quantity );
```

```
    theCurrentTransaction.commit();
    return True;


else
    theCurrentTransaction.rollback();
    return False;
```

From the client's perspective, `Inventory` and `Purchase` implement the transactional guarantees. `Inventory` may rely on these features in a database management system, rather than implement them itself. Such an object would be a transactional server—it has no recoverable state of its own, but needs to be part of the transaction so that the object with recoverable state (the database) can participate in transaction completion.

The type `Current` represents a pseudo-object; the code here looks like a conventional CORBA object invocation on `theCurrentTransaction`, but the operation is actually executed by a pseudo-object located within the ORB (conceptually, at least; remember that the boundaries of the ORB are frequently difficult to trace). Invoking `begin` on `theCurrentTransaction` creates a transaction context that is added by the ORB to every invocation signature until we invoke either `commit` or `rollback` on `theCurrentTransaction`.

While we're looking at Current, let's go over its IDL:

```
interface Current {
    void begin()
        raises( ... );
    void commit(in boolean report_heuristics)
        raises( ... );
    void rollback()
        raises( ... );
    void rollback_only()
        raises( ... );

    Status get_status();
    string get_transaction_name();
    void set_timeout(in unsigned long seconds);

    Control get_control();
    Control suspend();
    void resume(in Control which)
        raises( ... );
};
```

As we just pointed out, **begin** creates a new transaction, and its transaction context is associated with the client thread of control. If there already is a current transaction, the new transaction becomes a subtransaction of it. **commit** and **rollback** do what we said; note that the originating client controls access to the object reference to **current**, which is the target of the **commit** and **rollback** operations.

rollback_only sets the transaction status so that **rollback** is the only possible outcome, without forcing the **rollback** to occur immediately. **rollback_only**, **get_status**, and **get_transaction_name** are operations used internally by the TP system to stay organized; we're not going to describe them here. **get_control** and **suspend** return a control object that, when passed to **resume**, associates this transaction's context with our thread of execution. **suspend** also ceases the association of any context with our thread. That is, between a **suspend** and the **resume** with that same control object as an argument, invocations we make are not part of any transaction; with the **resume** invocation, the transaction resumes.

Continuing with our example: We first query inventory to see if we have enough widgets, or whatever. If we do, we issue invocations to reduce the quantity in inventory and add that same quantity to the purchase order. On **commit**, the two operations update "simultaneously," assuming that no exceptions are raised by objects theInventory and thePurchaseOrder.

If inventory is not sufficient, our example code does not try to fill the purchase order, and instead invokes **rollback** to terminate the transaction. We admit, we hadn't done anything to change the state of any transactional object so there isn't really anything to roll back. Imagine, however, that we were filling orders for widgets and handles, and we had already added 2000 widgets to the order and discovered we didn't have any handles, so we invoked rollback to cancel everything, widgets and handles together. (Of *course* widgets have handles. We thought everybody knew that!)

Current is associated with implicit propagation; there is another set of interfaces that you use if you require explicit control, but we won't detail them here.

We will spare you the details of most of the interfaces used by objects participating in the service, since you're probably going to be a user and not an implementor of the service. There is one, however, that reveals succinctly some key information on how the two-phase commit protocol works under the covers, so we'll go over it here. It is the **Resource** interface.

```
interface Resource {
    Vote prepare();
    void rollback()
        raises( . . . );
    void commit()
        raises( . . . );
    void commit_one_phase()
        raises( . . . );
    void forget();
};
```

prepare is invoked to begin the two-phase commit protocol on the resource. The resource responds with its vote on how to end the transaction: If no persistent data have been modified by the transaction, the resource returns **VoteReadOnly**. The transaction service will then ignore this resource for the rest of the processing of this transaction, and the resource can forget about the transaction. If the resource is prepared to commit—that is, the persistent data have already been written to stable storage (although they probably have not been made visible to the outside world)—it returns **VoteCommit.** The resource must still be prepared to roll back, however, since one of the other resources in the transaction may not have done so well with its own processing. If the resource is not prepared to commit, or if it has no knowledge of the transaction (it should assume that the knowledge was lost in a system crash, for instance), it returns **VoteRollback**. Like **VoteReadOnly**, this response relieves the resource of further responsibility for this transaction and it can forget that it ever existed.

In the event of failure, the OTS will attempt to continue the two-phase commit protocol. This requires recoverable servers to remember transaction state and be able to restore the proper copy of recoverable state from information recorded during prepare.

rollback and **commit** do what you think. **commit** raises a **NotPrepared** exception if the **prepare** operation didn't come first. **commit_one_phase** is like **commit** except it doesn't require a prior **prepare**; the resource can raise the **TransactionRolledBack** standard exception if it receives a **commit_one_phase** request and can't do it. **forget** is used to clean up after certain exception conditions.

This concludes our discussion of the Object Transaction Service. Before we leave this topic entirely, let's briefly skim the Concurrency Control Service, which supports the OTS with resource locks.

13.2 Concurrency Control Service

Frequently, a database will have to ensure that only one client at a time gets access to a record, or a file system will have to restrict write access to a file in order to prevent conflicting edits. This need is common enough that OMG established the Concurrency Control Service (CCS) to help take care of it. The service was designed specifically to service the OTS so it understands the transaction context, but the locking concept is general and the CCS can be useful in a more general way. If you are creating resources somewhere in your architecture and need to regulate access to them, the CCS may be just what you need. However, it's more likely (assuming that you're an end-user company and not a database vendor) that you will buy a facility like a database or file system and find that a locking facility is already part of it.

That's because the CCS isn't a concurrency control service at all, it's really a lock managing facility. Control is provided by the facility that uses the CCS such as a database, TP system, or file system, and these are typically items that end users buy rather than write.

Here's an analogy that might help: Imagine you're back in high school and it's the first day of gym class. The locker room is lined with lockers (of course), all without locks—this represents your DB system without the CCS. The gym teacher comes in with a box full of locks—this represents the CCS by itself: a bunch of locks in a box, which you could lock and unlock all day and never make any difference to anything. So you hang one lock on each locker, and suddenly things get useful, at least under the circumstances. Analogous to the locks in this story, the locks managed by the CCS are useful only when they're hung on an electronic "locker" with the right hooks, such as a database or TP system.

This means, for one thing, that if you want to add concurrency control to a system you already own and use (like a Unix file system, for example), the CCS is not going to help you out unless you plan to rewrite the internal file system code yourself. Using our analogy, the file system doesn't have any place for you to hang the locks, so you'd have to code that part—the entire resource control system—yourself.

The CCS is a well-designed and written facility, with five lock levels to enable fine-grained locking without undue overhead. If you're building a datastore facility and need to regulate access, this is the facility you should use for lock management. However, if you're planning to buy your database and TP system from an outside vendor, you'll access the CCS indirectly and never program to it. So, we're not going to describe it here. If you need to use the CCS, we're sure you won't have any trouble figuring it out from the OMG specifications or the doc set that comes with your vendor's implementation.

CHAPTER

14

CORBAservices, Part 4: Security and Licensing Services

14.1 Introduction

Security is expensive, and the cost of your CORBAsecurity implementation is just the tip of the iceberg. Once you've got it, you have to install it, configure it, give each of your users a login and password (and another and another, every time they forget), and maintain it. Small wonder, then, that people and companies rarely buy any more security than they need, and frequently either buy or install *less* than they should.

How much security is enough? It depends on what you're protecting. If you're protecting nuclear weapons secrets, it doesn't matter how secure your system is, it isn't secure enough. If you're protecting the calculations for a contract bid that might earn your company $500 profit if everything goes well, you probably don't want to spend *anything* on security unless that investment protects something else along the way. If you're protecting your e-commerce Website that does $5 million in business every week, hopefully you're serious about security and have specialists on staff who prepare (and justify!) a security budget, buy security products, install them, and see that they work as designed, 24×7.

Even though this chapter focuses on security for your CORBA systems, you shouldn't get the impression that your system will be safe if you only implement the things we present here. Attackers will go after your weakest link. If you've protected your running CORBA objects and your network messages with CORBAsecurity, attackers could still telephone your help desk, impersonate a legitimate user who has forgotten a password, and come away with a password that completely opens your system to them. Or, attackers may be insiders or office service people who carry away secrets on a floppy disk or backup tape. If this were a book on security, we'd discuss these overall aspects, but it's not: It's a book on CORBA and we don't have the space for a general security discussion. However, we had to say something about it—perhaps this short paragraph will be enough to get you started on a general security architecture, if you're not already working on one.

The good news about CORBAsecurity is that it's capable, flexible, and tailorable to different security needs. However, as we've seen in other aspects of CORBA, this flexibility also puts a responsibility on you to be a smart consumer, which means you'll need to educate yourself about security—find out what's in the specification, what's actually available in products on the market, what they do (and do not!) protect you against, how they can be configured, and what it takes to get them running, and to keep them running.

Here are the things we cover in this chapter, and why they're coming up the way they are:

Trust in distributed object systems. First, we'll look at our distributed object systems and identify the aspects that test our security systems. This will sets up the overall problem for us.

Security functionality. There's a lot more to security than just entering a password, or encrypting a message as it goes over the network. There are many basic security functions, which are the building blocks for almost all security systems including CORBAsecurity. We introduce these building blocks in Section 14.1.2.

CORBAsecurity. Once we have our building blocks, we start in Section 14.1.5 to show how CORBAsecurity uses them to build the two basic protection packages labeled Level 1 and Level 2, and the additional components: non-repudiation, and the various flavors of secure interoperability.

Firewalls. Next, we'll discuss firewalls and their relation to the rest of CORBAsecurity. Firewalls are covered in a separate OMG specification, and therefore get their own section.

Licensing. Finally, we'll cover licensing. This specification goes back a number of years, but implementations are still offered by a number of vendors.

So, off we go.

14.1.1 Trust in Distributed Object Systems

Security is an important issue in any distributed system, as information in transit is more vulnerable, and use of multiple machines introduces issues of trust and consistency between them. Distributed object systems are generally more complex than some traditional client-server systems, and the security issues can be more subtle.

Distributed object systems can be unlimited in scale and may be continually evolving. This means systems that:

- Have many components

- Have rich interactions between components

- Can introduce intricate boundaries of trust

Distributed object systems have many components. One of the key goals of OMG is to make it possible (in fact, easy) to build complex software systems from a set of CORBA objects. The components that a user or application programmer uses directly when interacting with a software system may only be the tip of the iceberg, with many more underlying objects in the distributed system coming into play through delegation. Also, because of subclassing, inheritance, or customization, the implementations of objects may change over time, often without the user or programmer knowing or caring.

There are rich interactions between components. Simple client-server architectures have straightforward interactions between components, which are usually well understood by users and programmers. In distributed object systems, the distinction between clients and servers is no longer a clear one—a server that implements a CORBA object might also act as a client of another object. Some objects may be implemented by delegating part of their implementation to another object, or (more generally) by using a set of objects connected in some arbitrary graph.

Users and programmers do not always understand—or even care about—all of the interactions that take place between objects that they invoke. Encapsulation hides the details of an object's implementation, including which method of implementation is selected in response to a particular invocation. So the proper use and understanding of a security architecture should not have to depend upon a full understanding of how objects interact "behind the scenes."

Boundaries of trust are more intricate. In a simple client-server system with relatively few components connected in straightforward ways, it is usually clear which of these components are trusted and by whom. For example, clients of a network file system will typically trust the server, but not vice versa.

With distributed object systems, however, things can be more complicated. The "natural" boundaries between objects provided by encapsulation may not always be the right ones to respect, as object boundaries are not always supported by underlying security protection mechanisms. For example, a user may trust an object with confidential data when its implementation runs on his or her local machine, but not if it is running on some unknown machine. Even if the implementation is running on a trusted machine, it may use other objects that run elsewhere or are not known to keep data confidential. CORBA-compliant systems have the flexibility to introduce and/or replace large numbers of components, and this very property leaves them vulnerable to Trojan Horses.

In an environment where users and programmers may not be aware of all the objects with which they are interacting, which objects (or collections of objects) can they trust? Similarly, where object implementations (or the CORBA implementation supporting them) make decisions about security, which other objects should they trust? An OMA security architecture should allow for environments where mistrust between objects is ubiquitous.

The trust that users and programmers have in objects, and that object implementations have in each other, also depends on the trust in the CORBA implementation and the boundary of trust between object implementations and CORBA implementation. Moving some security into the CORBA implementation could mean little trust is needed in most object implementations. In addition, using trusted tools to generate objects, or moving some security into runtime libraries, can reduce the trust needed in the part of the object implementation written by the application developer.

14.1.2 Security Functionality Introduction

Some people assume that if they encrypt their network communications, they're secure. This isn't true. There's a lot more to security than encryption and, in fact, encryption of your data as they travel over the wire is not even necessary for many security functions.

Here are the basic security functions that are the building blocks of CORBAsecurity:

Identification and authentication of principals. Human users and objects that need to operate under their own rights have to be *identified*—"Who are you?"—and *authenticated*—"Prove it!" At the simplest level, some security systems rely on a password for authentication (and this is certainly better than nothing at all). More sophisticated systems use a private key, or a biological characteristic, or a code generated by a chip enclosed in a card or ring.

Authorization and access control. *Authorization* looks at access from the user's point of view, deciding whether a user—either a person or an object acting on a person's behalf—can access an object, normally using the identity and/or other privilege attributes of the user (such as role, groups, security clearance). *Access control* looks at access from the object's point of view—what do the control attributes of the target object say about which principals, or principals with which attributes, may access it. Finer granularity of privileges can reduce the amount of damage any one principal can do, but that requires more resources to program, set up, and maintain.

Security auditing to make users accountable for their security related actions. Some people think that the best possible security system is one that can never be breached, but this isn't so. *Any* security system can be breached with enough effort (and penetration from the inside is one of the most difficult attacks to prevent). The best security systems take this into account and *log* security-relevant actions, allowing them to be replayed after breaches are discovered. This may help identify the perpetrator, allow the extent of the damage to be evaluated, and possibly enable all or some of it to be repaired.

Maintaining availability. Attackers do not have to breach security barriers to stage a *denial-of-service* attack; all they have to do is request a service, perhaps in a legitimate way although possibly with abnormal parameters, many more times than your site is prepared to handle. It is not difficult to automate a request for a Web page and issue it hundreds of times each minute, perhaps from different machines in different locations, rendering it difficult or impossible for legitimate users to get through. If the target is a commerce or financial trading Web site, for example, the consequences of a denial-of-service attack could be serious. If it is a healthcare provider or military installation, lives may be lost. Of course, Web servers are not the only type of service that is subject to this type of attack; almost any networked machine is vulnerable to some sort of attack of this type. Denial-of-service may be the hardest of any attack to defend against, although firewalls can protect servers from attacks that originate beyond the enclave. We admit, nothing in CORBAsecurity (or in just about any other security package either) except the Firewall specification does anything to protect against denial-of-service attacks.

Secure communications between objects. Once client and object have authenticated each to the other, secure communications protect both systems data (for example, security attributes of principals) and business data as they flow in transit, typically over insecure pathways. Distributed systems are vulnerable to attack when information is in transit. Information must be sent to the correct place and protected against corruption and replay; it may also need to be confidential. Systems data (including the security credentials themselves, and infrastructure information such as object identity) as well as application data need protecting. Security of communications must cover from end to end, and not rely totally on security in the communications services that do not cover important functionality at sending and receiving ends. In large systems, the communications model must be able to work between domains. The communication facility used by the security model must be capable of supporting a variety of authentication protocols or algorithms, and be capable of extending the set of protocols supported as new ones are developed.

Delegation. In an object system, when a client calls on an object to perform an operation, the object will often not complete the operation itself, but will call on other objects to do so. This will usually result in a chain of calls on other objects as shown in Figure 14.1. This complicates the access model, as access decisions may need to be made at each point in the chain. Different authorization schemes require different access control information to be made available to check which objects in the chain can invoke which further operations on other objects.

Non-repudiation. When you buy something over the Internet and pay in some valid way that nevertheless doesn't leave a trail (e.g., electronic cash, or barter), how can you prove that you paid? And, if you received whatever you bought electronically (e.g., music or software) over the Net, how could the merchant prove you received it if there were a dispute? These questions become crucial as transaction amounts grow, as they already have in business-to-business electronic commerce today. The answer is *non-repudiation*, a protocol in which both buyer and seller agree to trust a third party to be a certifying authority. The seller certifies to the certifying authority when he receives payment, and the buyer certifies that the goods have been delivered. The three parties (buyer, seller, and certifier) all agree that, forever into the future, if there is a dispute, the certifier's word about the transaction is the truth. Certification must be done by secure communication, and the authority's record system must be protected from tampering. Obviously this pattern holds for transactions other than sales, although sales are an easy scenario to describe.

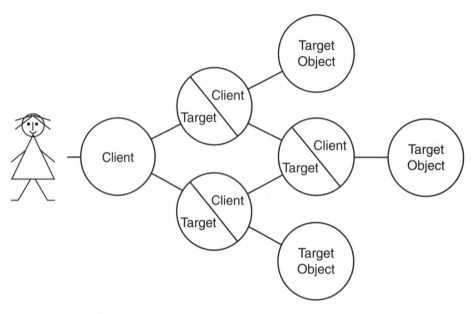

Figure 14.1   Delegation.

> **Cryptography.** Cryptography is used in support of many of the other functions. It is rarely visible directly outside the security services, except to provide encryption of data under direct object control.
>
> **Administrative tools.** Administration of security information about principals, server objects, and security policy configuration options, is also needed.

14.1.3 More on Security Functions

Many of these security functions are basic enough that we aren't going to present them in any more detail here: Identification and authentication, authorization and access control, are not CORBA specific and are presented well enough in basic security texts that we won't devote any more space to them here. Auditing is self-explanatory, at least in a basic way, and cryptography is a specialized area that deserves a book of its own (and has plenty already!). This leaves a few items that are, if not CORBA specific, at least applicable enough because of their relevance to networking and distributed systems: secure communications, delegation, and non-repudiation.

14.1.3.1 Secure Communications

There's so much misplaced emphasis on encryption that we want to cover the other, more important aspects of secure communications in this section.

When we make or receive an invocation, we want to know that we really are communicating with the server or client that we think we are. Assuring this involves *identification* ("Who are you?") and *authentication* ("Prove it!"). There are lots of ways to identify and authenticate, but the point here is that the method is irrelevant so long as it works; it's the result that is important. CORBAsecurity can use various methods to identify and authenticate, depending on your site's needs.

Integrity refers to keeping our message from being tampered with between sender and receiver. Encryption of the data on the wire is only needed in the cases where the data are of great value or threat, such as a sensitive company document, or a patient's HIV test results. However, in most cases, protecting the invocation from tampering is good enough. (For example, what fraction of your browser sessions occur with the lock locked in the lower left-hand corner?)

To assure integrity, we can sign our message. We sign a message by creating a checksum of the message, and we encrypt that checksum with a cryptographic key. This encrypted checksum is known as the *signature*. Tampering is evident after the signature is decrypted and does not match the checksum of the message.

Checksums are small and quickly calculated, so creating a signature for a message takes less time than encrypting the entire message. Therefore, this procedure meets the message integrity security requirement using minimal overhead.

Replay is a common attack, referring to an attacker recording a signed, checksummed (and perhaps even encrypted) invocation and reissuing it later, perhaps with his own originating IP address. To defend against replay, we can include a timestamp and address information in the message. To be effective, the timestamp and other information must be included in the signature so that any attempt at alteration will be evident.

Now that we've made sure that each party knows who the other one is, and that their messages are being transmitted accurately and protected from replay, it may make sense to take steps to keep certain data confidential. Here's where encryption comes in. There are many ways to encrypt data: public key, private key, each with its own set of variants (Kerberos is one standard of private key; RSA a standard of public key), and so on. We're not going to deal with these at all, since this part of security has nothing to do with CORBA. The CORBAsecurity specification can use just about any kind of encryption, and it references all of the important ones. That's all you really need to know about encryption.

14.1.3.2 Delegation

Typically in object systems, when a client invokes an object to perform an operation, the object does not complete the operation itself but instead calls upon other objects to do so. This results in a chain of calls like the ones shown in Figure 14.1. This complicates our access control model, because access decisions will have to be made at each link of the chain. Different authorization schemes will require different access control information to be made available at decision points, so that security systems can perform necessary checks.

In *Privilege Delegation*, the initiating principal's access control information (i.e., its security attributes) may be delegated past the directly invoked object to objects further down the chain, giving these objects the right to act on its behalf under specified circumstances. Privilege Delegation is not the only form of delegation, but it is the only one supported by the current CORBAsecurity specification, and so is the only one we will discuss here.

Oversimplifying once more, a number of Privilege Delegation modes are supported. Here's a summary:

No delegation. A client permits the intermediate to use its privileges only for access control decisions, not allowing them to be delegated, so the intermediate object cannot use these privileges when invoking the next object in the chain. The next object is invoked with only the intermediate object's own privileges, as shown in Figure 14.2.

Simple Delegation. A client permits the intermediate to assume its privileges, using them for access control decisions and delegating them to others. The target object receives only the client's privileges, and does not know who the intermediate is. When Simple Delegation is used without target restrictions, it is known as *impersonation*. Figure 14.3 shows Simple Delegation.

Combined and Composite Delegation Modes. There are three specified modes of delegation that allow the target object to distinguish, in some way, which privileges arise from the Principal and which from the intermediate object. Because we don't plan to define the security credential here (except to say that it's the token that carries privileges in an invocation), we won't distinguish among the three. Suffice it to say that these modes allow the target object and its security implementation to base access decisions on more information than is passed in Simple Delegation. Figure 14.4 is a diagram of Composite Delegation, the simplest of these three modes.

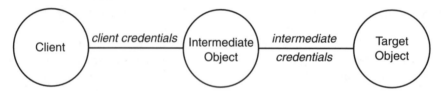

Figure 14.2   No delegation.

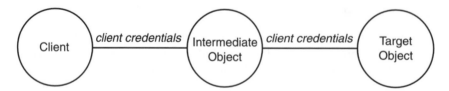

Figure 14.3   Simple delegation.

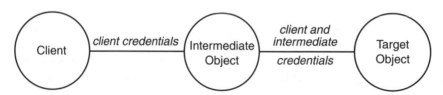

Figure 14.4   Composite delegation.

What might you want from a delegation facility, besides these modes? You'd probably want to control *which* objects your directly invoked object may delegate to. This capability is coming in a future version of CORBAsecurity, but it's not there now.

14.1.3.3 Non-repudiation

It's easy to grasp why non-repudiation is useful in the context of e-commerce, which is why we used this example in Section 14.1.2. However, non-repudiation is a lot more general than this so here is some more detail.

Although many CORBAsecurity functions are performed automatically by the ORB without the client or object having to do anything special or even being aware, non-repudiation services are always invoked explicitly by the application program. Invocations go through the ORB, of course, and will be subject to the usual security for invocations, but there is no automatic triggering of protection in non-repudiation the way there is for Level 1 security.

Two common types of non-repudiation evidence are the evidence of proof of creation of a message, and proof of receipt of a message.

Non-repudiation of Creation protects against an originator's false denial of having created a message. Non-repudiation services at the message originator construct evidence of Proof of Creation, and send it to a trusted third party where it is stored securely for subsequent retrieval.

Non-repudiation of Receipt protects against a recipient's false denial of having received a message (although it does not guarantee that the message has been read!). Non-repudiation services at the recipient construct evidence of Proof of Receipt, and send it to a trusted third party where it is, as before, stored securely for subsequent retrieval.

Other types of evidence and other event types are also covered by the service, but we will not go into detail on these here.

There are many more security functions, but we'd risk turning this into a security text if we described them all, so we'll stop here. Access Control Lists (abbreviated ACL), security administration, and Group Privileges are only a few of the things we've left out. In addition, we've only described the most basic aspects of the functions we have included. The OMG security specifications fill more than 600 pages, and perhaps now you can appreciate why.

We think that the descriptions we've presented so far, along with a little common sense and the experience you have with computing, will enable you to understand how CORBAsecurity lets you build an architecture from these functions and components.

14.1.4 Viewpoints on Security

Some people regard one or a few of the security functions listed in the previous section—especially encrypted communication—as a security architecture all by themselves, but we urge you to avoid this oversimplified outlook. Instead, look upon these functions as *building blocks* of a security architecture, which you can customize to meet your company's requirements using resources you can afford. In a way, this list of functions is a menu from which you will select items, taking only as much of each as you need, and flavoring it to your liking.

To make this easier, some of it has been done for you—CORBA defines two basic levels of security, one optional component (non-repudiation), and an assortment of protocols as conformance levels. Products list the conformance points that they meet, and the protocols that they support.

In the next section, we go over the conformance points for each level, the optional non-repudiation protocol, and the list of secure interoperability options. As we do, pay attention to the way this list cuts across the functions we just reviewed.

14.1.5 Conformance Points: CORBAsecurity Building Blocks

There are two main security functionality packages: Level 1 and Level 2.

14.1.5.1 Level 1 Security

Level 1 provides a first level of security for applications that are unaware of security, and for those having limited requirements to enforce their own security in terms of access controls and auditing. In terms of the security functions we listed previously, Level 1 security implementations must provide for the following, all at a basic level:

- **User (i.e., principal) authentication.** Allow users and other principals to be authenticated, although this may be done outside the object system.

- Provide security of the invocation between client and target object, including:

  - **Client/object authentication.** Establish trust between them, where needed, either by ORB-level security services or some other secure way such as secure lower-layer communications. Mutual authentication is not a requirement.

  - **Integrity and confidentiality.** Assure integrity and/or confidentiality of requests and responses.

  - **Access control.** Provide limited control of whether a particular client can access a particular object. At Level 1, access controls can be based on "sets" of subjects and "sets" of objects. Details of the Access Policy and how this is administered are not specified.

  - **Delegation.** At an intermediate object in a chain of calls, provide the ability to be able to either delegate the incoming credentials or use those of the intermediate object itself.

  - **Auditing.** Support auditing of a mandatory set of a system's security-relevant events listed in the specification.

- For security-aware applications, Level 1 security implementations must make the privileges of authenticated principals available for use in application access control decisions.

An ORB providing Security Functionality Level 1 may also conform to other security options. For example, it may also

- Support the optional non-repudiation protocol.

- Provide security replaceability using either of the replaceability options (which we discuss later in the chapter).

- Provide secure interoperability, a separate conformance point, using a subset of the specified protocols.

14.1.5.2 Level 2 Security

Level 2 provides more security facilities than Level 1, and allows applications to control the security provided at object invocation. It also standardizes administration of security policy, allowing an application's administering policy to be portable.

An ORB that supports Security Functionality Level 2 builds upon the basic functionality in Security Level 1, adding the following features and options:

- **User (principal) authentication.** Allow principals to be authenticated outside or inside the object system; for example, by a single-logon system.

- Provide greater security to invocations compared to Level 1 products in a number of ways:

  - **Client/object authentication.** Establish trust and message protection at the ORB level, so that security below this (for example, in the lower-layer communications) is not required (although it may be used for some functions).

  - **Integrity and confidentiality.** Allow additional integrity options to be requested, such as replay protection and detection of messages out of sequence.

  - **Access control.** Support the standard **DomainAccessPolicy** for control of access to operations on objects.

- **Auditing.** Support selective auditing of methods on objects.

- Allow applications to control the options used on secure invocations, including:

  - Choosing the required quality of protection of messages (subject to policy controls).

  - Changing the privileges in credentials.

  - Choosing which credentials are to be used for object invocation.

- **Delegation.** Specifying whether these can just be used at the target (e.g., for access control) or whether they can also be delegated to further objects.

- At Level 2, administrators can specify security policies using domain managers and policy objects. There is a standard policy management interface for each of the Level 2 policies.

- Level 2 applications can find out what security policies apply to them. This includes policies they enforce themselves (e.g., which events types to audit) and some policies the ORB enforces for them (e.g., default Quality of Protection, or delegation mode).

- ORBs (and optionally ORB Services) can find out what security policies apply to them. They can then use these policy objects to make decisions about what security is needed (check if access is permitted, check if auditing is required) or get the information needed to enforce policy (get QoP, delegation mode, etc.) depending on policy type.

- Security Level 2 implementations may conform to the same additional security options (non-repudiation, replaceability) as Level 1 implementations.

14.1.5.3 Optional Security Functionality: Non-repudiation

There is only one Optional Security Package, and it's non-repudiation. We've already covered it, so let's go on to the next topic.

14.1.5.4 Security Replaceability Packages

These packages specify how an ORB can be structured to allow incorporation of different Security services. There are two possibilities:

ORB Services replaceability package. This package specifies how an ORB uses interceptor interfaces to call on object services, including security services. It must use the specified interceptor interfaces and call the interceptors in the specified order. An ORB conforming to this does not include any significant security-specific code, as that is in the interceptors.

As we write this, the interceptor facility is being replaced in an RFP effort named, logically enough, "Portable Interceptors." One reason for this RFP is that the interceptor interfaces in the current CORBAsecurity specification are believed to be unimplementable. This RFP was in its final vote as we went to press in early 2000; watch for a revision of the ORB Services Replaceability Package some time after this.

Security Service replaceability package. Using this package, the ORB may or may not use interceptors, but all calls on Security services are made using specified replaceability interfaces. These interfaces are positioned so that the Security services do not need to understand how the ORB works (for example, how the required policy objects are located), so they can be replaced independently of that knowledge.

An ORB can provide Security by directly implementing the Security feature package specified as Level 1 or Level 2 without making use of any of the facilities provided by the Replaceability feature packages. In that case, however, the standard security policies defined in this specification cannot be replaced by others, nor can the implementation of the Security services be replaced (unless the ORB used other industry-standard replaceability interfaces, such as GSS-API, in place of the CORBA ones).

The specification calls an ORB that supports one or both of these replaceability packages, along with a few basic ORB operations, "Security Ready." Security Ready ORBs do not support any security functionality themselves, but are ready to host security functionality via the Security Replaceability package.

14.1.5.5 Common Secure Interoperability (CSI) Feature Packages

CORBAsecurity specifies three levels of secure interoperability, numbered 0 through 2. All levels can be used in distributed secure CORBA-compliant object systems where clients and objects may run on different ORBs and different operating systems. At all levels, security functionality supported during an object request includes mutual authentication between client and target and protection of messages—for integrity, and when using an appropriate cryptographic profile, also for confidentiality.

An ORB conforming to CSI Level 2 can support all the security functionality described in the CORBA Security specification. Facilities are more restricted at levels 0 and 1. The three levels are:

Identity-based policies without delegation (CSI level 0). At this level, only the identity (no other attributes) of the initiating principal is transmitted from the client to the target, and this cannot be delegated to further objects. If further objects are called, the identity will be that of the intermediate object, not the initiator of the chain of object calls.

Identity-based policies with unrestricted delegation (CSI Level 1). At this level, only the identity (no other attributes) of the initiating principal is transmitted from the client to the target. The identity can be delegated to other objects on further object invocations, and there are no restrictions on its delegation, so intermediate objects can impersonate the user. This is the impersonation form of simple delegation that we described a few sections back.

Identity- and privilege-based policies with controlled delegation (CSI Level 2). At this level, attributes of initiating principals passed from client to target can include separate access and audit identities and a range of privileges such as roles and groups. Delegation of these attributes to other objects is possible, but is subject to restrictions allowing the initiating principal to control their use. Optionally, composite delegation is supported, so the attributes of more than one principal can be transmitted. Therefore, it provides interoperability for ORBs conforming to all CORBA Security functionality.

An ORB that interoperates securely must provide at least one of the CSI packages.

14.1.5.6 Security Mechanism Packages

Far more than an encryption method, a security mechanism is the embodiment and implementation of the various security functions we've been discussing in this chapter. It also defines the handshaking sequence that allows ORBs to establish mutual trust when they first contact each other over the wire. Security mechanisms range from simple, implementing only a few of these mechanisms, to sophisticated, implementing many or perhaps all of them, with flexible options.

The security mechanism (also, unfortunately, referred to as a "security protocol") is half of what we need; the other half is a secure over-the-wire protocol. The two over-the-wire protocols in CORBAsecurity are SECIOP and SSLIOP. The CORBAsecurity specification defines the coupling of SECIOP with three security mechanisms: SPKM, GSS

Kerberos, and CSI/ECMA. These are explained, albeit briefly, just below. (It is possible to couple SECIOP to other mechanisms, but this has not been standardized.) SSL, unlike the other security mechanisms, defines its own over the wire protocol. OMG calls it SSLIOP, but it's just what you get when you run IIOP using the SSL security mechanism—there are no choices or options here. Figure 14.5 shows how these parts fit together.

An ORB that interoperates securely must do so using one of these four protocol packages. All of these security protocol packages are defined by bodies or companies outside of OMG; references to their specifications appear in Appendix A. SECIOP is defined by OMG in the CORBAsecurity specification, of course.

SPKM Protocol supports identity-based policies without delegation (CSI Level 0) using public key technology for keys assigned to both principals and trusted authorities. SPKM stands for Simple Public-Key GSS-API Mechanism, and it's an IETF specification. In CORBA, SPKM runs over the SECIOP wire protocol.

GSS Kerberos Protocol supports identity-based policies with unrestricted delegation (CSI Level 1) using secret key technology for keys assigned to both principals and trusted authorities. It is possible to use it without delegation (providing CSI Level 0). Kerberos originated in an MIT Project, but now it's defined by IETF specifications. (The name "Kerberos" comes from Greek mythology—it's the three-headed dog that guards the gates of Hades.) In CORBA, GSS Kerberos runs over the SECIOP wire protocol.

CSI-ECMA Protocol supports identity- and privilege-based policies with controlled delegation (CSI Level 2). It can be used with identity, but with no other privileges and without delegation restrictions if the administrator permits this (CSI Level 1), and can be used without delegation (CSI Level 0). For keys assigned to principals, it can use either secret or public-key technology. For keys assigned to trusted authorities, it uses public-key technology only. In CORBA, CSI-ECMA runs over the SECIOP wire protocol. This mechanism is based on an IETF-defined subset, known as "SESAME," of a larger ECMA standard.

SSL protocol only supports identity-based policies without delegation (CSI Level 0). In spite of this limitation, SSL is the most popular secure protocol used with CORBA. SSL defines its own protocol, and does not run over SECIOP.

Finally, the specification defines one more interoperability protocol:

SECIOP Plus DCE-CIOP Interoperability. An ORB with the Standard plus DCE-CIOP secure interoperability package supports all functionality required by the standard secure interoperability package, and also provides secure interoperability using the DCE Security services over the DCE-CIOP protocol that we discussed briefly in Chapter 6.

Security Mechanism	SPKM	GSS KERBEROS	CSI ECMA	SSL
Wire Protocol	SECIOP			SSLIOP

Figure 14.5 How security mechanisms and over-the-wire protocols fit together.

14.1.5.7 Security Over the Wire
and SECIOP

In order to make sense of the protocol options SECIOP and SSLIOP, we need a word or two on how security works over the wire.

CORBA specifies two over-the-wire security protocols, SECIOP and SSLIOP. Each protocol may give the connection between a CORBA client and CORBA server the ability to authenticate each other and give cryptographic integrity and confidentiality to its messages, if the security mechanism and all other factors allow. In order to be compliant with CORBAsecurity, an ORB must support either one or both of these protocols. It may, of course, support additional security protocols as well.

Both the SECIOP and SSLIOP protocols lie between the network transport layer (TCP/IP) and the GIOP protocol layers, alongside the IIOP layer as shown in Figure 14.6. IIOP provides no security and passes GIOP messages straight through to and from the TCP/IP layer. SECIOP and SSLIOP can both be thought of as cryptographic tunnels through which ORBs send CORBA GIOP messages.

SECIOP is a secure transport protocol that handles IETF General Security Service (GSS) mechanisms for CORBA. Depending on the particular mechanism selected, SECIOP gives authentication, integrity, and/or confidentiality to CORBA communication. SECIOP includes support for a variety of security mechanisms that can interact with existing "online" authentication mechanisms, such as Kerberos, DCE Security Servers, and Sesame systems. SECIOP also includes mechanisms that have support for public-key infrastructure (PKI) based systems, such as SPKM, or X.509 certificate-based systems.

When a client ORB initiates a connection with a server ORB, the two ORBs execute a series of steps as they come to agreement that each has provided adequate keys for the secure communication, and that they agree on the level and types of security (delegation, access control, and so on) that each will provide. This handshaking and negotiation follows a prescribed sequence also called a "protocol" (just to confuse this discussion even more!), which is defined by the security mechanism (GSS-Kerberos or whatever). During this handshaking phase, SECIOP executes the handshaking protocol and establishes a secure connection. During execution, as invocations and responses travel over the wire, the security "payload" in each message is a GSS token, defined by the IETF GSS that we mentioned in the previous paragraph. All three of the security mechanisms we mentioned—SPKM, GSS-Kerberos, and CSI/ECMA—produce GSS tokens, so SECIOP has no trouble supporting any one of them. The role of SECIOP is to transport these tokens, along with the invocations and responses, from client to server ORB and back. The ORB passes the entire message to the security service, which extracts and reads the token,

Figure 14.6 Layering of security protocols, network protocol, and network transport.

takes whatever security actions are necessary, and returns the invocation or response to the ORB assuming that security restrictions have been fulfilled.

SECIOP is versatile and extendible. Used with a capable security mechanism, SECIOP can go well beyond basic authentication, integrity, and confidentiality, and provide flexible privileges and delegation, such as Sesame systems. For extendibility, as new GSS mechanisms are devised, they can easily be inserted into an ORB supporting the SecurityReplaceable interfaces without changing the SECIOP protocol.

SSLIOP is a much more limited protocol than SECIOP. SSLIOP provides authentication, integrity, and confidentiality functionality based on the Secure Sockets Layer protocol (SSL). SSL is a secure transport protocol that only allows for a specific set of X.509 certificate-based public-key technologies, and it cannot support privileges or delegation.

14.1.6 Security Summary

Even without getting into details about the implementation or its underlying architecture, we've still included a lot of information in this presentation of CORBAsecurity. We hope you come away with an appreciation of the different functions that have to be executed to keep your systems secure, and how to assemble them—in the amounts that your company needs—to keep you as secure as you need to be, no more (too expensive) and no less (too dangerous).

This comprehensive and flexible security architecture, available in products from a number of vendors, is one of the benefits of CORBA. Along with its other architectural strengths, it reinforces the return you get for choosing CORBA as the architecture of your distributed object system.

14.2 Firewalls

Businesses protect their enterprise networks from attack by outsiders with firewalls. CORBA, with its location-transparent execution capability, looks like a security threat to a firewall, which may trap IIOP protocol and prevent CORBA invocations across its barrier. The Firewall Specification provides a number of standard ways for these invocations to be recognized and pass through, without removing the protection that firewalls are designed to effect.

The specification defines mechanisms for dealing with three types of firewalls.

TCP firewalls. This is the first example of a *transport-level* firewall; these perform access control decisions based on address information in TCP headers, typically host and port numbers. To facilitate this, IIOP requires a "well-known port number" assignment from the Internet Numbers Assignment Authority, or IANA. These ports have been assigned; the well-known port for IIOP is 683, and for IIOP/SSL it is 684.

SOCKS firewalls. The SOCKS protocol defines a proxy that serves as a data channel between a client and server communicating over either TCP or UDP. Following authentication of the client to the SOCKS proxy server, the client requests and the proxy server connects to the requested real server and the client starts passing data to it.

SOCKS is simple to implement for ORB vendors, who only have to relink their products with a SOCKS-ified TCP library. All differences between simple TCP and SOCKS TCP are taken care of by the library; APIs are identical. Requests are sent to the SOCKS proxy server instead of the target CORBA server; the proxy server in turn routes them to their destination.

GIOP Proxy firewalls. This is a new firewall type defined by the specification. Unlike the first two, it is an application-level firewall that understands the GIOP messages and CORBA headers. Because of this, it is the only one of the three that can perform object-level filtering. The specification also defines a *pass-through* connection that does not examine invocation data that may be, for example, encrypted and therefore opaque to the firewall. However, even this type of connection would be object specific and therefore more precise than either the TCP or SOCKS firewalls could provide.

It's common to have a client application notified when something happens; for example, financial displays need to be updated when data change, traders need to know when rates change ("If the prime rate falls .25%, let me know so I can sell all my stock"), data-caching objects must retrieve new data when the values they hold become obsolete.

In CORBA, when objects need to call back to the client that invoked them, they use the Event Service or Notification Service. In these, the objects at the server end act as clients and the client-side module instantiates an object that is called back in a reverse-direction invocation. Because standard GIOP connections carry invocations only one way, these callbacks require the establishment of a second connection for this traffic heading in the other direction. Since a firewall protecting client machines typically will not allowing incoming connections, this also prevents callbacks that are necessary for event-using applications to work.

To enable callbacks even through firewalls, the specification defines *bidirectional GIOP*, an extension to the GIOP protocol. Under the new specification, a GIOP connection is allowed to carry invocations in the reverse direction under certain restricted circumstances, chosen to maintain security: *if* the object reference for the target of the reverse invocation was sent to the remote server (now acting as client) over that same connection, and *if* ORBs at both ends have been enabled for bidirectional GIOP, then the reverse-direction traffic is allowed. So, when the client wants to be called back, it instantiates a callback object and sends its object reference to the remote server over its established GIOP TCP connection. The remote server sets up a client that, when it is triggered, invokes the callback object over the same connection in the reverse direction.

14.3 The Licensing Service

There are a lot of licensing models out there. The simplest is single-user licensing, but this is extended to concurrent-user, charge-per-hour, and many other models. There are also a number of licensing software products on the marketplace. So, following the example set by a number of other services (including the Naming Service, for example), the OMG did not establish yet another licensing model with this service.

Instead, the service provides a generic set of interfaces that can be used by virtually any vendor to provide access to his or her licensing software product regardless of its licensing model. Several major licensing software companies contributed to the specification, and all agreed that the interfaces met their needs.

We've bundled licensing into this chapter because of its obvious tie-in with, and use of, security.

One school of thought holds that licensing must be in place in order for software vending to be economic, especially in the distributed object environment where per-unit revenues may be small. OMG therefore prioritized this service in the early stages of CORBA development so that it could serve as such an enabler. If you are an end user, the message to you is that CORBA supports an environment where software diversity is encouraged because developers can be fairly compensated for what they produce. If you are a software provider, you should be encouraged to produce objects for this environment for the same reason.

If you're an end user, there's almost no reason for you to need details of the standard because you won't ever write software to it or deal with it directly. You'll either register using standard scripts, or dialog boxes, or by calling the vendor to put "money in the meter" (or whatever licensing mode you and your software employ). If you're a provider of licensed software, you'll get all the information you need from the documentation that came with the licensing software package you bought. Finally, if you're a provider of licensing software, you'll need a copy of the actual specification, and you get that from OMG directly. See Appendix A for contact information.

CHAPTER

15

CORBAservices, Part 5: Introduction to the Other CORBAservices and the CORBAfacilities

15.1 A Look Back

In the last four chapters, we examined six essential CORBAservices that we grouped into four service areas. These were Naming, Trader, Events, Notification (we admit, not officially grouped in the CORBAservices), Transactions (with some help from Concurrency), and Security. There are nine CORBAservices left to examine:

- LifeCycle
- Relationships
- Persistence
- Externalization
- Property
- Query
- Collections
- Licensing
- Time

There are also the CORBAfacilities to consider. In late 1995, OMG members adopted the "Common Facilities Architecture" that set out a surrounding architecture and roadmap for their eventual adoption. The document correctly foresaw that the area would divide broadly into two parts:

1. Horizontal (that is, generally applicable) facilities.

2. Vertical (that is, domain-specific) facilities.

The vertical facilities were divided into industry groups; for a look at the groups active in OMG today, look ahead to Chapter 19. The horizontal CORBAfacilities were divided into four major categories:

1. User Interface Common Facilities.

2. Information Management Common Facilities.

3. System Management Common Facilities.

4. Task Management Common Facilities.

When we wrote the first edition of this book, the CORBAservices and CORBAfacilities were almost new, and the idea of basing a distributed environment on open, standard services and facilities seemed like a sure win for *every* service. Now, however, after surveying the market with three years of experience, we can see that this isn't quite true: While some services and facilities are dramatic successes (it's almost impossible to write a CORBA application without the Naming Service), others have fallen by the wayside (it's almost impossible to *find* an implementation of the Collection Service). Others have developed, but not in the exact ways that we had expected or planned.

In this book, we're not going to discuss all of the services and facilities as equals. Our goal here is to help you design successful distributed enterprise applications, and we wouldn't succeed in that by pretending that you can use services that aren't available now and won't be in the future. We also believe that some of the less popular services have been neglected for good reasons, that you disregard at your peril! So, by discussing some of the possible differentiators in this chapter, we hope to make you aware of some characteristics of successful—and unsuccessful—services and facilities so that you can be a discerning judge of new service designs and products as they emerge.

We've examined the remaining CORBAservices (the ones on the preceding list) and divided them into four categories based on how they succeeded or failed. The next four sections deal with them, one category per section. In the final section, we analyze the CORBAfacilities in the same way.

15.2 Category 1: Success through Subclassing

Three services—Time, Property, and LifeCycle—make their mark on the OMA by providing the definition for what they do, rather than through their implementations.

The definition of UTC Time as set out in the Time Service is inherited throughout OMG specifications; obvious examples include the Security Specification and the AMI, but its use is truly ubiquitous.

Properties, as defined in the Property Service, are inherited and used in other OMG specifications where attributes might fit if only they could raise exceptions (which they do now, finally); for more of an explanation, see Chapter 18.

In your applications, use the Time Service definition of time and date wherever you can; it interoperates smoothly with the rest of CORBA and there are no Y2K problems associated with it. You can use properties when you need to **get** and **set** values that raise exceptions when something goes wrong until about the middle of the year 2000, but you should switch to IDL attributes as soon as CORBA 3 implementations come out with the new exception-raising capability.

Most interfaces in the LifeCycle Service were *designed* to be inherited—they're interfaces that are born by *your* objects; not services that you buy and invoke. See Chapter 16 for details. Since this is the major part of the service, we'll categorize it here. There are other parts—in particular, the Factory Finder interface—that are truly services and can be marketed as an implementation. Factory Finders are present on the market, from multiple vendors, so we could list it in the next category also if we chose.

15.3 Category 2: Gets Some Use

A few of these services get consistent use even though they're not popular enough to show on the usual market radar screen. We've already said that LifeCycle could fit here (or at least the Factory Finder part of it); Licensing is another one that could be included in this category, although these placements could be argued either way.

There is at least one serious, ORB-independent implementation of the Licensing Service, and it's important for the software marketplace. And, since the CORBA software marketplace is poised to take off with the advent of CORBA components, we expect that use of this service may grow.

15.4 Category 3: Getting a Tune-Up

Two of the services on our list fill a need, but the original version was so far from what implementers and users needed that they're getting tuned up: Persistence is one; Relationships is the other.

As we write this book, the Persistent Object Service has been deprecated and a new service definition has just been adopted in sync with CORBA components. Tailored to meet the needs of the component specification as well as noncomponent CORBA applications, the new specification takes advantage of a lot that has been learned since the original. The original specification, we guess, was a combination of too many ideas and did not allow practical implementations. For details about the new Persistent State Service, look ahead to Chapter 17.

The Relationship Service is the other one in this category. Business modelers use relationships all the time, but claim (with justification) that the model of OMG's current Relationship Service specification is not suitable for the uses they need to make of it. UML provides an alternative view of relationships, and a future business object environment may build something derived from this alternative definition into a facility. There are big problems associated with maintaining referential integrity in a distributed relationship system where referents are not all under the system's control, but OMG members are attempting to put together something that will be, at least, useful under controlled conditions. Don't look for this to show up as a revised Relationship Service, though; it's most likely to appear as part of a business object facility based on CORBA components.

15.5 Category 4: Lost in Translation

Finally, we come to three services with few or no implementations: Query, Collections, and Externalization. For each of these we guess that something got "lost in translation" on the way from concept to specification to implementation.

The Query Service is a grandiose one, but relatively under-specified. It defines a thin wrapper around a query engine that accepts input in standard languages defined elsewhere. (See Chapter 18 for details.) The Query Service is able to attempt an amazing amount in a thin specification, mostly because the details are in the query language specs that are included only by reference (or, perhaps, omitted altogether). Query Service functionality could be really useful, especially in large systems with gazillions of CORBA objects. However, the logistics would be formidable, and it's not clear that the investment in coding and setup would justify the benefits.

There are at least partial implementations of the Query Service available, so the concept seems viable. We don't know of any full implementations, nor of any sites that use the service for enterprise-wide queries.

The second entry in this category is the Collections Service, a thorough specification that includes every type of collection you could want or even think of. We were unable to locate *any* implementations of the Collection Service, and it's possible that the specification will be retired by the OMG if none comes to market soon. The specification seems to be a good one, with tight definitions and detail, and the concept seems sound, with Smalltalk (just for example) showing how useful collections can be and how much they can get used. We suspect that the concept just doesn't translate from a single-process implementation to the network. For one thing, it's impossible to guarantee "collection integrity"—since the objects in your collection are represented by their object references, destruction of an object would render your collection invalid and this could happen at any instant. In fact, remoteness makes a lot of the collection operations seem impractical to code in a general way, at least for people who have to get that report done before lunchtime. If you can make this work, code something up and tell OMG so they don't retire the spec!

Finally, we come to Externalization. This service serializes an instance's state in a standard format onto a physical medium such as a floppy disk that could be stored for a while, or, when you wanted, could be carried or sent to another machine where it would be internalized. The instance code has the responsibility for identifying which variables need to be externalized, and sending their values to a marshaling and disk-writing engine that was the purchasable service product. This engine was a CORBA object with standard interfaces, of course. To internalize (that is, reconstitute) the object at the other end, the Externalization Service object would locate a factory, create the instance, and feed it the state off the disk or whatever medium you had used.

The concept resembles Objects by Value, except that the Externalization specification's marshaling and execution are tailored to storage on external media rather than streaming and reconstitution on-the-fly. We've seen references to a few implementations on the market, but we think that at least some of these use a model that's more appropriate to today's environment than the one in the specification. Don't try to use this marshaling/streaming model for persistent storage either; it forces you to serialize and stash the entire state every time you go to disk, instead of storing only the bytes that changed as you can do with a well-designed persistence model. Frankly, we can't think of a lot of reasons to store objects on floppy disks (or any other permanent medium) for transport, and that may be the reason why this OMG specification doesn't get a lot of use.

15.6 The CORBAfacilities

OMG members disbanded the Common Facilities Task Force in June of 1997 and reassigned work in progress to a number of other task forces. This does not mean that the groups' efforts were not worthwhile, nor that they were discontinued (although some were, as we'll see). Rather, it allowed a reorganization of both the overall architecture and the organization's subgroups that allowed each individual effort to be worked on by the members who cared the most about it. And, since the successful efforts that came out of Common Facilities were spread in a number of diverse areas, this was necessary to keep them moving. Here are the four horizontal areas defined in the original Common Facilities architecture document, and what's happened to each of them:

The CORBA desktop or **User Interface Management Common Facility** had been partially populated by the Compound Document Display portion of OpenDoc, but this specification was left unsupported when Component Integration Laboratories closed up shop. (During this time, the Compound Document Interchange portion of Open-Doc filled part of the Information Management component as well.) In the meantime, various flavors of windows (X and proprietary) had taken over users' screens and there was little motivation or room in the market for a replacement, no matter how great its architecture was. Restricted by its nature to a single platform and a single operating system, the desktop benefits little from several of CORBA's main advantages. And, when your desktop application wants to talk to your distributed objects, there is nothing about its GUI implementation that keeps it from speaking CORBA and IIOP to your network, as millions of Windows and Unix-based clients prove every day around the world. As we go to press, OMG members are starting the process of retiring the Distributed Document Facility, OMG's name for OpenDoc.

Away from the desktop, the Printing Facility (processed by the ORBOS Task Force after the demise of Common Facilities) defined an architecture for a large-scale integrated document preparation and printing facility. With Xerox Corporation as a major contributor, the facility has a lot of experience in back of it, and it shows.

The **Information Management** component write-up in the Common Facilities Architecture document is so grandiose as to seem impossible; the wonder is that its vision has been fulfilled, and well done, too. OMG's Meta Object Facility (the MOF, presented in Chapter 22), standardizes a repository for metadata that fills many of the general requirements stated in the architecture; together with the XML Metadata Interchange (XMI), it provides a standard basis for model sharing that has been demonstrated on a network linking a dozen different modeling and design products. As for the rest of the Information Management architecture—generalized schemas of data interchange formats and the like—some are being worked on by specific industry groups where they have a need, while others are not, and this is as it should be.

The **Systems Management** effort also succeeded, for a while, with the adoption of the XCMF Systems Management Facility which had a market presence for some time. However, the specification (which was originally drawn up in 1995) concentrated in the same areas of instance management that the CCM fills now with much more sophisticated techniques, so the primary vendor of XCMF has recently withdrawn its product from the market and moved to retire the specification in OMG.

The **Task Management** effort recently chalked up a success with the adoption of the Workflow Facility by the Business Object Task Force on OMG's Domain side. Members of the Workflow Management Coalition participated in the effort, bringing that organization's work into OMG and carrying the resulting specification back to the rest of their group. We present more about this in Chapters 19 and 20.

While we're discussing facilities and services task forces, what happened to OMG's Object Services Task Force, the one responsible for the CORBAservices? In January, 1996, when OMG formed its Domain Technology Committee and started the Domain effort, the Object Services Task Force merged with the Object Request Broker Task Force to form the (take a deep breath) **Object Request Broker and Object Services Platform Task Force**, or ORBOS PTF. At the time, members justified the change by saying that the same members were doing the technical work on both the ORB and the services, and it didn't make sense to have two separate task forces. Members also knew that the amount of work on services had shrunk considerably—since that time, only three services have been adopted and two of these are revisions of prior versions: Interoperable Naming, the revised Persistence Service, and the Mobile Agents Facility (that we won't get a chance to cover in this book).

15.7 Trends in Services and Facilities

So what are the trends in Services and Facilities? We see four:

CORBA is concentrating on the server side, and on the clients that access them. No longer are OMG members planning to standardize a "CORBA Desktop"; CORBA is already accessible from *every* desktop. Standards development concentrates on the servers, and on the client code that accesses them—that is, the distributed systems where the advantages of CORBA translate to big savings for users.

Services are being packaged to ease programming. This makes CORBA accessible to more developers, especially those with business acumen and less systems skills. The packaging of persistence, transactionality, security, and event handling into the CCM container is one example of this; there will be more.

New platform developments concentrate on the "Middle Tier." CCM, objects-by-value, quality of service control, Java and Internet integration, the MOF, and a future business object facility combine to form a platform designed to handle business quantities using business rules. These developments keep CORBA in the forefront of the developing Application Server market.

Specialized services are being defined and used in vertical markets. OMG's Domain area is vital and growing rapidly, as we detail in Chapters 19 and 20.

In the next three chapters, we take a quick look at some of the minor services (yes, even though some are not wildly popular). Following that, we tour the CORBA-domains and, in Chapters 21 and 22, summarize UML and the MOF. Then, starting in Chapter 23, we (finally!) start the programming example.

CORBAservices, Part 6: LifeCycle and Relationship Services

16.1 The Object LifeCycle Service

The LifeCycle Service defines services and conventions for creating, deleting, copying, and moving objects. The conventions allow clients to perform lifecycle operations on objects in different locations, and to specify target locations where necessary, using standard interfaces and without violating the principal of location transparency built into CORBA. As you can imagine, this requires a number of new concepts. We'll present them in as logical an order as we can.

16.1.1 Factory Objects

Suppose we're running the IT department for a factory that makes widgets, and our sales staff crosses the country selling widgets by the truckload to huge retail and e-commerce emporia. (What do you mean, you've never bought a widget online?) One important object type in our system is the Sales Order that keeps track of a sale from start to finish, so every time a salesman makes a sale, we create a new instance. We've written and compiled our IDL, and written and compiled our program language code for the implementation, and we're ready for the next step.

The technical details for instance creation under the POA are straightforward, and we've already gone over them: The POA creates new object references, and the constructor for the servant class creates new servants. We can either call **create_reference** or **create_reference_with_id** on the POA if we don't want to activate the servant at creation time or, if **IMPLICIT_ACTIVATION** is set and the servant constructor has been invoked, we can invoke _this to activate the servant as an object and get back its new object reference.

Regardless of our POA policies and how we choose to associate servants with object instances, these are all *local* calls that let us create and activate new Sales Order instances only from the process running on the server machine, but our sales staff and office staff do not execute on this machine. Instead, they work online from laptops or desktops, and they need a remote operation to create new Sales Order objects on the server.

For this, we need a new CORBA object and we'll have to write it ourselves. It will have one operation that we will name, say, **create_new_sales_order**, that creates a new Sales Order object instance and returns its object reference. Inside this object, that runs on the server machine, we can either make local calls to the servant's constructor and invoke _this, or invoke the POA to **create_reference_with_id** if we're using one of the other POA policies to associate a servant with our new Object Reference. Being clever, we've made the sales order number an input parameter and, after the new instance is created but before returning, our object registers the new instance in the Naming Service with the number as its name.

This object with the **create_new_sales_order** method is a *factory object*. It is separate from the Sales Order object, even though it calls the Sales Order object constructor. It is started up automatically when our server initializes, has its own CORBA Object Reference, and is registered in the Naming Service (probably with the name "SalesOrderFactory"). Some people think there must be something magic-like about factory objects because the term "factory" sounds special, but, as you can tell from our discussion, there isn't.

Even if you're not remote, the factory pattern is useful for applications that do a lot of instance creation because of the way it packages up all of the creation operations under a single call. Of course if you're sure that every creation will be a local call, you could make the factory a Language object instead of a CORBA object. In our experience, however, every assumption that an object will only be invoked locally turns out incorrect.

You won't need a factory for every object on your system. Objects that are "one-of-a-kind"—your accounting system or object-oriented database, for example—do not need a factory because they're started during an installation procedure. (You might say that there's a factory working in the procedure, but this is moot because no client will ever have to call it.) Factory objects themselves are, most likely, started up at initialization time also. And objects that work together in your desktop application don't need factories because they all come into existence together when you start it up.

So what kind of objects might need to be created by a Factory object? Primarily, objects that are created, pass through a work stage where they accomplish something useful, and are deleted or archived when they are done. (Some systems skip the separate archival step and just let the instances hang around and be their own archive.)

You might find a Factory object very useful to create an object to represent an order for equipment at your plant: You invoke the Factory object to create an Order object each time a salesperson turns in a signed contract (as in our example). If you're an engineer designing a simulator for an oil refinery, your builder program might well invoke a Factory object each time you press a menu button for a new object, whether it's a storage tank, distiller, valve, or whatever.

As this description makes clear, there can be no such thing as a generic Factory object. And if there can be no standard factory, then there can be no standard interface for object creation either, so the specification does not prescribe one. (There is, sort of, a standard for specifying resources that may be needed in object creation, but we won't get to it in this book.)

16.1.2 Move, Copy, and Delete

Where the LifeCycle specifies standard interfaces is, rather, for:

- Moving an object
- Copying an object
- Deleting an object

If the object paradigm is new to you, these may not turn out to be the "services" you expected.

If you're the client programmer, things work as you would expect. You invoke **move**, **copy**, or **remove** on the affected object; in effect, ordering it to move, copy, or delete itself, and the object does it.

But what if you're the object implementation programmer? These invocations, suddenly, are coming right at you. To the object implementation programmer, the Life-Cycle operations **move**, **copy**, and **remove** are not a service but an *obligation*. Let's take a closer look at how this works.

16.1.3 Object and Interface Categories

The objects that bear CORBAservices interfaces divide into two distinct categories, and the types of interfaces themselves divide into three. For the objects, the categories are:

Specific objects. These bear the interface as their primary purpose (as the Naming Service bears the interface that resolves names).

Generic objects. These bear a CORBAservices interface incidentally (like a compound document object that bears the LifeCycle interface, although Move, Copy, and Delete are certainly not its primary purpose).

The three types of interfaces are:

Functional interfaces. These actually provide the service (including the Naming Service interface just mentioned as an example).

Participant interfaces. Born (and usually inherited by) generic objects participating in the service in some way, not usually as the primary provider.

Administrative interfaces. Used to administer the service in some way. We will see examples of all of these interface categories in the CORBAservices.

For LifeCycle, the **move**, **copy**, and **remove** operations constitute a participant interface born by generic objects. These CORBAservices were not standardized so that

ORB environments could provide LifeCycle services; rather, they standardize the interfaces that clients use to invoke LifeCycle services on generic objects—objects you build or buy, which need to be moved, copied, or deleted.

Typically, these objects will inherit the LifeCycle module as a component of their interface. Inheritance provides an easy way for an object to acquire interface components. Programmers should remember that, when an object inherits an interface, the programmer has an obligation to provide the functionality behind that interface.

The OMG membership recognized that these operations would be extremely implementation dependent, and did not attempt to provide anything more than an interface signature for them. **remove** involves a complete cleanup of all allocated resources; **copy** requires externalization of the object's state at the source, followed by creation of a new instance at the destination location, which initializes using that state; and **move** can be pictured as a copy followed by a remove of the original object, with the special condition that the original object reference now refers to the instance at the new location.

Here's how to get the maximum benefit from the LifeCycle CORBAservice: When you buy an object-oriented product with objects that must be created, moved, copied, or deleted, make sure the objects bear the standard LifeCycle interfaces. And if you build an application with objects like this, make sure they inherit the LifeCycle module and that you program the behavior this requires. When your network grows to tens of thousands of nodes and your system administrator discovers one day that he or she has to clean up a million objects, you'll really appreciate having every one of them respond to the same invocation for **remove**.

16.1.4 Location: Factory Finders

What do we really mean by *location transparency*? Typically, we mean that we've divided our environment into an application layer and an infrastructure level, and that all location dependencies are confined to the infrastructure level. We want location-transparent applications so that we only need to buy and install one version that will run anywhere; not because we don't care where a particular instance is running, because frequently we *do* care.

There are lots of reasons to care about an object's location. Your Accounting System object may work just fine on your mainframe or server, but not on Suzy's laptop, which lacks the horsepower and connectivity for that kind of application. And Suzy's Compound Document Report object will be much more useful on her laptop than on her desktop machine during her three-week sales trip to Australia.

To express the concept of location in an interface-independent way, the LifeCycle Service defines the **factory_finder** object. We'll use Suzy's report to illustrate how factory finders work.

Just before she takes off for her Australia sales trip, Suzy wants to copy her Report object onto her laptop. (Suzy appreciates the value of a backup copy, so she plans to leave the original on her desktop machine.) Of course, Suzy isn't a programmer, so she isn't going to code up a quick utility to move the object. Instead, she benefits from the standard environment that CORBA makes possible, including handy utilities like this one, which her system administrator provides on every desktop.

Using a Graphical User Interface, Suzy selects the Report object on her desktop machine and asks for a copy. The utility gives her a choice of locations, including her laptop and possibly a tape backup unit. The list includes all of the locations represented by Factory Finder objects set up by Suzy's system administrator. Note that even the concept of location is context dependent, and that the Factory Finder interface does not attempt to categorize what it means. This allows each application to set up factory finders that represent the important aspects of location for its own purpose.

Suzy selects her laptop from the list on her screen. The utility invokes the LifeCycle operation **copy** on her report, specifying the Factory Finder object representing her laptop as a parameter. Here's the IDL the utility uses:

```
interface LifeCycleObject {
    LifeCycleObject copy (
        in FactoryFinder there,
        in Criteria the_criteria)
    raises (NoFactory, NotCopyable,
        InvalidCriteria,
        CannotMeetCriteria);
}
```

Notice how generic this invocation is. Nothing in it refers specifically to a report, allowing the same interface to move any object from a scrollbar to a nuclear power plant. (Okay, okay, an OO representation of a nuclear power plant. And this probably requires the relationship service also, coming up in the next section.)

The target of the request is the original object. This way, the request always goes to an object that knows everything that has to be done to accomplish the copy. The return value is the Object Reference of the copy, which is returned to the utility. We expect that the utility will register the copy with a Naming Service, or represent it as an icon on the laptop's desktop, when the operation is complete. Criteria represent constraints on the creation process, described in the specification.

Do not assume that the Factory Finder object actually resides on Suzy's laptop. The specification only requires that the factory finder represent that location; its implementation may do this any way it likes. For example, the Factory Finder object may simply retrieve a pointer to Suzy's laptop from a database of location information. The Report object invokes the **find_factories** operation on the Factory Finder Object Reference it received in the copy invocation:

```
Factories find_factories (
    in Key factory_key
    )
    raises (no_factory);
```

The **factory_key** is a name, as defined by the Naming Service (Chapter 11). Note that it is supplied by the Report object rather than the client, to keep the invocation as generic as possible. The Report object supplies the name that represents its object type when it makes the invocation. When the operation completes, the Report object receives as a return value the Object Reference of a document factory, which will create a document on Suzy's laptop. The IDL allows the factory finder to return a list of factories in case there are more than one in its location, but in this example, we'll presume there is only one.

The Report object and the Factory object now work together to create a new Document object on Suzy's laptop, and duplicate the contents of the original report in the new instance. There is no standard interface for this part of the operation, since it is totally application dependent. In fact, it is not even required to be object-oriented or expressed in OMG IDL, although we expect this would have a lot of advantages.

16.1.5 Deleting or Moving an Object

Here is the IDL that LifeCycle objects inherit to allow deletion or moving:

```
void remove ()
    raises (NotRemovable);
void move (
    in FactoryFinder there,
    in Criteria the_criteria)
    raises (NoFactory, NotMovable,
        InvalidCriteria, CannotMeetCriteria);
```

The target of **remove** is the object itself; it is expected to clean up all of its mess before it goes away. If you are the programmer who built this object and allocated its resources, then you are expected to release them when you execute a remove. The client will not help you out here, so any memory leaks are your responsibility.

Of course, some objects are not removable, or at least not removable by just anybody. Your company would be in trouble if anyone on the network could kill the main accounting system just by dragging its icon over to the nearest trash can. For these objects, programmers have two choices: The objects can either not bear the LifeCycle interface, so that invocations return the standard exception **BAD_OPERATION** signaling an unsupported operation, or they can bear the interface but return the exception **NotRemovable**. A well-written client will check for both. Some objects may check the privileges of the invoker to determine whether a remove request is valid; the standard exception **NO_PERMISSION** is provided for this instance.

move is basically a **copy** followed by a **remove**, using the original Object Reference, and its signature reflects this: There's no return value, because there's no new value to return. If the operation fails for any reason, it will raise an exception.

We do have a word of advice about moving CORBA objects, however: DON'T EVER DO IT! (Except for **valuetype**s; move them about all you want.) We admit, with the POA there is a way to do it, but your original server ends up responsible for forwarding every invocation to the instance at the new location forever and ever. Moving of objects is an infrastructure responsibility that does not belong in application code. The LifeCycle service was written in 1993, two years before IIOP; if it were written now, the **move** operation would never have been included. Trust us, you don't need it.

16.2 The Relationship Service

OMG has a standard Relationship Service, and you might expect a discussion of it in a book such as this one. In fact, there is a fairly descriptive (and potentially amusing, in spots) discussion in the first edition of this book.

However, the service receives so little use that we did not reprint the description here. (We've placed the description on the Web site for this book, so you can read it if you're curious.) It's clear from the lack of use, and from the activity among OMG members to create an alternative relationship architecture, that there is a lot wrong with the way the original service is designed. For these reasons, we cannot recommend that you use it for general representation of relationships in your enterprise applications. (It is possible, of course, that there are good places to use it but we leave the discovery of those opportunities to you.)

The OMG members wanted a single service specification to meet needs for relationships everywhere they were needed. This was an admirable but unattainable goal. In brief, the current Relationship specification represents relationships as a set of connected first-class CORBA objects. The related objects do *not* take part in the relationship representation themselves; instead, they are represented by role and node objects that act as proxies and point to the related objects. Although the service represents the many types of relationships accurately in a formal sense, it suffers when translated into implementation. In fact, in separating the relationships from the related objects, it's possible that the Relationship Service sacrificed most of the advantages of CORBA. The resulting graph structure could have been created and stored in a database as easily as in a set of CORBA objects, or even more easily, and the Object Reference pointers to the related objects would still work (or not). In fact, the service as defined has no way to control "Relationship Integrity"; that is, there's no way for a node or role object to guarantee that the object it represents actually exists from instant to instant.

The UML specification (Chapter 21) contains its own representation of relationships. In addition, as we write this, OMG members are just beginning an effort to standardize a representation of relationships for business computing. Once this effort reaches the RFP stage, you will be able to follow it on the OMG Web site; the resulting specification will be posted for free download as are all OMG specifications. (See Appendix A for references.)

16.3 Summary

This completes our discussion of the LifeCycle and Relationship services. LifeCycle is a useful pattern, and its interfaces are inherited and used by many other services and user application objects. The Relationship Service has proved less successful, but relationship representations are needed so badly that members are working on alternative specifications as we write this.

In the next chapter, we'll explore the new Persistence Service, and the Externalization Service.

CHAPTER

17

CORBAservices, Part 7: Persistent State and Externalization Services

17.1 Introduction

Architecturally, there's a fundamental difference between the CORBAservices we've discussed so far and the ones in this chapter. None of the services up to now have concerned themselves with an object's internal state. In fact, OMG has done well keeping state private, a matter of concern only to the implementation. Even the BOA provided less in the way of state management than many applications needed, although the POA does this very well indeed. (We'll come full circle and tie the new Persistent State Service [PSS] to the POA before the end of this chapter.)

Storage and retrieval of state is an important part of programming virtually every application, and CORBA programmers want to use off-the-shelf products implementing standardized interfaces to persist their objects.

In the first edition of this book, we wrote hopefully about the first release of the Persistent Object Service (POS, an acronym which unfortunately collides with our Point-of-Sale programming example), in spite of its somewhat arcane design. Vendors could not overcome this handicap, however, and made few attempts at implementation; the specification languished and something had to be done to revive the concept of standardized persistence in CORBA.

Therefore, in mid-1997, OMG members initiated the process of replacing the POS with a totally new version, a 2.0 release. This process concluded in late 1999, just before we went to press, allowing us to include a writeup and short example of the newly named Persistent State Service (PSS) in this chapter. The new service specifies a very elegant architecture, and is expected to receive wide usage. This is the persistence that is required by the CCM, as we've already seen in Chapter 5.

After we're done with the PSS, we turn briefly to the Externalization Service (ES). This service serializes the state of an object into a standard format, allowing it to be stored on a removable medium and carried from place to place. Although this concept sounded handy when the spec was written, it must not have been handy enough because we never heard of any commercial implementations (although there may have been one or two). Networks, already popular in the mid-1990s when the spec was written, are everywhere now so it makes a lot more sense to bundle up an object's state and send it over the wire than to put it on a floppy disk. You can use a **valuetype** to do this, so we expect the Externalization Service to fade gradually into oblivion. We'll devote a page or two to the architecture of the service, but won't spend a lot of time on programming details.

17.2 The Persistent State Service

Architects and programmers spend a lot of time designing ways to make objects' states persistent. Vendors provide databases, both relational and object oriented, and transaction processing systems, sometimes at considerable cost, but the need for scalability and reliability in enterprise and Internet applications makes investment in these systems a wise move. We emphasized this point early in the book: Figure 2.8 breaks out persistence as the foundation layer in our four-tier overall architecture.

CORBA programmers have been maintaining objects' state persistent, even across activations, for years, so why standardize a PSS now? The benefits of the PSS stem from the way it packages up the persistence layer of your application. Once you've chosen a data storage format (database or file type) and PSS product that supports it, all your programmers have to do is declare their objects' state using one of the two ways the PSS gives them to do this. At build time, the PSS generates code to store and retrieve these objects when they're needed; at runtime, this code executes and values persist. This means that your programmers don't need to be persistence experts to use whatever datastore your company prefers: relational tables, object-oriented or object-relational databases, or flat files, all supported by the PSS specification. (Individual products will support some subset of these alternatives.) Some of these methods require training and experience in order to be used well, but this expertise is built into the PSS specification and product. Programmers can concentrate on business rules and logic, not database programming. A large part of CORBA 3 is about making services more accessible to programmers, so PSS fits right in.

Another reason to standardize PSS now: Persistence is one of the three key services provided by the CCM container. Components submitters wanted a to use a standard set of persistence service interfaces in their specification so the PSS is a response, in part, to their needs and wants. We've already seen, albeit at a high level, how the CCM uses the service we're about to describe. Even so, the PSS designers did not sacrifice generality in order to support components.

Transactional semantics are an important part of persistent storage. The PSS supports transactions, and we'll look at this aspect before we're done with this chapter.

Storage object structure will mirror your object structure, with *storage objects* for instances of a type (your shopping carts, for example) stored together in a *storage home*. Even this structure is generated and managed automatically.

The two ways of declaring state to the PSS are:

- Using the new *Persistent State Definition Language* (PSDL) defined by the specification

or

- Declaring state directly in your programming language, termed *transparent persistence*

We'll go over both of these methods.

If you have been paying attention to the architecture of each CORBAservice as we discussed them, you may have noticed that this is the first time that one intrudes on what the OMG refers to as "implementation detail"—the internals of your implementation. This is a departure for OMG specifications but, as applications become more complex, it's also a big help for programmers. Of course the CCM not only intrudes on the implementation; it *codes* large parts of the implementation, so by now this is not much of a surprise.

The PSS concerns itself *only* with the interfaces between a servant and the datastore that makes its state persistent. There is *no* interaction between the PSS and the client of the object incarnated by the servant.

17.2.1 PSS Basics

The PSS stores CORBA objects' state in datastores, which may be relational tables, object-oriented or object-relational databases, or flat files. A particular PSS implementation may support only a subset of these datastore types.

The PSS implements and manages the interaction between the state members of a storage object incarnation, shown in Figure 17.1 on the left-hand side, and the corresponding members of storage objects in a datastore shown on the right. Therefore, changes to the state of a storage object incarnation during execution automatically result in corresponding changes to the datastore.

Suppose you're running an e-commerce Web site and your shopping carts are CORBA objects. Each individual shopping cart needs its own storage. In the datastore, the storage for an individual shopping cart is termed a *storage object*. Storage for a group of shopping carts (possibly all of them, although you can split this up) resides inside a *storage home*. In Figure 17.1, the dots on the domino on the far right might represent storage objects for our shopping carts, while the rectangular domino boundary delineates their storage home. There will be additional storage homes for other storage object types; the other domino represents one. The surrounding oval represents the datastore that contains them. If this particular datastore is a relational database, then each storage home could be a table, and each storage object could be a row. The schema for each table has to correspond to the state of the type it represents; we will describe various ways of connecting things up shortly. Keep in mind that the representation in the datastore is generally static; we still need a representation in execution space to make things work.

Each storage object has an identifier unique within its storage home—its **short-pid**—and a global identifier, scoped to every catalog it may be implemented by on the left—its **pid**. You may set the **pid** and **short-pid** to identical types and values where scope allows. You identify and retrieve storage objects by their **pid**s.

In addition to a **pid** and **short-pid**, a storage object can have one or more **keys**. Each key consists of one or more state variables whose values, taken together, uniquely identify it in a storage home.

In order to update the storage objects in the datastore, they must be represented in code. The PSS represents them in a form analogous to the class/interface structure we've already seen in OMG IDL, and defines a new language for this: Persistent State Definition Language (PSDL). You declare the state variables for the smallest units of your program in *abstract storagetypes*. Then, you declare a *storagetype* (concrete; that is, not *abstract*) that *implements* one or more abstract storagetypes. This distinction was designed quite deliberately: abstract interfaces contain information important to the PSS user—that is, the servant programmer—while concrete interfaces collect information used by the PSS itself as it implements the storage functions in generated code.

Similarly, you declare an *abstract storagehome* that will be responsible for creating new instances of your abstract storagetypes. The corresponding concrete *storagehome* implements the operations that you declared in your abstract type. This structure means that your PSS work divides cleanly into two stages:

- First, you specify your storage objects' schemas—the objects' and servants' view of persistence, primarily the list of state variables—in abstract declarations.

- Second, you write specifications that the PSS uses to generate persistence implementation code.

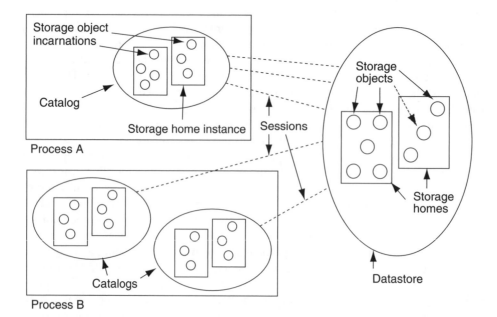

Figure 17.1 Relationships among storage objects, storage homes, storage object incarnations, storage home instances, and catalogs.

This architecture lets you specify the schema of an object *once*, and use it with various datastores and implementations as your application evolves; for example, from a small Web site to a large e-commerce emporium. It parallels the use of IDL in CORBA, where a single IDL interface can have multiple implementations.

If basic persistence functions are all you require, the PSS can generate all of the storage-home code for you. However, you are allowed to declare custom operations on storagetypes and storagehomes. If you do, you'll have to fill in the code for these yourself.

17.2.1.1 Declaring Abstract Types

Here's our shopping cart example, declared first in PSDL. PSDL is a superset of OMG IDL, adding five new constructs: **abstract storagetype, abstract storagehome, storagetype**, **storagehome,** and **catalog**. For brevity, we've included only our customer's account number, name, and address, and left out the state variables that hold the stuff that he bought. You can add these yourself as an exercise if you want. In this section, we declare the abstract interfaces as needed by our servant programmer:

```
// In file Cart.psdl:

abstract storagetype Cart {
    readonly state long cust_account_number;
    state string cust_full_name;
    state string cust_address;
};


abstract storagehome CartHome of Cart {

    Cart create (in long cust_acct_num,
                 in string cust_f_nam,
                 in string cust_addr)

};


catalog Emporium {
    provides CartHome cart_home;
};
```

To make our shopping cart a bit more realistic (but longer), we could have defined a few more related abstract storagetypes and included all of them in the concrete storagetype we're going to declare next. **abstract storagehome CartHome** bears the interface we'll use to create a shopping cart for each customer. **catalog Emporium** will connect our executing image with our datastore at runtime; details follow a few sections along.

abstract storagetype Cart defines the schema for our cart. In this example, we've chosen to declare all of our variables as state, but there's another way to do it:

An abstract storagetype can have state members and operations. In this PSDL taken from the example in the PSS specification, **abstract storagetype NamingContextState** defines persistent types for **CosNaming::NameComponent** and **Object** from our use of them in these operation declarations. We talk briefly about how to work with them in the next section.

```
// file NamingContextState.psdl
#include <CosNaming.idl>
abstract storagetype NamingContextState {
    Object resolve(in CosNaming::NameComponent n)
        raises(...);
    void bind(in CosNaming::NameComponent n, in Object obj)
        raises(...);
    etc...
```

An abstract storagehome can define operations as well, but we won't cover that in this book.

Don't look for a declaration of the **pid** here. It's not considered part of the storage object's schema, and doesn't appear in the PSDL declaration. **pid** values are actually set by the constructor in your programming language, and this operation only appears through the language mapping. There is a PSDL operation to locate and retrieve storage objects by **pid**, but we won't describe it in this chapter except to tell you here that you can do it.

Alternatively to PSDL, a PSS implementation that supports *transparent persistence* lets you specify storage objects directly in your programming language. Here is our cart declaration in Java:

```
// Java
public interface JCart {
    public long cust_account_number();
    public String cust_full_name();
    public void cust_full_name(String newName);
    public String cust_address();
    public void cust_address(String newAddress);
}
```

In transparent persistence, we don't have to declare storagehomes or catalogs—just one more step and we'll be done. There's a price to pay for this simplicity, however: We have a lot less control over the implementation, and in the way the values in our code are ultimately represented and stored in our datastore.

17.2.1.2 Declaring Concrete Types

There are a number of ways to define the concrete storagetypes and storagehome types that implement the abstract storagetypes and abstract storagehomes we've just declared in PSDL.

Perhaps the glitziest way is to buy a vendor's PSS fancy product with integrated interactive visual tools that let you map abstract storagehomes to tables in a relational database, and state variables in your abstract storagetypes to columns, with a couple of mouse clicks.

The "conventional" way (if there can be a convention for a specification that hadn't come to the market when we wrote this) to define your concrete storagetypes and storagehomes is to use more PSDL. All PSS products must let you declare your storagetypes and storagehome types using PSDL; fancier products may also write the PSDL for you using tools or other means, or read your PSDL and help you map it to your database. PSS products use these PSDL declarations to generate an implementation that persists your state variables. Here's what the PSDL looks like for our minimal shopping cart example:

// In file CartImpl.psdl

#include <Cart.psdl>

storagetype CartImpl implements Cart{};

storagehome CartHomeImpl of CartImpl implements CartHome{};

Your PSS product will generate implementation code in your programming language based on these declarations. In Java, for example, it would generate concrete Java classes for both **CartImpl** and **CartHomeImpl.** The class CartImpl would implement an interface representing **abstract storagetype Cart** (and, if we had declared any other abstract storagetypes that needed to go into it, each one of them would occur as an additional interface as well), while the class CartHomeImpl would implement the interface **create** to **create** a **Cart**. If we were going to define keys for our **Cart** (and the account number would be a great choice, except that we would probably define it to be the **pid** instead), we would do it here.

So, our Java version of **CartImpl** would have, for every settable state variable, two accessor methods (one read-only and one read-write), and one modifier method. If the state variable is read-only, only that accessor is generated.

For the **NamingContext** example in the previous section, the **NamingContextImpl** bears the signatures we declared in the PSDL file. Although we have to fill in the code that executes these operations, storage is simple: All of the state variables are connected to the datastore; we simply refer to them in our code and storage is automatic.

Regardless of the way we declared our state (as variables or in operations), the storage object implementation is a programming language object if we're working in an object-oriented language, or a function, in non-object-oriented languages. It's not a CORBA object, does not have a CORBA object reference, and can not be invoked remotely (at least not using CORBA).

The third alternative, transparent persistence, lets you define storage object implementations directly in your programming language, just as we defined our abstract storage objects in the previous section. Here is the Java for our cart implementation:

```
// Java
public class JcartImpl implements Jcart  {
    public long _cust_acct;
    public String _cust_name;
    public String _cust_addr;
    public long cust_account_number () {return _cust_acct };
    // etc
}
```

With transparent persistence, this is all you get. Specifically, only default storagehomes are available to you; you cannot define your own storagehome with keys and operations.

17.2.1.3 Connecting Things Up

To connect our programming language artifacts with their datastore counterparts, we need a session (as shown in Figure 17.1), or, if we don't want to explicitly manage connections ourselves, a session pool. We won't show any of the code here, but will tell you that the ORB provides the references you need through a call to `resolve_initial_references("PSS")`.

You control sessions, while the PSS controls session pools. If you are not using transactions, you may want to use sessions so that you can tune the system for performance. If you are using transactions, and especially if you're using a high-performance transaction monitor system, you will almost certainly use session pools because your system will already be tuned to perform best when left to its own devices.

The PSS specification uses the terms *storage object incarnation* and *storage object instance*. What's the difference? Both refer to a set of data in our execution space that is connected to the datastore via a session, but *storage object incarnation* refers to an independently accessible set of data with a **pid**, while *storage object instance* may refer to a dependent set of data that were extracted from a storage object incarnation and do not have their own **pid**. The storage object instance *may* have a **pid**; both of these entities are instances, but only the one with a **pid** is an incarnation.

For example, consider an **Employee,** which has an **EmployeeID** (that, for simplicity, we will use for both the **pid** and **short pid**), **Name**, and **Address**, where **Address** is another storage type with Street, City, and Zip, but no identifier. In this case, **Employee** would typically have an **EmployeeHome**, and an instance of **Employee** retrieved from an **EmployeeHome** would be an *incarnation*. Asking the **employee** for its **Address** would give out an embedded *storage object instance*, but not an incarnation because **Address** has no home and no life outside the **Employee** incarnation.

17.2.2   Persistent CORBA Objects

The simplest way to associate a CORBA object with a storage object is to bind the **ObjectID** of the CORBA object with the identity of the storage object. We've already seen how each storage object provides two external representations of its identity as octet sequences: a **pid** and a **short_pid.**

So, to associate the storage objects stored in storage home **CartHomeImpl** with CORBA objects representing each shopping cart, we would create for each one a CORBA object whose **ObjectID** was that cart's account number, and a storage object whose **short_pid** was also the cart's account number. Then, in our code's servant activation section, we would receive the account number from the POA as the ObjectID and invoke **find_by_pid** to associate the proper storage object with our storage object incarnation.

17.2.3 Transactional PSS

The PSS was designed to work with either transactional or non-transactional datastores. You have to create a session or session pool to connect your storage objects to their datastore, and this is where you tell your system if you want to operate transactionally. If you invoke **create_basic_session**, operation is not transactional, but if you invoke **create_transactional_session**, it is. Session pools may be either transactional or not; when you call **create_session_pool**, you have to input the pool's transactionality policy.

When you operate in transactional mode, reads and writes occur with transactional assurance. If you followed our presentation of the OTS in Chapter 13, you recall that a transaction could have many participants that all had the chance to vote either to commit or rollback at completion time, and the transaction could only commit if all voted that way. In transactional PSS stores, there is always only one participant: the storage object implementation. This means there is no need to coordinate multiple participants, so that transaction systems much simpler than those defined by the current OMG OTS may support PSS implementations perfectly well.

To allow these simpler implementations to qualify as conformant to the OTS specification, the PSS specification will add a qualifying appendix to the OTS defining a PSS-capable *lite* transaction service that does not need to support the registration of more than one resource per transaction, nor support distribution of a transaction over multiple ORBs. It also defines a *lite distributed* transaction service that supports distribution, but still only handles a single resource.

17.2.4 PSS: Summing Up

There are more details, especially for programmers, but we don't have the space to go into them here (or the time, since we're wrapping up our writing just as the PSS submission was posted on the OMG document server). We've covered the basic structure of the PSS and then some, so you should have a good idea of what the service can do for you and how you will use it once implementations come to market.

17.3 The Externalization Service

The Externalization Service (ES) comes in two parts. The first part packages up the state of a CORBA object into a stream, optionally using a standard format, suitable for recording onto a removable medium such as a floppy disk. (We were going to put a fortune-teller joke here, but enough's enough.) Later, in a separate step, the second part creates a running copy of the object somewhere else, reads the state off the floppy, and stuffs it into the object to produce a time- and space-warped copy of the original. The ES uses the relationship service to package up a group of related objects, and the LifeCycle factory interface to manage creation of the servant. Of course, the ES doesn't refer to the running implementation as a "servant" because it was specified years before the POA was defined.

There are a lot of similarities between the ES and **valuetype**s, but some key differences as well. The main similarities are that both package up an object's state, and use a stream for data. Differences include:

- Transmission method for the data stream (floppy disk for ES; network for **valuetype**s)

- Treatment of related objects (relationship service for ES; inclusion of **valuetype** instances in state for OBV)

- Type of the object produced (**valuetype**s were a new CORBA type, whereas the ES produced regular old CORBA objects)

- Factors of time and space (with ES, the user at the receiving end has to trigger creation of the copy and can do it whenever he wants, while **valuetype**s are instantiated immediately on receipt of the invocation or response that contains them)

All in all, the differences allow **valuetype**s to fit better into today's computing environment than the ES ever could, not surprising considering that **valuetype**s were designed by OMG only recently, while the ES was specified in the second generation of object services—quite a while back at least measured in Internet years.

We've read Web pages that claim implementations of the ES, but we know for certain that no implementation before mid-1998 used the standard IDL posted on OMG's Web site. We've followed up on some of these postings and found that they were either partial implementations, or premature announcement of intentions that hadn't been realized. We expect that there are one or two implementations out there now, but have to admit that the ES will never become the handy way of exchanging CORBA objects that submitters had in mind when they designed it. With the imminent availability of **valuetype**s as CORBA 3 ORBs come to market, it's likely that use of ES will shrink instead of expand. With this in mind, we will shrink our discussion of ES to correspond. Here we go:

The ES is built on a **Stream** object. There are three views of externalization, each with its own interface standardized by the service. They are the client's view, the externalized object's view, and the stream's view.

The client always invokes operations on the **Stream** object; never on the object being externalized or internalized. To externalize an object, you pass its object reference as an input argument to **externalize**. To internalize, you pass the identifier of the stream as input.

On externalization, the stream records the object's type. On internalization, the **Stream** object reads the type from the recording and invokes a factory object for that type to create an uninitialized instance, which then accepts the rest of the stream data. There is also a way to internalize state to a previously created instance (servant, in more current terminology).

You can't externalize any object that you want. In order to be externalizable and internalizable, an object's type must inherit and support the following interfaces, which are invoked by the **Stream** object:

- The LifeCycle Service (and must have a factory available to the Stream object)

- The identifiable object interface of the Relationship service

- The **streamable** interface, and the **StreamIO** interface, which it invokes on the stream object

When you purchase an implementation of the ES, you get **Stream, StreamFactory**, and **StreamIO** object implementations from your vendor. You will need many **Stream** and **StreamIO** instances in your system, since each represents a particular external representation of an object or group of related objects. If you are also building externalizable objects, you will have to inherit several interfaces and build implementations into your code.

There is a standard stream format, which makes it possible to externalize an object on one system and know for sure that you can internalize on any other system that can run your object type. It also makes it possible to wait for a long time while your system byte-swaps data needlessly if you specify standard format on the wrong system when you don't really need it. So, here's a little advice:

The standard format specifies a set of storage formats for basic datatypes. For integers, the standard is big-endian format; for floats, it's IEEE 754 format in either single or double precision depending on the data. If your machine uses these formats for its native representation, go ahead and specify standard format for all of your externalizations because it won't cost you anything—you're already there, so no translation will be performed.

If your machine is little-endian or uses non-IEEE floats, and you're sure you will only want to internalize on your same machine type, you can save some time by allowing externalization to use your native format, especially if your object is huge. Full-screen bitmaps and large binary datasets fit this description; if you're only externalizing a couple of bytes of personnel data or an 80-character string, then you might as well use standard format because the delay will not be noticeable. (This remark does not apply if you're externalizing a billion small objects at once!) Remember that use of native format means you cannot internalize on a machine with a different byte order or floating point format; if you're internalizing on a different machine, then you need to use standard format and pay the price to byte-swap here.

This is all we're going to say about the ES. If you're interested in the service interfaces, you can download them for free from the OMG Web site. There's a little more information in the first edition of this book, and in other first-generation CORBA books, so check them out also. However, we advise you to spend your time programming with **valuetype**s instead of the ES.

17.4 Summing Up: Making Objects Persistent

PSS is not the only OMG story on persistence, of course. The CCM, which we covered in Chapter 5, packages up a subset of PSS in its container and makes it available to the CCM programmer through a set of simplified interfaces, and OTS has been providing transactional persistence to CORBA programmers for years.

Persistence in CORBA has come a long way since we wrote the first edition of this book. For years, OTS was the main persistence tool in the CORBAservices. Since serious enterprise applications require transactional assurance, this satisfied an important part of the market but left the rest to fend for itself. With the new PSS and CCM, programmers have tools they can use for applications of almost any scale, from small to the enterprise and Internet. Until now, persistence was one of the least-used CORBA-services, but we think this was due to the poor design of the original specification. We also think that the new PSS defines a service that will get a lot more use.

The next chapter, on the Property and Query Services, is our last on the CORBAservices. The functions of both of these services are important in many applications, even though these services themselves are not widely available. It's worthwhile going over them all the same, because of the way their functions suggest standard ways of doing common tasks. All in all, the CORBAservices define a rich environment of standard functionality, and the packaging of this functionality in more convenient ways by CORBA 3 will magnify the productivity gains that the original services provided in the early days of CORBA.

chapter 18

CORBAservices, Part 8: Property and Query Services

If your system only has a few objects, they will be easy to keep track of, and life will be simple. Unfortunately, life isn't like this. A few objects are not enough to keep most systems going, so a small object system will likely either grow or die. Being die-hard optimists (we have to be, in this business), we'll assume that your system is going to grow, and that sooner or later, you'll have thousands, or hundreds of thousands, or maybe even gazillions of objects. And when you do, you'll have to keep track of them, sort them, organize them, and retrieve them. The Relationship Service will only go so far. Granted, it keeps our compound document in one piece no matter how complicated it gets, but an organization can have a whole bunch of documents. Consider the U.S. Congress, for example. Or maybe we'd better not. That belongs in a different book, by a different author—Stephen King, perhaps.

In this chapter, we'll consider two CORBAservices—the Query Service and the Property Service—designed to help you cope with large numbers of objects in various ways. There's a third service involved here implicitly—the Collection Service—that was specified shortly after the first edition of this book went to press. We have a couple of sentences to say about that service, too, here in the introductory section to this chapter.

The Object Property Service (OPS) lets you assign properties to an object. A property is like an IDL attribute, except it's defined dynamically by the client instead of statically in the IDL that defined the object's type. So, for instance, you can assign a property to each of your documents that records how important the document is to you. Or your network adminstration tool can assign a property to each object it manages, recording information about its registration status with the tool. These properties are associated with the object, but not part of the object's type.

The Object Query Service (OQS) attempts to unify your CORBA objects, OO databases, and relational databases into a single query target. (We say "attempts" because there are so few implementations on the market. We admit that query is an important function, and the implementations that exist can be very helpful.) It does this just the way you expect, by specifying a common interface to a set of OQS objects that query these different systems. Any information stored with an OQS front-end can participate.

When we wrote the first edition of this book, the Property and Query Services were brand new, and lots of people thought they would be widely available and frequently used. This hasn't happened, as we pointed out in Chapter 15. We've already speculated on possible reasons why, so we won't repeat that here. (Enough's enough, after all.)

The Property Service has proven useful around OMG where its interfaces are inherited or used as a pattern to define, well, properties that are associated with an object and can be set and retrieved. Why weren't IDL attributes used instead? If you examined the interface definitions for attributes and properties (at least the version of attributes before the CCM was adopted in late 1999), you would find that properties raise exceptions on failure to **set** and **get**, while IDL attributes did not. This led OMG members to inherit from the Property Service interface in several new OMG standards, instead of using attributes. For an example, look at the set of Product Data Management Enablers standardized by OMG's Manufacturing Task Force, described briefly in Chapter 20. Keep in mind that the inheriting service does not have to *use* an implementation of the property service; it can reimplement the functionality within its own code if that's the best way to work things. OMG requires that its *interfaces* be reused to avoid cluttering the specs with redundant and perhaps inconsistent interfaces that do the same thing, but functionality is at the decision of the implementor.

However, when the CCM specification was adopted in 1999, the definition of IDL **attribute**s was modified to allow them to raise exceptions of failures to **set** and **get**. The excuse for making this badly needed change in the CORBA components specification (which wasn't specifically about IDL attributes) was that components themselves needed attributes with exceptions; OMG members readily accepted the change and the only wonder was why it hadn't happened sooner. Look for IDL compilers and ORBs to implement this new feature in mid-2000 or soon after, as early CORBA 3 products come onto the market.

With this change to attributes, it is no longer necessary to inherit properties to raise exceptions on **set** and **get**, and this prime use of properties is gone forever. However, that was not necessarily a use of Property Service *implementations*, so we do not expect that this potentially useful service will see any less use.

The Collection Service is another matter. Adopted in late 1996, shortly after the first edition of this book came out, it defines a comprehensive set of collection objects—bag, set, and so on—and services in a scholarly, 138-page document. Unfortunately, in spite of the apparent quality of the specification and the utility of collections in language-specific local environments (such as the one Smalltalk provides), CORBA Collections never quite took off and we were unable to find even a single implementation available on the market as this book went to press. (Of course we're only talking about implementations of the OMG standard service; many vendors provide similar services in their own, nonstandard ways.) If no implementations show up soon, it's possible that

OMG members will retire the specification, so we've decided not to devote any space to it in this book.

By the way, the Collection Service did modify the Collection Query operations of the Query Service but, again, we're not going to describe this here because we haven't seen any implementations of this feature either. If you're interested in the changes, you can download the specification from the OMG Web site and read about the details there. For the URL, check the references in Appendix A.

18.1 The Property Service

Before we discuss properties, let's review **attribute**s for a second. An **attribute** is a variable declared in an object's IDL, containing a value that is permanently associated with an object. Good design practice dictates that an object's type definitions be kept as simple as possible, so IDL files tend to assign attributes to objects only where the attribute reflects a value intrinsic to the object and useful to (virtually) every instance.

Sometimes, however, we need to add an attribute-like element to an object whose IDL is already completely defined—objects we've purchased, or that were written by someone else, perhaps; or a personal label that few (or no) other users will ever need. For example, if we have a collection of document objects, and we've used an implementation of document that we bought from a vendor, we may want to label each document with an importance ranking that we can set to "very important" or "not very important." Or, we could have installed network control objects that we need to label with their positions in our network management system. These are just specific examples of a much more general problem. The point is, sometimes clients need to be able to add a label to an object, and being able to read or write the value of attributes already included in the established IDL definition is just not enough.

The Object Property Service extends the OMA, giving clients the ability to (sort of) hang properties on objects. Each property has a name and a value; the value is typed as an **any**, allowing anything the client wants (including **struct**s) to be stored and retrieved. More precisely, clients can dynamically create and delete properties, and **get** and **set** their values. Properties may be manipulated individually, or in batches using a special interface defined by the specification. An additional interface allows modes of properties to be set: **normal**, **readonly**, **fixed_normal** (cannot be deleted), and **fixed_readonly** (cannot be deleted or changed). An object can define properties to be **readonly** or **fixed_readonly** upon creation, and be assured that they will remain unchanged as long as the object exists.

One last thing: How are properties associated with objects? If the object was built after the Property Service was created, it can inherit the PropertySet or PropertySetDef interface and implement its functionality as part of the type. But what if it doesn't; that is, what if we have an immutable object? The service specification says, with characteristic precision, that "the association of properties with an object is considered an implementation detail" (and that's why we said "sort of" in our parenthetical remark in the last paragraph, and this also might be why the service isn't implemented or used much). The Relationship Service (that we "sort of" described in Chapter 16) tried to solve its similar problem by creating a role object that embodies the role and points to the related object—a proxy object that represents the actual object in the service. A similar proxy could serve here as well (or, we suppose, as poorly); in fact, an augmented role object could conceivably serve both purposes. But this is an implementation detail, of course.

18.1.1 Basic Property Service IDL

A **property** is a two-tuple of **<property_name, property_value>**.

property_name is a string that names the **property**; it is not a name as defined by the Naming Service. **property_value** is of type **any** and contains the value assigned to the **property**. If we don't need to define modes (**readonly** or whatever) for a **property**, this is the **struct** we use to define it. **properties** is defined as **sequence<Property>**, and will let us perform operations on more than one **property** at a time.

If we do want to assign modes, then we use the **PropertyDef**: a three-tuple of **<property_name, property_value, property_mode>**. Recall that **property_mode** can take the string values **normal, readonly, fixed_normal,** and **fixed_readonly**, **readonly** properties cannot be **set**, **fixed_normal** properties cannot be **delete**d, and **fixed_readonly** properties can neither be **set** nor **delete**d. You're right, a client could **delete** a **readonly** property and redefine a property with the same name but a different value; presumably, the definers of the service had a reason for providing such a nonrobust mode and there's a use for it somewhere. We recommend you avoid the **readonly** mode and use **fixed_readonly** instead. There's actually a fifth value, **undefined**. You can't set a property to have an undefined mode, but you can get this mode back from a **get_mode** request. And, as you might expect, **PropertyDefs** is defined as **sequence<PropertyDef>** to handle groups of properties with modes.

There is an extensive set of exceptions defined by the service to handle just about all of the situations that might arise when a client tries to **set** or **get** a **property** value, or define a new property, and something goes wrong. We won't list them all here; your vendor will give you a list when you get an implementation of the service so you'll have it when you need it.

Here's the **Property Set** interface in four different pieces.

18.1.1.1 Defining and Modifying Properties

These operations in the **PropertySet** interface let a client define or change the value of a property:

```
void define_property (
    in PropertyName property_name,
    in any property_value)
raises ( . . . );

void define_properties (
    in properties nproperties )
raises ( MultipleExceptions);
```

If the **property** already exists, the service checks the **property** type (the **any** type-code). If the new value has a different type, the attempt will fail; you have to delete the old property first using **delete_property** before you redefine it.

18.1.1.2 Listing and Getting Properties

Here's how we retrieve the values we set, or get a list of all **property_names** if we don't remember the ones we set or need to know which properties were defined on an object by someone else:

```
unsigned long get_number_of_properties ( );

void get_all_property_names (
    in unsigned long how_many,
    out PropertyNames property_names,
    out PropertyNamesIterator rest );

any get_property_value (
    in PropertyName property_name,
raises ( . . . );

boolean get_properties (
    in PropertyNames property_names,
    out Properties nProperties );

void get_all_properties (
    in unsigned long how_many,
    out Properties nproperties,
    out PropertiesIterator rest );
```

get_number_of_properties returns the number of properties in this **PropertySet**.

get_all_property_names returns all of the property names defined in the **Property-Set**. If there are more than **how_many**, the remainder are put into a **PropertyNames Iterator**. The iterator lets the client retrieve the rest of the names; we won't give details here.

get_property_value returns the value of the property you ask for, of course, assuming that it's there. **get_properties** returns values for all of the properties listed in **property_names** and sets the boolean flag to **true**. If retrieval fails for some of the properties, the boolean flag is set to **false**. In this case, you'll have to retrieve each property individually; this operation does not return mixed results.

get_all_properties returns all of the **properties** defined in the **PropertySet**; excess greater than **how_many** are returned in the iterator.

18.1.1.3 Deleting Properties

Here are the operations a client uses to delete one or more properties:

```
void delete_property (
    in PropertyName property_name)
raises ( . . . );
```

```
void delete_properties (
    in PropertyNames property_names )
raises ( MultipleExceptions );
```

```
boolean delete_all_properties ( ) ;
```

They work just the way you expect. **delete_all_properties** will not delete fixed properties; if deletion fails, the client can invoke **get_number_of_properties** or **get_all_property_names** to find out how many and which ones survived the attempted purge. There is no iterator for exceptions here!

18.1.1.4 Determining whether a Property Is Defined

is_property_defined returns **true** if it is, and **false** if it's not:

```
boolean is_property_defined (
    in PropertyName property_name )
raises ( . . . );
```

18.1.1.5 Getting and Setting Property Modes

There's a whole set of interfaces for getting and setting property modes. We've already talked about what the modes are and how they work; we're not going to include interface details here because there's little to be gained—when you're ready to code a client to manipulate property modes, you'll have the doc set for the service you're using and it will include all of these interface definitions.

There is one architectural issue: What about changing fixed mode properties? Does a property have an "owner" who can manipulate fixed mode properties when everyone else can't? What if there isn't, and you make a mistake when you set it on initialization? Is it frozen in place until the end of time (which, for most computers, is the next time the local power company decides to switch mains and sends you a 1- or 2-second outage as a byproduct)?

Perhaps you've already guessed the answer: The service says that this is an "implementation issue." The good news is that most implementations of the Property Service that you buy should provide a way to do this; the bad news is that it's not standardized, and code you write to manipulate fixed properties using one service may not port to another. Of course there are so few implementations of the Property Service that porting is not really an issue.

18.2 The Object Query Service

A powerful implementation of the Object Query Service could, conceivably, merge all of your CORBA objects, plus your OO databases, your relational databases, and even files on your system, into a database that you can search with a single query invocation. (The OQS doesn't actually merge the datastores, of course; it does the usual OMG thing and wraps each one with a standard interface layer, so they look the same to a client. That way, the service can transmit a single query through to all of them at once.)

If your query requirements are more modest, a smaller implementation of the OQS would still be capable of conducting queries of your set of CORBA objects. Or, perhaps, an OQS add-on to your OO database could add this capability and let you search through your CORBA objects, plus the objects in this one database.

We found few implementations of the Query Service on the market when we were writing this book. We spoke in Chapter 15 about some of the reasons why this might be so; whatever the reason, you may have to search to find one. Nevertheless, we think the architecture and goals of the Query Service are worth investigating so we'll spend a few pages looking at the general architecture and a few of its interfaces. There are at least one, and possibly several, vendors who provide OQS-like functionality to their customers in a product that resembles the OMG Query Service even if it doesn't quite conform, so apparently some people out there agree with us on this.

18.2.1 OQS Building Blocks

It turns out that we need only a few basic building blocks to construct a Query Service:

- First, we need a standard query language so that all of the objects in the system can both service your query and pass it on to additional objects or components.

- Second, we need a standard interface so that an object that holds a query can pass it to an independently built object for invocation.

- Third, we need to be able to query CORBA objects individually, or construct queryable collections of CORBA objects.

- Fourth, we need query managers which bear the standard interface we just mentioned, to perform and/or pass on the query.

The specification allows for a number of types of query managers. The diagram in Figure 18.1 shows a large-scale OQS installation that simultaneously queries a collection of CORBA objects, an OODB, and a relational DB. The query in the diagram is not an object; it's a string in the query language (more on this coming up) that gets passed from QE (query evaluator) to QE. There is a query object, but it's only used by service implementors so we won't mention it here except to warn you not to be confused by it if you read the OMG specification later. The dark bar at the top of each QE symbolizes the standard interface we mentioned in the second bullet in the preceding list.

Next we'll discuss each of the four standard building blocks in turn. When we're done, we still won't have enough to build our integrated system, so we'll see what else we have to add. Here we go:

18.2.2 Standardized Query Language

The OQS is, basically, a wrapper around a query engine that accepts queries in some language. When the specification was adopted, OMG members picked two incompatible languages for the standard:

- *SQL-92 Query*, the subset of SQL-92, which deals directly with query (that is, no schema, session, diagnostics, etc.)

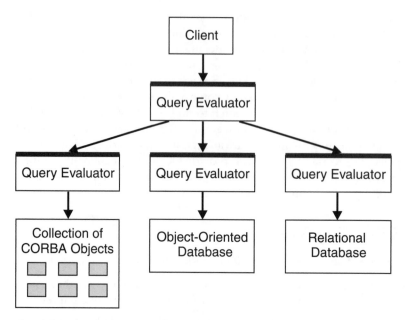

Figure 18.1   Nesting and federation of query evaluators.

- *OQL-93*, an adaptation of SQL-92 Query to cover all objects in the object model defined by the ODMG (Object Database Management Group)

Of these, SQL-92 is still current, but OQL-93 is not. However, since the OQS has not been revised, the OMG document on the books still points to OQL-93. We won't discuss the relative merits of various query languages here; if you find a query-service-like product that works for you, it will probably support only a single language anyhow. There are so few implementations on the market that porting is not an issue.

18.2.2.1 Standardized Interface

In order to pass a query from one QE to another, especially if the QEs are implemented independently by different vendors, they have to share a common interface. Of course, this is CORBA's strong point, so the interface is expressed in OMG IDL. It is

```
interface QueryEvaluator {
    readonly attribute sequence<QLType> ql_types;
    readonly attribute QLType default_ql_type;

    any evaluate (
        in string query,
        in QLType ql_type,
        in parameterlist params )
        raises ( . . . );
}
```

Looks simple, right? Of course, the devil is in the details, but we won't get to them in this book. A client can read the attribute **default_ql_type** to find the default query language for the QE, or the other attribute **ql_types** for a list of all of its other supported query languages. Then you just construct your query as a string in your chosen supported query language and pass it to the QE, specifying the language and a list of parameters, which are (you guessed it) implementation specific. When the query either completes or encounters an error, you get back either an **any** or an exception. The **any** type specification provides generality; the most common return type will probably be a collection of objects or records, but may differ for particular queries.

18.2.2.2 Querying Objects or Collections

If there's an Achilles' heel in OQS, it's here. In order to run a query over your CORBA objects, something has to know their interfaces and apply the predicate to them, and the specification is pretty loose on this aspect. You can benefit from query, but the lesson here is that it helps to design query-ability into your types before your system is cast in concrete. If you don't, you can still build query evaluators but they'll have to query interfaces you've designed for other purposes, instead of finding common evaluation interfaces on all of your instances. In any case, the bottom end of the query evaluator—the part that executes the query, not the part that accepts it—will be non-standard because the standard doesn't include these interfaces in its scope.

If you're familiar with collections of objects, then you're already familiar with the terms *set* and *bag*, for example. These are types of collections, and a collection is what the OQS gives you when it's done searching. Even though the OQS has never been the subject of an OMG Revision Task Force (the OMG group that is formed to maintain a specification), it was updated by the Collection Service when that specification was adopted. A section of that specification modified the queryable collection portion of the OQS to conform to its newly defined interfaces but, as far as we know, no implementations of this revision have ever come to market.

If you want to query a collection of CORBA objects, you need to buy a QueryableCollection object implementation from your OQS vendor. This object inherits, and supports, both the QueryEvaluator and Collection interfaces. Your client invokes the Collection interfaces to construct the group of objects you want to query, and then invokes the QueryEvaluator interface to execute the query. This query evaluator still has to query the objects in its collection, and perhaps others to evaluate whether or not they should be in its collection.

18.2.2.3 Query Evaluators/Managers

What about the objects that actually execute your query? All we've said about them so far is that they bear the QueryEvaluator interface, and that some instances also bear the Collection interfaces, and you want to buy them and not build them yourself. There's a lot more to it than this, however, especially if you want to construct a system that looks anything like Figure 18.1.

These are the things you buy, or already own, that actually make up the OQS. In Figure 18.1, consider the Query Evaluator (QE) on the right along with the native query system just below it. What's a native query system? One example is a database, and you know how huge they can be. Consider this QE to be a front-end to all of the query and processing power of your corporate database. You might also have one (or a hundred) smaller QEs frontending a collection of personal databases.

This is a really powerful concept: Any database or datastore can be integrated into your OQS. All it needs is a QE object with the QueryEvaluator interface on the top end and an interface into the database or datastore on the bottom. The QE object doesn't have to be supplied by the database vendor, although that is a logical first place to look for one. (Presumably, database vendors will see an advantage in having their products integrate into an enterprise's data storage this way.) By the way, the OQS writers were fully aware of this, and wrote the specification to take advantage of caching, indexing, and internal optimization mechanisms present in some native query systems.

In this architecture, the QE plays the role of integrator. It takes in a standardized query, through a standardized interface, and executes it on a particular domain with a particular query system. You'll need a different QE for each database type that you want to involve, plus a QueryableCollection QE for your CORBA objects, all responding to the same standard query language. Once you have all of these you'll be able to start a single query with a single invocation and have it passed to every database in your domain, just as Figure 18.1 illustrates.

Almost. You need one other thing, and that's the QE at the top that takes in the original query and passes it to all of the other QEs. Of course, it bears the QueryEvaluator interface to take in the query, and invokes the QueryEvaluator interface to pass it on.

The catch here is that the interfaces that let you connect the QEs like this, and scope a query to a particular set of QEs, are not part of the OQS standard. In just about all of the services we've described up to now, the scope or target of an operation was the object we invoked, but this is not the case here. This is a reasonable limitation for the standard; each installation will be unique, and the value of a standard is limited in this case. The general cases are covered: objects in relational or OO databases, which are already set up, and CORBA objects in collections, which are included in the OQS specification. But the programming interface you use to tell your upper-level QE that the target of the next query is whatever, is not part of the OMG OQS specification. How will you do this? Perhaps through a GUI that lets you check or uncheck a box for each potential target, or drag a database onto the query object icon, if you're a user. If you're a programmer, the provider will give you an API for this. Don't look in the OMG OQS specification for it.

What's the bottom line on query? A lot of the problem in implementing or running a query is finding, scoping, and accessing the CORBA objects you want to target, and making them queryable in the first place, and you can't cover all of this with a standard because it's site and installation specific. This lowers the gain from a standard, maybe to the point that it can't acquire critical mass and move the market, but it doesn't make it any less useful. Vendors with products that create and control their environment can capitalize on the mass of similar objects in their scope, and execute queries on them in a reasonably consistent way. If you need the functionality of Query, and you can find an implementation that looks good, try it out.

chapter 19

Introducing the CORBA Domains

When we wrote the first edition of this book in 1995, there was no domain activity in OMG. Instead, all of the standards work concentrated on the infrastructure—the ORB, IDL, language mappings, and the IIOP protocol.

However, the CORBA architecture was attracting the attention of knowledgeable workers in many businesses, who identified a number of advantages:

- OMG IDL provided a well-designed, stable, programming-language-independent way to define interfaces for standard components in any industry. The expectation (since come to pass) that IDL would become an international standard added to its luster.

- Components with OMG IDL interfaces could then be implemented on CORBA systems, so no roadblocks would be encountered on the way to market.

- Even if an implementor chose not to use CORBA, the language mappings defined standard and equivalent interfaces in all programming languages.

Inquiries from current and potential members led OMG to reorganize its structure in early 1996 with the formation of the Domain Technology Committee and the Architecture Board. The top-level OMG organization grew from the simple structure shown in Figure 19.1, to the multiheaded configuration shown in Figure 19.2.

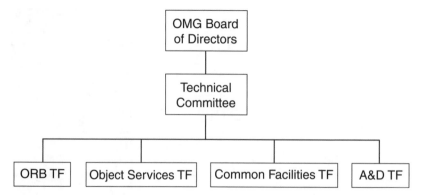

Figure 19.1 Original (pre-domain reorganization) OMG committee and subgroup structure.

19.1 OMG Process Basics

Here's how the OMG specification process works:

Technical work gets done in OMG member committees designated *Task Forces*. These groups are typically small enough to allow interaction, and organized by specialty so everyone in the room understands what's going on. A specification effort typically starts in a Task Force with the writing of a requirements document called a

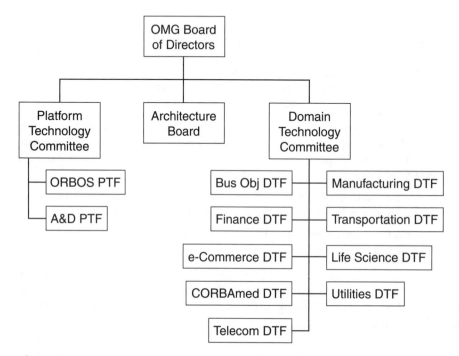

Figure 19.2 OMG committee and subgroup structure following domain reorganization in early 1996.

Request for Proposals or *RFP*, and continues with the technical evaluation of the various submissions that come in to OMG in response, and a Task Force vote to recommend that one of them be adopted as the OMG specification in that area.

Every Task Force is overseen by one of the *Technology Committees* (TC). There are only two, designated *Platform* and *Domain* (see the next section for details). The TCs charter Task Forces to, in effect, do the technical work for them in each specialized area; in turn, the Task Forces bring their RFPs to their parent Technology Committee for formal issuance and bring their technology recommendations for formal approval. (The creation of a specification actually requires an additional vote, by the OMG Board of Directors, acting on the recommendation of a TC.)

When a Task Force decides to adopt a specification in a particular area, its members start the process moving by writing an RFP stating the requirements. There's an art to writing an RFP: Task Force members have to specify *what they want* fairly tightly, or else they won't get it, but they have to leave loose the part about *how they want it done*, because a tight statement of the "hows" in the RFP could rule out clever solutions that the members might like very much, but just didn't happen to think of. The Task Force votes to recommend that its parent TC issue the RFP, and (virtually always) the TC does it.

Submitting companies respond to the RFP with documents called *submissions* (no surprise there). Submitters must meet a number of requirements:

- They must be OMG members, of either Domain, Platform, or Contributing Member category (depending on the TF and TC that issued the RFP).

- They must sign a *Letter of Intent* stating that they will, if their submission is voted the OMG specification, market a commercial implementation within a year.

- They must meet submission deadlines imposed by the RFP or those extended by the Task Force as the process goes along.

At the first deadline, companies submit *initial submissions*. Task Force members (and any OMG member company may be a member of every Task Force; all they have to do is show up for the meetings) evaluate the submissions at a meeting and over the following few months, while submitters prepare *revised submissions*. Frequently, submitting companies will get together (outside of OMG meetings) and merge their submissions during this period. At the OMG meeting following the revised submission deadline, the Task Force may vote to recommend one of the revised submissions (or the only one, if submitters have produced a single, consensus document, which happens frequently but not always) to its parent TC for adoption.

Before the TF's parent TC can vote on a submission, the Architecture Board (AB) has to certify that the submission is consistent with the OMA and with all of the other OMG specifications. If the submission fails to gain AB approval, it has to be revised and earn TF recommendation and AB approval in its new form.

Once the submission has been certified by the AB, it goes to the TC for a vote and, following this step (which is formally a recommendation to the OMG BOD), it goes to the BOD for its final vote. Before the BOD approves a specification, submitters must respond to a questionnaire from its Business Committee reaffirming the promise that they made in their letter of intent, to market an implementation within a year of adoption. With this requirement met, the BOD is very likely to vote to adopt the specification. (No submission that met all of these requirements has ever failed to gain BOD approval.)

How long does it take to produce an OMG specification? Because OMG is a consortium, and not a government-sanctioned standards organization, there is no requirement to achieve perfect consensus—majority vote decision-making is good enough. Recognizing this, OMG members can set deadlines for each stage of the process and expect that they will be adhered to pretty closely. Run at full speed, a specification effort can go from RFP to adoption in less than a year but this leaves little time for adjustment of submissions based on member feedback. Recognizing the value of this feedback, members typically set a timetable of a little over a year. Most RFPs add an additional revision step at the end to tie up loose ends and produce a specification that members are truly proud of; this results in an average process time of 14 to 18 months.

19.2 The 1996 Reorganization

As Figure 19.1 shows, OMG before 1996 was a simple organization with a single Technical Committee, two Task Forces, and no Architecture Board. In response to the influences we described in the introduction to this chapter, however, the reorganization in the beginning of 1996 split the Technical Committee into two, as we show in Figure 19.2: the Platform Technology Committee, charged with development of OMG infrastructure specifications including the ORB, IDL, IIOP, and the like; and the Domain Technology Committee, charged with development of specifications in vertical markets including Telecommunication, Healthcare, and more. (We'll give the entire list in the next section.) At the same time, the AB was created to oversee the OMA and ensure that new specifications were consistent with it and with each other, an important factor now that OMG had so many independent working bodies.

19.2.1 Who Votes Where?

OMG has a number of membership categories, each with its own set of privileges. By the way, OMG members are *companies*, not people, and the privileges of membership extend to *all* employees and/or students of the member. A SIG is a Special Interest Group that works in a technology area (typically) but does not recommend specifications to its parent TC. The acronym SC refers to Subcommittees, which look after procedural or non-specification areas such as Policies and Procedures, Liaison, and the Object Model. Subscription to OMG e-mail lists is restricted to members only except for a few "announcement" type lists; all categories of membership may subscribe to as many OMG e-mail lists as their already overloaded inboxes can handle, and have password access to the members-only parts of the OMG Web site.

Contributing Member. Votes in PTC, DTC, and all TFs, SIGs, and SCs. May submit in response to any RFP. May run for seat on BOD and AB.

Platform Member. Votes in PTC and all TFs, SIGs, and SCs. May submit in response to PTC RFPs. May run for seat on BOD and AB. This category was created in mid-1998.

Domain Member. Votes in DTC and all TFs, SIGs, and SCs. May submit in response to DTC RFPs. May run for seat on BOD and AB.

Influencing, Government, or University Member. Votes in all TFs and SIGs.

Auditing Member. May send one representative to attend every OMG meeting as an observer, but does not vote.

Analyst Member. May attend up to two meetings per year, and does not vote.

Two OMG member bodies, the AB and BOD, are special: Member representatives must be elected to voting membership in them. In all other bodies, voting rights are gained simply by making the commitment to join at a high enough level. Because OMG staff write neither software (OMG is not in the software business) nor specifications (members do this), the organization is able to keep membership fees low compared to other consortia. Current fees and a membership application are on OMG's Web site at www.omg.org/membership.

There are 10 elected members of the AB; the OMG's Director of Architecture is a permanent member and casts a tie-breaking vote. Five members of the AB are elected by the PTC, the other five by the DTC, for two-year terms. Interestingly enough, anyone from a Contributing, Platform, and Domain member company may run for AB election in *either* Technology Committee regardless of their membership category, so candidates frequently run for elections where they are unable to vote for themselves! AB members whose terms expire may run for reelection.

There are 32 members of the Board of Directors, who all hold three-year seats. One-third of the seats expire every year, and directors may be reelected. Only BOD members may vote to elect candidates to the board. OMG's CEO, Dr. Richard Soley, is Chairman.

In early 1999, OMG had about 800 members total. Of this, 96 joined as Contributing, 8 as Platform (relatively few because the category was only created recently), 92 as Domain, and about 200 as Influencing. About 100 Universities were members, and 10 Government agencies. The remainder (and quite a number, at that) are auditing members.

The important message in the membership numbers is that *the Domain category has grown, in less than three years, to equal or surpass the platform category by number and interest,* and remains the fastest growing part of the organization. Let's examine the Domain Task Forces (DTFs) and see what these new OMG members are doing.

19.3 Domains in the OMG

In late 1999, OMG had nine DTFs:

- Business Objects (BODTF)
- Finance (FDTF), which includes banking and insurance
- Electronic Commerce (ECDTF)
- Manufacturing (MfgDTF)
- Telecommunications (TelDTF)
- Transportation (TranspDTF)
- Healthcare (CORBAmed) DTF
- Utilities (UtilDTF)
- Life Science Research (LSRDTF)

There were also a number of groups forming, but not yet chartered as Task Forces, including the Enterprise Customer Interaction Systems (ECIS) SIG, active in

Call Center and associated technologies, a group in Retailing, a group in Space and Satellite technology.

Finally, the DTC has chartered a number of DSIGs that work in specific areas but do not intend to become Task Forces. These are:

- The C4I DSIG, short for Command, Control, Communications, Computers, and Intelligence, a military-oriented group and definitely international and not restricted to United States participation.

- The GIS DSIG, working in Geographic Information Systems (and nicknamed the "Palindromic SIG"); this group maintains a close liaison with the Open GIS Consortium, which creates standards in the GIS world.

- The Analytical Data Management DSIG, working in statistics, data collection, and data analysis.

- The Distributed Simulation DSIG, supported by the United States Distributed Military Simulation Office and responsible for shepherding the High Level Architecture (HLA), a respected Simulation architecture created by that office, to OMG specification through the Manufacturing Task Force. (Since SIGs can't recommend technologies to become OMG specifications, they have to ask some Task Force to conduct the votes for them. Since every OMG member can vote in every Task Force, this is not a problem.)

Between their start in early 1996 and the time this book was written in 2000, OMG Domain Task Forces adopted 25 technologies. As we pointed out, it takes about 14 to 18 months to produce an OMG specification, and the Domain side of OMG started with only three or four Task Forces, but the first specification arrived in September 1997 and the DTC has kept up production at the rate of a dozen or more specifications per year ever since. With the increase in the number of DTFs, the organization expects this rate to increase as well.

In this chapter, we'll list most of the adopted Domain specifications and RFPs in process at the time this was written in late 1999. In the next chapter, we'll isolate a few representative Domain specifications and present them in a little more detail. Our presentation will be organized by Task Force. For up-to-date information on OMG work in progress, surf to www.omg.org, look down the left-hand side of the homepage under the heading *Technology Process*, and click on the subheading *TC Work in Progress*. This page is a list of clickable links to pages describing each adoption process, and giving access (yes, even to nonmembers of OMG!) to all relevant documents including submissions still under evaluation.

19.4 Business Objects Domain Task Force

The BODTF is one of the original Domain Task Forces. It is working primarily on Business Objects and a Business Object Facility. An unsuccessful initial effort to establish a Business Object Facility in 1996–1997 resulted in the submission being withdrawn before an adoption vote completed, but a second effort is under way now—see Section 19.4.1.2 for details. In addition to this work, the BODTF also takes charge of some RFPs that work at Domain Level but don't fit neatly into any single domain.

Business Objects specifications that complete OMG's formal editing process will be posted on www.omg.org/library/cboindx.html; recently adopted Business Objects specifications can be downloaded from www.omg.org/techprocess/meetings/schedule/Technology_Adoptions.html.

19.4.1 Adopted Specifications

19.4.1.1 Common Business Objects: Task and Session

Task and *Session* are two fundamental concepts in computer-supported cooperative work. These, the first of the Common Business Objects (CBOs) to come out of the Task Force, will support CORBA-based groupware and already have been incorporated into another OMG specification, the Negotiation Facility from the ECDTF.

Efforts to establish more CBOs during 1998 did not receive support from OMG members even though submissions were received and reviewed. We suspect that members will want to have a little more experience actually using these concepts in a number of domains before they adopt something at a higher level. Without this experience, it's impossible to know beforehand whether or not a particular CBO design is the right foundation to build upon for your business object framework.

19.4.1.2 Workflow Facility

The Workflow Facility grew out of a cooperative effort of OMG and the Workflow Management Coalition (WfMC). In fact, the current specification is based on the WfMC's IDL interfaces and is formally supported by the WfMC; the only reason that WfMC did not submit their specification to OMG themselves is that they are not a software company and could not meet the commercial availability requirement. Instead, a group of companies that are members of both WfMC and OMG acted as submitters and took upon themselves the responsibility to market the commercial implementation. These companies are working on the implementations and preparing a maintenance revision, Workflow Facility 1.1.

A Workflow Management System provides procedural automation of a business process by managing the sequence of work activities and the invocation of human and IT resources associated with the various activity steps. Lifetimes of workflow-managed process range from minutes to days (or even months and years), depending upon their complexity and the duration of the various constituent activities.

Workflow is one of the Domain facilities we've chosen to highlight in Chapter 20, so look ahead to Section 20.2 for details.

19.4.2 RFPs in Progress

19.4.2.1 Business Object Facility-Related RFPs

When the initial Business Object Facility (BOF) effort finished in mid-1998 without adoption of a BOF specification, a number of OMG members immediately started a new effort. To maximize their chances of success, the advocates made sure to involve members of the Analysis and Design Task Force, and the ORBOS Task Force. Their plan starts with a UML-based foundation, and will build to a facility based on the forthcoming CORBA components architecture.

Work on the new Business Object foundation is well under way, with three RFPs issued in March, 1999 and a fourth ready for issue when these three complete. These four RFPs are grouped under the heading *Business Object Initiative* or BOI. The three RFPs have been recommended by the Analysis and Design Task Force and issued by the Platform Technology Committee. They are

> *The UML Profile for Enterprise Distributed Object Computing (EDOC) RFP.* This RFP asks for a UML profile, defined in terms of "well-formedness rules," "standard elements," semantics, and common model elements, that supports EDOC using CORBA. Information on this RFP is posted on www.omg.org/techprocess/meetings/schedule/UML_Profile_for_EDOC_RFP.html.

> *The UML Profile for CORBA RFP.* Even though UML and CORBA are both OMG specifications, they do not cover the same scope: UML is much broader than CORBA. This RFP asks for a UML profile for CORBA. UML designs done in this profile will be directly expressible in CORBA semantics; that is, in OMG IDL. Information on this RFP is posted on www.omg.org/techprocess/meetings/schedule/UML_Profile_for_CORBA_RFP.html.

> *The Human-Usable Textual Notation for the UML Profile for EDOC RFP.* Currently, the only official "language" for UML is the graphical notation defined in the UML specification. This RFP calls for a human usable (that is, readable and editable) notation. The RFP notes that this notation will be editable by machine as well. Information on this RFP is posted on www.omg.org/techprocess/meetings/schedule/UML_Textual_Notation_RFP.html.

There is a fourth RFP, *A Mapping of the UML Profile for EDOC to CORBA*, in draft and ready to be issued. However, since there is no way to define this specification until the UML Profile for EDOC is ready, the RFP is being held until the prerequisites are complete.

Using the results of these RFPs, and building on the CCM, OMG members expect to produce a standardized business object facility. This is at least several years in the future (speaking as we do in early 2000), but OMG members are hard at work already.

19.4.2.2 Document Repository Integration RFP

The BODTF does more than just the BOI. The Document Repository Integration RFP will establish standard interfaces for managing a heterogeneous set of document repositories. Functionality will include all or some of these items:

- Document Storage
- Document Identification

- Document Retrieval
- Document Integrity
- Document Tracking
- Document Renditions
- Document Revisions
- Query Over the Repository
- Document Delivery
- Notification of Changes to a Document
- Document Migration
- Document Archive
- Document Repository Backup

19.5 Finance Domain Task Force

Chartered early in the lifespan of the Domain Technology Committee, the Finance DTF includes companies representing Banking, Insurance, Financial Markets, and Accounting; of the financial trades, only Electronic Commerce resides in another TF. The first Financial Specification was the Currency Facility, with Party Management and General Ledger following close behind.

Finance specifications that have completed OMG's formal editing process can be downloaded from www.omg.org/library/cfinindx.html; recently adopted specifications can be downloaded from www.omg.org/techprocess/meetings/schedule/Technology_Adoptions.html.

19.5.1 Adopted Specifications

19.5.1.1 Currency Facility

The Currency Facility defines:

- A currency object
- Basic business object for currency, money, and exchange rate
- Calculation and formatting mechanisms for the use of money

Interfaces and operations to convert from one currency to another are included, but conversion rate setting is not—the specification assumes that each installation will connect its facility to a conversion-rate database of its choosing. The specification is careful to define dual representation functionality and interfaces for use in countries that are making the transition to the Euro during the three-year period starting in early 1999.

19.5.1.2 Party Management Facility

This isn't what you think; since either a person or a corporation (realizing that this concept has different names in different countries) can take part in a contract or agreement, the Finance DTF uses the general term "party" for this concept.

As you can imagine, people, organizations, and companies are represented in a myriad of different ways in computer systems. In the context of contract management, however, systems need to manipulate party information in a standard way regardless of the nature of the party, and of the ultimate storage type and data format. This facility provides that standard; if your system manipulates contracts and agreements, you've probably figured out the significance of this standard already.

With the establishment of a facility and, especially, agreement on the concept and representation of "party," OMG members are now proceeding to standardize Contract and Agreement objects and facilities, although these RFPs had not been issued as we wrote this chapter.

19.5.1.3 General Ledger Facility

The General Ledger (GL) Facility specifies General Ledger interfaces conformant with international accounting standards for double-entry bookkeeping. The GL interfaces comprise a framework that supports the implementation of accounting modules and applications, including Accounts Payable, Accounts Receivable, Payroll, and other standard accounting functions.

This lets application builders implement interoperable accounting applications. The set of GL services is as complete as possible in order to support the implementation of accounting clients that can interoperate with more than one GL Facility implementation.

There are seven interfaces in the facility. Here's a table listing all seven by name, along with each one's purpose and the primary application module—termed a "client" by the specification—that will use it:

INTERFACE	PURPOSE	PRIMARY GL CLIENT(S)
GL Arbitrator	Establish GL client session	All GL clients
GL Profile	Access to GL services	GL client session
GL BookKeeping	GL Transaction entry	GL data entry clients
GL Retrieval	GL Information Retrieval	GL reporting clients
GL LedgerLifeCycle	GL LifeCycle operations	GL administration clients
GL Integrity	GL Integrity checks	GL administration clients
GL FacilityLifeCycle	GL Facility LifeCycle operations	GL administration clients

Demonstrating OMG's worldwide participation, the GL facility submission was supported by the European Union's Esprit COMPASS project.

19.5.2 RFPs in Progress

With the Party Management Specification just under final vote, the Financial DTF had not had time to issue follow-up RFPs for contract and agreement by the time we wrote this chapter so we have no outstanding efforts under way to report on here.

19.6 Electronic Commerce Domain Task Force

Another well-established Domain Task Force with an world wide flavor, the Electronic Commerce DTF saw its Negotiation Facility become an OMG specification during 1999.

Electronic Commerce specifications that complete OMG's formal editing process will be posted on www.omg.org/library/ceindx.html; recently adopted Electronic Commerce specifications can be downloaded from www.omg.org/techprocess/meetings/schedule/Technology_Adoptions.html.

19.6.1 Adopted Specifications

By the time you read this, the Negotiation Facility should be an established OMG specification. It builds on the Task and Session Common Business Objects, and on the Notification Service.

19.6.1.1 Negotiation Facility

In order for a number of parties (and the number does not have to be two) to negotiate some outcome, they must *collaborate*. With this in mind, the Negotiation Facility starts out by defining a general framework for collaboration, which it then specializes into a number of negotiation scenarios. The framework itself is based on OMG's specifications and, in addition, the Document Object Model (DOM) of the W3C. For a pointer to the DOM specification, see Appendix A.

Figure 19.3, reproduced from the specification, shows the Negotiation Facility Framework.

The facility covers three collaboration models:

- Bilateral negotiation
- Multilateral negotiation
- Promissory commitment

In bilateral negotiation, two parties converge on an outcome. In multilateral negotiation, motions are made, seconded, amended, and voted. Promissory commitment deals with the rights of and obligations between participants, and the association of proof.

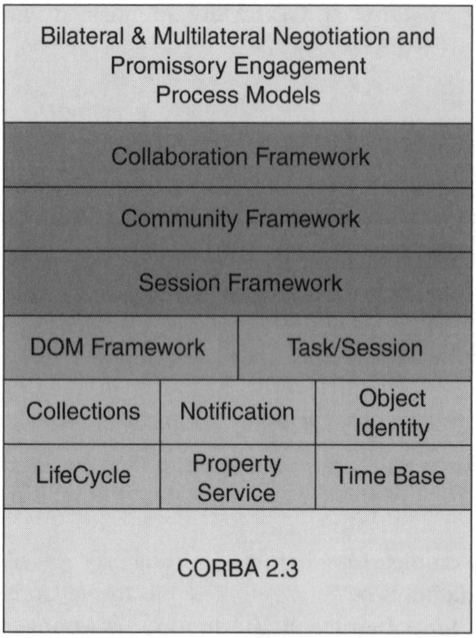

Figure 19.3 Negotiation Facility Framework composition.

Session, Community, and Collaboration Frameworks are defined generally enough to be useful beyond the context of the Negotiation Facility.

19.6.2 RFPs in Progress

19.6.2.1 Public Key Infrastructure RFP

This is more a security management RFP than a security functionality RFP. It defines, using IDL and CORBA, a Public Key Infrastructure (PKI); that is, a system for issuing, managing, and revoking digital certificates. Of course the system itself has to be secure, but it can manage this using standard CORBA security without (we presume) any modifications. For information on this recent effort, surf your browser to www .omg.org/techprocess/meetings/schedule/Public_Key_Infrastructure_RFP.html.

19.7 Manufacturing Domain Task Force

Another well-established Domain Task Force, the Manufacturing DTF had been a SIG for a number of years before the OMG Technical Committee reorganization and its members took advantage of its head start. Their first specification effort, in Product

Data Management (PDM), involved so many of the prominent PDM software vendors that it was assured of success. These companies continue to be involved, and are now collaborating as they build a set of interoperable implementations. While they do this, the task force is proceeding to additional standards in the realm of Enterprise Resource Planning (ERP).

Manufacturing specifications that complete OMG's formal editing process will be posted on www.omg.org/library/cmfgindx.html. Recently adopted Manufacturing specifications can be downloaded from www.omg.org/techprocess/meetings/schedule/Technology_Adoptions.html.

19.7.1 Adopted Specifications

19.7.1.1 Product Data Management (PDM) Facility

The PDM specification defines eight PDM Enablers which, taken together, provide a framework to carry out 11 PDM functions. The eight enablers are:

- Request for Engineering Action
- Engineering Change Order
- Manufacturing Implementation
- Document Management
- Product Structure Definition
- Effectivity of Products and Occurrences
- Configuration Management
- Test, Maintenance, and Diagnostic Information

The eight enablers support these eleven common PDM functions:

- Develop Strategic Product Plan
- Develop Product Business Plan
- Develop Product Definition
- Define Product Marketing Configuration and Rules
- Develop Product Design
- Develop Process Design and Procurement Agreements
- Coordinate Design Change
- Evaluate Product Design
- Implement Production Changes
- Develop Product Service Methods
- Develop Service Distribution Plan

19.7.1.2 Distributed Simulation High-Level Architecture (HLA)

OMG has a subgroup working on Distributed Simulation, but it's a SIG and is not able to recommend to the DTC that RFPs be issued or technology adopted as an OMG standard. So, when members of this group wanted to run a technology adoption process, they looked around for a friendly Task Force to run it as their "proxy." They needed a Task Force whose charter encompassed distributed simulation and they found it in Manufacturing, since their discrete event simulation was similar to that done in manufacturing studies.

The United States Government Distributed Military Simulation Office (DMSO) has established an architecture for distributed simulations. Termed the High Level Architecture, or HLA, it is expressed (in one form) in OMG IDL and CORBA. The DMSO joined OMG at the requisite Domain level of membership, and submitted the HLA for adoption as a Request for Comments (RFC).

The RFC process is an alternative to OMG's RFP process that works well when there is only one possible submitter for a specification; that is, there's no competition in the technology space. In this process, no Task Force writes or issues an RFP. Instead, an OMG member company submits its document (which has to be in the same form as an RFP submission, and meet all of the same types of requirements) to the OMG, which assign it to a TC and Task Force. If the Task Force and TC find that the submission meets basic requirements, OMG staff post the document for *public* comment for 90 days. If no significant negative comment is received during the 90-day period, the submission is reviewed by the AB and undergoes the same TC vote as if it had come in via the RFP process. This is followed by the usual Business Committee questionnaire process (since the commercial availability requirements are the same for RFC and RFP) and BOD vote.

The RFC process is quick when it works, but fragile: Once the process starts, the only way to change the submission is to withdraw it and start the process again from the beginning. Aware of this, the DMSO presented their initial draft submission to OMG members well before it was complete, and made modifications where necessary before they made their formal RFC submission.

As you might expect with so much advance work, the actual RFC adoption process ran smoothly and the HLA was adopted as an OMG specification.

The submission, which covers only a part of the DMSO HLA, is a massive 300-page document. Companies active in distributed simulation, especially military simulation, are already aware of the HLA (although some are not aware that it is an OMG specification) and don't need a two-paragraph summary. If you're working in this area but not aware of the HLA, you need a lot more than two paragraphs, so we'll just point you to the spec, which you may download for free, print out, and read in your spare time. It's at www.omg.org/cgi-bin/doc?mfg/98-06-06.

19.7.2 RFPs in Progress

19.7.2.1 Data Acquisition RFP

The Manufacturing DTF has one RFP in process, and a number of RFPs planned or in draft relating to ERP functionality.

In process now is an RFP for Data Acquisition in Industrial Systems. It will establish standard interfaces for access to data within industrial systems by other applications such as Utility Management Systems, Manufacturing Execution Systems, and Enterprise Resource Planning systems. This functionality includes:

- Discovery of Remote System and Device Schema
- Defining Data Access Requests
- Data Access/Retrieval
- Event Notification for Availability of Data
- Event Driven Data Upload for data types that are generated within and gathered from industrial systems.

This RFP is scheduled to complete in the second quarter of 2000. You can follow its progress at www.omg.org/techprocess/meetings/schedule/Data_Acquisition_RFP.html.

19.8 Telecommunications Domain Task Force

Telecommunications is an outstanding OMG Domains success story. Not only has the Telecoms DTF adopted more specifications than any other DTF; the impact of CORBA in the industry is unparalleled. More than 20 Telecoms design wins and success stories appear on the OMG Web site at www.corba.org; the Component Development Strategies newsletter for October, 1998 was devoted to the telecommunications industry and CORBA featuring more case studies; and a number of conferences on CORBA and Telecoms are held worldwide by independent conference organizers not affiliated with OMG.

Telecoms specifications that have completed OMG's formal editing process can be downloaded from www.omg.org/library/ctindx.html. Recently adopted Telecoms specifications can be downloaded from www.omg.org/techprocess/meetings/schedule/Technology_Adoptions.html.

19.8.1 Adopted Specifications

19.8.1.1 A/V Stream Control Facility

The A/V Stream Control Facility was the first Domain technology to be adopted by OMG. It defines a CORBA object framework for control of out-of-band streaming data transmission. That is, CORBA objects, controlled by IDL commands, set up the connection, set its properties, monitor it, and break it down when it's no longer needed. The ORB is not involved in the transmission of the actual streaming data. The specification is complete, covering stream topologies, multiple flows, stream description and typing, stream interface identification and reference, stream setup and release, stream modification, stream termination, multiple protocols, stream Quality of Service (QoS), flow synchronization, and interoperability. The specification provides hooks for security, but does not fill in any details.

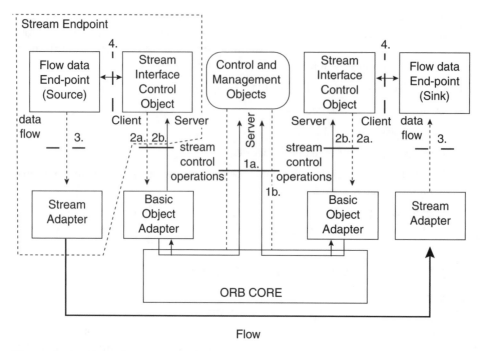

Figure 19.4 Example stream architecture.

Figure 19.4, reproduced from the specification, shows how the CORBA stream control object interacts with the stream source and adaptor to create the out-of-band data connection and route data over it. Currently, the specification covers streams of audio and video data.

19.8.1.2 Notification Service

We covered this service in Chapter 12, but it's worth putting this small section here to remind you that Notification is not officially a CORBAservice but rather a domain CORBAfacility, in spite of its general usefulness in the OMA.

19.8.1.3 CORBA/TMN (Telecoms Management Network) Interworking Facility and CORBA/IN (Intelligent Network) Interworking Facility

We admit, the CORBA/TMN Interworking Facility and the CORBA/IN Interworking Facility are two entirely different specifications, but for readers who are not Telecoms experts, this doesn't make a lot of difference.

There's a lot of standardized interoperability in the 279 pages of the CORBA/TMN specification. It provides Translation algorithms from ASN.1 to IDL, from GDMO to IDL, from IDL to ASN.1 and GDMO, and from SNMP SMI specifications to IDL. It also provides interworking between CORBA and both CMIP and SNMP, and a translation algorithm to GDMO. For the acronymically challenged, we'll point out that SNMP is the Simple Network Management Protocol; ASN.1 is Abstract Syntax Notation One; CMIP is the Common Management Interface Protocol; GDMO refers to the Guidelines for the Definition of Managed Objects; and SMI is SNMP Management Information (an acronym within an acronym—what did you expect at the end of this list?).

The CORBA/IN Interworking Specification provides a similar degree of interworking between CORBA and Telecoms Intelligent Networks; that is, long distance services, 800-number (toll-free) calling, and the like.

19.8.1.4 Log Facility

Telecoms networks need to log events. In a grossly oversimplified view, the Log Facility subscribes to CORBA event and notification service channels, filters the events it receives, and records the ones that pass through the filters. Subscribing clients may receive events generated by the log service for various happenings, or review the logs directly. The facility meets industry requirements for the log facility as stated in ITU-T X.735.

19.8.2 RFPs in Progress

Ever active, the Telecoms DTF had three RFPs in process when we wrote this chapter, and a number of others in draft. The RFP *Wireless Access for CORBA* started its way through the process in late 1999. Here are highlights of the three active RFPs.

19.8.2.1 Management of Event Networks RFP

If you have one, or a few, event channels, you can probably manage them without specialized tools. If, however, your network has thousands or more of these channels, collecting or dispatching events to networks of other Telecoms service providers, and you use them to maintain service levels to your paying customers, you probably want something more.

The Management of Event Networks RFP will standardize interfaces for a service to manage event network topology, Quality of Service, and subscription. It is at final vote stage in early 2000, as we go to press.

19.8.2.2 Service Access and Subscription RFP

When telephones were new, you didn't place calls yourself—an operator did it for you. (Is the phrase "Number please" more than a Trivia answer to you?!) With the advent of dial telephones, customers placed their own local calls, but still relied on operators for long distance. Now we place even overseas calls ourselves, but still rely on people when we order new service, or change our service configuration. This is about to change, and CORBA will be ready when it does.

The Service Access and Subscription RFP anticipates a business world in which "retailer" companies provide an electronic storefront where a consumer can order telecom or communications services. In a second step, the company passes the request on to one of a number of providers, which immediately provides it to the customer. (The concept of "retailer" comes from TINA-C specifications, but is not identical to the TINA-C retailer who is also a provider of service while the CORBA retailer is not.)

This RFP is scheduled to complete in early 2000. For details, surf your browser to www.omg.org/techprocess/meetings/schedule/Service_Access&Subscription_RFP.html.

19.8.2.3 CORBA/FTAM-FTP Interworking RFP

CORBA, with its active objects, usually doesn't get involved with files—either their contents, or manipulation. From the classic CORBA point of view, these data are an implementation detail hidden behind the interfaces.

But in a Telecommunications environment, many types of data are accumulated in files: billing data, performance data, and more. Then, from time to time, these files are transferred or copied from the service environment to a processing environment. Lacking a CORBA standard for file manipulation, this is done using ISO FTAM (File Transfer Access and Management) or FTP (File Transfer Protocol).

The FTAM-FTP RFP will establish a set of OMG IDL interfaces that allow Telecom applications to create, delete, copy, and manipulate attributes of files without leaving their CORBA environment. This RFP is scheduled to complete in early 2000. Details appear on the Web at www.omg.org/techprocess/meetings/schedule/CORBA-FTAM _FTP_Interw._RFP.html.

19.9 Transportation Domain Task Force

The Transportation DTF has been working for several years. Although Transportation includes many subdomains—Rail, Air, Trucking, Highways (especially the new field of Intelligent Highways), Marine, and all of these include both freight and passenger modes—only a few have "taken off" and the star of the show at OMG is Air Traffic Control.

Transportation specifications that complete OMG's formal editing process will be posted on www.omg.org/library/ctransindx.html. Recently adopted Transportation specifications can be downloaded from www.omg.org/techprocess/meetings/schedule/Technology_Adoptions.html.

19.9.1 Adopted Specifications

19.9.1.1 Air Traffic Control Human-Computer Interface Facility

Air Traffic Control facilities are made up of many modules, and the field obviously needs international standards since airplanes fly around the world and need to communicate with ground stations everywhere using the same equipment on the same frequencies (and even in the same language!).

Although the ground equipment does not travel this way, it also benefits from standards, and the recent move to upgrade this equipment (especially in the United States) is providing an opportunity to establish an industry-standards-based architecture. To this end, both the United States FAA and Europe's Eurocontrol are cooperating within OMG to establish ATC standards based on CORBA. First in this suite is the specification for Human-Machine Interface (HMI); more standards are on the way.

The ATC HMI specification actually prescribes the interface between the ATC system and the Display System, and not between the system and the air traffic controller person sitting at the console. (Display system interface specifications will follow later; GUI and display details are out of scope for CORBA and OMG.) Rather than define objects for airplane, track, beacon, and so on, the submitters chose to define a general CORBA-based communications mechanism that can transmit data about airplanes, beacons, and so on, that are defined for each individual system. The submitters explain that this enhances industry acceptance of CORBA because many companies can use it without reengineering their systems around narrow definitions of objects that currently differ from one manufacturer to another. As the industry defines standards for ATC objects, presumably the CORBA specifications will track these developments.

The specification is already implemented in commercial products in Europe.

19.9.2 RFPs in Progress

Transportation DTF does not have any RFPs outstanding, but they are drafting RFPs for Flight Planning and Air Traffic Surveillance. Watch for these on the OMG Web site.

19.10 Healthcare (CORBAmed) Domain Task Force

One of the most active Domains after Telecom, the Healthcare Task Force goes by the name CORBAmed. Their specification for the Person Identifier Specification, well known as PIDS, is used throughout the industry. Additional CORBAmed specifications also make progress in an industry known for its large number of competing standards organizations.

Healthcare specifications that have completed OMG's formal editing process can be downloaded from www.omg/org/library/cmedindx.html. Recently adopted Healthcare specifications can be downloaded from www.omg.org/techprocess/meetings/schedule/Technology_Adoptions.html.

19.10.1 Adopted Specifications

19.10.1.1 Person Identifier Service (PIDS)

Throughout your lifetime, you may have episodes of care provided by dozens or hundreds of healthcare providers, most of whom will assign and maintain patient IDs autonomously. These autonomously managed IDs allow the local organization to collect and use their records, but are not designed to correlate with other providers' record systems.

If a provider does not have a patient's complete record, things can go wrong. For example, redundant treatment can be administered (sometimes at considerable cost), or incompatible drugs prescribed. Increased specialization of providers increases fragmentation and distribution of patient records.

Healthcare information systems use various combinations of a person's identifying parameters to search for a record, and multiple systems—even within the same hospital or clinic—may use different parameter sets. The lack of a single client interface not only proliferates client code on desktop systems, but also prevents staff from using expertise acquired on one client to make better use of other clients also running in-house. Precise identification is important, but this task is difficult because identifying information does not always stay constant: Names and addresses change for many reasons: hair color comes in a bottle and changes with the fashion; height changes as people age; and even supposedly constant identifiers such as Social Security Numbers may be inadvertently duplicated, remembered wrong, or used fraudulently. Healthcare providers like it when software companies compete to provide better, faster, or cheaper matching algorithms, but they don't appreciate when vendor lock-in to a proprietary client interface increases their costs for a move up to the next level of ID-matching technology.

The PIDS specification defines the interfaces of a CORBA Person Identification Service that organizes person ID management functionality to meet healthcare needs. It:

- Supports both the assignment of IDs within a particular ID Domain and the correlation of IDs among multiple ID Domains

- Supports searching and matching of people in both attended-interactive and message-driven-unattended modes, independent of matching algorithm

- Supports federation of PIDS services in a topology-independent fashion

- Permits PIDS implementations to protect person confidentiality under the broadest variety of confidentiality policies and security mechanisms

- Enables plug-and-play PIDS interoperability by means of a core set of profile elements, yet still supports site-specific and implementation-specific extensions and customization of profile elements

- Defines compliance levels for several degrees of sophistication, ranging from small, query-only single ID Domains to large federated correlating ID Domains

PIDS Interoperability demonstrations have been held at two healthcare conferences, and a number of implementations are available on the market. One company has advertised a fee-based person identifier service, using their database, built on remote access via PIDS interfaces.

PIDS is one of the domain specifications that we've chosen to highlight. Our extended writeup starts in Section 20.3.

19.10.1.2 Lexicon Query Service

There are many ways to represent concepts in healthcare, ranging from "simple English" (or whatever your native language might be), to coding systems, to database schemas. The Lexicon Query Service attempts to provide a single interface that can query all—or almost all—of these systems. The specification gives this example to demonstrate the problem:

The question "Is penicillin an antibiotic?" could be presented to one system in the form "Does there exist a subtype relationship in which the concept code for antibiotic is the supertype and the concept code for penicillin is the subtype?" In another system, the question may be presented as "Is there a record in the drug database whose key is 'penicillin' that has the value of 'Yes' in the antibiotic column?"

All access to the lexicon is read-only. Only interfaces, and not lexicon (that is, dictionary entry) data are standardized; the medical community already has standards for the content.

19.10.2 RFPs in Progress

19.10.2.1 Clinical Observations Access Service RFP

As we went to press in early 2000, the Clinical Observations Access Service (COAS) RFP and Healthcare Resource Access Control RFP had both passed their final votes for adoption.

Observations can be just about anything: recordings of instrument data, X-ray or MRI images, physicians' scrawls on a chart or dictation into a recorder, and so on. The COAS submission says that just about all of these are fodder for their service when it defines an *observation* as "any measurement, recording, or description of the anatomical, physiological, pathological, or psychological state or history of a human being or any sample from a human being, and any impressions, conclusions, or judgments made regarding that individual within the context of the current delivery of healthcare."

According to the submission, all observations share these common features:

- They are made on a specific subject of care; e.g., patient, organ, population.

- They represent a snapshot of that subject in time, either at a particular time, or over some specified interval of time (time in this context includes the notion of both date and time).

- They are made, or recorded, by an instrument or a healthcare professional in some clinical context.

- They are given (by the patient, the healthcare institution, or society) some degree of confidentiality.

In this context, the submission defines interfaces for a comprehensive Clinical Observations server. It includes an information model.

In late 1999, the Clinical Observations Access Service had just completed all steps and been adopted as an official OMG specification; you can download it from www.omg.org/cgi-bin/doc?corbamed/99-03-25.zip.

19.10.2.2 Healthcare Resource Access Control (HRAC) RFP

Security is extremely important in healthcare—not only because healthcare providers and insurers properly feel that patient data should be safeguarded because their customers require it, but also because governmental penalties for security breaches can be severe.

The HRAC submission defines a Resource Access Decision (RAD) facility that can be consulted by security-aware objects before they process an invocation from a client. If the RAD approves, the object will return a response; otherwise, it returns a security exception to the client.

Since CORBA security decisions go down only to the object and interface level, but healthcare security potentially discriminates based on data content, CORBAmed felt that they needed to define content-based security management in a standard way, and the HRAC RFP and facility are the result.

This RFP completed its final vote in late 1999; for details, check out www.omg.org/techprocess/meetings/schedule/Healthcare_Resource_AC_RFP.html.

19.10.2.3 Healthcare Data Interpretation RFP

The Healthcare Data Interpretation Facility (HDIF) will provide a variety of intelligent transforms for clinical data. The RFP says this is necessary because:

> "Research in healthcare informatics continually produces viable decision support technologies that seldom achieve widespread use, because the field lacks a sufficient body of standard interfaces to enable easy integration of so-called intelligent systems into existing healthcare information systems. The research typically proceeds using some form of intelligence designed either as a stand-alone system or dependent on features of the local information systems. As a result, proven technologies remain isolated to the local provider that provides the testbed for the research. Having standard interfaces for intelligent clinical data transforms will provide a way to more easily integrate innovative technologies into multiple healthcare domains. Moreover, the HDIF will provide common interfaces for performing intelligent transforms on healthcare data distributed across disparate healthcare data domains."

In early 2000, revised submissions were posted on the OMG server, and the RFP was scheduled to complete by mid-year. You can follow developments at www.omg.org/techprocess/meetings/schedule/Healthcare_Data_Interpretation_RFP.html.

19.10.2.4 Clinical Image Access Service RFP

When computer images are used for primary diagnosis and patient care decision-making, they must be stored, retrieved, and viewed according to very strict standards such as

DICOM. After the decisions have been made, when images need to be consulted for lower-impact reasons, the extremely high resolution and image depth are no longer needed, but the industry lacks standards for this type of image access. This is the gap that the Clinical Image Access Service (CIAS) seeks to fill.

This RFP is scheduled to complete by mid-2000. For details, check out www.omg .org/techprocess/meetings/schedule/Clinical_Image_Access_Serv._RFP.html.

19.10.2.5 Medical Transcript Management RFP

This effort was undertaken by CORBAmed with participation by the American Association for Medical Transcription (AAMT), although it is not a joint effort. Transcription is a big part of healthcare data processing, with many incompatible systems. This RFP will set standards for interoperability in medical transcription. Details appear on the Web at www.omg.org/techprocess/meetings/schedule/Medical_Transcript_Mgmt._RFP.html.

19.10.2.6 Summary List Management Service (SLiMS) RFP

In Healthcare, a patient's Summary List contains his or her significant diagnoses, procedures, drug allergies, and medications, and is used by providers to get an overview of a patient's condition. Besides its impact on patient care, the Summary List is important because the U.S. Joint Commission of Accreditation of Healthcare Organizations (JAHCO) requires, as part of their Information Management Criteria (IM 7.4), that summary lists be up to date by the third outpatient visit for ambulatory care. Beyond this U.S. accreditation requirement, there has been international interest for a capability to manage patient summary lists.

The SLiMS RFP will define a service to create, update, and manage Summary Lists. The effort had just started when this chapter was written, so we cannot give you details about submissions (which hadn't been written yet!). We can tell you that the effort is scheduled to complete around the middle of the year 2000. Check it out at www.omg .org/techprocess/meetings/schedule/SliMS_RFP.html.

19.11 Utilities Domain Task Force

Another recently chartered group, the Utilities Domain Task Force comprises mainly electric power utilities, although water providers have recently shown interest also. With the recent trend to deregulate electric power provision and distribution especially in the United States, power companies need to interoperate as they work together to keep the grid supplied with electricity, and CORBA provides a ready way to make this work.

Utilities specifications that complete OMG's formal editing process will be posted on www.omg.org/library/cutilindx.html. Recently adopted Utilities specifications can be downloaded from www.omg.org/techprocess/meetings/schedule/Technology_ Adoptions.html.

19.11.1 Adopted Specifications

Since the Utilities DTF is a relatively young group, it hasn't placed any completed specifications into the OMG archives. However, its first RFP is progressing well and more are on the way, so look in the next section for the work in progress and stay tuned.

19.11.2 RFPs in Progress

19.11.2.1 UMS Data Access Facility RFP

Water, gas, and electric power utilities use specialized control systems called Utility Management Systems (UMS) for operations and operational decision support. The scope of control typically includes production facilities, bulk transmission networks, distribution networks, and supply points. Water Quality Management Systems (WQMS) in the water sector, and Energy Management Systems (EMS) or Distribution Management Systems (DMS) in the power sector, are examples of UMSs.

The most basic control system provides Supervisory Control and Data Acquisition (SCADA) functions. More sophisticated systems provide simulation and analysis applications that help the operators optimize performance, quality, and security of supply.

The Utilities DTF will cover UMS integration in at least two RFPs. This one, the first, covers the data analysis interface. The SCADA interface will be covered in a later RFP; more may be required before the specification suite is complete.

The Utility Management System Data Access Facility will improve the interoperability of UMS applications with other applications and systems. Specifically, the RFP asks for:

- A Utility Management System Data Access Facility that provides a uniform way to access the inputs and results of applications used for water, gas, or power operations.

- A mapping of the Electric Power Research Institute Common Information Model to this facility, for use in the power utility sector.

You can follow this effort on the OMG Web site at www.omg.org/techprocess/ meetings/schedule/UMS_Data_Access_Facility_RFP.html.

19.12 Life Science Research Domain Task Force

One of OMG's youngest Domain Task Forces (along with Utilities), the Life Science Research group includes drug and biotech companies and concentrates on areas relating to biochemistry and analysis of gene and protein sequences. It's a high-energy group; look for a lot of good work to come out of this task force.

Life Science Research specifications that complete OMG's formal editing process will be posted on www.omg.org/library/clsrindx.html. Recently adopted Life Science Research specifications can be downloaded from www.omg.org/techprocess/meetings/schedule/Technology_Adoptions.html.

19.12.1 Adopted Specifications

Because the Life Science Research DTF is so new, it hadn't completed any technology adoptions when we went to press although several were nearly complete. For a summary, read the next section; for details, check the OMG Web site.

19.12.2 RFPs in Progress

19.12.2.1 Biomolecular Sequence Analysis RFP

This first Life Science Research RFP will standardize interfaces for analysis and manipulation (but not display) of sequences of biological macromolecular components. This is a highly specialized area and we're not going to give an introduction to Biomolecular Sequence Analysis here. But, in short, here are the scope and basic requirements quoted directly from the RFP:

> "The objective of this RFP is to solicit proposals for specifications of services for the analysis of biological macromolecular sequence data and associated information, including facilities for their representation, manipulation, and analysis. This RFP specifically focuses on services for sequence analysis and does not cover graphical user interfaces (GUIs) for the display and visualization of these data.

> The development of methodologies for the analysis of biological macromolecular sequence data, including nucleic acid and protein sequences, is a central concern in the emerging scientific disciplines of computational biology, genomics, and bioinformatics. The goal of these analyses is to infer information concerning the structure, expression, and biological function of genes and their products. Despite many efforts over the years, the ability to consistently and precisely represent sequence and sequence-related information in a standardized form has eluded the computational biology community. The absence of such standards hinders the development of large-scale software architectures for directed, high throughput analysis of sequence data as is required in many applications in Pharmaceutical Drug Discovery, the Human Genome Sequencing Initiative, and basic research in comparative and functional genomics."

As we went to press, this RFP had just passed its Platform Technology Committee vote and needed only the approval of OMG's Board of Directors to become an official specification. If you work in a biotech field and you're interested in sequence analysis, you can read what will surely be a new OMG specification at these URLs: www.omg.org/cgi-bin/doc?lifesci/99-10-01, 99-10-03, 99-10-04, and 99-10-10.

19.12.2.2 Genomic Maps RFP

Once again, this is a specialized and technical RFP, so we'll let it speak for itself:

> "The blueprint for the cells of organisms is packaged in their chromosomes, which are essentially huge strings of DNA. Usually the complete DNA sequence

of a chromosome is not known in detail, but maps, i.e., high-level 'summaries' of the contents of a chromosome, are available or required. It is such maps that this RFP is concerned with.

Maps are very important tools for the molecular geneticist. They are used in large scale sequencing efforts such as the Human Genome Project. Maps are also of prime interest in disease gene hunting, the results of which are used in diagnosis of genetic defects and holds great promise for treatment of same. Maps are therefore of fundamental importance to the pharmaceutical industry.

Maps can be large and complex bodies of information, and they and their content can be of many different types. Current representations of maps are ad hoc, and are poor at representing the commonality between different types of maps and content. This renders the process of comparison and integration of information a tedious task."

This effort is just getting started as we write this. You can download the RFP, and follow the submissions, at www.omg.org/techprocess/meetings/schedule/Genomic_Maps_RFP.html.

19.13 Summary

OMG members' Domain work impresses both for its breadth and its depth. The breadth arises from the wide range of industries whose workers are attracted to CORBA and the OMG for quality, workable industry standards. The depth results from the knowledge and ability of these people. Even though this chapter is little more than a listing of specifications and work in progress, it demonstrates that the impression is correct. If you work in an industry that already has a task force working at OMG, we hope you'll follow up by checking out the Web pages listed here.

Another important impression is that the CORBA Domains standards book is very much a work in progress, and it's not too late to join OMG's member companies and help write the next set of chapters in your domain. We've already referenced OMG's membership Web pages; you can find out about OMG membership there, or send an e-mail to the author, siegel@omg.org, for an invitation to attend an OMG meeting as an observer. You can watch OMG members at work for a week and see if this kind of participation is worthwhile for you and your company.

Some CORBAdomain Specifications

20.1 Introduction

In the last chapter, we flew over all of OMG's Domain Specifications so quickly that our review was basically a list. In this chapter, we take a closer look but at only a few of the specifications. Our goal is to convey by example, the nature of the Domain Specifications: what they are, how they work, and, especially, how well they are designed and constructed. All were designed and approved by people working in their field, vendors and users together, and show the skill and balance that can only come from this kind of cooperative effort. We think that you'll learn a lot about all of OMG's Domain Specifications by reading about the two we've chosen for this chapter, even if neither one is relevant to your own area of business computing.

The two specifications we'll go over are:

Business Objects' Workflow Management Facility. There are a couple of reasons why this specification is important enough to start our tour. First, every office and plant environment—even virtual enterprises—route work from one person or station to another, and that's *workflow*. Second, this specification is noteworthy for the explicit cooperation between OMG and the Workflow Management Coalition during its creation. We'll discuss this a little more in our presentation.

CORBAmed's Person Identifier Service (PIDS). This started out inside CORBAmed as the "Patient Identifier Service," but took its final, more general name very quickly; after all, there's no difference between a patient and a person as far as identity is concerned. (Of course the patient is sick, but that doesn't affect his identity!) Many domains store and retrieve identifiers along with demographic information; with the more general name, it's clear that PIDS is intended to serve this need anywhere it occurs. This service definition has started to have an effect on the healthcare industry; we'll look at the anatomy of the service as well as its effects in this section of the chapter.

We've presented the two specifications in this chapter in quite different writing styles, to match their differing functional styles. The workflow facility is not a server in the conventional sense; instead, it is an engine: Once you program a workflow (using, it turns out, a proprietary part of the facility), this engine works as a unit to run the workflow as many times as you need. There are only a few standardized interfaces that you (or your master workflow system) use to interact with the facility, so we've concentrated on describing engine building blocks and functionality instead of interfaces. In contrast, PIDS is a server that is invoked by clients in many ways, providing differing functionality tuned to clients of widely ranging needs and scales. PIDS has many interfaces, each skillfully tuned to a particular use or range of uses. Keyed to interfaces, our presentation of PIDS presents this facet of the specification, but also mentions overall architecture in a number of places to emphasize the ways the interfaces work together, and with your system.

So, off we go with Workflow first.

20.2 The Workflow Management Facility Specification

The OMG specification defines workflow as "the automation of procedures where information and tasks are passed between participants according to a defined set of rules to achieve, or contribute to, an overall business goal." The information and tasks that are passed, by the way, may include physical documents and other things as well as computerized data.

Many businesses, including insurance companies and financial institutions, process paper and electronic (if they're lucky) forms in unbelievable quantities. Even a simple workflow management schema can keep basic forms processing organized; workflow schemas are predefined for the most part and, although they may branch depending on data content, rarely if ever need to be changed during processing. Of course, workflow engines that work this type of processing must be able to deal with volume, and users appreciate products' ability to do this!

At an intermediate level of workflow complexity, workflows may branch multiple times based on conditions encountered during execution, although unexpected conditions are rarely if ever encountered. These workflows take more effort to set up, but don't require heroic programming to deal with surprises.

Production and engineering workflow applications provide the most challenge since their schemas may need to be customized frequently and possibly changed during execution. Picture the processing of an Engineering Change Order (ECO) at a manufacturing plant: The ECO affects not only a particular part, but possibly also other parts in its subassembly or beyond. The extent of the effect depends on which part changed, and how it fits into its various assemblies. Automation of ECO processing can go a long way toward reducing costs and even errors, but workflow systems have to be flexible in order to cope with this type of task.

Of these three levels of complexity, OMG's Workflow Management Facility (WMF) can help with the first two, but does not deal directly with the third (although individual workflow engines may help here).

Figure 20.1, adapted from the OMG specification, shows how a generic workflow is composed of a series of discrete steps. Some of these steps may be done by people, others by computer applications, and still others by robots or other automatic means. In some workflows, paper documents or other stuff may be passed physically from station to station as the task progresses; in others, computer data may be passed, or all steps may access and process data in a common store.

We'll dissect Workflow Execution in more detail soon (in fact, the rest of this section will concentrate on this phase), but first a word about workflow *building*: Before we can execute a workflow schema, we have to define it and put it into executable form. Workflow folks call this *process definition* or one of any number of synonyms that we won't list here. While some workflow schemas may be easy to construct, most require considerable effort, and some are built during Business Process Engineering (BPE), which is typically a major undertaking for a company. In the process definition phase, a business process is analyzed (possibly using computerized tools), broken down into its basics, perhaps modeled, and ultimately put into a form executable by the company's workflow engine: that is, in terms of activities, applications, and business rules.

Regardless of a workflow's complexity, however, its construction has the delightful quality that it only has to be done *once*, although it will have to be maintained and possibly tuned-up from time to time. The workflow's *execution*, on the other hand, happens hundreds, or thousands, or perhaps millions of times typically over periods ranging from months to years. It made sense, therefore, for WfMC and OMG to start

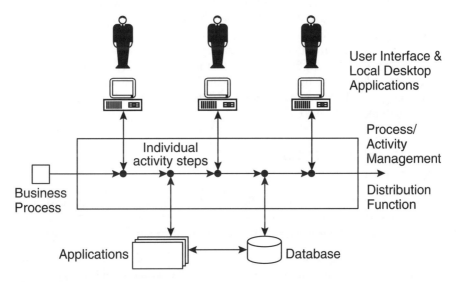

Figure 20.1   Workflow execution.

the workflow standardization process with the execution phase, take the big win, and postpone the standardization of workflow building until the execution phase implementation becomes established in the marketplace.

The big win for workflow users comes from this basic level of interoperability: Now that a workflow process running on one standards-compliant product can trigger and monitor a workflow process running on any other compliant product, users can define nested workflows that cover their entire enterprise no matter how large or complex. In fact, the OMG WMF provides this level of interoperability and then some, as we'll see in the next subsection.

Although the lack of workflow schema portability is not a show-stopper, it is definitely an inconvenience that grows along with the size of the workflow networks that an enterprise builds and maintains. In an ideal world, workflow schemas would be expressed in a standard way enabling them to be built on any workflow tool and executed on any other, similar to the way UML models can be exchanged among analysis and design tools. However, when the OMG Workflow Management Facility was specified, the WfMC had not finished standardizing their Process Definition Interchange interface; therefore, this function is not present in the OMG specification either. When it's done, the Process Definition Interchange will allow any compliant product to output its workflow schema in a format that any other compliant product can input and edit or execute. For companies with many diverse workflow engines and complex, interrelated workflows, this will allow them to build and maintain their schemas centrally, or edit them wherever they happen to be running when something breaks. We can expect that process interchange will be added to the OMG version in a major release upgrade, perhaps in a year or two, after the WfMC works out the details.

There are, of course, two ways that a workflow vendor can implement Process Definition Interchange. The easiest way, for a company that already has an engine implementation, is to build a module that translates their proprietary schema into the interchange format on output, and converts the standard format to their own on input. This allows interchange without increasing interoperability. The alternative is to evolve (perhaps over time) a product to store the schema in the interchange format and build a workflow engine that works directly on that schema in its standard metamodel. It is just a small step from here to standard IDL interfaces for these objects and a set of compliant products built to this model that interoperate at a deeper level, providing a very desirable alternative for sophisticated workflow customers. We admit, this speculation goes a little beyond current WfMC and OMG plans, but some big workflow users think it's the next logical step.

20.2.1 Workflow Objects and Interfaces

Here are the core interfaces and objects defined by the WMF. Figure 20.2 is a UML diagram showing the relationships among these classes. Check the diagram for key state variables and interfaces of these classes; we'll use this information in our discussion.

> **WfExecutionObject** is an abstract base class for WfProcess and WfActivity. You can resume(), terminate(), abort(), or suspend() a WfExecutionObject, which has an execution state and a few other key attributes.

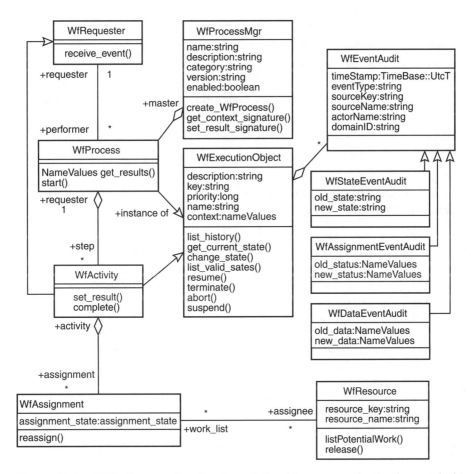

Figure 20.2 UML diagram showing the relationships among the fundamental objects making up the Workflow facility.

WfRequester bears the interface receive_event() that allows it to monitor a WfProcess once it's started; therefore, only WfRequesters are allowed to start() WfProcesses. WfActivity inherits the WfRequester interface; although some WfRequesters are not WfActivitys, virtually all are.

WfProcessMgr is the factory for a WfProcess. This object translates your schema into a running instance of a workflow. There is a separate WfProcessMgr for each schema; WfProcessMgr objects are started by the system and registered with the Naming Service so WfRequesters can find them.

WfProcess is an instance of a workflow schema. Once start()-ed by a WfRequester (probably a WfActivity), the WfProcess calls upon WfActivitys in turn to execute the workflow. It is a WfExecution object, but not a WfRequester.

WfActivity is a step in a WfProcess. It is a WfExecutionObject and a WfRequester. Most WfProcesses will be started by WfActivitys; it's natural for a step in one workflow to initiate processing of a remote workflow. However, many WfActivitys will never play the WfRequester role.

WfAssignment links activities to potential/actual WfResources.

WfResource is a person or thing that can do a WfActivity.

WfEventAudit is a common interface for recording workflow events. Several sub-types of this interface are defined to record change of the state of a workflow object, process data associated with it, and change in the assignment of resources to WfActivitys.

We'll go over the interoperability interfaces first, in enough detail to see how they work. Then we'll summarize the other functions.

20.2.1.1 Setting Up and Executing a Workflow Process

Suppose we want to run a workflow that spans two departments, each with its own machines and WMF-compliant workflow software. One workflow process will be the master: We start it to get the ball rolling; it does its stuff and, somewhere in the middle, starts up the subprocess in the other department, which does its thing and notifies the master process when it's done. The master process then takes over and finishes up.

We'll need to define the subprocess first; that way, when we define the master process there will be something for it to invoke. There will be a WfProcessMgr object instance associated with the subprocess. This process manager is the factory object for instances of the subprocess, and knows all about the subprocess definition. Each time our master process runs, it will create a new instance of the subprocess. This lets us run a separate instance of this workflow for each insurance claim form we process, for example, allowing our giant insurance enterprise to process many thousands of these simultaneously. The WfProcessMgr object is registered in our enterprise's Naming Service with a name that's known to the WfActivity in our master process that will trigger this remote workflow subprocess.

Now we can define our master workflow process schema. Let's presume that the first couple of steps execute locally, so we write these into our schema until we get to the place where we want to transfer execution to a workflow subprocess in the remote department. The WfActivity that executes this transfer of control will use the name we just mentioned to find the WfProcessMgr object that it needs in our Naming Service. Acting as a WfRequester, the WfActivity invokes the WfProcessMgr to create a new WfProcess with itself registered as the Requester; that is, all status reports from this new WfProcess will be addressed to the creating WfActivity.

The newly created WfProcess object bears the start() interface, which the WfActivity will invoke to start the workflow subprocess in the remote department. The WfProcess object remembers our requester's object reference and will notify when it changes state by invoking the WfActivity's receive_event() interface. Defined states include open.not_running.not_started, open.not_running.suspended, open.running, closed. completed, closed.terminated, and closed.aborted. Implementations are allowed to define substates of these states; check your product's documentation for details.

We can't pass the resources associated with the workflow directly—files, database entries, whatever—but we can pass a pointer to them into the workflow context which is a name-value pair list defined on our WfProcess object. You define which name-value pairs appear in the context array during process definition; there is no standard

IDL interface or GUI for this, so you should check the documentation of the WMF you purchase to see how you do it. You can get the context signature—that is, the list of defined names—from the WfProcessMgr object by invoking get_context_signature, logically enough. The update operation is set_process_context and the input is a list of name-value pairs that may contain multiple items. By defining whatever name-value pairs we need to identify passed resources during process definition, and setting the values (to filenames, or database keys, or whatever) just before the remote workflow process starts, we can couple the flows together as control gets transferred. By the way, at the conclusion of the process, we get a result structure back too, but the contents are not strictly defined by the specification. The structure is "derived from the process context and from the results of WfActivitys contained in the WfProcess."

WfProcess objects can extend beyond your workflow software; in fact, the way you integrate other applications into your workflow is by wrapping them with a WfProcess object. If you're automating an industrial process, you could write WfProcess interfaces onto the drivers for your industrial machinery and start each machine, in turn, from your workflow software as an assembly worked its way around the plant. Or, you could wrap your legacy applications with WfProcess interfaces and integrate their functions into your forms or accounts processing, or whatever. Since WfProcess objects are WfExecution objects by inheritance, they have a context that you can use to fine-tune resource assignments at runtime by calls to set_process_context (as we just explained) if you can't make all of your assignments at build time. They also have defined operations to start(), resume(), suspend(), and terminate(), as you would need on a controlled process.

Once we invoke start(), the remote workflow software is in control—although you get status changes back, the interfaces and semantics of WfActivity and WfResource objects are not defined tightly enough in the model to enable remote supervision of the workflow. If we've defined our workflow process well, it starts by looking in our context for the location of its input data, and goes on from there. When it completes, we get the result (we hope!) closed.completed, notifying us that all is well.

20.2.2 Additional Standard Features

Here are some more services you get from the WMF. WfExecutionObject is an abstract base class for both WfProcess and WfActivity that provides every instance of each one with these handy items:

Workflow Object Identification. WfProcess and WfActivity objects have both a name, assigned by the user, and a key, assigned by its WfProcessMgr. The key is unique among all created by the WfProcessMgr; it is not a CORBA object reference but provides a reference that lets you refer to this exact process at all times in the future, even after the CORBA object that implemented it has been deleted. There is also a description, another string, which you can set to whatever you like.

Process Context. We've already covered this. It's another one of these WfExecutionObject creations.

Priority. There's a priority that you can set from 1 (highest) to 5 (lowest), with 3 being "normal."

There's also a set of interfaces to navigate from a WfProcess to its WfActivitys, and to get the state of any of the WfActivitys, regardless of how deeply these are nested. A separate set of interfaces maintains a log of events during the workflow, and responds to queries.

20.2.3 WfMC and OMG

As we mentioned, WfMC and OMG worked together on this specification and continue to work together as more workflow items are added.

Because OMG requires that submitters to an RFP commit to marketing a commercial implementation of their submission if it is adopted, and WfMC is not a software vendor, the submission actually came into OMG from a group of WfMC members. However, they did this with the formal backing of WfMC and there is a note in the submission speaking of the organization's formal support.

In addition, WfMC has published a reference model (available on the Web; see Appendix B for a pointer). If you check out both the WfMC reference model and the adopted OMG workflow specification, you'll notice many similarities: Most of the figures are identical in the two documents, as are entire blocks of text. This is truly a cooperative effort between these two organizations.

20.3 Person Identifier Service (PIDS)

Throughout your lifetime, you may have episodes of care provided by dozens or hundreds of healthcare providers, most of whom assign and maintain patient IDs autonomously. That is, each organization simply assigns IDs that uniquely identify patients within its local ID Domain of ID values, with the result that these ID values are meaningless outside that system or organization. These autonomously managed IDs suit the purposes of recording and retrieval of service records for the local organization, but do not enable, or at least do not aid, correlation of health records among multiple venues. (At some healthcare providers, IDs proliferate like rabbits as the billing system assigns one ID, radiology assigns another, clinical systems yet another, and on and on.)

A typical healthcare information system allows a user to submit a search for a person's record using some combination of identifying parameters for that person. When the user must collect a patient's healthcare information from a different organization or from a disparately keyed system in the same organization, he typically must perform a new search in that other system—or ask a medical records person in the other organization to perform the search—in order to identify the person and retrieve the needed information.

In recent years, changes in the business of healthcare have made it both increasingly important and harder to access an individual's continuum-complete record of care. Risk-shared and capitation-based reimbursement policies make it absolutely necessary to avoid redundant treatments, while increased specialization of providers increases fragmentation and distribution of patient records.

Finally, organizational consolidation, growth, and flux exacerbate the problems associated with managing IDs as more and more large integrated delivery systems compete on the basis of population share.

The CORBA Person Identification Service (PIDS) organizes person ID management functionality to meet healthcare needs, by defining an extensive and flexible set of interfaces that support assignment and retrieval of patient (or person) IDs. In particular,

- PIDS supports efficient assignment and retrieval not only of quantities of IDs small enough to be monitored interactively, but also of batches so large that human intervention becomes impractical.

- PIDS supports both the assignment of IDs within a particular ID Domain and the correlation of IDs among multiple ID Domains.

- The PIDS architecture allows federation of PIDS installations in a topology-independent fashion.

- By standardizing the list of traits and their names, PIDS enables plug-and-play interoperability among independent implementations, but the service also allows site-specific and implementation-specific extensions to the list, along with customization of list elements.

- Installations may route PIDS queries to virtually any of the range of matching algorithms and software available on the market; fuzzy matching has become a highly competitive functional area, and PIDS' standardized interfaces allow products to compete on the basis of quality and price, rather than on vendor lock-in.

- The specification defines a range of compliance levels ranging from small, query-only single ID Domains to large, federated correlating ID Domains.

- A security architecture, working with CORBA security, enables PIDS implementations to protect person confidentiality under the broadest variety of confidentiality policies and security mechanisms.

The specification document also points out three areas that PIDS does not address:

- **Confidentiality policy.** PIDS will support whatever confidentiality policy your site requires; however, PIDS imposes no confidentiality policy of its own.

- **Retrieval of clinical data**. Although some clinical data double as identity criteria, PIDS is not a Computerized-Patient-Record application.

- **National Healthcare Identifiers (limited support).** When you examine it in detail, you discover that a national healthcare identifier (regardless of the nation that defines it) is just another identifier. Of course, large nations will issue some unbelievably large number of them, but we've already agreed that scalability is a requirement for PIDS, so this is already taken care of. The same goes for security. To make access to these IDs straightforward and consistent, PIDS defines them to be a standard list element, **NationalHealthId.**

20.3.1 PIDS Domain Reference Model

Identity domains are rarely correlated ad hoc; usually, there is some structure and a common configuration as shown in Figure 20.3, which the specification refers to as the Domain Reference Model. The overall organization could be a large healthcare provider that owns several hospitals and clinics. Within each hospital, a number of departments keep records by patient, and a highest-level system correlates these. (Although the department systems can use the master system most of the time, they must be able to function when it goes down. Therefore, all subsidiary systems are independent and capable of straying out of synchronization with the master ID system.) The master system may be the Healthcare Information System (HIS) in the hospital, but could be configured differently. Clinics and Group Practices maintain their own record systems, as do independent contract services. Taken together, all of these systems comprise the highest-level correlating ID domain.

The particular version shown in Figure 20.3 is probably an oversimplified view of such a complex system. Units that work together closely may need correlating ID domains (with accompanying PIDS software) defined around them, while the overall correlating domain may be little used, for example. The structure is right, however, and it at least suggests how PIDS is designed around a flexible architecture.

20.3.2 PIDS Datatypes

PIDS is built around a set of carefully defined datatypes. Let's review the essential ones:

The first problem PIDS deals with is *uniqueness*. Patient IDs, names of traits used for identification, and other quantities must be unique over the space of all of the correlated PIDS applications. Since any conceivable (or inconceivable!) combination of healthcare companies may federate in the future, the needed scope of uniqueness is the entire world. Attaining this uniqueness is a considerable endeavor; the specification does its part, but it will require constant vigilance by users to ensure that name collisions do not occur.

So that their solution could be applied to other healthcare (and non-healthcare) specifications, the authors placed their uniqueness solution in its own module: NamingAuthority. It's used throughout PIDS, but you should expect to see it used elsewhere as well. Here's what it does:

20.3.2.1 Domain Names: AuthorityID

To ensure (or, since I can hear the formalists protesting already, *mostly* ensure) that Patient IDs, trait names, and other names that we assign are unique, PIDS defines the

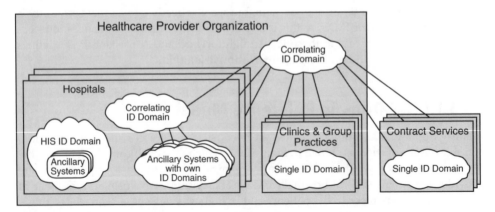

Figure 20.3   Example illustrating the PIDS Domain Reference Model.

qualified name: Qualified names are **struct**s that combine the name of our domain with the name string that we assign to something. Then, assuming that (1) our Domain Name is unique, and (2) we can keep our own house in order and not assign the same ID to two patients, or reuse the same trait name inconsistently within our domain, there will be no clashes even when we federate with companies we've never heard of.

By the way, the responsibility to keep your own naming house in order is a serious one. Careless clashes in patient IDs, trait names, or other identifiers will almost certainly have serious consequences down the road. When your company picks a Domain Name to start assigning IDs and names, it should simultaneously identify a responsible person and set up an organizational structure to keep names and IDs coordinated and recorded, for obvious reasons.

To ensure (again as much as practical) that Domain Names are unique, the Naming-Authority module recognizes four registration authorities or unique naming schemas; your organization can either register its Domain Name with one of these first two, or use one of the last two without registering. Registering is relatively simple and inexpensive; we think that the nonregistered Domain Names have enough drawbacks that every organization should pick from the first two choices on the following list:

ISO. The International Organization for Standards (ISO) defines a standard format, and provides registration authorities where an organization can register a place in a standard healthcare naming tree. The representation is defined in ISO/IEC Recommendation 8824-1.

DNS. Internet domains are recorded with a global authority (although they are assigned by a number of companies). A responsible person at each domain then maintains the subhierarchies.

IDL. With some qualifications because OMG is not a registration authority, the PIDS specification recognizes that the OMG **RepositoryID** name structure defines a unique name format.

DCE. Although DCE UUIDs are not registered, they are close enough to being guaranteed unique that the specification recognizes and allows their use when the name does not need to be recognizable outside of the domain. The form of the UUID—a 32-position hexadecimal number, divided into a few blocks by hyphens—is virtually unreadable to a person, so uniqueness is its only desirable attribute. (Of course there may be a planet someplace where hospitals and clinics have names like "**700DC518-0110-11CE-AC8F-0800090B5D3E**", but we haven't found it yet.)

There is also an OTHER authority (or nonauthority, actually), but you're only supposed to use it within a closed domain, such as when you're testing a PIDS installation and you don't have your own assigned Domain Name or whatever. Don't set up your clinic's permanent PIDS installation with an OTHER naming authority registration (or non-registration); a few years down the road when you've grown from a small-town clinic into a multistate HPO, you'll really regret it!

The combination of our Domain Name and its Registration Authority in a **struct** is an **AuthorityID.**

So, since our **AuthorityID** is unique in the world and we keep track of names that we assign in our own domain, the combination of our **AuthorityID** and every one of our

Assigned Names is unique as well. PIDS defines this combination to be a structure and calls it a *qualified name*; it is used for such things as traits. The **PersonID**, the basic PIDS person/patient identifier, also exists in a qualified form; more about this soon.

20.3.2.2 The PersonId and Related Types

There is a simple **PersonId** type defined by the IDL, and it's a string. You can only use it where the ID Domain is known because it was specified separately, or when you're working in the context of a known Domain. The Domain assigns the internal structure of the string; since these values are usually manipulated by machine, they're typically long and unreadable to you and me. The service also defines a sequence of **PersonId**s to be a **PersonIdSeq.**

When you combine a **PersonId** and an **AuthorityId**—that is, a Domain Name—into a **struct**, you get a **QualifiedPersonId**. With a **QualifiedPersonId**, you could always go back to the Domain it came from, where you could look up information about the person that it identified.

Each ID is assigned a state, which may take one of five values:

UNKNOWN. The service doesn't know if the ID exists or not, for whatever reason.

INVALID. An ID in this state can only be used in operations to create a new ID. If you query an entered ID and it comes back **INVALID**, you can't do anything else with it. (No, it does not mean that the patient is an invalid!)

TEMPORARY. This state comes in handy when you have to create an ID for a patient who will be cared for and have entries made for him in your system before you can enter all of the mandatory trait values. Perhaps he is unconscious and unable to answer questions, or there isn't time in an emergency. (We'll present trait values in the next section.) A temporary ID may be made permanent (but only after all of the required trait values are entered), merged, or deprecated.

PERMANENT. This is the usual working state of IDs; they must have values for all mandatory traits. **PERMANENT** IDs may be deprecated or merged (which makes them **DEACTIVATED**), but not made **TEMPORARY**.

DEACTIVATED. An ID that is not needed anymore can be Deprecated, which puts it into the **DEACTIVATED** state and enables it to be kept around for historical purposes. **DEACTIVATED** IDs may only be reactivated by Unmerging them.

Figure 20.4 show the states and the operations that transition from one to another.

20.3.2.3 Traits and Their Values

PIDS characterizes people by traits and associated values—no surprise there. To enable searches across the universe of PIDS installations, the specification defines a set of standard traits. First, two details about the trait:

Traits have traits themselves—they can be **mandatory**, **searchable**, and/or **read_only**. You have to supply values for all mandatory traits for an ID before it can be made **PERMANENT**. If you try to search on a trait that is not searchable, you receive an error. Similarly, you can't set a value for a **read_only** trait; that also returns an error.

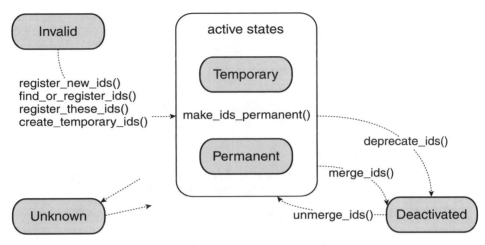

Figure 20.4 Transitions among the five possible states of a PIDS ID.

The trait name is a **QualifiedNameString** that combines your **AuthorityID** with the string name of the trait. When people at your site create whatever trait names they need, they don't have to appeal to some (nonexistent) central trait name authority for each one; the entire trait name, including the qualifier, is unique.

However, since PIDS defines three modules that define well-known sets of traits and PIDS-assigned **AuthorityID**s, you'll only need to define your own traits if these are not enough. The three modules are:

- **HL7Version2_3**
- **VCardTraits**
- **PersonIdTraits**

The **HL7Version2_3** module defines the traits you're familiar with if you've ever visited a doctor or been admitted to a hospital. Trait names in this module have **AuthorityID HL7**. Some familiar (and not so familiar) ones are **HL7/PatientName**, **HL7/PatientAddress**, **HL7/PhoneNumber_Home**, **HL7/PhoneNumber_Business**, **HL7/DateTimeofBirth**, **HL7/BirthPlace**, and **HL7/MothersMaidenName**.

The **vCardTraits** module defines 11 (!) different types of telephone numbers (home, work, car, cell, modem, etc.), e-mail address, and other fields, including a photograph. Trait names in this module have **AuthorityID vCard**.

The **PersonIdTraits** module defines some traits useful for the service; unlike the other two, it was defined by the PIDS specification itself. We'll list them all here, primarily because they indicate ways that PIDS helps companies keep track of the people in their database. Trait names in this module have **AuthorityID PIDS**.

INTERNAL_ID is the PIDS PersonId itself. By including it as a trait, it can be used for matching, *including* fuzzy matching, in the same way that all other traits are matched on. This enables, for example, using PIDS to look for a match for a unconscious person whose hospital ID was damaged along with him in an accident.

MERGED_IDS contains the set of other IDs that a person had, that have been merged into this one. These may be present in the system in the **DEACTIVATED** state, with the **preferred_id** field pointing to this **PersonId**.

DUPLICATE_IDS contains **PersonId**s that also refer to this same person, but have not been merged or deprecated.

CORRELATED_IDS contains **QualifiedID**s—that is, IDs in *other* domains, with their **AuthorityID**—that a person has been correlated with. These fields were set by the **Correlation Manager** that correlates between the two PIDS; thus, they are read-only by client applications.

EXTERNAL_IDS contains other IDs that a person may have, and may be set by client applications (unlike the **CORRELATED_IDS** field).

NATIONAL_HEALTH_IDS is a sequence because a person may have IDs in more than one country, or (presumably accidentally) have two IDs in one country. Each entry in the sequence contains a country code and a value.

NULL_TRAIT is useful if you have a trait but no value, or a value but no trait.

A trait's value is an **any**. Although many trait values are strings, other traits can be just about anything, including multimedia since a photograph, audio clip, even video with sound could be used for identification (with clever enough fuzzy matching algorithms!). The vCard trait set already includes a photograph. If your matching algorithm isn't up to matching on bitmaps, you might want to set this trait to non-**searchable**. By using an **any**, the PIDS specifiers avoided possible future obsolescence as traits become even more realistic.

20.3.3 Working with PersonIds and Domains

Now that we're familiar with PIDS artifacts and concepts, we can examine the things we can do with them and there are quite a few: We can create, populate, retrieve, and manage PersonIds, and we can manage and correlate across Domains.

PIDS defines six interfaces in all for this, with many operations. Four interfaces deal with retrieval of PersonIds via matching of traits: **IdentifyPerson**, **ProfileAccess**, **SequentialAccess**, and **IdentityAccess**. One interface provides functionality to manage IDs in a single Domain: **IdMgr**. One interface provides functionality to correlate IDs in multiple domains: **CorrelationMgr**. And finally, there's a navigation interface that provides access to all of these six interfaces (and a few other ones besides, that we won't expand upon in this brief discussion): **IdentificationComponent**. Even if you don't read the details on the first six interfaces, you should skip to Section 20.3.3.7 and read about **IdentificationComponent**, since it is the interface that collects all of the functionality you need for your Master Patient Index System, or your Registration System. Although the **IdentificationComponent** interface is the most general, we'll discuss it last because it uses all of the others to provide the actual services.

All of the PIDS operations on **PersonId**s accept and return data for multiple IDs in each call. This is not just for convenience, although it is a lot more convenient to retrieve an array than to loop around getting one ID on each call. More important, it minimizes network round-trips, a key factor in keeping service levels high. When you program your PIDS client application, use this feature not only to maximize the service you give your own users, but also to minimize your adverse impact on their coworkers by keeping down the number of round-trips and excess bytes you sling over the network.

20.3.3.1 The IdentifyPerson Interface

IdentifyPerson is the basic interface for finding candidates based on stuff you know. It does the job well, but only for one set of input data at a time.

IdentifyPerson has one operation, **find_candidates**. You input a trait profile—that is, a list of traits and the values you want to match, along with a confidence threshold. The service returns all of the candidates whose profiles match the one you input, to the specified confidence level or greater. Confidence levels range from 0.0 (lowest) to 1.0 (highest), but they're relative and only hold for the single set of candidates returned on a single call.

There's a lot of flexibility on how you get the matching candidates back, which is good because some systems hold hundreds of thousands of PersonIds (or more), and a minimal trait profile will match a large population. (Of course, a well-defined input trait profile will match only one candidate, or perhaps a few.) You can request to get all of the candidates as a sequence, or all as an iterator (which you retrieve in a set of subsequent calls), or you can request some number to come back in a sequence on the first call, and get the rest as an **iterator**. There's a little more flexibility than this, but we won't cover it in detail.

For even more ways to get candidates back, check out the **SequentialAccess** interface in Section 20.3.3.3.

20.3.3.2 The ProfilesAccess Interface

The **ProfilesAccess** interface returns or updates identity information for a person in the system. It has six operations:

get_traits_known takes a PersonId as input, and returns its known traits (but not their values) in a **TraitNameSeq**. This is one of the few operations in PIDS that operates on a single ID and does not have a corresponding "list" operation. However, it's likely that the list of known traits will be similar, if not identical, for all of the IDs in a Domain since they all come from the same form.

get_profile takes a PersonId and a list of traits as input, and returns a profile—that is, the list of those traits with their values—as output.

get_profile_list is similar to **get_profile**, but takes a set of PersonIds and returns a profile for each of them.

get_deactivated_profile_list takes a list of deactivated PersonIds and a list of traits, and returns a sequence containing the trait values for everyone on the list. If your system discards deactivated IDs instead of keeping them around, you'll get the **not_implemented** exception when you invoke this operation.

update_and_clear_traits modifies the profiles of existing IDs. You can specify which traits you want to clear, the ones you want to modify, and the ones you want to add. You can only change IDs that are in the **TEMPORARY** or **PERMANENT** states; if they're not, you'll get an **InvalidIds** exception. If the supported traits are read-only, you'll get a **NotImplemented** exception. CORBA security lets your administrator control who gets to make changes to the database, of course; you won't want just anyone updating your master patient index!

get_id_info returns a sequence of ID states—**TEMPORARY**, **PERMANENT**, whatever—for the IDs that you input.

20.3.3.3 The SequentialAccess Interface

Have you ever watched a clerk at a terminal scroll through a database of names, one screenful at a time, starting at a name close to the one he wants? **SequentialAccess** is the PIDS interface that supports this access style. It has six interfaces in all:

id_count_per_state returns the number of IDs in the entire database with the specified state or states; you can call it to find out how many IDs you'll have to deal with in all, excluding ones you're not interested in such as **DEACTIVATED** and **TEMPORARY** (for example). Databases for ancillary services—physical therapy, RMI, or whatever—may not contain that many names at least for a small clinic, while others or those at large institutions may contain thousands or hundreds of thousands. If the amount is small enough to stash locally, you may want to fetch them all instead of fetching IDs a screenful at a time.

So, you can either **get_all_ids_by_state** or, if this is too many (and it will be, most of the time), you can scroll through the list using **get_first_ids**, **get_last_ids**, **get_next_ids**, and **get_previous_ids**. The **next** and **previous** operations take a reference ID, so you can start or continue wherever you want in the list; all ask you how many you want although the last screenful may be a few patients short if you reach the end of the list.

How are the IDs ordered? PIDS doesn't say anything about this, appropriately enough, because it doesn't know which traits you will use in your particular installation. Your system architects will choose the traits, and your database and PIDS programmers will make the sorts work.

20.3.3.4 The IdentityAccess and Identity Interfaces

In some installations, the system will have to control access to Patient ID information on a per-patient, per-trait basis in addition to the usual per-client security. For example, the fact that a patient has AIDS may be okay to show the medical staff and certain business units, but not to other users who may nevertheless need all of the information except this one trait. CORBA security (and, actually, all general security architectures) is unaware of content, so this protection must be provided by the application itself.

PIDS standardizes interfaces for an Identity object that wraps a PatientID with access controls. Security at this level is applied by the application, and requires that all of your programmers be security aware and cooperate in maintaining the security of your system. Client applications use the **IdentityAccess** interface to retrieve the reference for an Identity object that wraps the PersonId object they're interested in, and then route their queries through it.

This type of security may be costly in terms of resources: In addition to the overhead of content-level security checks, applications will make more round-trips because this interface set does not have a set of sequence-based versions that batch queries. A new CORBAmed service, the Resource Access Decision facility, may help here.

20.3.3.5 The IdMgr Interface

IdMgr collects all of the write operations for PersonIds into a single interface. It also manages the transitions among the five ID states **UNKNOWN, PERMANENT, TEMPORARY, INVALID,** and **DEACTIVATED.**

Register_new_ids generates new IDs and binds profiles to them. **Find_or_register_ids** will look for each of the profiles you input, return the IDs of those it finds, and register new IDs for those it doesn't. You can specify a confidence threshold for the match. **Register_these_ids** is similar to **register_new_ids,** except that the client inputs the values for the new IDs. Some systems will require the IdMgr to create new ID values, while others will do this externally using a house-specified algorithm— PIDS supports both methods.

Create_temporary_ids creates new IDs for profiles input in the call that *may* be temporary: They definitely will be temporary if one or more mandatory traits are missing, but may be permanent if all required traits are present and the installation defaults to allow. The system does not search the database for a match on this call; every input profile receives a new ID.

Make_ids_permanent does just what you think. If your system uses an identifiable block of values for temporary IDs, it will create new IDs outside of this block for the permanent values; otherwise, it will just replace the **TEMPORARY** state of the IDs with **PERMANENT.**

And, finally, you can **merge_ids, unmerge_ids,** and **deprecate_ids.**

20.3.3.6 The CorrelationMgr Interface

The **CorrelationMgr** interface includes all operations for correlating IDs from one domain to another, including operations to cross-load IDs in batches, and find IDs in one domain that correspond to one passed in. The list of Domains covered by a **CorrelationMgr** is set administratively, outside of the standard interface set.

20.3.3.7 The IdentificationComponent Interface

This is a lot of interfaces to keep track of, even for a computer. To keep things manageable, PIDS defines the **IdentificationComponent** interface that collects object references for all of the six functional interfaces under one umbrella. This is the interface born by the client that accesses your Master Patient Index, or your Clinic Registration System, or other key ID-based application.

This lets a client navigate from one of these interfaces to any other: **IdentificationComponent** defines the object references of all of them to be **readonly** attributes of its own interface. Then, all of the six functional interfaces we've just discussed (plus a few more that we'll skip) *inherit* this interface and bear these attributes. This means that, once your client knows the object reference for any one of these interfaces, it can navigate to any other just by reading the value of its attribute.

Besides these object references, attributes on this interface also supply the Domain Name where it resides, and the list of traits that it supports, as well as its own unique name (useful when traversing a graph of linked domains, so you can tell if you return to one you've already visited).

Two additional interfaces support federation of PIDS domains, and event communication between them. These are advanced PIDS features that we won't discuss in any more detail except to emphasize that the architecture and feature list of PIDS contains much more than we've been able to cover.

20.3.3.8 Federating PIDS

In order to access one PIDS from another, your system has to be able to find it, and the standards for the lookup have to be pretty tight in order for this to work reliably. To maximize the chance of this working, PIDS specifies the ways in which installations use OMG's Naming and Trader Services in lookup and federation. In addition, PIDS uses the Notification Service (presented in Chapter 11) in a number of ways:

To start, the IdentificationComponent interface contains attributes that return to the client both a Naming Service and a Trading Service with PIDS pointers.

Next, the "kind" field (that is, after the dot) of each PIDS component name is standardized to specific strings representing the different types of PIDS components: Simple PIDS, Sequential Access PIDS, Identity Access PIDS, ID Domain Manager PIDS, and Correlation PIDS. Also, directory names that point to other domains are assigned standard names.

Finally, PIDS standardizes Trader component references and service types.

Architecturally, the standardized access to Naming and Trader Services and predictable assigned names for the parts of the PIDS service make federation of PIDS a straightforward and natural thing to do, far easier than if this part of the job were left for programmers and sysadmins to design and execute on their own. Look for PIDS installations that span multiple healthcare providers, not too far in the future.

20.3.3.9 PIDS Usage Patterns

PIDS' design and features demonstrate, in many ways, that people who understood CORBA and all of the things it can do specified the facility. There are many ways to integrate PIDS into a system, or use it to correlate IDs among a number of systems. One appendix to the specification, entitled "Interaction Patterns," demonstrates a variety of ways to use PIDS in a system, or to correlate a number of systems. We don't have space to repeat all of these here, so if you're interested in the entire range of possibilities that they show, you'll have to download the specification and read them all yourself. However, we will summarize a few here:

Figure 20.5 shows different ways that a pharmacy system could use PIDS. In this figure, PharmacyOrders is a hypothetical standard interface set, and DrugstoreChain is a proprietary interface. In the first variant, the pharmacy system is the integrator and calls standard (PIDS and PharmacyOrders) and proprietary (DrugstoreChain) interfaces directly. In the second, DrugstoreChain wraps, integrates, and conceals both stan-

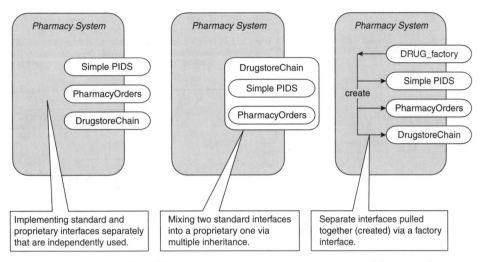

Figure 20.5 Some of the different ways that a pharmacy system could use PIDS.

dard interfaces behind its proprietary interfaces. DrugstoreChain could give itself a label *CORBA inside,* if it wanted to. We've heard of some products that do, in fact, have CORBA inside, but no label!)

Figure 20.6 shows a number of hospital systems accessing the lab observations server on the right-hand side. Since the server needs to organize records according to patient, but its record load is much smaller than the entire hospital record base, it implements only simple PIDS; that is, it implements the IdentifyPerson and Profile-Access interfaces and no others. The Patient Care application and other clients access lab results using CORBA interfaces, whether for PIDS functions or laboratory stuff. ADT (Admit/Discharge/Transfer) and other systems do not access the lab directly; instead, they work through the Patient Care application.

Other interaction patterns in the PIDS Appendix illustrate wrapping of legacy applications, correlation of multiple domains, use of Naming and Trader for federation, and other patterns. It's an informative collection of patterns, instructive whether your domain is healthcare or some other line of business.

20.3.4 Summarizing PIDS, and OMG's Domain Facilities

As we've walked through the PIDS specification, we've tried to cover its architecture and capabilities without (obviously) taking the time to provide anything near a documentation set for the service. We hope that you're impressed with the soundness and completeness of the architecture of the PIDS (as well as for the Workflow Facility) as we are. The OMG members have done a great job not only on these specifications, but also on the others that comprise the OMG Domain Specification Book.

The PIDS specification has been implemented by a number of companies, and interoperability demonstrations were run at the HIMSS conference using the network on the

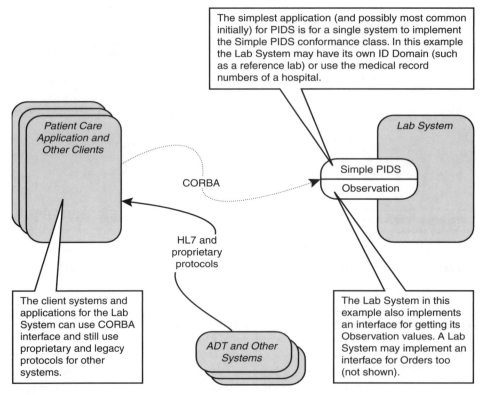

The simplest application (and possibly most common initially) for PIDS is for a single system to implement the Simple PIDS conformance class. In this example the Lab System may have its own ID Domain (such as a reference lab) or use the medical record numbers of a hospital.

Patient Care Application and Other Clients

Lab System

CORBA

Simple PIDS

Observation

HL7 and proprietary protocols

The client systems and applications for the Lab System can use CORBA interface and still use proprietary and legacy protocols for other systems.

ADT and Other Systems

The Lab System in this example also implements an interface for getting its Observation values. A Lab System may implement an interface for Orders too (not shown).

Figure 20.6 A number of hospital systems accessing the lab observations server shown on the right.

exhibition floor in both 1998 and 1999. As we write this, PIDS is poised to have a profound effect on commercial healthcare software, with products about to come onto the market just as healthcare providers are asking for them in their own purchasing requests. In the next edition, we expect to have a lot more news of successes in this area and others.

You can download all of these specifications for free from the OMG Web site; we've given references in Appendix A. And, if your company is interested in helping to define OMG specifications, you can come to the meetings and help. If your company belongs to OMG (see the Member List Web page to check), you can register and sign up; if it doesn't, you'll have to join before you can vote, but you can come as an observer first. Send me an e-mail (siegel@omg.org) to receive your invitation.

CHAPTER

21

Modeling CORBA Applications with UML

This chapter was written by Cris Kobryn,
a co-author of the UML specification.

The CORBA architecture provides a standard framework that you can flexibly extend to build robust distributed applications. This prefabricated architecture insulates you from the details of interprocess communication and distributed operating system services. However, it does not buffer you from the minutiae associated with real business applications, which can sometimes rival distributed operating systems in size and complexity.

Of course, you can use OMG IDL to specify your business objects and components. IDL is a pure specification language; it allows you to define the interfaces to objects without constraining their implementations. Consequently, you can use IDL to define the structure of your application and to separate the definitions of your business objects from their implementation details. By separating object specifications from their implementations, you obtain the benefits of information hiding, implementation neutrality, and platform independence.

For these reasons, IDL is an important tool for the application architect and programmer as well as for the system architect. However, IDL has some significant shortcomings. First, it does not allow you to specify object behavior or class relationships other than generalization. Consequently, you can specify the operations associated with an interface, but you cannot define methods, use cases, collaborations, state machines, workflows, or the various relationships typically associated with real business objects. Second, IDL is a textual language with no graphic representation. While this may be satisfactory for specifying simple structures, it is an undesirable limitation for defining complex structural relationships and behavior.

This chapter explores an alternative OMG specification language that addresses these shortcomings, the *Unified Modeling Language (UML)*. It provides an overview of the specification, focusing on the modeling language and the UML CORBAfacility. The chapter concludes with a discussion of the future evolution of UML.

21.1 What Is the UML?

The Unified Modeling Language is a language for visualizing, specifying, constructing, and documenting the artifacts of software systems. It is a general-purpose modeling language intended to be used with all major object methods and applied to all application domains. The multiple facets of the UML are explained here:

Visualizing. The UML's syntax is graphic, based on a rich set of graphic icons, symbols, and connectors. When properly applied, the graphic notation has a high semantic "signal-to-noise" ratio, so that a single UML diagram can concisely express what may otherwise require many pages of text.

Specifying. The UML's graphic syntax is matched by powerful semantics that allow you to specify static structure, dynamic behavior, and model organization. As previously explained, the UML's specification capabilities significantly exceed those of IDL.

Constructing. UML models can be directly mapped to various programming languages, protocols, and platforms. These mappings can support forward engineering; that is, the automated generation of executable code from object models. (UML also supports reverse and "round-trip" engineering, but these topics are beyond the scope of this chapter.)

Documenting. UML models can be used to produce documentation for all phases of the software lifecycle. UML diagrams can function as artifacts for requirements, analysis, design, testing, and project planning.

The UML represents the convergence of the best practices in object modeling. It is the proper successor to the object modeling languages of three leading object-oriented methods: Booch, Object Modeling Technique (OMT), and Objectory [Booch 94] [Jacobson 92] [Rumbaugh 91]. UML was designed to meet the following goals:

- Define an easy-to-learn but semantically rich visual modeling language.
- Unify the Booch, OMT, and OOSE modeling languages.
- Include the best ideas from other modeling languages.
- Support industry best practices for modeling.
- Address contemporary software development issues, such as scale, distribution, concurrency, and executability.
- Provide flexibility for applying different software processes.
- Enable model interchange and define repository interfaces.

The next section describes the benefits of modeling in general, and UML modeling in particular.

21.2 The UML Modeling Advantage

If you were commissioning a high-rise office building, you would expect your architect to provide you with detailed blueprints that describe the proposed structure from various views (e.g., elevations, site plans, floor plans, sections). These detailed plans allow you and the other stakeholders to evaluate how the proposed building will meet your needs, and will help the contractors to calculate their time and material costs. Similarly, if you were going to commission an aircraft, a ship, or a supercomputer you would expect an architect to produce detailed plans before you started work.

Those outside of the software profession may be surprised to learn that people commissioning large software systems do not always require detailed blueprints before they start a project. Software projects are frequently initiated with only high-level sketches ("conceptual architectures"), which consist of some simple box-and-line diagrams along with some informal prose. Of course, we recognize that software systems are substantially different from hardware and building systems in that they are far more malleable and dynamic. However, they are not so different that their builders wouldn't benefit from more thoughtful and detailed planning. The lack of detailed blueprints may be one of the major reasons that software systems tend to be less reliable and more difficult to estimate than their hardware and building counterparts.

The UML is a powerful language for specifying software blueprints. Consider the following simple analogy between building blueprints and UML software blueprints: The UML counterpart to a building is a physical system, the subject of a software model. An example of a physical system is an online car buying service, which includes software, hardware, and wetware (people). The UML analog for a building blueprint is called a *model*, which is an abstraction of a physical system with a certain purpose (e.g., allowing users to compare and buy cars on the Web). UML models show different viewpoints and can be decomposed into diagrams (e.g., class diagrams, use case diagrams, statechart diagrams) and model elements (e.g., classes, interfaces, components), just as building blueprints show different perspectives and can be broken down into plans and architectural elements.

If you are considering a major software project at your enterprise, you should consider using UML to specify your software blueprints. There are several advantages to this approach:

- It provides an excellent notation for software problem solving.
- It furnishes a rich set of abstractions for managing system complexity.
- It supports concurrent exploration of multiple solutions.
- In a manner similar to software prototyping, it facilitates project risk management.

From a business perspective, the ramifications of these advantages include reduced time-to-market, decreased development costs, and diminished risk.

In order to obtain the most benefit from UML, you should apply it using a rigorous software development process or method. Choose a method that is iterative, incremental, and also architecture-centric. By selecting a method that is iterative and incremental, you can synchronize the efforts of your modelers and your programmers, thereby increasing their efficiency. By choosing a process that is architecture-centric, you will increase the likelihood that your model is consistent with the physical system it represents, thereby improving the system's architectural integrity.

The UML is a general-purpose language that supports many methods over the full software lifecycle. Look for methods that show you how to apply UML modeling to business requirements analysis and testing, not just to software analysis and design. UML also supports many levels of sophistication in modeling techniques. Make sure that you select a method that matches the sophistication and culture of your development team.

The next section provides an overview of the UML specification, which includes language extensions for software development processes.

21.3 OMG UML Specification

Although the core of the UML specification is the definition of the language's syntax and semantics, it also includes related definitions for language extensions, constraints, and model interchange. The major sections of the specification are described here:

UML Semantics. Defines the semantics of the language using a metamodel. The language is organized by packages, and the metaclasses are described in a "semiformal" style that combines graphic notation, constraint language, and natural language. Both the semantics and graphic syntax (notation) are elaborated upon further in Section 21.4.

UML Notation Guide. Defines the graphic syntax for expressing the semantics described in the UML semantics specification.

UML Standard Profiles. Defines language extensions for software development processes and business modeling.

UML CORBAfacility Interface Definition. Defines a repository for models defined using UML. The facility enables the creation, storage, and change management of UML models. The facility is further described in Section 21.7. A feature new in UML 1.3 augments the UML CORBAfacility specification with an XMI DTD description for model interchange, described in the next chapter.

Object Constraint Language (OCL). Defines the syntax and semantics of the OCL, a declarative language for specifying object constraints.

The following sections describe the modeling language and the UML CORBAfacility in more depth.

21.4 The Modeling Language: Syntax and Semantics

In keeping with the principles of good language design, the UML's syntax and semantics are defined separately. The semantics constructs are the foundation for the syntactic constructs, since there is a well-defined unidirectional mapping from the syntax to the semantics. Consequently, we discuss the UML semantics first.

The UML semantics are defined with a metamodel that is decomposed into several logical packages: Foundation, Behavioral Elements, and Model Management. Figure 21.1 shows these packages as folder icons, with the dependencies between them illustrated as dashed arrows. The package at the tail of the arrow (the client) depends upon the package at the head of the arrow (the supplier). The top-level packages are decomposed into subpackages, indicated by nesting the folders. For example, the Foundation

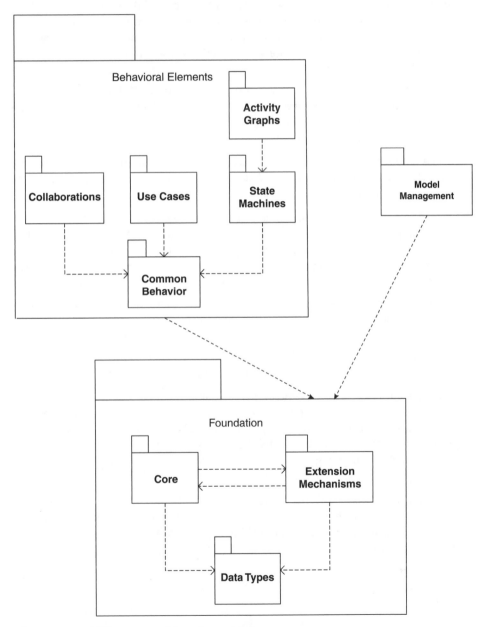

Figure 21.1   UML metamodel package structure.

package consists of the Core, Extension Mechanisms, and Data Types subpackages. The scopes of the top-level packages are:

Foundation. Defines the semantics for static structural models. The Foundation package supports various structural diagrams, including class diagrams, object diagrams, component and deployment diagrams. It consists of the Core, Extension Mechanisms, and Data Types subpackages.

Behavioral Elements. Defines the semantics for behavioral models. This package supports various behavioral diagrams, including use case diagrams, sequence diagrams, collaboration diagrams, statechart diagrams, and activity diagrams. It consists of the Common Behavior, Collaborations, Use Cases, State Machines, and Activity Graphs subpackages.

Model Management. Defines the semantics for managing UML models. This package supports various grouping constructs, including packages, models, and subsystems. It has no subpackages, but in the future, it may be grouped with other packages that are also general mechanisms.

The metamodel is described in a semiformal manner using a combination of graphic notation (UML), constraint language (OCL), and natural language (English). The description is presented in three complementary views:

Abstract Syntax. Defines the semantic constructs, where complex constructs are built from simple constructs. The abstract syntax is presented in UML class diagrams that show the metaclasses that define constructs along with their metarelationships. The diagrams also present a limited number of well-formedness rules (mostly multiplicity and ordering constraints) and short informal descriptions in natural language.

Well-Formedness Rules. Specify the constraints on each semantic construct (except for multiplicity and ordering constraints) as a set of invariants on an instance of the metaclass. These rules are expressed in both OCL and English.

Semantics. Defines the detailed meanings of the constructs using natural language. The constructs are organized into logical groups that are defined together.

UML's graphic notation is the concrete syntax that is mapped onto the semantics. The notation is defined in terms of four basic graphic constructs: icons, two-dimensional symbols, paths (connectors), and strings. At its most basic level, a UML diagram is a graph containing "boxes" (icons and two-dimensional symbols) connected by "lines" (paths) and labeled with strings.

UML supports the following diagrams:

Structural diagrams. Show the static structure of the model. Structural diagrams present the entities that exist (e.g., classes, interfaces, components, nodes), their internal structure, and their relationships to other entities. The kinds of structural diagrams include:

- Class
- Object
- Component
- Deployment

Behavioral diagrams. Show the dynamic behavior of the model. The kinds of behavioral diagrams include:

- Use case

- Sequence

- Collaboration

- Statechart

- Activity

Model Management diagrams. Show how models are organized into packages, models, and subsystems. These grouping constructs are typically applied to the various structural diagrams. When a structural diagram is dominated by package constructs, it is sometimes referred to as a "package diagram."

21.5 A Class Diagram Example: The POS System

Although a UML tutorial is beyond the scope of this chapter, we include a simple example showing how you can use UML to define IDL interfaces and modules. Figure 21.2 is a class diagram that shows a subset of the interfaces and classes for the Point-of-Sale (POS) tutorial example as presented in the first edition of this book. (There is very little change between that and this edition, so you can look at this edition's IDL to interpret the figure if you allow for minor discrepancies. If you want to compare exactly to the original edition's IDL, check out this book's Web site where both versions of the code are available. For the Web site URL, see Appendix A.) Some of the **get** and **set** operations are considered implicit, and are not shown in the UML version.

In this diagram, the POS IDL module is shown as the package labeled "Point-of-Sale." IDL interfaces are shown as rectangles labeled with the keyword **IDLinterface**. We have chosen to model the IDL interfaces as a stereotype of the Class base model element, rather than use the standard **interface** construct. The reason for this is that a UML interface is defined as a named set of operations that characterize the behavior of a model element. Since IDL interfaces include attributes as well as operations, we found it convenient to define a stereotype that does the same. In this example, we follow the convention that all interface names are prefixed with the letter **I**, such as **IPOSterminal**, **IInputMedia**, and **IOutputMedia**. The attributes of the IDL interfaces are shown in the middle compartment of the rectangle, and the operations are shown in the lower compartment. For example, the attributes of the **IStore** IDL interface are **totals** and **POSlist**, and its operations are **initialization**, **login**, **getPOStotals**, and **updateStoreTotals**.

The IDL interfaces are realized by (i.e., are implemented by) classes, which are shown as rectangles without special keywords. For example, the POSterminal class realizes the **IPOSterminal** IDL interface. The realization relationship is shown by a dashed line with a closed triangular arrowhead connected to the specified element, and the tail connecting to the realized element.

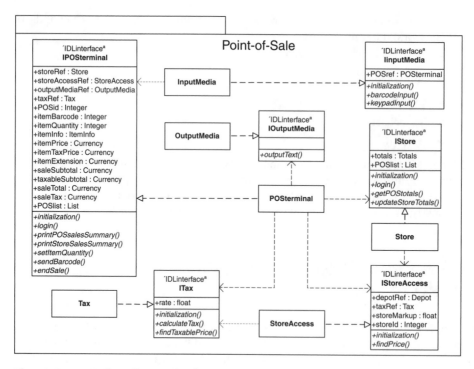

Figure 21.2   A Class diagram for the POS example.

The IDL interfaces are also used by the various classes. For example, the `Store` class uses the **IStoreAccess** IDL interface. The usage relationship is shown by a dependency arrow, a dashed line with an open arrowhead.

This rather mechanical translation of IDL to UML only shows you a small subset of the specification capabilities of UML. In order to appreciate UML's expressive power, you should consider the elaboration of the POS example with relationships between the various classes and the specification of behavior with use cases, collaborations, statecharts, and activity graphs. Since this exercise is beyond the scope of this overview, we suggest that you check out some of the many books that feature UML notation for more complete examples.

21.6 Metamodel Architecture

The UML metamodel is one of the layers of a four-layer metamodel architectural pattern. The other layers in this pattern are the meta-metamodel layer, the model layer, and the users objects layer. The metamodel layer is derived from the meta-metamodel layer, which for UML is defined by the Meta Object Facility's meta-metamodel. In particular, metaclasses in the UML metamodel are instances of the MOF meta-metaclasses. This architectural pattern is shown in the class diagram in Figure 21.3. In this diagram, the various model layers are shown as package symbols with a triangle symbol in the upper-right corner. (Models can alternatively be shown by inserting the keyword

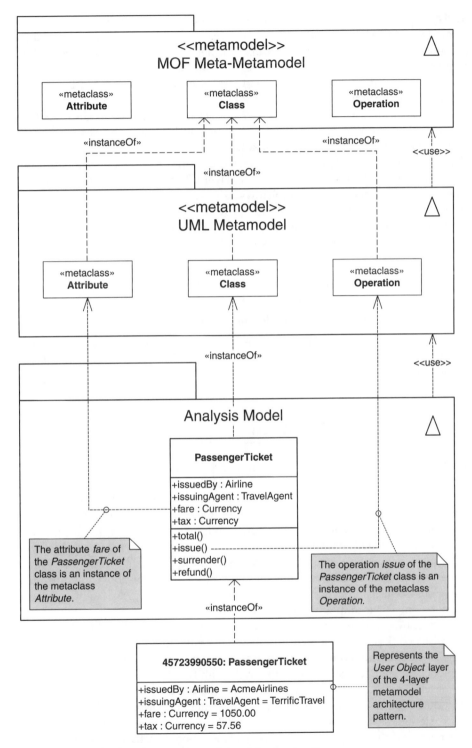

Figure 21.3   The four-layer metamodel architectural pattern.

model above the model name). The models that are also metamodels (i.e., MOF Meta-Metamodel and UML Metamodel) are stereotypes on the Model base element and are indicated with the keyword **metamodel**. The metaclasses in the MOF Meta-Meta-model and UML Metamodel layers are shown as **metaclass** stereotypes on the Class base model element. Instance-of metarelationships between elements in the various metamodel layers are shown by the **instanceOf** keyword on the dependency arrows. The instance in the lowest layer (the user objects layer) represents an executable instance, which is shown by underlining its name and including the class name after the colon: **45723990550: Passenger Ticket.**

The **instanceOf** metarelationships between the various metamodel elements imply usage dependencies between the metamodel layers. These are shown explicitly with the **use** keyword on the dependency arrows between the models.

The metamodel architectural pattern is a proven infrastructure for defining the precise semantics required by complex models that need to be reliably stored, shared, manipulated, and exchanged across tools. There are several advantages associated with this approach:

- It recursively refines the semantic constructs at each metamodel layer, resulting in more concise and regular semantics.

- It provides an infrastructure for defining future metamodel extensions.

- It architecturally aligns the UML metamodel with other standards based on a four-layer metamodeling architecture (e.g., the XMI Facility for stream-based model interchange).

21.7 The UML CORBAfacility

The UML specification specifies the IDL interfaces for an object analysis and design facility consistent with the modeling language we just described. The relationship of the UML CORBAfacility (or UML Facility for short) to the rest of the Object Management Architecture (OMA) is shown in Figure 21.4. In this UML depiction of the OMA, the Object Request Broker, the major architectural groupings, and the various facilities and services are represented as UML subsystems. A subsystem is shown as a package symbol with a nesting symbol (an upside-down fork) in the upper-right corner. (Subsystems can alternatively be shown by inserting the keyword «subsystem» above the subsystem name.) Subsystems can have interfaces, which are shown using the "lollipop" short-hand notation. For example, the CORBAfacilities and CORBAservices architectural groups are shown as subsystems without explicit interfaces, and the UML Facility and the Persistence Service are shown as subsystems with interfaces. The XMI Facility, which is metadata and has no interfaces, is modeled as a stereotype of the Component base model element. It is shown as a rectangle with two smaller rectangles projecting from the left side, and is marked by the keyword **metadata.**

At its most basic level, the UML Facility is a repository for UML models. It enables the creation, storage, sharing, and manipulation of UML models. The facility enables development of clients that support a wide variety of model-based activities, including:

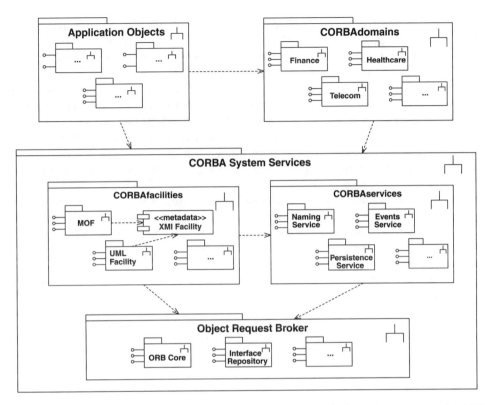

Figure 21.4 The Object Management Architecture including the UML and MOF CORBAfacilities.

- Drawing and animating UML models
- Enforcing software process (method) guidelines
- Applying software metrics
- Generating queries and reports
- Automating software lifecycle activities (e.g., design wizards, forward engineering)

The UML Facility provides two set of interfaces: *generic* and *tailored*. Both sets of interfaces enable the creation and manipulation of UML models. The generic interfaces are general purpose and provide basic browser-type functionality. They also serve as the foundation for the tailored interfaces that are specifically typed to UML metamodel elements.

21.8 UML Futures

The speed at which the UML has been adopted and applied is encouraging. Developers are using UML for a wide range of business and scientific applications in a variety of domains. UML is being applied to enterprise information systems as well as commercial products and embedded real-time systems. It is being used for domains ranging from finance and health to telecommunications and e-commerce.

As software continues to evolve, so will the UML. It is a "living language" in the same sense that human languages such as English and Japanese "live" to adapt to the needs of changing cultures. Future revisions of the language will provide better support for physical and executable models. Requirements for more robust ("heavyweight") extension mechanisms, diagram interchange, and model change management will drive improvements in physical models. Advances in statechart and activity graph modeling will accelerate the evolution of executable models.

The trends toward distributed enterprise architectures and component-based development are also driving many other improvements. The demands of distributed enterprise architectures are helping us improve how we model systems-of-systems, distribution, and concurrency. Similarly, advances in component-based development are helping us refine how we model interfaces, classes, and components. We can look forward to UML not only tracking, but also enabling, these and other advances in software development.

Implementing Metamodels and Repositories Using the MOF

*This chapter was written by Sridhar Iyengar,
a co-author of the MOF specification.*

Within the OMG's Object Management Architecture, the use of IDL and the COR-BAservices to specify distributed interoperable applications is now the norm. These technologies help in implementing object interoperability using standardized Object Interfaces specified in OMG IDL. However, there has historically been a lack of standard modeling techniques and application development and management infrastructure within the OMA. The increased complexity involved in the process of designing and implementing distributed object applications has been an additional motivation for standardization of application infrastructure. The use of metadata repositories for data administration (1980s), data warehouse management and year 2000 inventory management (mid-1990s), and more recently for managing distributed object components, frameworks, and business objects (late 1990s) is indicative of the growing role of metadata in the enterprise.

The OMG Object Analysis & Design Task Force (ADTF) was chartered in 1995 to address the problems of lack of standardization in these areas. Soon after, OMG members responded with the Unified Modeling Language (UML) and the Meta Object Facility (MOF) in November 1997. You've just read our overview of UML and how it can be used to model CORBA applications in the previous chapter. In fact, UML is the most widely known and implemented metamodel and has been formally defined using the MOF. In addition, OMG members have standardized a set of CORBA Interfaces used to manipulate UML repositories known as the *UML CORBA Facility,* which we just described in Section 21.7. These CORBA Interfaces are derived from the MOF-to-IDL mapping, which is part of the MOF specification.

The OMG standard for metamodeling and metadata repositories is the MOF, which is fully integrated with UML and, in fact, uses the UML notation for describing repository metamodels. In March 1999, the OMG standardized XMI—XML Metadata Interchange—a specification used to interchange metadata among tools, repositories, and applications in a vendor- and middleware-neutral way. XMI allows the interchange of metadata using the W3C eXtensible Markup Language (XML) among MOF-compliant applications. The MOF, XMI, and UML form the core of the OMG metadata management as well as component-based development architecture.

This chapter focuses on the use of MOF-based metamodeling, a formal technique for designing and implementing modeling languages such as UML, and metadata repositories that are used for tool and application integration in distributed object environments. The MOF provides modeling constructs and a set of CORBA interfaces that can be used to define and manipulate a set of interoperable metamodels and their implementations.

22.1 The OMG Metadata Architecture

Even before the adoption of the MOF, the OMA had several metadata specifications: the CORBA Interface Repository, the Trader Service, and the COS Naming Service. However, these specifications did not have a unifying metadata architecture. The MOF formally introduced the four-layered, object-oriented metamodeling architecture that is shown in Figure 22.1 using the UML package diagram notation. You can expect that, over the next few years, many of OMG's unaligned metadata specifications will gradually evolve to the MOF-based architecture. The MOF is the most fundamental layer (the M3 or Meta-Meta Model layer) of the four, defining the modeling primitives such as MOF::Class (MetaClass) and MOF::Attribute (MetaAttribute) needed for defining object-oriented metamodels. Metamodels defined using the MOF (such as UML and the emerging Common Warehouse Metamodel—CWM) are at the metamodel (or M2) layer. The metamodel layer describes modeling concepts in a particular domain.

In the case of UML, modeling concepts include Package, Class, Collaboration, and Usecase. In the case of a data warehousing metamodel such as the emerging Common Warehouse Metamodel, concepts include Table, Column, Cube (for multidimensional databases), and Transformation.

The dependency arrow between the M3 and M2 layers implies an "instance-of" relationship, indicating that metamodels can be stored and managed in a MOF repository in an implementation sense. The dependency can also be used to imply "The Metamodel is-defined-by the MOF." Figure 21.3 in Chapter 21 shows a more complete example of the metamodel architectural pattern using the UML notation. The next layer is the Model or M1 layer, which typically corresponds to application models. In this example, we've described a stock trading application using UML. This model has concepts such as Stockshare and Askprice, and can be managed in a UML repository or an XML document allowing multiple developers to share, use, and exchange consistent definitions of these key quantities. Finally, the user objects layer is referred to as the M0 level and typically corresponds to the information captured in an operational database for a specific stock trade.

While the layers appear complicated, they are primarily an artifact useful in the analysis and design phase of designing and implementing complex model-driven sys-

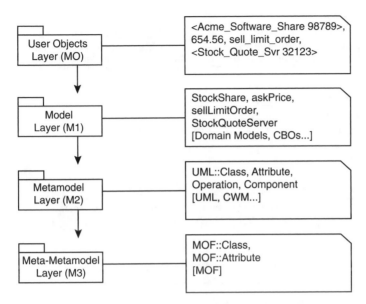

Figure 22.1   The OMG four-layer metamodeling architecture.

tems. At runtime, all of these models are CORBA, Java, or COM objects. The traversals across the levels happens by navigating these relationships or by invoking operations on MOF objects.

Metamodeling has been used over the years in metadata repositories for a number of reasons:

- Metamodeling provides the basis for recursive definition of semantic constructs.

- Metamodeling provides the basis for introspection and reflection of not just attributes and operations, but also relationships, constraints, and additional semantics. The MOF Reflective module specifies metadata reflection within the OMG architecture.

- Metamodeling provides an architectural basis for extending existing metamodels and introducing new ones in a coherent manner.

- Metamodeling can be used to architecturally align metamodels in different but related domains to maximize reuse. This technique was used in the alignment of the modeling concepts in UML and the MOF as well as in the design of new MOF-based metamodels.

- Metamodeling can be used to ease tool and application integration by formally describing the tool and application models as metamodels. You can then relate the concepts and subtype the concepts in these related metamodels, and still get a cohesive view across the metamodels.

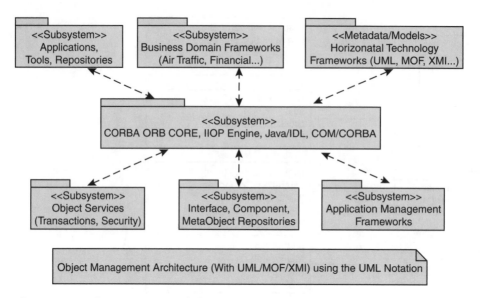

Figure 22.2 The MOF, UML, and XMI as part of the OMA.

Figure 22.2 shows the runtime architecture of the MOF and how it fits within the OMA. Once again, we've used the UML notation to architecturally depict the dependencies between the various components and/or subsystems.

In Figure 22.2 Metadata (XMI) and Metamodels (UML, MOF) are shown as horizontal technology frameworks (CORBAfacilities) that provide modeling and metamodeling services in the OMA. These services and modeling frameworks can be used to implement various metadata repositories, component repositories, application development frameworks, and similar modules. These frameworks have been modeled as UML subsystems using the <<subsystem>> UML notation. The arrows imply either CORBA interface calls between the various systems or, in some cases, interchange of metadata using XMI that may not have to use CORBA.

Within this architecture, the roles of the MOF, XMI, and UML are as follows:

- The MOF defines one or more metamodels and their CORBA interfaces for manipulating metadata in a distributed environment.

- XMI provides an XML-based metadata interchange format. The XMI specification defines a MOF to XML mapping for specifying XML Document Type Definitions (DTDs) and XML streams.

- UML is used to design and analyze the metamodels or models that are implemented using CORBA.

The OMG metadata architecture is concretely expressed in Figure 22.3, which shows how application development tools, repositories, and CORBA work together. Tools and applications can be implemented in any programming language supported by

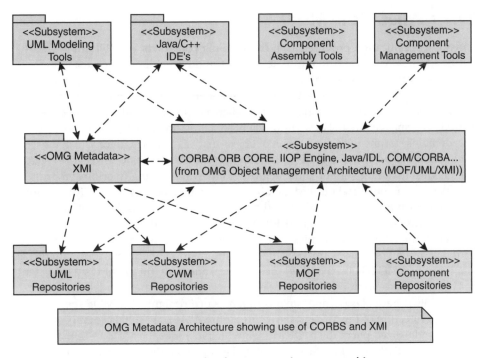

Figure 22.3   A CORBA application development environment architecture.

CORBA, and can directly manipulate the metadata. In addition, tools and repositories that use XMI can also exchange metadata as XML documents without necessarily using CORBA. A typical scenario would be for a designer to create a UML model that represents the problem domain and manage it in a MOF-compliant UML repository. A Java IDE could read the classes and interfaces in the model using a Java program and automatically generate the Java Class and Interface definitions (or even implementations, if the model is precise enough). These could be passed to a deployment tool that reads XML documents that describe the deployment metadata. This metadata would be used to configure the application components. Such as scenario is quite common in component-based runtime architectures such as the CORBA Component Model, Java-Soft EJB, or Microsoft COM+ environments.

The UML-based modeling tools shown in Figure 22.3 can store and manage models in a UML repository (which could be a flat file, or relational or object-based repository) using CORBA interfaces. Once the model has been saved, a second tool could use XMI to read this information and refine the model with additional detail (for example, providing actual Java code that corresponds to an implementation), and a third tool could use CORBA to manipulate the same metadata. This could happen over a network, thus enabling collaboration in a virtual development environment.

We will now dive a little deeper into the architecture of the MOF itself, to give you a better understanding of how to design and implement metamodels.

22.1.1 What Is the MOF?

The MOF specification provides a set of modeling constructs and IDL interfaces that can be used to define and manipulate a set of interoperable metamodels. The MOF enhances metadata management and interoperability in distributed object environments in general, and in distributed development environments in particular.

The MOF also defines an abstract model called a meta-metamodel (Because the MOF is used to define metamodels!) with sufficient semantics to describe metamodels in various domains starting with the domain of object analysis and design for which the UML metamodel has been defined. Since its adoption, the MOF has been used to specify metamodels in a range of domains including data warehousing (work in progress for the OMG Common Warehouse Metadata RFP), business objects, the CORBA Component Model (in final vote at OMG), and proprietary metamodels. Integration of metamodels across domains is required for integrating tools and applications across the lifecycle using common semantics. The abstract model is, in essence, a metalanguage with rich semantics (classes, relationships, constraints, and operations) but with precise mappings to OMG IDL (in the MOF specification) and XML (in the XMI specification).

The MOF is an evolution of object-oriented repository and metamodeling research in Unisys, IBM, Oracle, DSTC, and other companies that designed the MOF specification.

The architecture of the MOF is shown in Figure 22.4. The MOF is composed of two major standardized parts: the MOF Model, which includes the MOF-to-IDL mapping; and the MOF Reflective Interfaces. (A MOF Facility, included in early versions of the specification, was deprecated in version 1.3 but is still shown in Figure 22.4.)

22.1.2 The MOF Model

The MOF Model is the built-in meta-metamodel and is the abstract language for defining metamodels. You use the UML notation to design and describe MOF-based metamodels. The key modeling concepts in the MOF are:

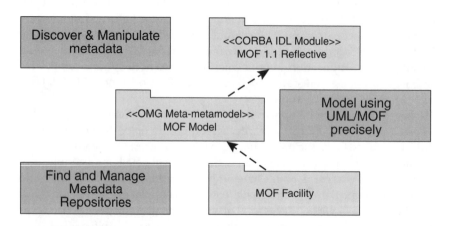

Figure 22.4 The MOF architecture.

Classes, which can have attributes, references, and operations to model state, relationships, and behavior. The MOF supports multiple inheritance as well as constraints. References allow direct navigation from one class to another.

Binary Associations (Relationships), which are links between Class instances and can model relationships between two classes in a model, or between classes in separate models. The latter is typically used to integrate tools and applications supplied by multiple vendors. Associations have two AssociationEnds that can have constraints on multiplicity (cardinality), aggregation (shared or composite), and semantics.

Packages, which are collections of related Classes, Associations, and Packages (nested packages are supported by the MOF) and typically correspond to metamodels. Packages can be composed by importing or inheriting from other packages.

Data Types for describing state or parameters. The MOF supports all the CORBA data types.

Constraints, which are used to define well-formedness rules in OCL or other languages.

Figure 22.5 shows the MOF model using UML notation.

By design, the MOF model is well-aligned with the UML metamodel, making it possible to use UML-compliant modeling tools to design MOF-based metamodels.

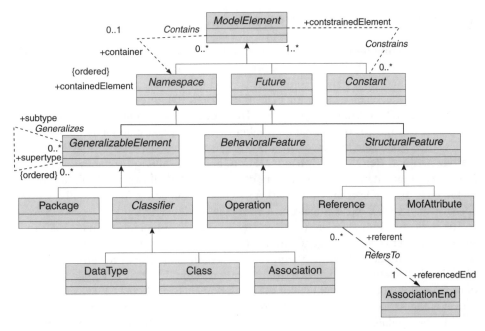

Figure 22.5 The MOF model.

22.2 The MOF and CORBA: MOF-to-IDL Mapping

The MOF-to-IDL mapping provides a standard set of templates that can be used to map a MOF metamodel to a corresponding set of OMG IDL Interfaces. For a given metamodel (that corresponds to certain types of metadata), the resulting IDL interfaces are for CORBA objects that correspond to the metadata. The IDL interfaces are typically used to store and manage metadata in a repository.

The main mapping algorithms are as follows:

A **Package** in a metamodel maps onto an IDL interface for a package proxy that is used to manipulate the package contents (packages, classes, and associations).

A **Class** in a metamodel maps onto two IDL interfaces: one for the Class object that provides factory operations for meta objects, and the other for the interfaces that support the attributes, operations, and references in the metamodel.

An **Association** in the metamodel maps to an IDL interface for a metadata association proxy object.

The semantics of the mapping are defined precisely enough to allow interoperability between metadata repositories from multiple vendors. In fact, it is possible to generate the CORBA server implementation for a metadata repository from a well-formed MOF-based metamodel.

22.2.1 The MOF CORBA Interfaces

The MOF CORBA interfaces come in two categories: they may be tailored to a specific metamodel based on the MOF IDL mapping, or Reflective. The MOF Model itself has tailored interfaces that can be used to create and manipulate models. Similarly, for a given metamodel (such as UML or EDI), the tailored IDL interfaces can be generated based on the MOF IDL mapping patterns. These interfaces reflect the metamodel structure and are roughly proportional in number to the complexity of the metamodel.

The MOF Reflective Interfaces, on the other hand, are a fixed set of four interfaces: **RefbaseObject**, **RefObject**, **RefAssociation**, and **RefPackage**, as shown in Figure 22.6. These four interfaces form the core of the MOF that allows manipulation of any metadata in any MOF-compliant CORBA server. The Reflective Interfaces allow introspection of any MOF-based metadata across metamodel layers.

The Reflective Interfaces are used by general-purpose metadata management tools such as browsers and report generators, and are a bit cumbersome to use compared to the tailored interfaces. They also require a deep understanding of the structure of the MOF itself. The ability of the MOF to integrate metamodels that have been independently developed takes advantage of the modeling concepts in the MOF as well as the power of the Reflective Interfaces. The Reflective Interfaces have all the machinery you need to manipulate arbitrary metadata: create, delete, update, invoke, and introspect metadata.

The interface **MOF::RefBaseObject:meta_object()** allows traversal across meta levels. The **Refpackage** interface is used to manipulate Packages, Classes, and Associ-

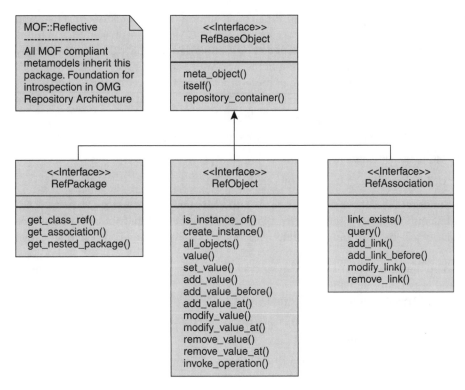

Figure 22.6   MOF Reflective Interfaces.

ations. **RefObject** is used to manipulate Objects and Classes. **RefAssociation** is used to manipulate links between Objects.

Next we'll review the latest OMG metadata standard, XMI-XML Metadata Interchange, adopted in March 1999 as a vendor- and middleware-neutral standard for exchanging metadata among tools, applications, and repositories. Once we have done that, we will use a simple EDI model to demonstrate how to use the MOF and XMI along with UML to design and implement MOF-based repositories and tools that also support XMI as a metadata interchange mechanism.

22.2.2 XMI Overview

XMI, which stands for *XML Metadata Interchange*, is the OMG standard used for interchanging metadata among tools, applications, and repositories. While XMI was initially defined to exchange UML models, the architecture of XMI is generic and can be used to interchange any metadata described using the MOF. In fact, because of the extensibility of XMI and MOF, you can even exchange metadata where the tool needs to go beyond what is in the standard. Many tools have a need for these extensions for their legacy needs or to provide value-add over competing tools.

When the UML and MOF were standardized by OMG in November 1997, an important piece of work was not completed. At that time, only CORBA-based access to metadata was supported; due to time constraints as well as lack of consensus, no file- or stream-oriented interface was specified. The OMG Stream-based Model Interchange Format (SMIF) RFP was issued to solve this problem. XMI was proposed by Unisys, IBM, and several other companies, and was adopted by the OMG. The XMI specification allows easy exchange of metadata among tools, repositories, and applications using XML.

XMI integrates three key industry standards:

- XML (eXtensible Markup Language), a W3C standard

- MOF, which we've just covered

- UML, described in the previous chapter

The integration of these three standards into XMI marries the best of OMG and W3C metadata and modeling technologies, allowing developers of distributed applications to share object models and metadata over networks anywhere. The benefits of XMI over traditional interchange mechanisms stem from the ubiquity of XML technology, the inherent extensibility of both XML and MOF, and the fact that XML is human readable and easy to implement.

The XMI specification consists primarily of:

- A set of XML Document Type Definition (DTD) production rules for transforming MOF-based metamodels into XML DTDs.

- A set of XML document production rules for encoding and decoding MOF-based metadata.

- Design principles for generating XMI-compliant DTDs.

- Design principles for generating XMI-compliant XML documents. (XMI documents are XML documents. No extensions to XML have been proposed or used.)

- Concrete XML DTDs for the MOF (to exchange metamodels) and UML (to exchange models).

Starting with versions MOF 1.3 and UML 1.3 of these two specifications, the DTDs and streams will be maintained as part of the MOF and UML specifications.

22.3 Using MOF and XMI to Implement Metamodels

The process used in defining and implementing MOF- and XMI-based systems is straightforward. First you need to thoroughly understand the domain before you design a model or a metamodel. Use a UML-compliant tool (or you can do it manually or programmatically) to define your metamodel. If you are familiar with the Class Diagram part of UML, you know enough to define MOF-based metamodels.

Apply the MOF-to-IDL mapping rules to generate the OMG IDL interfaces. If your project uses advanced programming tools, they will automate not only IDL generation but also CORBA server generation. Use Reflective Interfaces to write generic tools and Tailored (generated) Interfaces to write more concrete tools.

If you need to exchange metadata using a stream- or file-based mechanism, use the MOF-to-XML mappings defined in the XMI spec to automatically generate an XML DTD that can be used to validate the metadata that is being exchanged between systems.

We will use a simple EDI model (we will pretend it is a metamodel!) to show how the concepts in the MOF apply to metadata as well as data within the constraints of what you can model in the MOF. For more complex examples, check out the MOF 1.1, MOF 1.3, XMI, and UML 1.3 specifications on the OMG server. You'll find URLs for these references in Appendix A.

22.3.1 The EDI Model

Figure 22.7 is a simple model of an EDI system that shows Customers purchasing products over the Web. We've purposely used a model different from UML and the MOF to demonstrate the MOF's generality. By the way, this model was used in the XMI proof-of-concept demonstrations during the OMG XMI adoption process in November 1998. This model uses all the major MOF modeling constructs.

22.3.2 The OMG IDL for Portions of the EDI Model

Once the model in Figure 22.7 has been designed and verified as being MOF compliant (either by hand or automatically by a UML/MOF-based modeling tool), the model can be imported into a MOF repository server and the MOF-to-IDL mapping can be applied.

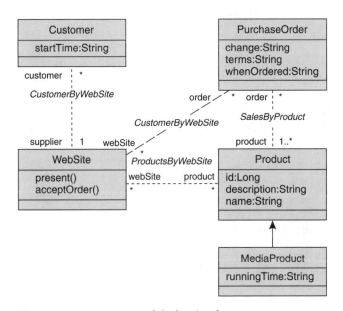

Figure 22.7 A MOF model of a simple EDI system.

The following IDL fragment shows the generated IDL for the Customer Class. **CustomerClass** is the factory interface that inherits **Reflective::RefObject**. The object interface is **Customer**, which inherits **CustomerClass**. The EDI model, generated IDL, XML DTD, and the XML stream for the model can be found on this book's Web site. This shows how relationships and the more complex mappings are handled.

```
interface CustomerClass : Reflective::RefObject
  {
    readonly attribute CustomerSet all_of_type_customer;
    readonly attribute CustomerSet all_of_class_customer;
    Customer create_customer (
      in string start_time)
      raises (Reflective::MofError);
  };
  interface Customer : CustomerClass
  {
    string start_time ()
      raises (Reflective::MofError);
    void set_start_time (in string new_value)
      raises (Reflective::MofError);
    WebSite supplier ()
      raises (Reflective::MofError);
    void set_supplier (in WebSite new_value)
      raises (Reflective::MofError);
  }; // end of interface Customer
```

22.3.3 The XML DTD for Portions of the EDI Model

Once the EDI model has been loaded (or registered) in a MOF repository, if there is a need to exchange EDI metadata (or in some cases, data), an XMI-compliant XML DTD can be generated. This DTD would be used to validate the contents of the message to be validated by either an XML parser in a Web browser or part of an application.

Here is a fragment of the XML DTD generated for the Customer Class. The complete DTD is found on this book's Web site.

```
<!--  _____  -->
<!-- METAMODEL CLASS: EDI.Customer                        -->
<!--  _____  -->
<!ELEMENT EDI.Customer.startTime (#PCDATA|XMI.reference)*>
<!ELEMENT EDI.Customer.supplier (EDI.WebSite)?>
<!ENTITY % EDI.CustomerProperties '((EDI.Customer.startTime)?)' >
<!ENTITY % EDI.CustomerAssociations '(EDI.Customer.supplier?)' >
<!ELEMENT EDI.Customer ( %EDI.CustomerProperties;
        ,(XMI.extension* ,   %EDI.CustomerAssociations; ) )?>
<!ATTLIST EDI.Customer %XMI.element.att; %XMI.link.att; >
```

22.3.4 The XML Document for Portions of the EDI Model

This example was generated by applying the MOF-to-XML DTD mapping rules in the XMI spec. How did we get the EDI model into a MOF repository server? Very simply: We loaded an XML document into a MOF repository server in the first place. The way we generated the XML document corresponding to the EDI model was by applying the MOF-to-XML stream mapping rules to the EDI model. A fragment of the Customer Class appearing as an XML document is shown below. This document was of course validated against the MOF 1.3 XML DTD that is part of the MOF 1.3 specification. This example will also show clearly that DTDs are how you specify the schema in XML, while the document itself appears as an XML stream. Work is under way within the World Wide Web Consortium (W3C) to unify these two syntaxes as part of the XML Schema work. When this work completes, the XMI specification will be extended to support the W3C adopted specification.

When the XMI specification was adopted by OMG, the XML Namespaces work was still in progress. One of the directions for improving the readability of XMI is to use XML Namespaces. Another feature being considered is to use default values in the XML stream so that the stream is more compact.

```
<!-- _____ -->
<!-- Contents of Class: Customer                        -->
<!-- _____ -->
<Model.Class xmi.id='a2'>
    <Model.ModelElement.name>Customer</Model.ModelElement.name>
    <Model.ModelElement.annotation> </Model.ModelElement.annotation>

<!-- Portions deleted for simplicity                    -->
<Model.Class.isSingleton xmi.value='false'/>
    <Model.Namespace.contents>
    <Model.Attribute xmi.id='a3'>

<Model.ModelElement.name>startTime</Model.ModelElement.name>
    <Model.ModelElement.annotation> </Model.ModelElement.annotation>
    <Model.Feature.visibility xmi.value='public_vis'/>
    <Model.Feature.scope xmi.value='instance_level '/>
      </Model.StructuralFeature.multiplicity>
    <Model.StructuralFeature.isChangeable xmi.value='true'/>
    <Model.Attribute.isDerived xmi.value='false'/>
    <Model.TypedElement.type>
    <Model.DataType xmi.idref='a17'/> <!-- EDI.String -->
      </Model.TypedElement.type>
      </Model.Attribute>
    <Model.Reference xmi.id='a28'>

<Model.ModelElement.name>supplier</Model.ModelElement.name>
    <Model.ModelElement.annotation>From Rose
</Model.ModelElement.annotation>
```

```
<Model.Feature.visibility xmi.value='public_vis'/>
<Model.Feature.scope xmi.value='instance_level '/>
<Model.StructuralFeature.multiplicity>
<XMI.field>1</XMI.field>
<XMI.field>1</XMI.field>
<XMI.field>false</XMI.field>
<XMI.field>false</XMI.field>
  </Model.StructuralFeature.multiplicity>
<Model.StructuralFeature.isChangeable xmi.value='true'/>
<Model.TypedElement.type>
<Model.Class xmi.idref='a14'/> <!-- EDI.WebSite -->
  </Model.TypedElement.type>
<Model.Reference.referencedEnd>
<Model.AssociationEnd xmi.idref='a25'/>

<!-- EDI.CustomerByWebSite.supplier -->
  </Model.Reference.referencedEnd>
    </Model.Reference>
    </Model.Namespace.contents>
    </Model.Class>
```

22.4 Futures

22.4.1 The MOF

The MOF specification has evolved over the last two years based on the experience of various MOF implementors. The main enhancements from MOF 1.1 to MOF 1.3 made it easier to manage complex metamodels and their relationships to other metamodels (or parts of them) by introducing a package clustering concept. The MOF model itself has remained stable.

Some of the features being considered for future versions of the MOF include:

- MOF Schema Evolution and Versioning
- Support for mappings between metamodels
- Support for higher order relationships
- Tighter integration with UML and XML
- Mappings from the MOF to Java and COM to enable better interoperability with Java- and COM-based metadata repositories
- Integration with Naming and Directory Services

22.4.2 XMI

The XMI specification was adopted in March of 1999, but the designers are already looking at enhancements to make it more usable over a wide range of technology and business domains. XMI is already being used to specify metadata interchange standards for middleware, data warehousing, document management, and other application areas. During the next several years, you will see the use of XMI expand into business domains.

Some of the features being considered in the future for the XMI include:

- Use of XML Namespaces to improve management of multiple XML metamodels
- Improving the readability of the DTDs and documents
- Shrinking the size of documents through better choice of default values
- Better integration with W3C XML Schema efforts
- Maintaining the tight integration with UML and MOF specifications as they evolve

22.5 Summing Up

The introduction of MOF, UML, and XMI into the OMA is a big step forward for OMG and the software industry. Now you can analyze, model, and design applications with UML; manage, discover, and integrate your application metadata using the MOF; and interchange metadata among tools and applications in both CORBA and non-CORBA environments using XML. Figure 22.8 summarizes these roles of XMI, UML, OMF, and XML within the OMG environment.

Using UML and the MOF, you can implement software designs at a higher level of abstraction and precision. In addition, the MOF and XMI automate the definition and implementation of standard metadata repositories with common interchange formats for specific technology and business domains. This integration of OMG and W3C metadata and modeling standards eases the modeling, discovery, management, and sharing of metadata over the Internet and networks everywhere.

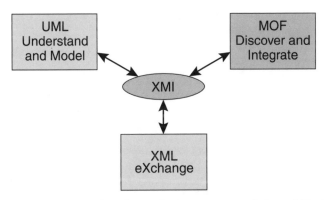

Figure 22.8   Roles of XMI, the UML, MOF, and XML within OMG.

CHAPTER
23

The Tutorial Example: Overview and Scenario

In at least one respect, CORBA programming is like mountain climbing, or skiing, or playing the guitar—no matter how much you read about it, you can't really appreciate it until you've actually done it. Even the detailed description you find in a technical specification can only carry you so far. To really understand CORBA, you'll have to write and compile some code, link and run some modules, and finally connect all of your distributed objects and get them to work together.

The rest of this book is devoted to a tutorial example of CORBA programming. We hope you'll spin the CD that comes with the book (or, even better, work the example by typing code in yourself) and work along with us, but you're free to just read along and assume that everything "really works" if that suits you better. But, if you actually work the example, when you've finished you'll not only be in a better position to decide if CORBA is the architecture for your enterprise, you'll also be ready to start work on your first project.

The authors have chosen this example with care. The scenario models a distributed environment, and demonstrates CORBA interoperability in a natural way. The example is close enough to real life that we were able to create computer objects that model real-world objects. And, we've tried to use "best-practice" wherever we could: IDL style follows the OMG style guide recommendations; code is commented and indented to show modularization, and so on. (In fact, the IDL for this edition was revised by the author of the OMG's IDL style guide.)

We have deliberately kept our *solution* as simple as possible, because the objective of the exercise is to teach you CORBA programming and the advantages of object-oriented architecture within the OMA. Therefore, while the objects and interfaces are real and fully developed, the functionality within them is only a shell or model, and is usually implemented in only a few lines of code. This way, as you work the exercise, you'll spend almost all of your time working on the things that this book is really supposed to be about. It would take a lot of programming time to turn the example code into a real-life application, and you wouldn't learn any more about CORBA by doing it. (You'd probably learn less, since you'd be concentrating on side issues. You would learn a lot about retailing, but that's a different book by an entirely different set of authors.) There's a partial list of things we left out in Section 23.4.

This chapter poses a realistic although somewhat simplified three-site distributed computing problem, and Chapter 24 performs a first-level Object-Oriented Analysis and Design (OOA&D) on it. Neither chapter discusses any CORBA aspects, coding conventions, data typing, or language issues. These "implementation details" have been left to the next steps, as they would be in a real-life programming exercise.

Because this book is written for both architects and programmers, we've deliberately avoided the "Hello, World" approach. We agree that it's a great way to teach programming, but we don't think it's a good way to approach projects complex enough to need an architect at the start. Our example illustrates a lot more than just basic CORBA programming (which is well covered along the way, of course): Objects in the example resemble their counterparts in the real world, and the natural way that we progress from problem statement, through analysis and design, to programming, demonstrates how you can do the same thing in your enterprise when you choose CORBA as your interoperability infrastructure. Our multi-language, multi-ORB treatment demonstrates, directly, how CORBA fits naturally into heterogeneous environments, including your enterprise along with the networks and systems of your customers and suppliers. The example gives you, in addition to experience with most of the basic CORBA programming techniques, an understanding of how CORBA supports complex, multilevel enterprise applications. Once you've completed the example and grasp the big picture, you can move on to study specialized topics from advanced books. If you're an architect, you can sharpen your A&D skills with a book on UML; if you're a programmer, you can study advanced techniques using a book that (in all likelihood) will be devoted to a single language rather than the three we treat here. Just keep in mind, as you specialize, how broadly applicable CORBA is and how much of the IT spectrum is covered by its various parts.

Do not assume that the problem statement, OOA&D, and coding were produced by the authoring team on the first pass. The truth is far from this; instead of using the older "waterfall" approach where each level is analyzed in excruciating detail and frozen before progressing to the next, we used an iterative procedure. After we stated the problem as well as we could at first, we started to design and found that we had forgotten some details in the statement or found that we wanted something different. Similarly, after doing some coding, we found that we wanted to change some design, which in turn, led us to change the problem statement a bit. Since you only get to see our final product, you may get the impression that this is the first version we came up with, but please take our word that this is far from the case. Of course, after the first two iterations, the changes became smaller and smaller, but you should be just as prepared to deal with this "spiral" type of development as we were. Although this OOA&D has little to do with CORBA as such, it is a normal part of the development cycle for any object-oriented system and essential for the enterprise-scale systems that benefit most from CORBA. This chapter didn't spring full-blown into our heads, and you shouldn't expect the same in your own projects.

23.1 Example Roadmap

We figured that if all you wanted was a single-platform, single-language development environment, you'd probably be reading a different book. Instead, you're reading this book to find out about how CORBA ORBs and objects work in diverse heterogeneous environments, and how all of the CORBA components fit together. In addition, you want the answers to the questions that are difficult, or sometimes impossible, to answer without firing up the development environment and ORB and getting your hands on the code: Which code is common to every environment and product? Which code is common to every ORB product that implements C++, or Java, or COBOL? Which parts of your code port easily, and which require more effort? How does a POA server differ from a BOA server?

With those questions in mind, we structured this half of the book to bring these answers out into the open. We admit, this means you'll have to put out a little more effort to trace your way through the example, but the advantage is worthwhile. Common code is presented only once, isolated in its own sections of the book, for everyone to read and study together. These sections are followed by shorter sections for each product, where the differences (and advantages!) of each product are brought out.

Figure 23.1 is a map of the rest of the book. It shows, by the splitting and rejoining of the paths, which sections are common and which are language or product specific. Here is a little more detail:

The IDL is common to every implementation: The code that is determined by the language mapping and may be produced by an IDL compiler is common to all implementations in each programming language.

The code that implements the functionality set down in the analysis and design is also common to all implementations in each programming language.

Only the code that takes care of details such as connecting an object to the ORB and object initialization is different for each ORB. The BOA ORBs in the book show less commonality than the POA ORBs will as they appear on the market during the year ending in early 2000. (We have included both a C++ and a Java POA ORB in the example. Since POA code ports from one ORB to another, you will be able to use this code on POA ORBs from other vendors as they become available.)

This book is arranged to take advantage of all of this commonality. Here's how to work your way through the example. Follow along on Figure 23.1 as you read though the rest of this section.

Everyone should read Chapters 23, 24, 25, and 26. The material in these chapters (Okay, except for Chapter 25) applies equally to every ORB and programming language: It's where we divide the problem into objects, assign each one its jobs to do, and set down the OMG IDL interfaces for each one.

At this point, we're almost ready to split by programming language, but not quite. When you read the A&D in Chapter 24, you'll discover that it makes very clear what the objects do, but not how they do it. There's a good reason for this: The A&D is con-

	C++	Java	COBOL
Starting Up	Chapter 23: Scenario		
	Chapter 24: Analysis and Design		
	Chapter 25: ORBs supporting C++, Java, COBOL, and other languages		
	Chapter 26: Coding and Compiling the IDL		
	26.4 BEA C++ · 26.5 Exprsft C++, Java · 26.6 IBM C++, Java · 26.7 DAIS Java · 26.8 Orbix C++, Java · 26.9 COBOL · 26.10 Visi C++, Java		
The Depot	Section 27.1: Language-Independent Overview		
	Section 27.2: C++ Mapping Code	Section 28.1: Java Mapping Code	Section 29.1: Getting Started
	Section 27.3: Coding Functionality in C++	Section 28.2: Coding Functionality in Java	Section 29.2: COBOL
	27.4 Exprsft · 27.5 IBM · 27.6 Orbix · 27.7 Inpr · 27.8 BEA	28.3 Exprsft · 28.4 IBM · 28.5 DAIS · 28.6 Orbix · 28.7 Inpr	29.3: ORBIX COBOL
The Store	Section 30.1: Language-Independent Overview		
	Section 30.2: C++- Mapping Code	Section 31.1: Java Mapping Code	Section 32.1: Getting Started
	Section 30.3: Coding Functionality in C++	Section 31.2: Coding Functionality in Java	Section 32.2: COBOL
	30.4 Exprsft · 30.5 IBM · 30.6 Orbix · 30.7 Inpr · 30.8 BEA	31.3 Exprsft · 31.4 IBM · 31.5 DAIS · 31.6 Orbix · 31.7 Inpr	32.3: ORBIX COBOL
The POS	Section 33.1: Language-Independent Overview		
	Section 33.2: C++ Mapping Code	Section 34.1: Java Mapping Code	Section 35.1: Getting Started
	Section 33.3: Coding Functionality in C++	Section 34.2: Coding Functionality in Java	Section 35.2: COBOL
	33.4 Exprsft · 33.5 IBM · 33.6 Orbix · 33.7 Inpr · 33.8 BEA	34.3 Exprsft · 34.4 IBM · 34.5 DAIS · 34.6 Orbix · 34.7 Inpr	35.3: ORBIX COBOL
Run	36.2 BEA C++ · 36.3 Exprsft C++, Java · 36.4 IBM C++, Java · 36.5 Orbix C++, Java · 36.6 Inpris C++, Java · 36.7 COBOL · 36.8 DAIS Java		

Figure 23.1   Example roadmap. Use this to plot your path through the example, based on the programming language and specific ORB you choose. Because of the way CORBA works, the planning, analysis, design, and IDL coding are common to all languages, and most of the coding is language-specific but not ORB-specific. Only the last part of each module—Depot, Store, and POS—includes ORB-specific code and procedures.

cerned with the problem space, while algorithms and methods belong in the solution space. However, since algorithms and methods are mostly language independent, we still need to set them down before we get into the language-dependent sections, and we chose to use the first section of each C++ chapter (the first of the language-specific chapters for each module) to do this. So, for each component (Depot, Store, and POS), there's an overview section covering its functionality and coding, which applies regardless of language. For the Depot, it's Section 27.1; for the Store, it's Section 30.1; and for the POS, it's Section 33.1. Regardless of your language, read this just before you dive into the coding sections.

Now we split things up by programming language. (You don't have to work or read just a single language! You can learn a lot about the suitabilities of a particular language by comparing it to other languages working the same problem. This book gives you a great opportunity to compare three languages side by side without having to do any of the work yourself. To compare even more languages, get a copy of the first edition of this book, which works almost the same example in C and Smalltalk. It's not exactly the same as the example here: We've updated the IDL to conform to the OMG style guidelines in this edition and added the POA ORBs. Also, the first version uses a home-grown Naming service instead of the OMG standard one.)

Each language chapter starts with two sections common to all of its ORBs, and concludes with individual sections for each ORB environment.

Therefore, if you're working in C++, regardless of the ORB, you work through Section 27.2 where you write or import the C++ code generated by the language mapping, which is common to all ORBs, and Section 27.3, where you write the code implementing the functionality dictated by the A&D, which is also common. Then you skip to the one section in the back half of the chapter that discusses the ORB you've chosen, to add the ORB-specific code and learn how to compile, link, and activate your object.

If you're working in Java, from Section 27.1 (the Depot overview), you skip to Section 28.1 to write or import the code generated by the Java mapping and IDL compiler, and Section 28.2 to write the code implementing the functionality dictated by the A&D. Then you skip to the one section in the back half of Chapter 28 that discusses the ORB you've chosen, to add the ORB-specific code and learn how to compile, link, and activate your object.

If you're working in COBOL, from Section 27.1 (the Depot overview) you skip to Section 29.1 and work your way straight through the chapter because we have only one COBOL implementation in this book. It is arranged in about the same way as the others, so you can make some comparisons to the other languages.

At this point, regardless of the ORB, you have the Depot code completed and running and it's time to start on the Store object.

Chapters 30, 31, and 32 discuss the Store object coding using a structure that exactly parallels the treatment of the Depot.

Chapters 33, 34, and 35 do the same for the POS and its associated objects.

Finally (whew!), we're ready to fire up all the objects and run our retail domain. This is covered in a single chapter, Chapter 36, with a section for each ORB.

What if you're using an ORB that isn't covered in this book? That's okay; there are lots of great ORBs, and we can't possibly cover all of them, even in 870 pages. If you're using C++, Java, or COBOL, you can still use all of the common components before you either start out on your own or look around for help. If you're using C or Smalltalk, look in the first edition of this book where the example—with the few changes we mentioned above—is worked in those languages.

If you're using a different language entirely—Ada, perhaps, or Objective C, or Lisp (a language that is about to get an official OMG language mapping), you need somewhere to go for more information and we have just the place:

OMG has set up a homepage on the Web for information about this book and its example. We purposely made the copyright for the example very liberal, freely allowing educational use by any person or company. All ORB vendors that have implemented the example, whether they're included in this book or not, may post their implementations on their Web site and give the OMG a URL to point to from the book's homepage. Information about the book itself, about the example in general, and pointers to the implementations that we know about are included on the book's homepage at www.omg.org/library/corfun/corfun.html. If you have an ORB and you've implemented the example in any language, send an e-mail to the author at siegel@omg.org to get your example's URL listed on the page.

If you want, you can choose different ORBs for your Depot, Store, or POS objects. We didn't have time to test every possible combination of ORBs and programming languages, but we did check a number of possibilities without running into any trouble. You may have to load remote Naming services manually, as did we, in order to get your ORBs in touch with each other, but this is not an impediment to interoperabilty. (When implementations of the Interoperable Naming Service come on the market, you will be able to skip this step.) To watch ORBs interoperate using a different demo program, surf over to www.corba.net.

23.2 Problem Overview

A chain of grocery stores is changing its information handling. It is installing intelligent cash registers, called Point-of-Sale (POS) terminals, with barcode readers and receipt printers. These POS terminals are all connected to a single store computer that contains information common to all POSs in the store but is potentially different from information in other stores (such as markup, tax policy, and store totals). The store computer answers requests and stores summary data for the POS terminals. All store computers for stores in the chain are, in turn, connected to the central office's depot, which supplies item information to the store such as cost before markup and descriptive information to be printed on receipts. The depot also keeps track of each store's inventory and will, eventually, schedule deliveries to the store based on the inventory.

To expand on this description, we will first give a detailed set of tasks that will be performed by the overall system and its parts. We then specify what is explicitly excluded from the problem. After these detailed parts, we specify a set of objects along with some "desk-checking" information to convince ourselves that we understand the problem.

23.3 Detailed Problem Statement

Here is a "management level" problem statement, stating the rough information flow as a series of tasks:

A. A chain food store has several POS stations connected to a store computer. A cashier turns on the POS station and logs in to the store computer stating that the POS system is ready for business—the store computer obviously performs some security checks to make sure the POS station and the cashier are who they say they are. The store computer runs continuously and is connected to a continuously running central depot computer. It is the job of the Depot to keep track of all inventory and to respond to requests with the chain's cost for each item, as well as the taxable status for an item (food, clothes, other). All taxation is calculated at the local store.

B. Each POS station is connected to a barcode scanner and keypad. The barcode scanner outputs a number to the POS station. The keypad can transmit one of five choices to the POS station:

1. Log in a new cashier.

2. Print a slip showing the total sales for this POS station since the last login.

3. Print a slip showing the total sales for the entire store since the store computer started.

4. Indicate a quantity that applies to the next scanned item. Two or more of these in a row without intervening barcode input are resolved by forgetting all but the last quantity. Once a barcode is input, the quantity for the next item is automatically set to 1; that is, if any barcode comes in without a preceding quantity, its quantity is 1.

5. Total a sale (a series of one or more grocery items). [Once a sale has started (either a quantity or barcode entered), the only legal input is another quantity or the Total choice. Reports or logins are disabled.]

C. The store has multiple items, each of which has a barcode. A customer brings a basket of items to a cashier at one of the POS stations. The cashier, who runs each item over a barcode scanner, may enter a quantity greater than 1 via the keyboard for each barcoded item when more than one of the same item is being purchased. (That is, duplicate items do not necessarily pass under the scanner.) The POS station then prints the sum of all sales to finish the sales slip. The cashier rips off the printed sales slip and gives it to the customer. The cashier bags the order, collects the money, and tells the customer to have a nice day, whether the customer is smiling or not.

D. In order to print each line of the sales slip and to tell the central depot about its inventory, each POS station sends barcode numbers and quantity to the store computer, which passes them on to the central depot, getting back at least the chain's cost for the item, the tax type for the item, and the item name. The store computer then adds on a store-specific constant percentage markup for an individual item, which is then reported back to the POS station and printed as the customer's per-item price for the sales slip. The store computer also returns the taxable price for each item to the POS so that it can figure out the tax at the end. The POS station calculates the amount of the (possibly) multiple items for a single line of the sales slip. A single line printed on the sales slip has the barcode, the item name, the sales price for each item, the quantity of each item, and the total sales price for the line.

E. The store computer keeps track of the total amount of sales during the day. From any POS station, the store manager can ask for a daily report. The POS station reports the total sales since the store computer started. (There is no special console for the store computer; any POS can get the store totals.)

F. The POS station keeps a running tally of all its sales since its login time. The cashier can ask for this running total at any time except during a sale.

G. The taxes are calculated at the store level to allow for varying jurisdictions' rates. The chain management provides a standard tax object that calculates a flat tax for everything that is taxable. In the example, the total taxable amount is calculated by adding up the individual taxable amounts per item. The taxable amount per item is either 0 or the full value of the item. The taxes are always calculated on a final taxable sales total, not on an item-by-item basis, to avoid cumulative rounding errors.

H. For the purpose of this example, an item is either taxable or not taxable, and the sum of all taxable items is multiplied by the constant percentage for its jurisdiction to arrive at the tax. This is very simplistic but will do for the example. In real life, each store may have a different tax object that inherits from the basic object but that calculates taxes in a different way. The reason for calculating taxes on the total instead of each item is that rounding of individual items to the penny might lead to a different result from the rounding of the total sales. Again, a simplification for the sake of the example.

23.4 Problem Issues Explicitly Ignored

Here are some of the scenarios and issues that were explicitly left out of the problem statement but would probably be accounted for in any real application. You can probably think of more.

A. Customer returns an item.

B. Customer takes a previously scanned item out of the sale.

C. Customer decides to abort the entire sales transaction.

D. Accounting periods—totals by day aren't kept, dates aren't printed, summations are never zeroed except for POS total when a new cashier logs in (which implies that another cashier is logging out). Similarly, the running store totals are not kept persistently since the beginning of time or ever reset except at store computer startup.

E. The Depot does not yet automatically schedule a delivery when the store's inventory for a given item falls below the low-water mark.

F. Communications lines and computers never go down. In particular, a store never releases a StoreAccess object servicing any POS station that has called in since the beginning of the store computer's startup.

G. The store does not cache its own inventory or the price of items.

H. Shutting down the Store or Depot.

I. Arithmetic overflow on the running sums.

J. No optimization is done on store and item cost/quantity database.

K. The POS station does not keep track of multiple items in case there is a sale of "n-items/currency-price" that is different from the individual item price.

L. Does not deal with amount tendered nor calculate change. The sociological implications may be profound, but let's pretend we live in an era when knowing how to calculate change was a requirement for being a cashier, instead of (perhaps) a requirement for being a manager.

M. Cashiers are not identified by numbers, and security when a new cashier logs in is ignored (although a comment shows where it might be placed).

N. All barcodes are always scanned correctly, and no price will have to be entered by hand. (This would require a completely parallel path to set price, taxes, sums, etc. This would double the amount of code, without teaching anything more about CORBA.)

O. Inventory count going negative in the Depot is ignored. In real life, it would not be ignored.

P. At the Depot in the current state of development, the store ID is ignored, and all stores are serviced from a single database—in real life, each store would have its own database at the Depot.

23.5 Use Cases

Use cases are a technique used in OOA&D to help determine whether the design is complete. They are analogous to "walk-through" design techniques of the past. Another way of defining a use case is as a "business rule"—it states what will happen in the business. In particular, use cases identify specific actions that start the "system" working.

If everything is specified properly in the objects, you should be able to "desk-check" the working of the system for each use case by looking at the objects defined here and walking through the implementation specified. This is not a foolproof method, but it does turn up a lot of design flaws before you get to the coding stages.

23.5.1 Initialization

Here are three similar initialization use cases that cover the functionality we're interested in:

1. Turn on a POS station.
2. Turn on a store computer.
3. Turn on the Depot computer.

Each of these starts up the related object and calls its initialize operation in some system-dependent manner.

23.5.2 Login-to-POS

1. A new cashier comes to a running POS station and types L on the (simulated) keypad.

2. The keypad calls the login operation of the related POS station.

23.5.3 Request-a-report (two types)

1. A person types P or S on the keypad at a legal time.

2. The keypad calls the **print_POS_sales_summary** or **print_store_sales_ summary** operation on the related POS station.

23.5.4 Perform-a-sale

1. (Optional) the operator enters Qn on the keypad, indicating a request for multiple items for the next barcode. The keypad calls the **item_quantity** operation on the POSTerminal object with input argument **n**.

2. The operator runs a grocery item over the barcode scanner. The (simulated) scanner calls operation **send_barcode** on the POSTerminal object with input argument the number from the scanner. Much happiness ensues while objects call other objects. Two possible outcomes:

   a. Barcode not recognized—scan ignored, cashier tries again. (For the sake of simplicity, we assume success eventually.)

   b. Barcode recognized. All the correct calculations ensue, and a line of a sales slip is printed. If this is the first line, print out the name of the store.

3. Repeat steps 1 and 2 until the cashier enters T at the keypad, at which time the keypad calls the **end_sale** operation on the POSTerminal object with no arguments. It enjoys itself updating all the numbers, printing out extra lines at the end of the sales slip, including subtotal, taxes, and grand total.

23.6 Deployment

When the system is finally deployed, we expect the following configuration: Each POS station is a separate computer in a LAN within the store. It contains the POSTerminal object, the InputMedia and the OutputMedia objects. The Store object, the StoreAccess objects it creates, and the Tax object reside on a separate computer in the same LAN, but on a different computer from the POS stations. The Depot is on a separate computer reachable by WAN.

Of course, you'll be able to test your prototype on a single computer, and the instructions in Chapter 36 will tell you how. And, you will be able to run in distributed mode also; all you need are enough networked computers and IIOP-enabled ORBs, such as any of the ones presented here.

CHAPTER

24

The Tutorial Example: Analysis and Design

This chapter presents a somewhat more formal object-oriented analysis and design for the problem statement in Chapter 23. We didn't use a formal OOA&D methodology for this, nor did we use any computerized tool except our word processor, but we did have a lot of experience to draw upon. We strongly recommend that you pick a methodology before designing your first OO project, and probably a computerized tool as well, although we are not going to give you any advice here on which one to pick. Of course, we suggest that your tool be based in UML!

As you read the object descriptions in this chapter, you will see the many places where neither the problem statement nor the design are completely realistic. We intended them only to be vaguely suggestive of real-world problems that have distributed components. We have designed input and output objects, for example, that are extremely simple, since making them realistic would not teach you anything more about CORBA. We likewise made the Tax objects very simple, intending only to show how CORBA objects might be used; they are not intended to be realistic for any application, because a realistic set of Tax objects would probably be larger than the rest of this simple application and would have little to do with CORBA.

This level of design defines some local variables (objects' state) and enough implementation discussion to reassure ourselves that we have indeed captured all the information processing needs of the system. Specifically, we have provided enough information to show that the points in the detailed object descriptions yield the desired results without too much arm-waving.

457

This level of design also intentionally has few explicit references to CORBA, although it does identify which state variables are IDL attributes (that is, variables that are publicly available through the generated CORBA accessor interfaces, obviating the need to explicitly declare operations that access these variables). The design explicitly recognizes that the resulting system will likely be distributed. That fact subtly influences the selection of objects; in particular, the particular object definitions tend to minimize the network traffic. As with all distributed applications, this aspect should not be over- or underemphasized since the particular deployment of objects tends to change over time and early decisions may well be changed, yielding performance that may be subaverage, much less suboptimal.

We made one other concession to CORBA in this otherwise general object-oriented design: naming conventions. In converting this design to IDL in Chapter 26, to avoid confusion we used the same names used in this chapter wherever possible. To do this, we had to anticipate a naming convention for IDL identifiers. In this regard, we chose the conventions used in OMG specs. It makes little difference which conventions you use in your own work. What's important is that you *have* a convention because it helps greatly in reading code. Briefly, the OMG conventions specify that "types" (objects, structures, sequences, and so forth) start with uppercase letters, continue with lowercase letters, have no underscores, and the first letters of words in the middle of identifiers are uppercase (examples: InputMedia, StoreTotals). Other identifiers are lowercase with underscores separating words (examples: total_sales, calculate_tax), with the exception that constants are all uppercase with underscores separating words (example: CLOTHES). Acronyms usually spelled in uppercase stay that way (example: print_POS_sales_summary). Conventions for other identifiers in the particular programming languages will vary, of course, but the IDL names will carry through even to the languages.

In Chapter 26, we will start implementation by extracting the potentially distributed aspects of the design into a set of CORBA interfaces expressed in IDL. The IDL will not have many of the local variables or local operations needed to express a complete system design. The IDL will contain only those object interfaces, attributes, and datatypes that need to be public in a distributed environment.

Finally, talking about datatypes, this level of design does not specify datatypes except in general terms, such as "reference to," "list of," "structure containing," and so forth, vaguely at that. All details of that sort are left to Chapter 26 and individual language mappings. Some of the "local variables" mentioned in the analysis might be turned into IDL datatypes and have their names changed to satisfy those conventions (as mentioned), but we don't consider that here.

24.1 Overview

One thing we needed to do was to divide our problem space into a number of objects. In keeping with the principles of object orientation, we wanted them to correspond as much as possible to real-life objects; this also helps us divide the functionality in a natural way. The major objects were easy to determine, but it took our programmers and designers a few iterations before the objects supporting the POS were fully stable. (Designing by committee can be so much fun!) The objects in the final design are:

- InputMedia Object
- OutputMedia Object
- POSTerminal Object
- Store Object
- StoreAccess Object
- Tax Object
- Depot Object

Figure 24.1 shows how these objects connect to make everything work. This is an invocation diagram, not an inheritance diagram.

The full definition of each object is given in the rest of this chapter. Each section gives one object definition, with a short glossary definition (an object is a "thing"), a list of state variables (some identified as CORBA attributes), a list of operations, and implementation details for each operation.

24.2 InputMedia Object

Glossary

InputMedia is (simulates) a keypad device and a barcode reader device for the purpose of the demo. Operationally, the devices are a single keyboard that routes

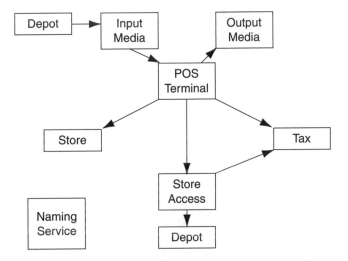

Figure 24.1   Objects in the POS example problem. Arrows indicate direction of an invocation.

its output to either "barcode_input" (line is all numeric, simulating a barcode scanner) or to "keypad_input" (line starts with a letter).

State Variables

POSRef: Reference to the POSTerminal object that this input device services.

(local): Local variables to help scanning input line from the terminal that is simulating the input devices.

Operations

Initialization

Description: Start up the device at system startup time, but only after starting the POSTerminal object.

Parameters: None; no return.

Called from: Startup.

Implementation:

    1. Find the POSTerminal object reference, POSRef.

barcode_input

Description: A simulated barcode reader—it presents the scanned barcode.

Parameters: Input "item" (a string representing the barcode); no return.

Called from: Startup.

Implementation:

    1. Simulated by input from a line-oriented input device. Any number followed by a return is treated as coming from a barcode reader. It calls operation "send_barcode" on the POSTerminal object with input argument the barcode string from the scanner.

keypad_input

Description: A simulated keypad reader—it presents input from a clerk.

Parameters: Input "cmd" (a string representing input from a POS's keypad); no return.

Called from: InputMedia client.

Implementation:

    1. Simulated by input from a line-oriented input device. Any line beginning with the following letters and ending with return have the following meaning and call the appropriate operation on its POS reference. Other keypad input is ignored.

      L   Login a new cashier—Call "login" operation of the POSTerminal object with no arguments.

      P   Print a POSTerminal sales total (i.e., sum of all sales since last login)—Call "print_POS_sales_summary" operation on the

POSTerminal object with no arguments.

S   Print a store sales total (i.e., sum of all sales in entire store since the computer was turned on)—Call "print_store_sales_summary" operation on the POSTerminal object, no arguments.

Qn   (That is, a Q followed by a number) The next barcode scanned is to be replicated this many times—Call the "item_quantity" operation on the POSTerminal object with input argument "n".

T   End of sale, calculate subtotals, taxes, grand total—Call the "end_sale" operation on the POSTerminal object with no arguments.

2. After calling the operation, wait for return, then read a new line, starting from step 1. (We must wait since we are using simulated input = simulated output device. The simulation wouldn't need to wait if the devices were real and separate.)

24.3 OutputMedia Object

Glossary

OutputMedia is (simulates) a sales tape printer and/or a screen showing current status of a sale. The output device is simulated by simple, line-oriented output to a console terminal. A more realistic UI object might have multiple methods with multiple parameters given different meanings, but that is not deemed necessary for the purpose of the example.

State Variables

None

Operations

output_text

Description:	Output the "string_to_print" to the media.
Parameters:	Input "string_to_print"; no return.
Called from:	POSTerminal operations: "print_POS_sales_summary", "print_store_sales_summary", "send_barcode", "end_sale".

Implementation:

Like the description says, man!

24.4 POSTerminal Object

Glossary

POSTerminal represents the terminal controller. It handles interaction with the media devices (InputMedia and OutputMedia objects), remembers the state of ongoing sales calculations, allows new cashiers to log in, and delivers reports about the POS station or the store.

State Variables

storeRef:	Reference to the Store object.
storeAccessRef:	Reference to the StoreAccess object.
outputMediaRef:	Reference to the OutputMedia object connected to the POSTerminal.
taxRef:	Reference to the Tax Calculator object.
POSId:	Identification of this POSTerminal.
itemBarcode:	From barcode scanner.
itemQuantity:	From keypad; one (1) otherwise.
item_info:	A structure returned from the Depot via the "find_price" operation, containing at least the following:

item	Should be the same as itemBarcode.
item_type	The tax type of the item for use by the Tax object.
item_cost	Wholesale cost before markup.
name	Text description of the item suitable for printing on a receipt.
quantity	Remaining quantity in the store's inventory (should match what's on the store's shelves).

item_price:	Price to customer, including store's markup; set by operation find_price.
item_tax_price:	Amount of this item that is taxable; set by operation find_price.
itemExtension:	Calculated internally from quantity times price.
saleSubtotal:	Running total of itemExtension.
taxableSubtotal:	Running total of taxable itemExtension.
saleTotal:	Sum of final saleSubtotal + tax.
saleTax:	Tax on this sale.
POSList:	Sequence of structures representing all POSTerminals and their totals.

Operations

Initialization

Description:	Startup the POSTerminal.
Parameters:	None.
Called from:	Startup.

Implementation:

    1. Find storeRef, outputMediaRef, taxRef, and POSId.

login

Description: Tell the POSTerminal object and thus the Store object that a new cashier is starting; retrieve reference to a StoreAccess object for use by the POS later.

Parameters: None; no return.

Called from: InputMedia operation "keypad_input".

Implementation:

1. Set itemQuantity to 1, all other values to 0.

2. Register new POS/cashier by calling "login" operation on storeRef object with input parameter POSId. (Since there is no security for this demo, there are no security parameters or failure returns.) This operation returns a reference to a StoreAccess object to be used by this POSTerminal.

print_POS_sales_summary

Description: Tell the POSTerminal object to print a slip of its POSTotal and POSTaxTotal.

Parameters: None; no return.

Called from: InputMedia operation "keypad_input".

Implementation:

1. Ignore this command if itemBarcode or saleSubtotal is nonzero, since that means the POSTerminal is in the middle of a sale.

2. Obtain this POS's "Total" and "TaxTotal" by calling the Store operation "get_POS_totals", getting a sequence of all the store's POSes and then selecting the POS information for this POS's POSId. (We recognize that this is a relatively poor use of object-oriented methods—encapsulation, in particular—because we are obtaining from the Store much information we don't need, and we have to search through that information to find the information pertaining to us. We decided to leave the design at this level because we wanted to stop adding more methods in order to keep the example simpler.)

3. Format "Total" and "TaxTotal" and call the "output_text" operation on the outputMediaRef object with the formatted string being an input argument.

print_store_sales_summary

Description: Tell the POSTerminal object to print a slip of the store's total, and the store's tax total, and the similar totals for each POS station in the store since each POS station logged in.

Parameters: None; no return.

Called from: InputMedia operation "keypad_input".

Implementation:

1. Ignore this command if itemBarcode or saleSubtotal is nonzero, since that means the POSTerminal is in the middle of a sale.

2. Call "_get_totals" operations on storeRef object to get the store's total and tax total.

3. Format the store's total and tax total and call "output_text" operation on outputMediaRef object, with the formatted string being an input argument.

4. Call operation "get_POS_totals" of the storeRef object to get a sequence of structures, POSList, about all the POS stations in the store.

5. For each structure in the sequence (representing a POS), format the POS's id, POS's total sales, and POS's total taxes; use that formatted string as an input argument on a call on the "output_text" operation on outputMediaRef object.

item_quantity

Description: Sets the quantity to be applied to the next barcode message. Note that successive calls to this operation overwrite the previous call. Also, the local variable itemQuantity is reset to 1 after a barcode is read and processed so that the next barcode will be processed with the (default) quantity 1.

Parameter: Input "quantity"; no return.

Called from: InputMedia operation "keypad_input".

Implementation:

1. Set itemQuantity to "quantity".

send_barcode

Description: Informs POSTerminal of a grocery item scanned by the barcode scanner. The POSTerminal object then sends messages to the StoreAccess object (which sends to the Depot object) about the inventory reductions and to get retail and taxable price as well as information to complete the sales receipt.

Parameters: Input "item"; no return.

Called from: InputMedia operation "barcode_input".

Implementation:

1. Copy "item" to local itemBarcode.

2. Call "find_price" operation on storeAccessRef object with input arguments itemQuantity and itemBarcode; and output arguments item_price, item_tax_price, and structure item_info.

3. If return from 2 is the exception BarcodeNotFound, zero out itemBarcode, set itemQuantity to 1, and return. (Thereby requiring operator to rescan. The operator only notices this when the receipt maker doesn't

go ka-chunk. Very annoying. In future versions, we should add a beep for error. Put it on the wish list. Hah!) If there is no exception, continue.

4. Calculate itemExtension from item_price and itemQuantity, then accumulate into saleSubtotal.

5. Call "output_text" operation of the outputMediaRef object with input argument of a formatted string including itemBarcode, item_info.name, itemQuantity, item_price, and itemExtension, putting asterisk after bar code if item is taxable (i.e., item_tax_price not 0).

6. Accumulate product of item_tax_price and itemQuantity into taxableSubtotal.

7. Set itemQuantity to 1.

end_sale

Description:	Tell the POSTerminal object to complete the sale by calculating tax on taxable items, completing the printing of the sales slip, reporting the sale to the store, and preparing for a new command.
Parameters:	None; no return.
Called from:	InputMedia operation "keypad_input".

Implementation:

1. Call "output_text" operation of outputMediaRef object with input argument a formatted string of taxableSubtotal.

2. Call "calculate_tax" operation of taxRef object with input arguments taxableSubtotal; returns saleTax.

3. Call "output_text" operation of outputMediaRef object with input argument a formatted string of saleTax.

4. Calculate saleTotal as sum of saleSubtotal and saleTax.

5. Call "output_text" operation of outputMediaRef object with input argument a formatted string of saleTotal.

6. Call operation "update_store_totals" of storeRef object with input arguments saleTotal, saleTax, and POSId.

7. Set to 0: itemBarcode, saleSubtotal, saleTaxableSubtotal.

8. Set itemQuantity to 1.

24.5 Store Object

Glossary

The Store object is the traffic keeper and accountant for the store. It deals with multiple POSes, logging them in, keeping track of their sales, and reporting totals on the store and the POSes.

State Variables

totals:	(CORBA Attribute, read-only) a structure consisting of two numbers collected since the store computer last started:

	StoreTotal:	Running sum of total sales (including taxes) for all POSes.
	StoreTaxTotal:	Running sum of total taxes for all POSes.

storeId:	The identifier of this store.
POSList:	A sequence of structures about POSTerminal objects that have logged into the store. Each structure contains the id of the POSTerminal, the total sales reported by that POSTerminal since last login, and the total taxes collected by that POSTerminal since last login.

Operations

Initialization

Description:	Start up the store when the store computer starts.
Parameters:	None; no return.
Called from:	Startup.
Implementation:	

1. Set StoreTotal and StoreTaxTotal to 0.
2. Set POSList sequence to indicate no logged in POSes.

login

Description:	Register a new cashier/POS with the store and start keeping track of sales and tax totals for that POSTerminal. (Note: This is also where security would go if there were any.) Create a StoreAccess object and return its reference.
Parameters:	Input "id" (i.e., POS id); return reference to StoreAccess object.
Called from:	POSTerminal operation "login".
Implementation:	

1. If there is no POSTerminal with "id" already in the sequence,
   a. Create a StoreAccess object.
   b. Add another POSInfo structure to the POSList sequence, setting its POSId, zeroing the totals, and setting its StoreAccess reference.
2. If there is already a POSTerminal in the sequence with POSId the same as "id", just zero out the totals.
3. Return the StoreAccess object reference.

get_POS_totals

Description:	Return, in the output parameter, the state of the store's current knowledge of the registered POSTerminals (POSList).

Parameters: Output "POS_data"; no return.

Called from: POSTerminal operations "print_POS_sales_summary", "print_store_sales_summary".

Comment: A better encapsulation-design would be to return just a list of POS totals rather than the POSList which contains a lot of other information. We didn't do that because we wanted to keep the number of methods down for this example.

Implementation:

     Set POS_data values to current values in POSList.

update_store_totals

Definition: Accumulate the parameters into the store state and into the POS state kept by the store.

Parameters: Input "id" (i.e., id of POS caller), "price", "taxes"; no return.

Called from: POSTerminal operation "end_sale".

Implementation:

1. Search POSList sequence for structure containing a POS id equal to parameter "id".

    a. If not found, there is a major inconsistency in the operation of the entire system. (Notify MIS manager [hopefully in bed] by beeper—not implemented in demo.) The demo dies.

    b. If found, add "price" and "taxes" to corresponding fields in the structure found.

2. Add "price" to StoreTotal and add "taxes" to StoreTaxTotal.

_get_totals

Parameters: None; returns the structure "totals".

Called from: POSTerminal operation "print_store_sales_summary".

Implementation:

     Note: This operation name is automatically generated for the Store object by IDL compilers since it refers to an IDL attribute. It is declared read-only, so only the store can set it.

_get_store_id

Parameters: None; returns the storeId.

Called from: StoreAccess "find_price".

Implementation:

     Note: This operation name is automatically generated for the Store object by IDL compilers since it refers to an IDL attribute. It is declared read-only, so only the store can set it.

24.6 StoreAccess Object

Glossary

The StoreAccess object is a surrogate for the Store, acting as a Store to avoid having the store overloaded with individual POS Terminals. The StoreAccess object deals only with a single terminal, providing access to the grocery item database.

State Variables

depotRef:	Reference to chain's Depot object.
taxRef:	Reference to Local Tax Calculation object.
storeMarkup:	Percentage markup (Note: this is constant for all items in the store. This is quite unrealistic, but to do otherwise would require a local database for all items with markup for each, or at least a designator from the Depot as to loss-leader, small, medium, high, or something like that. Definitely not needed for this CORBA demo.)
store_id:	Store identification number, used to identify self to central office depot.

Operations

Initialization

Description:	Start up StoreAccess object.
Parameters:	None; no return.
Called from:	Store operation "login".
Implementation:	

    1. Set depotRef, taxRef, and storeMarkup.

find_price

Description:	Given input parameters, tell Depot about inventory reduction and ask it for ItemInfo (the information about the barcode in the database). Calculate the output parameters from the ItemInfo's cost, the markup, and the tax type, the latter using the taxRef object.
Parameters:	Input "item" (a barcode), and "quantity"; output "item_price", "item_tax_price", and "item_info"; no return value.
Exception:	BarcodeNotFound.
Called from:	POSTerminal operation "send_barcode".
Implementation:	

    1. Call "find_item_info" operation of depotRef object with input arguments local variable "store_id", passing through received arguments "item", and "quantity"; output argument is passed through argu-

ment "item_info" which returns (among other things) the item's cost and item's type.

2. If step 1 yields a BarcodeNotFound exception, raise exception BarcodeNotFound. Else (i.e., bar code was found), continue.

3. Calculate "item_price" as item's cost times storeMarkup.

4. Call "find_taxable_price" operation on taxRef object with input arguments "item_price" and the item_type, receiving back output argument "item_tax_price".

24.7 Tax Object

Glossary

The Tax object is the repository of information concerning the tax status of items in the store. For the purposes of the demo, it implements a flat tax method, where clothes and food are not taxable but everything else is taxed via a straight percentage of sales price.

State Variables

Rate: Percentage charged.

Operations

Initialization

Description: Start up when Store system starts.

Parameters: None; no return.

Called from: Startup.

Implementation:

Set Rate. (For the example, it's stored in the server itself as a constant.)

calculate_tax

Description: Calculate tax on parameter amount and return the result.

Parameters: Input "taxable_amount"; returns tax on that amount.

Called from: POSTerminal operation "end_sale".

Implementation:

Multiply "taxable_amount" by Rate, round it, return it.

find_taxable_price

Description: Determine how much, if any, of the item's price is taxable in this jurisdiction. In this case, food and clothes are not taxable, but everything else is 100% taxable.

Parameters: Input "item_price", "item_type"; return taxable price.

Called from: StoreAccess operation "find_price".

Implementation:

1. If "item_type" is "FOOD" or "CLOTHES", return 0.
2. Else return "item_price".

24.8 Depot Object

Glossary

The Depot object represents the inventory for the grocery store chain. It contains information about items for sale in all the stores. It currently responds only to queries. (For future editions, it might print out a reorder slip or sing a song.)

State Variables

(Ideally: Multiple stores, each with its own database. Practically, for this example, each store uses the same database.)

The database contains multiple items, each with a structure indexed by its barcode:

- itemName
- inventoryCount
- itemCost
- taxType

Operations

Initialization

Description: Started after system boot time at corporate headquarters.

Parameters: Name of the data file containing all information about the goodies.

Called from: Startup.

Implementation:

Initialize access to database (perhaps read it all into memory).

find_item_info

Description: Look up the information and return the values asked for. If the barcode asked for is not found in the database, raise an exception.

Parameters: Input "store_id", "item" (a barcode), "quantity"; output parameter "item_info", a structure containing the database information about the grocery item corresponding to the barcode in "item".

Exception: BarcodeNotFound.

Called from: StoreAccess operation "find_price".

Implementation:

1. Ideally, look up a different database for each "store_id". For the sake of the example's simplicity, all stores use the same database.

2. Search for key "item". If not found, raise exception BarcodeNot-Found and quit. Else, continue.

3. Reduce database quantity for "item" by "quantity".

4. From database, set values in output parameter "item_info", a structure.

CHAPTER

25

ORB Product Descriptions

25.1 ORB Products Overview

Right here, we start a very different part of the book. We're finished with the general, specification-level discussion of the example. Everything from here on deals with real products and real code—products you can buy and load, IDL and programming language code you can write and compile, ORBs you can connect to (and connect to each other!), and clients and object implementations you can run.

The example we presented in the last two chapters is worked in the rest of this book in three programming languages, using a grand total of 11 ORB environments from seven vendors. Each ORB and environment has been tuned by its vendor and technical team to be the best it can be for the users they have targeted. As you will see in the next three chapters, this can lead to products that differ markedly yet still conform completely to the OMG specifications and interoperate fully over the network.

25.1.1 ORBs and Language Support

Most ORBs support more than one programming language; several work the example in more than one so you can see this for yourself right in this book. Another way a company can support different languages is with separate ORBs (that interoperate via IIOP, of course, and sometimes also using a vendor-specific protocol), so watch for this configuration on the market also.

There are so many ORBs available, in so many languages, that it's almost impossible to maintain an up-to-date list of all the ORBs, languages, and features. Fortunately, that doesn't keep some people from trying and there are several Web sites that do a good job. We've listed a few in the references in Appendix A; the longest list we've seen so far includes over 70 ORBs and about 14 programming languages (including the six official OMG-mapped languages).

25.1.2 ORB Features and the Programming Example

One important feature of an ORB development environment is its ability to automate parts of the development process and to hide details of, for example, how objects connect and work together. For the typical development tool, the more automation and simplification, the better.

Unfortunately, though, it's difficult to learn the details about something when everything is hidden under the covers. Since the differences in the products appear on the surface, and the similarities that enable integration are sometimes hidden, when we work the example we're going to dig under the surface layer of these ORB environments in order to teach you how CORBA works. This way, you'll be in a better position to take advantage of CORBA everywhere it fits into your enterprise. In addition, you'll be much less likely to get into trouble from misunderstanding what CORBA can and cannot do.

All of the companies and developers who helped write this book agreed to make the example heuristic; that is, to expose the OMG-standardized components of CORBA that enable objects to work together: IDL interfaces, language mappings, where objects reside and run, how they connect. And, for every ORB, these components are brought out into the open even though they are handled automatically in various ways by the products in this book and many other ORB products on the market. This presentation starts in Chapter 26 and continues through the end of this book. If the working of the example seems primitive, that's because it was made so deliberately, just this once, for your benefit. Learn the details this time through and then let your ORB environment handle them for you and your development staff as you apply CORBA to real-world problems and projects.

25.1.3 Advanced ORB Product Features

The advanced features of ORBs and their development environments are crucial, too, because they determine the usability of the product and the productivity of the programmers and users who depend on it. The designers of the CORBA specification knew this; that's why CORBA specifies the interface and protocol layers very tightly while saying virtually nothing about the development layer above them. This allows development environments the freedom to flourish without spoiling the portability and interoperability the standard confers. There's no reference implementation for CORBA. Instead, all of the products you see here, and many others, are written to conform to the CORBA specifications, and are still able to offer a wide range of development and runtime enhancements.

In this chapter, the vendors of these ORBs present details of their products. This is the one place in this book where you can learn what these products can do when they're not in "teaching mode." It's a great place to start an investigation leading to the purchase of one—or more!—ORBs and programming environments for your company. All of the ORBs support the OMG specifications for CORBA and a number of CORBA-services, but some may meet your company's needs or wants better than others. There's also a good possibility that different groups in your company—engineering, R&D, finance—may benefit from different ORBs and environments. Finally, with CORBA, you can allow them this freedom without sacrificing interoperability!

These are not the only ORBs available, of course—many other vendors offer ORBs and development environments that conform to the OMG specifications and have the potential to fit well in your enterprise. We're limited to 11 ORBs mostly by space and time restrictions; don't overlook a good product just because it's not included in this book. OMG offers several easy ways to find out about additional ORBs. You can either contact OMG directly (see Appendix A) and ask for the CORBA products directory, or you can surf to the OMG homepage (www.omg.org). There are two places on the homepage to look: either the CORBA products directory online, or the CORBA Fundamentals and Programming homepage with pointers to updated versions of example code and advice for every ORB vendor who has notified OMG that he or she has working example code on the Web (including all seven vendors in this book, plus many more).

In the rest of this chapter, the vendors that have contributed to the example in this book present details of their product to you in their own words. In the first edition, we split this part of the book into chapters by programming language; this made sense when most ORBs supported only one programming language, but doesn't anymore with so many working the example in several. So, you'll find all of the descriptions in this one chapter, sorted alphabetically by company name. (We were going to use a hashing algorithm to determine order but decided that didn't make sense!)

25.2 BEA WLE

WLE is one of BEA System's extensive suite of middleware products. It is a rich, sophisticated deployment framework for your CORBA objects.

25.2.1 Overview

The following is a brief summary of the operations and features of BEA WLE (formerly known as BEA M3).

- You program WLE objects in C++ or Java using CORBA 2.2 interfaces. You use OMG IDL to define your objects' interfaces. You can develop your objects using standard, off-the-shelf tools. WLE runs your objects in server processes that it manages.

- Your objects communicate with each other via the BEA WLE CORBA/IIOP ORB.

- Various types of clients—including Java, Active/X, Web application servers such as BEA's WebLogic Express or WebLogic Server, and standard CORBA clients—can invoke your server objects. Clients that meet the IIOP specification can communicate with a WLE server whether they use the BEA WLE ORB or some other ORB.

- On the server side, a highly scalable, reliable communications system can grow to handle a very large number of clients. An IIOP Listener process—combined with the ORB—acts as a high-speed switch to pool communications across a cluster of WLE servers and route the IIOP messages through the WLE infrastructure.

- The WLE deployment services confer your seemingly normal objects in server processes with the runtime qualities that mission-critical applications require—including transaction integrity, security, scalability, performance, high availability, and location transparency.

- WLE Manager provides a complete infrastructure for dynamically configuring, monitoring, and tuning your distributed applications. With WLE's Java-based console, you can administer your applications virtually anywhere. Or, you can monitor your application from off-the-shelf SNMP-based management stations, such as HP's OpenView or IBM's Tivoli.

25.2.2 Architecture

WLE is an Object Transaction Monitor (OTM), which is not just an ORB with transactions, just as a transaction monitor is not just a mechanism for doing two-phase commit. An OTM is a deep integration of an ORB with the "engine" of a TP monitor. These existing BEA technologies are melded in WLE, building on each other's strengths to produce more than just the sum.

The ORB element of WLE evolved from the BEA ObjectBroker product, which was the first commercial ORB. It was already known for its ability to handle large applications (for example, one with over 4 million transactions a day) with all the programming advantages of the CORBA object model.

The BEA engine element of WLE is an evolution of the BEA TUXEDO product, a widely used TP monitor in open systems. As with any successful TP monitor, BEA TUXEDO first dealt with the large scale requirements of mission-critical, enterprise-wide applications; only then could transactions even be considered. Such an ambitious infrastructure requires years of development, and the BEA TUXEDO engine certainly has that, evolving since 1983. As a result of such a long lifetime, the engine has not only the features customers need for large applications, but also has the code stability you would expect of a mission-critical tool.

WLE (code named "Iceberg" while in development) is an integrated deployment framework for your objects. Like its namesake, 90 percent of the "Iceberg" lies beneath the surface. All these "under the waterline" services are functions that WLE brings to your application—you don't have to develop them yourself. The 10 percent "above the waterline" is the programming environment you use; this visible part is standard CORBA, with WLE's TP Framework and Helper Objects to make it easy.

25.2.3 Your Objects in a WLE Environment

WLE's *raison d'être* is to run your application components in a mission-critical manner—managing bet-your-business objects is the goal. This section looks at your application objects in such an environment.

25.2.3.1 Server-Side Constructs

WLE implements a hierarchy of logical constructs to provide a runtime environment for your objects; each level of construct implements a different control and management function. These management functions begin inside your application objects and extend to a monitoring system that can span hundreds of computer systems. Here is how these under-the-waterline management structures are organized:

Your objects. The WLE system manages your CORBA objects within server processes. You combine your object's implementation with a CORBA skeleton and a group of classes that you inherit from the WLE TP Framework. This framework orchestrates certain kinds of behavior for your object.

Server processes. Your objects execute in WLE server processes. The TP Framework and the Portable Object Adapter (POA) work with the objects in each server process to manage their lifecycle and protect your transactions. WLE can manage many different types of objects within a server process. When a request is routed to a particular server process, its CORBA 2.2-compliant POA routes the invocation to a previously activated object, if one is available. Otherwise, the TP Framework and the POA work together to *activate* the requested object in any available server process. Activation includes loading the object's state from permanent storage— usually from a database.

Server process groups. Server processes belong to server process groups. To get the scalability, availability, and performance that mission-critical applications require, multiple copies of your object implementations can run in different processes of process groups. When a request comes in for a particular object, WLE instantiates the object in one of these processes. It can gracefully shut down and move process groups, run backups of them, and load-balance across them. For additional fault tolerance, you can run backup groups. The same server processes can run in different groups on different machines for further load balancing.

Domains. WLE's highest level of management is the domain, the unit of monitoring and administration. You define administrative domains to more efficiently manage large distributed environments. WLE manages the collection of computers and server process groups as a single unit. You can assign domains based on application function, security needs, or geography.

25.2.3.2 The TP Framework

WLE's TP Framework manages the action in the server processes. It is the primary orchestrator of your objects' activities—the central figure in your objects' lives. You can think of the TP Framework as an encoded design pattern for well-behaved object-based applications. It calls your objects and the WLE services at the right time, in the right sequence. When you use the TP Framework, your objects become managed, transactional, robust, persistent, and high-performing. The framework maximizes the reuse of scarce system resources by your objects.

The TP Framework embodies good transaction processing programming practices. This means that you don't have to learn—or remember to use—them. You inherit these "best practices" when your code inherits the TP Framework's attributes, so the TP Framework can turn even average programmers into great mission-critical application developers. Here are the main activities the TP Framework orchestrates:

Activates and deactivates objects. The Framework works with the POA to bind object implementations to a servant. It also activates and deactivates objects when requests arrive and when they are complete. This ensures that your objects' resources and state are efficiently managed.

Synchronizes object caches with the DBMS prior to transaction commits. This makes object *durability* the responsibility of the DBMS, rather than the programmer.

Handles transactions with the Transaction Coordinator. It can also start transactions if none exist.

Notifies objects of system events. e.g., server shutdown.

The TP Framework is itself CORBA compliant, using CORBA in a particular fashion. This BEA framework is one of the sources for the CORBA Component specification, contributing to the Component Container model. Users of the WLE framework will find CORBA Components quite a natural way of doing things when it becomes available. Enterprise JavaBeans (EJB) is a Java version of CORBA Components optimized specifically for the Java programmer. BEA will use its EJB implementation (in the BEA WebLogic Server) in CORBA Components so you will have multiple choices for your implementation strategy.

25.2.3.3 How WLE Manages Object State

When a method invocation arrives, WLE's ORB works with the Framework and the POA to locate—or *activate*—and invoke an instance of your object. This is the easy part. The question that has plagued object programmers is: When do you *deactivate* objects? By definition, objects include *state*; that is, the data the object's methods work on. If you don't deactivate them, you end up loading more and more objects into memory—until your system grinds to a halt.

One of the secrets of creating a resource-efficient system is to keep objects around (or *active*) only when they are actually being used. The rest of the time they are dormant, even though they appear to be active to clients. To optimize response time and scalability, the TP Framework must control the number of objects that are active in the system at once. So, it invokes your object's *deactivate* method. When the TP Framework calls this method, your object "flushes" its state to a persistent storage mechanism—usually to one or more databases.

The TP Framework supports four models of memory management. Once an object is activated, these are the choices for when to deactivate it:

Per method call. The TP Framework deactivates your object after you return from each method invocation.

On transaction boundaries. The TP Framework interacts with the *Transaction Coordinator* on behalf of your objects. Your object is notified at the end of a transaction with the opportunity to vote on the outcome of the transaction. The Framework will deactivate your object when the transaction completes or rolls back. Until then, your object can respond to multiple object invocations.

On process boundaries. The TP Framework deactivates your object only when your server process terminates. You typically use this policy for long-running, non-transactional objects.

Application controlled. The preceding three models are automatically controlled by the TP Framework. You also have the ability to explicitly deactivate the object based on some application logic.

25.2.4 WLE's ORB Communications

The foundation of WLE's features is in its internal server-side communications subsystem. Instead of connecting clients directly to the servers that run objects they invoke, WLE separates client communication management from message routing and object invocations. Clients use logical object references—WLE routes the invocations to the right objects over a high-speed software switch. This minimizes the server resources required to support large numbers of clients. It also allows load-balancing requests across processes and servers as well as relocating objects during planned or unplanned outages.

The WLE ORB is a CORBA-compliant, interobject communication bus. This ORB is linked directly into your server processes. Behind the scenes, the ORB embeds a high-performance, highly reliable server-side *message switch* to dispatch requests to and from clients and server objects. This switching technology is also used in BEA TUXEDO. The tight integration between the ORB and this switch provides the performance, scale, and availability exhibited by WLE.

The WLE server-side ORB provides a client communications handler system that is designed to support tens—or even hundreds—of thousands of IIOP-based clients. *Listeners* assign clients to *IIOP Handlers* during their bootstrap process. *Handlers* funnel client communications and optimize server resource utilization. Large production environments can run many handlers, often distributed across multiple servers. Listeners balance the incoming client loads across these handlers. The result is a system that can handle a very large number of simultaneous client connections.

Handlers manage client communications—clients don't connect directly to server objects. Clients use their assigned handler for all requests to any object in the domain, regardless of the object's location. WLE routes the request to the object best able to service it. CORBA object references contain the location and identifier of objects. WLE uses them to locate the object you want to invoke and further uses the object's type and unique identifier to route your requests optimally. This allows any standards-compliant IIOP client to invoke an object, while providing for very efficient server-side communications. And WLE can locate (and relocate) objects anywhere in the network at its discretion. This enables it to manage the scale and availability of server objects. It can even move entire server process groups, if necessary, without impacting clients or requiring them to get new object references. In summary, WLE's various communications mechanisms collaborate to create a fast, highly scalable, flexible, and fault-tolerant communications infrastructure.

25.2.5 Clients

Theoretically, there is no difference between clients and servers in the eyes of the ORB—clients can be servers and servers can be clients. This is accurate from a communications point of view, but it not true when referring to the platform that supports the objects. Desktop machines need a lightweight environment that supports a few call-back objects, manages a few outgoing connections, and initiates secure operations, perhaps with transactions. In contrast, the server platform must support millions of objects, tens of thousands of clients, and implement the services that ensure business transactions are completed quickly and securely.

You don't want a featherweight system managing your key transactions on servers, and you don't want a large management environment on your clients. Consequently, the client and server infrastructures of WLE are very different. The server side is a rich, robust, deployment environment. Objects can be invoked from clients running on either a WLE client ORB or an off-the-shelf commercial CORBA ORB.

Clients of a WLE system come in many flavors, currently including:

- Clients that use WLE's own C++ CORBA/IIOP client-side ORB. This ORB runs on Windows NT, Windows 95/98, AIX, Digital Unix, HP-UX, Solaris, with others on the way.

- Clients running other IIOP-based ORBs in any language. This includes Java ORBs and Java clients.

- ORB-enabled Web browsers (e.g., Netscape Communicator).

- OLE/COM clients—using CORBA-compliant COM/CORBA interworking—including BEA's own ActiveX Client.

- Web-based application servers, such as BEA's WebLogic Server.

25.2.6 WLE Deployment Services

The WLE Deployment Services provide the platform support that server-side, mission-critical applications need. These services manage your application objects and server processes to maximize your application's performance, scale, distribution, and availability. They also ensure the security and integrity of your objects and data. Some of these services require no programming at all. For example, fault management, dynamic load balancing, and object location are totally transparent to your clients and objects. Other services require some level of programmer involvement.

WLE's TP Framework and client-side Environmental Objects let you use the Deployment Services with a minimal amount of programming. Most of the time, you will use them to interact with the services instead of using the CORBA APIs yourself—after all, this lets WLE do the work, not you.

25.2.6.1 Fault Management

"What goes up, must come down," so you need to have contingency plans for failures of computers, processes, clients, and networks. In a distributed client/server environment, thousands of independent processors and processes must cooperate to run the application. Many malfunctions can happen. WLE automatically considers such contingencies and keeps the application running in the face of failures in two ways. It ensures that there are no single points of failure by providing replicas of server process groups that can keep going when something breaks, and it restores the running application to good condition after failures occur.

Here is a list of potential failures in distributed application environments and what WLE does to recover from the problem:

Clients terminate. Clients join and leave applications—sometimes voluntarily, sometimes because of failures. WLE tracks clients; it can tell if they leave the application abnormally (for example, because of failures). When clients terminate for whatever reason, WLE releases their operating system resources, as well as the transactions and objects they've invoked.

Server processes terminate. Server processes join and leave applications, too—a normal event that WLE was designed to manage. Sometimes, however, a bug can cause a server process to exit abnormally—or, the server may crash. This is a much more serious problem than when a client fails—many clients and services may be dependent on the failed server class process.

WLE lets you define *replica server processes* that can take over the load. These server processes can be on the same computer or on different computers. When a server process fails, WLE cleans up any inprocess requests and sends a failure indication back to the client or object that originated it. WLE will then forward requests to the replica server processes and will also try to restart server processes that abnormally fail—your operator can specify the number of times it tries.

Computers crash. When a computer crashes, you lose all unsaved data, open sessions, and running processes (except persistent resources). Clients that use the computer as an entry point to the network will hang. Network failures can also make computers appear to have failed. These failures can be permanent or temporary (for example, caused by an overloaded computer or transient network problem). WLE monitors the status of all the computers in its domain. You can specify *backup computers* for groups of server processes. When computer failures occur, WLE reroutes requests to replica server processes in these computers.

Maintenance requires planned outages. Sometimes you need to take a computer out of service for maintenance. WLE can migrate server processes gracefully to a backup computer so that the primary computer can be turned off without impacting the running application.

Networks fail. Networks can fail—they can also be overloaded to the point that they can appear to have temporarily failed. The larger the network, the more likely you are to encounter these failures. Network failures can disrupt a distributed application. During these failures, WLE *partitions* the network into two domains: one on either side of the failure. It then manages each part of the network separately. This management scheme lets the application continue to run despite the failure. When the network is fixed, WLE reintegrates the distributed environment—it heals itself.

Transactions deadlock. In a distributed environment, deadlocks can occur when two components have locked resources while they wait for each other's locks to release. In this situation, WLE times out one of the transactions and rolls it back, thus releasing its locks and breaking the deadlock condition.

As you can see, WLE automatically recovers from many types of failures. However, some failures—often the most serious ones—require operator intervention to determine what has actually failed. The operator can use WLE tools to recover from these failures. The Event Log, for example, contains information about important events across the entire domain (multiple computers), including failures.

25.2.6.2 Transaction Management

An important, integrated feature of WLE is transaction management. WLE is responsible for implementing the mechanisms that guarantee data integrity and error recovery in your distributed, heterogeneous, object-based client/server applications.

WLE protects your transactions' integrity by providing a complete infrastructure for ensuring that database updates are done accurately, even across a variety of *resource managers*, such as databases. WLE includes a CORBA-compatible *Object Transaction Service (OTS)* based on BEA TUXEDO's proven distributed transaction log and XA technology. The Transaction Service implements the CORBA-defined *Transaction Coordinator* that orchestrates your business transactions. These transactions can start from the client, include objects that access a variety of XA-compliant databases, incorporate BEA TUXEDO services, and even update CICS, IMS, and OSI/TP-based applications through BEA Connect.

You can use the OTS objects via the standard CORBA APIs. Alternatively, you can let the TP Framework do this work for you. The TP Framework works with the Transaction Coordinator to make transactions nearly transparent, and certainly foolproof. If you want, you can initiate and end transactions or you can let WLE do it automatically for you. You decide how objects participate in transactions by setting a transactional policy for each of your object classes at design time. The transactional policy indicates to the TP Framework how you want it to include your objects in transactions.

25.2.6.3 The Security Service

It may seem like an oxymoron, but security is essential for open access to applications. The Internet has driven this point home. Enterprises are now extending the applications beyond the corporate walls. They want their customers and suppliers to also access some—but probably not all—of their applications' functions.

To meet these requirements, WLE provides CORBA-compatible authentication, as well as authorization and encryption. Clients authenticate themselves using their *SecurityCurrent* Helper Object. After obtaining an *authorization credential*, clients can then invoke the objects for which they are authorized. Behind the scenes, WLE checks their authorization credentials to permit or deny them access. The Security Service uses the client's credentials to provide three incremental levels of secure access for application objects. Clients provide no information, some information, or specific information about the user, depending on which of these security levels you choose for your application.

25.2.6.4 The Object Location Service

The Object Location Service is responsible for providing object location transparency. This lets WLE distribute objects across processes and machines at its discretion—and, therefore, allows you to dynamically scale your application and recover from failures. This service—like the Load Balancing Service we will discuss next—are infrastructure services, not application controlled services: You never need to call them.

Server process groups are the first step in the location service. An object is associated with a server group, which is a logical, not physical location. The current location of a server group is stored in each computer in the domain. If an operator migrates the server group elsewhere, WLE propagates changes to all computers. Thus, each computer can do rapid routing to the correct computer without having to do "locate" requests.

Once in a computer hosting the server group, WLE consults the *Active Object Map* for that computer. The Active Object Map maintains a memory cache of locations of active objects to obtain ultrafast performance. If the object is active in a server process, control is dispatched to it immediately. If the object isn't already active, WLE turns to its Load Balancing service to determine where the object should be activated.

25.2.6.5 The Load Balancing Service

WLE provides two levels of load balancing: the IIOP Listener/Handler subsystem (discussed earlier) and the *Load Balancing Service*. This dual load-balancing system creates a funnel that maximizes application performance and scalability, while using computer resources efficiently.

The Listener/Handler subsystem balances client connections across handlers. Handlers can be distributed across multiple computers. Larger environments may even allocate some computers to be entirely Listener/Handler machines. This specialization allows these computers to be tuned for communications-handling activities. The handlers concentrate users over network connections; therefore, servers don't need to incur a network connection per user, as with less sophisticated configurations. In a large, enterprise-sized configuration in which handler machines are separate from server machines, there is at most one connection between a server machine and each handler machine, optimizing resources on the server machine. This is particularly important with thousands or tens of thousands of clients. This funneling mechanism frees WLE to dynamically distribute and scale application objects.

On the object side, within a server group, the Load Balancing Service intelligently distributes invocations for inactive objects across available server processes. Its goal is to optimize response time and resource utilization. If WLE receives a request for an inactive object, it analyzes the load conditions of the various server processes. It looks for the least busy location that can run the object and service the request; this determination is made on a per-request basis, not per-client connection, allowing maximum balancing. This activity is transparent to your objects—they just magically scale and handle large client loads.

25.2.6.6 The LifeCycle Service

The *LifeCycle Service* manages a system of *Factory Finders* and *object factories* that let you create and locate objects. On startup, servers register factories with a systemwide Factory Finder. (There can be several Factory Finder servers, all kept synchronized, to spread the load.) When a client starts, it accesses a Factory Finder to find factories that can give it object references of particular types. The client uses a factory to obtain an object reference for a new or existing object, which it then uses normally. The Factory Finder is recommended by the CORBA LifeCycle Service as a pattern of use of a naming service.

Using the Factory Finder pattern aids scalability in several ways. Multiple factories for a given class of objects reduce the load on each; the Factory Finder alternately chooses between available factories, a feature not available in the CORBA Naming Service where one name equals one reference. Next, by consistently getting fresh object references from factories at the beginning of a session, clients allow dynamic reconfiguration to happen more easily. Finally, WLE's LifeCycle Service provides an especially useful *factory-based routing* feature. The (user-written) factory can do application-specific load balancing and even use alternate object implementations.

25.2.7 BEA Manager: Run Anywhere, Manage Anywhere

WLE automates many of the key management functions in a distributed system. Consequently, it requires minimum operator intervention. For example, WLE automatically starts and stops objects, manages them through failure and planned-outage situations, allocates system resources, and balances loads. Of course, you also need to manually manage and control some aspects of your applications. WLE's MIB-instrumented environment lets you monitor, tune, and configure your applications dynamically. You can manage your distributed applications centrally (or decentrally, if you prefer). Your system administrators have a choice of operations consoles: (1) They can manage applications using the Java-based console; (2) They can use an off-the-shelf management environment of their choice; or (3) They can use BEA Manager's programmatic interface, which is used to automate operations functions in unattended environments.

25.3 Vertel's Expersoft: CORBAplus

25.3.1 Overview

Vertel's Expersoft has been developing tools to support distributed object computing for over 10 years. Vertel's Expersoft delivered its first distributed object tool, called "XShell," in 1991. This product evolved into Extended C++ and is still used in production today.

Vertel's Expersoft, armed with five years of real-world, distributed object computing experience, shipped its CORBAplus for C++ product in May of 1996. The CORBAplus product is a CORBA 2.0-compliant Object Request Broker, with many of the extensions from the Extended C++ product.

Today, CORBAplus spans the desktop, across the World Wide Web, to the backend Enterprise Severs with their family of products. Figure 25.1 shows the range of products and how they may be deployed. At the front end, CORBAplus ActiveX Bridge allows Excel, Visual Basic, and other Microsoft COM components to speak CORBA. Web browsers running CORBAplus, Java Edition applets give anyone with Internet access the ability to obtain CORBA services. In the back end, scalable, dependable heavy-duty servers rely upon CORBAplus for C++ with features such as asynchronous communications to deliver those services in a reliable, efficient, and scalable manner. The enterprise-capable infrastructure depends upon services such as Naming and Trader to facilitate object location. Notification services are required to distribute events from suppliers of information to the consumers of that information).

For complete, information regarding Vertel's Expersoft's products, please visit its Web site at www.expersoft.com.

25.3.2 Products

Since the first edition of this book, there have been many additions to the CORBAplus product line. The suite of Vertel's Expersoft CORBAplus products now consists of:

- CORBAplus for C++
- CORBAplus, Java Edition
- CORBAplus, ActiveX Edition
- Event Service
- Relationship Service
- Trader Service
- Notification Service

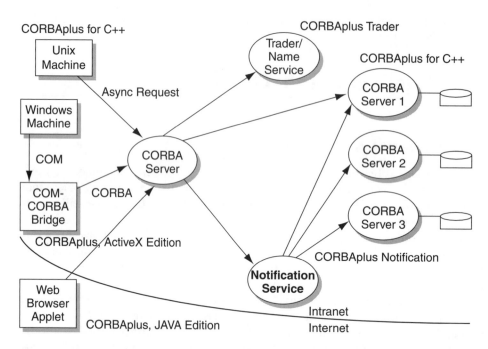

Figure 25.1 CORBAplus Components, how the different pieces of the CORBAplus product line can be used.

25.3.2.1 CORBAplus for C++

CORBAplus for C++ is a fully CORBA 2.0-compliant Object Request Broker. As shown in Figure 25.1, CORBAplus for C++ is suitable for development at any tier in a distributed system. A client application may decide to use standard CORBA-defined services or one of the many extensions such as asynchronous communications, as shown. This would allow the client application to send a request to the CORBA Server and immediately continue processing. The middle-tier CORBA Server would be busy handling the request, contacting backend servers, while the client application is handling the user of the system. CORBAplus supports many additional features, some of which are just now (in early 1999) becoming part of the CORBA specification. These include:

Asynchronous processing. The asynchronous request/response capability of CORBAplus enables an application developer to issue requests without blocking or polling for the response. This is important for requests that take a long time to execute or for applications that make multiple requests in parallel. Asynchronous request/response guarantees that the application won't block, allowing developers to leverage two-way operations without adding the extra complexity associated with multithreading or bidirectional callback architectures.

CORBAplus asynchronous invocations allow clients to make non-blocking requests on a server. The server is not aware of the calling semantics employed by the client.

In general, developers can make any IDL operation asynchronous by adding a pragma directive to the IDL. The IDL compiler generates asynchronous client implementations in addition to the typical synchronous implementations. Client applications may then make synchronous requests on the server, as usual, or make asynchronous requests simply by passing an additional reply-handler parameter.

Asynchronous invocations can be made in single and multithreaded applications. Asynchronous calls may have any legal return type, parameters, and contexts, and they may also raise exceptions.

Interceptor support. CORBAplus supports premarshaling interceptors that allow the clients to add information to a request, unbeknownst to the client application, which can then be extracted by the server, again without the server application being aware. This capability is very important if it is required to send client context information to a server, to perhaps check an access control list for security.

Pass by value. CORBAplus Rogue Wave Integration extends the CORBA standard by allowing both user-defined C++ objects and Tools.h++ objects to be passed-by-value across a CORBA interface. With no limitations to parameter types, CORBAplus accelerates development by eliminating the need to translate familiar types into CORBA types.

Connection event handlers. There are times when a server application needs to know if clients are connected to it. While CORBA goes to great lengths to hide this information, it is necessary for certain applications. CORBAplus allows developers to install either "connection" or "disconnection" event handlers. The event handlers will get an ID of the client that connected or disconnected from the server. This allows for the implementation of efficient distributed garbage collection by the server application. Without this, an inefficient pinging mechanism is required, which has been shown to be unscalable.

Implementation of CORBA::Current. A server object implementation will, at times, need to know information about the client that made the request. For any request, it is possible to get the file descriptor that the request was read from, the port the client is listening on, and the host ID where the client is running. With this information, a Server application can transparently maintain session information for a particular client. Coupled with the connection event handlers, the server can monitor the client and if the client should go away, the server will detect this and clean up any outstanding resources.

Active blocking for synchronous invocations. Single-threaded CORBAplus applications will not block or deadlock while waiting for CORBA response events. When CORBAplus issues a two-way request, it associates an event with the response and dispatches the event loop for the time-out period associated with the request. This allows the client to process events, such as incoming GUI or CORBA requests, while synchronous calls wait for responses. This feature allows developers to avoid writing threaded clients and servers, in most cases, without sacrificing concurrency.

Configurable Governor. The CORBAplus Governor allows developers to specify a runtime limit on the memory usage for a particular Object server. By imposing a memory limit on the incoming event buffer, CORBAplus developers can ensure that their machines and processes are not brought to a halt when their objects are flooded or backlogged with requests. This type of feature is present in today's Web servers but is typically not seen in most ORB implementations. The Governor allows applications to behave predictably under flooded or backlogged periods of time. Without this feature, applications will fail abnormally or behave unpredictably under flooded or backlogged conditions.

CORBAplus provides a static method on the BOA class to specify the number of bytes in the pool of memory a server process allocates for incoming requests. The server then divides the request memory pool evenly among the channels it uses to communicate with clients. When a channel exceeds its share of memory, the event service stops listening until the server processes enough buffered requests to allow it to dip back below its allotment.

Object servers built without a governor can potentially become backlogged by excessive use and large numbers of one-way calls, or can be delayed by blocking activity. Machines running these Object servers would be likely to run out of memory and could hang. Applications would encounter failures on operations that require memory, such as malloc, new, etc.

Dynamic Type Manager. CORBAplus allows you to take full advantage of the capabilities offered by CORBA's dynamic architecture (DII and DSI) from a C++ environment. Using the CORBAplus Dynamic Type Manager (DTM) class, it's possible to issue or receive dynamic responses using types that were unknown at compile time. The DTM allows the application to change with the business while requiring minimum maintenance; applications can manipulate user-defined IDL datatypes (including structs, sequences, and object references) at runtime from C++. The CORBAplus DTM is portable across all supported platforms.

Without the DTM class, developers must either avoid using complex datatypes, recompile applications with the user-defined type #included, or write complicated operating-system-specific code to malloc and free the space associated with manipulating unknown types at runtime.

Open Event Loop Library. The CORBAplus Open Event Loop library provides a mechanism for applications to participate in event servicing. Specifically, it provides an API for installing and removing system event handlers, appending and removing events from the event queue, and allowing other events to be processed while waiting for a blocked operation to complete. The CORBAplus Open Event Loop and associated XpsEventService C++ class make it easy to integrate CORBAplus with Windowing systems (Microsoft, X11, XT), third-party or in-house event-based packages, and legacy event-based applications.

The Open Event Loop is portable across platforms and eliminates the need for developers to write low-level socket code, allowing integration with existing libraries that use custom socket coding. The CORBAplus event loop can accept external file descriptors or user-defined Windows events along with an associated handler method to invoke. The internal event loop can be replaced with a developer-defined event loop, ensuring the greatest possible event loop integration with the lowest development cost.

Portable CORBA Threading Library. CORBAplus is much more than just thread safe. CORBAplus for C++ includes portable threading libraries, making it easy to build servers that support high concurrency, high scalability, and OS portability without requiring developers to implement low-level OS threading.

CORBAplus ships with both single-threaded and multithreaded libraries that provide high-level direct support for many of the common threading patterns used within typical CORBA Servers. The product includes a portable C++ class library that sits on top of native system threads, supporting Threads, Thread Pools, and Mutexes via a high-level OO abstraction. The thread-per-invocation, -object, or -session models can also be supported.

25.3.2.2 CORBAplus, Java Edition

CORBAplus, Java Edition is an implementation of CORBAplus for the Java language. It provides full CORBA-compliant client/server development and runtime capability for Java environments. Because it is written completely in Java, it adds all the inherent benefits of the Java language to those of the CORBA standard. Developers can create a single distributed Java application that is open, flexible, and interoperable across heterogeneous platforms, object models, and languages.

CORBAplus, Java Edition enables interoperable distributed object applications for Internet/intranets and proprietary enterprise computing environments through a Java implementation of the Internet Inter-ORB protocol (CORBA's IIOP standard).

The CORBAplus, Java Edition runtime is pure Java and therefore portable across any platform hosting a Java Virtual Machine. For Internet/intranet browser-based Java applications, the CORBAplus, Java Edition runtime provides full CORBA client/server support and may be downloaded on demand to the target. There is no need for CORBAplus to be preinstalled on the target platform.

As shown in Figure 25.1, CORBAplus, Java Edition can be used either from a Web browser or as a standalone front-end application.

25.3.2.3 CORBAplus, ActiveX Bridge

Vertel's Expersoft's CORBAplus, ActiveX Bridge is an enterprise-class desktop connectivity solution for developing ActiveX applications that span global networks. It provides seamless integration between CORBA applications and applications running on Microsoft Windows desktops. Using the CORBAplus, ActiveX Bridge, developers can take full advantage of the CORBA architecture to build distributed object applications and maintain compatibility with the Microsoft Windows desktop. In Figure 25.1, it would be possible for a spreadsheet program to retrieve information from the back-end servers as well as automatically be notified if a change has occurred and show the change immediately in the spreadsheet.

CORBAplus, ActiveX Bridge supports all of the bidirectional interworkings specified in CORBA 2.0:

- COM to CORBA
- CORBA to COM

- Automation to CORBA
- CORBA to Automation
- Dual Interface to CORBA
- CORBA to Dual Interface

CORBAplus, ActiveX Bridge is fully compliant with the COM-CORBA Interworking Specification, Part A, of the Object Management Group (OMG). It provides complete, bidirectional interoperability between ActiveX (COM, DCOM, Automation, Dual Interface) and CORBA object systems, and supports the OMG Internet Inter-ORB Protocol (IIOP) for communication across the network. An easy-to-use graphical interface provides access to all product functionality, and Just-In-Time (JIT) compilation technology achieves the utmost in performance and simplicity.

25.3.2.4 Trader Service

The Vertel's Expersoft CORBAplus Trader Service is a linked trader conformance class Trader Service. The book you are reading now provides a great overview of the Trader Service in Chapter 11. In Figure 25.1, the middle-tier CORBA Server would use the Trader Service to locate the desired backend CORBA Server based on some offer properties. Each time the middle-tier CORBA Server requests an offer, depending upon the properties that it is looking for, the Trader Service may return zero to three offers.

The Vertel's Expersoft CORBAplus Trader Service comes complete with a persistent Trader Service which persists all options, Trader links and exported offers, libraries to build clients and servers, examples of how to use the Trader Service, documentation, and a GUI administration tool.

The administration tool that comes with the Trader Service allows you to view/modify the attributes of the Trader Service, add/edit Service Types, view the offers in the Trader Service, view/modify/edit any Trader Service links to federate the trading space, and issue queries against a Trader Service and view the offers that are returned. Figure 25.2 is a screen capture of the administration tool showing the Import Attributes for a Trader Service.

25.3.2.5 Notification Service

The Vertel's Expersoft CORBAplus Notification Service is an implementation of the essential features of the CORBA Notification Service. The Notification Service is persistent, which means it will "remember" supplier and consumer connections, as well as the events in the Event Channel. It also provides full support for Generic and Structured events along with QoS properties. The QoS parameters allow you to set the connection and event reliability to either "best effort" or "persistent." You can also specify timeouts on the events to limit the lifetime of the event in the system to ensure that consumers do not receive stale information.

The Notification Service is the enterprise class version of the original Event Service specification. It is designed to meet the needs of more demanding applications. The book you are reading now provides an excellent overview of the Notification Service and its many capabilities in Chapter 12.

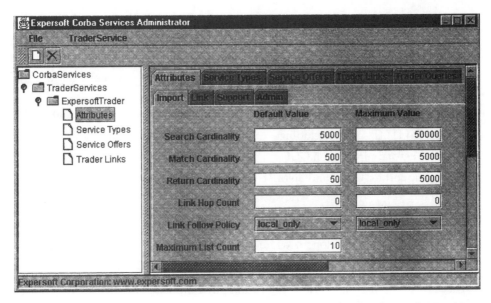

Figure 25.2   Sample screen capture of the Vertel's Expersoft CORBAplus Trader Service.

25.4 IBM WebSphere Product Family

IBM does not market the C++ and Java ORBs used for the IBM implementation of the example as independent products. They are bundled with offerings from the WebSphere product family. IBM WebSphere Application Server is built on open, reusable technologies that leverage your existing resources, shorten development cycles and ease your administrative burden. The Standard Edition lets you use Java servlets, JavaServer Pages and XML to quickly transform static Web sites into vital sources of dynamic Web content. The Advanced Edition is a high-performance EJB server for implementing EJB components that incorporate business logic. The Enterprise Edition integrates EJB and COBRA to build high-transaction, high-volume e-business applications.

The standard Edition, for Web site builders, provides:

- Support for JavaServer™ Pages, including:
  - Support for specifications .91 and 1.0
  - Extended tagging support for queries and connection management
  - An XML-compliant DTD for JSPs
- Support for the Java™ servlet 2.1 specification including automatic user session and user state management

- High speed pooled database access using JDBC for DB2™ Universal Database® Oracle and Microsoft® SQL Server
- XML server tools, including a parser and data transformation tools
- A Web site analysis tool for developing traffic measurement to help improve the performance and effectiveness of your Web sites
- Machine translation for dinamic language translation of Web page content
- An IBM HTTP server, including:
  - A new administration GUI
  - Support for LDAP and SNMP connectivity

- Tivoli Ready™ modules
- Additional integration with IBM VisualAge® for Java to help reduce development time by allowing developers to remotely test and debug Web-based applications
- V3.01 adds support for national languages for Windows NT and AIX

The Advanced Edition, for Web application programmers, provides all the features of the Standard Edition, plus:

- Full support for the Enterprise JavaBeans™ (EJB) 1.0 specification, both session and entity beans
- Deployment support for EJBs, Java servlets and JSPs with performance and scale improvements, including:
  - Application-level partitioning
  - Load balancing

- Enhanced support for distributed transactions and transaction processing
- Improved management and security controls, including:
  - User and group level setup
  - Method level policy and control

The Enterprise Edition, for Web enterprise architects, includes all the features of the Advanced Edition, plus:

- Full distributed object and business process integration capabilities
- IBM's world-class transactional application enviroment integration (from TXSeries™)
- Full support for the Enterprise JavaBeans (EJB) 1.0 specification
- Complete object distribution and persistence
- Support for MQSeries®
- Complete component backup and restore support
- XML-based team development functions
- Integrated Encina application development kit

The Enterprise Edition, which consists of the Component Broker product, is an enterprise implementation for distributed objects, and implements many of the OMG specifications discussed in this book. An overview of Component Broker is provided in the following sections.

25.4.1 IBM Component Broker Overview

IBM Component Broker represents a significant step toward truly distributed object applications deployed in large-scale commercial scenarios. It provides the infrastructure needed to design, implement, deploy, and manage new object applications in multicomputer networks, and at the same time exploits the best in existing systems.

25.4.1.1 Standard Interfaces to Facilitate Reuse

The concept that different implementations can be provided behind well-designed interfaces is central to successful deployment of systems. Reuse of object material from a variety of sources requires that there be widespread agreement on a set of standard interfaces to shape and facilitate development of such reusable material. The Object Management Group (OMG) has defined the standards needed to begin this process in its comprehensive Management Architecture (OMA). IBM Component Broker is an available large-scale infrastructure based on OMG standards to support the use of reusable components.

25.4.1.2 Standard Interfaces to Facilitate Distribution

The concept that objects in one system can communicate with objects in another system across a network is central to the successful deployment of distributed object systems. In a typical enterprise application scenario, the systems used to support object infrastructure will be supplied by different manufacturers, designed to different platform architectures, and managed to different operational guidelines. The OMG has defined the standards needed to facilitate communications between dissimilar systems platforms in Common Object Request Broker Architecture (CORBA). IBM Component Broker is based on CORBA standard interfaces for distribution of object communications (GIOP/IIOP) within networks.

25.4.1.3 Standard Interfaces to Facilitate Management

The concept that objects can be designed to represent a mission-critical business model and then be deployed in a configuration of networked systems determined by operational considerations, such as:

- Security of access

- Usage demand patterns
- Proximity to existing systems

is central to the successful deployment of distributed object systems. The industry is rapidly coming to agreement on standard interfaces for managing such configurations. IBM Component Broker is a commercially available large-scale, cross-platform infrastructure to facilitate management of distributed object applications based on many years of accumulated industry expertise.

25.4.1.4 Tight Integration to Facilitate Operational Reuse

The concept that objects built to standard interfaces can be well integrated with existing systems is central to successful deployment of enterprise-wide distributed object systems. For many applications, operational reuse of programs and data, possibly deployed years ago, cannot be re-implemented using object technology for a variety of very practical reasons. IBM Component Broker is a commercially available large-scale object infrastructure to facilitate operational reuse of database and transactional applications such as those in existing software such as IMS, DB2, CICS, and vendor software systems.

25.4.2 The Component Broker Programming Model

Component Broker applications are collections of client views of a set of business objects managed by the Component Broker runtime environment, CBConnector. It is anticipated that, over time, enterprises will develop and deploy an expanding set of business objects, distributed across a network of Component Broker and other CORBA servers to represent their active business model. As new business objects are added and existing business objects used in new ways, the set of end-user (client) views of the business model will expand to provide new applications. In the Component Broker programming model, each business object has a number of visible client interfaces and an implementation executing in the CBConnector runtime environment according to the OMG CORBA architecture.

Business object interfaces are defined in OMG Interface Definition Language (IDL). Using the CBToolkit Object Builder tools, both client views and implementation skeletons are automatically generated in Java or C++ according to specification. Client views may also be generated with Microsoft ActiveX interfaces for access from Visual Basic programs or ActiveX container applications such as word processors or spreadsheets. Distribution of and communications among client views and Component Broker business objects is achieved using an IBM CORBA-compliant Object Request Broker.

Objects in a business model created using these facilities typically fall into one of several categories defined within the Component Broker Programming Model. Briefly, they are defined according to their intent within the model:

Application objects represent states that encapsulate process or flows of interaction (e.g., conversations and workflow) between clients and business objects in the server.

Business objects represent basic external objects in the enterprise model, which may be used directly or composed into higher-level objects.

Composed Business objects represent higher-level external objects that are dynamically composed from lower-level business objects in the same or different CBConnector runtime environments.

State objects represent persistent states upon which basic business objects are built at execution time.

By separating the types of information about the object, Component Broker objects are assured of long-lasting models and extensibility for the future. The CBToolkit Object Builder provides the necessary facilities for defining and generating your objects within these major categories and other minor categories.

25.4.2.1 Component Broker Object Builder

Using the CBToolkit Object Builder it is possible to import existing object designs from design and modeling tools such as Rational Rose or Select OMT, for extension and refinement and for implementation using Component Broker frameworks. Much of the Component Broker programming model is itself also expressed in Rational Rose notation so that it is easy to see how your enterprise business objects are derived from standard frameworks and how they can be extended. Over time, your libraries of related business object componentry will accumulate within the Object Builder team development environment for easy reuse and adaptation for future applications.

Once object designs have been satisfactorily refined, they must be converted into real implementations and associated client views. Object Builder provides the facilities to generate these components according to the programming model outlined previously. For example, business object skeletons are generated for completion with appropriate business logic in a chosen object-oriented language.

25.4.2.2 The Managed Object Framework

The skeletons are automatically generated using the Component Broker Managed Object Framework so that access to standard CORBA services (such as LifeCycle, Naming, and Transactions) and CBConnector management facilities is straightforward. The use of frameworks in this way by the Object Builder ensures that complexity is minimized and productivity is maximized as business objects and their client views are developed. Each of the frameworks provided may be individually customized to enhance this process.

25.4.2.3 Support for Persistent Data and Legacy Systems

The State Objects needed to provide initial and persistent state for business objects are also generated using Object Builder. These must be customized where existing systems are providing the data source. For example, access to IBM CICS transactions might provide the data source for certain business objects within an enterprise model.

Object Builder provides facilities for mapping transaction interactions to State Object attributes. Metadata such as BMS map definitions and COMMAREA structures involved in such interactions are retained for future reuse. Object Builder also provides the corresponding mappings for relational database tables and other significant resources into State Object attribute values.

25.4.2.4 Generating Component Broker Business Objects and Their Client Views

Once the necessary definitions for business objects have been completed and refined, Object Builder automatically invokes the appropriate compilers to generate executable materials for business objects and their client views. On Microsoft Windows NT platforms and on IBM AIX platforms, the award-winning IBM VisualAge compilers are recommended for use with Component Broker. As an option for Microsoft Windows platform users, CBToolkit Object Builder will also invoke Visual C++ and Visual J++ compilers.

25.4.2.5 Completing the Component Broker Development Cycle

After business objects have been defined and implemented using Component Broker frameworks as outlined, they must be validated for deployment using the CBToolkit trace and debugging facilities. From a CBToolkit development platform (e.g., IBM AIX or Microsoft Windows NT) it is possible to step through business logic encapsulated within Server Objects to ensure their correct execution within the deployment environment (e.g., Microsoft Windows NT, IBM AIX, or IBM OS/390 servers). Critical components in both client and server systems automatically create debugging traces when configured to do so.

The final necessary step in the process used to develop Component Broker applications is to package the Server Objects and their client views for easy installation and validation on their target platforms. CBConnector management runtime facilities assist in completing this final step.

25.4.3 Executing Distributed Object Solutions Using Component Broker

Once a business model has been implemented as a set of objects, it must be deployed in an execution environment that enables efficient access by large numbers of end users. CBConnector is the execution runtime environment of Component Broker. In a CBConnector world, thousands of clients may access business objects distributed in a network of hundreds of runtime environments.

Every business object is defined by its interfaces, expressed in OMG Definition Language (IDL), and realized in server memory by its implementation in Java or C++. Instances of business objects are created on demand by client requests and given object references for access by clients in accordance with CORBA specifications. The instances created within CBConnector runtime are partitioned according to their need (if any) for access to existing systems and the management policies assigned to them. One or more partitions or instance containers may exist at any time within CBConnector runtime environment, and each is under the control of its Application Adapter.

Instances of business objects are known to Component Broker as "managed objects" because they have been implemented using the Managed Object Framework and can be controlled by CBConnector in well-defined ways. This framework not only simplifies the construction of business objects, but also implements a number of inherited behaviors that ensure their orderly runtime performance.

25.4.4 Component Broker Object Services

The implementation of business objects will often involve access to standard CORBA object services. CBConnector provides an implementation of services for lifecycle, identity, naming, security, events, notification, query, concurrency, and transactions—other services will be added over time as they are agreed upon at OMG. The runtime for these services exists within CBConnector runtime environments as a set of automatically instantiated objects available to enterprise business objects according to their needs as follows:

LifeCycle services provide for basic object creation, copy, move, and destruction within the managed domains of CBConnector runtimes.

Identity services provide the mechanism for uniquely identifying object instances from their object references within the managed domains of CBConnector runtime environments.

Naming services provide a mechanism for locating named business objects or collections of them within a network. The Component Broker naming service is based upon DCE Naming standards.

Security services provide authentication checks for clients wishing to access business objects and authorization checks at the class, instance, or method level. The CBConnector implementation is based on DCE Security standards.

Event and Notification services provide business objects with an asynchronous mechanism for communicating with other business objects and for automatic notification of changes from one object to another.

Query services provide an important subset of the OMG Object Query Service interfaces for data retrieval from an underlying database.

Concurrency services provide the locking mechanism that enables sharing of business object state between active clients. This service is used in conjunction with the persistence and transaction services.

Transaction services provide the mechanism for identifying sets of changes to business objects as atomic units of work that may be committed or rolled back as required.

These services are made available to business objects in CBConnector runtime environments via interfaces provided by the Managed Object Framework. This approach not only simplifies the process of accessing CORBA services, but also ensures integrity within the server environment according to specified "policies" at development time.

25.4.4.1 CBConnector Client Enabling

A number of different types of client are supported by facilities. The concept of "thin" clients to CBConnector runtime environments is realized by automatically downloading Java applets and business object proxy interfaces to Web Browsers, such as Netscape, on demand from end-user machines. Java applications may also act as CBConnector clients from stand-alone Appletviewers on a wide range of user platforms. In support of other Web Browser scenarios, CBConnector also provides a gateway for HTML requests to be translated into business object requests flowing over IIOP connections and for the handling of their responses.

For Microsoft Windows desktop systems, CBConnector enables access to business objects by providing ActiveX interfaces to business objects that are callable from Visual Basic, Word Processors, Spreadsheets, and other ActiveX component containers. This capability translates COM interface calls into object requests flowing over IIOP connections into CBConnector runtime environments and handles their response as required.

25.4.5 IBM Summary

The development of Object Technology has reached a level of maturity suggesting that it is now the technology of choice for new computer applications. The Websphere product family's integrated support for serving both CORBA and Sun's Enterprise JavaBeans (EJB) object models may make it the ideal choice for deployment of your server applications.

25.5 Inprise VisiBroker Middleware Products

VisiBroker provides the ease of use, the scalability, and the flexibility required to confront the many challenges of today's complex, heterogeneous application environments. VisiBroker makes good on the promise of the Object Management Group's (OMG's) standard: leveraging emerging Internet technologies, enabling application reuse to improve time to market, and providing a solid, industry standard foundation for mission-critical applications.

The Inprise VisiBroker family of products provides an integrated suite of tools and services to enable the development, deployment, and management of flexible, scalable, and secure distributed object applications throughout your organization, your intranet, and across the Internet.

25.5.1 VisiBroker for Java and C++

VisiBroker for Java, and VisiBroker for C++ provide the means to build and deploy distributed applications that are open, flexible, and interoperable across a wide range of platforms. VisiBroker allows you to take advantage of the opportunities presented by Web-, Internet-, and intranet-based technologies while leveraging the component reuse fostered by object-oriented computing— reducing development cycles and lowering costs. With native support for CORBA's Internet Inter-ORB protocol (IIOP) and ongoing leadership by Inprise staff in the OMG's standards process, VisiBroker enables the development and deployment of truly distributed applications for enterprise computing environments.

VisiBroker provides a unique Smart Agent architecture that provides high availability and fault tolerance needed in mission-critical applications. It also uses sophisticated thread management to maximize the efficiency of heavily loaded VisiBroker applications. Advanced connection management in VisiBroker allow you to maintain control over important network resources.

VisiBroker's modular design provides the ability to plug in additional capabilities and functionality—such as security and transactions—while leveraging the power of the other VisiBroker capabilities. VisiBroker provides OMG IDL interfaces to system utilities for complete control of the ORB through industry-standard interfaces. Finally, customized ORB interactions are supported in VisiBroker through Interceptors and Object Wrappers.

25.5.2 VisiBroker Integrated Transaction Service

Inprise's VisiBroker Integrated Transaction Service (VisiBroker ITS) is the next-generation transaction-management solution for delivering reliable, high-performance distributed object applications. It delivers the features of a traditional TP monitor while meeting the requirements of distributed object applications. VisiBroker ITS simplifies the complexity of distributed transactions by providing an implementation of the CORBA Transaction Service, recovery and logging; integration with databases and legacy systems; and administration facilities—all within a single, integrated architecture.

VisiBroker ITS is built specifically to meet the needs of the new application architecture. Unlike other solutions on the market, VisiBroker ITS is a fully integrated CORBA solution—a reliable, high-performance, fully CORBA-compliant transaction service that's tightly integrated with an underlying Object Request Broker (ORB). Implemented on top of Inprise's award-winning, industry-standard VisiBroker ORB, the Transaction Service leverages the power of the ORB to perform such tasks as multithreading and connection management.

25.5.3 VisiBroker SSL Pack

VisiBroker SSL Pack is an option to Inprise's VisiBroker ORB that provides an introductory level of security. By using SSL Pack, developers can add authentication and encryption capabilities to their distributed applications. Based on industry standards such as RSA's BSafe libraries, SSL comes in two flavors, Java and C++ to, work with the corresponding versions of VisiBroker.

SSL Pack supports the use of digital certificates from vendors such as Verisign. It also includes support for HTTPS, which allow you to have secure applets running in your Web browser without having to do any client-side setup.

The Java version of the SSL Pack works with both Netscape Navigator Versions 3.x and above and Microsoft's Internet Explorer versions 3.x and above. Additionally, the Java version of the SSL Pack can work with both Java applications and Java applets.

For Java applets, no client-side administration is required. For Java applications, a client-side installation is provided.

25.5.4 VisiBroker Gatekeeper

VisiBroker Gatekeeper allows your enterprise computing environment to extend beyond your corporation's firewall. By transparently providing a proxy mechanism between applets and server objects, VisiBroker Gatekeeper allows applets to escape the limitations of Java "sandbox" security without compromising functionality such as callbacks. Support for HTTP tunneling is also built into Gatekeeper providing even more flexibility to companies concerned with firewall administration and configuration.

VisiBroker Gatekeeper enables your VisiBroker applications to work within your network infrastructures and environments while maintaining their integrity.

25.5.5 VisiBroker Naming Service

VisiBroker Naming Service helps developers cope with the increasing complexity of large-scale distributed computing. Providing a mechanism to associate meaningful names to individual object implementations, VisiBroker Naming Service reduces the complexity of locating and retrieving objects from the thousands of objects available.

The VisiBroker Naming Service is a CORBA-compliant solution ensuring the flexible, heterogeneous interoperability required by today's enterprise computing environments.

25.5.6 VisiBroker Event Service

The VisiBroker Event Service is an implementation of the OMG's CORBA Event Service specification and extends the capabilities of the VisiBroker ORB to include alternative communication mechanisms needed by event-based tasks. Through support for asynchronous invocations, VisiBroker Event Service allows the decoupling of the traditional clients and servers and transforms applications into information suppliers and information consumers. This supplier-consumer model reduces server traffic and improves scalability without impacting development efforts.

25.5.7 VisiBroker for OS/390

VisiBroker for OS/390 allows organizations to gain a competitive advantage by enabling new business opportunities based on distributed Internet/intranet applications to be developed and deployed in a mainframe environment. While ensuring that mission-critical applications continue to operate securely on the trusted mainframe platform, VisiBroker for OS/390 provides the reuse needed to integrate existing applications into the emerging distributed environment. VisiBroker for OS/390 allows enterprises to bring critical applications to production faster by reducing the time needed to develop and to deploy new applications. Support for the CORBA standard ensures that investments in skills and application development will be preserved as the needs of the business change.

VisiBroker for OS/390 provides a complete environment for developing CORBA applications on your mainframe systems that can be accessed from any language on any platform through industry-standard IIOP protocols.

VisiBroker for OS/390 applications maintain all of the benefits, the scalability, and the reliability provided by the VisiBroker architecture and, in addition, provide tight integration with mainframe security. VisiBroker extends the reach of these proven mainframe capabilities to your distributed applications without compromising security or reliability.

25.5.8 Inprise AppServer

Inprise Application Server builds on a proven foundation of VisiBroker, the Integrated Transaction Service (ITS), and industry standards such as CORBA, IDL, C++, Java, and HTML. It integrates the heterogeneous enterprise environment including Web servers, database servers, multiple languages, multiple platforms, and legacy environments. Enterprise applications can be developed utilizing technologies already in place, which enables companies to focus on timely and cost-effective solutions.

Inprise Application Server includes Inprise AppCenter, which provides robust distributed application management tools for ensuring a reliable production environment and less downtime. Developers and administrators can use the Java-based console to model, monitor, and manage distributed applications. Operators can then use the Pure Java AppCenter Console to monitor and manage individual objects, groups of objects, and customized views of the whole application. The AppCenter management tools ensure that business can be conducted in a stable 24×7 environment.

25.5.9 Future Outlook

The next major release of VisiBroker will be VisiBroker 4.0, due out Q3 1999. Amongst other things, this release will support the Portable Object Adapter (POA), valuetypes (OBV), GIOP 1.2, and a new Interceptor API. Inprise is also making use of VisiBroker for Java in its upcoming EJB implementation. For more information on VisiBroker and other distributed object technology products from Inprise, please visit www.inprise.com.

25.6 IONA Orbix

25.6.1 Introduction

IONA Technologies is committed to Making Software Work Together. One of the major challenges facing organizations today is the integration of diverse IT systems across language, platform, and network boundaries. IONA addresses this challenge through the provision of middleware products and services, most notably the Orbix product suite. Over 4000 organizations around the world currently use IONA's products to integrate today's diverse software systems.

25.6.2 Product Overviews

25.6.2.1 Orbix

Overview

IONA's Orbix provides organizations with a proven standards-based approach to making diverse, cross-platform computer systems work together. The latest release, Orbix 3, is a faster, more powerful, and robust version of IONA's flagship product. It offers new features that promote ease of use, flexibility, and scalability all in one box. It gives developers the tools they need to build middleware applications across traditional IT language, platform, and networking boundaries. Through its compliance with the CORBA standard, Orbix 3 allows IT systems to evolve over time by offering support for new and existing technologies. The result is a middleware solution that protects and enhances any investment in IT.

Orbix 3 is currently available on Microsoft NT/Windows 95, Sun Solaris, HP-UX 10-20 (ANSI C++, C-Front), and HP-UX 11 (ANSI). Features included in Orbix 3 are, among others, COM-CORBA integration using OrbixCOMet, location transparency and load balancing using OrbixNames, rapid application development with the Orbix Code Generation Toolkit, and built-in Internet security using Orbix Wonderwall.

COM-CORBA Integration with Orbix COMet Desktop

OrbixCOMet Desktop is an exciting development that combines the best of CORBA and COM (Microsoft's Component Object Model), giving developers the ability to build systems using both COM and CORBA components. This high-performance bidirectional dynamic bridge enables COM applications—written using tools such as Visual Basic, PowerBuilder, Delphi, MS Office, or Active Server Pages—to access CORBA applications running on Windows, Unix, and the mainframe. In January 1998, IONA Technologies and Microsoft entered into a technology agreement under which Microsoft provides IONA with the source code for COM.

Location Transparency and Load Balancing with OrbixNames

OrbixNames is IONA's implementation of the CORBA Naming Service. It acts as a central repository of objects that clients use to locate server applications. A CORBA server that holds an object reference can register it with OrbixNames, giving it a fixed name that can be used by any client to subsequently find that object. If the server is moved, it can associate its new object reference using the same fixed name, providing location transparency to the client. OrbixNames extends the CORBA naming model, providing load balancing of servers through replication. Developers can choose from a variety of server-side selection algorithms to optimize the performance of their system in deployment.

Rapid Application Development with the Orbix Code Generation Toolkit

Orbix's code generation toolkit is a powerful addition to any CORBA programmer's toolkit. Ready-to-run scripts called "Genies" aid in the development of Orbix and OrbixWeb applications. This Rapid Application Development (RAD) tool dramatically reduces development time by automating many repetitive coding tasks. IONA's Genies are easy to extend and customize to suit the exact requirements of your task. Alternatively, you can write your own Genie that can be used with IONA's Code Generation Tool. Using this tool you can autogenerate gateways to COTS (commercial off-the-shelf) applications, create demos quickly, or easily modify your existing CORBA applications.

Built-in Internet Security with Orbix Wonderwall

IONA's industry-leading IIOP firewall technology, Orbix Wonderwall, provides the protection required for Internet CORBA systems. Wonderwall filters IIOP messages to provide fine-grained access control for backend objects and also provides transparent traversal on the client side. Wonderwall features a powerful logging facility for tracing the history of suspicious message exchanges. Orbix and OrbixWeb support callbacks using bidirectional IIOP and both ORBs integrate with OrbixSSL, which provides authentication, privacy, and integrity for IIOP traffic on the Internet.

25.6.2.2 OrbixWeb

Overview

OrbixWeb is IONA's award winning Java-CORBA development environment that provides Java developers with a powerful middleware solution that enables the creation of compelling applications tying Java technology to other broadly used platforms including the Mainframe, Unix, and Windows. OrbixWeb 3 offers Java developers the tools they need to build rich applications that integrate Java and the Internet with the rest of the organization's IT systems. Building CORBA systems for the Internet requires technology that provides a secure infrastructure, and is capable of scaling from thin clients to back-end servers. It also requires a portable pure-Java ORB with the flexibility to allow you to configure and deploy large-scale Web-enabled Internet systems. OrbixWeb 3 gives Java programmers the power to access, through a common interface, applications written in languages such as C++, COBOL, and PL/1.

Orbix Wonderwall is included in OrbixWeb 3. Orbix Wonderwall, IONA's IIOP firewall technology, provides the protection needed for Internet CORBA systems. Wonderwall filters IIOP messages to provide fine-grained access control for backend objects, as well as transparent traversal on the client side. In addition, version 3.1 delivers new GUI tools; complete support for the most popular Java RAD tools, including Symantec's Visual Café; enhanced debugging tools; and support for enterprise services such as transactions and security. OrbixWeb 3 is available on Windows NT, Hewlett-Packard UX, and Sun Solaris platforms.

25.6.2.3 OrbixOTM—Orbix for the Enterprise

Overview

OrbixOTM is Orbix for the Enterprise, an integrated suite of enterprise middleware services. OrbixOTM provides components with a rich set of services including systems management, directory services, security, and transactions. It combines the component service infrastructure of an application server with the robustness and extensibility of the market-leading Orbix middleware. OrbixOTM is an application container that provides an environment into which multi-language components can be developed, integrated, and deployed.

OrbixOTM 3, the latest release of the OrbixOTM application container, introduces Java client and server support for OrbixOTM services and consolidates encryption and firewall technologies to guarantee fully secure middleware applications for the Internet. OrbixOTM 3 features include:

Java client and server functionality for OrbixOTM Services, including:

Management

SSL Security

Transactions

Names

Secure CORBA Internet link through combined middleware, firewall, and standard encryption technology. Firewall access control for Internet CORBA communication is provided via Orbix Wonderwall, which has been upgraded to support SSL V3.0. The OrbixOTM 3 SSL-based container security mechanism can now be used in conjunction with Wonderwall, providing both access control and data privacy for Internet Inter-ORB Protocol (IIOP) requests.

Extended enterprise middleware integration. The integration of OrbixCOMet with OrbixOTM 3 offers organizations a more flexible approach to building integrated enterprise systems. OrbixCOMet allows Windows applications to communicate with nonWindows platforms and allows organizations to combine CORBA and COM-based applications.

Manageability. The ability to track, monitor, and actively intervene in server behavior (OrbixManager).

Directory Service/Deployment Support. Naming and load-balancing services for component lookup and system optimization (OrbixNames).

Security. Data privacy and integrity for secure Internet communication and e-commerce transactions (OrbixSSL).

Messaging. Decoupled communication to enable scaling and asynchronous message delivery (OrbixEvents).

Transactionality. Guaranteed system integrity and consistency through a full Object Transaction Service (OrbixOTS).

OrbixOTM 3 will be shipping from Q2 1999, with initial availability on the Windows NT, HP-UX, and Sun Solaris platforms.

25.6.2.4 Orbix for OS/390

Overview

Orbix for OS/390 enables developers to build applications that transparently leverage mainframe resources, transactions, applications, and data from anywhere in the network. As a result, the mainframe can be completely integrated with other corporate resources such as Unix, Windows, OS/2, and even Java. Orbix on the mainframe is being used in production today by organizations revitalizing their legacy data to deliver new levels of performance and interoperability. Orbix for OS/390 is available in two versions, one for the traditional mainframe (batch and TSO) environment and one for the newer Unix Services environment. The Orbix IMS Adapter and Orbix CICS Adapter permit new Orbix servers to be developed and deployed within the respective environment in COBOL, and enable the retrofitting of existing IMS and CICS programs into a CORBA framework without any need for change.

Recent additions to the OS/390 product family include Orbix SSL, Orbix Manager support, and a PL/I language binding and object adapter. These new products enhance the effectiveness of the Orbix for OS/390 family by enabling the integration of traditional proprietary mainframe systems with new technologies such as Application Servers or e-business tools. The mainframe can, therefore, be a full peer partner in the dynamic world of modern IT.

Orbix for OS/390 gives you the power to integrate mainframe resources—transparent flexibility to deploy critical systems on the mainframe and migrate noncritical systems, the benefits of a service-based architecture via CORBA's interface definition language, and the ability to harness both CICS and IMS deployment environments.

Technical Features of Orbix for OS/390

Orbix for OS/390 is a full implementation of the Orbix C++ product (features include an IDL compiler that runs on this platform).

- Includes Orbix COBOL support.
- DB/2 and SAF demos included.
- JCL/PROCs for Orbix program development.
- ISPF and TSO support for the Orbix utilities.
- Configuration files are stored in native file formats.

25.6.2.5 Messaging

Overview

OrbixTalk is IONA's messaging support service for distributed systems. It is quick to build, massively scalable and offers a choice of reliable or guaranteed semantics through its unique MessageStore persistence technology. OrbixEvents, an implementation of the OMG's Event Service, allows clients to communicate with application objects using events. Suppliers generate events, and consumers receive them. Orbix Notification is an implementation of the CORBA notification service. Orbix Notification brings standards-based Quality of Service to messaging for the first time. It extends IONA's messaging product set to offer content-based filter and routing of messages.

25.6.3 History

IONA Technologies was founded in 1991 with the vision of Making Software Work Together. The company was founded by Chris Horn, Annrai O'Toole, and Sean Baker, all of whom had been active in the distributed computing field prior to founding the company.

Orbix, released in 1993, was the culmination of over a decade of research and development, and has since become the leading CORBA middleware solution. The Orbix product family has been continually extended, and now runs on more than 15 platforms including mainframe, Unix, Windows, and the Internet, and encompasses transactions support, messaging, security, and system management—all the prerequisites of large-scale enterprise development.

IONA Technologies is headquartered in Dublin, Ireland, with its U.S. headquarters in Waltham, Massachusetts, and has offices around the globe. IONA Technologies (IONAY) was launched on the U.S. NASDAQ market on February 26, 1997. It was the fifth largest software IPO in the exchange's history.

25.6.4 Services and Partners

IONA Professional Services provides comprehensive training and consulting services worldwide. IONA's partner marketing program now includes over 400 systems integrators, consultants, and software vendors who are committed to IONA and Orbix. In addition, IONA is working with many of the world's leading IT companies such as Microsoft, Sun Microsystems, Compaq, Hewlett-Packard, NEC, Oracle, Symantec, PLATINUM, and Silicon Graphics to deliver the best middleware solutions available.

25.6.5 More Information

For more information on IONA Technologies, visit their Web site at www.iona.com, or to order an evaluation of IONA's Orbix product suite, go to their Web Store at www.iona.com/online/ or e-mail info@iona.com.

25.7 Merant: Supporting CORBA in COBOL

Mainframe COBOL and CORBA may initially appear to be technologies that are orthogonal to each other. However, it should be remembered that the underlying goal of CORBA is the use of an object model to solve the problem of developing distributed components written in different languages within a heterogeneous environment. Given the large investment that many corporations have in mature technologies such as COBOL, it is not just desirable but vital for CORBA to support COBOL. Without a COBOL enabling for CORBA, an enterprise would be left high and dry, and not be able to take advantage of its investment in the more historic technologies.

At the time of writing, the only ORB supporting the OMG COBOL language mapping is Iona's Orbix. However, it is expected that other ORB vendors will probably also extend their ORB functionality into this arena. This will come about as a natural extension to ORB functionality as they are ported to mainframes where COBOL support is required due to its prolific usage within that context.

Alternative solutions may also be applied in some instances where direct support of COBOL is not available. The COBOL compiler vendor, Micro Focus, supports a wrapping technology within its NetExpress product for a COBOL application presenting a well-defined callable interface. This involves the automatic generation of C++ wrappers around the COBOL, thus enabling it to be distributed as a C++ object. It may also, of course, be used to generate Orbix COBOL wrappers.

25.7.1 IONA Technologies: Orbix

Orbix, from IONA Technologies, is currently not only the leading ORB in the market, but is also the first to support the OMG COBOL language mapping. Initially, Orbix started its product life as an ORB with a specific emphasis on C++; however, as its horizon has expanded into the mainframe arena, the addition of COBOL support has been added to the matrix of other languages and features that it now supports.

For a more general overview of Orbix, see the description of Orbix in Section 25.6.

The Iona implementation of the COBOL Language mapping is known as OrbixCOBOL. It is an implementation of the Dynamic COBOL Language mapping as specified by OMG, and is available, not only for MVS, but also for other platforms such as Windows NT.

25.7.2 OrbixCOBOL Components

The OrbixCOBOL support consists of the following two components:

- An implementation of the Dynamic COBOL Mapping functions. This is basically a collection of functions that can be called using a standard COBOL CALL statement. Together they provide COBOL application developers with a completely portable ORB development environment.

- gencbl: The OrbixCOBOL generation utility that extracts Interface details from the Orbix Interface Repository and generates COBOL copy files. The generated COBOL copy files may be used in conjunction with the mapping routines to provide complete CORBA support in COBOL for a specific interface.

25.7.3 Creating an OrbixCOBOL Application

OrbixCOBOL allows COBOL application developers to quickly and easily create distributed COBOL applications. The complete development cycle for distributed Orbix-COBOL applications is typically as follows:

1. Define the interface, using the standard Interface Definition Language (IDL).

2. Compile the IDL and populate the Interface Repository using the standard Orbix IDL compiler. The –R command-line option directs it to put all the interface details into the Orbix Interface Repository.

3. Generate COBOL support files using the `gencbl` utility. This will result in the following files being generated:

   `<interface-name>.cpy`—The complete parameter layout for all operations and attributes within the interface.

   `<interface-name>X.cpy`—Internal support data for the interface.

   `<interface-name>D.cpy`—Operation selection code for the interface implementation.

4. Implement the interface in COBOL.

5. Write a server trigger that will handle server initialization and then inform Orbix when initialization has been completed and the server is ready to accept requests.

6. Register the server with Orbix.

7. Write a client that will connect to, and use, the server.

25.7.4 An Alternative Strategy: Wrapping COBOL

If an ORB does not support the OMG COBOL Language mapping, does that mean that COBOL application developers are locked out? No, because a viable alternative approach is to wrap the COBOL using a language binding that is supported, such as C or C++.

Hand-crafting a wrapper around legacy COBOL is not only a tedious task, but is also potentially very error prone. Luckily, there are tools available that can be used to automate this process. The NetExpress COBOL development environment, which is available from Micro Focus, provides support for several popular CORBA implementations.

When processing a COBOL application that presents a well-defined callable interface for ORB support, NetExpress may be used to do the following:

- Generate IDL that describes the interface to the COBOL application.

- Generate wrappers around the COBOL for a variety of different CORBA implementations. The wrappers will not only provide specific ORB support, but will also convert COBOL datatypes that cannot be described using IDL into types that can.

For further details, refer to www.microfocus.com/.

25.7.5 The Real Challenge

In a pure academic world, the ideal approach for the development and deployment of distributed applications is fundamentally a revolutionary one: "All legacy should be discarded and new distributed applications should be properly designed from scratch."

Meanwhile, back in the real world, a migration path is needed from current legacy solutions into the world of distributed business solutions. While some may be able to afford the luxury of designing and deploying new systems without giving any real consideration to legacy, most will find that they have to retain their current investment and reuse it in order to stay within budget and also meet tight time constraints. It is very ironic that Object Technology purists who advocate that reuse is one of the key benefits of OO are not prepared to endorse the reuse of legacy as a viable strategy.

There are many corporations out there that have a heavy investment in legacy systems, many of which are written in COBOL. It will be vital for them to be able to migrate these well-proven systems forward so that they can be Web enabled. However, one vital point to recognize is that having a COBOL mapping for CORBA or a COBOL mapping for any other distribution technology is not a complete solution. The challenge within this arena is the transformation of legacy business logic into a format that is suitable for distribution. For example, you should never expose 12 CICS transactions by defining an IDL interface with 12 operations that match the 12 CICS transactions exactly. What really needs to be done is the definition of an IDL interface that describes the service that is to be provided. This can then be implemented using your 12 CICS transactions. The fact that it is implemented using CICS, or some other technology, should always be completely hidden from anybody using it. This is a basic principle that should always be adhered to when migrating COBOL into a CORBA environment.

The real challenge facing COBOL application developers who wish to migrate legacy systems into a distributed architecture using the CORBA COBOL Language mapping is understanding how to transform their business logic into a form that can be distributed.

Today, tools are starting to emerge that may be used to both pull apart legacy systems and automatically extract reusable segments of business logic, or identify business services and automatically encapsulate them with well-defined interfaces.

Details regarding such tools are beyond the scope of this current publication. However, they should still be recognized as a vital part of the story for COBOL application developers who wish to consider using CORBA as a business solution for their enterprise. For details of transformation technology solutions such as these, contact Micro Focus, or refer to their Web page at www.microfocus.com.

25.8 PeerLogic DAIS

25.8.1 Implementing Distributed Solutions

DAIS, the Enterprise ORB, is designed to simplify the development, deployment, and operation of large-scale, mission-critical, distributed systems. To implement these solutions in today's highly distributed and complex environments, developers must resolve not only communication issues between mixed hardware and software, but security and data integrity issues as well. Adding to the complexity, distributed communication can be implemented in a variety of ways with synchronous, asynchronous, and broadcast mechanisms. Distributed solutions must also maximize the benefits of new technologies while continuing to allow integration with legacy systems.

Understanding the issues is one challenge; however, evolving a well-architected solution that will work for businesses in the real world is another. The number of standards and products available in today's marketplace further complicates this. Consider solving a jigsaw puzzle when all the pieces have been mixed up with other puzzles. Not only do you have to discover which pieces fit together; you have to ensure that the pieces you select solve your particular puzzle.

The Object Management Group's (OMG) Common Object Request Broker Architecture (CORBA) is an excellent choice for integrating legacy systems with each other and with the latest development tools. The CORBA architecture is based on standards, emphasizes portability and interoperability between ORB products, and supports a wide variety of development languages across a wide range of hardware platforms. Its component architecture allows development teams to focus on areas of expertise, develop new skills, and, more importantly, evolve existing systems. For example, imagine a team of C language developers working on a legacy database system. The CORBA IDL C mapping that DAIS supports allows existing C developers to learn CORBA using a language and system they are familiar with to build CORBA components that fully participate in distributed environments. Once encapsulated, the legacy database can be accessed by existing applications and new applications implemented with other technologies such as Web browsers, word processors, spreadsheet applications, and mail systems. However, the success of this scenario depends largely on the strength of the ORB implementation, its ability to integrate both new and old technologies, and its ability to be managed as part of a larger system.

25.8.2 Origins

Initially developed by ICL, DAIS is now developed by PeerLogic, Inc. The agreement, completed in August 1998, supported strategic initiatives for both companies. ICL, undergoing a major shift in direction, was adopting a strategy to focus on systems and services. PeerLogic, founded in 1986 and a pioneer in the market for Message-Oriented Middleware (MOM), was expanding its enterprise middleware offering. With the acquisition of DAIS, PeerLogic added an industrial-strength ORB to its advanced messaging middleware product line and strengthened its product offering to provide a more complete enterprise computing solution.

DAIS originated from the ANSA research program, which had a significant influence on both the OMG architecture and the ISO Open Distributed Processing Reference Model. The product, launched in October 1993, won the British Computer Society award for technical innovation in 1994 when it was used to demonstrate a prototype heterogeneous DBMS system. Although only a prototype, this system illustrated how component layers encapsulate underlying complexities. The DAIS ORB implicitly handled the network and platform layers, while the applications presented a single view of the distributed business data. Today, this may appear trivial; however, in 1993 the concept of ORBs and object technology was still new and little understood.

Today, components are essential, and when layered they provide levels of transparency to handle security, data integrity, and system management. DAIS has evolved from a rich set of core features, largely inherited from the ODP model, to focus on key CORBA services such as Event, Transactions, and Security. DAIS was the first CORBA ORB to support the concept of Trading; the first ORB to demonstrate a CORBA security with Level 2 conformance; and the first ORB to supply a native CORBA Transaction Service implementation without relying on third-party software. More recently, it was the first ORB to support the CORBA Portable Object Adapter (POA).

25.8.3 Core ORB Features

DAIS is a high-performance, distributed ORB that includes features designed for application resilience, manageability, and scalability.

25.8.3.1 Capsule Management

Capsule management enables CORBA objects to be organized as part of a containment tree, the root of which is the capsule object. The term "capsule" was inherited from ODP and is analogous to the application process. Each DAIS application contains a capsule object that is the root of a containment tree. The tree contains nodes for each CORBA object created by the application. Using DAIS, application developers have the option to exploit the containment tree to create explicit relationships (parent, child) and maintain integrity between objects. In order to exploit these features, DAIS supports the Extended Object Adapter, which is similar but more powerful than the simple Basic Object Adapter supported by CORBA. With the arrival of the Portable Object Adapter, developers now have a choice as to which model they wish to implement. It is likely that the POA will include some of the features of the capsule architecture since the capsule architecture has certain manageable and scalable properties that allow a process to be handled as an object. The capsule object can be remotely managed along with all of the objects contained within its containment tree. DAIS provides specific services that exploit capsule management to dynamically create processes and objects on demand. When the capsule object receives a request to terminate a process, all objects in the containment tree are closed in an orderly fashion.

25.8.3.2 Role of Transparencies and Interceptors

When invocations are made on DAIS CORBA objects, the requests are subject to a number of transparencies that resolve all the underlying issues associated with the request. DAIS supports a number of transparencies in addition to the standard marshaling of data supported by all ORBs. Transparencies match the attributes of the request against the attributes of the target object and select the necessary resources to support the binding between the two.

> **DAIS can optimize the code sequence when it detects calls where the invocation is made on an object in the same process.** Such calls do not invoke any network routines.

DAIS supports a number of network protocols. Each capsule (application process) builds a set of protocols supported by the host machine. This allows it to dynamically switch from one protocol to another when handling or invoking requests between different objects. For example, an object may use IPC for a local request, TCP for a remote request, and IIOP for another. The network protocol set for a set of DAIS applications is configurable. Since IIOP is the CORBA standard, some environments may choose to configure it as the single protocol. However, the remaining protocols are still relevant for backward compatibility and performance tuning.

DAIS also has built-in transparencies for recovery. A client request may fail or time out because the target object is not responding or because the server application has crashed. In the event of a crash, an alternative server may be available to handle the request, and DAIS will direct the original client request to the backup server.

DAIS supports a number of specialized transparencies that are called "interceptors." DAIS uses interceptors when the ORB supports additional features such as transactions and security. Interceptors act on specific requests and perform additional tasks based on information supplied with the request. For example, in the case of security, interceptors may examine a request for appropriate credentials to authenticate the user and determine whether the request itself has the right to bind to the object, and vice versa. It will also determine whether the request has any confidentiality or integrity constraints. Transactional requests require a transaction context that is both supplied and later processed by a set of interceptors that exist throughout the life of the transaction. Transactional interceptors will exist in each transactional application to handle the events of the two-phase commit process. The existence of additional transparencies creates additional overheads to the request. However, the DAIS architecture is designed to minimize additional network invocations by handling extra tasks either within the same process or in the same host environment.

25.8.3.3 Concurrency and Threads

DAIS maintains a strong threads architecture. Even before thread APIs were widely adopted, DAIS provided a nonpreemptive, lightweight, multithreading model that was portable across all hardware platforms. This model enabled multithreaded applications to run on operating systems such as Windows 3.11. Threads allow ORBs to handle multiple concurrent requests on one or more objects within the same process. With the emergence of preemptive multithreaded programming and support across most platforms, DAIS now offers both thread models, which can be selected dynamically at runtime. Although DAIS uses threads implicitly, developers can configure the size of the thread pool for each process and control the maximum concurrency of each object. In addition, DAIS supports a set of thread APIs that can be called explicitly. In the preemptive model, the thread APIs mask the underlying operating system APIs so that applications remain portable. However, an experienced thread developer may not wish to learn a new set of APIs and may call the native thread APIs in the same DAIS application.

25.8.4 DAIS ORB Services

Built on top of the DAIS ORB are a number of services designed to provide superior performance, flexibility, and key enterprise functionality. A number of these services are implementations of standard CORBA services. Here a brief outline of each of these services is given next.

25.8.4.1 Interface Repository

The DAIS Interface Repository Service is an implementation of the CORBA Interface Repository and is supplied as part of the DAIS runtime. It provides a central repository for IDL interfaces and can be used to provide definitions of CORBA objects relevant to the system. More importantly, it can be used in conjunction with the Dynamic Invocation Interface (DII) and Dynamic Skeleton Interface (DSI) to build applications that determine how to handle components at runtime. An application with no knowledge of a component's services can query the Interface Repository to determine how it can interact with the component, and then use DII to create invocations on that component. The converse is also true. An application can act as the component itself by querying the Interface Repository and using DSI to respond to queries on its own implementation of a component. The application of this technology makes it possible to build generic components or build application-specific interceptors.

25.8.4.2 Trader Service

The DAIS Trader Service provides a directory for advertising and dynamically locating services offered by objects. Even though many of the concepts adopted by the CORBA Trader specification originated from the DAIS Trader Service, the DAIS Trader Service predates the CORBA Specification and consequently is not fully CORBA conformant. A Trader Service provides a comprehensive mechanism for locating objects based on constraints provided by the caller. Constraints allow the Trader to distinguish between objects that have the same type, but different characteristics. This concept is not included in the Naming Service architecture, which is the CORBA alternative for discovering objects. The DAIS Trader exploits capsule management services to support recovery and process automation ("objects on demand"), functionality not included in the CORBA Trader. DAIS Trader domains can be organized logically and linked together for scalability and fault tolerance. For example, Trader domains can be organized to suit network attributes so that a local service will always be used in preference to a similar remote service. Also, trading domains can be linked so that if an object is not available to satisfy a local request, the Trader can resolve the request by locating an object outside the local domain. A DAIS Trader can be mirrored (secondary trading), so that if the Trader fails, a secondary Trader will automatically handle the requests. The DAIS Trader is currently supplied as part of the DAIS runtime environment.

25.8.4.3 Naming Service

The DAIS Naming Service is an implementation of the CORBA Naming Service. Like the DAIS Trader Service, it allows objects to discover each other. The difference between a Naming Service and a Trader Service is that a Naming Service has a one-to-one binding with an object, and a Trader Service has a one-to-many binding. In effect, the Naming Service is like the telephone directory "white pages," and the Trader service is like the telephone directory "yellow pages."

25.8.4.4 Event Service

The DAIS Event Service is an implementation of the CORBA Event Service. In addition to the CORBA Event Service, it supports mechanisms that exploit the underlying network properties. Events involve the delivery of messages from one or more message suppliers to one or more message consumers. By exploiting the multicast properties of TCP/IP, DAIS delivers messages to one or more consumers in a single network call.

25.8.4.5 Object Transaction Service

The Object Transaction Service is an implementation of the CORBA Transaction Service. A set of object invocations is grouped as an atomic unit that will either succeed or fail. In the event of failure, the ORB initiates recovery mechanisms. In terms of determining what is recoverable, DAIS supports both CORBA resources and X/Open XA resources. The significance of the DAIS implementation is its underlying architecture. DAIS OTS is designed for performance and implements the CORBA concept of interposed management. Each DAIS capsule (application process) that supports transactions has a local Transaction Manager (Interposed Manager) that propagates transactional data on the back of the object invocations that make up the transaction. This minimizes network costs. Other performance gains are made through configuration. DAIS supports local or remote logging, and checked or unchecked transactions. The very nature of distributed transactions makes them complex to manage. Although a Transaction Monitor can recover itself, the time it takes to handle recovery will impact downtime. DAIS has configuration options that enable comprehensive system testing and establish whether the applications are handling sensible transactions.

25.8.4.6 Security Service

The DAIS Security Service was the first CORBA security Level 2 implementation. DAIS security authenticates users based on combinations of individual rights, group rights, and roles. Message protection is supported and employs both symmetric and asymmetric algorithms. As with all DAIS implementations, an emphasis is placed on manageability, scalability, and performance. The organization of DAIS security is divided into security domains. Each host environment participating in a domain runs a number of replicated security components that handle security issues for applications running on that host. This model minimizes the number of network invocations. Unique to DAIS is a set of GUI management tools, developed in Java, for configuring and managing DAIS security. The configuration of security domains simplifies management. DAIS, which supports CORBA Level 2 security, handles two distinct styles of applications: "security aware" and "security unaware." A security-unaware component is developed and tested in a nonsecure ORB environment. It can then be moved on to a secure ORB environment with no modification for integration, testing, and subsequent rollout. A security-aware application is one that can modify security policy by explicitly communicating with security components. In "security unaware" applications, policy is applied generally at the domain level or specifically on methods supported by a component. A security-aware application offers an additional level in that it can dictate policy based on the values of parameters handled by a component. For example, a generic component that handles multiple bank accounts will have rights to access only the single account of the user making an inquiry.

25.8.4.7 Language Bindings

DAIS supports a wide range of languages and development environments to simplify legacy integration and provide powerful Internet, intranet, and desktop solutions. DAIS applications can be developed in C, C++, COM2CORBA, Eiffel, and Java, using a wide variety of development tools such as Visual Basic and Delphi. Support for the C language provides access to most development tools and legacy languages such as COBOL and FORTRAN. Using DAIS, companies can leverage existing skill sets of C and C++ developers, create an environment that allows developers to migrate to distributed computing, and adopt and integrate technologies such as COM and Java at a controlled pace.

J^2 is a complete implementation of the DAIS ORB in Java. Designed for use with Internet applications, J^2 supports the concept of HTTP tunneling in order to communicate with CORBA applications outside the scope of the browser. J^2 was the first ORB to support the Portable Object Adapter (POA), which will revolutionize the way server objects are handled in CORBA.

COM2CORBA builds on the CORBA/COM mapping. It automates the process of generating COM components from IDL. The IDL can be generated to produce two types of COM components. OLE Automation servers are generated when a Microsoft application is acting as a client. ActiveX controls are generated when the Microsoft application is providing the implementation.

DAIS language mappings allow developers to use the native development environments with which they are most familiar. Standard compilers and tools associated with the host platform environment are used. For example, a Visual Basic (VB) developer may not want to work with CORBA IDL. The automated process that DAIS uses to generate COM components allows the VB developer to simply reference the COM component and use the object browser to verify its properties and methods. The developer does not have to work outside the Visual Basic development environment.

Given the relevance of key technologies such as Java and COM, example implementations of GUIs implemented in Java (exploiting J^2) and Visual Basic (exploiting COM2CORBA) are supplied as part of the tutorial defined in this book. Full details of running these examples can be found in Chapter 36.

25.8.5 The Future

PeerLogic recognizes that enterprise computing requires flexible solutions that will allow you to change and evolve your business, migrate to new technologies, and leverage existing investment in systems, applications, and personnel. Large-scale, mission-critical business systems are being implemented in increasingly distributed and complex environments that span corporate networks and the Internet. Future systems will combine best-of-breed technologies and will bridge a number of standard architectures such as CORBA, COM, and the emerging Enterprise JavaBeans model. Each of these architectures has its own security and transaction models, and the future challenge is to enable these architectures to work together. PeerLogic's DAIS is a high-performance, distributed ORB that delivers key enterprise functionality and a proven architecture for integrating legacy systems with new technologies. An extremely robust implementation of the OMG's CORBA standard, DAIS provides PeerLogic with a leading CORBA ORB and the first ORB to deliver enterprise-strength distributed solutions. For more information, please visit PeerLogic's Web site at www.peerlogic.com.

CHAPTER

26

Coding and Compiling the IDL

26.1 Coding the IDL

If you're serious about working the example, now is the time to sit down at your computer. In the first half of this chapter, we start with the Analysis and Design (A&D) developed in Chapters 23 and 24 and generate the OMG IDL file containing all of our objects' interfaces. In the second half, we compile it into client stubs and object skeletons using the IDL compiler that comes with your chosen ORB product.

In some sense, this chapter is the "answer book" for the problem given in Chapters 23 and 24. If you enjoy a challenge, you might want to try generating an IDL file yourself from those chapters, and compare the results to what we present here. (If you do this, you may want to switch to our version of the file before you start coding, to get operation and parameter names into synch.) If this is all new to you, just follow along one section at a time.

Regardless of how you do it, you'll need all of the IDL stored as files in order to compile it in the last half of the chapter. If you're working along, you should type it in by hand as you work your way through the example. Or, if you prefer, just read the IDL files off of the CD. However, we recommend that you study the chapter even so, since real-life problems usually don't come with answers on a CD in the back.

Ready to start typing? Here we go.

26.2 Introduction to IDL Coding

The A&D gives a lot of guidance in writing the IDL. We did this on purpose; we knew during the design phase what the next step would be. Because the A&D specifically states object, attribute, and operation names, the main things we need to do here are to translate the A&D constructs to IDL, and define the modularity of the components.

Here are the assumptions that were "built in" to the A&D as we wrote it, to enable easy transformation into IDL:

- Each object defined in the A&D will be defined as an IDL interface.

- State variables are assumed to be implementation details and will not be part of the IDL unless the A&D states they are attributes or parameters to operations.

- To help illustrate IDL syntax, we will use a variety of IDL constructs to specify our objects.

- We will use the OMG's IDL style guide for identifier formation (that is, how you make up variable names). Interfaces, datatypes, and exceptions start with capitals; if they consist of more than one word, we will capitalize the start of each word (no spaces). Names of operations, parameters, and structure elements will be all lower-case with underscores to separate words. Acronyms (like "POS") will stay all capitals no matter where they are used. Constants and enumeration values will be all capitals with underscores to separate words. It doesn't really matter whether you use this or any other style. What does matter is using a style consistently.

Readers of the first edition will notice that the main change to the IDL has been to conform to the new OMG IDL style guide. The other change was to use the standard OMG Naming Service now that it's widely available.

First, let us consider how to best modularize the IDL that represents these objects. We define each object as an IDL interface and group logically related interfaces within IDL modules. In creating these groupings, we have made some assumptions on how the system will be deployed. We know from the A&D that object instances will exist on separate computers:

- Each **POS** station is a separate computer in a LAN within the store. It contains the **POS** object, the **InputMedia** and the **OutputMedia** objects.

- The **Store** object, the **StoreAccess** objects it creates, and the **Tax** object reside on a separate computer in the same LAN, but on a different computer from the POS stations.

- The **Depot** object is on a separate computer reachable by WAN.

This deployment strategy suggests that we create three modules, one for each computer system. The analysis suggests these three:

```
module POS
{
        interface POSTerminal;
        interface InputMedia;
        interface OutputMedia;
};
```

```
module AStore
{
      interface Store;
      interface StoreAccess;
      interface Tax;
};

module CentralOffice
{
      interface Depot;
};
```

The next step in completing the IDL is to add the operations and supporting datatypes to each module. We will address each module in turn, filling in the details of the IDL as we go.

26.2.1 POS Module

The POS module is composed of three interfaces and several data types. Together, these components make up the point-of-sale terminal software. The objects are discussed in the following three sections, and the complete POS module is shown in Section 26.2.1.4.

26.2.1.1 InputMedia Object

The **InputMedia** object is described in the A&D in Section 24.2 in enough detail to define almost completely the IDL file we're about to generate. We won't reprint the A&D here; it's close at hand, and we have to conserve paper someplace. Be sure you flip back to Section 24.2 and compare the A&D to the IDL here.

The A&D defines three operations for InputMedia:

initialization
keypad_input
barcode_input

As described, the Initialization operation is not invoked by other components in the system, so it need not be part of **InputMedia**'s public IDL interface. **keypad_input** and **barcode_input** are, however, both invoked by a client. They will be part of the **Input-Media** interface.

The A&D states that the operation **barcode_input** takes one input parameter, **item**, which represents the scanned barcode. IDL has a **typedef** construct for defining synonyms to existing types, allowing us to define a datatype, **Barcode**, to represent the barcode. The **Barcode** type is used by both the **POS** and **InputMedia** interfaces so we will define it outside the scope of InputMedia. The IDL for **Barcode** is:

typedef string Barcode;

keypad_input operation also has a single input parameter; in this case, "a string representing input from the POS's keypad." The IDL string type is used for both barcodes and keypad input. Neither **keypad_input** nor **barcode_input** return a value, so the IDL must declare their return value **void**.

InputMedia does not contain any attributes, so the **POS** module is now:

```
module POS
{
        typedef string Barcode;
        interface InputMedia
        {
                typedef string OperatorCmd;

                void        barcode_input(in Barcode item);
                void        keypad_input(in OperatorCmd cmd);
        };
};
```

26.2.1.2 OutputMedia Object

As stated in the A&D, Section 24.3, **OutputMedia** has a single operation and no attributes. The operation, **output_text**, has one input argument. This argument is a string to be printed, and it is represented with CORBA's **string** type. Here is the complete IDL for the OutputMedia interface:

```
interface OutputMedia {

        boolean        output_text(in string string_to_print);

};
```

26.2.1.3 POSTerminal Object

The A&D for the POSTerminal object, Section 24.4, defines several operations, including an Initialization method. As with the **InputMedia**, we do not anticipate remote invocations of the initialization operation, so it will not be defined in the IDL. Each of the other operations is invoked by **InputMedia** based on specific user inputs. The implementation discussions do not specify a need for any attributes, so the POSTerminal IDL shown here contains only the following operations:

```
login
print_POS_sales_summary
print_store_sales_summary
send_barcode
item_quantity
end_of_sale
```

26.2.1.4 The Complete POS Module

This module completely defines the **POS** in IDL. Note that we have added the type **POSId**; it is used by the operation **login** in the **Store** interface.

```
module POS
{
    typedef long   POSId;
    typedef string Barcode;

    interface InputMedia
    {
        typedef string OperatorCmd;

        void barcode_input(in Barcode item);
        void keypad_input (in OperatorCmd cmd);
    };

    interface OutputMedia
    {
        boolean output_text(in string string_to_print );
    };

    interface POSTerminal
    {
        void login();
        void print_POS_sales_summary();
        void print_store_sales_summary();
        void send_barcode (in Barcode item);
        void item_quantity(in long quantity);
        void end_of_sale();
    };
};
```

26.2.2 AStore Module

The IDL for the **AStore** module is derived from the A&D for the **Store** (Section 24.5), **StoreAccess** (Section 24.6), and Tax (Section 24.7) objects. The IDL for each interface is presented in segments in the next three sections, and the completed module is shown in Section 26.2.2.4.

26.2.2.1 Store Object

The **Store** handles messages to Initialize, log in a POS, and to report totals, but once again the A&D operation "Initialize" will not be represented in IDL. The A&D further specifies that the **Store** will track running totals from all POSTerminals and will contain an attribute that contains these totals.

We used a single struct attribute, instead of two independent attributes, to avoid possible inconsistencies. This is an example of a problem that comes up frequently in the design of distributed systems, where multiple clients can access a single server for both update and retrieval, so we'll point it out here. Consider the following scenario:

1. POS 1 calls the **get** operation for the store total.

2. POS 2 calls **UpdateStoreTotals**, which changes both the store total and the store tax total.

3. POS 1 calls the **get** operation for the store tax total.

Even if POS 1 calls the **get** operation for the store tax total immediately after the **get** for the store total, there can be no guarantee that the totals are consistent, because POS 2 is an independent object and can submit an update at any time. Granted, the probability is slight under light load conditions as we have in this example, but accounting systems are not supposed to report inconsistent results under any conditions.

To avoid this problem, we define a struct with two fields, the store total and store tax total, and a single IDL attribute of the **struct** type.

```
struct StoreTotals {
    float    store_total;
    float    store_tax_total;
};
readonly attribute StoreTotals totals;
```

By combining the two values into a single **struct**, which is retrieved via a single operation, the A&D guarantees that the result will be consistent for single-threaded servers (which cannot execute multiple requests simultaneously). Extending this guarantee to multithreaded servers requires thread control via locks and semaphores, which we will neither define nor explain here. They are extremely useful tools for distributed applications, but we're afraid they just won't fit into this book.

POSTerminals invoke **Store**'s operation **login** to start a session with the store. The **login** operation assigns a **StoreAccess** object to the POS and returns a reference to the **StoreAccess** object. This can be expressed in IDL as:

```
StoreAccess login(in POS:: POSId id);
```

Note that **login**'s return type is the reference to the **StoreAccess** object. CORBA semantics dictate that **login** return an object reference, not a copy of the actual object implementation. We will see in later chapters how this is accomplished in C++, Java, and COBOL.

To complete the **Store** IDL, we create definitions for the **StoreId** attribute and the operation **get_POS_totals**, which reports store totals. From the A&D, **get_POS_totals** returns "the state of the store's current knowledge of all of the registered POS stations."

To support this requirement, we define a structure that represents the state of a POS object and a sequence type of these structures. We do not know, nor do we wish to hard-code, the maximum number of POS objects that can use a Store object, so an IDL "unbounded" sequence type (an unbounded sequence can dynamically change size at run time) is used.

```
struct POSInfo {
    POS::POSId  id;
    StoreAccess store_access_reference;
    float        total_sales;
    float        total_taxes;
};
```

```
typedef sequence <POSInfo> POSList;
```

The **POSInfo** struct was defined to contain all information that the Store maintains about each **POSTerminal**, including a reference to the POS's **StoreAccess** object. **POSInfo** is defined in the **AStore** module as shown in Section 26.2.2.

The last step is to add **update_store_totals**, which completes the IDL for the **Store**:

```
interface Store {
    struct StoreTotals
    {
        float    store_total;
        float    store_tax_total;
    };

    readonly attribute AStoreId store_id;

    StoreAccess login( in  POS::POSId id);
    void           get_POS_totals( out POSList POS_data);
    void           update_store_totals( in  POS::POSId      id,
                                        in  float           price,
                                        in  float           taxes);
};
```

26.2.2.2 StoreAccess Object

The **StoreAccess** object is, from the A&D Section 24.6, "the intermediary between the POS and the central Depot concerning access to the grocery item database. One such object is created for each POS that logs in to the Store." The A&D indicates that **StoreAccess** has two operations and several state variables. None of the state variables was specified as an attribute. Of the operations, only **find_price** needs to be part of the IDL interface, because it is the only operation invoked by remote clients.

The A&D states that **find_price** accepts inputs to specify the item and outputs the price, taxable price, and an "item info." It also must raise an exception, **BarcodeNot-Found**, if it cannot locate the item in the database.

We discussed IDL exceptions in Section 3.3.1.4; now (finally!), we'll use one. We'll define **BarcodeNotFound**, in the **AStore** module, to contain the offending barcode as follows:

```
exception BarcodeNotFound {POS:: Barcode item;};
```

The **find_price** operation also has an output parameter of type **ItemInfo**, defined in the A&D as "a structure containing at least ItemInfo.item, ItemInfo.item_type, Item-Info.item_cost, and ItemInfo.name." These types are used by several interfaces, so we will put the following declaration in the **AStore** module:

```
enum ItemTypes {FOOD, CLOTHES, OTHER};
struct ItemInfo {
    POS::Barcode    item;
    ItemTypes       item_type;
```

```
float        item_cost;
string       name;
long         quantity;
};
```

ItemTypes is expressed as an IDL enumerated list. Its three identifiers represent the set of item types carried by stores in our system (as defined in the A&D, of course). ItemInfo is defined as stated in the A&D, plus an additional member, which contains the quantity in inventory for the item (barcode).

The **find_price** operation can now be defined as follows:

```
void find_price(in  POS::Barcode item,
           in  long          quantity,
           out float         item_price,
           out float         item_tax_price,
           out ItemInfo      item_info)
      raises (BarcodeNotFound);
```

The IDL interface **StoreAccess** just wraps that operation in braces:

```
interface StoreAccess {
     void find_price(in  POS::Barcode item,
                in  long          quantity,
                out float         item_price,
                out float         item_tax_price,
                out ItemInfo      Item_info)
           raises (BarcodeNotFound);
};
```

26.2.2.3 Tax Object

The Tax object performs tax services for the Store object. The A&D Section 24.7 states that it contains the operations:

```
Initialize
calculate_tax
find_taxable_price
```

Two state variables are defined in the A&D, but because they are not attributes, they do not appear in the IDL. And, as usual, Initialize will not be part of the IDL.

Both IDL operations return floating point numbers that represent the tax and taxable price for an item, respectively. The IDL for the Tax object is:

```
interface Tax {
     float calculate_tax( in float taxable_amount );

     float find_taxable_price(
           in float         item_price,
           in ItemTypes item_type);
};
```

26.2.2.4 Complete AStore Module

The completed IDL for the module AStore is:

```
module AStore
{
    enum ItemTypes {FOOD, CLOTHES, OTHER};
    typedef long AStoreId;

    struct ItemInfo
    {
        POS::Barcode    item;
        ItemTypes       item_type;
        float           item_cost;
        string          name;
        long            quantity;
    };

    exception BarcodeNotFound { POS::Barcode item; };

    interface StoreAccess; // forward reference

    struct POSInfo
    {
        POS::POSId  id;
        StoreAccess store_access_reference;
        float       total_sales;
        float       total_taxes;
    };

    typedef sequence <POSInfo> POSList;

    interface Tax
    {
        float calculate_tax( in float taxable_amount);
        float find_taxable_price( in float item_price,
                            in ItemTypes item_type);
    };

    interface Store
    {
        struct StoreTotals
        {
            float   store_total;
            float   store_tax_total;
        };

        readonly attribute AStoreId store_id;

        readonly attribute StoreTotals totals;
```

```
        StoreAccess login( in POS::POSId id);
        void get_POS_totals( out POSList POS_data);
        void update_store_totals( in  POS::POSId   id,
                                  in  float        price,
                                  in  float        taxes);
    };

    interface StoreAccess
    {
        void     ind_price( in   POS::Barcode     item,
                            in   long             quantity,
                            out  float            item_price,
                            out  float            item_tax_price,
                            out  ItemInfo         item_info)
                raises (BarcodeNotFound);
    };
};
```

26.2.3 CentralOffice Module

The **CentralOffice** module contains the single interface **Depot**. **Depot** has a single operation, **find_item_info**, which selects and returns an **ItemInfo** structure based on three input arguments. Note that **find_item_info** uses types defined in the **AStore** and **POS** modules, so we must scope references to the type names as shown here. The A&D, in Section 24.8, also states that **find_item_info** raises the exception **Barcode-NotFound** when given an invalid barcode (formal argument **item**). Based on these observations, the complete IDL declaration for **CentralOffice** is as follows:

```
module CentralOffice {

    interface Depot {
        void FindItemInfo(
            in  AStore::AStoreId    store_id,
            in  POS::Barcode        item,
            in  long                quantity,
            out AStore::ItemInfo    item_info)
        raises (AStore:: BarcodeNotFound);
    };
};
```

26.2.4 The IDL Files

In preparation for compiling the IDL, we must partition it into one or more source files. IDL source files are typically named with the suffix .idl, although this may vary between IDL compilers. We'll put the IDL for each module into a single file, since we have only a few dependencies. (If we had an object that was inherited by a number of different modules, we might put its IDL into a file by itself for easier inclusion.)

Here is the skeleton of each file. If you've been typing in the IDL as we went along, edit your files to reflect this structure.

File `POS.idl`

```
#ifndef _POS_IDL_
#define _POS_IDL_

module POS {
...
};

#endif
```

File `Store.idl`

```
#ifndef _STORE_IDL_
#define _STORE_IDL_

#include "pos.idl"

module AStore {
...
};

#endif
```

File `Central.idl`

```
#ifndef _CENTRAL_IDL_
#define _CENTRAL_IDL_
#include "pos.idl"
#include "store.idl"

module CentralOffice {
...
};

#endif
```

The IDL compiler supports C++ style preprocessing, so we use "cpp" conditional, define, and include directives. Each file is bracketed by the lines:

```
#ifndef <name>
#define <name>

...
#endif
```

where **\<name>** is replaced by a (hopefully) unique preprocessor string derived from the file name. For example, **_POS_IDL_** is used in the file POS.idl. These three lines protect against multiple-declaration errors.

Notice also that Central.idl and Store.idl use the cpp #include statement so the IDL compiler will know of constructs from the other modules.

If your files contain the IDL given at the end of each module section in this chapter, bracketed by the module structure we just presented, then you're ready to compile your stubs and skeletons starting in the next section.

26.3 Compiling the IDL

The IDL files that we've just completed represent the fulfillment of the promise we made at the beginning of this book: They completely specify the interfaces of all of the objects in our system, and can (and will!) be implemented in several programming languages, on a wide variety of platforms. And, when implemented on IIOP-enabled ORBs such as the ones in this book, they will interoperate with objects from any other IIOP ORB, transparent to differences in programming language, platform, or other factors.

Now it's time to compile these IDL files into client stubs and object implementation skeletons. Many IDL compilers generate various header files and "starter" files for your client and object implementation code, in addition to stubs and skeletons. Your ORB vendor will tell you, in the next half of this chapter and in your documentation, which files are output by the IDL compiler and what you're supposed to do with them.

Here is a listing of the programming languages that each ORB uses to work the example and the section in this chapter where its IDL compiler is presented. Keep in mind that almost all of these ORBs implement multiple languages. ORBs working the example in C++ are:

- Vertel's Expersoft CORBAplus for C++ (Section 26.5.1)
- IBM Component Broker (Section 26.6)
- IONA Orbix for C++ (Section 26.8.1)
- Inprise VisiBroker for C++ (Section 26.10.1)
- BEA WLE (Section 26.4)

ORBs working the example in Java are:

- Vertel's Expersoft CORBAplus, Java Edition (Section 26.5.2)
- The IBM ORB for Java (Section 26.6)
- PeerLogic DAIS (Section 26.7)
- IONA OrbixWeb (Section 26.8.2)
- Inprise VisiBroker for Java (Section 26.10.2)

The ORB working in COBOL is:

- IONA OrbixCOBOL (Section 26.9).

Now's the time to skip ahead to the section on your ORB and IDL compiler, unless you prefer to read about compiling the IDL for more than one of these ORBs. Follow the instructions it gives you to compile the IDL. Some compilers add **#pragma** directives as IDL comments; these give the compiler additional information it needs without spoiling the "standardness" of the IDL. The **#pragma**s are ignored by other compilers so you still end up with a standard file that can be compiled by any standard IDL compiler.

When you've finished compiling the IDL, turn to Chapter 27 where we'll start coding the Depot object.

26.4 Compiling the IDL for BEA WLE

BEA WLE provides an IDL compiler using the (surprise!) idl command. The compiler produces stub files (.h and .cpp) and skeleton files (.h and .cpp).

In addition to taking the IDL input file, the compiler optionally takes an Implementation Configuration File (.icf) that gives the WLE infrastructure some special information about the server. The compiler puts this special information in the skeletons (hidden) so that the WLE infrastructure can more efficiently perform routing to this server. See the BEA Depot section 27.4 for information for creating the entire application, including the names of stubs and skeletons and use of the ICF for the Depot.

A convenience feature of the WLE compiler is help in getting started writing an implementation. If you have just defined an IDL file (abc.idl) with interfaces (**foo** and **bar**), running

```
idl -i abc.idl
```

will generate two files, abc_i.h and abc_i.cpp, that contain the outline for your implementation. The .h file contains the definition of the foo and bar implementation classes, including the signatures of the methods you need to provide. The .cpp file contains (empty) method definitions. You add specific data and private methods to the classes in the .h file and then the method code in the .cpp file.

26.5 Compiling the IDL with CORBAplus

This section introduces the CORBAplus IDL compilers for the CORBAplus for C++ and CORBAplus, Java Edition products. This section describes the idlc and idlj compilers and the files that are produced. Specific implementation details are covered later in the different implementation sections. At the end of this section you should feel comfortable with running the compilers and know what each of the generated files are for.

We are going to cover just enough so you can understand how the examples are compiled. We are only going to scratch the surface in terms of the options we could use, so please refer to the product documentation if you need more detailed information.

26.5.1 idlc Tutorial

This tutorial has been written for Unix; however, usage differences between Unix and Windows will be pointed out as we go. Before going too far, to actively follow along you must install CORBAplus for C++ on your computer. You will need to set up two environment variables: PBHOME and PBTMPDIR. PBHOME is used to specify the CORBAplus installation directory, and PBTMPDIR is used to specify where CORBAplus should write its temporary files. PBTMPDIR is typically either the same as PBHOME or /tmp. If you are installing CORBAplus on a Windows-based computer, then these environment variables can be set up automatically for you during the installation.

The tutorial walks us through the process of compiling the **POS** IDL file. You will need to repeat the same steps to compile the **Store** and **Depot** IDL files.

The output generated from idlc can be tailored to meet specific needs, but for most users, and certainly for this example, the default options for idlc are most appropriate. idlc accepts your IDL files and produces four files. These files contain the CORBA C++ language mapping for the IDL constructs found in your IDL file. Let's look at an example of how to compile the POS.idl file and the files generated by the IDL compiler.

```
%idlc POS.idl
```

That's all there is to compiling an IDL file. The idlc compiler will produce the following files:

```
POS.h
POS.C
POS_s.h
POS_s.C
```

In case you are wondering, you will never change the generated files. You will include the header files into your applications and compile and link the source files. If you ever accidentally change your IDL file, just recompile the IDL to generate new source and header files and recompile your application.

The idlc compiler breaks up the IDL file into client-side files and server-side files. Only the POS.h and POS.C are required for the client, but the server will require all four files. The POS.h header file declares the C++ types associated with the IDL defined in the IDL specification. POS.h, which is sometimes referred to as the "interface header file," declares a C++ class for every IDL interface. The POS.h provides remote access to objects through stubs that correspond to the IDL-defined interfaces. A CORBAplus client program includes this header file and makes a request by calling one of the stub routines on an object reference. Of course, you will never know that you are using a generated stub; you just see an object with the correct interface.

For object implementations, the header file POS_s.h provides a C++ base object implementation class for every interface construct in the IDL file. A CORBAplus object implementation class is then derived from this base class. The derived class is where you specify the implementation for each IDL operation, which were translated into C++ virtual functions—if you were really curious.

The POS.C file contains client-side and server-side implementations of types declared in POS.h, including interface stub class implementations used by CORBAplus client programs.

The implementation file POS_s.C contains the implementations of the operation dispatch methods required by the object implementations.

On a Windows platform, idlc can generate file names with a .cpp extension, which is more suitable for some development tools such as Visual C++. The idlc command to change the file suffix is:

```
%idlc -Cext=cpp POS.idl
```

This will generate the following files:

```
POS.h
POS.cpp
POS_s.h
POS.cpp
```

The last topic we cover in this tutorial will give you a more concrete example of how to start writing your implementation class. The POS_s.h contains the base class that you must derive from. The name of the base class has the following naming convention:

```
ModuleName_InterfaceName_base_impl
```

You would see this if you opened up the POS_s.h file. You would create another file and define your own class, like:

```
// POS Terminal Implementation
#include <POS_s.h>
class POSTerminalImpl : public virtual POS_POSTerminal_base_impl {
private:

    ...
public:
    // implement the virtual functions
    // ...
};
```

26.5.1.1 Compiling the POS Example

To compile the example, a top-level makefile is provided for both Solaris and NT. To compile everything on Solaris you would execute the following command:

```
%make -f Makefile.unix.xps
```

To compile everything on NT you would execute the following command:

```
%make -f Makefile.win.xps
```

This top-level Makefile just steps into each of the subdirectories and calls the Makefile.unix.xps or Makefile.win.xps depending upon your platform.

26.5.2 idlj Tutorial

This tutorial is the same regardless of hardware platform. Again, to actively follow along you should install the CORBAplus, Java Edition product. This tutorial assumes that the product has been properly installed and your CLASSPATH has been updated.

At the time of this writing, CORBAplus, Java Edition supports JDK 1.1.x. Besides the CORBAplus, Java Edition CLASSPATH settings and the usual JDK CLASSPATH settings, you will need to add the following to your CLASSPATH:

```
<book installation directory>/classes
```

The idlj compiler has many different options that may be useful to your application, but for this tutorial just the basic compiler options are demonstrated. As described in other sections of the book, the IDL-to-Java mapping is pretty clear about what classes are generated for each IDL type, and what the names for those classes must be. So, for the POS.idl file to compile this with the idlj compiler, you execute the following command:

```
%idlj POS.idl
```

This causes the POS.idl file to be compiled, placing the generated code in a directory below the IDL directory. The directory structure below the IDL directory will, of course, follow the package hierarchy.

Because the IDL-to-Java mapping is very explicit about the generated files, that's really all there is to it, unless you need other options on the compiler. For example, perhaps you would like to generate the Java code to a directory that is not below the IDL directory. The idlj compiler can handle this with the –base_dir option.

26.5.2.1 Compiling the POS Example

To compile the example, a top-level Makefile is provided for both Solaris and NT. To compile everything on Solaris you would execute the following command:

```
%make -f Makefile.unix.xps
```

To compile everything on NT you would execute the following command:

```
%cpjemake all
```

For NT, we did not want to assume you had access to make, so we provided a batch file to compile the example.

26.6 Compiling the IDL in IBM Component Broker

The IBM Component Broker comes with an object builder that guides the user all the way from object model to a final business object implementation. It contains a code generator that generates additional code to make the user-written business object manageable by the Component Broker runtime. The output of the code generator consists of IDL files, C++ implementations, Java implementations, and makefiles. The makefiles contain rules to invoke the IDL compiler to generate C++ and Java bindings, and rules to run the C++ compiler, C++ linker, and the Java compiler. The results are C++ shared libraries and Java .jar files for both the client and server.

Since our example does not involve the use of the object builder, we'll show you how to generate language bindings from the command line. The IDL files from the example may be used unmodified.

For the C++ ORB, invoke the IDL-to-C++ compiler as follows:

```
idlc -ehh:uc:sc pos.idl
idlc -ehh:uc:sc store.idl
idlc -ehh:uc:sc central.idl
```

The command line flags hh, uc, and sc tell the IDL-to-C++ compiler to emit .hh, _C.cpp, and _S.cpp files:

```
pos.hh   pos_C.cpp pos_S.cpp
store.hh store_C.cpp store_S.cpp
central.hh central_C.cpp central_S.cpp
```

The .hh header files contain the C++ declarations for the corresponding IDL files. They are included for use by both the client and server code. The _C.cpp files contain the stub code to be compiled and linked with the client. The _S.cpp files contain the skeleton code to be compiled and linked with the server. Note that the _S.cpp file #include the corresponding _C.cpp file, since the server-side bindings also require the client-side bindings.

For the IBM Java ORB, invoke the IDL-to-Java compiler as follows:

```
java com.ibm.idl.toJava.Compile -fall pos.idl
java com.ibm.idl.toJava.Compile -fall store.idl
java com.ibm.idl.toJava.Compile -fall central.idl
```

The -fall option tells the IDL-to-Java compiler to generate all the .java files needed for both the client side and server side, as defined by the IDL-to-Java mapping specifications. Unlike C++, many .java files are generated for each .idl file. Although not shown here, the -d dir option may be used to redirect the output to a different directory.

26.7 Compiling the IDL with DAIS

26.7.1 Getting Started

In order to implement the primer example in Java using DAIS, you must have DAIS J^2 installed on your machine. The CD accompanying this book contains a special installation program that will install DAIS J^2 SDK for Windows 32-bit platforms, DAIS Name Service, and Dais Primer Example. Full details on the installation of this can be found in Chapter 36. Although the DAIS sections in this book presume you are running on a Windows platform, it should not be difficult to apply the semantics to the operating system on which you are developing DAIS applications.

The DAIS CORBA compiler is a standard CORBA compiler and requires no modifications to the IDL described in this chapter—it is simply a matter of locating the IDL and compiling it. The DAIS Java implementation is the first to include the Portable Object Adapter (POA), and the DAIS implementation of the primer example illustrates implementations using the POA.

26.7.2 Locating the IDL

Under the primer directory are a number of subdirectories, two of which are called IDL and classes. The IDL directory contains the three IDL files:

```
POS.idl
Store.idl
Central.idl
```

The IDL will generate Java files, which in turn are compiled by the Java compiler into class files. This work will be carried out in the IDL directory. All class files will be copied or moved to the classes directory, which is where we will run the final applications.

26.7.3 Compiling the IDL

Open a console session and change directory to <installation root>\Primer\ java\IDL. A default installation would have set this to c:\Dais32\Primer\ java\IDL. You should be able to list the IDL files described in the previous section.

At this point, you may feel it is logical to compile all three IDL files, but there is a shortcut unique to the Java mapping that is worth a comment. The Central.idl file contains the following preprocessor statements:

```
// Include interface definition for store and POS objects.
#include "POS.idl"
#include "Store.idl"
```

The normal behavior of a preprocessor copies these files into the central.idl file. Since public Java classes are generated in files of the same class name, compiling Central.idl will generate all the Java files for POS.idl, Store.idl, and Central.idl. Let's compile Central.idl.

```
stubgen -lJava Central.idl
```

- *Stubgen is the name of the DAIS IDL compiler.* It supports a number of parameters and by simply typing stubgen, with no arguments a list of valid parameters can be obtained.

- *The -l parameter defines the required language mapping.* The compiler is split into two components, a front end and a back end. The front end is the same for all DAIS software developer kits. Depending on the DAIS SDKs installed you may have one or more back-end components installed. There is one for each language mapping. DAIS currently supports five language mappings:

Java	(-ljava)
C++	(-lc++)
COM	(-lcom)
Eiffel	(-leiffel)
C	(-lc) - the default

The DAIS J^2 SDK accompanying this book only supports the Java mapping.

■ *The final argument is the IDL file name.*

If you have problems compiling this file, it could be related to an incorrect PATH setting, which will fail to locate stubgen. In order to call stubgen from a command line, your PATH environment variable should be set to include the DAIS bin directory

```
Set PATH=%PATH%;<DAIS ROOT Installation>/bin
```

where <DAIS ROOT Installation> describes where you installed DAIS. For example, a default installation would require a PATH setting of:

```
Set PATH=%PATH%;C:Dais32/bin
```

26.7.4 Compiling the Java Files

One of the great aspects of the Java mapping in conjunction with the POA is that it standardizes the precise classes, class names, and package structures. All the files generated by the DAIS IDL compiler conform to the standard. Because each of the IDL files defined modules, you should be able to view the following files and subdirectories in the IDL directory:

```
POS.idl
Store.idl            →   IDL files
Central.idl


CentralOffice
Astore               → client side packages
POS


POA_CentralOffice
POA_AStore           → server side packages
POA_POS


mk_Central.bat       → build file for compiling all the java files
```

As we are dealing with a lot of files, and the target directory for the class files in this example is the classes directory, copy all the generated Java files, maintaining their package structure, to the classes directory. Perhaps the simplest way to do this is to use **copy** and **paste** through the Windows Explorer utility. The classes directory should look now look like this:

```
CentralOffice
Astore            → client side packages
POS


POA_CentralOffice
POA_AStore        → server side packages
POA_POS


mk_Central.bat    → build file for compiling all the
                     java files
```

Run the copy of the mk_Central.bat file located in the classes directory. If you have problems compiling, it may relate to an incorrect CLASSPATH setting, which will fail to pick up the DAIS ORB Java classes. The CLASSPATH environment variable should be set to pick up the following class directories:

```
Set
CLASSPATH=%CLASSPATH%;<installation root>\lib\daisorb.jar;<installation
root>\lib\daissrv.jar; <installation root> \lib\daissrvx.jar;<installation
root>\Primer\classes
```

A default installation would require a CLASSPATH setting of:

```
Set
CLASSPATH=%CLASSPATH%;C:\DAIS32\lib\daisorb.jar;C:\DAIS32\lib\daissrv.jar;
C:\DAIS32\lib\daissrvx.jar;C:\DAIS32\Primer\classes
```

Once the Java files have been compiled into their associated class files, we are ready to look at implementation details. Strictly speaking, the classes folder should only contain class files, so it might be good practice to delete all the .java files from the classes directory.

26.8 Compiling the IDL in Orbix

You don't need to modify the standard IDL files to use them with Orbix; just compile them with the Orbix IDL compiler. There are no special configuration files required apart from the IDL, the generated code produced by the IDL compiler, and your own client and server code. We'll discuss compiling the IDL for Orbix C++ first, then for OrbixWeb for Java.

Note that the IDL compiler for Orbix 3 and later versions includes a powerful code generation tool that can create a complete functioning client and server from an IDL file. This greatly reduces the time it takes to get a CORBA project started, because you can immediately start modifying working code, rather than building clients and servers from scratch. The code generation tool can also be customized to generate code specific to your application based on the contents of an IDL file.

26.8.1 Orbix C++

You compile each IDL file to generate C++ code corresponding to the IDL that can be used by clients and implemented at the server side. The Orbix IDL compiler is run from the command line as follows (the makefiles with the demonstration code do this automatically):

```
idl -B Pos.idl
idl -B Store.idl
idl -B Central.idl
idl -B NamingService.idl
```

The -B flag is required to produce server-side skeleton support—the BOAImpl classes. You will find out about these when we describe how to code the example in C++. The file NamingService.idl is the IDL for the standard CORBA Naming Service, and is supplied with Orbix 3 and later (for earlier versions you need to download a copy of OrbixNames).

The IDL compiler for each platform produces code tailored to the C++ compiler on that platform. For example, an IDL module is mapped to a C++ `namespace` for compilers that support namespaces, and to a C++ `class` for compilers that do not. The IDL compiler generates three output files for each IDL file. For example, from `Store.idl` it produces the following files:

`Store.hh`: Header file containing declarations of all the C++ types corresponding to the IDL. This is included (using `#include`) in both client and server C++ code.

`StoreC.cc`: Client stub code. This is the code that turns client C++ calls into remote CORBA invocations. Compile this file and link the resulting object file with your client using your normal C++ compiler and linker.

`StoreC.cc`: Server skeleton code. This is the code that dispatches CORBA invocations as C++ calls on your server objects. Compile this file and link the resulting object file with your server using your normal C++ compiler and linker.

Note that the default extensions for C++ code files vary depending on the platform; for example, `.cpp` on Windows, `.cc` on Solaris, and `.C` on HP-UX. The default extension for generated header files is always `.hh`. You can change the extensions for generated files by passing command line switches to the IDL compiler.

The IDL compiler also provides a switch, `-S`, to generate a starting point file for the server-side C++ class that implements an interface. This generates a header and code file containing the C++ signatures of the IDL operations for each interface. You can use this switch, or write your classes from scratch, or use the more powerful Orbix code generation toolkit to generate a complete skeleton client and server to get your project started.

26.8.2 OrbixWeb

As with Orbix, each IDL file can be compiled to generate Java code corresponding to the IDL that can be used by clients and implemented at the server side. The OrbixWeb IDL compiler is run from the command line as follows (the makefiles with the demonstration code do this automatically):

```
idl  Pos.idl
idl  Store.idl
idl  Central.idl
```

(Note: There is no need to build the Naming Service IDL as the `org.omg.COSNaming` package comes prebuilt in the OrbixWeb runtime, although we could rebuild it had we wished to.)

Alternatively, the following command could also have been used:

```
idl  -N Central.idl
```

The `-N` flag tells the IDL compiler to build all the included files; by default, only IDL types contained in files specified on the command line will have Java code generated. Please refer to Appendix A of the OrbixWeb Programmer's Guide for a more exhaustive discussion of the flags available with the OrbixWeb IDL compiler.

The IDL compiler generates up to nine Java objects for each IDL type; we've explained this already but now you can see the files in your directory, and browse through them if you want. (Don't you dare edit them!) For example, from `Store.idl` it produces the following files:

```
java_output\AStore\AStoreIdHelper.java
java_output\AStore\BarcodeNotFound.java
java_output\AStore\BarcodeNotFoundHelper.java
java_output\AStore\BarcodeNotFoundHolder.java
java_output\AStore\ItemInfo.java
java_output\AStore\ItemInfoHelper.java
java_output\AStore\ItemInfoHolder.java
java_output\AStore\ItemTypes.java
java_output\AStore\ItemTypesHelper.java
java_output\AStore\ItemTypesHolder.java
java_output\AStore\POSInfo.java
java_output\AStore\POSInfoHelper.java
java_output\AStore\POSInfoHolder.java
java_output\AStore\POSListHelper.java
java_output\AStore\POSListHolder.java
java_output\AStore\Store.java
java_output\AStore\StoreAccess.java
java_output\AStore\StoreAccessHelper.java
java_output\AStore\StoreAccessHolder.java
java_output\AStore\StoreAccessPackage
java_output\AStore\StoreHelper.java
java_output\AStore\StoreHolder.java
java_output\AStore\StorePackage
java_output\AStore\Tax.java
java_output\AStore\TaxHelper.java
java_output\AStore\TaxHolder.java
java_output\AStore\TaxPackage
java_output\AStore\_StoreAccessImplBase.java
java_output\AStore\_StoreAccessOperations.java
java_output\AStore\_StoreAccessSkeleton.java
java_output\AStore\_StoreAccessStub.java
java_output\AStore\_StoreImplBase.java
java_output\AStore\_StoreOperations.java
java_output\AStore\_StoreSkeleton.java
java_output\AStore\_StoreStub.java
java_output\AStore\_TaxImplBase.java
java_output\AStore\_TaxOperations.java
java_output\AStore\_TaxSkeleton.java
java_output\AStore\_TaxStub.java
java_output\AStore\_tie_Store.java
java_output\AStore\_tie_StoreAccess.java
java_output\AStore\_tie_Tax.java
java_output\AStore\StorePackage\StoreTotals.java
java_output\AStore\StorePackage\StoreTotalsHelper.java
java_output\AStore\StorePackage\StoreTotalsHolder.java
```

The output of the Java IDL compiler is explained in Chapter 8, Section 1.

As with Orbix, the OrbixWeb code generation toolkit can also be used to generate a complete Java client and server to get your project started.

26.9 Compiling the IDL with OrbixCOBOL

This section gives an overview of the COBOL support provided by Iona within its OrbixCOBOL product. To help you to understand how it is used, we will briefly step through the process of turning IDL into an executable COBOL client and COBOL server with some references to our tutorial examples to illustrate it. However, before we start, it is worth pausing for a moment to note that Iona does in fact provide more than just basic COBOL support—it also provides a CICS and IMS adapter. Now that should make life really easy for you if you just happen to be a true-blue COBOL application developer.

The complete programming cycle for an OrbixCOBOL Server and Client can be viewed as a six-step process. Here is a quick summary of those six steps:

1. Define your interface using IDL.

2. Generate COBOL support files.

3. Implement your interface in COBOL.

4. Write a server base that handles server initialization and informs Orbix when initialization has been done and the server is ready to accept requests.

5. Register your server with Orbix.

6. Write your client that will interface to your server.

For our tutorial, we already have our interface defined and have the complete IDL ready for processing. Since no special IDL directives are required for COBOL, and only pure OMG IDL is supported, you do not have to make any changes, additions, or deletions.

The next step is to use the Orbix IDL compiler to place your interface details into the Orbix Interface Repository. You do this using the standard IDL compiler with the `-r` option. Normally the IDL compiler is used to just generate C++ stubs. However, by using the `-r` option we are parsing the IDL and placing the interface details into the repository instead. The following command line illustrates this:

```
idl -r pos.idl
```

If this also results in C++ stubs being generated, you can ignore them. You do not need them.

Once you have all your interface details placed into the Orbix Interface Repository, you use the `gencbl` utility, which is supplied as part of the OrbixCOBOL package, to generate the support files required for each of the interfaces. When running this utility, you use the name of the interface, not the name of the module that contains the IDL. This means that you would use the following three commands for the interfaces that were contained within the `pos.idl` file.

```
gencbl InputMedia
gencbl OutputMedia
gencbl POSTerminal
```

One other sanity point worth mentioning is that the gencbl utility uses the standard Orbix Interface Repository server IR.EXE, so you need to ensure that it is running with the –L option. If it was started before you inserted your IDL into the Interface Repository, you will need to stop and restart it; otherwise, it may not find your interface.

Each interface that you process with the gencbl utility will result in the following COBOL support files being generated for you:

<interface>S.xxx This is the main COBOL server implementation source code. This file contains stub paragraphs for all of your callable operations. The generation of this file will overwrite any previous contents, so you should rename it and make any changes to the renamed version. The best option is to change the .xxx suffix to a more standard name such as .cbl.

<interface>SV.cbl This is the COBOL server base. If you are handling several interfaces within one server, you may want to merge several of these into one module.

<interface>.cpy This copybook contains data definitions used for working with operation parameters and return values.

<interface>X.cpy This copybook contains data definitions to be used by the Orbix COBOL runtime system to support the interface. This copybook is automatically copied in by the <interface> copybook, so you do not have to worry about it.

<interface>D.cpy This copybook contains procedural code for performing the correct paragraph for the requested operation. This copybook is automatically copied into your <interface>S.xxx source module, so you do not have to worry about it.

<user-defined>.cpy One of these copybooks will be generated for each of your user-defined types such as structs and typedefs. These are used as necessary by the <interface> copybook and are also available for your use. When these copybooks are generated, the user-defined name is truncated to eight characters. If the file name is still not unique within the interface, then it is made unique through the use of a three-digit numeric suffix.

Once you've generated all of these files, you fill in the interface implementation details within the generated <interface>S.xxx that you have first renamed to <interface>S.cbl. You then compile it and the server base module <interface>SV.cbl and link them both with the standard OrbixCOBOL library coa.lib to produce your executable server. You do this using the appropriate standard COBOL compiler for your environment. Currently, both MVS and NT are supported.

To run it, you register your executable server with Orbix using the standard mechanisms. This would be done using either the putit command line interface or the GUI interface. For more details on this, refer to the standard Orbix documentation. The main point here is that there are no additional registration requirements for an Orbix server written in COBOL.

The development and deployment of an executable Orbix Client written in COBOL is easy: You simply use the generated COBOL copy file <interface>.cpy in conjunction with the standard OrbixCOBOL routines. This is done by copying the COBOL copy file into your COBOL client, writing code that sets up the parameters for the call you want to make, and using the standard ORBEXEC routine to invoke the implementation. We'll show this in detail in the COBOL tutorial in the rest of the book.

26.10 VisiBroker

26.10.1 VisiBroker for C++

The IDL compiler that comes with VisiBroker for C++ has the following options (shown when you simply type idl2cpp):

```
usage: idl2cpp [-options] files...
where options are:
  -version                     Print version
  -root_dir<dir_string>        Specify directory to write all generated code to
  -hdr_dir<dir_string>         Specify directory to write generated headers to
  -src_dir<dir_string>         Specify directory to write generated source to
  -client_ext<ext_string>      Specify client file extension -'none' for none,default:'_c'
  -server_ext<ext_string>      Specify server file extension -'none' for none,default:'_s'
  -hdr_suffix<suf_string>      Specify header file suffix - default:'hh'
  -src_suffix<suf_string>      Specify source file suffix - default:'cc'
  -no_exceptions               Suppress exception generation
  -no_tie                      Suppress generation of tie code
  -ptie                        Generate ptie code
  -obj_wrapper                 Generate typed object wrapper code
  -no_stdstream                Suppress generation of class stream operators
  -pretty_print                Generate _pretty_print methods
  -type_code_info              Generate type code information
  -virtual_impl_inh            Generate virtual interface impl. inheritance
  -export<tag_string>          Generate export tags (WinNT/95)
  -export_skel<tag_string>     Generate export tags in skeletons (WinNT/95)
  -incl_files_code             Generate code for included files
  -corba_inc<include_file>     Use include_file instead of 'corba.h'
  -impl_base_object<o_str>     Use o_str instead of 'CORBA::Object'
  -map_keyword<keyword>        <replacement> Replace 'keyword' with 'replacement'
  -preprocess_only             Send preprocessed source to stdout; do not compile
  -no_preprocess               Do not preprocess the source
pre-processor options:
  -C                           Retain comments in output
  -D                           Define a macro
  -H                           Print the pathnames of included files
  -I<directory>                Specify an[other] directory in the include path
  -P                           Suppress #line pragmas
  -U                           Undefine a macro
```

For the purposes of our example, the following IDL2CPP commands will do the trick:

```
idl2cpp -src_suffix cpp -hdr_suffix h -root_dir ..\pos POS.idl
idl2cpp -src_suffix cpp -hdr_suffix h -root_dir ..\store Store.idl
idl2cpp -src_suffix cpp -hdr_suffix h -root_dir ..\central Central.idl
```

Of course, the -root_dir option can be specified differently and you can also change the suffixes if you prefer other ones.

For ease of file management, only four files are output for each .IDL file (unlike in Java where there must be one file per public class). For instance, the POS.idl file would generate the following files:

```
pos_c.h      // Client-side header file
pos_c.cpp    // Client-side implementation file
pos_s.h      // Server-side header file
pos_s.cpp    // Server-side implementation file
```

The files are placed in the root directory you specified (otherwise, it puts them into the current directory). Make sure that the .h files are somewhere in the INCLUDE directory for your compiler. You should compile the preceding files to obtain two object files: pos_c.obj and pos_s.obj (under Win32). When you write your CORBA application, make sure you link the object files into the appropriate code (either the client side or the server side).

As you can see, the IDL compiler supports many options. If your particular application requires advanced code-generation features, the VisiBroker IDL compiler should be able to support your requirements.

26.10.2 VisiBroker for Java

The IDL compiler that comes with VisiBroker for Java has the following options (shown when you simply type idl2java):

```
usage: idl2java [-options] files...

where options include:
  -package <name>         The package name into which to generate code
  -idl2package <idl> <pkg> Put defns in scope <idl> into the specified Java
                          package.  (Sample use: -idl2package ::CORBA org.omg.CORBA)
  -version                Print version
  -portable               Generate portable stubs/skeletons (using DII/DSI)
  -strict                 Generate code which can run on any compliant ORB
  -smart_stub             Generate smart stub support
  -obj_wrapper            Generate ObjectWrapper support
  -incl_files_code        Generate code for included files
  -all_serializable       Make all data types implement java.io.Serializable
  -serializable <idl>     Make the data type specified by the absolute <idl> name
                            implement java.io.Serializable
  -root_dir <dir_path>    Generate code into the specified directory
  -no_comments            Suppress comments in generated code
  -no_examples            Suppress generation of example code
  -no_tie                 Suppress generation of tie code
  -no_stub                Suppress generation of stub code
  -no_skel                Suppress generation of all skeleton code
  -no_toString            Suppress generation of toString() methods
  -no_bind                Suppress generation of bind() methods
  -deprecated_skel        Generate deprecated version of skeleton
  -map_keyword<keyword> <replacement> Replace 'keyword' with 'replacement'
  -narrow_compliance      Generated narrow() methods exhibit standard CORBA semantics
  -no_narrow_compliance   Generated narrow() methods exhibit 3.2 semantics (default)
```

```
    -preprocess_only          Send preprocessed source to stdout; do not compile
    -no_preprocess            Do not preprocess the source
pre-processor options:
    -C                        Retain comments in output
    -D                        Define a macro
    -H                        Print the pathnames of included files
    -I<directory>             Specify an[other] directory in the include path
    -P                        Suppress #line pragmas
    -U                        Undefine a macro
```

For the purposes of our example, the following IDL2JAVA commands will produce the necessary files:

```
idl2java central.idl -root_dir ..\ -no_examples
idl2java pos.idl -root_dir ..\ -no_examples
idl2java store.idl -root_dir ..\ -no_examples
```

The IDL2JAVA translator will generate the corresponding package hierarchy for the Java mapping (e.g., an IDL module corresponds to a Java package). We specify not to produce examples, but you may want them to simplify development (as the shell will be created).

For POS.IDL, the IDL2JAVA IDL translator will produce the following files:

```
POS.POSIdHolder.java
POS.POSIdHelper.java
POS.BarcodeHolder.java
POS.BarcodeHelper.java
POS.InputMedia.java
POS.InputMediaHolder.java
POS.InputMediaHelper.java
POS._st_InputMedia.java
POS._InputMediaImplBase.java
POS.InputMediaOperations.java
POS._tie_InputMedia.java
POS.OutputMedia.java
POS.OutputMediaHolder.java
POS.OutputMediaHelper.java
POS._st_OutputMedia.java
POS._OutputMediaImplBase.java
POS.OutputMediaOperations.java
POS._tie_OutputMedia.java
POS.POSTerminal.java
POS.POSTerminalHolder.java
POS.POSTerminalHelper.java
POS._st_POSTerminal.java
POS._POSTerminalImplBase.java
POS.POSTerminalOperations.java
POS._tie_POSTerminal.java
POS.InputMediaPackage.OperatorCmdHolder.java
POS.InputMediaPackage.OperatorCmdHelper.java
```

You can ignore the _tie_ files unless you want to implement the interfaces using the TIE approach. You could have suppressed the generation of the _tie_ files by specifying –no_tie as an option to IDL2JAVA.

You should be able to compile each `.java` file as long as `vbjorb.jar` and `vbjapp.jar` are in your CLASSPATH. These two `.jars` are part of VisiBroker for Java.

Similar output will be generated from other IDL files—it really depends on its contents.

The files ending with `ImplBase` are the ones you need to inherit from and provide an implementation.

Once you have compiled the `.java` files (including the ones for your application), place them into a directory specified in your CLASSPATH (or in a `.jar` file).

CHAPTER 27

The Depot

27.1 Language-Independent Overview

This section is for everyone, regardless of which programming language you're using. It adds implementation detail to the requirements set out in the A&D, which we left out on purpose when we were writing it; at that point, we were primarily concerned with analyzing and stating the *problem*, and implementation details would have been an unnecessary and annoying distraction. Now, with the problem thoroughly analyzed (keeping in mind that, for any real-life problem, we would actually iterate through the entire A&D implementation procedure a number of times, spiraling in on an optimal solution), we are free to concentrate on the *solution*, and it is appropriate for us to focus now on algorithms, data flow, file formats, and other implementation details.

When CORBA started being used for enterprise-level solutions, one of the primary concerns of users was its *scalability*—that is, the ability to add more load to the system (usually more clients and more requests) in a graceful fashion, without hitting hard limitations that make further growth impractical. Although our retailing example will start running with only a few POS terminals, a single Store, and a single Depot, of course we're planning to grow into a mega-merchant with hundreds of stores, each with dozens of POS terminals, plus telemarketers selling directly into customers' homes, and an e-commerce Web site taking millions of hits per day, all running off a common database containing our stock tally and an application server enforcing business rules for pricing as well as tax calculation.

This is *not* going to happen with the implementation we've chosen for our tutorial example and we'll tell why, and what you can do about it, in the first section of this chapter. Our tutorial concentrates on basic CORBA techniques, and exposes the classic CORBA interfaces. When you're finished, you'll understand how CORBA works and how CORBA objects can correspond, one for one, to objects in the real world. But, we don't want you to take our *implementation* as your pattern for enterprise implementations because we have *not*—out of consideration for you while you're learning the basics—tuned it for enterprise throughput. If we had, trust us, first-timers would not be able to learn the basic structure of CORBA while working through it because too much of it gets wrapped up and specialized for scalability and robustness.

After we've covered general implementation and scalability aspects in the next section, we'll proceed to the example.

Of course, the Depot object has to execute the functionality prescribed in our A&D in every language, so we'll work out the language-independent details in this section—algorithms, file formats, data flow details—and then split into language-specific chapters. The Store and POS chapters are organized just like this one. Figure 23.1 showed this organization in some detail.

Before we head into the Depot, we'll review how the rest of the next nine chapters are organized. We've divided the code for each module into three parts, based on what it does and where it comes from:

- *Code generated from the IDL by the language mapping.* For each language, this code is the same for all ORBs because the language mapping is an OMG standard.

- *Code that executes the functionality of the module.* For each language, this code is common to all ORBs because we've used good programming practice to write portable code.

- *Code that takes care of system and ORB-dependent details.* This is the only code that differs, for a given language, from one ORB to another and only for BOA ORBs. (Code for POA ORBs ports, as we've mentioned and point out again later in the chapter.)

To emphasize commonality of the different CORBA implementations in this book, the common code from the first two parts is presented only once, in its own sections. Chapters presenting C++ language coding start with the language-independent overview, and the common code is presented in Sections 2 (for the IDL-derived code) and 3 (for the common functionality) of those chapters. Java and COBOL chapters start right out with common code in Sections 1 (IDL-derived) and 2 (common functionality).

The implementors have done their best to maximize the amount of common code and minimize the amount of ORB-specific code. The new POA specification will give you totally portable code on the server side (with expanded capability as well), but, as we write this book, there are only a few POA-based ORBs on the market, so for now, we've implemented the example mostly using the BOA. There *is* a POA implementation in this book for both C++ and Java, and you'll find it as you look through. But, even if you're not using one of these POA ORBs now, your ORB will come out with a POA soon, and when it does, you can use this code because it ports directly from one ORB to another, of course—that's what POA means (Portable Object Adapter, remember!).

If you read the first edition of this book you'll recall that we used a substitute Naming Service that we called the "Pseudo-Naming Service" because, at the time, not all vendors had a Naming Service. Now they do, so we've modified the example in this edition to use it and, since we're being standard, the Initialization Service at startup as well.

27.1.1 Scalability and CORBA Implementation Design

Most of us learned the facts of life about searching for a piece of information very early in our careers. The easiest way of storing information is in a "flat file" (structured as an array), and the easiest way of finding an item is by starting at the beginning of the array and checking each element in turn. The cost of that search algorithm is a linear function of the size of the array. One way to speed things up is to get a faster disk and a faster computer. That's insufficient when the number of elements gets large, so we can change the algorithm to a binary search, reducing search time to a logarithmic function of the size, a major reduction. However, as the number of items becomes very large, we can't make further improvements in the algorithm or get faster equipment. More disks don't make things faster and the single computer design point is a bottleneck. That is, as the problem gets bigger, we hit a hard limit and there's no good way to move forward. It's tempting for us software people to blame the hardware, but that's not the problem. The problem is the original design decision to store the information in an array because that's the easiest way. That design decision effectively limits our ability to grow. Most of us know now that there are much more efficient ways of storage: partitioned databases, hashing, indexes, and parallel access to the same database, to name a few. Using these techniques, it is possible to continue to grow by adding more disks and more computers, using more disk space to help in the search, and executing the search in parallel. The programming task isn't as easy, but being able to grow is worth the work. Of course, this is now second nature to all of us; these standard techniques are packaged as part of any database and the high-level programming task actually is easier. There are still limits, but they are incredibly higher than simple, linear search. Design decisions have many effects.

Scalability isn't solved by faster round-trips or shorter messages for requests. While fast messaging is useful, it has the same limitations as speed and memory within the computer. Even getting message time down to zero doesn't do much (if anything) for scalability because the in-computer aspects dominate. Faster messaging and shorter messages are, of course, important. They are another dimension of performance measurement, useful in all applications, especially for real-time applications.

Scalability in an enterprise similarly requires using multiple resources to divide the work. Adding more resources will increase capacity *if the basic design allows it*. Since computer resources are essentially memory and speed, these are the design points for scalability. While we can add more memory, there are limits to that, as well as costs. So, one software attack point is use of memory. If you are memory bound (or likely to become so), use memory for an object only when necessary and, when finished, give it up so other objects can use it. There is overhead in initializing and storing object state to and from memory, but that overhead is offset (in many cases) by increased sharing of the memory. For speed, one software solution is parallelism. Whenever feasible, make it such that any one of several processes or machines can execute an object. To do this, there is overhead in deciding where to direct individual requests and in coordinating state among several machines, but, again, in large applications this is more than made up for by increased parallelism.

Not coincidentally, both memory and machine usage techniques for scalability involve careful object state management. Managing the state of an object means keeping track of where that state exists, in long-term storage on disk or in short-term storage in memory, and in transferring the state to achieve maximum resource utilization. Again, not coincidentally, careful state management for scalability has other benefits: easier recoverability after errors, avoidance of single points of failure, transactional behavior, dynamic configuration, and others.

All these benefits require extra work from programmers, but they are absolutely necessary for enterprise-level programming. You can write good CORBA-based programs or bad CORBA-based programs. CORBA gives you the ability to do distributed computing but, like most other tools, you have to use it skillfully.

One of the first tools you should use for memory management of object state is the POA, but you have to use its features well. It's also possible to use the POA (or any other tool) to produce bad memory utilization, depending on the nature of your objects. The POA allows you to program using several patterns that have implications for memory utilization. Here are a few:

- Explicitly activate an object (that is, create a servant for it and initialize its state) at server initialization and keep state in memory until server termination. You can hand out references to such objects, and when the POA receives requests on those objects it will immediately dispatch to the servant's methods. This pattern is useful for an object that has little state and that gets a large number of requests per second. Specifically, such an object doesn't need much memory (the same concept as "little state") and won't take much time to initialize and save state since it's done only once (instead of many times per second). Of course, you can explicitly activate and deactivate at any time, not just at server initialization, but the timing is always under your control so you should carefully consider how soon you can possibly deactivate the object. An object of this sort is sometimes called "stateful"; that is, its state is in memory between requests.

- Creating a POA that uses a Servant Manager gives you much more control over memory use for objects that have a great deal of state. You can hand to clients object references for objects that are not active (that is, are not present in memory). When a request comes in for an object that is not active, the POA will call your servant Manager to create a servant and initialize state (perhaps from disk). The POA then invokes the method on your servant to fulfill the request. Depending on the kind of Servant Manager you have written, one possibility is that the object is immediately deactivated after the method call completes. The Servant or Servant Manager saves state to disk, deletes the Servant (freeing up memory resources), and waits patiently to repeat the procedure. This particular pattern is often called "stateless," meaning that object state is not kept in memory between requests. The object does have state, of course, but that state is usually kept on disk, not in memory.

- An alternate kind of Servant Manager doesn't immediately deactivate the object, thus keeping the state in memory once the object has been activated (that is, leaving it "stateful"). The trick for good memory management then is to find the earliest time possible to deactivate the object. For example, the client might call a method on the object that means "I'm finished with you for a while, go stand in the corner." That method would save its state and tell the POA to deactivate the object. Another good time to deactivate such an object might be at the end of a transaction. An object that takes active part in a transaction needs to stay active until the transaction terminates (rolls back or commits); it's then safe to deactivate.

There's a lot you can do with present-day (that is, 1999 and pre-POA) products as well, although the techniques won't port as easily as POA-based ones. If you're using a BOA ORB today, check your documentation for the instance management techniques that your vendor has provided to support scalability. They will have different names for different vendors' products, but you'll recognize them by the way they work now that you've read this section and found out what they (and you) have to do. Scalability has always been important to CORBA, and products have always been able to support scalable implementations even though the initial set of techniques wasn't standardized. In fact, it was this experience, collected by multiple vendors, that is embodied in the POA specification.

What does all of this mean for the example in this book? Well, the example implementation in the book is not intended to show enterprise-level techniques. It is intended to show the absolute simplest way for beginners to use CORBA. It is a teaching tool, not a template for betting your business. The object implementations do the simplest state management possible: They set object state at startup and keep it in memory for the duration of the application. (In POA terms, this is the first choice mentioned earlier: preactivate the objects and leave them active.) None of the common code tries to minimize in-memory state. This has the follow-on result that the objects can be run on one, and only one, machine. Since only one object implementation has the state in memory, that's the implementation that everybody has to use. No parallelism is possible.

Why did we do it that way? A couple of reasons: First, the POA isn't yet universal (although it's coming, and soon). Next, state management is highly idiosyncratic now, and not particularly simple. Saving and restoring state takes code that is not CORBA-specific and that may well require a database package, which we really don't want to ship as part of the example. Therefore, we produced code that is easy to understand (honest, it's trivial if you think about it for a couple of days) and only involves CORBA. For the same reason, we didn't try to dress up the user interface: It's not CORBA either, and not important for the CORBA learning process.

What specifically would we do to make the example scale better? Keep in mind what this means: A dozen or fifty huge warehouses, hundreds of stores, thousands of POS terminals, and millions upon millions of items in (and out of) stock. First, the Depot high-level design is fine, but we'd have more than one Depot implementation available and that implementation would be much different. A "Depot object" would be started only when needed (in POA terms, it would use a Servant Manager) and terminate immediately. It would read and write state—probably for only a single item— to one of multiple, partitioned databases using the database's control mechanisms to provide synchronization. That way, if there were several hundred stores trying for access at the same time, we could achieve considerable parallelism for the Depot. Although the example is a retail store and a store doesn't usually have very many cash registers (quaint old term, isn't it?) we might imagine a situation in which there are thousands of client terminals (say, for example, e-commerce). Our example design creates one StoreAccess object per terminal; the pedagogical reason is showing the creation of an object on the fly. Rather than doing that, we could change the high-level design to allow the Store object to be more intelligent. It would handle terminals directly, using more intelligent state management. There could then be multiple Store implementations for the same store as with the Depot. Alternately, there might be a single Store object that keeps simple state in memory, as now, and a much more intelligent StoreAccess object that handles a large number of terminals. There are many options.

The POA already gives you these options in a portable manner. When they become available, the CCM and the Persistent State Service will further ease the process of writing enterprise-level, scalable applications. Components will help decide when to bring state into memory and when to write it to disk, and will integrate with the Persistent State Service to help do the actual transfer more easily and portably, both among CORBA vendors and among database/persistence vendors. That will be the next step in your learning process. The example in the next edition of the book, based on these next-generation CORBA products, will contain code that's probably no longer but gives a lot more realism and functionality.

27.1.2 Language-Independent Depot Implementation Details

We've purposely structured this example to illustrate as many facets of CORBA as we could, in a reasonably realistic way. Look for these CORBA features in the Depot:

- Passing of object references between objects
- Use of the Naming Service
- Use of **in** and **out** parameters (sorry, we don't have an **inout** parameter)
- Raising of a CORBA exception

The Depot component is implemented as a server called `Depot_Server`. This server creates a single CORBA object of **interface Depot**, which is then registered with the Naming Service using the name `Depot`.

The Depot interface defines just one operation:

```
void find_item_info(
    in AStore::AStoreId store_id,
    in POS:: Barcode item,
    in long quantity,
    out AStore:: ItemInfo item_info)
    raises (AStore:: BarcodeNotFound);
```

Using an `out` parameter called **item_info, find_item_info()** returns the **ItemInfo** (that is, **item_type, item_cost, name**, and so on) of the item specified by the item parameter. To fulfill this requirement, the Depot needs to have a database giving the following data for each item type handled by the depot:

```
Barcode     name     quantity     item_cost     item_type
```

For simplicity, this data is stored in a text file called `depot.dat`. In a full commercial implementation of the Depot, this data would almost certainly be stored by a database management system. An example line of this data file is

```
102345    Pasta      2      12.38     FOOD
```

When the Depot is started, it reads this file and stores the data in an in-memory search structure. The details of this search structure (and in particular, its efficiency) need not concern us here since this is straightforward programming that is independent of any CORBA concerns. It could be a binary search tree, or a simple linear list. In fact, the different language implementations presented in this book use totally different algorithms for the search, thus demonstrating the separation of interface and implementation that we have been emphasizing. You'll find details of each algorithm in the language-specific sections of this and the next two chapters.

The actions of the operation **find_item_info()** can be summarized as follows:

- Take the item parameter (of type **POS::Barcode**) and use it to look up the search structure for the **ItemInfo** record. If the item cannot be found in the search structure, return immediately with an exception of type **AStore:: BarcodeNotFound**.

- Use the **store_id** parameter of the call to update statistics for the specified store. For simplicity, this updating has not been carried out in the sample code.

- Use the **quantity** parameter of the call to reduce the count of the chosen item held in stock by the Depot. For simplicity, this updating has not been carried out in the sample code.

The code for **FindItemInfo()** can be written without using any special CORBAfacilities, and in particular, without invoking on any other CORBA objects in the network.

27.1.3 Accessing the Naming Service

In this section we are going to discuss and explain the reasons why we decided to wrap the standard CORBA Naming Service in an object with simpler interfaces called the NsPublisher.

We decided to wrap the Naming Service interfaces in order to factor out code that is common to all parts of the tutorial (and may be useful in other CORBA applications as well). We noticed that we were following the same pattern of calls each time we used it: Every time we bound a name, we wrote call to `bind` and checked for exceptions; if we found one, we called `rebind` and checked for exceptions again, and then returned. We followed a similar pattern when we resolved names. Instead of repeating all of this code in multiple places in the example (so that we would have to change it everywhere if we wanted to change it anywhere), we put it all into an object that we could call with a simple invocation—a wrapper. We named the Wrapper object `NsPublisher`. Because we use, underneath the wrapper, the standard OMG Naming Service, we retain all of the benefits of standardization: The vendor provides the implementation; if our enterprise maintains a site-wide installation, we access it; and our code will port from one vendor's implementation to another.

The model that the Naming Service is built on is one that is very familiar to most people: It is a database of associations between a name and some information (in this case, an object reference). The same concept allows access to the data contained in this file by typing in the name of the file as "Chap27.doc" or "c:\primer\Chap27.doc" depending on whether I want to access a file in absolute or relative notation. Therefore, the name is being used as the "key" to access some interesting information stored somewhere.

Although the Naming Service is one of the most important CORBAservices, it is not absolutely vital for users to understand all the workings of this service before they write an application. For example, it is not necessary to understand the organization of a hard disk in order to edit a file.

Normally, the most difficult part of writing a CORBA application is getting an initial reference to the CORBA object that we want to use. Once an object's reference has been found, actually using the CORBA object becomes trivial. One of the key design goals of CORBA is to allow a user to access a remote service/object in a manner that is consistent with making a normal in-process call to a native object; in other words, a user shouldn't need or want to be able to distinguish the following piece of C++ code as an inprocess or distributed call:

```
interestingObj_ptr->someMethod();
```

Although the Naming Service IDL is fairly straightforward (see Chapter 11 for a discussion of the API in more detail), most normal (i.e., non-administrative) users only need to be able to extract and retrieve information from the Naming Service. An administrator will take care of maintaining the Naming Service, ensuring consistency (equivalent to checking a hard disk for errors), creating the structure into which objects are populated (equivalent to creating the directory structure on a hard-disk), federating Naming Services (equivalent to linking a Directory structure together), and so forth.

All we require, as users, is to be able to populate the Naming Service with object references (from the server side) and to be able to extract references from the Naming Service (from the client side).

For use on the client side of a CORBA application we need to write a method that we will call nsResolve, that has the following inputs:

- The *NamingContext* in which to search for the name. This is equivalent to the current working directory.

- The *name of the object* whose reference we are looking for (e.g., "Chap27.doc"). Just like a file name, a Naming Service name is split into two components: the *id* component (equivalent to "Chap26") and the *kind* component (equivalent to "doc").

This nsResolve method needs to return the following:

- The object reference that was associated with this name

On the server side of a CORBA application, we need to write a method that we will call nsBind, that has the following inputs:

- The NamingContext in which to bind the name (equivalent to the working directory).

- The object reference to put into the Naming Service (equivalent to the contents of a file).

- The name to associate with this object reference binding (equivalent to a file name). Again, this name has two components, the id and the kind.

This `nsBind` method doesn't need to return any information, but if it fails, it needs to raise an exception, which it does.

27.2 Getting Started With C++ Coding

Now we need to code the functionality of the `Depot` object. The IDL interface for the Depot was shown in Section 26.2.3. In this section, we'll implement this interface in C++. We'll first discuss the common code and then send you off to the section on your specific ORB for final coding, compilation, and linking.

Since this is the first example code we've seen for C++, here are a few comments that apply to all C++ code in this book. We have adopted the convention that **interface Xx** is implemented by C++ class `XxImpl`; hence, **interface Depot** will be implemented by class `DepotImpl`. The code for the Depot is given in the `Central` directory, and all file names given here are relative to that directory. The IDL definition for Depot can be found in a file named `Central.idl` (in the `IDL` directory).

Some of the book's example ORBs use the BOA coding style (before CORBA 2.2) and some use the POA (CORBA 2.2 and later). Since the majority use the BOA, the common codes sections here and in later chapters show its use in a relatively common interpretation (since BOAs differ). ORBs using the POA will note the differences. In addition, the names of the client stub and server skeleton "include" files generated by different ORBs' IDL compilers are different; this common code shows only one possibility. Also, the skeleton base class names for BOA ORBs vary and we show only one version; the POA skeleton class name is standardized.

The final convention for these chapters is that we show no error checking or debugging output in order to make the logical flow easier to understand. The code on the CD has error checking in appropriate places, to demonstrate CORBA's exception-handling ability, but we don't continue to explain it or go over it in the text here once we've covered the basics.

The overall system requires only one object of **interface Depot.** This is created in a server called `Depot_Server`, and the code for this is also given here.

The remainder of this section explains the code in the following order:

- The C++ binding for the Depot IDL
- The code for the server `Depot_Server`
- The declaration and then implementation of class `DepotImpl`

27.2.1 C++ Binding for the Depot

The IDL for the Depot is:

```
#include "POS.idl"
#include "Store.idl"
```

```
module CentralOffice
{
  interface Depot {
    void find_item_info(
        in  AStore::AStoreId      store_id,
        in  POS::Barcode          item,
        in  long                  quantity,
        out AStore::ItemInfo      item_info)
        raises (AStore::BarcodeNotFound);
  };
};
```

The C++ mapping results in the following signature for a client invoking the Depot's single operation:

```
void find_item_info ( AStore::AStoreId   store_id,
                      const char *       item,
                      CORBA::Long        quantity,
                      AStore::ItemInfo_out item_info);
```

For example, if we have a reference to the Depot interface, depot_ref, a very simple call might be:

```
Astore::ItemInfo_var returned_item_info;
depot_ref->find_item_info( 12, "pencil", 18, returned_item_info);
```

The types for the three parameters store_id, item, and item_info, are taken from the two included IDL files. Note that the declaration of the **ItemInfo** structure from the Store is mapped to a C++ class, Astore::ItemInfo_var, which allows the system to manage memory for us, as we explained in Chapter 7. The class Astore::ItemInfo_out is likewise a convenience for management of out parameters in the more recent version of the C++ mapping. Earlier versions used AStore::ItemInfo*& item_info instead, as you will see in some vendors' code.

27.3 Coding Functionality in C++

Now that we've briefly reviewed the C++ code produced by the language mapping, it's time to start coding the functionality dictated by our analysis and design.

27.3.1 The Depot_Server

The primary actions of this main() routine are to:

- Initialize the ORB by calling ORB_init() and BOA_init() (lines 11–12).
- Find the system's Naming Service object (lines 14–17).
- Create an instance of class DepotImpl, passing it the name of the data file passed in by the command-line parameter (lines 20–21); then initialize the Depot by loading from its database (line 24).

- Register the Depot in the Naming Service (line 25) so that stores can find it.

- Call the `impl_is_ready()` function on the BOA to inform it that the implementation is ready to accept incoming operation calls (line 28); in this case, operations call on the `DepotImpl` object.

Here is the code. Most of the actions of the `main()` function in the actual file are coded within a `try` block, and the corresponding `catch` clause reports any exceptions that are raised.

```
// Filename: Depot_Server.cpp
1   #include "DepotImpl.h"
2   #include <iostream.h>
3   #include <stdlib.h>
4   #include <vendor naming service files>
5   #include "primer_utils/NsPublisher.h"
6
7   int main(int argc, char** argv)
8   {
9       DepotImpl *theDepot;
10
11      CORBA::ORB_ptr orb   = CORBA::ORB_init(argc, argv, "PRIMER_ORB");
12      CORBA::BOA_ptr boa   = orb->BOA_init(argc, argv, "PRIMER_BOA");
13
14      CORBA::Object_var obj =
15          orb->resolve_initial_references("NameService");
16      CosNaming::NamingContext_var naming_service    =
17          CosNaming::NamingContext::_narrow(obj);
18
19      // Create a new Depot
20      const char* depot_data_file = argv[1];
21      theDepot = new DepotImpl(depot_data_file);
22
23      // Load the files in.
24      theDepot->loadDepot();
25      NsPublisher::nsBind(obj, theDepot, "Depot", "Primer_Example");
26
27      // Wait for incomming requests.
28      boa->impl_is_ready();
29
30      delete theDepot;
31      return 0;
32  }
```

27.3.2 Depot Implementation: Class Declaration

The class definition of `DepotImpl` is shown in this subsection. The member function `find_item_info()` corresponds to the operation of the same name; its parameters and return type are dictated by the standard mapping from IDL to C++. In addition, class `DepotImpl` adds other members required at the implementation level. Here, a member variable of type `DepotData` and a constructor are added. C++ type `DepotData` will be explained later in this chapter. In general, any number of member functions and variables can be added at this implementation stage.

```
   // filename: DepotImpl.h
1  #include <Central_s.h>
2  #include <DepotData.h>
3
4  // The super class of your implementation class
5  // depends on the output of your ORBs IDL compiler.
6  class DepotImpl : public CentralOffice_Depot_base_impl
7  {
8  private:
9      DepotData m_items;
10     CORBA::String_var m_data_file;
11     static void _abort(const char *msg);
12
13 public:
14 DepotImpl(const char* data_file);
15
16     void loadDepot();
17
18     void find_item_info(
19         AStore::AStoreId    store_id,
20         const char*         item,
21         CORBA::Long         quantity,
22         AStore::ItemInfo_out item_info
23     );
24 };
```

Other important details here include: In line 6, `DepotImpl` inherits from a BOA (Basic Object Adapter, introduced in Chapter 5) class generated by the IDL compiler. This gives instances of class `DepotImpl` the support they require to be CORBA objects. The name of the base class varies between the C++ ORBs using the BOA; line 6 shows one example. The base class name has been standardized for the POA. Only servers (server `Depot_Server` here) are concerned with Object Adapter classes; clients are not aware of them.

In line 1, the file `Central_s.h` is included; it contains the C++ definition of the IDL interface. It is automatically generated from the `Central.idl` file, which holds the definition of the **Depot** interface. This filename will vary for the various vendors.

27.3.3 Depot Implementation: Class Implementation

The implementation of class `DepotImpl` (file name `DepotImpl.cpp`) includes the following header files:

```
#include <iostream.h>
#include <fstream.h>
```

```
#include <stdlib.h>
#include <stdio.h>
#include "DepotImpl.h"
```

It also defines the following variables at the global level:

```
const int    NITEMTYPES=3;
const char *itemtypestext[NITEMTYPES] = {"FOOD","CLOTHES","OTHER"};
```

The last of these contains the string representation of the general classifications of the goods the Depot handles.

The _abort member function is a convenience routine for error exits and is included in all the implementation classes in the example (not just the Depot).

The constructor for class DepotImpl is coded as follows. Its parameter is the name of the file containing the Depot's data. The only action of the constructor is to save the name of the file.

```
DepotImpl::DepotImpl(const char* data_file)
    : m_data_file(CORBA::string_dup(data_file))
{
    // Nothing else to do
}
```

The DepotImpl object holds a search structure describing the items that it handles. This is held in its m_items member variable, which internally contains structures of type AStore::ItemInfo. The variable m_items is populated by reading lines from the data file passed as a parameter on the constructor.

The member variable m_items is of type DepotData, a C++ class that is used in the implementation of the Depot interface. m_items is used to store and then efficiently find descriptions of the items that the Depot stocks. Class DepotData is not directly related to any IDL definition since it does not need to be directly accessed by remote clients. It is explained later in this section.

After constructing class DepotImpl, the main program calls its member function loadDepot to read each line of the data file. Each item of a line is read into a C++ object of type Astore::ItemInfo, which can hold the description of one stock item. That ItemInfo object is then inserted into the m_items variable using the insert() function of class DepotData. The loadDepot code follows:

```
1   void DepotImpl::loadDepot() {
2       AStore::ItemInfo loaditem;
3       loaditem.item = new char[30];
4       loaditem.name = new char[40];
5       char tempstring[30];
6       int i;
7
8       ifstream is(m_data_file, ios::in|ios::nocreate);
9
10      while (!is.eof())
11      {
12          is >> loaditem.item;
13          is >> loaditem.name;
```

```
14          is >> loaditem.quantity;
15          is >> loaditem.item_cost;
16          // Read in the string containing the itemtype and convert it to
17          // an enumerated value
18          is >> tempstring;
19          i=0;
20          while (i<NITEMTYPES && strcmp(tempstring,itemtypestext[i]) != 0)
21              i++;
22          if (i < NITEMTYPES)
23          {
24              loaditem.item_type=AStore::ItemTypes(i);
25              m_items.insert(loaditem);
26          }
27      }
28 }
```

It starts (lines 2 to 4) by creating and initializing a structure of type `AStore::Item-Info`. It then opens the data file (line 8) and loops (line 10) until each line has been processed. Each line is read in the following order: item barcode, item name, stock level, item cost, and item type. The first four of these are easily read (lines 12 to 15). The item type is read as a string (line 18), and then converted into an enumerated value (of type `AStore::ItemTypes`). This conversion is done by comparing (line 20) the string read with each of the strings in the `itemTypesText` variable, which holds the strings `"FOOD"`, `"CLOTHES"`, and `"OTHER"`. If a match is found, the index into the `itemTypesText` array is converted (line 24) into an enumerate constant of type `AStore::ItemTypes`.

The code for the member function `find_item_info()` is shown next. The in parameters to this function include the `Barcode` of the item (which is mapped to `const char*` in C++), and there is an out parameter (`item_info`) of type `AStore::Item-Info`. The function searches for the `Barcode` using the `m_items` member variable, using its `locate()` function. This function returns a boolean to indicate whether the item has been found. If the item has been found, the `item_info` parameter will be updated to contain details of the found item. Otherwise, the `find_item_info()` function raises a `BarcodeNotFound` exception back to the client that called it.

```
1  void DepotImpl::find_item_info(
2      AStore::AStoreId    store_id,
3      const char*         item,
4      CORBA::Long         quantity,
5      AStore::ItemInfo*&  item_info)
6  {
7      item_info = new AStore::ItemInfo;
8      if ( m_items.locate(item, *item_info) == 0)
9      {
10         throw AStore::BarcodeNotFound(item);
11     }
12 }
```

On line 7, the out parameter `item_info` is initialized to a new `AStore::Item-Info` structure. (Note that the out parameter `item_info` is mapped slightly differently in a recent C++ binding update to allow better memory management. Some of the implementations have the new binding `Astore::ItemInfo_out`.) The in parameter `item` is then used to search for the required item in the `Depot`'s search structure (line 8). If the item is found, the `item_info` parameter will have been updated, and the actions of the function are complete. If the item is not found, an exception is thrown in line 10.

Class `DepotImpl` uses class `DepotData` as the type of its member variable `m_items`. Class `DepotData` is used as a transitory store and quick-search facility for the items known to the `Depot`. The remainder of this subsection shows the implementation of this class, which is declared as follows:

```
// Filename DepotData.h
#include <Central_s.h>
class TreeNode;

class DepotData {
    TreeNode *m_root;
    unsigned long _locateNode(const char* bc, TreeNode * &ret_node);
public:
    DepotData() : m_root(0) {};
    unsigned long locate(const char* bc,AStore::ItemInfo &i);
    void          insert(const AStore::ItemInfo &i);
};
```

As well as a constructor, class `DepotData` defines member functions `insert()` and `locate()`. The former adds an item description, and the latter searches for an item and updates its second parameter to contain all of the information known about it. `locate()` returns a boolean to indicate the success or failure of the search.

To store its data, the `DepotData` class uses a binary search tree (member variable `m_root`), the nodes of which are of class `TreeNode` (another C++ class that is not directly related to the IDL definitions). `TreeData` is declared as follows:

```
// Filename: TreeNode.h
#include <Central_s.h>

class TreeNode {
public:
    TreeNode *m_left, *m_right;
    AStore::ItemInfo m_item;

    TreeNode() : m_left(0), m_right(0) {}
};
```

`TreeData` holds its left (`m_left`) and right (`m_right`) pointers and an item of type AStore::ItemInfo. It provides a simple constructor to initialize its left and right pointers. For simplicity, the two pointers and the item pointer are public, but it would also have been easy to add access functions to set and get these values.

The code for `locate()` and `insert()` is in file DepotData.cpp. Let's discuss the code for the function `DepotData::insert()` first.

```
1  #include "DepotData.h"
2  #include "TreeNode.h"
```

```
 3
 4   void DepotData::insert(const AStore::ItemInfo &i) {
 5       TreeNode *temp;
 6       const char *s = i.item;
 7       if (!_locateNode(s,temp)) {
 8           TreeNode *new_node=new TreeNode;
 9           new_node->m_item=i;
10           if (m_root==0) {
11               m_root=new_node;
12               return;
13           }
14           if (strcmp(i.item,temp->m_item.item)<0)
15               temp->m_left=new_node;
16           else
17               temp->m_right=new_node;
18       }
19       else {
20           temp->m_item=i;
22       }
23   }
```

The first action of this function is to find the correct position for the new data in its binary search tree. This is done on line 7 using the private member function _locate-Node(). This returns the boolean value false if the item being inserted does not already exist in the binary tree. Line 7 also tests the return value of _locateNode(). If the item is not already present, line 8 creates a new node of the binary tree, and line 9 assigns it to its m_item member variable (the left and right pointers will be automatically set to zero by the constructor of TreeNode).

The next step is to attach the new node to the existing binary tree. If the tree is currently empty, line 11 makes the new node the root node. Otherwise, line 14 tests whether the new node should be added to the left or to the right of the correct node position (the correct position is returned as the second (reference) parameter of _locateNode()). Line 15 attaches the new node to the left; line 17 attaches it to the right.

Finally, if _locateNode() indicates that the item is already recorded in the binary tree, line 20 replaces the old value with the new value.

The private function _locateNode() performs the normal binary search algorithm, branching to the left if the sought-after position is less than the current node and to the right if it is greater. The code, without further explanation, is as follows:

```
unsigned long DepotData::_locateNode(const char* bc, TreeNode *
&ret_node) {
    int compare;
    ret_node=m_root;
    if (ret_node==0) return 0;

    compare=strcmp(bc,ret_node->m_item.item);
    while (compare!=0) {
        if (compare<0) {
            if (ret_node->m_left==0) {
```

```
                   return 0;
             }
         else
             ret_node=ret_node->m_left;
     }
     else {
         if (ret_node->m_right==0)
         {
             return 0;
         }
         else
             ret_node=ret_node->m_right;
     }

     compare=strcmp(bc,ret_node->m_item.item);
 }
 return 1;
}
```

The `DepotData::locate()` function is coded using the private function `_locateNode()`:

```
1  unsigned long DepotData::locate(const char* bc,AStore::ItemInfo &i) {
2      TreeNode *t;
3      unsigned long status = _locateNode(bc,t);
4      if (status)
5          i=t->m_item;
6      return status;
7  }
```

Line 3 attempts to find the item in the binary tree; if it is present, the parameter i is updated to point to the `AStore::ItemInfo` structure found. The boolean return value indicates whether the item was found.

27.3.4 NsPublisher: Wrapping the Naming Service

The various sections of the sample application connect to each other by use of the CORBA Naming Service. As we pointed out in Chapter 4, the CORBA standard way of "bootstrapping"—that is, finding an initial object reference to get started—is to use the `CORBA::resolve_initial_references` operation, asking for an object reference for a system-wide Naming Service. Specifically, after first obtaining an ORB reference, each section in the common code has the following statements:

```
CORBA::Object_var obj = orb->resolve_initial_references("NameService");
CosNaming::NamingContext_var naming_service =
        CosNaming::NamingContext::_narrow(obj);
```

Using this initial Naming Service reference, a server registers itself when started by giving the Naming Service an identifying name and a corresponding object reference.

Code needing to connect to the servers correspondingly asks the Naming Service to find an object reference corresponding to a particular name.

As we pointed out in Section 27.1.4, we're going to wrap the Naming Service in an object named NsPublisher. We'll put all of the Naming Service access and error handling into this one object, and call it whenever we need to bind or resolve a name. This way, our code will be less cluttered and we benefit from our thorough coding in NsPublisher every time we invoke it.

The wrapper function that helps us register a name and corresponding reference is (ignoring the usual error checking) the following:

```
1   void NsPublisher::nsBind(CORBA::Object_ptr nsObj,
                              CORBA::Object_ptr bindObj,
                              const char * id,
                              const char * kind )
    {
2       CosNaming::NamingContext_var ns =
            CosNaming::NamingContext::_narrow(nsObj);

3       CosNaming::Name_var name = NULL;

4       name = new CosNaming::Name(1);
5       name->length(1);
6       name[(CORBA::ULong)0].id = id;
7       name[(CORBA::ULong)0].kind = kind;

8       try
        {
9           ns->bind(name, bindObj);
        }
10      catch(CosNaming::NamingContext::AlreadyBound ab)
        {
11          ns->rebind(name, bindObj);
        }
    }
```

The first parameter, nsObj, is the reference that the caller has found for the initial Naming Service. The common code finds this reference in the main program and passes it to the classes that need it so that they can pass it to nsBind (and nsResolve, below). The parameter bindObj is the object reference that is going to be bound (or registered, or advertised—whatever term you like). Parameter id is the name to be associated with bindObj. Parameter kind is used to further identify and distinguish id; it is used in the name structure required by the Naming Service.

The Naming Service's structure name is a sequence of structures, each structure containing an identifying string (id) and second string (kind) that further qualifies the id. One of the purposes of this wrapper class is to centralize the creation of this structured name. The code to do this is in lines 3–7. Once the structured name is created from the simple strings supplied by our code, line 9 invokes the Naming Service to bind the name to the object reference. In this simplified example, it is possible that a server crashes and is later restarted; it will try to bind a name that was bound before (since the Naming Service is still running). Lines 10 and 11 take care of that case by ignoring the previous binding and replacing it with the one now needed.

The wrapper function to look up the name is similar:

```
1   CORBA::Object_ptr NsPublisher::nsResolve (CORBA::Object_ptr nsObj,
                                                const char * id,
                                                const char * kind)
    {
2       CORBA::Object_ptr resolveObj = NULL;
3       CosNaming::NamingContext_var ns      =
            CosNaming::NamingContext::_narrow(nsObj);
4       CosNaming::Name_var name = NULL;
5       try
        {
6           name = new CosNaming::Name(1);
7           name->length(1);
8           name[(CORBA::ULong)0].id = id;
9           name[(CORBA::ULong)0].kind = kind;
10          resolveObj = ns->resolve( name );
        }
11      catch (const CORBA::UserException&)
        {
12          cerr << "CORBA::UserException caught" << endl;
13          throw NsPublisherException(
                "NsPublisher::resolve - CORBA User Exception");
        }
14      return resolveObj;
    }
```

The `try` block surrounding line 10 (the actual lookup operation) traps exceptions returned by the Naming Service. The most likely such exception is that the name is not found. This is usually a programming error. You can generate such an error by starting a POS client and giving it a store number that does not have a server. Because the POS terminal can't find a store with that number, it complains. The messages in the client window will look something like:

```
prompt>POS_client 44 99
Creating POSTerminalImpl
CORBA::UserException caught
NsPublisher::resolve - CORBA User Exception

prompt>
```

The "Creating" line is written by the client main program. The first error message is produced in `nsResolve` (line 12) and the second in the invoking code when it receives the exception thrown in line 13. The exception thrown is defined in file `NsPublisher.h` and has the same structure as a CORBA-defined exception; the code receiving the exceptions uses normal exception handling to deal with it.

27.4 Implementing the Depot Application Using CORBAplus for C++

This section describes the Vertel's Expersoft CORBAplus implementation of the Depot. The CORBAplus implementation of the Depot component will only need a small number of recurring changes. The primary places where the Depot implementation differs from the common source base are the base class names, the use of CORBAplus' event loop object, and the include files.

A makefile is provided for both Unix and Windows platforms. See Section 26.1.1.1 for details on how to build the Depot component.

27.4.1 Changes to the Depot Server Component

27.4.1.1 CORBAplus Include Files

A typical CORBAplus server will need the following include files:

```
#ifdef WIN32
#include <pbroker/winsvc/winsvc.h>
#else
#include <pbroker/unixsvc/unixsvc.h>
#endif
#include <pbroker/corba/orb.h>
#include <pbroker/corba/boa.h>
#include <pbroker/corba/naming/naming.h>
#endif
```

The first set of include files will include either the Windows version of the CORBAplus event loop or the Unix version of the CORBAplus event loop. The orb.h and boa.h bring in the definitions for the CORBAplus ORB and BOA, respectively, and naming.h brings in the definitions required to use the Naming Service.

27.4.1.2 BOA::obj_is_ready

The first task is to notify the BOA that the object is ready to receive events, which is accomplished with the boa->obj_is_ready call. The obj_is_ready method returns control to the caller, so many objects can be readied in this fashion:

```
#ifdef EXPERSOFT
        boa->obj_is_ready( theDepot, nil);
```

27.4.1.3 CORBAplus Event Loop

When we talk about the CORBAplus event loop in the context of a client or server, we are not referring to the OMG-specified Event Service, but instead a process local event loop.

The XpsEventService class is very flexible, and we only show one possible use of it. See the CORBAplus documentation for a complete listing of methods available on XpsEventService. The event loop allows the application process to detect and dispatch incoming requests such as method invocations from remote clients. In the example, we call eventService.mainloop, which will enter an infinite loop dispatching events. The mainloop method will not return control to the caller. There are other methods of the XpsEventService class that will return if more control is required by the application.

```
XpsEventService eventService;
eventService.mainloop();
```

Those are all the necessary changes specific to the Depot server. Next, we will look at the implementations.

27.4.1.4 Base Class Names

idlc, The CORBAplus IDL compiler, generates a base implementation class for each IDL interface. Implementation classes, such as DepotImpl, are derived from this base class. The naming convention followed by idlc is to append the string _base_impl to the interface name. Thus, for the interface Depot, declare DepotImpl as:

```
#include <Central_s.h>
class DepotImpl : public CentralOffice_Depot_base_impl {
      ...
}
```

Notice that we included Central_s.h. The CORBAplus idlc compiler will generate all implementation-specific bindings into a file called <ModuleName>_s.h.

27.4.1.5 Use of _out Classes for CORBA out and inout Arguments

For some IDL types, the C++ mapping defines a pointer-reference parameters type for the inout or out parameter passing modes. The C++ mapping requires that all operations support arguments of the IDL type's C++ type equivalent, as well as its _var counterpart. To ensure that types can be passed as out parameters by either their true type or their var type, CORBAplus generates an out helper class. The out classes are used in the generated operation signatures so that the memory management behavior is correct regardless of whether the var or non-var types are passed as parameters to the operation. In this example, since AStore::ItemInfo is a variable length structure, an out parameter will be generated, but you can think of it as AStore::ItemInfo *&. For example, the signature of find_item_info is

```
void find_item_info(
      AStore::AStoreId store_id,
      const char* item,
      CORBA::Long quantity,
      AStore::ItemInfo_out item_info
   );
```

but the implementation of `find_item_info` is the same as described previously in Section 27.2.4.

27.4.2 Compiling and Running

Finally, you will need to compile and link the `Depot_Server` program. The object file for the main program should be linked with object files for all the implementations that may be instantiated in your program. Both Unix and Windows makefiles are provided. We assume that you have installed CORBAplus for C++ and have `PBHOME` and `PBTM-PDIR` environment variables configured correctly. The easiest way to build the `Depot_Server` is to use the makefiles `Makefile.unix.xps` or `Makefile.win.xps`, which are located in the `Central` directory.

To build the Solaris version, at an xterm, type:

```
%make -f Makefile.unix.xps
```

To build the Windows version, at a command window, type:

```
%nmake -f Makefile.win.xps
```

27.4.2.1 Running the NamingService

To start the CORBAplus Naming Service open a Unix shell or Windows command tool and execute the following:

```
pbnamed -pbportr 6004 -pbtrace
```

The `-pbportr` option will instruct the Naming Service to listen on the specified port number even if the port is thought to already be in use. This is helpful if you start and try to restart the Naming Service. Without this option, you will get an error stating that the port is already in use.

The `-pbtrace` option will print trace information when clients access the Naming Service so you can watch what is happening.

Another useful tool is the Naming Service explorer, `nsexplr`, which can be found in the `%PBHOME\bin` or from the CORBAplus program group. This tool is only available on Windows but can access a Naming Service anywhere. Naming Service Explorer will allow you to graphically view your name space and make modifications if necessary. (This service anticipates some of the functionality defined by the Interoperable Naming Service, described in Chapter 11.)

27.4.2.2 Running the Depot_Server

To start the Depot program, execute the following command lines, each in its own window:

```
%pbnamed -pbtrace -pbportr 6004
%.\central\Depot_Server depot.dat -pbinit NameService\
iiop://localhost:6004/NameServiceRoot
```

CORBAplus URL Notation

The CORBAplus URL notation is very flexible and is used in these examples to provide the initial object reference to the Naming Service. The URL notation is broken up into the following structure:

```
iiop://<hostname>:<port number>/<alias>
```

The hostname is the hostname or IP address of where the server is running. The port number is the port on which the server is listening. The alias is the process local name associated with the object. Again this anticipates, although not exactly, the `corbaname` and `corbaloc` URL object reference formats defined in the new Interoperable Naming Service and mentioned in Chapter 11.

27.4.2.3 Windows Platforms and Visual C++ Project Settings

It is important to point out the Visual C++ project settings so you can build your own projects from scratch. If you have Visual C++, start it now and follow along. Otherwise, read through the steps and make a mental note so that you can find the information here when you need it. This information assumes Visual C++ 5. CORBAplus for C++ is certified with Visual C++ 6.0, but not everyone has converted so these instructions will need to be modified slightly for those using Visual C++ 6.0.

Select the **File->New** menu option. You will be presented with a dialog box where you should select "**Win32 Console Application**". Be sure to select the location and project name before you press the OK button.

Select the **Project->Setting**... menu option. You will be presented with a dialog box. Next select the **C/C++** tab. Table 27.1 has all the necessary project settings. Any settings that are specific to this example are pointed out.

Select the **Tools->Options**... menu item. In the dialog box, select the **Directories** tab. Under "**Show directories for:**" select **Include Files.** Add the full path to `%PBHOME\include`, but do not use `%PBHOME%`; instead substitute the path. We have found that Visual C++ will not expand this using environment variables. Next select **Library Files:**. Again, add the full path to `%PBHOME%\lib`, expanding `%PBHOME%`.

There are all the settings for Visual C++. You will just need to add files to this project and you are ready to build CORBAplus applications.

27.5 IBM Implementation of the Depot

This section explains how to compile and run the Depot server in the IBM ORB. Since this is the first of three servers discussed in depth, we will include some overview and general background information that will not be repeated when the other servers are discussed in later chapters.

Table 27.1 Visual C++ Project Settings for Vertel's Expersoft's CORBAplus

SELECTED TAB	CATEGORY	ENTRY LABEL	SETTING
C/C++	General	Preprocessor Definitions	USE_XPS_DLL EXPERSOFT (only necessary for this example)
	Code generation	Use runtime Library	Multithreaded DLL
	Optimizations	Optimizations	Either: Disable (Debug) or Default
	Precompiled headers		Not using precompiled headers
	Preprocessor	Additional include directories	Add any additional include paths for this specific project. Typically: <path to idlc generated header files>
Link	General	Object/library modules	Add CORBAplus libraries. Assuming single-threaded applications: corba.lib pbroker.lib winsvc.lib If you are using the Naming Service, then add: naming.lib

27.5.1 Overview of Code Changes for IBM

There are three types of changes that need to be made:

- The #include statements for header files that are generated by the IDL compiler need to be modified to match the filename given to the file by the IBM IDL compiler. For example, the name of the header file emitted for central.idl is central.hh.

- Implementations inherit from the implementation class emitted by the IBM IDL compiler. In this example, a Skeleton class is used for implementation (as opposed to a Tie class). The name of the Skeleton class emitted by the IBM IDL compiler has the form of <BaseClassName>_Skeleton. These classes are generated by the IDL compiler.

- Initialization of the IBM ORB in the server main() program.

27.5.2 Specific Changes to the Depot C++ Code

27.5.2.1 DepotServer.cpp

Near the start of the file, include the header for the CORBA Naming Service being used. For the IBM implementation, a simple Naming Service has been implemented in the `primer_utils` directory to the IDL interface defined in the `CosNaming.idl` IDL file. So, we include:

```
#include <CosNaming.hh>
```

The ORB and BOA initialization calls near the beginning of `main()` have been modified to specify that the ORB being initialized is the IBM ORB. This is indicated by the final string parameters "DSOM" and "DSOM_BOA", respectively, in the calls:

```
CORBA::ORB_ptr orb  = CORBA::ORB_init(argc, argv, "DSOM");
CORBA::BOA_ptr boa  = orb->BOA_init(argc, argv, "DSOM_BOA");
```

The remaining code in the server that is unique to the IBM implementation is related to server registration. The IBM ORB maintains a persistent Implementation Repository of defined servers. Each server is registered in the Implementation Repository with a record describing the server's characteristics. The record is keyed by the server's UUID or the server's alias (an optional unique string name, which is more user friendly than a UUID string). The class `ImplDef` defines the data for this record. Typically, the Implementation Repository would be managed as part of server installation and administration and would be used by the ORB daemon to find and activate server processes when necessary. For simplicity in this example, we have avoided the server administration and use of the daemon for activation. The `DepotServer` assumes that it has not been registered previously (by an administrator or by a previous execution) and therefore creates an `ImplDef` to register itself.

```
CORBA::ImplDef * imp = new CORBA::ImplDef ();
imp->set_protocols("SOMD_TCPIP");
```

The only field of the implementation record (instance data on the `ImplDef`) that the server sets is the field that defines which protocols can be used to access the server. In this case, the TCP/IP protocol is specified. Other fields that would commonly be defined for an implementation include the path name of the server executable and the server alias. (`<path>/Depot_Server.exe` and `Depot_Server`, respectively, would be appropriate for this server.) The call to `impl_is_ready` passes the `ImplDef` as a parameter:

```
boa->impl_is_ready (imp, 0);
```

The second parameter is optional and is not normally included. It is used in this example to indicate that the server does not wish to use the daemon for activation. By default, servers use the daemon for activation, and communication with the daemon occurs under the impl_is_ready call to report that the server is active. Specifying the second parameter here has two effects. First, it prevents communication of server status to the daemon. Second, it causes object references that are generated by this process to map directly to this process rather than the daemon.

27.5.2.2 DepotImpl.h

The `DepotImpl.h` file includes the header file generated by the IDL compiler for the Central IDL file using the name assigned by the IBM ORB's IDL compiler:

```
#include <Central.hh>
```

The parent class for the `DepotImpl` is specified to be `Depot_Skeleton` (the name generated by the IDL compiler). This parent class provides the server-side support needed by an IBM ORB object implementation:

```
class DepotImpl : : virtual public CentralOffice::Depot_Skeleton
```

27.5.2.3 DepotData.cpp, TreeNode.h

Include the IBM header file generated by the IDL compiler, with the line:

```
#include <Central.hh>
```

27.5.3 Compiling an IBM ORB Client or Server

The IBM ORB has specific unique binaries for various operating systems/compiler combinations. This example code and makefiles were implemented on Windows NT/ Microsoft C++. Client and server code must be linked with the client or server stubs generated by the IDL compiler. For an interface defined in `Foo.idl` you should link servers with `Foo_S.cpp` and clients with `Foo_C.cpp`. When a process is both a client and server you only need to link the server code, which includes the client code.

You also need to link with the IBM ORB's library (`emororm.lib`).

In this example, the Central IDL file includes the POS and Store IDL files, so our Depot needs to be linked with the generated code for each of these files: `Central_S.cpp`, `POSS_c.cpp`, and `Store_S.cpp`. The Depot is also a client of the Naming Service, so it needs to be linked with `CosNaming_C.cpp`.

27.5.4 Running the IBM ORB

This example is very easy to run because it has been coded in a way that does not require the administrative tasks of server registration or daemon communication. While these are features that normally you would want to take advantage of, it is not necessary to describe them for this example.

There is some minimal configuration for running on your system that is required. This is limited to modification of stanzas in the `SOMCBENV.ini` file included with the ORB installation. Specifically, two stanzas must be modified: The `HOSTNAME` should be set to your system's `TCPIP HOSTNAME`, and you need to specify the file that will be used to contain the stringified object reference of the root naming context. The `Name_Server` included in the `primer_utils` directory of this example is coded to write its object reference to the filename `PNS.dat`. To enable the `resolve_initial_references` call for the ORB, the stanza in the `SOMCBENV` file must be modified to point to the `PNS.dat` file.

27.6 Orbix Implementation of the Depot

This section explains how to compile and run the Depot server in Orbix. Since this is the first of the Orbix servers discussed in depth, we will include some overview and general background information that will not be repeated when the other servers are discussed later.

27.6.1 Overview of Code Changes for Orbix

There are four types of changes that need to be made:

- `#include` Orbix header files.
- Inherit your base classes from `BOAImpl` classes generated by the IDL compiler.
- Add a `CORBA::Environment` parameter to the signature of IDL operation, in the implementation classes.
- Initialize Orbix in the server `main()` program.

A note on Environment parameters: The CORBA specification provides two ways to handle exceptions: using native C++ exceptions or using `CORBA::Environment` parameters. The latter is for compilers that do not support C++ exceptions. Orbix requires the `CORBA::Environment` parameter to be present, even if native C++ exceptions are supported (which provides portability between such compilers). However, when C++ exceptions are supported (as assumed in these examples), you can ignore this parameter completely in your code. You simply need to include it in the implementation function signatures to override the correct virtual functions. You do *not* need to pass it in client code, or make any use of it in server code.

27.6.2 Specific Changes to the Depot C++ Code

27.6.2.1 Depot_Server.cpp

At the start of the file, include the Orbix version of the CORBA Naming Service header file:

```
#include <NamingService.hh>
```

Modify the initialization section at the beginning of `main()` as follows:

```
CORBA::ORB_ptr orb  = CORBA::ORB_init(argc, argv, "Orbix");
CORBA::BOA_ptr boa  = orb->BOA_init(argc, argv, "Orbix_BOA");
```

```
char* server_name = "Depot_Server";
boa->setServerName(server_name);
boa->setNoHangup(1);
```

The changes to ORB_init() and BOA_init() indicate that the ORB you are using is Orbix.

setServerName() is required before you create objects in an Orbix server; server _name corresponds to the server name registered in the Implementation Repository (see below).

setNoHangup() is an optional call; it ensures that the server will not time out while clients are still connected. By default, in Orbix a server may time out if clients are connected but are not making any calls.

Finally, update the call to impl_is_ready to include the server name. This is required for servers that may be run manually. It is not required if a server is only launched automatically by the Orbix daemon, since the daemon will supply the name at launch time.

```
boa->impl_is_ready(server_name);
```

27.6.2.2 DepotImpl.h

Include the header file generated by the IDL compiler for the Central IDL file:

```
#include <Central.hh>
```

Add an inheritance for class DepotImpl from class DepotBOAImpl (generated by the IDL compiler). This provides the server-side support needed by an Orbix object.

```
class DepotImpl : public CentralOffice::DepotBOAImpl
```

27.6.2.3 DepotData.cpp, TreeNode.h

Include the Orbix header file generated by the IDL compiler, with the line:

```
#include <Central.hh>
```

27.6.3 Compiling an Orbix Client or Server

Compile clients and servers using your normal C++ compiler. To enable CORBA, you need to link them with some IDL-generated code. For IDL file Foo.idl you should link servers with FooS.cpp and clients with FooC.cpp. When a process is both a client and server, you only need to link the server code, which includes the client code. (The suffix for the generated code varies depending on your system; for example, .cpp, .C, .cxx, .cc.)

You also need to link with the Orbix library, and may need to link with some system libraries depending on your system (e.g., network libraries.) For examples of how to compile and link Orbix applications on your system, look at the demos that ship with Orbix.

In our example, the Central IDL file includes the POS and Store IDL files, so our Depot needs to be linked with the generated code for each of these files: CentralS.cpp,

POSS.cpp, and StoreS.cpp. The Depot is also a client of the Naming Service, so it needs to be linked with NamingServiceC.cpp.

The code on the CD has makefiles to build the example, and detailed instructions on how to compile and run them.

27.6.4 Running Orbix

Orbix provides a daemon that allows clients to find servers in the system. In CORBA terms, this daemon implements the Implementation Repository. You must run it on each host that runs Orbix servers (but not necessarily on those that run only clients). The daemon is the program called orbixd in the Orbix bin directory; on Windows systems there are also GUI and NT service versions of the daemon.

The orbixd daemon, the Orbix utilities, and any clients or servers you may run require some configuration information. This is usually provided in a configuration file called Orbix.cfg. On Windows systems you can also use the Registry. You can configure Orbix by editing the Orbix.cfg file and setting the environment variable IT_CONFIG_PATH, or you can use the GUI configuration tool that is supplied with Orbix to do this. See your Orbix installation instructions and documentation if you need further information.

27.6.5 Registering Servers

Each Orbix server must be registered with the orbixd daemon, either using the putit command or the GUI server manager tool. The server that creates the Depot object is called Depot_Server, and it can be registered as follows:

```
putit Depot_Server <path_to_Depot_Server_executable>
```

This example also requires the Naming Service, which should be registered as follows:

```
putit NS <path_to_OrbixNames_executable>
```

You must provide an absolute pathname to putit. You can optionally include any number of command-line arguments for the server, which will be useful for some of our later examples. Once registered, a server can be launched manually (for example, from the command line or in a script), or started automatically by the Orbix daemon when a client uses one of the objects in the server. All of the CORBA BOA *activation modes* are supported: shared, unshared, per-method-call, and persistent, and some useful variations to these are provided.

In the case of our Depot server, you need to run it once manually so that it can register its objects with the Naming Service (using the same command-line arguments as you register with the daemon). After that, clients can find the objects via the Naming Service, and the Orbix daemon will automatically launch the server.

The putit command is one of a set of utility commands that help programmers and administrators to manage servers. Other commands list and remove registered servers, and to list the set of currently running servers. Each of these commands is implemented using an IDL interface to the Orbix Implementation Repository. There is also a graphical server manager tool that provides the same functionality via a GUI, and uses the same IDL interface. This interface is published so you can write your own server management tools if you wish.

27.6.6 Implementing an IDL Interface in Orbix

You implement each IDL interface with a C++ class, which redefines each of the member functions that correspond to the attributes and operations of the IDL interface. (If you want, you can provide more than one implementation of the same interface.) There are two ways to associate a C++ implementation class with an IDL interface, by inheritance or by delegation, also known as the BOAImpl and TIE approaches, respectively.

27.6.6.1 The BOAImpl Approach: Using Inheritance

Your C++ implementation class inherits from a BOAImpl class generated by the IDL compiler. For example, to implement the interface Depot, you write a C++ class that inherits from DepotBOAImpl (where BOA refers to the Basic Object Adapter, presented back in Chapter 5). By convention, the implementation class is called DepotImpl:

```
class DepotImpl : public DepotBOAImpl
{
     // add member variables
public:
     // redefine all of the member functions that
     // correspond to IDL operations and attrs.
};
```

When you create instances of class DepotImpl in your server, they automatically become CORBA objects available to clients. For example:

```
Depot_var my_first_depot = new DepotImpl;
```

Three C++ classes are associated with each IDL interface. For example, for interface Depot, the three classes are:

- Depot, the C++ mapping of the IDL interface Depot, *used by clients*. It provides each IDL operation or attribute as a C++ function.

- DepotBOAImpl, which provides server-side support for implementation classes using inheritance. The IDL compiler generates this class. The implementation class (for example, DepotImpl) inherits from DepotBOAImpl to indicate that it is implementing the **Depot** IDL interface.

- DepotImpl, which is the implementation class that provides the behavior behind the IDL interface. This class can have any name you wish; only the server uses it. The client uses the class Depot, and is not concerned with server-side classes DepotBOAImpl and DepotImpl.

This is one example of how the client is isolated from implementation details, including the name of the implementation class.

27.6.6.2 The TIE Approach: Using Delegation

In some cases, you may not want your implementations to inherit from a BOAImpl class. In this case you can use delegation to associate your implementation with the interface, using the Orbix TIE macros as follows:

```
class DepotImpl // note no inheritance
{
     // add member variables
public:
     // define all of the member functions that
     // correspond to IDL operations and attrs.
};
DEF_TIE_Depot(DepotImpl)
```

When you want to create an instance of your implementation, you also need to create a TIE object to associate it with a CORBA interface, like this:

```
DepotImpl* my_first_depot = new DepotImpl;
Depot_var my_depot_tie = new TIE_Depot(DepotImpl)(my_first_depot)
```

You can choose either of these two approaches when writing your applications. The BOAImpl approach is simpler, because there is just one implementation object that includes the CORBA functionality and your implementation code. The TIE approach is more flexible, because the CORBA server functionality is completely separated from your implementation class, and you are not obliged to use any particular inheritance.

27.7 Implementing the Depot Package Using VisiBroker for C++

The Inprise VisiBroker implementation of the Depot component will only need a small number of changes. There will be a number of recurring changes that will be required to the common code for each component implemented using the VisiBroker libraries.

A makefile is provided with the implementation that you should use to compile and link the program. The code provided has been written using the Microsoft Visual C++ 5.0 compiler. The Inprise C++ Builder 3.0 compiler can also be used to compile and link the program if you are using the correct VisiBroker libraries and header files.

There are two libraries provided with the VisiBroker C++ product. The first library is a single-threaded version of VisiBroker, and the second is a multithreaded version. The library names (under Win95/98/NT) are orb.dll and orb_r.dll, respectively. The VisiBroker product is supported on many platforms, including Solaris, HP-UX, AIX, and others.

27.7.1 Changes to the Depot Server Component

The Naming Service is used to register the Depot; therefore, the Depot server acts as a client to the Naming Service. The following preprocessor directive must be used to include the Naming Service definitions:

```
#include <CosNaming_c.hh>
```

The VisiBroker idl2cpp compiler uses "_c" suffix to denote files that represent definitions that clients should use. The "_s" used by the idl2cpp compiler represents definitions that should be used by servers.

In VisiBroker the osagent daemon can be used to facilitate locating an instance of the Naming Service. Make sure you have an osagent daemon running within your subnet. (See the VisiBroker documentation for further information on the osagent.) The common code:

```
CORBA::Object_var obj = orb->resolve_initial_references("NameService");
CosNaming::NamingContext_var naming_service =
CosNaming::NamingContext::_narrow(obj);
```

can be replaced with:

```
CosNaming::NamingContext_var naming_service =
CosNaming::NamingContext::_bind();
```

27.7.2 Changes to the Other Depot Components

The Depot implementation code in VisiBroker does not require much change from the common code. The few required changes are with the skeleton class name that must be derived by the implementation and the header file that must be included for the Depot definition.

The Depot skeleton file must be included when writing the DepotImpl class. This can be done as follows in the DepotImpl.h file:

```
#include <Central_s.hh>
```

This file will include the definition of the Depot skeleton that the DepotImpl class will inherit from. The class inheritance declaration should be as follows:

```
class DepotImpl : public _sk_CentralOffice::_sk_Depot
```

In VisiBroker, the _sk_ prefix is used for skeleton code in which you should subclass in your implementation. Here, _sk_CentralOffice::_sk_Depot indicates that the Depot skeleton is in the module CentralOffice. If you look at the IDL, you will see that this is the case.

The inherited skeleton code is required by the implementation (DepotImpl) in order to unmarshal incoming requests and invoke the implementation's function. The skeleton is also responsible for sending back the return value(s) (i.e., result, out, and inout parameters) back to the client. The skeleton code is generated by the IDL compiler and should not be modified.

The `DepotData.h` and `TreeNode.h` files also require that the file `Central_s.hh` be included.

27.7.3 Compiling the Depot Package

When setting up your build environment under a different compiler/platform, you should only have to change the makefiles to reflect the compiler, linker, libraries, and paths on your system.

To run the build of this program, you should do the following:

- Compile the IDL for the Depot
- Build the Depot

I will assume that you will be using the 'nmake' program. If you are using 'gmake' or some other build system, you should use the equivalent commands. Step 1 is simply a matter of compiling all the IDL files. This should be run from the root project directory, and only be run once for the entire project:

```
prompt> nmake idl
```

This will run `idl2cpp` on the IDL files and produce four files for each .idl file, two files for the stub(s), and two files for the skeleton(s). The two files are the `.hh` and `.cpp` files. You should never have to modify the files generated by an IDL compiler. I know of a site that sets the files generated by the IDL compiler to 'read-only' in order to prevent the developers from modifying these files.

To compile the Depot server, change to the `central` directory and compile the depot:

```
prompt> nmake compile
```

This will produce the object files for the different components. You will not be able to link the program until all the other packages have been implemented. If you have already implemented and compiled the other packages, you can link the program by typing the following in the `root` project directory:

```
prompt> nmake link
```

This will produce an executable (`.exe` files under Win95/98/NT). In the `central` directory, you will find a file named `Depot_Server.exe`, which you can run to bring up the Depot and make Depot objects available to clients.

27.8 Implementing the Depot Using BEA WLE

BEA's WLE is intended for high-throughput production systems, strongly recommending the use of certain patterns now introduced into the CCM. As mentioned in Section 27.1.2, the common implementation was not designed for large-scale production use (to keep the code simple). To stay faithful to the goal of commonality, we can't show you what the recommended BEA WLE implementation looks like. We can, however, show you one of the possibilities by simply moving some of the common code from one place to another. The pattern of scalability shown is "delay activating an object until it is needed." We can't show more advanced techniques without changing the common code beyond recognition, but this one change may give you a flavor of the BEA WLE approach and a small part of what the CCM has in store.

27.8.1 IDL-Generated Files

Since the names of C++ "include" files have not been standardized by OMG, each ORB must state what files its IDL compiler produces. The WLE IDL compiler produces four files for C++: a definition file and code file each for stub and skeleton, with a _c suffix referring to files used by the client and _s referring to files used by the server. In the case of `Central.idl`, the files are `Central_c.h`, `Central _c.cpp`, `Central_s.h`, and `Central_s.cpp`.

27.8.2 POA

Since WLE uses the POA, the name of the skeleton base class for an interface has been standardized. More significantly, the CORBA 2.2 POA makes a strong, necessary distinction between an implementation class instance (a servant) and an object (as we pointed out in Chapter 5). Many BOAs have the server instantiate the implementation class and return the pointer to that class as an object reference. (The BOA obviously must convert the pointer to an object reference.) The POA, on the other hand, allows an object reference to be created with or without creating a servant, thereby allowing considerable flexibility and scaling opportunities. An application must make explicit use of POA features to create an object reference. The other important concept for the POA (not in the BOA) is the Object ID. The Object ID is the real identifier of the object within a given POA. The POA uses the Object ID as part of its algorithm for accessing the object. A servant might use the Object ID to decide what data makes up the object—for example, using it as a key to a database. For the POA, an object is not active until the POA has both a servant pointer and an associated Object ID.

27.8.3 Server

BEA's WLE is intended for production systems that have high throughput needs. As mentioned in the BEA WLE overview, BEA strongly recommends the use of certain patterns, similar to the CCM patterns. Most of the design decisions of the example application are contrary to these patterns, so we have made small changes to the common code to show some of the recommended pattern use. We could have matched the common code exactly (and did, initially), but it would go against our own documentation and the future direction of the CCM; we don't want people to even *think* those unscalable thoughts. Unfortunately, the example's major coding decisions make it impossible to achieve *any* scalability—the objects are kept in memory at all times, defeating any attempt at scaling because only one server can be associated with, say, the Depot. This is reasonable for an example, but we'd like to note that this code shouldn't be used as the basis of an enterprise-level application. It is strictly a demonstration of the simplest techniques.

The BEA WLE version of the example uses most of the common code, modified slightly for the TP Framework (TPF) described in Section 25.2.3.2. The primary structural difference for a WLE server concerns the main program; it is supplied by the TPF. This means that a server writer doesn't have to activate the ORB or POA; the TPF `main()` creates the kind of POA needed and does the attendant administrative functions. A user ties into the main program functions by supplying an object called `Server` with three methods: `initialize`, `create_servant`, and `release`. Method `initialize` is invoked by the TPF main program to allow the user to do server-specific initialization; this is code that would otherwise be in the `main()`, such as registration with a Naming Service or factory finder. Similarly, `release` performs server-specific shutdown. Method `create_servant` is invoked by the TPF when it needs a servant to satisfy a request. (At this point the TPF is partially delegating the POA's invocation on the `PortableServer::ServantManager` established by the TPF.)

Specifically for the Depot, in `Depot_Server.cpp`, we don't use `main()`; we define the `Server` class. Some of the `main` code is moved to the `Server` class and some to `DepotImpl.cpp`, for database initialization. In addition, we do not create the `Depot` instance immediately as in the common code; instead, we create only a reference to the `Depot` object. This allows delaying the activation of the `Depot` object until the latest possible time, with benefits as explained in the BEA WLE overview. This is the one scalability factor that doesn't upset the common design very much.

None of the BEA WLE example code uses the common code's `NsPublisher::bind` operation. Instead, the code uses a LifeCycle `FactoryFinder` (a single line of code) to register a name. Since a `FactoryFinder` itself acts a Naming Service with a single level of names, this is an exact analog to the common code. (Although we are registering a Depot reference with the `FactoryFinder`, we really are using it as a simple Naming Service for simplicity. This is not recommended for anything but super-simple cases. For a real application, we would add a factory interface to the Depot.) As explained in the BEA WLE overview, the CORBAservices LifeCycle `FactoryFinder` pattern is more scalable than a simple Naming Service.

All these differences take longer to explain than to code. The code for `Server::initialize`, (the analog of the `main` program startup code) to create the Depot object reference and register it is:

```
1 CORBA::Boolean Server::initialize(int argc, char* argv[]) {
2     depot_as_factory_ref = TP::create_object_reference(
          CentralOffice::_tc_Depot->id(),    // Interf Repos Id
          argv[1],                           // Data file is ObjectId
          CORBA::NVList::_nil()              // No special needs
          );
3     TP::register_factory(depot_as_factory_ref, "Depot");
4     return CORBA_TRUE;
  }
```

Line 1 shows that the `initialize` function receives the command-line parameters passed through from `main`. WLE's TP class is a wrapper for many of the POA functions and for the `FactoryFinder`. In this case, line 2 uses one such function to create the object reference for the Depot. The parameters are the Interface Repository ID (`_tc_Depot` is part of the standard mapping for C++) and the Object ID (the name of the Depot file passed on the command line). This Object ID will be used later, when the object is activated. Line 3 registers the Depot reference.

When the Depot reference is invoked for the first time, the TPF needs to get a servant, which it does by invoking `Server::create_servant` (the analog of the `main` code that creates a `DepotImpl`).

```
1 Tobj_Servant Server::create_servant(const char* intf_repos_id)
2 {  return new DepotImpl(); }
```

In this case, there is only one implementation class in the server, so our application knows that the only reason for a call on it is to return a `DepotImpl` servant (see Chapter 30 for a variation). The returned value in line 2 is a `Tobj_Servant`, a specialization of the `PortableServer::Servant` class. As a result, a TPF servant is a `PortableServer` servant, with two extra methods defined in the skeleton, `activate_object` and `deactivate_object`, of which only the first is used, described under DepotImpl.

Finally, the `Server` class has a release method that is called when the server shuts down (the analog of the `main` program shutdown code). In this case, the only action necessary is to "unregister" the Depot from the system-wide `FactoryFinder`. This particular piece of bookkeeping is more important for a production-level system like BEA WLE because the infrastructure continues running even after individual servers shut down (perhaps the servers are merely to be moved), and we should clean up carefully to preserve resources. The code is simple.

```
1 void Server::release(){
2    if (CORBA::is_nil(depot_as_factory_ref.in()))
3        return; // cleanup not necessary
4    TP::unregister_factory(depot_as_factory_ref.in(), "Depot");
   }
```

27.8.4 DepotImpl

The POA mapping specifies a skeleton (base) class whose name is "`POA_`" followed by the fully qualified name of the interface. The implementation class inherits from this base class. For the example, the `DepotImpl` class definition inherits from the standard POA skeleton as follows:

```
class DepotImpl : public POA_CentralOffice::Depot { ...
```

For an WLE server, the TPF (and CORBA components) recommends that we separate the functions of creating a servant and initializing state for an object. This results in two differences from the common code. First, the constructor for `DepotImpl` simply creates the instance. Second, the servant class (`DepotImpl`) has an inherited method from the skeleton, `activate_object`. This method is invoked by the TPF when it is time to (duh…) activate the object; that is, to initialize its state. Thus, the common code is all in the WLE DepotImpl, just slightly rearranged to help scalability. Again, the specific code differences are minimal.

```
1   void DepotImpl::activate_object( const char* object_id ) {
2       m_data_file = CORBA::string_dup(object_id);
3       loadDepot(); }
4   DepotImpl::DepotImpl() {}
```

Line 1 starts the `activate_object` method; the TPF invokes it with a parameter that is the stringified Object ID. Recall that we had set the name of the data file as the Object ID when we created the object reference. This is where it is used: copy the data file name to the class's member data (line 2). We then call the common `loadDepot` to read the data file (line 3). Line 4 shows the constructor doing nothing (just constructing).

27.8.5 Creating the Application

The WLE code on the CD-ROM includes a setup command file and a makefile. The setup file takes care of the administrative aspects for an WLE domain (see Section 35.3 for details).

Specific directions: After you have copied the BEA-WLE tree from the distribution CD, change to the BEA-WLE directory and type `WLEsetup`. The setup file will create a subdirectory, "working", with some administrative files and another sub-subdirectory for administration. It will then completely generate the application by running the makefile.

The makefile completely builds all parts of the application by invoking further makefiles in each component directory. The makefiles were tested on a Windows NT 4.0 system using Microsoft Visual C++ 5.0. Fairly simple changes to the setup file and makefiles (directory paths, etc.) will make it possible to use the same code on any of the Unix systems supported by WLE.

The component makefiles contain two WLE-specific commands, `idl` and `build-objserver`. The `idl` command optionally takes an implementation configuration file (ICF) as a second parameter. This file is similar to the configuration file in the CCM, differing in syntax at this point because it preceded Components. The ICF tells the TPF how to treat the implementations in the server. There are two options of importance, the transactional model and the activation model. The example application has no transactions, so we specify a transactional model of "never". The activation model for the Depot object is "process", meaning that once an object has been activated, it stays active until the process shuts down. Since these models are not the default, they are specified in the file `Central.icf`.

```
module POA_CentralOffice {
    implementation DepotImpl {                  // name of implementation class
        activation_policy ( process );          // once activated, stay active
        transaction_policy ( never );           // will never use a transaction
        implements ( CentralOffice::Depot );    // interface used
        };
};
```

The `idl` command in the makefile thus boils down to the following (ignoring directory considerations):

```
idl Central.idl Central.icf
```

The `buildobjserver` command is used to create the server main for the TPF and to include all the correct libraries (so you don't have to remember them). Again, the command in the makefile boils down to:

```
buildobjserver -o Depot_Server.exe -f <list of .obj files>
```

CHAPTER

28

Depot Implementation in Java

28.1 Implementation Summary

This chapter begins with the standard approach to implementing the Depot application in Java. It follows on from the Depot Overview described in Section 27.1, which you should read first. The sections have the following outline:

- Review of the IDL, in which we will describe the mapping of types supported by the **Depot** interface.

- Implementation of the CORBA Object **Depot** covering both POA and non-POA implementations.

- Implementation of the main application class for both POA and non-POA implementations, which covers the use of the ORB, object adapter, and Naming Service components. We examine these components in more detail in this chapter, as the Depot application is the first one to be implemented.

- Sections for each ORB vendor, covering ORB-specific details.

By the end of this chapter, the Depot application will consist of two code modules, which will either be

```
DepotImpl.java
DepotServer.java
```

or

```
DepotPoaImpl.java
DepotPoaServer.java
```

The decision as to which you will develop will depend on whether the ORB you are developing with supports the Portable Object Adapter (POA) or not. As the names suggest, the Impl classes are implementations of the CORBA IDL **Depot** interface, and Server classes implement the main application routines. Whether you developing with an ORB that supports the POA or not, it is worth working through each of the common code sections in order to appreciate the differences between the object adapters.

28.1.1 Mapping the CentralOffice.IDL to Java

Let's review the IDL for **Depot**. It represents a single interface that supports a single operation:

```
module CentralOffice
{
  interface Depot {
    void find_item_info(
              in  AStore::AStoreId store_id,
              in  POS::Barcode    item,
              in  long                 quantity,
              out AStore::ItemInfo item_info)
      raises (AStore::BarcodeNotFound);
  };
};
```

The IDL for Depot illustrates a number of Java mapping features. We first described these in Chapter 8. Here we'll see how they're used in live code.

Modules. IDL modules map straight onto Java packages. As the interface Depot belongs to module **CentralOffice**, our implementation of this class must also belong to a Java package called `CentralOffice`.

Interfaces. The IDL compiler will generate a number of Java classes that represent the client and server view of the interface. However, the developer is required to provide the CORBA Object implementation. There are two approaches, implementation via inheritance and implementation by delegation (commonly known as the "TIE" approach). Both the `DepotImpl` and `DepotPoaImpl` classes are examples of implementation via inheritance, where the class is derived from an abstract 'skeleton' class generated from the IDL.

Operations, parameters, and basic types. The **Depot** interface supports a single operation, `find_item_info`, which the Implementation class must implement. The operation supports a number of parameters that illustrate the use of in parameters, out parameters, and the mapping of basic IDL types such as **long**; template types such as **string**; and constructed types such as **struct**s and enumerated types. The operation also introduces the concept of user exceptions (`AStore::Barcode-NotFound`).

IDL typedefs in Java. The parameters **store_id** and **quantity** are both examples of IDL **long** types. Of the two, **store_id** is interesting because it is an example of a user-defined data type constructed using the `typedef` statement in module AStore. In the mapping for C++, a corresponding `typedef` would generate a user-defined type `AStore::StoreId`, but in Java no corresponding statement exists and the standard mandates that any IDL basic types should resolve to the corresponding primitive Java type. So, both **store_id** and **quantity**, like all IDL **long** types, map to Java `int`.

Template types. The parameter **item** is an example of an unbounded string type (`POS::Barcode` is a user-defined type that is actually a **string**). Since the type `POS::Barcode` is another example of a typedef, the Java mapping rules mandate that this must map to the corresponding primitive type in Java. So, item is an unbounded IDL string that maps onto `java.lang.String`.

Constructed types. The parameter **item_info** is an example of a structure defined in IDL as **AStore::ItemInfo**. The data elements of this structure include an enumerated type. The precise details of both these constructed types are explained in Chapters 29 and 30 as part of the Store application implementation. The significant point about structures and enumerated types is that they have no natural mapping in Java. The standard maps both types onto Java classes of the same name:

Astore::ItemInfo maps onto a Java class `Astore.ItemInfo`.

Astore::ItemType maps onto a Java class `Astore.ItemType`.

Holder classes. In Chapter 8 we introduced `Holder` classes that enable Java to pass modified arguments back to the caller, and here we're going to see them in code. To support **out** and **inout** parameters in Java, the Java mapping defines appropriate `holder` classes for each type. The **item_info** is of type **AStore::ItemInfo**, so the IDL compiler will generate a holder class `AStore.ItemInfoHolder`. This class is used in the implementation of the method `find_item_info` to satisfy the final argument. You don't have to do any of the work for this; it's all been done for you and shows up in the IDL compiler output where you can examine it if you're curious. Here's a cut-down version of `AStore.ItemInfoHolder`; to see the rest, examine the files generated by your IDL compiler:

```java
package AStore;

public final class ItemInfoHolder
    implements org.omg.CORBA.portable.Streamable
{
    public AStore.ItemInfo value;

    public ItemInfoHolder()
    {
    }
    public ItemInfoHolder (AStore.ItemInfo initial)
    {
        value = initial;
    }
}
```

Helper classes. In Java, any user-defined IDL type will have a corresponding `helper` class. For example, `AStore.ItemInfoHelper` is the `helper` class for `AStore.ItemInfo`. Helper classes, as the name suggests, support ancillary methods such reading and writing from streams, and insertion and extraction from the IDL **any** type. They also support the `narrow` method that we will use in the Depot server application. We will explain its use later.

Exceptions. The Depot interface raises user exception **AStore::BarcodeNotFound**. In Java, user exceptions map onto their own class. Hence, **AStore::BarcodeNot-Found** maps onto a class `AStore.BarcodeNotFound`. The specifics of this class are defined in Chapter 30 as part of the Store application implementation. In Java, a user exception is derived from a generic class called `org.omg.UserException`. This class is derived from the generic Java exception class, `java.lang.Exception`. While an implementation may raise specific user exceptions, the ORB will raise system exceptions, which map to the class `org.omg.SystemException`. A CORBA system exception is derived from the generic Java class `java.lang.RuntimeException`.

In the code examples, whenever a CORBA invocation is made it is protected by checking for CORBA system exceptions; CORBA user exceptions, if applicable; and Java exceptions, if applicable.

28.2 Orb-Independent Java Coding II Functionality

Now that we've examined the mapping of the Depot interface, we're ready to implement it in Java.

28.2.1 Implementing DepotImpl.java

As mentioned earlier, `DepotImpl.java` is an example of implementation via inheritance. The Java class defined next satisfies all the requirements of a CORBA object implementation in Java.

```
package CentralOffice;

import CentralOffice.*;

import java.io.*;
import java.util.*;

class DepotImpl extends _DepotImplBase {

  public void find_item_info(int store_id,
                             String item,
                             int quantity,
```

```
                              AStore.ItemInfoHolder item_info)
      throws AStore.BarcodeNotFound
   {
   } // find_item_info

} // DepotImpl
```

The class inherits from `_DepotImplBase`, which is the skeleton class generated for IDL interface Depot. It supports a single method, `find_item_info`. The last parameter of this method uses a Holder class to match the behavior of an out parameter. The class doesn't do a lot at this point, but we will develop the implementation as we go.

28.2.2 Implementing DepotPoaImpl.java

Like `DepotImpl.java`, this is an example of implementation via inheritance. For a POA implementation, the files generated by the IDL compiler have a subtly different hierarchy and naming convention. `DeptPoaImpl.java` is derived from an abstract skeleton class `DepotPOA`.

```
package CentralOffice;


import CentralOffice.*;

import java.io.*;
import java.util.*;

class DepotPoaImpl extends DepotPOA {

  public void find_item_info(int store_id,
                             String item,
                             int quantity,
                             AStore.ItemInfoHolder item_info)
     throws AStore.BarcodeNotFound
   {
   } // find_item_info

} // DepotImpl
```

Apart from the class name, the structure of this class and the `DepotImpl` class is the same.

28.2.3 Common Depot Implementation Code

It is time to deal with the full Java implementation details of Depot. This component encapsulates a simple database that supplies product item information to connected stores. You may develop your own implementation; the code developed here is a simple example so that we can focus on aspects related to CORBA. Although the code extracts will refer to `DepotImpl.java`, they equally apply to `DepotPoaImpl.java`.

The Depot database of products is defined in a simple text file called depot.dat. The Depot component will process this file and cache the values in a hashtable, which will be processed by the find_item_info method. You can see how easy it would be to substitute a more robust and scalable implementation of the database behind the interfaces of the Depot as our retail empire grows. This is one of the significant advantages of the CORBA architecture. To load the database, we need to introduce a new method and add some private data members to the DepotImpl class. Let's examine this method. For clarity, all class data members have a m_ prefix.

```java
void loadDepot() {

BufferedReader inStream = null;

    Properties x = System.getProperties();
    Properties prop = new Properties(System.getProperties() );
    string filename = prop.getProperty("primer.depotfile");

    if( filename != null && filename.length() > 0 )
        m_filename = filename;

    File datFile = new File(m_filename);
    if( !datFile.exists() ) abort("Error: Could not find " + m_filename );

    try {
        inStream = new BufferedReader ( new FileReader( datFile ) );
    } catch (java.io.FileNotFoundException exc ) {
        abort("File " + m_filename + " could not be opened" );
    }

    String line = null;
    StringTokenizer    st;

    System.out.println("\n\n------------ Depot Inventory ----------");
    System.out.println("Barcode\t\tName\t\tQty\t\tCost\t\tType");


    try {
        while(( line = inStream.readLine() ) != null ) {

            ItemInfo itemInfo = new ItemInfo();

            st = new StringTokenizer( line );

            itemInfo.item = st.nextToken();
            itemInfo.name = st.nextToken();
            itemInfo.quantity = Integer.parseInt( st.nextToken() );
            itemInfo.item_cost = Float.valueOf(
               st.nextToken() ).floatValue();
            String Token = st.nextToken();
            if( Token.equals("FOOD") ) {
```

```
                itemInfo.item_type = ItemTypes.FOOD;
        } else if( Token.equals("CLOTHES") ) {
                itemInfo.item_type = ItemTypes.CLOTHES;
        } else {
                itemInfo.item_type = ItemTypes.OTHER;
        }

        m_depotDictionary.put( itemInfo.item, itemInfo);

        System.out.print(itemInfo.item + "\t\t" );
        System.out.print(itemInfo.name + "\t\t" );
        System.out.print(itemInfo.quantity + "\t\t" );
        System.out.print(itemInfo.item_cost + "\t\t" );
        System.out.println(Token );


    }
  } catch( java.io.IOException exc ) {
      abort("Error while reading " + m_filename );
  }
} // loadDepot
```

- The first task for this method is to establish whether the user has provided an alternative database file. If this is the case, then this file will exist in the system properties. The property is set by passing an argument to the Java Virtual Machine when the application is started. We reference the property list through the prop variable and search for a property called `primer.depotfile`.

- If this property exists, reassign the `m_filename` data member. Note that this variable has already been initialized to the default `depot.dat` file name.

- Check that the file exists and open it for processing (`inStream` variable).

- The file is processed line by line using a `StringTokenizer`. We want to store the data in the form of the IDL type **Astore::ItemInfo**, which is the type returned by `find_item_info`. This introduces the Java classes `Astore.IntemInfo` (structure), `Astore.ItemType` (enumerated type). A structure maps onto an object in Java with public data members and no access methods. Hence, all data members are assigned directly:

```
        itemInfo.item = st.nextToken();
        itemInfo.name = st.nextToken();
        itemInfo.quantity = Integer.parseInt(st.nextToken());
        itemInfo.item_cost =
Float.valueOf(st.nextToken()).floatValue();
```

AStore.ItemTypes is used to enumerate three product item types ("CLOTHES", "FOOD", "OTHER"). The class uses static data members, one for each item type, as the only means of creating an instance of an enumerated object. For example:

```
if( Token.equals("FOOD") ) {
                itemInfo.item_type = ItemTypes.FOOD;
} else if( Token.equals("CLOTHES") ) {
```

```
                          itemInfo.item_type = ItemTypes.CLOTHES;
    } else {

                          itemInfo.item_type = ItemTypes.OTHER;
        }
```

■ Once each record has been processed, it is added to the hashtable defined by the m_depotDictionary variable. In order to show a list of available product items when the example is run, the code prints a summary of product item details.

You may notice that the code introduces another method called abort. The method has been added to all the implementation classes in Java. It is a simple, consistent way of dealing with terminal errors. It is not designed for a real system, but suits the purposes of the example. On any terminal error, we call abort and close the application. The code for this method is:

```
private void abort( String msg ) {
    System.err.println(msg);
    try {
    Thread.currentThread().suspend();
    } catch( Exception e ) {}
    System.exit(1);
} // abort
```

The class is now ready for processing queries on product information, which means we need to provide an implementation for find_item_info. The code for this method is:

```
public void find_item_info(int store_id,
                           String item,
                           int quantity,
                           AStore.ItemInfoHolder item_info)
    throws AStore.BarcodeNotFound
  {
    ItemInfo i = (ItemInfo) m_depotDictionary.get(item);

    if(i == null){
      throw new AStore.BarcodeNotFound(item);
    }

item_info.value = new ItemInfo( i.item,

i.item_type,
i.item_cost,
i.name,
i.quantity);

  } // find_item_info


} // DepotPoaImpl
```

The implementation is very simple because the `load_table` method loaded the hashtable with data in the format we require. The caller of the method provides the barcode reference in the item parameter. The code uses this to search the hashtable:

```
ItemInfo i = (ItemInfo) m_depotDictionary.get(item);
```

The hashtable returns a generic object and we cast it to its correct type. We create a copy of this to return to the caller. The rationale behind copying the value is that the implementation is unaware of how it was called:

1. Was it called on remote CORBA Depot object reference?
2. Was it called on local CORBA Depot object reference?
3. Was it called directly (i.e., an invocation on the DepotImpl instance as opposed to CORBA Depot object reference)?

In Case 3, if we did not return a copy, the caller could amend the record details, which would update the database in the hashtable. We want only the implementation, and not the client, to control the database. Depending on the ORB implementation, which could optimize the marshaling of local invocations, a caller could update the database. Case 2 may have the same results as Case 3. In Case 1, a remote invocation will produce a copy, and so this cannot happen. In cases where the implementation controls the state of the encapsulated data, it is good practice to return explicit copies.

- If the barcode is found, assign the `Astore.ItemInfo` data into the `holder` class, which is returned to the caller.
- If the barcode is not found, throw the IDL user-defined exception `Astore.BarcodeNoFound`. This exception is defined to contain a string description of the barcode. Hence, when we create the exception we initialize it with the item value:

```
throw new AStore.BarcodeNotFound(item);
```

To complete the implementation, we require a constructor that initializes the hashtable for the database. The `DepotImpl` class now has the following structure, which applies equally to the `DepotPoaImpl` class:

```
package CentralOffice;

import AStore.*;
import CentralOffice.*;

import java.io.*;
import java.util.*;

class DepotImpl extends _DepotImplBase {

    private String     m_nsName = "Depot";
    private String     m_filename = "depot.dat";
    private Dictionary m_depotDictionary = null;

    private void abort( String msg ) {
```

```
        // see earlier description
    } // abort

    DepotImpl(){
        m_depotDictionary = new Hashtable( 20 );
    }  // Constructor

void loadDepot() {
        // see earlier description
    }  // loadDepot

    public void find_item_info(int store_id,
                               String item,
                               int quantity,
                               AStore.ItemInfoHolder item_info)
        throws AStore.BarcodeNotFound
    {
        // see earlier description
    }  // DepotImpl
```

28.2.4 Handling CORBA Objects in an Application

An application that handles CORBA object implementations requires two fundamental components: an ORB, and an object adapter. In a distributed world, objects need to advertise themselves if they are to make themselves known to perspective clients. One solution to this problem is to use the CORBA Naming Service. Before we develop the main application code, let's summarize how the application will use these components.

ORB. The ORB is fundamental to all CORBA applications in that it must be initialized before any CORBA calls can be processed. It is an example of a pseudo-object and is only relevant to the application that created it. Any attempts to pass this object to a distributed application that subsequently calls it will fail. In Java, the ORB object belongs to the package `org.omg.CORBA`. There is a comprehensive set of methods supported by the ORB object; we described these in Chapters 4 and 5 and is worth both a look back and a reference to your ORB's documentation for the rest of the discussion.

Object adapters. The object adapter manages the lifecycle of CORBA objects within a server. Like the ORB, it is a pseudo-object. The CORBA standard recognizes two object adapters of which the newer Portable Object Adapter (POA) deprecates the original Basic Object Adapter (BOA). The first Java ORBs came into existence before the POA had been finalized, but with the knowledge that the BOA would be deprecated. As an intermediate step, the ORB took on the role of the object adapter in the early revisions of the Java mapping. At the time we wrote this chapter, most but not all Java ORB products on the market used the BOA. As a result, this chapter contains both POA and BOA implementations—BOA code to help you with implementations using products current when the book first comes out, and POA code to show you how to code with this new feature and to help you program with future products (including future versions of *all* of the ORBs in this book!).

Naming Service. The Naming Service is a standard CORBA service that offers methods to advertise and discover CORBA objects in a distributed environment. All the example applications use the Naming Service and it seemed appropriate to introduce a class that encapsulated everything about the Naming Service.

This class describes how to use the Naming Service and the components it supports. We will discuss its implementation in Section 28.2.6.

28.2.5 Implementing DepotServer.java

It's time to get into the code. The DepotServer.java class is the main application class and we can perform ORB initialization in a number of places. Since this is a simple application, all of the relevant tasks are performed in main. So let's have a look at the code in its entirety:

```java
package CentralOffice;

public class DepotServer {

private static final String m_usageString =
    "Usage : java  CentralOffice.Depot [vendor specific options] \n";

private static void abort( String msg ) {
        System.err.println(msg);
        System.exit(1);
}  // abort

public static void main(String args[]){

    DepotImpl theDepot  = null;
    org.omg.CORBA.ORB orb = null;

    if( args == null ) {
      abort(m_usageString);
    }

    System.out.println("Depot.main ()");

    try {
      System.out.print("Depot.main () initialising ORB.......");

    orb = org.omg.CORBA.ORB.init(args,null);

      System.out.print("Depot.main () resolving root
      NamContext.......");

      org.omg.CORBA.Object obj = null;
      try {
          obj = orb.resolve_initial_references("NameService");
```

```
    } catch( org.omg.CORBA.ORBPackage.InvalidName exc ) {
        abort(
"ERROR: The ORB could not resolve a reference to the NameService");
    }


    System.out.print(
"Depot.main () creating new depot,connecting to ORB.......");

theDepot = new DepotImpl();
theDepot.loadDepot();

orb.connect(theDepot);

PrimerUtils.NsPublisher.nsBind(obj, theDepot, "Depot", "Primer_Example"
);

System.out.println("Depot is ready" );


    }


catch (org.omg.CORBA.SystemException se) {
        System.out.println ("Caught CORBA.SystemException : "  + se);
        se.printStackTrace();
    }

    catch( java.lang.Exception jle ) {
      jle.printStackTrace();
      abort("Caught java.lang.Exception : " + jle);
    }

  }  // main

} // DepotServer
```

- The class has two static methods: `main` and `abort`. The `abort` method has the same functionality as the `abort` method for the implementation class. It terminates the application in the event of a terminal error. The class defines one private data member, which is a usage string.

- The `main` method encapsulates all of the CORBA-related details. The first job of an ORB application is to initialize the ORB through a static method `org.omg.CORBA.ORB.init()`. This method returns an instance of the ORB. The `init` method has a number of implementations:

```
public static ORB init(Strings[] args, Properties props);
public static ORB init(Applet app, Properties props);
public static ORB init();
```

(Don't get confused about overloading. OMG IDL methods *cannot* be overloaded, but this is not IDL. It's Java, and overloading works fine in Java, even in CORBA applications. Just don't try to overload a CORBA Java invocation!)

As you can see, `init` caters to a variety of application types. In the code example, we chose to call the method that handles command-line arguments with a null property string. This is because it lets us tune the behavior of the ORB based on runtime arguments. Some ORBs mandate this, some do not. Check the ORB-specific code sections to see what arguments are required for your ORB.

Once we have a reference for the ORB, we can use it as a bootstrap to connect to standard CORBA Services. As we showed in Chapter 4, the ORB provides the method `resolve_initial_references`, which returns object references for services we need to bootstrap. We need an object reference for the Naming Service now, so it's time for us to use it. Here's the call:

```
obj = orb.resolve_initial_references("NameService");
```

Since the ORB deals with generic services, the method returns an object of type `org.omg.CORBA.Object`. Before the application can make invocations on the Naming Service, this object must be narrowed to the correct type. The object narrowing is handled by the `nsPublisher` class that was mentioned earlier.

■ Once we have the ORB running we can create the `Depot` object and load the database:

```
theDepot = new DepotImpl();
theDepot.loadDepot();

orb.connect(theDepot);
```

The final statement introduces the basic object adapter, which is encapsulated by the ORB. The `connect` method is the application's way of stating that the Depot component is ready to receive invocations. Without this statement, the ORB would not pass incoming requests onto the Depot component. If at any time the Depot wanted to block incoming calls, it could call the `disconnect` method on the ORB.

■ At this point, the only way a Store application will be able to call the Depot component is if it can find it. The Depot Server application advertises the object in the Naming Service using the `nsPublisher` class.

■ The Depot Server application is ready and has nothing further to do. Not quite true: Depending on the ORB you are using, the `main` application thread needs to allow the application to wait or loop to process incoming requests on the Depot. This can be done in a number of ways and each ORB vendor has submitted alternative ways of handling this as part of the ORB-specific code.

28.2.6 Implementing NsPublisher.java

Since we covered the Naming Service in Chapter 11, and introduced the NsPublisher functionality in Chapter 26, we're just going to jump into the Java implementation now. Here's the outline of the class:

```
Package PrimerUtils;
```

```
import org.omg.CosNaming.*;
import org.omg.CosNaming.NamingContextPackage.*;

public class NsPublisher
{
    public static void nsBind ( org.omg.CORBA.Object nsObj,
                                org.omg.CORBA.Object bindObj,
                                String id,
                                String kind )
    throws java.lang.Exception, org.omg.CORBA.SystemException
    {
      // Details to follow
    } // bind method

    public static org.omg.CORBA.Object nsResolve (
                                org.omg.CORBA.Object nsObj,
                                String id,
                                String kind )
     throws java.lang.Exception, org.omg.CORBA.SystemException
    {
      // Details to follow
          } // resolve method
} // NsPublisher class
```

- As a CORBA service, the Naming Service would usually belong to the package org.omg in Java. However, this may not be the case for the ORB you are developing with.

- NsPublisher supports two static methods. The nsBind method registers an object reference and its name in the Naming Service. The nsResolve method queries the Naming Service with the specified name and returns the associated object reference.

- The first argument for the nsBind method is a CORBA object, which will be the Name Server object reference returned by the ORB method resolve_ initial_references. The second argument is the CORBA object to be registered in the Naming Service. The next two string arguments combine to make a unique NameComponent that the object will be identified with.

- The first argument for the nsResolve method is a CORBA object, which, like the nsBind method, is the Name Server object. The next two string arguments combine to make a NameComponent that will be used to locate the target object.

Here is the implementation of the nsBind method:

```
public static void nsBind ( org.omg.CORBA.Object nsObj,
                            org.omg.CORBA.Object bindObj,
                            String id,
                            String kind )
    throws java.lang.Exception,
           org.omg.CORBA.SystemException
{
```

```
String exPrefix = "NsPublisher.bind:";
NamingContext ns = NamingContextHelper.narrow(nsObj);

if ( ns == null )
        throw new NullPointerException( exPrefix +
        " object is null or not of NamingContext type");
    if ( bindObj == null )
        throw new NullPointerException( exPrefix +
        " null object reference parameter passed");
    if ( id == null )
        throw new NullPointerException( exPrefix +
        " null String ID passed");
    if ( kind == null )
        throw new NullPointerException( exPrefix +
        " null String ID passed");

    NameComponent []  name = null ;

    try {
        name = new NameComponent[1];
        name[0] = new NameComponent( id, kind);

            try {
                ns.bind( name, bindObj);
            }
            catch(AlreadyBound ab) {
                ns.rebind(name, bindObj );
            }
        }
    catch (org.omg.CORBA.SystemException se) {
        se.printStackTrace();
        throw new Exception( exPrefix + " CORBA System Exception " +
        se.toString() );
    }
    catch (org.omg.CORBA.UserException ue) {
        ue.printStackTrace();
        throw new Exception( exPrefix + " CORBA User Exception " +
        ue.toString() );
    }

} // bind method
```

- The first task of this method is to create a string prefix for error messages.

- The first job of this class is to narrow the generic CORBA object to its correct type. All CORBA objects support the concept of narrowing, which will generate a type-specific object reference from a more generic type. In Java, `Helper` classes are generated by the IDL compiler to perform such tasks. The Naming Service is actually an object reference of type `CosNaming::NamingContext`, and so the compiler will generate `CosNaming.NamingContextHelper`. (If you're using the standard OMG package, it will actually be `org.omg.CosNaming.Naming-ContextHelper`.)

■ If the `narrow` fails, a null reference is returned. One reason for failure could be that the actual object passed is not a `CosNaming.NamingContext` object. The code ensures that none of the parameters are null.

■ The `bind` operation of the Naming Service is the method that advertises an object reference against a unique Name. A Name is made up of one or more `NameComponents`. Hence the first parameter to bind is a sequence of `Name-Component`. In the examples we only bind to one Name and so the parameter required is an array of `NameComponent` with a length of 1. A `NameComponent` is made up of two strings, `ID` and `Kind`. `ID` is the main part of the name, while `Kind` is the analogue of a file name extension (the part of the name after the dot). The `ID` for the depot component is `Depot` and the `Kind` value for the all the example code is `Primer_Example`. Both these values are set in the main method of `DepotServer` class.

■ Once the array has been created, the `bind` operation is called with the array as the first parameter and the target object as the second parameter.

■ The exception handling covers CORBA system exceptions for events such as Naming Service that may not be running. The code covers general CORBA user exceptions and specifically checks for objects that are already bound. When this occurs we attempt a `rebind`, as a simple recovery expedient. In the event that any of the example applications close down, they may or may not handle the process of unbinding from the Naming Service. When the application restarts, it will attempt to bind to the Naming Service and this may cause the exception `AlreadyBound`. To cope with this scenario, the application calls the `rebind` method, which replaces the original reference. Whether this is the correct approach for a commercial system will depend on the ORB you develop with. The ORB-specific sections may deal with this in more detail.

Here is the implementation of the `nsResolve` method:

```
public static org.omg.CORBA.Object nsResolve (
                              org.omg.CORBA.Object nsObj,
                              String id,
                              String kind )
    throws java.lang.Exception, org.omg.CORBA.SystemException
    {
        String exPrefix = "NsPublisher.nsResolve:";
        org.omg.CORBA.Object resolveObj = null;

        NamingContext ns = NamingContextHelper.narrow(nsObj);

        if ( ns == null )
          throw new NullPointerException( exPrefix +
          " object is null or not of NamingContext type");
        if ( id == null )
          throw new NullPointerException( exPrefix +
          " null String ID passed");
```

```
        if ( kind == null )
          throw new NullPointerException( exPrefix +
          " null String ID passed");

    NameComponent [] name = null ;

    try
    {
        name = new NameComponent[1];
        name[0] = new NameComponent( id, kind);

        resolveObj = ns.resolve( name );
    }
    catch (org.omg.CORBA.SystemException se)
    {
        se.printStackTrace();
        throw new Exception( exPrefix + " CORBA System Exception " +
        se.toString() );
    }
    catch (org.omg.CORBA.UserException ue)
    {
        ue.printStackTrace();
        throw new Exception( exPrefix + " CORBA User Exception " +
        ue.toString() );
    }

    return resolveObj;

} // resolve method
```

- Like the `nsBind` method, this method validates the parameters and creates the `NameComponent` array.

- The `resolve` method is invoked on the Naming Service, and if successful will return the required object reference.

- If any CORBA system exceptions or CORBA user exceptions are raised, then the application throws an appropriate exception.

28.2.7 Implementing DepotPoaServer.java

This section covers the differences between a `DepotServer.java` and `Depot-PoaServer.java`, the latter of which is an implementation using the POA. This section illustrates the fundamental differences between the BOA and POA architectures. Let's take a look at the `DepotPoaServer.java` class in its entirety:

```
package CentralOffice;

public class DepotPoaServer {
```

```java
private static final String m_usageString = "Usage : java
CentralOffice.Depot [vendor specific options] \n";


private static void abort( String msg ) {

        System.err.println(msg);
        System.exit(1);
}   // abort

public static void main(String args[]){

  DepotPoaImpl theDepot  = null;
  org.omg.CORBA.ORB orb = null;

  if( args == null ) {
    abort(m_usageString);
  }

  System.out.println("Depot.main ()");

  try {
    System.out.print("Depot.main () initialising ORB.......");


    orb = org.omg.CORBA.ORB.init(args,null);

   org.omg.CORBA.Object pobj = orb.resolve_initial_references
   ( "RootPOA" );

   org.omg.PortableServer.POA  poa =
   org.omg.PortableServer.POAHelper.narrow( pobj );

   org.omg.PortableServer.POAManager poa_mgr = poa.the_POAManager();


   System.out.print("Depot.main () resolving root NamContext.......");

   org.omg.CORBA.Object obj = null;
   try {
       obj = orb.resolve_initial_references("NameService");
   } catch( org.omg.CORBA.ORBPackage.InvalidName exc ) {
       abort("ERROR: The ORB could not resolve a reference to the
       NameService");
   }

   System.out.print("Depot.main () creating new depot,connecting to
   ORB.......");

   theDepot = new DepotPoaImpl();
   theDepot.loadDepot();
```

```
        poa_mgr.activate();

        PrimerUtils.NsPublisher.nsBind(obj, theDepot._this(), "Depot",
        "Primer_Example" );

        System.out.println("Depot is ready" );

    }

    catch (org.omg.CORBA.SystemException se) {
        System.out.println ("Caught CORBA.SystemException : "  + se);
        se.printStackTrace();
    }

    catch( java.lang.Exception jle ) {
        jle.printStackTrace();
        abort("Caught java.lang.Exception : " + jle);
    }

  } // main

} // DepotPoaServer
```

The structure, as you would expect, is similar to `DepotServer`, and so we will focus on specific issues relating to the POA. We covered the POA in a general way in Chapter 5, but here we'll see it in live code so we'll review some before we get started. Here we go:

- The POA is a hierarchical structure, the root of which is called the "root POA." This object can manage objects much like the ORB is doing in the `Depot-Server.java` class. To keeps the concepts simple and minimize the code changes between the two approaches, the example applications use the root POA to manage all the object implementations. This will illustrate the basic POA concepts.

- A reference to the root POA, like the Name Server reference, is obtained through the ORB:

```
org.omg.CORBA.Object pobj = orb.resolve_initial_references("RootPOA");
org.omg.PortableServer.POA poa =
                org.omg.PortableServer.POAHelper.narrow(pobj);
```

The string `"RootPOA"` identifies which reference the ORB is expected to resolve. The ORB returns a generic object that must be narrowed to the correct type. In this case, a POA object is of type `org.omg.PortableServer.POA`.

- A POA object uses a POA manager to handle the active state of the POA. An application can use a POA manager to control whether or not the POA queues or discards incoming object requests. A reference to a POA manager object is obtained through the `POAManager` method:

```
org.omg.PortableServer.POAManager poa_mgr = poa.the_POAManager();
```

- Once a reference to the POA manager is obtained, the code resolves the Naming Service reference and instantiates the `DepotPoaImpl` object. Although this code is similar to the `DepotServer` implementation, the underlying architecture isn't. In the `DepotServer.java` class, a `DepotImpl` object was created where the object and its object reference are indistinguishable. The POA architecture defines an instance of `DepotPoaImpl` as a *servant*. A servant is an implementation that can serve as one or more object references associated with the implementation. This key difference allows a one-to-many relationship between object references and implementation. The POA can distinguish between each object reference, and each object reference can hold unique state within the implementation. In our example, though, we only require one object reference for the servant:

```
theDepot = new DepotPoaImpl();
theDepot.loadDepot();
```

  By default a servant will be associated with the root POA. If an application required the servant to be administered by an alternative POA, then the servant implementation would have to explicitly handle this. The `DepotPoaImpl` instance is created and is implicitly managed by the root POA. It then loads the product item details.

- At this point, the `Depot` object is ready and a call is made to the POA manager in order to activate the POA. This is similar to the `ORB.connect` method, as it enables an object adapter to process incoming calls for the target object:

```
poa_mgr.activate();
```

- The only task that remains is to advertise an object reference for the servant in the Naming Service using the `nsPublisher` class:

```
PrimerUtils.NsPublisher.nsBind(obj, theDepot._this(), "Depot",
"Primer_Example" );
```

  The servant method `_this()` is invoked, which returns a CORBA object reference. An attempt to register the servant itself will fail! A servant is not derived from `org.omg.CORBA.Object`.

This completes the common code section. In the rest of this chapter, each ORB vendor presents any changes necessary to port the common code to the vendor-specific ORB environment, and tells how to compile and link the Depot executable. As we mentioned in Section 28.2.5, one thing these sections will deal with is how the main application thread is suspended in order to wait for incoming requests from Store applications. Because this is the first coding chapter for Java, it includes procedure details that will be used but not repeated in Chapters 31 and 34.

28.3 Implementing the Depot Package Using CORBAplus, Java Edition

The Vertel's Expersoft CORBAplus, Java Edition implementation of the Depot component requires a small change to the PrimerUtils/NsPublisher.java. See the following section for details and instructions on how to build the example using the CORBAplus, Java Edition product.

28.3.1 NsPublisher.java

The `NsPublisher.java` file requires a small change in the import files. The modified lines are:

```
//import org.omg.CosNaming.*;
//import org.omg.CosNaming.NamingContextPackage.*;
import com.expersoft.CORBA.CosNaming.*;
import com.expersoft.CORBA.CosNaming.NamingContextPackage.*;
```

The Java mapping does not specify the package for the Naming classes. Vertel's Expersoft felt that placing the CosNaming in the Vertel's Expersoft package provided the most flexibility to the end user.

28.3.1.1 Compiling the Depot

The first step is to make sure all the IDL files are compiled. Chapter 25 covered the high-level build procedure, so here we will look at the individual steps.

After setting the Java classpath, `cd` to the `idl` directory in the sample and invoking the IDL compiler to process the IDL files:

```
idlj central.idl
idlj store.idl
idlj pos.idl
```

the `idlj` compiler will just compile IDL-to-Java files. We still need to compile the generated Java files with the Java compiler. Here are the steps to do that:

```
cd .\CentralOffice
javac -d ..\..\classes *.java
cd ..\POS
javac -d ..\..\classes *.java
cd ..\AStore
javac -d ..\..\classes *.java
cd ..\
```

The next step is to compile the Depot Java source files. Chapter 25 covered the high-level build procedure, so here we will look at the individual steps. You will need to `cd` into the `CentralOffice` directory. Here are the steps to compile the Depot server:

```
javac -d ..\classes DepotImpl.java
javac -d ..\classes DepotServer.java
```

28.3.1.2 Executing the Depot

Before the `DepotServer` can be started, you need to make sure you have a Naming Service running. To start the CORBAplus, Java Edition Naming Service, execute the following:

```
java NameService.NameServer -pbtrace -pbport 6004
```

This will start the `NameService` on port 6004. The `-pbtrace` option will cause the `NameService` to print progress information to the console so you can see when binds or resolves are executed. The Naming Service must be started before any of the POS examples are executed.

To start the `DepotServer`, change directory to the Classes subdirectory and execute the following:

```
java CentralOffice.DepotServer -pbinit NameService
         iiop://localhost:6004/NameServiceRoot
```

28.4 Implementing the Sample Using IBM ORB for Java

The IBM ORB for Java is currently not available as a standalone package; it is being bundled as part of the Component Broker family of software. Here are the steps needed to make the sample run under the IBM ORB for Java. The changes are simple enough that the steps needed for the complete sample, not just the Depot, are described here.

28.4.1 Changes to the Java Code for IBM

The files `DepotServer.java`, `StoreServer.java`, and `PosServer.java` should be modified in two places, one for ORB initialization and the other for control of the main thread. The file `PosClient.java` should be modified for ORB initialization. Note that the `BOOTSTRAPHOST` and `BOOTSTRAPORT` properties should be set to the host name, and the port number, of the IBM ORB that is running with a Name Server. Currently, the Name Server is only available from the IBM C++ ORB; again not available as a standalone package, but this is not a problem in the interoperable CORBA architecture. After setting these properties, the IBM ORB for Java contacts the C++ ORB, so that `resolve_initial_references` will work and you have full access to the Naming Service from your Java application.

Here are the changes needed for ORB initialization:

```
// Some ORB vendors prefer to initialize the ORB using different ORB
// initialization interfaces.  See the vendor specific portions of
// the text for more information.
java.util.Properties props = new java.util.Properties();
props.put("org.omg.CORBA.ORBClass", "com.ibm.CORBA.iiop.ORB");
props.put("BOOTSTRAPHOST", "hostname");
props.put("BOOTSTRAPORT", "port");
orb = org.omg.CORBA.ORB.init(args,props);
```

Here are the changes needed for main thread control:

```
// For non-gui server applications, some ORB vendors require that the main
// thread not exit and others allow the main thread to exit and continue
// processing requests.  For a server application with a GUI, typically the
```

```
// main thread is used to run the GUI.  See the vendor specific sections of
// the text which describes how each ORB behaves with respect to the main
// thread.
Thread.currentThread ().suspend ();
```

28.4.2 Compiling

Since the IBM ORB for Java does not yet support the POA, first remove all files having to do with the POA. These are files with names like `*Poa*.java`.

After setting the Java classpath, `cd` to the `idl` directory in the sample and invoke the IDL compiler to process the IDL files. The `-d` option specifies the destination directory for the output files. The `-f all` option tells the compiler to emit both server-side and client-side bindings.

```
java com.ibm.idl.toJava.Compile -d .. -f all central.idl
java com.ibm.idl.toJava.Compile -d .. -f all pos.idl
java com.ibm.idl.toJava.Compile -d .. -f all store.idl
```

Finally, `cd` to each code subdirectory and invoke the `javac` command on all the `.java` files:

```
cd Astore
Javac *.java
cd ../CentralOffice
Javac *.java
cd ../Pos
Javac *.java
```

28.4.3 Running

Other than ensuring that an IBM ORB with Name Server is available and running, there are no other special rules. The servers and the client may be started via the `java` command, like any other Java program.

28.5 DAIS-Specific Implementations Details for the Depot Application

28.5.1 Amendment Summary

DAIS supports the Portable Object Adapter. At this point, if you have been following the common code sections, you should have the following Java code modules:

CentralOffice\DepotPoaServer.java   Requires two amendments for DAIS

CentralOffice\DepotPoaImpl.java_   Requires no amendments for DAIS

PrimerUtils\NsPublisher.java   Requires one amendment for DAIS

The first amendment to `DepotPoaServer` is only required in early versions of DAIS J[2] where `resolve_initial_references` does not recognize the Naming Service. This means using an alternative method to discover the Naming Service. This amendment is not required if you have a GR (general release) version. If you are not sure whether this change is applicable to you, don't make any changes at this point. When the application is run, it may abort with the error:

```
"ERROR: The ORB could not resolve a reference to the NameService"
```

This may occur because your Naming Service is not running, or because your version of DAIS J[2] is an early release.

The second amendment to `DepotPoaServer` is essential. The common code section asserted that each ORB vendor could decide how the main application thread would suspend so that the application does not terminate. There is no definitive answer to this. We offer a simple solution in DAIS, and summarize a couple of alternatives.

The one amendment to the `NsPublisher` class is an optional amendment. It involves an additional method to unbind an object reference from the Naming Service. It is used to illustrate the tidy termination of a CORBA application.

The following subsections deal with each of these changes in turn.

28.5.1.1 Alternative to resolve_initial_references

The class `DepotPoaServer` requires a single amendment that is highlighted in the following code:

```
org.omg.CORBA.Object obj = null;
try {
obj = orb.resolve_initial_references("NameService");
} catch( org.omg.CORBA.ORBPackage.InvalidName exc ) {
        if ((obj = DaisSpecific.ResolveNameService.resolve(orb))==null
           abort(
"ERROR: The ORB could not resolve a reference to the NameService");
}
```

At the point where the common code resolves the Naming Service reference, a `catch` statement already tests for the exception `org.omg.CORBA.ORBPackage .InvalidName` and resolves to abort the application. At this point, we insert a statement to call `DaisSpecific.ResolveNameService`, an alternative class that returns a reference for the Naming Service. If this routine cannot resolve the Naming Service (returns null), then it will abort as well. This class is not part of the product, but is supplied for use with the primer examples. In case you are interested, the implementation for this class is described next. It introduces the DAIS Trader Service, which is an alternative to the Naming Service.

```
package DaisSpecific;

import org.omg.CosNaming.*;
import Trader;
import TraderHelper;
```

```
public class ResolveNameService
{
    ResolveNameService () {}

    public static org.omg.CORBA.Object resolve(org.omg.CORBA.ORB orb)
    {
      try
      {
       org.omg.CORBA.Object trader_obj;
       trader_obj = orb.resolve_initial_references("DAIS_Trader");

       Trader trader_ref = TraderHelper.narrow( trader_obj );

       TraderPackage.OffersHolder offers =
           new TraderPackage.OffersHolder();

       trader_ref.lookup ( "CosNaming_NamingContext","/" ,"",
                  TraderPackage.LookUpPolicy.lookup_random, offers);

         return (offers.value[0]).offer_ref;
      }
      catch ( org.omg.CORBA.UserException ue )
      {
          System.out.println(
          "DaisResolveNameSrv.resolve () :  UserException " + ue);
          ue.printStackTrace();
      }
      catch ( org.omg.CORBA.SystemException se )
      {
          System.out.println(
          "DaisResolveNameSrv.resolve () :  SystemException " + se);
          se.printStackTrace();
      }
      catch( Exception e)
      {
          System.out.println(
          "DaisResolveNameSrv.resolve () :  Java Exception " + e);
          e.printStackTrace();
      }

      return null;
    } // method resolve
} // class ResolveNameService
```

- The class is specific to DAIS and it belongs to the package `DaisSpecific`.
- The class uses the Naming Service and DAIS Trader Service, and so the associated packages for these are imported. The DAIS implementation of the Naming Service exploits the DAIS Trader Service, which is our preferred method of

advertising CORBA objects. This is because the DAIS Trader Service is a much richer implementation. The Naming Service relies on a running DAIS Trader Service and actually stores all its references in the DAIS Trader. One of those references is the Naming Service itself. Querying the Trader Service is an alternative for discovering the Naming Service.

- The class `ResolveNameService` has one task: to obtain the Naming Service object reference from the DAIS Trader. It supports a single static method, `resolve`. It takes one argument, the ORB. Like the ORB method `resolve_initial_references`, it returns a generic CORBA object.

- The DAIS Trader reference can be resolved through the ORB method `resolve_initial_references`, so the following code should be familiar:

```
org.omg.CORBA.Object trader_obj;
trader_obj = orb.resolve_initial_references("DAIS_Trader");

Trader trader_ref = TraderHelper.narrow( trader_obj );
```

- Next, we invoke the `lookup` operation on the Trader. This is analogous to the Naming Service `resolve` operation. However, they have two subtle differences. A Naming Service associates a single object reference against a unique `Name` made up of one or more Name Components (a structure with two string identifiers). It is a one-to-one relationship between the `name` and the object. A Trader Service associates one or more object references against a single Interface Type Name (a single string identifier). While the `resolve` operation accepts a `Name` in order to return a single object reference, the `lookup` operation accepts a single type description in order to return a sequence of offers, which contains one or more object references. Let's have a closer look at the `lookup` operation:

```
trader_ref.lookup (      "CosNaming_NamingContext",
                         "/" ,
                         "",
TraderPackage.LookUpPolicy.lookup_random,
                         Offers
    );
```

- The first parameter resolves to a string representing the type Name. For the Naming Service this is an identifier `CosNaming_NamingContext`.

- The second parameter defines the context in which to search for the type. Contexts allow the Trader to organize objects into logical hierarchies. The root of this hierarchy is "/". Specifying the context in the lookup operation dictates where the search will begin for the target type. Specifying the root context means that it will search all contexts for an object reference of type `CosNaming_NamingContext`.

- The third parameter defines any properties to be used in the `lookup` operation. Properties are dynamic attributes. Because one or more instances of an IDL interface will advertise themselves against the same type name, they can exhibit independent properties that allow them to differentiate themselves. A simple example of this is a client that requires a printer service. The Trader could be used to advertise all the printers on the system under the generic type name "Printer". The printers may each exhibit a property that identifies their location; for example, "Location '5th Floor'". A client has the option of printing on a specific printer by matching the property, or leaving it up to the Trader to randomly choose a printer, by specifying an empty property string. As far as the Naming Service is concerned, there is only one instance and an empty property string will suffice.

- The fourth parameter dictates the `lookup` policy. The Trader can return a single object reference or a sequence of object references that match the criteria. Continuing with the printer example, a client application could choose to select a number of printers. Since we are only interested in one Naming Service, the policy `lookup_random` is chosen. This will always return a single object reference.

- The final parameter is an `out` parameter that contains a `holder` class containing a sequence of offers. The value of the `holder` class is an array of offers of length 1, as only one offer is returned. The offer type is a structure that not only contains the object reference, but type, context, and property information associated with the object. For this example, we are only interested in the Naming Service object reference that is returned by the `resolve` method.

```
return (offers.value[0]).offer_ref;
```

- The code implements the usual exception handling that is illustrated in the common code. If an exception occurs, the routine returns a null reference.

28.5.1.2 Handling Application Main Thread

Once the application has created the Depot component and advertised it in the Naming Service, it must wait for incoming requests. However, since the application is a nonGUI application, the main thread must not terminate as this will cause the application to close. We need to keep the main thread busy.

One way of doing this is to call the ORB method `run()`. It has no parameters and explicitly hands control to the ORB. The routine returns when it detects a tidy shutdown. The same effect can be achieved by simply calling suspend on the main thread.

In the case of the Depot application, applying either of these solutions will have the following effect. The only way to terminate the application would be to interrupt it (Cntl C). Since Java does not support signal handling, nothing is closed in a tidy manner. For this example, the consequences are minimal. The Naming Service is left with a stale reference because there was no way for the application to unbind. When the application is restarted, it will `rebind` to the Naming Service as a consequence of failing to `bind`. This behavior may not suit all application scenarios and the following is a simple expedient to illustrate how a Java server can unbind a reference in the Naming Service. Instead of terminating the main thread, the application provides a simple user interface with one option to exit the application. The main thread blocks awaiting a response from the user:

```
System.out.println("Depot is ready" );

System.out.println("Type exit to terminate application");
java.io.BufferedReader in = new java.io.BufferedReader( new
java.io.InputStreamReader(System.in));
String exitString = "exit";
while ( exitString.compareTo(in.readLine()) != 0 )
{
    System.out.println("Type exit to terminate application");
}
```

When the Depot Server application is ready to be closed, the user types `exit`. The main thread can then proceed to do the necessary tidying. In the case of the Depot server, the code could unbind the Depot component from the Naming Service. All interaction with the Naming Service has been via the NsPublisher class, and so we amend this class to support an additional unbind method. We will look at its implementation later. The code required to complete the DepotPoaServer class is shown here:

```
PrimerUtils.NsPublisher.nsUnbind(obj, "Depot", "Primer_Example" );
```

As mentioned earlier, this is a simple but effective solution. The DAIS Trader, Node Manager, and Factory services offer more resilient solutions, because they can remotely control the lifecycle of an application. In such a situation it may useful to use the ORB.run() method.

28.5.1.3 Amending the NsPublisher Class

The amendment to this class is the addition of a method to unbind references from the Naming Service. The implementation has a similar format to the other two methods. The only difference is that it invokes the unbind method on the Naming Service. The method takes a single argument, which is an array of type CosNaming.NameComponent.

```
public static void nsUnbind ( org.omg.CORBA.Object nsObj,
                              String id,
                              String kind )
      throws java.lang.Exception, org.omg.CORBA.SystemException
{
    String exPrefix = "NsPublisher.nsUnbind:";

    NamingContext ns = NamingContextHelper.narrow(nsObj);

    if ( ns == null )
        throw new NullPointerException( exPrefix + " object is null or
        not of NamingContext type");
    if ( id == null )
        throw new NullPointerException( exPrefix + " null String ID
        passed");
    if ( kind == null )
        throw new NullPointerException( exPrefix + " null String ID
        passed");
```

```
NameComponent []  name = null ;

try
{
    name = new NameComponent[1];
    name[0] = new NameComponent( id, kind);

    ns.unbind( name );
}
catch (org.omg.CORBA.SystemException se)
{
    se.printStackTrace();
    throw new Exception( exPrefix + " CORBA System Exception " +
    se.toString() );
}
catch (org.omg.CORBA.UserException ue)
{
    ue.printStackTrace();
    throw new Exception( exPrefix + " CORBA User Exception " +
    ue.toString() );
}

return;

} // unbind method
```

This completes the amendments to the Depot application. You are now ready to build the Depot server.

28.5.1.4 Compiling the Depot Server

Open a console session and change directory to `<installation root>\primer\java`. A default installation would mean changing directory to `c:\Dais32\primer\java`. It should contain the `CentralOffice` package directory, where we have been implementing the Depot server. To compile the application, we simply have to compile the main application class.

```
javac   CentralOffice\DepotPoaServer.java
```

This will also compile any dependent Java files, and so it produces the following class files:

```
.\CentralOffice\DepotServer.class
.\PrimerUtils\NsPublisher.class
.\DaisSpecific\NsPublisher.class
```

These files should be moved into their associated subdirectories under the `Classes` directory. For example, the `DepotPoaServer.class` and `DepotPoaImpl.class` files should be copied to the directory `classes\CentralOffice`.

28.5.1.5 Running the Depot Server

For a complete description on installing, building, and running the primer example, look ahead to Chapter 36. The DAIS installation contains an easy-to-use GUI for configuring and running the full example. The following details will suffice for running the Depot server. Before running the Depot server, an instance of the DAIS Trader Service must be started, followed by an instance of the Naming Service.

The Depot server can be started from the `classes` directory in the following ways:

1. `java CentralOffice.DepotPoaServer`
2. `java -D"primer.depotfile=<alternative depot file>"`
   `centralOffice.DepotPoaServer`

where `<alternative depot file>` is the path and file name of another product item database, which must be in a similar text format to the default `depot.dat` file located in the `Classes` directory.

28.6 Description of the OrbixWeb Implementation of the Depot Server

This section explains how to build and execute the Depot using OrbixWeb 3.x. Since this is the first of the OrbixWeb servers to be discussed, we will give some extra details and background information that will not be repeated in later sections of the book (although we may refer the reader back to this section).

28.6.1 Changes to the Java Code for OrbixWeb

The code that was shown and described in the previous sections will build and run with OrbixWeb as is; in other words, no changes are required.

Changes that could be made, however, are :

```
// in file DepotServer.java
IE.Iona.OrbixWeb._OrbixWeb.ORB(orb).impl_is_ready("CentralSrv",0);
```

and

```
// in file DepotServer.java
int timeout = 5 *1000; // 5 seconds or whatever timeout value you want
IE.Iona.OrbixWeb._OrbixWeb.ORB(orb).impl_is_ready("CentralSrv",timeout);
```

The next 2 changes must be made together:

```
// in file DepotServer.java theDepot = new
DepotImpl("depotPrimerExample");
```

```
// file DepotImpl.java
DepotImpl(String marker){
     super(marker);
```

```
m_depotDictionary = new Hashtable( 20 );

}  // Constructor
```

The `impl_is_ready` method basically means that the implementation (server) is ready to receive remote invocations. The form that we are using takes two parameters:

- **A `String` that contains the name of this server process.** This parameter is discussed in greater detail later in this section.

- **An `int` time-out value.** When `impl_is_ready` is called it passes control to the ORB runtime to receive incoming invocations. When the ORB is waiting for an incoming invocation it starts a timer. If it receives an invocation before the timer times out, then it will process the invocation, reset the timer to the time-out value, and wait for the next invocation. If no invocation is received before the timer times out, then the `impl_is_ready` command will return.

The first time this method is used it contacts the Orbix daemon process and registers itself as the "`CentralSrv`" server process in the Implementation Repository (described later). A zero time-out value is specified, so no invocations will be processed.

The first call to `impl_is_ready` ensures that any object references produced by this server contains the Orbix daemon's port number. In this case, the first time a client tries to contact a server the invocation will go to the daemon process. If the server is not currently running, the daemon will launch an instance of that server and tell the client to reinvoke the method on the new server. If a server is currently running, the daemon simply redirects the client to the running server (this hand-shaking process only takes place when a client tries to contact a server for the first time; all subsequent invocations made by the client go directly to the server process).

The desirable side effects of this process are:

- All the information contained in an IOR is now fixed and persistent for any given object (unless we move the server to a new host or change its server name or marker name).

- It is not necessary to rebind a server's name into the Naming Service every time the server start because, as stated previously, the information in an IOR rarely changes.

- The servers in our system do not have to be running all the time. It is possible and generally advisable to have the Orbix daemon process launch the servers when they are needed.

- The port number that a server uses is hidden behind a single-fixed port number (the Orbix daemon's, generally port 1570). We don't have to manage the allocation of server port numbers (since the daemon does this for us), which would quickly become unmanageable in a system with a large number of server processes.

The second call to `impl_is_ready` allows the programmer to specify a time-out value as the second parameter to the method. If no remote invocation is sent to the process before the timer times out, the `impl_is_ready` command will return and the server process can shut down. Remember, however, that this process will be restarted by the daemon process if a client makes another invocation on the server.

The last two changes made allow a marker name to be assigned to an implementation object. A marker name acts as a unique identifier for an OrbixWeb object within a server process. The significance of this marker will be explained in the last part of this section.

28.6.2 Running the Orbix/OrbixWeb Daemon

The Orbix daemon process is the Activation agent for CORBA servers. It also provides the functionality for the Implementation Repository. An instance of this process must be started on each host that requires automatic launch of servers (it is not necessary to run it on the client host). If the server is persistently launched (that is, always running whether started by a person or by a script at boot time), then it is not always necessary to have a daemon running although it may be desirable. There are currently two forms of this daemon process:

- An `orbixd` native executable process
- An `orbixdj` Java executable

Both of these two daemons can launch either binary or Java executable servers. The Java version is necessary because the goal of OrbixWeb was to make all the main components of the Java ORB available in pure Java form.

The Java version of the daemon can be run using the `orbixdj.bat` file on Windows or the `orbixdj` shell script on Unix. These files should be in the OrbixWeb installation `bin` directory. In order to run the `orbixdj`, there must be a copy of the file `OrbixWeb.properties` somewhere in the system's `Classpath` environmental variable. Normally this file is in the `OrbixWeb` installation Classes directory. This file contains the default configuration for all the OrbixWeb components of the system. The `owconfig` script must be used to edit this configuration.

28.6.3 Compiling OrbixWeb Clients and Servers

A wrapper executable (`owjavac.exe` on Windows or `owjavac` on Unix) is supplied in the OrbixWeb installation to hide some of the details of this process. Basically, this executable wraps the call to the Java compiler and passes it the correct parameters in order to build a Java class that uses OrbixWeb components (i.e., it sets up the classpath that the compiler uses and passes it the correct output directory, among other things). It is not, however, mandatory. Any valid Java compiler can be used. For example, the following two commands are equivalent:

```
owjavac DepotImpl.java

c:\jdk1.1\bin\javac.exe -classpath
"C:\Iona\OrbixWeb3.1c\classes;c:\jdk1.1\lib\classes.zip" -d
"C:\Iona\OrbixWeb3.1c\classes" DepotImpl.java
```

The `classpath` passed to the `javac` command must contain the path to the OrbixWeb installation classes directory (as shown in the second command). Otherwise, the compiler won't be able to find the OrbixWeb Java classes.

28.6.4 Registering Servers in the Implementation Repository

A server process can be registered in the Orbix daemon's Implementation Repository. This repository stores information about the mapping between a server name (e.g., CentralSrv) and the executable process that implements this server. This allows the daemon to launch an inactive server when a client first invokes on it. This registration can be done using the putit command line utility.

Some examples of using the putit command are:

```
putit -persistent persistentServer

putit -j CentralSrv CentralOffice.DepotServer

putit cppDepot depotServer.exe
```

The first example shows the command used to register a persistent server. A persistent server is a server that can only be launched explicitly by a user (either on the command line or as an NT Service or as a Unix inetd process); it cannot be launched by the orbixd (mainly because the daemon doesn't know which executable implements the server!).

The second example shows the registration of a Java server, the CentralSrv process that implements the Depot. This is the command used to register our Java Depot server in the Implementation Repository. Once this command has been issued, the daemon will launch a new Java process if an invocation is made on a dormant CentralSrv server process.

Finally, the third example shows the registration of a binary executable process. Again, this depotServer executable will be run if an invocation is made on a dormant cppDepot server.

The servers defined in the second and third examples can also be launched persistently/manually by a user.

The putit command belongs to a set of command-line utility commands that allow users and administrators to manage servers (i.e., access and modify the Implementation Repository). There are also other commands to list (lsit) registered server, remove (rmit) servers from the Implementation Repository, list all the currently active (psit) servers , and so forth. There is also a GUI version of these utilities available (the ServerManager).

Each of these commands is implemented in the Orbix daemon process using the IT_daemon IDL interface, so it is also possible to call these methods from within your own processes.

In addition to the putit command, it is also possible to change the launch right and access right for a server process using the chmodit command:

```
chmodit i+jones CentralSrv
chmodit i+all CentralSrv
chmodit l+jones CentralSrv
chmodit l+all CentralSrv
```

Lines 1 and 3 give the user "jones" invocation and launch rights for this server. Similarly, lines 2 and 4 gives all users invocation and launch rights.

28.6.5 Implementing an IDL interface in OrbixWeb

The example in this section shows the Depot IDL interface being implemented using class inheritance. This implementation model is called the ImplBase approach and uses direct class inheritance (an IS-A model as the Implementation object, `DepotImpl`, IS-A CORBA object).

Class inheritance in Java is deliberately limited to single inheritance. Since our `DepotImpl` class inherits from `CentralOffice._DepotSkeleton` we cannot also derive from, say, `java.lang.Thread` or possibly some other legacy class that we want to expose to the world.

In order to overcome this issue there is also a delegation implementation model available in OrbixWeb. To support this, the OrbixWeb IDL compiler produces two Java objects. In the case of our Depot example, these objects are:

_tie_Depot.java: This is a Java class that provides the CORBA functionality in order to receive incoming CORBA invocations and translate them into native Java method calls (similar to the `_depotSkeleton` class). It also defers or delegates processing of these requests to a Java object that implements the `_DepotOperations` Java interface (described next).

_DepotOperations.java: This Java interface is used as a reference to the Implementation object. It also provides the method names and signatures that an object must implement in order to be an object of the Depot IDL interface type. Note that this model uses Java interface inheritance, so our implementation class could have also been derived from `java.lang.Thread` or some other legacy class.

This approach is called the TIE approach (the CORBA object, in this case an instance of `_tie_Depot`, is tied to the Implementation object, an instance of `_DepotOperations`) and provides a delegation model for the IDL interface implementation. This is a HAS-A relationship as the CORBA object, `_tie_Depot`, HAS-A reference to the Implementation object, an implementation of `_DepotOperations`.

The code changes required for this approach are minor. In the file `DepotImpl.java`, line 12, needs to be changed to the following:

```
class DepotImpl implements _DepotOperations {
```

and in file `DepotServer.java`, the following code need to be inserted instead of the original lines 52–53:

```
_DepotOperations _dImpl = new DepotImpl();
_dImpl.loadDepot();
theDepot = new _tie_Depot (_dImpl);
```

The remainder of the code remains exactly the same and, as all client code is isolated from the server implementation, no changes are needed on the client side.

It is possible for both ImplBase and TIE approach implementations of the same IDL interface to coexist in the same server process. In fact, multiple implementations of an object using the same implementation model can coexist in the same server process. This might seem strange, but it could be used to support different size/time tradeoffs in our implementations.

28.6.6 Accessing the Naming Service

A complete set of command-line utilities is available in the OrbixWeb installation to access the Naming Service. The utilities are named using the following scheme: `<util type>ns`, where `<util type>` is the nearest equivalent Unix-style command. For example, to list the contents of the Naming Service's root Naming context, type the following command:

```
lsns
```

To list the contents of a particular Naming Context, type:

```
lsns id1-kind1.id2-kind2
```

Similarly, to view the contents of a Name/Object reference binding, the following command can be used:

```
catns Depot-Primer_Example
```

Other commands to view and modify the Naming Service (e.g., `rmns`, `putns`, etc.) are also available.

With all the Orbix command-line utilities, it is possible to access a service on a remote machine by adding the `-h <hostname>` switch to the command. For example,

```
catns -h nsHost Depot-Primer_Example
putit -h nsHost -j CentralSrv CentralOffice.DepotServer
```

There is also a GUI executable available to view and manage the Naming Service.

28.6.7 Binding to Remote Objects

Finally, in addition to resolving names to object references using the Naming Service, it is also possible to obtain references to remote CORBA objects using the Orbix/OrbixWeb `bind` mechanism.

In the Java Helper class generated for an IDL interface by the IDL compiler, there is the definition of a Java method called `bind`. (It is also possible to turn this feature off by using the -jOMG IDL compiler switch.) This method is of the form:

```
// from DepotHelper.java
public static final Depoit bind(String markerServer, String host)
```

The first parameter is a colon-separated string that allows the user to specify an object in a server process. If no marker name is supplied (i.e., the `markerServer`

String begins with a "`:`"), then any instance of the type of object (in this case, `Depot`) will be found.

The second parameter is a string signifying the host name of the remote host on which that this server process is running.

For example, the client for the Depot server could use the following code to obtain a reference to the `DepotImpl` object, instead of using the `nsResolve` method:

```
String hostname = // put in the hostname you are running the depot on
Depot dRef = DepotHelper.bind(":CentralSrv", hostname);
```

or

```
String hostname = // put in the hostname you are running the depot on
Depot dRef = DepotHelper.bind("depotPrimerExample:CentralSrv",
                              hostname);
```

28.7 Implementing the Depot Package Using VisiBroker for Java

The Inprise VisiBroker implementation of the Depot component does not require any changes to the common code. There are only a few things that need to be done with your platform's environment variables. I will describe what needs to be changed on the Win95/98/NT system.

I recommend that you use JBuilder2 or JDK 1.1.2 or later for this demo. The build system provided with the demo makes use of the JDK.

The `CLASSPATH` environment variable must be modified: Click on the System icon in the Control Panel. Go to the `Environment` tab and add the root directory of your project to the `CLASSPATH` entry. Make sure that the VisiBroker ORB jar (`vbjorb.jar`) and the VisiBroker Naming Service jar (`vbjcosnm.jar`) files are also in your `CLASS-PATH`. These files should be located in VisiBroker's `lib` directory. You must also make sure that the VisiBroker `bin` directory is listed in your `PATH` environment variable.

The build system is very simple to use. At the root level of the project, you will find a batch file named `vbmake.bat`. To compile the IDL, type the following at the project's root directory:

```
prompt> vbjmake idl
```

This will invoke the idl2java compiler, which will produce the stubs, skeletons, and many other helper files. You must recompile an IDL file each time you make a change to the file.

Once you have compiled the IDL files, you are ready to compile the program. You can do so by typing

```
prompt> vbjmake all
```

in the root project directory, or you can go to each directory (that is, CentralOffice, POS, and AStore) and type `vbjmake all`. If you call `vbjmake.bat all` from the root directory, it will call `vbjmake.bat all` in each subdirectory for you.

The usage help for the IDL compiler is displayed when you type `idl2java` without any arguments (make sure that the VisiBroker `bin` directory is listed in your PATH environment variable). The `vbjc` program in the VisiBroker `bin` directory is a replacement for the `javac` JDK command. You don't need to use `vbjc` to compile your VisiBroker code, but it will help set the environment for you.

CHAPTER

29

Depot: Overview and COBOL Language Coding

29.1 Getting Started

This chapter presents the implementation of the Depot server using Orbix COBOL. Since this is the only implementation of the COBOL language mapping presented in this book, the convention used in other language mapping chapters of separating the common code from specific implementation examples is not necessary. However, we still present the details of several routines that are common to all of the COBOL tutorial examples in this book.

Before you jump into the details of how Depot is implemented using COBOL, you should first read the language-independent description of the functionality for Depot in Section 27.1. There you will find an overview of the Depot implementation, so if you have not read it yet, take the time to do so now.

This chapter is divided into four distinct areas of focus. First we examine a common Database Implementation that is used by both Depot and an implementation of a lightweight Naming Service. Then we see how the depot-init routine loads the contents of the DEPOT.DAT file into our Database Implementation. After that, we look at the Naming Service that we'll use in all of the COBOL tutorials, and also review in detail the two routines that will be used for accessing it. Finally, we look at the details of the actual Depot implementation itself.

29.2 Database Implementation

29.2.1 Overview

In this section we will quickly review the common database routines that are provided for both the `Depot` server and our lightweight Naming Service. Since the topic is really beyond the scope of the CORBA COBOL tutorials, we won't be looking at the actual implementation in too much detail. However, in order to gain a complete understanding of the tutorials, a basic understanding of what is going on is desirable. Those readers whose disposition has blessed them with enough curiosity to wonder how a cyclic in-memory list can be implemented in COBOL may review the sample code at their leisure.

At its core, the database implementation consists of a set of callable routines that allow you to create a cyclic list in memory, add an element to the list, or look up an element within the list. The actual implementation here is a very simple in-memory singly linked circular list.

Here is the layout of each element:

```
01 db-entry.
        03 db-next              pointer.
        03 db-data              pointer.
        03 db-key               pic x(40).
```

The first item is a pointer to the next element. The second is a pointer to the arbitrary data associated with a key. The third and final item is a 40-byte textual key associated with the data. This key will be used to search the list.

The externally callable common routines are `db-init`, `db-insert`, and `db-lookup`. We'll examine the functionality of each of these briefly, but will not go into any actual implementation detail since that is really off topic and does not enlighten you on how you should write CORBA applications using COBOL.

These routines will be used by the `Depot` server to load the contents of the `DEPOT.DAT` file into a list using the barcode for each item within the file as the key. This then will permit `Depot` to search for item details using the item's barcode as a search key.

Our Naming Service implementation will also use these routines to hold lists of Object References and associate each one with a unique textual name so that it can be looked up. When we wrote this example, there was no Naming Service available for our COBOL CORBA development environment, and we chose not to access a Naming Service written in another language (although we could have, and one of the Java implementations uses a C++ Naming Service). So we wrote our own, using a subset of the standard Naming Service IDL, to ease your transition to a full version when one comes on the market.

29.2.2 Db-init

This routine is used to initialize the list within working storage. It accepts no input parameters and returns no values. All it does is initialize the list internally within COBOL working storage. This is a very simple call that is called during an initialization phase.

29.2.3 Db-insert

This routine accepts two input values. The first is a 40-character key associated with the list item. The second is a pointer to the arbitrary data that is to be inserted into the cyclic list. Upon completion, the item is added into the cyclic list. If an element with exactly the same key is found, it is replaced.

29.2.4 Db-lookup

This routine accepts one input value, a 40-character key that is to be used to search the current list. If an element with the specified key is found, then the pointer to the arbitrary data associated with it is returned to the caller. If it is not found, then NULL is returned.

29.3 Loading the Database Implementation

29.3.1 Overview

When the Depot server is first started, it calls a depot-init routine to initialize our database using the contents of the DEPOT.DAT file. Later, when we look at the Depot server in detail, we'll see where the call to this routine is actually made, but for now let's take a look at how it works. Its functionality can be summed up in the following three steps:

1. Initialize our database implementation.
2. Open the DEPOT.DAT file for access.
3. Load the data from the file into the database.

Let's briefly look at each of these steps in more detail.

29.3.1.1 Database Initialization

The actual initialization of our database is very simple. We just call the db-init routine that we described in the previous section. Here is the COBOL code that makes this call:

```
*-------------------------------------------------------------
*      Initialize the database
*-------------------------------------------------------------
       call "db-init"
```

29.3.1.2 Opening the DEPOT.DAT File

The next step is to use the standard COBOL OPEN statement to open the DEPOT.DAT file. In the event of an I/O error when opening the file, an appropriate error message will be displayed.

```
*-------------------------------------------------------------
*    Open DEPOT.DAT
*-------------------------------------------------------------
     move "DEPOT.DAT"          to dat-file-name
     OPEN input fd-dat-file

     if ws-dat-file-status not = 78-IO-GOOD
        display
           "depot: Unable to open DEPOT.DAT file, status="
                 ws-dat-file-status
        exit program
     end-if
```

29.3.1.3 Loading the Database

The next step is to use a COBOL READ statement to access each of the records within the DEPOT.DAT file and insert them into our database. For each record we access, the CBL_ALLOC_MEM routine is used to dynamically access memory for the record. The db-insert routine is then used to add it to our database.

When we finally reach the end of the file, the call to our READ statement fails and we exit the PERFORM. The file is closed and the routine returns control to the caller.

```
*-------------------------------------------------------------
*    Load DEPOT.DAT into database
*-------------------------------------------------------------
     display "Loading product database ..."
     READ fd-dat-file NEXT
     perform until ws-dat-file-status not = 78-IO-GOOD
        move length of lk-depot-dat-rec to ls-lth
        move 0                      to ls-flags
        call "CBL_ALLOC_MEM" using ls-ptr
                                 by value ls-lth
                                          ls-flags
        set address of lk-depot-dat-rec to ls-ptr
        move ws-depot-dat-rec        to lk-depot-dat-rec
        move ws-barcode              to ls-key
        call "db-insert" using ls-key
                              by value ls-ptr
        display " " ws-desc
        READ fd-dat-file NEXT
     end-perform

     close fd-dat-file
     exit program
```

29.4 COBOL Implementation of a Lightweight Naming Service

In a real distributed system, the Naming Service is a fundamental element; without it, scalability would be an issue. However, for the sake of simplicity and also the opportunity to start you off with an example of a COBOL implementation of a simple IDL interface with two basic operations, we've used a lightweight Naming Service in these COBOL tutorials.

The complete description of the externally accessible interface for this Naming Service is contained within the NS IDL file. Internally this file contains a simple interface that supports only two Naming Service operations: `bind` and `resolve`.

For the sake of brevity, this simple tutorial implements those operations by keeping object references within a simple cyclic list that can be accessed via a name value. However, a more serious implementation may choose to replace this implementation with a real Naming Service. Details regarding the implementation of our cyclic list were presented in Section 29.2.

To start you off, we present the complete NS IDL, then follow that with the Orbix COBOL copy file that is generated for the interface contained within the IDL file. After that, we review the actual implementation. Finally, we look at two common routines (`ns-bind` and `ns-rslv`) that are used by all of the COBOL tutorials within this book to locate and interface to our Naming Service.

29.4.1 Our Naming Service IDL

The following is the complete Naming Service IDL used within this tutorial. It is a subset of the OMG Naming Service IDL, but contains just two operations.

```
interface NamingContext
{
   typedef string Istring;
   struct Name {
       Istring id;
       Istring kind;
   };

   void   bind(   in Name n, in Object obj);
   Object resolve(in Name n);
};
```

29.4.2 The Mapping for Our Naming Service Interface

When the IDL is compiled by the Orbix IDL compiler, the −R option is used to populate the Orbix Interface Repository with the details. The Orbix COBOL `gencbl` utility is then used to generate a COBOL copy file for a specific IDL interface. The actual name of the generated COBOL copy file will be the name of the IDL interface truncated to

8 bytes. This limitation on the name is to ensure that it will be compatible with COBOL development environments that cannot handle COBOL copy files with names longer than 8 bytes. In this specific case, the generated COBOL copy file is called `NamingCo.cpy`. Its contents are as follows:

```
*******************************************************************
*
*   Interface:  NamingContext
*
*   Generated by gencbl
*
*******************************************************************

*******************************************************************
*
*   Defined Operations
*
*******************************************************************


*
*   Operation   :  bind
*   Parameters  :  in struct NameComponent
*                  in objref obj
*
 01 NAMINGCONTEXT-BIND-ARGS.
    03 N.
       05 IDL-ID                      POINTER.
       05 KIND                        POINTER.
    03 OBJ                            POINTER.


*
*   Operation   :  resolve
*   Parameters  :  in struct NameComponent
*   Returns     :  objref
*
 01 NAMINGCONTEXT-RESOLVE-ARGS.
    03 N.
       05 IDL-ID                      POINTER.
       05 KIND                        POINTER.
    03 RESULT                         POINTER.


*******************************************************************
     COPY NAMINGCX.
*******************************************************************
 01 NAMINGCONTEXT-OPERATION            PICTURE X(8).
    88 NAMINGCONTEXT-BIND                 VALUE "bind ".
    88 NAMINGCONTEXT-RESOLVE              VALUE "resolve".


 01 NAMINGCONTEXT-OPERATION-LENGTH     PICTURE 9(09) BINARY
                                          VALUE 8.
```

The NAMINGCO COBOL copy file contains the parameter layouts for the two operations defined within our Naming Service interface and an operation area. For the Orbix implementation of COBOL, it also pulls in another copy file called NAMINGCX.CPY. This includes product-specific details for the Naming Service interface. The contents of this file are completely opaque to users, so you need not worry about what is inside of it.

29.4.3 Implementing Our Naming Service with Orbix COBOL

Having looked at the COBOL copy file generated for the interface, we now move on to take our first look at an actual implementation. Here we see how the combination of the generated COBOL copy file and the set of callable routines enables us to produce a complete implementation of our Naming Service server. We start by looking at the main program that registers the interface with the ORB, then go on to look at the implementation of a dispatcher for incoming requests. Finally, we review the implementation of each of the two operations.

29.4.3.1 The Naming Service Server

The Naming Service server is responsible for performing all the initialization required to enable the Naming Service server to receive and process inbound requests.

When first started, the server initializes the database. After that, it registers its interface with the ORB.

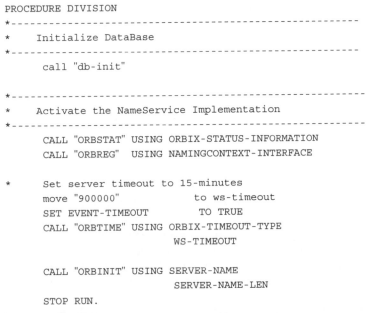

```
PROCEDURE DIVISION
*-----------------------------------------------------------
*     Initialize DataBase
*-----------------------------------------------------------
        call "db-init"


*-----------------------------------------------------------
*     Activate the NameService Implementation
*-----------------------------------------------------------
        CALL "ORBSTAT" USING ORBIX-STATUS-INFORMATION
        CALL "ORBREG"  USING NAMINGCONTEXT-INTERFACE

*     Set server timeout to 15-minutes
        move "900000"              to ws-timeout
        SET EVENT-TIMEOUT          TO TRUE
        CALL "ORBTIME" USING ORBIX-TIMEOUT-TYPE
                             WS-TIMEOUT

        CALL "ORBINIT" USING SERVER-NAME
                             SERVER-NAME-LEN
        STOP RUN.
```

Details of the db-init call were presented in Section 29.2.

The first interaction with the ORB is an ORBSTAT call. This is used to register an ORBIX-STATUS-INFORMATION area as the COBOL working storage in which all status information is recorded for any calls made within this program. This is a pre-defined area within a standard COBOL copy file called CORBA.CPY. This copy file contains common definitions such as this, and must always be copied into the working storage of any program using OrbixCOBOL. This allows us to check for an exception after each call by looking at a status field within this block. We'll be discussing this mechanism for exception handling in more detail later when we review the Depot implementation.

Next, an ORBREG call is used to register the details of the interface for this specific server. The interface details specified on the call were generated by the Orbix gencbl utility within the generated COBOL copy file, and are totally opaque to the user. The name of the parameter with all the interface details is always <interface-name>-INTERFACE.

Finally, we set a timer using ORBTIME, then call ORBINIT so that the server may proceed to receive and process inbound requests. In this specific example we set the timer to run for an arbitrary 15 minutes. Note that the actual value is in milliseconds. Once ORBINIT has been called, it will never return until either the timer expires or the server is terminated. As inbound requests are received they are passed to the dispatcher.

29.4.3.2 The Naming Service Dispatcher

As mentioned earlier, once a server has called ORBINIT, it will wait within that call for all inbound requests. When one is received, it will be passed directly to an entry point within the server that is called DISPATCH.

The following code is the dispatcher for our Naming Service. For each inbound request it receives, it determines which specific operation has been requested and then calls the appropriate code to process it:

```
ENTRY "DISPATCH".
    CALL "ORBSTAT" USING ORBIX-STATUS-INFORMATION
    CALL "ORBREQ"  USING REQUEST-INFO
    CALL "STRGET"  USING OPERATION-NAME
                         NamingContext-OPERATION-LENGTH
                         NamingContext-OPERATION
    COPY NAMINGCD.
    EXIT PROGRAM
```

Once again we do an ORBSTAT call to establish the status area for exception handling. After that we use an ORBREQ call to obtain the details of the inbound request. The details returned will include the name of the requested operation; however, it will be in a CORBA string format, so we use a call to STRGET to extract the string value. In this case we extract it into a NamingContext-OPERATION area. (The Naming Context-OPERATION area is defined within the standard NAMINGCO.CPY COBOL copy file that is generated by the Orbix Gencbl utility.)

Finally, the code within a generated COBOL copy file called NAMINGCD.CPY is used to perform the requested operation. (The COBOL copy file, NAMINGCD.CPY is also generated by the Orbix Gencbl utility.)

The following is the code generated within the NAMINGCD copy file. It expects the operation name to be set in the NamingContext-OPERATION field, which is defined within the NAMINGCO copy file (as illustrated earlier on), and uses the level 88 COBOL values associated with this field to select the correct COBOL paragraph:

```
EVALUATE TRUE

    WHEN NAMINGCONTEXT-BIND
        PERFORM DO-NAMINGCONTEXT-BIND

    WHEN NAMINGCONTEXT-RESOLVENAME
        PERFORM DO-NAMINGCONTEXT-RESOLVE

END-EVALUATE
```

29.4.3.3 Naming Service Method: Bind

This bind routine accepts two input parameters: an Object Reference and an associated Object name. The Object Reference is inserted into a database using the supplied Object name as a key:

```
*============================================================
*    bind
*============================================================
DO-NamingContext-Bind.
    display "NS: bind invoked"

    CALL "ORBGET" USING NamingContext-Bind-Args

    move length of lk-data  to ws-lth
    move 0                  to ws-flags
    call "CBL_ALLOC_MEM" using ws-data-ptr
                                by value ws-lth
                                          ws-flags
    set address of lk-data  to ws-data-ptr
    call "OBJDUP"   using object-ref in
                          NamingContext-Bind-args
                          lk-object
    PERFORM CHECK-STATUS

    move length of ws-txt   to ws-txt-lth
    call "STRGET"       using IDL-ID in
                              NAMINGCONTEXT-BIND-ARGS
                              ws-txt-lth
                              ws-txt
    call "db-insert" using ws-txt
                          by value ws-data-ptr
    display "    Bind  for " ws-txt(1:30)
    CALL "ORBPUT"     USING NamingContext-Bind-Args
    .
```

For every operation implementation, an ORBGET routine is first called to populate a parameter area with all the operation's input parameters. This parameter area is defined within the generated COBOL copy file for the Naming Service interface.

For this operation, storage is allocated for one cyclic list element, then initialized. Next, a duplicate of the Object Reference passed in as an input parameter is inserted into the list element using the OBJDUP function. It is necessary to use ORBDUP to ensure that the correct reference count is maintained for the Object Reference.

The STRGET function is used to get the actual value of the Object Name passed in as a CORBA string within the structure. The value is extracted from its opaque CORBA string format and converted into a COBOL string using this function.

The db-insert function is then used to add the new element into the cyclic list using the Object Name as its key.

Upon completion of all processing, the operation implementation makes an ORBPUT call to return control back to the caller along with any output values set up within the parameter area by the operation. Since there are no output parameters for this operation, none were placed into the parameter area for return to the caller.

29.4.3.4 Naming Service Method: Resolve

The resolve routine takes an Object Name supplied as an input parameter and uses it as a key into the database. If an entry associated with the key is located, then the Object Reference within it is returned to the caller. Otherwise, a NULL is returned:

```
*============================================================
*     resolve
*============================================================
DO-NamingContext-Resolve.
     display "ns: Resolve invoked"
     CALL "ORBGET"  USING NamingContext-Resolve-Args

     move length of ws-txt to ws-txt-lth
     call "STRGET"    using IDL-ID in
                            NAMINGCONTEXT-RESOLVE-ARGS
                            ws-txt-lth
                            ws-txt
     call "db-lookup" using ws-txt
                            returning ws-data-ptr
     if ws-data-ptr not = null
         display "    Match for " ws-txt(1:30)
         set address of lk-data
                    to   ws-data-ptr
         set result   to    lk-object
     else
         set result   to    null
         display "    No Match for " ws-txt(1:30)
     end-if

     CALL "ORBPUT"  USING NamingContext-Resolve-Args
     .
```

Once again the initial call to ORBGET is made to populate the parameter area defined within the generated COBOL copy file for the Naming Service interface with all the input parameters for this operation.

The STRGET function is used to get the actual value of the Object Name passed in as a CORBA string within the structure. The value is extracted from its opaque CORBA string format and converted into a COBOL string using this function.

The db-lookup function is then used to locate any elements within the cyclic list associated with the supplied Object Name. If none are found, a NULL value is set up for the caller. Otherwise, the associated Object Reference is set up for return to the caller.

Finally, now that all processing has been completed, ORBPUT is called to return the results back to the caller. In this instance the result of the operation is defined as an Object Reference, so an actual Object Reference, or a NULL value, is returned to the caller.

29.4.4 Common Routines for Interfacing to Our Naming Service with Orbix COBOL

Two common routines are provided to simplify the access of our Naming Service for all of the COBOL tutorials. These are ns-bind, which constructs an Object Reference and caches it into our Naming Service, and ns-rslv, which locates a specific Object Reference within our Naming Service. (If you've been following the implementation in C++ and Java, you'll recall that these languages defined an object, NsPublisher, which wrapped the calls to the Naming Service and error checking. Don't look for that here; we haven't written a parallel NsPublisher routine in COBOL.)

Each of the preceding externally callable routines also utilizes one internal common routine called ns-ns that returns the object reference for our Naming Service.

Since we'll be using these routines within each of the COBOL tutorials, let's now review each of them in more detail.

29.4.4.1 ns-ns

The sole objective of this routine is to return the Object Reference of our Naming Service. Only the common routines ns-bind and ns-rslv will ever call it:

```
PROCEDURE DIVISION.


*------------------------------------------------------------
*      Return Object Reference if I already have it
*------------------------------------------------------------
       if yes-object-ref
           exit program returning obj-ref
       end-if


*------------------------------------------------------------
*      Initialize
*------------------------------------------------------------
       CALL "ORBSTAT"        USING ORBIX-STATUS-INFORMATION
```

```
     *-------------------------------------------------------------
     *      Create Object Reference
     *-------------------------------------------------------------
     *
     *      Get HOST Name
     *
            move length of host-name to host-name-lth
            call "ORBHOST" using host-name-lth host-name


     *-------------------------------------------------------------
     *      Get Object Reference for Naming Service
     *-------------------------------------------------------------
     *
     *      Get Naming Service Object Reference
     *
            CALL "ORBREG" USING NamingContext-INTERFACE
            string ":\"                 delimited by size
                  host-name             delimited by space
                  ns-txt                delimited by size
                  into obj-txt
            call "OBJSET" using obj-txt, obj-ref
            PERFORM CHECK-STATUS

            set yes-object-ref to true

            exit program returning obj-ref
               .
```

Initially this routine checks to see if the Object Reference has previously been cached within working storage. If it has, then that value is returned directly to the caller. Otherwise, it proceeds with the following processing to obtain our Naming Service Object Reference.

A call is made to ORBSTAT to register the status information area for this program. Next, an ORBHOST is called to obtain the host name for the local machine. After that, an ORBREG call is made to register the start of activity for our Naming Service.

A stringified object reference is constructed using the host name. This assumes that, for the tutorial, the Naming Service will be running off the same host. In real life this is not at all realistic, but this has been done here to keep the tutorials simple.

Finally, an OBJSET call is made to convert the stringified object reference into a real Object Reference. This Object Reference is then returned to the caller.

29.4.4.2 ns-bind

This routine is called by all of the COBOL tutorials to construct a unique Object Reference for the caller, then cache it within our Naming Service using a unique name provided by the caller. The input parameters provided by the caller are:

- The name of the server that supports the interface
- The name of the interface

■ The unique name that is to be used as a key within the Naming Service for the cached Object Reference

```
PROCEDURE DIVISION using lk-server-name
                          lk-interface-name
                          lk-bind
                            .


*-------------------------------------------------------------
*      Initialize
*-------------------------------------------------------------
       CALL "ORBSTAT"  USING ORBIX-STATUS-INFORMATION

*
*      Set up bind name
*
       move length of lk-server-name to ws-lth
       call "STRSET" using IDL-ID
                         in NamingContext-Bind-args
                         ws-lth
                         lk-bind-name
       PERFORM CHECK-STATUS

*-------------------------------------------------------------
*      Create Object Reference
*-------------------------------------------------------------
*
*      Get HOST Name
*
       move length of host-name to host-name-lth
       call "ORBHOST" using host-name-lth host-name

*
*      Build stringified Object reference
*
       move spaces               to obj-txt
       string ":\"               delimited by size
              host-name          delimited by space
              ":"                delimited by size
              lk-server-na       delimited by space
              ":::IR:"           delimited by size
              lk-interface-name delimited by space
                        into obj-txt

*
*      Construct actual Object Reference
*
       CALL "OBJSET" using obj-txt
                        obj IN
                           NamingContext-Bind-args
       PERFORM CHECK-STATUS
```

```
*------------------------------------------------------------
*       Cache Object Reference in NameService
*------------------------------------------------------------
        call "ns-ns" returning ns-obj

*
*       Cache the reference
*
        set NamingContext-Bind  to true
        call "ORBEXEC" using ns-obj
                            NamingContext-Operation
                            NamingContext-Bind-args
        PERFORM CHECK-STATUS

        exit program
        .
```

Once again we find the standard ORBSTAT routine being called to register the status exception area within this program's working storage.

Next, we set up the actual bind name by converting the text into an opaque CORBA string using STRSET, and placing that converted value into the bind parameter list.

Next, ORBHOST is used to get the host name of the local host. The returned value is then used along with the supplied server name and interface name to construct a stringified Object Reference for the caller's interface. OBJSET is then used to convert it into a real Object Reference.

The internal ns-ns routine is then called to obtain our Naming Service Object Reference.

Finally, ORBEXEC is called to invoke the bind operation within the instance of our Naming Service that we previously obtained an Object Reference for. Note that the first parameter on this routine is the Object Reference of the object that we are invoking an operation on, the second parameter is the name of the operation we are invoking, and the third parameter is the parameter area for the operation.

You may have also noticed that we checked the status of each call with a perform of a CHECK-STATUS paragraph. For the moment we will just pass over this. Don't worry, we'll discuss the details of this method of exception handling later on within this chapter when we look at the Depot implementation.

29.4.4.3 ns-rslv

This routine is called by all of the COBOL tutorials to extract an Object Reference from our Naming Service using a unique name provided by the caller:

```
PROCEDURE DIVISION using lk-name.


*------------------------------------------------------------
*       Activate the Depot Implementation
*------------------------------------------------------------
        CALL "ORBSTAT" USING ORBIX-STATUS-INFORMATION
```

```
 *
 *     Set up resolve name
 *

       move length of lk-name to ws-lth
       call "STRSET" using IDL-ID
                           in NamingContext-RESOLVE-args
                           ws-lth
                           lk-name
       PERFORM CHECK-STATUS


 *
 *     Locate Object ref within NS
 *

       call "ns-ns" returning ns-obj

       set NamingContext-Resolve  to true
       call "ORBEXEC" using ns-obj
                           NamingContext-Operation
                           NamingContext-Resolve-args
       PERFORM CHECK-STATUS

       exit program returning result in
                           NamingContext-Resolve-args
```

We start by once again calling the standard ORBSTAT routine to register the status exception area within this program's working storage.

Next, we set up the actual resolve name by converting the text into an opaque CORBA string using STRSET, and placing that converted value into the resolve parameter list.

The ns-ns routine is then called to obtain the Naming Service Object Reference.

ORBEXEC is then called to invoke the Resolve operation within the instance of our Naming Service that we previously obtained an Object Reference for. The extracted Object Reference is then returned to the caller. Now that was easy!

29.5 COBOL Implementation of Depot

We are now ready to look at the implementation details for the Depot server. The complete description of the externally accessible interface for depot is contained within the Central IDL file. If you look inside this file, you will see that it contains just one IDL interface, **Depot**. Since each specific IDL interface will always result in one COBOL copy file, we will be generating just one COBOL copy file containing the complete layout of all the parameters for each of the operations within the interface. We'll now have an actual illustration of this.

We first present the complete IDL contained within the Central IDL file, then follow that with the Orbix COBOL copy file that is generated for the **Depot** interface contained within it. After that, we complete this chapter with a review of the actual implementation details.

29.5.1 The Complete Depot IDL

Here is the complete Central IDL, which contains one IDL interface that is implemented within the module:

```
// Include interface definition for store and POS objects.
#include "POS.idl"
#include "Store.idl"

#pragma prefix "omg.org"

module CentralOffice
{
  interface Depot {
    void find_item_info(
            in  AStore::AStoreId store_id,
            in  POS::Barcode    item1,
            in  long            quantity1,
            out AStore::ItemInfo item_info)
      raises (AStore::BarcodeNotFound);
  };
};
```

You may notice that there are some types that are actually defined within other IDL files. The rule that all COBOL types are rolled back to their basic types still holds in this case. Users do not have to include a COBOL copy file for either the **Store** or **Pos** interfaces; the COBOL copy file generated for this interface is all that is required.

29.5.2 The Mapping for the Depot Interface

As mentioned earlier, the Orbix COBOL mapping for the **Depot** interface illustrated previously generates a COBOL copy file called depot.cpy. It contains:

```
*************************************************************
*
*   Interface:   Depot
*
*   Generated by gencbl
*
*************************************************************


*************************************************************
*
*   Defined Operations
*
*************************************************************


*
*   Operation  :  find_item_info
```

```
     *   Parameters :   in long store_id
     *                  in string item1
     *                  in long quantity1
     *                  out struct AStore::ItemInfo item_info
     *   Raises     :   BarcodeNotFound
     *
      01 DEPOT-FIND-ITEM-INFO-ARGS.
          03 STORE-ID                PICTURE S9(09) BINARY.
          03 ITEM1                   POINTER.
          03 QUANTITY1               PICTURE S9(09) BINARY.
          03 ITEM-INFO.
             05 ITEM                 POINTER.
             05 ITEM-TYPE            PICTURE S9(09) BINARY.
                88 FOOD                 VALUE 0.
                88 CLOTHES              VALUE 1.
                88 IDL-OTHER            VALUE 2.
             05 ITEM-COST            COMPUTATIONAL-1.
             05 IDL-NAME             POINTER.
             05 QUANTITY             PICTURE S9(09) BINARY.


      *************************************************************
          COPY DEPOTX.
      *************************************************************
      01 DEPOT-OPERATION             PICTURE X(15).
         88 DEPOT-FIND-ITEM-INFO        VALUE "find_item_info".

      01 DEPOT-OPERATION-LENGTH      PICTURE 9(09) BINARY
                                        VALUE 15.
```

The DEPOT COBOL copy file contains the parameter layouts for the one operation within the **Depot** interface and an operation area. Notice that the IDL typedefs within the IDL interface have been rolled back to their basic COBOL definitions.

For the Orbix implementation of COBOL, it also pulls in another copy file called DEPOTX.CPY. This includes product-specific details for the Depot interface. The contents of this file are completely opaque to users, so you need not worry about what is inside it. These generated interface details are passed in as a parameter on the ORBREG routine using the label DEPOT-INTERFACE. It is a mechanism for passing details of the interface in for a dynamic mapping just before we commence to interact via that interface as either a client or an object implementation. We shall see this within the implementation details presented in the following section.

29.5.3 Implementing the Depot with Orbix COBOL

Let's look at the actual implementation of the Depot server written using Orbix COBOL. As we review the details, notice that the pattern introduced with our Naming Service is repeated here. The server consists of:

- A main program that registers the interface, a dispatcher for receiving all inbound requests.

- The actual implementation of the operations.

You will find this basic pattern repeating itself throughout all the COBOL tutorials. The best place to begin is to review the main program. This is the primary entry point into the server. After that we move on to look at the details of the dispatcher, then the implementation of the interface.

29.5.3.1 The Depot Server

When first started, the Depot server needs to perform all the initialization required to enable it to receive and process inbound requests for the Depot IDL interface. To do this, it initially performs some basic initialization, then registers the Depot interface with the ORB. Here is the actual code that does all this:

```
PROCEDURE DIVISION.
*-----------------------------------------------------------
*     Perform DEPOT Initialization
*-----------------------------------------------------------
      call "depot-init"


*-----------------------------------------------------------
*     Activate the Depot Implementation
*-----------------------------------------------------------
      CALL "ORBSTAT" USING ORBIX-STATUS-INFORMATION
      CALL "ORBREG"  USING DEPOT-INTERFACE
```

It begins with a call to the depot-init routine. Since we have already reviewed this routine, we do not need to illustrate it explicitly here. Nevertheless, in order to understand what is going on, let's briefly review what it does:

- First, it initializes a cyclic in-memory list using the db-init routine that was discussed earlier in this chapter.

- It then proceeds to open the DEPOT.DAT file and load its contents into the cyclic list. The db-insert routine, described earlier in this chapter, is used to insert each item. As each item is loaded into the list, the barcode for each is used as the key. This enables us to access items from the list using just their barcodes.

Once the db-init routine has completed all its processing, we may proceed with the actual ORB initialization. This starts with the standard ORBSTAT call to register the ORBIX-STATUS-INFORMATION area as the working storage in which all status information is to be recorded for this program. We do this to enable exception handling within a COBOL context. We will discuss exception handling in more detail later in the chapter. The ORBIX-STATUS-INFORMATION area, which we specified as a parameter on the call, is defined within the standard CORBA.CPY copy file. Remember that this copy file must be included within the working storage of all COBOL programs that use the Orbix COBOL routines.

After the ORBSTAT call, ORBREG is called to register the details for the depot interface that the Depot server will support. The DEPOT-INTERFACE parameter used on the ORBREG call is defined for you within the COBOL DEPOT.CPY copy file that was generated for the Depot interface. In fact, it's actually within the DEPOTX.CPY copy file, which is embedded inside the DEPOT.CPY copy file.

Next we need to call ns-bind to create a unique Object Reference for the Depot interface, then register it with our Naming Service. (The ns-bind routine was discussed and illustrated in detail earlier in this chapter.) However, before it is possible for the construction of a valid Object Reference within an Orbix COBOL context, the ORBINIT call must be invoked. Here we face an interesting Catch-22 dilemma. By default, ORBINIT will run forever when called and send all inbound requests to the Depot server's dispatcher until the server is terminated. Therefore, if we call ORBINIT we will not be able to call the initialization routines. How do we resolve this? The answer is to set a timer so that an initial call to ORBINIT times out immediately. We can then call the ns-bind routine, reset the ORBINIT timer, and call it again. The following code illustrates this solution:

```
*
*       Set server timeout to 0 just to get it going
*

        move "0"            to ws-timeout
        SET EVENT-TIMEOUT        TO TRUE
        CALL "ORBTIME" USING ORBIX-TIMEOUT-TYPE
                             WS-TIMEOUT

        CALL "ORBINIT" USING SERVER-NAME
                             SERVER-NAME-LEN


*
*       Now Cache its object reference in the
*       NameService
*

        CALL "ns-bind" using server-name
                             server-name
                             server-name
```

As you can see, the ORBIX ORBTIME call is used to set a 0 time-out for the ORBINIT call so that it will time out and return immediately when called. This then enables us to call ns-bind to create the Depot Object Reference, and then cache it within our Naming Service. The ns-bind routine expects three different parameters to be passed to it: the server name, the interface name, and a unique name to cache the Object Reference under. Since there will only ever be one Depot server, we can actually use the same value for all three parameters in this case.

We can now reset the timer for ORBINIT, then call it once again so that the server may proceed to receive and process inbound requests. In this specific example, we set the timer to run for an arbitrary 15 minutes. Note that the actual timer value specified is in milliseconds:

```
*
*       Now wait for up to 15 minutes for inbound requests
*

        move "900000"           to ws-timeout
```

```
        SET EVENT-TIMEOUT        TO TRUE
        CALL "ORBTIME" USING ORBIX-TIMEOUT-TYPE
                             WS-TIMEOUT
        CALL "ORBINIT" USING SERVER-NAME
                             SERVER-NAME-LEN
        PERFORM CHECK-STATUS
        STOP RUN.
```

Orbix COBOL Exception Handling

You may have noticed that we made a call to a paragraph called CHECK-STATUS just after the call to the ORBINIT routine within the last code illustration. This is done to check for an exception being raised in response to the ORBINIT call. Let's take a closer look at this mechanism for exception handling.

If you wish to perform CORBA exception handling within a COBOL context, you need to check the completion status after each call. To do this, you first need to make an ORB-STAT call to register a standard status information area before making any other calls. The area registered by this call is a standard area contained with the CORBA.CPY COBOL copy file, and always has the label ORBIX-STATUS-INFORMATION. All programs that wish to interface to CORBA must include this copy file within their working storage.

Once the ORBSTAT call has been made, you may check the status area after each call to determine if the call was successful. This is done within the COBOL tutorials using a generic paragraph of COBOL code that is performed as follows:

```
CALL "ORBTIME" USING ORBIX-TIMEOUT-TYPE
                     WS-TIMEOUT
PERFORM CHECK-STATUS


The contents of the CHECK-STATUS paragraph is as follows:


*============================================================*
*     Exception Handler                                      *
*============================================================*
 CHECK-STATUS.
     IF EXCEPTION-NUMBER NOT = 0
         DISPLAY "Call failed; Exception = "
                 EXCEPTION-NUMBER
         MOVE LENGTH OF WS-TXT TO WS-TXT-LTH
         CALL "STRGET" USING EXCEPTION-TEXT
                             WS-TXT-LTH
                             WS-TXT
         DISPLAY WS-TXT
     END-IF
     .
```

When this paragraph is performed, the EXCEPTION-NUMBER area within the registered ORBIX-STATUS-INFORMATION area is checked. If it is not 0, an exception has been detected. The exception number will be displayed. Then the textual description for the exception is obtained using a call to STRGET to convert the CORBA opaque string description into COBOL string. This is then displayed.

Throughout all of the Orbix COBOL tutorial examples within this book, you will find that this common mechanism for exception handling is used. The basic pattern applied is that each COBOL program makes an initial call to ORBSTAT to register the standard ORBIX-STATUS-INFORMATION status area in the local working storage. The status of each call may then be checked with a simple PERFORM CHECK-STATUS COBOL statement.

29.5.3.2 The Depot Dispatcher

Once the ORBINIT call has been invoked, the server waits within it for all inbound requests. Every inbound request received is then passed directly to an entry point within the server that has an entry point called DISPATCH.

The following code is the dispatcher for the Depot interface. Here we obtain details for the current request and use that information to determine which specific Depot operation has been requested, and then perform it. In fact, in the case of the Depot interface only one operation is supported, so we could bypass all this processing and call the operation directly. However, for the sake of illustrating how to determine which operation has been requested, the dispatcher code has been included:

```
ENTRY "DISPATCH".
    CALL "ORBSTAT"      USING ORBIX-STATUS-INFORMATION.
    CALL "ORBREQ"       USING REQUEST-INFO.
    CALL "STRGET"       USING OPERATION-NAME
                              DEPOT-OPERATION-LENGTH
                              DEPOT-OPERATION.

    COPY DEPOTD.

    GOBACK. .
```

After the initial ORBSTAT call is made to establish the status area for exceptions, an ORBREQ call is used to obtain the details of the inbound request:

- The REQUEST-INFO parameter on the ORBREQ call is defined within the standard CORBA.CPY copy file. Remember, this should always be included within your working storage.

The actual name of the requested operation is then extracted from the CORBA String type into a DEPOT-OPERATION area by a call to STRGET.

- The OPERATION-NAME parameter is an item within the REQUEST-INFO area that was populated by the previous ORBREQ call.

- The DEPOT-OPERATION area is defined within the DEPOT.CPY COBOL copy file that is generated by the Orbix Gencbl utility.

Finally, the code within a generated COBOL copy file called DEPOTD.CPY is used to perform the requested operation. This file is generated by the Orbix Gencbl utility, and expects the operation name to be set in the DEPOT-OPERATION field, which is defined within the DEPOT.CPY copy file (as illustrated earlier). It uses the level 88 COBOL values associated with this field to select the correct COBOL paragraph. The actual contents of the DEPOTD.CPY copy file are:

```
EVALUATE TRUE

    WHEN DEPOT-FIND-ITEM-INFO
        PERFORM DO-DEPOT-FIND-ITEM-INFO

END-EVALUATE
```

Since the Depot interface only supports one operation, there is only one WHEN statement to select it within the generated code. This is all a bit redundant because the one operation could be called directly. Nevertheless, it does illustrate the principle of operation selection within a dispatcher.

29.5.3.3 Depot Method: Find-Item-Info

Finally, we have reached the implementation of the one operation defined within the Depot interface. It is the Find-Item-Info routine and is used to search the list of items we loaded during initialization for a specific one. If found, it returns the details to the caller. If not found, it raises an exception. Details regarding the implementation of the db-lookup routine were covered in Section 29.2.

Here is the actual code for the implementation of the method:

```
DO-DEPOT-FIND-ITEM-INFO.
    CALL "ORBGET"        USING DEPOT-FIND-ITEM-INFO-ARGS.

    move length of ws-key  to    ws-key-lth
    call "STRGET"             using item1
                                   ws-key-lth
                                   ws-key
    display "Depot: Looking up - " ws-key
    call "db-lookup" using ws-key
                     returning ws-ptr
    if ws-ptr not = NULL

*       Set up return values
        set address of lk-depot-dat-rec to ws-ptr
        display "        Found it      "
                "item=" lk-desc
        move length of lk-barcode  to ws-key-lth
        call "STRSET"         using item in item-info
                                   ws-key-lth
                                   lk-barcode
        evaluate lk-item-type
            when "CLOTHES"
                set clothes   to true
            when "FOOD    "
                set food      to true
            when other
                set idl-other to true
        end-evaluate
        move lk-cost          to item-cost
        move length of lk-desc to ws-key-lth
        call "STRSET"         using idl-name
                                   ws-key-lth
```

```
                                    lk-desc
          move lk-quantity       to quantity in item-info

*         Subtract quantity from current quantity
          subtract quantity1 from lk-quantity
      else
          display "      Not found"
          CALL "ORBERR" USING DEPOT-BARCODENOTFOUND-EXID
                              DEPOT-BARCODENOTFOUND-E-LENGTH
                              DEPOT-BARCODENOTFOUND
      end-if

      CALL "ORBPUT"     USING DEPOT-FIND-ITEM-INFO-ARGS
      .
```

We always start a method implementation with an ORBGET call. This needs to be done to populate the parameter area for this operation with all the input parameters contained within the inbound request. In this case, this includes the store identifier, the unique barcode for the item, and the number of items of that type that are being processed. The DEPOT-FIND-ITEM-INFO-ARGS area used as a parameter on the ORBGET call is defined within the COBOL copy file generated for the Depot interface. You can refer back to the listing of the contents of this copy file in Section 29.5 to see the complete layout of the parameter area. It contains all the parameters used by the operation in one COBOL group item. Note that the ORBGET call will only populate the IN and INOUT parameter areas.

The STRGET routine is then used to obtain the value of the item's barcode that was passed in as a parameter to the operation. It will convert it from its received opaque CORBA string format into a COBOL text string. It is then used on a db-lookup call to locate the details for this item within the Depot's in-memory cyclic list. (The db-lookup routine was discussed in detail in Section 29.2.)

If the details for the requested item are found, the item's details are placed into the parameter return area. This includes using the STRSET routine to establish the textual description of the item in the parameter return area as a CORBA string. You may also observe that the number of items within the database entry for the item is reduced by the quantity requested.

If the details for the requested item are not found, then the ORBERR routine is called to raise the BarcodeNotFound user-defined exception.

When a method implementation has completed its processing, the ORBPUT routine should always be called. This is done to return all the accumulated results for the operation back to the caller. All the OUT, INOUT, and RESULT parameter values within the DEPOT-FIND-ITEM-INFO-ARGS area that was specified on the ORBPUT call will be returned to the caller. Note that ORBPUT should always be called even when there are no return values.

Now that we have reached the end of this method implementation, we have also reached the end of the COBOL tutorial for the Depot server. Congratulations! If you've been working along as you read this, you have successfully completed your first CORBA server written entirely in COBOL.

CHAPTER

30

The Store

30.1 Language-Independent Overview: Store Implementation

This section focuses on the implementation of the Store application and is applicable to everyone. Without getting into language-specific issues, it builds on the A&D and IDL chapters, adding implementation detail relating to the store application. At the end of this section, we will be ready to explore the language-specific sections that follow.

The implementation of the Store application provides a home for the following CORBA components:

- Store object
- Tax object
- Store Access object

These components handle the following IDL data types:

- Structures
- Sequences of structures
- Enumerated types
- Attributes

The Store application makes requests on the following remote services:

- CORBA Naming Service
- Depot Server

The Store, like the Depot, is implemented as a separate server executable. Unlike the Depot, however, there can be multiple Store objects in the system. For identification purposes, each one is given a unique name that it registers with the Naming Service on startup. This name is derived from an ID given on the command line. One other value that a Store needs is the markup rate to be used for prices, which is given as the second parameter on the command line. A valid call to start the store application would be:

```
Store_Server 1.10 26
```

This will cause the markup rate to be 10 percent and the object to be named "Store_26." (This will work fine in the example, but the low markup will probably result in financial failure for anything except a grocery store with one-day average turnover. For a more realistic demo, choose a markup between 50 and 100 percent. To simulate a commune or co-op with recruit volunteers and unpaid staff, try 5.)

On startup, the Store application will carry out a number of tasks that are common to all the example modules, such as initializing the ORB and resolving the Naming Service reference. In addition to this, it will create instances of the `Store` object and `Tax` object. Both the `Store` and `Tax` objects are then advertised in the Naming Service. At this point the application has nothing to do but wait for invocations on the `Store` and `Tax` objects.

The `Store` object waits for invocations on its `login` method. The implementation of this method creates a new instance of a Store Access object for each POSTerminal that logs in. A POSTerminal uses the Store Access object to process requests on products. In order to keep account of each terminal and the associated Store Access object, the Store object maintains a list of POSTerminal details, which is implemented as an array of the IDL structure type `AStore::POSInfo`. The Store object processes this list in order to tally up the POSTerminal and Store totals.

The Store Access object depends on the `Depot` and `Tax` objects in order to process requests from POSTerminals; hence, it exhibits both client and server behavior. When a Store Access object is created, it obtains references to the Depot and Tax components from the Naming Service.

A `Tax` object is solely used by Store Access objects to calculate the local tax on each product that is processed. It may seem strange that this object is advertised in the Naming Service, as it is used by another component in the same application. The Store application itself could provide the Store Access object with a reference to the Tax object. The point here is simply one of component portability and reuse. The implementation of the Store Access object makes no assumption as to the location of the Tax object. It will always resolve it through the Naming Service. Hence, the Tax object could equally reside inside the Store application or in its own application. In fact, in the first edition of this book, the Tax object was implemented both ways!

This concludes the language-independent discussion of the Store object implementation. If you're working the example in C++, continue with the next section. If you are working in Java, skip to the beginning of Chapter 31. If you're working in COBOL, skip to Chapter 32.

30.2 C++ Generated from the Store IDL Definitions

In this section, we'll describe the code generated from the IDL by the C++ language mapping. We'll cover the module in parts, quoting each IDL fragment just before we discuss it. To examine the complete AStore Module IDL in one piece, flip back to Section 26.2.2.4.

30.2.1 C++ Language Mapping for the Store Module Types

The Astore Module starts by declaring a number of types used throughout the Store code, so we'll start by describing the C++ types that correspond to these IDL definitions. Here are these IDL declarations:

```
enum ItemTypes {FOOD, CLOTHES, OTHER};
typedef long AStoreID;

struct ItemInfo
{
  POS::Barcode      item;
  ItemTypes         item_type;
  float             item_cost;
  string            name;
  long              quantity;
};

exception BarcodeNotFound {POS::Barcode item;};

interface StoreAccess; // /forward reference

struct POSInfo
{
  POS::POSId        id;
  StoreAccess       store_access_reference;
  Float             total_sales;
  float             total_taxes;
};

typedef sequence <POSInfo> POSList;
```

Since IDL **enum**s map to C++ enums, the **ItemTypes** enum mapping is straightforward. It is:

```
enum ItemTypes { FOOD, CLOTHES, OTHER, _ItemTypes = CORBA::enum32 };
```

The **enum** maps to an opaque type that forces a 32-bit enumeration, as its type suggests. You should not reference the enumerator _ItemTypes in your application, nor should you assume that all languages start their enumeration with zero as C++ does. So, to portably pass FOOD, use FOOD and not zero.

The mapping for **struct ItemInfo** contains a number of interesting types:

```
class ItemInfo_var { ...}
struct ItemInfo {
    POS::Barcode_var item;
    ItemTypes item_type;
    CORBA::Float item_cost;
    CORBA::String_var name;
    CORBA::Long quantity;
};
```

struct ItemInfo in IDL maps to a C++ `struct` (`ItemInfo`) plus a class used for memory management (`ItemInfo_var`). Because the element **POS::Barcode** is actually typedef'd to a string, `ItemInfo` is a variable length structure. **POS::Barcode** maps to its _var type to automate its memory management. The class `ItemInfo_var` manages the memory of the entire structure. When `ItemInfo_var` goes out of scope, it is deallocated along with the structure itself.

The next element is our user defined exception, **BarcodeNotFound**. This maps to a C++ class, which inherits from `CORBA_UserException`:

```
class BarcodeNotFound : public CORBA_UserException {
public:
    POS::Barcode_var item;
};
```

Because the data element of this exception, **POS::Barcode**, is actually a **string**, the mapping uses the `POS::Barcode_var` class to automate memory management.

The forward reference for **interface StoreAccess**, necessary because the POSInfo structure references this type before the StoreAccess is defined, does not map directly so we'll skip it here.

The next element is a definition for **struct POSInfo**, with a mapping similar to **struct ItemInfo** that we just described:

```
struct POSInfo {
    POS::POSId id;
    StoreAccess_var store_access_reference;
    CORBA::Float total_sales;
    CORBA::Float total_taxes;
};
class POSInfo_var { ... };
```

As before, we get both a `struct` (`POSInfo`) and a class (`POSInfo_var`). The second element, an object reference to a Store Access object, is of variable length and therefore maps to a `StoreAccess_var` type. The use of a _var type, which automates memory management (as we've seen a number of times), ensures that `CORBA::release` is called on the `StoreAccess` when the `POSInfo` structure goes out of scope.

The next element in the Store IDL file is typedef for **POSList** sequence, which maps to two C++ classes:

```
class POSList_var { ... };
class POSList { ... };
```

The C++ mapping of sequences was discussed earlier, so we won't go over that again. For this particular instance, the mapping generates a POSList_var class which manages the memory of the sequence, plus a POSList class which is the actual implementation of the sequence.

30.2.2 Tax Interface

The first interface in the Store module, **interface Tax**, contains two operations:

```
interface Tax
{
  float calculate_tax( in float  taxable_amount);

  float find_taxable_price(in float  item_price,
                           in ItemTypes item_type);

};
```

Here's how they map in C++:

```
class Tax : virtual public CORBA_Object {
public:
     // USER Tax VIRTUALS
     virtual CORBA::Float calculate_tax(
                  CORBA::Float taxable_amount) = 0;
     virtual CORBA::Float find_taxable_price(
                  CORBA::Float item_price,
                  ItemTypes item_type) = 0;
}
```

As with all interfaces, the Tax class uses virtual public inheritance from CORBA_Object, and declares pure virtual methods matching the operations defined n the IDL file. Since this interface uses primitive types only, its mapping to C++ is straightforward.

30.2.3 Store Interface

interface Store is more interesting because it declares a new structure, **StoreTotals**, scoped to the Store interface. The Store also contains two readonly attributes and three operations.

```
interface Store
{
  struct StoreTotals
  {
    float   store_total;
    float   store_tax_total;
  };
  readonly attribute AStoreId store_id;

  readonly attribute StoreTotals totals;
```

```
   StoreAccess login(              in POS::POSId id);

   void    get_POS_totals(         out POSList  POS_data);

   void    update_store_totals(    in  POS::POSId id,
                                   in float  price,
                                   in float  taxes);
};
```

We'll start with the mapping of **struct StoreTotals**, which is

```
class Store : virtual public CORBA_Object {
public:

     struct StoreTotals {
         CORBA::Float store_total;
         CORBA::Float store_tax_total;
     };
     class StoreTotals_var { ...};
};
```

Since the structure elements are of type **float**, the mapping is simple. The interesting aspect of this structure is that it was defined within an interface, which forces its type to be directly visible only to the Store interface. To do this, C++ defines the struct within the public section of the Store class. As with both of the structs that we've already described, we also get a _var class to help with the memory management, this time within the public section of the Store class.

The rest of the class contains the attribute and operation mappings, which are:

```
// USER Store VIRTUALS
virtual AStoreID store_id() = 0;
virtual StoreTotals totals() = 0;
virtual StoreAccess_ptr login(POS::POSId id) = 0;
virtual void get_POS_totals(POSList *& POS_data) = 0;
virtual void update_store_totals(POS::POSId id,
                                 CORBA::Float price,
                                 CORBA::Float taxes) = 0;
```

The **readonly attribute**s **store_id** and **total**s map to methods with the same name as the attribute returning their respective types. Because these are readonly attributes, only the **get** operations are generated. There is no way to set these attributes from an external client; we must set these in program code (which, of course, is why we defined them readonly).

The login operation returns a StoreAccess_ptr which is the object reference type for the **StoreAccess interface**. The **POS::POSId** type is fixed by the typedef in **module POS**.

The get_POS_totals operation returns a void but specifies that the POSList is returned as an out parameter. The out parameter maps to a *& because the client is expecting the server to populate this with a value. Therefore passing a reference to a pointer allows the ORB to allocate the memory for the sequence, and update the pointer held by the client to point to it. In the latest C++ mapping, the POSList *& has been replaced with `POSList_out`. `PosList_out` is a class that is used to make sure that memory is released correctly. Whether your ORB uses `POSList *&` or `POSList_out` will have no affect on your application code when you call this method.

The `update_store_totals` operation uses only primitive types, or typedefs to primitive types, which makes it straightforward.

30.2.4 StoreAccess Interface

The **StoreAccess interface**, the last interface defined in the `Store.idl` file, contains a single operation that can raise an exception:

```
interface StoreAccess
{

    void    find_price(    in          POS::Barcode item,
                           in          long         quantity,
                           out         float        item_price,
                           out         float        item_tax_price,
                           out         ItemInfo     item_info)
        raises (BarcodeNotFound);
};
```

in C++, find_price looks like this:

```
class StoreAccess : virtual public CORBA_Object        {
public:
    // USER StoreAccess VIRTUALS
    virtual void find_price (const char* item,
                        CORBA::Long quantity,
                        CORBA::Float& item_price,
                        CORBA::Float& item_tax_price,
                        ItemInfo *& item_info) = 0;
    };
```

There are no surprises here. The only piece that may look odd is the fact there is no mention of the `BarcodeNotFound` exception. The C++ mapping does not require that the method indicate this with a `throw` clause, even though the implementation is expected to throw this exception if it occurs.

This concludes our look at the C++ mapping of the Store module. Next we will look at the actual implementation.

30.3 Programming the Store: Common Functionality in C++

We are now ready to present the common implementation of the Store package for C++. The first subsection provides the physical layout of this package. Each Store component is explained in a following subsection.

30.3.1 Introduction

The components of the Store package are

COMPONENT	DESCRIPTION
Store_Server	Main control for Store server
StoreAccessImpl	POS session manager
StoreImpl	Representation of a store
TaxImpl	Representation of a store's regional tax

Each component will be looked at in turn. You should note that we define a component as a C++ .h/.cpp pair. In general, you can think of a component as one class and its closely related classes and functions. (No, these are not CORBA components!)

30.3.2 Store Server Component

The Store Server component contains the C++ entry-point function main(). The Store Server's first task is to initialize the ORB and the (basic) object adapter as follows:

```
CORBA::ORB_var orb  = CORBA::ORB_init(argc, argv);
CORBA::BOA_var boa  = orb->BOA_init(argc, argv);
```

Since the current version of CORBA does not solve the bootstrap problem, the ORB is responsible for providing a set of initial references. A reference to the Naming Service is obtained in this way:

```
CORBA::Object_var obj =
orb->resolve_initial_references("NameService");

CosNaming::NamingContext_var naming_service =
    CosNaming::NamingContext::_narrow(obj);
```

The reference obtained is then checked for validity using the is_nil() function (defined in the CORBA package). For example:

```
if (CORBA::is_nil(naming_service)) {
    // Error cannot resolve or narrow naming service
    return 1;
}
```

The Store server then uses the two mandatory command-line arguments to get the store number that this server will represent, and the markup for this store.

Each Store server is responsible for creating a single instance of a Store and a Tax component. The Store and Tax objects are then bound to the Naming Service so that other CORBA objects can reference them. The name given to the Store and Tax objects are Store_<store number> and Tax_<store number>, respectively. For example, if the store number command-line argument is 5, then the Store object is bound with the name Store_5 in the Naming Service. Similarly, the Tax object is bound with the name Tax_5.

The Naming Service Publisher static helper (described earlier) is used to bind the two objects to the Naming Service previously resolved:

```
long storeId = atol(argv[2]);
float markUp = atof(argv[1]);

store = new StoreImpl(naming_service, storeId, markUp);

tax = new TaxImpl(markUp);

// Publish Store and Tax objects into the Naming Service
char regStoreStr[256];
char regTaxStr[256];
sprintf(regStoreStr,"Store_%ld", storeId);
sprintf(regTaxStr,"Tax_%ld", storeId);

try {
NsPublisher::nsBind(obj, store, regStoreStr, "Primer_Example");
NsPublisher::nsBind(obj, tax, regTaxStr, "Primer_Example" );
}
catch(const NsPublisherException& nse) {
    cerr << nse.toString() << endl;

    delete store;
    delete tax;

    return 1;
}
```

The NsPublisherException is caught whenever one of the parameters to NsPublisher::nsBind is nil.

The last significant task the Store server accomplishes is to invoke:

```
boa->impl_is_ready()
```

Before I explain the preceding call, let's step back and describe what has happened. At this point, the Store server has obtained a reference to the Naming Service and has bound two CORBA objects to it: Store and Tax. This means that another CORBA object can query the Naming Service and obtain a reference to these two objects made available by the current process.

Since we bound the Object References (TaxImpl and StoreImpl) to the Naming Service, the ORB should have made the instance(s) ready to accept incoming requests. The way this is accomplished is vendor specific.

Now, when a peer wishes to obtain a reference to a Tax or Store object, it queries the Naming Service for the reference. The reference obtained should point to a valid object (note, I said 'should') that can be invoked upon.

It is possible that the reference obtained from the Naming Service points to a CORBA object that is no longer valid. If this is the case, the NsPublisher will throw an exception, which we will catch and report.

30.3.3 Store Access Component

The Store Access component is used to manage POS sessions. It acts as an intermediary between the POS and the central depot with respect to the item's database access.

As with most classes used in this book, we have opted for simplicity rather than completeness. For this reason we only provide the functions required to implement the IDL interfaces and to create instances of these types.

The StoreAccessImpl component has one constructor and a single public member function, find_price. Both are described next.

30.3.3.1 StoreAccessImpl Constructor

The StoreAccessImpl constructor has the following signature:

```
StoreAccessImpl(CosNaming::NamingContext_ptr ns,
    AStore::Store_ptr store, CORBA::Float markup);
```

Therefore, it takes three parameters:

- A pointer to a CosNaming::NamingContext
- A pointer to a Store
- A markup value

The CosNaming::NamingContext is used to obtain the Store's associated Tax object as follows:

```
char refstr[256];
AStore::AStoreId id = store->store_id();
sprintf(refstr,"Tax_%ld",id);

CORBA::Object_var obj;

// Resolve Tax
try {
    obj = NsPublisher::nsResolve(ns, refstr, "Primer_Example");
}
catch(const NsPublisherException& nse) {
    _abort(nse.toString());
}

m_tax = AStore::Tax::_narrow(obj);
```

Since each Store object is bound to the Naming Service at the same time as its corresponding Tax object, we can be assured that they are both there. In reality you will want to use a Transaction Service to assure something like this.

The Depot and Store objects bound in the Naming Service are resolved in a similar way:

```
// Resolve Depot
try {
     CORBA::Object_var obj = NsPublisher::nsResolve(ns, "Depot",
"Primer_Example");
}
catch(const NsPublisherException& nse) {
     _abort(nse.toString());
}


m_depot = CentralOffice::Depot::_narrow(obj);



// Make sure all the _narrow calls succeeded
if (CORBA::is_nil(m_tax) || CORBA::is_nil(m_depot))
{
     // We'll just exit for the demo, in real life it would be better
     // to raise an exception.
     _abort("ERROR: StoreAccess failed to narrow objects from Naming
Service");
}


m_store = AStore::Store::_duplicate(store);
```

StoreAccessImpl instances are created by the StoreImpl component when someone 'logs on' to a POSTerminal. Therefore, each POSTerminal points to an instance of a StoreAccessImpl object. In the IDL we see that StoreAccess provides one operation, find_price.

30.3.3.2 StoreAccessImpl::find_price

The POSTerminal calls this operation when the barcode for an item is read (and the optional quantity has been input). The signature for this function is:

```
void StoreAccessImpl::find_price(const char *item,
                    CORBA::Long quantity,
                    CORBA::Float& itemPrice,
                    CORBA::Float& itemTaxPrice,
                    AStore::ItemInfo*& iInfo);
```

Remember that the IDL for this function specifies that the last three parameters are out parameters. The code implementation of this operation is:

```
void StoreAccessImpl::find_price(const char *item,      CORBA::Longquantity,
CORBA::Float& itemPrice,
CORBA::Float& itemTaxPrice,
AStore::ItemInfo*& iInfo) {

     m_depot->find_item_info(m_store->store_id(), item, quantity,
     iInfo);

     itemPrice    = m_storeMarkup * iInfo->item_cost;

     itemTaxPrice = m_tax->find_taxable_price(itemPrice,
```

```
iInfo->item_type);
}
```

This function simply asks the central depot for information on the item. The relevant information is returned by `find_item_info` in the `AStore::ItemInfo` parameter. The `Depot::find_item_info` operation could have had a return type of `AStore::ItemInfo` instead of using a single `out` parameter.

The item price is calculated as the store's markup value multiplied by the cost of the item (as reported by the central depot). Of course, the `Tax` reference previously obtained is used to calculate the tax on this item.

If the central depot cannot find an item corresponding to the barcode, then it will throw a `AStore::BarcodeNotFound` exception, which will be propagated to the client. This is generally not good practice. The exception should be caught and re-thrown by `StoreAccessImpl::find_price`.

30.3.4 Store Component

The `Store` component represents a store. It has a constructor, three functions, and two read-only attributes (which are mapped to C++ accessor functions).

30.3.4.1 StoreImpl Constructor

The `StoreImpl` constructor signature is:

```
StoreImpl(CosNaming::NamingContext_ptr ns, AStore::AStoreId storeID,
CORBA::Float storeMarkup);
```

The constructor's implementation is pretty straightforward:

```
StoreImpl::StoreImpl(CosNaming::NamingContext_ptr ns,
AStore::AStoreId storeID,
CORBA::Float storeMarkup)
: m_POSTerminals(10) // start with space for 10 POSs
{
        m_ns = CosNaming::NamingContext::_duplicate(ns);
        m_storeTotal    = 0;
        m_storeTaxTotal = 0;
        m_storeMarkup   = storeMarkup;
        m_storeID       = storeID;

    // initialize m_POSTerminals to indicate no POS Logins have been
        received
    CORBA::ULong len      = m_POSTerminals.length();

    for (CORBA::ULong i = 0; i < len; i++) {
        m_POSTerminals[i].id = EMPTY;
    }
}
```

The preceding code simply initializes StoreImpl's member variables. The number of POSTerminals is initially set to 10. The status of each POSTerminal is also set to EMPTY, meaning that no one has logged in to the terminal yet.

A copy of the CosNaming::NamingContext is kept so that when we create StoreAccessImpl objects (when someone logs in), then StoreAccessImpl can obtain the corresponding Tax and central depot references (see above).

The member variable m_POSTerminals is defined in the IDL to be an unbounded (dynamic) sequence of POSInfo structs:

```
typedef sequence <POSInfo> POSList;
```

POSList is mapped to a C++ class that provides the ability to get and set the length of the sequence. It also allows for insertion and access of its elements using the [] operator (that is, the operator [] has been overloaded to return a C++ reference to the POSInfo object at the specified index location in the sequence). The POSList class has the following form:

```
class  POSList {
public:
    ...
POSList(CORBA::ULong _max=0);void length(CORBA::ULong _len);
CORBA::ULong length() const;
AStore::POSInfo& operator[](CORBA::ULong index)
    ...
private:
AStore::POSInfo * data;
    ...
};
```

The POSList class is defined for you in the stub code generated by your vendor's IDL compiler.

30.3.4.2 StoreImpl::store_id

This function is trivial and returns the store's id, as was assigned in StoreImpl's constructor.

30.3.4.3 StoreImpl::totals

This function returns a AStore::Store::StoreTotals structure that contains two fields: store_total and store_tax_totals. The implementation of this function simply assigns StoreImpl's member variables, m_storeTotal and m_storeTax-Total, to the structure it creates and returns.

30.3.4.4 StoreImpl::login

The login function is invoked by the POSTerminal when a new cashier logs in at a POSTerminal. This member function is implemented as:

```
AStore::StoreAccess_ptr StoreImpl::login(CORBA::Long id) {

    CORBA::ULong loc = _locatePOSEntry(id);

    m_POSTerminals[loc].id          = id;
    m_POSTerminals[loc].total_sales = 0;
    m_POSTerminals[loc].total_taxes = 0;

    // check to see of a StoreAccess object exists for this
    // m_POSTerminal
    // allocate new one if needed.
    if (CORBA::is_nil(m_POSTerminals[loc].store_access_reference))
    {
        // create a local instance of the SToreAccess Object
        m_POSTerminals[loc].store_access_reference =
            new StoreAccessImpl(m_ns, this, m_storeMarkup);

        if (CORBA::is_nil(m_POSTerminals[loc].store_access_reference))
            cerr << "Store_i::Login: Unable to create StoreAccess
            object for POS Login" << endl;
    }

    return
  AStore::StoreAccess::_duplicate(m_POSTerminals[loc].store_access_reference);
  }
```

The _locatePOSEntry function is private to StoreImpl. You will not find it in the IDL file. All that _locatePOSEntry does is to iterate through the list of POSTerminals and return the index to the next available one.

The next available POSTerminal is then initialized to a new cashier's session. If there was no Store Access reference previously associated with this POSTerminal, then we create a new StoreAccessImpl instance and assign it to the POSTerminal.

The login function returns a duplicate pointer of the AStore::StoreAccess that is associated with the POSTerminal at this Store. A duplicate was made so that the reference count is properly maintained. This is important to do when you pass pointers around.

30.3.4.5 StoreImpl::get_POS_totals

The signature for this function is:

```
void get_POS_totals(AStore::POSList*& posData);
```

In the IDL definition for this function, the posData parameter is an out parameter. All that this function does is to create a duplicate of the AStore::POSList member variable m_POSTerminals (which, if you remember, is a AStore::POSList).

30.3.4.6 StoreImpl::update_store_totals

The signature for this function is:

```
void StoreImpl::update_store_totals(CORBA::Long id,
```

```
CORBA::Float price,
    CORBA::Float taxes)
```

Every parameter is an in parameter. This function is invoked by the POSTerminal at the end of a sale. The store keeps track of its totals as well as the POSTerminal's totals this way.

30.3.5 Tax Component

The Tax component keeps track of the regional tax rate for a particular store. It is responsible for calculating the tax for a store as well as providing the taxable price for an item (since some items may not be taxable in some regions).

The tax rate is set at 5 percent for this demo, but in reality you would have your application set this value to the current tax rate in the jurisdiction of your store.

The implementation of this class is straightforward:

```
const CORBA::Float region_rate = 0.05;


TaxImpl::TaxImpl()
{
    // set tax rate applied to taxable goods
    m_regionRate = region_rate;
}


CORBA::Float TaxImpl::calculate_tax(CORBA::Float taxableAmount)
{
    return taxableAmount*m_regionRate;
}


CORBA::Float TaxImpl::find_taxable_price(CORBA::Float itemPrice,
    AStore::ItemTypes itemtype)
{
    CORBA::Float taxprice;

    if (itemtype == AStore::OTHER)
        taxprice = itemPrice;
    else
        taxprice = 0.0;

    return taxprice;
}
```

As you can see, the implementation of this class has very little to do with CORBA (although the flexibility that the design gives to the application is very relevant!). The TaxImpl class is a subclass of the TaxImpl skeleton, which is responsible for unmarshaling CORBA requests to the implementation and for returning the results back to the client (the way that this is done is beyond the scope of this book).

30.4 Implementing the Store Using CORBAplus for C++

This section describes the CORBAplus implementation of the Store. The Vertel's Expersoft CORBAplus implementation of the Store components will only need a small number of recurring changes. The primary places where the Store implementation differs from the common source base are the base class names, the use of CORBAplus' event loop object, and the include files.

A makefile is provided for both Unix and Windows platforms. See Section 26.5.1.1 for details on how to build the Store component.

The CORBAplus-specific implementation issues are:

- CORBAplus#includes
- Base class name
- BOA::obj_is_ready
- CORBAplus event loop
- Use of _out classes for CORBA out and inout arguments

Each of these issues was already described in detail in Section 27.3. This section will look at the four files that make up the Store component: Store_Server.cpp, StoreAccessImpl.cpp, StoreImpl.cpp, and TaxImpl.cpp.

30.4.1 Store_Server.cpp

Nearly all CORBAplus applications will be required to include the following header files:

```
#ifdef EXPERSOFT
#ifdef WIN32
#include <pbroker/winsvc/winsvc.h>
#else
#include <pbroker/unixsvc/unixsvc.h>
#endif
#include <pbroker/corba/orb.h>
#include <pbroker/corba/boa.h>
#include <pbroker/corba/naming/naming.h>
#endif
```

The first set of include files will include either the Windows version of the CORBAplus event loop or the Unix version of the CORBAplus event loop. The orb.h and boa.h bring in the definitions for the CORBAplus ORB and BOA, respectively, and naming.h brings in the definitions required to use the Naming Service.

30.4.2 StoreAccessImpl.cpp

The StoreAccessImpl requires very few changes. The portion of code that is different is shown here:

```
void StoreAccessImpl::find_price(
    const char* item,
    CORBA::Long quantity,
    CORBA::Float& item_price,
    CORBA::Float& item_tax_price,
#ifdef EXPERSOFT
AStore::ItemInfo_out item_info
        // can be thought of as Store::ItemInfo*& item_info

#endif

)
{ ...
```

The reason for the _out parameter is discussed in Section 27.3.1.5.

30.4.3 StoreImpl.cpp

The only change from the common code is again in the generated out parameter.

```
void StoreImpl::get_POS_totals(
#ifdef EXPERSOFT
    AStore::POSList_out POS_data

    // is equivalent to: AStore::POSList*& POS_data
#endif

)
{ ...
```

Remember from Section 27.3.1.5 that the out parameter is generated so memory management is handled correctly, regardless of whether you pass an _var or the non_var equivalent. Programmatically, it is the same as a reference to a pointer.

30.4.4 TaxImpl.cpp

TaxImpl requires no modifications from the common code base.

30.4.5 Compiling and Running

Finally, you will need to compile and link the Store_Server program. The object file for the main program should be linked with object files for all the implementations that may be instantiated in your program. Both Unix and Windows makefiles are provided. See Section 26.5.1.1. for a description of how to build the example. It is assumed that you have installed CORBAplus for C++ and have PBHOME and PBTMPDIR environment variables configured correctly. The easiest way to build the Store_Server is to use the makefiles Makefile.unix.xps or Makefile.win.xps, which are located in the Store directory.

To build the Solaris version, at an xterm type:

```
%make -f Makefile.unix.xps
```

To build the Windows version, at a command window type:

```
%nmake -f Makefile.win.xps
```

See Section 27.4.2.1 for a description of how to run the Naming Service. You must have a Naming Service running before trying to start the Store_Server.

30.4.5.1 Running the Store_Server

Assuming you are following along, you must have a Naming Service running and you must start the Depot_Server before starting the Store_Server. The Store_Server will use the Naming Service to publish objects and will use the Naming Service to obtain a reference to the Depot_Server. The Store_Server is started with the following command line:

```
%Store_Server 1.1 1 -pbinit NameService
iiop://localhost:6004/NameServiceRoot
```

30.5 IBM Implementation of the Store

The types of changes required for the IBM implementation of the Store are the same as those described for the IBM implementation of the Depot in Section 27.4. You may wish to refer back to that section for review. The remainder of this section simply describes how the same types of changes are made for the implementation of the Store.

30.5.1 Detailed Changes to the C++ Code

30.5.1.1 StoreServer.cpp

Near the start of the file, include the header for the CORBA Naming Service being used. For the IBM implementation, a simple Naming Service has been implemented in the primer_utils directory to the IDL interface defined in the CosNaming.idl IDL file. We include:

```
#include <CosNaming.hh>
```

The ORB and BOA initialization calls near the beginning of main() have been modified to specify that the ORB being initialized is the IBM ORB. This is indicated by the final string parameters "DSOM" and "DSOM_BOA", respectively, in the calls:

```
CORBA::ORB_ptr orb  = CORBA::ORB_init(argc, argv, "DSOM");
CORBA::BOA_ptr boa  = orb->BOA_init(argc, argv, "DSOM_BOA");
```

The remaining code in the server that is unique to the IBM implementation is related to server registration. The IBM ORB maintains a persistent Implementation Repository of defined servers. Each server is registered in the Implementation Repository with a record describing the server's characteristics. The record is keyed by the server's UUID or the server's alias (an optional unique string name, which is more user friendly than a UUID string). The class `ImplDef` defines the data for this record. Typically the Implementation Repository would be managed as part of server installation and administration, and would be used by the ORB daemon to find and activate server processes when necessary. For simplicity in this example, we have avoided the server administration and use of the daemon for activation. The `Store_Server` assumes that it has not been registered previously (by an administrator or by a previous execution) and therefore creates an `ImplDef` to register itself:

```
CORBA::ImplDef * imp = new CORBA::ImplDef ();
imp->set_protocols("SOMD_TCPIP");
```

The only field of the implementation record (instance data on the ImplDef) that the server sets is the field that defines which protocols can be used to access the server. In this case, the TCP/IP protocol is specified. Other fields that would commonly be defined for an implementation include the pathname of the server executable and the server alias (`<path>/Store_Server.exe` and "`Store_Server`", respectively, would be appropriate for this server). The call to `impl_is_ready` passes the `ImplDef` as a parameter:

```
boa->impl_is_ready (imp, 0);
```

The second parameter is optional and is not normally included. It is used in this example to indicate that the server does not wish to use the daemon for activation. By default, servers use the daemon for activation, and communication with the daemon occurs under the `impl_is_ready` call to report that the server is active. Specifying the second parameter here has two effects. First, it prevents communication of server status to the daemon. Second, it causes Object References that are generated by this process to map directly to this process rather than the daemon.

30.5.1.2 StoreAccessImpl, StoreImpl, TaxImpl

You'll need to modify each of the `.h` and `.cpp` files for your object implementations in the same way:

Include IBM header files. In each of the .h files, include the Naming Service header file and the generated headers for `Central.idl` and `Store.idl`. In `StoreAccessImpl.h`, `StoreImpl.h`, `TaxImpl.h` add the lines:

```
#include <CosNaming.hh>
#include <Central.hh>
#include <Store.hh>
```

Implementations inherit from their <classname>_ Skeleton classes. Each implementation class (`StoreAccessImpl`, `StoreImpl`, `TaxImpl`) must inherit from the corresponding `<classname>_Skeleton` class (`StoreAccess_Skeleton`, `Store_Skeleton`, `Tax_Skeleton`) generated by the IBM IDL compiler. For example, in `StoreAccessImpl.h` modify the class as follows:

```
class StoreAccessImpl :
public virtual ::AStore::StoreAccess_Skeleton
```

Make the corresponding changes in each of the header files: `StoreAccessImpl.h`, `StoreImpl.h`, and `TaxImpl.h`.

30.5.2 Compiling and Linking

As with the `Depot`, you need to link the `Store` server with `Central_S.cpp`, `POSS_C.cpp`, `Store_SS.cpp`, and `CosNaming_C.cpp`. You also need to link with the IBM ORB's library (`emororm.lib`).

30.6 Orbix Implementation of the Store

The changes are essentially the same as those described for the `Depot` in Section 27.6. You should review the material in that section before continuing, and refer back to it if you need explanation of the changes.

The rest of this section is a detailed file-by-file description of what needs to change.

30.6.1 Detailed Changes to the C++ Code

30.6.1.1 StoreServer.cpp

At the start of the file, include the Orbix Naming Service header file.

```
#include <NamingService.hh>
```

Modify the initialization section at the beginning of `main()` as follows:

```
CORBA::ORB_ptr orb  = CORBA::ORB_init(argc, argv, "Orbix");
CORBA::BOA_ptr boa  = orb->BOA_init(argc, argv, "Orbix_BOA");
char* server_name = "StoreServer";
boa->setServerName(server_name);
boa->setNoHangup(1);
```

Finally, update the call to `impl_is_ready` to include the server name:

```
boa->impl_is_ready(server_name);
```

30.6.1.2 StoreAccessImpl, StoreImpl, TaxImpl

You'll need to modify each of the `.h` and `.cpp` files for your object implementations in the same way:

Include Orbix header files. In each of the .h files, include the Naming Service header file and the generated code for Central.idl, which includes Store.idl. In StoreAccessImpl.h, StoreImpl.h, TaxImpl.h add the lines:

```
#include <NamingService.hh>
#include <Central.hh>
```

Inherit from BOAImpl classes. Inherit each of your implementation classes (Store-AccessImpl, StoreImpl, TaxImpl) from the corresponding IDL-generated server classes (StoreAccessBOAImpl, StoreBOAImpl, TaxBOAImpl). For example, in StoreAccessImpl.h modify the class as follows:

```
class StoreAccessImpl : public  AStore::StoreAccessBOAImpl
```

Make the corresponding changes in each of the header files. StoreAccessImpl.h, StoreImpl.h, and TaxImpl.h.

Add CORBA::Environment parameters. Each IDL operation defined on your objects needs a final CORBA::Environment parameter. You can completely ignore this parameter when using C++ exceptions, but it needs to be present to match virtual function signatures. You'll need to modify both .h and .cpp files to change the signatures.

For example, in StoreAccessImpl .cpp and .h files add the parameter indicated in **bold** as follows:

```
void find_price(const char* item,
                CORBA::Long quantity,
                CORBA::Float& item_price,
                CORBA::Float& item_tax_price,
                AStore::ItemInfo*& item_info
                ,CORBA::Environment&
);
```

You'll need to do this for each implementation class. Here's the complete list of functions to change:

```
StoreAccessImpl: find_price
StoreImpl: store_id, totals, login, get_POS_totals, update_store_totals
TaxImpl: calculate_tax, find_taxable_price
```

30.6.2 Compiling and Linking

As with the Depot, you need to link the Store server with CentralS.cpp, POSS.cpp, StoreS.cpp, and NamingServiceC.cpp. You also need to link with Orbix libraries. See the demos with your copy of Orbix for an example of all the libraries required on your system.

30.6.3 Registering the Server

As with the Depot, you'll need to register the server with the orbixd daemon, either using the putit command or the GUI server manager tool. The Store server requires two command-line parameters: a store number (integer) and a markup (floating point number), which must be included in the registration. Using the putit command, you would register the server like this:

```
putit StoreServer <path_to_executable > <store_number> <markup>
```

Once registered, a server can be started manually (through the operating system's normal command-line interpreter), or it will be started automatically by the Orbix daemon when a client uses one of the objects in the server. The daemon knows the command-line arguments to pass when automatically launching the server because they are included in the registration information.

You need to run the server once manually so that it can register its objects with the Naming Service. You should use the same command-line arguments as you register with the daemon.

30.7 Implementing the Store Package Using VisiBroker for C++

The Inprise VisiBroker implementation of the Store component will only need a small number of changes. There will be a number of recurring changes that will be required to the common code for each component implemented using the VisiBroker libraries.

Refer to Section 27.7 for a full description on how to build a component. The following text will assume that you are familiar with the information contained in that section.

30.7.1 Changes to the Store Server Component

The Naming Service is used to register the Store; therefore, the Store server acts as a client to the Naming Service. The following preprocessor directive must be used to include the Naming Service definitions:

```
#include <CosNaming_c.hh>
```

Once again, in VisiBroker the osagent daemon can be used to facilitate locating an instance of the Naming Service. Make sure you have an osagent daemon running within your subnet (see the VisiBroker documentation for further information on the osagent). The following common code:

```
CORBA::Object_var obj = orb->resolve_initial_references("NameService");
CosNaming::NamingContext_var naming_service =
CosNaming::NamingContext::_narrow(obj);
```

can be replaced with:

```
CosNaming::NamingContext_var naming_service =
CosNaming::NamingContext::_bind();
```

30.7.2 Changes to the Other Store Components

As with the Depot component, the Store implementation code in VisiBroker does not require much change from the common code. The few required changes are with the skeleton class name that must be derived by the implementation and the header file that must be included for the Store definition.

The Store skeleton file must be included when writing the `StoreImpl` class. This can be done as follows in the `StoreImpl.h` file:

```
#include <Central_s.hh>
```

This file will include the definition of the Store skeleton that the `StoreImpl` class will inherit from. The class inheritance declaration should be as follows:

```
class StoreImpl : public _sk_AStore::_sk_Store
```

In VisiBroker, the `_sk_` prefix is used for skeleton code, which you should subclass in your implementation. Here, `_sk_AStore::_sk_Store` indicates that the Store skeleton is in the module `AStore`. If you look at the IDL, you will see that this is the case.

The preceding changes must also be done to the other components in the Store package: `StoreAccessImpl` and `TaxImpl`.

30.7.3 Compiling the Store Package

When setting up your build environment under a different compiler/platform, you should only have to change the makefiles to reflect the compiler, linker, libraries, and paths on your system.

To run the build of this program, do the following:

1. Compile the IDL for the Store.

2. Build the Store.

This will produce an executable (`.exe` files under Win95/98/NT). In the store directory, you will find a file named `Store_Server.exe`, which you can run to bring up the Store and make `Store` and `Tax` objects available to clients.

30.8 BEA Implementation of the Store

The BEA WLE implementation of the Store component has practically identical changes to the common code as explained in Section 27.7. Object References and implementations are in the new POA standard style; the main program code is split between the `Server` class and the `StoreImpl` class; there is a slightly different use of Naming

Services. Building the Store component is done at the same time as all other components by using the "WLEsetup" command described in Section 36.2.

30.8.1 The Store Server

As with the Depot, the initialization code of the main program is moved, some into class `Server::initialize` and some into `StoreImpl::activate_object`. The important code segments for the `Server` class follow:

```
1 CORBA::Object_var store_as_factory_ref;
2 CORBA::Object_var tax_as_factory_ref;
3 char regStoreStr[256];
4 char regTaxStr[256];
5 extern Tobj::FactoryFinder_ptr factory_finder = 0;

6 CORBA::Boolean Server::initialize(int argc, char* argv[]) {
7     CORBA::ORB_ptr orb = CORBA::ORB_init(argc, argv, "");
8     Tobj_Bootstrap bootstrap(orb,"");
9     CORBA::Object_var fact_finder_oref =
            bootstrap.resolve_initial_references("FactoryFinder");
10    factory_finder =
      Tobj::FactoryFinder::_narrow(fact_finder_oref);

11    long storeId   = atol(argv[2]);
12    double markUp  = atof(argv[1]);
13    sprintf(regStoreStr,"Store_%ld", storeId);
14    sprintf(regTaxStr,  "Tax_%ld",  storeId);

15    char storeObjectId[20];
16    sprintf(storeObjectId, "%5i%10f", storeId, markUp);

17    store_as_factory_ref = TP::create_object_reference(
               AStore::_tc_Store->id(),      // Interf Repos Id
               storeObjectId,                // Object Id
               CORBA::NVList::_nil()         // No special needs
               );
18    tax_as_factory_ref = TP::create_object_reference(
               AStore::_tc_Tax->id(),        // Interf Repos Id
               regTaxStr,                    // Object Id
               CORBA::NVList::_nil()         // No special needs
               );
      }

19    TP::register_factory(store_as_factory_ref, regStoreStr);
20    TP::register_factory(tax_as_factory_ref, regTaxStr);

21    return CORBA_TRUE;
   }
```

For `Server::initialize`, lines 3–4 and 11–14 are the same as in the common code. Some of the variables are declared in static storage so that when server shutdown invokes the `release` function, it can unregister the references. Lines 7–10 get a static Factory Finder reference that is used later by the `nsPublisher::resolve` static function (explained in Section 27.7.3).

Lines 15–16 save the command-line parameters for use as the Object Id for the `Store` object in the Object Reference creation of line 17. This Object Id will be used when the `Store` object is first activated. (This is the same technique as for the `Depot` reference.) Line 18 creates the Object Reference for the `Tax` object. Lines 19–20 register the `Store` and `Tax` objects, the same as in the common code but with the BEA WLE Factory Finder instead of the less scalable Naming Service.

The Naming Service code exactly parallels the code shown for the `Depot`; it merely unregisters the references, two of them this time. The `Server::create_servant` code is similarly parallel, the only difference being that since this server has implementations for three objects, the `create_servant` class uses the repository id (passed as a parameter from the framework) to determine which servant to return.

```
1 Tobj_Servant Server::create_servant(const char* intf_repos_id) {
2     if (!strcmp(intf_repos_id, AStore::_tc_Store->id()))
3         return new StoreImpl();
4     if (!strcmp(intf_repos_id, AStore::_tc_StoreAccess->id()))
5         return new StoreAccessImpl();
6     if (!strcmp(intf_repos_id, AStore::_tc_Tax->id()))
7         return new TaxImpl();
8     return 0; // unknown interface
  }
```

30.8.2 StoreImpl

For the POA, the skeleton class name is standardized as explained in Section 27.3.3. The formation is the same for all three of the `Store`-related classes. For the `Store` implementation, for example, we use:

```
class StoreImpl : public POA_AStore::Store {...
```

The constructor for `StoreImpl` in the BEA WLE example code does nothing more than create the instance with room for up to 10 POSTerminals. Recall that this constructor is called from the TP framework:

```
StoreImpl::StoreImpl() : m_POSTerminals(10) {}
```

As with the `Depot`, all initialization that is in the common code's constructor is delayed until the first invocation on the object, where it is executed in response to the framework telling the servant to initialize its object state:

```
1 void StoreImpl::activate_object( const char* object_id ) {
2     sscanf( object_id, "%5i%10f", &m_storeID, &m_storeMarkup );
3     m_storeTotal    = 0;
4     m_storeTaxTotal = 0;
5     CORBA::ULong len = m_POSTerminals.length();
6     for (CORBA::ULong i = 0; i < len; i++) {
7         m_POSTerminals[i].id = EMPTY; }
```

```
8 }
```

The Object Id that was put into the Object Reference for the Store at initialization time is passed into the `activate_object` method by the framework. The method reads the store number and the markup directly into the servant's private storage in line 2, as in the common code but using a different source for the information. Lines 3–7 are the same as the common code.

The only other difference from the common code for `StoreImpl` is in the `login` method, which returns a reference to a `StoreAccess` object. This difference arises from using the POA, just as when we created references for the `Depot`, the `Store`, and the `Tax` objects. In addition, we use the same technique the POA makes possible in creating just the reference for `StoreAccess`. The `StoreAccess` object won't be initialized until its first invocation, so we carry the store number and markup in the `ObjectId` of the Object Reference. The code is parallel to that creating the `Store` reference, so we present it without further comment:

```
// create and save a reference to the StoreAccess Object
char storeAccessObjectId[20];
sprintf(storeAccessObjectId, "%5i%10f", m_storeID, m_storeMarkup);
CORBA::Object_var objref = TP::create_object_reference(
    AStore::_tc_StoreAccess->id(),    // Interf Repos Id
    storeAccessObjectId,              // Object Id
    CORBA::NVList::_nil() );          // No special needs
m_POSTerminals[loc].store_access_reference =
    AStore::StoreAccess::_narrow( objref );
```

30.8.3 StoreAccessImpl

As with `StoreImpl`, the common code in `StoreAccessImpl`'s constructor is moved to `StoreAccessImpl::activate_object`. Once there, the only difference is in getting the Store's Object Reference. Since the `StoreImpl` C++ pointer is not an Object Reference in the POA, we obtain the Store's object reference by lookup in the `NsPublisher` as for the Depot and the Tax object. The invocation parameters for `NsPublisher::resolve` is different than the common code, as explained in Section 27.7.3.

30.8.4 TaxImpl

BEA WLE `TaxImpl` has no differences from the common code (other than skeleton base class name and include file name, as for all ORBs). However, `TaxImpl` has one interesting characteristic that is different from other objects in the example: It is stateless. That is, it keeps no in-memory or on-disk information between method invocations. It operates only on the basis of information passed to it in parameters.

This fact allows BEA WLE to use the memory model that often helps in scalability. Recall that the BEA WLE initialization of `Store_Server` created a `Tax` Object Reference only; it did not create a servant (an instantiation of the implementation class `TaxImpl`). As a result, no resources (memory) in the server are used for `Tax` until an invocation on the `Tax` object is made. When the BEA WLE framework receives an invocation, it asks the `Server::create_servant` method (described earlier) to create a servant for the purposes of servicing the invocation. So far, this is the same as for the other objects. In the case of Tax, however, we use the Implementation Configuration File (a forerunner of the CORBA components packaging file) to describe the Tax object as using the "method" memory model. This means that when the method is finished, the framework gets rid of the Tax servant and its memory.

In the case of Tax, there is no saving in doing this (since its resources during execution are minuscule), but we show it to illustrate the point. For many applications, the savings are significant; for example, if the method reads a large record from a database, performs lengthy work on it, perhaps doing other disk accesses and method invocations, and finally writing the record back to disk. This is the so-called "stateless" behavior: State is on the disk until needed, not in memory. It is the single most effective way that application code can directly affect scalability (other ways are provided by the infrastructure).

Specification of memory models is done in the Store.icf file. The memory models for Store and StoreAccess are both "process," the same as for Depot, but for Tax it is "method":

```
implementation TaxImpl {
    activation_policy ( method );
    transaction_policy ( never );
    implements ( AStore::Tax );
    };
```

Coding the Store in Java

In this chapter, we present the Java language code for the Store module. We first present the Java language mappings for the types defined in the Store Module. We then present the implementation of the common functionality. Finally, we split into ORB-specific sections as before.

Before you read this, you should review Section 29.1. We've put enough detail into this chapter for Java programmers to understand what's going on without having to read the language-specific section for other programming languages. Wherever applicable, we also contrast the difference between C++ and Java, to help those who are already familiar with C++ but new to Java.

31.1 Java Mapping of Data Types for Store

The Java mappings for the Store module are in separate files in the directory AStore, with a name like AStore/Store.java, the exact names for your product were listed in its section of Chapter 28, produced by your IDL compiler so you won't have to type them in yourself. However, you will need to be aware of their form (some of which are dictated by the standard OMG IDL/Java language mappings) and how they are used.

The Store is composed of several data types and three classes that implement the IDL interfaces **Tax**, **Store**, and **StoreAccess**. They are discussed in Chapter 24 in the analysis and design, and declared in the IDL file `Store.idl`.

The mappings for the data types are described in this section, while the implementation classes are described in the next section.

Several key items to note about the Java mapping for these data types are:

- IDL built-in types such as **float** translate to Java primitive types, such as `float`.

- CORBA modules are mapped to Java packages.

- **Sequence**s are mapped into `arrays` in Java.

- **Enum**s and **Struct**s are mapped into Java `classes`, with a corresponding `Helper` and `Holder`.

- **Typedef**s are not mapped into Java. Java users need to chase down and use the base types of **typedef**s.

- Unlike C++, the Java runtime provides automatic garbage collection. There is no need to call `_duplicate()` or `_release()` on object references.

31.1.1 Java Mappings for ItemTypes

The first type in the Astore module is the **enum ItemTypes**:

```
module AStore
{
    enum ItemTypes {FOOD, CLOTHES, OTHER};
```

whose Java mapping looks like this:

```
package AStore;
public final class ItemTypes {
    public static final int _FOOD = 0;
    public static final ItemTypes FOOD =
            new ItemTypes(_FOOD);
    public static final int _CLOTHES = 1;
    public static final ItemTypes CLOTHES =
            new ItemTypes(_CLOTHES);
    public static final int _OTHER = 2;
    public static final ItemTypes OTHER =
            new ItemTypes(_OTHER);
    public int value() {
        . . .
    }

    public static ItemTypes from_int (int value) {
        . . .
    }
}
```

Unlike C++, Java does not directly support the **enum** type as a language construct. An IDL **enum** type is mapped into a Java class. So the IDL **AStore::ItemTypes** is mapped into the Java class AStore.ItemTypes.

Each member of the **enum** is represented by a static final class variable, i.e., a constant, of the same name. For ItemTypes, these are FOOD, CLOTHES, and OTHER. They may be used wherever an **enum** member is needed. For example:

```
// Initialize myItemTypes to FOOD.
AStore.ItemTypes  myItemTypes = AStore.ItemTypes.FOOD;
```

Each member of the **enum** is also assigned a distinct integer value, and given the same name prefixed by "_". For ItemTypes, these are _FOOD, _CLOTHES, and _OTHER. Given an instance of AStore.ItemTypes, its integer value may be obtained by calling the value() method. This integer value is useful within a switch statement. For example:

```
AStore.ItemTypes myItemTypes = ...; // somehow, get an ItemTypes
switch(myItemTypes.value()){
    case AStore.ItemTypes._FOOD:
             . . .
    case AStore.ItemTypes._CLOTHES:
          . . .
    case AStore.ItemTypes._OTHER:
          . . .
}
```

Note the lack of public constructors. This is deliberately designed so that the user has no way of creating an instance of ItemTypes that does not correspond to one of the **enum** members. There are only three ways that the user can get a hold of an instance of ItemTypes. The first, as shown, is to use the static final variables FOOD, CLOTHES, or OTHER that correspond to the **enum** members. The second is through the from_int(int) method supported by ItemTypes. The input to from_int() has to be one of _FOOD, _CLOTHES, or _OTHER, or an exception will be thrown. Finally, the third is by passing around an instance obtained via the first two ways.

In order to pass ItemTypes as an inout or out parameter, an AStore.ItemTypesHolder class is also emitted by the IDL-to-Java compiler. Like all Holder classes, the value instance variable holds the inout or out parameter:

```
public class ItemTypesHolder
package AStore;
        implements org.omg.CORBA.portable.Streamable {
    public ItemTypes value;
    public ItemTypesHolder () {}
    public ItemTypesHolder (ItemTypes initial) {
        value = initial;
    }
    . . .
}
```

Finally, an AStore.ItemTypesHelper class is also emitted as part of the IDL-to-Java mapping. This class is not very useful to us as users, but it is needed to support the marshaling and demarshaling of ItemTypes as it is passed between client and server.

31.1.2 Java Mappings for AStoreId

The IDL for AStoreID is:

typedef long AStoreId;

Since Java does not support **typedef**, **AStoreId** is mapped to its base type, an integer. Therefore, wherever an **AStoreId** is needed in Java, an "int" is used, except for passing it as an out or inout parameter, in which case an org.omg.CORBA.IntHolder is passed.

31.1.3 Java Mappings for ItemInfo

The IDL for ItemInfo is:

```
struct ItemInfo
    {
    POS::Barcode    item;
    ItemTypes       item_type;
    float           item_cost;
    string          name;
    long            quantity;
    };
```

A **struct** in IDL is mapped into a Java class containing public fields whose names correspond to the IDL struct member names. For ItemInfo, it looks like:

```
package AStore;
public final class ItemInfo {
      public java.lang.String item;
      public AStore.ItemTypes item_type;
      public float item_cost;
      public java.lang.String name;
      public int quantity;

      public ItemInfo () {}

      public ItemInfo (java.lang.String _Item, AStore.ItemTypes
              _item_type, float _item_cost,
           java.lang.String _name, int _quantity) {
          item = _item;
          item_type = _item_type;
          item_cost = _item_cost;
          name = _name;
          quantity = _quantity;
      }
}
```

Note that the type for the member **item** is `java.lang.String`, the base type for `POS::BarCode`. Also note the constructor that takes all the members' types as arguments. It can be used to construct an instance of `ItemInfo`. For example:

```
AStore.ItemInfo myItemInfo = new AStore.ItemInfo("0-471-12148-7",
AStore.ItemTypes._OTHER, (float)49.95,
"CORBA Fundamentals and Programming", 50000);
```

There is also a no-argument constructor that can be used to create a new instance of the structure without initializing its fields. However, the user needs to initialize these fields before making use of the instance. The user also needs to be aware that strings can not be initialized to `null`, because this is prohibited by the IDL-to-Java mappings. Here is an example using the no-argument constructor:

```
AStore.ItemInfo myItemInfo = new AStore.ItemInfo();
myItemInfo.item = "0-471-12148-7";
myItemInfo.item_type = AStore.ItemTypes._OTHER;
myItemInfo.item_cost = (float)49.95;
myItemInfo.name = "CORBA Fundamentals and Programming";
myItemInfo.quantity = 50000;
```

The `ItemInfoHolder` and `ItemInfoHelper` classes are also emitted by the IDL to Java compiler. Their functions are similar to those for **enum**s, so we will not discuss them further.

31.1.4 Java Mappings for BarcodeNotFound

The IDL-to-Java mapping for user exceptions is very similar to that of structs, except that the exception class inherits from `org.omg.CORBA.UserException`. The IDL for the exception **BarcodeNotFound** is:

exception BarcodeNotFound { POS::Barcode item; };

The mapping for `BarcodeNotFound` exception looks like:

```
package AStore;
public final class BarcodeNotFound extends
            org.omg.CORBA.UserException  {
    public java.lang.String item;
    public BarcodeNotFound () {}
    public BarcodeNotFound (java.lang.String _item) {
        item = _item;
    }
}
```

Like `structs`, the members of the exception are mapped into public fields of the exception class. There is also a constructor that takes all member types as parameters, and a no-argument constructor. The corresponding `Holder` and `Helper` classes are also generated.

31.1.5 Java Mappings for POSInfo

The mapping for **POSInfo**

```
struct POSInfo
  {
    POS::POSId  id;
    StoreAccess  store_access_reference;
    float        total_sales;
    float        total_taxes;
  };
```

is typical to that of the mapping of a **struct**, as shown next. Note that the Java type of **id** is an int, the underlying type of POS::POSId.

```
package AStore;
public final class POSInfo {
      public int id;
      public AStore.StoreAccess store_access_reference;
      public float total_sales;
      public float total_taxes;

      public POSInfo () {}

      public POSInfo (int _id, AStore.StoreAccess
         _store_access_reference, float _total_sales,
          float _total_taxes) {
         id = _id;
         store_access_reference = _store_access_reference;
         total_sales = _total_sales;
         total_taxes = _total_taxes;
      }
  }
```

The Helper and the Holder are also generated.

31.1.6 Java Mappings for POSList

The IDL for POSList is:

typedef sequence <POSInfo> POSList;

The IDL-to-Java mapping for a **sequence** is an array of the underlying type of the sequence. Therefore, wherever **POSList** is needed in Java, an array of POSInfo is used. For example:

```
// Create a new POSLISt sequence with length 2.
AStore.POSInfo [] mySeq = new AStore.POSInfo[2];
mySeq[0] = new AStore.POSInfo(...);
mySeq[1] = new AStore.POSInfo(...);
```

In addition, the Holder and Helper for the sequence are also generated.

31.1.7 Java Mappings for StoreTotals

Our final type in the Astore module is **AStore::Store::StoreTotals**:

```
interface Store
{
    struct StoreTotals
    {
      float    store_total;
      float    store_tax_total;
    };
```

whose mapping looks like this:

```
package AStore.StorePackage;
public final class StoreTotals {
     public float store_total;
     public float store_tax_total;
     public StoreTotals () {}
     public StoreTotals (float _store_total, float
        _store_tax_total) {
        store_total = _store_total;
        store_tax_total = _store_tax_total;
     }
}
```

Types defined in an interface are mapped into Java as belonging to the package "<interface>Package" or interface "Package". Therefore, the Java package for Store-Totals is "AStore.StorePackage" instead of "AStore.Store". The latter introduces a conflict in Java because the package name "AStore.Store" coincides with the interface of the same name.

31.2 Functionality Common to All Java ORBs

Now we need to code the functionality of the Store classes. These are the implementations of the Tax, Store, and StoreAccess interfaces. There's almost nothing ORB-specific about these, so we'll present all in this section. If you're working the example by hand, you'll need to type all of this code into your program files as we go along. At the end of this section, we'll send you off to the section on your specific ORB for final coding, and compilation.

There are two versions of implementations for Store, one for ORBs that support the Portable Object Adapter (POA) and one for ORBs that do not. For ORBs that support the POA, the implementation classes are TaxPoaImpl, StorePoaImpl, and StoreAccessPoaImpl. They all belong to the module Astore, and are stored in the directory of the same name. The suffix "PoaImpl" is used to distinguished the implementation class from the corresponding interface class, as generated by the IDL compiler. Each implementation is derived from its corresponding POA skeleton class, whose name is POA_module.Interface. For example, the POA skeleton for AStore.Store is POA_AStore.Store. The POA skeletons are stored in the directory POA_AStore.

For ORBs that do not yet support the POA, the implementation classes are `Tax-Impl`, `StoreImpl`, and `StoreAccessImpl`. The suffix "`Impl`" is used to distinguish the implementation class from the corresponding interface class, as generated by the IDL compiler. Each non-POA implementation class is derived from a base "`ImplBase`" class generated by the IDL compiler.

The POA implementations and the non-POA implementations are almost identical, except that:

- POA implementations are derived from their POA skeletons, while non-POA implementations are derived from their `ImplBase` classes, as described earlier.

- POA implementations pass `_this()` instead of `this` when passing themselves around either as parameters or as return values.

- POA implementations are activated in the ORB differently from non-POA implementations.

We will only describe the POA versions of the implementations, reiterating the differences where applicable. The only exception is the server `main()` program. The POA version is called `StorePoaServer`, and the non-POA version is called `StoreServer`. Because of the differences in how the server communicates with the ORB to activate the implementations, both versions will be presented.

31.2.1 Introduction

The source code for the Store that will be presented has been partitioned into the following files:

FILE NAME	CONTENTS
`StorePoaImpl.java`	The implementation of `AStore::Store`
`StoreAccessPoaImpl.java`	The implementation of `AStore:StoreAccess`
`TaxPoaImpl.java`	The implementation of `AStore::Tax`
`StorePoaServer.java`	The main program, POA version
`StoreServer.java`	The main program, non-POA version

In our implementation, each Store executes a single instance of the `StorePoaImpl` and `TaxPoaImpl` classes. The `StorePoaImpl` object constructs a separate instance of `StoreAccessPoaImpl` for each point-of-sale (POS) terminal. For simplicity, all `StorePoaImpl`, `TaxPoaImpl`, and `StoreAccessPoaImpl` instances execute within a single process.

The following sections describe the logic of the three classes and the `main()` program.

31.2.2 TaxPoaImpl Class

TaxPoaImpl.java is the implementation of the IDL interface Tax defined in Store.idl. It is derived from the TaxPOA skeleton base class generated by the IDL compiler, and contains members and member functions called out in the analysis and design, Chapter 24. To support the A&D requirements, we have added a private data member and a constructor. We have also added an abort helper function that we use to print out an error message and exit the server process when an unrecoverable error is encountered.

We started with the following observations:

- Tax needs a data member that corresponds to the state variable Rate in the A&D. Therefore, we declared m_regionRate, which will be a "private" data member of TaxPoaImpl. For simplicity, we will initialize it inside the constructor.

- The state variable taxTotal called out in the A&D is actually calculated by calculate_tax each time it is invoked. Because there is no need to keep this value across calls, it was implemented as an automatic variable of calculate_tax.

- We know from the A&D that the StoreAccess object will use the Tax object to calculate item prices. The requirement for this is derived from the statement in the A&D for the StoreAccess object: Call find_taxable_price operation on taxReference object with input arguments item_price and item_tax_type, receiving back output argument item_tax_price. To support this requirement, the server will create an instance of TaxPoaImpl, and register the instance with the Naming Service so clients (such as StoreAccess) can connect to it. We don't have to be concerned about it in the implementation of TaxPoaImpl.

Here is the complete implementation for TaxPoaImpl:

```
01 package AStore;
02
03 class TaxPoaImpl extends TaxPOA {
04
05     private static final float region_rate = (float)0.05;
06
07     private float m_regionRate;
08
09     private void abort( String msg ) {
10         System.out.println(msg);
11         System.exit(1);
12     }  // abort
13
```

31.2.2.1 Constructor

```
14     TaxPoaImpl(){
15
```

```
16          // set tax rate applied to taxable goods
17          m_regionRate = region_rate;
18
19   }  // Constructor
20
```

The TaxPoaImpl constructor accepts no arguments. It merely sets the internal private variable m_regionRate to the constant region_rate, currently set at 5 percent.

31.2.2.2 calculate_tax

```
21      public float calculate_tax(float taxable_amount){
22
23          return taxable_amount*m_regionRate;
24      }  // calculate_tax
25
```

The member function calculate_tax computes the tax from m_regionRate and the input argument taxable_amount. It then returns the tax amount.

31.2.2.3 find_taxable_price

```
26      public float find_taxable_price(float item_price, ItemTypes
        item_type){
27
28          float taxprice;
29
30          if ( item_type == ItemTypes.OTHER)
31              taxprice = item_price;
32          else taxprice = (float)0.0;
33
34          return taxprice;
35      }  // find_taxable_price
36
37  }  // TaxPoaImpl
```

find_taxable_price encapsulates the algorithm for computing the taxable price of an item. In our implementation, the full price of items of type OTHER is taxed; the other item types (FOOD and CLOTHES) are not taxed. Therefore, find_taxable_price returns either the value of the input argument price for item type "OTHER" or 0.0 for all other item types.

31.2.3 StorePoaImpl Class

The StorePoaImpl class is more sophisticated than the taxPoaImpl class in that it services all POSTerminals in the Store and keeps track of sales information for the Store. POS objects "log in" to the Store to activate a session with a StoreAccess instance. `StorePoaImpl` also contains methods for obtaining sales information. Here is the implementation of this class:

```
001 package AStore;
002
003 class StorePoaImpl extends StorePOA {
004
005     private float      m_storeTotal;
006     private float      m_storeTaxTotal;
007     private float      m_storeMarkup;
008     private int        m_storeID;
009     private org.omg.CORBA.Object m_ns;
```

To implement `StorePoaImpl`, we first add private data members as specified in the A&D. These members are `m_storeTotal`, `m_storeTaxTotal`, `m_store-Markup`, `m_storeID`, and `m_ns`, the Name Server.

```
010     private POSInfo []    m_POSTerminals;
```

The private data member `m_POSTerminals` stores one `POSInfo` for each terminal that has logged in.

```
011     private Store m_storeRef = null;
```

The private data member `m_storeRef` stores a pointer to the Object Reference for the `StorePoaImpl`. It is specific to the POA implementation. In the nonPOA version, the Java keyword `this` is used instead of `m_storeRef`.

```
012
013     private static final int EMPTY= -1;
```

The private constant `EMPTY` is used to indicate the slots in `m_POSTerminals` that are not yet in use.

```
014
015     private void abort( String msg ) {
016         System.out.println(msg);
017         System.exit(1);
018     } // abort
```

The `abort` method is used whenever an unrecoverable error is encountered. It simply prints an error message and terminates the server process.

31.2.3.1 LocatePOSEntry

```
019
020     private int LocatePOSEntry(int Id){
021         int loc = EMPTY;
022         int availloc = EMPTY;
023         int len = m_POSTerminals.length;
024
025         // locate POSId or first available slot
```

```
026      int i = 0;
027      while ( loc == EMPTY && i < len){
028        if ( m_POSTerminals[i].id == Id)
029          loc = i;
030        else if ( availloc == EMPTY && m_POSTerminals[i].id == EMPTY)
031          availloc = i;
032        else i++;
033      }
034
035      // If we did not find POSId, then use the available slot or
036      //append new slot at end of m_POSTerminals
037      if ( loc == EMPTY){
038        if ( availloc != EMPTY)
039          loc = availloc;
040        else {
041          // expand m_POSTerminals array by one
042          POSInfo [] temp = new POSInfo[len+1];
043          for (int j=0; j < len ; j++)
044            temp[j] = m_POSTerminals[j];
045
046          temp[len ] = new POSInfo(EMPTY, null, (float)0.0,float)0.0);
047          m_POSTerminals = temp;
048          loc = len;
049        }
050      }
051      return loc;
052   } // LocatePOSEntry
053
```

This private method encapsulates the details of searching the `m_POSTerminals` sequence for an available entry. It detects when an entry for the specified POS ID exists and reuses that slot, preventing the creation of a new `StoreAccess` reference when one already exists.

When a new entry needs to be created, the length of the sequence may have to be incremented, if it is already full. The only way to accomplish this in Java is to create a new and larger array, and copy the contents of the old into the new. We adopt the simple solution of allocating a new array whose size is just one element larger than the existing one.

31.2.3.2 Constructor

```
054   StorePoaImpl(org.omg.CORBA.Object ns, int storeID, float
      storeMarkup){
055
056     System.out.println("StorePoaImpl.CTOR() : ");
057
058
059     System.out.print("StorePoaImpl.CTOR()  : initialising
        object......");
```

```
060
061      m_storeTotal = (float)0.0;
062      m_storeTaxTotal = (float)0.0;
063      m_ns = ns;
064      m_storeMarkup = storeMarkup;
065      m_storeID = storeID;
066      m_storeRef = this._this();
067
068      // start with spaces for 10 POSs
069      m_POSTerminals = new  POSInfo[10];
070      for (int i=0; i < m_POSTerminals.length; i++){
071        m_POSTerminals[i] = new POSInfo(EMPTY, null,
           (float)0.0,(float)0.0);
072      }
073
074
075  } // Constructor
```

StorePoaImpl's constructor implements the processing defined as the operation Initialize in the Store Analysis and Design. The constructor sets the instance members m_storeTotal and m_storeTaxTotal to 0. It also sets m_ns, m_storeID, and m_storeMarkup to the values of the in parameters.

The last activity of the constructor is to initialize the sequence m_POSTerminals. Recall that m_POSTerminals was defined in the IDL to be an unbounded (dynamic) sequence of POSInfo structs.

typedef sequence <POSInfo> POSList;

POSList is mapped to a Java array of PosInfo. To create an initial sequence of 10 empty POSInfos, the constructor first creates an array of 10 POSInfo, and assigns them to m_POSTerminals. It then creates 10 empty POSInfos, and places them into the array. The constant EMPTY is passed to the constructor of each POSInfo being created, to indicate an empty slot.

31.2.3.3 store_id

```
076
077   public int store_id(){
078      return m_storeID;
079   }  // StoreId
080
```

This is the accessor for the attribute store_id.

31.2.3.4 totals

```
081   public AStore.StorePackage.StoreTotals totals() {
082
```

```
083      return new AStore.StorePackage.StoreTotals(m_storeTotal,
         m_storeTaxTotal);
084   }  // totals
085
086
```

This is the accessor for the attribute totals.

31.2.3.5 Login

```
087   public StoreAccess login(int id) {
088
089      int loc = LocatePOSEntry(id);
090
091      m_POSTerminals[loc].id = id;
092      m_POSTerminals[loc].total_sales = (float)0.0;
093      m_POSTerminals[loc].total_taxes = (float)0.0;
094
095      // check to see if a StoreAccess object exists for this
096      // m_PosTerminal allocate new one if needed
097      if ( m_POSTerminals[loc].store_access_reference == null
098   ){
099
100         // create servant instance of the StoreAccess object
101         StoreAccessPoaImpl storeAccess = new StoreAccessPoaImpl(m_ns,
            m_storeRef, m_storeMarkup);
102         // Extract CORBA object reference from servant
103         m_POSTerminals[loc].store_access_reference =
            storeAccess._this();
104
105      }
106
107      if (m_POSTerminals[loc].store_access_reference == null
108   ){
109         System.err.println(
            "Store::Login: Unable to create StoreAccess object for POS Login");
110      }
111
112      return m_POSTerminals[loc].store_access_reference;
113   }  // login
```

Login assigns a StorePoaAccessImpl object to the POS and resets the POS totals
to 0. Login first calls the private member function LocatePOSEntry to obtain a slot
in the m_POSTerminals sequence. It then initializes the id, total_sales, and
total_taxes fields to 0.

Login next checks to see if a StoreAccess object exists, and, if needed, constructs
a new instance. It then returns a reference to the StoreAccess object.

31.2.3.6 get_POS_totals

```
114
115    public void get_POS_totals(POSListHolder POSData){
116        // Return a copy of m_POSTerminals
117        POSData.value = new POSInfo[m_POSTerminals.length];
118        for (int i=0; i < m_POSTerminals.length; i++){
119            POSInfo info = m_POSTerminals[i];
120            POSData.value[i] = new POSInfo(info.id,
               info.store_access_reference,
121                            info.total_sales, info.total_taxes);
122        }
123    }  // GetPOSTotals
124
```

This method returns the m_POSTerminals sequence to the caller. Note that the argument is an out parameter. In Java, we return out parameters by assigning the parameter to the value field of the Holder instance. In order to maintain local/remote transparency, we return a new copy of m_POSTerminals.

31.2.3.7 update_store_totals

```
125    public void update_store_totals(int Id, float Price, float Taxes){
126
127        int i = LocatePOSEntry(Id);
128
129        if ( i != EMPTY){
130          m_POSTerminals[i].total_sales  += Price;
131          m_POSTerminals[i].total_taxes  += Taxes;
132          m_storeTotal                   += Price;
133          m_storeTaxTotal                += Taxes;
134
135        } else
136          System.err.println(
           "Store::UpdateStoreTotals: Could not locate POS Terminal " + Id);
137
138    }  // UpdateStoreTotals
139
140
141 } // StorePoaImpl
```

This method is called to update the running totals for the POS terminal specified by the input parameter id. It calls LocatePOSEntry to locate the entry in m_POSTerminals, then updates both the POS totals and the store totals. If the terminal cannot be found, it prints an error message.

31.2.4 StoreAccessPoaImpl Class

StoreAccess provides a mechanism for managing POS sessions. It is the intermediary between the POS and the central depot concerning access to the grocery item database. Here is its implementation:

```
01 package AStore;
02
03 class StoreAccessPoaImpl extends.StoreAccess POA {
04
05    private CentralOffice.Depot m_depot;
06    private Store              m_store;
07    private Tax                m_tax;
08    private float              m_storeMarkup;
09
10    private void abort( String msg ) {
11    System.err.println(msg);
12    System.exit(1);
13    } //abort
14
```

31.2.4.1 Constructor

```
15    StoreAccessPoaImpl(org.omg.CORBA.Object ns, Store store, float
      markup){
16
17       System.out.println("StoreAccessPoaImpl.CTOR() :");
18
19       m_storeMarkup = markup;
20
21       int id = store.store_id();
22
23       String refstr = "Tax_" + id;
24
25       System.out.print("StoreAccessPoaImpl.CTOR() : " +
26                        "resolving reference to Tax.....");
27       try {
28          org.omg.CORBA.Object obj = PrimerUtils.NsPublisher.nsResolve
             (ns, refstr, "Primer_Example");
29          m_tax = TaxHelper.narrow(obj);
30       } catch( Exception exc ) {
31           abort("ERROR: Cannot resolve " + refstr +
             " in Name Service");
32       }
33
34       System.out.print("StoreAccessPoaImpl.CTOR() : " +
35                        "resolving reference to depot.....");
36
37       try {
38           org.omg.CORBA.Object obj = PrimerUtils.NsPublisher.nsResolve
```

```
                          (ns, "Depot", "Primer_Example");
39          ·        m_depot = CentralOffice.DepotHelper.narrow(obj);
40          } catch( Exception exc ) {
41              abort("ERROR: Cannot resolve Depot in Naming Service");
42          }
43
44          m_store = store;
45
46      }  // Constructor
```

The StoreAccessPoaImpl constructor first sets m_markup, the markup for the store, from its input parameter. It then uses the store input parameter to find its ID, by calling store.id(). This allows it to find, via the Name Server, the Tax object for the store, which it stores in m_tax. Since there is only one depot, it uses the Name Server again to find the distinguished depot instance, and stores it in m_depot. Finally, it initializes m_store with the store object.

31.2.4.2 find_price

```
47
48      public void find_price(java.lang.String item, int quantity,
49                              org.omg.CORBA.FloatHolder item_price,
50                              org.omg.CORBA.FloatHolder item_tax_price,
51                              ItemInfoHolder item_info) throws
                                BarcodeNotFound {
52
53          System.out.print("StoreAccessPoaImpl.find_price() : " +
54                              "calling Depot::find_item_info.....");
55
56          m_depot.find_item_info(m_store.store_id(), item, quantity,
            item_info);
57
58          item_price.value = m_storeMarkup * item_info.value.item_cost;
59          item_tax_price.value = m_tax.find_taxable_price(item_price.value,
60          item_info.value.item_type);
61
62      }  // FindPrice
63  }  // StoreAccessPoaImpl
```

This method computes the price and taxable price for the given quantity of the item specified by the barcode. It first uses the find_item_info() method of the depot to find information about the item. This information is also returned as an ItemInfo struct, via the item_info out parameter. The price, item_price, is computed as the cost times markup percent as required in the A&D:

Calculate ItemPrice as item's cost times storeMarkup.

As an out parameter, item_price is of type org.omg.CORBA.FloatHolder, holding a float value.

The taxable price is returned via the item_taxable_price out parameter, whose value is determined by calling the find_taxable_price() method on the Tax object.

The A&D and IDL specify that `find_price` should raise a `BarcodeNotFound` exception if the input barcode is not known to the `Depot`. Because the `find_item_info()` method of the `Depot` implementation itself raises this exception, we simply let the exception propagate to the caller.

31.2.5 StorePoaServer

`StorePoaServer` is the POA implementation of the server main program. Here is its complete implementation:

```
001 package AStore;
002
003 public class StorePoaServer {
004
005   private static void abort( String msg ) {
006   System.err.println(msg);
007   System.exit(1);
008   }  // abort
```

The method `abort()` is used to print an error message and exit the server process.

```
009
010   public static void main (String[] args) {
011
012     if ( args.length < 2){
013       abort("usage: StorePoaServer <Markup> <Store Number> <vendor
             specific options>");
014     }
015
016     int storeId = 0;
017     try {
018       storeId = Integer.parseInt(args[1]);
019     } catch(NumberFormatException e){
020       abort("Unrecognizable Store Number: " + args[1]);
021     }
022
023     float markup = 0;
024     try {
025       markup = Float.valueOf(args[0]).floatValue();
026     } catch(NumberFormatException e){
027       abort("Unrecognizable markup: " + args[0]);
028     }
029
```

The `StoreServer` program expects the user to supply a markup percent and a store number as command-line parameters. The main program first validates that the correct number of arguments were supplied, and then extracts the arguments into local variables `storeId` and `markup`, with appropriate error checking.

```
030
031     try {
```

```
032
033         System.out.println("StorePoaServer.main() : starting");
034
035         System.out.print(
             "StorePoaServer.main() : initialising ORB...");
036
037         // Some ORB vendors prefer to initialize the ORB using
038         // different ORB initialization interfaces.  See the
039         // vendor specific portions of the text for more info.
040         org.omg.CORBA.ORB orb = org.omg.CORBA.ORB.init(args,null);
041
042         // Standard CORBA method for creating root POA and POA manager
043         org.omg.CORBA.Object pobj = orb.resolve_initial_references(
             "RootPOA" );
044
045         org.omg.PortableServer.POA  poa = org.omg.PortableServer.POA
             Helper.narrow( pobj );
046
047         org.omg.PortableServer.POAManager poa_mgr =
             poa.the_POAManager();
048
049         System.out.print(
             "StorePoaServer.main() : getting NS reference...");
050
```

It then initializes the ORB and the POA by calling the methods
`org.omg.CORBA.ORB_init` and calling the ORB's `resolve_initial_refer-`
`ences("RootPOA")` method. It finds the POA manager by calling the `the_POAMan-`
`ager()` method of the POA.

```
051         org.omg.CORBA.Object obj = null;
052         try {
053         obj = orb.resolve_initial_references("NameService");
054         } catch( org.omg.CORBA.ORBPackage.InvalidName exc ) {
055       abort(
             "ERROR: The ORB could not resolve a reference to the NameService");
056         }
```

Next, it finds the Name Server by calling the ORB's `resolve_initial_refer-`
`ences("NameService")`. The Name Server is needed as a parameter to create an
instance of `StorePoaImpl`.

```
057
058         System.out.print(
             "StorePoaServer.main() : creating new store,tax...");
059
060         // Instantiate the Store and Tax servants
061         StorePoaImpl store = new StorePoaImpl(obj, storeId, markup);
062
063         TaxPoaImpl tax = new TaxPoaImpl();
064
```

```
065        System.out.print(
              "StorePoaServer.main() : connecting objects to ORB...");
066
067        // Activate the poa_manager. By default, it will
068        // manage and pass requests onto the implementations
069        poa_mgr.activate();
```

The main program then constructs local (within the current address space) instances of `StorePoaImpl` and `TaxPoaImpl`, and activates the POA manager by calling the `activate()` method of the POA manager. This allows client-initiated method calls to be dispatched to these implementations.

```
070
071        // Publish Store and Tax objects into the Naming Service only
072        // after connecting them to the ORB.
073        PrimerUtils.NsPublisher.nsBind(obj, store._this(), "Store_" +
              storeId, "Primer_Example" );
074        PrimerUtils.NsPublisher.nsBind(obj, tax._this(), "Tax_" +
              storeId, "Primer_Example" );
075
076        System.out.println("Store Server Listening...");
```

Next, the main program publishes the `StorePoaImpl` and `TaxPoaImpl` instances to the Name Server, via the `PrimerUtils.NsPublisher.nsBind()` utility method. By registering with the Name Server, the main program allows a `POSTerminal` implementation to find, via the Name Server, the instance of Store implementation that was just created, and a `StoreAccess` implementation to find the instance of the Tax implementation.

```
077        // For non-gui server applications, some ORB vendors require
078        // that the main thread not exit and others allow the main
079        // thread to exit and continue processing requests.  For a
080        // server application with a GUI, typically the main
081        // thread is used to run the GUI.  See the vendor-specific
082        // sections of the text which describes how each ORB
083        // behaves with respect to the main thread.
```

Finally, the main program must enter an event loop, which detects and dispatches requests from (possibly remote) clients. This activity is specific to individual ORBs, and the code is not shown.

```
084
085      }
086      // used to catch CORBA System exceptions that could result from
087      // initialization or narrow of object references.
088      catch (org.omg.CORBA.SystemException se) {
089        se.printStackTrace();
090        abort("Caught CORBA.SystemException : "  + se);
091      }
092
093      // used to catch Java exceptions such as a null object
094      // reference being returned
```

```
095      // from the narrow operation.
096      catch( java.lang.Exception jle ) {
097  jle.printStackTrace();
098  abort("Caught java.lang.Exception : " + jle);
099      }
100
101  } // main
102 } // class StorePoaServer
```

For error recovery, the main program code is encapsulated in `try`/`catch` blocks, so that all exceptions are caught and a message is printed for error reporting.

31.2.5.1 StoreServer Class

The `StoreServer` class contains the server main program for non-POA implementations:

```
001 package AStore;
002
003 public class StoreServer {
004
005   private static void abort( String msg ) {
006  System.err.println(msg);
007  System.exit(1);
008   }  // abort
009
010   public static void main (String[] args) {
011
012     if ( args.length < 2){
013       abort("usage: StoreServer <Markup> <Store Number> <vendor
             specific options>");
014     }
015
016     int storeId = 0;
017     try {
018       storeId = Integer.parseInt(args[1]);
019     } catch(NumberFormatException e){
020       abort("Unrecognizable Store Number: " + args[1]);
021     }
022
023     float markup = 0;
024     try {
025       markup = Float.valueOf(args[0]).floatValue();
026     } catch(NumberFormatException e){
027       abort("Unrecognizable markup: " + args[0]);
028     }
029
030
031     try {
032
033       System.out.println("StoreServer.main() : starting");
034
```

```
035        System.out.print("StoreServer.main() : initialising ORB...");
036
037        // Some ORB vendors prefer to initialize the ORB using
038        // different ORB initialization interfaces.  See the
039        // vendor specific portions of the text for more info.
040        org.omg.CORBA.ORB orb = org.omg.CORBA.ORB.init(args,null);
041
042        System.out.print(
             "StoreServer.main() : getting NS reference...");
043
044        org.omg.CORBA.Object obj = null;
045        try {
046        obj = orb.resolve_initial_references("NameService");
047        } catch( org.omg.CORBA.ORBPackage.InvalidName exc ) {
048   abort(
             "ERROR: The ORB could not resolve a reference to the NameService");
049        }
050
051        System.out.print(
             "StoreServer.main() : creating new store,tax...");
052
053        // Instantiate the Store and Tax objects
054        StoreImpl store = new StoreImpl(obj, storeId, markup);
055
056        TaxImpl tax = new TaxImpl();
057
058        System.out.print(
             "StoreServer.main() : connecting objects to ORB...");
059
060        // Connect the Store and Tax objects to the ORB so they are
061        // ready to be remotely called.
062        orb.connect (store);
063        orb.connect (tax);
064
065        // Publish Store and Tax objects into the Naming Service only
066        // after connecting them to the ORB.
067        PrimerUtils.NsPublisher.nsBind(obj, store, "Store_" + storeId,
             "Primer_Example" );
068        PrimerUtils.NsPublisher.nsBind(obj, tax, "Tax_" + storeId,
             "Primer_Example" );
069
070        System.out.println("Store Server Listening...");
071        // For non-gui server applications, some ORB vendors require
072        // that the main thread not exit and others allow the main
073        // thread to exit and continue processing requests.  For a
074        // server application with a GUI, typically the main
075        // thread is used to run the GUI.  See the vendor-specific
076        // sections of the text which describe how each ORB
077        // behaves with respect to the main thread.
078
```

```
079      }
080      // used to catch CORBA System exceptions that could result from
081      // initialization or narrow of object references.
082      catch (org.omg.CORBA.SystemException se) {
083        se.printStackTrace();
084        abort("Caught CORBA.SystemException : "  + se);
085      }
086
087      // used to catch Java exceptions such as a null object reference
088      // being returned from the narrow operation.
089      catch( java.lang.Exception jle ) {
090  jle.printStackTrace();
091  abort("Caught java.lang.Exception : " + jle);
092      }
093
094    } // main
095 } // class StoreServer
```

The only differences between the non-POA version and the POA version are:

- There is no need to find the root POA or the POA manager.

- The instances created are `StoreImpl` and `TaxImpl`, instead of `StorePoaImpl` and `TaxPoaImpl`.

- `orb.connect()` is used to make the instances known to the ORB, so that the ORB can dispatch method requests to these implementations.

31.2.6 Implementation Summary

If you've been typing in the code as you went along, your Store code is nearly complete. You're ready to make just a few adjustments for your specific ORB, and prepare to run your Store objects. You won't be able to test them until you've completed a few more chapters, but this does represent additional progress.

31.2.7 Connecting to the ORB, and Starting the Store Object

Once more, we have a few ORB-specific adjustments to make before our objects are complete. That code is presented in the remainder of this chapter, along with reminders of product-specific procedures to create and fire up your objects.

Next you need to go to the section in this chapter on your specific ORB product and follow its procedures to get your objects ready and running. After you've finished, go to Section 33.1, the language-independent section for the POSTerminal.

31.3 Implementing the Store Package Using CORBAplus, Java Edition

The Vertel's Expersoft CORBAplus, Java Edition implementation of the Store component requires a small change to the PrimerUtils/NsPublisher.java. This change was covered in Section 28.3.1. Please refer to that section for details on the NsPublisher.java difference. This section contains information on how to start the Store application.

31.3.1 Executing the Store

```
%java AStore.StoreServer 1.1 1 -pbinit NameService
iiop://localhost:6002/NameServiceRoot
```

To start the StoreServer, you first specify the markup. In the preceding example we selected 10 percent, but your store may require more (if you want to stay in business!). You also specify a Store Number or ID. In addition, you need to specify where the Naming Service is running. This is accomplished in CORBAplus with the pbinit option passing a URL to the Naming Service.

31.4 Implementing the Store Using IBM ORB for Java

Please refer to Section 28.4 for instructions.

31.5 DAIS-Specific Implementation Details for the Store Application

31.5.1 Amendment Summary

DAIS supports the Portable Object Adapter (POA). At this point, if you have been following the common code sections, you should have the following Java code modules:

- AStore\StorePoaServer.java   Requires two amendments for DAIS
- AStore\StorePoaImpl.java   Requires no amendments for DAIS
- AStore\StoreAccessImpl.java   Requires no amendments for DAIS
- AStore\TaxPoaImpl.java   Requires no amendments for DAIS

The amendments are similar to those applied to the Depot Server application, which are documented in detail in Section 28.5. A summary of the changes is covered here. The first amendment to StorePoaServer is only required in early versions of DAIS J[2] where resolve_initial_references, does not recognize the Naming Service. This means using an alternative method to discover the Naming Service. This amendment is not required if you have a GR (general release) version. If you are not sure whether this change applicable to you, don't make any changes at this point. When the application is run, it may abort with the error:

```
ERROR: The ORB could not resolve a reference to the NameService
```

This may occur because your Naming Service is not running, or because your version of DAIS J^2 is an early release.

The second amendment to StorePoaServer is essential. The common code section asserted that each ORB vendor could decide how the main application thread would suspend so that the application does not terminate.

The following subsections will deal with each of these changes in turn.

31.5.2 Alternative to Resolve_Initial_References

The class StorePoaServer requires a single amendment that is shown in bold in the following code:

```
org.omg.CORBA.Object obj = null;
try {
obj = orb.resolve_initial_references("NameService");
} catch( org.omg.CORBA.ORBPackage.InvalidName exc ) {
    if  ((obj = DaisSpecific.ResolveNameService.resolve(orb))==null)
     abort("ERROR: The ORB could not resolve a reference to the
NameService");
}
```

At the point where the common code resolves the Naming Service reference, a catch statement already tests for the exception org.omg.CORBA.ORBPackage. InvalidName and resolves to abort the application. At this point, we insert a statement to call DaisSpecific.ResolveNameService, an alternative class that returns a reference for the Naming Service. If this routine cannot resolve the Naming Service (returns null), then it will abort as well. This class is not part of the product but is supplied for use with the primer examples. If you are interested in the implementation of this class, it is documented in the Java implementation of the Depot server.

31.5.3 Handling the Application Main Thread

Once the application has created the Store and Tax components and advertised them in the Naming Service, it must wait for incoming requests. At this point, we implement a simple user interface with a single option to exit the application. By terminating the application in this way, the main thread can remove references in the Naming Service before exiting. The alternative is to suspend the main thread and interrupt the application (Cntl 'C'). Since Java does not support signal handling, nothing is closed in a tidy manner.

```
System.out.println("Store Server Listening...");

System.out.println("Type exit to terminate application");
java.io.BufferedReader in = new java.io.BufferedReader( new
java.io.InputStreamReader(System.in));
String exitString = "exit";
while ( exitString.compareTo(in.readLine()) != 0 )
{
        System.out.println("Type exit to terminate application");
}

PrimerUtils.NsPublisher.nsUnbind(obj, "Store_" + storeId,
        "Primer_Example" );
PrimerUtils.NsPublisher.nsUnbind(obj, "Tax_" + storeId,
        "Primer_Example" );
```

As mentioned earlier, this is a simple yet effective solution. The DAIS Trader, Node Manager, and Factory services offer more resilient solutions because they can remotely control the lifecycle of an application. This completes the amendments to the Store application. You are now ready to build the Store server.

31.5.4 Compiling the Store Server

Open a console session and change the directory to <installation_root> \primer\java. A default installation would mean changing directory to "c:\Dais-Primer\primer\java". It should contain the AStore package directory, where we have been implementing Store Server. To compile the application we simply have to compile the main application class.

```
javac    AStore\StorePoaServer.java
```

This will also compile any dependent Java files, and so it produces the following class files:

```
AStore\StorePoaServer.class
AStore\StorePoaImpl.class
AStore\StoreAccessPoaImpl.class
AStore\TaxPoaImpl.class
```

These files should be moved into their associated subdirectories under the classes directory. All the above classes should be moved to the .\classes\AStore directory.

31.5.5 Running the Store Server

Before running the Store server, an instance of the DAIS Trader Service must be started, followed by an instance of the Naming Service. An instance of the Depot server should also be running.

The Store server is started from the `classes` directory. It requires two parameters, the Store markup price and the Store identifier. Both are numeric values:

```
java AStore.StorePoaServer 10 1
```

Once we have tested all the applications together, it is possible to run a number of instances of the Store application with different identifiers. Different configurations for the primer example are discussed in Chapters 23 and 26.

31.6 The OrbixWeb Implementation of the Store

Background information on how to code OrbixWeb clients and servers can be found in Section 28.6, which discusses on the OrbixWeb implementation of the `Depot`. You should review this material before continuing with this section.

31.6.1 Changes to the Java Code for OrbixWeb

Once again, the code will build and run as is, but the following changes could be made:
Add the extra `impl_is_ready` calls just after the `orb.init()` call and just after the `System.out.println("Store Server Listening...");` call.

```
// in file StoreServer.java
IE.Iona.OrbixWeb._OrbixWeb.ORB(orb).impl_is_ready("StoreSrv",0);
```

and

```
// in file StoreServer.java
int timeout = 5 *1000; // or whatever timeout value you want
IE.Iona.OrbixWeb._OrbixWeb.ORB(orb).impl_is_ready("StoreSrv",timeout);
```

The following changes must be made together:

```
// in file StoreServer.java
StoreImpl store = new StoreImpl("storePrimerExample",obj, storeId,
markup);


TaxImpl tax = new TaxImpl("taxPrimerExample");


// file StoreImpl.java
StoreImpl(string marker,
          org.omg.CORBA.Object ns,
          int storeID,
          float storeMarkup){
     super(marker);
// the remainder of the constructor is the same as the original
```

```
}   // Constructor



// file taxImpl.java
taxImpl(string marker){
      super(marker);
// the remainder of the constructor is the same as the original

}   // Constructor
```

Again, these changes are made for the same reasons as discussed in Section 28.6 where we discussed the OrbixWeb implementation of the Depot.

31.6.2 Registering Servers in the Implementation Repository

The Server that creates the `Store` and `Tax` objects in this case is called `StoreSrv`. It can be registered in the Orbix daemons' Implementation Repository using the following commands:

```
putit -j StoreSrv AStore.StoreServer
chmodit i+all StoreSrv
chmodit l+all StoreSrv
```

As before, a server that is registered in this fashion can also be run manually from the command line. However, if a client makes an invocation on this server and it is not currently running, then the Orbix daemon will launch the process.

31.6.3 Binding to Remote Objects

The client for the Store Server could use the following code to obtain a reference to the Impl objects instead of the `nsResolve` method:

```
String hostname = // put in the hostname you are running the depot on
Store sRef = StoreHelper.bind(":StoreSrv", hostname);
Tax tRef = TaxHelper.bind(":StoreSrv", hostname);
```

or

```
String hostname = // put in the hostname you are running the depot on
Store sRef = StoreHelper.bind("depotPrimerExample:StoreSrv",hostname);
    Tax tRef = TaxHelper.bind("taxPrimerExample:StoreSrv",hostname);
```

31.7 Implementing the Store Package Using VisiBroker for Java

The Inprise VisiBroker implementation of the Store component does not require any changes to the common code. The information contained in Section 28.7 can be used to build the Store package as well.

Store: COBOL Coding

32.1 Getting Started on the Store

This chapter presents the implementation of the Store using Orbix COBOL. As in Chapter 29, the convention used in other Store chapters of separating the common code from specific implementation examples is not necessary because Orbix COBOL is the only implementation of the COBOL language mapping presented in this book.

Before proceeding any further and jumping into the details of how Store is implemented using COBOL, you should first read the language-independent functionality of Store back in Section 30.1. There you will find an overview of the Store implementation, so if you have not yet read it, we suggest that you do before you read on.

32.2 COBOL Implementation of Store

The complete description of the externally accessible interfaces for Store are contained within the Store IDL file. Internally, this file actually contains three IDL interfaces: **Store, StoreAccess,** and **Tax.** Along with these interface definitions you will also find some data structures that are defined at a global level. This presents us with an interesting question: Since we only generate COBOL copy files for specific interfaces, how are global **typedef**s handled? In fact, it actually opens up a deeper question: The concept of a typedef just does not exist within standard COBOL syntax, so how can **typedef**s be mapped at all? The answer is simple: All types within interfaces are rolled back to their basic types, so IDL **typedef**s are not mapped to any specific COBOL data items in their own right. Each specific IDL interface will always result in one COBOL copy file containing the complete layout of all the parameters for each of the operations within the interface. We'll see specific illustrations of this in a moment.

To start us off, let's look at the COBOL copy files that are generated for the **Tax** interface. After that we move on to look at the COBOL copy files generated for the **Store** and then the **StoreAccess** interfaces. Finally, we look at the implementation details of the **Store** server and each of its three interfaces.

32.2.1 The Mapping for the Tax Interface

Here is the IDL for the **Tax** interface within the **AStore** module:

```
enum ItemTypes {FOOD, CLOTHES, OTHER};

interface Tax
{
    float calculate_tax      (in float      taxable_amount);
    float find_taxable_price (in float      item_price,
                              in ItemTypes item_type);
};
```

The Orbix COBOL mapping for this interface, the first of the three Store interfaces, results in a COBOL copy file called `tax.cpy` being generated. Its contents are as follows:

```
*******************************************************************
*
*   Interface:  Tax
*
*   Generated by gencbl
*
*******************************************************************

*******************************************************************
*
*   Defined Operations
*
*******************************************************************


*
*   Operation  :   calculate_tax
*   Parameters :   in float taxable_amount
*   Returns    :   float
*
  01 TAX-CALCULATE-TAX-ARGS.
     03 TAXABLE-AMOUNT             COMPUTATIONAL-1.
     03 RESULT                     COMPUTATIONAL-1.
```

```
*
* Operation  :  find_taxable_price
* Parameters :  in float item_price
*               in enum AStore::ItemTypes item_type
* Returns    :  float
*
 01 TAX-FIND-TAXABLE-PRICE-ARGS.
    03 ITEM-PRICE                 COMPUTATIONAL-1.
    03 ITEM-TYPE                  PICTURE S9(09) BINARY.
       88 FOOD                    VALUE 0.
       88 CLOTHES                 VALUE 1.
       88 IDL-OTHER               VALUE 2.
    03 RESULT                     COMPUTATIONAL-1.


 **********************************************************************
        COPY TAXX.
 **********************************************************************
 01 TAX-OPERATION                 PICTURE X(19).
    88 TAX-CALCULATE-TAX          VALUE "calculate_tax".
    88 TAX-FIND-TAXABLE-PRICE     VALUE "find_taxable_price".


 01 TAX-OPERATION-LENGTH          PICTURE 9(09) BINARY
                                  VALUE 19.
```

The TAX COBOL copy file contains the parameter layouts for the two operations within the **Tax** interface and an operation area. For the Orbix implementation of COBOL, it also pulls in another copy file called TAXX.CPY. This includes product-specific details for the Tax interface. The contents of this file are completely opaque to users, so you need not worry about what is inside it. These generated interface details are passed in as a parameter on the ORBREG routine using the label TAX-INTERFACE. It is a mechanism for passing details of the interface in for a dynamic mapping just before we commence to interact via that interface as either a client or an object implementation. We shall see this in the implementation details later in this chapter.

32.2.2 The Mapping for the Store Interface

Here is the IDL for the **Store** interface within the **AStore** module:

```
typedef long AStoreId;

interface StoreAccess; // /forward reference

interface Store
{
  struct POSInfo
  {
```

```
        POS::POSId  id;
        StoreAccess  store_access_reference;
        float        total_sales;
        float        total_taxes;
    };

    typedef sequence <POSInfo> POSList;

    struct StoreTotals
    {
      float    store_total;
      float    store_tax_total;
    };

    readonly attribute AStoreId StoreId;
    readonly attribute StoreTotals Totals;

    StoreAccess login(in  POS::POSId id);
    void        get_POS_totals(out POSList    POS_data);
    void        update_store_totals(in  POS::POSId id,
                        in  float    price,
                        in  float    taxes);
  };
```

The Orbix COBOL mapping for this interface, the second of the three **Store** interfaces, results in a COBOL copy file called STORE.CPY being generated. Its contents are as follows:

```
*******************************************************************
*
*   Interface:  Store
*
*   Generated by gencbl
*
*******************************************************************


*******************************************************************
*
*   Attribute Access Operations
*
*******************************************************************
*
*   Attribute  :  readonly long StoreId
*
 01 STORE-STOREID-ARGS.
    03 RESULT                         PICTURE S9(09) BINARY.


*
*   Attribute : readonly struct AStore::Store::StoreTotals Totals
*
 01 STORE-TOTALS-ARGS.
    03 RESULT.
```

```
        05 STORE-TOTAL                    COMPUTATIONAL-1.
        05 STORE-TAX-TOTAL                COMPUTATIONAL-1.


*****************************************************************
*
*  Defined Operations
*
*****************************************************************


*
*  Operation   :  login
*  Parameters  :  in long id
*  Returns     :  objref
*
 01 STORE-LOGIN-ARGS.
        03 IDL-ID                         PICTURE S9(09) BINARY.
        03 RESULT                         POINTER.


*
*  Operation   :  get_POS_totals
*  Parameters  :  out sequence <struct AStore::Store::POSInfo>
*
 01 STORE-get-pos-totals-ARGS.
        03 POS-DATA-1.
           05 POSINFO.
              07 IDL-ID                   PICTURE S9(09) BINARY.
              07 STORE-ACCESS-REFERENCE POINTER.
              07 TOTAL-SALES              COMPUTATIONAL-1.
              07 TOTAL-TAXES              COMPUTATIONAL-1.
        03 POS-DATA-SEQUENCE.
           05 SEQUENCE-MAXIMUM            PICTURE 9(09) BINARY.
           05 SEQUENCE-LENGTH             PICTURE 9(09) BINARY.
           05 SEQUENCE-BUFFER             POINTER.
           05 SEQUENCE-TYPE               POINTER.


*
*  Operation   :  update_store_totals
*  Parameters  :  in long id
*                 in float price
*                 in float taxes
*
 01 STORE-UPDATE-STORE-TOTALS-ARGS.
        03 IDL-ID                         PICTURE S9(09) BINARY.
        03 PRICE                          COMPUTATIONAL-1.
        03 TAXES                          COMPUTATIONAL-1.


*
* Typecode definitions used in the interface Store
* Use this data item for retrieving or setting the type
* information for ANYs or SEQUENCES.
*
```

```
01 STORE-TYPE                        PICTURE X(111).
        COPY CORBATYP.
     88 STORE-POSINFO                   VALUE "..........".
     88 STORE-POSLIST                   VALUE "..........".
     88 STORE-STORETOTALS              VALUE "..........".


01 STORE-TYPE-LENGTH                 PICTURE 9(09) BINARY
                                        VALUE 111.


* * * * * * * * * * * * * * * * * * * * * * * * * * * * * * * * * * * * * * * *
        COPY STOREX.
* * * * * * * * * * * * * * * * * * * * * * * * * * * * * * * * * * * * * * * *
01 STORE-OPERATION                   PICTURE X(20).
     88 STORE-GET-STOREID              VALUE "_get_StoreId".
     88 STORE-GET-TOTALS              VALUE "_get_Totals".
     88 STORE-LOGIN                   VALUE "login".
     88 STORE-GET-POS-TOTALS          VALUE "get_POS_totals".
     88 STORE-UPDATE-STORE-TOTALS     VALUE "update_store_totals".


01 STORE-OPERATION-LENGTH            PICTURE 9(09) BINARY
                                        VALUE 20.
```

The STORE COBOL copy file contains the parameter layouts for the two-accessor routines for the read-only attributes and the three operations, **typecode** definitions, and an operation area. For the Orbix implementation of COBOL, it also pulls in another copy file called STOREX.CPY that includes product-specific details for the Store interface. As we saw for the previous Tax interface, the contents of this file are completely opaque to users.

You will also notice that we have something here that we have not seen before. There are **typecode** definitions, and a CORBATYP copy file with **typecode**s of all the basic IDL types. Because the get-POS-totals operation within this interface contains a parameter that is a sequence of some other type, we need to be able to hold a specific **typecode** in the sequence to identify what it is a sequence of. These **typecode**s are included to allow us to do just that. When we get down to looking at the implementation details we'll see how all of this works.

32.2.3 The Mapping for the StoreAccess Interface

Here is the IDL for the **StoreAccess** interface within the **AStore** module:

```
enum ItemTypes {FOOD, CLOTHES, OTHER};

struct ItemInfo
{
    POS::Barcode    item;
    ItemTypes       item_type;
    float           item_cost;
    string          idl_name;
    long            quantity;
```

```
};

exception BarcodeNotFound { POS::Barcode item; };

interface StoreAccess
{
   void      find_price( in  POS::Barcode item1,
                         in  long         quantity1,
                         out float        item_price,
                         out float        item_tax_price,
                         out ItemInfo     item_info)
      raises (BarcodeNotFound);
};
```

The Orbix COBOL mapping for this interface, the third of the three Store interfaces, will result in a COBOL copy file called storeacc.cpy being generated. Note that for Orbix COBOL, the size of the name for generated COBOL copy files is restricted to eight characters, so the **StoreAccess** interface name has been truncated to storeacc. Its contents are as follows:

```
****************************************************************
*
*  Interface:  StoreAccess
*
*  Generated by gencbl
*
****************************************************************


****************************************************************
*
*  Defined Operations
*
****************************************************************


*
*  Operation   :  find_price
*  Parameters  :  in string item1
*                 in long quantity1
*                 out float item_price
*                 out float item_tax_price
*                 out struct AStore::ItemInfo item_info
*  Raises      :  BarcodeNotFound
*
01 STOREACCESS-FIND-PRICE-ARGS.
      03 ITEM1                        POINTER.
      03 QUANTITY1                    PICTURE S9(09) BINARY.
      03 ITEM-PRICE                   COMPUTATIONAL-1.
      03 ITEM-TAX-PRICE               COMPUTATIONAL-1.
      03 ITEM-INFO.
         05 ITEM                      POINTER.
         05 ITEM-TYPE                 PICTURE S9(09) BINARY.
            88 FOOD                      VALUE 0.
```

```
            88 CLOTHES                     VALUE 1.
            88 IDL-OTHER                   VALUE 2.
        05 ITEM-COST                   COMPUTATIONAL-1.
        05 IDL-NAME                    POINTER.
        05 QUANTITY                    PICTURE S9(09) BINARY.


    ***************************************************************
          COPY STOREACX.
    ***************************************************************
     01 STOREACCESS-OPERATION          PICTURE X(11).
        88 STOREACCESS-FIND-PRICE          VALUE "find_price".

     01 STOREACCESS-OPERATION-LENGTH   PICTURE 9(09) BINARY
                                           VALUE 11.
```

The STOREACC COBOL copy file contains the parameter layouts for one operation and an operation area. As we saw with the other two Store interfaces, the Orbix implementation of COBOL pulls in another copy file called STOREACX.CPY that includes product-specific details for the **StoreAccess** interface. The contents of this file are completely opaque to users.

32.2.4 Implementing the Store with Orbix COBOL

Now let's look at the actual implementation of the Store server written using Orbix COBOL. We'll start by reviewing the main program that is used to register the three Store interfaces with the ORB. After that we'll look at the dispatcher that is responsible for receiving all inbound requests and dispatching them to the correct interface implementation. We then turn our attention to each of the interfaces (**Tax**, **Store**, and **StoreAccess**) and look at the details of each of their implementations.

32.2.4.1 The Store Server

The Store server is responsible for performing all the initialization required to enable it to receive and process inbound requests for each of the three Store IDL interfaces (**Tax**, **Store**, and **StoreAccess**).

The Store server initially receives a unique Store Identifier as a command-line argument. It then proceeds to register the Store interfaces with the ORB. For the sake of simplicity we won't focus on the syntax of COBOL command-line argument processing here.

```
        PROCEDURE DIVISION.
        *------------------------------------------------------------
        *    Initialize
        *------------------------------------------------------------
            perform get-args.


        *------------------------------------------------------------
        *    Activate the Implementation
        *------------------------------------------------------------
```

```
CALL "ORBSTAT" USING ORBIX-STATUS-INFORMATION
CALL "ORBREG"  USING STORE-INTERFACE
CALL "ORBREG"  USING STOREACCESS-INTERFACE
CALL "ORBREG"  USING TAX-INTERFACE
```

We start by performing the GET-ARGS paragraph to process the store identifier received as a command-line parameter. After that, the standard ORBSTAT call is used to register the ORBIX-STATUS-INFORMATION area as the COBOL working storage in which all status information is to be recorded for this program. As we discussed in more detail in Chapter 29, this area contains the return status for all calls, and may be checked to determine if an exception has been raised. The ORBIX-STATUS-INFORMA-TION area, which we specified as a parameter on the call, is defined within the standard CORBA.CPY copy file. Remember that this copy file must be included within the working storage of all COBOL programs that use the Orbix COBOL routines.

After the call to ORBSTAT, the ORBREG call is used to register the details for each of the three interfaces that the Store server will support. This means that we have three instances of the call. The interface-specific parameters used on each of the ORBREG calls are defined for you within the interface-specific COBOL copy files generated for each of the three Store interfaces.

Once the ORBREG calls have been completed, the server needs to call initialization routines for the **Tax** and the **Store** interfaces. Along with some basic initialization, these routines will also construct unique object references for each of the interfaces, then register them with the Naming Service. However, before it is possible for such routines to be able to construct valid Object References within an Orbix COBOL context, the ORBINIT call must first be invoked. By default, ORBINIT will run forever when called and send all inbound requests to the Store server's dispatcher until the server is terminated. Therefore, if we call ORBINIT, we will not be able to call the initialization routines. We have seen this problem before within the previous Depot tutorial in Section 29.5.3.1, so we shall solve it here just as we did there by setting a timer so that an initial call to ORBINIT times out. We can then call the initialization routines, reset the ORBINIT timer, and call ORBINIT once again. This is illustrated in the following code:

```
*
*
*     Set server timeout to 0 just to get it going
*
      move "0"            to ws-timeout
      SET EVENT-TIMEOUT       TO TRUE
      CALL "ORBTIME" USING ORBIX-TIMEOUT-TYPE
                           WS-TIMEOUT
      PERFORM CHECK-STATUS

      CALL "ORBINIT" USING SERVER-NAME
                           SERVER-NAME-LEN
      PERFORM CHECK-STATUS



*
*     Now Initialize
*
```

```
        CALL "Tax-Init"   using StoreId server-name
        CALL "Store-Init" using Markup StoreId server-name
```

As you can see in the preceding code segment, the ORBIX ORBTIME call is used to set a 0 time-out for the ORBINIT call so that it will time out, and return immediately when called. This then enables us to perform the required initialization for the **Tax** and **Store** interfaces. We won't look at the details of these initialization routines here; instead, we'll review them each as we review the implementation details for the interfaces later on.

Having completed the interface-specific initialization, we can now reset the timer for ORBINIT, then call it again so that the server may proceed to receive and process inbound requests. In this specific example we set the timer to run for an arbitrary 15 minutes. Note that the actual value specified is in milliseconds.

```
    *
    *       Now wait for up to 15 minutes for inbound requests
    *
            move "900000"               to ws-timeout
            SET EVENT-TIMEOUT           TO TRUE
            CALL "ORBTIME" USING ORBIX-TIMEOUT-TYPE
                                 WS-TIMEOUT
            CALL "ORBINIT" USING SERVER-NAME
                                 SERVER-NAME-LEN
            PERFORM CHECK-STATUS
            STOP RUN.
```

32.2.4.2 The Store Dispatcher

After the ORBINIT call has been called within the main program for the second time, it waits for all inbound requests, and when one is received, it passes it directly to the DISPATCH entry point within the Store server. If the server only supported one interface, then the implementation of that interface could have the DISPATCH entry point, and needs to only determine which operation has been requested. However, since the Store server supports three interfaces, it needs a generic dispatcher that will determine which of the three interfaces has been requested for each inbound request.

```
            IDENTIFICATION DIVISION.
            PROGRAM-ID.                         DISPATCH.

            DATA DIVISION.
            WORKING-STORAGE SECTION.

              COPY CORBA.

            01 WS-INTERFACE-TEXT         PICTURE X(64).
            01 WS-INTERFACE-TEXT-LEN     PICTURE 9(9) BINARY
                                         VALUE 64.


    *=============================================================
    *     Store DISPATCHER
    *=============================================================
```

```
        PROCEDURE DIVISION.
              CALL "ORBREQ"  USING REQUEST-INFO.
```

As requests are received within the dispatcher, an ORBREQ call is made to populate a data area called REQUEST-INFO with the specific details for the inbound request. The layout of the REQUEST-INFO area is defined within the generic COBOL copy file CORBA.CPY. As mentioned previously, all COBOL programs using Orbix COBOL are required to specify this COBOL copy file within their working storage area. This is illustrated in the previous COBOL code fragment.

Once the request details have been obtained, the string that identifies which interface the request is for is used to call the correct interface implementation. The following code shows you how this is done:

```
        *
        *      Determine which interface has been called
        *

              CALL "STRGET"  USING INTERFACE-NAME
                                   WS-INTERFACE-TEXT-LEN
                                   WS-INTERFACE-TEXT
              EVALUATE WS-INTERFACE-TEXT
                  WHEN "Store"
                      call "STORE"

                  WHEN "Tax"
                      call "TAX"

                  WHEN "StoreAccess"
                      call "STACCESS"

              END-EVALUATE
```

Since the interface name is held in the REQUEST-INFO block as a CORBA String, the actual textual description is obtained by using the STRGET function to convert it into COBOL text. The returned textual interface name is then used to call the specific interface implementation that has been requested for this request.

Let's look at the implementation details for each of the Store interfaces in turn.

32.2.4.3 The Tax Interface Implementation

The first Store interface we'll look at in detail is the Tax interface. The best way to start is to look at how the state of the Tax interface is held and how its initialization is performed. We then look at how it invokes the correct COBOL paragraph for inbound requests, and finally look at the actual implementation of the two operations defined within the interface.

Tax Instance State

When an instance of an interface is created, it may consistently retain information within its working storage as long as that logical instance remains available to clients. We can rightly view this as the state of the instance. For the Tax interface, its state will be held within the following structure:

```
DATA DIVISION.
    WORKING-STORAGE SECTION.

    01 Tax-state.
        03 Store-id                    pic 9(9) binary.
        03 rate                        comp-1.
        03 tax-name                    pic x(32).
```

The values held here include the unique identifier for the store, the tax rate, and the character representation of the unique name for this instance of the Tax interface.

Initialization for the Tax Interface

As previously discussed, the main program for the Store server will call the `Tax-Init` entry point when it is performing the initialization required for the Tax interface. When that call is made, it will pass as parameters the Store identifier and the name of the Store server. Here is the actual code that is called:

```
*=============================================================
*      Tax-Init
*=============================================================
 Tax-init.
 Entry "Tax-Init" using lk-store-Id
                       lk-server-name
                       .

        move lk-Store-Id      to Store-Id
        move lk-Store-Id      to ws-99

        move "Tax_"           to tax-name
        move ws-99            to tax-name(5:2)

        CALL "ns-bind" using lk-server-name
                             ws-interface-name
                             tax-name

        move .05              to rate
        exit program
        .
```

Within the preceding initialization code for the Tax interface, the following occurs:

■ The unique Store identifier is saved in the state area, and also used to construct a unique name for this Tax instance called `Tax_nn` (where nn is the unique Store identifier).

■ The `ns-bind` code is called to create the object reference for the Tax instance, then cache it within the Naming Service. The `ns-bind` routine was discussed in detail in Chapter 29.

■ A tax rate of `.05` is established for this instance of the Tax interface. Since the objective here is to focus on how to code a CORBA interface in COBOL, a simplistic approach to obtaining the rate has been taken. Here a hard-coded value is set during initialization. A more realistic example would have done this differently.

Processing Inbound Tax Requests

Once the generic dispatcher has received an inbound request for the Tax interface, it will be passed to the Tax implementation. Here we need to determine which specific operation within the Tax interface has been requested, and call it:

```
IDENTIFICATION DIVISION.
PROGRAM-ID.                         TAX.
     . . .

PROCEDURE DIVISION.
     CALL "ORBSTAT"  USING ORBIX-STATUS-INFORMATION.
     CALL "ORBREQ"   USING REQUEST-INFO.
     CALL "STRGET"   USING OPERATION-NAME
                           TAX-OPERATION-LENGTH
                           TAX-OPERATION.
     COPY TAXD.
     GOBACK.
```

The code used to identify the specific operation requested within the Tax interface is very similar to the code within the previous generic dispatcher. After the usual call to ORBSTAT to establish the status area, an ORBREQ call is used to obtain the details of the inbound request.

The actual name of the requested operation is held in the OPERATION-NAME item within the REQUEST-INFO area. It is converted using the STRGET routine from its CORBA String format into a COBOL text value and placed into the TAX-OPERATION area. (The TAX-OPERATION area is defined within the TAX.CPY COBOL copy file that was generated by the Orbix Gencbl utility.)

Finally, the code within a generated COBOL copy file called TAXD.CPY is used to perform the requested operation. (The COBOL copy file, TAXD.CPY, is generated by the Orbix Gencbl utility. It expects the operation name to be set in TAX-OPERATION, and uses this to select the correct COBOL paragraph for the requested operation.)

Tax Method: Calculate-Tax

The first of the Tax interface's operations, Calculate-Tax, takes the Taxable-Amount supplied as an input parameter, and multiplies it by the Tax rate established during the initialization of the Tax interface. The result is then returned as the operation's output.

```
*-------------------------------------------------------------
*    CalculateTax
*-------------------------------------------------------------
 DO-TAX-CALCULATE-TAX.
     display "Tax: Calculate-Tax"
     CALL "ORBGET"           USING TAX-CALCULATE-TAX-ARGS
     compute result in TAX-CALCULATE-TAX-ARGS =
```

```
                  (TAXABLE-AMOUNT
                  in TAX-CALCULATE-TAX-ARGS * rate)
        CALL "ORBPUT"            USING TAX-CALCULATE-TAX-ARGS
        .
```

As we have already seen in Chapter 29, we always start a method implementation with an ORBGET call. This needs to be done to populate the parameter area for the operation with all the input parameters contained within the inbound request. In this case, this will be the taxable amount. The TAX-CALCULATE-TAX-ARGS area used as a parameter on the ORBGET call is defined within the COBOL copy file generated for the Tax interface. You can refer back to the illustration of the contents of this copy file in Section 32.2.1, to see the complete layout of the parameter area. It contains all the parameters used by the operation in one COBOL group item. Note that the ORBGET call will only populate the IN and INOUT parameter areas.

For this operation, the tax rate is calculated and then placed into the RESULT area. Once a method implementation has completed its processing, the ORBPUT routine is always called. This is done to return all the accumulated results for the operation back to the caller. All the **out**, **inout**, and result parameter values within the TAX-CALCULATE-TAX-ARGS area that was specified on the ORBPUT call will be returned to the caller. Note that ORBPUT should always be called even when there are no return values.

Tax Method: Find-Taxable-Price

The second of the Tax interface's operations, Find-Taxable-Price, is used to return the actual amount that is to be taxed. It will take the Item-Price and Item-type as input. If the Item-Type is OTHER, then the full value of the item is taxable; otherwise, a zero taxable value is returned.

```
      *-------------------------------------------------------------
      *    FindTaxablePrice
      *-------------------------------------------------------------
       DO-TAX-FIND-TAXABLE-PRICE.
           display "Tax: Find-Taxable-Price"
           CALL "ORBGET"  USING TAX-FIND-TAXABLE-PRICE-ARGS
           if idl-other
               move Item-Price in TAX-FIND-TAXABLE-PRICE-ARGS
                       to result in TAX-FIND-TAXABLE-PRICE-ARGS
           else
               move 0.0 to result in TAX-FIND-TAXABLE-PRICE-ARGS
           end-if
           CALL "ORBPUT"  USING TAX-FIND-TAXABLE-PRICE-ARGS
           .
```

The standard ORBGET routine is called to obtain the inbound parameters and insert them into the specified parameter operation area, TAX-FIND-TAXABLE-PRICE-ARGS. This area is defined within the generated COBOL copy file for the Tax interface.

If the Item-Type, which was received as an input parameter, is IDL-Other, the Item-value is set as the output value. Otherwise, the output value is 0. The standard ORBPUT routine is then used to return the output values back to the caller.

32.2.4.4 The Store Interface Implementation

Now let's look at the **Store** interface. We'll follow the pattern we started when we looked at the **Tax** interface, by looking at how the state of the **Store** interface is held and also how its initialization is performed. We then move on to see how it invokes the correct paragraph for inbound requests, and finally look at the actual implementation of the two attributes and three operations defined within the interface.

Store Instance State

The state of all implementations of the **Store** interface is held within the following structure within COBOL working storage. Since it's one of the more complicated interfaces, its state is larger:

```
DATA DIVISION.
WORKING-STORAGE SECTION.

78 MAX-POSLIST-ENTRIES              value 12.

01 Store-state.
    03 PosArray occurs MAX-POSLIST-ENTRIES.
        05 access-id                pic 9(9) binary.
        05 StoreAccess-ref          pointer.
        05 ws-Total-Sales           comp-1.
        05 ws-Total-Taxes           comp-1.
    03 array-count                  pic 9(9) binary.
    03 totals.
        05 StoreTotal               comp-1.
        05 StoreTaxTotal            comp-1.
    03 Depot-ref                    pointer.
    03 Tax-ref                      pointer.
    03 Store-Markup                 comp-1.
    03 Store-id                     pic 9(9) binary.
    03 Store-name                   pic x(32).
    03 Tax-Name                     pic x(32).
```

Within the state area we keep track of each instance of the **StoreAccess** interface created by the **Store** interface. This includes the unique Object Reference, and also the Sales and Taxes that have been collected for each. (For this simple example we only support a maximum of 12 instances of the **StoreAccess** interface.) We also keep totals for the entire store. The unique object references for the store's associated Tax object and the Depot object are also kept here along with the store's markup and unique identifier. Finally, the textual representation of the Store and Tax object names are also retained here.

Initialization for the Store Interface

As previously discussed, the main program for the Store server calls the Store-Init entry point when it is performing the initialization required for the Store interface. When that call is made, it will pass as parameters the markup value for this instance of store, the unique store identifier, and the name of the Store server. These values are used when constructing a unique object reference for the Store interface.

```
*==============================================================
*    Store-Init
*==============================================================
 store-init.
 Entry "Store-Init" using lk-markup
                          lk-StoreId
                          lk-server-name
                          .

      move lk-storeid       to    store-id
      move lk-storeid       to    ws-99
      move lk-markup        to    store-markup
      move 0                to    array-count

      move spaces           to    store-name
      string lk-server-name delimited by space
             "_"            delimited by size
             ws-99          delimited by size
                      into   store-name

      move "Tax_"           to    tax-name
      move ws-99            to    tax-name(5:2)
      call "ns-rslv" using tax-name
                        returning tax-ref

      move "Depot"          to ws-data
      call "ns-rslv" using ws-data
                        returning Depot-ref

      CALL "ns-bind" using lk-server-name
                           ws-interface-name
                           store-name

      move 0                to StoreTotal     in totals,
                               StoreTaxTotal in totals

*
*     Initialize POS access to indicate no login's
*     have been received
*
      move 0                    to array-count
      perform varying ws-i from 1 by 1
            until ws-i > MAX-POSLIST-ENTRIES
         move 0                   to access-id(ws-i)
         set StoreAccess-ref(ws-i) to null
      end-perform

      exit program
            .
```

Within the preceding initialization code for the Store interface, the following occurs:

- The parameter values received are saved within the state area for this instance of the interface.

- A unique name for this instance of the Store interface is then constructed using the server name combined with the unique Store identifier.

- The ns-rslv routine is used to obtain object references for both the Tax interface within this server and the Depot interface that is running within a different server. (The ns-rslv code is discussed in detail in Chapter 29.)

- The ns-bind code is then called to create the object reference for the Store interface and then cache it within the Naming Service. (The ns-bind code is also discussed in detail in Chapter 29.)

- The StoreTotals and StoreTaxTotals values within the state area are initialized to zero.

- Finally, the array of StoreAccess object references within the state area are initialized to NULL.

Processing Inbound Store Requests

Once the generic dispatcher has received an inbound request for the **Store** interface, it will be passed to the Store implementation. Here we need to determine which specific operation within the Store interface has been requested, and call it.

```
IDENTIFICATION DIVISION.
      PROGRAM-ID.                    STORE.
            . . .


      PROCEDURE DIVISION.

          CALL "ORBSTAT" USING ORBIX-STATUS-INFORMATION.
          CALL "ORBREQ"  USING REQUEST-INFO.
          CALL "STRGET"  USING OPERATION-NAME
                               STORE-OPERATION-LENGTH
                               STORE-OPERATION.
          COPY STORED.

          GOBACK.
```

The code used to identify the specific operation requested within the Store interface is more or less the same as the code used for the previous Tax interface. After the usual call to ORBSTAT to establish the status area for exception handling, an ORBREQ call is used to obtain the details of the inbound request.

The actual name of the requested operation is held in the OPERATION-NAME item within the REQUEST-INFO area that was previously filled in by the call to ORBREQ. It is converted using the STRGET routine from its CORBA String format into a COBOL text value and placed into the STORE-OPERATION area. (The STORE-OPERATION area is defined within the STORE.CPY COBOL copy file that was generated by the Orbix Gencbl utility.)

Finally, the code within a generated COBOL copy file called `STORED.CPY` is used to perform the requested operation.

Store Attribute Accessor: Get-StoreId

The **StoreId** attribute is read-only, so it only has a `Get` accessor routine that is used to obtain its current value:

```
*------------------------------------------------------------
*     Get-StoreId
*------------------------------------------------------------
DO-STORE-GET-STOREID.
      CALL "ORBGET"                    USING STORE-STOREID-ARGS
      move store-id to result in store-storeid-args
      CALL "ORBPUT"                    USING STORE-STOREID-ARGS
      .
```

This is a very simple accessor function that returns the current value. We start by making the mandatory ORBGET call. The required `Store-Id` is then taken from the state area and placed into the result area for this operation and ORBPUT is used to return it to the caller.

Store Attribute Accessor: Get-Totals

The **Totals** attribute is read-only, so it only has a `Get` accessor routine that is used to obtain its current values:

```
*------------------------------------------------------------
*     Get-Totals
*------------------------------------------------------------
DO-STORE-GET-TOTALS.
      CALL "ORBGET"                    USING STORE-TOTALS-ARGS
      move StoreTotal in Totals
                 to Store-Total in STORE-TOTALS-ARGS
      move StoreTaxTotal in Totals
                 to Store-Tax-Total in STORE-TOTALS-ARGS
      CALL "ORBPUT"                    USING STORE-TOTALS-ARGS
      .
```

This accessor function is very similar to the previous one. Once again we start by calling ORBGET. The `StoreTotal` and `StoreTaxTotal` values are then taken from the state area and placed into the output parameter area for this operation. Finally, ORBPUT is used to return them to the caller. The only difference between this accessor function and the previous one is that the previous one returned a single value, and this one returned two values contained within a structure.

Store Method: Login

The first of the three Store interface operations, `Login`, is used to create an instance of the `StoreAccess` interface within the Store server on behalf of a unique POS (Point of Sale) terminal:

```
*------------------------------------------------------------
*     Login
```

```
     *-------------------------------------------------------------
      DO-STORE-LOGIN.
          display "Store: Login"
          CALL "ORBGET"                    USING STORE-LOGIN-ARGS

          perform varying ws-i from 1 by 1
                  until ws-i > array-count
                    or access-id in posarray (ws-i) =
                        idl-id in STORE-GET-POS-TOTALS-ARGS
          end-perform
          if array-count = MAX-POSLIST-ENTRIES
              display "Store::Login - POSList overflow"
              set result in STORE-LOGIN-ARGS to NULL
          else
              if ws-i > array-count
                  add 1 to array-count
                  move array-count to ws-i
              end-if
              move 0.0 to ws-Total-Sales(ws-i),
                          ws-Total-Taxes(ws-i)
              move idl-id in STORE-LOGIN-ARGS
                          to access-id(ws-i)
              call "new-StoreAccess" using store-markup
                                           store-id
                                           ws-i
                                           target
                            returning StoreAccess-ref(ws-i)

              CALL "OBJDUP" using StoreAccess-ref(ws-i)
                                     result in STORE-LOGIN-ARGS
          end-if

          CALL "ORBPUT"                    USING STORE-LOGIN-ARGS
          .
```

As usual, we start with a call to the standard ORBGET routine to populate the parameter area with all the input parameters for this operation. In this case, it is the unique POS Identifier. The code then proceeds to search the array of StoreAccess details held within the Store state (COBOL working storage) until it either matches one, or exceeds the current count of entries.

If all the entries have already been used, a message will be displayed informing the user that all the POS entries are in use, and a NULL StoreAccess object reference will be set up in the return area.

If the entry is available, then the TotalSales and TotalTaxSales in the Store-Access entry within the state area are initialized to 0. The new-StoreAccess routine is then called to obtain a new instance of the StoreAccess object. For the moment we'll postpone looking at the details of the new-StoreAccess routine. At this stage we just need to understand that it will return an Object Reference for a new instance of the StoreAccess interface. When we look at the implementation of the StoreAccess interface later on, we'll look at this in more detail. Once we have the

Object Reference for the new instance of `StoreAccess` cached within our state area, we use `ORBDUP` to set up a copy of it in the return area.

Finally, we finish by calling `ORBPUT` to pass back the `StoreAccess` object reference to the caller.

Store Method: Get-POS-Totals

The second of the three Store interface operations, `Get-POS-Totals`, is used to return a sequence of all of the current `StoreAccess` details recorded within the state (working storage) of this instance of the `Store` object. This operation will be the first time we have encountered the manipulation of a CORBA sequence type as a parameter within our COBOL tutorial:

```
*-------------------------------------------------------------
*     GetPOSTotals
*-------------------------------------------------------------
DO-STORE-GET-POS-TOTALS.
       CALL "ORBGET"          USING STORE-GET-POS-TOTALS-ARGS


*
**   Set up the initial sequence attributes
*
       MOVE MAX-POSLIST-ENTRIES TO SEQUENCE-MAXIMUM OF
                                   STORE-GET-POS-TOTALS-ARGS
       MOVE 0                  TO SEQUENCE-LENGTH OF
                                   STORE-GET-POS-TOTALS-ARGS


*
**   Set the type of the sequence using generated typecode
*
       SET STORE-POSINFO          TO TRUE
       CALL "STRSET" USING SEQUENCE-TYPE OF
                              STORE-GET-POS-TOTALS-ARGS
                           STORE-TYPE-LENGTH
                           STORE-TYPE
*
**   Allocate a buffer of the correct size to hold the data
*
       CALL "ORBALLOC"  USING WS-SEQ-BUFF-LEN
                              SEQUENCE-BUFFER OF
                                 STORE-GET-POS-TOTALS-ARGS


*
**   The sequence is now initialized and could be
**   sent back to the client in this state.  The current
**   length of the sequence is zero.
*
       perform varying ws-i from 1 by 1
              until ws-i > array-count
          move access-id(ws-i) to idl-id
                           in store-get-Pos-Totals-args
          set Store-Access-Reference
```

```
                                      in store-get-Pos-Totals-args
                       to StoreAccess-Ref(ws-i)
          move ws-Total-sales(ws-i) to total-Sales
                                      in store-get-Pos-Totals-args
          move ws-Total-taxes(ws-i) to total-Taxes
                                      in store-get-Pos-Totals-args


     *
     **   Now store this element of the sequence.  If the
     **   current length exceeds the maximum length then
     **   the SEQSET routine will automatically reallocate
     **   the data buffer to ensure it is large enough to
     **   hold all the data.
     *
              CALL "SEQSET" USING POS-DATA-SEQUENCE OF
                                  STORE-GET-POS-TOTALS-ARGS
                                  WS-I
                                  POS-DATA-1 OF
                                  STORE-GET-POS-TOTALS-ARGS
              MOVE WS-I        TO SEQUENCE-LENGTH OF
                                  STORE-GET-POS-TOTALS-ARGS
              PERFORM CHECK-STATUS
          end-perform

          CALL "ORBPUT"        USING STORE-GET-POS-TOTALS-ARGS
          .
```

As always, we start off with a call to the mandatory ORBGET routine. In this case, there are no input parameters to be placed into the parameter area, but we should still always make the call.

The first thing to do is to construct the sequence that is to hold the StoreAccess details that are to be returned. The SEQUENCE-MAXIMUM is set to the maximum size possible, and SEQUENCE-LENGTH is set to 0. The SEQUENCE-TYPE is then set using a call to STRSET to set the typecode value for the sequence. Finally, ORBALLOC is used to create a buffer large enough to hold the sequence data. The empty sequence is now ready. Note that in this specific example, the method of sequence construction is a bit more complicated than the mechanism described in the latest CORBA mapping for COBOL. This is because the new, simpler approach has not yet been implemented; hence, the example uses the older, more complicated mechanism. In the newer mapping, all of the preceding is done with just one call to SEQALLOC.

Each StoreAccess element found within the Store state will have its details inserted into one instance of a sequence element. SEQSET will then be called to insert the sequence element into the sequence buffer.

Finally, ORBPUT is called to return the sequence to the caller.

Store Method: Update-Store-Totals

The third of the three Store interface operations, Update-Store-Totals, is used to locate a specific StoreAccess element held in this Store's state and update its totals with the input values supplied. The accumulated totals for the entire store are also updated with input values.

```
     *-------------------------------------------------------------
     *      UpdateStoreTotals
     *-------------------------------------------------------------
      DO-STORE-UPDATE-STORE-TOTALS.
          CALL "ORBGET"    USING STORE-UPDATE-STORE-TOTALS-ARGS

          perform varying ws-i from 1 by 1
                  until ws-i > array-count
                      or access-id in posarray (ws-i) =
                          idl-id
                            in STORE-UPDATE-STORE-TOTALS-ARGS
          end-perform
          if array-count = MAX-POSLIST-ENTRIES
              display "Store::UpdateStoreTotals: "
                      "Could not locate POS Terminal "
                      idl-id in STORE-UPDATE-STORE-TOTALS-ARGS
          else
              add price in STORE-UPDATE-STORE-TOTALS-ARGS
                                      to ws-Total-sales(ws-i)
              add taxes  in STORE-UPDATE-STORE-TOTALS-ARGS
                                      to ws-Total-taxes(ws-i)
          end-if

          add price in STORE-UPDATE-STORE-TOTALS-ARGS
                                  to StoreTotal in Totals
          add taxes  in STORE-UPDATE-STORE-TOTALS-ARGS
                                  to StoreTaxTotal in Totals

          CALL "ORBPUT"    USING STORE-UPDATE-STORE-TOTALS-ARGS
          .
```

Once again we start off with a call to the ORBGET routine to populate the parameter area with all the input parameters for this operation. For this operation, this includes the specific identifier for a StoreAccess instance, and the price and tax values that are to be used for the update.

The array of StoreAccess elements held within the Store's state is searched for an entry that matches the identifier passed in as a parameter. If not found, an error message is issued; otherwise, the totals in the StoreAccess element are updated. The accumulated totals for the entire store are also updated.

Finally, ORBPUT is called to return to the caller.

32.2.4.5 The StoreAccess Interface Implementation

The last of the three interfaces we'll look at in detail is the **StoreAccess** interface. We once again follow the pattern we used for the previous two interfaces. This means that we start off by looking at how the state of the **StoreAccess** Interface is held and also how its initialization is performed. We then move on to see how it invokes the correct paragraph for inbound requests, and finally look at the actual implementation of the one operation defined within the interface.

StoreAccess Instance State

The state of the **StoreAccess** instance is held in the following structure within COBOL working storage:

```
DATA DIVISION.
WORKING-STORAGE SECTION.

01 StoreAccess-State.
   03 depot-ref            pointer.
   03 tax-ref             pointer.
   03 ws-store-id          pic 9(9) binary.
   03 tax-name            pic x(32).
   03 markup              comp-1.
```

The StoreAccess State includes the object references for the associated **Tax** interface within the same Store server, and also the Depot interface, which is within a different server. Also held here is the unique POS identifier for this StoreAccess. Finally, the markup for the store and the textual name for the associated instance of the Tax interface are also retained here.

Initialization for the StoreAccess Interface

Within the previous implementation of the **Store** interface we discovered that each time the **Store** interface's Login operation is called by a POS server, a new instance of the **StoreAccess** interface is created. The Login operation does this by calling new-StoreAccess. This is the implementation of that function, so we'll now look at it in detail:

```
*===============================================================
*     Access-Init
*===============================================================
 access-init.
 Entry "new-StoreAccess" using lk-markup
                              lk-Store-Id
                              lk-storeAccess-id
                              lk-store-ref
                            .

      CALL "ORBSTAT"   USING ORBIX-STATUS-INFORMATION
      CALL "ORBREQ"    USING StoreAccess-Interface

      move lk-markup        to markup
      move lk-Store-Id      to ws-store-id
      move lk-store-id      to ws-99
      move lk-storeAccess-id to StoreAccess-marker

      move "Tax_"           to    tax-name
      move ws-99            to    tax-name(5:2)
      call "ns-rslv" using tax-name
                         returning tax-ref

      move "Depot"          to ws-data
      call "ns-rslv" using ws-data
```

```
                                returning Depot-ref

     *
     **   Get the stringified object reference string
     *

          move length of store-text to store-text-lth
          CALL "OBJGET" USING lk-store-ref
                              store-TEXT
                              store-TEXT-lth


     *
     **   Decompose the stringified object reference to get at
     **   the host and server name.  We don't care about the
     **   other components of the reference.
     *
          UNSTRING STORE-TEXT DELIMITED BY ":\" OR ":" OR SPACE
              INTO WS-DUMMY-TEXT
                   WS-HOST-TEXT
                   WS-SERVER-TEXT
                   WS-DUMMY-TEXT
                   WS-DUMMY-TEXT
                   WS-DUMMY-TEXT
                   WS-DUMMY-TEXT
          END-UNSTRING


     *
     **   Now create a stringified object reference to represent
     **   this account
     *
          MOVE SPACES            TO WS-OBJ-STRING
          STRING ":\"               DELIMITED BY SIZE
                 WS-HOST-TEXT       DELIMITED BY SPACE
                 ":"                DELIMITED BY SIZE
                 WS-SERVER-TEXT     DELIMITED BY SPACE
                 ":::IR:"           DELIMITED BY SIZE
                 WS-StoreAccess-txt DELIMITED BY SPACE
                              INTO WS-OBJ-STRING
          END-STRING


     *
     **   Build reference with a marker
     *
          CALL "OBJSETM" USING ws-obj-string
                               storeAccess-marker
                               storeAccess-ref
          perform check-status

          exit program returning storeAccess-ref

          .
```

When first called, the new-StoreAccess routine is called with the unique identifier for the Store, its markup, the store's object reference, and the unique identifier

for this new instance of the StoreAccess interface. The initialization performed will then be as follows:

- ORBREG is called to register the start of activity for an instance of the StoreAccess interface.

- The input parameter values are saved within the StoreAccess State within working storage.

- The ns-rslv routine is called to obtain the object references for both the Tax interface within this server and also the Depot interface that is running within a different server. (The ns-rslv code is discussed in detail in Chapter 29.)

- A unique Object Reference for this instance of the **StoreAccess** interface is created. This is done by first converting the Store object reference into its stringified format, and picking out the host and server names. These are then used together with the StoreAccess identifier to create its stringified Object Reference. Finally, OBJSETM is use to construct a unique Object Reference for this instance of StoreAccess. Note that this mechanism has been simplified in the latest CORBA mapping for COBOL through the use of an OBJNEW function. However, for the tutorial example we are using the currently available implementation of the mapping.

Finally, the new Object Reference for this new instance of StoreAccess is returned to the caller.

Processing Inbound Store Requests

After the generic dispatcher has received an inbound request for the **StoreAccess** interface, it will be passed to the StoreAccess implementation. This is where we need to determine which specific operation within the **StoreAccess** interface has been requested, and call it:

```
IDENTIFICATION DIVISION.
PROGRAM-ID.                               STACCESS.
        . . .


PROCEDURE DIVISION.

        CALL "ORBSTAT"  USING ORBIX-STATUS-INFORMATION.
        CALL "ORBREQ"   USING REQUEST-INFO.
        CALL "STRGET"   USING OPERATION-NAME
                              STOREACCESS-OPERATION-LENGTH
                              STOREACCESS-OPERATION.
        COPY STOREACD.

        GOBACK.
```

The code used to identify the specific operation requested within the **StoreAccess** interface is more or less the same as the code used for the previous **Tax** and **Store** interfaces. The standard ORBREQ call is used to obtain the details of the inbound request. The actual name of the requested operation is extracted from the CORBA String type into the STOREACCESS-OPERATION area by a call to STRGET. Finally, the code within a generated COBOL copy file called STOREACD.CPY is used to perform the requested operation.

Note that the base names for COBOL copy files are restricted to 8 bytes. This means that in instances such as this where the actual interface name exceeds 8 bytes, the name is truncated. This restriction is imposed by the mapping to ensure that it can be used in all COBOL development environments, including some mainframe environments, where the names of COBOL copy files are restricted to 8 bytes in length.

StoreAccess Method: Find-Price

The one and only `StoreAccess` operation, `Find-Price`, accepts an item barcode as input along with a count of the items being transacted. It locates the details for the item, then returns the total value, the tax, and the details of the item as output. If it fails to find the item, an exception is raised.

```
*-------------------------------------------------------------
*    FindPrice
*-------------------------------------------------------------
DO-STOREACCESS-FIND-PRICE.
    display "StoreAccess: findPrice"
    CALL "ORBGET"  USING STOREACCESS-FIND-PRICE-ARGS.


*
*    Call Depot::FindItemInfo to get item details
*
    move ws-store-id
                to store-Id
                    in Depot-Find-Item-Info-args
    set item1 in Depot-Find-Item-Info-args
                to item1 in STOREACCESS-FIND-PRICE-ARGS
    move quantity in STOREACCESS-FIND-PRICE-ARGS
                to quantity1
                    in Depot-Find-Item-Info-args
    set Depot-Find-Item-Info  to true
    call "ORBEXEC" using Depot-ref
                        Depot-Operation
                        Depot-Find-Item-Info-args
    if exception-number not = 0
        display "  unable to find item - Exception = "
                exception-number
        perform check-status
        CALL "ORBERR" USING
                        STOREACCESS-BARCODE-NOT-F-EXID
                        STOREACCESS-BARCODE-NOT-LENGTH
                        STOREACCESS-BARCODE-NOT-FOUND
    else
        move item-info   in Depot-Find-Item-Info-args
                    to item-info
                        in STOREACCESS-FIND-PRICE-ARGS
        set idl-Name in STOREACCESS-FIND-PRICE-ARGS
                    to idl-Name
                        in Depot-Find-Item-Info-args
        set item      in STOREACCESS-FIND-PRICE-ARGS
```

```
                       to item in Depot-Find-Item-Info-args


*
*          Calculate the price based on cost + store
*          specific markup percentage
*
           compute item-price in STOREACCESS-FIND-PRICE-ARGS
              = item-cost in Depot-Find-Item-Info-args +
                (item-cost
                   in Depot-Find-Item-Info-args * markup)


*
*          Call the tax server to obtain taxable amount of
*          price
*
           move item-price in STOREACCESS-FIND-PRICE-ARGS
                   to Item-Price
                      in Tax-Find-Taxable-Price-ARGS
           move item-Type in STOREACCESS-FIND-PRICE-ARGS
                   to Item-Type
                      in Tax-Find-Taxable-Price-ARGS
           set TAX-FIND-TAXABLE-PRICE  to true
           call "ORBEXEC" using Tax-ref
                               Tax-Operation
                               Tax-Find-Taxable-Price-ARGS
           perform check-status
           move result in Tax-Find-Taxable-Price-ARGS
                   to Item-Tax-Price
                      in STOREACCESS-FIND-PRICE-ARGS
      end-if

      CALL "ORBPUT"  USING STOREACCESS-FIND-PRICE-ARGS
      .
```

The standard ORBGET routine is called to populate the parameter area with all the input parameters for this operation. This includes the unique barcode for the item and the number of items of that type that are being processed.

The Find-Item-Info operation within the **Depot** interface is called with a call to ORBEXEC to obtain the details of the requested Item. If it is not found, then an exception will be raised by Find-Item-Info. In response to such an exception, ORBERR will be called to raise an exception for the caller of this operation.

If the item information is successfully located, the returned details are set up in the output area for this operation. The total cost is then calculated by adding in the store markup to the price of the item. The Find-Taxable-Price operation within the **Tax** interface is called with a call to ORBEXEC to obtain the taxable price, and the returned value is then set up in the operation's output area.

Finally, ORBPUT is called to return all the accumulated results to the caller.

Now that we have reached the end of this method implementation, we have also reached the end of the COBOL tutorial for the Store server. Congratulations!

Programming the POSTerminal in C++

33.1 Language-Independent Overview

This is the last module—the physical points-of-sale (POS) terminals in each store. Once more, this section is for everyone, regardless of which programming language you're using. It adds implementation detail to the A&D for the POS, going as far as it can without becoming language-specific—algorithms, file formats, data flow details. At the end of this section, we'll split into language-specific chapters.

Here are the CORBA features used for the first time (well, almost) in this module:

- CORBA objects with a user interface, making CORBA calls in response to user input
- CORBA object with only client interfaces—no BOA linkage
- Local CORBA objects (okay, okay, not for the first time)

We avoided use of a Graphical User Interface (GUI) for simplicity (well, not completely), even though we believe that this is the best way to access most applications, including ones based on CORBA. If you're looking for a programming exercise, try modifying your POS module to use a GUI. This will make a more impressive-looking demo, even though it doesn't have much to do with CORBA. It will, at least, demonstrate that CORBA and the GUI that you choose can run together in the same module.

There is one POS for each sales position in the store, and each POS is used by one salesperson. Its inputs come from a barcode reader and from a keypad, and it outputs printed receipts for the customers of the store.

An implementation of the POS must handle these two inputs, communicate as required with the `Store` object local to its store, print receipts, and record brief sales statistics. In this book, the POS is implemented as a CORBA client called `POS_Client` for C++ and `PosClient` for Java, and a server called `POS_Server` for C++ and `PosServer` for Java. This client and server form a unit, and this pair should be run on each physical POSTerminal.

The `POS_Server` server contains a single object of interface **OutputMedia** that prints receipts. It has one operation defined as follows:

```
interface OutputMedia
{
    boolean output_text(in string string_to_print );
};
```

The implementation of the **OutputMedia** object is therefore very straightforward, and in particular it does not interpret the strings that it prints.

Internally, `POS_Client` contains two CORBA objects, one each of interfaces **POSTerminal** and **InputMedia**. The `POSTerminal` object implements the main functionality of the POSTerminal; in particular, it communicates with the `Store` object to find prices, it records statistics, and it prints receipts by invoking the **output_text()** operation on the `OutputMedia` object in `POS_Server`.

The **InputMedia** object in `POS_Client` handles the inputs. It has two operations, one to accept inputs from the barcode reader and the other to accept inputs from the keypad, defined as follows:

```
interface InputMedia
{
    typedef string OperatorCmd;
    void barcode_input(in Barcode item);
    void keypad_input (in OperatorCmd cmd);
};
```

Since our development machines are not equipped with these special input devices, the code in this book uses a simple input reader. This reads lines of input from a normal computer keyboard and passes them to the **InputMedia** object. Strings of digits are interpreted as barcodes, and are passed to **barcode_input()**; other input is passed, uninterpreted, using **keypad_input()**.

The `POS_Client` process creates the **POSTerminal** and **InputMedia** objects, and gives the **InputMedia** object a reference to the `POSTerminal` object so that it can make operation calls on it. These two objects are always collocated in this example, showing how CORBA supports distribution transparency; objects are used in the same way whether they are local or remote.

The relationship between the components on each POSTerminal is shown in Figure 33.1. The **OutputMedia** object is in a separate server that runs on the same machine as the corresponding **POSTerminal** and **InputMedia**. Once it is created, the **OutputMedia** object is registered with the CORBA Naming Service. The **POSTerminal** object uses the

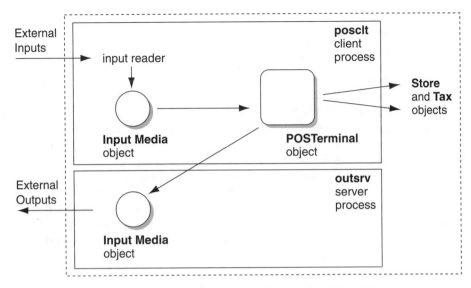

Figure 33.1   Components of each POSTerminal and their relationships.

Naming Service to find the **OutputMedia**, **Store**, and **Tax** objects it needs (it uses one of each of these three types). These three objects are named as follows within the CORBA Naming Service:

OutputMedia object. `"OutputMedia_"` appended with the point-of-sale identifier (decimal number).

Store object. `"Store_"` appended with the store identifier (decimal number).

Tax object. `"Tax_"` appended with the store identifier (decimal number).

Each Store is given a unique identifier in the system, and each POS is given a unique identifier within its Store.

The **POSTerminal** interface defines six operations:

```
interface POSTerminal
{
    void login();
    void print_store_sales_summary();
    void print_POS_sales_summary();
    void send_barcode (in Barcode item);
    void item_quantity(in long quantity);
    void end_of_sale();
};
```

Each of these is invoked by the **InputMedia** object, which is collocated with the **POSTerminal** object. The **InputMedia** object sends barcodes to the **POSTerminal** object using the **send_barcode()** operation. Keypad input is parsed by the **InputMedia** object and sent to the **POSTerminal** object using one of the five other operations.

The implementation of **login()** requires the **POSTerminal** object to invoke the **login()** operation on its **Store** object. In order to be able to implement the

print_POS_sales_summary() operation, the **POSTerminal** object must record its own sales and tax totals; the implementation of this operation outputs these values using the **OutputMedia** object.

The implementation of the **print_store_sales_summary()** operation communicates with the local **Store** object to find the store's sales and tax totals and also the sales and tax figures for each **POSTerminal** connected to the store. This data is then formatted and output, again via the **OutputMedia** object.

The **item_quantity()** operation is called by the **InputMedia** object when the salesperson uses the keypad to indicate that more than one instance of an item is being purchased. The **POSTerminal** must remember this value (the **quantity** parameter) and use it on the next invocation of the **send_barcode()** operation. It then communicates with the **Store** object to find information about the item being purchased; in particular, the price. A line describing the purchase is then output via the **OutputMedia** object.

The **end_of_sale()** operation communicates with the **Tax** object to calculate the tax due on the overall sale, and then it outputs a sales summary, via the **OutputMedia** object, at the end of the receipt.

It is also important that the **POSTerminal** object knows whether it is currently logged on to the **Store** object. It should ignore all other operation calls until the **login()** operation has been called.

33.1.1 Command-Line Arguments

Each physical POSTerminal contains one `POS_Client` client and one `POS_Server` server. Each one needs to know its unique *POS number* so that it can distinguish itself from the other POSTerminals. Therefore, these two programs take a POS number as a command-line argument. In addition, the **POSTerminal** object in the `POS_Client` must know which `Store` object to communicate with; hence, the `POS_Client` program also takes a **Store** number as a command-line argument. The **POSTerminal** object appends this Store number to the string `"Store_"` when searching for the correct Store using the CORBA Naming Service. The command-line arguments are:

- `POS_Client`: `Store_number`, `POS_number`, and optionally any vendor-specific options
- `POS_Server`: `POS_number`, and optionally any vendor-specific options

This concludes the language-independent discussion of the POS implementation. If you are coding in C++, keep reading. For Java, skip to Chapter 34; for COBOL, go to Chapter 35.

33.2 C++ Generated from the POS IDL Definitions

This section, and the one that follows, present C++ language code for the Store module that is common to every C++ language ORB.

The declarations we present here are probably in a file with a name like POS.h (the exact name for your product was listed in its section of Chapter 27), produced by your IDL compiler so you won't have to type them in yourself. However, you will need to be aware of their form (which is dictated by the standard OMG IDL C++ language mapping) when you connect with the stubs and skeletons. This section contains the details you need to know.

When we finish coding the common functionality, we'll split into ORB-specific sections as before.

The POS IDL module starts out with the definitions:

```
module POS
{
    typedef long   POSId;
    typedef string Barcode;
```

These become, in C++:

```
namespace POS     // or class POS

    typedef CORBA::Long        POSId;
    typedef char*              Barcode;
```

The two typedef definitions translate into C++ equivalents of the same name. The types become CORBA::Long (a 32-bit type) and char*, respectively. Each of the three IDL interfaces—**InputMedia**, **OutputMedia**, and **POSTerminal**—translate into a C++ class. We'll discuss these next, one per subsection.

33.2.1 InputMedia

Interface **InputMedia** is defined as:

```
interface InputMedia {
    typedef string OperatorCmd;
    void barcode_input(in Barcode item);
    void keypad_input(in OperatorCmd cmd);
};
```

It is translated into the following C++:

```
class InputMedia :public CORBA::Object
public:
    virtual void barcode_input(const char* item=0);
    virtual void keypad_input(const char* cmd=0);

;
```

Since interface **InputMedia** defines the new type OperatorCmd, this typedef is translated into its equivalent in C++. Each of the two operations **barcode_input()** and **keypad_input()** are translated into public member functions. The C++ parameter types are straightforward translations of their IDL counterparts.

33.2.2 OutputMedia

Interface **OutputMedia** is defined as:

```
interface OutputMedia {
    boolean output_text (in string string_to_print);
};
```

It is translated into the following C++:

```
class OutputMedia : public CORBA::Object
public:
    virtual CORBA::Boolean output_text(const char* string_to_print=0);
;
```

As usual, the operation **output_text()** is translated into a public member function of the same name. The return type becomes CORBA::Boolean, which is defined in the header file CORBA.h.

33.2.3 POSTerminal

Interface POSTerminal is defined as:

```
interface POSTerminal {
    void login();
    void print_POS_sales_summary();
    void print_store_sales_summary();
    void send_barcode (in Barcode Item);
    void item_quantity (in long quantity);
    void end_of_sale();
};
```

It is translated into the following in C++:

```
class POSTerminal : public CORBA::Object
public:
    virtual void login ();
    virtual void print_POS_sales_summary ();
    virtual void print_store_sales_summary ();
    virtual void send_barcode
                    (const char* item);
    virtual void item_quantity
                    (CORBA::Long quantity);
    virtual void end_of_sale ();
;
```

Each of the IDL operations is translated into a public member function. The parameter to operation **send_barcode()** translates to the simple string type in C++, which is char*. The parameter to function item_quantity() is the 32-bit type CORBA::Long.

This completes the presentation of the C++ declarations generated by the IDL compiler. Now we need to implement the functionality of these interfaces. We'll do that in the next section.

Table 33.1 Components making up the POSTerminal

COMPONENT	DESCRIPTION
PosTerminalImpl	Implementation of **POSTerminal** Interface
InputMediaImpl	Implementation of **InputMedia** Interface
OutputMediaImpl	Implementation of **OutputMedia** Interface
POS_Server	Main control for POS Server
POS_Client	Main control for POS Client

33.3 Common POS Implementation in C++

There's almost nothing ORB-specific about the functionality, so we'll do it all in this section. If you're working the example by hand, type this code into your code files as we go along. At the end of this section, we'll send you off to the section on your specific ORB for final coding, compilation, and linking. Since this is the last module (Hooray!), the only thing left to do after this is to run it; that's in Chapter 36.

The POSTerminal is made up of the components shown in Table 33.1.

Each of the interfaces is implemented by a C++ class.

Two separate processes are created to instance these implementations. The first is POS_Client. It holds one object of type POSTerminal and one object of type Input-Media. The latter accepts input from the user and communicates it to the POSTerminal object. This is an example of a local call (within a single address space) between two CORBA objects. The second process is POS_Server, which holds a single object of type OutputMedia. This object is invoked by the POSTerminal object when it wishes to output a line of the sales receipt.

This section explains the implementation of the components of the POSTerminal in the following order:

1. The **POS** client (POS_Client)

2. The **output media** server (POS_Server)

3. The declarations and then implementations of each of the IDL interfaces, in turn

   InputMedia (InputMediaImpl)

   POSTerminal (PosTerminalImpl)

   OutputMedia (OutputMediaImpl)

The code for these is given in the POS directory, and the file names used in this section are relative to that directory.

33.3.1 Implementation of the POS_Client

Here is the code for the POS client, based on the requirements we set down in Chapter 25:

```
1 #include "InputMediaImpl.h"
2 #include "POSTerminalImpl.h"
```

```
 3 #include <stdlib.h>
 4 #include <iostream.h>
 5
 6 // Include Naming Service.
 7 // Each ORB implementation will provide a different header file
 8 // to include.
 9
10
11
12 int main(int argc, char **argv)
13 {
14    if (argc<3) {
15       cerr << "usage: " << argv[0] <<
16          " <Store Number> <POS Number> <vendor specific options>"
17          << endl;
18       return 1;
19    }
20
21    CORBA::ORB_ptr orb;
22    POS::POSTerminal_var ter;
23
24    try {
25       orb  = CORBA::ORB_init(argc, argv);
26
27       CORBA::Object_var obj =
28             orb->resolve_initial_references("NameService");
29       CosNaming::NamingContext_var naming_service =
30             CosNaming::NamingContext::_narrow(obj);
31
32       if (CORBA::is_nil(naming_service)) {
33          cerr << "ERROR: cant narrow naming service" << endl;
34          return 1;
35       }
36
37       cout <<"Creating POSTerminalImpl" << endl;
38       ter = new POSTerminalImpl(naming_service,
39                atol(argv[1]), atol(argv[2]));
40       cout << "Terminal started" <<endl;
41
42    }
43    catch(const CORBA::Exception& ) {
44       cerr << "ERROR Starting POSTerminal Media" << endl;
45       return 1;
46    }
47
48    POS::InputMedia_var input;
49    char caBuff[255];
50
51    try {
52       input = new InputMediaImpl(ter);
53    }
```

```
54      catch(const CORBA::Exception& ) {
55         cerr << "Error starting InputMedia" << endl;
56      }
57
58      cout << "Command Summary :-" << endl;
59      cout <<
60        "L : Login    P : POS Sales Summary    S : Store Sales Summary"
61        << endl;
62      cout <<
63        "T : Total    Q : Quantity            X : Exit"
64        << endl << endl;
65
66      do {
67         cout << "Enter code, command (L,P,Q,S,T) or X to exit : ";
68
69         try {
70            cin.getline(caBuff,250);
71            Int c = cin.gcount();
72
73            for( int ic = 0; ic< c; ic++ ) {
74               if( caBuff[ic] == '\r' ) caBuff[ic] = '\0';
75            }
76
77            if ((caBuff[0] >= '0') && (caBuff[0] <= '9'))
78               input->barcode_input(caBuff);
79            else
80               input->keypad_input(caBuff);
81         }
82         catch(const CORBA::Exception& ) {
83            cerr << "ERROR using Input Media" << endl;
84            caBuff[0] = 'x';
85         }
86      }
87      while (caBuff[0] != 'x' && caBuff[0] != 'X');
88      return 0;
89 }
```

The main function of the POS_Client process starts by initializing the ORB (line 25). It then obtains a reference to the root NamingContext (lines 27–34). Specifically, it calls the ORB's resolve_initial_reference() method, passing the string "NameService" to request the root NamingContext. Since this call returns type CORBA:Object, the object must be narrowed; in this case, it is narrowed to type Cos-Naming::NamingContext_var. Before continuing, a check is made that a non-nil reference has been obtained for the NamingContext.

On line 38, a CORBA object of type POSTerminal is created (by creating a C++ object of class POSTerminalImpl). The constructor arguments to this are the reference to the root NamingContext (this is necessary because the POSTerminalImpl object needs to communicate with the Naming Service), the Store identifier number, and the POS identifier number. Any exceptions thrown while locating the Naming Service or creating the POSTerminal object are caught at line 43.

On line 48, the main function creates its InputMedia object, giving it an object reference for the POSTerminal object. In a real implementation of the system, the InputMedia object would receive input events from the POS's special hardware (the barcode reader and the keypad); however, in our simple implementation, the main function reads the input from the normal keyboard and passes it to the InputMedia object. A menu is first output to the user (lines 58 to 64), and the main function enters a loop on line 66. Once the prompt is written (line 67), a line of input is read on line 70. Each such line is tested, and if it begins with a decimal digit (the test is made on lines 77), the input is treated as a barcode, and is forwarded to the InputMedia object (on line 78) by calling its barcode_input() operation. Otherwise, it is treated as a keypad input and passed without interpretation to InputMedia object by calling its keypad_input() operation. Exceptions thrown while reading input are caught at line 82. The exit condition to terminate (input character x or X) is tested at line 87.

33.3.2 Implementation of the Output Media Server (POS_Server)

The main function of this server simply creates an object of type OutputMediaImpl, and then calls the standard impl_is_ready() function to inform the ORB that this server is ready to accept incoming operation calls to its objects (in this case, calls to the OutputMediaImpl object):

```
1.  #include "OutputMediaImpl.h"
2.  #include <stdlib.h>
3.  #include <iostream.h>
4.  #include <stdio.h>
5.
6.  // Include Naming Service.
7.  // Each ORB implementation will provide a different header file
8.  // to include.
9.
10. #include <NsPublisher.h>
11.
12. int main(int argc, char* argv[])
13. {
14.     if (argc<2) {
15.         cerr << "usage: " << argv[0] <<
16.             " <POS Number> <vendor specific options>" << endl;
17.         return 1;
18.     }
19.
20.     POS::OutputMedia_ptr outputMedia;
21.
22.     try {
23.         CORBA::ORB_ptr orb  = CORBA::ORB_init(argc, argv);
24.         CORBA::BOA_ptr boa  = orb->BOA_init(argc, argv,"");
25.
26.         CORBA::Object_var obj =
```

```
27.                    orb->resolve_initial_references("NameService");
28.        CosNaming::NamingContext_var naming_service =
29.                CosNaming::NamingContext::_narrow(obj);
30.
31.        if (CORBA::is_nil(naming_service)) {
32.            cerr << "ERROR: cant narrow naming service" << endl;
33.            return 1;
34.        }
35.
36.        long posID = atol(argv[1]);
37.
38.        outputMedia = new OutputMediaImpl();
39.
40.        // Publish OutputMedia to the Naming Service
41.        char regStr[256];
42.        sprintf(regStr,"OutputMedia_%ld", posID);
43.
44.        try {
45.            NsPublisher::nsBind(naming_service,
46.                    outputMedia, regStr, "Primer_Example" );
47.        }
48.        catch(const NsPublisherException& npe) {
49.            cerr << npe.toString() << endl;
50.            return 1;
51.        }
52.
53.        // Everything is ok at this point.
54.        // Wait for incomming requests.
55.        boa->impl_is_ready("POS_Server");
56.
57. }
58.    catch (const CORBA::Exception& )
59.    {
60.        cout <<
61.         "CORBA::Exception caught. ERROR Starting OutputMedia  Server"
62.          << endl;
63.        return 1;
64.    }
65.    return 0;
66. }
```

At line 10 an ORB-specific file is included. The included code defines the NSPub-lisher class. As previously explained, this class is a wrapper for the NamingCon-text instance. The ORB is initialized on lines 26 and 27. The root NamingContext is located (lines 28 to 33). The OutputMedia object is created on line 38. At line 42 a unique registration string is created containing the POSId of this instance, and at line 45 the NSPublisher class is used to bind the instance in the NamingContext to the registration string. The impl_is_ready() function is passed the server name (line 55). The server is then ready to accept operation invocations on its objects.

33.3.3 InputMedia Implementation: Class Declaration

Interface **InputMedia** is implemented by the C++ class `InputMediaImpl`. The sole member variable is a pointer to the `POSTerminal` object that is to be used; this variable is initialized by the constructor. The two member functions correspond to the two operations of the InputMedia IDL interface:

```
#include "POS.hh"

class InputMediaImpl:
        // inherits from orb specific skeleton class
        public virtual ::POS::InputMedia_Skeleton;

private:
    POS::POSTerminal_var  m_POSTerminalRef;
    static void _abort(const char *msg);


public:
    InputMediaImpl(POS::POSTerminal_ptr pTer);
    virtual void barcode_input (const char* item);
    virtual void keypad_input (const char* cmd);
;
```

33.3.4 InputMedia Implementation: Class Implementation

The `InputMediaImpl` has a private `_abort` method that is coded to simply print the `msg` parameter to standard error and exit.

```
#include <iostream.h>
#include <stdlib.h>
#include <ctype.h>
#include "InputMediaImpl.h"


void InputMediaImpl::_abort(const char* msg) {
    cerr << msg << endl << flush;
    exit(1);
}
```

The constructor of `InputMediaImpl` is coded simply by initializing the `m_POSTerminalRef` member variable to the value passed as a parameter. The parameter is duplicated because the destructor of the `m_POSTerminalRef` object reference will automatically release (reduce the reference count by 1) the object that it references.

```
InputMediaImpl::InputMediaImpl(POS::POSTerminal_ptr pTer)
{
    // we will comunicate with the following terminal
```

```
      m_POSTerminalRef = POS::POSTerminal::_duplicate(pTer);
}
```

The `barcode_input()` operation is coded simply by calling the `send_barcode()` operation on the `POSTerminal` object, and then checking for any errors.

```
void  InputMediaImpl::barcode_input(const char *item)
{
   try
   {
      m_POSTerminalRef->send_barcode(item);
   }
   catch (const AStore::BarcodeNotFound &)
   {
      _abort("Error in Sending barcode");
   }
}
```

The `keypad_input()` function is passed a command (defined to be of type `POS::InputMedia::OperatorCmd`, which is a string). It tests the first character and uses the function shown in Table 33.2 to recognize the command to be executed. The `InputMedia` object itself does not process commands; instead, it simply calls the correct operation on the `POSTerminal` object.

The characters q and Q are followed by the actual quantity setting, as a string of digits. These digits are converted to an integer value before calling the `item_quantity()` operation on the `POSTerminal` object. The other commands are not followed by any input values.

Table 33.3   POSTerminal Commands and Functions

CHARACTERS	MEANING	FUNCTION TO CALL ON THE POSTERMINAL OBJECT
L or l	Login	`Login()`
P or p	Print POS sales summary for this POS	`print_POS_sales_summary()`
S or s	Print store sales summary for the whole store	`Print_store_sales_summary()`
T or t	End the sale of items to this customer	`End_of_sale`
Q or q	Set the quantity of the item being purchased	`Item_quantity()`

The `keypad_input()` function has therefore been coded as follows:

```
void  InputMediaImpl::keypad_input(const char *cmd)
{
    char *pStr = new char[255];
    strcpy(pStr, cmd);
    try {
        long lTot = 0;
        switch(toupper(*pStr)) {
            default : cerr << "Invalid entry" << endl;
            break;
            case 'X': break;
            case 'L': m_POSTerminalRef->login();
            break;
            case 'P': m_POSTerminalRef->print_POS_sales_summary();
            break;
            case 'S': m_POSTerminalRef->print_store_sales_summary();
            break;
            case 'T': m_POSTerminalRef->end_of_sale();
            break;
            case 'Q': {
                char* temp_pStr = pStr;
                while(*(++temp_pStr) == ' ');
                lTot = atol(temp_pStr);
                m_POSTerminalRef->item_quantity(lTot);
            }
            break;
        }

        delete [] pStr;

    }
    catch(const CORBA::Exception& ) {
        delete [] pStr;
        cerr << "CORBA::Exception caught in InputMediaImpl::keypad_input"
          << endl;
        _abort("Error in transmitting command");
    }

}
```

In order to simplify the `switch` statement, the function `toupper()` is used to convert the first input character to uppercase. The switch condition for `Q` converts the rest of the input line to an integer value, and then passes this to the `item_quantity()` operation.

33.3.5 POSTerminal Implementation: Class Declaration

The code for the **POSTerminal** interface is shown next. Its member functions correspond to the IDL operations defined in its interface, with the addition of a constructor. Its member variables will be explained shortly.

```
#include "POS.hh"
#include "Store.hh"
#include "PNS.hh"

//-----------POSTerminal -------------
    class POSTerminalImpl :
            // inherits from orb specific skeleton class
            public virtual   ::POS::POSTerminal_Skeleton
  {

  private:
    POS::Barcode_var  m_itemBarcode;
    CORBA::Long    m_itemquantity;
    AStore::Tax_var     m_taxRef;
    AStore::Store_var  m_storeRef;
    AStore::StoreAccess_var m_storeAccessRef;
    POS::OutputMedia_var    m_outputMediaRef;
    CORBA::Float m_itemExtension;
    CORBA::Float  m_saleSubTotal;
    CORBA::Float  m_saleTaxableSubTotal;
    CORBA::Float  m_POSTotal;
    CORBA::Float  m_POSTaxTotal;
    CORBA::Long   m_id;

    unsigned char _loggedIn();
    static void _abort(const char *msg);

  public:
    POSTerminalImpl(CosNaming::NamingContext_ptr naming_service,
                CORBA::Long storeid,  POS::POSId id);

    void login ();
    void print_POS_sales_summary ();
    void print_store_sales_summary ();
    void send_barcode (const char* item);
    void item_quantity (CORBA::Long quantity);
    void end_of_sale ();
    };
```

The member variables of class `POSTerminalImpl` are explained in Table 33.3.

Table 33.3 Member Variables of Class POSTerminalImpl

NAME	DESCRIPTION
m_itemBarcode	The current barcode (identifying the item currently being purchased at this POSTerminal).
m_itemquantity	This is the number of items of a given type that are currently being purchased. This variable is

Continued

Table 33.3   *(Continued)*

NAME	DESCRIPTION
	initialized to 1, and it is changed by the `item_quantity()` operation. The `send_barcode()` operation, which signals to the POSTerminal that an item is being purchased, assesses this variable to determine how many of this item are being purchased. The variable is then reset to value 1.
m_taxRef	The object reference of the `Tax` object. This is initialized in the constructor of the `POSTerminal` object, by searching for the correct Tax object using the Naming Service.
m_storeRef	The object reference of the `Store` object. This is initialized in the constructor of the `POSTerminal` object, by searching for the correct `Store` object using the Naming Service.
m_storeAccessRef	The object reference of the `StoreAccess` object. The `login()` operation on the `POSTerminal` logs the `POSTerminal` into the `Store` object. The Store object returns an object reference to a newly created `StoreAccess` object, through which the `POSTerminal` subsequently accesses the store information.
m_outputMediaRef	The object reference of the `OutputMedia` object to which to print receipts and reports. This is initialized in the constructor of the `POSTerminal` object, by searching for the correct `OutputMedia` object using the Pseudo-Naming Service.
m_saleSubTotal	The sales total so far for the sale to the current customer.
m_saleTaxableSubTotal	The sales tax so far for the sale to the current customer.
m_POSTotal	This POS's total sales since power up.
m_POSTaxTotal	This POS's total tax since power up.
m_id	This POS's identifier (a unique number within the Store that the POS uses). This is passed to the process as a command-line argument.

33.3.6 POSTerminal Implementation: Class Implementation

The main actions of each of the member functions are as follows. The description of each function is followed by the C++ code to implement it.

33.3.7 POSTerminalImpl()

POSTerminalImpl has a private _abort method that is coded to simply print the
msg parameter to standard error and exit:

```
#include <stdio.h>
#include <iostream.h>
#include <stdlib.h>
#include "POSTerminalImpl.h"
#include <NsPublisher.h>


void POSTerminalImpl::_abort(const char* msg) {
   cerr << msg << endl << flush;
   exit(1);
}
```

This constructor initializes the m_taxRef, m_storeRef, and m_outputMediaRef
member variables by binding to the correct Tax, Store, and OutputMedia objects,
respectively. It uses the Naming Service to find each object, using the following strings,
respectively: "Tax_"<Store_identifier>, "Store_"<Store_identifier>,
"OutputMedia_"<POS_identifier>. Finally, it initializes the other member variables:

```
POSTerminalImpl::POSTerminalImpl(CosNaming::NamingContext_ptr ns,
        CORBA::Long storeid, POS::POSId id){
// Load in the stringified object references from the files and
// construct references to these objects
   char caStr[512];
   sprintf(caStr, "Tax_%ld", storeid);
   CORBA::Object_var taxObj;
   try {
      taxObj = NsPublisher::nsResolve(ns, caStr, "Primer_Example");
   }
   catch(const NsPublisherException& npe) {
     _abort(npe.toString());
   }

   m_taxRef = AStore::Tax::_narrow(taxObj);


   sprintf(caStr, "Store_%ld", storeid);
   CORBA::Object_var storeObj;
   try {
      storeObj = NsPublisher::nsResolve(ns, caStr, "Primer_Example");
   }
   catch(const NsPublisherException& npe) {
     _abort(npe.toString());
   }

   m_storeRef = AStore::Store::_narrow(storeObj);


   sprintf(caStr,"OutputMedia_%ld", id);
   CORBA::Object_var outputObj;
```

```
try {
    outputObj = NsPublisher::nsResolve(ns, caStr, "Primer_Example");
}
catch(const NsPublisherException& npe) {
    _abort(npe.toString());
}
m_outputMediaRef = POS::OutputMedia::_narrow(outputObj);
// Make sure all the _narrow calls succeeded
if( CORBA::is_nil(m_taxRef) || CORBA::is_nil(m_storeRef)
  || CORBA::is_nil(m_outputMediaRef) ) {
    // Just exit for the demo, in real life it would be better
    // to raise an exception.
      _abort("ERROR: POSTerminal failed to narrow objects"
          "from Naming Service");
}
// Initialize the member variables to their appropriate values
m_itemBarcode = (char*)0;
m_storeAccessRef = AStore::StoreAccess::_nil();
m_id = id;
m_POSTaxTotal = m_POSTotal = 0.0;
m_saleTaxableSubTotal = m_saleSubTotal = 0.0;
}
```

33.3.8 login()

This function calls the **login()** operation on the **Store** object, tests for errors, and then initializes the member variables to their correct state for the start of a sales session for a customer. The return value of the **login()** operation is assigned to the **m_StoreAccessRef** member variable. The **login()** operation on the store is called, and this returns a reference to a **StoreAccess** object, which is used when the **POSTerminal** subsequently needs to find the price of an item. The first few lines ensure that the **login()** function has no effect if the **POS** is already logged in.

```
void POSTerminalImpl::login{
    if (!CORBA::is_nil(m_storeAccessRef)) {
        cerr << "Cant log in twice" << endl;
        return;
    }

    // Get a reference to the StoreAccess object for this POS
    try
    {
        m_storeAccessRef = m_storeRef->login(m_id);
    }
    catch (const CORBA::Exception& )
    {
        _abort("CORBA::Exception caught. Error in Login");
    }

    m_saleSubTotal = m_POSTotal = m_POSTaxTotal = 0.0;
    m_itemQuantity = 1;
}
```

33.3.9 print_POS_sales_summary()

The result of calling this function is the writing of a single line to the receipt containing the POS total sales and the POS total tax. The output is constructed using the **sprintf()** library function, and output using the **output_text()** operation of the **OutputMedia** object.

This function returns immediately without doing any work if the **POSTerminal** is currently handling a sale. That is, we do not allow the sales totals to be printed while a customer's items are being rung up. The function determines whether it is handling a sale by testing the m_itemBarcode and m_saleSubTotal member variables. If either of these is nonzero, then the terminal must be handling a sale.

```cpp
void POSTerminalImpl::print_POS_sales_summary() {
    if (!_loggedIn())
        return;
    if ((m_itemBarcode != 0) || (m_saleSubTotal != 0.0))
        return;
    char caOpStr[255];
    sprintf(caOpStr,"%25s %8.2f\n%25s %8.2f\n",
                "Point of Sale Total := ",
                m_POSTotal, "Tax Total := ",m_POSTaxTotal);
    try
    {
        m_outputMediaRef->output_text(caOpStr);
    }
    catch (const CORBA::Exception& )
    {
        _abort("CORBA::Exception caught. Error printing Sales Summary");
    }
}
```

33.3.10 print_store_sales_summary()

This function communicates with the POSTerminal's Store object, calling **StoreTotal()** and **StoreTaxTotal()**, to find the Store's sales totals, and it then outputs these using the **output_text()** operation on the **OutputMedia** object (again, it uses the standard **sprintf()** function to construct the string to output).

It then calls the Store's **GetPOSTotals()** operation to find the sales totals for each of the **POSTerminal** objects connected to the **Store**. Once this operation call returns, the function iterates (using a **for** statement) through the sequence returned in the operation's parameter. To process the sequence, the function determines its length using the **length()** function, and then it constructs a string to output for each entry. There will be one entry for each **POSTerminal** connected to the Store.

The function also returns immediately if the **POSTerminal** is currently handling a sale.

```cpp
void POSTerminalImpl::print_store_sales_summary () {
    if (!_loggedIn()) return;
    if ((m_itemBarcode != 0) || (m_saleSubTotal != 0.0)) return;
    char caOpStr[255];
```

```
        // Find and output the total sales and tax for the store
        AStore::Store::StoreTotals tots;
        try {
            tots = m_storeRef->totals();
        }
        catch(const CORBA::Exception& ) {
            _abort("CORBA::Exception caught. Error finding store Totals");
        }

        sprintf(caOpStr,"%s %7.2f\n%s %7.2f\n",
            " Total Sales :=",tots.store_total,
            " Total Tax   :=",tots.store_tax_total);
        try {
            m_outputMediaRef->output_text("STORE TOTALS");
            m_outputMediaRef->output_text(caOpStr);
        }
        catch(const CORBA::Exception& ) {
            _abort("CORBA::Exception caught. Error with Output Media");
        }

        // Output the Totals for each POS in turn
        AStore::POSList_var pList;
        try {
            m_storeRef->get_POS_totals(pList);
        }
        catch(const CORBA::Exception& ) {
            _abort("CORBA::Exception caught. Error Getting Store Totals");
        }

        for (CORBA::ULong i = 0; i < pList->length(); i++)
        {
            if (pList[i].id > 0) {
                sprintf(caOpStr,"%15s %ld\n%15s %9.2f\n%15s %9.2f\n",
                  "POS   I.D.  :=",pList[i].id," Total Sales :=",
                  pList[i].total_sales," Total Tax :=",
                  pList[i].total_taxes);

                try {
                    m_outputMediaRef->output_text(caOpStr);
                }
                catch(const CORBA::Exception& ) {
                    _abort("CORBA::Exception caught. Error with Output Media");
                }
            }
        }
    }
}
```

33.3.11 send_barcode()

This function handles the purchasing of one or more items of a given type by the current customer. The parameter to the function specifies the barcode of the item being purchased. The number of these items that are being purchased is determined by the object's m_itemquantity member variable. This defaults to 1, but it may have been changed by a preceding call to the item_quantity() operation.

The function's first action is to find the price and other information of the item described by the barcode (using the find_price() operation on the StoreAccess object). If any error occurs (the user-defined BarcodeNotFound exception or a system exception is raised when calling the find_price() operation), it is reported on the standard error output and the purchase quantity is reset to the default of 1.

If all goes well, the price variable passed to the call to find_price() will have been updated to be the price of the item. This is multiplied by the quantity and assigned to the itemExt variable, which in turn is used to update the m_salesSubTotal member variable (which is the record of the amount being spent by the current customer). Then a line is output to summarize the item sale. sprintf() is once again used to construct this output line, which is output using the output_text() operation on the OutputMedia object. The output line gives the item quantity, item barcode, item name, item cost, and total cost (that is, the item cost multiplied by the item quantity). Taxable items are marked with an asterisk on the output lines of the receipt.

Finally, the tax subtotal (m_saleTaxableSubTotal) is updated to reflect the purchase by this customer. The taxablePrice variable (updated as an out parameter by the find_price() operation) is multiplied by the quantity of the current item being purchased, and then added to the m_saleTaxableSubTotal member variable.

```cpp
void POSTerminalImpl::send_barcode(const char *item)
{
    if (!_loggedIn())
        return;

    AStore::ItemInfo_var itemInf;
    CORBA::Float price;
    CORBA::Float taxablePrice;
    m_itemBarcode = item;

    try
    {
        m_storeAccessRef->find_price(m_itemBarcode, m_itemQuantity,
            price, taxablePrice, itemInf);
    }
    catch (const AStore::BarcodeNotFound &)
    {
        m_itemQuantity = 1;
        cerr << "Invalid Barcode Found" << endl;
        return;
    }
    catch(const CORBA::Exception&) {
        _abort("CORBA::Exception caught. Error in find Price");
    }

    CORBA::Float itemExt = (float)m_itemQuantity * price;
    m_saleSubTotal += itemExt;
```

```
char caOpStr[255];
char * szFmtStr;
szFmtStr = "%3d %10s %20s %7.2f %7.2f %s";
sprintf(caOpStr, szFmtStr, m_itemQuantity,
    (const    char*)m_itemBarcode,
    (const char*)itemInf->name, price, itemExt,
    ((taxablePrice > 0.0) ? " *" : "") );
try { m_outputMediaRef->output_text(caOpStr); }
catch (const CORBA::Exception &)
{
    _abort("CORBA::Exception caught. Error with Output Media");
}
m_saleTaxableSubTotal +=
        taxablePrice *   (CORBA::Float)m_itemQuantity;
m_itemQuantity = 1;}
```

33.3.12 item_quantity()

This function simply changes the m_itemquantity member variable, which is used by the next call to the send_barcode() function:

```
void POSTerminalImpl::item_quantity(CORBA::Long quantity){
    if (!_loggedIn())
        return;

    if (quantity > 0)
        m_itemQuantity = quantity;
}
```

33.3.13 end_of_sale()

This function signals that all of the purchases for the current customer have been rung up. It outputs (via the **OutputMedia** object) the total taxable sales made on this occasion, and then it uses the **CalculateTax()** operation of the **Tax** object to determine the corresponding tax. This value is then output, also using the **OutputMedia** object.

The tax value returned by the **CalculateTax()** operation is also used by the **end_of_sale()** function to determine the overall tax total of this sale (m_saleTax + m_saleSubTotal).

The function next outputs the total sale value. Once this is finished, the **POS** can inform the store of the total sale value and total price of this sale using the Store's **UpdateStore-Total()** operation. Finally, the member variables are reset to initial values:

```
void POSTerminalImpl::end_of_sale() {

    char caOpStr[255];
    if (!_loggedIn())
        return;
```

```
sprintf(caOpStr,"Taxable Sub-Total := %8.2f",
    m_saleTaxableSubTotal);
m_outputMediaRef->output_text(caOpStr);
CORBA::Float saleTax =
    m_taxRef->calculate_tax(m_saleTaxableSubTotal);
sprintf(caOpStr,"Taxes            := %8.2f",saleTax);
m_outputMediaRef->output_text(caOpStr);
CORBA::Float saleTotal = saleTax + m_saleSubTotal;
sprintf(caOpStr,"Total            := %8.2f",saleTotal);
m_outputMediaRef->output_text(caOpStr);
m_POSTotal += saleTotal;
m_POSTaxTotal += saleTax;

try {
    m_storeRef->update_store_totals(m_id,saleTotal,saleTax);
}
catch(const CORBA::Exception& ) {
    _abort("CORBA::Exception caught. Error Ending sale");
}

m_saleSubTotal = m_saleTaxableSubTotal = 0;
m_itemQuantity = 1;
m_itemBarcode = (char*)0;
return;
}
```

Class `POSTerminalImpl` also declares a private function `_loggedIn()`. This returns a boolean indication of whether the `login()` operation has been called. Since the effect of the `login()` operation is to set the `m_storeAccessRef` member variable, the return value of `_loggedIn()` can be determined by whether the `m_store-AccessRef` object reference is `nil`. The code is as follows:

```
unsigned char POSTerminalImpl::_loggedIn(){
    if (CORBA::is_nil(m_storeAccessRef)) {
        cerr << "Need to log in first" << endl;
        return 0;
    }
    else
        return 1;
}
```

33.3.14 OutputMedia Implementation: Class Declaration

Interface **OutputMedia** is implemented by class `OutputMediaImpl`, as shown here:

```
class OutputMediaImpl :
            // inherits from orb specific skeleton class
            public virtual ::POS::OutputMedia_Skeleton {
```

```
private:
    static void _abort(const char *msg);
public:
    OutputMediaImpl();
    virtual CORBA::Boolean output_text
                    (const char* string_to_print);
};
```

Its single member function, **output_text()**, corresponds to the operation in the IDL interface definition.

33.3.15 OutputMedia Implementation: Class Implementation

OutputMediaImpl has a private **_abort** method that is coded to simply print the msg parameter to standard error and exit.

```
#include <stdlib.h>
#include <iostream.h>
#include "OutputMediaImpl.h"

void OutputMediaImpl::_abort(const char* msg) {
    cerr << msg << endl << flush;
    exit(1);
}
```

The constructor of OutputMediaImpl is coded as follows:

```
OutputMediaImpl::OutputMediaImpl(){
}
```

The implementation of the **output_text()** function simply prints a single message on standard output:

```
CORBA::Boolean OutputMediaImpl::output_text(
                    const char * stringToPrint)
{
    // Check if the string passed exists and if so, output it
    if (stringToPrint)
        cout << stringToPrint << endl;
    return (CORBA::Boolean) TRUE ;
}
```

33.3.16 Implementation Summary

If you've been typing in the code as you went along, your POS code is nearly complete. You're ready to make just a few adjustments for your specific ORB, and compile and link your POS objects.

33.4 Implementing the POS Using CORBAplus for C++

This section describes the CORBAplus implementation of the POS. The Vertel's Expersoft CORBAplus implementation of the POS component will only need a small number of changes that have already been discussed for the other components. The primary places where the POS implementation differs from the common source base are the base class names, the use of CORBAplus' Event loop object and the include files.

A makefile is provided for both Unix and Windows platforms. We'll give details on how to build the POS component in Section 33.4.5.

The PowerBroker-specific implementation issues are:

- PowerBroker `Includes`
- Base class name
- `BOA::obj_is_ready`
- PowerBroker event loop
- Use of `_out` classes for CORBA `out` and `inout` arguments

Each of these issues was already described in detail in Section 27.4.

33.4.1 InputMediaImpl

The `InputMediaImpl.cpp` source file requires no changes from the common code base. The `InputMediaImpl.h` include file has a couple of modifications from the common code base. The differences in the include files result from the names of the files generated from the `idlc` compiler.

The first difference is:

```
#ifdef EXPERSOFT
#include <POS_s.h>
#include <Store.h>
#else
```

As described in Chapter 26, CORBAplus `idlc` by default generates header files with a `.h` extension and an `_s` suffix for all server side `includes`.

The second difference is in the name of the Servant base class:

```
class InputMediaImpl

#ifdef EXPERSOFT
    : public POS_InputMedia_base_impl
#else
```

CORBAplus follows the naming convention of:

```
<ModuleName>_<InterfaceName>_base_impl.
```

33.4.2 POS_Server.cpp

The POS_Server.cpp source file has the two standard differences that we saw in the other components: CORBAplus-specific include files and use of the CORBAplus event loop class. For completeness, those are listed again here:

```
#ifdef EXPERSOFT
#ifdef WIN32
#include <pbroker/winsvc/winsvc.h>
#else
#include <pbroker/unixsvc/unixsvc.h>
#endif
#include <pbroker/corba/orb.h>
#include <pbroker/corba/boa.h>
#include <pbroker/corba/naming/naming.h>
#endif
```

The other difference from the common code base is, again, in the CORBAplus event loop. Look back to Section 27.3.1.3 for a discussion of the CORBAplus event loop. Again for completeness, the difference is shown here:

```
#ifdef EXPERSOFT
        boa->obj_is_ready( outputMedia, nil);
        XpsEventService eventService;
        eventService.mainloop();
#else
```

The mainloop method will distribute CORBA events and never return control to the caller.

33.4.3 POS_Client

The only difference from the common code in the POS_Client is in the include files, which was discussed in the previous section on POS_Server.

33.4.4 OutputMediaImpl

There are only two differences from the common code in this include file: the necessary include files and the name of the base servant class.

To include the definitions from the POS IDL file, a CORBAplus implementation must include the generated file, POS_s.h.

In the POS_s.h will be the class definition that the OutputMediaImpl must derive from. OutputMediaImpl is defined as:

```
class OutputMediaImpl  : public POS_OutputMedia_base_impl
```

Those are all of the changes necessary for the OutputMediaImpl header file. Next we will look at the source file.

33.4.4.1 OutputMediaImpl.cpp

The `OutputMediaImpl` class implementation does not require any changes from the common code. All the changes were captured in the `OutputMediaImpl` include file.

33.4.4.2 POSTerminalImpl.h

You should be starting to see a pattern here. The include file usually has some differences because of the names of the files generated from the CORBAplus IDL compiler. This is no exception. We have include file name differences, and the base servant class name is different from the common code base.

The necessary include files are:

```
#ifdef EXPERSOFT
#include <pbroker/corba/naming/naming.h>
#else


// Include Store type information via the skeleton.
// The file to include depends on the output of
// your ORBs IDL compiler.
#ifdef EXPERSOFT
#include "Store.h"
#include "POS_s.h"
#endif
```

The `naming.h` include file has all the definitions to use types defined in the Cos-Naming module. The other include files were generated from the CORBAplus IDL compiler and contain all the required definitions.

The base servant class name is:

```
// The super class of your implementation class
// depends on the output of your ORBs IDL compiler.
class POSTerminalImpl : public POS_POSTerminal_base_impl
```

33.4.4.3 POSTerminalImpl.cpp

The `POSTerminalImpl` source file does not require any changes from the common code base.

33.4.5 Compiling and Running

Finally, you will need to compile and link the `POS_Client` and `POS_Server` programs. The object file for the main program should be linked with object files for all the implementations that may be instantiated in your program. Both Unix and Windows makefiles are provided. See Chapter 26 for a description of how to build the example. It is assumed that you have installed CORBAplus for C++ and have `PBHOME` and `PBTMPDIR` environment variables configured correctly. The easiest way to build the

POS_Client and POS_Server is to use the makefiles Makefile.unix.xps or Makefile.win.xps, which are located in the POS directory.

To build the Solaris version at an xterm, type:

```
%make -f Makefile.unix.xps
```

To build the Windows version at a command window, type:

```
%nmake -f Makefile.win.xps
```

See Section 27.3.2.1 for a description of how to run the NameService. You must have a Naming Service and Store_Server running before trying to start the POS_Client and POS_Server.

33.4.5.1 Running the POS_Server

```
%POS_Server 1 -pbinit NameService iiop://localhost:6004/NameServiceRoot
```

The POS_Server option is the POS_Number that it will service.

33.4.5.2 Running the POS_Client

```
%POS_Client 1 1 -pbinit NameService
iiop://localhost:6004/NameServiceRoot
```

The POS_Client options are:

```
POS_Client <Store Number POS_Client should connect to> <POS ID>
```

33.5 IBM Implementation of the POS

The types of changes required for the IBM implementation of the Store are the same as those described for the IBM implementation of the Depot in Section 27.5. You may wish to refer back to that section for review. The remainder of this section simply describes how the same types of changes are made for the implementation of the Store.

In C++, the POSTerminal itself consists of one client and one server. The server contains the OutputMedia object, and the client contains the InputMedia and POSTerminal objects.

33.5.1 Changes to the C++ Code

33.5.1.1 POSClient.cpp

Near the start of the file, include the header for the CORBA Naming Service being used. For the IBM implementation, a simple Naming Service has been implemented in the primer_utils directory to the IDL interface defined in the CosNaming.idl idl file. We include:

```
#include <CosNaming.hh>
```

The ORB and BOA initialization calls near the beginning of main() have been modified to specify that the ORB being initialized is the IBM ORB. This is indicated by the final string parameters "DSOM" and "DSOM_BOA", respectively, in the calls.

```
CORBA::ORB_ptr orb  = CORBA::ORB_init(argc, argv, "DSOM");
CORBA::BOA_ptr boa  = orb->BOA_init(argc, argv, "DSOM_BOA");
```

33.5.1.2 POSServer.cpp

Near the start of the file, include the header for the CORBA Naming Service being used:

```
#include <CosNaming.hh>
```

The ORB and BOA initialization at the beginning of main() is modified to indicate the IBM ORB as follows:

```
CORBA::ORB_ptr orb  = CORBA::ORB_init(argc, argv, "DSOM");
CORBA::BOA_ptr boa  = orb->BOA_init(argc, argv, "DSOM_BOA");
```

An ImplDef is created for this server and used to register the server activation:

```
CORBA::ImplDef * imp = new CORBA::ImplDef ();
imp->set_protocols("SOMD_TCPIP");
boa->impl_is_ready (imp, 0);
```

33.5.1.3 InputMediaImpl, OutputMediaImpl, POSTerminalImpl

You'll need to modify each of the .h and .cpp files for your object implementations in the same way:

Include IBM header files. Each implementation header file includes the necessary IDL-generated header files.

InputMediaImpl.h includes Store.hh.

OutputMediaImpl.h includes POS.hh.

POSTerminalImpl.h includes POS.hh and CosNaming.hh.

Implementations inherit from their <classname>_ skeleton **classes.** Each implementation class (InputMediaImpl, OutputMediaImpl, POSTerminalImpl) inherits from the corresponding IDL-generated <classname>_Skeleton class. For example, in InputMediaImpl.h:

```
class InputMediaImpl : public _sk_POS::_sk_InputMedia
```

Make the corresponding changes in each of the implementation class header files.

33.5.2 Compiling and Linking

The POS server is linked with the client stubs for Central.idl, Store.idl, and Cos-Naming.idl. These are Central_C.cpp, Store_C.cpp, and CosNaming_C.cpp, respectively. Since it serves the POS implementation, it is linked with the server stub for the POS.idl, POS_S.cpp.

The POS client is linked with the client stubs Central_C.cpp, Store_C.cpp, and CosNaming_C.cpp. It is linked with the server stub POS_S.cpp because it implements the POSTerminal interface.

As before, you also need to link with IBM ORB library eomororm.lib.

33.6 Orbix Implementation of the POS

The changes are essentially the same as those described for the Depot in Section 27.6. You should remind yourself of the material in that section before continuing, and refer back to it if you need explanation of the changes.

In C++, the POSTerminal itself consists of one client and one server. The server contains the OutputMedia object, and the client contains the InputMedia and POSTerminal objects. It would be straightforward to run the client and the server code in one process (with or without Orbix support for lightweight threads).

33.6.1 Changes to the C++ Code

33.6.1.1 POSClient.cpp

At the start of the file, include the Orbix Naming Service header file:

```
#include <NamingService.hh>
```

Modify the initialization section at the beginning of main() as follows:

```
CORBA::ORB_ptr orb  = CORBA::ORB_init(argc, argv, "Orbix");
```

33.6.1.2 POSServer.cpp

At the start of the file, include the Orbix Naming Service header file:

```
#include <NamingService.hh>
```

Modify the initialization section at the beginning of main() as follows:

```
CORBA::ORB_ptr orb  = CORBA::ORB_init(argc, argv, "Orbix");
CORBA::BOA_ptr boa  = orb->BOA_init(argc, argv, "Orbix_BOA");
char* server_name = "POSServer";
boa->setServerName(server_name);
boa->setNoHangup(1);
```

Finally, update the call to impl_is_ready to include the server name:

```
boa->impl_is_ready(server_name);
```

33.6.1.3 InputMediaImpl,
OutputMediaImpl, POSTerminalImpl

You'll need to modify each of the `.h` and `.cpp` files for your object implementations in the same way.

Include Orbix header files. Each implementation header file needs to include the necessary IDL-generated header files.

> In `InputMediaImpl.h`, include `Store.hh`.
>
> In `OutputMediaImpl.h`, include `POS.hh`.
>
> In `POSTerminalImpl.h`, include `POS.hh` and `NamingService.hh`.

Inherit from BOAImpl classes. Inherit each of your implementation classes (`InputMediaImpl`, `OutputMediaImpl`, `POSTerminalImpl`) from the corresponding IDL-generated `BOAImpl` class. For example, in `InputMediaImpl.h`:

```
class InputMediaImpl : public POS::InputMediaBOAImpl
```

Make the corresponding changes in each of the header files.

Add `CORBA::Environment` **parameters.** As for the Depot and Store, each IDL operation defined on your objects needs a final `CORBA::Environment` parameter. You can completely ignore this parameter when using C++ exceptions, but it needs to be present to match virtual function signatures. You'll need to modify both `.h` and `.cpp` files to change the signatures.

Here's the complete list of functions to change:

```
InputMediaImpl: barcode_input, keypad_input.
OutputMediaImpl: output_text.
POSTerminalImpl: login, print_POS_sales_summary, print_store_sales
  _summary, send_barcode, item_quantity, end_of_sale.
```

33.6.2 Compiling and Linking

As with the Depot, you should link the POS client and server with `CentralS.cpp`, `POSS.cpp`, `StoreS.cpp`, and `NamingServiceC.cpp`. In fact, you could link the POS client with the client versions of some of these files (`CentralC.cpp`, `StoreC.cpp`), but it does no harm to link with the server versions, and you must link the client with `POSS.cpp` because it implements the **POSTerminal** interface. Even though this interface is not remotely called, the client needs the definition of `POSTerminalBOAImpl`.

As before, you also need to link with Orbix libraries. See the demos with your copy of Orbix for an example of all the libraries required on your system.

33.6.3 Registering the Server

As for the Depot, you'll need to register the POS server with the `orbixd` daemon. The POS server is called `POSServer` and requires one command-line parameter: a POS number (integer), which must be included in the registration. Using the `putit` command you would register the server like this:

```
putit OutputSrv <path_to_executable > <POS_number>
```

Once registered, the server can be started manually or automatically by the Orbix daemon when a client uses one of the objects in the server. You need to run the server once manually so that it can register its objects with the Naming Service. You should use the same command-line arguments as you register with the daemon.

You don't have to register the client. This is the key difference between a server and a client, since clients can implement CORBA objects just like servers. The user (or some non-CORBA agent) always runs a client, whereas a server is registered and may be launched by the daemon. The client requires two command-line arguments: Store number and POS number. These should correspond to the arguments you used when registering the Store and POS servers.

33.7 Implementing the POS Package Using VisiBroker for C++

The Inprise VisiBroker implementation of the POS component will only need a small number of changes. There will be a number of recurring changes that will be required to the common code for each component implemented using the VisiBroker libraries.

Please refer to Section 27.7 for a full description on how to build a component. The following text will assume that you are familiar with the information contained in that section.

33.7.1 Changes to the POS Server Component

The Naming Service is used to register `OutputMedia` objects. The POS server acts as a client to the Naming Service; therefore, the following preprocessor directive must be used to include the Naming Service definitions:

```
#include <CosNaming_c.hh>
```

Once again, in VisiBroker the `osagent` daemon can be used to facilitate locating an instance of the Naming Service. Make sure you have an `osagent` daemon running within your subnet (see the VisiBroker documentation for further information on the `osagent`). The following common code:

```
CORBA::Object_var obj = orb->resolve_initial_references("NameService");
CosNaming::NamingContext_var naming_service =
CosNaming::NamingContext::_narrow(obj);
```

can be replaced with:

```
CosNaming::NamingContext_var naming_service =
CosNaming::NamingContext::_bind();
```

33.7.2 Changes to the POS Client Component

The POS Client is also a client to the Naming Service (indirectly, through POSTerminalImpl). You should make the same modifications as you did with the POS Server component in the POS Client component.

33.7.3 Changes to the Other POS Components

As with the Depot and Store components, the POS implementation code in VisiBroker does not require much change from the common code. The few required changes are with the skeleton class name that must be derived by the implementation, and the header file that must be included for POS component definitions.

The POSTerminal skeleton file must be included when writing the POSTerminalImpl class. This can be done as follows in the POSTerminalImpl.h file:

```
#include <Store_s.hh>
#include <POS_s.hh>
```

Since the POSTerminal uses definitions from both the Store module and the POS module, both header files are included. The other components in the POS package may not be required to include both header files, only the POS_s.hh header file.

This file will include the definition of the POSTerminal skeleton that the POSTerminalImpl class will inherit from. The class inheritance declaration should be as follows:

```
class POSTerminalImpl : public _sk_POS::_sk_POSTerminal
```

The preceding changes must also be applied to the other components in the POS package: InputMediaImpl and OutputMediaImpl.

33.7.4 Compiling the POS Package

When setting up your build environment under a different compiler/platform, you should only have to change the makefiles to reflect the compiler, linker, libraries, and paths on your system.

To run the build of this program, you should do the following:

- Compile the IDL for the POS
- Build the POS

I will assume that you will be using the nmake program. If you are using gmake or some other build system, you should use the equivalent commands. Step 1 is simply a matter of compiling all the IDL files. This should be run from the root project directory, and only be run once for the entire project.

```
prompt> nmake idl
```

This will run idl2cpp on the IDL files and produce four files for each .idl file, two files for the stub(s) and two files for the skeleton(s). The two files are the .hh and

.cpp files. You should never have to modify the files generated by an IDL compiler. I know of a place that sets the files generated by the IDL compiler to 'read-only' in order to prevent the developers from modifying these files.

To compile the POS Server and POS Client, change to the POS directory and compile the POS package.

```
prompt> nmake compile
```

This will produce the object files for the different components. You will not be able to link the program until all the other packages have been implemented. If you have already implemented and compiled the other packages, you can link the program by typing the following in the root project directory:

```
prompt> nmake link
```

This will produce a few executables (.exe files under Win95/98/NT). In the POS directory, you will find two files named POS_Server.exe and POS_Client.exe.

33.8 Implementing the POS Using BEA WLE

The BEA WLE implementation of POS is very different from the implementation of the Depot and the Store. Those two packages are "managed" servers: they are started, monitored, restarted, and stopped by the WLE management tools. There could be many instances of each such server on a single machine or spread across multiple machines. Invocations on them use the WLE engine for rapid dispatch because of the special properties of such servers. POS, on the other hand, is a client. It isn't started at boot time and if it dies, it shouldn't be restarted. It shouldn't be replicated and it is not subject to other performance enhancements.

Since the clients don't need the attributes supplied by a WLE server, it doesn't use the TP Framework. The POS client handles all communication with the ORB and must prepare to operate as a server also, for the three POS objects included. This isn't difficult, but it is different from doing the same thing as the BOA in the common code. This section shows direct use of the CORBA-compliant POA.

(As an aside, we've folded in the functions of the POS::OutputMedia servant into the POS_Client process, just like the POS::InputMedia and POS::POSTerminal servants. Recall that the common code's reason for having POS::OutputMedia in a separate server is that it was supposed to emulate a cash register tape. The common code used a separate window to start the server, and the implementation wrote its output directly to that server's window. In a production system such as BEA WLE, servers don't have windows. They are run as detached processes; indeed, since there might be many copies of the servers running and because they can be on different machines, no single window could be assigned. If there were truly a cash register tape attached to a specific machine, this wouldn't be a problem; we'd run the server on that machine and write to that specialized device. However, a client is different from a pure server: It has a window (a user starts it from an existing window) and the user inputs to that window. The example's emulation of the POSTerminal is fulfilled just as well if the output appears in that same input window. Operationally, this means there is no POS_Server.cpp file and no separate process. The example didn't show anything special for the POA_Server anyway, so no example features are lost. (The POS::Output-putMedia servant is included in POS_client.exe.)

33.8.1 POS_Client

WLE code for the POS differs by using the POA. The way of creating object references is different. The non-common code segments using the POA are:

```
1   PortableServer::POA_ptr root_poa;
2   POS::POSTerminal_var ter;
3   POS::InputMedia_var input;

4   orb  = CORBA::ORB_init(argc, argv, "BEA_IIOP");
5   root_poa = PortableServer::POA::_narrow(orb->
        resolve_initial_references("RootPOA"));
6   root_poa -> the_POAManager() -> activate();
7   Tobj_Bootstrap bootstrap(orb,"");
8   CORBA::Object_var fact_finder_oref =
        bootstrap.resolve_initial_references("FactoryFinder");
9   factory_finder =
        Tobj::FactoryFinder::_narrow(fact_finder_oref);

    // Create a servant for OutputMedia and and activate it
10  OutputMediaImpl* out_servant = new OutputMediaImpl();
11  PortableServer::ObjectId_var temp_Oid = root_poa ->
        activate_object ( out_servant );
12  CORBA::Object* oref = root_poa->create_reference_with_id(
        temp_Oid, POS::_tc_OutputMedia->id() );
13  POS::OutputMedia_var output =
        POS::OutputMedia::_narrow( oref );

    // Create a servant for POSTerminal and activate it
14  POSTerminalImpl* ter_servant = new POSTerminalImpl(
        output, atol(argv[1]), atol(argv[2]));
15  temp_Oid = root_poa ->activate_object ( ter_servant );

16  oref = root_poa->create_reference_with_id(
        temp_Oid, POS::_tc_POSTerminal->id() );
17  ter = POS::POSTerminal::_narrow( oref );

    // Create a servant for InputMedia and activate it
18  InputMediaImpl* input_servant = new InputMediaImpl(ter);
19  PortableServer::ObjectId_var temp_Oid =
        root_poa->activate_object ( input_servant );
20  CORBA::Object* oref = root_poa->create_reference_with_id(
        temp_Oid, POS::_tc_InputMedia->id() );
21  input = POS::InputMedia::_narrow( oref );
```

Although it looks very different, it's mostly the same difference repeated. Line 5 gets the root POA, which has policies that are sufficient for this example. Line 6 activates the POAManager for the root POA, meaning that the POA can start accepting requests.

Lines 7–9 find the factory finder (similar to what we did for the `Store` initialization in a previous chapter), pretty much the same function as the Naming Service; see Section 33.7.3 below for further explanation.

Lines 10–13, 14–17, and 18–21 are completely parallel for the three objects that are implemented in this process, so we explain only the first. Line 10 creates a new instance of the `OutputMediaImpl` servant. (This would have been sufficient for the common code BOA, but is just the start for the POA.) The next three statements activate the object and create an object reference for the `OutputMedia` object. (There are other ways of doing this, but a small variation on what's shown is guaranteed to work in all types of POAs, not just the root POA.) Line 11 activates the object; that is, it associates the servant with an ObjectId, so that whenever the POA receives a request with that Object Id, it will invoke that servant. Since this is the root POA, the POA itself generates the Object Id; for these objects, we don't care what it is, just that it's unique. We use the Object Id returned by the POA to create an object reference in line 12 and then narrow the reference to an `OutputMedia` object reference in line 13. This is a little longer than some vendors' BOA, but it is standardized (meaning portable, which the BOA isn't) and it offers many more possibilities than the BOA. Once you see the pattern, it's easy.

33.8.2 POSTerminal

The code for BEA WLE `POSTerminal` differs in two places. The first is in the constructor:

```
POSTerminalImpl::POSTerminalImpl(POS::OutputMedia_ptr p_output,
                                 CORBA::Long storeid,
                                 POS::POSId id)
```

The first parameter is a reference to the `OutputMedia` object instead of the common code's pointer to a helper function for the Naming Service. Since we have included the `OutputMedia` in this server and know where it is, we don't need to look it up in `POSTerminal`, so we pass it directly into the constructor. The second difference is in the lookup for references.

33.8.3 Finding Object References

POSTerminal and **StoreAccessImpl** differ in the use of the helper function **NsPublisher::resolve** for finding other object references. As noted in the `Depot` section, we don't use the **NsPublisher::bind** function at all since there is an equivalent function available as one statement of code using the TP Framework's Factory Finder (**TP::register**). Since we then look up the object references in a Factory Finder, the **resolve** function signature and code are different. The **resolve** code is shown next. Line 2 shows the variation of the signature from the common code: The only parameter is the name to look up since that's what the Factory Finder uses, rather than the complex structure of the Naming Service. Line 3 does the lookup.

```
1 Tobj::FactoryFinder_var factory_finder;

2 CORBA::Object_ptr NsPublisher::nsResolve(const char * id){
```

```
3   resolveObj = factory_finder->find_one_factory_by_id(id);
4   return resolveObj; }
```

In order to use this single statement, however, the main program had to save the reference to the Factory Finder in static storage. As mentioned in the BEA WLE overview, BEA supplies a small library to each supported client platform to use in making connections with a BEA WLE domain. This small library is necessary because CORBA does not yet have an interoperable way of getting references from an ORB on a machine different from the one being used by the client. What we really would like is something like an extended **ORB::resolve_initial_references** that will get us boot information from an ORB on a different machine. The Interoperable Naming Service, discussed in Chapter 11, is adding this feature to standard CORBA but it won't appear in products until about mid-2000 or so. In the meantime, BEA WLE supplies this small workaround. No matter what platform you use, you can get references to a BEA WLE domain. You do this using the *Bootstrap object*.

Both the Store server and POS client contain this code; in this chapter it's statements 7–9 in the POS_Client section. Line 7 initializes the Bootstrap object using the ORB on this machine and a string pointing to a Listener in the BEA WLE domain. In this case, we've provided a null string, signifying that an environment variable (part of administrative setup for the client) supplies that machine name. Line 8 uses the bootstrap object to get a reference to a Factory Finder, just like **ORB::resolve_initial_reference**. Line 9 narrows, as usual.

CHAPTER

34

Coding the POS in Java

34.1 Java Generated from the POS IDL Definitions

As we've seen, OMG IDL maps rather easily to Java due to the fact that the Java object model provides many similar architectural constructs such as the specialized interface class type, multiple interface (type) inheritance, strong type management, and a well-defined exception-handling system. There are some differences, however, wherever IDL relies on C++-oriented features such as typedefs, which don't exist in the Java language. Details are provided later in this chapter.

This section and the one that follows present Java language code for the **POS** module that is common to every CORBA-compliant Java ORB.

The classes that we present here are probably in a file with a name like `POS\PosClient.java` and `POS\PosServer.java` (the exact name for your product was probably listed in its section of Chapter 26), produced by your IDL compiler so you won't have to type them in yourself. However, you will need to be aware of their form (which is dictated by the standard OMG IDL Java language mapping) when you connect with the stubs and skeletons. This section contains the details you need to know.

When we finish coding the common functionality, we'll split into ORB-specific sections as before.

Recall that the POS components of the example are defined in an IDL module called **POS**:

```
module POS
{

    typedef long   POSId;
    typedef string Barcode;

    interface InputMedia
    {
       typedef string OperatorCmd;

       void      barcode_input(in Barcode    item);
       void      keypad_input( in OperatorCmd cmd);
    };

    interface OutputMedia
    {
       boolean    output_text( in string    string_to_print );
    };

    interface POSTerminal
    {
       void  login();
       void  print_POS_sales_summary();
       void  print_store_sales_summary();
       void  send_barcode(     in Barcode    item);
       void  item_quantity(    in long      quantity);
       void  end_of_sale();
    };

};

#endif /* _POS_IDL_ */
```

This is translated into the following Java interface classes:

```
package POS;


public interface InputMedia extends org.omg.CORBA.Object {
    void barcode_input(String item);
    void keypad_input(String cmd);
}

public interface OutputMedia extends org.omg.CORBA.Object {
    boolean output_text(String string_to_print);
}

public interface POSTerminal extends org.omg.CORBA.Object {
    void login();
    void print_POS_sales_summary();
```

```
void print_store_sales_summary();
void send_barcode(String item);
void item_quantity(int quantity);
void end_of_sale();
}
```

The two **typedef** definitions are translated into Java native language equivalents, since Java does not support the notion of type aliasing via a **typedef** keyword. The types are "unwound" to their primitive type and become `java.lang.int` (a 32-bit type) and `java.lang.String`, respectively. Each of the three IDL interfaces—**Input-Media**, **OutputMedia**, and **POSTerminal**—are translated into a Java interface class that inherits the `CORBA.Object` interface methods. These will be discussed in turn in the remainder of this subsection.

Recall from Chapter 11 that for each of the IDL types, whether object references, primitive types (such as **CORBA::float**), or structured types, the IDL-to-Java compiler also generates `Helper` and `Holder` classes. For example, an `InputMediaHelper` class is generated that provides the `narrow` operation, which allows a client that needs to obtain an `InputMedia` reference to typecast a `CORBA.Object` reference into an `InputMedia`. Likewise, the `InputMediaHolder` class allows a client to receive an `InputMedia` object reference as an **out** parameter.

Java supports access keywords (`public` and `private`) much like the C++ language does. For a Java class, the `public` keyword allows objects outside this package to instantiate and then call methods on the objects within this package.

Each of the three IDL interfaces—**InputMedia**, **OutputMedia**, and **POSTerminal**—is translated into a Java Interface class. These will be discussed in turn in the remainder of this subsection.

34.1.1 InputMedia

Interface InputMedia is defined as:

```
typedef string Barcode;

interface InputMedia
{
    typedef string OperatorCmd;

    void      barcode_input(in Barcode    item);
    void      keypad_input(in OperatorCmd cmd);
};
```

It is translated into the following Java Interface class:

```
package POS;
public interface InputMedia extends org.omg.CORBA.Object {
    void barcode_input(String item);
    void keypad_input(String cmd);
}
```

The IDL interface **InputMedia** defines a new type (**OperatorCmd**); this typedef is mapped to the Java native type `java.lang.String`. The IDL interface **InputMedia** is mapped to a public Java Interface class. Each of the two IDL operations **barcode_input(...)** and **keypad_input(...)** are translated into abstract public methods of the Java interface.

34.1.2 OutputMedia

Interface **OutputMedia** is defined as:

interface OutputMedia
{
   boolean   output_text(in string   string_to_print);
};

It is translated into the following Java Interface class:

```
package POS;
public interface OutputMedia extends org.omg.CORBA.Object {
    boolean output_text(String string_to_print);
}
```

As usual, the operation (**output_text()**) is translated into an abstract public method of the same name. The return type becomes a native Java `boolean` type. The input value of IDL type string is mapped to a `java.lang.String` type.

34.1.3 POSTerminal

Interface **POSTerminal** is defined as:

interface POSTerminal
{
   void login();
   void print_POS_sales_summary();
   void print_store_sales_summary();
   void send_barcode(in Barcode   item);
   void item_quantity(in long   quantity);
   void end_of_sale();
};

It is translated into the following Java Interface class:

```
package POS;
public interface POSTerminal extends org.omg.CORBA.Object {
    void login();
    void print_POS_sales_summary();
    void print_store_sales_summary();
    void send_barcode(String item);
    void item_quantity(int quantity);
    void end_of_sale();
}
```

Each of the IDL operations is translated into an abstract public method. The parameter to operation **send_barcode()** translates to the Java `java.lang.String` string type. The parameter to function **item_quantity()** is the 32-bit type **CORBA:: Long,** which is mapped to the native Java int type.

This completes the presentation of the Java interfaces generated by the IDL compiler. Now we need to implement the functionality of these interfaces. We'll do that in the next section.

34.2 Common POS Implementation in Java

There's almost nothing ORB-specific about the functionality, so we'll do it all in this section. If you're working the example by hand, type this code into your code files as we go along. At the end of this section, we'll send you off to the section on your specific ORB for final coding and compilation.

The point-of-sale (POS) terminal is made up of the following components: **POSTerminal, InputMedia**, and **OutputMedia**. Each of these IDL interfaces is implemented by a Java class and an instance of each is created.

Two separate processes are created. The first is a client, which holds one object of type PosTerminal and one object of type InputMedia. The latter accepts input from the user and communicates it to the PosTerminal object. This is an example of a local call (within a single address space) between two CORBA objects. The second process is a server that holds a single object of type OutputMedia. This object is invoked by the PosTerminal object when it wishes to output a line of the sales receipt.

There are two versions of implementations for the POS module, one for ORBs that support the Portable Object Adapter (POA), and one for ORBs that do not. For ORBs that support the POA, the implementation classes are InputMediaPoaImpl, OutputMediaPoaImpl, and POSTerminalPoaImpl. They all belong to the module POS, and are stored in the directory of the same name. The suffix "PoaImpl" is used to distinguish the Implementation class from the corresponding Interface class, as generated by the IDL compiler. Each implementation is derived from its corresponding POA Skeleton class, whose name is "POA_module.Interface". For example, the POA skeleton for InputMediaPOA. The POA skeletons are stored in the directory POA_POS.

For ORBs that do not yet support the POA, the Implementation classes are InputMediaImpl, OutputMediaImpl, and POSTerminalImpl. The suffix "Impl" is used to distinguish the Implementation class from the corresponding Interface class, as generated by the IDL compiler. Each non-POA Implementation class is derived from a base "ImplBase" class generated by the IDL compiler.

The POA implementations and the non-POA implementations are almost identical, except that:

- POA implementations are derived from their POA skeletons, while non-POA implementations are derived from their ImplBase classes, as described earlier.

- POA implementations pass _this() instead of this when passing themselves around either as parameters or as return values.

- POA implementations are activated in the ORB differently from non-POA implementations.

Table 34.1 POS Source Code Files and Their Contents

FILE NAME	CONTENTS
`InputMediaPoaImpl.java`	Implementation of `POS::InputMedia`
`OutputMediaPoaImpl.java`	Implementation of `POS::OutputMedia`
`POSTerminalPoaImpl.java`	Implementation of `POS::POSTerminal`
`PosPoaServer.java`	The main program, POA version
`PosServer.java`	The main program, non-POA version
`PosPoaClient.java`	The main program, POA version
`PosCˇlient.java`	The main program, non-POA version

We will only describe the POA versions of the implementations, reiterating the preceding differences where applicable. The only exceptions are the client and server main programs. The POA version is called `PosPoaServer`, and the non-POA version is called `PosServer`. The client versions are `PosPoaClient` and `PosClient`. Because of the differences in how the server communicates with the ORB to activate the implementations, both versions will be presented.

The source code for the POS that will be presented has been partitioned into the files listed in Table 34.1.

The following sections describe the logic of the three classes and the client and server programs.

34.2.1 Implementation of InputMediaPoaImpl Class

Here is the complete implementation for InputMediaPoaImpl class. The InputMediaPoaImpl is the implementation of the **POS::InputMedia** CORBA interface. It is derived from the `InputMediaPOA` skeleton base class generated by the IDL compiler, and contains members and member functions called out in the analysis and design presented in Chapter 24. To support the A&D requirements, we have added a private data member and a constructor. We have also added an `abort` helper function that we use to print out an error message and exit the server process when an unrecoverable error is encountered.

34.2.2 InputMedia Implementation: Class Implementation

```
1
2 package POS;
```

```
3
4 import java.io.*;
5 import java.util.*;
6 import java.lang.*;
7
8
9 class InputMediaPoaImpl extends InputMediaPOA {
10
11 private POS.POSTerminal m_POSTerminalRef;
12
13 private static final String cmdSummary =
14     "Command Summary :\n" +
15     "L : login\n" +
16     "P : POS Sales Summary\n" +
17     "S : Store Sales Summary\n" +
18     "T : Total\n" +
19     "Q num : Quantity\n" +
20     "X : Exit\n\n\n";
21
```

Line 2	Puts the InputMedia implementation into the same Java package as the generated Java classes from the IDL compiler.
Lines 4–6	Necessary Java imports for the implementation.
Line 9	Shows the class declaration for the `InputMediaPoaImpl`. Notice that it extends the `InputMediaPOA` class, which is generated by the IDL compiler. For non-POA implementations, line 9 would read: `class InputMediaImpl extends POS._InputMediaImplBase {` Here the actual class name was changed to differentiate the POA version from the non-POA version and it extends the `POS._InputMediaImplBase` class, which was also generated by the IDL compiler.
Line 11	The sole instance variable to the POSTerminal object that is to be used; this variable is initialized in the constructor.
Lines 13–20	Sets up a string that will be used repeatedly to output the command summary.

34.2.2.1 abort()

```
22 private void abort( String msg ) {
23
24     System.out.println(msg);
25     System.exit(1);
26 } // abort
27
28
```

Lines 22–26	abort is a helper method used to print out a message and then exit the server. As mentioned previously, this is not usually the preferred method of error handling, but in the interest of keeping the example understandable, we opted for this approach.

34.2.2.2 InputMediaPoaImpl()

```
29 InputMediaPoaImpl( POS.POSTerminal pTer) {
30
31     m_POSTerminalRef = pTer;
32
33     System.out.println(cmdSummary);
34 } // Constructor
35
```

Lines 29–34	The constructor takes a POS.POSTerminal object reference. By using the interface type (POS.POSTerminal), the constructor does not haveto know whether the implementation is POA version or a non-POA version or a stub object. This is why the type of all object references is always the interface type.The object reference is saved in the InputMedia implementation object to be used later. The constructor also prints the command summary to the console.

34.2.2.3 Barcode_input()

```
36 public void barcode_input(String item){
37
38     try
39     {
40         m_POSTerminalRef.send_barcode(item);
41
42     }
43     // For a mission critical application this is where recovery
44     // would normally take place.
45     catch(org.omg.CORBA.SystemException se)
46     {
47         se.printStackTrace();
48
49         abort("SystemException sending barcode" + se);
50
51     }
52 } // barcode_input
53
```

Lines 36–52	The barcode_input method is the implementation of the IDL operation. This method takes a string representation of the barcode and uses the saved POSTerminal object reference to

forward the barcode. Recall that the POSTerminal is responsible for interfacing with Store and Tax objects. The InputMedia just accepts and validates the input and sends it along.

Line 45	Notice that we catch a general CORBA SystemException. In an application where aborting on errors is not an option, you would have to deal with the exception. For example, a COMM_FAILURE exception would indicate that you could not communicate with the server process. Perhaps a reasonable thing to do would be to log the error and notify the person running the POSTerminal. If an INV_OBJREF is returned, this would indicate that the process received the message but there was no object that was associated with the object reference. This may mean that the object reference you are holding is 'stale'. One possible solution would be to go back to the Naming Service and get the reference again. An object reference can become stale if the server is restarted or the object is moved from host to host.

34.2.2.4 Keypad_input()

```
54 public void keypad_input(String cmd){
55
56      String pStr = cmd.toUpperCase();
57      StringTokenizer tokens = new StringTokenizer(pStr);
58      int lTot = 0;
59
60
61      // skip first token
62      tokens.nextToken();
63
64      try
65      {
66          if(pStr.startsWith("X"))
67          return;
68
69          else if(pStr.startsWith("L"))
70              m_POSTerminalRef.login();
71
72          else if(pStr.startsWith("P"))
73              m_POSTerminalRef.print_POS_sales_summary();
74
75          else if(pStr.startsWith("S"))
76              m_POSTerminalRef.print_store_sales_summary();
77
78          else if(pStr.startsWith("T"))
79              m_POSTerminalRef.end_of_sale();
80
81          else if(pStr.startsWith("Q"))
82          {
```

```
83
84              lTot = Integer.parseInt(tokens.nextToken());
85
86              m_POSTerminalRef.item_quantity(lTot);
87          }
88
89      else{
90          System.out.println("InputMediaImpl.keypad_input Invalid
            Entry");
91          System.out.println(cmdSummary);
92      }
93  }
94  // For a real application this is where recovery would normally
95  // take place.
96  catch(org.omg.CORBA.SystemException se)
97  {
98      se.printStackTrace();
99
100     abort("InputMediaImpl.keypad_input : " +
101         " CORBA.SystemException transmitting command" + se);
102
103 }
104 catch(java.lang.NumberFormatException fe)
105 {
106     System.out.println("InputMediaImpl.keypad_input : " +
107         "NumberFormat Exception " + fe);
108
109     System.out.println(cmdSummary);
110
111     fe.printStackTrace();
112 }
113 catch(java.util.NoSuchElementException nse)
114 {
115
116     System.out.println("InputMediaImpl.keypad_input : " +
117         "NumberFormat Exception " + nse);
118     System.out.println(cmdSummary);
119
120     nse.printStackTrace();
121 }
122 } // keypad_input
123 } // InputMediaImpl
124
```

Lines 54–122   The `keypad_input` method is passed a command (defined to be of type `POS::InputMedia::OperatorCmd` which is a string). It tests the first character and uses the following list to recognize the command to be executed. The `InputMedia` object itself does not process commands; instead, it simply calls the correct operation on the POSTerminal object.

CHARACTERS	MEANING	POSTERMINAL FUNCTION TO CALL
l **or** L	login	`login()` Line 70
p **or** P	Print POS sales summary for this POS	`print_POS_sales_summary()` Line 73
s **or** S	Print store sales summary for the whole store	`print_store_sales_summary()` Line 76
t **or** T	End of the sale of items to this customer	`end_of_sale()` Line 79
q **or** Q	Set the quantity of the item being purchased	`item_quantity()`

The characters q and Q are followed by the actual quantity setting, as a string of digits; for example, Q4<cr>. These digits are converted to an integer value before calling the `item_quantity()` operation on the `POSTerminal` object. The other commands are not followed by any input values.

Note that in order to simplify the `switch` statement, the function `toUpperCase()` is used to convert the first input character to uppercase in line 56. The switch condition for Q converts the rest of the input line to an integer value, and then passes this to the `item_quantity()` operation.

34.2.3 Implementation of OutputMediaPoaImpl Class

Here is the complete implementation of the `OutputMediaPoaImpl` class. The `OutputMediaPoaImpl` is the implementation of the `POS::OutputMedia` CORBA interface. This class is used to represent the output device. In this example, it simply prints to a console window.

34.2.3.1 OutputMedia Implementation: Class Implementation

```
1 package POS;
2
3
4 class OutputMediaPoaImpl extends OutputMediaPOA
5 {
6
```

Line 1	Puts the InputMedia implementation into the same Java package as the generated Java classes from the IDL compiler.
Line 4	Shows the class declaration for `OutputMediaPoaImpl`. Notice that it extends the `OutputMediaPoa` class,

which is generated by the IDL compiler. For non-POA
implementations line 4 would read:class OutputMediaImpl
extends POS._OutputMediaImplBase { Here the actual
class name was changed to differentiate the POA version
from the non-POA version and it extends the POS.
_InputMediaImplBase class, which was also generated by the
IDL compiler.

34.2.3.2 Abort()

```
7 private void abort( String msg ) {
8     System.out.println( msg );
9     System.exit(1);
10 } // abort
11
```

Lines 7–10	Helper method used to print out a message and then exit the server.

34.2.3.3 OutputMediaPoaImpl()

```
12 OutputMediaPoaImpl(){
13
14 } // Constructor
15
```

Lines 12–15	Default constructor.

34.2.3.4 Output_text()

```
16
17 public boolean output_text (String string_to_print){
18
19 // Check if the string passed exists and if so, output it
20   if (string_to_print != null)
21         System.out.println(string_to_print);
22
23   return true;
24 } // output_text
25 } // OutputMediaPoaImpl
26
```

Lines 17–24	The output_text takes in a string that needs to be printed. This implementation checks to make sure the string is not null, and if not, it uses the Java standard System.out.println to display the information.

The very observant reader might ask why you would need to check that the string is null. The Java CORBA Language specification says that you cannot pass null for a string parameter to an operation, so technically you should never receive a null. This is true, but to maintain strict object location transparency it is good practice to check that the parameter is not null.

34.2.4 Implementation of PosTerminal Class

The code for the POSTerminal interface is shown next. Its member functions correspond to the IDL operations defined in its interface, with the addition of a constructor.

34.2.4.1 POSTerminal Implementation: Class Implementation

```
1
2 package POS;
3
4 class POSTerminalPoaImpl extends POSTerminalPOA {
5
6 private String m_itemBarcode;
7 private int m_itemQuantity;
8 private AStore.Tax m_taxRef;
9 private AStore.Store m_storeRef;
10 private AStore.StoreAccess m_storeAccessRef;
11 private POS.OutputMedia m_outputMediaRef;
12
13 private float m_saleSubTotal;
14 private float m_saleTaxableSubTotal;
15 private float m_POSTotal;
16 private float m_POSTaxTotal;
17 private int m_id;
18
```

Line 2	Puts the POSTerminal implementation into the same Java package as the generated Java classes from the IDL compiler.
Line 4	Shows the class declaration for POSTerminalPoaPoaImpl. Notice that it extends the POSTerminalPOA class, which is generated by the IDL compiler. For non-POA implementations line 4 would read: `class POSTerminalImpl extends POS._POSTerminalImplBase {` Here the actual class name was changed to differentiate the POA version from the non-POA version and it extends the POS._InputMediaImplBase class, which was also generated by the IDL compiler.
Lines 6–17	The member variables of class POSTerminalPoaImpl are explained in the following table.

NAME	DESCRIPTION
m_itemBarcode	The current barcode (identifying the item currently being purchased at this point-of-sale terminal).
m_itemQuantity	This is the number of items of a given type that are currently being purchased. This variable is initialized to 1, and it is changed by the ItemQuantity() operation. The SendBarcode() operation, which signals to the POSTerminal that an item is being purchased, assesses this variable to determine how many of this item are being purchased. The variable is then reset to value 1.
m_taxRef	The object reference of the Tax object. This is initialized in the constructor of the POSTerminal object, by searching for the correct Tax object using the Naming Service.
m_storeRef	The object reference of the Store object. This is initialized in the constructor of the POSTerminal object, by searching for the correct Store object using the Naming Service.
m_storeAccessRef	The object reference of the StoreAccessobject. The Login() operation on the POSTerminal logs the POS terminal into the Store object. The Store object returns an object reference to a newly created StoreAccess object, through which the POSTerminal subsequently accesses the store information.
m_outputMediaRef	The object reference of the OutputMedia object to which to print receipts and reports. This is initialized in the constructor of the POSTerminal object, by searching for the correct OutputMedia object using the Naming Service.
m_saleSubTotal	The sales total so far for the sale to the current customer.
m_saleTaxableSubTotal	The sales tax so far for the sale to the current customer.
m_POSTotal	This POS's total sales since power up.
m_POSTaxTotal	This POS's total tax since power up.
m_id	This POS's identifier (a unique number within the Store that the POS uses). This is passed to the process as a command-line argument.

34.2.4.2 abort()

```
19 private void abort( String msg ) {
20   System.err.println(msg);
```

```
21   System.exit(1);
22 }
23
```

Lines 19–23   Helper method used to print out a message and then exit the server.

34.2.4.3 POSTerminalPoaImpl()

```
24 POSTerminalPoaImpl(org.omg.CORBA.Object ns,
25                                    int StoreId,
26                                    int Id)
27 {
28
29 String str = null;
30
31 try {
32   m_itemBarcode = null;
33   m_itemQuantity = 0;
34
35   str = "Tax_" + StoreId;
36
37   try {
38   org.omg.CORBA.Object obj = PrimerUtils.NsPublisher.nsResolve(ns,
    str, "Primer_Example");
39       m_taxRef = AStore.TaxHelper.narrow(obj);
40   } catch( Exception exc ) {
41       abort("ERROR: Cannot resolve " + str + " in Naming Service");
42   }
43
44   str = "Store_" + StoreId;
45
46   try {
47       org.omg.CORBA.Object obj =
          PrimerUtils.NsPublisher.nsResolve(ns, str, "Primer_Example");
48       m_storeRef = AStore.StoreHelper.narrow(obj);
49   } catch( Exception exc ) {
50       abort("ERROR: Cannot resolve " + str + " in Naming Service");
51   }
52
53   str = "OutputMedia_" + Id;
54
55   try {
56       org.omg.CORBA.Object obj =
          PrimerUtils.NsPublisher.nsResolve(ns, str, "Primer_Example");
57       m_outputMediaRef = POS.OutputMediaHelper.narrow(obj);
58   } catch( Exception exc ) {
59       abort("ERROR: Cannot resolve " + str + " in Naming Service");
60   }
61
62   m_storeAccessRef = null;
```

```
63      m_itemExtension = 0;
64      m_saleSubTotal = 0.0f;
65      m_saleTaxableSubTotal = 0.0f;
66      m_POSTotal = 0.0f;
67      m_POSTaxTotal = 0.0f;
68      m_id = Id;
69
70
71      }
72      catch(org.omg.CORBA.SystemException se)
73      {
74
75          se.printStackTrace();
76
77          abort("POSTerminalPoaImpl.CTOR() : CORBA.SystemException " +
78          "trying to resolve " +
79          str + " Primer Example : " +
80          se);
81
82      }
83      catch(Exception ue)
84      {
85
86          ue.printStackTrace();
87
88          abort("POSTerminalPoaImpl.CTOR() : Exception " +
89          "trying to resolve " +
90          str + " Primer Example : " +
91          ue);
92      }
93
94  } // Constructor
95
96
```

Lines 35–42	This section of code is obtaining a reference to the Tax object. It first constructs the name of the Tax object, which must match the name as it is known in the Naming Service. It then calls the utility class to resolve that name in the naming context passed to the constructor. If it is successful, it will return a generic `CORBA.Object`, which must be narrowed to the expected interface. In this case, we were hoping for an object reference to a Tax object, so in line 39 we use the `TaxHelper` to narrow the generic object reference. If any errors occur, the catch block on line 40 will print out an error message and abort.
Lines 44–51	This section of code is obtaining a reference to the Store object. It first constructs the name of the `Store` object, which must match the name as it is known in the Naming Service. It then calls the utility class to resolve that name in the naming context passed to the constructor. If it is successful, it will return a generic `CORBA.Object`, which must be narrowed to the expected

interface. In this case, we were hoping for an object reference to a Store object, so in line 48 we use the StoreHelper to narrow the generic object reference. If any errors occur, the catch block on line 49 will print out an error message and abort.

Line 53–60	This section of code is obtaining a reference to the OutputMedia object. It first constructs the name of the OutputMedia object, which must match the name as it is known in the Naming Service. It then calls the utility class to resolve that name in the naming context passed to the constructor. If it is successful, it will return a generic CORBA.Object, which must be narrowed to the expected interface. In this case, we were hoping for an object reference to a OutputMedia object, so in line 48 we use the OutputMediaHelper to narrow the generic object reference. If any errors occur, the catch block on line 58 will print out an error message and abort.
Lines 72–92	Catch blocks to catch exceptions. The CORBA System exceptions will be thrown as a result of trying to resolve the various object references.

34.2.4.4 loggedIn()

```
97 boolean loggedIn(){
98
99 if (m_storeAccessRef == null) {
100
101  return false;
102 }
103 else{
104
105  return true;
106 }
107 } // loggedIn
108
```

Lines 97–107	The loggedIn method is a helper method that determines whether the POS terminal has logged in. It does this by checking to see if the m_storeAccessRef is null, which it will be if the POS terminal is not logged in. Note that the Java mapping does not require the use of the CORBA:is_nil method because null is a legal value for an object reference.

34.2.4.5 login()

```
109 public void login(){
110
111 if(m_storeAccessRef != null)
112 {
113        System.out.println("Can't log in twice");
114        return;
```

```
115 }
116
117 try
118 {
119
120        m_storeAccessRef = m_storeRef.login(m_id);
121
122 }
123 catch(org.omg.CORBA.SystemException se)
124 {
125
126   se.printStackTrace();
127
128   abort("POSTerminalPoaImpl.Login() : CORBA.SystemException " +se);
129 }
130
131
132
133
134 } // login
135
```

Lines 109–134   The `login` method is the implementation of the IDL **login** operation. The `login` method is responsible for obtaining an object reference to the `StoreAccess` object. The `login` method will first check to see if it already has a reference to the `StoreAccess` object on line 111, and if so, just return printing a message saying you cannot log in twice. On line 120, we call the `login` method on the `Store` object, passing the ID for this POSTerminal, to get an object reference to a `StoreAccess` object. Used in this way, the `Store` acts as a factory for `StoreAccess` objects. The catch block on lines 123–129 looks for generic CORBA system exceptions and abort if one is caught.

34.2.4.6 print_POS_sales_summary()

```
136 public void print_POS_sales_summary(){
137
138 if(!loggedIn()) {
139
140   return;
141 }
142
143 if((m_itemBarcode != null || m_saleSubTotal != 0.0)){
144
145   return;
146 }
147
148 String caStr;
```

```
149
150 caStr = "Point of Sale Total: " + m_POSTotal +
151 " Tax Total: " + m_POSTaxTotal;
152
153 try
154 {
155
156  m_outputMediaRef.output_text(caStr);
157
158 }
159 catch(org.omg.CORBA.SystemException se)
160 {
161  se.printStackTrace();
162  abort("POSTerminalPoaImpl.PrintPOSSalesSummary() :" +
163  "SystemException " + se);
164
165 }
166 } // print_POS_sales_summary
167
```

Lines 136–166	The `print_POS_sales_summary` method is the implementation of the IDL **print_POS_sales_summary** operation. The result of calling this method is the writing of a single line to the receipt containing the POS total sales and the POS total tax. The output string is constructed using the `m_POSTotal` and `m_POSTaxTotal` member variables.

The first order of business to check to see that the POSTerminal is logged in on line 138. If not, then this method prints nothing and just returns.

Note that this method also returns if the POSTerminal is currently handling a sale. That is, we do not allow the sales totals to be printed while the customer's items are being rung up. The method determines whether it is handling a sale by testing the `m_itemBarcode` and `m_saleSubTotal` member variables on line 143. If either of these is nonzero, then the terminal must be handling a sale.

34.2.4.7 print_store_sales_summary()

```
168 public void print_store_sales_summary(){
169
170 if(!loggedIn()){
171
172  return;
173 }
174
175 if( m_itemBarcode != null || m_saleSubTotal != 0.0 ){
176
177  return;
178 }
179
```

```
180 String caOpStr = null;
181
182 AStore.StorePackage.StoreTotals tots = null;
183
184 try {
185
186  tots = m_storeRef.totals();
187
188 }
189 catch(org.omg.CORBA.SystemException se) {
190
191  se.printStackTrace();
192  abort("POSTerminalPoaImpl.print_store_sales_summary() : " +
193  "SystemExceptionfinding store totals: " + se);
194
195 }
196
197 caOpStr = "Total Sales := " + tots.store_total + "\n" +
198 "Total Tax := " + tots.store_tax_total;
199
200 try {
201
202  m_outputMediaRef.output_text("STORE TOTALS");
203  m_outputMediaRef.output_text(caOpStr);
204
205 }
206 catch(org.omg.CORBA.SystemException se) {
207  se.printStackTrace();
208  abort("POSTerminalPoaImpl.print_store_sales_summary() : " +
209  "systemException with Output Media: " + se);
210
211
212  AStore.POSListHolder PL;
213
214 try
215 {
216
217  PL = new AStore.POSListHolder();
218  m_storeRef.get_POS_totals(PL);
219  AStore.POSInfo[] posinfo = PL.value;
220
221  for(int i = 0; i < PL.value.length; i++)
222  {
223         if(posinfo[i].id > 0)
224         {
225             caOpStr = "\tPOS I.D. : " + posinfo[i].id + "\n" +
226             "\t\tTotal Sales : " + posinfo[i].total_sales +
227             "\t\tTotal Tax : " + posinfo[i].total_taxes;
228             m_outputMediaRef.output_text(caOpStr);
229         }
230  }
231
```

```
232 }
233 catch(org.omg.CORBA.SystemException se)
234 {
235  se.printStackTrace();
236
237  abort("POSTerminalPoaImpl.print_store_sales_summary() : " +
238  "SystemException getting Store Totals: " + se);
239
240 }
241 } //print_store_sales_summary
242
```

Lines 168–241	The print_store_sales_summary method is the implementation of the IDL **print_store_sales_summary** operation. The method communicates with the Store reference to obtain the totals for the Store that the POS is logged in to.
General Overview	Again, the first order of business to check to see that the POSTerminal is logged in on line 170. If not, then this method prints nothing and just returns.

This method also returns if the POSTerminal is currently handling a sale. That is, we do not allow the sales totals to be printed while the customer's items are being rung up. The method determines whether it is handling a sale by testing the m_itemBarcode and m_saleSubTotal member variables on line 143. If either of these is nonzero, then the terminal must be handling a sale.

Line 186	We use the saved Store object reference to get the Store totals. Recall from the Store interface definition that **StoreTotals** was defined to be a structure that contained the store total sales and the tax total for the store. Because this was defined as an IDL attribute of the store interface, no user exceptions can be thrown. The call to the totals() operation is wrapped in a try/catch block to catch any CORBA system exceptions.
Line 197	After the totals for the Store have been returned, construct the proper output string with the returned information.
Lines 202–203	Using OutputMedia object reference, display the totals for the store.
Lines 212–241	Next, the details on each POS logged into the Store must be displayed to the OutputMedia. A POSListHolder is constructed. Recall that IDL compiler-generated Holder classes are used for IDL **inout** and **out** parameters.

On line 218, we use the Store reference to obtain a list of all the POSs currently logged into the Store. When the get_POS_totals operation returns, the value of the POSListHolder object will be modified to hold a sequence of POSInfo structures.

Line 219 extracts the POSInfo structure from the Holder object. This is not required, but it is good programming practice as it makes the code that follows easier to read because it does not need to typecast. Recall that the value variable is of type CORBA Object.

Because every IDL sequence translates to a Java array, in lines 221–230 a loop is set up to loop for every POSInfo structure returned and construct the proper output string. This output string is then sent to the OutputMedia object reference.

Line 233 is the catch block for CORBA system exceptions. This catch block is used to help determine if there were any problems with the get_POS_totals operation.

34.2.4.8 send_barcode()

```
243 public void send_barcode(String item){
244
245 if (!loggedIn()){
246
247  return;
248 }
249
250 String caOpStr = null;
251
252 AStore.ItemInfoHolder ItemInf = new AStore.ItemInfoHolder();
253 org.omg.CORBA.FloatHolder price = new org.omg.CORBA.FloatHolder();
254 org.omg.CORBA.FloatHolder taxablePrice = new org.omg.CORBA
    .FloatHolder();
255 m_itemBarcode = item;
256 float itemExt;
257
258 try
259 {
260
261  m_storeAccessRef.find_price(m_itemBarcode,m_itemQuantity,
262  price,taxablePrice,ItemInf);
263
264  itemExt = (float) (m_itemQuantity * price.value);
265  m_saleSubTotal += itemExt;
266  caOpStr = "\n\tQuantity=" + m_itemQuantity +
267  "\n\tBarcode =" + m_itemBarcode +
268  "\n\tItemInf =" + ItemInf.value.name +
269  "\n\tprice =" + price.value +
270  "\n\tItemExt =" + itemExt +
271  ((taxablePrice.value > 0.0) ? " *" : "") ;
272
273 }
274 catch (AStore.BarcodeNotFound bnf)
275 {
276
277  m_itemQuantity = 1;
278  System.out.println("POSTerminalPoaImpl.send_barcode
    ( " + item + ") : " +
279  "Invalid Barcode Found: " +bnf);
280  return;
281
```

```
282 catch(org.omg.CORBA.SystemException se)
283 {
284
285   se.printStackTrace();
286
287   abort("POSTerminalPoaImpl.send_barcode ( " + item + ") : " +
288   " SystemException in findPrice " + se);
289
290 }
291
292 try
293 {
294
295   m_outputMediaRef.output_text(caOpStr);
296
297 }
298 catch (org.omg.CORBA.SystemException se)
299 {
300   se.printStackTrace();
301
302   abort("POSTerminalPoaImpl.send_barcode ( " + item + ") : " +
303   "SystemException Output Media" + se);
304
305 }
306
307 m_saleTaxableSubTotal += (taxablePrice.value * (float)m_itemQuantity);
308 m_itemQuantity = 1;
309
310 } // send_barcode
311
```

Lines 243–310	The `send_barcode` method is the implementation of the IDL `send_barcode` operation. This method handles the purchasing of one or more items of a given type by the current customer. The parameter to the method specifies the barcode of the item being purchased. The number of the items that are being purchased is determined by the object's `m_itemQuantity` member variable. This defaults to 1, but it may have been changed by a preceding call to the `item_quantity()` operation.
Lines 252–254	These lines create the `Holder` classes that are required by the IDL-to-Java language mapping for IDL **out** and **inout** parameters. Because all of these parameters are IDL out parameters, the equivalent `Holder` object must be created, but they are not required to be initialized with any values. The `find_price()` method will modify the value member of the `Holder` object.
Lines 258–274	The method's first action is to find the price and other information of the item described by the barcode (using the `find_price()` operation on the `StoreAccess` object). If any error occurs (the user-defined `BarcodeNotFound` exception or a system exception is raised when calling the `find_price()`

operation), this is reported on the standard error output (and the purchase quantity is reset to the default of 1).

If all goes well, the price variable passed to the call to find_price() will have been updated to be the price of the item. This is multiplied by the quantity and assigned to the itemExt variable, which in turn is used to update the m_saleSubTotal member variable (which is the record of the amount being spent by the current customer). Then the output string is constructed to summarize the item sale. The output line gives the item quantity, item barcode, item name, item cost, and total cost (that is, the item cost multiplied by the item quantity). Note that taxable items are marked with an asterisk on the output lines of the receipt.

Line 295	After the output string has been constructed, it is output to the OutputMedia object using the output_text method. This method is wrapped in a try/catch block to make sure the OutputMedia received the message to print.
Lines 307–308	Finally, the tax subtotal (m_saleTaxableSubTotal) is updated to reflect the purchase by this customer. The taxablePrice variable (updated as an out parameter by the find_price() operation) is multiplied by the quantity of the current item being purchased, and then added to the m_saleTaxableSubTotal member variable).

34.2.4.9 item_quantity()

```
312 public void item_quantity(int quantity){
313 if (!loggedIn()){
314
315  return;
316 }
317
318 if (quantity > 0)
319  m_itemQuantity = quantity;
320
321 } // item_quantity
322
```

Lines 312–321	This method simply changes the m_itemQuantity member variable, which is used by the next call to the send_barcode method.

34.2.4.10 end_of_sale()

```
323 public void end_of_sale(){
324 String caOpStr;
325
326 if (!loggedIn()){
327
328  return;
329 }
```

```
330
331 try {
332
333   caOpStr = "Taxable Sub-Total := " + m_saleTaxableSubTotal;
334
335   m_outputMediaRef.output_text(caOpStr);
336
337   float saleTax = m_taxRef.calculate_tax(m_saleTaxableSubTotal);
338
339   caOpStr = "Taxes := " + saleTax;
340
341   m_outputMediaRef.output_text(caOpStr);
342
343   float saleTotal = saleTax + m_saleSubTotal;
344
345   caOpStr = "Total := " + saleTotal;
346
347   m_outputMediaRef.output_text(caOpStr);
348
349   m_POSTotal += saleTotal;
350   m_POSTaxTotal += saleTax;
351
352   m_storeRef.update_store_totals(m_id,saleTotal,saleTax);
353
354
355 }
356 catch(org.omg.CORBA.SystemException se) {
357   se.printStackTrace();
358
359   abort("POSTerminalPoaImpl.end_of_sale() : " +
360   "SystemException Ending sale: " + se);
361
362 }
363
364 m_saleSubTotal = m_saleTaxableSubTotal = 0;
365 m_itemQuantity = 1;
366 m_itemBarcode = null;
367 return;
368
369
370
371 } // end_of_sale
372
373
374
375 } // POSTerminalPoaImpl
376
```

| Lines 323–375 | This method signals that all of the purchases for the current customer have been rung up. It outputs (via the `OutputMedia` object) the total taxable sales made on this occasion, and then it |

	uses the `calculate_tax()` operation of the `Tax` object to determine the corresponding tax. This value is then output, also using the `OutputMedia` object.
Line 337–350	The tax value returned by the `calculate_tax()` operation is also used by the `end_of_sale()` function to determine the overall tax total of this sale (`m_saleTax + m_saleSubTotal`).
Lines 352–366	The method next outputs the total sale value. Once this is finished, the POS can inform the store of the total sale value and total price of this sale, using the Store's `update_store_total()` operation. Finally, the member variables are reset to initial values.

34.2.5 Implementation of the POA Version of the POS Client

Here is the code for the POA version of the POS client. The implementation is based on the requirements we set down in the analysis and design presented in Chapter 24. Recall that we are going to present two versions of the POS Client: a POA version and a non-POA version.

```
1 package POS;
2
3 import java.io.*;
4
5 public class PosPoaClient {
6
7 private static String m_usage = "usage: PosClient <Store Number> <POS
  Number> <vendor specific options>";
8 private static void abort( String msg ) {
9 System.out.println( msg );
10 System.exit(1);
11 }
12
```

Lines 1–12	The POA version of the POS client is placed in the POS package. The first portion of the implementation should be pretty straightforward. There really is nothing CORBA-specific just yet. The class name is `PosPoaClient`, but there is nothing significant about the name. We use 'Poa' in the name just to differentiate it from the non-POA version. CORBA does not dictate any naming conventions for the clients and servers.

```
13 public static void main(String[] args){
14
15
16 System.out.println("PosClient.main()");
17
```

```
18 if(args.length < 2)
19 {
20 abort( m_usage );
21 }
22
23 int storeid = 0;
24 int posid = 0;
25 try {
26 storeid = Integer.parseInt(args[0]);
27 posid= Integer.parseInt(args[1]);
28 } catch( NumberFormatException nfe ) {
29
30 nfe.printStackTrace();
31 abort(m_usage);
32 }
33
34 org.omg.CORBA.ORB orb;
35
36 POS.POSTerminal Ter = null;
37 POS.InputMedia InPut = null;
38
```

Lines 13–38	The `main` method is the starting point for the CORBA client, as it is for any Java application. The start of the `main` method is just reading command-line options and initializing runtime variables.
Line 34	This is the first place where there is a CORBA-specific item. This line is declaring a variable called `orb` of type `org.omg.CORBA.ORB`. We will assign this later on. How you obtain the `orb` reference can be vendor specific, so be sure to check out the vendor-specific section for the particular CORBA ORB you are using.

```
39 try
40 {
41
42 System.out.print("PosClient.main() : initialising ORB...");
43
44 // Some ORB vendors prefer to initialize the ORB using different ORB
45 // initialization interfaces. See the vendor specific portions of
46 // the text for more information.
47 orb = org.omg.CORBA.ORB.init( args, null);
48
49 // Standard CORBA method for creating root POA and POA manager
50 org.omg.CORBA.Object pobj = orb.resolve_initial_references( "RootPOA"
);
51
52 org.omg.PortableServer.POA poa = org.omg.PortableServer
   .POAHelper.narrow( pobj );
53
```

```
54 org.omg.PortableServer.POAManager poa_mgr = poa.the_POAManager();
55
```

Lines 39–55	This section of code is responsible for initializing the ORB and the POA Manager.
Line 47	Most vendors will support the `org.omg.CORBA.ORB.init` method as a way to initialize the ORB. There are many ways to initialize the ORB, this is just one way. It depends upon whether you are initializing an application or an applet. See the vendor's documentation for the different ways to initialize the ORB. Upon successfully initializing the ORB, you will get back an ORB reference that you will use to do further initialization.
Line 50	Once you have a reference to the ORB, you can then obtain a reference to the root POA pseudo object. This is held by the ORB implementation and you obtain a reference to it just as you would any initial ORB service, using `resolve_initial_references` and specifying "RootPOA" as the reference that you are interested in. Upon successful completion, the ORB will return a generic CORBA object reference that must be narrowed.
Line 52	This line uses the generic CORBA object reference and the `POAHelper` class to narrow the object reference to a reference to the POA. The `POAHelper` class is provided by the ORB vendor. The CORBA specification requires that the `narrow` operation be available from the `Helper` class. Recall that `narrow` is a distributed type-safe downcast. In line 50 you requested a reference to the `RootPOA`, but you were returned a generic object reference. In line 52 you need to find out if it really returned to you a reference to the `RootPOA`. If `narrow` succeeds, then you have a reference to the `RootPOA`.
Line 54	Using the reference to the `RootPOA`, you obtain a reference to the `POAManager` using the `the_POAManager` method on the POA class. We will see how we use the `POAManager` later on in the client application.

That's it for this section of the code. You now have the ORB initialized and a reference to the `POAManager`. You are now ready to start creating objects.

```
56 System.out.println("PosClient.main() : " +
57 "resolving root NameContext...");
58
59 org.omg.CORBA.Object obj = null;
60 try {
61 obj = orb.resolve_initial_references("NameService");
62 } catch( org.omg.CORBA.ORBPackage.InvalidName exc ) {
63 abort("ERROR: The ORB could not resolve a reference to the
   NameService");
64 }
65
66 System.out.println("PosClient.main() : " +
```

```
67 "creating new Terminal...");
68
69 // Instantiate servant
70 POSTerminalPoaImpl TerServant = new POSTerminalPoaImpl( obj, storeid,
   posid );
71 Ter = TerServant._this();
72 // Activate the poa_manager
73 // By default it will manage and pass requests onto the
      implementation
74 poa_mgr.activate();
75
76 System.out.println("PosClient is ready" );
77
78
79 }
80 catch(org.omg.CORBA.SystemException se)
81 {
82
83 se.printStackTrace();
84
85 abort("PosClient.main() SystemException " + se);
86
87 }
88 catch(java.lang.Exception jle){
89
90 jle.printStackTrace();
91
92 abort("PosClient.main() exception " + jle);
93
94 }
95
96
```

Line 61	The POS Client will require a reference to the Naming Service and does this, as we saw in line 50, using resolve_initial_ references using the CORBA defined "NameService" string. If the ORB can return a reference to the NameService, it will do so. Well, to be completely accurate, it will return a generic CORBA object reference to the root Naming Context within the NameService. This reference is used by the POSTermainPoaImpl to get references to Store and Tax objects. Note that if "NameService" is not a recognized service name, then the ORB will throw the CORBA InvalidName exception.
Line 70	This line creates the POSTerminalPoaImpl object. The POSTerminalPoaImpl take the reference to the root Naming Context, and the storeid and posid that came from the command line. Note that just instantiating the POSTerminalPoaImpl object has not made it a distributed object just yet.
Line 71	The _this method is used to implicitly activate the object. Implicit activation of an object involves allocating a system-

	generated Object ID and registering the servant with that Object ID in the Active Object Map.
Line 74	The `poa_mgr.activate` causes the ORB to activate all the implementations, allowing requests to be passed to the implementations. Up to this point you have done two separate activities—initialize the ORB and POA and initialize the object implementations—but you have not tied the two activities together. This is what `poa_mgr.activate` is used for. It ties the object implementations to the ORB, so it can start passing requests to them.
Lines 80–96	The rest of this section is just catching any possible CORBA exceptions.

This section, essentially, completes the work required to start a CORBA application. There are just a couple of other items in the next section, but these could have been done in this section. From here on, it is going to start to look more like a standard Java application than a CORBA application.

```
97  // The PosClient's main thread blocks reading input from the user.
98
99  BufferedReader in = new BufferedReader( new
      InputStreamReader(System.in));
100
101 String response = "";
102
103 try
104 {
105 InputMediaPoaImpl inputServant = new InputMediaPoaImpl(Ter);
106 InPut = inputServant._this();
107 do
108 {
109 System.out.println(
110 "Enter code, command (L,P,Q,S,T) or X to exit : ");
111
112 try {
113
114 response = in.readLine().trim();
115 // if the length is zero then the user just typed return or space
         and return
116 if( response.length() == 0 ) continue;
117 response = response.toUpperCase();
118 }
119 catch(java.io.IOException ioe){
120 System.out.println("PosClient.main() : Error reading input " +
121 ioe);
122
123 ioe.printStackTrace();
124
125 continue;
```

```
126
127 }
128 if(Character.isDigit(response.charAt(0)))
129 InPut.barcode_input(response);
130 else
131 InPut.keypad_input(response);
132 }
133 while (!response.startsWith("X")) ;
134
135
136 }
137 catch(org.omg.CORBA.SystemException se) {
138
139 se.printStackTrace();
140
141 abort("PosClient.main() : " +
142 "CORBA SystemException using InputMedia: "+
143 se);
144 }
145 catch( java.lang.Exception jle ) {
146
147 jle.printStackTrace();
148 abort("PosClient.main() : " +
149 "java.lang.Exception using InputMedia: "+
150 jle);
151 }
152
153 System.exit(1);
154 } // Main
155 } // PosClient
```

Lines 97–155	This section of code goes into an infinite loop, getting input from the user. On line 105, the InputMediaPoaImpl object is created and passed a reference to the POSTerminalPoaImpl object. In a real implementation of the system, the InputMedia object would receive input events from the POS's special hardware (the barcode reader and the keypad); however, in our simple implementation the main function reads the input from the normal keyboard and passes it to the InputMedia object.
Lines 107–133	This section is the infinite loop. Line 114 reads input from the keyboard, and line 117 converts everything to uppercase. Line 128 checks to see if the input is a character or a digit. If it's a digit, it assumes it is a barcode and is forwarded to the InputMedia object by calling its barcode_input operation. Otherwise, it is treated as a keypad input and is passed without interpretation to InputMedia object by calling its keypad_input operation. If the user enters "x", the client application is exited.

34.2.6 Implementation of the Non-POA Version of the POS Client

Here is the code for the non-POA version of the POS client. The implementation is based on the requirements we set down in Chapter 24. While there are many similarities in the non-CORBA portion of the application, the section of the code that deals with the initialization of the ORB and object implementation is significantly different to justify a new section in to discuss it. We will keep our comments brief on the non-CORBA sections if they are not significantly different from the POA version.

```
1 package POS;
2
3 import java.io.*;
4
5 public class PosClient {
6
7 private static String m_usage = "usage: PosClient <Store Number> <POS
  Number> <vendor specific options>";
8 private static void abort( String msg ) {
9 System.out.println( msg );
10 System.exit(1);
11 }
12
13 public static void main(String[] args){
14
15
16 System.out.println("PosClient.main()");
17
18 if(args.length < 2)
19 {
20 abort( m_usage );
21 }
22
23 int storeid = 0;
24 int posid = 0;
25 try {
26 storeid = Integer.parseInt(args[0]);
27 posid= Integer.parseInt(args[1]);
28 } catch( NumberFormatException nfe ) {
29
30 nfe.printStackTrace();
31 abort(m_usage);
32 }
33
34 org.omg.CORBA.ORB orb;
35
36 POS.POSTerminal Ter = null;
37 POS.InputMedia InPut = null;
38
39 try
```

```
40 {
41
42 System.out.print("PosClient.main() : initialising ORB...");
43
44 // Some ORB vendors prefer to initialize the ORB using different ORB
45 // initialization interfaces. See the vendor specific portions of
46 // the text for more information.
47 orb = org.omg.CORBA.ORB.init( args, null);
48
49 System.out.println("PosClient.main() : " +
50 "resolving root NameContext...");
51
52 org.omg.CORBA.Object obj = null;
53 try {
54 obj = orb.resolve_initial_references("NameService");
55 } catch( org.omg.CORBA.ORBPackage.InvalidName exc ) {
56 abort("ERROR: The ORB could not resolve a reference to the
   NameService");
57 }
58
59 System.out.println("PosClient.main() : " +
60 "creating new Terminal...");
61
62 Ter = new POSTerminalImpl( obj, storeid, posid );
63
64 System.out.println("PosClient is ready" );
65
66 // Connect the POSTerminal object to the ORB so it is ready to
      receive remote calls
67 orb.connect( Ter );
68
69 }
```

Line 47	Up to this point, everything is the same as in the POA version. Even line 47 is the same. Regardless of POA or no POA, you still have to initialize the ORB, and this commonly done with `org.omg.CORBA.ORB.init`.
Line 54	As before, we need to obtain an object reference to the Naming Service, which will be used later. Note, however, that we do not resolve an initial reference to a `RootPOA`.
Line 62	Here we instantiate the non-POA version of the `POSTerminal` object.
Line 67	The `orb.connect` call explicitly connects the `POSTerminalImpl` object to the ORB so the ORB can start passing requests up to the object. It is very similar to the `poa_mgr.activate`, but in this case we have to explicitly state which objects we are connecting to the ORB.

```
70 catch(org.omg.CORBA.SystemException se)
71 {
72
73 se.printStackTrace();
74
75 abort("PosClient.main() SystemException " + se);
76
77 }
78 catch(java.lang.Exception jle){
79
80 jle.printStackTrace();
81
82 abort("PosClient.main() exception " + jle);
83
84 }
85
86
87 // The PosClient's main thread blocks reading input from the user.
88
89 BufferedReader in = new BufferedReader( new
InputStreamReader(System.in));
90
91 String response = "";
92
93 try
94 {
95
96 InPut = new InputMediaImpl(Ter);
```

Line 96	This line is the only other line that differs from the POA version. The non-POA version just instantiates the objects and does not require the call to `_this`. The code that follows can just use `InPut` directly.

```
97 do
98 {
99 System.out.println(
100 "Enter code, command (L,P,Q,S,T) or X to exit : ");
101
102 try {

103
104 response = in.readLine().trim();
105 // if the length is zero then the user just typed return or space
and return
106 if( response.length() == 0 ) continue;
107 response = response.toUpperCase();
108 }
109 catch(java.io.IOException ioe){
110 System.out.println("PosClient.main() : Error reading input " +
111 ioe);
```

```
112
113 ioe.printStackTrace();
114
115 continue;
116
117 }
118 if(Character.isDigit(response.charAt(0)))
119 InPut.barcode_input(response);
120 else
121 InPut.keypad_input(response);
122 }
123 while (!response.startsWith("X")) ;
124
125
126 }
127 catch(org.omg.CORBA.SystemException se) {
128
129 se.printStackTrace();
130
131 abort("PosClient.main() : " +
132 "CORBA SystemException using InputMedia: "+
133 se);
134 }
135 catch( java.lang.Exception jle ) {
136
137 jle.printStackTrace();
138 abort("PosClient.main() : " +
139 "java.lang.Exception using InputMedia: "+
140 jle);
141
142
143 System.exit(1);
144 } // Main
145 } // PosClient
```

As you can see, there is not a great deal of difference between POA and non-POA versions of the client applications, but we felt that since the POA will be new to most readers, that it was worth breaking out the different versions and showing explicit differences. So, now on to the servers.

34.2.7 Implementation of the POA Version of the POS Server

Here is the code for the POA version of the POS server. The implementation is based on the requirements we set down in Chapter 24. Recall that we are going to present two versions of the POS Server: a POA version and a non-POA version.

The main function of this server simply creates an object of type OutputMedia to print messages to the POSTerminal.

```
1 package POS;
2
3 public class PosPoaServer {
4
5
6 private static void abort( String msg ) {
7 System.out.println( msg );
8 System.exit(1);
9 } // abort
10
11 public static void main(String[] args){
12
13 System.out.println("PosPoaServer.main()");
14
15 if(args.length < 1)
16 {
17 abort("usage: PosPoaServer <POS Number> <vendor specific options>" );
18 }
19
```

Lines 1–19	The POA version of the POS server is placed in the POS package. The first portion of the implementation should be pretty straightforward. There really is nothing CORBA-specific just yet. The class name is PosPoaServer, but there is nothing significant about the name. We use 'Poa' in the name just to differentiate it from the non-POA version. CORBA does not dictate any naming conventions for the clients and servers.

```
20 System.out.println("Using POS Number: " + args[0]);
21 int posID = 0;
22 try {
23 posID = Integer.parseInt(args[0]);
24 } catch( NumberFormatException nfe ) {
25 nfe.printStackTrace();
26 abort("usage: PosPoaServer <POS Number> <vendor specific options>" );
27 }
28
29 org.omg.CORBA.ORB orb = null;
30 POS.OutputMediaPoaImpl outPut = null;
31
```

Lines 20–31	The main method is the starting point for the CORBA server, as it is for any Java application. The start of the main method is just reading command-line options and initializing runtime variables.
Line 29	This is the first place where there is a CORBA-specific item. This line is declaring a variable called orb of type org.omg.CORBA.ORB. We will assign this later on. How you obtain the orb reference can be vendor specific so be sure to check out the vendor-specific section for the particular CORBA ORB you are using.

```
32 try
33 {
34
35 System.out.println("PosPoaServer.main() : initialising ORB...");
36
37 // Some ORB vendors prefer to initialize the ORB using different ORB
38 // initialization interfaces. See the vendor specific portions of
39 // the text for more information.
40 orb = org.omg.CORBA.ORB.init( args, null);
41
42 // Standard CORBA method for creating root POA and POA manager
43 org.omg.CORBA.Object pobj = orb.resolve_initial_references( "RootPOA"
);
44
45 org.omg.PortableServer.POA poa =
   org.omg.PortableServer.POAHelper.narrow( pobj );
46
47 org.omg.PortableServer.POAManager poa_mgr = poa.the_POAManager();
48
```

Lines 32–48	This section is responsible for initializing the ORB and POA Manager.
Line 40	Most vendors will support the `org.omg.CORBA.ORB.init` method as a way to initialize the ORB. There are many ways to initialize the ORB; this is just one way. It depends upon whether you are initializing an application or an applet. See the vendor's documentation for the different ways to initialize the ORB. Upon successfully initializing the ORB, you will get back an ORB reference that you will use to do further initialization.
Line 43	Once you have a reference to the ORB, you can then obtain a reference to the root POA pseudo object. This is held by the ORB implementation and you obtain a reference to it just as you would any initial ORB service, using `resolve_initial_references` specifying `"RootPOA"` as the reference that you are interested in. Upon successful completion, the ORB will return a generic CORBA object reference that must be narrowed.
Line 45	This line uses the generic CORBA object reference and the `POAHelper` class to narrow the object reference to a reference to the POA. The `POAHelper` class is provided by the ORB vendor. The CORBA specification requires that the `narrow` operation be available from the Helper class. Recall that `narrow` is a distributed type-safe downcast. In line 50 you requested a reference to the `RootPOA`, but you were returned a generic object reference. Therefore, in line 52 you need to find out if it really returned to you a reference to the `RootPOA`. If narrow succeeds, then you have a reference to the `RootPOA`.
Line 47	Using the reference to the `RootPOA`, you obtain a reference to the `POAManager` using the `the_POAManager` method on the `POA` class. We will see how we use the `POAManager` later on in the server application.

That's it for this section of the code. You now have the ORB initialized and a reference to the POAManager. You are now ready to start creating objects.

```
49 System.out.println("PosPoaServer.main() : resolving root
   NameContext...");
50
51 org.omg.CORBA.Object obj = null;
52 try {
53 obj = orb.resolve_initial_references("NameService");
54 } catch( org.omg.CORBA.ORBPackage.InvalidName exc ) {
55 abort("ERROR: The ORB could not resolve a reference to the
   NameService");
56 }
57
58 System.out.println("PosPoaServer.main() : creating new
   OutputMedia...");
59
60 outPut = new OutputMediaPoaImpl();
61
62 System.out.println("PosPoaServer.main() : connecting object to
   ORB...");
63
64 // Activate the poa_manager
65 // By default it will manage and pass requests onto the
   implementation
66 poa_mgr.activate();
67
68 System.out.println("PosPoaServer.main() : publish OutputMedia
   reference to Name Service...");
69
```

Lines 53	The POS server will require a reference to the Naming Service and does this, using resolve_initial_references and the CORBA-defined "NameService" string. If the ORB can return a reference to the NameService, it will do so. Well, to be completely accurate, it will return a generic CORBA object reference to the root Naming Context within the NameService. This reference is used to publish the OutputMedia object into the NameService. Note that if "NameService" is not a recognized service name, then the ORB will throw the CORBA InvalidName exception.
Line 60	This line creates the OutputMediaPoaImpl object. As you can see, even though OutputMediaPoaImpl is a CORBA object, the instantiation of the object is just like any other Java object.
Line 66	The poa_mgr.activate causes the ORB to activate all the implementations, allowing requests to be passed to the implementations. Up to this point you have done two separate activities: initialize the ORB and POA and initialize the object implementations but, you have not tied the two activities together. This is what poa_mgr.activate is used for. It ties the object implementations to the ORB, so it can start passing requests to them.

```
70 // Publish OutputMedia to the Naming Service only after it is ready
      to receive requests
71 PrimerUtils.NsPublisher.nsBind(obj, outPut._this(), "OutputMedia_" +
   posID, "Primer_Example" );
72
```

Line 71	This line binds the `OutputMediaPoaImpl` object into the Naming Service. The name used, as defined in the requirements, is `OutputMedia_<POSTerminalID>`. This naming convention allows each `POS` terminal to locate its specific `OutputMedia` object.

```
73 System.out.println("PosPoaServer is ready" );
74
75 // For non-gui server applications, some ORB vendors require that the
      main
76 // thread not exit and others allow the main thread to exit and
      continue
77 // processing requests. For a server application with a GUI,
      typically the
78 // main thread is used to run the GUI. See the vendor specific
      sections of
79 // the text which describes how each ORB behaves with respect to the
      main
80 // thread.
81
82 }
```

Lines 73–82	As discussed in the previous server implementations, some vendors require that the main thread of execution not exit and others allow the main thread to exit. The ORB has spawned threads to do its work. Some ORB vendors spawn daemon threads and others do not. See the sections on your specific ORB for details.

```
83 // used to catch CORBA System exceptions that could result from
84 // initialization or narrow of object references.
85 catch (org.omg.CORBA.SystemException se) {
86 se.printStackTrace();
87 abort("Caught CORBA.SystemException : " + se);
88 }
89
90 // used to catch Java exceptions such as a null object reference
      being returned
91 // from the narrow operation.
92 catch( java.lang.Exception jle ) {
93 jle.printStackTrace();
94 abort("Caught java.lang.Exception : " + jle);
95 }
96
97 } // main
98 } // PosPoaServer
99
```

34.2.8 Implementation of the Non-POA Version of the POS Server

Here is the code for the non-POA version of the POS server. The implementation is based on the requirements we set down in Chapter 24. This section will primarily point out the differences between the POA and non-POA versions. As you will see, the difference is small, but significant.

The main function of this server simply creates an object of type OutputMedia to print messages to the POSTerminal.

```
1 package POS;
2
3
4 public class PosServer {
5
6
7 private static void abort( String msg ) {
8 System.out.println( msg );
9 System.exit(1);
10 } // abort
11
12 public static void main(String[] args){
13
14 System.out.println("PosServer.main()");
15
16 if(args.length < 1)
17 {
18 abort("usage: PosServer <POS Number> <vendor specific options>" );
19 }
20
21 System.out.println("Using POS Number: " + args[0]);
22 int posID = 0;
23 try {
24 posID = Integer.parseInt(args[0]);
25 } catch( NumberFormatException nfe ) {
26 nfe.printStackTrace();
27 abort("usage: PosServer <POS Number> <vendor specific options>" );
28 }
29
30 org.omg.CORBA.ORB orb = null;
31 POS.OutputMediaImpl outPut = null;
32
33 try
34 {
35
36 System.out.println("PosServer.main() : initialising ORB...");
37
38 // Some ORB vendors prefer to initialize the ORB using different ORB
39 // initialization interfaces. See the vendor specific portions of
```

```
40 // the text for more information.
41 orb = org.omg.CORBA.ORB.init( args, null);
42
43 System.out.println("PosServer.main() : resolving root
   NameContext...");
44
45 org.omg.CORBA.Object obj = null;
46 try {
47 obj = orb.resolve_initial_references("NameService");
48 } catch( org.omg.CORBA.ORBPackage.InvalidName exc ) {
49 abort("ERROR: The ORB could not resolve a reference to the
   NameService");
50 }
51
52
53 System.out.println("PosServer.main() : creating new OutputMedia...");
54
55 outPut = new OutputMediaImpl();
56
57 System.out.println("PosServer.main() : connecting object to ORB...");
58
59 orb.connect(outPut);
60
```

Line 59	This is the primary difference between the POA and non-POA versions. The non-POA version takes the ORB reference that was returned from `org.omg.CORBA.ORB.init` and uses it to `connect` object implementations to the ORB. Once an object is connected to the ORB, it can start to receive messages. Note that it is important to connect the object with the ORB before publishing its object reference with the Naming Service. Otherwise, there is a window where remote objects can get a reference to this object before the object is capable of receiving messages.

```
61 System.out.println("PosServer.main() : publish OutputMedia reference
   to Naming Service...");
62
63 // Publish OutputMedia to the Naming Service only after it is ready
      to receive requests
64 PrimerUtils.NsPublisher.nsBind(obj, outPut, "OutputMedia_" + posID,
   "Primer_Example"
);
65
66 System.out.println("PosServer is ready" );
67
68 // For non-gui server applications, some ORB vendors require that the
69 // main thread not exit and others allow the main thread to exit
70 // and continue processing requests. For a server application with
71 // a GUI, typically the main thread is used to run the GUI. See the
72 // vendor specific sections of the text which describes how each
```

```
73 // ORB behaves with respect to the main thread.
74 }
75 // used to catch CORBA System exceptions that could result from
76 // initialization or narrow of object references.
77 catch (org.omg.CORBA.SystemException se) {
78 se.printStackTrace();
79 abort("Caught CORBA.SystemException : " + se);
80 }
81
82 // used to catch Java exceptions such as a null object reference
      being returned
83 // from the narrow operation.
84 catch( java.lang.Exception jle ) {
85 jle.printStackTrace();
86 abort("Caught java.lang.Exception : " + jle);
87 }
88
89 } // main
90 } // PosServer
91
```

34.3 Implementing the POS Package Using CORBAplus, Java Edition

The Vertel's Expersoft CORBAplus, Java Edition implementation of the POS component requires a small change to the PrimerUtils/NsPublisher.java. This change was covered in Section 28.3.1. Please refer to that section for details on the NsPublisher.java difference. This section contains information about how to start the Store application.

34.3.1 Executing the POS

The POS program is broken up into two programs, POSClient and POSServer.

To execute the POSClient program, change directory to the classes subdirectory and execute the following:

```
java POS.POSClient <StoreNumber> <POSNumber> -pbinit NameService
iiop://localhost:6004/NameServiceRoot
```

To execute the POSServer program, change directory to the classes subdirectory and execute the following:

```
java POS.POSServer <StoreNumber> <POSNumber> -pbinit NameService
iiop://localhost:6004/NameServiceRoot
```

34.4 Implementing the POS Using the IBM ORB for Java

Please refer to Section 28.4 for instructions.

34.5 DAIS-Specific Implementation Details for the POS Client and Server Applications

34.5.1 Amendment Summary

DAIS supports the Portable Object Adapter (POA). At this point, if you have been following the common code sections, you should have the following Java code modules:

`POS\PosPoaServer.java`	Requires two amendments for DAIS
`POS\OutPutMediaImpl.java`	Requires no amendments for DAIS
`POS\PosPoaClient.java`	Requires one amendment for DAIS
`POS\PosTerminalImpl.java`	Requires no amendments for DAIS
`POS\InputMediaImpl.java`	Requires no amendments for DAIS

The amendments are similar to those applied to the `Depot` server application, which are documented in detail in Section 28.5. A summary of the changes is covered here.

The first amendment applies to `PosPoaServer` and `PosPoaClient` and is only required in early versions of DAIS J^2 where `resolve_initial_references` does not recognize the Naming Service. This means you need to use an alternative method to discover the Naming Service. If you are not sure whether this change is applicable to you, don't make any changes at this point. When the application is run, it may abort with the error:

```
"ERROR: The ORB could not resolve a reference to the NameService"
```

This may occur because your Naming Service is not running, or because your version of DAIS J^2 is an early release.

The second amendment to PosPoaServer is essential. The common code section 34.2.7 pointed out that each ORB vendor could decide how the main application thread would suspend so that the application does not terminate.

The following subsections will deal with each of these changes in turn.

34.5.2 Alternative to resolve_initial_references

The classes `PosPoaServer` and `PosPoaClient` both require a single amendment, which is highlighted in the following code:

```
org.omg.CORBA.Object obj = null;
try {
obj = orb.resolve_initial_references("NameService");
} catch( org.omg.CORBA.ORBPackage.InvalidName exc ) {
    if  ((obj = DaisSpecific.ResolveNameService.resolve(orb))==null)
        abort("ERROR: The ORB could not resolve a reference to the
NameService");
}
```

At the point where the common code resolves the Naming Service reference, a
`catch` statement already tests for the exception `org.omg.CORBA.ORBPackage`
`.InvalidName` and resolves to abort the application. At this point, we insert a
statement to call `DaisSpecific.ResolveNameService`, an alternative class that
returns a reference for the Naming Service. If this routine cannot resolve the Naming Service (returns null), then it will abort as well. This class is not part of the product, but is supplied for use with the primer examples. If you are interested in the
implementation of this class, it is documented in the Java implementation of the
`Depot` server.

34.5.3 Handling the Application Main Thread

Once the `PosPoaServer` application has created the `OutPutMedia` component and
advertised it in the Naming Service, it must wait for incoming requests. At this point,
we implement a simple user interface with a single option to exit the application. By
terminating the application in this way, the main thread can remove references in the
Naming Service before exiting. The alternative is to suspend the main thread and interrupt the application (`Cntl-C`). Since Java does not support signal handling, nothing is
closed in a tidy manner.

```
System.out.println("PosPoaServer is ready" );

System.out.println("Type exit to terminate application");
java.io.BufferedReader in = new java.io.BufferedReader( new
            java.io.InputStreamReader(System.in));
String exitString = "exit";
while ( exitString.compareTo(in.readLine()) != 0 )
{
    System.out.println("Type exit to terminate application");
}

PrimerUtils.NsPublisher.nsUnbind(obj, "OutputMedia_" + posID,
                "Primer_Example" );
```

As mentioned earlier, this is a simple but effective solution. The DAIS Trader, Node
Manager, and Factory services offer more resilient solutions because they can remotely
control the lifecycle of an application. This completes the amendments to the Store
application. You are now ready to build the Store server.

34.5.4 Compiling the PosPoaClient and PosPoaServer Applications

```
javac    POS\PosPoaServer.java
javac    POS\PosPoaClient.java
```

This will also compile any dependent Java files, and so it produces the following class files:

```
POS\PosPoaServer.class
POS\OutputMediaPoaImpl.class

POS\PosPoaClient.class
POS\PosTerminalPoaImpl.class
POS\InputMediaPoaImpl.class
```

These files should be moved into their associated subdirectories under the `classes` directory, so all of the preceding classes should be moved to the `.\classes\POS` directory.

34.5.5 Running the PosPoaClient and PosPoaServer Applications

Before running the `PosPoaServer` application, the following servers should be started in the order described:

- An instance of the DAIS Trader should be running.

- An instance of the Naming Service should be running.

The `PosPoaServer` is started from the `classes` directory. It requires one parameter, an identifier describing which POS terminal it is associated with:

```
java POS.PosPoaServer 1
```

Before running the `PosPoaClient`, in addition to the what we just discussed, all the following servers should have been started in the order described:

- An instance of the `DepotPoaServer` should be running

- An instance of the `StorePoaServer` should be running

- An instance of the `PosPoaServer` should be running

The `PosPoaClient` is started from the `classes` directory. The first parameter defines an identifier describing the associated POS terminal. The second parameter identifies the associated `Store` server. Both are numeric values.

```
java POS.PosPoaClient 1 1
```

Once we have tested all the applications together, it is possible to run a number of associated POS clients and servers with different identifiers. Chapter 36, Section 4 discusses different configurations for the primer example.

34.6 The OrbixWeb Implementation of the POS

Background information on how to code OrbixWeb clients and servers can be found in Section 28.6. You should review this material before continuing with this section.

34.6.1 Changes to the Java Code for OrbixWeb

Once again, the code will build and run as is, but the following changes could be made:

Add extra `impl_is_ready` calls just after the `orb.init()` call and just after the `System.out.println("PosServer is ready");` call:

```
// in file PosServer.java
IE.Iona.OrbixWeb._OrbixWeb.ORB(orb).impl_is_ready("OutputSrv",0);
```

and

```
// in file PosServer.java
int timeout = 5 *1000; // or whatever timeout value you want
IE.Iona.OrbixWeb._OrbixWeb.ORB(orb).impl_is_ready("OutputSrv",timeout);
```

The following changes must be made together:

```
// in file PosServer.java
outPut = new OutputMediaImpl("outputPrimerExample");

// file OutputMediaImpl.java
OutputMediaImpl(string marker){
        super(marker);
// the remainder of the constructor is the same as the original

}  // Constructor
```

Again, these changes are made for the same reasons as discussed in Section 28.6.

34.6.1.1 Registering Servers in the Implementation Repository

The Server that creates the `Store` and `Tax` objects in this case is called `StoreSrv`, and it can be registered in the Orbix daemons' Implementation Repository using the following commands:

```
putit -j OutputSrv POS.PosServer
chmodit i+all OutputSrv
chmodit l+all OutputSrv
```

As before, a server that is registered in this fashion can also be run manually from the command line. However, if a client makes an invocation on this server and it is not currently running, then the Orbix daemon will launch the process.

34.6.1.2 Binding to Remote Objects

For example, the `PosClient` could use the following code to obtain a reference to the `OutputMediaImpl` object instead of the `nsResolve` method:

```
String hostname = // put in the hostname you are running the depot on
OutputMedia oRef = OutputMedia.Helper.bind(":OutputSrv", hostname);
```

or

```
String hostname = // put in the hostname you are running the depot on
OutputMedia oRef =
  OutputMedia.Helper.bind("outputPrimerExample:OutputSrv", hostname);
```

34.7 Implementing the POS Package Using VisiBroker for Java

The Inprise VisiBroker implementation of the POS component does not require any changes to the common code. The information contained in Section 28.7 can be used to build the `Store` package as well.

POS: COBOL Coding

35.1 Getting Started on the POS

This chapter presents the implementation of POS using Orbix COBOL. As with the Depot and Store COBOL chapters, the convention used in other POS chapters of separating the common code from specific implementation examples is not necessary because Orbix COBOL is the only implementation of the COBOL language mapping presented in this book.

Before you proceed any further and jump into the details of how POS is implemented using COBOL, you should first read the language-independent functionality of POS in Section 33.1. There you will find an overview of the POS implementation, so if you have not read it yet, turn back there first before you read on.

35.2 Mapping of POS IDL to COBOL

The complete descriptions of the externally accessible interfaces for POS are contained within the POS IDL file. This file is similar to the Store IDL file in that it also contains three IDL interfaces: **InputMedia**, **OutputMedia**, and **POSTerminal.** Along with these interface definitions you will also find several typedefs that are defined at a global level. As we observed in Chapter 32, all types within interfaces are unrolled back to their basic types, so IDL typedefs are not mapped to any specific COBOL data items in their own right. This means that each specific IDL interface will be mapped to one COBOL copy file that will contain the complete layout of all the parameters for each of the operations within the interface. We shall see illustrations of this in a moment when we review the COBOL copy files generated for each of the POS interfaces.

Within this chapter we shall repeat the pattern we used in the previous two COBOL chapters. We will start by showing you the Orbix COBOL copy files that are generated for each of the three interfaces. After that we'll look at the implementation details of the POS server and each of its interfaces. Finally, we'll complete the chapter with a review of the POS client's details.

35.2.1 The Mapping for the InputMedia Interface

Here is the IDL for the **InputMedia** interface that is contained within the POS module:

```
typedef string Barcode;

interface InputMedia
{
  typedef string OperatorCmd;

    void      barcode_input(in Barcode      item);
    void      keypad_input( in OperatorCmd cmd);
};
```

The Orbix COBOL mapping for this **InputMedia** interface will result in a COBOL copy file called `INPUTMED.CPY` being generated. The names for generated COBOL copy files are restricted to 8 bytes. As a result, the interface name has been truncated to `INPUTMED` and used as the file name. The contents of the generated copy file for this implementation will be:

```
*************************************************************
*
*   Interface:   InputxMedia
*
*   Generated by gencbl
*
*************************************************************


*************************************************************
*
*   Defined Operations
*
*************************************************************


*
*   Operation  :  barcode_input
*   Parameters :  in string item
*
```

```
01 INPUTXMEDIA-BARCODE-INPUT-ARGS.
   03 ITEM                       POINTER.


*
*  Operation  :  keypad_input
*  Parameters :  in string cmd
*
 01 INPUTXMEDIA-KEYPAD-INPUT-ARGS.
    03 CMD                       POINTER.


*************************************************************
   COPY INPUTXMX.
*************************************************************
01 INPUTXMEDIA-OPERATION          PICTURE X(14).
   88 INPUTXMEDIA-BARCODE-INPUT    VALUE "barcode_input".
   88 INPUTXMEDIA-KEYPAD-INPUT     VALUE "keypad_input".

01 INPUTXMEDIA-OPERATION-LENGTH  PICTURE 9(09) BINARY
                                 VALUE 14.
```

Here we find that we have the parameter layouts for the two operations within the InputMedia interface and an operation area. As we have seen in the previous COBOL chapters, the Orbix implementation of COBOL also pulls in another copy file called INPUTMEX.CPY. This includes product-specific details for the InputMedia implementation that are completely opaque to users.

35.2.2 The Mapping for the OutputMedia Interface

Here is the IDL for the **OutputMedia** interface that is contained within the POS module:

```
interface OutputMedia
{
   boolean    output_text(in string  string_to_print );
};
```

The Orbix COBOL mapping for this **OutputMedia** interface will result in a COBOL copy file called OUTPUTME.CPY being generated. Once again, the name has been truncated to 8 bytes. Its contents will be as follows:

```
*************************************************************
*
*  Interface:  OutputMedia
*
*  Generated by gencbl
*
*************************************************************


*************************************************************
*
*  Defined Operations
```

```
     *
     ********************************************************
     *
     *  Operation   :   output_text
     *  Parameters  :   in string string_to_print
     *  Returns     :   boolean
     *
       01 OUTPUTMEDIA-OUTPUT-TEXT-ARGS.
          03 STRING-TO-PRINT                POINTER.
          03 RESULT                         PICTURE 9(01) BINARY.
             88 RESULT-FALSE                VALUE 0.
             88 RESULT-TRUE                 VALUE 1.


     ********************************************************
       COPY OUTPUTMX.
     ********************************************************
       01 OUTPUTMEDIA-OPERATION             PICTURE X(12).
          88 OUTPUTMEDIA-OUTPUT-TEXT        VALUE "output_text".

       01 OUTPUTMEDIA-OPERATION-LENGTH      PICTURE 9(09) BINARY
                                            VALUE 12.
```

In the preceding COBOL copy file we can see that it contains the parameter layout for the one operation within the **OutputMedia** interface and an operation area. For the Orbix implementation we once again find another copy file called OUTPUMX.CPY that includes product-specific details for the OutputMedia implementation, which has contents that are completely opaque to users.

35.2.3 The Mapping for the POSTerminal Interface

Here is the IDL for the **POSTerminal** interface that is contained within the POS module:

```
interface POSTerminal
{
    void  login();
    void  print_POS_sales_summary();
    void  print_store_sales_summary();
    void  send_barcode(in Barcode    item);
    void  item_quantity(in long      quantity);
    void  end_of_sale();
};
```

The Orbix COBOL mapping for this **POSTerminal** interface will result in a COBOL copy file called POSTERMI.CPY being generated. Its contents will be as follows:

```
     ********************************************************
     *
```

```
*  Interface:  POSTerminal
*
*  Generated by gencbl
*
**********************************************************

**********************************************************
*
*  Defined Operations
*
**********************************************************

*
*  Operation  :  login
*
 01 POSTERMINAL-LOGIN-ARGS.
   03 FILLER                    PICTURE X(01).


*
*  Operation  :  print_POS_sales_summary
*
 01 POSTERMINAL-PRINT-POS-SAL-ARGS.
   03 FILLER                    PICTURE X(01).


*
*  Operation  :  print_store_sales_summary
*
 01 POSTERMINAL-PRINT-STORE-S-ARGS.
   03 FILLER                    PICTURE X(01).


*
*  Operation  :  send_barcode
*  Parameters :  in string item
*
 01 POSTERMINAL-SEND-BARCODE-ARGS.
   03 ITEM                      POINTER.


*
*  Operation  :  item_quantity
*  Parameters :  in long quantity
*
 01 POSTERMINAL-ITEM-QUANTITY-ARGS.
   03 QUANTITY                  PICTURE S9(09) BINARY.


*
*  Operation  :  end_of_sale
*
 01 POSTERMINAL-END-OF-SALE-ARGS.
   03 FILLER                    PICTURE X(01).
```

```
********************************************************************
    COPY POSTERMX.
********************************************************************
01 POSTERMINAL-OPERATION              PICTURE X(26).
   88 POSTERMINAL-LOGIN                  VALUE "login".
   88 POSTERMINAL-PRINT-POS-SALES-SU
                   VALUE "print_POS_sales_summary".
   88 POSTERMINAL-PRINT-STORE-SALES
                   VALUE "print_store_sales_summary".
   88 POSTERMINAL-SEND-BARCODE         VALUE "send_barcode".
   88 POSTERMINAL-ITEM-QUANTITY        VALUE "item_quantity".
   88 POSTERMINAL-END-OF-SALE          VALUE "end_of_sale".


01 POSTERMINAL-OPERATION-LENGTH   PICTURE 9(09) BINARY
                                  VALUE 26.
```

In the preceding code we can see that this COBOL copy file contains the parameter layouts for the six operations within the **POSTerminal** interface and an operation area. And, as always, we have a product-specific copy file called POSTERMX.CPY that includes product-specific details for the POSTerminal implementation that are completely opaque to users.

35.3 Implementing the POS with Orbix COBOL

Now let's look at the actual implementation of the POS server written using Orbix COBOL. We'll start by reviewing the main program that is used to register the three POS interfaces with the ORB. After that we'll look at the dispatcher that is responsible for receiving all inbound requests and dispatching them to the correct interface implementation. We will then turn our attention to each of the interfaces (**InputMedia, OutputMedia,** and **POSTerminal**) and look at the details of their implementation. Finally, we'll finish by examining the details of the POS client.

35.3.1 The POS Server

The POS server initialization carries out all the processing required to enable the POS server to receive and process inbound requests for each of the three IDL interfaces **InputMedia, OutputMedia,** and **POSTerminal**.

The server starts off by receiving two command-line parameters. The first of these is the unique identifier for the Store server that it is to communicate with. The second is a unique numeric Identifier for this instance of the POS server. It will then register the three POS interfaces with the ORB. We will not be reviewing the syntax of COBOL command-line argument processing here. This will enable us to stay focused on CORBA. If you are really curious to see how that works, you may look at the tutorial source code.

```
      PROCEDURE DIVISION.

*-------------------------------------------------------------
*    Initialize
*-------------------------------------------------------------
      perform get-args.


*-------------------------------------------------------------
*    Activate the Implementation
*-------------------------------------------------------------
      CALL "ORBSTAT" USING ORBIX-STATUS-INFORMATION
      CALL "ORBREG"  USING PosTerminal-INTERFACE
      CALL "ORBREG"  USING OutputMedia-INTERFACE
      CALL "ORBREG"  USING InputMedia-INTERFACE
```

Once the GET-ARGS paragraph has been performed to receive and process the command-line arguments, the ORBSTAT routine is called to register the ORBIX-STATUS-INFORMATION area as the COBOL working storage in which all status information is to be recorded for this program. As discussed in Section 29.5.3.1.1, this area will contain the return status for all calls and is checked to determine if an exception has been raised. The ORBIX-STATUS-INFORMATION area, which we specified as a parameter on the call, is defined within the standard CORBA.CPY copy file. Remember that this copy file must be included within the working storage of all COBOL programs that use the Orbix COBOL routines.

After the ORBSTAT call, ORBREG calls are used to register the details for each of the three interfaces that the POS server will support. The interface-specific parameters used on each of the ORBREG calls are defined for you within the implementation-specific COBOL copy files generated for each of the three Store interfaces.

Once the ORBREG calls have been completed, the server needs to call initialization routines for the implementations. Along with some basic initialization, these routines will also construct unique object references for each of the implementations, then register them with the Naming Service. However, before it is possible for such routines to be able construct valid object references within an Orbix COBOL context, the ORBINIT call must be first invoked. By default, ORBINIT will run forever when called and send all inbound requests to the Store server's dispatcher until the server is terminated. Therefore, if we call ORBINIT, we will not be able to call the initialization routines. We solved this problem before in Section 29.5.3.1, and we'll solve it here just as we did there by setting a timer so that an initial call to ORBINIT times out. We can then call the initialization routines, reset the ORBINIT timer, and call ORBINIT once again:

```
*
*    Set server timeout to 0 just to get it going
*
      move "0"                    to ws-timeout
      SET EVENT-TIMEOUT           TO TRUE
      CALL "ORBTIME" USING ORBIX-TIMEOUT-TYPE
                           WS-TIMEOUT
      PERFORM CHECK-STATUS

      CALL "ORBINIT" USING SERVER-NAME
                           SERVER-NAME-LEN
```

```
          PERFORM CHECK-STATUS

     *
     *    Now Cache object references in the NameService
     *
          move posId              to ws-99
          move "Om_"              to om-name
          move ws-99              to om-name(4:2)
          CALL "ns-bind" using server-name
                              omi-name
                              om-name
          CALL "Pos-Init"   using posid StoreId server-name
          CALL "Input-Init" using posid StoreId server-name


     *---------------------------------------------------------
     *    Start client
     *---------------------------------------------------------
          start "inclt" using pos-args
```

As can be seen within the preceding code segment, the ORBTIME call is used to set a zero time-out for the ORBINIT call so that it will time out, and return immediately when called. This then enables us to perform the required initialization. ns-bind is called directly to create and cache the object reference for the OutputMedia object. We then call initialization routines that do the same, along with some other initialization for the InputMedia and POSTerminal implementations. We won't be looking at the details of that initialization right away. Instead, we'll review it as we review the implementation details for each of the interfaces later on.

Once the initialization has been completed, we start the POS Client running as a separate thread within the POS server. It could just as easily be run as a separate process, but for the sake of simplicity within this chapter, we are starting it as a separate thread within this process. Later on, once we have completed our review of the implementation of the three POS server interfaces, we shall be reviewing the details of this POS Client.

Having completed the initialization, we now find that we are ready to start listening for inbound requests. To do this we simply reset the timer for ORBINIT, then call it so that the server may proceed with its request processing. We once again set the timer to run for an arbitrary 15 minutes. The actual value specified is in milliseconds.

```
     *---------------------------------------------------------
     *    Now wait for inbound requests
     *---------------------------------------------------------
     *
     *    Now wait for up to 15 minutes for inbound requests
     *
          move "900000"            to ws-timeout
          SET EVENT-TIMEOUT        TO TRUE
          CALL "ORBTIME" USING ORBIX-TIMEOUT-TYPE
                              WS-TIMEOUT

          CALL "ORBINIT" USING SERVER-NAME
                              SERVER-NAME-LEN
          STOP RUN.
```

35.3.2 The POS Dispatcher

As we just saw in Section 29.5.3.2, when an Orbix COBOL server has made the ORBINIT call, it will wait within that call for all inbound requests. Each one that is received will then be passed directly to an entry point within the server called DIS-PATCH. Because the POS server is like the Store server and has three interfaces, it needs a generic dispatcher that will determine which of the three interfaces has been requested for each inbound request. The following is the code for the POS dispatcher. You will find it to be almost identical to the Store dispatcher.

```
IDENTIFICATION DIVISION.
PROGRAM-ID.                   DISPATCH.

DATA DIVISION.
WORKING-STORAGE SECTION.
    COPY CORBA.
    . . .
PROCEDURE DIVISION.

    CALL "ORBSTAT" USING ORBIX-STATUS-INFORMATION.
    CALL "ORBREQ"  USING REQUEST-INFO.
```

As requests are received, an initial ORBSTAT is done to register the status area. An ORBREQ call will then be made to insert details for the inbound request into a data area called REQUEST-INFO. The layout of this area is defined within the generic COBOL copy file called CORBA.CPY. All COBOL programs using Orbix COBOL are required to specify this COBOL copy file within their WORKING-STORAGE area, as illustrated earlier.

Once the request details have been obtained, the string that identifies which interface the request is for is used to call the correct interface implementation. The following code shows you how this is done:

```
*
*       Determine which interface has been called
*
        CALL "STRGET"   USING INTERFACE-NAME
                              WS-INTERFACE-TEXT-LEN
                              WS-INTERFACE-TEXT
        EVALUATE WS-INTERFACE-TEXT
            WHEN "OutputMedia"
                call "OM"

            WHEN "POSTerminal"
                call "POSTERM"

            WHEN "InputxMedia"
                call "IM"

        END-EVALUATE

        EXIT PROGRAM
```

Since the string is passed into the REQUEST-INFO block as a CORBA String, the actual textual description is obtained by using the STRGET function call. This will convert the Opaque CORBA String into a COBOL text value. The returned textual interface name is then used to call the interface that has been requested for this call.

35.3.3 The OutputMedia Implementation

Now let's turn our attention to the first of the three POS server interfaces: **Output-Media**. This will include an overview of how it invokes the correct COBOL paragraph for inbound requests, and also the actual implementation of the one operation defined within the interface.

35.3.3.1 OutputMedia Interface State

The OutputMedia interface is a very simple interface. It does not retain any state, so it will also not require a specific initialization entry point to be called. Instead, a call is made directly to ns-bind within the main initialization code for the POS server to create an object reference for this implementation, and then store that reference in the Naming Service.

35.3.3.2 Processing Inbound OutputMedia Requests

When the generic POS server Dispatcher has received an inbound request for the **OutputMedia** object, it will be passed to the **OutputMedia** implementation. Here the code will determine which specific operation within the **OutputMedia** implementation has been requested, and call it. In fact, since there is only one operation, we could call it directly; however, for the sake of illustration we shall assume more than one.

```
PROCEDURE DIVISION.
      CALL "ORBSTAT" USING ORBIX-STATUS-INFORMATION.
      CALL "ORBREQ"  USING REQUEST-INFO.

      CALL "STRGET"  USING OPERATION-NAME
                           OUTPUTMEDIA-OPERATION-LENGTH
                           OUTPUTMEDIA-OPERATION.
      COPY OUTPUTMD.

      GOBACK.
```

Like all the other operation selectors that we have seen, an initial ORBSTAT call is made to establish the status area. An ORBREQ call is then used to obtain the details of the inbound request. The actual name of the requested operation is extracted from the CORBA String type into an OUTPUTMEDIA-OPERATION area by a call to STRGET. (The OUTPUTMEDIA-OPERATION area is defined within the OUTPUTME.CPY COBOL copy file that is generated by the Orbix Gencbl utility.) Finally, the code within a generated COBOL copy file called OUTPUTMD.CPY is used to perform the requested operation.

(The COBOL copy file OUTPUTMD.CPY is generated by the Orbix Gencbl utility. It expects the operation name to be set in OUTPUTMEDIA-OPERATION, and uses this to select the correct COBOL paragraph.)

35.3.3.3 OutputMedia Method: Output-Text

The one and only operation within the OutputMedia implementation, Output-Text, will take a text string supplied as input and display it:

```
*--------------------------------------------------------
*     OutputText
*--------------------------------------------------------
 DO-OUTPUTMEDIA-OUTPUT-TEXT.
     CALL "ORBGET" USING OUTPUTMEDIA-OUTPUT-TEXT-ARGS

     move length of ws-data to ws-data-lth
     call "STRGET"     using String-To-Print
                             ws-data-lth
                             ws-data

     display ws-data

     CALL "ORBPUT" USING OUTPUTMEDIA-OUTPUT-TEXT-ARGS

     .
```

As we have already seen, we always start a method implementation with an ORBGET call. This needs to be done to populate the parameter area for the operation with all the input parameters contained within the inbound request. In this case, this will be the string that is to be displayed. The OUTPUTMEDIA-OUTPUT-TEXT-ARGS area used as a parameter on the ORBGET call is defined within the COBOL copy file generated for the **OutputMedia** interface. You can refer back to the illustration of the contents of this copy file to see the complete layout of the parameter area. It contains all the parameters used by the operation in one COBOL group item. The ORBGET call will only populate the **in** and **inout** parameter areas.

The STRGET routine is called to convert the opaque CORBA string into a COBOL text string. The COBOL text is then displayed.

Once a method implementation has completed its processing, the ORBPUT routine is called. This is done to return all the accumulated results for the operation back to the caller. All the **out**, **inout**, and result parameter values will be returned to the caller. In this case, there are no values to be returned; however, ORBPUT should always be called just to return control back to the caller.

35.3.4 The POSTerminal Implementation

Now let's look at the details of the second of the three POS server interfaces: **POSTerminal**. This will include a look at how the state of the **POSTerminal** instance is held and how its initialization is performed. We'll also see how it invokes the correct

COBOL paragraph for inbound requests, and finally look at the actual implementation of the six operations defined within the interface.

35.3.4.1 POSTerminal Instance State

The state of the POSTerminal implementation is held in the following structure within the COBOL working storage of each instance:

```
1 pos-State.
      03 PosTotal                    comp-1.
      03 PosTaxTotal                 comp-1.
      03 saleSubtotal                comp-1.
      03 saleTaxSubtotal             comp-1.

      03 itemBarCode                 pic 9(9) binary.
      03 ws-quantity                 pic 9(9) binary.

      03 access-ref                  pointer.
      03 store-ref                   pointer.
      03 tax-ref                     pointer.
      03 om-ref                      pointer.

      03 store-name                  pic x(32).
      03 om-name                     pic x(32).
      03 tax-name                    pic x(32).
      03 pos-name                    pic x(32).
```

The values held within the state for the POSTerminal are:

- Totals for POS and Store sales both with and without tax.

- The current item barcode and the number of items of that specific type.

- Object references for other implementations accessed by methods within the POSTerminal implementation. The textual names under which these object references are cached within the Naming Service are also held here.

35.3.4.2 Initialization for the POSTerminal Interface

Within the main program for the POS server, a call to the Pos-Init entry point is made when it is performing its primary initialization. When that call is made, it will pass as parameters the unique POS and store identifiers along with the name of the POS server. Here we will see initialization performed that is specific to the POSTerminal implementation:

```
*=============================================================
*     Pos-Init
*=============================================================
 Pos-Init.
```

```
Entry "Pos-Init" using lk-pos-id
                        lk-store-Id
                        lk-server-name
            .

    move 0.0                    to PosTotal         in pos-state
    move 0.0                    to PosTaxTotal       in pos-state
    move 0.0                    to saleSubTotal      in pos-state
    move 0.0                    to saleTaxSubTotal   in pos-state
    move 0                      to itemBarCode       in pos-state

    move lk-pos-Id      to PosId
    move lk-store-id    to storeId

    move lk-pos-id      to ws-99
    move "Pos_"         to pos-name
    move ws-99          to pos-name(5:2)
    call "ns-bind" using lk-server-name
                         ws-posterm-name
                         pos-name

    move lk-store-id    to ws-99
    move "Store_"       to store-name
    move ws-99          to store-name(7:2)

    move lk-pos-id      to ws-99
    move "Om_"          to om-name
    move ws-99          to om-name(4:2)

    move lk-store-id    to ws-99
    move "Tax_"         to tax-name
    move ws-99          to Tax-name(5:2)

    call "ns-rslv" using store-name returning store-ref
    call "ns-rslv" using tax-name   returning tax-ref
    call "ns-rslv" using om-name    returning om-ref

    move 1              to ws-quantity
    set access-ref      to null
    exit program
        .
```

Within the preceding initialization code for the POSTerminal implementation, the following occurs:

- The Store, POS total, and item barcode fields are initialized to zero.

- The textual names used to cache object references within the Naming Service are set. These are Store_nn for the Store implementation within the Store server, Om_nn for the OutputMedia implementation within this server, and Tax_nn for the Tax implementation within the Store server.

- The `ns-rslv` routine is used to obtain the object references for the three implementations, `Store`, `OutputMedia`, and `Tax`. (The `ns-rslv` code is discussed in detail in Section 29.4.3.4.)

- Finally, the current item quantity is set to 1, and the **StoreAccess** object reference is set to NULL. The **StoreAccess** object reference will be established by the `Login` operation when a cashier logs in to the Store.

35.3.4.3 Processing Inbound POSTerminal Requests

When the generic POS server Dispatcher has received an inbound request for the **POSTerminal** interface, it will be passed to the `POSTerminal` implementation. Here the code will determine which specific operation within the **POSTerminal** interface has been requested, and call it. We have seen code like this before, but for the sake of the completeness of this example we have included it here:

```
PROCEDURE DIVISION.
        CALL "ORBSTAT" USING ORBIX-STATUS-INFORMATION.
        CALL "ORBREQ"  USING REQUEST-INFO.

        CALL "STRGET"  USING OPERATION-NAME
                             POSTERMINAL-OPERATION-LENGTH
                             POSTERMINAL-OPERATION.
        COPY POSTERMD.

    GOBACK.
```

After the usual `ORBSTAT` call to establish the status area, an `ORBREQ` call is used to obtain the details of the inbound request. The actual name of the requested operation is then extracted from the CORBA String type into a `POSTERMINAL-OPERATION` area by a call to `STRGET`. (The `POSTERMINAL-OPERATION` area is defined within the `POSTERMI.CPY` COBOL copy file that is generated by the Orbix `Gencbl` utility.)

Finally, the code within a generated COBOL copy file called `POSTERMD.CPY` is used to perform the requested operation. It is generated by the Orbix `Gencbl` utility, and expects the operation name to be set in `POSTERMINAL-OPERATION` so that it can use it to select the correct COBOL paragraph. Its actual contents are:

```
EVALUATE TRUE

    WHEN POSTERMINAL-LOGIN
        PERFORM DO-POSTERMINAL-LOGIN

    WHEN POSTERMINAL-PRINT-POS-SALES-SU
        PERFORM DO-POSTERMINAL-PRINT-POS-SALES

    WHEN POSTERMINAL-PRINT-STORE-SALES
        PERFORM DO-POSTERMINAL-PRINT-STORE-SAL

    WHEN POSTERMINAL-SEND-BARCODE
```

```
           PERFORM DO-POSTERMINAL-SEND-BARCODE

      WHEN POSTERMINAL-ITEM-QUANTITY
           PERFORM DO-POSTERMINAL-ITEM-QUANTITY

      WHEN POSTERMINAL-END-OF-SALE
           PERFORM DO-POSTERMINAL-END-OF-SALE


  END-EVALUATE
```

35.3.4.4 POSTerminal Common Routines: Do-Output

Before we get down to the specific implementation details of each of the operations within the interface, we shall first pause for a moment to review the Do-Output paragraph, which is used by several of the **POSTerminal** operations to send the contents of the ls-out-txt area in working storage to the Output-text operation in the Output-Media implementation:

```
      *=============================================================
      *    Do-Output
      *=============================================================
       Do-Output.
           move length of ls-out-txt to ls-out-lth
           call "STRSET" using STRING-TO-PRINT
                                   in OUTPUTMEDIA-OUTPUT-TEXT-args
                               ls-out-lth
                               ls-out-txt
           if 88-output-media-no-init
               CALL "ORBREG" USING OutputMedia-Interface
               set 88-output-media-init to true
           end-if

           set OUTPUTMEDIA-OUTPUT-TEXT  to true
           call "ORBEXEC" using om-ref

                               OutputMedia-Operation
                               OUTPUTMEDIA-OUTPUT-TEXT-args

           perform check-status

           .
```

First we convert the COBOL text within the ls-out-txt area into a CORBA string type, then establish this value within the parameter area for the Output-text operation within the OutputMedia implementation.

Next, if we have not previously used the OutputMedia implementation within this program, we call the ORBREG routine to register the fact that we are about to start using it.

Finally, we use the ORBEXEC routine to call the Output-text routine within the OutputMedia implementation. We use the OutputMedia object reference that we cached within the POSTerminal State when we first initialized the POSTerminal implementation.

35.3.4.5 POSTerminal Method: Login

We are now ready to review the POSTerminal operations. The first of the six, Login, will log the POS terminal into an instance of the Store by calling the Store object's Login operation to create a new instance of the StoreAccess object. The Object Reference for the new StoreAccess object will be saved within the POSTerminal State:

```
     *-------------------------------------------------------------
     *    Login
     *-------------------------------------------------------------
     DO-POSTERMINAL-LOGIN.
         CALL "ORBGET" USING POSTERMINAL-LOGIN-ARGS

         if 88-login
             display "Not allowed to login twice "
         else
             display "Starting store login ..."

             move posid
                     to IDL-ID in store-login-args
             perform store-init
             set store-login  to true
             call "ORBEXEC" using store-ref
                                   store-Operation
                                   store-login-args
             perform check-status
             if exception-number = 0
                 set access-ref in pos-state
                     to result in store-login-args
                 display "POS::Login - logged into store - "
                         posid
                 move 0.0 to saleSubtotal      in pos-state,
                             PosTaxtotal       in pos-state,
                             PosTotal          in pos-state
                 move 1   to ws-quantity       in pos-state
                 set 88-login                  to true
             end-if
         end-if

         CALL "ORBPUT" USING POSTERMINAL-LOGIN-ARGS
         .
```

The mandatory ORBGET is first called (as it always should be) to populate the parameter area for this operation within the generated COBOL copy file for this implementation with all the input parameters for this operation.

If a login has already been done, another will not be permitted.

If there is no current login, the unique POS identifier will be extracted from the current state and set up as the input parameter for a call to the login operation in the Store object. The ORBEXEC routine is then called to invoke that operation. We use the Store object reference that we obtained during the initialization of this specific implementation.

As long as no exception has been raised, the returned object reference for the newly created instance of the StoreAccess object is cached within the state. Since the state area is also used to keep track of totals, these values are initialized to zero and a flag is set to indicate that a login is now in progress.

Finally, the mandatory ORBPUT routine is called to pass control back to the caller of this operation. In this instance, there are no return values that get passed back to the caller. Even in cases such as this, the ORBPUT routine should still be called.

35.3.4.6 POSTerminal Method: Print-POS-sales-summary

The second of the six operations, the Print-POS-sales-summary routine, will display the totals for this POSTerminal:

```
*------------------------------------------------------------
*     PrintPosSales
*------------------------------------------------------------
DO-POSTERMINAL-PRINT-POS-SALES.
    display "PosTerminal: Print-Pos-Sales-Summary"
    CALL "ORBGET" USING POSTERMINAL-PRINT-POS-SAL-ARGS

    if 88-no-login
        display "You must first login"
    else
        if saleSubTotal in pos-state not = 0
             OR
           itemBarCode  in pos-state not = 0
         display "POSTerminal_Print-POS-Sales-Summary - "
                    "ignored, sale in progress"
        else

            move "Point of Sale Total:"   to ls-out-txt
            move PosTotal             to ls-out-value
            move ls-out-value         to ls-out-txt(22:12)
            perform do-output

            move "Tax Total             :"   to ls-out-txt
            move PosTaxTotal in pos-state to ls-out-value
            move ls-out-value         to ls-out-txt(22:12)
            perform do-output

        end-if
    end-if

    CALL "ORBPUT" USING POSTERMINAL-PRINT-POS-SAL-ARGS
    .
```

As always, the ORBGET routine is called to populate the parameter area with all the input parameters for this operation. In this case, there are no input parameters, but the call should still be made.

As long as there is a current login, and there is no sale currently in progress, then the POS totals are extracted from the State and formatted for display. The actual output is sent to the `OutputMedia` object using the common `Do-Output` paragraph that we reviewed earlier.

Finally, `ORBPUT` is called to pass control back to the caller of this operation.

35.3.4.7 POSTerminal Method: Print-store-sales-summary

The third of the six operations, the Print-store-sales-summary routine, will obtain the store totals from the `Store` object and display them:

```
*-------------------------------------------------------------
*      PrintStoreSales
*-------------------------------------------------------------
DO-POSTERMINAL-PRINT-STORE-SAL.
        display "PosTerminal: PrintStoreSalesSummary"
        CALL "ORBGET" USING POSTERMINAL-PRINT-STORE-S-ARGS

        if 88-no-login
            display "You must first login"
        else
            if saleSubTotal in pos-state not = 0
                  OR
               itemBarCode  in pos-state not = 0
             display "POSTerminal_PrintStoreSalesSummary - "
                     "ignored, sale in progress"
            else


*
*               Print Store Totals
*

                perform store-init
                set STORE-GET-TOTALS  to true
                call "ORBEXEC" using store-ref
                                     store-Operation
                                     STORE-TOTALS-ARGS
                perform check-status
                move "Total sales        :"   to ls-out-txt
                move STORE-TOTAL in STORE-TOTALS-ARGS
                                     to ls-out-value
                move ls-out-value    to ls-out-txt(22:12)
                perform do-output
                move "Total taxes        :"   to ls-out-txt
                move STORE-TAX-TOTAL in STORE-TOTALS-ARGS
                                     to ls-out-value
                move ls-out-value    to ls-out-txt(22:12)
                perform do-output
            end-if
        end-if
```

```
       CALL "ORBPUT" USING POSTERMINAL-PRINT-STORE-S-ARGS
       .
```

Once again we find the usual call to the ORBGET routine to populate the parameter area with all the input parameters for this operation. This is another instance when there are no input parameters.

Next we check the current login and sale status. If there is no current login, or if there is a sale currently in progress, then nothing will be displayed.

If there is a current login, and if there is no sale in progress, then we use the ORBEXEC routine to call the Get-totals operation within the Store implementation. For this call we use the object reference for the Store object that we cached within the State area during initialization. The returned store totals are formatted and displayed using the common Do-output paragraph to send the output to the Output-text operation within the OutputMedia implementation.

Finally, ORBPUT is called to pass control back to the caller of this operation.

35.3.4.8 POSTerminal Method: Send-barcode

The fourth of the six operations, the Send-barcode routine, initiates a sales transaction for a specific item. It does this by first looking for the details of the item within the Store using the barcode that has been passed in as an input parameter. When found, the total value for the item and its tax will be added into the current transaction totals:

```
*------------------------------------------------------------
*    SendBarCode
*------------------------------------------------------------
DO-POSTERMINAL-SEND-BARCODE.
       CALL "ORBGET" USING POSTERMINAL-SEND-BARCODE-ARGS

       if 88-no-login
           display "You must first login"
       else
           set ITEM1 in STOREACCESS-FIND-PRICE-ARGS
               to item in POSTERMINAL-SEND-BARCODE-ARGS
           move ws-quantity
               to quantity1 in STOREACCESS-FIND-PRICE-ARGS
           perform storeAccess-init
           set STOREACCESS-FIND-PRICE  to true
           call "ORBEXEC" using access-ref
                               STOREACCESS-OPERATION
                               STOREACCESS-FIND-PRICE-ARGS
           if exception-number not = 0
               display "BarCode not found"
               move 1      to ws-quantity
               perform check-status
           else
               compute tmpTotal = (ws-quantity *
                       item-Price
                           in STOREACCESS-FIND-PRICE-ARGS)
```

```
                  add tmpTotal      to saleSubTotal

                  MOVE LENGTH OF WS-TXT TO WS-TXT-LTH
                  CALL "STRGET" USING idl-name in
                                    STOREACCESS-FIND-PRICE-ARGS
                                WS-TXT-LTH
                                WS-TXT
             move ws-quantity      to ws-99
             move ws-99            to ls-out-txt
             move ws-txt           to ls-out-txt(4:8)
             move ITEM-COST in STOREACCESS-FIND-PRICE-ARGS
                                   to ls-out-value
             move ls-out-value     to ls-out-txt(14:8)
             move tmpTotal         to ls-out-value
             move ls-out-value     to ls-out-txt(23:8)
             perform do-output

                  compute tmpTotal = (ws-quantity *
                        item-Tax-Price
                           in STOREACCESS-FIND-PRICE-ARGS)
                  add tmpTotal      to saleTaxSubTotal

             move 1                to ws-quantity
          end-if
        end-if

          CALL "ORBPUT" USING POSTERMINAL-SEND-BARCODE-ARGS
             .
```

Once again we start off with a call to ORBGET to populate the parameter area with the input parameters for this operation. In this case, the barcode of the item that is to be processed is passed in as a CORBA string.

If a login has not already been done, then no processing is permitted.

If a login has been done, then the barcode is put into the parameter area for the Find-Price operation within the StoreAccess implementation. ORBEXEC is then called to execute the Find-Price operation. The object reference used for the Store-Access object was previously cached within the POSTerminal State. This was done when the Login operation within this POSTerminal instance called the Login operation within the Store object to create a new instance of the StoreAccess object.

If an exception is detected, a message will be issued to the caller announcing that the item was not found. The exception details will also be displayed by the CHECK-STATUS paragraph.

If the item is found, and its details are returned, then the full value of the sale for this item is added to the sale subtotal area, and its taxable value is added to the tax subtotal area. The name of the item and the sale and taxable value is also displayed to the caller. The name is extracted from the item's details using the STRGET routine to convert it from its CORBA string format into a COBOL text string. The DO-OUTPUT paragraph is used to issue the sale details via the OutputMedia object. We covered the details of this DO-OUTPUT paragraph earlier.

Finally, we finish by calling ORBPUT to pass control back to the caller of this operation.

35.3.4.9 POSTerminal Method: Item-quantity

The fifth of the six operations, the Item-quantity routine, is used to establish the current number of items for the current transaction within the POSTerminal state area:

```
*----------------------------------------------------------
*     ItemQuantity
*----------------------------------------------------------
DO-POSTERMINAL-ITEM-QUANTITY.
     display "PosTerminal: Item-Quantity"
     CALL "ORBGET" USING POSTERMINAL-ITEM-QUANTITY-ARGS

     if 88-no-login
         display "You must first login"
     else
         if quantity in POSTERMINAL-ITEM-QUANTITY-ARGS > 0
             move quantity
                 in POSTERMINAL-ITEM-QUANTITY-ARGS
                     to ws-quantity in pos-State
         end-if
     end-if

     CALL "ORBPUT" USING POSTERMINAL-ITEM-QUANTITY-ARGS
```

We start with a call to the standard ORBGET routine to populate the parameter area with all the input parameters for this operation. For this operation it will be a count of the number of items.

If a login has not already been done, then no processing is permitted.

If a login has been done, then the number of items passed in will be placed into the POSTerminal State area.

Finally, ORBPUT is called to pass control to the caller of this operation.

35.3.4.10 POSTerminal Method: End-of-sale

The final operation of the six, the End-of-sale routine, will complete the current sale transaction and display the details of the completed sale.

```
*----------------------------------------------------------
*     EndOfSale
*----------------------------------------------------------
DO-POSTERMINAL-END-OF-SALE.
     display "PosTerminal: EndOfSale"
     CALL "ORBGET"    USING POSTERMINAL-END-OF-SALE-ARGS

     if 88-no-login
         display "You must first login"
     else
```

```
        if saleSubTotal in pos-state = 0
          display "EndOfSale ignored, "
                  "there is no sale in progress"
        else
          if ws-quantity in pos-state not = 1
            display "EndOfSale ignored, "
                    "transaction in progress"
          else

            move " Taxable Subtotal   :"      to ls-out-txt
            move saleTaxSubtotal in pos-state
                                    to ls-out-value
            move ls-out-value       to ls-out-txt(22:12)
            perform do-output

            move saleTaxSubtotal in pos-state
                 to TAXABLE-AMOUNT
                    in TAX-CALCULATE-TAX-ARGS
            perform tax-init
            set tax-calculate-Tax   to true
            call "ORBEXEC" using tax-ref
                                  tax-Operation
                                  tax-calculate-Tax-args
            perform check-status
            move result in tax-calculate-Tax-args to ls-tax

            move " Tax               :"      to ls-out-txt
            move ls-tax             to ls-out-value
            move ls-out-value       to ls-out-txt(22:12)
            perform do-output

            move " Total             :"      to ls-out-txt
            move ls-tax             to tmpTotal
            add saleSubtotal in pos-state   to tmpTotal
            move tmpTotal           to ls-out-value
            move ls-out-value       to ls-out-txt(22:12)
            perform do-output

            move posid
                 to idl-id
                    in store-update-Store-Totals-args    -
            move tmpTotal
                 to price
                    in store-update-Store-Totals-args
            move ls-tax
                 to taxes
                    in store-update-Store-Totals-args
            perform store-init
            set store-Update-Store-Totals  to true
            call "ORBEXEC" using store-ref
                            store-Operation
```

```
                          store-update-Store-Totals-args
              perform check-status

              add tmpTotal            to PosTotal
              add ls-tax              to PosTaxTotal

              move 0.0 to saleSubtotal       in pos-state,
                          saleTaxSubtotal    in pos-state
                move 1    to ws-quantity      in pos-state
                move 0    to itemBarCode
              end-if
           end-if
        end-if

           CALL "ORBPUT"    USING POSTERMINAL-END-OF-SALE-ARGS
           .
```

Initially, we start with the standard ORBGET routine to populate the parameter area with all the input parameters for this operation. In this case, there are no input parameters; however, the call should still be made.

Next we check the current login, transaction, and sale status. If there is no current login, or if there is a sale or transaction in progress, then no end-of-sale processing will be performed.

If there is a current login, and if there is no sale or transaction in progress, then we proceed with the end-of-sale processing. First, the taxable subtotal is displayed. Then we take the value and set it up as a parameter for the calculate-tax operation within the Tax object. ORBEXEC is then called to calculate the actual amount of the tax. The returned value is then displayed along with the total value of the sale. Another ORBEXEC is then used to call the Update-Store-Totals operation within the Store object to update the totals for this sale within Store. The totals within the POSTerminal state for a sale are then reset to zero.

Finally, ORBPUT is called to pass control back to the caller of this operation.

35.3.5 The InputMedia Implementation

Having covered the first two POS server interfaces in detail, we are now ready to turn our attention to the third: **InputMedia**. Here we will take a peek at how the state of this InputMedia implementation is held and how its initialization is performed. We'll also see how it invokes the correct COBOL paragraph for inbound requests, and finally take a look at the actual implementation of the two operations defined within the interface.

35.3.5.1 InputMedia Interface State

The state of the InputMedia implementation is held in the following structure within the COBOL working storage of each instance:

```
01 Input-state.
   03 Pos-ref                    pointer.
```

```
03 Pos-id                      pic 9(9) binary.
03 Pos-Name                    pic x(8).
03 Input-name                  pic x(32).]
```

The values held here include the unique identifier for the POS server that was passed into the server as a command-line parameter, the object reference for the POSTerminal object, and the names used to cache the POSTerminal and Input-Media Object references within the Naming Service.

35.3.5.2 Initialization for the InputMedia Interface

Within the main program for the POS server, a call to the Input-Init entry point is made when it is performing its primary initialization. When that call is made, it will pass as parameters the unique POS and store identifiers along with the name of the POS server. Here we shall see initialization performed that is specific to the Input-Media implementation:

```
*===========================================================
*    Input-Init
*===========================================================
 Input-init.
 Entry "Input-Init" using lk-posId
                         lk-storeid
                         lk-server-name
                         .

     move lk-posId          to pos-id
     move lk-posid          to ws-99
     move spaces            to pos-name
     string "Pos_"          delimited by size
            ws-99           delimited by size
                            into pos-name
     call "ns-rslv" using pos-name
                          returning pos-ref

     move spaces      to input-name
     string "Input_"       delimited by size
            ws-99          delimited by size
                       into input-name
     CALL "ns-bind" using lk-server-name
                          ws-input-media
                          Input-name
     exit program
            .
```

Within the preceding initialization code for the InputMedia implementation, the following occurs:

■ The unique POS identifier that was passed in is saved and then used to construct a unique name for the POSTerminal object called Pos_nn (where nn is the unique POS identifier). This value is then used as a parameter on the ns-rslv routine to obtain the object reference for the POSTerminal object. (The ns-rslv code is discussed in detail in Section 29.4.3.4.)

■ The unique POS identifier is then used to construct a unique name for this InputMedia object called Input_nn (where nn is the unique POS identifier). The ns-bind code is then called with this value as one of the parameters to create the new object reference for this InputMedia object and cache it within the Naming Service. (The ns-bind code is also discussed in detail in Section 29.4.3.3.)

35.3.5.3 Processing Inbound InputMedia Requests

When the generic POS server Dispatcher has received an inbound request for the InputMedia object, it will be passed to the InputMedia implementation. Here the code will now determine which specific operation within the **InputMedia** interface has been requested, and call it. This is more or less the same code we used for the other two interfaces within the POS server:

```
PROCEDURE DIVISION.
      CALL "ORBSTAT" USING ORBIX-STATUS-INFORMATION.
      CALL "ORBREQ"  USING REQUEST-INFO.

      CALL "STRGET"  USING OPERATION-NAME
                           INPUTMEDIA-OPERATION-LENGTH
                           INPUTMEDIA-OPERATION.
      COPY INPUTMED.

      GOBACK.
```

After the standard ORBSTAT call to establish the status area, an ORBREQ call is used to obtain the details of the inbound request. The actual name of the requested operation is then extracted from the CORBA String type into an INPUTMEDIA-OPERATION area by a call to STRGET. (The INPUTMEDIA-OPERATION area is defined within the INPUTMED.CPY COBOL copy file that is generated by the Orbix Gencbl utility.)

Finally, the code within a generated COBOL copy file called INPUTMED.CPY is used to perform the requested operation. It is generated by the Orbix Gencbl utility, and expects the operation name to be set in INPUTMEDIA-OPERATION so that it can use it to select the correct COBOL paragraph. The actual code within the generated copy file that will select the correct paragraph for the incoming operation is:

```
EVALUATE TRUE

    WHEN INPUTXMEDIA-BARCODE-INPUT
        PERFORM DO-INPUTXMEDIA-BARCODE-INPUT

    WHEN INPUTXMEDIA-KEYPAD-INPUT
        PERFORM DO-INPUTXMEDIA-KEYPAD-INPUT

END-EVALUATE
```

35.3.5.4 InputMedia Method: Barcode-Input

The first of the two operations, the `Barcode-Input` routine, takes a barcode supplied as an input parameter by the POS client, and uses it to invoke the `Send-Barcode` operation on the **POSTerminal** object:

```
*------------------------------------------------------------
*     BarCodeInput
*------------------------------------------------------------
 DO-INPUTMEDIA-BARCODE-INPUT.
     CALL "ORBGET" USING INPUTMEDIA-BARCODE-INPUT-ARGS

     move item in INPUTXMEDIA-BARCODE-INPUT-ARGS
          to item in POSTERMINAL-SEND-BARCODE-ARGS
     perform pos-init
     set PosTerminal-send-BarCode  to true
     call "ORBEXEC" using pos-ref
                         PosTerminal-Operation
                         PosTerminal-send-BarCode-args
     perform check-status

     CALL "ORBPUT" USING INPUTMEDIA-BARCODE-INPUT-ARGS
     .


*===========================================================*
*     PosTerminal-Init
*===========================================================*
 POS-INIT.
     if 88-pos-no-init
        CALL "ORBREG"  USING PosTerminal-Interface
        set 88-pos-init    to true
     end-if
     .
```

We start off with the mandatory ORBGET routine to populate the parameter area with all the input parameters for this operation. In this case, that will be the barcode. The received value is set up within the parameter area of the `Send-Barcode` operation in the POSTerminal implementation.

Just prior to the ORBEXEC call, the POS-INIT paragraph is performed to call the ORBREG routine to register the start of activity on the POSTerminal implementation within this program. This routine has been coded to ensure that the call is only performed the first time. For successive calls, nothing will happen.

ORBEXEC is called to invoke the `Send-Barcode` operation within the POSTerminal implementation. The first parameter used on this call is the unique object reference for the instance of the POSTerminal object within this server. Remember that we obtained this object reference during the initialization of this InputMedia object and retained it within its state area in its COBOL working storage. The second parameter identifies the specific operation that has been requested. The third parameter is a parameter area containing all the parameters for the operation. Here you insert the barcode as input prior to the ORBEXEC call. Upon completion, any output parameter values will have been set up for you. In this case, there are no output values.

The standard CHECK-STATUS paragraph is performed to check the completion status of the ORBEXEC call. For a more detailed discussion on exception handling, look back to Section 29.5.3.1.1.

Finally, ORBPUT is called to pass control back to the caller of this operation.

35.3.5.5 InputMedia Method: Keypad-Input

The second of the two operations, the Keypad-Input routine, will take a keypad character supplied as an input parameter by the POS client. It will then examine the received character and use it to determine which POSTerminal operation should be called. The range of valid characters is as follows:

- L or l—Login
- P or p—Print POS sales summary
- S or s—Print store sales summary
- T or t—End of sale
- Q or q—Item quantity

Any other characters will be ignored.

```
      *------------------------------------------------------
      *     KeyPadInput
      *------------------------------------------------------
       DO-INPUTMEDIA-KEYPAD-INPUT.
           CALL "ORBGET" USING INPUTMEDIA-KEYPAD-INPUT-ARGS

           move length of ws-data to ws-data-lth
           call "STRGET" using cmd
                                   in INPUTMEDIA-KEYPAD-INPUT-ARGS
                               ws-data-lth
                               ws-data
           evaluate ws-data(1:1)
             when "L"
             when "l"
               perform pos-init
               set PosTerminal-login  to true
               call "ORBEXEC" using pos-ref
                               PosTerminal-Operation
                               PosTerminal-login-args
             perform check-status
             when "P"
             when "p"
               perform pos-init
               set PosTerminal-Print-Pos-Sales-Su  to true
               call "ORBEXEC" using pos-ref
                               PosTerminal-Operation
                               PosTerminal-Print-Pos-Sal-args
```

```
                   perform check-status
               when "S"
               when "s"
                   perform pos-init
                   set PosTerminal-Print-Store-Sales  to true
                   call "ORBEXEC" using pos-ref
                                      PosTerminal-Operation
                                      PosTerminal-Print-Store-S-args
                   perform check-status
               when "T"
               when "t"
                   perform pos-init
                   set PosTerminal-End-Of-Sale  to true
                   call "ORBEXEC" using pos-ref
                                      PosTerminal-Operation
                                      PosTerminal-End-Of-Sale-args
                   perform check-status
               when "Q"
               when "q"
                   perform pos-init
                   move function numval(ws-data(2:10))
                          to quantity
                          in PosTerminal-Item-Quantity-args
                   set PosTerminal-Item-Quantity  to true
                   call "ORBEXEC" using pos-ref
                                      PosTerminal-Operation
                                      PosTerminal-Item-Quantity-args
                   perform check-status
               when other
                   display "input ignored"
           end-evaluate

           CALL "ORBPUT" USING INPUTMEDIA-KEYPAD-INPUT-ARGS
           .
```

The ORBGET routine is called to populate the parameter area with all the input parameters for this operation. In this instance, it will be a character that identifies the specific function that is to be executed.

The STRGET routine is used to convert the input parameter from its opaque CORBA string format into COBOL text. The character is then examined. If recognized, an appropriate operation within the POSTerminal implementation will be called; otherwise, it will be ignored.

When the character is recognized, the POSTerminal operation requested will be called using the ORBEXEC routine. Prior to ORBEXEC, the POS-INIT paragraph will be performed to ensure that the initial ORBREG call has been made. (ORBREG should only ever be called the first time activity for the POSTerminal implementation is initiated. This paragraph will not call it for successive calls.) After the ORBEXEC call, the CHECK-STATUS paragraph will be performed to handle any exceptions raised.

Finally, ORBPUT is called to pass control back to the caller. Now *that* was easy.

35.3.6 The POS Client Implementation

The POS Client may of course be run as a separate process. However for the sake of simplicity, it is actually run within this chapter as a separate thread within the POS server, and is started during its initialization phase.

The POS Client will locate the object reference for the `InputMedia` object within the Naming Service. It then presents a very simple textual menu of options. When valid input is received, it will invoke the appropriate operation within the `InputMedia` implementation to perform the requested function.

35.3.6.1 POS Client: Initialization

The following code is used to initialize the POS Client when it is first called:

```
WORKING-STORAGE SECTION.
    COPY CORBA.
    . . .


PROCEDURE DIVISION using pos-args.


*-----------------------------------------------------------
*     Initialize
*-----------------------------------------------------------
    move posId        to ws-99
    move "Input_"     to input-name
    move ws-99        to input-name(7:2)


*-----------------------------------------------------------
*     Activate the Implementation
*-----------------------------------------------------------
    CALL "ORBSTAT" USING ORBIX-STATUS-INFORMATION

*
*     Get Object Reference
*
    call "ns-rslv" using input-name
                         returning in-obj
```

Initially we construct the textual name that was used to cache the object reference for the `InputMedia` object within the Naming Service. In this case, the value is `Input_nn`, where nn is the unique identifier for POS that is passed in as a parameter value.

We then make a call to `ORBSTAT` to establish the standard status area `ORBIX-STATUS-INFORMATION` that is defined within the standard COBOL copy file called `CORBA.CPY` (as always, the CORBA.CPY file must be specified within the working storage of all programs that interface to Orbix COBOL).

Finally, the `ns-rslv` routine (which was discussed in detail in Section 29.4.3.4) is used to obtain the object reference of the `InputMedia` object.

35.3.6.2 POS Client: Core Logic

The POS Client will display a menu of options, then loop accepting command requests, or item barcodes until an X character is entered to terminate it:

```
*==========================================================
*    Get User Input
*==========================================================
      display "Command Summary :-"
      display "L : Login    P : POS Sales Summary    "
              "S : Store Sales Summary"
      display "T : Total    Q : Quantity             "
              "X : Exit"
      display "<barcode> : Item "

      perform until exit
          display "Enter barcode, command (L,P,Q,S,T) "
                  "or X to exit : "
          accept ws-input

          if ws-input(1:1) = "x" or "X"
              exit perform
          end-if

          if ws-input(1:1) is numeric
              move length of ws-input to ws-lth
              call "STRSET" using item in
                            INPUTXMEDIA-BARCODE-INPUT-ARGS
                                ws-lth
                                ws-input
              PERFORM CHECK-STATUS
              set INPUTXMEDIA-BARCODE-INPUT  to true
              call "ORBEXEC" using in-obj
                            INPUTXMEDIA-OPERATION
                            INPUTXMEDIA-BARCODE-INPUT-ARGS
              PERFORM CHECK-STATUS
          else
              move length of ws-input to ws-lth
              call "STRSET" using cmd in
                            INPUTXMEDIA-KEYPAD-INPUT-ARGS
                                ws-lth
                                ws-input
              PERFORM CHECK-STATUS
              set INPUTXMEDIA-KEYPAD-INPUT  to true
              call "ORBEXEC" using in-obj
                            INPUTXMEDIA-OPERATION
                            INPUTXMEDIA-KEYPAD-INPUT-ARGS
              PERFORM CHECK-STATUS
          end-if
      end-perform
      goback
```

Prior to entering the main loop, a full display of all the options supported is displayed. Once issued, a loop is entered until a X character is detected as input. Within this loop, the following sequence will occur:

1. An invitation to enter input will be issued, then a COBOL ACCEPT statement will be used to receive input from the user. If the input is either a lower- or uppercase 'X' character, the POS client will be terminated.

2. If the input is numeric, it will be handled as a barcode. The STRSET routine will be used to establish it as a CORBA string input parameter within the parameter area for the Barcode-input operation within the InputMedia implementation. ORBEXEC is then called to process the specified barcode.

3. If the input is not numeric, it is handled as keypad input. The STRSET routine will be used to establish it as a CORBA string input parameter within the parameter area for the Keypad-input operation within the InputMedia implementation. ORBEXEC is then called to process the specified character.

Now that you have reached the end of the implementation details for the POS Client, you have also reached the end of this COBOL tutorial. Congratulations! You have stepped through the implementation details for a complete CORBA server and client written entirely in COBOL.

CHAPTER 36

Running the Example

36.1 Congratulations!

You've finished all of the coding, and you're ready to run the CORBA foundation for your retail empire. (Well, at least your pretend retail empire; this example would need a lot of work before it could ever support a real store!)

In this chapter, each vendor presents the steps you need to take to fire up your objects in the proper order, register them with the Naming Service, connect them up, and run them. The end result is the same in every case, but the commands differ because many refer to files and their names are not standardized by OMG.

A few of the sections in this chapter—for BEA, IONA, and Inprise—include sample input and output. We've left the samples in their own sections because they're surrounded by commands and prompts for each product's directory configuration. However, since the input and output are the same regardless of ORB and platform, you can look at these sections to see how the program runs regardless of your ORB. Or, if you haven't worked the example yourself but want to see what the output looks like anyhow, you can turn to one of these sections.

36.2 Running the Example in BEA WLE

In the section describing the BEA WLE code for the Depot, we gave instructions on how to build the application (Run the command file WLEsetup). That file also sets up administrative files to describe the application; all servers are set up to run on a single machine. A textual description of the configuration of the application, ubb, is put into the "working" subdirectory and then the setup file executes a tmloadcf ubb command to generate a binary version of the configuration. (You need to have administrator privileges.)

Briefly, the ubb file contains a description of the administrative and application-specific servers that WLE will use to start and monitor the application. Having a complete description of the configuration of an application is necessary for enterprise-level scaling and reliability by enabling monitoring and resource optimization. The setup file generates the configuration to have three specific application servers. One Store server has command-line parameters that specify store 26 with a markup factor of 1.5; another Store server specifies store 37 with a markup factor of 2.0. The Depot server has a command-line parameter specifying the location of the Depot data file. You can examine the ubb file using a type command or a text editor.

If you wish to run the application in a different process than the WLEsetup command (logging in later, for example), change to the "working" directory and issue the command setenv; this will set the environmental variables without having to regenerate the whole application.

When you are ready to start the application, issue the command tmboot -y. This will boot the entire application from the configuration file information. You will receive output stating that nine processes have been started, including the three application servers we are interested in. What are the other six processes? They provide WLE runtime services (for example, Factory Finder and Listener) and, more importantly, the monitoring services that give your application the scalability and reliability you want. WLE isn't convenient for simple demos; it is entirely appropriate for the enterprise.

Since tmboot starts the entire application, you are now ready to start one or more clients, from the same, or any other, window on the same machine. Change to the POS directory to start up a POS client. You might type POS_client 26 12 to identify yourself as terminal 12 (or any other number) connecting to store 26. Or, you can try POS_client 37 145 for store 37, terminal 145. You can run as many clients as you wish, opening new windows to do so or running the client, exiting, and starting a new client. After running multiple clients for a particular store, you might issue the S input command to the POSTerminal to see the summary of information for Store and its multiple terminals.

When you are finished experimenting, you should issue the tmshutdown -y command to tell WLE to shut down the application. This frees resources on your workstation.

The following is a capture of a short session with some suggested input you might try. We don't show the output from the tmboot command because that is rather lengthy and not significant for the example. It shows two runs of POS_client for store 26, from terminal 12 and from terminal 145 (to show that the store does keep track of multiple terminals). Each possible input command is represented.

```
E:\Primer\BEA-WLE\POS >tmboot -y
...<omitted output>
E:\Primer\BEA-WLE\POS>POS_client 26 12
```

```
Creating POSTerminalImpl
Terminal started

Command Summary :-
L : Login    P : POS Sales Summary    S : Store Sales Summary
T : Total    Q : Quantity             X : Exit

Enter code, command (L,P,Q,S,T) or X to exit : L
Enter code, command (L,P,Q,S,T) or X to exit : 102345
   1    102345              Pasta   18.57   18.57
Enter code, command (L,P,Q,S,T) or X to exit : T
Taxable Sub-Total :=     0.00
Taxes             :=     0.00
Total             :=    18.57
Enter code, command (L,P,Q,S,T) or X to exit : X


E:\Primer\BEA-WLE\POS>POS_client 26 145
Creating POSTerminalImpl
Terminal started

Command Summary :-
L : Login    P : POS Sales Summary    S : Store Sales Summary
T : Total    Q : Quantity             X : Exit

Enter code, command (L,P,Q,S,T) or X to exit : L
Enter code, command (L,P,Q,S,T) or X to exit : Q3
Enter code, command (L,P,Q,S,T) or X to exit : 234234
   3    234234              Pen     12.47   37.40  *
Enter code, command (L,P,Q,S,T) or X to exit : 789789
   1    789789              Peas    11.02   11.02
Enter code, command (L,P,Q,S,T) or X to exit : T
Taxable Sub-Total :=    37.40
Taxes             :=     1.87
Total             :=    50.29
Enter code, command (L,P,Q,S,T) or X to exit : P
  Point of Sale Total :=     50.29
           Tax Total :=      1.87


Enter code, command (L,P,Q,S,T) or X to exit : S
STORE TOTALS
 Total Sales :=    68.86
 Total Tax   :=     1.87

 POS   I.D.  := 12
 Total Sales :=    18.57
 Total Tax   :=     0.00

 POS   I.D.  := 145
 Total Sales :=    50.29
 Total Tax   :=     1.87

Enter code, command (L,P,Q,S,T) or X to exit : X
```

```
E:\Primer\BEA-WLE\POS>
```

36.3 Running the Example in Vertel's Expersoft CORBAplus

This section contains information on how to run the example using CORBAplus for C++ and CORBAplus, Java Edition.

36.3.1 Running the Example Using CORBAplus for C++

There are two ways to start the example: You can either start each application one at a time or execute the scripts that will automatically start each process.

36.3.1.1 Starting Each POS Application

Each application must be started in its own window. Applications should be started in the following order:

```
Pbnamed -pbportr 6002 -pbtrace
./central/Depot_Server  depot.dat -pbinit NameService
    iiop://localhost:6002/NameServiceRoot
./store/Store_Server 1.1 1 -pbinit NameService
    iiop://localhost:6002/NameServiceRoot
./pos/POS_Server 1 -pbinit NameService
    iiop://localhost:6002/NameServiceRoot
./pos/POS_Client 1 1 -pbinit NameService
    iiop://localhost:6002/NameServiceRoot
```

The preceding commands assume you are running the example on Solaris, but it is very similar if you are executing the example on NT.

36.3.1.2 Script to Start the POS Application

There is a script file for both Solaris and NT that can be executed to start the POS example. This will simplify the starting of the example.

For Solaris type:

```
%runxps_cpp
```

This script will start each application in its own xterm. The script pauses 10 seconds between starting up each application to give the previous application time to start and register with the Naming Service.

For NT, there is a batch file of the same name. The batch file pauses between starting up each application. After each application is running and registered with the Naming Service, press any key in the main window to start the next application.

36.3.2 Running the Example Using CORBAplus, Java Edition

There are two ways to start the example: You can either start each application one at a time or execute the scripts that will automatically start each process. Both the scripts and the individual command lines assume you have the CLASSPATH set up correctly to point to the classes directory of the POS example.

36.3.2.1 Starting Each POS Application

Each application must be started in its own window and should be started in the following order:

```
pbnamed -pbport 6002 -pbtrace
java CentralOffice.DepotServer depot.dat -pbinit NameService
    iiop://localhost:6002/NameServiceRoot
java AStore.StoreServer 1.1 1 -pbinit NameService
    iiop://localhost:6002/NameServiceRoot
java POS.PosServer 1 -pbinit NameService
    iiop://localhost:6002/NameServiceRoot
java POS.PosClient 1 1 -pbinit NameService
    iiop://localhost:6002/NameServiceRoot
```

36.3.2.2 Script to Start the POS Application

There is a script file for both Solaris and NT that can be executed to start the POS example. This will simplify the starting of the example.

For Solaris type:

```
%runxps_java
```

This script will start each application in its own xterm. The script pauses 10 seconds between starting up each application to give the previous application time to start and register with the Naming Service.

For NT, there is a batch file of the same name. The batch file pauses between starting up each application. After each application is running and registered with the Naming Service, press any key in the main window to start the next application.

36.4 Running the Example Using IBM Java and C++ ORBs

36.4.1 Running the Example Using the IBM C++ ORB

IBM currently does not offer a stand-alone C++ ORB for general release. It is embedded into a series of products, including Component Broker, part of the Websphere family of products. We have not provided information about how to compile or run the sample stand-alone, because this information is not useful without a stand-alone IBM C+ ORB. However, we have included a makefile.ibm on the CD as an example of how to compile the sample if you had an IBM ORB embedded into your product.

36.4.2 Running the Example Using the IBM ORB for Java

The sample modified to run on the IBM Component Broker, part of the IBM Websphere family of products, is presented below. At this time, we are unable to include with the sample a copy of the IBM ORB for Java shipped with Component Broker. In addition, Component Broker only supports servers that can be managed through its systems management. Running the stand-alone servers, like the PosServer, within a Component Broker installation is an unsupported configuration. We have decided to include the instructions because they are relatively straightforward, and they may be of benefit to some readers. However, these instructions may not work for all installations.

To run the Java sample, you will need to have installed a version of Component Broker Server, and have the Name Server running on that installation. Please consult the Component Broker documentation for instructions to start the Name Server. Assuming that you have the Name Server Already running, you can compile and run the Example as follows:

To set up your CLASSPATH, do the following, assuming that <IBM directory> is the IBM's directory on the CD, such as j:\ExampleCode\Java\IBM:

on NT:

```
    set BOOKDIR= <IBM directory>
    set
CLASSPATH=%BOOKDIR%\classes;%BOOKDIR%;%BOOKDIR%\idl;%SOMCBASE%\lib\
somojor.zip;%CLASSPATH%
```

on AIX:

```
    export BOOKDIR= <IBM directory>
    export
CLASSPATH=$BOOKDIR/classes:$BOOKDIR:$BOOKDIR/idl:$SOMCBASE/lib/somojor.
zip:$CLASSPATH
```

To compile:
on NT:

```
    run comp.bat in <IBM directory>
```

on AIX:
We did not provide a shell script. Please follow the commands in the .bat files provided for NT. They are self-explanatory.

To start the servers:
First, make sure that your Component Broker Name Server is started. cd to the "classes" sub-directory, and
on NT:

```
start java CentralOffice.DeportServer <host>
start java AStore.StoreServer 1.1 1 <host>
start java POS.PosServer 1 <host> &
start java POS.PosClient 1 1 <host>
```

on AIX:

```
java CentralOffice.DepotServer <host>&
java AStore.StoreServer 1.1 1 <host> &
java POS.PosServer 1 <host> &
java POS.PosClient 1 1 <host>&
```

If you are running the sample on a different machine than the Name Server, you'll need to specify the host where the Name Server is located.

The above is just an example to start a new Store and POS Client. You can start multiple stores with multiple POS terminals.

36.5 Running the Example in IONA Orbix

36.5.1 Compiling the Code

Makefiles are provided with the example code. Edit the file `Makedefs.win.orbix` or `Makedefs.unix.orbix` to set the paths and compiler flags for your system. The files already have settings for a standard Orbix installation on NT and Solaris, respectively. For other platforms, check the makefile definitions in the demos that ship with Orbix for the proper directories and compiler flags.

Once you have edited the appropriate `Makedefs` file, just type:
Windows:

```
nmake -f Makefile.win.orbix
```

Unix:

```
make -f Makefile.unix.orbix
```

36.5.2 Running the Example

You need to perform the following steps. Each step is explained in more detail in the following sections.

1. Make sure Orbix and OrbixNames are installed and configured, and the Orbix daemon is running.

2. Register the servers.

3. Run the servers manually to register themselves in the Naming Service.

4. Run the client.

Steps 1–3 need only be done once. Once the servers are registered with the Orbix daemon and the Naming Service, running the client will look up the Naming Service, and then use the Orbix daemon to automatically launch the server if it's not already running. The servers will time out if unused for around 60 seconds, but they will be automatically relaunched anytime you run the client.

36.5.2.1 (Step 1) Configure Orbix and OrbixNames

Install and license Orbix and OrbixNames per the instructions that ship with the product. OrbixNames is bundled with Orbix from version 3.0 onward; if you have an older version, contact info@iona.com to find out how to get a copy of OrbixNames.

If you installed Orbix in a non-standard directory, you need to set the environment variable IT_CONFIG_PATH to the location of the configuration directory. If you installed in the default IONA directory, you don't need to do this.

You need to ensure that the Orbix daemon (orbixd) is running, and Name Server is registered with orbixd. You can do this using graphical tools, or from the command line. We'll show the command-line method here; check the user documentation for details of the graphical tools.

The commands are

Windows:

```
start orbixd
putit NS c:\iona\bin\ns.exe
```

Unix:

```
xterm -e orbixd&
putit NS /opt/iona/ns
```

Note: The location of the ns executable may vary by platform, or if you've installed OrbixNames in a nonstandard place. Make sure you use the correct absolute path name.

You can verify that the daemon is running and Naming Service is registered using the utilities pingit (pings the Orbix daemon) and lsns (lists the Naming Service root context). For example:

```
pingit
[208: New Connection (hermit,IT_daemon,*,aconway,pid$7,optimised) ]
Trying to contact hermit and it's running.
lsns
[Contents of root]
    lost+found   (Context)
    ObjectGroups   (Context)
[0 Objects, 2 Contexts]
```

36.5.2.2 (Step 2) Register the Servers with Orbix

Each server needs to be registered with the Orbix daemon, along with any command-line parameters that are to be passed to the server.

For the POS example, the parameters required are

Depot_Server: `data_file` (note this should be an absolute path to the file)

Store_Server: `mark_up store_number`

POS_Server: `POS_number`

Here are the commands to register the servers with `markup` = 1.5, `store number` = 1, and `POS number` = 2:

Windows:

```
set ROOT=c:\<directory containing example code >
putit Depot_Server   "%ROOT%\central\Depot_Server.exe %ROOT%\depot.dat"
putit Store_Server   "%ROOT%\store\Store_Server.exe 1.5 1"
putit POS_Server     "%ROOT%\pos\POS_Server.exe 2"
```

Unix sh:

```
ROOT=/<directory containing example code >
putit "Depot_Server"   "$ROOT/central/Depot_Server.exe $ROOT/depot.dat"
putit "Store_Server"   "$ROOT/store/Store_Server.exe 1.5 1"
putit "POS_Server"     "$ROOT/pos/POS_Server.exe 2"
```

You must provide an *absolute* path name when registering a server, not a *relative* path name.

36.5.2.3 (Step 3) Register Objects in the Naming Service

The POS servers register their objects in the Naming Service so clients (and other servers) can find them. Since some servers depend on others, they must be run in the correct order the first time they are started.

To run the servers, run the same commands registered with `putit` in step 2 directly from the command line. Once started, a server will wait for requests from clients, so run them in the background.

Windows:

```
start %ROOT%\central\Depot_Server.exe %ROOT%\depot.dat
start %ROOT%\store\Store_Server.exe 1.5 1
start %ROOT%\pos\POS_Server.exe 2
```

Unix:

```
xterm -e $ROOT/central/Depot_Server.exe $ROOT/depot.dat o&
xterm -e $ROOT/store/Store_Server.exe 1.5 1 &
xterm -e $ROOT/pos/POS_Server.exe 2 &
```

Note that the servers will time out fairly quickly if a client does not use them. Don't worry! The Naming Service and Orbix daemon keep persistent records of all registrations on disk. When clients look up a name and want to use an object, the daemon will automatically restart the server.

By default, Orbix times out inactive servers and restarts them as needed. In your applications you can set your own time-outs or disable time-outs entirely if you wish. Look for `impl_is_ready` and `setNoHangup` in the Orbix documentation for more details. There is no need to repeat the preceding steps more than once. After the first run, the names are stored persistently in the Naming Service, so you can proceed directly to running the client, even if some or all of the servers have timed out.

36.5.2.4 (Step 4) Run the Client

To run the client, pass the same store and POS numbers you used when registering and running the servers.

Windows:

```
%ROOT%\pos\POS_Client.exe 1 2
```

Unix:

```
$ROOT/pos/POS_Client.exe 1 2
```

Once the client is running you'll get a simple prompt. First, log in to the store by typing L. Then enter a few barcodes—you can find the valid barcodes in the `depot.dat` data file. Q lets you enter a quantity for the next barcode (instead of reentering the barcode many times). T totals your entries; after you've totaled you can output the POS or store totals with P or S.

If you just look at the client window, it may seem like nothing is happening. That's because all the output from the system goes to the `OutputMedia` object, which is implemented in the POS server. Our simple implementation just sends output to the C++ `cout` stream. If you started the POS server directly from the command line, you can see this output in the window where you started it. If the Orbix daemon automatically started the server for you (which is more likely), then you can see the output in the window where the `orbixd` is running. There is some sample output for the client and POS server in the next section. The lines in square brackets are messages from the Orbix runtimes. You can disable these messages, or request more detailed output—see `setDiagnostics` in the Orbix documentation for more details.

36.5.3 Example Output

36.5.3.1 Client Output

Here's a sample client session; the corresponding output from the POS server is shown in the following section.

```
Creating POSTerminalImpl
[264: New Connection (hermit,IT_daemon,*,aconway,pid$7,optimised) ]
[264: New IIOP Connection (HERMIT:1578) ]
Terminal started
L : Login     P : POS Sales Summary   S : Store Sales Summary
T : Total     Q : Quantity            X : Exit
```

```
Enter code, command (L,P,Q,S,T) or X to exit : L [250: Retrying
connection to host "hermit" port 1588] [250: Retrying connection to host
"hermit" port 1588]
[250: New IIOP Connection (hermit:1588) ]
Enter code, command (L,P,Q,S,T) or X to exit : 102345 [250: Retrying
connection to host "hermit" port 1592] [250: New IIOP Connection
(hermit:1592) ]
Enter code, command (L,P,Q,S,T) or X to exit : q3
Enter code, command (L,P,Q,S,T) or X to exit : 234234
Enter code, command (L,P,Q,S,T) or X to exit : 789789
Enter code, command (L,P,Q,S,T) or X to exit : 123
Invalid Barcode Found
Enter code, command (L,P,Q,S,T) or X to exit : 923988
Enter code, command (L,P,Q,S,T) or X to exit : t
Enter code, command (L,P,Q,S,T) or X to exit : p
Enter code, command (L,P,Q,S,T) or X to exit : s
Enter code, command (L,P,Q,S,T) or X to exit : q10
Enter code, command (L,P,Q,S,T) or X to exit : 423552
Enter code, command (L,P,Q,S,T) or X to exit : t
Enter code, command (L,P,Q,S,T) or X to exit : p
Enter code, command (L,P,Q,S,T) or X to exit : s
Enter code, command (L,P,Q,S,T) or X to exit : x
```

36.5.3.2 Server Output

In our example, all the servers were launched by the daemon. Here's the output from the daemon corresponding to the client input in the preceding section. We have omitted the start-up messages from other servers for brevity, since the POS server is where the action is. All of the following output is from the POS server, except for the final disconnect messages from other servers when the client exits.

```
[POS_Server: New Connection (hermit,IT_daemon,*,aconway,pid!3,optimised) ]
[POS_Server: New IIOP Connection (HERMIT:1580) ]
[POS_Server: Server "POS_Server" is now available to the network ]
[ Configuration tcp/1586/cdr ]
[POS_Server: New IIOP Connection (hermit:1592) ]
   1     102345          Pasta    18.57   18.57
   3     234234            Pen    12.47   37.40   *
   1     789789           Peas    11.02   11.02
   1     923988         Persil    18.51   18.51
Taxable Sub-Total :=     37.40
Taxes             :=      1.87
Total             :=     87.37
   Point of Sale Total :=     87.37
            Tax Total :=      1.87


STORE TOTALS
  Total Sales :=    87.37
  Total Tax   :=     1.87
```

```
POS    I.D.  := 2
Total Sales :=      87.37
Total Tax   :=       1.87


  10     423552                Pencil   3.52   36.25   *
Taxable Sub-Total :=      36.25
Taxes             :=       1.76
Total             :=      37.01
  Point of Sale Total :=     124.38
           Tax Total :=       3.63


STORE TOTALS
Total Sales :=  124.38
 Total Tax   :=     3.63


 POS    I.D.  := 2
 Total Sales :=     124.38
 Total Tax   :=       3.63


[Store_Server: End of IIOP Connection (hermit:1588) ]
[POS_Server: End of IIOP Connection (hermit:1592) ]
[orbixd: End of Connection (hermit,250,*,aconway,pid%0) ]
[ NS: End of IIOP connection (hermit:1402) ]
```

36.6 Running the Example in Inprise VisiBroker

This section describes how to build and run the example using Inprise's VisiBroker. VisiBroker for C++ v3.3 was used in conjunction with MS Visual C++ 5.0. The Java version was built using VisiBroker for Java v3.4 and JDK 1.2.1. For the Java version, make sure that you have all the necessary JAR files in your classpath, and that you have the classes directory of the example in your classpath as well.

36.6.1 Building the Code

The makefiles we've provided will let you build the C++ version of the example; for the Java version, look for Windows/DOS batch files instead. Here are the steps required to build the C++ code:

1. Go into the root source directory (where you will find the Makedefs.visibroker file).

2. Edit the Makedefs.visibroker file to reflect your environment (especially the VBROKERDIR variable).

3a. Under Windows, type nmake -f Makefile.visibroker.

3b. Under Unix, type make -f Makefile.visibroker.

   This will compile all of the IDL files and C++ or Java source.

To build the Java example, you should run/edit `makeall`. The Java class files will reside in the `classes` directory of the example.

36.6.2 Starting the Servers

In order to run the example, you must have the Smart Agent and the Naming Service running. It is important to start the Smart Agent first. To start the Smart Agent, run the `osagent` program. To start the C++ Naming Service under Windows, run:

```
NameExtF myNameService myLogFile
```

To start the C++ Naming Service under Unix, run:

```
CosNamingExtFactory myNameService myLogFile
```

If you only have the Java version of VisiBroker, then run (entering all on a single line)

```
vbj -DORBservices=CosNaming
com.visigenic.vbroker.services.CosNaming.ExtFactory myNameService
myLogFile
```

to start the Java Naming Service. (Make sure vbjcosnm.jar and the other VisiBroker jar files are in your classpath).

Once you have these two services running, it is time to start the three servers in the example. We will assume that you have the Depot data file stored at `c:\example\data\depot.dat`. We'll use a markup of 25% at store number 3. The POS number will be 17. If the location of your `depot.dat` file (which can usually be found in either the `CentralOffice` or `classes` directory) is different, please insert the right path in the steps that follow.

Here is what you need to do to set it all up in C++:

1. Start the Depot server by typing `Depot_Server c:\example\data\depot.dat` in the `central` directory.
2. Start the Store server by typing `Store_Server 1.25 3` in the `store` directory.
3. Start the POS server by typing `POS_Server 17` in the `pos` directory.

Here is what you need to do to set it all up in Java. Run these in the `classes` directory:

1. Start the Depot server by typing `vbj CentralOffice.DepotServer`.
2. Start the Store server by typing `vbj AStore.StoreServer 1.25 3`.
3. Start the POS server by typing `vbj POS.PosServer 17`.

36.6.3 Running the Example

Now that you have the servers running and registered with the Naming Service (this part is done automatically for you by the servers), you are ready to start running the POS client. You may want to take a look at the `depot.dat` file in order to know what items are sold in your store, along with their barcodes.

In C++, run the POS client by typing `POS_Client 3 17` in the pos directory. In Java, run the POS client by typing `vbj POS.PosClient 3 17` in the `classes` directory.

Here is a sample run for the Java example:

```
C:\primer\java\classes>vbj POS.PosClient 3 17
PosClient is ready
Command Summary :
L      : login
P      : POS Sales Summary
S      : Store Sales Summary
T      : Total
Q num  : Quantity
X      : Exit

Enter code, command (L,P,Q,S,T) or X to exit :
L
Enter code, command (L,P,Q,S,T) or X to exit :
Q 2
Enter code, command (L,P,Q,S,T) or X to exit :
923988
Enter code, command (L,P,Q,S,T) or X to exit :
Q 5
Enter code, command (L,P,Q,S,T) or X to exit :
789789
Enter code, command (L,P,Q,S,T) or X to exit :
T
Enter code, command (L,P,Q,S,T) or X to exit :
P
Enter code, command (L,P,Q,S,T) or X to exit :
S
Enter code, command (L,P,Q,S,T) or X to exit :
X

C:\primer\java\classes>
```

On the POS server, we see:

```
PosServer is ready

        Quantity=2
        Barcode =923988
        ItemInf =Persil
        price   =15.425
        ItemExt =30.85

        Quantity=5
        Barcode =789789
        ItemInf =Peas
        price   =9.1875
        ItemExt =45.9375
Taxable Sub-Total := 0.0
```

```
Taxes := 0.0
Total := 76.7875
Point of Sale Total: 76.7875   Tax Total: 0.0
STORE TOTALS
Total Sales := 76.7875
Total Tax := 0.0
        POS I.D. : 17
                Total Sales : 76.7875          Total Tax   : 0.0
```

This output comes from the activity of the barcode reader and store clerk.

36.7 Running the Example in OrbixCOBOL

The OrbixCOBOL example on the CD-ROM includes a makefile that automates the building, registration, and running of the OrbixCOBOL tutorial. Once the example has been built, all that you need to do is to register the executables with Orbix before you run it. The following command line will automate this for you:

```
nmake reg
```

When run, this will execute the following commands to register the details of the tutorial with Orbix:

```
putit NamingContext 'pwd'/NS/ns
putit Depot 'pwd'/Central/Depot
putit Store 'pwd'/Store/Store 2
putit Pos 'pwd'/pos/possrv 2 2
```

Once all the details have been registered with Orbix, you are ready to run the example. This may be done using the following command line:

```
nmake run
```

This will start the tutorial example using the following sequence:

1. First it will start the lightweight Naming Service with the following simple command:

   ```
   ns\ns
   ```

2. It will then start the Depot:

   ```
   central\depot
   ```

3. An instance of Store is then started with a unique store ID number for this instance of the Store supplied on the command line:

   ```
   store\store 2
   ```

4. Finally, we start a POS server with two command-line parameters. The first identifies the unique Store ID that it will connect to, and the second is the unique identifier for this POS server:

   ```
   pos\possrv 2 2
   ```

In order to keep the example simple, the POS server will also start a simple character-based POS client for you. So you may now turn on your store's "Open" sign and start your first day of business as the proud owner of a COBOL store.

36.8 Running the Example in PeerLogic DAIS

36.8.1 Summary

The CD that accompanies this book contains an installation program that will install the DAIS J^2 Software Development Kit, DAIS Naming Service, Primer Example applications, and associated documentation. When you install any of the options, you are agreeing to a restricted user license. The license is displayed during the installation. Please read the license carefully before installing the products. The only dependency is that you are running a Windows 32-bit with JDK 1.1, which is required for developing the Java applications. If you are interested in other platforms and products, or have any comments, please contact PeerLogic at the URLs or addresses given in Appendix A.

Have fun and enjoy.

36.8.2 Installation

The installation program is called `Dais32Setup.exe` and can found on the CD that accompanies this book. When you run this installation program, it will guide you through a number of dialogs that are briefly explained next.

- **Welcome Dialog.**

- **License Agreement.** Please read this carefully before accepting the terms and conditions. A copy of the license agreement is installed if you choose to continue with the installation.

- **User detail.** Please enter your name and company details.

- **Select Components.** To run and develop the Primer Example, you must install J^2, Naming Service, and Primer Example files. It is advisable to install the manuals, which contain valuable information to accompany the book. The manuals are in PDF format and require Adobe Acrobat Reader 3.0.

- **Select Destination Directory.**

- **Select "ProgMan" Group.** The installation will by default create a program manager group called "DAIS" with icons for running the DAIS tools and services.

- **Post Installation Options.** The installation will automatically set up environment details. If you choose not to do this, then you must set up the following details manually:

```
Set  DAIS=<installation directory>
```

For example a default installation would be:

```
Set DAIS=c:\Dais32
```

```
Set
CLASSPATH=%CLASSPATH%%DAIS%\lib\daisorb.jar;%DAIS%\lib\daissrv.jar;%DAIS
%\lib\daissrvx.jar%DAIS%\Primer\classes

Set PATH=%PATH%;%DAIS%/bin
```

36.8.3 What Next?

One of the first things you can do, once the product is installed, is run our version of the Primer Example. It will introduce you to the DAIS environment and services and demonstrate CORBA in a variety of ways. Under the DAIS program group, locate an application called "Primer Control." This application will help you to configure and run the DAIS environment, the DAIS Naming Service, and the Primer Example itself, in four simple steps. In a distributed environment, applications and services can run anywhere on the network. For simplicity, the Primer Control application presumes that you are running on a single platform.

Step 1

This configures the DAIS environment. All DAIS applications participate in Trading Domains. A Trader allows CORBA components to advertise and discover each other. Configuring to run in a Trading Domain requires you to set up the Trader on your host machine. Follow the instructions to default all the options. This step must be completed before any DAIS application can be run. Once you become a little more familiar with DAIS, you will notice that this step has just run the Config Editor tool, which is also available under the DAIS program group. This step only needs to be performed once.

Step 2

The DAIS J^2 Beta product required an extract, which is redendent with copy of J^2 that accompanies this book. The application, exhibits step2, but notice that this step is no longer required and is disabled.

Step 3

The Primer Example, as you will discover, uses the CORBA Naming Service to advertise CORBA components. The DAIS implementation of this CORBA Service uses the DAIS Trader to provide the backbone. This step will run an instance of both these services on your local host. You will also find options under the DAIS program group for starting either of these services manually.

Step 4

This will run a set of applications on your local host, which are the subject of the "Analysis and Design" sections of the book. The Options button associated with step 4 allows you to configure different scenarios for the example. By default, the example runs, as it would, if you had followed the "Analysis and Design" sections and implemented a set of non-GUI Java applications using DAIS J^2.

What you see is four command consoles. The first of these is the Depot Application server that will display a list of products. The second is a single instance of a Store

Application server that uses the Depot server to get product information. The remaining two consoles are the POS input terminal and POS output terminal, which are associated with the Store. The input terminal provides a simple user interface for purchasing goods from the store. A list of processed items is shown on the output terminal. The system demonstrates a three-tier model in action. In a real system, a barcode reader would process real products. In this system, the Depot server displays a list of valid barcodes, which you can use with the POS input terminal.

Be aware that the Primer Control application is a simple way of getting you started. You should close down the example applications before repeating step 4 to avoid multiple instances sharing the same parameters. If you wish to run multiple instances of the Store applications and associated POSTerminals, use the "Options dialog" of the Primer Control application.

If all goes well you have just run a comprehensive CORBA example, which will help you understand the programming elements of this book.

36.8.4 Running GUI Versions of the POSTerminal

Non-GUI applications do not have a very intuitive interface, nor are they very exciting. To demonstrate that CORBA can integrate with the latest tools and technologies, we have provided two GUI implementations of the POSTerminal. The GUI applications integrate the roles of the POS input and output mediums. The first GUI is implemented as a Java GUI application, the second is implemented as a Visual Basic application. The latter demonstrates the language independence of IDL, and was built using DAIS COM2CORBA. To run these applications, select the Primer Control Options button and configure the number of instances you require under the POS dialog tab. Select OK or Apply to confirm your changes. Repeat step 4, but remember to close any running instances of the example first.

36.8.4.1 Running Web Versions of the POSTerminal

The Internet is a powerful communication tool, but organizations find it difficult to use because of the technology gap between existing and new technologies. To demonstrate how CORBA can bridge that gap, we have implemented a POSTerminal as a Java applet. With the right plug-in in your Web browser you should be able to run this applet. Browsers such as Netscape already support a standard JVM for running Java applets, but Microsoft Explorer, for example, does not currently support a standard JVM and requires the Sun Java plug-in. The HTML provided for the example will detect whether your Explorer browser has the plug-in, and supplies details on how to download it.

36.8.4.2 Introducing JGUARD

If you are used to running applets you will be aware of the "sandbox" security mechanisms the JVM is subject to. By default, this prevents Java applets from communicating with other applications outside the Web browser, and so the applet POSTerminal will not be able to communicate with the other elements of the POS system. In reality you would normally download applets from a Web server, which runs under its jurisdiction. DAIS supplies JGUARD, a Web server that enables you to develop and run CORBA applications that can interact with Java applets through a Web browser. The JGUARD application can be found in the DAIS bin directory. To run it, simply start a command console session and type JGUARD. Since JGUARD is effectively a Web server, no other Web server applications should be running on your machine. To download the applets, JGUARD must know where they are. It has its own directory structure, the home of which is called "webroot". Have a look at the webroot directory, which would be c:\Dais32\webroot for a default installation. It contains a number of examples, including Primer, which contains HTML files and the compiled class POSGuiApplet. For efficiency, the applet class runs with a set of Java archives in the webroot/jar directory. These archive files contain the ORB and ORB Services, the Naming Service, and the IDL compiled classes associated with the Store application.

If you wish to run the POSTerminal applet under your Web browser, ensure that the following are running:

- JGUARD
- An instance of the Trader, and an instance of the Naming Service
- Instances of the Depot and Store servers

Using Netscape

From your Web browser, use the following URL:

```
http://<host_name>/Primer/PosGuiApplet.html
```

where <host_name> is the name of your machine. This will load the applet from the webroot.

Using Internet Explorer 4

From your Web browser, use the following URL:

```
http://<host_name>/Primer/PosGuiApplet-ie4.html
```

where <host_name> is the name of your machine. This will load the applet from the webroot.

36.8.5 Running Other DAIS Examples

If you wish to run other DAIS examples that are installed with DAIS J^2, refer to the "Getting Started with DAIS J" guide for details.

36.8.6 Developing the Primer Example in Java

If you have read the "Analysis and Design" sections of the book, you may wish to implement your own versions of the POS system, which is documented in the earlier chapters. As you develop each application you can test against the existing solutions provided. This is one advantage of a component-based model like CORBA. Note that if you start your applications using the "Primer Control" application, it can be configured to run the applications from an alternative directory. Select the Options button and locate the Classes tab dialog. The Primer directory contains a Java subdirectory. This contains all the implemented elements of the example POS system. The classes subdirectory contains all the compiled classes used in the example, and this directory should be added to your class path (a default installation would have done this for you). If you are going to develop your own code, you may wish to back up these directories, but the example can be reinstalled from the CD.

If you choose to develop your own applets that can run under JGUARD, then the class files should be copied to a suitable directory under the webroot directory. This is the default home for JGUARD. Have a look at the HTML files under "webroot" in order to understand how the applet is loaded. You will notice that it uses archives of the DAIS ORB and services, including the Primer Example IDL class files (AStore), which are located under the webroot/jar directory. This is done purely for efficiency so you only need to copy your own POS applet classes to the webroot/directory. Developing GUI applications in Java is beyond the scope of this book, but there is sample code that can be examined.

There is a subtle difference between the Java GUI application and the Java GUI applet. The application simply wraps the non-GUI POSTerminal input and POSTerminal output applications, which are described in the book. It contains CORBA objects for the `POS::Terminal`, `POS::InputMedia`, and `POS::OutputMedia`. These objects would be fine in the real world where they may be embedded in separate hardware elements, but they are redundant for a GUI application that incorporates all three elements. For example, the Java application awkwardly deals with a reimplementation of the POS CORBA components to direct them to GUI elements instead of standard output. The GUI applet, on the other hand simply dispenses with these objects and communicates with the Store server directly.

36.8.7 Developing the Primer Example Using COM2CORBA

If you have development tools that support COM development, it is possible to create your own POSTerminal implementations like the Visual Basic application located under the Primer/COM directory. The IDL for the Store and Naming Service have been compiled using COM2CORBA, which automatically generates "in process COM Automation servers." They exist as two dll files under the `Primer/Com/idl` directory and were registered during the installation. From tools like Visual Basic, it is possible to build a COM client that calls the automation server. Although this installation does not provide you with the COM2CORBA product, it does have the two DLLs. Under the Primer/COM directory is a single form called "frmPOS.frm". If you familiar with Visual Basic you can rebuild the project to include this form and examine how the application uses COM to communicate with the Java implemented Depot and Store servers. The COM directory also contains a user document called "PosGuiDoc.dob". You can use this to create a Visual Basic Active X DLL that can be called from the Internet Explorer 4 Web browser. For both these applications, follow the ReadMe.txt file under the Primer/COM directory.

36.9 In Conclusion

This may be the last page of this book, but it's only the beginning of CORBA 3.

Over the next few years, we're going to watch CORBA 3 products come to market and reach maturity: ORBs will implement the POA (in addition to the ones in this book that already do!), asynchronous invocation, Quality of Service control, objects by value, interoperable naming, CORBA Components, and the other features we've written about. A future edition of this book may implement the parts of the POS example as CORBA Components!

As this happens, we'll update the Web site for this book regularly. It's at www.omg.org/library/corfun/corfun.html.

You can look there any time you want for updates to the example code for newer versions or additional vendors' ORBs, pointers to the vendors' Web sites, updates to chapters in the book that we've referenced to the Web site, or other news that we think may be interesting to readers. For copies of the OMG specifications (Free!) or information on current OMG adoption efforts, check out the OMG Web site following the pointers in Appendix A.

We know from our experience around the OMG that CORBA programming skills are very much in demand. If you've worked the example in this book, you've acquired a solid foundation and are in a good position to continue with books or lessons on advanced CORBA skills. We wish you the best in your CORBA career!

Contact Information and References

A.1 Contact Information

A.1.1 BEA Systems

BEA Systems, Inc.
2315 North First Street
San Jose, CA 95131
(800) 817-4BEA (U.S. Toll-Free)
(408) 570-8000 phone
(408) 570-8901 fax
www.beasys.com

A.1.2 Expersoft Corporation

Expersoft Corporation,
   a Vertel Company
5825 Oberlin Drive
San Diego, CA 92121
Sales:
E-mail: sales_info@vertel.com
(800) 810-8095 (U.S.A. Toll-Free)
(858) 824-4100 phone
(818) 227-1400 phone
(858) 824-4110 fax
(818) 598-0047 fax
www.vertel.com

A.1.3 IBM Corporation

IBM Direct
4111 North Side Parkway
Atlanta, GA 30321
(800) 426-2255 phone
(800) 242-6329 fax

A.1.4 Inprise, Inc

Inprise Corporation
951 Mariners Island Boulevard
San Mateo, CA 94404-1547
(831) 431-1000 phone
(650) 358-3099 fax
www.inprise.com

A.1.5 IONA Ltd

Training: training@iona.com
Sales: sales@iona.com
FTP site: ftp.iona.com
World Wide Web: www.iona.com/

A.1.5.1 IONA Technologies PLC

The IONA Building
Shelbourne Road
Dublin 4
Ireland
+353 1 637 2000 phone
+353 1 637 2888 fax

A.1.5.2 IONA Technologies, Inc.

200 West St
Waltham, MA 02451
(781) 902-8000 phone
(781) 902-8001 fax
Toll Free: 1-800-672-4948

A.1.5.3 IONA Technologies Japan Ltd.

Aoyama KK Bldg 7/F
2-26-35 Minami Aoyama
Minato-ku, Tokyo
Japan 107-0062
+813 5771 2161 phone
+813 5771 2162 fax

A.1.6 Merant Ltd

Merant, Ltd.
The Lawn
Old Bath Road
Newbury
England RG14 1QN
011 44 1 635 32 646 phone
011 44 1 635 32 595
U.S. Main Office
701 East Middlefield Road
Mountain View, California 94043
(650) 938-3700 phone
(650) 404-7414 fax

A.1.7 PeerLogic Inc

PeerLogic, Inc.
555 De Haro Street
San Francisco, CA 94107-2348
800.PEER.601 (733-7601)
(415) 626-4545 phone
(415) 626-4710 fax
E-mail: info@peerlogic.com

A.1.8 Object Management Group

There are many reasons why you might want to contact OMG: You might want to download a specification, find out about membership for your company or upcoming meetings, research a specification effort in progress, or as a technical question about a specification. (OMG does *not* respond to questions about particular products; for those questions, contact the vendor directly.)

If you don't know whom to contact at OMG for your question, email it to either info@omg.org or the author, siegel@omg.org.

To get started with OMG, try the organization's home page:

www.omg.org

You can send snail mail, telephone, or FAX the OMG at

Object Management Group
250 First Avenue
Needham, MA 02494
(781) 444-0404 phone
(781) 444-0320 fax

A.1.8.1 OMG Specifications

All information about specification work in progress is available from

www.omg.org/techprocess/meetings/schedule/index.html

or the shorter alias

www.omg.org/schedule

For information on upcoming meetings, surf to

www.omg.org/techprocess/meetings/

To download OMG specifications (always free), you may have to try several places. Within a year of adoption, every specification is edited by OMG's professional staff editors from the original submission into a formal document. Editing does not affect technical content; it removes rationale helpful for approval during the adoption process, removes tentative words such as "proposed" (appropriate in a submission but no longer necessary in the specification), and replaces the word "submission" with "specification". URLs for the formal documents are:

www.omg.org/library/c2indx.html for CORBA core;

www.omg.org/library/clangindx.html for the IDL language mappings;

www.omg.org/library/csindx.html for the CORBAservices;

www.omg.org/library/specindx.html#domain for the Domain specifications;

www.omg.org/uml/ for UML;

www.omg.org/techprocess/meetings/schedule/techtab.html#mof

for the MOF; and

www.omg.org/library/idlindx.html for IDL text files.

Until a submission has been edited and placed in one of these URLs, you will have to refer to the original submission if you want to get a head start on implementation, or just find out what's coming up. While the specification effort is under way, you will always find the latest documents on the Work in Progress page already cited. During the hiatus between adoption and publication of the formal document, you can find adopted submissions listed on

www.omg.org/techprocess/meetings/schedule/tech2a.html

A handy page which points to most of the various specifications in all of their varied forms on the OMG Web site is

www.omg.org/techprocess/meetings/schedule/adopt.html

A.1.8.2 Learning about CORBA from OMG

The OMG's starting page for learning about CORBA is named *CORBA for Beginners* and its URL is

www.omg.org/corba/beginners.html

It points to pages and sites that will help you get started with CORBA: Tutorials, writeups, books and magazines, non-OMG CORBA discussion email lists, demos, FAQs, and links collections. Later in this section, we'll list some of our own favorite link collections.

A.1.8.3 About OMG Membership

If all of this talk about CORBA has made you curious about what happens at an OMG meeting, why not go to one and find out? OMG's policy is to allow guests to attend a meeting or two. If you're interested, you can either fill out the form at

www.omg.org/techprocess/meetings/guest.html

or email the author directly (siegel@omg.org).

A.1.8.4 Is your company a member already?

To find out if your company is already an OMG member, check the list at

www.omg.org/cgi-bin/membersearch.pl

If it is, you can take advantage of the member services listed on

www.omg.org/members/

For a summary of membership benefits, check out

www.omg.org/membership/benefits.html

A.1.8.5 Technical Questions about OMG Specifications

If you have a technical question about an OMG specification (and not about a CORBA product), there are two ways to get it answered: If you're an OMG member, go to the 'Ask the Experts" forum on the Web site at

www.omg.org/members/askexperts.html

and ask your question there. You'll have to type in the OMG member username and password; Ask the Experts is an OMG member benefit. If you work for an OMG member company or organization and don't know the password, email info@omg.org and ask for the name of your company's primary contact with OMG; you can then contact that person for the password.

If you're not an OMG member, email webtech@omg.org . Currently, your author is the moderator for technical questions on both experts and webtech.

If you find something that you're pretty sure is wrong with an OMG specification, write an email note and send it to issues@omg.org . This will get your issue registered in the official OMG issues database, and it will be considered the next time the specification that you referenced is addressed by a Revision Task Force. If you're in the middle of implementing a compliant commercial product and a bug or ambiguity in the specification is keeping you from meeting your schedule, point this out in your note. You don't have to be an OMG member to submit issues. But, this is not the place to ask for enhancements. The best way to work for an enhancement to an OMG specification is to join up and lead the effort at OMG meetings.

A.2 This Book

This book's home page lives on the OMG Web site at

www.omg.org/library/corfun/corfun.html

This one page serves for both this and the first edition; everything we provide via the web starts here. You'll find URLs to updated versions of the example when vendors adapt to new releases as well as updated sample ORBs to download, and pointers to example implementations from vendors not included in the original text. We've posted the original chapter on the Relationship Service, edited out of the second edition; additional material may get posted as time goes by. Another important downloadable item: Generic language code and IDL for this edition's example in C++ and Java, and the original edition's example in C, C++, and Smalltalk.

A.3 CORBA Link Collections

There are many CORBA link collections. It's probably impossible to give a complete list, so we'll give a representative two as examples. The first is maintained by Cetus, at

www.cetus-links.org/oo_corba.html

The second is maintained by Junichi Suzuki in Japan; it's won an award from Links2Go and lives at

www.yy.cs.keio.ac.jp/~suzuki/object/dist_comp.html

There are others, so don't stop your surfing at these two.

A.4 References

A.4.1 Chapter 1

Guttman, Michael, and Mattews, Jason, *The Object Technology Revolution*: John Wiley and Sons, Inc., New York, 1995.

A.4.2 Chapter 2

The source code to OpenDoc, and other information about it, appears on URL

www-4.ibm.com/software/ad/opendoc/index.html

OMG Work in Progress appears on URL

www.omg.org/techprocess/meetings/schedule/index.html

A.4.3 Chapter 3

OMG Technology Adoptions appear on URL

www.omg.org/techprocess/meetings/schedule/adopt.html

A.4.4 Chapter 5

As this book went to press, three BOI RFPs were in process. They were:

www.omg.org/techprocess/meetings/schedule/UML_Profile_for_EDOC_RFP.html
www.omg.org/techprocess/meetings/schedule/UML_Profile_for_CORBA_RFP.html
www.omg.org/techprocess/meetings/schedule/UML_Textual_Notation_RFP.html

At least one additional BOI RFP is planned. All of this will appear on the Work in Progress page, already cited.

A.4.5 Chapter 6

The Real-time CORBA submission appears at URL

www.omg.org/cgi-bin/doc?orbos/99-02-12

A.4.6 Chapter 7

We've already cited the Cetus-links URL mentioned in the text but here it is again:
www.cetus-links.org/oo_corba.html

A.4.7 Chapter 11

The Naming Service specification appears at URL
www.omg.org/cgi-bin/doc?formal/97-12-10

The Interoperable Naming Service specification was being revised as we went to press. We wrote the chapter from the latest interim documents available, which were

www.omg.org/cgi-bin/doc?ptc/99-09-01
www.omg.org/cgi-bin/doc?ptc/99-09-02

Neither of these was an adopted OMG specification at the time. When OMG adopts a revision of the specification, we will post it on the book's Web site.

The Trader Service specification appears at URL
www.omg.org/cgi-bin/doc?formal/97-12-23

A.4.8 Chapter 12

The Event Service specification appears at URL
www.omg.org/cgi-bin/doc?formal/97-12-11

The Notification Service specification appears at URL
www.omg.org/cgi-bin/doc?telecom/98-11-01

A.4.9 Chapter 13

The OTS specification appears at URL
www.omg.org/cgi-bin/doc?formal/97-12-17

The OTS specification was modified in the Asynchronous Messaging specification which appears at URL
www.omg.org/cgi-bin/doc?orbos/98-05-05

and by the Persistent State Service which appears at URL
www.omg.org/cgi-bin/doc?orbos/99-07-07

Additional TP standards and specifications are defined in the following three documents:

Distributed Transaction Processing: the TxRPC Specification. X/Open Document P305, The Open Group Ltd., Reading, UK.

Distributed Transaction Processing: the XA Specification. X/Open Document C193, The Open Group Ltd., Reading, UK.

Distributed Transaction Processing: the XATMI Specification. X/Open Document P306, The Open Group Ltd., Reading, UK.

For an introduction to transaction processing, read Jim Gray and Andreas Reuter, *Transaction Processing: Concepts and Techniquest.* San Francisco, Morgan Kaufman, 1992.

Ed Cobb's original article *Objects and Transactions: Together at Last* appeared in Object Magazine, January 1995, SIGS Publications, New York.

A.4.10 Chapter 14

The Security Service specification appears at URL
www.omg.org/cgi-bin/doc?formal/98-12-17

The *OMG White Paper on Security* appears at URL
www.omg.org/cgi-bin/doc?1994/94-04-16

Here are references for the four protocols used in SECIOP:

SPKM, the Simple Public-Key GSS-API Mechanism, is defined in Internet Draft draft-ietf-cat-spkmgss-06.txt, www.ietf.org, Jan. 1996.

The GSS Kerberos protocol is defined in IETF RFC 1510 and RFC 1964, available from
www.ietf.org/rfc/

The CSI-ECMA Protocol is defined in ECMA-235, available at URL
www.ecma.ch/stand/ECMA-235.htm . ECMA, Geneva, Switzerland, 1996.

The SSL Protocol is defined in //ietf.cnri.reston.va.us/internet-drafts/draft-freier-ssl-version3-01.txt

The Licensing Service specification appears at URL
www.omg.org/cgi-bin/doc?formal/97-12-19

A.4.11 Chapter 16

The Lifecycle Service specification appears at URL
www.omg.org/cgi-bin/doc?formal/97-12-13

The Relationship Service specification appears at URL
www.omg.org/cgi-bin/doc?formal/97-12-16

We've posted the Relationship Service chapter from the first edition on this book's Web site. Surf to www.omg.org/library/corfun/corfun.html and follow the pointers to the chapter.

OMG's Work in Progress page, www.omg.org/schedule, will contain information on the anticipated business relationships RFP when and if it is issued.

A.4.12 Chapter 17

The Persistent State Service appears at URL
www.omg.org/cgi-bin/doc?orbos/99-07-07

The Externalization Service appears at URL
www.omg.org/cgi-bin/doc?formal/98-12-16

A.4.13 Chapter 18

The Property Service appears at URL
www.omg.org/cgi-bin/doc?formal/97-12-20

The Query Service appears at URL
www.omg.org/cgi-bin/doc?formal/97-12-18

SQL-Query, the subset of SQL-92 that deals directly with query, is defined in *Database Language – SQL*, American National Standard x3.135-1992, ANSI, January 1992.

OQL-93 is defined by the Object Database Management Group in R.G.G. Cattell, T. Atwood, J. Duhl, G. Ferran, M. Loomis, and D. Wade, *the Object Database Standard: ODMG-93 v 1.2*. San Mateo, CA: Morgan Kaufman, 1993. This is not the current version of the ODMG standard (their Web site, www.odmg.org, references both a 2.0 and a 3.0 version), but is the version referenced in the OMG Query Service.

The Collection Service appears at URL
www.omg.org/cgi-bin/doc?formal/97-12-24

A.4.14 Chapter 20

The DOM is defined by the W3C, and appears at URL
www.w3.org/TR/WD-DOM-Level-2/
The Workflow Facility Specification appears at URL
www.omg.org/cgi-bin/doc?bom/98-06-07
The Workflow Management Coalition lists available documents at URL
www.aiim.org/wfmc/mainframe.htm
The WfMC Reference Model cited in the chapter is available at URL
www.aiim.org/wfmc/standards/docs/tc003v11.pdf
The PIDS Facility Specification appears at URL
www.omg.org/cgi-bin/doc?formal/99-03-05

A.4.15 Chapter 21

G. Booch, *Object-Oriented Analysis and Design with Applications* (2nd ed.). Addison Wesley Longman, 1994.

I. Jacobson, et al. *Object-Oriented Software Engineering: A Use Case Driven Approach*. Addison Wesley Longman, 1992.

J. Rumbaugh, et al. *Object-Oriented Modeling and Design*. Prentice Hall, 1991.

J. Siegel, et al., *CORBA Fundamentals and Programming*, First Edition, John Wiley, New York, 1996.

OMG Unified Modeling Language Specification v. 1.3 final draft, *Object Management Group, document ad/99-06-08*, June 1999 available at URL

www.omg.org/cgi-bin/doc?ad/99-06-08

A.4.16 Chapter 22

The MOF 1.1 Specification appears at URL
ftp://ftp.omg.org/pub/docs/ad/97-08-01.pdf
The MOF 1.3 Specification appears at URL
ftp://ftp.omg.org/pub/docs/ad/99-09-05.pdf
The XMI 1.1 Specification appears at URL
ftp://ftp.omg.org/pub/docs/ad/99-10-12.zip
The UML 1.3 Specification appears at URL
ftp://ftp.omg.org/cgi-bin/doc?ad/99-06-08

About the Web Site

OMG and the author maintain a Web site for this book and the first edition at www.omg.org/library/corfun/corfun.html. Here, we've collected all of the material, information, and pointers that we have about the book and the example. You'll find pointers to Web sites for all of the companies that contributed to the example, and to additional ORBs that work the example even though they're not in the book. This is also where we've posted the writeup of the Relationship Service from the first edition, which was cut from this version. We may post other material from the first edition as well, in response to readers' requests.

If you work for a company that markets an ORB, and you work the example in this book, post your work on your Web site and send the author an e-mail with the URL. We'll post a pointer to your site. (Send your note to siegel@omg.org) We've intentionally set the copyright on the example to allow unlimited use for teaching purposes, so you don't need explicit permission to do this. We'd like to see this example get wide use. Just don't use it to run a real retail emporium; it's not nearly robust enough for that. See Chapter 26 for a list of the things we left out, that you'd need in a real POS application!

Let us know if you do something interesting with the book, such as using it as a textbook in a college course or CORBA training. This information helps us tailor later editions to your needs and, if we can, we may post some of the more interesting uses and ideas on the Web site. Thanks!

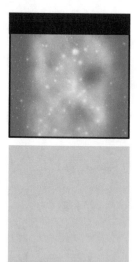

What's on the CD-ROM?

We've put a lot of material onto the CD-ROM that comes with this book.

First, it contains almost everything you need to compile and run the example (except for the computer, of course!). For every one of the ORBs presented in the book, for every programming language it's presented in, the CD-ROM contains all source code, IDL files (only #includes and pathnames have been changed where necessary; all of the IDL is the same), and makefiles or the equivalent for the ORB's target platform or platforms. Some vendors have provided evaluation ORBs as well. By the way, many vendors provide evaluation ORBs on their Web sites so check these out too if you're online; these are kept up-to-date while the CD-ROM is frozen in time sometime in early 2000.

We've also included generic versions of the example in both C++ and Java. These versions are as close to standard CORBA as we could get (since the BOA is loosely defined, for one thing). If you're going to port the example to an ORB not in the book, these provide a good starting point although many of the vendors' code sets are very close also. And if you're porting to a POA ORB, you might want to start with a POA version.

We had space left after we put all that on, so we included OMG specifications as well: We started with all of CORBA 2.3 (the current version as we went to press), the language mappings, and the CORBAservices. Then we added the Domain specifications, UML, the MOF, and XMI. Finally, we put on the latest versions of the submissions that are being collected into the CORBA 3.0 book. All are in pdf format; to view them, you'll need to install a pdf browser which Adobe makes available for free. We've put the Windows and Solaris versions on the CD-ROM; for other operating systems you can download browsers from Adobe's Web site www.adobe.com.

Don't get discouraged if you find some of the specifications hard to read. They're aimed at ORB and service *implementors*; not at CORBA object programmers or end-users. Many have introductory sections aimed at a more general audience, so look around for these and spend some time with the technical sections if you feel the need.

Index